OZ CLARKE
WINE ATLAS

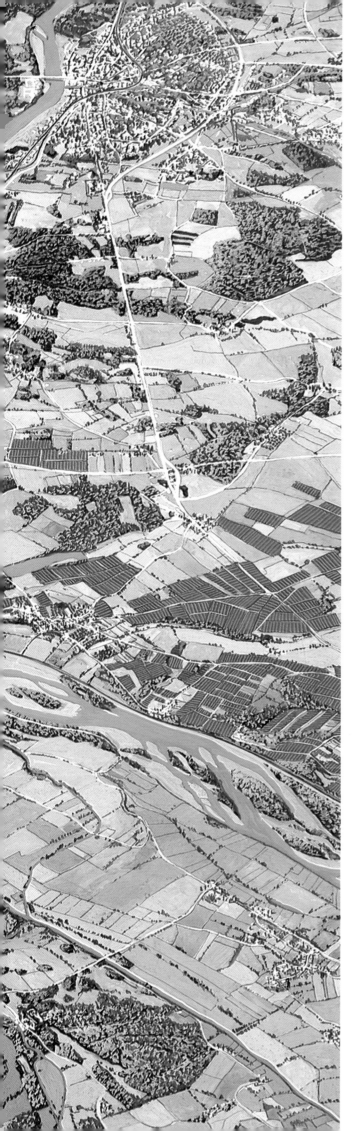

OZ CLARKE
WINE ATLAS

WINES AND WINE REGIONS OF THE WORLD

REVISED AND UPDATED

PANORAMIC MAPS PAINTED BY

KEITH & SUE GAGE

PAVILION

Printed for WHSmith in 2009

Produced by Pavilion Books
An imprint of Anova Books Company Ltd
10 Southcombe Street
London W14 0RA

www.anovabooks.com
www.ozclarke.com

This Second Edition first published in 2002
Reprinted with revisions in 2007 by Pavilion Books
Copyright © 2007 Pavilion Books
Text copyright © 1995, 2002, 2007 Oz Clarke
Maps and artwork copyright © 2007 Pavilion Books

A CIP catalogue for this book is available from the
British Library

ISBN-13: 9-781862-058729
Colour separations by Alliance Graphics Ltd
Printed and bound by CT Printing, China

*Page 1: Vineyards are arguably at their most beautiful
after the harvest, when the leaves take on the brilliant
russets and yellows of fall – these ones are in the
Alexander Valley in northern California.*
*Pages 2–3: Detail from the panoramic map of Sancerre
and Pouilly in the Loire Valley.*

Editorial Director and Chief Editor Fiona Holman
Art Director and Art Editor Nigel O'Gorman
Chief Cartographer Andrew Thompson

Assistant Editors Cécile Landau, Helen Spence,
Jo Turner
Additional Editorial Assistance and Research Lorna
Bateson, Lucy Bridgers, David Moore, Maggie Ramsay,
Nick Skinner, Phillip Williamson
Desktop Publishing Keith Bambury
Index Angie Hipkin

Consultant Editor Margaret Rand
Regional Consultants Nicolas Belfrage MW, Jim Budd,
Bob Campbell MW, Liz Eyre, Giles Fallowfield, Peter
Forrestal, Rosemary George MW, Antony Gismondi,
Olivier Humbrecht MW, Tom Hyland, James Lawther
MW, Jonathan Livingstone-Learmonth MW, Angela
Lloyd, Wink Lorch, Dan McCarthy, Dave McIntyre, Sally
Marden, Richard Mayson, Jasper Morris MW, Stuart
Pigott, Victor de la Serna, Stephen Skelton
Consultant Geologist Professor Jake Hancock

Panoramic Cartography Keith and Sue Gage
Panoramic Map Editor Wink Lorch
Panoramic Maps digitally updated Andrew Thompson
Illustrations Aziz Khan, Trevor Lawrence, Coral Mula,
James Robins
Studio Photography Nigel James

Further acknowledgments, including those for the first
edition, are on page 336

CONTENTS

INTRODUCTION 8

THE WORLD OF WINE

THE VINE & ITS ENVIRONMENT 10

WORLD CLIMATE & VINEYARDS 12

SITING THE VINEYARD 14

THE IMPORTANCE OF SOIL 16

THE IMPACT OF WATER 18

THE MODERN VINEYARD 20

GRAPES OF THE WORLD 22

THE MODERN PICTURE 25

WINES & WINE REGIONS OF THE WORLD

LIST OF PANORAMIC MAPS 27

FRANCE 28

THE WINE REGIONS OF FRANCE 30

BORDEAUX 32

THE MEDOC & HAUT-MEDOC 36

GRAVES & PESSAC-LEOGNAN 42

ST-ÉMILION, POMEROL & FRONSAC 44

BORDEAUX SWEET WINES 48

REST OF BORDEAUX 50

BURGUNDY 52

UNDERSTANDING THE MAPS

There are two styles of map in this Atlas: the
handpainted panoramic vineyard maps, which
are the main feature, and the more conventional
regional and country maps.

▪The panoramic maps These are detailed artists'
renderings of the world's great vineyard areas. In
many areas, the vineyards have never been
mapped before. In every case we have checked
locations with local organizations and/or
individual winemakers, but total accuracy is
almost impossible as plantings are changing all
the time. In some New World areas massive
planting is taking place, while in some outlying
European areas vineyards are being grubbed up.
As well as vineyards, general landscape features,
such as forests, rivers and mountains, have been
painted as accurately as possible. All the
panoramic maps have an element of perspective
and this inevitably introduces slight distortion; a
vineyard or village in the north, at the top of a
map, will appear smaller than one in the
foreground. Scale bars indicate distances covered
from east to west. However, because of the effect
of perspective, total distances are given from

north to south. Map colours are appropriate
for late summer, just before the grape
harvest. The vineyards have been painted
bright green, with surrounding land
often yellow or brown as other crops
have usually been harvested by this
time. Field boundaries and vine row
directions are mainly notional.

Where annotation is shown, it is
minimal so as not to spoil the effect.
More detail is given on the key maps
that accompany the most detailed maps.
Wineries are located at the main installation,
not necessarily the tasting or visitors' centre.
Selected châteaux, wineries and vineyards shown
on the key maps are the author's personal
selection.

▪Other wine maps Wine regions shown on these
maps are official growing areas (the panoramic
maps show planted vineyard areas). To the best
of our knowledge, boundaries are correct at the
time of going to press. If you have more up-to-
date information we would be delighted to hear
from you.

CHABLIS 56

CÔTE DE NUITS 58

CÔTE DE BEAUNE 61

CÔTE CHALONNAISE 64

MÂCONNAIS 66

BEAUJOLAIS 68

CHAMPAGNE 70

HEART OF CHAMPAGNE 74

ALSACE 76

HEART OF ALSACE 78

THE LOIRE VALLEY 80

ANJOU-SAUMUR 84

TOURAINE 86

SANCERRE & POUILLY 88

THE RHÔNE VALLEY 90

NORTHERN RHÔNE 92

SOUTHERN RHÔNE 96

JURA & SAVOIE 99

PROVENCE 100

LANGUEDOC-ROUSSILLON 102

CORSICA 105

SOUTH-WEST FRANCE 106

VINS DE PAYS 108

GERMANY 110

THE WINE REGIONS OF GERMANY 112

MOSEL-SAAR-RUWER 114

MIDDLE MOSEL 116

SAAR-RUWER 118

THE RHINE VALLEY 120

AHR & MITTELRHEIN 122

RHEINGAU 123

NAHE 126

RHEINHESSEN 128

PFALZ 130

FRANKEN 132

BADEN-WÜRTTEMBERG 135

HESSISCHE BERGSTRASSE 138

SAALE-UNSTRUT & SACHSEN 139

SWITZERLAND 140

VALAIS 142

AUSTRIA 144

NIEDERÖSTERREICH 146

BURGENLAND 148

A little chapel sits on the peak of the hill of Hermitage in the northern Rhône Valley. The steep granite hill has excellent exposure to the sun and is possibly the oldest vineyard site in France.

The panoramic map of the heart of the Rheingau region, Germany.

The coastal hills of Tuscany south-east of Grosseto in the Maremma are buzzing with activity. Many producers, from Tuscany and beyond, are rushing in to buy up existing vineyards as well as suitable new land for planting.

ITALY 150
THE WINE REGIONS OF ITALY 152
NORTH-WEST ITALY 154
PIEMONTE 156
BAROLO & BARBARESCO 158
NORTH-EAST ITALY 160
TRENTINO-ALTO ADIGE 162
VENETO 164
FRIULI-VENEZIA GIULIA 166
CENTRAL ITALY 168
TOSCANA 170
CHIANTI 172
BRUNELLO DI MONTALCINO 174
VINO NOBILE DI MONTEPULCIANO 176
BOLGHERI 178
SOUTHERN ITALY 180
SARDEGNA 182
SICILIA 183

SPAIN 184
THE WINE REGIONS OF SPAIN 186
NORTH-EAST SPAIN 188

CATALUNYA 190
RIOJA 192
ARAGÓN & NAVARRA 194
NORTH-WEST SPAIN 196
RIBERA DEL DUERO 198
CENTRAL SPAIN 200
SOUTHERN SPAIN 202
JEREZ 204

PORTUGAL 206
THE WINE REGIONS OF PORTUGAL 208
NORTHERN PORTUGAL 210
THE DOURO VALLEY 212
CENTRAL & SOUTHERN PORTUGAL 214
MADEIRA 216

ENGLAND 218

CZECH REPUBLIC & SLOVAKIA 219

HUNGARY 220

BLACK SEA STATES 222

ROMANIA 224

WESTERN BALKANS 226

BULGARIA 228

GREECE & EASTERN MEDITERRANEAN 230

NORTH AMERICA 232
THE WINE REGIONS OF NORTH AMERICA 234
CALIFORNIA 236
NORTH COAST 238
NORTH CENTRAL COAST 248

SOUTH CENTRAL COAST	250
CENTRAL & SOUTHERN CALIFORNIA	254
SOUTHERN & MID-WEST STATES	255
PACIFIC NORTHWEST	256
WASHINGTON STATE	258
OREGON	260
EAST COAST	262
NEW YORK STATE	264
CANADA	266
BRITISH COLUMBIA	267
ONTARIO	269

SOUTH AMERICA & MEXICO — 270

URUGUAY	272
CHILE	273
CENTRAL VALLEY/MAIPO VALLEY	276
CENTRAL VALLEY/RAPEL VALLEY	278
ARGENTINA	280
MENDOZA	282

AUSTRALIA — 284

THE WINE REGIONS OF AUSTRALIA	286
SOUTH AUSTRALIA	288
BAROSSA VALLEY	290

COONAWARRA	292
CLARE VALLEY	294
VICTORIA	296
YARRA VALLEY	298
NEW SOUTH WALES	300
HUNTER VALLEY	302
WESTERN AUSTRALIA	304
MARGARET RIVER	306
TASMANIA	308
QUEENSLAND	309

NEW ZEALAND — 310

NORTH ISLAND	312
HAWKES BAY	314
SOUTH ISLAND	316
MARLBOROUGH	318

SOUTH AFRICA — 320

STELLENBOSCH & PAARL	323

NORTH AFRICA — 326

ASIA — 327

INDEX	328
PICTURE CREDITS & ACKNOWLEDGMENTS	336

Chardonnay vineyards belonging to Leeuwin Estate in the Margaret River region of Western Australia. Chardonnay from this high-flying winery was one of the first in Australia to exhibit Burgundian-style complexity and concentration.

Detail from the panoramic map of the Heart of Mendoza, Argentina.

INTRODUCTION – SECOND EDITION

California is at the very heart of progress in the world of wine, but it doesn't forget tradition, and it carefully cossets some of the oldest vines in existence. The grapes off this 100-year-old Zinfandel vine at Lytton Springs in Dry Creek Valley are used to make superb red wine by Ridge.

I FEEL AS THOUGH I'VE COME FULL CIRCLE. My first visits to wine regions were all about vineyards. I didn't get inside many wineries, unless I had wheedled an intro – which just occasionally I managed to do. Most winery owners had more sense than to let me in – I was a student, after all, and a thirsty one. But it didn't matter. It meant that I spent the time ambling and clambering through the vineyards, dallying in them, picnicking in them, and sometimes sleeping in them. Instead 'of standing wide-eyed and bemused amongst the barrels in a dusty *cave*, I was outdoors acquainting myself with what really mattered – the soil, the vines, the rain, the wind and the sun.

By the time I began to write about wine, it was the 1980s – the most frantic, frenetic, frenzied decade the world of wine had yet seen, when the Old Order was stood upon its head and the New World tyros blazed their trail across the globe, convinced they had unlocked all the secrets that wine could hold, and that wherever they chose, whenever they wished, they and their bag of winemaker's tricks could create wines of genius and delight. Well, up to a point they could. But their whole focus was on the winery, not the vineyard. Interestingly, as they seemed to be winning the argument of new versus old, Europe, and France in particular, was putting together a golden decade of great vintages, based on the genius that lay in the soils and the climatic conditions of her best vineyards. Taste the classics that Europe produced in the 1980s versus the bluster and bravado of the 1980s New World offerings, and there's no doubt the old still held sway then.

But the 1990s saw a shift of emphasis again. No longer was I always ushered straight to the winery to admire the forest of stainless steel and the barns full of barrels, and regaled with tales of cultured yeasts and self-draining fermenters. Winemakers became less cocky, less convinced that you could achieve anything you wanted with just the right equipment, the right chemicals, and the skills to use them. New World winemakers started drawing back from the mixture of brilliant innovation and control freakery that had characterized their earlier efforts. And as the Old World quietly set about learning a few of these tricks to try on the fruit from their ancient hills and valleys, the New World realized that the key to their making wine which could equal the best in Europe lay not in the pages of the wine making manual, the sensitivity of the crusher–destemmer or the particular grain of oak the barrel maker used – it lay under their feet, in the vineyard.

It was this move back towards the vineyard that persuaded me to write the first edition of this Atlas the better part of a decade ago, and this second edition has been prompted by the astonishing rate of change that the world of wine is experiencing again. And, above all else, that change is focused on the vineyards. The number of new plantings in such places as New Zealand, Australia, Chile and North America is remarkable. Regions that hardly had a vine, like New Zealand's Central Otago, Australia's Limestone Coast or Chile's Casablanca Valley, are now fully fledged, exciting and self-confident producers creating wines of real individuality, thanks to the special nature of their climate and soil. At the same time ancient vineyard areas of Europe like the south of Italy, Portugal's Alentejo, Spain's Priorat and Ribera del Duero and Greece are being revitalized by modern methods in the winery and the vineyard. So, I've set out to re-evaluate all the vineyards of the world – some task! I've revised all the original text and written completely new sections where areas and countries warrant it; and, as well as six totally new maps, every existing map has been updated to reflect the state of the world's vineyards as they are now. In some instances, as in Australia's Clare Valley or New Zealand's Marlborough, the effects are dramatic with a doubling of land under vine.

Yet, with all this hectic change, the eternal truths of what makes wine good and special have never been more evident. Every good winemaker in every country in the world knows that the final limiting factor on wine quality is the quality of the grapes. And every winemaker knows that some regions grow better grapes than others, some areas within those regions are more suitable, some small patches of the very same field are better than others – and some growers care more about their work and will always produce the finest fruit.

And so I'm back where I began. And once more, you're far more likely to find me out amongst the vines than seated at the tasting table. Sure, I'll taste – try to stop me – but I'll taste when I have seen the vines, their soil, their place, the wine's place. If I'm in Côte-Rôtie, I want to climb to the highest point on the slope from whose grapes the juice always runs blackest and sweetest. I want to stand with my face held up to the sun, imagining how it creeps into view at dawn and fades with the evening shadows. I want to feel the poor stony soil crumble beneath my feet and touch the twisted, tortured trunk of the vine which each year struggles to survive on this barren slope and ripen its tiny crop. If I'm in Margaux, I want to tread the warm, well-drained gravel outcrops and then step off into the sullen clay swamps nearby and, with this single step, I'll know why the gravel-grown grapes are precious and the clay-clogged ones are not. I want to see the Andes water gushing down off the mountains into the fertile vineyards of Chile's Maipo Valley. I want to feel the howling mists chill me to the bone in California's Carneros, and then feel the warm winds of New Zealand's Marlborough tugging at my hair. I want it all to make sense.

And I hope this Atlas will help. I was convinced I wanted to write the first edition as soon as I saw the prototype panoramic map. It was a map of Chablis. I saw the town, the little valleys, I saw which hills were high, which were low, which faced the sun, and which were protected from the wind. I had never seen a map before that made me exult in the sense of place like this one. Suddenly it was blindingly obvious why the Grand Cru wines were riper, fatter, more intense, why the Premier Cru wines were better than basic Chablis. I had walked through all the vineyards, but this new perspective was shattering. It was as though I was hovering in a helicopter directly above the vines, able to dip down and swoop in and out of every tiny twist in the slope, through every gully, round every outcrop of rock. The roads and railways I had travelled, the rivers and hilltops I'd used for reference – all were set out before me.

What we have tried to achieve in these brilliant maps is a grand aerial tour of the world's vineyards. Focusing minutely on areas where there are particularly exciting features dictating the character of the wine, but also taking a broader regional view to put the world's great vineyards into context. And in my writing, I have tried to achieve a distillation of all the travelling I have done since student days. Some villages and their vines seem unchanged since then and may still be unchanged a hundred years from now. Has anything much really changed in the quiet communities of Burgundy's Côte d'Or, in the hamlets high up in Portugal's Douro Valley towards the Spanish border, in the friendless huddles of huts on Spain's bleak La Mancha plain? In other places, there were no vines at all when I first passed through, yet now they stretch as far as the eye can see. The North Fork of Long Island, New York, was all potatoes when I first went there. A 100-ha (250-acre) vineyard now carpets the English North Downs near Dorking, making my childhood memories of pastureland and copses of tall, dark trees seem ever so remote. Some places seem to have slipped into poverty and decline. Others have a Klondike air as the gaze of fashion turns upon them and their wines, and every available scrap of land is planted up with vines. I just hope that when the dust settles in Coonawarra or Hawkes Bay, the right vines will have been planted on the right soils by the right people. And in this age when change has come faster than ever before in the world of wine, it is equally certain that within the decade some of those now in decline will be fired by a new confidence and popularity; others now considered so chic will be struggling in the tough real world as their first flush of fame dissolves; and yet others, at this moment mere pastureland or rocky mountainside, will become flourishing vineyards producing wines whose flavours may be entirely different to anything yet achieved on this planet.

And through all this will run the constant theme: the relationship between the land and its climate, the grape varieties planted, and the commitment of the winemakers concerned.

These elements have always been intrinsically connected, yet frequently the relationship has been an insincere one because the history of wine is littered with examples of human endeavour failing to match the quality of a site. To say that a piece of land is a great vineyard site is only to say that it has the potential to produce great wine, so long as the right grapes are planted and the desire for greatness burns brightly in the breasts of the growers.

But just as the massive advances in winemaking technology made available excellent wine from areas that had never before excelled, so the dramatic progress made in vineyard management and the manipulation of the vine, enabling it to perform well in less than perfect mesoclimates, has made the definition of a great site today far more wide-reaching than ever before. Wine styles that were lauded a generation ago may not be so widely appreciated now: the rich, heady exotic Chardonnays from Australia's Hunter Valley or the Napa Valley in California that ushered in a new age of wine a mere generation ago are snubbed by many wine lovers today. The slavish attempts to ape Red Burgundy that produced so many light and feeble Oregon and New Zealand Pinot Noirs have been replaced in those areas by a robust self confidence in the different characters their Pinot Noirs possess. Wines that are lapped up with enthusiasm these days have flavours that weren't possible a generation ago. The south of Italy was derided for producing truckloads of coarse, high alcohol hooch fit only for a distant blending tank. Now the Negroamaros and Primitivos of Puglia and the Nero d'Avolas of Sicily are regarded as exciting examples of new technology marrying into old vineyards and old vine varieties. Argentina's perfumed Malbecs, South Africa's tangy Sauvignon Blancs, Canada's Icewines – none of these flavours were thought possible a generation ago.

The world of wine has moved at breakneck speed since the 1980s, and if the vineyard men and women and the winemakers, the committed wine merchants and the enthusiastic wine consumers were allowed to get on with things unhindered, all would be well. But there is a cloud on the horizon threatening the world of well-tended vineyards, well-ripened fruit and finely flavoured wines. Profit – or should I say profit as the overriding principle. Wine has never been thought of as a cash cow. But as the wealthy nations of northern Europe, North America, and Asia turn increasingly to wine as their drink of choice, often at the expense of spirits and beer, the brewers and distillers, and the venture capitalists and entrepeneurs can all smell the unlikely aroma of excessive profit in the wine world's air. As I write, vast wine conglomerates are being created crossing continents, meshing traditions and individuals into a disturbingly homogeneous whole ruled by profit, not by flavour, ruled by market share and corporate identity, not by the human passion and commitment that has created all the world's great wines so far.

Well, this Atlas stands for something I hope is more permanent than the unsightly couplings of multinational money makers and brand builders. In this Atlas I've tried to show the world of wine in all its natural, timeless beauty. A vineyard evolves. It is not about political wrangling, about special interest pleading protectionist legislation, about copywriters' fantasies or the market share of a brand. It is about a piece of soil, the sun, the wind and the rain, and the happy chance of men and women wanting to love that place, cherish it and, through their vines and the wines they make, bring it to its fullest expression. Wherever those vineyards are, whether they are great or small, famous or unknown, I dedicate this new edition of the Atlas to them and to those who care for them.

The frontiers of wine are being pushed back all the time, but you can't push much further southwards than these vineyards on Bannockburn Heights overlooking Lake Dunstan in the Central Otago region of New Zealand's South Island. This is the world's most southerly wine region, and, unless someone pushes even further south in Chile or Argentina, likely to remain so.

Author's Acknowledgements

Heartfelt thanks go to all who have helped to produce this Atlas. An illustrated work of reference is by definition a team effort – and you can't beat the team I've had! Editors, designers, cartographers, DTP experts, researchers, regional consultants (sharing their insights and expertise with great generosity) – and especially Fiona Holman, my long-standing and long-suffering editor, Nigel O'Gorman (art director) and Andrew Thompson (chief cartographer). A full list of acknowledgements can be found on page 336.

THE VINE & ITS ENVIRONMENT

WHEN DID YOU LAST SEE A WILD VINE? The answer, almost certainly, is never. Not a European wild vine, anyway, because such vines are probably extinct. The European wild vine is a species from which cultivated vines were bred several millennia ago. The story of wine is the story of the taming of the vine. Vines, if they're allowed to, will rampage over everything in their path in their drive to find sunlight. They will produce leaves and fruit many yards from their trunks, and if you made wine from their grapes it would be thin, dilute stuff, short on flavour and high on acidity – because the vine doesn't exist to produce wine. It exists to produce grapes and reproduce itself. So when man intervenes and diverts the vine from its original purpose, he has a fair bit of work on his hands.

The grower must consider every detail of the vine's environment: the draining capability of the soil and the minerals present in it, the angle of the slope to the sun, the amount of sunshine and rainfall in that particular spot, the strength of the wind and the likelihood of frost. If he is French he will refer to the whole package – climate, soil and exposure – as *terroir*. Every *terroir* is unique, he will say, and imparts its own character to its wine. His New World counterpart would, until recently, have dismissed this as nonsense. There are mesoclimates – the climatic conditions affecting a whole vineyard – yes, and there are micro-climates, which are the conditions pertaining to the individual vine, but what really matters at the end of the day is how you make the wine.

Now that is changing. Now the buzzword in every serious New World region is – you guessed it – *terroir*. Sometimes it is merely a marketing tool: in a world awash with decent-to-good wine, *terroir* is seen as the key to distinguishing one Merlot or Shiraz from another. Of course the New World has great *terroirs*: they turn up just as frequently as in the Old World. And where *terroir* is most influential is in a marginal climate – a place where it is only just warm enough to ripen those particular grapes. Long, cool ripening seasons give subtle flavours with a good balance of fruit, alcohol and acidity. But what is cool for one vine variety is warm for another: even the finest *terroir* is wasted if the choice of vine is inappropriate – or if the viticulture is geared to quick results and high yields.

The setting sun intensifies the bronzed foliage of the vines at Clayvin Vineyard in Marlborough, New Zealand, long after the harvest is over. Irrigation is crucial here; the barren hills beyond show clearly just how dry the region naturally is.

The vine's environment is so complex and finely balanced that to alter one part of it affects everything else. Pruning, drainage, soil type and exactly the right amount of sun and rain at the appropriate times are all vital to its development.

A warm climate may become cooler at higher altitudes; in a cool climate, however, lower altitudes don't always help, as cold air collects in the valley floor, increasing the risk of frost. Slopes are generally better than flat land, because drainage is better and they enjoy more sun. Then there is the question of which way the slope faces: in the northern hemisphere due south is marvellous, but east-facing slopes catch the morning sun, west-facing slopes the warmer afternoon sun. And while shelter from the wind makes a vineyard warmer, a breeze can dry the grapes after a shower and prevent rot.

And soil is important. In cool damp areas, free-draining, warm soils are crucial; in hot areas less so.

CASE STUDY OF A VINEYARD

St-Estèphe is in the north of the Haut-Médoc, and the deep, undulating gravel beds that mark out the best parts of the region are getting a bit sparser here. As a result there are only five Classed Growth châteaux in the commune, and vineyards here are far more likely to make Cru Bourgeois wine than Grand Cru Classé. One of these châteaux, Cos d'Estournel, is in the south of St-Estèphe, and faces Château Lafite-Rothschild (in Pauillac) across the tiny Jalle du Breuil stream that divides the two communes. The land immediately around the stream is low-lying and damp, and not planted with vines, but then the ground rises, gravel takes over again, and there is Cos d'Estournel, the best property of the commune.

The photograph on the right shows the sloping Cos d'Estournel vineyards. You can see just how dense the gravel is there. This is quite warm, heat-retaining soil and, as a result, some 60 per cent of the vineyard is planted with Cabernet Sauvignon. It drains well, but there is enough sand in it to ensure that it holds some humidity in summer to protect the vines from drought. And while the photograph doesn't show the Gironde (the river is just over a mile away), its estuary affects the climate of the whole region, softening the extremes of both winter and summer. And look how closely the vines are packed in. Growing them cheek by jowl in this way reduces yields and increases concentration. It's all part of making the vine work hard for its living.

1. BUDBREAK

Northern Hemisphere:
March to April.
Southern Hemisphere:
September to October.
In early spring the vine
wakes up after the
dormant winter months.
Sap rises and the pruned
shoots drip with 'tears'.
Some varieties of vine
bud earlier than others;
warm, sheltered vineyard
sites and warm soil will
also bring vines on faster.
Generally, the air
temperature needs to reach
an average of 10°C (50°F).
The earlier the budding the
greater the danger from spring frosts.

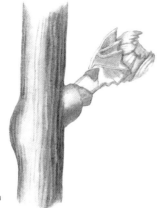

2. FIRST FOLIAGE

Northern Hemisphere:
April to May.
Southern Hemisphere:
October to November.
Shoots and leaves emerge, followed by miniature bunches
of flower buds. Frost is a
major danger now. Most
European wine nations
have dates after which
they breathe easy and
decide that the frost risk
is finally past. In
Germany they don't
relax until the middle of
May – after the Three
Kings of May (11–13
May) and Cold St Sophie
(15 May) are past.

3. FLOWERING

Northern Hemisphere:
May to June.
Southern Hemisphere:
November to December.
Flowering lasts about 10 days, and the ideal average
temperature is between 18 and 20°C (64 and 68°F).
The perfect weather is frost-free, sunny, dry and still.

5. CHANGING COLOUR (*VÉRAISON*)

Northern Hemisphere:
August.
Southern Hemisphere:
January to February.
The grapes are developing well, and two months or so
after flowering they begin to change colour (*véraison*).
Sugar levels inside the grapes start to rise and the
acid balance begins to change. From being small,
green, and as hard as bullets, the grapes soften,
assuming either golden or red colouring, and grow
larger: they should double in size by harvest. Dangers
now are rot and mildew.

4. SETTING

Northern Hemisphere:
June to July.
Southern Hemisphere:
December to January.
This is when the flowers develop
into miniature grapes. The
success or failure of the
flowering will begin to be
apparent: unfertilized flowers will
just drop off. In hotter climates, lack
of water and excessive heat can
affect set. In cool climates, wind, rain
and low temperature are problems.

VINE PESTS AND DISEASES

Growers have to be on their guard: nature may have provided ideal
conditions for their vineyards, only to hit them with a whole battery of
diseases and pests. The photograph shows the insect currently on the Napa
Valley's Least Wanted list: the Glassy Winged Sharpshooter, which
spreads Pierce's Disease. This is a virus disease which kills vines, and for
which treatment is so far impossible. Other virus diseases include leaf roll
and fan leaf. Fungal diseases like downy mildew, powdery mildew, black
rot and grey rot can be controlled by
fungicides or Bordeaux mixture
(lime and copper sulphate). You can
tell when a grower has been using
copper sulphate: the wooden posts
in the vineyard will be stained a faint
blue. Insect parasites, like moth
caterpillars and various mites,
beetles and nematodes, can all be
fought with varying degrees of
difficulty. But the only answer to the
vine's biggest enemy, the aphid
phylloxera, is to graft the vines on to
resistant rootstock.

6. RIPENING

Northern Hemisphere:
August to October.
Southern Hemisphere:
February to April.
There are vine varieties suitable for both hot and cold
regions and they ripen at vastly different rates. Hot-
country red wine varieties would hardly even change
colour by vintage time if grown in a cool German
Riesling vineyard. Some vines are happy ripening fast,
others will only give their best if the ripening period is
as long and as cool as possible. Experts differ as to
whether or not fruit flavour is improved by a long, cool
ripening season: some claim the faster the better
between *véraison* and actual harvest; others believe
that long, sunny autumns are perhaps the most
important factor in increasing flavour intensity. The aim
is to build sufficient sugar in the grape while keeping
acidity in balance and, for reds, getting the right
amount of tannin and colour.

WORLD CLIMATE & VINEYARDS

This is the devastation hailstorms can cause. These vines in Mendoza, Argentina, have been stripped bare of foliage and fruit by a sudden midsummer hailstorm. Many Argentine vineyards now have protective nets against the hail that forms high in the sky above the Andes.

IF IT WEREN'T FOR THE GULF STREAM warming up the west coast of France, we'd have no Classed Growth Médoc reds. If it weren't for the sea fogs cooling down the west coast of California, we'd have no Napa Valley Cabernets. If it weren't for the cold Benguela current from the Antarctic soothing the fevered brow of the Western Cape, South Africa would be far too hot to make exciting table wines. And thank goodness for the rain-shadows of Washington State in the United States, of Marlborough in New Zealand and Alsace in France, which create a long, dry autumn that lets fruit hang confidently on the vine and ripen magnificently against all odds. Thank goodness, too, for the tempering effects of Lakes Ontario and Erie on the Canada/US border. Without these huge lakes, there'd be no Ontario wine industry and no grapes would ripen in Ohio or upstate New York.

But on the other hand – damn those late spring frosts that appear out of the calm April night skies and decimate the crop in Chablis; damn the drought that creeps up unnoticed in Australia's New South Wales, stressing the hardiest vines almost beyond endurance. Damn the cyclonic storms of autumn that sweep in on Gisborne and Hawkes Bay in New Zealand and dump a month's rain in an hour on vines so tantalizingly, agonizingly close to perfect ripeness. And, for that matter, damn the damp grey clouds that sit like sullen duennas over the South Downs of England from spring to autumn, spoiling the chances of decent cricket and a decent wine vintage.

It's the world's climate in all its variety. One thing that becomes ever more evident as the debate on global warming rages is that all the climates of the world are interlinked, and whatever happens in one place will set off chain reactions that will affect conditions right round the world.

All the way through this Atlas I'll be talking about climate conditions and how they affect individual vineyards around the world. The elements of climate that are most relevant to viticulture are temperature – obviously you need a certain amount of warmth to ripen grapes; variability of day and night temperatures; continentality, or the difference between winter and summer temperatures; actual sunlight; rainfall and an area's relative humidity; and wind.

The best vineyard sites have traditionally been fairly cool ones, with a measure of summer rainfall and long, dry autumns, or those with Mediterranean climatic conditions, with winter rainfall, relatively high temperatures and, ideally, moderating maritime breezes. In the Old World grape growers have slowly discovered the best conditions over the centuries. In the New World, every year brings the discovery of new and exciting sites for vines. But most wine regions are either on the cool edges of warm continents, or the warm edges of cool continents. Look at the map and you'll see what I mean.

Growers are bringing greater and greater subtlety to their understanding of climate and its effects on vines – and an increasing awareness of how difficult it is to replicate the climate of one region in another region half the world away. A pair of first-class Bordeaux producers, making wine in Chile, kicked off by trying to find a rainfall pattern similar to that of Bordeaux: a wet spring, followed by water stress right up to the harvest. This, they reckoned, would give wines of more Bordelais style than are commonly made in Chile. Did it? No, it did not. Not only was the resulting wine not at all like good Bordeaux, it wasn't much like good Chilean either.

The difficulty of matching one climate to another has been particularly observed by Australian researchers keen to plant finicky Italian grape varieties like Sangiovese or Nebbiolo. They have found it almost impossible – well, absolutely impossible,

actually – to find exact replicas of the Tuscan or Piedmontese climates in Australia. It all boils down to a question of the relative continentality of climates; the warmth at different stages of spring and autumn, the sort of weather in the final month before the harvest, even the relative humidity in the afternoons during that month. These sorts of detail didn't matter too much when everybody was planting Chardonnay and Cabernet Sauvignon, because these grapes are so adaptable that they'll cope with pretty well any conditions you throw at them. (Making really great wine from either variety, of course, is a different matter altogether.) But now growers are moving on to trickier grapes that don't travel so easily, and life's not so simple any more.

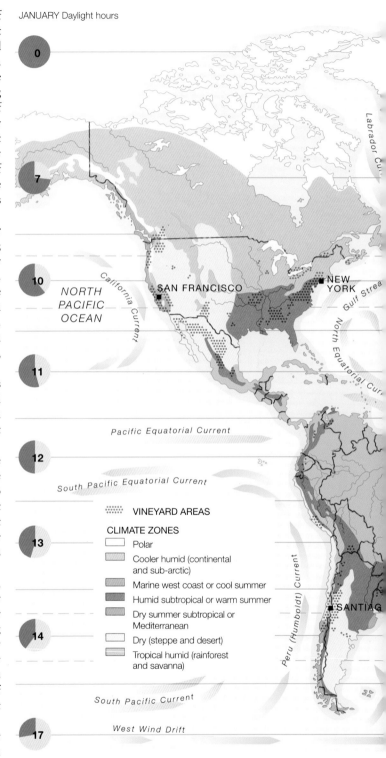

JANUARY Daylight hours

0

7

10

NORTH
PACIFIC
OCEAN

SAN FRANCISCO

NEW YORK

11

Pacific Equatorial Current

12

South Pacific Equatorial Current

13

14

SANTIAG

Peru (Humboldt) Current

South Pacific Current

17

West Wind Drift

Labrador Cur

Gulf Strea

North Equatorial Cur

California Current

░░░░ VINEYARD AREAS

CLIMATE ZONES

Polar

Cooler humid (continental and sub-arctic)

Marine west coast or cool summer

Humid subtropical or warm summer

Dry summer subtropical or Mediterranean

Dry (steppe and desert)

Tropical humid (rainforest and savanna)

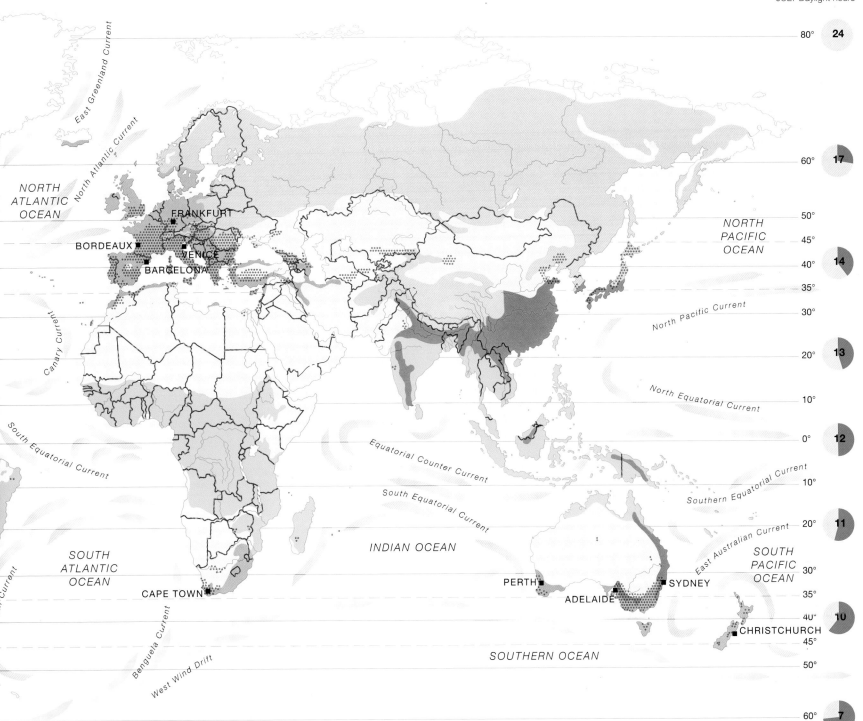

JULY Daylight hours

80° **24**

60° **17**

50°
45°

40° **14**

35°
30°

20° **13**

10°

0° **12**

10°

20° **11**

30°

35°
40° **10**
45°

50°

60° **7**

NORTH
ATLANTIC
OCEAN

East Greenland Current

North Atlantic Current

Canary Current

South Equatorial Current

SOUTH
ATLANTIC
OCEAN

Benguela Current

West Wind Drift

FRANKFURT
BORDEAUX
VENICE
BARCELONA

INDIAN OCEAN

Equatorial Counter Current

South Equatorial Current

CAPE TOWN

NORTH
PACIFIC
OCEAN

North Pacific Current

North Equatorial Current

Southern Equatorial Current

East Australian Current

SOUTH
PACIFIC
OCEAN

PERTH
ADELAIDE
SYDNEY

CHRISTCHURCH

SOUTHERN OCEAN

Just looking at the figures doesn't tell you enough. For a start, at any given latitude, the Northern Hemisphere will be warmer than the Southern, partly because of the Gulf Stream and partly because the northern land masses are greater. And yields may be higher in some New World regions not just because the soils may have higher potential vigour, but because greater sunlight in the spring encourages more flowers to form on each cluster. This can be controlled by water stress at the right moment – but what might be an optimum yield in Australia's Margaret River or Chile's Central Valley might not be ideal in Bordeaux or Tuscany.

Now that great winemaking is global, we're all learning that no one country has all the answers.

RAINFALL PATTERNS

It's not just the amount of rainfall that matters, it's the pattern. Bordeaux gets most of its rain in winter, with enough from April to August to keep the vines happy, though slightly less from August to September would be better: not for nothing is one of the standard anti-mildew sprays known as Bordeaux mixture. In San Francisco the reverse is true: lack of summer rain means irrigation is necessary, as is the case for many Southern Hemisphere vineyards. Adelaide sees far less rain than Barcelona in summer, and although Santiago, Cape Town and Perth all have some rainy winter months, their all-important growing season is extremely dry.

SITING THE VINEYARD

So I'm a grower – I can choose the exact vines I want. I can survey the whole region to find the soil type that suits them. I can get all my meteorological data together, telling me precisely whether I've got a cool, warm or hot climate to contend with, and I can adjust my methods and aspirations accordingly. There's only one thing that's almost guaranteed to upset my most detailed calculations – the weather. The wretched, fickle, heartless weather. That's why, from bud-break to harvest, you can spot a winemaker by his furrowed brow and narrowed eyes. He's got stuck like that, from perpetually trying to see what's coming over the horizon.

Since I can't control the weather, I have to rely on a system of checks and balances to soften its extremes. In a cool climate, the problems are ones of frost, rain, wind and early autumns. For a start, let's be sure we have a south-facing slope. South-east and south-west are probably fine, too. But *not* north. But nothing is ever perfect, and each advantage quite often has an associated snag. For example, a supposedly ideal south-facing slope may be the warmest of all, great for ripening the grapes in a cool climate. But it will also

be where the snow melts first. In a harsh winter, snow actually keeps the ground relatively warm, and the sites which lose their protective covering of snow too early can then be exposed to damaging frost.

But planting vineyards on a slope has few disadvantages – except that they are more difficult, and therefore more expensive, to work. If I want to get twice as much sunlight onto my vines I have to plant them on a 26° (58 per cent) slope that faces the sun rather than on the flat. Conversely, if I am in a very hot climate, I can plant on an equivalent slope facing away from the sun, and get 50 per cent less sunlight. But if my slopes are so steep that I am forced to terrace them, then all my vines are effectively planted on flat land. In Portugal's Douro Valley, this isn't a problem – there's plenty of sunshine to go round – but in Germany, where every half-hour of sunshine counts, terraces are increasingly a thing of the past.

Woods near vineyards are also to be reckoned with. A good, thick wood can shelter vines from cold winds, but can also shade them from warming sunshine. A large expanse of water at the foot of a slope can reflect light back onto the vines. Conveniently, this effect is

Burgundy's Le Montrachet could contest the title of World's greatest white vineyard, and it's just this little patch of land sloping down to the wall. Beyond the wall is Bâtard-Montrachet – nearly as good – and beyond that is the flatter Puligny-Montrachet – not nearly as good – all in the space of a few hundred metres.

SOLVING THE CLIMATE PROBLEM
Two very different problems nature poses are the risk of frost and the lack of water. Many marginal ripening areas run the risk of spring frosts destroying the vinebuds. One way to combat these is to operate heaters known as smudge pots on days and nights when frost threatens. These are at Nevis Bluff in New Zealand's Central Otago – the world's southernmost wine region. Mountadam estate (far right) is in the very dry Barossa Ranges in South Australia. All winter rain has to be collected into reservoirs which provide irrigation water during the growing season, without which it would be impossible to establish a vineyard.

CHOOSING A SITE

SEA
Cold coastal currents can often cause temperature inversions which lead to fogs, as in San Francisco.

COAST
The area next to the coast will usually get more rain due to moisture-laden maritime breezes. However, there are dry zones on the west coasts of America, Africa and Australia.

RIVERS AND LAKES
Water stores heat, thereby raising the temperature of the surrounding area, as well as reflecting sunshine onto nearby slopes.

TOWN
A group of buildings warms the air and helps keep the valley frost-free.

ASPECT TO SUN
Because of the inclination of the earth, south-facing slopes in the northern hemisphere and north-facing slopes in the southern hemisphere will receive more direct sunshine than others.

SLOPE ANGLE
An adequate slope is needed to gain the most benefit from the sunshine and to encourage good air circulation which prevents frosts and fogs.

SHELTER
Wooded hills shelter the vines from winds.

most marked when the sun is low (in the spring and autumn), extending the growing season by a crucial few extra weeks. But water doesn't just reflect heat: as the sun heats up the earth, very useful cooling breezes come off the water. As for the sea, the Gulf Stream warms all France's west coast, including Bordeaux, while the Pacific acts as a massive air conditioner in California, Chile, Australia and New Zealand, pushing cold air far inland to regions that otherwise would be way too hot. I should remember, too, that while I may want the long ripening season given by the early springs and late autumns of a lower latitude, I may not want the high temperatures that go with it. At higher latitudes I lose the heat and the long growing season, but I gain daylight hours, so what I lose in warmth I gain in photosynthesis – which itself speeds ripening.

IDEAL VINEYARD SITES

There is no such thing as a vineyard that can excel at everything. Many big commercial vineyards in the New World prove that they are reasonable at most things, but excellence is usually very site specific, and it is usually only one or two vine varieties that shine. The Mosel Valley in Germany is cold, windswept and situated so far north hardly any grape variety will ripen there. Except one. The cold-resistant, cool-climate-loving Riesling. But even then, the site has to be exceptional. The Urziger Würzgarten site is dizzily steep, angled south and composed of a mixture of red sandstone and heat–retaining red slate. Add in the reflected warmth from the river and the result is a superb site. For Riesling. There's no point planting Syrah or Cabernet here. They wouldn't ripen.

On the other hand, there would be no point planting Riesling on the Gimblett Gravels in Hawkes Bay, New Zealand, because despite being a cool area, it's too warm for Riesling. Most of Hawkes Bay, except for Gimblett Gravels, is too cool and wet for Cabernet and Syrah. In an area that frequently has its vintage diluted and delayed by autumnal rains, the Gimblett Gravels provide some of the most free-draining conditions of any vineyard in the world as well as extra warmth. Cabernet and Syrah can ripen here virtually every year. As soon as you step off the gravels into clay, they can't.

TWO CONTRASTING VINEYARDS
Far left: The steep Urziger Würzgarten vineyard slopes down to the river Mosel in Germany. Believe it or not, there are steeper vineyards than this in the Mosel, but not many that are warmer. Riesling has been grown on this site for hundreds of years.
Left: In contrast, there were no vines at all in the Gimblett Gravels area of Hawkes Bay in New Zealand until the 1980s. Most parts of Hawkes Bay are too cool and wet to fully ripen varieties like Cabernet and Merlot, but the warm, free-draining Gimblett Gravels speed maturing sufficiently to ripen the crop.

HILLTOP

In a cool climate this may be too cold for vines.

SHADED HILLSIDE

The side of the hill facing away from the sun may, in a cool climate, be too cold to make good wine. In a hot climate it may be ideal.

INLAND

Rainfall is lower inland, particularly if there is a coastal range of hills nearby forming a rain-shadow. The climate is likely to be one of hotter summers and colder winters.

VALLEY

Frost will occur on the valley floor, and valley winds may also be a problem.

WIND-BREAK

A line of trees acts as an effective barrier to winds.

EXPOSED PLATEAU

This land is too windy for growing vines.

FLAT VALLEY LAND

On flat valley floors the soil is often too clayey and poorly drained for fine wines. However, these conditions may be overcome, as in the Napa Valley, California.

THE IMPORTANCE OF SOIL

The stony soils of Stoneleigh Vineyard in the Wairau River valley of Marlborough, on South Island, New Zealand. These free-draining soils contribute significantly to the intense flavour of the local white wines.

MY VIEW ON WHAT SOIL contributes to a wine is going to depend to a large extent upon whether I was brought up with an Old or New World wine philosophy. So, let's say I come from California. I used to think soil just held the vine upright; to me it was the climate that mattered. Now I'm coming round to the idea of 'dirt'. It's obvious now that there has to be a synergy between grape variety and place, and that the soil structure affects the development of the root system, which in turn affects flavour. I do soil analyses now before I plant, and I dig holes to look at root spread. And I'm in love with my land. You see how the slope just falls away on that hillside vineyard over there? It's the most beautiful thing. And there's a breeze there every afternoon when there won't be one anywhere else. The French call this whole soil and climate thing 'terroir'. And sure it matters. But only so that I get the best fruit that I can to then craft into the ultimate wine. *My* ultimate wine.

On the other hand I'm an Old World grower – perhaps from Alsace in France. I grow Riesling and Gewürztraminer in several Grand Cru sites, and the wines taste different from each vineyard. If I were to take up an extreme position I would say that you should be able to reconstruct the geology of the vineyard from the taste of the wine; that I want you to taste the *terroir* in the wine, and not even the grape variety or (God forbid) the winemaker's personality.

These positions may sound extreme, but the New World one in particular has softened significantly in the last few years, and many winemakers now point out qualities that soils give their wines. But the idea of *terroir* winning out over grape flavour is largely confined to France. They invented the concept; they're unwilling to let go.

But one thing we can agree upon is drainage. How dull. But how fundamental. You see, a well-drained soil is a warm soil, and a wet soil is a cold one. It's the temperature of the soil, much more than that of the air, that decides when a vine is going to start budding in

the spring – and that's one of the factors that decides what vines can be planted where. Soil temperature also influences a wine's acidity: cold soils give more acidic wines, since heat burns off acidity.

A well-drained soil has bigger particles. There are four basic particle sizes: coarse sand, fine sand, silt and clay. Gravel and stones, of course, are bigger still; there, water pours through very quickly, but essential nutrients are washed away and it must be fertilized before it will bear decent fruit. At the other end of the scale is clay, with particles of 0.002mm or less in diameter. Heavy clay can hold water so tightly that a vine can't get at it. Well-drained, warm gravelly soil can make more water available to the vine than a wet clay one. So in areas of heavy rain, like Bordeaux, well-drained gravelly soil has advantages over non-draining clay. Until there's a drought, you say. Well, even then a gravelly soil can be better. In poor soils (and stony soil with big particles is poor soil) the vine's roots have to plunge deeper so that in a hot, dry summer they are more likely to be able to find moisture; vines whose roots are mostly within the first metre of soil are far more likely to suffer in droughts.

But I'd hate to give you the idea that one type of soil is automatically better than another; soils that heat up quickly in the spring also get colder in the winter, and are more affected by frost; in hot climates they can reflect too much heat onto the grapes, and burn them. Small amounts of organic matter in the soil, be it gravelly or clay soil, can also help to even out water availability. And a cold clay soil can not only help to hold back an early-ripening vine, like Merlot, it can give the wine more structure and solidity, too.

Then there's the question of pH. Alkaline soils, with a pH of seven or more, tend to be young soils. They are high in calcium, from shells left behind when the sea receded, and they tend to produce wines high in acidity. Champagne's soil is like this. There's a lot of alkaline soil in Europe. But the New World, particularly

CASE STUDY OF A VINEYARD

There is no single soil type that is ideal for wine. And to prove it, many different soils have proved themselves perfect for particular grape varieties in particular climates. So acidic granite produces great Syrah in Hermitage and the best Gamay in Beaujolais; limestone seems to suit Chardonnay in many places, including Champagne, Chablis and the Côte d'Or; and the rich grey-blue marl of Barolo retains water and is cold – ideal for the longer, slower ripening of Nebbiolo in a warm climate. Schist can give rich, spicy reds in the Rhône's Côte-Rôtie and Portugal's Douro Valley. Clay soil reduces bouquet but gives structure to a wine, so in Alsace it is favoured for the broader, more aromatic grape varieties like Gewürztraminer, rather than for the more subtle Riesling. In Germany's Mosel Valley, steep slate slopes impart a haunting beauty to Riesling wines. However, the warm, black basalt soils of Forst and Deidesheim in the Pfalz provide Rieslings that are far more exotic and fleshy.

Clockwise, from top left: 1. *Clay is not considered the best soil for growing vines. The small flat clay particles fit together closely, keeping water locked between them, and surface water tends to stagnate. One of the only advantages of a clay soil is that in a hot region it can hold enough water to sustain the vine right through a long, dry summer. This recently ploughed clay soil in Slovenia glistens with moisture in the sun.*
2. *The Mosel Valley's dark slate soil absorbs heat and helps the Riesling to ripen in a cool climate. In a hot climate, it could reduce acidity, but here in the Brauneberger Juffer Sonnenuhr vineyard it aids ripening and adds a minerality to the flavour.*
3. *Chalk soil is able to hold good amounts of water which is then released to the vine during the summer. Here in Jerez in southern Spain this is important because winters are usually wet, while summers are blisteringly hot and dry.*
4. *There doesn't seem to be any soil at all in these Grenache vineyards of Château de Beaucastel in Châteauneuf-du-Pape in southern France. On the surface there isn't. Instead, you have round stones called* galets *that absorb heat during the day and then release it after dusk, pushing the grapes to super-ripeness.*

Australia, has older soils and the pH may be pretty neutral, though old rocky soils can be acidic. California's Napa Valley is generally more acidic than the young alluvial gravel of Bordeaux. The wines of Napa are thus less acidic than those of Bordeaux.

So can soil affect the flavour of the wine? Yes. Stonier soils give lighter, more perfumed wines; richer soils with more clay give more solid wines. But what about particular 'mineral' flavours? Elsewhere in this Atlas, I talk about the specific smoky tang that Riesling acquires on slate soil. It's not imagination: I could pick it out for you, blind. And, although it's true that only a minute percentage of the ions from the minerals and trace elements assimilated by the vine from the soil will find their way into the finished wine, it is also true that the same grape grown by my Alsace friend on different soils will taste different. At least, it will if he keeps yields down and encourages his vines to root deep into the bedrock. Because the influence of soil on wine is most noticeable when yields are low, where the climate is marginal, and where vines are deeply rooted.

On this last point my Alsace friend will be especially vociferous. He'll stress that the right sort of viticulture for the first five years of a vine's life – dense planting and ploughing to cut the surface roots – will force the roots to search deep, down below the topsoil. That, they say, is the only way to get an expression of *terroir* into the wine, and if you don't work the right way in the first five years you've had it, because the root system will be established, and no matter what you do in later years, you will never get a *terroir* wine.

But back to California: yes, these days I want to make a *terroir* wine, but I want Merlot plus *terroir*, or Cabernet plus *terroir*; I don't want *terroir* expressed through Merlot or Cabernet, with the grape variety as a sort of neutral vector. Because at the end of the day I'm Californian, and Californian wines taste first and foremost of fruit. I suppose you could say I'm a product of my *terroir*. How's that?

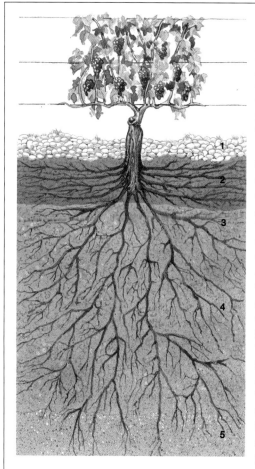

BELOW THE VINE

1. STONES
Pebbles and stones lying on the surface help to retain heat within the topsoil. They also reflect sunlight, and therefore warmth, back onto the vines.

2. TOPSOIL
This is the main root zone, and is about 15–30cm (6–12in) thick in most soils. Topsoil is formed from a mix of weathered bedrock, organic matter from decaying plants and animals, and fertilizers.

3. SUBSOIL
This is pure, weathered bedrock, which lays the foundations for the all-important tap roots that stabilize the vine.

4. BEDROCK or PARENT MATERIAL
The bedrock is the underlying geology. Since soils are formed from broken-down and weathered rock, the bedrock has a great influence on the characteristics of a soil. The bedrock can only be used by roots if it is well-pored or fissured.

5. WATER TABLE
The water table is the level beneath which the rock is saturated with ground-water. If it is only a few yards from the surface, it can serve as a good source of water for a vine, provided it is not stagnant.

GLOSSARY OF COMMON VINEYARD SOIL TERMS

Acid soil A soil with a low pH value. These soils tend to occur mostly in wetter climates where high rainfall leaches the calcium out of the soil. The rootstock and vine variety can be chosen for their sympathy with soil pH values.

Alkaline soil A soil with a high pH value, often due to the presence of calcium (see Calcareous soil) or salt.

Alluvial deposits (alluvium) Materials deposited from rivers, usually gravels, sands and silts, such as are found in the Graves area of Bordeaux and Marlborough in New Zealand.

Basalt soil A warm dark, fertile soil, formed from volcanic rock. It is usually alkaline, being rich in calcium and sodium.

Calcareous soil A soil with a high calcium content, which comes from a limestone geology. Chalk is a form of limestone. It has a high pH (alkaline) and usually has good aeration, drainage and structure. Many vines do well when grown on a calcium-rich soil, particularly the Chardonnay grape, as in Chablis and parts of the Côte d'Or.

Chalk A form of limestone with a characteristic white or pale colour and alkaline pH (see Calcareous soil and Limestone). It has proved good for vines growing in cooler and wetter climates, such as the Champagne region of France.

Clay The smallest size of soil particle. Soils rich in clay particles are usually cold and acidic with poor drainage, and can have a tendency to waterlogging.

Colluvial deposits (colluvium) Weathered rock and soil debris which have slid down slopes and been deposited at a lower level.

Gravel The French word for gravel, *graves*, has given its name to the Graves area of Bordeaux. Pebbles covering the ground retain heat and are freely drained.

Granite An igneous rock whose crystals are large enough to be seen with the naked eye. It can form rock masses which reflect the sun's heat, such as the hill of Hermitage.

Limestone Sedimentary rock made of calcite (calcium carbonate), typically pale in colour and with a high pH. Chalk (see Calcareous soil) is a form of limestone.

Loam A usually fertile soil, which is composed of equal proportions of clay, silt and sand particles.

Loess A layer of wind-blown silt that covers the topsoil.

Marl A sedimentary mixture of clay and limestone. Some marl contains more clay than limestone; some contains more limestone than clay.

Organic matter Humus, which is derived from living organisms, usually plants and fallen leaves, and manure.

pH A measure of acidity or alkalinity. The lower a soil's pH number, the more acidic it is. Soils that have a pH number above seven are alkaline.

Sand Large, granular soil particles, which are made up of weathered rock and quartz. A soil that contains a large proportion of sand is warm and drains freely, but is poor in nutrients and somewhat acidic.

Schist Coarsely grained, crystalline rock, which retains heat and crumbles easily. Rich in potassium and magnesium, but low in organic nutrients, it occurs most notably in Portugal's Douro Valley.

Scree The slope of debris found at the bottom of a cliff which has fallen due to erosion and weathering. It consists of various-sized fragments of rock and is usually steep.

Silt With particles larger than clay but smaller than sand, silt holds water well and is relatively fertile, as is the case in the Napa Valley.

Slate A hard rock formed from shales and clays put under great pressure. Its heat-retaining qualities provide an excellent environment for vines, sometimes passing on metallic flavours, as in the Bernkastel wines that are produced in Germany's Mosel Valley.

Terra rossa When the calcium is leached out of limestone, it can form a reddish soil, the staining coming from dehydrated iron compounds. It is usually associated with Mediterranean climates, which have very dry summers and wet winters that enable the leaching and hydrating processes to occur. However, its most famous manifestation is in the Coonawarra region in South Australia.

THE IMPACT OF WATER

Irrigation systems were in place in South America long before the arrival of Europeans. The Incas were experts at it and, by the 16th century, somewhere like Mendoza in Argentina was already using Andes snow-melt water for irrigation. With water so plentiful, most vineyards in Mendoza, like these at Trapiche, still follow the old method of channeling river water between the rows, literally flooding the vineyard.

I<small>T'S THE HOT TOPIC</small> of the 21st century: something so fundamental to life – and for most of us, so readily available – that we've tended to take it for granted. The factors that determined where vineyards were planted were principally soil and climate and, historically, ease of transport to centres of population – in other words, the wine-drinkers. Water didn't come into it. In Europe vines relied on rainfall, and viticultural techniques were adapted to whether rain was too plentiful or too scarce. Irrigation wasn't allowed, except for experimental vineyards or for getting young vines established.

In New World countries, where rainfall patterns do not follow the European model and where there is no such thing as a blanket ban on irrigation, if you could water your vines, you did. Even in Australia's Barossa Valley, where dry farming is the tradition, in the past you irrigated your young vines by hand until they were established enough to survive without irrigation. In Chile, you took advantage of snow-melt water pouring off the Andes in spring to get you through an otherwise impossibly dry summer. Modern techniques of computer-controlled irrigation have refined matters even further. The fact is that, today, very few of us doubt the assumption that if we want water, we can have it. We take it for granted.

This is a very complacent and comfortable picture compared with what might be the scenario in the future. We all know that the globe is warming up, and that there will be more rain for some and less for others. We also know that the world's population is increasing, and what that means is greater demand for water – not just for growing food, but for washing cars and watering golf courses, too. And while vines are relatively low users of water –

cotton and rice, for example, use around 35 per cent more, and growers in Chile's Casablanca Valley might use one litre per second to irrigate 5 hectares, while grass for cattle needs more like 1 litre per second for half a hectare – wine production worldwide is rising. If you live in California or Australia, having a vineyard near you won't affect your ability to fill your swimming pool – people take priority over vines any day. But if you want to plant a vineyard in California or Australia, the proximity of lots of houses may well affect your ability to get water rights for your vines. And in Europe, the hard line on irrigation taken by the EU is softening: irrigation is creeping into Italy, Spain, Portugal and just about everywhere else that needs a quick aqueous top-up once in a while.

Getting permission to irrigate in Europe is no longer that difficult. If a region petitions the authorities, they are unlikely to say no. Getting the water itself might, however, be trickier: all Portugal's water comes from Spain, for example, and while agreements are in place to ensure that both sides are happy, some Portuguese are pretty cynical about what might happen if push came to shove. In Spain, water is already short in Cataluña, and there is talk of diverting water from France.

In California, water availability is less of a limiting factor on planting vineyards than other environmental issues, like land use and development, and even the cutting down of oak trees and the health and happiness of endangered species. But the United States certainly has water problems, and they are not going to go away. In the south-west of the USA, there are huge aquifers filled with water from rainier periods in the globe's history, but these reserves are now being drained much faster than they are being refilled. There are plans to buy water from Canada; theoretically, Canada

BUYING WATER IN THE BAROSSA

Martin and Sally Pfeiffer are lucky: salinity on their Barossa vineyard, Whistler Wines, is far less serious than in some parts of the Valley and, in addition, they've managed to organize a water supply generous enough to allow for some future expansion of plantings. Even so, they've had to keep pace with a changing situation. When they bought the land back in 1982, not only did it come with a small stock dam already in place, but the Valley had no water licensing requirements at all. These days you can neither sink a bore nor dig a dam without a licence – these requirements came into effect in the mid-1990s – and if you want more water than nature can provide you'll need to be a member (which means being a shareholder) in a private water scheme called Barossa Infrastructure Ltd, or BIL.

The Pfeiffers' property covers 32ha (80 acres) and so far they've planted 13ha (32 acres). Any further expansion will incur extra costs. 'A pump shed and automation control cost us A$25,000. Then there's another A$25,000 for installing and supplying water for every 10 acres of vineyard. We installed a 10-megalitre [1 megalitre = 1,000,000 litres] storage dam with a Water Resources licence through the BIL scheme, and that dam cost A$20,000. Then there's the A$100,000 for costs for BIL capital, which is spread over 15 years, so that works out at A$6666 per year. In addition, there's the A$10,000 per year water usage charge for BIL water.'

So where does the BIL water come from? 'From the River Murray, which is some 80km away to the east,' says Martin. 'The company has leased water rights to access this water and, in future, it may purchase the rights.' BIL has an agreement with the state water company, SA Water, which allows it to fill a reservoir in the winter, and supply it to shareholders in the summer when the vines need it. The Pfeiffers'

membership of the BIL scheme entitles them to 10 megalitres of premium water, which is available all year round, and 10 megalitres of off-peak water, which is available only from April to October. They use the slightly cheaper off-peak water to fill the dam.

As for how much water is dripped on to the vines throughout the hot Barossa summer – well, the Pfeiffers say they normally apply around 0.5–0.75 megalitres per hectare per year for red grapes, and 1–1.5 megalitres for whites. 'Our water usage has not reduced yet, because the vines are only young and establishing deep root systems,' says Martin. 'In future years we'll be looking to reduce. But we've set aside about 20 per cent of the Shiraz to be dry grown with no irrigation, and we'll be looking to produce a Reserve Whistler Shiraz from the 2002 vintage.'

But as always in the Barossa, there's the question of salinity. 'It's not so bad on my property,' says Martin, 'because vines and supplementary watering are relatively new to the land. But I do have some effects, particularly in the Merlot, which seems to be the most sodium- and choride-susceptible variety I have planted. Where I had difficulty establishing Merlot, I have planted salt-tolerant Ruggeri rootstock and grafted Merlot on to it.

'Salinity in groundwater varies dramatically depending on where your property is in the Barossa, and some areas within the Valley – mine, for example – have no or little groundwater. Salinity varies from 100–3500 parts per million (ppm), averaging around 1000–1200 ppm. At above 2000ppm you can see surface crusting. But even moderate salinity can reduce yields by 20 to 30 per cent – in badly affected areas vines can even die – and with salt levels slowly rising, it was important for us to have access to supplementary water.'

opposes these plans, but at the time of writing this opposition seems less than determined.

Pretty well wherever you are, if you want to take water from a river, or any source except your own rain-filled dam, you need permission. In Australia, for example, you cannot plant a vineyard unless you have previously bought a water licence, and inevitably there's a price tag attached: between A$400 and A$4000 per hectare, depending on region. Water rights can be traded, too: the cost of this is relatively low for the moment, at around A$5000 per megalitre. The infrastructure of irrigation – the pumps, pipes and so on – is more expensive, amounting to about A$10,000 per hectare. In Australia millions of hectares of land are suitable for vines, but if you can't get water rights or water then you might as well forget it.

No wonder people go to extreme lengths when they see a piece of land they just know would be great for wine: when Chilean company Errázuriz found a must-have site for new vines, it pumped water from 5km (3miles) away.

NOT ALL WATER IS GOOD WATER

Water availability is, however, only part of the problem. Water quality, especially in Australia, is just as important. Australia's problem is salinity. Not all of Australia suffers in the same way: the Murray basin is the worst affected, but for 'Murray basin' read 'much of South-East Australia'. (And where does most of Australia's wine come from? Correct. South-East Australia.) If you take a look at the map on page 287, you'll see that the Murray rises in the far south-eastern corner of the country and flows more or less north-west before changing its mind and draining into the sea south-east of Adelaide. The Murray provides most of the irrigation water for Australia's vineyards. Right now, the Murray is carrying 18.1 tonnes of salt to the sea every five minutes. Per day, that's 5212 tonnes of salt. That's just what reaches the sea. Far more is being drawn off by the irrigation pumps every single day.

Much of the Australian landmass was once an inland sea, and the water table is naturally saline. Clearance of the native trees, which grew in profusion before the first European settlers arrived, allowed the water table to rise. And, as always, we only properly understood the problem once it was too late to go back.

It was between World Wars One and Two that much of the damage was done. Huge areas of land were made available to 'soldier settlers' returning to a depressed economy – and there were government incentives to encourage them to clear it for pasture and arable farming. Well, once the scrub and forest were cleared, the topsoil simply blew away: billowing clouds of dust would hang for days over Melbourne, literally hundreds of miles away from land that had been cleared up the Murray River.

And while Melbourne was coughing and spluttering and complaining about the state of its washing, back up the Murray, the saline water table was quietly creeping upwards.

Vines don't like salt. At salt concentrations of over 1200 parts per million they suffer stress, though some rootstocks, notably Ramsey and Dog Ridge, are more salt-resistant. Roots, however, are generally less affected by salt than leaves, so irrigating vines using drip irrigation, which goes straight to the roots, is much kinder and safer than applying salty water by sprinkler, which wets the leaves and quickly leads to defoliation. Australia's relentless and vital search to find ways of coping with poor water quality is the main reason that its irrigation techniques are so advanced.

There are remedies for salinity: planting native trees is one; the carrying away of salty drainage water from below the roots is another. Reverse osmosis, a technique that takes salt out of water,

is used in the Middle East but is hugely expensive. The trouble is, vines exacerbate the problem since they suck the water out of the soil and leave the salt behind, resulting in the build-up of salt.

But planting indigenous species – often the scrubby Mallee gums – means waiting for nature to do the job for you and push the salty water down beyond the reach of vines and other crops. And that's a very slow process indeed. In the past 15 to 20 years, the federal government has invested millions of dollars in reafforestation schemes, with varying degrees of success. The cheapest option of all is to wait for rain. Heavy rain will at least flush out the Murray and dilute the salt in your own dam; you can then give your vines lots of water while the quality is high, and later revert to your normal policy of giving them only enough to keep them alive.

Since grapes are such a high-value crop, producers can take their own measures and justify them economically. But in some cases wheat and sheep farmers are simply having to abandon their land – the problem is that serious. At the moment, 2.5 million ha (6.2 million acres) of Australia are already wrecked by excessive salinity. That sounds a lot. Well, it is: it's considerably larger than Wales, slightly smaller than Albania. And I can sort of hear you saying, 'well, it's not that big, then.' OK. Projections are that by the middle of this century, 15.5 million ha (38.3 million acres) of Australia will be lost to salt. That's considerably bigger than England. That's bigger than Greece; bigger than New York State, or the states of Georgia or Illinois. Does that sound serious enough?

Salinity can be a problem in other places as well, including the South of France and even parts of Chile, where water quality is normally very good. And in Penedès on Spain's Mediterranean coast, there's a town – called Sitges (if you're thinking of visiting) – where even the tap water is salty. Just don't make tea with it.

Australia's greatest river, right in the heart of the vineyard area at Renmark, South Australia. The Murray mops up all the water from the west side of the Great Dividing Range and then begins its extremely languid and serpentine route of 2600km (1616 miles) until it reaches the sea, south of Adelaide. By that time it hasn't got much water left, because it's all been extracted for irrigation. Well over half the vineyards in Australia rely upon the Murray and its tributaries, the Lachlan and the Murrumbidgee, for their water. Without the rivers, there would be no modern Australian wine industry.

THE MODERN VINEYARD

You can't get much more modern than this – the striking new Sileni winery in Hawkes Bay, North Island, New Zealand. In the foreground, young wines have just been planted for the first time in the virgin soil.

THIS IS THE MOMENT OF DECISION for the grape grower. He has picked the most favourable spot the landscape has to offer; he has analysed the soil and observed the climate. He has decided which vine varieties will cope best with both. Now he must plant. But before he can put a single vine in the soil, there is one more thing he must do. Virtually all the vines these days are grafted on to phylloxera-resistant rootstock, to protect them from one of the most devastating of all vine pests. But because the rootstock comes from a different vine species, it throws another element into the equation. He must choose a rootstock that is compatible with the soil, the climate and with his vines: some are more vigorous than others, some are more resistant to drought or cold and so on. So his choice of rootstock will affect the style and quality of his wine.

Then he must decide how densely to plant his vines. Higher densities reduce the yield per vine – from 5000 vines per hectare (2000 per acre) up to 10,000 (4000) is common in Europe. Vines spaced more widely develop bigger (though not deeper) root systems, and larger canopies, and can thus ripen a larger crop per vine, which can be more appropriate to certain climates and soils: Californian and Australian growers often settle for 1100 to 1600 vines per hectare (450 to 650 per acre).

Pruning, training and canopy management are all aimed at making the vine produce the optimum-sized crop. In a cool climate on poor soil, for example, the vine can ripen fewer grapes than in a warm climate on deep, rich soil, so you should prune harder to reduce the number of fruiting buds. Then you train the vine in order to make it bear its bunches of grapes where you want them: partially exposed to the sun so that they'll ripen; with good air circulation so that they won't rot; high enough off the ground to avoid frost, or low enough to benefit from the heat stored in the soil.

1. Winter pruning is the grower's most effective way of controlling yield. Here at Château Margaux in Bordeaux the pruner removes the previous year's growth, leaving only enough buds to produce a strictly limited yield.

5. In cooler parts of the world, the risk of frost lasts right through springtime. In the coolest of all, you may even risk a pre-harvest frost, too. You can lose a whole year's crop in one cold snap. Here, smudge pots blaze in the pre-dawn chill at Torlesse, in Waipara, South Island, New Zealand.

VINE MANAGEMENT

This is now accepted as fundamental to the eventual quality of the wine. The aim is to nurture a healthy plant that will deliver a crop of healthy grapes at whatever quantity and quality level the grower desires, by choosing a highly productive or a less productive clone, and planting it on a vigorous or less vigorous rootstock. To create competition and reduce crop levels, the vines can be closely planted. On non-vigorous soils, such as the Médoc gravel banks, a simple training system will suffice. On fertile, productive soils, like most New Zealand vineyard sites, training the vine through different trellising and pruning methods can transform the quality of the fruit.

Double Guyot: This simple system is the most common one used in Bordeaux and involves training two canes along a wire, one to each side of the vine. The number of buds left on each cane after pruning will dictate the probable size of the crop.

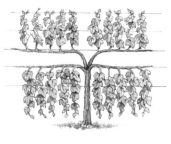

Scott Henry: Developed by an Oregon vineyard owner, this system is popular in the New World as it increases yields and ripeness. By training the canopy vertically, the fruit is exposed more effectively to sunlight and air circulation and the canopy area available for photosynthesis is increased.

9. Irrigation is essential in many hot, dry New World vineyards. It is especially important when establishing young vines like these ones at Cowra in New South Wales. The drip irrigation system is widely used nowadays – the amount of water can be controlled carefully as each vine has its own water supply.

13. At last the grapes are ripe and ready to be picked. Increasingly this is done by machine and here at the Graham Beck winery in Robertson, South Africa, a mechanical harvester brings in the Cabernet Sauvignon. Arguments rage as to whether or not machines are as good as human pickers.

2. Chip budding, making an incision in the existing vine, as here, and grafting into it a bud of the new variety, is the quickest way of transforming an inferior vine variety into a better one.

3. Virtually all vines are grafted on to phylloxera-resistant rootstock, to protect them from one of the most devastating of all vine pests. These young vines are now ready to plant.

4. You know that winter is coming to an end in California's Napa Valley when the vineyards erupt in a blaze of yellow wild mustard, which is then ploughed in to provide nutritious organic fertilizer.

6. Several of the most important estates in Burgundy are investigating organic methods of grape-growing. In the great Romanée-Conti vineyard in Vosne-Romanée, Côte de Nuits, phacelia is planted to cleanse the soil and rid it of nematodes.

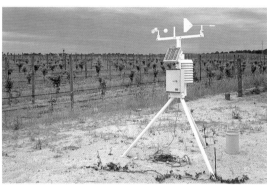

7. Predicting the weather is notoriously difficult, but collecting data on weather conditions can certainly help you make a more informed guess. This weather station is at Penfolds' new vineyards at Robe on the South Australia coast, west of Coonawarra.

8. There may be restrictions on new plantings in traditional countries like France, but in Australia, if you can find water, you can plant. New plantings at Brown Brothers' vineyard at Banksdale, Victoria, start to develop as the summer warms up.

10. One of the best ways to improve quality is to reduce the size of your crop by cutting off less ripe bunches. The time to do this is when the grapes change colour in midsummer. The best bunches change colour first, so you keep those and chop the others.

11. The Okanagan Valley in British Columbia is a cool region. Usually cool regions have quite enough moisture for the vine, but the Okanagan is almost desert-dry, so Cedar Creek are providing some overhead irrigation at their Cresta Ranch vineyard.

12. Once the grapes begin to ripen, the word rapidly spreads round the bird community. Flocks of birds can devastate a crop in a matter of hours, so Tuck's Ridge in Mornington Peninsula, Victoria, cover their vines with nets to keep the birds out.

14. Human pickers are definitely the preferred form of harvesting in Burgundy's top vineyards. Anne-Claude Leflaive, a top white winemaker, checks out the quality of the Chardonnay grapes from her Puligny-Montrachet Le Clavoillon vineyard.

15. These lads are happy. The sun's shining and the grapes are healthy, ripe – and harvested. Wineries often have contracts with growers for some of their grapes and here Peter Leske (right) of Nepenthe in the Adelaide Hills, South Australia, clearly approves of the Cabernet Sauvignon grown by Simon Green.

16. I can feel the damp chill in the air as the vines take a well-earned midwinter rest at Trittenheim in the Mosel Valley, Germany. A cold winter is important to allow the vine a dormant period and to destroy pests and infections in the vineyard.

GRAPES OF THE WORLD

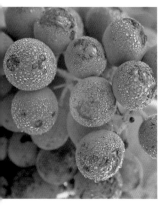

Most of the world's leading grapes end up with just one generally accepted name. However, the great Syrah or Shiraz grape has two names, Syrah being the French version and Shiraz the Australian one. Under either name it makes some of the world's most richly flavoured reds and the wines usually choose one name or the other, according to whether producers feel their style is restrained (Syrah) or rumbustious (Shiraz).

THERE ARE THOUSANDS AND THOUSANDS of grape varieties in the world. So why does it often feel as if you're being offered a choice of only Chardonnay or Cabernet Sauvignon when you buy a bottle of wine? How come those thousands sometimes seem to have been narrowed down to two? There are several answers. Most grape varieties are used for dessert grapes or raisins, or are rarely grown, or are the wrong species for winemaking. And of the 1000 or so varieties that are at all significant for wine, only about 30 have international relevance – which leaves hundreds of obscure, but possibly excellent, local varieties to be discovered by the adventurous wine drinker.

Virtually all those 1000 varieties are of the same species, *Vitis vinifera*, the species most people mean when they refer to wine vines. And yet *vinifera* is only one branch of the vine family; there are dozens of others growing in diverse climates all over the world, from the *Vitis amurensis* of Siberia to the *Vitis cariboa* of the tropics. They all produce grapes – indeed America's first settlers made wines from the native *Vitis labrusca*, *Vitis riparia* and *Vitis berlandieri*. The flavour of these wines has often been described as foxy, although a cross between hawthorn blossom and nail varnish might be more accurate.

You can still taste them in parts of North America, Austria and on Madeira. Some are OK – but you can see why *vinifera* won the day.

A few decades ago Chardonnay was seen as a Burgundian or Champagne grape; now it's grown in almost every wine region with aspirations. Such movements of vines are not new – merely faster than they used to be. Vine cuttings have been transported vast distances over the centuries. Missionaries took cuttings from Spain to the Americas. The Syrah of the Rhône and Australia (where it is called Shiraz) is believed to have come from Shiraz in Persia. And many of the vines we think of as Italian are, in fact, Greek in origin.

Why would people bother to take cuttings of a favourite variety to a country that probably already had plenty of its own vines? Because it has always been recognized that the crucial factor in the flavour of a wine is grape variety. Every grape has its own flavour, though most need specific climatic conditions to give their best. Thus Cabernet Sauvignon grown in too cold a climate produces thin, grassy wine; too hot and it risks being baked and raisiny. But when the worldwide movement of vines creates a chance combination of right vine, right climate and right soil, that's when classic wine styles are established.

CABERNET FRANC
To see this grape merely as Cabernet Sauvignon's less important sibling is to do it a disservice. It gives good, but not great, wines as a varietal (although it is the main grape by quite a long way in Château Cheval Blanc, which is about as great as red wine can get). But its value as a blending grape in Bordeaux is enormous, because it is less tannic and acidic than Cabernet Sauvignon on its own. It's an early ripener, so it also does well in the cool Loire Valley.

CABERNET SAUVIGNON
This is the world's most famous red grape because Bordeaux was the world's most famous red wine, and when local producers worldwide decided to improve their quality, they looked to Bordeaux for inspiration. Luckily Cabernet Sauvignon is up to the challenge and seems to relish travelling almost as much as nestling on the gravel banks of its spiritual home in Bordeaux's Médoc region. Thick-skinned and slow to ripen yet rot-resistant if caught by autumn rains, it will provide deep colour, reasonable tannin, a universally recognizable aroma and flavour of blackcurrants, black cherry and plum anywhere it is grown (except in the coolest and the very hottest sites). Cabernet Sauvignon has become a byword for full-flavoured, reliable red wine.

CHARDONNAY
The world's favourite white grape is so adaptable it makes everything from light, dry sparkling wine to sweet, botrytized dessert wine, but its dry, oak-aged incarnation, based on the great wines of Burgundy's Côte d'Or, is the best-known style, found from Chile to China, and from California to New South Wales. Clearly the vine is happy in a wide range of soils and climates though, as an early ripener, it buds early, which can be a problem in frost-prone regions like Chablis and Champagne. Otherwise, it is resistant to cold and yields well virtually anywhere. The wine has such an affinity with new oak (which adds a rich, spicy butteriness) that it can be easy to forget what its varietal flavour is. Unoaked, cool-climate Chardonnay is pale, appley and acidic; these flavours gradually soften towards melon and peach as the climate warms. Simple Chardonnays are made to be drunk young, and certainly most New World examples should not even be aged for a few years. But in Burgundy, Chardonnay makes one of the most long-lived of all white wines.

CHENIN BLANC
This versatile white grape is capable of producing wines that are dry or sweet, still or sparkling, and for drinking now or for cellaring for a decade or more. However, it has yet to reach great heights away from the Loire Valley in France. Here, on chalky soils and in distinctly cool climates, it can produce some of the most individual wines to be found anywhere in the world. In both dry and sweet styles, all highly acidic when young, these wines can, and should, be put away for years. In New Zealand and Western Australia some delicious dry examples are surfacing, and in South Africa a few adventurous growers are also starting to take the grape seriously.

GEWÜRZTRAMINER
The name means 'spicy Traminer' and that spice is a smell of roses, lychees, sometimes mangoes, often with a dab of cold cream and a dusting of ginger – a nose that, as you might guess, wants plenty of acidity on the palate. But Gewürztraminer can lack acidity, and needs a cool climate to keep a tendency to high sugar levels in check. At its best in Alsace, followed by New Zealand and Italy's Alto Adige, the vine buds early and is susceptible to frosts. But if it survives these and is then affected by noble rot in a warm autumn, superb sweet wines can result.

GRENACHE NOIR
Varietal Grenache used to be very rare, yet this variety covers mile upon mile of vineyards in Spain (where it's called Garnacha Tinta), the South of France, California and parts of Australia. It is still mostly a blending grape: in Rioja and Navarra in Spain, its burly fruit fills out the rather more restrained Tempranillo. Throughout southern France, but especially in the southern Rhône, its high strength and juicy, peppery character is crucial in many blends, notably Châteauneuf-du-Pape. But in Australia growers are rediscovering old vineyards of dry-farmed Grenache and making superb deep wines, and Garnacha dominates the blend in Spain's Priorat, producing super-rich monsters full of tar and figs.

MALBEC
This vine is now associated largely with Argentina, where it makes lush, damsony, violet-scented wines. Its homeland was Bordeaux, where its job was primarily to soften Cabernet Sauvignon. In Cahors' drier, hotter vineyards, Malbec (here known as Cot or Auxerrois) can produce deep, damsony wine that becomes dark and tobacco-scented with age. Chile and Australia do well with Malbec.

MERLOT
This red grape, with its rich, plummy fruit, its fondness for oak-aging and its tendency to mature in bottle relatively quickly, is a natural partner for Cabernet Sauvignon. But bottling it on its own and writing 'Merlot' on the label is currently the fastest way to sell a bottle of red wine. It has become so fashionable simply because it's so easy to drink: it is supple, luscious, low in

COMPOSITION OF A GRAPE

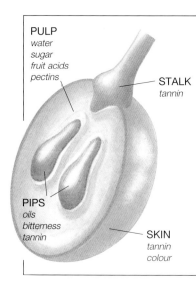

PULP
water
sugar
fruit acids
pectins

STALK
tannin

PIPS
oils
bitterness
tannin

SKIN
tannin
colour

When it comes to imparting flavour to its wine, the actual juice of the grape rarely has very much to offer. Muscat juice is sweet and perfumed – that's why we eat Muscat grapes as well as make wine from them – but most of the great wine grapes of the world are no fun at all to eat. At best, a ripe wine grape has a sugary, neutral-flavoured, colourless pulp. Much of the character of a wine comes from its skin. As the grape ripens, the skin matures: its tannins become less aggressive, its colour deepens and all the perfume and flavour components build up. The trick is to try to ripen the grape so that sugar, acid, tannin, colour and flavour are all in balance at the time it is harvested. Both the pips and the stalks are very bitter, which is why modern winemakers usually de-stalk the grapes and avoid crushing the pips.

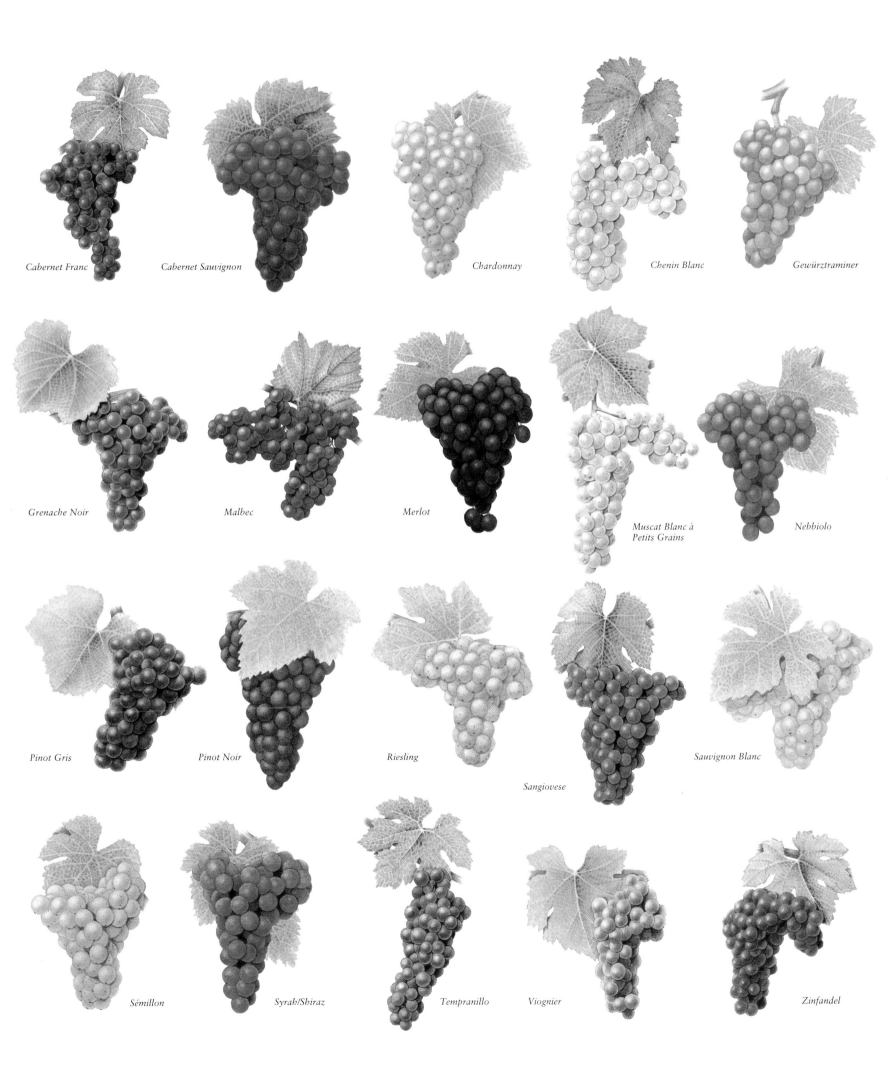

Cabernet Franc

Cabernet Sauvignon

Chardonnay

Chenin Blanc

Gewürztraminer

Grenache Noir

Malbec

Merlot

Muscat Blanc à
Petits Grains

Nebbiolo

Pinot Gris

Pinot Noir

Riesling

Sangiovese

Sauvignon Blanc

Sémillon

Syrah/Shiraz

Tempranillo

Viognier

Zinfandel

Sangiovese grapes in Errázuriz's Las Vertientes vineyard in the Aconcagua Valley. These are the first plantings of the variety in Chile and signs are promising.

tannin and dark in colour – red wine without tears. With Cabernet Sauvignon it forms the basis of the Bordeaux blend, and all around the world where the Bordeaux red-wine model has been copied, Merlot has been planted. But it can ripen almost too quickly in hot climates and give too much crop in fertile soils. On its own, it can be found almost everywhere: north-eastern Italy, southern France, Hungary, California, Chile, New York and Washington states, and in New Zealand and Australia.

MUSCAT BLANC À PETITS GRAINS
The aristocrat of the Muscats, this low-yielder is prone to mutation, but makes intensely grapy wines of more delicacy and elegance than any of its cousins. It comes in all colours from white to brownish red, and can make fortifieds the colour of burnt toffee, but is seldom red enough to make a proper red wine. It is scattered throughout France (especially in the *vins doux naturels* of Roussillon and the Rhône, and the fragrant, dry wine of Alsace) and Italy, where it creates Asti and scented wines in the Alto Adige. In Australia and Greece, it makes intense, fortified wines.

NEBBIOLO
I always hear a shrug of resignation in this name. Why? Probably because it comes from *nebbia*, the Italian word for fog. I imagine those north-western Italian winemakers of centuries back shaking their heads over their late-ripening vine and indulgently naming it after the fog that was invariably around when they picked in late October. Today, growers plant Nebbiolo high up the slopes, so it can make the most of autumn sunshine. And it can make the most sensational wines. Barolo and Barbaresco are the stars: strange and unyielding yet richly fragrant; tannic yet pale; bullish but perfumed with violets. Nebbiolo is attracting attention in Australia, but finding ideal sites is proving tricky.

PINOT GRIS
Some of Europe's most exotic white wines ooze from this grape in Alsace, Germany and Hungary. Yet cross the Alps and you'll find northern Italy producing oceans of light, innocuous and rather pricy dry whites without the unctuous honey and raisin richness that is so exciting further north. It's all to do with yields and attitude: Italians view white wine as a palate cleanser; northern Europeans see it as their chance for vinous glory and coax every ounce of character they can from grapes like Pinot Gris. High in extract and sugar yet low in acidity, it shouldn't age, but it does – brilliantly. You'll find a few patches of it in

Burgundy, and a good deal in Romania, Oregon and New Zealand.

PINOT NOIR
If you're a grower, this is the most tantalizing of all vines – and the most disobliging, the most unforgiving and yet the most rewarding. This red vine likes a cool climate but, because it buds and ripens early, is highly susceptible to spring frosts, while in too hot a region it just produces solid, baked-tasting or flabby wines. So why plant it? Because when you get it just right – as the best growers in Burgundy's Côte d'Or often do – the wines are sensual, fragrant, silky yet slightly savage, not so much intellectually impressive as unforgettably pleasurable. Planted worldwide, until recently Pinot Noir has strongly resisted attempts to create great flavours. Now exciting reds are appearing from California and Oregon, Chile, South Africa, Australia and New Zealand, thrillingly different from anything produced in Burgundy. Germany has some in a more Burgundian mould; Switzerland and Italy seldom hit the mark. And if it doesn't ripen, it can be used for fizz, as usually happens in Champagne.

RIESLING
This marvellous grape deserves a better deal. Responsible for some of the most heavenly, aristocratic and elegant wines, and grown under tortuous conditions, it is nonetheless disdained and dismissed throughout most of the world. Yet in the Mosel and Rhine Valleys of Germany, stunning results are achieved by growers prepared to limit yield and caress the grapes to ripeness. Water-white wines as fleeting as gossamer share honours with sweet wines of such intensity as to strike the most babble-mouthed drinker dumb. This cold-resistant, late-ripening vine is also a superb performer elsewhere. Austria produces wonderful Riesling, and both Alsace and Australia make superb examples quite unlike those of Germany and completely unlike each other. Italy and Eastern Europe could and sometimes do make good ones. In the US, the Pacific North-West and New York State both have some decent stuff, and New Zealand is home to a few stunners.

SANGIOVESE
The workhorse red grape of Tuscany, Sangiovese also plays a part further south in Italy as well as north in Emilia-Romagna, where it produces oceans of light red wine for the trenchermen of Bologna. However, Tuscany is Sangiovese's heartland and, in various clonal manifestations, it is the main grape of Chianti and Vino Nobile di Montepulciano, and the sole

grape of Brunello di Montalcino. With its thick skin and numerous pips it can make raw, lean wine if picked before it is fully ripe, and only the best vineyards regularly excel with it. Blended with Cabernet, it can make a fascinating, stylish bitter-cherry-and-chocolate red wine. Elsewhere, growers in Australia and Chile are taking Sangiovese seriously, and early examples show promise. But California is drawing back from Sangiovese, having found it more difficult than expected.

SAUVIGNON BLANC
If you ask most wine drinkers where Sauvignon Blanc comes from, there's a fair chance they'll say New Zealand. Yet there wasn't a single Sauvignon vine in New Zealand as recently as 1970. It's just that the wonderfully tangy, aggressive flavours of New Zealand Sauvignon have completely outpaced those of its original sources, the Loire Valley and Bordeaux in France. Outside New Zealand, good examples in this style come from South Africa and sometimes Chile; Australian versions tend to be riper and more melony, and unoaked Bordeaux ones are tangy but not strongly grassy. Fermented and aged in oak, Sauvignon Blanc is totally different – toasty, nutty and long-lasting. Bordeaux is the home of this style as well, but the method has now spread worldwide.

SÉMILLON
Thick-skinned, prone to overcropping and lacking any particular aroma, Sémillon is not, on the face of it, a white grape destined for international fame. Yet plant it in Sauternes, let botrytis get to it, then blend it with Sauvignon Blanc, and you have one of the world's greatest sweet wines. When barrel-fermented and dry, this Sémillon-Sauvignon blend is another world classic. Used on its own, Sémillon can be too low in acidity, although Australia has made varietal Semillon (without the accent, here) a speciality, and invented a new classic wine style in the process.

SYRAH/SHIRAZ
Heat is what this red vine likes: in a hot, dry climate, planted in poor soil, it'll be as happy as a sandboy. Syrah also needs decent weather when flowering, as it is prone to *coulure*, or poor fruit-set, when bunches of smaller berries drop off. It loves the northern Rhône: those impossible slopes, the granite soil, and serious growers who limit yields – perfect. Australia also provides hot, dry conditions and Shiraz responds magnificently. It has only recently become fashionable, but Spain, Chile and Argentina make excellent examples, and now there are

exciting ones also coming from South Africa, Italy, New Zealand and even a few from Switzerland.

TEMPRANILLO
I really don't know where Spain would be without Tempranillo. All its major red-wine regions rely on it, and yet it performs very differently in the various regions and adopts different names too. In its heartland, Rioja, as long as it isn't overcropped, it gives fruit, perfume and ageability. In Navarra, it plays second fiddle to Garnacha. It is fairly important, but less exciting, as Ull de Llebre in Penedès, yet extremely dark, rich and fragrant as Tinto Fino in the low-yielding vineyards of Ribera del Duero, and as Cencibel in the La Mancha and Valdepeñas regions. Elsewhere in Spain it's known as Tinto Madrid or Tinto de Toro, while the Portuguese call it Aragonez or Tinto Roriz. Tempranillo is attracting more interest worldwide, and is becoming a focus of attention in both Australia and South America.

VIOGNIER
Just a few years ago, there was hardly a wine lover who'd heard of Viognier. Now it has the aura of a supermodel: flouncing, petulant and perfumed; riding its popularity for all its worth before someone says, hang on, is it really that good? Well, yes and no. The grape of Condrieu and Château-Grillet, it can produce wines of heady mayflower perfume and peach and crème fraîche flavours – when it's allowed to get really ripe. This is the key to Viognier, one of the things that makes it tricky. Without super-ripeness, it can lack flavour. It is found in varying quantities all over the south of France, while Australia, California and South America are also getting in on the act with increasing success.

ZINFANDEL
The United States imported the first cuttings of this versatile red vine from Europe in the 19th century; they appear to have been the same as the Primitivo variety of southern Italy or Croatia's obscure Crljenak. 'Zin', however, has become a Californian speciality, used for red, white or 'blush' wines, ranging from dry to a sweet, late-harvest style, to 'port' wines. But its best expression is as a richly fruity red, full of blackberry or plum flavours. For this, it needs a fairly cool climate and not too much irrigation, since yields can be high. Sugar levels can be high, too, giving a baked, port-like taste. The most intense blackberry and pepper flavours come from old vines. Not just confined to California, Mexico, Chile, South Africa and Australia also make good Zinfandels.

THE MODERN PICTURE

A COUPLE OF THOUSAND YEARS AGO, this map of the world of wine would have looked very different, with both winemaking and consumption being highest in the Middle East and the Eastern Mediterranean, and Greece and Italy not far behind. The rest of Western Europe would hardly have registered at all – and the New World hadn't yet been discovered. The adoption of Islam, with its ban on alcohol, by most Middle Eastern and North African countries has meant that, although vineyards still flourish there, hardly any produce wine grapes, and the centre of wine production has shifted to Western Europe, mainly to Italy, France and Spain.

But the greatest growth today is outside Europe in the New World – in South America, South Africa and Australasia – and most recently in China, which now has more vines than Argentina and Chile combined. The vineyards outside Europe now account for 40 per cent of the world's total.

A WORLD AWASH WITH WINE

In the first edition of this book we talked of declining production and vineyard area in the biggest wine-producing countries (the green areas on our map). Well, those declines have now stabilized: Italy's vineyards, for example, shrank by about a quarter between the early 1980s and the late 1990s, but this has now steadied. The same thing has happened in Spain. Production is growing again – in spite of EU policies to control the situation. The EU ban on new plantings has been extended to 2010, so potential production should, in theory, stay the same. But let's look at the Spanish region of Castilla-La Mancha to see what is actually happening.

The region's vineyards cover nearly 560,000 hectares (1,383,700 acres) – around half of all Spain's vineyards are here. And producers there are keen to make better quality wine – something we're all in favour of, aren't we? That means planting better grape varieties and managing the vineyards more efficiently. It also means introducing irrigation, which has been legal here since 1996. The result is that some vineyards can quadruple their yields with no trouble at all. When irrigation becomes legal in southern France and southern Italy (as it surely will) yields will shoot up there, too.

In the New World, there are no restrictions on planting, and the area under vine is growing fast to meet increasing export demands: Australia had 90,000ha (222,400 acres) in 1997 and now has 164,000ha (405,200 acres). The USA's 1997 figure of 337,000ha (832,700 acres) has risen to 398,000ha (983,400 acres). Chile's vineyard, having steadily declined since the 1970s, is also on the increase again thanks to successful exports. The decline of the huge vineyard of Argentina has stopped and South Africa's vineyard area is expanding slightly. Add to this the fact that none of the New World countries have regulations restricting irrigation and yields, unlike Europe, and you end up with large-scale production increases.

The question is, of course, who is going to drink the stuff? Consumption, which was generally falling in the mid-1990s, is creeping up again, but not yet fast enough to keep pace with production. Countries like Argentina, South Africa, France, Italy and Spain make far more wine than the locals will drink, and the current picture worldwide is that 20 to 30 per cent more wine is made each year than is drunk. There are countries like Britain and Canada that record significant year-on-year increases in wine consumption of largely imported wines; yet many living in the USA remain stubbornly immune to the allure of wine and its per capita wine consumption remains one of the lowest in the English-speaking world. But it is the huge population of China that remains the big unknown. If this rapidly developing nation raised its per capita wine consumption to even 1/10th of that of the USA, then no-one need worry further about a global surplus. It's a changing world out there.

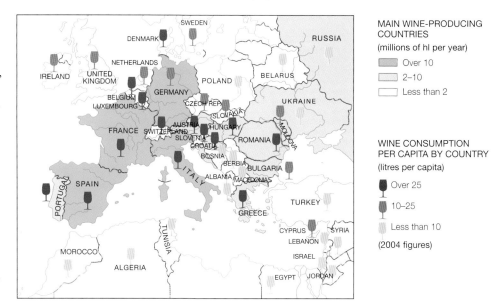

MAIN WINE-PRODUCING COUNTRIES
(millions of hl per year)
- Over 10
- 2–10
- Less than 2

WINE CONSUMPTION PER CAPITA BY COUNTRY
(litres per capita)
- Over 25
- 10–25
- Less than 10

(2004 figures)

WINES & WINE REGIONS OF THE WORLD

LIST OF PANORAMIC MAPS

FRANCE
Bordeaux   32–33
Southern Haut-Médoc   38–39
Médoc & Northern
    Haut-Médoc   40
Graves & Pessac-Léognan   42–43
St-Émilion, Pomerol &
    Fronsac   44–45
Bordeaux Sweet Whites   49
Burgundy   53
Chablis   56–57
Côte de Nuits   58–59
Côte de Beaune   62–63
Côte Chalonnaise   65
Mâconnais   67
Beaujolais   68
Champagne   70–71
The Aube Region   73
Heart of Champagne   74–75
Alsace   76–77
Heart of Alsace   79
Anjou-Saumur   84–85
Touraine   86–87
Sancerre & Pouilly   88–89
Northern Rhône   93, 95
Southern Rhône   96–97
Provence   100–101
Languedoc-Roussillon   102–103

GERMANY
Mosel-Saar-Ruwer   114–115
Middle Mosel   116–117
Saar-Ruwer   118–119
The Rhine Valley   121
Rheingau   124–125
Nahe   126–127
Rheinhessen   129
Pfalz   131
Franken   132–133
Baden   137

SWITZERLAND
Valais   142–143

AUSTRIA
Niederösterreich   146–147
Burgenland   148–149

ITALY
Barolo & Barbaresco   158–159
Alto Adige   162–163

Veneto   164–165
Friuli-Venezia Giulia   166–167
Chianti Classico   172–173
Brunello di Montalcino   174–175
Vino Nobile
    di Montepulciano   176–177
Bolgheri   178–179

SPAIN
Penedès   190–191
Rioja   192–193
Ribera del Duero   198–199
Jerez   204–205

PORTUGAL
The Douro Valley   212–213
Madeira   216–217

NORTH AMERICA
California North Coast   238–239
North Sonoma   240–241
Russian River Valley   242–243
Napa Valley, Sonoma Valley
    & Carneros   244–245
Heart of Napa   246–247
California South Central Coast   251
Santa Maria &
    Santa Ynez Valleys   252–253
Washington State   258–259
Oregon   260–261
New York State   264–265

SOUTH AMERICA & MEXICO
Maipo Valley, Chile   276–277
Rapel Valley, Chile   278–279
Mendoza, Argentina   282–283

AUSTRALIA
Barossa & Eden Valleys   290–291
Coonawarra   293
Clare Valley   295
Yarra Valley   298–299
Lower Hunter Valley   302–303
Margaret River   306

NEW ZEALAND
Hawkes Bay   314–315
Marlborough   318–319

SOUTH AFRICA
Stellenbosch & Paarl   324–325

FRANCE

Nobody does it better – or do they? France has built her reputation on such wines as Champagne, from the cool, chalk hills of the North (main picture) and on the top wines of Bordeaux, like Château Margaux (above). But nowadays outside competition is forcing France to look to her laurels.

We've had our tiffs. I've stormed off and formed fleeting, flirtatious liaisons with other nations around the world. But true love is true love. I've always come back to France. Other countries can do some things better but when it comes to wine, no country can do so many things as well as France. My love of France, my respect for her natural genius in wine is deepened, not diminished, by contact with her rivals in Europe and elsewhere. The more I learn about wine in Chile, Australia, California, Italy, Spain or New Zealand, the more I appreciate France.

But then, France is lucky. Her geographical situation is ideally suited to many of the grape varieties that make great wine and her geological make-up has provided numerous sites perfectly suited to the measured ripening of these varieties. This combination provides a wide array of areas that achieve a precise balance between too much heat and too little, between too much rain and too little. The result is that the great varieties like Cabernet Sauvignon, Pinot Noir, Syrah, Chardonnay and Sauvignon Blanc will generally creep towards ripeness rather than rush headlong. Just as with an apple, slowly ripened fruit gives the most delicious flavour, the balance between sugar and acidity and perfume is most perfectly achieved.

Nowadays, modern vineyard technology can mimic such conditions up to a point in warmer areas, and perfect cool cellar and winemaking conditions could be created as easily at the equator as at the North Pole. But such developments are only a generation old. France's other priceless natural asset has always been her winemaking conditions. For two thousand years before the advent of refrigeration techniques, most major French wine areas were sufficiently cool by vintage time for the wines to ferment in a controlled way without artificial help, preserving the delicous, but fragile, balance of the fruit. Other great wine nations, such as Italy and Spain, the United States and Australia, had few areas that could rely on such luck.

France also enjoyed her position at the crossroads of Europe and she has a longer on-going tradition of fashioning wines to suit the export markets than her competitors round the Mediterranean. These days, it's true, newer countries and regions seem intent on stealing her thunder and proving that, whatever France can do, they can do better. Well, sometimes they can and sometimes they can't. We're in a fascinating period at the moment as France, with one eye on the New World, redefines her ideas of what makes a wine great, and what makes her wines different from all others. And my love for France? A few lovers' tiffs can't destroy the Real Thing.

THE WINE REGIONS OF FRANCE

WE'RE STANDING ON THE BROW of the Montagne de Reims in the Champagne region of northern France. The pale spring sun hardly takes the edge off the damp westerly gale, scudding in over the soggy plains. We're just about at the northern limit beyond which the classic grape varieties will not ripen, but it feels as though we're way past it. Back in town we descend, windswept, into the cool chalky cellars dreaming of a good log fire and a hot toddy. No such luck. We have the 'clear wines', the *vins clairs*, to taste. They cut our gums with the raw attack of a hacksaw slicing through a crab-apple. Undrinkable. Yet once local magicians have been to work, this reedy, rasping liquid will be transformed into Champagne, the world's classic sparkling wine. No riper grapes, no less sour wine, no warmer, more protected slopes would do.

So let's flee to the other end of France to the parched terraces teetering above the Mediterranean at Banyuls, just yards from the Spanish border. Let's go at vintage time and protect ourselves from the searing sun and scorching wind that shrivel Grenache grapes half-way to raisins on the vine. In the warmish cellars we taste the thick, sweet juice of these ripened grapes, then try the wines of a year old, then two years, five, ten, always getting deeper, more chocolate-rich, more treacly, more damson dark. Banyuls Grand Cru, the nearest thing in France to vintage port. No less ripe grapes, no less luscious wine, no cooler, less sheltered sites would do.

These are the two extremes of France. In between, almost every conceivable type of wine is made, from the driest to the richest of whites, from rosés as ethereal as sweet pea's bloom to ones as ruddy as a butcher's cheeks, from carefree reds to toss back from the jug, to reds as solemn as temples. All of these I'll try to show you in the following pages. We've got maps for all the significant areas in France, and detailed maps of the most exciting and important. The object of the maps is to make the vineyards come alive, to put them in the context of the valleys and mountainsides they inhabit, of the towns they surround and the rivers they front.

France's vineyards can be roughly divided into three. On the Atlantic coast, from the Loire Valley, down through Bordeaux and on to the western Pyrenees, the climate is maritime. The Gulf Stream moderates the climate but rain carried in on the westerly winds is a continual problem. In the Loire, mesoclimate and well-drained soils are crucial to decent wine. In Bordeaux, though the Landes pine forests draw off much rain, free-draining gravel beds

are vital for the great Cabernet Sauvignon to ripen. This influence spreads up the Dordogne, Lot, Garonne and Tarn rivers, lessening until the Mediterranean influence takes over east of Toulouse.

The grape varieties, the styles of wine, the food, the lifestyle and the landscape all change. The vine grows naturally and easily right round the warm, inland Mediterranean. Summers are hot and dry; winters are mild. Close to the sea, breezes ameliorate the sun's heat but don't interfere with the ripening of the grapes. Otherwise, the heat is tempered by regular westerly and northern winds and by planting vines up towards the mountain ranges that crowd in on the coastal plains. Vast amounts of ordinary wines are made out of grapes like the red Carignan and Cinsaut and the white Macabeo and Ugni Blanc. When vines grow this easily, winemakers must tame their vigour if they want quality. Old vines and infertile stony soils reduce the yields, and then some magnificent wines ensue. The *vins doux naturels*, from Banyuls in the Pyrenees to Beaumes-de-Venise and Rasteau in the Rhône Valley are heady and sweet. The Languedoc-Roussillon region is undergoing a revolution based on old, dark, savage reds from the varieties of the South, as well as bright, exciting, modern wines from international varieties led by Cabernet, Merlot, Syrah and Chardonnay. Provence is still nervously nibbling at the revolution on her doorstep, but the reds and whites of the Rhône Valley are roaring and prancing with a self-belief in their stupendous qualities that is a joy to behold.

Above Lyon, the climate changes again, becoming more continental as the Mediterranean influence wanes. To the west, in the upper reaches of the Loire, the Atlantic influence flickers and dies. Winters become harsher, summers hotter. Vineyards stretch much further north on this eastern side of France, but grapes don't ripen that easily. Autumn storms often herald the end of summer a crucial week or so before the vintage is ready, so mesoclimates are all-important here. In Burgundy sheltered south-east-facing slopes protected from the wet westerlies and angled to every ray of sun are at a premium. The scattered mountain sites of Savoie and Jura hack out their small warm mesoclimates from forest and rock. Alsace squeezes up against the Vosges mountains whose peaks and forests to the west provide a rainshadow, making the region one of the sunniest and driest parts of France. And then there's Champagne: a few unlikely but ideal sites allow Pinot and Chardonnay to ripen just enough to make the magical drink that is Champagne.

The stark, steep, hot vineyards of the northern Rhône are perfect for Syrah.

THE CLASSIFICATION SYSTEM FOR FRENCH WINE

The French have the most far-reaching system of wine quality control. The key factors are the 'origin' of the wine, its historic method of production and the use of the correct grapes.

QUALITY CATEGORIES

Wine is divided into two groups – quality wine (AC and VDQS) and table wine (*vin de pays* and *vin de table*).

• **Appellation d'Origine Contrôlée (AC, AOC)** This covers the main wine regions of France and is slowly being extended. The seven most important requirements are as follows: *Suitable land* Vineyard land is minutely defined. *Grape* Only grape varieties traditionally regarded as suitable can be used. *Degree of alcohol* Wines must reach a minimum (or maximum) degree of natural alcohol. *Yield* A maximum permitted yield is set for each AC, but the figure may be altered each year. *Vineyard practice* AC wines must follow rules about pruning methods and density of planting. *Winemaking practice* Each AC wine has its own rules. Typically, chaptalization – adding sugar during fermentation to increase alcoholic strength – is accepted in the North but not in the

South. *Tasting and analysis* Since 1974 wines must pass a tasting panel. *Varietal labelling* The AC authorities aim to restrict the use of a grape variety's name on the label of AC wines unless this is a long-established practice. They argue that the uniqueness of French wines lies in *terroir*, not grape. Meanwhile, expect the *vins de pays* – which can and do use varietal names on their labels – to increase their market share.

• **Vin Délimité de Qualité Supérieure (VDQS)** This group is, in general, slightly less reliable in quality and is being phased out. No more *vins de pays* are being upgraded to VDQS, and occasionally existing ones are upgraded to AC.

• **Vin de Pays** This category gives a regional definition to basic blending wines. The rules are similar to AC but allow more flexibility for yields and grape varieties. Quality can be stunning, and expect fruit, value and competent winemaking.

• **Vin de Table** 'Table wine' is the title for the rest. There's no quality control except for basic public health regulations. *Vins de pays* are available for about the same price and offer a far better drink.

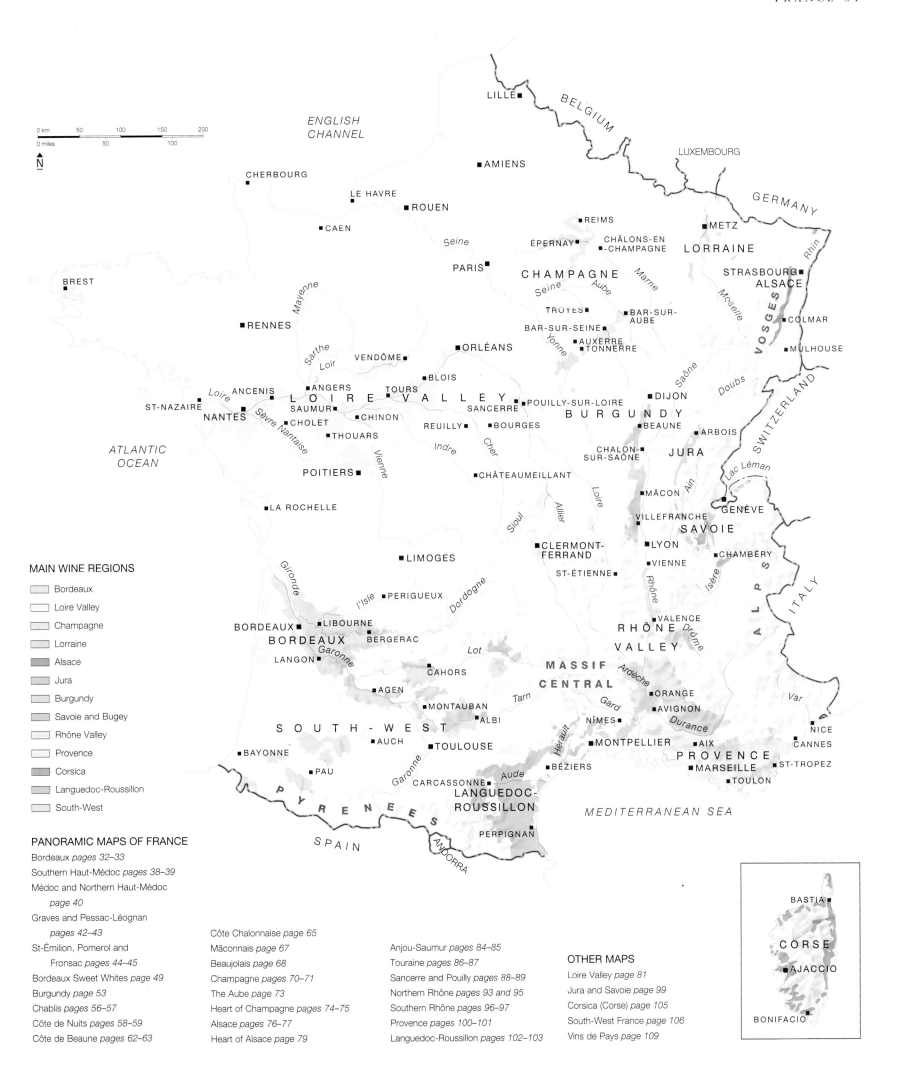

MAIN WINE REGIONS

- Bordeaux
- Loire Valley
- Champagne
- Lorraine
- Alsace
- Jura
- Burgundy
- Savoie and Bugey
- Rhône Valley
- Provence
- Corsica
- Languedoc-Roussillon
- South-West

PANORAMIC MAPS OF FRANCE

Bordeaux pages 32–33
Southern Haut-Médoc pages 38–39
Médoc and Northern Haut-Médoc page 40
Graves and Pessac-Léognan pages 42–43
St-Émilion, Pomerol and Fronsac pages 44–45
Bordeaux Sweet Whites page 49
Burgundy page 53
Chablis pages 56–57
Côte de Nuits pages 58–59
Côte de Beaune pages 62–63

Côte Chalonnaise page 65
Mâconnais page 67
Beaujolais page 68
Champagne pages 70–71
The Aube page 73
Heart of Champagne pages 74–75
Alsace pages 76–77
Heart of Alsace page 79

Anjou-Saumur pages 84–85
Touraine pages 86–87
Sancerre and Pouilly pages 88–89
Northern Rhône pages 93 and 95
Southern Rhône pages 96–97
Provence pages 100–101
Languedoc-Roussillon pages 102–103

OTHER MAPS

Loire Valley page 81
Jura and Savoie page 99
Corsica (Corse) page 105
South-West France page 106
Vins de Pays page 109

BORDEAUX

I CAN'T HELP IT. I love Bordeaux. It isn't the most friendly of wine regions. It isn't the most beautiful. Its wines can be pig-headed and difficult to understand when they are young, and some can be pretty harsh when they're still in barrel. But you know what they say about your first time. Bordeaux was my first time. My first ever wine visit, my first ever vineyards.

And Bordeaux was my first wine-tasting. And Bordeaux was my first great wine. First, first, first. I suppose it's not so strange for someone brought up in England. When I was at university, great wine was red, and great red wine was Bordeaux. Of course, we tried other wines from time to time, especially when money ran short, but if we were being treated to dinner by our richers and

betters, we felt short-changed if the red wines weren't Bordeaux. Every winetasting session would always end up as a passionate discussion of the minutiae of different Bordeaux properties and vintages as we lapped up every scrap of knowledge we could. So it was only natural that one summer vacation I would optimistically jump into my Mini and, armed with a precious introduction to the late Peter Sichel at Château d'Angludet in Margaux, head off to what I hoped would be wine drinkers' nirvana.

Bordeaux is as much a story of politics and history as it is a story of wine. Look at the map. To the left I had expected great rolling hills and dales all covered in vines. Jovial bucolic cellar masters and their swains ever keen to swap a tale and share a jar. Villages and towns bustling with the busy activities of wine. I should have gone anywhere but Bordeaux. At first I found no vineyards at all.

Bordeaux was a splendid, haughtily magnificent place – well, the centre was; the rest was sprawling suburbia and industrial estates. And as I drove out towards

AC WINE AREAS

1. Médoc
2. Haut-Médoc
3. St-Estèphe
4. Pauillac
5. St-Julien
6. Listrac-Médoc
7. Moulis
8. Margaux
9. Pessac-Léognan
10. Graves
11. Cérons
12. Barsac
13. Sauternes
14. Côtes de Bordeaux-St-Macaire
15. Bordeaux Haut-Benauge or Entre-Deux-Mers Haut-Benauge
16. Ste-Croix-du-Mont
17. Loupiac
18. Cadillac or Premières Côtes de Bordeaux
19. Entre-Deux-Mers
20. Graves de Vayres
21. Premières Côtes de Bordeaux
22. Côtes de Bourg
23. Côtes de Blaye and Premières Côtes de Blaye
24. Fronsac
25. Canon-Fronsac
26. Pomerol
27. Lalande-de-Pomerol
28. St-Émilion
29. St-Émilion satellites (Lussac, Montagne, St-Georges, Puisseguin)
30. Côtes de Castillon
31. Bordeaux-Côtes de Francs
32. Ste-Foy-Bordeaux

TOTAL DISTANCE
NORTH TO SOUTH
144KM (89½ MILES)

BORDEAUX/BORDEAUX SUPÉRIEUR AC

OTHER AC BOUNDARIES

VINEYARDS

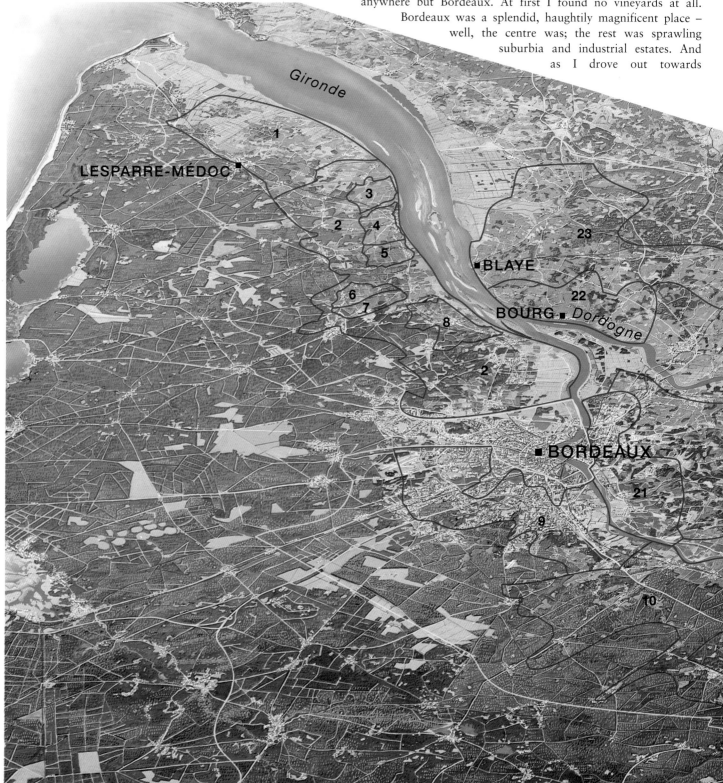

Margaux, the little villages seemed sullenly asleep and the land damp, low-browed and devoid of vines. I did find the vines; of course I did once I got to Margaux; I did find friendly if not exactly gregarious people, and across these broad, undulating acres, I did find some amazing châteaux – the grand houses at the centre of many estates – but the Médoc, with the best will in the world, isn't exactly a sylvan paradise. Once those vines start, that's all you get where the soil's at all suitable – vines. I found a few hills and dales around St-Émilion but even there it is mostly just a carpet of vines. The Graves isn't quite so wall-to-wall because many of its best vineyards are now buried under suburbia and an airport.

No great scenery, just vines, vines, vines. And that is the key to why Bordeaux, at the beginning of the new millennium, can claim the title of the World's Greatest Wine Region. Look at the map again. Although there are numerous places in France, the rest of Europe, America and the southern hemisphere that can boast brilliant wines, most are produced in tiny quantities. Bordeaux has great swathes of land suited to different sorts of wine and currently there are some 123,000ha (303,929 acres) of vines. There are about 9800 properties in all, with an average vineyard holding of 17ha (42 acres), which is high compared to many other parts of Europe. Over 40 per cent of the producers bottle their own wine, the rest being sold in bulk; and co-operatives produce a quarter of the wine. The region produces a staggering total of around 800 bottles of wine. Every year.

CLIMATE AND SOIL

Most of the area on the map grows vines to a greater or lesser extent, but it is only certain favoured localities that regularly achieve exceptional quality. The sea to the west gives some clues. The Gulf Stream draws in warm tropical currents up this western shore of France, crucially ameliorating temperatures near the coast. Yet the Bay of Biscay is also notoriously stormy. Only the vast stretches of Landes pine forest to the west break the salt-laden westerly winds and suck down much of the rainfall that could otherwise ruin a vintage. The consequence is a pattern of generally hot summers and long, mild autumns still only just warm enough to fully ripen the local grape varieties. But there's a fair amount of rainfall too and here's where the gravel and the limestone slopes come in

WHERE THE VINEYARDS ARE *This map shows the greatest fine wine area of the world in all its glory. Although there are vineyards on virtually every segment of the map, with the exception of the great pine forests of the Landes that spread their protective shield along the Bay of Biscay to the west, the best vineyards are those situated close to the rivers Garonne and Dordogne, and the Gironde estuary. The important Garonne vineyards start around Langon, with the Graves region which follows the left bank up to Bordeaux. Sauternes and Barsac are clustered round the river Ciron, while the best vineyards to the south of the city are Pessac-Léognan. The Médoc runs like a tongue of land northwards from the city, with the best vineyards between Macau and St-Estèphe, close to the Gironde. Across the estuary, at Bourg and Blaye, are vineyards more famous in Roman times, and following the Dordogne east towards Libourne, Fronsac has also enjoyed greater renown. However, Pomerol, next to Libourne, and St-Émilion have never been more famous. Lesser vineyards spread out from St-Émilion, and the area between the Dordogne and the Garonne – Entre-Deux-Mers – is a source of much decent red and white wine.*

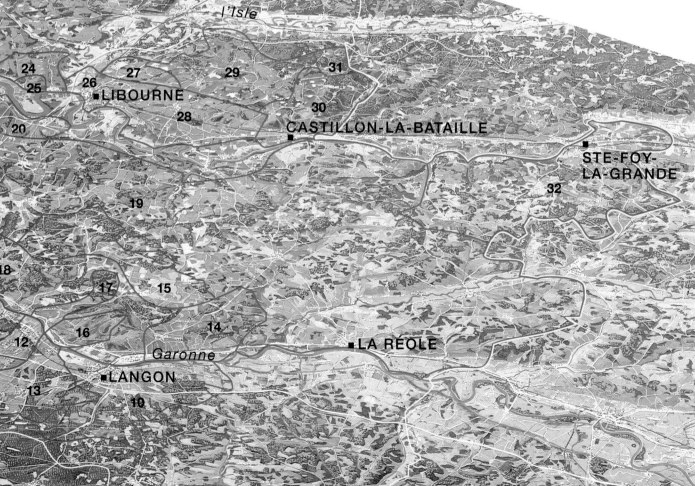

The tower in the vineyards of Château Latour – one of the landmarks of the Médoc.

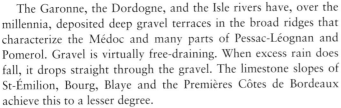

The Garonne, the Dordogne, and the Isle rivers have, over the millennia, deposited deep gravel terraces in the broad ridges that characterize the Médoc and many parts of Pessac-Léognan and Pomerol. Gravel is virtually free-draining. When excess rain does fall, it drops straight through the gravel. The limestone slopes of St-Émilion, Bourg, Blaye and the Premières Côtes de Bordeaux achieve this to a lesser degree.

Vines put down deep roots in gravel and limestone as they search for scant supplies of nutrients. In a climate only just warm enough to ripen the crop, an excess of water would bloat the grapes and fatally retard ripening. There are years when even the efficient draining gravel and limestone can't stop the crop being deluged, but the best vineyards, those that prune severely to restrict yield, and have enough mature vines with deep roots in gravel or limestone, have an amazing record of producing good wines in years that should be write-offs. In years of drought, though clay

soils hold water better, mature vines with roots stretching far into deep gravel beds will conserve enough water to survive the torrid heat and give a decent crop.

RED GRAPE VARIETIES

Most of the greatest wines of France rely upon a single grape variety for their personality and quality. Hardly any Bordeaux wines do. There can be up to five different varieties used for red wines, and not many good properties use fewer than three. White wines come from five main grapes and almost all properties use at least two. But this is a model of simplicity compared to the early 19th century when over 30 red and almost as many white varieties were planted in the region.

The taste is only one part of the reason for planting several different varieties. Simple farming practicality is at least as important. Although the Gironde estuary and the Dordogne and Garonne rivers contribute stability of day and night-time temperatures, spring frosts do still occur. And though the Gulf Stream broadly acts as a warm water heater for the entire coastal region round Bordeaux, maritime climates are very fickle, and June is often plagued with clouds and damp weather. Though Bordeaux generally enjoys the warm hazy autumns typical of a mild maritime climate, the Bay of Biscay can still send over torrential rainstorms in the months of September and October for several days at a time.

Spring frost can kill young buds on the vine, so all the Bordeaux varieties bud at different times. A farmer might thus lose some of his crop, but not all. Good weather at the flowering period around June is crucial because that is when the size of the crop is decided. Bordeaux varieties flower at slightly different times: a few days of rain might decimate the potential Merlot harvest, while leaving the Cabernet crop unaffected. And they all ripen at different times. Rain might catch the Merlot and Cabernet Franc crop, but afterwards the sun often returns and it can bring the slower-maturing Cabernet Sauvignon or Petit Verdot to super-ripeness.

But of course taste does matter, and each variety not only contributes its own flavour but also complements the flavours of the others to produce the inimitable Bordeaux style. And each variety does more or less well on different types of soil and in different climatic conditions. Part of the skill for a Bordeaux proprietor is knowing what patch of land to plant with which variety, and then working out how much of each will make up the best final blend. In an area like the Haut-Médoc, where, in the best vineyards, the old timers say the soil 'changes with every step', it all helps to explain why seemingly identical neighbouring properties produce wines that are always fascinatingly different.

Cabernet Sauvignon is the most famous red variety, contributing a powerful colour, a sinewy structure of tannin and a dark, brooding fruit that takes years to open out to blackcurrant, black cherry, cedar and cigars. It doesn't like damp clay and performs best on deep, well-drained gravel in the Left Bank regions. It is the king of the Haut-Médoc's top vineyards, important in Pessac-Léognan, but much less important in the cooler clays of St-Émilion and Pomerol on the Right Bank.

Merlot is the king in St-Émilion and Pomerol, and indeed is the most widely planted variety in Bordeaux. It thrives in rich but cool, damp clay, it gives high yields yet ripens early and produces succulent juicy wines of high alcohol and good colour. In Pessac-Léognan and the Médoc it is planted on less well-drained soils and softens and fattens the austere beauty of Cabernet Sauvignon.

The lesser red varieties are the perfumed yet lighter-bodied Cabernet Franc, used as a seasoning in the Médoc, but important in St-Émilion and Pomerol particularly on limestone soil; Malbec, a

---

THE SOIL OF THE MÉDOC

This is a Cabernet Sauvignon vine in the Médoc. The diagram shows how the layers of soil give the vine's roots depth and moisture without over-feeding them. The soil is well-drained, which prevents the vine roots from suffering 'wet feet'.

1 consists of pebbles, which help to keep the plant warm, but offer very little in the way of nourishment.

2 is composed of marl, a limy clay, which is highly fertile and retains moisture well. This gives the plant an extra boost of minerals and moisture, but the layer is thin enough not to provide a drainage problem.

3 is compacted sand, which the smaller roots cannot penetrate. The major roots go down into the next layer.

4 is a thick layer of gravelly sand with organic matter, which holds water and nutrients in a form which the root can easily absorb. Most of the plant's nutrients come from this layer.

5 is composed of compacted sand, which, again, is difficult to penetrate.

6 consists of well-defined layers of red and yellow sand, which cannot retain moisture.

7 consists of small ellipses of grey sand. These retain a certain amount of moisture, which the roots exploit.

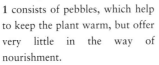

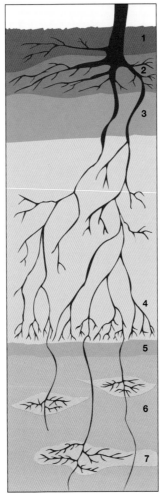

juicy richly flavoured grape, now in decline; and Petit Verdot, an excellent late ripener, full of perfume, colour and tannin, but notoriously tricky to grow.

WHITE GRAPE VARIETIES

Sémillon is the most important white variety, and is particularly important in Graves and Sauternes. On its own the wine can be a bit flat and waxy, but it gains marvellous complexity when blended with Sauvignon Blanc and aged for a year or two. In Sauternes its susceptibility to noble rot makes it the favourite sweet wine grape.

Sauvignon Blanc is a trendy grape, but in Bordeaux by itself it rarely achieves the exciting flavours it can attain in the Loire or New Zealand. Blended with Sémillon, it adds a mouthwatering tang and an acid backbone that can work tremendously well.

Muscadelle is an aromatic grape that can add a spiciness to dry whites, and a grapy richness to sweet whites. Colombard adds a crucial green fruity zest to whites, especially in the Bourg and Blaye areas. Ugni Blanc is Cognac's distilling grape and, though still grown in Bordeaux, produces pretty thin stuff.

WINEMAKING IN BORDEAUX

The styles of wines the various grapes produce depend upon the amounts of each in the blend, the siting of the vineyard, and the ambitions and talents of the producer. Splendid sites are in a minority, as are ambitious producers. Only about 40 per cent of growers bottle their own wine, the rest simply selling the grapes, the juice or the wine to merchant houses, or to the co-operatives who account for 25 per cent of the total Bordeaux production.

Consequently, basic Bordeaux Rouge or Bordeaux Blanc will generally be a light, simple wine from the less-favoured hinterland of Bordeaux. To be honest, such land is better suited to whites which, when carefully made, are refreshing and appetizing. Red grapes rarely ripen fully in such soil, and basic Bordeaux Rouge is usually thin, often raw, and just occasionally appetizing.

However, even in these lesser areas an ambitious proprietor can do a great deal to improve his or her wine. Modern trellising and pruning systems are dramatically improving the quality of grapes in the Entre-Deux-Mers. Severe pruning and then rigid selection of only the best grapes means that even a property in a basic appellation can cream off any superior juice and bottle it separately. Replacement of old wooden and cement vats with stainless steel allows a proprietor to maximize whatever fruit and freshness his wine possesses. And the use of new oak barrels for fermenting whites and/or aging wines of either colour dramatically deepens and intensifies the flavour of the wine. Throughout the hinterland, the best proprietors are now striving to improve their wines by these methods. In the top areas such methods are commonplace, and so they should be, because the great Bordeaux wines are expensive and we should expect the proprietor to have done his best on our behalf.

THE CHÂTEAU SYSTEM

The word 'château' is a grand sounding title. Its literal translation is 'castle', and if you have visions of turrets, high fortified walls and portcullis gates guarding the moat – well, that's all right. There are a few châteaux like that in Bordeaux, but very few. The idea of a 'château' coming to represent a particular wine grew up in the 18th century when the wealthy businessmen and parliamentarians of Bordeaux began to hanker for magnificent estates at which to relax and indulge in a bit of showing off. The Médoc was the area most of those grandees chose to explore, and there are many stunning properties right the way north through the vineyard areas,

but understandably, the most impressive are generally found closer to the city of Bordeaux itself.

Almost all of these properties developed vineyards too, and by 1855 a hierarchy had sufficiently developed for a famous classification to be made that still largely holds good today (see page 36). What also began to happen was the adoption of the title 'château' for an estate's wines, even when there was no imposing building deserving the name. In recent years the use of the word 'château' has spread throughout Bordeaux as a mark of supposed superiority and individuality. A property in a famous area like, say, Pauillac or St-Émilion can still get a good price for its wine even when sold anonymously in bulk. In the lesser appellations, the price for bulk wine is likely to be miserable. Any proprietor determined to improve his wine, and thus his selling price, will find that calling his estate 'Château Something' is the first step in adding value to his wine, however uncastle-like his farmhouse may be.

This is what a château should look like: all towers and gateways and courtyards. These are part of Château d'Yquem; the oldest parts of the building date from the late 14th century.

APPELLATIONS AND CLASSIFICATIONS

There are three levels of AC in Bordeaux, as well as numerous classifications that have sprung up in the last 180 years or so.

- **General regional AC** 'Bordeaux' is the basic AC, covering red, white, rosé and sparkling wines from the Gironde *département*. Wines with a higher minimum alcohol level can use 'Bordeaux Supérieur'.
- **Specific regional ACs** These are the next step up the ladder and cover large areas, for instance Entre-Deux-Mers for whites, and Haut-Médoc for reds. They often apply to one colour of wine only.
- **Village ACs** Within a few of the regional ACs the most renowned villages have their own appellations, e.g. St-Estèphe, Pauillac, St-Julien, Margaux, Listrac and Moulis in the Haut-Médoc, Pessac-Léognan in the Graves, and Barsac and Sauternes.
- **The 1855 Classification** The famous 1855 Classification of Gironde wines was conceived for the Exposition Universelle in Paris to cover Bordeaux red and sweet white wines. It was simply a list drawn up in a couple of days, based on the prices wines were fetching on the current market and intended for a single event: it was never meant to be a permanent guide. Apart from Château Haut-Brion in the Graves, all the red wines are from the Médoc (see pages 36–41) while the sweet whites of Sauternes and Barsac (see pages 48–9) were separately classified. It continues to be a remarkably accurate guide to the wines of the Haut-Médoc, and the only change to the list since 1855 has been the promotion of Château Mouton-Rothschild from Second to First Growth in 1973. It is difficult to understand why it is still so accurate, since the classification applied to the château name, not to the vineyards it owned, and some of these vineyards are now completely different from those of 1855. A Classed Growth château can annex land from a non-classified estate, and hey presto, that land is suddenly Classed Growth land. However, if a non-classified château buys land from a Classed Growth, that land loses its right to Classed Growth status. Nowadays the better properties receive the highest prices, regardless of their classification.
- **Other classifications** Graves had to wait until 1953 for its reds and 1959 for its whites (see pages 42–3). Pomerol has no classification, although St-Émilion does – and it is revised every ten years or so to take account of both improving properties and declining ones, though it was temporarily suspended in 2007 (see pages 44–7). Finally, the Crus Bourgeois of the Médoc and Haut-Médoc is a grouping of over 400 properties below the Classed Growth level: this classification also suffered a legal challenge in 2006 and is currently suspended.

One of the world's priciest wines, based on Merlot grown on heavy clay soils.

THE MÉDOC & HAUT-MÉDOC

RED GRAPES
Cabernet Sauvignon is the main variety, performing brilliantly on the warm gravelly Médoc soils. Lesser varieties are the softer perfumed Cabernet Franc, Merlot planted on cooler, less well-drained soils, Malbec (in the Bas-Médoc) and the rarely used Petit Verdot.

CLIMATE
The soothing influence of the Gulf Stream sweeping along the Atlantic coast produces long, warm summers and cool, wet winters. The Landes pine forests act as a natural windbreak, sheltering the vineyards. Heavy rains can be a problem at vintage time.

SOIL
The topsoil is mostly free-draining gravel mixed with sand, the subsoil is gravel with sand plus some limestone and clay. The best vineyards are on the gravel outcrops.

ASPECT
Generally low-lying and flat with the main relief provided by gravel ridges and low plateaus, especially in the Haut-Médoc. Most, though not all, of the top vineyards are on very gentle rises facing east and south-east towards the Gironde estuary.

THE BEST PLACE to get a good look at the Médoc is from the middle of a traffic jam. I'd recommend about 9am or 5.30pm on a nice bright spring day, sitting patiently on the lofty span of the Pont d'Aquitaine that sweeps across the Garonne river north of the city of Bordeaux.

And look north, as far as the eye can see – out there are the great vineyards of Margaux and Cantenac; further on – from this height they should still be visible – are St-Julien, Pauillac and even St-Estèphe. Ah, bliss. Please God keep the traffic snarled up a little longer while I pause to dream.

I'm afraid dreams are your best bet. You are getting by far the best view of the land that is the Médoc, home to many of the greatest red wines in the world. But there's not much to see even from the bridge. There are the industrial estates, the sprawling suburbs, the scrubby-looking trees and the mud flats glumly following the Garonne's shores round towards Macau and Margaux. But the vineyards? Don't great vineyards need slopes and hills and precious perfect exposures to the sun? It's difficult to believe that in this flat, marshy-looking pudding of a place these unique pre-conditions exist, but they do.

The highest spot in the Médoc – all 80km (50 miles) long of it – is only 43m (141ft) above sea level. That's at the village of Listrac-Médoc, not even one of the best places. Look it up on the map on

THE 1855 CLASSIFICATION OF RED WINES
This is the original 1855 list brought up to date to take account of name changes and divisions of property as well as the promotion of Château Mouton-Rothschild in 1973. Properties are listed alphabetically, followed by their commune name in brackets.
- **Premiers Crus (First Growths)** Haut-Brion (Pessac/Graves); Lafite-Rothschild (Pauillac); Latour (Pauillac); Margaux (Margaux); Mouton-Rothschild (Pauillac) – since 1973.
- **Deuxièmes Crus (Second Growths)** Brane-Cantenac (Cantenac); Cos d'Estournel (St-Estèphe); Ducru-Beaucaillou (St-Julien); Durfort-Vivens (Margaux); Gruaud-Larose (St-Julien); Lascombes (Margaux); Léoville-Barton (St-Julien); Léoville-Las-Cases (St-Julien); Léoville-Poyferré (St-Julien); Montrose (St-Estèphe); Pichon-Longueville (Pauillac); Pichon-Longueville-Comtesse-de-Lalande (Pauillac); Rauzan-Gassies (Margaux); Rauzan-Ségla (Margaux).
- **Troisièmes Crus (Third Growths)** Boyd-Cantenac (Cantenac); Calon-Ségur (St-Estèphe); Cantenac-Brown (Cantenac); Desmirail (Margaux); Ferrière (Margaux); Giscours (Labarde); d'Issan (Cantenac); Kirwan (Cantenac); Lagrange (St-Julien); la Lagune (Ludon); Langoa-Barton (St-Julien); Malescot-St-Exupéry (Margaux); Marquis d'Alesme-Becker (Margaux); Palmer (Cantenac).
- **Quatrièmes Crus (Fourth Growths)** Beychevelle (St-Julien); Branaire (St-Julien); Duhart-Milon-Rothschild (Pauillac); Lafon-Rochet (St-Estèphe); Marquis-de-Terme (Margaux); Pouget (Cantenac); Prieuré-Lichine (Cantenac); St-Pierre (St-Julien); Talbot (St-Julien); la Tour-Carnet (St-Laurent).
- **Cinquièmes Crus (Fifth Growths)** d'Armailhac (Pauillac); Batailley (Pauillac); Belgrave (St-Laurent); de Camensac (St-Laurent); Cantemerle (Macau); Clerc-Milon (Pauillac); Cos-Labory (St-Estèphe); Croizet-Bages (Pauillac); Dauzac (Labarde); Grand-Puy-Ducasse (Pauillac); Grand-Puy-Lacoste (Pauillac); Haut-Bages-Libéral (Pauillac); Haut-Batailley (Pauillac); Lynch-Bages (Pauillac); Lynch-Moussas (Pauillac); ; Pédesclaux (Pauillac); Pontet-Canet (Pauillac); du Tertre (Arsac).

page 38. Can you spot this Mount Everest of the Médoc? Me neither. And all the best vineyards are located between 4m (13ft) above sea level (parts of Château Montrose in St-Estèphe and other good properties in Pauillac, St-Julien and Margaux creep down this close to the slimy edge of the Gironde estuary) and 29m (95ft) (Pauillac's Château Lynch-Moussas outstretches Château Pontet-Canet to reach these giddy heights). Amazingly, this pathetic 25m (82ft) spread is enough to provide growing conditions for Cabernet Sauvignon, Cabernet Franc, Merlot and Petit Verdot vines that the entire wine world envies and would give anything to possess.

Right. Let's get off this bridge – if we can – and head up towards Margaux. But keep your eyes peeled for two things – drainage ditches, and those times when you suddenly realize that the land is almost imperceptibly rising up a metre or two. You might also look right to check whether you can see the glistening waters of the Gironde because the saying is that all the best vineyards in the Médoc are within sight of the estuary. And thinking about this, I realize that there's hardly a single top vineyard without a view of the water.

Those drainage ditches are critical because, before Dutch engineers arrived in the 17th century, the Médoc was a desolate, dangerous, flood-prone swamp. The Dutch, being, I suppose, world experts on matters of drainage, dug the great channels that still slant east across the Médoc to the Gironde and created dry land where bog existed before. The slight rises in the land show where gravel ridges, washed down from the Massif Central and Pyrenees millennia ago, provide islands of warm free-draining soil rising out of the clay. Remember that the Médoc is not a particularly warm place, and that the Cabernet Sauvignon, the main grape of the region, takes a long time to ripen. It needs these deep gravel beds that warm up quickly in spring if it is going to do well in most years. Indeed in parts of Margaux, the fine gravel is mixed with white pebbles which, they say, helps the ripening process by reflecting the light on to the grapes.

I'm taking the D2 road up from Bordeaux because I never fail to thrill when the woodland sweeps aside and a broad, very gentle slope to my right displays the excellent Château la Lagune. Almost immediately I plunge into more woods, but deep in a glade to my left is the fairytale keep of Château Cantemerle whose gravel crest spreads out beyond the trees.

MARGAUX
A moment more and we're in the appellation area of Margaux, but not in its heart. There is a fair bit of sand and clay in many of the vineyards at Labarde and at Cantenac, but there are some fine properties, particularly on the south-west-facing slope round Château Brane-Cantenac. However, this is one of the thankfully few areas where the validity of the 1855 classification as a guide to the quality of the wines is questionable, although from about 1996 many of the underperforming properties have begun to get their act together. It's no good having lovely vineyards if you don't put heart and soul – and, I fear, bank balance – into the creation of great wine, and for most of the late 20th century, châteaux round here with great potential seemed to lack the will to excel. A new generation taking over, some much-needed investment, and occasionally the purchase of the property by a well-funded outsider can all turn things round, and fine Cantenac properties like Brane-Cantenac, Cantenac-Brown, Kirwan and Prieuré-Lichine are witness to this.

There is only one Classed Growth in the backwoods behind Cantenac: the Fifth Growth Château du Tertre, sitting on a knoll of gravelly soil just north of the little village of Arsac. Though the wine doesn't immediately show its charming side, with a little maturity du Tertre opens out into a delightful blend of blackcurrant fruit and violet perfume far more consistently than do many of the properties with higher classifications and supposedly better sites nearer the Gironde estuary.

Châteaux Monbrison and d'Angludet aren't classified at all. Yet, due to the determination of their respective proprietors, the wines they produce, from supposedly inferior soil, can easily rival many Classed Growth Margaux wines. It is possible that Margaux has even more potentially great vineyard land than Pauillac or St-Julien to the north. Thank goodness for the new generation of proprietors and winemakers doing their best to prove this could be the case.

Altogether there are five villages in the Margaux appellation totalling 1425ha (3521 acres) of vines and including a grand total of 21 Classed Growths, but the greatest Margaux vineyards begin around the village of Issan, and continue on to the little town of Margaux itself. We're on a broad plateau here, gently sloping east to the river, and the ground seems white with pebbles and even the gravelly soil is frequently a pale sickly grey. But that's excellent for the vines. The soil offering very few nutrients, the vines send their taproots deep below the surface.

As a result the wines of Margaux are rarely massive – though Châteaux Rauzan-Ségla and Margaux can be deep and chewy – yet they develop a haunting scent of violets and a pure perfume of blackcurrants that is as dry as those sun-bleached pebbles, yet seems as sweet as jam.

The Margaux vineyards continue north to Soussans, yet they become darker, the clay more evident and suddenly we dive into marshy woodland and they've gone. A matter of 5m (16ft) or so difference in the height of the land and we lose all that gravel and are left with damp cold clay. We're now in a kind of no-man's-land until we reach St-Julien about 12km (8 miles) ahead. There are vineyards here, around Lamarque and Cussac, the best being accorded the appellation Haut-Médoc, but they lack the brilliance of Margaux, crucially because the vineyards lack the depth of gravel and the drainage.

MOULIS AND LISTRAC

There are, however, two small appellations just west of Arcins that do have gravel and can produce excellent wine – Moulis and Listrac-Médoc. Neither of these villages has any Classed Growth properties, but looking at the excellent vineyard sites of Moulis in particular, you could be excused for thinking that the growers there were a little unlucky. Above all, over near the railway, around the village of Grand Poujeaux there are some splendid deep gravel ridges that would definitely have qualified for honours if they had been within the boundaries of such major villages as Margaux or St-Julien. Never mind; it allows us as wine drinkers that rare

This is not exactly what I mean when I say that the best Médoc châteaux have a view of the water. Château Pichon-Longueville just happens to have a gorgeous ornamental lake. The fairytale architecture of the château dates from 1851.

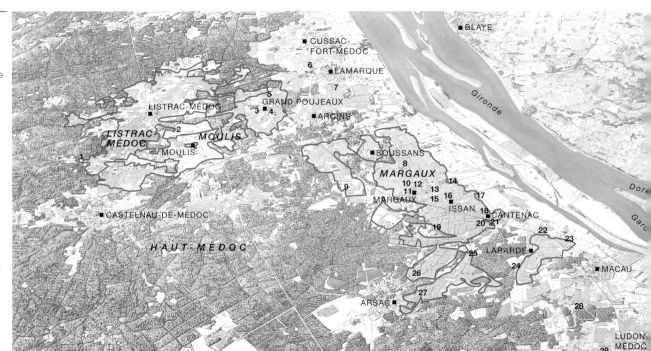

AC WINE AREAS AND SELECTED CHÂTEAUX

1. Ch. Mayne-Lalande
2. Ch. Clarke
3. Ch. Poujeaux
4. Ch. Chasse-Spleen
5. Ch. Maucaillou
6. Ch. Tour-du-Haut-Moulin
7. Ch. Malescasse
8. Ch. Labégorce-Zédé
9. Ch. Bel Air-Marquis d'Aligre
10. Ch. la Gurgue
11. Ch. Ferrière
12. Ch. Lascombes
13. Ch. Malescot-St-Exupéry
14. Ch. Margaux
15. Ch. Rauzan-Ségla
16. Ch. Palmer
17. Ch. d'Issan
18. Ch. Prieuré-Lichine
19. Ch. Brane-Cantenac
20. Ch. Kirwan
21. Ch. Desmirail
22. Ch. Siran
23. Ch. Dauzac
24. Ch. Giscours
25. Ch. d'Angludet
26. Ch. du Tertre
27. Ch. Monbrison
28. Ch. Cantemerle
29. Ch. la Lagune

MARGAUX = AC WINE AREAS

— AC BOUNDARIES

experience in Bordeaux – relatively bargain-priced wine of classic quality. The leader of this group of gravel-based wines is Château Chasse-Spleen – splendidly dark and sturdy, but beautifully ripe at its core. Other high grade wines also come from such châteaux as Maucaillou and Poujeaux.

Moulis is the better of these appellations, with a fine ridge of gravel running through its midst. Listrac-Médoc has some gravel, too, but is a crucial mile or so further away from the mild influence of the Gironde, and is located another 20m (66ft) higher. Higher vineyards are cooler vineyards and in a marginal climate like the Médoc, even 20m (66ft) makes a difference.

Whereas the Moulis wines are generally marked by an attractive precociousness, a soft-centred fruit and smooth-edged structure, Listrac wines are always sterner, more jut-jawed and less easy to love – though a greater percentage of Merlot in the blend is making them more supple these days. The quality is there all right, but the style is rather old-fashioned and reserved. Even a supremely well-equipped and well-financed property like Château Clarke, that strains every sinew to make a spicy, ripe-fruited, oak-scented 'modern' classic, is often ultimately defeated by nature, its wine demanding the traditional decade of aging that most Listracs have always needed in order to shine.

ST-JULIEN

You have to change gear when you cross the wet meadows and the drainage channel beneath Château Beychevelle and enter the St-Julien AC. You change down a gear to navigate the left turn and upward sweep of the road, as suddenly the vineyards surge into existence once more. But you change gear up in wine terms, up into the highest gear in the red wine world, because St-Julien and its neighbour Pauillac have more great red wines packed tight within their boundaries than any other patch of land on earth.

The St-Julien appellation is only 899ha (2221 acres) but it has 11 Classed Growths – while Pauillac has 1204ha (2975 acres) and 18 Classed Growths, including three First Growths. Here the Cabernet Sauvignon, aided and abetted by the Merlot and the Cabernet Franc (and in some châteaux, the Petit Verdot), exploits the deep gravel banks and the mellow maritime climate to produce grapes of an intensity and, above all, a balance between fruit and tannin, perfume and acid, that you simply don't find elsewhere. Add to this some of the world's highest prices for wine, which in itself is no good thing, though when the profit is re-invested in an almost obsessive care of the vineyard, superior winery equipment and row upon row of fragrant new oak barrels in which to age the wine, well, your pockets have to be deep. But you buy not only superb quality, you buy enviable consistency too.

WHERE THE VINEYARDS ARE *This map tells part of the tale of the Médoc immediately. The wide Gironde estuary provides a warming influence to the east, the pine forests to the west protect the region from salt-laden winds coming off the Bay of Biscay and draw off much of the rain from the clouds in wet weather. But the other part of the Médoc's story, the soil, isn't so apparent. All the best vineyards in the Médoc are sited on gravelly soil.*

Where there are concentrations of vineyards, as there are around the little town of Margaux, this is because the banks of warm gravelly soil that are crucial for the ripening of the Cabernet Sauvignon dominate the landscape. Where the vineyards are piecemeal, the gravel will have been largely displaced by damp clay. Such vineyards as there are on this type of soil will generally be planted with the earlier-ripening Merlot, but results are rarely thrilling.

Macau and Ludon in the south have good vineyards, but the fireworks only really start at Labarde, one of the five villages that make up the Margaux AC. The best vineyards are concentrated around Cantenac and Margaux itself. North of Soussans, the vineyards become scrappier, as the gravel banks largely disappear until re-emerging at Château Beychevelle in the St-Julien AC. Haut-Médoc is the highest AC these vineyards are permitted to claim.

West of Arcins there are two small but high quality ACs – Moulis and Listrac. There are no Classed Growths here, but there are several châteaux of high enough quality, especially on the gravel ridge around the village of Grand Poujeaux. The islands in the estuary have vineyards, but they only qualify for the basic Bordeaux AC and aren't much good. I know. I've picked their grapes. I couldn't wait to get back to dry land.

■MACAU

SOUTHERN HAUT-MÉDOC

N

TOTAL DISTANCE NORTH TO SOUTH 18KM (11 MILES)

 VINEYARDS

Château Beychevelle looks merely attractive from the roadway. Seen from the gardens and lawns that run down towards the Gironde, it is a stunning piece of 18th-century architecture. The villages of Margaux, St-Julien and Pauillac may consist largely of featureless vine monoculture, but the numerous enchanting and occasionally magnificent châteaux buildings do add a distinct air of romance and sophistication.

And I'm all for that, because otherwise, I'm afraid we're back to the same basics as in Margaux further south – drainage and gravel. These impoverished soils really make the vine reach deep into the earth for nutrients, and, despite modern fertilizers and certain vine clones bred for high yield making their presence felt, such infertile soil naturally keeps the volume of the harvest down.

We're in a cool climate here, remember. Gravel is a warm, well-drained soil and a small crop ripens more quickly when those autumn rain clouds start to build up out in the Bay of Biscay.

That drainage channel we drove over close to Château Beychevelle is very important, because there is a whole ridge of vineyards running westwards towards St-Laurent whose soils are a little heavier than is usual for St-Julien, and yet whose angle to the south and slope down towards the drainage channel help to produce excellent wines. Châteaux Gruaud-Larose and Branaire are the most significant of the properties here. However, for the true genius of St-Julien – of wines of only middling weight that develop a haunting cigar, cedar and blackcurrant fragrance as they age – we need to go back to the slopes near the Gironde where three gravel

MÉDOC AND NORTHERN HAUT-MÉDOC

TOTAL DISTANCE
NORTH TO SOUTH
25KM (15½ MILES)

 VINEYARDS

N

0 km   1   2
0 miles   1

WHERE THE VINEYARDS ARE *This is the most concentrated area of fine red wine in Bordeaux. Gravel banks begin at Château Beychevelle, at the bottom of the map, and are most impressive close to the waterfront in the St-Julien and Pauillac ACs, where the best properties get the full benefit of the warm estuary and the best drainage.*

Pauillac ends very abruptly at Château Lafite-Rothschild. A drainage channel and meadow create an interlude, but then there's another low bank covered with vines and we are in the large AC of St-Estèphe. Three of St-Estèphe's five Classed Growths are found here but generally this AC has more clay than gravel, so few of the wines achieve the brilliance of Pauillac.

From Blanquefort, on the northern outskirts of Bordeaux, to St-Seurin, north of the St-Estèphe AC, wines not covered by the main village ACs are allowed the title Haut-Médoc. The vineyards become patchy as suitable land is more difficult to find. North of St-Seurin are the vineyards of the Médoc AC, occasionally good but rarely thrilling.

ESPARRE-MÉDOC

ST-SEURIN-DE-CADOURNE ■

ST-ESTÈPHE ■

PAUILLAC ■

ST-JULIEN ■

■ ST-LAURENT-MÉDOC

outcrops push their way eastwards and downwards towards the estuary. Château Ducru-Beaucaillou and the three Léoville properties occupy these slopes. Great wines all.

PAUILLAC

You can't tell where you leave St-Julien and enter Pauillac, the vines are so continuous. Well, yes you can – there's another little stream helping to drain famous vineyards like Château Latour. Where the road crosses the stream, there's the boundary. And there is a change in wine style; Cabernet Sauvignon becomes even more dominant in Pauillac, the wines are darker and take longer to mature and yet have a more piercing blackcurrant fruit that mingles with the cedar and cigar box fragrance. Certainly the extra percentage of Cabernet Sauvignon deepens the colour of the wine, but is only possible because Pauillac has the deepest gravel beds in the whole Médoc, stretched out across two broad plateaux to the south and north of the town of Pauillac. And there's some iron in the gravel and a good deal of iron pan as subsoil. No one's ever proved it, but a lot of growers reckon iron in the soil gives extra depth to a red wine.

You certainly get your depth in Pauillac. Pauillac has 18 Classed Growths in total and three of the 1855 Classification's five First Growths, each playing a different brilliant variation on the same blackcurrant and cedarwood theme as well as a host of other excellent properties. Once again, the adage that the best vineyards have a view of the river holds sway, because the buffeting of tides and currents that piled up those vital gravel banks has obviously left the deepest ridges close to the estuary. But the ridges go a long way back in Pauillac, and standing on tiptoe you can still just about see the river from properties like Pontet-Canet and Grand-Puy-Lacoste. In fact, these two properties give some of the purest expressions of blackcurrant juice and cedar perfume of any châteaux in Pauillac.

Every signpost in St-Julien and Pauillac bears yet another name dripping with the magic of memorable vintages. How much longer can this parade of excellence go on? Not much longer, I'm afraid. Cruising north past Château Lafite-Rothschild, past its unusually steep, well-drained vineyards, there's one more drainage stream ahead of us, and one long slope running along its north bank.

ST-ESTÈPHE

Here we're in St-Estèphe, and despite the quality of these frontline St-Estèphe vineyards like Châteaux Cos d'Estournel and Lafon-Rochet facing Pauillac over the Jalle du Breuil stream, from now on, the gravel begins to fade and clay begins to clog your shoes. We're

further north and ripening is slower here than in, say, Margaux. There's much more of the earlier-ripening Merlot planted to try to provide fleshy flavour from the clay soils. And despite the size of the St-Estèphe appellation, at 1233ha (3046 acres) only a whisker smaller than Margaux, a mere five properties were classified in 1855. The best wines are very good – full, structured and well-flavoured – but if you sometimes wonder whether they don't lack a little scent, whether they don't carry with them the vaguest hint of the clay beneath the vines, you're not wrong.

HAUT-MÉDOC

St-Estèphe marks the northern end of the great Médoc villages. Yet from the very gates of Bordeaux at Blanquefort, right up to St-Seurin-de-Cadourne, about a mile north of St-Estèphe, there are patches of land outside the main villages where a decent aspect, some good drainage and sometimes some gravel occur. Often these vineyards are interspersed with woodland, and almost all of these can carry the Haut-Médoc AC. There are even five Classed Growths within the Haut-Médoc AC, but, these apart, few wines exhibit the sheer excitement of the riverfront gravel bed wines. Good proprietors make good wine. For great wine, you need a bit more help from the Almighty.

MÉDOC

North of St-Seurin lies the Bas-Médoc (Lower Médoc), though its appellation is simply Médoc to spare the locals' egos. It's a flat but relaxing landscape covering 5743ha (14,191 acres) of vines, right up to the tip of the Médoc peninsula, though vineyards do peter out north of Valeyrac. There is much evidence of the marsh the whole area was before the Dutch started draining it in the 18th century. It's not ideal wine country, though there are a few gravel outcrops and some sandy clay. Between them they produce a good deal of decent red wine and, occasionally, as at Châteaux Potensac or Tour Haut-Caussan, something really good.

The Médoc side of the broad Gironde estuary is fringed with these little stilted fishing huts. The very edge of the shore is not planted with vines: appellation boundaries begin just slightly inland.

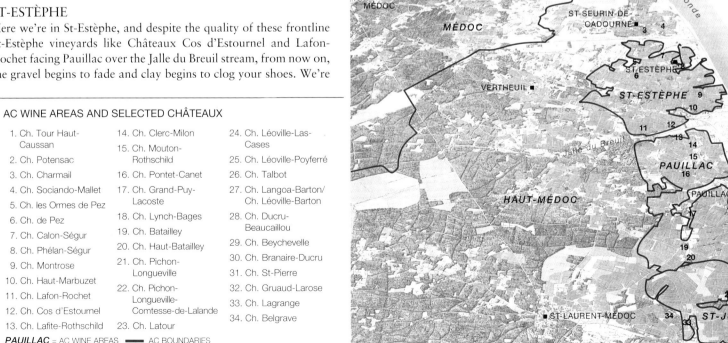

AC WINE AREAS AND SELECTED CHÂTEAUX

1. Ch. Tour Haut-Caussan
2. Ch. Potensac
3. Ch. Charmail
4. Ch. Sociando-Mallet
5. Ch. les Ormes de Pez
6. Ch. de Pez
7. Ch. Calon-Ségur
8. Ch. Phélan-Ségur
9. Ch. Montrose
10. Ch. Haut-Marbuzet
11. Ch. Lafon-Rochet
12. Ch. Cos d'Estournel
13. Ch. Lafite-Rothschild

14. Ch. Clerc-Milon
15. Ch. Mouton-Rothschild
16. Ch. Pontet-Canet
17. Ch. Grand-Puy-Lacoste
18. Ch. Lynch-Bages
19. Ch. Batailley
20. Ch. Haut-Batailley
21. Ch. Pichon-Longueville
22. Ch. Pichon-Longueville-Comtesse-de-Lalande
23. Ch. Latour

24. Ch. Léoville-Las-Cases
25. Ch. Léoville-Poyferré
26. Ch. Talbot
27. Ch. Langoa-Barton/Ch. Léoville-Barton
28. Ch. Ducru-Beaucaillou
29. Ch. Beychevelle
30. Ch. Branaire-Ducru
31. Ch. St-Pierre
32. Ch. Gruaud-Larose
33. Ch. Lagrange
34. Ch. Belgrave

PAUILLAC = AC WINE AREAS ■■■ AC BOUNDARIES

0 km   1   2
0 miles   1

GRAVES & PESSAC-LÉOGNAN

NORTHERN GRAVES
AND PESSAC-
LÉOGNAN

TOTAL DISTANCE
NORTH TO SOUTH
25KM (15½ MILES)

VINEYARDS   N

0 km   1   2
0 miles   1

I WONDER HOW MANY of the famous old Graves vineyards I've walked over – and never knew it. How many have I driven over, how many have I taken the train through, spent the night in – even landed in an aeroplane in – and never known. Dozens, I reckon, because most of the famous Graves vineyards of a century or so ago have long since been eaten up by the sprawling expansion of the city of Bordeaux, and the development of the airport complex.

At the beginning of the 20th century, there were 168 wine properties in the three major communes closest to the city of Bordeaux – Talence, Pessac and Mérignac. Now there are only ten. Mérignac had 22 properties in the 19th century, but that was before the international airport, the hotels and the industrial parks. Now there are just two Mérignac properties left, gamely holding back the tidal waves of progress.

Well, you can't have it both ways. The Graves region was the centre of fine wine production in Bordeaux for hundreds of years, because it reached right to the very outskirts of the city. In the days when transport was both difficult and dangerous, this proximity to the town was of crucial importance. Bordeaux became rich and powerful partly by establishing itself as the chief supplier of French wine to northern Europe, and later to America. So the city naturally gets bigger. Remove a few vineyards, build a few houses, cut down some more forest, plant some more vineyards. It was a natural progression.

What the city builders didn't know – or didn't care about – was that the unique gravelly soil that gives the Graves region its name

doesn't stretch out to infinity. It is only present in the zone closest to the heart of Bordeaux. Look at Talence and Pessac on the map. They've got the best soil in the Graves but there's hardly room for a row of vines among the crowded rows of suburban villas. Look at the town of Léognan. At last, signs of a few vineyards appear. A mere couple of miles further south, and the gravel starts to disintegrate into sand and clay. Good wines abound in these southern reaches of the Graves, all the way down to Langon, but no great ones.

The Graves region technically begins north of Bordeaux, at the Jalle de Blanquefort, the southern boundary of the Médoc. It then continues round and through the city for 56km (35 miles), ending just south of Langon. Vines cover about 5500ha (13,590 acres), as against more than 10,000ha (24,710 acres) a hundred years ago. Of these, 1610ha (3978 acres) are in the Pessac-Léognan AC, 337ha (833 acres) are used for the production of the rare semi-sweet Graves Supérieures, and the remainder are AC Graves. Since 1987, the traditional superiority of the soil immediately to the south and west of the city has been rewarded with a separate appellation, Pessac-Léognan, which covers ten communes. All the 16 Graves Classed Growths are inside the Pessac-Léognan borders.

It is here in Pessac-Léognan that the deep ancient gravel banks predominate, washed down over the millennia from the Pyrenees, and the excellent quality of the reds produced on such soil is no new phenomenon: Samuel Pepys was noting in his diary in 1663 that he had come across 'a sort of French wine called Ho Bryan that hath a good and most particular taste that I ever met with'. I'm not sure about the grammar, but the gist of this tasting note is that he'd found a wine called Haut-Brion that was an absolute smasher. Haut-Brion is still the leading Pessac-Léognan château and one of Bordeaux's greatest wines. In 1663 it provided the first example of a single property's name being recommended in the English language, and it is fair to assume it was the best (or the best marketed) Bordeaux wine being made then.

BORDEAUX

PESSAC

TALENCE

LÉOGNAN

LA BRÈDE

PODENSAC

RED WINES

In those days Graves wine would almost certainly have been red. The protective pine forests to the west, the warming Garonne river to the east and the pale, well-drained gravel soil, as well as the fact that the Graves vineyards are in any case the most southerly in Bordeaux – all these factors would have helped the grapes to ripen earlier than in the Médoc or in St-Émilion.

Most Bordeaux reds were pale and thin (until they were blended with something else) and vineyards that could produce ripe grapes were much prized. Even today, Pessac-Léognan has a reputation for producing good reds in less good years because of its ability to ripen Cabernet Sauvignon and Merlot grapes that little bit earlier, before the autumn winds sweep in off the Bay of Biscay. In the genuinely hot Bordeaux years, like 1982, 1989, 1990, 2000 and 2003, the vines are likely to suffer from that rare phenomenon in a cool area like Bordeaux: heat stress. For classic Graves flavours – a mellow earthiness, a soft-edged, yet cool plum and blackcurrant fruit and, as the wine matures, a thrilling tobacco-cedar scent – cooler vintages like 1996 and 2004 are the ones to seek out.

WHITE WINES

Just over a quarter of the vineyard area is planted with white grapes – Sémillon and Sauvignon and, here and there, a little Muscadelle to add a hint of exotic spice to the wine if necessary. With the exception of minute amounts of brilliant wine from properties like Châteaux Haut-Brion, Laville-Haut-Brion and Domaine de Chevalier, white Graves was a byword for decades for flat, sulphurous, off-dry liquids, the result of antediluvian winemaking. Even most of the Classed Growths produced dull, mediocre wine. However, the explosion of demand for good white during the 1980s, and the consequent spiralling of price

for such wines as white Burgundies and white Loire Sauvignons, persuaded the more forward-looking growers to make a bit more effort. After all, Sémillon and Sauvignon Blanc are both good grape varieties and complement each other brilliantly, and both the gravelly Pessac-Léognan soil and the sandier southern Graves soil are suitable for high quality white wine production.

All that was needed was the will to improve, the know-how and some investment, and during the 1980s and 1990s, led by Domaine de Chevalier, Châteaux de Fieuzal, la Louvière and Smith-Haut-Lafitte, almost all important properties modernized their wineries, and most began using new oak to ferment and to age their wines. Although Graves and Pessac-Léognan are best known for their red wines, the modern white equivalents are easily of the same quality, and are now without any doubt some of France's most exciting wines.

THE 1959 CLASSIFICATION OF THE GRAVES

The Graves classification came out first in 1953, but for red wines only. White wines were added in 1959. The properties are listed alphabetically, followed by their commune name in brackets. Bouscaut (Cadaujac); Carbonnieux (Léognan); Domaine de Chevalier (Léognan); Couhins (Villenave d'Ornon) – white only; Couhins-Lurton (Villenave d'Ornon) – white only; de Fieuzal (Léognan) – red only; Haut-Bailly (Léognan) – red only; Haut-Brion (Pessac) – red only; Latour-Martillac (Martillac); Laville-Haut-Brion (Talence) – white only; Malartic-Lagravière (Léognan); la Mission-Haut-Brion (Talence) – red only; Olivier (Léognan); Pape-Clément (Pessac) – red only; Smith-Haut-Lafitte (Martillac) – red only; la Tour-Haut-Brion (Talence) – red only.

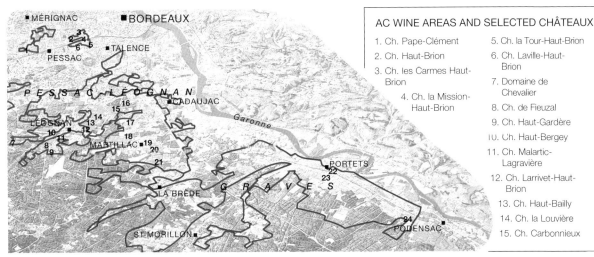

AC WINE AREAS AND SELECTED CHÂTEAUX

1. Ch. Pape-Clément
2. Ch. Haut-Brion
3. Ch. les Carmes Haut-Brion
4. Ch. la Mission-Haut-Brion
5. Ch. la Tour-Haut-Brion
6. Ch. Laville-Haut-Brion
7. Domaine de Chevalier
8. Ch. de Fieuzal
9. Ch. Haut-Gardère
10. Ch. Haut-Bergey
11. Ch. Malartic-Lagravière
12. Ch. Larrivet-Haut-Brion
13. Ch. Haut-Bailly
14. Ch. la Louvière
15. Ch. Carbonnieux
16. Ch. Couhins-Lurton
17. Ch. Smith-Haut-Lafitte
18. Ch. de Rochemorin
19. Ch. Latour-Martillac
20. Ch. la Garde
21. Ch. de Cruzeau
22. Ch. Vieux-Château-Gaubert
23. Ch. Rahoul
24. Ch. de Chantegrive

GRAVES = AC WINE AREAS

— AC BOUNDARIES

WHERE THE VINEYARDS ARE *I'm always surprised when I visit Pessac-Léognan and Graves at how few vineyards there are in such an illustrious pair of wine regions. Lots of suburban villas, lots of pine forests, quite a few meadows and a few orchards, but surprisingly few big chunks of vineyard land. Is it me, I wonder? Am I looking in the wrong places? Well, this map reveals in graphic detail the fact that this famous vineyard area, which was the original source of the Bordeaux wines that were shipped to northern Europe from the 12th century onwards, really doesn't have all that many vineyards. The vines now cover only just over half the area they did a hundred years ago. Many of the vines that have disappeared in the last century were in the area at the top left of*

the map, now covered with housing and also Bordeaux's airport at Mérignac. The most important surviving estates in the suburbs of Bordeaux are Château Pape-Clément in Pessac and Châteaux Haut-Brion and la Mission-Haut-Brion in Talence, and these are tiny sploshes of green surrounded by houses on all sides.

The other highly important vineyard area of Pessac-Léognan is distributed between the small villages of Léognan, Cadaujac and Martillac. South of here the less gravelly, sandier soils spread down the left bank of the Garonne, past the sweet wine enclaves of Cérons, Sauternes and Barsac, finally petering out just south of Langon. The vineyards in the hilly region on the opposite bank of the Garonne are those of the Premières Côtes de Bordeaux.

Château Smith-Haut-Lafitte is benchmark white Pessac-Léognan, a truly brilliant blend of finely focussed fruit and oak.

St-Émilion, Pomerol & Fronsac

RED GRAPES
Merlot does best on the cooler, heavier clays of St-Émilion and Pomerol, with greater or lesser amounts of Cabernet Franc and Cabernet Sauvignon on gravel outcrops. There is a minuscule amount of Malbec.

CLIMATE
The maritime influence begins to moderate, producing warmer summers and cooler winters. It is drier than the Médoc with frequent, sometimes severe frosts.

SOIL
A complex pattern shows gravel deposits, sand and clay mixed with limestone. The top vineyards are either on the côtes around St-Émilion or on the gravel outcrops of Pomerol/Figeac.

ASPECT
Generally flat, especially in Pomerol, the land rises steeply in the côtes south and south-west of St-Émilion. Elsewhere the slopes are at best moderately undulating.

Pomerol is a world of small vineyards and unassuming houses that just happen to make world-famous wines. This is Le Pin, which is about as famous – and as small – as they get.

WHAT A DIFFERENCE 31km (19 miles) makes. I head east from Bordeaux on the N89 away from the prosperous, cosmopolitan city and, by the time I cross the Dordogne River into the Libournais wine region, I am in a totally different world.

The main town, Libourne, has none of the majesty and grandeur of the city of Bordeaux, no quays telling of an illustrious trading past. Although Libourne does have a quay, with wine merchants' offices huddled together beneath some willow trees at the edge of the Dordogne, it is a toytown affair compared to Bordeaux. Libourne's narrow streets and folksy market square could be in any one of a hundred towns in France.

The vineyards, too, have none of the charming sylvan air of so many of the Graves properties, carefully carved from the encroaching woodland all about, nor the proud self-confidence of the great Médoc estates. The Libournais is packed with vines: indeed, there's room for little else, so much so that in this region you get few of the copses and meadows that offer a welcome break from vineyards in the Médoc. But, unlike the Médoc, this is down-to-earth vine-growing, with nothing vainglorious or self-indulgent. St-Émilion has 5565ha (13,750 acres) of vines, yet these are divided between more than 1000 growers. Pomerol has a mere 770ha (1903 acres), and the average holding is only 4ha (10 acres). A successful Médoc property is likely to average 40ha (99 acres). So we're going to look in vain for the startling architectural follies that bring the dull Médoc landscape to life. With few exceptions, a sturdy no-nonsense farmhouse is all we'll get in the Libournais. Even the ultra-expensive, minuscule quantity super-cuvées that have become so fashionable have been sardonically termed *garagiste* or 'garage' wines with good reason.

But there are redeeming features in this region. Founded in the 11th century (though originally settled in Roman times) the town of St-Émilion is a jumble of old houses, squeezed into a cleft in the limestone plateau looking out over the flat Dordogne valley. The coarsely cobbled streets are narrow and steep and the whole town has been declared an ancient monument to preserve it for posterity. Indeed, the whole St-Émilion appellation was proclaimed a World Heritage Site by UNESCO in 1999.

And then there are the flavours. I'm almost tempted to say 'and then there is the flavour', because the joy of almost all the great wines of Pomerol and St-Émilion lies in the dominance of one grape – Merlot. Bordeaux reds are famous for their unapproachability in youth and their great longevity. That reputation has been built by the grandees of the Médoc where Cabernet reigns supreme. Cabernet Sauvignon wines are tough and aggressive when young, but Merlot wines exhibit a juicy, almost jam-sweet richness just about from the moment the grapes hit the vat. Bordeaux without tears? You want Pomerol or St-Émilion. Their best wines will age just as long as the best Médocs, it's simply that they're so attractive young that most of them never get the chance.

There is some Cabernet Sauvignon planted here – perhaps 6 per cent or so – but the lack of warm gravel soils in most of the Libournais means that it rarely ripens properly despite the climate being rather warmer and more continental than in the Médoc. Château Figeac in St-Émilion and Vieux-Château-Certan in Pomerol are two exceptions that manage to ripen it well. In Pomerol and St-Émilion, the Cabernet Franc gives far better results than Cabernet Sauvignon, especially where there is a decent amount of limestone in the soil and subsoil: the great Château Cheval Blanc has almost 60 per cent Cabernet Franc.

Though vines have been grown here since Roman times, the emergence of St-Émilion as one of Bordeaux's star turns is fairly recent and Pomerol's soaring reputation is a good deal more recent still. History and geography have conspired against both areas. The

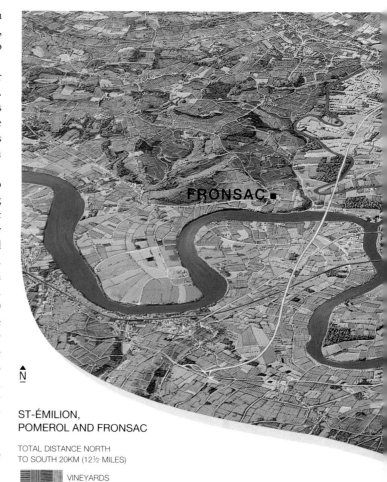

FRONSAC

N

ST-ÉMILION, POMEROL AND FRONSAC

TOTAL DISTANCE NORTH TO SOUTH 20KM (12½ MILES)

VINEYARDS

majority of Bordeaux's export trade has always been carried on from Bordeaux itself. Those 31km (19 miles) may seem trivial now, but until the 1820s there were no bridges across the Garonne and Dordogne rivers between Bordeaux and Libourne. Few Bordeaux merchants felt the need to make the short but tiresome journey to the Libournais when they had the Graves and the Médoc on their doorstep. A band of Libourne merchants did grow up to ship their local wines, but they were generally regarded with disdain and Libournais wines were accorded little respect and low prices.

When the Paris–Bordeaux railway opened in 1853, with a station in Libourne, this freed local producers from the thrall of Bordeaux's merchants. Ever since, a mainstay of Libourne's trade has been the network of consumers in northern France, Belgium and Holland who happily soak up whatever wine is available, undeterred by the fact that not a single Libournais wine was included in Bordeaux's 1855 Classification.

CLASSIFICATIONS
St-Émilion is divided into two appellations: basic St-Émilion AC and St-Émilion Grand Cru AC. The latter now has its own classification system (see page 47), which includes a mechanism for promoting or demoting wines during an intended revision every decade, making it potentially one of the best systems of its kind. The classification has two categories: Premier Grand Cru Classé, divided into Groups A and B, and Grand Cru Classé. These revisions have worked reasonably well but in 2006 legal challenges put the whole thing on hold. My view was that most demoted châteaux deserved their fate and that those which were seriously run put their shoulder to the wheel and got promoted back. Effort instead of lawsuits every

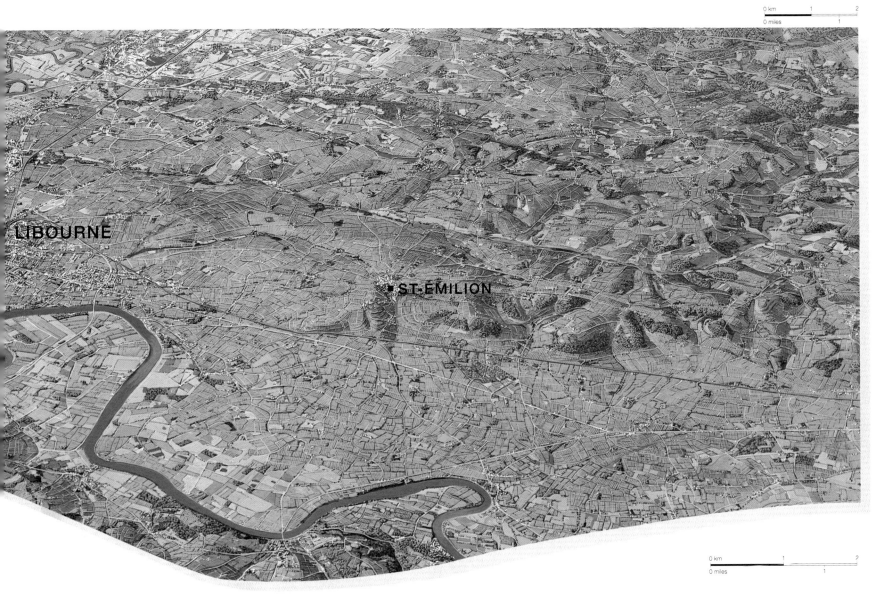

WHERE THE VINEYARDS ARE

The Libournais covers the area north of the Dordogne river. Libourne became important as the shipping port for all the wines produced on the banks of the Dordogne and is still the base for the main companies shipping St-Émilion, Pomerol and Fronsac. The slopes and hills to the west of Libourne are those of Fronsac and Canon-Fronsac. This attractive region was an obvious place for the Libourne business community to build its estates and, until the 19th century, Fronsac wines were seen as leading lights in the area. The area east of the town is now more important. Pomerol and St-Émilion also produce wines of much higher quality. From the air Pomerol appears as a uniform carpet of vines. But below the surface is an array of soil types giving different characteristics to its wines, and excellent quality overall. South of St-Émilion, a cleft in the plateau creates the south and east-facing slopes of the côtes area of St-Émilion, home of many of St-Émilion's finest wines.

AC WINE AREAS AND SELECTED CHÂTEAUX

1. Ch. Fontenil
2. Ch. Grand Renouil
3. Ch. Latour à-Pomerol
4. Ch. Trotanoy
5. Ch. le Pin
6. Ch. l'Eglise-Clinet
7. Ch. Petit-Village
8. Vieux-Château-Certan
0. Ch. Lafleur
10. Ch. la Fleur-Pétrus
11. Ch. la Conseillante
12. Ch. Pétrus
13. Ch. l'Évangile
14. Ch. Gazin
15. Ch. Cheval Blanc
16. Ch. Figeac
17. Ch. Angélus
18. Ch. Beau-Séjour Bécot
19. Ch. Magdelaine
20. Ch. Canon
21. Ch. Belair
22. Ch. Canon-la-Gaffelière
23. Ch. Ausone
24. Ch. Valandraud
25. Ch. Pavie
26. Ch. Pavie-Macquin
27. Clos de l'Oratoire
28. Ch. Troplong-Mondot
29. La Mondotte
30. Ch. Tertre-Rôteboeuf
31. Ch. Monbousquet

POMEROL = AC WINE AREAS
— AC BOUNDARIES

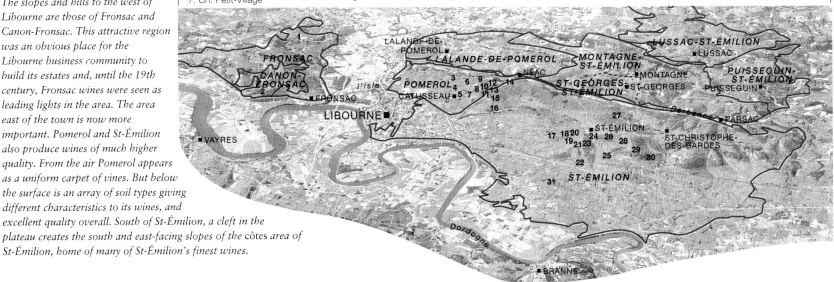

Ch. Angélus produces sumptuous, heady wines, from vineyards that mostly lie at the foot of the côtes area of St-Émilion, on limestone-clay plus sand.

time. Let's hope the whole thing blows over, but with lawyers involved I'm not holding my breath. Pomerol has no classification system, and doesn't seem to need one, since its wines are now the most expensive in Bordeaux. This is a remarkable achievement. Pomerol was only officially delimited as an AC in 1928 and I've read books published after World War Two that sniffily dismissed Pomerol as a subdivision of neighbouring St-Émilion. Those writers, clearly, had never tasted it.

The intensively farmed Libournais is an exclusively red wine region. There are a few white wines made over towards Bergerac, east of St-Émilion, but what concerns us are the totally red wine regions of Fronsac, Pomerol and St-Émilion and their satellites.

ST-ÉMILION

There aren't many vineyards where you can stumble upon well-preserved Roman archaeological remains, but you're quite likely to in the *côtes* vineyards clinging to the steep slopes directly to the south of the town of St-Émilion. Much of St-Émilion's wine is still stored in caves which were dug into the limestone rock in Roman times. There is no doubt that wine was being made in St-Émilion by the Romans, and you can trace its modern history as far back as 1289, when Edward I, King of England and Duke of Gascony, specified boundaries for St-Émilion, encompassing eight communes in all, that are virtually unchanged today. With the exception of a few planted on flat, alluvial-rich river land near Libourne, the St-Émilion vineyards still adhere to historic boundaries.

Though influenced by the nearness of the Bay of Biscay, St-Émilion's climate is more continental than the Médoc's to its north-west. Although there are more extreme temperature drops at night in St-Émilion, warmer daytime temperatures and fewer summer-to-autumn rains in most years mean an early harvest in most vintages.

The only areas of warm gravel soil in the region are the small St-Émilion *graves* zone next to Pomerol, and some gravel residue down by the Dordogne. The lack of it elsewhere retards ripening, and explains today's dominance of the Merlot grape in St-Émilion. Merlot is an early-ripener and quite at home in cool, damp, fertile clays. Even where the soils are warmer and better-drained, Cabernet Franc is the preferred variety, rather than Cabernet Sauvignon.

One major reason for the growers' enthusiasm for Cabernet Franc, or Bouchet as they call it locally, is the pervasive presence of limestone in many of the best St-Émilion vineyards. Just as Cabernet Franc thrives in the Loire valley on very limey soils, so do Merlot and Cabernet Franc on the plateau that surrounds the town of St-Émilion,

and the steep slopes that fall away towards the Dordogne river plain. Nearly all the best wines come from these slopes of the plateau, directly south and south-west of the town of St-Émilion. The ground slowly drops away to the north and west of the town and the unspectacular land produces attractively soft, but not memorable wines. The soils here are called *sables anciens* or 'ancient sands'. Vines grown in sand usually produce wines with loose-knit gentle flavours, and that's exactly what you get here.

But hold on. Just before we come to the border with the Pomerol AC on the D245, there's a dip for a stream, after which the ground seems to rise in a series of waves towards the north. Just for a moment, the deep gravel topsoil which is so important in most of Bordeaux rears its head. These *graves* soils only cover around 60ha (148 acres) out of the whole AC, but two of the most magnificent of all St-Émilions – Château Figeac and Château Cheval Blanc – are here and pack these vineyards with more Cabernet Sauvignon and Cabernet Franc than Merlot. The results are stunning.

ST-ÉMILION SATELLITES

Four small appellations – Montagne, St-Georges (part of the commune of Montagne), Lussac and Puisseguin – are based north of the Barbanne river, which acts as the northern boundary for St-Émilion and Pomerol. Their wines used to be sold as St-Émilion, but since 1936 they have only been allowed to hyphenate St-Émilion to their names. The wines are similar to St-Émilion – fairly soft though a bit earthy sometimes – but they never quite gain the perfume and sheer hedonistic richness of a really good St-Émilion.

POMEROL

There isn't much to see in Pomerol apart from fields, vines and a tall church spire. Bordeaux often seems determined to prove that the dullest-looking vineyards can produce the most memorable flavours. In which case Pomerol, only 12km (8 miles) square, squeezed into the virtually flat land to the north and east of Libourne, is a *tour de force*. But let's look below ground.

Luckily, in this very small area there is a surprising diversity of soil types which contribute to the fascinating array of flavours the Pomerol wines offer. As for grapes, the juicy Merlot is king here. These are among the most luscious, heady and sensuous red wines in the world and, though Cabernet Franc and the odd few rows of Cabernet Sauvignon help out, Merlot bestrides Pomerol in brilliant braggart fashion. Every grape has its perfect vineyard site. For Merlot, it's Pomerol.

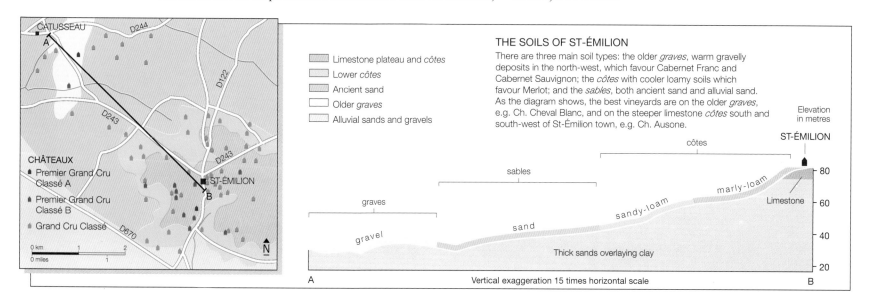

CATUSSEAU   D244

D122

D243

CHÂTEAUX
▲ Premier Grand Cru Classé A
▲ Premier Grand Cru Classé B
▲ Grand Cru Classé

ST-ÉMILION

D243

D670

0 km   1   2
0 miles   1

N

Limestone plateau and *côtes*
Lower *côtes*
Ancient sand
Older *graves*
Alluvial sands and gravels

THE SOILS OF ST-ÉMILION

There are three main soil types: the older *graves*, warm gravelly deposits in the north-west, which favour Cabernet Franc and Cabernet Sauvignon; the *côtes* with cooler loamy soils which favour Merlot; and the *sables*, both ancient sand and alluvial sand. As the diagram shows, the best vineyards are on the older *graves*, e.g. Ch. Cheval Blanc, and on the steeper limestone *côtes* south and south-west of St-Émilion town, e.g. Ch. Ausone.

Elevation in metres

côtes

ST-ÉMILION

sables

graves

marly-loam

sandy-loam

Limestone

sand

80

60

gravel

40

Thick sands overlaying clay

20

A   Vertical exaggeration 15 times horizontal scale   B

The easy equation is clay and Merlot. Merlot that has been grown on clay gives the sort of structure that most of the Merlot grown worldwide does not attain, and there is a lot of clay in Pomerol. Given that the climate here is basically the same as that of St-Émilion – relatively warm in Bordeaux terms – the Merlot shoots to super-ripeness in most vintages. At the heart of Pomerol lies the great Château Pétrus, with its thick clay soil, mixed up with a bit of sand and a thick but broken crust of iron pan. Around it lies a plateau which is a mere 35m (115ft) high – a mix of cloggy clay with gravel and chunks of rusty hardpan, stretching for nearly 2km (1 mile) from Château Trotanoy in the west to Château Cheval Blanc over the border in St-Émilion. Just about all the greatest Pomerols come from this tightly packed patch of land. This is the centre of the *appellation*, but there's more to Pomerol. Gravel now begins to play a bigger part than clay, as the vineyards spread out from the centre, and the wines lose the richness of the greatest Pomerols, yet they continue to blow kisses of soft-centred pleasure across the stern brow of Bordeaux. When the vineyards reach the town of Libourne, and stretch across its northern suburbs, the gravel becomes sandier, then sand and sandy clay take over. These vineyards produce nice wines still, but they are predictably enjoyable, rather than swirling with exotic abandon.

LALANDE-DE-POMEROL

North of Pomerol, over the Barbanne river, is the appellation of Lalande-de-Pomerol, which has 1171ha (2893 acres) planted with vines. In general, the sandy gravel soils here produce attractive, slightly leaner versions of the Pomerol style, but the commune of Néac, whose wines used to be sold under its own name, has a plateau of good gravelly soil producing wine of a very decent Pomerol flavour and weight.

THE 1996 CLASSIFICATION OF ST-ÉMILION

St-Émilion was first classified in 1954 and allowed for a revision every ten years, so that it would be possible to promote or demote châteaux according to their performance. The 2006 classification is currently suspended, so we've regretfully had to continue with the 1996 classification below. The most significant changes in 2006 were the promotion of Pavie-Macquin and Troplong-Mondot to Premier Grand Cru Classé status. There are two St-Émilion appellations: St-Émilion Grand Cru AC and simple St-Émilion AC for the non-classified wines.
- **Premiers Grands Crus Classés (First Great Growths)**
A: Ausone, Cheval Blanc; **B:** Angélus, Beau-Séjour Bécot, Beauséjour Duffau-Lagarrosse, Belair, Canon, Clos Fourtet, Figeac, la Gaffelière, Magdelaine, Pavie, Trottevieille.
- **Grands Crus Classés (Great Classed Growths)** l'Arrosée, Balestard-la-Tonnelle, Bellevue, Bergat, Berliquet, Cadet-Bon, Cadet-Piola, Canon-la-Gaffelière, Cap de Mourlin, Chauvin, Clos des Jacobins, Clos de l'Oratoire, Clos St-Martin, la Clotte, la Clusière, Corbin, Corbin-Michotte, la Couspaude, Couvent des Jacobins, Curé-Bon, Dassault, la Dominique, Faurie de Souchard, Fonplégade, Fonroque, Franc-Mayne, Grand-Mayne, Grand-Pontet, Les Grandes Murailles, Guadet-St-Julien, Haut-Corbin, Haut-Sarpe, Lamarzelle, Laniote, Larcis-Ducasse, Larmande, Laroque, Laroze, Matras, Moulin-du-Cadet, Pavie-Decesse, Pavie-Macquin, Petit-Faurie-de-Soutard, le Prieuré, Ripeau, St-Georges-Côte-Pavie, la Serre, Soutard, Tertre-Daugay, la Tour-du-Pin-Figeac (Giraud-Bélivier), la Tour-du-Pin-Figeac (Moueix), la Tour-Figeac, Troplong-Mondot, Villemaurine, Yon-Figeac.

FRONSAC AND CANON-FRONSAC

Fronsac is a delightful region of tumbling hills, bordered by the Dordogne and Isle rivers just to the west of Libourne. This rolling countryside comes as something of a relief after the flat monoculture of Pomerol and most of St-Émilion, and rates as my top picnic spot in the Libournais. But the wines, which were more highly regarded than those of St-Émilion until the mid-19th century, with a few exceptions, resolutely fail to shine. The vineyards are good, particularly the south-facing limestone bluffs of the Canon-Fronsac subdivision. There's been a lot of investment recently in the area, and Merlot, Cabernet Franc and Malbec all suit the terrain. And yet... The wines have some of Pomerol's plummy richness, some of its mineral backbone, and develop some Médoc-like cedar perfume with maturity, but most still fail to find their own personality.

THE WORLD'S GREATEST RED WINE?

Vision. Passion. Money. And a good pair of Wellington boots. That's what you need to make the greatest red wine in the world. A decent vineyard would help, of course, packed with a brilliant, unique soil and subsoil, but that's where the boots come in. Château Pétrus occupies a tiny buttonhole of land at the heart of Pomerol that is just about the thickest, most squidgy clay I've ever had the temerity to tread upon. Rule number one on visiting Pétrus: don't wear a decent pair of shoes because you'll never be able to clean the clay off.

On the surface, this clay is mixed with some sand, but as the soil gets deeper it turns into cake-like clay before becoming entangled with a rock called *crasse de fer* – a resolute, tough layer of rusty hardpan, nuggets of which have crumbled off over the millennia. Does it give a mineral quality to the wine? Swathed deep in the lush velvet embrace that old Merlot vines can impart, I think there is a streak of mineral cool, brilliantly counterbalancing the kasbah scent and sensuous fruit of Pétrus.

The vineyards are now a mere 11.5ha (28 acres), from an original 7ha (17 acres). But as early as 1878 it won a gold medal at the Paris Exhibition, the first Pomerol estate to do so. Pétrus's modern fame is the result of the happy coincidence of two visionaries – Madame Loubat, who owned the property until her death in 1961, and the late Jean-Pierre Moueix, a well-known Libourne merchant and the creator of Pomerol's current reputation. She knew her wine was Bordeaux's finest, he believed her and made it his life's quest to prove it to the world.

He succeeded brilliantly and carried the whole of Pomerol upward with Pétrus. His son Christian now manages the property and is the impassioned carrier of the Pétrus flame. He keeps the yields as low as possible, partly by thinning his valuable crop every July; he has even introduced a gravel ditch drainage system that allows such dense clays to ooze away the moisture they don't need. He supervises the replanting of one hectare of vines every eight or nine years, keeping the average age to 40 years, and preserving for as long as possible the 60-year-old vines that bleed their tiny amounts of concentrated nectar into the final blend.

If the weather is wet at vintage time, he supervises the deployment of blowers that are used in order to drive off the extra moisture that would dilute his precious juice. He puts the entire Moueix picking team of 180 people into the vineyards at a moment's notice – and only in the afternoon when any dew has evaporated. They can clear the entire vineyard in only two or three afternoons, allowing him to pick at optimum ripeness and to minimize the risk of bad weather. But above all, he has inherited his father's vision, and his father's love for this tiny fragment of blue-tinted messy mud that produces the greatest red wine in the world. The Wellington boots he bought himself...

You don't have to have a fine château to make great wine in Pomerol. This is Château Pétrus, one of the grandest of all red Bordeaux wines.

BORDEAUX SWEET WINES

 WHITE GRAPES
Sémillon, the variety most prone to noble rot, is blended with much lesser amounts of Sauvignon Blanc, and sometimes a little Muscadelle.

 CLIMATE
This is milder and wetter than Graves. The crucial factor for the growing of grapes for sweet wine is the combination of early morning autumnal mists rising off the Garonne and the Ciron rivers and plentiful sunshine later in the day – humidity and warmth being ideal conditions for promoting noble rot.

SOIL
The common theme here is clay with varying mixtures of gravel, sand and limestone. Both Sémillon and Sauvignon Blanc vines can do well in all these conditions.

ASPECT
The landscape ranges from moderately hilly around Sauternes, Bommes and Fargues to lower, more gentle slopes towards the river in Barsac and Preignac.

IT'S A FRUIT FARMER'S nightmare. Here I am, desperately trying to ripen my grapes in the supposedly warm days of an early autumn in the southerly reaches of the Bordeaux area – and every morning this great cloud of mist rises off the surface of the local river and creeps up the slopes of my vineyard. How can my grapes ripen in the morning sun when they're shrouded in chilly mist? How can I keep them free of disease when they're blanketed with damp fog every morning? Well, at least by the end of the morning the sun has blazed its way through the mist and burnt it all away. Heat now courses through my vineyards – but it's hardly an improvement because the hotter the day becomes, the more the humidity left over from the fog makes the air as clammy as a Turkish bath. Trying to avoid rot breaking out all over the vines is a virtual impossibility.

Which, in this case, is the whole point of the exercise. I'm talking about the vineyards of Sauternes and Barsac here. They make some of the world's greatest sweet wines. And the only way they can get their grapes sufficiently full of sugar is to encourage them to rot on the vine. But this isn't any old kind of rot: it's a very particular version called noble rot, or *pourriture noble* – or botrytis if you like. And Sauternes and Barsac are two of the few places in the world where it is a natural occurrence.

If you look at the map, you'll see the little river Ciron sneaking past Sauternes and Bommes, then turning to the north-east as its valley widens out and fills with vines, until it hits the major river Garonne between Barsac and Preignac. The Ciron is a fairly short, ice-cold river that rises from deep springs in the nearby Landes. The Garonne is much warmer, especially by the end of the summer, and the collision of two water flows of very different temperatures creates the mist, particularly in early morning, which drifts back up the Ciron valley. However, this mist just by itself is no good. Why Barsac and Sauternes are so special is that by the time those mists become daily occurrences in autumn, the Sémillon and Sauvignon (and occasionally Muscadelle) grapes in the vineyards should be fully ripe, and turning plump and golden. If the grapes are unripe, noble rot won't develop, although the closely related black rot, sour rot and grey rot will – and simply destroy the grapes.

NOBLE ROT
Noble rot is different. Instead of devouring the skin and souring the flesh inside, the spores latch on to the skin and gradually weaken it as the grape moves from ripeness to overripeness. The skin becomes a translucent browny gold but the grape is still plump and handsome. Not for long. If the warm humid weather continues, the skin is so weakened by the noble rot that it begins to shrivel. The water content in the grape dramatically reduces while the sugar, glycerine and acidity content is concentrated by dehydration. A noble-rotted grape looks horrible – wizened, maybe coated with furry fungus. It feels horrible too. Pick one and it will dissolve into a slimy mess between your fingers, the skin so weakened it can hardly contain the flesh. But persevere. Put that nasty gooey pulp into your mouth, and instead of the sourness most rotten fruit displays, this is intensely, memorably, syrupy sweet, sweeter than any grape left to ripen in the normal way.

That's the magic of noble rot. This sugar level may be twice the level achieved through natural ripening. When the thick golden juice ferments into wine, the yeasts cannot work at alcohol levels much higher than 14 to 15 degrees. But that grape may have been picked with potential alcohol levels of 20 to 25 degrees. As the yeasts slow down and become comatose in their own giddy creation of alcohol all that remaining sugar stays put in the wine as natural sweetness. Great sweet wines like port and liqueur Muscat are made by adding brandy to fermenting wine to stun the yeasts into inactivity, but infection by noble rot is the classic method to produce totally natural sugar levels high enough to create such superbly liquorous sweet wine. Without attack by noble rot, the great sweet wines of Sauternes and Barsac would not exist.

The trouble is, noble rot does not attack all the grapes on a bunch at the same time, and sometimes doesn't attack them at all, even in a particularly suitable mesoclimate like that of Sauternes and Barsac. There are three stages of noble rot. The first is the 'speckled grape' phase when the grape is fully ripe and begins to exhibit speckles on its golden skin. Then there is a 'full rotted stage' when the colour quickly changes to purple brown and the grape seems to collapse in on itself. You can make good sweet wine from grapes at this stage. But if you hang on a few days longer, and if the autumn weather stays sunny and warm, the grapes reach the third 'roasted' stage – shrivelled and covered in fungus. The sugar and acid concentrations and certain chemical changes in the juice at this stage are what give the dramatic flavour of great Sauternes.

The best producers are after these 'roasted' berries. The pickers go through the vines picking off 'roasted' berries, if necessary one by one. This is time-consuming and very expensive. They have to go through the vineyards again and again as the individual grapes rot. There may be as many as ten of these *tries* as they are called, and the

This is luscious golden wine at its most delectable. Château d'Yquem's perfectly sited vineyards flow downwards from one of the highest points in Sauternes.

THE 1855 CLASSIFICATION OF SAUTERNES

This is the original list but brought up to date to take account of name changes and divisions of property. The châteaux are listed alphabetically, followed by their commune name within brackets.

- **Premier Cru Superieur (Superior First Growth)** d'Yquem (Sauternes).
- **Premiers Crus (First Growths)** Climens (Barsac); Clos Haut-Peyraguey (Bommes); Coutet (Barsac); Guiraud (Sauternes); Lafaurie-Peyraguey (Bommes); Rabaud-Promis (Bommes); de Rayne-Vigneau (Bommes); Rieussec (Fargues); Sigalas-Rabaud (Bommes); Suduiraut (Preignac); la Tour-Blanche (Bommes).
- **Deuxièmes Crus (Second Growths)** d'Arche (Sauternes); Broustet (Barsac); Caillou (Barsac); Doisy-Daëne (Barsac); Doisy-Dubroca (Barsac); Doisy-Védrines (Barsac); Filhot (Sauternes); Lamothe-Despujols (Sauternes); Lamothe-Guignard (Sauternes); de Malle (Preignac); de Myrat (Barsac); Nairac (Barsac); Romer-du-Hayot (Fargues); Suau (Barsac).

WHERE THE VINEYARDS ARE *The heart of sweet winemaking in France is the strip of land that runs along both sides of the river Ciron in the centre of the map. About 2278ha (5629 acres) of vineyards spread over five communes make up the Sauternes appellation. One of these communes, Barsac, to the north of the Ciron and with about one quarter of the Sauternes vines, can call its wine either Barsac or Sauternes. The mesoclimate that creates noble rot is more important than the soil, which alternates between gravel and sand and clay. Barsac is relatively flat, and relies upon its proximity to the Ciron and the Garonne for the noble rot conditions to develop. The wines are particularly fragrant, but are rarely as luscious as those of the other villages. Preignac, to the south, is also fairly flat, but its major property – Château Suduiraut – is on a small hillock right next to Sauternes' greatest property, Château d'Yquem.*

All the top properties in Bommes, Fargues and Sauternes itself are spread over little hillsides. They get the benefit of noble rot in the autumn and better conditions to produce ultra-ripe grapes. The result is wines of a more intense, luscious character. The map also shows the other areas of sweet wine production in Bordeaux: Cérons and across the Garonne in Cadillac, Loupiac and Ste-Croix-du-Mont.

whole process of picking can drag on for more than two months. At the end of it all, a property like Château d'Yquem will produce perhaps one glass of wine from each vine. A top red Bordeaux property gets nearer a bottle a vine. No wonder Yquem is one of the most expensive wines in the world. It deserves to be.

Sémillon is the most important sweet wine grape, since its thick skin is particularly suited to noble rot and its wine has a propensity towards lanolin and waxy fatness when it ages. Add the lusciousness of noble rotted residual sugar and the result is smooth, rich and exotic. Most vineyards also have perhaps 20 per cent Sauvignon Blanc because it rots too and imparts an acidity and crispness that gives an exciting lift to the unctuous Sémillon. Muscadelle is occasionally used to add a honeyed texture, but is mainly planted in vineyards further from the Ciron where rot develops less well, and some extra richness is much needed. Botrytis only develops regularly in Barsac and Sauternes. Cérons, north of Barsac, makes a mildly sweet wine, though without real lusciousness, and most producers here make dry wines to sell as AC Graves. Across the Garonne are three sweet wine areas within the larger Premières Côtes de Bordeaux AC – Cadillac, Loupiac and Ste-Croix-du-Mont. In good years the wines are excellent, but noble rot develops only patchily here, and sweetness is more likely to come from shrivelling by the sun – in less than top years the wines are mildly sweet at best.

SAUTERNES AND OTHER SWEET WHITE WINE REGIONS

TOTAL DISTANCE NORTH TO SOUTH 18KM (11MILES)

 VINEYARDS

AC WINE AREAS AND SELECTED CHÂTEAUX

1. Ch. Nairac	8. Ch. Gilette	15. Ch. Lafaurie-Peyraguey	21. Ch. d'Arche
2. Ch. Caillou	9. Ch. Bastor-Lamontagne	16. Ch. Raymond-Lafon	22. Ch. Lamothe-Guignard
3. Ch. Coutet	10. Ch. de Malle	17. Ch. la Tour-Blanche	23. Ch. Guiraud
4. Cru Barréjats	11. Ch. Rabaud-Promis	18. Ch. Clos Haut-Peyraguey	24. Ch. de Fargues
5. Ch. Climens	12. Ch. Suduiraut	19. Ch. d'Yquem	
6. Ch. Doisy-Daëne	13. Ch. Sigalas-Rabaud	20. Ch. Rieussec	
7. Ch. Doisy-Védrines	14. Ch. Rayne-Vigneau		

SAUTERNES = AC WINE AREAS

— AC BOUNDARIES

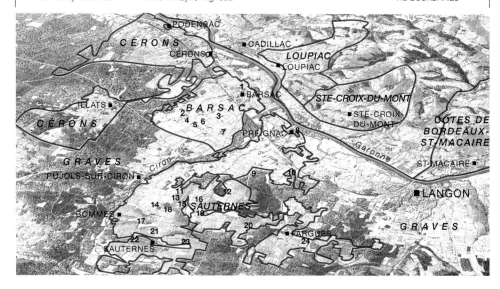

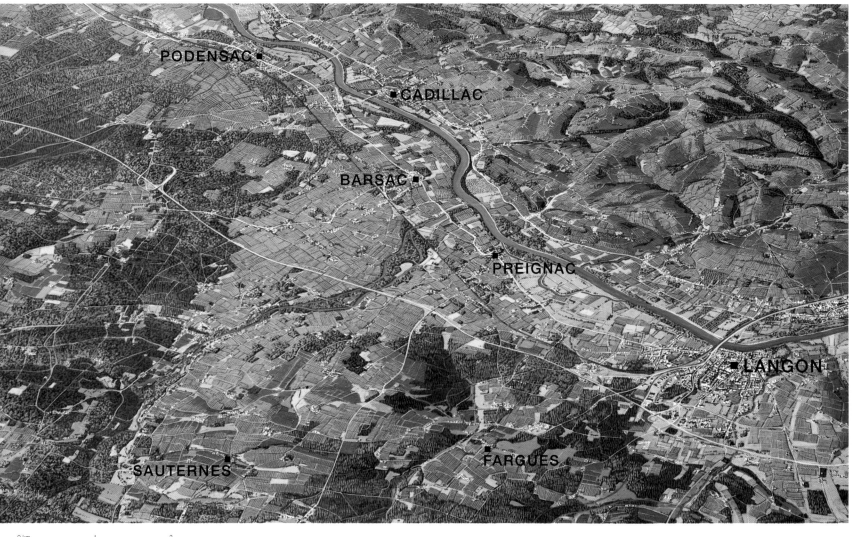

REST OF BORDEAUX

Entre-Deux-Mers: the landscape here is far more rustic and relaxed than that found in the ordered, tidy Haut-Médoc.

Some of the outlying vineyard areas of Bordeaux were famous centuries ago, when the Médoc was just a marsh. And there are other areas, with little reputation so far, which could be shining stars within a generation, given a little luck and a good deal of effort and investment. But when you lose a reputation, or when you fail to adapt to the changing tide of fashion, it's difficult to make up the lost ground. Stand on the high ground above the town of Blaye on the right bank of the Gironde estuary and you're standing among vineyards that were established by the Romans and highly regarded by the English when they were masters of Aquitaine. But Blaye wines are little regarded today. Take the ferry from Blaye across the Gironde to Lamarque, between the world-famous appellations of Margaux and St-Julien, and there you can stroll between the vines of the superstars of present-day Bordeaux, estates that didn't exist when the wines of Blaye were famous.

PREMIÈRES CÔTES DE BLAYE, CÔTES DE BLAYE
On the right bank of the Gironde Blaye is now rather a forlorn region. It is a pleasant enough place with its uplands facing the Gironde, mixing vineyards with forests, pasture and arable land, but it doesn't take an Einstein to realize that the vine plays a subsidiary role here to other agricultural pursuits. Out of about 60,000ha (148,258 acres) of agricultural land, only about 9500ha (23,474 acres) are planted with vines. Of these, nearly 90 per cent are red, and the Merlot grape dominates with 75 per cent. This makes sense, as Cabernet Sauvignon has a tough time ripening here. Even if the Romans did like to sit on the quayside at Blaye watching the sun set in the west, they should have noticed that the wind got up rather too frequently and that it blew straight into their faces, rather cold and wet. Consequently many of the best vineyard sites are on fairly steep slopes, soaking up whatever sun there is and draining off the drizzle when necessary.

The clay and limestone soils *can* ripen Merlot and it may be global warming or simply making more effort, but recent vintages have revealed a number of attractively gentle, Merlot-based wines. Premières Côtes de Blaye is the main appellation for both reds and whites but some of the top, quality-driven reds use the Blaye AC. One maverick property is the imaginative, indeed inspired, estate of Haut-Bertinerie which uses 75 per cent Cabernet Sauvignon in its red – but then the owners have installed the revolutionary rapid-ripening 'Lyre' training system in their vineyards. Blaye needs more properties like Haut-Bertinerie.

Sauvignon Blanc is the dominant white grape at 42 per cent but performs well in the far north of the *appellation*. Colombard actively improves the perfume and acidity of the whites which are generally sold as Côtes de Blaye.

CÔTES DE BOURG
Bourg is a smaller area directly upstream of Blaye on the right bank of the Dordogne where it flows into the Gironde. The steep sandstone slopes and plateau with occasional patches of gravel are much more intensely cultivated with vines than the Blaye region just to the north, with 3847ha (9506 acres) of red varieties and just 21ha (52 acres) of white. I often taste the rather brusque reds and think, well, yes, there is something there, a dark dry fruit, a hint of blackcurrant tumbled in rough earth that tells me – yes, Bourg reds could be splendid if the will and investment were there.

Recent tastings show wines with a bit more polish indicating investment in stainless steel tanks and new oak barrels, as well as reduction in yields. The good quality co-operative at Tauriac does its best and there are one or two star turns like the brilliant Château Roc de Cambes showing the potential of the region.

BORDEAUX–CÔTES DE FRANCS
Côtes de Francs has got the star every small, unsung appellation needs. In fact it has three stars, and more could well follow. It's a tiny area tacked on to the eastern end of the St-Émilion satellite appellations. Indeed, growers used to sell their wines as St-Émilion. Although the region gained its own appellation in 1967, there were just a few vineyards and a fairly moribund co-operative to make use of it. No one knew why it deserved special attention.

Not quite true. George Thienpont, a relation of the owners of Vieux-Château-Certan, one of the greatest of all the Pomerol estates, could see why. He bought Château Puygueraud and Château Claverie. And the owners of Château Angélus, newly promoted St-Émilion Premier Grand Cru Classé, and the Hébrard family, formerly shareholders in Château Cheval Blanc, one of the greatest St-Émilions, could also see why. And so they bought the ancient Château de Francs.

The limestone and clay soil is good for growing vines. The mesoclimate is reckoned to be the driest and highest in all Bordeaux, but the height means it isn't all that hot and the deep, cool limestone clays mean the best vineyards are all angled towards the sun. These prescient families had the resources to invest in this unknown quantity regardless of Côtes de Francs' lack of reputation. Their wines are now showing wonderful fruit and character, and sometimes outshine many of the more famous St-Émilions just a mile or two to the west. The wines are almost all red, and Merlot is the dominant grape, but there are a few white vines as well.

CÔTES DE CASTILLON
Côtes de Castillon wines are all red and this area has shot to new stardom faster than any other area of Bordeaux. Money and expertise have piled in and the best properties share the characteristics of the St-Émilion Côtes wines. But some of the vineyards are on flatter, clay-rich soil near the river Dordogne and, despite their good coarse fruit, these wines rarely lose that clay-clod quality. It's amazing how a certain earthiness relentlessly hounds the fruit in wines from those Bordeaux vineyards that are dominated by clay, with the exception of the rare, great sites of Pomerol and St-Émilion. Even so, the Merlot is the grape you have to have for clay here, and over two-thirds of the plantings are Merlot, with the easy-ripening Cabernet Franc making up the bulk of the rest. When you move away from the Dordogne, northwards, you are quickly into a world of quite steep slopes, often woodland, sometimes pasture, but just as likely to be covered with a sweep of vines. There's good limestone in the clays here, and there's a good limestone subsoil too. Merlot and Cabernet Franc enjoy that, and the increase in quality as you move up into the woods is dramatic. This is where thrilling reds are being made, led by such high-profile St-Émilion producers as Stephan von Neipperg of Canon-la-Gaffelière. With this sort of investment and imaginative wine-making quality is leaping ahead, but so, unfortunately, are prices.

ENTRE-DEUX-MERS
Cross over the Dordogne at the little town of Castillon-la-Bataille, remembering just for a brief moment that it was here that the English finally lost control of Aquitaine to the French in 1453, and we're in what is Bordeaux's most charming rural area – the Entre-Deux-Mers. The name means 'between two seas' and refers to the two rivers – the Dordogne and the Garonne – that make an 80-km (50-mile) long wedge from the borders of the Gironde *département* as they head north-west, getting closer and closer together until they finally join and together become the Gironde estuary just north of the city of Bordeaux. This is a landscape of

charming little villages, friendly *prix-fixe* family restaurants full of good humour and rough-and-ready food. The roads dip and twist through forest, pasture and orchard, streams with nowhere much to go glint in the sun and tease and taunt you to bring your *charcuterie* and flagon of wine to the water's edge and dally the day away.

And there's lots of wine to choose from. The Entre-Deux-Mers is the great well from which most simple red, white and pink Bordeaux is drawn. Most of it is sold under the Bordeaux or Bordeaux Supérieur title, and the most important producers are the co-operative cellars spread through the region. Some of the white wine uses the Entre-Deux-Mers appellation, and there are other small, unexceptional appellations adjoining the Entre-Deux-Mers.

Graves de Vayres in the north-west, which faces Fronsac across the Dordogne is, as its name implies, a gravelly outcrop in a zone where gravel is pretty rare. Three-quarters of the vines here are red and you would expect something a bit out of the ordinary, but in fact most of the wine is simply pleasant AC Bordeaux. Ste-Foy-Bordeaux is another small area in the north-east, while St-Macaire and Haut-Benauge are minor zones primarily for white wines in the south of Entre-Deux-Mers. Most growers in these appellations are quite happy to declare their wine as simple AC Bordeaux.

PREMIÈRES CÔTES DE BORDEAUX

To the south-west of the Entre-Deux-Mers, bordering the Garonne, there is a recognizable and definable leap in quality. Here in the Premières Côtes de Bordeaux appellation, which stretches in a long, narrow strip from the city of Bordeaux in the north to St-Macaire

opposite Langon at the southern end of the Graves, the land rises to a majestic limestone escarpment high above the Garonne. The plateau and the flowing slopes are thick with vines, and the views across the river to the Graves and Sauternes appellations are some of the most magical in all Bordeaux.

This is an area beginning to rediscover its glorious past. Along with the Graves, these vineyards provided much of the wine that first made Bordeaux famous in the Middle Ages. The Premières Côtes were thought of until recently as an appellation for semi-sweet wines but all the action now is in reds, rosés and dry whites (though as yet the whites can only use the simple Bordeaux AC). It may be because the views are heavenly or it may be that the vineyard sites are excellent, especially those south of Langoiran, but there is now a lot of investment here, in modern winemaking equipment and imaginative winemaking. The reds are marked by a character that is unusually juicy and 'come-hither' for Bordeaux, while the dry whites have an extra intensity increasingly emphasized by oak-barrel maturation.

It's not inconceivable that the steeply sloping vineyards overlooking the Garonne around the villages of Cadillac, Loupiac and Ste-Croix-du-Mont (all enclaves in the Premières Côtes – see also map on page 49), whose appellations are for sweet wines, will gradually convert to red or dry white wine production. It depends so much on fashion. A few good Sauternes vintages, a bit of razzmatazz for dessert wines, and the growers can make a living. When sweet wines go out of vogue the growers can make a better living out of dry whites, or reds.

Some of Bordeaux's top winemakers are now producing splendidly fresh, fruity wines in Entre-Deux-Mers.

Château de Barbe in the Côtes de Bourg. Beyond lie the waters of the Gironde and the vineyards of Margaux. It was wines from these Bourg vineyards close to the water that made the area of Bourg famous 2000 years ago.

BURGUNDY

BURGUNDY. I LUXURIATE IN THAT NAME. I feel it roll around my mouth and my mind like an exotic mixed metaphor of glittering crusted jewels, ermine capes, the thunder of trumpets and the perfumed velvet sensuality of rich red wine. And it has been all those things, because Burgundy is not just the name of a wine.

In the 14th and 15th centuries, Burgundy was a Grand Duchy, almost a kingdom, spreading up eastern France, encompassing Belgium, to the shores of the North Sea. Its power and wealth rivalled that of the throne of France itself. Burgundy was the pomp and circumstance of jewels and ermine and trumpet voluntaries, as well as the flowering of arts and architecture and the subtle but pervasive influence of some of France's greatest monastic establishments.

These may have faded, but one part of Burgundy's glorious history remains: its remarkable ability to provide the soul and the stomach with the sustenance of great food and great wine. Look at the map opposite, at the town of Mâcon, right in the centre. To the east of Mâcon lie the rich farmlands of the Saône valley packed with vegetables and fruit, but most famous for the chickens of Bresse. To the west of Mâcon as the hills of the Morvan rise up towards the central plateau of France, the small town of Charolles has given its name to the local Charollais cattle that provide France's finest beef.

And between these two extremes of mountain and plain, as the ridges slope down towards the flat valley floor, vineyards, providing every sort of wine for the feast, from the gurgling reds of Beaujolais in the south to the intense, beetle-browed giants of the Côte de Nuits reds in the north, from the round, supple Chardonnays of the southern Mâconnais to the steely-eyed austerity of Chablis in the far north. The Mâconnais, Chalonnais and Auxerrois areas also produce excellent fizz. Only sweet wines are lacking, though the sweet blackcurrant liqueur Crème de Cassis of Nuits-St-Georges goes some way towards redeeming this.

GRAPE VARIETIES

Pinot Noir has had more exasperated expletives hurled at it than just about all other great grapes put together. It is a tantalizingly difficult grape to grow successfully, its juice is tantalizingly difficult to ferment into wine, then mature to just the right age, but, ah, when it works, there's no grape like it.

The Côte d'Or is its heartland, although some is grown in the Yonne, and a fair amount in the Mâconnais and Chalonnais. It's a very ancient vine, and prone to mutation. It buds early and ripens early, but is an erratic yielder and is prone to rot. If this all sounds as if it's more trouble than it's worth, well you'd be right – were it not capable of the most astonishing marriage of scent and succulence, savagery and charm when grown by an expert in one of Burgundy's best sites.

Of the other red varieties, Gamay makes deliciously juicy wines in Beaujolais, less good ones in the Mâconnais, and is a marginal producer in the Côte d'Or. César and Tressot are two old Yonne varieties, the latter now virtually extinct.

Chardonnay is grown with such success around the world that it is easy to forget that Burgundy is where it made its reputation. It can, in the right circumstances, still produce its greatest wine here, particularly on the limestone slopes of the Côte de Beaune. However, it performs reliably well all over Burgundy. It buds early, making it prone to frost in Chablis, but it ripens early too and is a consistent yielder of generally ripe grapes. This allows it to produce lean but balanced wines in Chablis, marvellously full yet savoury and refreshing wines in the Côte d'Or, chalkier yet attractive wines in the Côte Chalonnaise and plumper, milder wines in the

The Grands Crus are the best-sited vineyards in the Chablis appellation, and produce the ripest wines.

Mâconnais. Of the other white grapes, Aligoté is quite widely grown, especially in the northern Côte Chalonnaise, and produces a sharp lemony wine, sometimes with a soft smell of buttermilk. Pinot Blanc and Pinot Gris are occasionally found.

THE YONNE REGION

The Chablis or Yonne region is, in fact, about 160km (100 miles) north of Beaune and it used to be at the centre of a vast vineyard area supplying Paris with basic *vin ordinaire*. The Yonne was one of several regions east of Paris which churned out oceans of what must have been very thin, mean reds and whites to slake the capital's thirst. None of the areas was very suitable for viticulture, and when the railways came and made possible the transport of enormous amounts of cheap wine from the Mediterranean coast, demand for these raw northern brews disappeared.

Only the very best survived, and the most famous is Chablis, centred round the little town of the same name and a few surrounding villages, where suitable mesoclimates and limestone and clay soil allow the Chardonnay grape to creep to ripeness and create highly individual wine. Elsewhere in the Yonne, mainly south-east of Auxerre, several varieties, mostly red Pinot Noir and white Chardonnay and Aligoté, are increasingly grown, but are only accorded the Bourgogne AC, the best of them like Vézelay and Epineuil also using their village name on the label. Many of their grapes now go to make very good Crémant de Bourgogne fizz. The village of St-Bris now has an appellation for its Sauvignon Blanc.

CÔTE D'OR

Dijon, right at the top of the map, is at the northern end of the world-famous Côte d'Or, divided into the Côte de Nuits and Côte de Beaune, and from here, right the way south to Lyon, there is an almost unbroken vista of vines, comprising the Burgundy region. However, because we are fairly far north here, the southern warmth only begins to dominate around Mâcon, so mesoclimates of vineyards facing towards whatever sun there is are crucial for ripening grapes.

WHERE THE VINEYARDS ARE *The Burgundy region relies crucially upon the slopes of the mountains in the west to provide suitable vineyard land. The Saône Valley to the east is rich, fertile agricultural land and as such is not fit for fine wine production. You can see vineyards down by the river Saône, but they produce regional Bourgogne AC at best, and more generally vin de pays. The mountains rising to the west are the beginnings of the Massif Central that runs like a broad backbone down the centre of France. These hills and dales are generally too high and too exposed to westerly winds and rain to be warm enough to ripen grapes.*

The ridge below which the slopes drop away to the plain provides ideal protection from wind and angles the land towards the south and east to gain maximum warmth from the sun. Between Dijon and Chagny in the north lies the narrow but high quality sliver of vineyards known as the Côte d'Or and divided into the Côte de Nuits in the north and Côte de Beaune in the south. Burgundy's greatest reds and whites are produced here in these world-famous wine villages.

West of Chalon-sur-Saône the local climates become less protected and the Côte Chalonnaise reflects this with vineyards appearing only sporadically in the best sites. However passing Tournus to Mâcon, Villefranche and Lyon the warmer south allows the vineyards to spread away from the protective hills, though the finest Mâconnais whites and Beaujolais reds still come from the steep slopes to the west of the vineyards between Mâcon and Villefranche.

The inset map shows the Yonne region, a northern outpost of Burgundy, whose best known wine is Chablis.

AUXERRE

EPINEUIL
TONNERRE
CHABLIS

ST-BRIS
IRANCY

Serein

Yonne

DIJON

2

BEAUNE

3

CHAGNY

CHALON-SUR-
SAÔNE

4

5

5

TOURNUS

5

5

MÂCON

6

Saône

BELLEVILLE

6

VILLEFRANCHE-
SUR-SAÔNE

Rhône

LYON

CHARMES-CHAMBERTIN
Grand Cru
APPELLATION CHARMES-CHAMBERTIN CONTRÔLÉE
Bernard DUGAT-PY
Propriétaire - Viticulteur à
GEVREY-CHAMBERTIN
FRANCE

BIENVENUES-BATARD-MONTRACHET
GRAND CRU
Louis CARILLON et Fils

DOMAINE
MICHEL LAFARGE
BOURGOGNE
PINOT NOIR
APPELLATION CONTRÔLÉE

WINE AREAS

1. Chablis and the Yonne

2. Côte de Nuits and Hautes-
   Côtes de Nuits

3. Côte de Beaune and
   Hautes-Côtes de Beaune

4. Côte Chalonnaise

5. Mâconnais

6. Beaujolais

TOTAL DISTANCE
NORTH TO SOUTH
176KM (109 MILES)

■■■ REGIONAL AC
BOUNDARIES

VINEYARDS

N

The village of Auxey-Duresses, tucked into the mouth of a valley in the hills just above Meursault in the Côte de Beaune, can be a good source of fairly gentle, fruity reds and soft, dry, nutty whites.

The Côte d'Or, which is divided into the Côte de Nuits in the north between Dijon and a point just south of Nuits-St-Georges, and the Côte de Beaune which continues southwards past Beaune to a point just west of Chagny, consists of east- to south-east-facing, well-drained slopes on alkaline ground, mixing rich marls and pebbly limestone for the best results. The map on page 53 shows the hills stretching away to the west, and the tiny strip of vines hugging the ridge – these hills provide crucial protection from the prevailing westerly wind as well as drawing off a lot of the moisture from the clouds before they reach the Côte d'Or. Pinot Noir dominates the Côte de Nuits, while the Côte de Beaune vineyards have a mixture of Pinot Noir and Chardonnay. Scattered vineyards just to the west of the Côte d'Or, in the area called the Hautes-Côtes, can make good, light wine in warm years.

CÔTE CHALONNAISE
South of Chagny and west of Chalon-sur-Saône, the protective ridge of mountains breaks down somewhat, and this region, the Côte Chalonnaise, is more sparsely planted with vines, the vineyards generally nestling into south- and south-east-facing mesoclimates and leaving the more exposed land free for grazing and orchards. Chalonnais reds and whites can be good, but their less perfect vineyard conditions show in the wines' relative leanness. Traditionally, much of this wine was transformed into sparkling wine, Crémant de Bourgogne, but increased demand for red Pinot Noir and white Chardonnay still wines has encouraged producers to make more efforts to ripen their grapes and use them for still wine, while investment by some of the region's leading producers in new oak barrels for making the wine has also greatly improved standards.

MÂCONNAIS
South-west of Tournus and west of Mâcon, the vineyards begin to spread out. This is the Mâconnais, increasingly a white Chardonnay region, though Gamay and Pinot Noir are also grown for red wines. The best vineyards are still those closest to the ridge of hills in the west, and famous wines like Pouilly-Fuissé are dependent on steep slopes and well-drained limestone soils for their quality. The flatter land that spreads out towards the Saône is mirrored by softer, less defined wines, usually selling under the title Mâcon Blanc, or Mâcon Blanc-Villages. They are, in general, a very mild interpretation of Chardonnay character, but a new generation of young growers is beginning to show what the area could achieve with more effort.

In the south of France, in Eastern Europe and obviously in the New World, winemakers are producing excellent, tasty, fairly priced Chardonnays from land that supposedly lacks the advantage of Burgundian *terroir*. The new wave of growers is beginning to realize that a Burgundian birthright is a big plus in the wine world, but that the world does not owe them a living just because of it. As it is, however, production today is still largely in the hands of highly efficient co-operative groups that are intent on supplying decent, though not spectacular, wine, but the new single domaine wines are set to revolutionize the region and redefine the quality potential.

BEAUJOLAIS
The soil, the architecture, certainly the wine style, change quite abruptly just south of the Pouilly-Fuissé *appellation* as we plunge into Beaujolais. Here, almost all the wines are red (there

is just a little rosé and occasional Beaujolais Blanc from Chardonnay grapes) and the grape is the Gamay. Once again the western slopes play their part, providing good southerly and easterly aspects, protection from wind and good drainage. The soils on the slopes to the north-west and west of Belleville are granite-based and provide the generally unregarded Gamay grape with a rare chance to shine. These slopes harbour the ten Crus – the communes that produce the best Beaujolais wines, and use their own names on the label, rather than that of Beaujolais. Intermingled with the Crus, and spreading southward, are the communes that make Beaujolais-Villages, while the broader, clay-dominated vineyards reaching down to Lyon provide simple quaffing Beaujolais in vast quantities.

MERCHANTS, GROWERS AND CO-OPERATIVES

Burgundy's vineyards are some of the oldest in France, established by the Romans, if not by the Gauls before them, nurtured through the centuries by the monasteries, and subsequently by the great power of the Duchy of Burgundy itself. Once large homogeneous estates, Burgundian vineyard holdings are nowadays incredibly fragmented due to the Napoleonic laws which decreed that every inheritance be equally divided between all offspring. Yet the reputation of the wine from the main villages and vineyards continued to grow.

To cope with an increasingly erratic supply, a merchant class grew up, based primarily in the town of Beaune, but also in Nuits-St-Georges, whose job was to seek out sufficient small parcels of the well-known vineyard names to make up into saleable and marketable quantities. These merchants would buy from numerous growers and blend the wines and bottle them

in their cellars. Honest merchants made up good wines, dishonest merchants didn't. So no change there, then! But however good the blending, in a region like Burgundy where nuance of flavour should be everything, those nuances were lost. In the Mâconnais and Beaujolais smallholders were more likely to band together into co-operatives. These might well then sell on their blends to merchants, but several in the Mâconnais, like those at Clessé, Lugny, Viré and Azé, have established strong reputations of their own, as has the excellent Buxy co-operative in the Côte Chalonnaise.

Burgundy's reputation for much of the 20th century was created and maintained by these *négociants*, or merchant houses, and most of the 'Meursault' or 'Beaune' or 'Nuits-St-Georges' you find will be from a merchant. But in the Côte d'Or, a region that has made more efforts than any other to define precisely why its different parcels of land are special, it is worth seeking out individual growers' wines.

A lazy grower will still produce poor wine, but a committed grower will give you an expression of himself and the soil he works that is rare and precious in the modern world.

The village of Chambolle-Musigny in the Côte de Nuits produces classically elegant, perfumed Pinot Noir. These grapes are from Comtes Georges de Vogüé's vines in Les Petits Musigny vineyard.

CRÉMANT DE BOURGOGNE

To say that the vineyards of Burgundy are ideally suited for the production of sparkling wine is only true up to a point. Their prime objective is the production of still wines – some of the world's most perfumed reds and some of the most majestic and complex whites from the best vineyards in the centre and north, and pleasantly rounded, fruity reds and gentle whites from the southern vineyards. But Burgundy is a marginal vine-growing area. The weather is unpredictable, and frequently the wine produced is too thin and unripe to make enjoyable drinking on its own. But it's just fine as a sparkling wine base.

The Côte Chalonnaise, especially Rully with its exposed limestone slopes, used to be the centre for Crémant de Bourgogne and, further north, Nuits-St-Georges even boasted several well-known brands. But the best producers are now in the Auxerrois region of the Yonne where excellent white and rosé is produced, particularly at the Caves de Bailly, and in the Mâconnais where co-ops like Lugny and Viré use much of their Chardonnay and Pinot Noir grapes to produce excellent Champagne-method sparkling wine.

But there is a difference between here and Champagne: marginal Burgundy may be, but it's not as marginal as Champagne. The base wine is always just that little bit riper and rounder than the tooth-scouringly acid base wine of Champagne, and so when the wine, complete with sparkle, is finally poured it will taste just that little bit riper and rounder than Champagne. This can be a good thing , but somehow it also means that Crémant de Bourgogne never quite hits the heights of Champagne.

APPELLATIONS AND CLASSIFICATIONS

There are five basic levels of AC in Burgundy.

- **General regional ACs** 'Bourgogne' is the basic catch-all AC covering red, white, rosé and sparkling wines which do not qualify for one of the higher ACs. This category includes Bourgogne Passe-Tout-Grains, a mix of Pinot Noir with the inferior Gamay, and Bourgogne Grand Ordinaire which doesn't really deserve an AC at all.

- **Specific regional ACs** These are a half-way house between general regional appellations and single village ACs, for example, Chablis or Beaujolais. The Bourgogne Hautes-Côtes de Nuits and Hautes-Côtes de Beaune ACs apply to certain villages or communes in the hills to the west of the main Côte d'Or vineyards. Côte de Beaune-Villages and Côte de Nuits-Villages apply to villages, blended or separate, in their respective parts of the Côte d'Or.

- **Village ACs** These apply to wine of a single village or commune and there is a growing move to include vineyard names on the label, even if they're not top rank, for example, Meursault 'le Cromin'. The majority of village wines are still blends of several vineyards within the village.

- **Premiers Crus (First Growths)** Despite the name, these are the second best vineyard sites in Burgundy. Even so they include some of the region's finest wines. The village name on the label will be followed by the vineyard name, for example Gevrey-Chambertin 'Combe-aux-Moines'.

- **Grands Crus (Great Growths)** These are Burgundy's tiptop vineyards and are found only in Chablis and the Côte d'Or. They are so carefully and jealously delineated that every single row of vines is separately assessed. The reds are mostly in the Côte de Nuits and almost all the whites are in Chablis and the Côte de Beaune. Except in Chablis, a Grand Cru vineyard name will stand alone on the label without the name of the village – for example, Chambertin from the village of Gevrey-Chambertin. Indeed, many of the Côte d'Or villages have hyphenated their own name to the name of their most famous vineyard. Grand Cru and Premier Cru classifications apply only to the vineyard and the potential for quality such a site possesses. The human element is not counted, and while a good grower can maximize a site's potential, a bad grower or winemaker can equally ruin a Premier Cru or Grand Cru through lousy viticulture or lousy winemaking.

Nuits-St-Georges lacks any Grand Cru vineyard, but has excellent Premiers Crus as good as some Grands Crus.

CHABLIS

 WHITE GRAPES
Chardonnay is the only grape allowed for Chablis.

CLIMATE
The maritime influence lessens as you go east and the winters become longer and colder, summers warmer and drier. Hail storms and spring frosts are the greatest hazards to vines in this northerly region.

SOIL
The soil is a mixture of marly limestone and clay with two main types: Kimmeridgian and Portlandian.

ASPECT
The exposure and angle of the slope are critical in this northern region. The best vineyard sites are on the south-east- and south-west-facing slopes of hills along the banks of the Serein.

IT'S SO COLD! As I scramble up the damp slopes of the Grand Cru vineyards looming above the little river Serein, the freezing air worms its way under my coat and seems to settle very precisely inside my joints. I stumble down the stairs to the producers' cellars and an eternal truth is revealed: if hot air rises, cold air descends. From the mist-wreathed woodland above the vineyard slopes to the grey charmless tarmac of the town streets, the cold finally tumbles down the stairwell like a cloud of invisible ice, into the cellars where the wine is fermented and matured. Ah, the rigours of Chablis in early spring.

This chill austerity in the climate, in the vineyards, in the little town and its maturation cellars too, gives Chablis its uniqueness. Its glinting, cold green mineral attack allows Chablis a special hauteur in a modern wine world caught in a feeding frenzy for the heady flavour of ripeness and warmth. This niche is one that the growers and producers of Chablis would do well not to desert in the face of those hot-blooded flavours of Chardonnay from warmer climes.

Chablis' vineyards are right at the limit beyond which the Chardonnay grape will not ripen. The Kimmeridgian limestone clay – a soil with fossilized oyster shells – present in all the traditional Chablis vineyard sites, gives a very particular character to the wines. Modern moves to increase Chablis' vineyard area, to increase yields in the vineyards – never a quality option in areas where the vine struggles to ripen – and to maximize the use of the malolactic fermentation to produce a soft, easy dry white wine merely serve to dilute Chablis' personality. No wonder the price is often no different from a supposedly inferior Mâcon-Villages; the flavours become virtually interchangeable, so why should one pay more?

Let's look at the heart of Chablis to see why it became famous in the first place. The appellation initially intrigued me because it is the first vineyard area you come across as you roar down the Autoroute du Soleil from Paris. But Chablis gives little indication in its wines or geography of being anything to do with the warm south. It comprises a small, chilly, isolated jumble of vineyards in the frost-prone valley of the river Serein about 160km (100 miles) north of Beaune, the wine capital of Burgundy's Côte d'Or.

This northern outpost of the Burgundy region is virtually all that is left of the extensive Yonne vineyards that used to supply the bulk of Paris' everyday wine, before the railways brought warmer and more suitable wine regions within easy reach, though there is a new lease of life in such outlying villages as Épineuil, Irancy and Vézelay. I've never read a complimentary word about those old Yonne wines (which must have been feeble in the extreme) but

Chablis survived – just – because the grape it grows is the great Chardonnay of white Burgundy fame. Huddled along the banks of the tiny river Serein, angled towards the south-west and protected from the harsh winds of this semi-continental climate, there are a few slopes of Kimmeridgian limestone that can, in a good summer, produce sublime dry white wine. Its fame was such that the name Chablis has been coined indiscriminately throughout the world to label dry (and not so dry) white wines, made from whatever grape was to hand. True Chablis is a dry white wine that comes only from these vineyards, and only uses the Chardonnay grape.

There has been considerable expansion recently, and Chablis now has about 3155ha (7796 acres) of vines. This is a tenfold increase since the 1950s when Chablis was at its nadir. Much of this increase has merely been the return of good vineyard to production, but some of the new plantings are on barely suitable soil.

GRANDS CRUS AND PREMIERS CRUS

However, despite the general expansion, the Grands Crus have remained virtually unchanged and command a long, steep, south-west-facing slope of vines rising up at between 150 and 250m (492 and 820ft) from the river Serein opposite the town of Chablis. If we remember that this is a cold, inhospitable region in which to grow grapes, the mesoclimates created by aspect to the sun and the warming influences of the river and the town are all-important. Frost has always been a far greater problem in Chablis than elsewhere in Burgundy and the Grands Crus were always the worst hit, for the narrow Serein Valley tends to trap cold air masses. Various protection methods are now used to combat the worst effects of the frost but in the 1950s the viability of these great vineyards was called into question. In 1956 Les Clos, which produces the nuttiest, most honeyed of all the Grands Crus, was being used as a ski slope.

THE CHABLIS VINEYARDS

Chablis' Grand Cru vineyards sit lower down the south-west-facing slopes opposite the town where more sunshine means better ripening. The soil of the Grand Cru vineyards is rich in lime which enables the Chardonnay grapes to remain acid while ripening thoroughly.

■ Grands Crus
■ Premiers Crus
■ Chablis
□ Petit Chablis

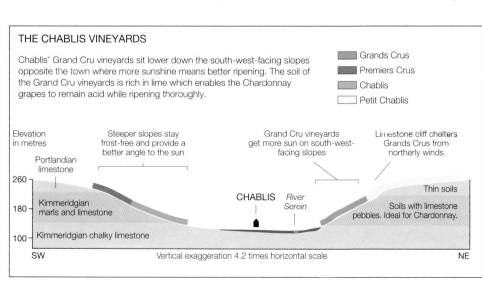

There are seven different Grand Cru vineyard sites covering 100ha (247 acres), all contiguous, but all subtly different. Their true characters only become evident with a judicious marriage of low yields in the vineyards and a few years' bottle aging. The modern tendency to use new oak barrels for both fermenting and aging can produce delicious results but usually blurs the distinctions between each site. A newly established Grand Cru Syndicate looks determined to preserve these distinctions. There has been a massive expansion of Premier Cru sites with the result that the words 'Premier Cru' on a Chablis label no longer guarantee a wine much superior to a basic Chablis. However, there are some excellent Premier Cru sites, usually not quite so

steep as the Grands Crus, and often with a more south to south-east aspect, thereby missing some of the warm afternoon sun. Those on the Serein's east bank are best though there are other fine ones directly south-west of the town.

CHABLIS AND PETIT CHABLIS
Simple Chablis is made further away from the town of Chablis itself, its quality depending upon the mesoclimate and the determination of the grower. Petit Chablis – the lowest form of Chablis from the least suitable sites – is being systematically, and cynically, upgraded to Chablis, a move that does nothing for the reputation of the region.

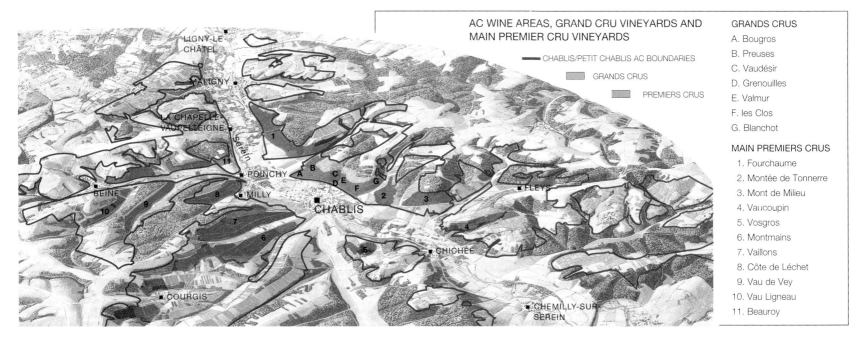

AC WINE AREAS, GRAND CRU VINEYARDS AND MAIN PREMIER CRU VINEYARDS

— CHABLIS/PETIT CHABLIS AC BOUNDARIES

GRANDS CRUS

PREMIERS CRUS

GRANDS CRUS
A. Bougros
B. Preuses
C. Vaudésir
D. Grenouilles
E. Valmur
F. les Clos
G. Blanchot

MAIN PREMIERS CRUS
1. Fourchaume
2. Montée de Tonnerre
3. Mont de Milieu
4. Vaucoupin
5. Vosgros
6. Montmains
7. Vaillons
8. Côte de Léchet
9. Vau de Vey
10. Vau Ligneau
11. Beauroy

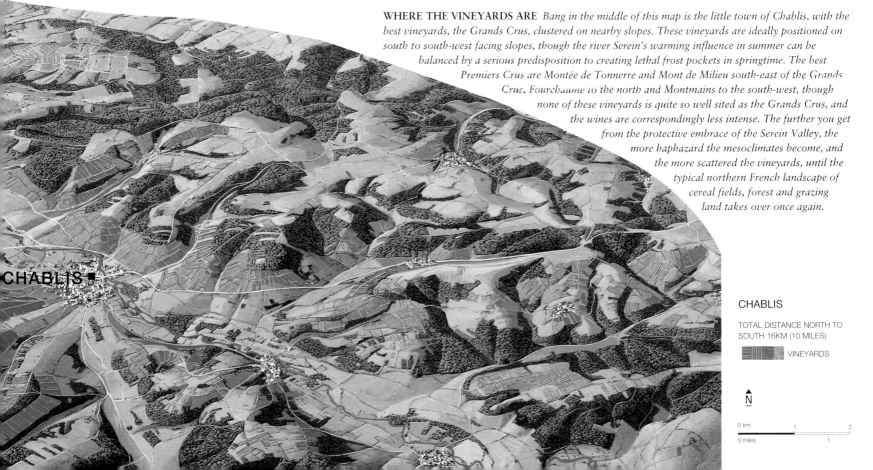

WHERE THE VINEYARDS ARE *Bang in the middle of this map is the little town of Chablis, with the best vineyards, the Grands Crus, clustered on nearby slopes. These vineyards are ideally positioned on south to south-west facing slopes, though the river Serein's warming influence in summer can be balanced by a serious predisposition to creating lethal frost pockets in springtime. The best Premiers Crus are Montée de Tonnerre and Mont de Milieu south-east of the Grands Crus, Fourchaume to the north and Montmains to the south-west, though none of these vineyards is quite so well sited as the Grands Crus, and the wines are correspondingly less intense. The further you get from the protective embrace of the Serein Valley, the more haphazard the mesoclimates become, and the more scattered the vineyards, until the typical northern French landscape of cereal fields, forest and grazing land takes over once again.*

CHABLIS

TOTAL DISTANCE NORTH TO SOUTH 16KM (10 MILES)

VINEYARDS

N

0 km   1   2
0 miles   1

CÔTE DE NUITS

 RED GRAPES
Pinot Noir is the only grape allowed in non-generic wines.

WHITE GRAPES
Among the few Côte de Nuits whites Chardonnay is the main grape, though some of the best examples use Pinot Blanc.

CLIMATE
This is sunnier in the growing season than Bordeaux but the autumns are cool and the winters long and cold. Spring frosts and hail can cause problems. The Hautes-Côtes are less protected from the prevailing westerly winds and can get heavy rain.

 SOIL
The Côte d'Or is basically a limestone ridge where weathering has produced a stony scree-like limestone and clay topsoil, especially on middle slopes, which provides the best drainage for the vines.

ASPECT
The top vineyards are situated on the middle slopes at 250–300m (820–984ft) where the steeper gradients, as well as the soil structure, facilitate drainage. The south- or south-east-facing aspect of the best sites also enhances exposure to the sun and therefore ripening in these northern vineyards.

CÔTE DE NUITS AND HAUTES-CÔTES DE NUITS

TOTAL DISTANCE NORTH TO SOUTH 28KM (17½ MILES)

VINEYARDS

N

MY FAVOURITE PLACE in the Côte de Nuits, one of the world's greatest vineyard regions, isn't the most famous. It's in the village of Prémeaux, just to the south of the town of Nuits St-Georges. Here you can step off the N74 road into the vines right below the marvellous Clos Arlot vineyard. At this point, the Côte de Nuits is little more than 90m (295ft) across, one side to the other. Admittedly this is the narrowest part, but the point is that the Côte de Nuits, which includes many of the most famous red wine names in the world, is a mere sliver of land snaking its way in and out of an east-facing escarpment that marks the eastern edge of the Morvan hills. The Côte lies between 250 and 350m (820 and 1148ft) above sea level. The escarpment is limestone, which continues down the slope to the plain. On this slope, over the millennia, soil has been created through a mixture of eroded limestone, pebbles and clays. An outcrop of rich dark marlstone is particularly in evidence in the middle of the slope at around the 275m (902ft) mark. All the greatest vineyards are situated within 25m (82ft), more or less, of this height and face mainly east or south-east.

PINOT NOIR'S HOMELAND
The really top vineyards are planted with red Pinot Noir. Indeed the whole Côte de Nuits is overwhelmingly a red wine slope, with

WHERE THE VINEYARDS ARE *There are a lot of vineyards on this map. But the ones that really matter, the world-famous red wine vineyards of the Côte de Nuits, are few in number and precisely delineated. The Côte de Nuits begins where the hills rise up south of Dijon. The N74 road runs due south and, with a few exceptions in Gevrey-Chambertin, Morey-St-Denis and Nuits-St-Georges, marks the eastern boundary of good vineyard land. All the best vineyards occupy a thin band of this east-facing escarpment between Gevrey-Chambertin and Nuits-St-Georges. Here the aspect to the sun, the drainage afforded by the slopes and the protection provided from wind and rain by the hills to the west, all combine to create what many consider to be the Pinot Noir grape's spiritual home. The vineyards to the west, in the mountains, are the Hautes-Côtes de Nuits. They are higher and less well protected than those of the Côte de Nuits. The wines made here are generally pleasant but are often on the light side.*

just a little rosé being made at Marsannay in the north, and a few bottles of rare white being made at Morey-St-Denis, Nuits-St-Georges, Vougeot and, most famously, Musigny at Chambolle-Musigny. Otherwise Pinot Noir rules. White grapes prefer impoverished, easy-draining limestone soils, and in the Côte de Beaune to the south there are various instances of limestone dominating the slopes. But here in the Côte de Nuits, limestone merely seems to temper the rich marl soil and reduce its fertility. Over-fertile soil never produces great wine, but this mixture seems just right.

CÔTE DE NUITS CLASSIFICATIONS
The great vineyards start in the north at the village of Gevrey-Chambertin and form an almost unbroken line through Morey-St-Denis, Chambolle-Musigny and Vougeot to Vosne-Romanée. Many of the Nuits-St-Georges vineyards are also very good, though none are classified as Grand Cru. Over the centuries vines in the very best sites have

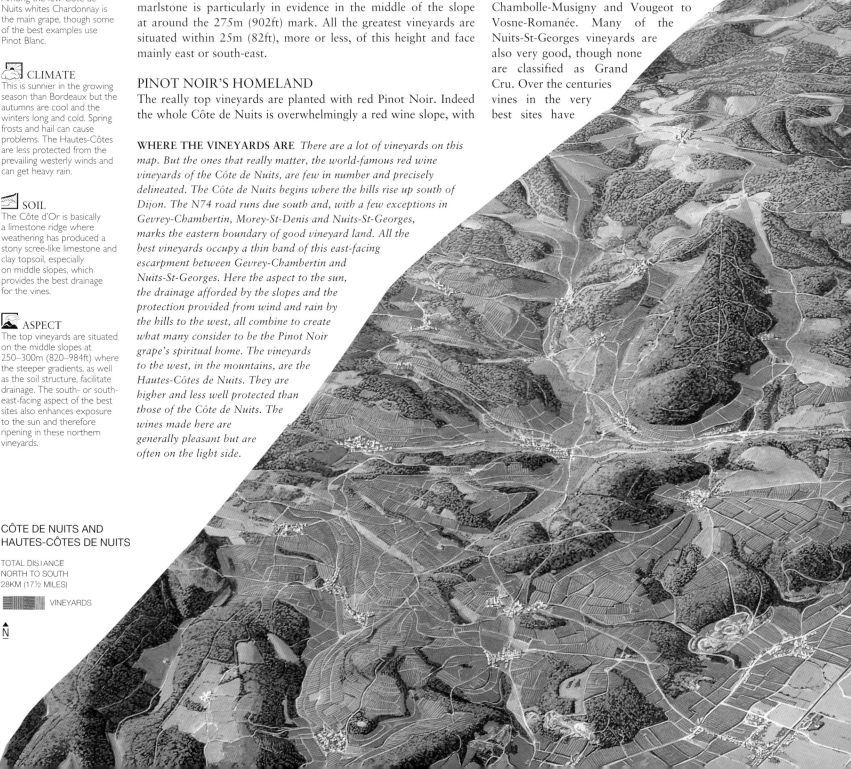

consistently ripened earlier than those too high up the slope or on flatter ground at the bottom. So a minutely accurate system of vineyard classification has evolved. The Grands Crus are so carefully and jealously delineated that every single row of vines is separately assessed. The same goes for the second rank of vineyards, the Premiers Crus.

There are numerous instances of certain rows of vines being excluded from the higher appellation and condemned to the third tier – the village appellation. Even so, the village AC is still only applied to decent land, which almost always lies between the N74 and the escarpment to the west. Some vineyards, in the north at Brochon and Fixin, and in the south between Prémeaux-Prissey and Corgoloin, use the collective appellation Côte de Nuits-Villages. Less suitable land, such as the flatter vineyards to the east of the N74 (better suited to cattle and vegetables), is relegated to regional or generic appellations – Aligoté, Bourgogne, Bourgogne Passe-Tout-Grains and Bourgogne Grand Ordinaire – a good deal more Ordinary than Grand.

But the good Côte de Nuits Burgundies are very grand indeed. Red wines from a cool area like Burgundy should be delicate, not monumental, but that relatively rich soil, sloped east and south-east, can, when the summer is warm and the grape grower careful to limit his yield, produce wines of disturbing, heady brilliance. These can often be dark and brooding when young, especially those from Gevrey-Chambertin, but may break out into glorious exotic scents as they age, in particular at Vosne-Romanée and Chambolle-Musigny, finally maturing into a state of delectable decay, when all the savagery, sweetness and scent melds into a dark, ripe autumn richness of quite astonishing beauty. From the

Some of Burgundy's top vineyards are surrounded by a wall, or clos in French. Clos St-Jacques, above, is perhaps Gevrey-Chambertin's best Premier Cru.

VILLAGE ACS, GRAND CRU AND MAIN PREMIER CRU VINEYARDS

1. MARSANNAY

2. FIXIN
   Main Premiers Crus: Clos du Chapitre, Clos de la Perrière.

3. GEVREY-CHAMBERTIN
   Grands Crus: Chambertin, Chambertin-Clos de Bèze, Chapelle-Chambertin, Charmes-Chambertin, Mazoyères-Chambertin, Griotte-Chambertin, Latricières-Chambertin, Mazis-Chambertin, Ruchottes-Chambertin.

Main Premiers Crus: les Cazetiers, Clos St-Jacques, Clos des Varoilles, Combe aux Moines, aux Combottes, Estournelles St-Jacques, Lavaut St-Jacques.

4. MOREY-ST-DENIS
   Grands Crus: Bonnes-Mares (part), Clos des Lambrays, Clos de la Roche, Clos St-Denis, Clos de Tart.
   Main Premiers Crus: la Bussière, Clos des Ormes, les Milandes, les Monts Luisants, les Ruchots.

5. CHAMBOLLE-MUSIGNY
   Grands Crus: Bonnes-Mares (part), Musigny.
   Main Premiers Crus: les Amoureuses, les Baudes, les Charmes, les Cras, les Fuées, les Sentiers.

6. VOUGEOT
   Grand Cru: Clos de Vougeot.

7. VOSNE-ROMANÉE
   Grands Crus: Grande-Rue, Richebourg, la Romanée, la Romanée-Conti, Romanée-St-Vivant, la Tâche, and (in the commune of Flagey-Échézeaux) Échézeaux, Grands-Échézeaux.
   Main Premiers Crus: les Beaux Monts, aux Brûlées, les Chaumes, Clos des Réas, Cros Parantoux, aux Malconsorts, les Suchots.

8. NUITS-ST-GEORGES
   Main Premiers Crus: aux Boudots, aux Bousselots, les Cailles, aux Chaignots, Clos des Argillières, Clos Arlot, Clos des Corvées, Clos des Forêts-St-Georges, Clos de la Maréchale, Clos des Porrets-St-Georges, les Damodes, aux Murgers, aux Perdrix, les Porrets-St-Georges, les Pruliers, la Richemone, Roncière, les St-Georges, aux Thorey, les Vaucrains, aux Vignes Rondes.

GRAND CRU VINEYARDS

PREMIER CRU VINEYARDS

VILLAGE AC BOUNDARIES

Looking eastwards from the vineyards of Nuits-St-Georges over the town. The autumnal gold of the vine leaves complements the glistening tiles on the church spire.

best growers, the nuances of flavour detectable in wines from vines only yards apart offer a marriage between the hedonistic and the intellectual that hardly any other wines ever manage. From a bad grower or merchant, there are few bigger, nor more expensive, disappointments than a thin, lifeless wine masquerading under these great names.

VILLAGES OF THE CÔTE DE NUITS

If you look at the top of the map on pages 58-59, you can hardly spot a vine. There used to be loads of vineyards to Dijon's south-west, but the city's suburban sprawl has swallowed them up. In any case, they were mostly planted with Gamay to make cheap quaffing wine for Dijon, not classy Burgundy. Chenôve still has a few vines on the slope just north of Marsannay, but Marsannay is the first serious village. It used to be famous for rosé, but is now an increasingly useful supplier of good, perfumed, though lightweight reds and some pleasant whites. The slopes at Couchey, Fixin and Brochon might look pretty suitable for vines: they grow Pinot Noir, but little of great excitement ever comes to light. Fixin's heavy clay soils can give good sturdy reds in a hot year.

The real fireworks start at Gevrey-Chambertin. Here the rich marl soil comes properly into play, with red clays peppered with stones, and outbreaks of rich subsoil through a thin layer of topsoil on the higher sites. The narrow east- and south-east-facing slope under its protective forest brow continues almost unbroken between Gevrey-Chambertin and Nuits-St-Georges. Here the Pinot Noir really shows what it can do.

Those village names, by the way. Over the centuries, the best Côte d'Or villages found that they had one vineyard above all whose wines people sought. The village of Gevrey had Chambertin,

the village of Chambolle had Musigny, and so on. So, to grab a little reflected glory from their greatest vineyard – and a little more profit from allying their less exciting wine with that of the star performer – wine producers hyphenated the vineyard name to that of the village for their wines.

So. Back to Gevrey-Chambertin. This village distinguishes itself with nine Grands Crus – the most of any Côte d'Or commune – safely protected from the wet westerlies by the Montagne de la Combe Grizard. The lesser vineyards spread down to and, unusually, across the N74, where a pebbly subsoil is supposed to provide enough drainage. Maybe. The potential for riches at every level in Gevrey is high but the variation among producers is dramatic. It's a problem of popularity. Chambertin, which can be so sensuously savage at its best, is one of France's most famous reds. Wines with Chambertin in their title are not difficult to sell.

Morey-St-Denis is a good deal less famous, but the vineyards are just as good. There are five Grands Crus, on slightly steeper slopes with a little more limestone in evidence and, indeed, one steep, infertile site – Monts Luisants – that is famous for a beefy white. The reds, led by Clos de la Roche, have a sweet, ripe, fruity depth and a chocolaty softness.

Chambolle-Musigny is set into a little gully in the hillside, so there is a brief loss of protection for the vines and the Grand Cru, Bonnes-Mares, ends abruptly north of the village. The other Grand Cru, Musigny, doesn't commence till the south-east-facing slope begins again near Vougeot. At its best, Chambolle-Musigny can be hauntingly perfumed.

The chief wine of Vougeot is the 50-ha (124-acre) walled Grand Cru, Clos de Vougeot. This runs right down to the N74, on to considerably lower and more alluvial soil than any other Grand Cru. Add to this 80 different proprietors all eager to exploit the famous name, and you have a recipe for some decidedly rum bottles of Clos de Vougeot. At its best, though, it is fleshy and rich.

Directly above the fine, higher vines of Vougeot are those of Grands Crus, Échézeaux and Grands-Échézeaux. Their parent village, Flagey, is in fact down in the plain, and they are considered to be part of Vosne-Romanée. Lucky them, because the other six Vosne Grands Crus, especially La Tâche and La Romanée-Conti, are the most famous and expensive of all Burgundies. Intoxicating in their spice and heady scent, thrilling in their depth of dark fruit, they really do lead the way. The red clays spattered with pebbles undoubtedly put the other Vosne Grands Crus and Premiers Crus on a special level.

Nuits-St-Georges might seem hard done by to be Vosne's neighbour – it has no Grands Crus at all. Instead it has 38 Premiers Crus. In the valley to the west the protective curtain is broken, and many of the vineyards are on flat alluvial soil. But south of Nuits down to Prémeaux, the slopes steepen, narrow, and veer back towards the south-east. Here great wines are made, Grands Crus in all but name.

THE HAUTES-CÔTES DE NUITS

Up in the hills behind the Côte de Nuits slopes, planted in carefully selected sites, are the vines of the Hautes-Côtes de Nuits appellation. In warm years, the Hautes-Côtes de Nuits vineyards with the best aspect and drainage can make light, pleasant, mostly red, wine from Pinot Noir. But the word 'Hautes' or 'high' is important. We're far north here for a major red wine area. Red grapes usually need more heat to ripen than white – and the higher you get above sea level, the cooler the sun's rays become and the more exposed you are to wind and rain. That makes for thin wine most years.

CÔTE DE BEAUNE

I'M NOT A GREAT RESPECTER of traditions and reputations just for the sake of them. In the world of wine, I often think that there are more ill-deserved reputations and baseless traditions than the other way round. But I have to say, the first time I trekked up the narrow lane from the main road (the N6) at the village of Chassagne-Montrachet, patted the crumbling stone wall on the left rather gingerly with my hand, and then sneaked into the vineyard of le Montrachet, my heart was thumping with excitement.

Le Montrachet is quite possibly the greatest white wine vineyard in the world. But why? I tasted the grapes from its vines, then crossed the lane to taste the grapes of Bâtard-Montrachet – another of the great Grand Cru vineyards – only 9m (30ft) lower down. They were different. Le Montrachet's grapes seemed to have more intensity, more vibrant personality before they'd even been picked off the vine. I clambered over the wall above le Montrachet to the adjacent Chevalier-Montrachet vineyard. It's a matter of a couple of yards, but the stony soil of Chevalier gives more austere grapes, which in turn gives leaner, haughtier, yet still superlative wine.

Since then, on other occasions I've scratched away at the soil of le Montrachet, and know that it is stonier and less rich than that of its neighbours, except for the ultra-stony Chevalier-Montrachet. I've noticed how the slope is just that little bit steeper as it gently changes angle from an easterly to a south-easterly aspect. I've felt my face warmed by early morning sun, in the midst of its vines. I've sweltered under blazing midday sun; and in high summer, late into the evening, as the surrounding vineyards are cooling in the shade, I've felt the sun's rays still streaking towards me across le Montrachet's tiny clump of vines, as it sinks into a dip in the hills.

Mesoclimate. The perfect conjunction of soil, angle of slope, and aspect to the sun, providing just that bit more chance for these northern grapes to ripen to perfection. In every commune on the Côte d'Or the endlessly changing geological and climatic conditions create little plots of vineyard, some only a few hectares

broad, that give wines of more power, personality or finesse than those of their neighbours. This is what makes the Côte d'Or so fascinating, yet so exhausting a region to get to know.

Whereas the most famous wines of the Côte de Nuits, directly to the north of the Côte de Beaune, are all red, most of the world-renowned wines of the Côte de Beaune are white. And that's down to those mesoclimates again. In fact, 75 per cent of the Côte de Beaune wines are red. The fertile, red-tinged soils and, periodically, the marl that is such a feature of the Côte de Nuits, occupy the majority of the slopes, and in these cases Pinot Noir predominates. But the slopes here are less extreme, and the red Côte de Beaune wines, even from the one red Grand Cru vineyard of Corton, right next to the Côte de Nuits, have a rounder charm and less savage power than those of the Côte de Nuits itself. Wines from Aloxe-Corton, Beaune, Volnay and, in a rougher way, Pommard, are all marked by perfume rather than by power.

The whites at their best, however – from Chardonnay grapes planted where limestone dominates the darker clays – are marked by virtually every characteristic you could ask of a dry white wine. I say dry, because there is no sugar left in wines like Corton-Charlemagne, Meursault, Puligny-Montrachet, Chassagne-Montrachet, or the host of others that the different villages make. Yet the honey and butter lusciousness, the cream, the wafted scent of grilled nuts still warm from the fire, the cinnamon and nutmeg spice that ripples through the orchard fruits – all these flavours, plus the taut backbone of mineral, of herb, of smoke from a forest glade, are there. I can remember bottles like these drunk twenty years ago as clearly as if my glass were being refilled in front of me this very minute.

What is equally exciting is that, if you seek out good producers, you really can taste the difference in wines which come from neighbouring patches of vines. The Burgundian system of delineating each vineyard plot with distinctive characteristics is the most comprehensive in the world. Meursault-Perrières does have stonier soil than its neighbour Meursault-Charmes; the wine is tauter, it promises more, and will perhaps give more sublime satisfaction in time. That's how it should be. And fairly frequently, that's how it is.

 **RED GRAPES**
Pinot Noir is the only permitted grape in non-generic wines.

WHITE GRAPES
Chardonnay is the official grape, though there may still be some Pinot Blanc and Pinot Gris.

CLIMATE
The slopes are gentler here, providing less shelter from the westerly winds, so rainfall is higher than further north and heavy rain can be a problem. The temperatures are marginally milder than in the Côte de Nuits.

SOIL
The soil structure is basically similar to the Côte de Nuits, but with limestone outcrops more in evidence and these are often where the best vineyards, such as le Montrachet, are sited.

ASPECT
These are some lower slopes and more gentle gradients than in the Côte de Nuits but the south- to south-east-facing aspect of many vineyards is even more critical here.

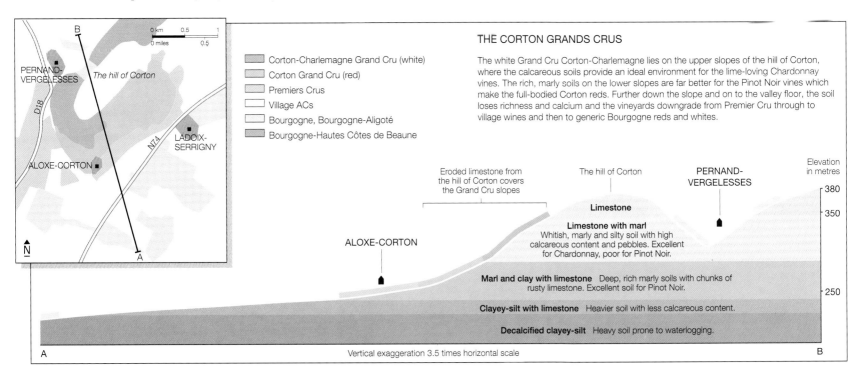

THE CORTON GRANDS CRUS

The white Grand Cru Corton-Charlemagne lies on the upper slopes of the hill of Corton, where the calcareous soils provide an ideal environment for the lime-loving Chardonnay vines. The rich, marly soils on the lower slopes are far better for the Pinot Noir vines which make the full-bodied Corton reds. Further down the slope and on to the valley floor, the soil loses richness and calcium and the vineyards downgrade from Premier Cru through to village wines and then to generic Bourgogne reds and whites.

Corton-Charlemagne Grand Cru (white)
Corton Grand Cru (red)
Premiers Crus
Village ACs
Bourgogne, Bourgogne-Aligoté
Bourgogne-Hautes Côtes de Beaune

The entrance to the Hôtel-Dieu in Beaune, scene of the annual Hospices de Beaune charity wine auction. Ornate tiled roofs such as this are found all over Burgundy.

VOLNAY-SANTENOTS-DU-MILIEU
1996
Domaine des Comtes LAFON

CÔTE DE BEAUNE CLASSIFICATIONS

As in the Côte de Nuits, the top vineyard sites are given the status of Grand Cru, but the procession of Grands Crus at around the 275m (902ft) mark isn't repeated in the Côte de Beaune, and there are only two groups of Grands Crus – one in the north, at Aloxe-Corton, and one in the south straddling Puligny-Montrachet and Chassagne-Montrachet. Apart from these two, the best vineyards for both red and white wines are Premiers Crus. The same detailed examination of the vines, row by row took place to determine the status of a plot of land because, in this cool area, the slightest nuance can make the difference between great and merely good wine. An almost imperceptible dip in the field, a scarcely registered change in slope angle or exposure to the sun, a brief streak of clay running across a limestone ridge – all these tiny details combine to form the great imponderable the French call *terroir*. And of all the French areas to take *terroir* seriously, the Côte d'Or, with its obsessive classification, is the most passionate.

Below these levels are the village appellations, and though many of these are on flatter, alluvial land, the quality is still pretty good. Sixteen villages can use the title Côte de Beaune-Villages for their reds, rather than their own village name, but these days this option is rarely exercised except by merchants keen to make up a blend. Côte de Beaune is a tiny red and white appellation from a slope west of Beaune. The least good vineyards only qualify for the Bourgogne, Bourgogne Passe-Touts-Grains or Bourgogne Grand Ordinaire ACs.

VILLAGES OF THE CÔTE DE BEAUNE

The Côte de Beaune really begins with the great hill of Corton, and three villages share its slopes – Ladoix, Aloxe-Corton and Pernand-Vergelesses. This impressive, proud crescent of vines swings right round from east to west with the pale, weathered limestone soils of Corton and Corton-Charlemagne producing white wine right up to the forest fringe at 350m (1148ft). The lower slopes produce round, succulent red Corton; in general the east-facing slopes are best for red, the west-facing for white.

Savigny is tucked into the valley just north-west of Beaune with less protected and, indeed, some north-facing vineyards, but its reds and whites are generally good. Beaune is more famous and the style of its wine is more traditionally soft and mellow; excellent red and white Premiers Crus reach down towards the town itself. Pommard and Volnay have steep, uneven slopes climbing up into the scrub-covered hills. They jig in and out, creating numerous different aspects to the sun, affording erratic protection for the vines. This means that the mesoclimate becomes particularly important, especially for the demanding Pinot Noir which dominates Pommard and Volnay. These are often jealously delimited by wall enclosures.

The heart of the Côte de Beaune runs from Meursault to Chassagne-Montrachet. Here, between 240 and 300m (788 and 984ft), with a few fine vineyards as high as

350m (1148ft) round the hamlet of Blagny, the Chardonnay revels in the spare stony soils and the limestone outcrops jutting to within inches of the surface, delights in the dips and curves of the east- to south-east-facing slopes and produces a fascinating array of brilliant flavours. All are minutely but recognizably different, and every one, when created by a serious producer, is a triumphant vindication of the notion of *terroir*. At Chassagne-Montrachet the soils become heavier again, spreading south-west to Santenay and then trailing away further west to Maranges, and more red than white is grown once again.

HAUTES-CÔTES DE BEAUNE

You can see numerous vineyards in the hills behind the Côte de Beaune. These are included in the appellation Hautes-Côtes de Beaune. It's a heavenly part of Burgundy, with twisting country lanes, ancient avenues of trees, and a tranquillity conducive to relaxing with the very best of Burgundies. But these slopes are a crucial 50 to 100m (164 to 328ft) higher than those of the Côte de Beaune, are less perfectly angled to the sun and less protected from wind and rain. They produce pleasant light reds and whites when the weather's warm – just right for a picnic in one of the high meadows.

WHERE THE VINEYARDS ARE *The Côte de Beaune is less of a single strip of land directly beneath an escarpment than the Côte de Nuits. In the Côte de Beaune there are several large re-entrants into the hills harbouring major vineyard sites; the vineyards themselves slope more gently and expansively towards the plain, and the soil structures are far less homogeneous, veering between austere barren limestone and rich marly limestone. With the exception of Volnay, whose delicate reds come largely from light, stony soils, it is the heavier soils that produce red wines. The lighter, limestone-based soil produces peerless whites such as at Puligny-Montrachet, Chassagne-Montrachet and Meursault. The hill of Corton at the top of the map is unusual in that it has two Grands Crus, one for red and one for white wine. Historic Beaune is regarded as the wine capital of Burgundy. Excellent villages like St-Aubin, St-Romain and Auxey-Duresses are less well-known and less popular. The vineyards right up in the hills to the west are the Hautes-Côtes de Beaune.*

CÔTE DE BEAUNE AND HAUTES-CÔTES DE BEAUNE

TOTAL DISTANCE
NORTH TO SOUTH
25KM (15½ MILES)

▓▓▓▓▓ VINEYARDS

N

VILLAGE ACS, GRAND CRU VINEYARDS AND MAIN PREMIER CRU VINEYARDS

1. LADOIX
   Grands Crus: Corton (part), Corton-Charlemagne (part).

2. PERNAND-VERGELESSES
   Grands Crus: Corton (part), Corton-Charlemagne (part).
   Main Premiers Crus: Ile des Vergelesses, les Vergelesses.

3. ALOXE-CORTON
   Grands Crus: Corton (part), Corton-Charlemagne (part).
   Main Premiers Crus: les Chaillots, les Maréchaudes, les Valozières.

4. CHOREY-LÈS-BEAUNE

5. SAVIGNY-LÈS-BEAUNE
   Main Premiers Crus: aux Guettes, les Lavières, aux Serpentières, les Vergelesses.

6. BEAUNE
   Main Premiers Crus: les Avaux, les Boucherottes, les Bressandes, les Cents Vignes, Champs Pimont, le Clos des Mouches, le Clos de la Mousse, Clos du Roi, les Cras, les Epenotes, les Fèves, les Grèves,

les Marconnets, les Teurons, les Toussaints, les Vignes Franches.

7. POMMARD
   Main Premiers Crus: les Arvelets, les Boucherottes, Clos Blanc, Clos de la Commaraine, Clos des Epeneaux, les Grands Epenots, les Petits Epenots, les Pézerolles, les Rugiens-Bas, les Rugiens-Hauts.

8. VOLNAY
   Main Premiers Crus: les Angles, Clos de la Bousse d'Or, les Caillerets, Champans, Clos des Chênes, Clos des Ducs, les Santenots, Taillo Pieds.

9. MONTHELIE
   Main Premiers Crus: les Champs Fulliot, les Duresses, sur la Velle.

10. MEURSAULT
    Main Premiers Crus: les Charmes,

les Perrières, les Genevrières, les Gouttes d'Or, le Porusot. Certain red wines can also be sold as Volnay or Blagny.

11. AUXEY-DURESSES
    Main Premiers Crus: Climat du Val, Clos du Val, les Duresses.

12. ST-ROMAIN

13. PULIGNY-MONTRACHET
    Grands Crus: Bâtard-Montrachet (part), Bienvenues-Bâtard-Montrachet, Chevalier-Montrachet, le Montrachet (part).
    Main Premiers Crus: le Cailleret, le Champ Canet, Clavaillon, les Combettes, les Demoiselles,

les Folatières, la Garenne, les Pucelles, les Referts, la Truffière.

14. ST-AUBIN
    Main Premiers Crus: le Charmois, la Chatenière, en Rémilly.

15. CHASSAGNE-MONTRACHET
    Grands Crus: Bâtard-Montrachet (part), Criots-Bâtard-Montrachet, le Montrachet (part).
    Main Premiers Crus: les Baudines, la Boudriotte, Cailleret, les Champs Gains, les Chaumées,

les Chenevottes, Clos St-Jean, les Embasées, la Grande Montagne, les Grandes Ruchottes, les Macherelles, la Maltroie, Morgeot, la Romanée, les Vergers.

16. SANTENAY
    Main Premiers Crus: Beauregard, le Clos des Mouches, le Clos de Tavannes, la Comme, Grand Clos Rousseau, les Gravières, la Maladière, Passetemps.

17. MARANGES

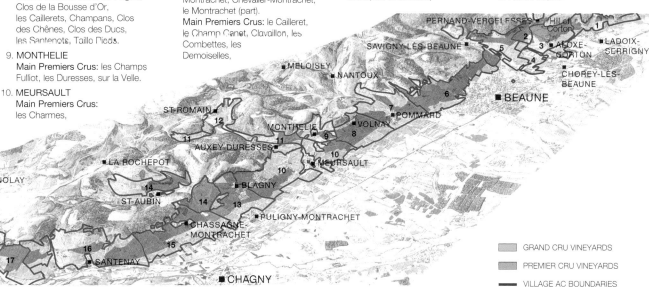

GRAND CRU VINEYARDS

PREMIER CRU VINEYARDS

VILLAGE AC BOUNDARIES

0 km   1   2
0 miles   1

CÔTE CHALONNAISE

RED GRAPES
The main grape is Pinot Noir.

WHITE GRAPES
The main grape is Chardonnay with some Aligoté at Bouzeron.

CLIMATE
It is less sheltered from westerly winds here than in the Côte d'Or, but though it is cooler the Côte Chalonnaise can also be drier. Getting enough sun to ripen the grapes is the main problem.

SOIL
The soils here are based on limestone or a mixture of limestone and clay.

ASPECT
In this scattering of low hills, a good aspect is vital for ripening, and the best sites are on south-, south-east- and east-facing slopes at about 220–350m (722–1148ft).

The steep limestone slopes of Montagny are at last fulfilling their potential for high-quality white wines.

I KNOW ALL ABOUT the prevailing westerly winds in the Côte Chalonnaise. A few years ago, in high summer, I was nosing about the Burgundian vineyards trying to work out what was what, and ended up at dusk with no hotel booking. How exciting, I thought. A night under the stars, warmed by the balmy August zephyrs. I hardly bothered with a blanket but plonked myself down on the broad ridge of vineyards, just south of Bouzeron and drifted off to sleep with a little smile of contentment playing on my lips. Then the wind got up. Wow. Balmy August zephyrs? Atlantic gale more like, as I stumbled freezing back to the car and spent a miserable rest of the night waiting for an early, and chilly dawn.

It made me appreciate just what a crucial job Burgundy's high hills do in protecting their vineyards against the prevailing westerlies. In the Côte d'Or, the range of hills is relatively unbroken from Dijon in the north to Santenay in the south. But then they trail unconvincingly away to the west, and what takes their place around the town of Chagny is a hotchpotch of disjointed hillocks, offering rare shelter from the wind and occasional sloping land angled towards the sun. This is the Côte Chalonnaise. A jumbled collection of mesoclimates, growing the same grapes as the Côte d'Or to the north, occasionally making wines of similar quality, but rarely with their richness, roundness or perfume. A poor relation? Yes. But consider what they are a poor relation to. The greatest Pinot Noir and Chardonnay vineyards in France, possibly in the world? A poor relation to these isn't so bad.

Even so, you have to choose your sites carefully here. The best are on limestone-dominated slopes, slanted, sometimes steeply, to between south-east and south-west to catch every available ray of sun. Most vines are planted at between 220 and 350m (722 and 1148ft) above sea level – much the same as in the Côte d'Or – but, with the shining exception of the top section of the famous Corton hill, no exciting Côte d'Or vineyards are set above 300m (984ft). The leanness that characterizes many Chalonnais wines is easily explained by this relatively high altitude, less-than-perfect wind protection, and the lack of gently angled, continuously south-east-facing slopes.

BOUZERON
The leanness doesn't matter at Bouzeron, the most northerly Chalonnais appellation, because Bouzeron has made its reputation with a lemon-sharp, peppery, yet buttermilk-scented dry white from the Aligoté grape. There is some Chardonnay and Pinot Noir sold

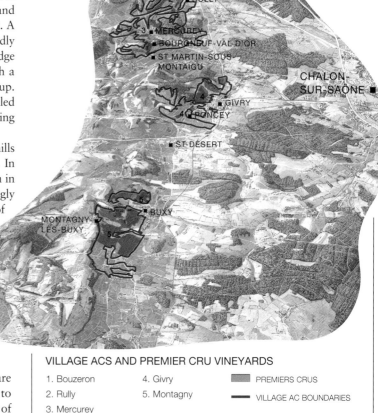

VILLAGE ACS AND PREMIER CRU VINEYARDS

1. Bouzeron	4. Givry	▰ PREMIERS CRUS
2. Rully	5. Montagny	— VILLAGE AC BOUNDARIES
3. Mercurey		

simply as Bourgogne, but Aligoté is the main wine here. Wine from old vines, marked *vieilles vignes*, generally has a little more Chardonnay-like richness to it.

RULLY
Rully has traditionally been seen as a sparkling wine area, but now deserves better. The light, lean wines from some steepish limestone slopes have the delicacy and acidity much prized by fizz-makers, but a better understanding of vineyard practice and winemaking, and a bit of self-confidence, have been injected into the area by merchant houses like Rodet. These have brought forth light but cherry-scented Pinot Noir reds, and lean-limbed but tasty Chardonnays, especially with oak barrel-aging. Some of the better vineyards have Premier Cru status, but it doesn't mean that much.

MERCUREY
Mercurey to the south is the largest Chalonnais village appellation, with just under 90 per cent of it being red wine from Pinot Noir. Again, we're not talking about really big-boned wines here – the leanness still comes through – but there is a considerable difference in perfume and style between the lighter wines from the limestone slopes and the chunkier ones from the clay vineyards. The whites have rarely been special but, as in Rully, efforts by leading growers, as well as the main merchant houses like Faiveley and Rodet, have greatly improved the whites and added more flesh to the reds. There are a fair number of Premier Cru vineyards, the best south-facing slopes being located to the north of the town.

GIVRY
Givry has an impressive ring of south-east-facing vines rising to the west of the town. Although the soil here begins to shift away from the

friable limestone of the north towards a more fertile mix of clay and sandy limestone, Givry's best sites give a red wine of reasonable depth and considerable flavour in warm years. After a few years' aging, these wines can develop an almost sweet strawberry and cherry fruit. Those sheltered slopes do pay off. There is a little white from Chardonnay but none of it is that exciting.

MONTAGNY

Several miles south, again on steep slopes and in the clefts of little valleys, the all-white Montagny appellation is at last producing interesting Chardonnay wines from what is clearly excellent vineyard land. Montagny whites used to be bone dry and stony-flavoured and not much fun to drink. Now, with better vinification and the judicious use of oak barrels, they can be excellent, dry, yet softly toasty whites. The most important producer of Montagny is the go-ahead

WHERE THE VINEYARDS ARE *Although the Côte Chalonnaise is south of the Côte de Beaune, and you'd expect the climate therefore to be warmer, it doesn't quite work like that. There is no regularity to the landscape in the Chalonnais, there is little shelter from the wind, particularly the westerlies, and the vineyards are frequently at a higher altitude than those to the north. In addition, the marl and limestone that form the basis of the Côte d'Or soils dwindle as we head south towards the Mâconnais.*

Even so, it is easy to see on the map where the best vineyard sites are. The little cleft of Bouzeron, and the well-protected south-east-facing slopes of Rully are particularly good for white wine. Mercurey is more spread out, with the best red wines coming from the protected south-facing slopes to the north of the town. To the south, the villages of Bourgneuf-Val d'Or and St-Martin-sous-Montaigu are included in the appellation, with the latter producing the better wines. Givry has one particularly good south- to south-east-facing swathe of vines. Montagny occupies a relatively small but well-protected area of the southern Chalonnais.

co-operative at Buxy. Not only has the co-operative created high quality white from Montagny where only potential existed before, but it has transformed the quality of basic Chalonnais reds and whites. These used to be sold simply as Bourgogne but, in 1990, after considerable lobbying from Buxy, a new Bourgogne-Côte Chalonnaise appellation was created. The southern Chalonnais continues to develop and will produce exciting wines in the future, but it still lacks the prerequisite for real progress – the emergence of a bevy of good individual estates. The Mâconnais, to the south, is developing precisely that.

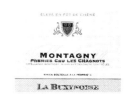

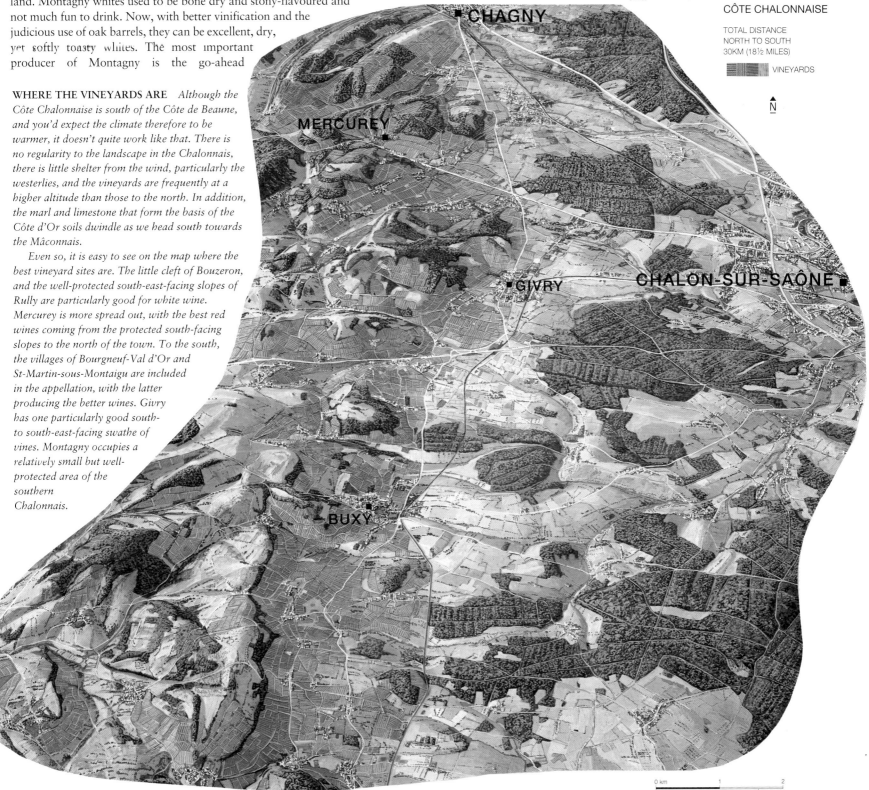

CÔTE CHALONNAISE

TOTAL DISTANCE
NORTH TO SOUTH
30KM (18½ MILES)

VINEYARDS

N

CHAGNY

MERCUREY

GIVRY

CHALON-SUR-SAÔNE

BUXY

0 km · 1 · 2
0 miles · · 1

MÂCONNAIS

 **RED GRAPES**
Gamay is the main variety, followed by Pinot Noir.

WHITE GRAPES
Chardonnay is the main grape, with small amounts of Aligoté.

CLIMATE
The Mediterranean influence begins to be felt with higher temperatures and occasional storms. Overall, annual rainfall is higher than in the Côte d'Or to the north. Spring frosts can be a problem.

SOIL
There are two basic types of soil: limestone, favoured by the white vines, and a mix of clay and sand, favoured by the reds.

ASPECT
This is a region of low hills cut by a series of transverse valleys which usefully create south-, south-east- and south-west-facing slopes with good exposure to the sun.

YOU CAN APPROACH the Mâconnais at 270km (168 miles) per hour – on the TGV train from Paris that drops its dazed travellers at Mâcon station before surging onward to Lyon and the Mediterranean. Or you can approach the Mâconnais at half the speed, or slightly less if you're a law-abiding citizen, on the Autoroute du Soleil. Or you can approach it at whatever ambling, easy-going pace that the farmers' droning tractors, the smallholders' wheezing Deux Chevaux and the odd roaming sheep, cow and goat will let you – by the country roads that twist and turn through the charming rural backwaters at the southern end of the Côte Chalonnaise, gradually dropping down to the blander, broader spaces of the Mâconnais.

I'd take the time to meander, if I were you. The Mâconnais stretches north to south for about 50km (31 miles) from the southernmost tip of the Côte Chalonnaise to the border with the Beaujolais region at St-Vérand. It isn't the most startling of landscapes, being mainly a continual vista of gently rolling hills and dales. Vines share the land with other crops and with Charollais cattle. The wines aren't the most startling of wines either. But something does happen here, amid the orchards, the meadows and the rather four-square spreads of vineyard land.

The air that can seem so damp and chill right the way through northern France, and most poignantly so in Burgundy's Côte d'Or, seems warmer here, friendlier, more benign. The fogs here seem more like wisps of white cotton, rather than the palls of grey misery further north. The sun spreads itself more broadly in a sky that is wider and coloured increasingly with the azure of the South stretching into infinity. And the houses – these are what finally tell you you're leaving the North behind. The angular, defensive rooftops and storm-coloured slates give way to the warm, rounded terracotta tiles of Provence. The roofs become almost flat, and open porches and verandahs or *galeries* face southwards towards the sun. The heart-warming South begins here in the Mâconnais.

But does the Mâconnais produce wines worthy of its position at the portals of the South? It definitely could – in an increasing number of instances, it does – but in general, Mâconnais wines suffer from what is, I suppose, an understandable identity crisis.

GRAPE VARIETIES

Until quite recently, most of the 6500ha (16,061 acres) of Mâconnais vineyards produced red wine, mainly from Gamay, but with some Pinot Noir being grown too. There has not been one single famous Mâcon red wine in living memory. Most of the Gamays are earthy and rough, with acidity dominating their meagre fruit. From the villages of Igé in the centre of the region and Mancey in the north, occasional full-bodied reds emerge. Local producers absorb much of the Pinot Noir to make sparkling Crémant de Bourgogne, and now under 9 per cent of the Mâconnais vines are red. Most of the still red Mâcon wine is sold as Mâcon Supérieur, which has a slightly higher minimum alcohol level than straight Mâcon.

Not surprisingly, and reflecting the explosion of worldwide interest, the Chardonnay grape now occupies 90 per cent of the Mâconnais vineyards (there is just a little Aligoté too). Indeed, there is a village called Chardonnay here, near Tournus in the north of the region, that tradition claims as the birthplace of the Chardonnay vine. There is no reason why this shouldn't be true as Chardonnay is the traditional white grape round here.

But the locals have taken an awfully long time to show any great pride in their famous offspring and the wines were rarely exciting. Only now are we seeing a gentle flowering of single estates showing just how good Mâconnais Chardonnay can be.

THE POUILLY APPELLATIONS

Certainly the Mâconnais region has some of the best Chardonnay vineyards in France – those of Pouilly-Fuissé. This wine became rather too famous for its own good, primarily because of its phenomenal success on the American market, and this had the usual consequences of overproduction with a lowering of quality, and scary price hikes.

Yet the beautifully angled vineyards that carpet the lower slopes of the magnificent rock of Solutré, and its near twin, the rock of Vergisson in the south of the region, are of a superb quality. An increasing number of growers here produce delectable examples of Chardonnay under the Pouilly-Fuissé banner, with the round, oatmealy softness of a Meursault fattened out and honeyed by the Mâconnais' warmer southern sun. But most Pouilly-Fuissé is still made by co-operatives and sold under merchants' labels. Such wines are simply pleasant dry Chardonnay at best, and a good deal less than that at worst.

Pouilly-Fuissé comes from five villages – Chaintré (generally regarded as the least good), Solutré, Vergisson, Pouilly and Fuissé. The nearby villages of Loché and Vinzelles, between Pouilly-Fuissé and Mâcon, have attached Pouilly to their names to share a bit of the glory, but, though their wines can be pleasant, the vineyards are flatter and more fertile and thus are less capable of growing the best Chardonnay grapes.

ST-VÉRAN

A more recent Mâcon appellation is St-Véran which lies right on the border with the Beaujolais region. Vineyards in the southern part of the appellation around the villages of St-Vérand, Chânes, Chasselas, Leynes and St-Amour-Bellevue can produce either white St-Véran, which has mopped up most of what used to be called Beaujolais Blanc or red St-Amour, one of the top Beaujolais Crus, and it is not uncommon to find producers here who make both wines. Wines from here are usually rather stony in character. There is another section of St-Véran vineyards north of Pouilly-Fuissé, on the outskirts of the villages of Davayé and Prissé, and these wines are much fuller and fatter.

THE ROCK OF SOLUTRÉ

If I were to be in the Mâconnais on Midsummer's Day, I'd head for the massive jut-jawed rock of Solutré that rears out of the vineyards round Pouilly-Fuissé like a shark's snout breaking through the billowing green waves. The local inhabitants celebrate the longest day of the year by lighting a great bonfire of old vines and pruned branches, in honour of the Gauls' victorious battle for independence that took place near here in AD511. Standing at the base of this magnificent rock, and looking up its near-vertical face, you can see why, in this gently rolling landscape, with the broad Saône plain to the east, the Gauls chose this natural fortress. Then look down, at your feet, and think back another 15,000 years. Here, a massive deposit of Stone Age remains was discovered, in 1866, at the base of the rock. Among the remains was a metre-thick layer of about 1000 horse skeletons. It seems the prehistoric inhabitants of Solutré herded wild horses up the gentle eastern slope, and stampeded them over the cliff at the western end. Then they ate them.

The quality of St-Véran is fairly good – the wine is light and dry, rarely made with any oak, and often has a hint of muskiness quite common in the southern Mâconnais. If you want to check out the discreet charm of the Mâconnais at a fair price, St-Véran is a good place to start.

MÂCON BLANC

Although there is a simple Mâcon Blanc appellation, the white wine most commonly found is Mâcon-Villages. The best 26 villages can add their own name to the appellation – as in Mâcon-Lugny or Mâcon-Pierreclos. In 1999 local growers in Viré and Clessé, long regarded as two of the best of the Mâcon villages, successfully petitioned for their own appellation, called Viré-Clessé.

Production of Mâcon Blanc is dominated by one of France's most efficient networks of co-operative cellars, which are responsible for 60 per cent of all Mâconnais wine. Their organizational clout has brought about much of the region's prosperity. The standard of wine produced is generally decent to boot and the co-operatives also produce some of France's best sparkling wine, as Crémant de Bourgogne. But to really understand the potential of these pleasant vineyards set amid meadows, copses and glades, you must try the wines of the small but growing band of individual growers. Fiercely committed to raising standards, they vehemently oppose high yields and machine harvesting – and their Chardonnay wines show just how good the Mâconnais could be.

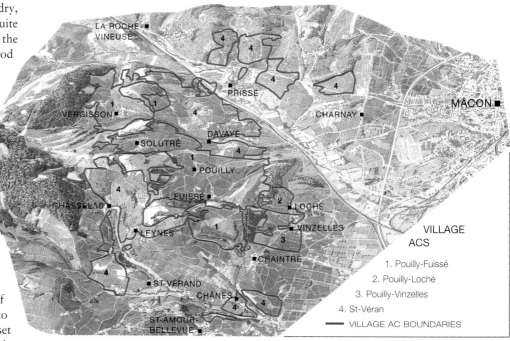

VILLAGE ACS

1. Pouilly-Fuissé
2. Pouilly-Loché
3. Pouilly-Vinzelles
4. St-Véran
— VILLAGE AC BOUNDARIES

0 km   1   2
0 miles   1

SOUTHERN MÂCONNAIS

TOTAL DISTANCE NORTH
TO SOUTH 13KM (8 MILES)

VINEYARDS

N

WHERE THE VINEYARDS ARE

The map shows the intensively planted southern section of the Mâconnais that contains the region's most famous vineyards, those of Pouilly-Fuissé. You can see how beautifully angled the vineyards are to the south-east, below the rocks of Vergisson and Solutré. Further south the St-Véran vineyards, around the village of St-Vérand, catch all the afternoon sun with their south-westerly exposure. The village of St-Amour-Bellevue marks the northern end of the Beaujolais region. St-Véran vineyards are also found to the north-east of Pouilly-Fuissé, especially in the communes of Davayé and Prissé. The next best wines in the Mâconnais come from the communes allowed to attach their name to the Mâcon appellation, for both red and white.

0 km   1   2
0 miles   1

BEAUJOLAIS

NORTHERN
BEAUJOLAIS

TOTAL DISTANCE
NORTH TO SOUTH
23KM (14 MILES)

░░░░ VINEYARDS

N

0 km   1   2
0 miles   1

I LIKE TO THINK OF BEAUJOLAIS as a state of mind rather than a place dependent on contours, kilometres and map references. In my mind this is a magical haven of hills, of a bucolic way of life far removed from the drab conformity of city life. That doesn't need a map of time and place, just a vaguely remembered sketch of the head and heart. I would still rather take the map below and say, do you see how that track rises from Chiroubles up to the forest rim above the village? Well, scramble up there and you can picnic in blissful solitude. Or do you want the best view out over the fat, prosperous Saône Valley and on, to the snowy peaks of the Alps?

Or would you like the most succulent frogs' legs in France, and juicy-pink *entrecôtes*, washed down with fragrant Côte de Brouilly straight from the jug? Follow me. Yes, I like to pretend that Beaujolais is all about dream-time hills, romantic peasant life. But it isn't. And perhaps it never was, because in the days immortalized by Chevallier in his famous novel *Clochemerle*, Beaujolais was a beautiful, but poverty-stricken region. Its job was to provide the basic jug wine of Lyon, France's second city. The Lyonnais had monumental thirsts, but were used to paying little for their tipple.

BEAUJOLAIS NOUVEAU

Things all changed with the advent of Beaujolais Nouveau. What a stroke of genius. Beaujolais has been drunk as young as possible in Lyon since the vineyards were first planted. But first the Parisians caught on to the idea, in the 1950s, then the British joined them in the 1970s, then the Americans, then the Japanese... By the 1980s Beaujolais Nouveau had been sold and oversold as the concept of the first wine of the year's harvest, released on the third Thursday in November, gushing, purple-pink and hardly old enough to have forgotten the flavour of the grape upon the vine. This euphoric state couldn't last forever, and few of the traditional Beaujolais markets, like Northern Europe, now take much notice of Nouveau Day. With the result that much of the prosperity of the region has faded as producers try to find a new way forward for Beaujolais – a wine that lives and dies by its joyous youthful fruit. Beaujolais Nouveau now accounts for just one-third of all Beaujolais and almost every country in the wine world has become adept at producing its own versions of bright, easy, drink-me-quick reds.

Administratively Beaujolais is considered part of Burgundy or La Grande Bourgogne but as far as wine goes the two regions are completely different. The dominant grape in Beaujolais, and the only one used for Beaujolais, is Gamay, barred from all but the most basic wines in the rest of Burgundy because of the raw, rough flavours it tends to produce on alkaline soils. But in Beaujolais the soils are different, and here the Gamay can produce bright, juicy-ripe glugging wine difficult to beat for sheer uncomplicated pleasure. This should be particularly so in the gently rolling, southerly vineyards nearest Lyon, where rich clay and limestone soils grow the light, easy reds sold simply as Beaujolais or Beaujolais Nouveau. But yields are far higher than they used to be and so many of the wines lack the fruit and perfume that made Beaujolais famous in the first place.

THE BEAUJOLAIS METHOD OF FERMENTATION

If we think of Beaujolais Nouveau as merely some modern marketing man's creation, well it is and it isn't. The hoopla of

0 km   1   2
0 miles   1

Nouveau Day in November can often obscure details like whether we actually *like* the wine. But the release of the first wine of the vintage has always been a cause for merrymaking throughout wine regions the world over. Far from being a modern phenomenon, the Nouveau celebrations take us right back to the heart of tradition! They may have been hijacked by marketing men but they've been there ever since the first wine harvest. However, not all red grapes are suitable for the Nouveau treatment. Luckily Beaujolais' Gamay grape naturally has a bright strawberry and peach flavour that is accentuated when vinified by the Beaujolais method.

Grapes are harvested by hand and then, instead of being crushed, whole bunches are piled into a vat. Those at the bottom break, the juice seeps out and begins to ferment as usual, warming the vat and giving off carbon dioxide that rises like a blanket to the top. This encourages the unbroken grapes to begin to ferment inside their skins. Since the colouring and flavouring components in the skin are next to the flesh, this 'whole grape fermentation' or carbonic maceration extracts these elements, yet doesn't extract much of the bitter tannin near the surface of the skin. After four to seven days the grapes split, spilling their dark, fruity, but not bitter, juice into the vat. This mixes with the traditionally fermented juice at the bottom of the vat to create a red wine strong on perfume and colour but low in tannin. This juice is drawn off and the rest of the grapes are pressed. This pressing gives rather more tannin, but thanks to carbonic maceration, colour and fruit perfumes still dominate. This method is used with varying success all around the world by people wanting to create reds to drink very young.

WHERE THE VINEYARDS ARE *This map shows the northern part of the Beaujolais region, yet covers all the most important vineyard sites: these are the ten Beaujolais Crus and most of the 39 communes making Beaujolais-Villages. To the west of the railway line in the rolling hills with vineyards facing in all directions, it's a virtual monoculture of vines, while in the east the flat Saône valley is almost entirely farmland. As you head west, the flatter, reasonably fertile but less well-drained soils make straightforward Beaujolais; the gentler slopes make Beaujolais-Villages; while all the top Beaujolais Cru vineyards lie on the steeper, inhospitable granite outcrops from the Monts du Beaujolais where Gamay performs at its best until around 400m (1312ft), when ripening becomes a problem even this far south and vineyards revert to Beaujolais-Villages once more.*

THE BEAUJOLAIS CRUS

The northern part of Beaujolais – covered by the map below – contains the potentially superior vineyards. The most important of these are the ten Beaujolais Crus, or 'growths', which account for 25 per cent of all Beaujolais; each has its own appellation contrôlée. The Cru vineyards are reckoned to produce wine with an identifiable character, and most have a granite subsoil, which is rarely associated with fine wine – Hermitage in the Rhône valley, south of Lyon, being a notable exception.

St-Amour is the most northerly commune, actually sharing its vineyards with the Mâconnais St-Véran appellation. Going south come Juliénas, Chénas and Moulin-à-Vent, all capable of producing well-structured wines. The perfumed wines of Fleurie and Chiroubles come next, followed by Morgon, whose best wines develop a delightful cherry perfume. Régnié, with its sandy soils, is the newest Cru, though so far it has not really justified its right to be a Cru, but Brouilly, the largest Beaujolais Cru, and Côte de Brouilly can produce delightful gluggable wines.

BEAUJOLAIS-VILLAGES

Thirty-nine other communes, mostly in the north of the region between Vaux-en-Beaujolais and St-Amour-Bellevue on the border with the Mâconnais region, qualify for Beaujolais-Villages status. This appellation is for wines that are better than basic Beaujolais but supposedly less fine than Crus. But what do we mean by fine?

Frankly, we're not after the longevity and complexity that may characterize the greatest reds from Bordeaux, Burgundy or the Rhône. What we want is the uncomplicated cherub-cheeked, red-fruit ripeness and spicy blossom perfumes of the best ordinary Beaujolais. But we want those fruits to be riper, those perfumes more heady, and the wine's soft-centred, smooth consistency to leave lingering trails in the memory long after the flavour fades.

These are the blessings of youth. There is hardly a Brouilly, a St-Amour or a Chiroubles that should be aged for even as long as a couple of years. An occasional bottle of Morgon, Juliénas, Fleurie or, particularly, Moulin-à-Vent does begin to resemble a charming mild-mannered Côte de Beaune Burgundy after five to ten years' age, but these are the exceptions. But, as in the rest of Beaujolais, yields are generally too high even in these top vineyards, and a grape like the Gamay can only aspire to class if yields are kept low.

Beaujolais is almost the only place in the world that can produce memorable wine from the Gamay grape, and has over 60 per cent of the world's plantings. These juicy-looking grapes are from the Côte de Brouilly Cru at the southern end of the region.

 RED GRAPES
Gamay is the only variety allowed for Beaujolais, accounting for 99 per cent of the Beaujolais vineyards.

 WHITE GRAPES
A tiny amount of Chardonnay is planted for white Beaujolais (0.9 per cent of the vineyards).

CLIMATE
Warmer and sunnier than northern Burgundy, the region is partly protected by the Monts du Beaujolais from prevailing westerly winds.

SOIL
The most important aspect is the granite subsoil which influences all the northern zone and on which Gamay thrives. Further south nearer Lyon, the soil is richer, primarily clays and limestone, and is less suited to Gamay.

 ASPECT
The vineyards lie between 150 and 500m (492 and 1640ft) and face all directions. Fleurie and Moulin-à-Vent have many south-east-facing vineyards which are protected by the hills to the north-west.

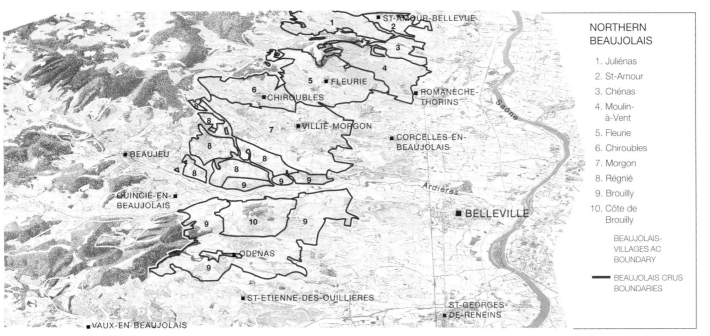

ST-AMOUR-BELLEVUE

FLEURIE

CHIROUBLES

ROMANÈCHE-THORINS

VILLIÉ-MORGON

CORCELLES-EN-BEAUJOLAIS

BEAUJEU

Saône

Ardières

QUINCIÉ-EN-BEAUJOLAIS

BELLEVILLE

ODENAS

ST-ETIENNE-DES-OUILLIÈRES

ST-GEORGES-DE-RENEINS

VAUX-EN-BEAUJOLAIS

NORTHERN BEAUJOLAIS

1. Juliénas
2. St-Amour
3. Chénas
4. Moulin-à-Vent
5. Fleurie
6. Chiroubles
7. Morgon
8. Régnié
9. Brouilly
10. Côte de Brouilly

—— BEAUJOLAIS-VILLAGES AC BOUNDARY

━━ BEAUJOLAIS CRUS BOUNDARIES

CHAMPAGNE

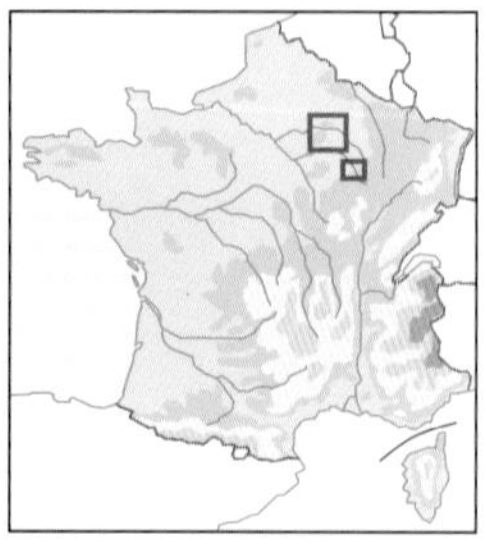

RED GRAPES
Pinot Noir and Pinot Meunier account for just under three-quarters of all Champagne grapes.

WHITE GRAPES
Chardonnay accounts for a little over one-quarter of the vineyards.

CLIMATE
Cold, wet, continental climate but the northerly latitude gives more daylight hours in the growing season than Provence. Rain and late spring frosts are the main enemies.

SOIL
Shallow topsoil as little as 15cm (6in) in places covering subsoil largely of chalk up to 200m (656ft) thick.

ASPECT
Mainly east- and south-east-facing vineyards, that lie between 100 and 200m (328 and 656ft) high, and are protected by thickly wooded hilltops.

North-facing Pinot Noir vines above Verzenay on the Montagne de Reims. Why Pinot Noir should ripen so well in such a spot is by no means clear.

THEY WEREN'T PAYING THE AREA round Reims and Épernay north-east of Paris any compliments when they called it Champagne. They weren't thinking of glittering first night parties, of dandies and dancing girls, the hectic celebrations of a Grand Prix winner or the tingling joyful tension of a lover with warm words in his mind and brave deeds in his heart.

The word 'Champagne' comes from the Latin *campania* meaning 'open, flat countryside', and I sometimes feel this is a positive understatement as I urge the car onwards. Driving through the pale, lonely plains to the east of Reims, the sea of corn enlivened by an occasional steepling grain silo, I feel more as if I were in the depths of the Oklahoma prairie than trying to make a dinner date in the heart of one of the world's greatest wine regions. As I plough through the flat sugar-beet fields of the Pas de Calais, still saturated by squalls from the English Channel, past the giant slag heaps of long-dead coal mines and once more out on to the chalky windswept plains to the north of Reims, I don't scent the slightest possibility of any vines ever ripening under such inhospitable conditions. It is simply too cold, too windy, too rainy for growing grapes.

And they don't. This whole expanse of north-eastern France is a desolate, underpopulated province of broad cornfields and dark forbidding forests, which experienced some of the fiercest fighting in World Wars One and Two. And in what many historians reckon may have been the bloodiest battle ever to take place, Attila the Hun was finally turned back east of Reims near Châlons-en-Champagne.

CLIMATE AND SOIL

But in this flat landscape there is one brief eruption of low hills – a grouping of cliffs, slopes and valleys of ancient chalk. These hills do provide just the amount of protection and privileged mesoclimate that the grape vine needs. Take a look at the map. The Montagne de Reims is one of these. The Côte des Blancs is another. The cleft where the Marne river pushes its way westward towards Paris is a third. And little pockets like the Côte de Sézanne and the Aube (see page 73) further south can also provide suitable conditions for ripening the vine. Just.

Yet this knife-edge between ripeness and unripeness is what gives the wine of Champagne its peculiar suitability to form the base for a sparkling wine. And the cold autumns and icy winters that grip the whole region in a joyless embrace are what, by chance, created the now famous bubbles in the first place.

High acidity is crucial in the base wine for a good fizz. If you can lengthen the ripening time of the fruit as much as possible so that it only creeps to maturity in the golden days of autumn, you are going to retain high acidity, yet have physically mature grapes. The flavours that these give are infinitely superior to those obtained from grapes grown in warmer climates simply picked early. All you then get is green, raw unripeness. You can't make great wine out of that.

In the few favoured vine-growing mesoclimates of Champagne, the annual mean temperature is about 10.5°C (51°F), a half degree above what is generally regarded as the minimum required to ripen any high-quality grape variety, although training the vines close to the ground will increase the temperature somewhat. The number of hours of sunshine in the growing season are actually as high in Champagne as in the considerably warmer vineyards of Alsace. But whereas Alsace, sheltered behind the Vosges mountains, has much higher temperatures and less rain due to its continental climate, Champagne's days are cooled by the damp Atlantic breezes that sweep in unhindered from the west.

And those winds often bring rain – and at the wrong time too. Although the total annual rainfall is lower than in regions like Bordeaux, Burgundy and the Loire, nearly 60 per cent of it falls in the summer and early autumn, with July and August being particularly hard hit when the rain causes mildew and rot among the ripening grapes. But this is where the importance of the right soil comes in. With the exception of the southerly Aube, Champagne's vines are planted on a thick chalk subsoil. The topsoil differs within the region – the Montagne de Reims has a kind of brown coal lignite and some gravel, the Vallée de la Marne has far more sand, and the Côte des Blancs has clay – but this topsoil is frequently so thin that the chalk keeps breaking through.

The chalk is porous and fissured, holding enough water to nourish the vine but not drown it. The vine roots burrow into the soft, almost spongy, stone thus anchoring the plant against climatic extremes above ground. Since the chalk is so close to the surface, it is relatively warm, and indeed, may even reflect sunlight back on to the vine, aiding the grapes' final struggle for ripeness as autumn drifts towards winter.

FROM STILL WINE TO SPARKLING

This rather sombre scenario means that wines with truly ripe, sun-filled flavours simply aren't part of the Champagne repertoire, although historically the region's reputation was based on still red wines. These must have been pretty feeble and thin and I'm glad I didn't have to rely on them for washing down my Sunday roast. But highly acidic grapes, picked just as winter set in, would have fermented slowly and inefficiently. As the freezing winter air filled the wine cellars, the yeasts would simply have become

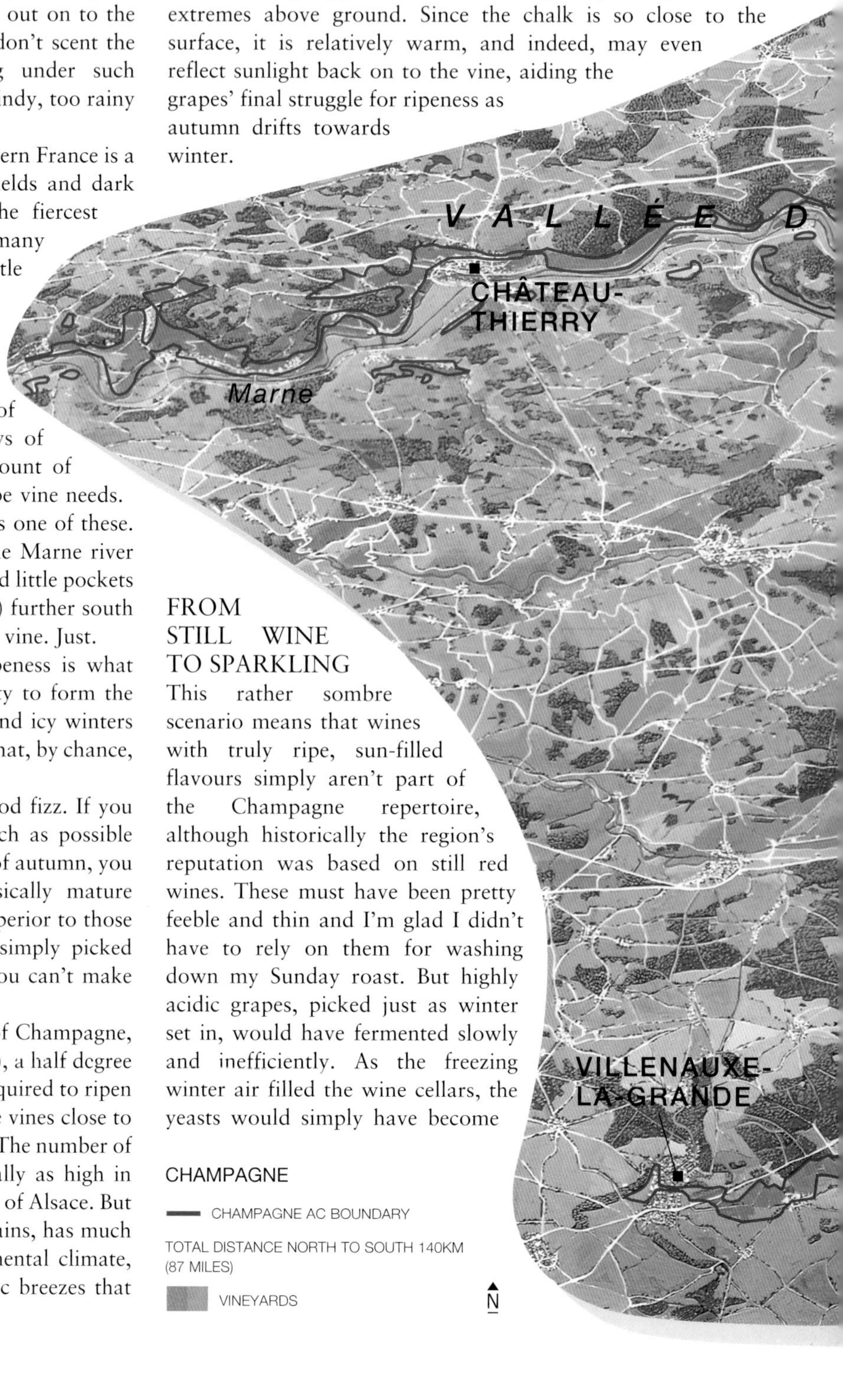
VALLÉE D
CHÂTEAU-THIERRY
Marne
VILLENAUXE-LA-GRANDE
CHAMPAGNE
CHAMPAGNE AC BOUNDARY
TOTAL DISTANCE NORTH TO SOUTH 140KM (87 MILES)
VINEYARDS
N

too cold to go on with their job: they'd have packed it in and gone into hibernation. In the days before central heating they'd have lain dormant until the following spring had warmed the cellars up and – hey presto – they'd have finished off their fermentation with a final brisk burst of bubbles to emerge as still wines.

The English and the Parisians used to buy a lot of Champagne wine. Since young wine was prized more than old, until modern times it would be shipped to them in barrel during the winter. Once the spring came, it would begin bubbling again.

Traditionally much effort was put into ridding the wines of their bubble, but in England, in the carefree period after Charles II's Restoration in 1660, and in the pleasure-mad days in France that followed the death of Louis XIV in 1715, a vogue developed for frivolous sparkling wines that may have upset connoisseurs of those times, but has ensured Champagne's fame ever since. No-one then understood exactly why the fizziness came and went. The English managed to preserve the bubbles rather longer into the summer because they had developed particularly strong

Nearly all Champagne is a blend of different vineyards – and usually all the better for it.

REIMS

MONTAGNE DE REIMS

A MARNE **DAMERY**

ÉPERNAY **AY** *Marne*

PIERRY **CHOUILLY**

CÔTE DES BLANCS

VERTUS

BERGÈRES-LÈS-VERTUS

SÉZANNE

CÔTE DE SÉZANNE

WHERE THE VINEYARDS ARE *The map shows all the important Champagne vineyards, except for the Aube (see page 73). In a region this far north suitable soils, good aspect to the sun and protection from wind and rain are all crucial. Many of the best vineyard sites are on the Montagne de Reims. Interestingly, many villages here appear to face north yet the forested hilltop, the chalk soil, and warm air currents and numerous east- and south-east-facing sites provide good conditions. The Vallée de la Marne vineyards start at Mareuil-sur-Ay and continue west past Château-Thierry. However, the best sites are between Mareuil and Damery, on steep south-facing slopes. There are numerous vineyards on the south banks of the Marne but few are outstanding. The third great area is the Côte des Blancs. This chalky, east-facing slope runs south from Chouilly to Bergères-les-Vertus. Most of the finest Chardonnay wine comes from these slopes, open to the sun's rays for most of the day, yet protected to the west from wind and rain. There are several other good sites just south of Épernay, in particular at Pierry. Further south, the Côte de Sézanne, with its chalky, east-facing slopes and forested hilltops also provides classic Champagne conditions.*

glass bottles and they used cork rather than rags soaked in oil as a stopper. Bottles would still burst, but not half as often as did the weaker French bottles. Gradually, in the latter part of the 17th century the English, and the French – led by Dom Pérignon, who was in charge of the cellars at Hautvillers Abbey between 1670 and 1715 – worked out how to control the fizz and then how to start it going again in a still wine.

The reputation of Champagne is based on this last achievement. By adding a little yeast and sugar to a still wine and then corking the bottle tightly, the wine re-ferments in the bottle and the bubbles dissolve, waiting to burst forth when the bottle is opened. This is the traditional 'Champagne method' of making sparkling wine and is used across the world for top class bubbly. Others have since improved upon Dom Pérignon's methods for creating a reliable sparkling wine, but he was perhaps more important for formulating other principles that are now accepted as fundamental to quality in Champagne. Above all, he saw the need to restrict yields to achieve ripeness, and to blend together the wines of different vineyards and communes to produce the best end result.

THE CLASSIFICATION OF CHAMPAGNE VINEYARDS

In the marginal climate of Champagne, there are few vineyard sites that can produce an attractive, multi-faceted wine in most years. However, the three grape varieties used for Champagne, each grown on different sites, can contribute a more rounded flavour to a final blend. Older 'reserve' wines held back from the previous year may also be added for extra flavour. As a result, Champagne is usually a blend of different wines, often from all over the region, and most of it is sold as non-vintage. A vintage is 'declared' only in especially good years, and the wines made from a selection of the best grapes. The so-called 'de luxe' cuvées are also blends from different vineyards, unless they come from a single grower.

Merchant houses – the most important are in Reims, Épernay and Ay – and co-operatives handle most Champagne production, buying grapes from the growers based on a guideline price per kilo, determined by a tribunal of officials, growers and producers and renegotiated every three or four years. Prices are fixed by a system known as the *échelle des crus*, or 'ladder of growths' whereby villages, rather than individual vineyards, are classified according to quality on a scale ranging from 100 per cent down to 80 per cent. There are 17 villages accorded the title Grand Cru, and these receive 100 per cent of the agreed grape price per kilo. The 41 villages with Premier Cru status receive between 90 and 99 per cent. All the other less-favoured villages receive between 80 and 89 per cent.

GRAPE VARIETIES

Not only are some vineyards better than others, but they are also better suited to particular grape varieties. Three varieties are grown in Champagne – two red, Pinot Noir and Pinot Meunier, and one white, Chardonnay. The total vineyard is 32,178ha (79,512 acres): Pinot Noir covers 12,253ha (30,277 acres); Pinot Meunier 10,869 ha (26,857 acres); and Chardonnay 8953ha (22,123 acres).

Just south of Reims is the Montagne de Reims with vineyards on its northern, eastern and southern slopes. Pinot Noir dominates these vineyards, especially those in the Grand Cru villages, and much of the backbone for the Champagne blends comes from these grapes and from those grown in the Aube region. Pinot Noir is also used for the rare still wines of Champagne such as Bouzy Rouge which is light but perfumed with strawberry fruit.

Chardonnay dominates the chalky, east-facing slopes of the Côte des Blancs south of Épernay. The other particularly successful areas for Chardonnay are the village of Villers-Marmery at the eastern end of the Montagne de Reims, and the Côte de Sézanne to the south. Chardonnay from the northern sites adds zest and lively, lean fruit to the Champagne blend, while that from the less chalky Côte de Sézanne is likely to add a creamy, honeyed roundness. Blanc de Blancs Champagne is from 100 per cent Chardonnay.

Pinot Meunier is the Champagne workhorse. In general it is planted in the lower-lying vineyards because it buds late, thus avoiding the worst of the frost. Most villages grow some, with the exception of the top Côte des Blancs communes, and Bouzy in the Montagne de Reims. It is particularly prevalent west of Épernay in the Vallée de la Marne where the valley vineyards are susceptible to frost. Blended with the other two varieties it can add a pleasant, mildly perfumed quality that softens the more austere, slow-developing characteristics of Pinot Noir and Chardonnay.

THE CHALK OF CHAMPAGNE

There is a thick, billowing seam of chalk that runs across northern France to Calais and across southern England. This is the subsoil for the Champagne vineyards. There are two main sorts: micraster, found on the lower slopes and the plain, and belemnite, found in all the best vineyards and on the upper slopes. Chalk has a perfect balance between porosity and water retention and is able to nourish vines equally well in dry or wet years. Its brilliant whiteness helps the soil's ability to reflect sunlight back on to the vines, and chalk retains heat well, vital factors in such a northerly vineyard region. Chalk is also alkaline, which in turn produces grapes with high acid levels – perfect for sparkling wine. In addition, the region's *caves* or cellars, dug deep into the chalk, mainly in the towns of Reims and Épernay, are cold and damp, providing an ideal environment for storing bottles while the Champagne inside undergoes its second fermentation. This is because the slower the yeasts set to work, the smaller the bubble and the more persistent the fizz in the finished wine.

The cru vineyards The best vineyards are found on the chalk slopes covered with downwash material from the upper slopes. The high proportion of calcium in the chalk prevents the vines from taking up iron and this is compensated for by the perennial use of fertilizers.

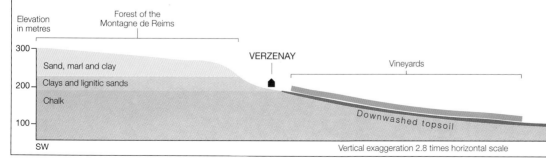

THE AUBE (CÔTE DES BAR)

Lying well south of Troyes, the former capital of the Comtes de Champagne, the vineyards in the Aube *département* have long been hampered with the problem that they are situated in the Champagne region but only just, and in the Burgundy region, well almost. The first scattered outposts of Burgundian vineyards begin across the departmental border at Chatillon-sur-Seine less than 20 kilometres (12 miles) away and the Aube's gently rolling landscape feels quite different to the heart of Champagne around Épernay a good 110km (70 miles) to the north. At least now the A26 *autoroute* between Reims and Dijon slices between the two main Aube towns of Bar-sur-Aube and Bar-sur-Seine so that we can see the region's dual personality for ourselves.

As it happens, the Aube's vineyards are a lot closer to the Chablis vineyards (only 40km/25 miles to the south-west) than any of the main Champagne districts, and they also lie on soil similar to Chablis' but the Burgundians rejected all overtures from the Aube growers. When the Marne growers further north (i.e., in the classic districts of the Montagne de Reims, the Vallée de la Marne and the Côte des Blancs) started to delimit Champagne's boundaries at the beginning of the twentieth century in an attempt to control the quality of the grapes being used, some of the Aube growers petitioned for their region to be included within the Champagne-producing area. The Aube was only included as an official Champagne district after several years of violent resistance by the Marne growers and until 1927 when the Champagne *appellation* came into being, the Aube had to be content with the demeaning title of 'Champagne Deuxième Zone'. In other words, it was thought of as inferior.

Although increasingly untenable, this is an attitude that you still come across in a few of the more snobbish *grande marque* houses based in Reims and Épernay, even though they use Aube grapes in their non-vintage brands. However, partly because some of the leading winemakers from the big houses are increasingly open about the merits of the region, these days there is less ill-informed prejudice against the Aube vineyards. In fact, this area, nowadays also called the Côte des Bar, is one of Champagne's most important sources of full-flavoured, ripe Pinot Noir grapes. Nearly 87 per cent of the Côte des Bar's 6817ha (16844 acres) of vines are planted with Pinot Noir, and it thus accounts for very nearly half (49 per cent) of Champagne's supply of this variety.

Despite past schisms, the links between Burgundy and the Côte des Bar are more than just close proximity. The Côte des Bar soils are the same as Chablis', the best sites having Kimmeridgian limestone clay subsoils, and there's a good smattering of Portlandian limestone, Chablis' other soil, as well. Even the weather has more in common with Chablis than with Champagne. Greater maximum heat in the Côte des Bar is balanced by more extreme cold and the general effect is of riper, rounder, slightly raspberryish, yet earthy fruit.

This slightly red-fruit flavour is especially marked in a local oddity, the Rosé des Riceys. This is a still rosé wine, aged in cask, and made only in the warmest years. Although the cask-aging drives out any richness, there is a core of curious sweetness as though you'd left a punnet of raspberries to wither and shrivel in a hot desert wind.

Although more growers bottle their own wine today, most Côte des Bar wines either head north for blending into the Champagnes produced by the biggest houses or are sold by the large co-operative, the Union Auboise at Bar-sur-Seine, whose Devaux Champagne blend puts many a *grande marque* to shame.

Vines and sunflowers share the slopes at Essoyes in the Aube, or Côte des Bar, a source of round, early-maturing Champagnes ideal for softening the more austere wines from elsewhere in the region.

WHERE THE VINEYARDS ARE *The Aube or Côte des Bar is the least known of Champagne's four main districts, but in many ways it is the most attractive to explore. While the principal Champagne districts to the north around Épernay are affected by breezes sweeping in unhindered from the Atlantic, the Côte des Bar has a more continental climate and is particularly prone to frost. The landscape resembles the outlying areas of Chablis more than the main Champagne areas themselves. Most of the land is broad and rolling but there are also low, wooded hills with relatively steep slopes and, where the aspect is broadly south-facing, patches of vines planted among pasture and other crops. The best examples are to the east of Bar-sur-Seine, along the valley to Champignol-lez-Mondéville and Urville, and beneath the forest between Polisy and Les Riceys. North of Bar-sur-Seine, in this cool part of France, the land flattens out and becomes far too exposed for grapes to ripen.*

Aube · BAR-SUR-AUBE · URVILLE · CHAMPIGNOL-LEZ-MONDÉVILLE · BAR-SUR-SEINE · POLISY · ESSOYES · Seine · LES RICEYS

— CHAMPAGNE AC BOUNDARY

TOTAL DISTANCE NORTH TO SOUTH 44KM (27 MILES)

VINEYARDS

N

HEART OF CHAMPAGNE

BEFORE WE GO ANY FURTHER, let's remind ourselves of the one factor that dominates all others in Champagne. The cold. In all my trips to Champagne, whatever the time of year, there's hardly a day when I haven't felt cool dampness underfoot as I first step into the vineyard of a morning. It's a rare evening when I haven't been glad I'm wearing a jacket as the sun sets behind a forested hill and leaves me in its mildly chilly shade. And at vintage time, since I often spend a day or two in the region as the grapes are coming in, I have rarely squeezed a Chardonnay or a Pinot Noir berry off the vine and exalted in its sweetness. They're just not ripe enough.

In this part of France we're just about at the limit for ripening grape varieties like Chardonnay or Pinot Noir, even in the hottest of years. At the best of times only the most perfect locations are going to manage it. Fortunately, in Champagne, there is a whole cluster of just such places.

There are three main zones at the heart of Champagne, each best suited to a different grape, producing quite different styles of wines. Remember, in most cases, it is the blending of wines from various vineyards across the region that creates the finest Champagne. There *are* excellent single-vineyard Champagnes, but the sum of the parts in Champagne is almost always better than anything the individual components can manage alone.

MONTAGNE DE REIMS

Nowhere is this more true than in the Montagne de Reims. Look at the map. Reims is the city at the top, and the group of forested hills just to its south constitutes the Montagne de Reims. In a cold area like Champagne, surely only the most protected southerly sites will ripen the grapes properly? But remarkably, some of the darkest-coloured, hardest-to-ripen Pinot Noir grapes, and some of the longest-lived wines in the Champagne region come from vineyards that are on the *north* side of the Montagne de Reims.

How is it that villages such as Mailly-Champagne, Chigny-les-Roses and Verzenay, located on these northern slopes, are able to produce such deep, sturdy wine? One explanation is the possible warming effect of the nearby city of Reims, and its thermal blanket of warm air that protects the vines in winter and aids ripening in summer. But I don't think that that fully explains matters. Most of the good vineyards don't actually *face* north, and those that do ripen on average only eight days later than those that don't. Directly south of Reims – where the vines would have to face due north – there *aren't* any vines. They do appear on slopes to the south-west,

Startlingly stormy sunlight over the vineyards of Cuis, on the northern edge of the Côte des Blancs.

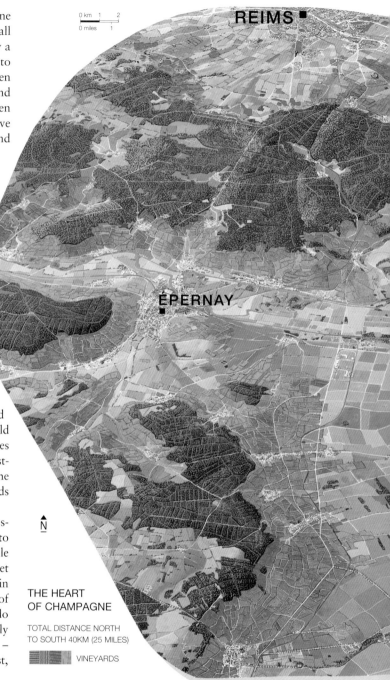

REIMS

ÉPERNAY

0 km 1 2
0 miles 1

N

THE HEART OF CHAMPAGNE

TOTAL DISTANCE NORTH TO SOUTH 40KM (25 MILES)

▓▓▓▓ VINEYARDS

on what is known as the 'petite Montagne', but the good vineyards of Écueil, Sacy and Villedommange face virtually due east, with some slopes even inclined towards the south.

South-east of Reims, between Rilly-la-Montagne and Mailly-Champagne, many vines *do* face north, but, unlike elsewhere on the Montagne, most of these are on the almost flat lower slopes and get a share of the cool but long summer's day sun. However, these villages are renowned for austere, slow-maturing Pinot Noir wines. With the exception of the remarkable Vilmart wines from Rilly, I've never found them that enjoyable, yet their reputation comes largely because this sturdy, lean backbone provides a crutch for softer, blander wines in many Champagne houses' blends.

The best villages here lie between Verzenay and Bouzy where the slopes curve round from north to south. They are protected by the forested hilltop but the best sites also have an east-to-south aspect. Three other important factors help: exposure to morning sun, a chalk soil that reflects and stores heat, and the protection

WHERE THE VINEYARDS ARE *In a cool northern area like Champagne, it's as important to look at the land that isn't covered with vines as that which is. All the flat land here is arable. It couldn't support grapes because it's too exposed to wind and rain and doesn't catch enough sun. Only rarely do vineyards venture out into the plain although, oddly, some of the better ones on the northern face of the Montagne de Reims are on flattish slopes. All the best grapes are grown on sites first planted centuries ago and the map shows us why. The eastern and southern parts of the Montagne de Reims are protected by forested hilltops, and round Ambonnay and Bouzy there's a natural south-facing amphitheatre, ideal for ripening mainly Pinot Noir. Between Avenay and Damery the Marne Valley has steep, south-facing chalky slopes protected from wind and rain and sited to soak up the sun. South of Épernay there are good sites at Pierry, Mancy and Grauves, but the real class act is the east-facing chalk slope of the Côte des Blancs, protected, well-drained and angled towards the sun – just what a northern vineyard needs.*

narrower and wetter, and the chalk becomes a thin strip rather than a broad band, with sandy clays increasingly taking over, and most of the vineyards are on this sedimentary layer. Neither Pinot Noir nor Chardonnay will ripen under these conditions, but the less fussy Pinot Meunier will, and dominates plantings in this area. Vines grow on both sides of the valley, with the northern banks being superior. Exceptions include the south bank village of Leuvrigny which provides Pinot Meunier for Krug, Deutz and Roederer – three quality-conscious Champagne houses – and in the hinterland, the villages of le Breuil, and, closer to Épernay, Pierry and Grauves. But these are virtually part of the Côte des Blancs, the third great Champagne zone.

CÔTE DES BLANCS

It's easier to understand what's special about the Côte des Blancs – a long, east- and south-east-facing slope of chalky soil stretching from the Butte de Saran in the north just outside Épernay to below the town of Vertus in the south. For about 15km (9 miles) there's nothing but vines, and the vast majority of these are Chardonnay. Chardonnay doesn't find it easy to ripen in Champagne. But the grape loves chalky soil and long warm days without too much rain. The Côte des Blancs provides both better than anywhere else in the region, and the result is the most regularly high-yielding of all the Champagne zones, but also the most reliably attractive wines.

Many of the wines are sold unblended as Blanc de Blancs Champagne, made only from Chardonnay, but grapes from the villages of Cramant, Avize, le Mesnil-sur-Oger and Vertus also give many Champagne blends a fragrance and fresh, lemony zing. If the wine is young and the bubbles dance and twirl around your mouth, that will be the Côte des Blancs talking. And if the wine is old and a soft, toasty foam creams and coils around your tongue, that will be the Côte des Blancs talking too.

from westerly winds and rain offered by the Montagne de Reims. Such a combination allows villages like Bouzy in particular, with its warm, south-facing amphitheatre of vines, and Verzenay to a lesser extent, to produce deep-flavoured Pinot Noir wines against the odds.

VALLÉE DE LA MARNE

The Marne Valley begins where the Montagne de Reims' southern slopes sidle down to join the river between Avenay and Mareuil-sur-Ay. Meandering west for the first 10km (6 miles) or so, between Mareuil and Damery, you come to a sweep of vineyards, dipping and diving in and out of the hilly slopes, but above all maintaining a marvellous south-facing aspect for the vine carpet that swoops down from the hills above Épernay to the broad valley floor.

This area, in particular the slopes around Ay, can produce beautiful Pinot Noir wines, but west of Damery the valley gets

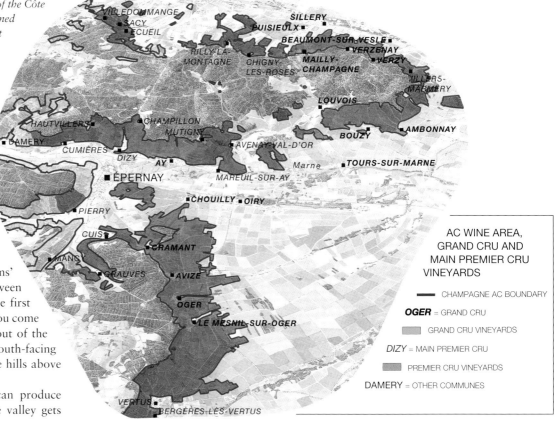

AC WINE AREA, GRAND CRU AND MAIN PREMIER CRU VINEYARDS
— CHAMPAGNE AC BOUNDARY
OGER = GRAND CRU
GRAND CRU VINEYARDS
DIZY = MAIN PREMIER CRU
PREMIER CRU VINEYARDS
DAMERY = OTHER COMMUNES

ALSACE

RED GRAPES
Pinot Noir is the only red grape, occupying about 9 per cent of the plantings.

WHITE GRAPES
Riesling is the most widely planted, followed closely by Pinot Blanc and then Gewurztraminer, Pinot Gris and Sylvaner, whilst Muscat trails far behind. Negligible amounts of Chasselas are used in Edelzwicker, and Chardonnay in Crémant.

CLIMATE
Despite the northerly latitude, the region benefits from plentiful sun and low rainfall caused by its location in the rain shadow created by the Vosges mountains.

SOIL
The region divides into three main zones – mountain, mid-slopes, and foothills and plains. The best sites are on the middle slopes which are limestone based with marly clay and sandstone topsoils.

ASPECT
The vineyards are sited between 170 and 420m (558 and 1378ft) with the best sites on the well-drained, sheltered steep middle slopes.

Rangen de Thann, just to the west of Cernay in the south, produces remarkable wines and is one of Alsace's top Grand Cru vineyards.

Y OU ONLY HAVE TO STAND in the middle of the steeply sloping vineyards to the west of Colmar to realize there's something special about Alsace. Over to the west, dark clouds pile ominously above the mountains; yet here, where the Riesling and Gewurztraminer vines climb gamely up towards the wooded brows of the Vosges eastern foothills, the sky is as clear and blue as dreams, the sunshine is warm and mellow, the air is pure and sweet with the perfume of flowers and alive with the twittering chatter of insects. In these vineyards, grapes for some of the most heady and exotic wines in Europe ripen in the summer sun.

The vineyards of Alsace sit in a rain shadow created by the Vosges mountains that rise high above the Rhine Valley. Most of the rain brought by the westerly winds falls over these mountains and forests. By the time the clouds reach the vineyards they have just enough rain left to cast a few refreshing showers on the vines and then evaporate into the warm air. Alsace is almost as far north as vineyards can go in France – only Champagne is marginally further north. Yet that rain shadow allows Colmar to be the second driest spot in France, beaten only by Perpignan, down on the Spanish border. Perpignan cooks under torrid skies. Not so Alsace. Perpignan produces rough-and-ready hot-climate reds; Alsace, because of cooler northern temperatures, allied to day after day of clear skies, can provide the ripeness – and therefore the higher alcoholic strength – of the warm south but also the perfume and fragrance of the cool north.

The enigma goes much further than climatic conditions. Politically Alsace has been caught between two inimical philosophies. The Rhine is southern Germany's great waterway. Nowadays it forms a natural frontier as it runs northwards from Basel on the Swiss border but, in less peaceful times, the river, and the flat farmland on both its banks, formed an obvious battleground whenever the French and Germans went to war. The frontier then was seen as the Vosges mountains to the west, on whose eastern foothills all Alsace's vineyards are planted. Prussia gained control of Alsace in 1870, France won the region back in 1918; by 1940 Alsace was again under German occupation, before finally reverting to France in 1945.

After several generations of confused national identity, the region has settled into a reasonably contented dual personality. The Alsatian people maintain proudly, even ferociously, that they are as French as any Frenchman can be. Yet most of the names of their villages are German and the villages themselves look as though they've stepped off the set of some German operetta; most family surnames are German (though Christian names are usually French), and the local Alsace dialect has far more in common with German than French.

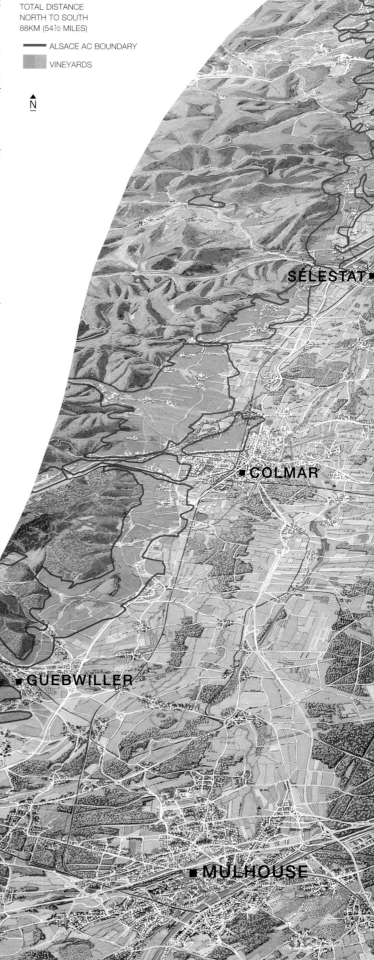

ALSACE

TOTAL DISTANCE
NORTH TO SOUTH
88KM (54½ MILES)

———— ALSACE AC BOUNDARY

▨ VINEYARDS

N

SÉLESTAT

COLMAR

GUEBWILLER

CERNAY

MULHOUSE

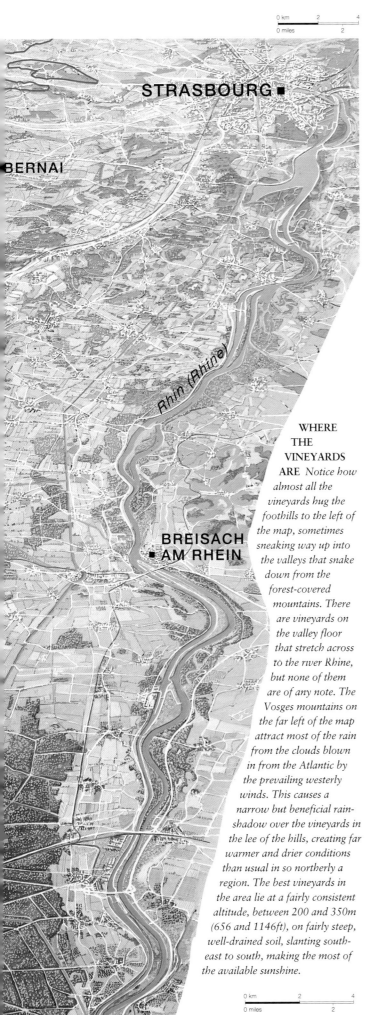

STRASBOURG ■

BERNAI

BREISACH
■ AM RHEIN

Rhin (Rhine)

WHERE THE VINEYARDS ARE *Notice how almost all the vineyards hug the foothills to the left of the map, sometimes sneaking way up into the valleys that snake down from the forest-covered mountains. There are vineyards on the valley floor that stretch across to the river Rhine, but none of them are of any note. The Vosges mountains on the far left of the map attract most of the rain from the clouds blown in from the Atlantic by the prevailing westerly winds. This causes a narrow but beneficial rain-shadow over the vineyards in the lee of the hills, creating far warmer and drier conditions than usual in so northerly a region. The best vineyards in the area lie at a fairly consistent altitude, between 200 and 350m (656 and 1146ft), on fairly steep, well-drained soil, slanting south-east to south, making the most of the available sunshine.*

GRAPE VARIETIES AND WINE STYLES

The grape varieties that make Alsatian wine are, for the large part, not typical in the rest of France. Her two most famous grapes – Riesling and Gewurztraminer, though enthusiastically planted in Germany and much of Central Europe, are conspicuous by their absence elsewhere in France. Sylvaner doesn't appear elsewhere in France and is on the decline in Alsace; Pinot Gris and Pinot Blanc are tolerated at best in a very subordinate role in Burgundy. Only the red Pinot Noir, Burgundy's best red grape, and the white Muscat, planted in the fortified wine appellations around the Mediterranean, have genuine legitimacy in France. In Germany, however, Riesling, Gewurztraminer, Pinot Blanc aka Weissburgunder and Pinot Gris aka Ruländer or Grauburgunder and even Sylvaner, in the Franken and Rheinhessen regions, are regarded as producing most of that country's greatest wines.

The dual personality of Alsace is reflected by the wines too. Alsace's French grape varieties take on a Germanic perfume, while the German grapes proudly distance themselves from the flavours one would find over the border in Germany itself.

Traditionally the difference has been more marked with Riesling because nearly all Germany's great Rieslings were sweet, whereas all those of Alsace were dry. Nowadays, Germany makes increasing amounts of dry Rieslings, many very good, but they are generally taut and lean as well as subtly scented. Alsace's best Rieslings, on the other hand, are fat and round in the mouth, yet marvellously dry, streaked with cold lime pith acidity, yet thick with glycerine ripeness. Alsace Riesling does best in the hillier Haut-Rhin in the south of the region on sheltered sites with sandy-clayey loams that warm up quickly in the spring.

The two countries' other wines are also distinctive. Germany's Gewurztraminer is generally made with a certain fat sweetness and perfume. Alsace goes for the perfume of freshly plucked tea roses and the ripeness of lychee and mango. Gewurztraminer needs a long, ripening season and loves Alsace's sunny, dry weather which continues well into the autumn. Germany's Ruländer is attractively honeyed and sweetish, though it is also appearing in a full oaky style under the Grauburgunder label, whereas Alsace Pinot Gris revels in spicy, musky, honeyed and exotic flavours. Most Alsace Pinot Noir is pale and floral, whereas Germany is making a number of Spätburgunders with impressive Burgundian depth. Alsace Muscats have a light, dry grapy perfume rather than the heady but weighty hothouse flavours preferred in the Muscats from France's far south.

Kaysersberg: the 'Hansel and Gretel' architecture found in Alsace could fool anyone into thinking they were in Germany. They wouldn't be far wrong – Germany is just over the Rhine to the east.

APPELLATIONS AND CLASSIFICATIONS

- **Alsace AC** The general AC covering the whole region. It appears on all labels. Any of the permitted grape varieties may be used. Currently, there is no intermediate level between AC and Grand Cru, but work is being done on a Premier Cru and there's talk of a 'Villages' level, too.
- **Alsace Grand Cru AC** This AC covers certain special vineyards (see page 79) and, with one exception, Zotzenberg, is allowed only for wines made from Gewurztraminer, Muscat, Pinot Gris and Riesling.
- **Crémant d'Alsace AC** This AC is for sparkling wine produced over the whole region and made in the traditional method usually from Pinot Blanc or Riesling.
- **Vendange Tardive** Late-harvested wine made from very ripe Gewurztraminer, Riesling, Pinot Gris and occasionally Muscat.
- **Séléction de Grains Nobles** A higher category than Vendange Tardive made from even riper grapes of the same varieties.

HEART OF ALSACE

THOUGH ALSACE'S WINE REGION stretches north to the border with Germany at Wissembourg and south almost to Mulhouse, a distance of about 110km (68 miles), virtually all the finest wines come from a central section of vineyards in the Haut-Rhin *département* west of Colmar, a miraculously preserved medieval market town which is rightly called the Wine Capital of Alsace. Good wines are made in the north of Alsace, in the Bas-Rhin *département*, but they rarely have the ripeness or intensity of those from the vineyards of the Haut-Rhin, which lie further south.

The vineyards that twist in and out of the folds in the Vosges eastern foothills are dotted with magical little villages that make you rub your eyes in disbelief at their unspoilt charm. And they're not some kind of Walt Disney copy – these are real working villages. Those tilting gabled houses are inhabited by the people who tend the vines and make the wine; those rickety wooden doors do lead down to cellars that have housed the vats and barrels for hundreds of years.

The vineyards on these slopes also date way back, as the Romans had planted most of the lower foothills with vines by the 2nd century. There are specific vineyards like Goldert in the village of Gueberschwihr and Mambourg in Sigolsheim, whose documented reputation stretches back to the eighth century, when Alsace was ruled by the Franks, and these ancient vineyards now form the core of the present Grand Cru system of wine classification in Alsace.

GRANDS CRUS

Grand Cru means 'great growth' and is intended to apply to particular patches of land that have traditionally produced the finest grapes. A similar system in Burgundy has produced famous names like le Montrachet and Chambertin which have, for centuries, enjoyed global renown. However, hardly any of the Alsace Grand Cru names are known except to a few devoted fans, and it wasn't until 1983 that a provisional list of Grand Cru sites was produced. Alsace's turbulent history has much to do with this, since it takes a fair bit of time to build the reputation of a Cru, and in the critical 19th and 20th centuries, when areas like Burgundy and Bordeaux were advancing their fame, Alsace was concentrating on expanding its vineyards into the flat, over-fertile soils of the plain nearer the Rhine in order to produce cheap wines.

After World War Two, when Alsace finally reverted to France, the winemakers determinedly set out to achieve appellation contrôlée status for their region and decided to do so by concentrating their efforts on the single appellation – that of Alsace, which was finally granted only in 1962 – but with the different grape names prominently displayed on the best wines to indicate what flavours the drinker should expect. This labelling by grape variety may seem commonplace now, because of the influence of New World wines, but it was novel in France, where more and more precise delineation of the origin of a wine was at the heart of the appellation system.

The people with the power to market and promote Alsace as a wine region of quality were the big merchant houses and, since their objective was to produce large quantities of wine at various but consistent levels of quality, they needed to blend from numerous different vineyards and hardly ever named the actual vineyard site, preferring to promote their own names as brands. This worked well enough, but in the 1980s, when export markets like Britain and the United States became increasingly interested in single-vineyard wines from the top European wine regions, conflict between the merchants, the growers, and indeed the co-operatives became inevitable. Despite owning large tracts of Grand Cru vineyards, the leading merchant houses of Beyer, Trimbach and Hugel are most unwilling even now to put vineyard names on their wines and, indeed, they do not market Grand Cru wines, preferring to emphasize their companies' reputations instead.

Their position is understandable and not solely self-interested, because houses like Hugel have been most influential in promoting the quality classifications of Vendange Tardive for wines from super-ripe grapes, and Sélection de Grains Nobles for wines from grapes affected by noble rot. However, the concept of superior vineyard sites is crucial in marginal vineyard regions where only the most favourable mesoclimates can truly excel. Good drainage and a good aspect to the sun are vital in any vineyard area at the limits of the vine's ability to ripen.

At present there are 51 Grand Cru sites covering 8 per cent of Alsace vineyards, but they represent only 4 per cent of Alsace's total wine production. Basic maximum yields are lower than for simple Alsace wines, but are still high at 55hl/ha and serious growers never reach these figures. Current law states that only four 'noble' grapes planted in these sites are entitled to the Grand Cru appellation – Gewürztraminer, Riesling, Pinot Gris and Muscat – apart from the Grand Cru Zotzenberg for Sylvaner; but in future each local area may be allowed to nominate other varieties that perform particularly well in a given site. There is no doubt that many of the best sites, exploited by the best growers, do produce unique personalities in the wine that dominate varietal character, especially in Rieslings. Those Grands Crus that genuinely deserve a special reputation, and whose vines are tended with care and respect, will eventually establish top reputations for themselves and be able to charge top prices. But there are still numerous wines sporting Grand Cru labels that offer nothing special. But then, Alsace is still in the throes of re-organizing its classification system.

Currently, there is no intermediate level of quality between the great 'Grand Cru' vineyards and the simple Alsace AC. Work is now being done on establishing a group of Premier Cru vineyards, below Grand Cru, and these might eventually cover 2000–3000ha of land. There is also talk of a 'Villages' classification between Premier Cru and AC. And if all this sounds familiar, you're right. Burgundy operates just such a system and, from a good producer, it gives a reliable pointer to relative quality levels.

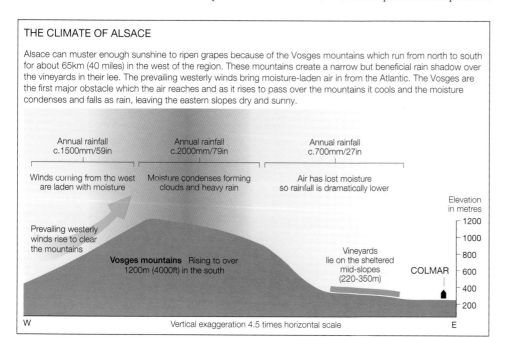

THE CLIMATE OF ALSACE

Alsace can muster enough sunshine to ripen grapes because of the Vosges mountains which run from north to south for about 65km (40 miles) in the west of the region. These mountains create a narrow but beneficial rain shadow over the vineyards in their lee. The prevailing westerly winds bring moisture-laden air in from the Atlantic. The Vosges are the first major obstacle which the air reaches and as it rises to pass over the mountains it cools and the moisture condenses and falls as rain, leaving the eastern slopes dry and sunny.

Annual rainfall c.1500mm/59in

Annual rainfall c.2000mm/79in

Annual rainfall c.700mm/27in

Winds coming from the west are laden with moisture

Moisture condenses forming clouds and heavy rain

Air has lost moisture so rainfall is dramatically lower

Prevailing westerly winds rise to clear the mountains

Elevation in metres

1200
1000
800
600
400
200

Vosges mountains Rising to over 1200m (4000ft) in the south

Vineyards lie on the sheltered mid-slopes (220-350m)

COLMAR

W

Vertical exaggeration 4.5 times horizontal scale

E

0 km   1   2
0 miles   1

WHERE THE VINEYARDS ARE *There is not a single top-quality Alsace vineyard that doesn't rely on the protection of the Vosges mountains. The reason that most of the very best Alsace vineyards are in the central block of foothills between Bergheim and Gueberschwihr is that the Vosges mountains are at their highest and broadest at this point. Further north, the mountains are substantially lower and do not provide such an efficient rainshadow. Good wines are made in the northerly Bas-Rhin region of Alsace, but they rarely have the ripeness or intensity of those from the vineyards of the Haut-Rhin shown here. The map clearly demonstrates how the vines sweep up towards the wooded hilltops, yet peter out towards the flat valley floor. If you look at the location of the Grands Crus, all of them are either in the lee of the hills or else, as in the case of Froehn and Mambourg, on large outcrops of steeply sloping land away from the foothills. The excellent drainage and the favourable aspect to the sun provided by the slopes are crucial, particularly in a vineyard area such as Alsace, which is at the limits of the vine's ability to ripen.*

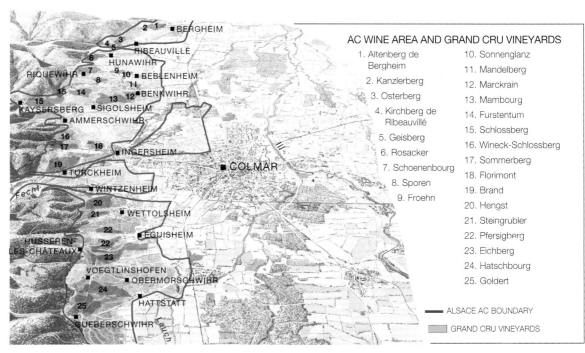

AC WINE AREA AND GRAND CRU VINEYARDS

1. Altenberg de Bergheim
2. Kanzlerberg
3. Osterberg
4. Kirchberg de Ribeauvillé
5. Geisberg
6. Rosacker
7. Schoenenbourg
8. Sporen
9. Froehn
10. Sonnenglanz
11. Mandelberg
12. Marckrain
13. Mambourg
14. Furstentum
15. Schlossberg
16. Wineck-Schlossberg
17. Sommerberg
18. Florimont
19. Brand
20. Hengst
21. Steingrubler
22. Pfersigberg
23. Eichberg
24. Hatschbourg
25. Goldert

—— ALSACE AC BOUNDARY

▨ GRAND CRU VINEYARDS

0 km 1 2
0 miles 1

AROUND COLMAR

TOTAL DISTANCE
NORTH TO SOUTH
27KM (17 MILES)

▦ VINEYARDS

▲
N

THE LOIRE VALLEY

I SOMETIMES WONDER WHETHER the Loire River is just too long for its own good. It starts brightly enough, cascading and splashing out of the Ardèche gorges only 50km (31 miles) west of the Rhône at Valence, full of purpose and vivacity. Gambolling and churning its way northwards, it seems to be tiring even as it reaches the site of its first decent vineyards – those of the Côtes du Forez and Côte Roannaise, both of which make a very passable imitation of good Beaujolais from the Gamay grape. But by the time the river gets to Pouilly and Sancerre, sites of its first world-famous wines, the initial breezy seaward flow has slowed to a walk.

As the river makes its great arc northwards to Orléans past the haunting Sologne marshes, and then loops wearily south and west, through Blois, Tours, Angers, Nantes and finally to the Atlantic at St-Nazaire, the walk slows to an amble, the motion of the water so listless that the valley seems caught in a reverie, completely unconcerned about reaching its destination on the turbulent shores of the Bay of Biscay. Great gravel banks push through the river's surface, children paddle in the shallows, parents picnic and gossip on the warm pebbles (mind you, in winter it's a different story with treacherous currents and a tendency to flood). It doesn't seem as though the lazy summer Loire has the character to be a great wine river, home of some of the most thrilling and individual wines in France. But behind its dozy exterior, the Loire Valley does have exactly the character required.

GRAPE VARIETIES

The Loire is predominantly a white grape region, producing enormous quantities of wine from Melon de Bourgogne – one of the world's most neutral white grape varieties. As its name suggests, the grape was originally from Burgundy, but it is no longer grown there and is far more famous as Muscadet. Its virtue, when grown in the maritime climate near Nantes, is that it retains freshness, which makes it an exceptionally good partner to the local seafood.

Sauvignon Blanc needs a relatively cool climate if it is to express its trademark pungency, its bright green, grassy, gooseberry freshness and slightly smoky perfume. In Sancerre and Pouilly, in the hands of a good winemaker, Sauvignon Blanc excels at such mouth-tingling crispness. But Loire Sauvignon Blanc can also be associated with a pungent 'cat's pee' smell, a sure sign that the fruit was not ripe when picked. Sauvignon needs its green streak; the skill is in marrying that with proper ripeness.

Chenin Blanc needs warmth – it's raw and harsh when unripe. Few other places in the world take Chenin Blanc seriously, but here in the Loire Valley it can reach heights undreamed of elsewhere. The *tufa* soil (a type of chalky limestone) keeps acidity levels high, enabling the greatest dry and sweet Chenins to last for decades, when they mature to a honeyed, minerally richness. Chenin is used for everything from sparkling wines to botrytized sweet ones. While most dry Loire Chenin Blanc is made for drinking young, those from Vouvray and Savennières age brilliantly. Still Vouvray can, in fact, be searingly dry when young and needs aging – often at least two decades or more. Then there's the mildly sweet *demi-sec*, with its gorgeous nuances of honeysuckle and quince. And when the autumn is kind and lasts long, then great sweet wines are made, from grapes that have either been affected by noble rot or dehydrated by heat.

Cabernet Franc, used largely as a seasoning grape in Bordeaux, is the main red wine grape grown in the Loire. In Bourgueil, St-Nicolas-de-Bourgueil and Chinon, its mouthwatering perfume and smooth texture makes some of France's most lovely red wines. At its best, Cabernet Franc has an unmistakable and hugely appealing raspberry fruit and a summery tang of blackcurrant leaves. Delicious young, its wines can also be very long-lived. It is used for rosés, too.

Pinot Noir, the great grape of Burgundy, is grown in the Loire in Sancerre and Menetou-Salon where, in ripe years, it makes wines with good fruit and structure. Most red Sancerre, however, is made to be drunk young. Some Pinot Noir goes into rosé production.

Gamay makes fresh, juicy Beaujolais-like reds and rosé wines designed to be drunk young. The Teinturier Gamay (red-fleshed, as opposed to the Gamay Noir à Jus Blanc) is also grown in Touraine, but its wines are robust, solid and unaromatic.

PAYS NANTAIS

Since the river's flow can be so mild, let's begin by looking at the vineyards at its western seaward end, and then push our way upstream aided by the brisk westerly winds, to Sancerre and Pouilly, several hundred miles away. Well, I have to admit these wines of the Pays Nantais, as the western section is called, are indeed the mildest, the least memorable of the entire river. But they are also some of the most famous, for this is the home of Muscadet and the four Muscadet appellations, which between them make up the fifth highest volume of French wine production, after Vin de Pays d'Oc, Bordeaux Rouge, the Vins de Pays Aude and Hérault.

Muscadet is famous because it is so irreproachably, ultra-gluggably anonymous. At best it has a quenching freshness, a hint of lemon and pepper, a hint of apricot, and if you're lucky, a hint of cream. But we're talking about hints here – the one thing Muscadet never does is taste of a good deal of anything. And that is the basis for its success.

Muscadet isn't the name of an area: it's the local name for the Burgundian grape variety of Melon de Bourgogne. Because this was the only variety in the Nantes region to survive the devastating frosts of 1709–10, it was enthusiastically adopted by local growers. For more than two centuries the Muscadet, and its more acidic neighbour the Gros Plant, did an excellent job of providing cheap, light white wine to accompany the superb local seafood.

But Parisians eat seafood too – from autumn to spring there are oyster stalls all over Paris' *boulevards* – and they adopted Muscadet as their seafood wine. Then, during the 1970s and '80s the export

The Loire Valley was the playground of the Valois kings and the French court in the 15th and 16th centuries. Château de Chenonceau on the river Cher is just one of many outstanding Renaissance palaces built during the golden age of French culture.

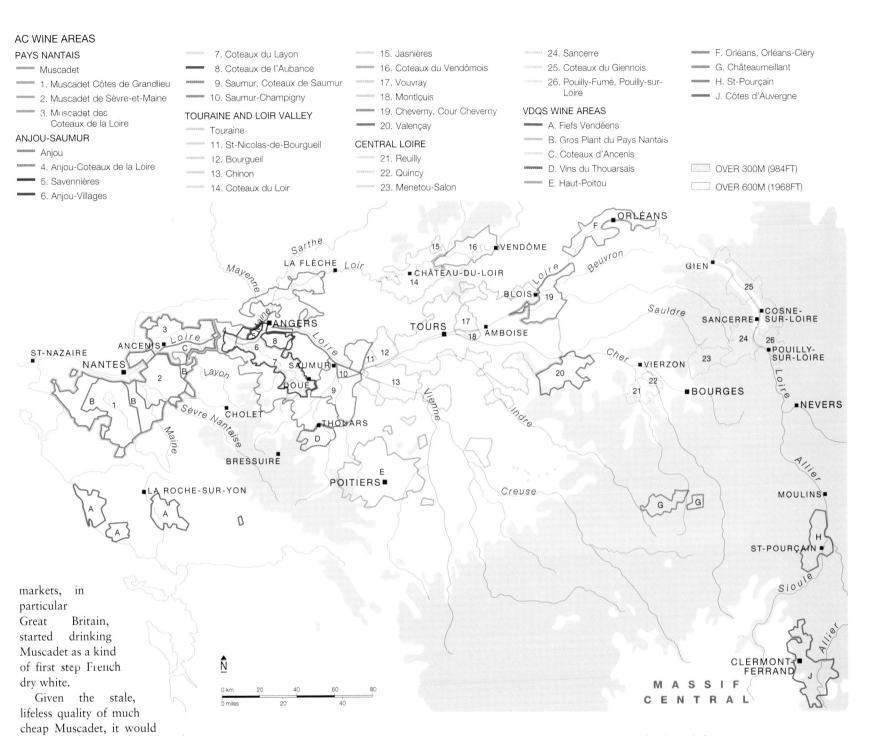

AC WINE AREAS

PAYS NANTAIS
Muscadet
1. Muscadet Côtes de Grandlieu
2. Muscadet de Sèvre-et-Maine
3. Muscadet des
Coteaux de la Loire

ANJOU-SAUMUR
Anjou
4. Anjou-Coteaux de la Loire
5. Savennières
6. Anjou-Villages

7. Coteaux du Layon
8. Coteaux de l'Aubance
9. Saumur, Coteaux de Saumur
10. Saumur-Champigny

TOURAINE AND LOIR VALLEY
Touraine
11. St-Nicolas-de-Bourgueil
12. Bourgueil
13. Chinon
14. Coteaux du Loir

15. Jasnières
16. Coteaux du Vendômois
17. Vouvray
18. Montlouis
19. Cheverny, Cour Cheverny
20. Valençay

CENTRAL LOIRE
21. Reuilly
22. Quincy
23. Menetou-Salon

24. Sancerre
25. Coteaux du Giennois
26. Pouilly-Fumé, Pouilly-sur-Loire

VDQS WINE AREAS
A. Fiefs Vendéens
B. Gros Plant du Pays Nantais
C. Coteaux d'Ancenis
D. Vins du Thouarsais
E. Haut-Poitou

F. Orléans, Orléans-Cléry
G. Châteaumeillant
H. St-Pourçain
J. Côtes d'Auvergne

OVER 300M (984FT)
OVER 600M (1968FT)

markets, in particular Great Britain, started drinking Muscadet as a kind of first step French dry white.

Given the stale, lifeless quality of much cheap Muscadet, it would be easy to say that this mirrored the sluggish brown estuarial waters of the river as it oozes through St-Nazaire. But Muscadet need not be a poor drink – it is only the exploitation of an easily remembered name by greedy merchants that makes it so. Good Muscadet, especially from the delightful jumbled rolling countryside of the Sèvre-et-Maine area south-east of Nantes, can be an absolute charmer – relatively neutral in taste, but with a streak of grapefruit and pepper assertiveness and a mild creaminess too.

Because of the innate neutrality of the grape, the best examples are left on their yeast lees, and are undisturbed before being bottled directly off the lees – thereby capturing a little of the yeasty creaminess and also some of the natural carbon dioxide in the wine. These wines are labelled 'sur lie' and their blend of freshness, neutrality and soft texture make them the perfect seafood wine. The tangy, acid Gros Plant du Pays Nantais, from the flat vineyards whipped by the salty ocean gales to the south-west of Nantes, can

equal Muscadet as the perfect accompaniment to seafood. And if I had to choose one city in France in which to enjoy brilliant seafood, Nantes would take some beating.

ANJOU-SAUMUR
We need to head upstream – past Ancenis, where, surprisingly, the Alsace grape Pinot Gris makes a little, vaguely sweet wine under the title Malvoisie – before we really begin to discover the fascinating variety that belies the river's somnambulent appearance. This brings us to Anjou, with its plantations of the thoroughly difficult, exasperating, but sometimes majestically rewarding Chenin Blanc grape variety.

Much of Anjou isn't ideal for the vine – remember that the Loire Valley is as far north as the vine can ripen on the west coast of France, and most of Anjou is planted with cereal crops and vegetables, which are able to withstand the wind and rain better than

any grape vines can. Those vines planted away from the various river valleys on exposed land are unlikely to produce anything but the most basic wine, generally the palest of pale whites – or a pale pink from various struggling reds. This explains why much of the cheap Anjou Rosé to be found skulking among the pink wines on every merchant's shelf is so poor – the grapes are grown on exposed sites that would be better suited to cabbages, and they just never ripen.

But there are sheltered vineyards, usually facing towards the south-west, ideally planted on limestone or slate soils, that can produce some absolute stunners. Most brilliant of these, and most unexpected, are the sweet Chenin wines (see below) that emerge from the folds of the river banks along the Layon Valley, and to a lesser extent, the Aubance Valley, both of which are formed by southern tributaries of the Loire river.

Generally, however, the Chenin Blanc makes medium or dry wines in Anjou. The climatic feature that allows the grapes to ripen at all along the cool Loire Valley is a generally warm early autumn that, with luck, pushes the late-ripening Chenin Blanc to a decent level of maturity. The most famous of these whites is the dry Savennières, perched on the north side of the Loire, just to the west of Angers, a gaunt, austere wine with the distant beauty of an ice maiden. Most of the rest of Anjou's whites come from vineyards spread across the fields south of the Loire. The regulations allow for up to 20 per cent of Chardonnay and Sauvignon Blanc in the blend, but increasingly producers prefer to use just Chenin Blanc, making sure it is properly ripe before picking it.

But for those grapes that fail to ripen properly, there is still a haven: in the eastern part of Anjou, bordering on Touraine, is Saumur, one of France's chief production centres for sparkling wine (see box, facing page). The soils around Saumur are more chalky

than in the rest of Anjou, which encourages a certain leanness in the wines. This, combined with cool ripening conditions, often produces just the sort of acid base wine that sparkling wine manufacturers like.

Red wines are less successful in most of Anjou because the largely clay soils don't ripen the grapes sufficiently, but there are pockets of decent Gamay and Cabernet Franc – the best of these Cabernet Franc vineyards claiming an Anjou-Villages appellation – while the Saumur-Champigny vineyards to the south-east of the town can make delightful fragrant reds of varying weights.

SWEET WINES OF THE LAYON VALLEY

Across from Savennières the Layon river joins the Loire, and it is along the Layon's northern banks that the Chenin grape produces some of the finest sweet wines in France. Even so, it is often a long wait to achieve the necessary overripeness, but good sites allied to meticulous producers can manage it on a regular basis.

Most great sweet wines are made when the grapes are attacked by the noble rot fungus. For the last few miles before the two rivers join, the influence of both causes morning mists to form along the Layon and its little tributaries. This humidity rising from the streams in warm autumns provides perfect conditions for the development of noble rot, which, as in Sauternes (see page 48), helps to concentrate the grapes' sweetness to a remarkable degree. A combination of climate, the Chenin Blanc grape and those growers with nerves of steel means that sweet wines can be made here even in the most difficult of years. These luscious wines can be utterly magical.

In particular at Chaume, Quarts de Chaume and Bonnezeaux, a perfect sheltered south to south-west exposure allows grapes every

Right: the castle and fortifications of Chinon stand proudly above the Vienne, a tributary of the Loire, but the river meanders lazily past, and the sandbanks make a perfect perch for a local fisherman.

The river Layon is a tributary of the Loire: Chenin Blanc from vineyards along its banks is rich and sweet.

chance to ripen, then rot. Even so, noble rot doesn't happen uniformly. Often the pickers have to comb the vines again and again, picking the grapes that have nobly rotted, sometimes grape by grape, and leaving the rest to develop the welcome fungus.

Coteaux du Layon covers 25 communes in the Layon Valley. Coteaux du Layon-Villages covers six of the best seven villages between Faye d'Anjou and St-Aubin de Luigné and the seventh, Chaume, has recently been promoted to its own appellation, joining those of Quarts de Chaume and Bonnezeaux, with their perfect conditions and slopes for when the autumn weather holds.

Both the Coteaux de l'Aubance and the Coteaux de la Loire make reasonable sweetish white wines.

TOURAINE

The best Loire reds come from Touraine, a few miles to the east where the breezes seem to soften and the air to mellow. Touraine *appellations* St-Nicolas-de-Bourgueil, Bourgueil and Chinon use the Cabernet Franc grape to create gorgeously refreshing, tangy reds – wonderful young, but also capable of staying fresh for decades.

However, I have to admit that when I'm in Touraine, I find it difficult to concentrate on the wines, because there are more spectacular castles here than anywhere else in France. These bear testament to the Valois kings who, from the 15th century onwards, used Touraine for rest and relaxation. Many châteaux are open to visitors and, though I don't normally have time for sightseeing, I have seen a few of these beauties, Chenonceau, Amboise and Azay-le-Rideau among them. And in any case, the only other famous wine in Touraine is Vouvray. Cheap Vouvray is a peculiarly nasty sulphurous brew of no virtue whatsoever. But the appellation has been undergoing a revival. From a committed producer the dry, medium, sweet, or fizzy white wines of Vouvray can be a revelation, each of them fit for sipping on the balustrades of some of the most grandiose châteaux.

Vineyards are spread sparsely through the rest of Touraine, and as we follow the Loire up past Blois to Orléans, they become almost non-existent. Given that Orléans is the vinegar capital of France, this may be no bad thing, and it certainly makes one wonder what the local wines used to be like. Yet a tiny wine industry does survive here, and from one or two producers, including Clos St-Fiacre who make an excellent Chardonnay (here called the Auvernat), the wine can be rather good. This is also the hang-out of several producers of a pleasant, pale, smoky pink wine called Gris Meunier – from the Pinot Meunier grape, famously used in the Champagne blend. The strangest things do crop up along the Loire Valley.

CENTRAL VINEYARDS

As we turn south from Orléans up the Loire past the minor wine towns of Gien and Cosne, to the mainstream appellations of Sancerre and Pouilly-Fumé – regarded by many as the quintessential Sauvignon Blanc styles – we come across a few plots of Chasselas. This is basically an eating grape – indeed it was grown for the dining-tables of Paris in the 19th century – though it is used for wine in Alsace, Germany and Switzerland. Chasselas makes wine of just about no discernible character and yet here, in the fancy vineyards of Pouilly, in a world crying out for good Sauvignon Blanc, you still find the odd plot of Chasselas. Weird, but most of Pouilly is more than capable of looking after itself, making high-quality, high priced Sauvignon Blanc.

Sancerre across the river also concentrates on Sauvignon whites. Recently, though, top Sancerre producers have been paying increased attention to Pinot Noir, a traditional variety in the area.

By reducing yields they have produced some remarkably full bodied reds, showing how dilute most other red Sancerres are.

Menetou-Salon adjoins Sancerre and makes delicious Sancerre lookalikes (white, rosé and red) but a bit cheaper. Going further west still, past the historic town of Bourges, brings you to Reuilly with its light reds and rosés. But Reuilly, along with its neighbour Quincy, are much better at making good, snappy Sauvignon whites, filled with the aroma of gooseberries and green grass.

UPPER LOIRE

We could continue up the river, eyes peeled for any signs of life beneath its placid surface, for another 160km (100 miles) and more until, past Roanne in the Loire gorge, it finally shows fitful signs of life. But if we do, we won't find too many vines trailing down to the water's edge. There's little wine of consequence produced between Pouilly and Roanne, except for some made around St-Pourçain close to the Allier, a Loire tributary.

Honest Gamays from the Côte Roannaise plus the occasional rosé are helped by association: the famous Troisgros restaurant at Roanne often serves the bright, Gamay red as its house wine. Past the Loire gorge, the Côtes du Forez red is similar in style – but it doesn't have a world-famous local chef to trumpet its charms.

THE SPARKLING WINES OF THE LOIRE

It would be easy to look upon the Loire Valley sparkling wine industry simply as a mechanism for soaking up large amounts of otherwise undrinkable local wines, since most of the best sparklers are made from a very acid base wine. But this wouldn't be fair, any more than it would be fair to describe Champagne in those terms. Although in a warm year the late-ripening Chenin Blanc can make excellent still wine, in the all-too-frequent cool years this high acid variety simply doesn't get ripe enough. So a cool year provides the perfect material for sparkling wines.

The best sparkling wines are made by the traditional method (as used in Champagne), that is, with a second fermentation in the bottle, and tend to come from cool vineyards of limestone-dominated soils and subsoils. Both Saumur and Vouvray, which produce the two most important sparkling wine appellations in the region, are predominantly limestone areas. Vouvray and its neighbouring appellation of Montlouis use only Chenin Blanc for their fizz and, if you give the bottles a few years to soften, they attain a delicious nutty, honeyed quality, yet retain the zing of Chenin acidity.

Saumur Mousseux is usually based on Chenin but may include other varieties like Chardonnay, Sauvignon and Cabernet Franc. Saumur Mousseux made from 100 per cent Chenin is often too lean, so the addition of Cabernet, and Chardonnay in particular, brings a very welcome softness. Crémant de Loire, an appellation created in 1975 covering Anjou and Touraine, stipulates lower vineyard yields and requires 150kg (330lb) of grapes to make one hectolitre of juice, rather than the 130kg (287lb) permitted for Saumur. This lower yield of juice means the grapes are not pressed so savagely and so the bitter elements present in the skins and pips are not extracted. The appellation also stipulates a longer aging period before release, giving a gentler foaming mousse and attractive hints of yeast and honey. The wines are generally superior to Saumur, but the title of Crémant de Loire sounds rather generic and catch-all, and so it hasn't had the success it deserves.

Occasionally in Saumur you'll find a Cabernet Franc-based fizzy red, grassy and full of fruit, ideal for picnic glugging by the riverbank.

ANJOU-SAUMUR

RED GRAPES
Groslot is used for rosé, mainly Cabernet Franc and a little Cabernet Sauvignon for the reds. Gamay is also planted in Anjou.

WHITE GRAPES
Chenin Blanc is the main grape, with increasing amounts of Chardonnay and Sauvignon Blanc.

CLIMATE
A mild maritime climate moderated by the influence of the Gulf Stream produces warm summers and mild autumns and winters. Ripening can be a problem.

SOIL
In Anjou the soil is predominantly dark slate, schist and clay with areas of more permeable shale and gravel which favour the Cabernet grapes. Much of Saumur is limestone characterized by pale outcrops of a chalky freestone known as *tuffeau blanc*.

ASPECT
In this area of low hills specific aspect to the sun is vital for ripening. The best sites are on the steeper slopes and face south-west, south or south-east.

SINCE 1985, ANJOU HAS HAD A DECENT RED WINE in which to incorporate its name – Anjou-Villages AC – from a grouping of 46 Anjou villages south of Angers deemed to have better than average vineyard sites. Only Cabernet Franc and Cabernet Sauvignon may be used for Anjou-Villages and, by a lucky coincidence, the 1988, '89 and '90 vintages were excellent, giving the appellation a great start, while most of the vintages since the mid-1990s have been equally good. The dry, fruity wines need at least three to four years aging.

These hinterland villages spread across the indeterminate rolling agricultural land running from west of Angers across to Saumur, and centred on Brissac-Quincé, needed all the help they could get to make decent wine. The sweet wines of the Layon Valley (see page 83), the small, high-class, dry white appellation of Savennières, west of Angers, and the sparkling and red wines of Saumur are among the several enclaves of high-quality wine in Anjou. Despite these,

WHERE THE VINEYARDS ARE *The border between Anjou and the Muscadet region of Nantais is just to the west of the map and these wild, open acres enjoy the mixed blessing of a maritime climate. They avoid the extremes of temperature of a continental climate and, in general, enjoy a reasonably balmy autumn, but they also get the damp, westerly winds that drive inland from the Bay of Biscay. Some Coteaux de la Loire is grown in these vineyards, but it's hard work. Then see how dramatically things change where the Layon river joins the Loire at Chalonnes.*

On the Loire's north bank, suddenly there are sufficient plateaux to protect vineyards beneath them – and Savennières immediately benefits from this protection. The Layon meanders in to join the Loire from the south-east. Its northern banks have ridges of hills and forests to protect the vines and allow the long autumn ripening that the grapes need to make great sweet wine (see page 83). The land becomes wooded and undulating from here, right across to Saumur. This creates myriad mesoclimates where even a late-ripening variety like Chenin Blanc has a chance to build up sugar. At Saumur in the east of the region we are into the chalky freestone subsoil which also dominates Touraine and gives excellent conditions for white grapes.

the image of the province has been relentlessly dragged down for decades by the mediocrity of most Anjou Rosé and the over-sulphured, off-dry Anjou Blanc.

The drift away from rosé wines by the drinking public forced the Anjou winemakers to rethink. Many of the vineyards in Anjou are too exposed, and the soil is too cool and moist for them to be able to produce anything special, and, apart from ripping up their vines, growers have little choice but to continue growing the uninspiring Groslot for rosés or late-ripening Chenin for whites.

The trouble is, much of Anjou isn't particularly suited to grape-growing – the great open spaces full of cereals and sunflowers and vegetables bear witness to that. But modern methods of viticulture and winemaking can and do help. There is a small amount of Anjou-Gamay made by the Beaujolais method of fermentation – carbonic maceration (see page 68). It makes a fairly rustic, but juicy, purplish red, much of which is drunk as Primeur in November, just after the vintage.

For the Cabernet-based wines the problem is how to get enough colour and flavour from grapes that rarely ripen fully in Anjou without risking bitter, tannic harshness from unripe skins and pips. The solution is to lower the yields, de-leaf and, for top producers, to pick selectively. Micro-oxygenation is also being used to extract colour and flavour. Similarly the best white producers concentrate on getting their Chenin Blanc ripe and using stainless steel and cold fermentation. Some also ferment in new wood. There is, however, a big gap between the best and the worst, and more than ever, you need to look for the producer's name rather than the appellation.

SAVENNIÈRES

The one dry Anjou white which has always been revered, if not exactly fêted, is Savennières. The vineyards don't amount to more than 124ha (306 acres) looking out over the islands and channels of the wide Loire towards the mouth of the Layon river, but they can produce the Loire's best dry whites. When this appellation was granted in 1952 the permitted yield was set artificially low, and the

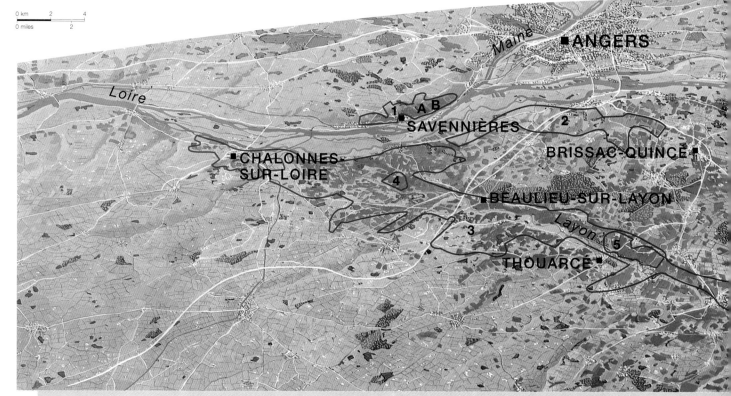

minimum alcohol level extremely high, because the wine was then generally sweet, and good sweet French wines always have very low permitted yields and ambitiously high minimum alcohol levels.

Today, Savennières is almost always dry, and the restrictions are a mixed blessing. On the slate and clay soils, high alcohol is only possible most years because of the low yield, and it is this rare, high ripeness level from the tricky Chenin grape that gives Savennières wine the ability to age and improve for a generation or more. There are two small Grands Crus – Coulée-de-Serrant, which makes the subtlest and most refined wine and la Roche-aux-Moines, whose wines are lighter but also extremely good – whose steep slopes rising up from the Loire (see right) and excellent exposure to the sun further intensify the taut, but fathoms-deep, flavour of these wines.

SAUMUR

Saumur is important both for its sparkling white wines and its Cabernet Franc reds. The soil changes as you head south-east from Angers to Saumur. The dark clay, slate and schist of Angers has been replaced mostly by limestone, especially a layer of chalky freestone called *tuffeau blanc*. This freestone layer is over 50m (164ft) thick in places, and not only provides a completely different subsoil for vines, in particular along the south bank of the Loire where the red grape vineyards are situated, but it also offers the perfect medium for wine cellars. This rock was quarried to build many of the region's châteaux and the excavations left behind numerous caves which have been adapted over the centuries for growing mushrooms, aging wine or even as dwellings.

Champagne in north-eastern France is founded on chalk, its vines grow on chalk, and its wines mature in cool, underground chalk cellars. It is very similar in Saumur, where there are reckoned to be 1000km (620 miles) of underground passages and cellars. Sparkling Saumur is based on Chenin grapes, but both Chardonnay and Sauvignon Blanc are allowed to constitute up to 20 per cent of the blend as they are in still Saumur Blanc. Up to 60 per cent of red grapes are permitted in white sparkling Saumur and 100 per cent in the rosé. Interestingly, there is also an occasional, rare sweet Chenin called Coteaux de Saumur produced at the eastern end of Anjou.

Still Saumur Rouge is based on Cabernet Franc, though Cabernet Sauvignon and the rare Pineau d'Aunis can also be used. On Saumur's chalky soils the Cabernet Franc grape does best, producing light but often attractively grassy reds, and, in the small Saumur-Champigny area, especially on the freestone plateaux east and south-east of the town, this is often married to a keen, mouthwatering blackcurrant and raspberry fruit.

Savennières' top two vineyards – Coulée de Serrant in the foreground and la Roche-aux-Moines with its château in the distance – lie on steep slopes above the Loire.

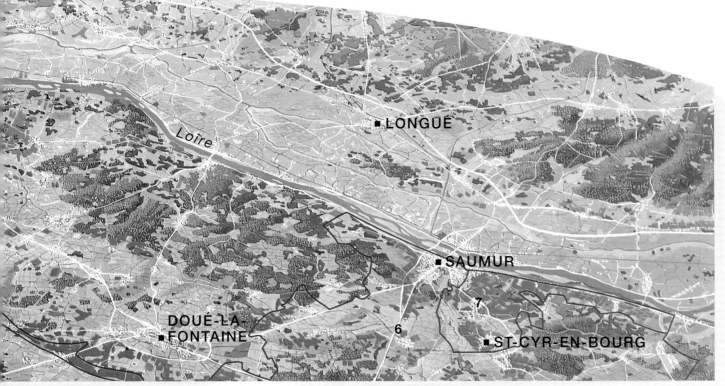

Loire

■ LONGUÉ

■ SAUMUR

7

6

DOUÉ-LA-FONTAINE

■ ST-CYR-EN-BOURG

AC WINE AREAS

1. Savennières
   A. la Roche-aux-Moines
   B. Coulée-de-Serrant
2. Coteaux de l'Aubance
3. Coteaux du Layon
4. Quarts de Chaume
5. Bonnezeaux
6. Saumur
7. Saumur-Champigny

TOTAL DISTANCE
NORTH TO SOUTH
40KM (25 MILES)

▬ AC BOUNDARIES

▨ VINEYARDS

N

0 km   2   4
0 miles   2

TOURAINE

 RED GRAPES
Gamay accounts for two-thirds of Touraine red wines, though the quality grape is Cabernet Franc. Other lesser varieties are Cabernet Sauvignon, Malbec (Cot), Pinot Noir and Pineau d'Aunis.

 WHITE GRAPES
Chenin Blanc dominates, but Chardonnay and Sauvignon Blanc are both fairly widely planted.

CLIMATE
The climate is similar to Anjou-Saumur but with rather lower rainfall. Early autumn is usually sunny, favouring late-ripeners such as Chenin Blanc.

SOIL
The flatland near the river is mostly sandy alluvial flood-plain with outcrops of sandy gravel; the slopes and plateaux are mostly limestone and chalky freestone (*tuffeau blanc*) with some clay.

ASPECT
The vineyards are at 40 to 100m (130 to 328ft), usually on south-facing slopes.

This Vouvray grower is checking to see that his grapes are at least partially affected by botrytis – crucial if he decides to make a sweet wine.

THIS IS ABOUT THE ONLY TIME in this book I'm going to give lumps of granite and slabs of brick and mortar precedence over the flavour of the wines or the contours of the vineyard sites, because Touraine, with its array of peerless châteaux, is different. Why were these Renaissance masterpieces built along the banks of the Loire, and its tributaries the Cher, the Indre and the Vienne, which join the main river to the west of Tours? What were they used for and by whom?

Proximity to Paris, and climate, provide the keys. As the Loire flows down from Orléans to Tours and Saumur, its vast forests are full of game for hunting, and its fertile river valley is ideally suited to growing fruit and vegetables. It was this natural abundance of the land, and the mild, benign climate that made this middle section of the Loire the obvious choice for the Court of France to use as a playground, a place to build holiday homes – well, holiday castles, this being the Court – and to relax from the rigours of ruling.

The legacy is some truly magnificent châteaux – from a whole hatful I will pick just a few. The dream-like Azay-le-Rideau – where Balzac found inspiration for several of his novels – is set serenely on an island in the middle of the Indre river. Part of Chenonceau, a château of an extraordinary haughty grandeur, actually straddles the river Cher. Chambord, east of Blois, is the largest of them all, with 440 rooms and 365 fireplaces – one for each day of the year. Ruined Chinon, on the Vienne river, towers above the pretty gabled town where Rabelais learned to drink deep and long, where Richard the Lionheart died, and where Joan of Arc first pumped some courage into the veins of her King, Charles VII of France.

Most of Touraine is so suitable for vegetables, flowers, cereals – and virtually anything else you could want to plant – that the vine, accustomed to thriving in infertile conditions, is often conspicuous by its absence. The cattle fatten contentedly on lush river meadows, the forests are still thick with game. In early summer the whole region seems to blaze with flowers. By late summer the trees are weighed down with France's best pears and apples, cherries, nuts and plums. And early autumn – well, early autumn generally sees a wonderfully calming warmth bathing the valley. It's too late to have any effect on vegetables or fruit, but it is what makes fine wine possible in these vineyards of France's north-west.

The Chenin Blanc, the Loire's native white grape, is late-ripening, and desperately needs the late autumn of this region to get past its initial thin, sour state. Chardonnay and Sauvignon Blanc both ripen more easily and are quite widely planted, especially Sauvignon Blanc. The reds also need the extra warmth of autumn, and are primarily made from the Bordeaux grapes – Cabernet Franc, Cabernet Sauvignon and Malbec (or Cot as it is called here). The Gamay grape variety, though more used to the hot summer weather of Beaujolais in southern Burgundy, is equally important in Touraine's reds.

WINE AREAS

Our map covers the heart of Touraine, and its most famous wines. These comprise Vouvray, to the east of Tours, and the group of red wines – Chinon, Bourgueil and St-Nicolas-de-Bourgueil – which lie to the west.

Touraine is a general appellation for reds, whites, pinks and sparklers, and covers the less-favoured vineyard areas. Three superior villages – Mesland, Amboise and Azay-le-Rideau – can tack their own name on to the basic Touraine AC.

South-east of Blois, the strange Romorantin grape makes fairly hairy wine at Cour-Cheverny. North of Tours on the Loir (sic) river, Jasnières makes unforgiving, but occasionally rewarding, stone-dry whites from the Chenin.

VOUVRAY AND MONTLOUIS

However, to see just how good the Chenin grape can be, we need to come back to the Loire, to the vineyards of Vouvray that lie above the low chalky cliffs lining the north bank of the river. Using only Chenin Blanc, Vouvray comes in a welter of styles, and the sparkling version is the best of the Loire fizzes.

The still wines can be searingly dry, pushing anyone's sensitive gums to the limit when young, but undergoing a magical transformation over 20 or 30 years. Vouvray can also be sumptuously rich, developing more and more nuances of flavour for half a century or longer. Or it can be anywhere between: the mildly sweet *demi-sec* (when made carefully by a committed producer) is a heavenly balance between high acid, mellow quince and honeysuckle fruit.

A word of caution: cheap, anonymous Vouvray *demi-sec* is likely to be poor stuff. If you do want a similar style to Vouvray but at a lower price, Montlouis, south-east of Vouvray, is more likely to provide good examples. Vouvray's wide variety of styles is due to soil and to climate. Those low cliffs are of an unusual chalky limestone, with a topsoil made of a mix of clay and gravel, and sometimes flint. This limestone base means the wines retain acid even in the hottest years. When the autumn is late – and sometimes this season can continue into November – great sweet wines are possible either through dehydration of the grapes by heat (as in 2003), or by noble rot (as in 2005).

In less warm years, *demi-sec* is the more popular style. When the autumn fails, only the dry version is possible, and most wines will end up being made into fizz.

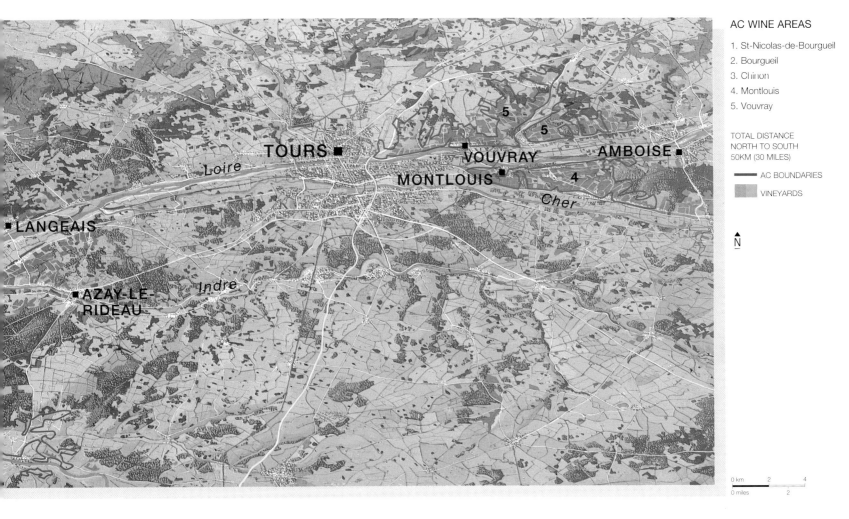

AC WINE AREAS

1. St-Nicolas-de-Bourgueil
2. Bourgueil
3. Chinon
4. Montlouis
5. Vouvray

TOTAL DISTANCE
NORTH TO SOUTH
50KM (30 MILES)

━━━ AC BOUNDARIES

▨ VINEYARDS

▲
N

CHINON, BOURGUEIL & ST-NICOLAS-DE-BOURGUEIL

The Loire's best reds (as well as a little rosé) come from the trio of villages at the western end of the map, where the Vienne river slides in from the south-east to join the Loire. The reds of Chinon, Bourgueil and St-Nicolas-de-Bourgueil are remarkable wines, because so much of their character seems to lie in a fresh, joyous raspberry fruit, and a summer scent of warm earth and stone, and yet they can age as well as all but the best wines from Bordeaux. There is a tiny amount of white Chinon made from Chenin Blanc.

Again, climate and soil give some clues. The Cabernet Franc, the dominant grape here, doesn't need as much warmth to ripen as the Cabernet Sauvignon (though a few producers use a little of this too). Consequently the mild summer is sufficient to produce a pleasant, light-bodied, red fruit character. When the autumn is good, the wines dramatically deepen in colour and strength, yet never lose their gorgeous soft-centred raspberry and sweet earth perfume, sometimes heightened by a haunting scent of violets.

This whole area has less rain than its neighbours, but Bourgueil in particular has a warm, dry mesoclimate because its best vineyards are protected from cold, wet, northerly winds by a 120m (394ft) high wooded plateau.

The deepest, darkest wines are from the *coteaux* slopes of chalky freestone and limestone clay soil that run up towards the plateau. Below these, good wines come from gravelly soils, while there are outcrops of sandy gravel on the Loire banks that give light, easy-drinking flavours. Often the best results come from blending the wines from the different soils, since Bourgueil from the *coteaux* alone can be rather aggressive and joyless, requiring years of maturity to show its underlying fruit and perfume.

WHERE THE VINEYARDS ARE *This map shows the heart of the Loire, where the best red wines are produced, as well as excellent whites, dry or sweet, and fine fizz. The reds come from the western end, where the river Vienne joins the Loire from the south-east. The area between the river, St-Nicolas-de-Bourgueil and Bourgueil is mostly flat, alluvial flood-plain, but there are a few outcrops of sandy gravel producing light Bourgueil reds. However, all the best Bourgueil comes from the vineyards you can see beneath the wooded brow of hillside to the north. This plateau protects the vines and provides Bourgueil with a particularly dry mesoclimate. The lower slopes here are relatively gravelly, the higher slopes, especially those to the north-east of Bourgueil, are limestone clays over chalky freestone and produce the deeper, darker reds.*

Chinon's best reds come from the slopes directly to the east of the town where clay and gravel mix with limestone, and from the more chalky slopes to the north and west. There are also sandy soils along the banks of the river Vienne planted with vines that yield lighter reds and rosés. The Vouvray vineyards mostly lie on plateaux above the chalky cliffs between Tours and Noizay. The wines of Montlouis come from vineyards planted on a gently sloping, sandy clay plateau above reasonably chalky subsoil that inclines southwards towards the river Cher.

St-Nicolas-de-Bourgueil can be divided into two main vineyard types: those planted on gravel terraces, and others planted on limestone slopes. Increasingly there are separate bottlings for wines from the different soils.

Chinon's reds are generally more perfumed and approachable from a young age, especially from sandy soils. Those from the limestone slopes need a little more time, while wines from the gravel are in-between. However, their precocious charm doesn't stop the best of them aging at least as well as a good-quality Médoc from Bordeaux.

SANCERRE & POUILLY

 RED GRAPES
Such reds and rosés as there are, mainly from Sancerre, will be produced from Pinot Noir.

WHITE GRAPES
Sauvignon Blanc is king here, occupying the best sites throughout the region. There is a little Chasselas planted on inferior sites in Pouilly and sold under the Pouilly-sur-Loire appellation. Some Pinot Gris is used in Reuilly for rosé.

 CLIMATE
As the maritime influences wane, summers are longer and warmer, winters cooler and drier. Frost can be a problem early in the year. Shelter from the prevailing north-east wind is important.

 SOIL
The soil here is limestone-based with the shallow, pebbly, Kimmeridgian formations of Sancerre producing the best vineyards. Flinty deposits in Sancerre and Pouilly are supposed to affect the wine's flavour.

ASPECT
The hills rise to around 350m (1148ft). Deep crevices in the slopes produce favourable south and south-westerly aspects.

I'M ALWAYS HEARTILY GLAD to see the great mound of Sancerre looming up in front of me on the banks of the Loire. At last. A landmark in the featureless centre of France, a reference point I can relate to. I've approached Sancerre from all directions, but usually from the empty, disorientating acres of waterways and marshland which make up the Sologne, the setting for Alain-Fournier's wonderful novel, *Le Grand Meaulnes*.

This area, more than any other, conveys the sense of isolation that pervades France's lonely heart. And then up looms the hill of Sancerre: beautiful buildings, ramparts, a town square full of bustle and bars and restaurants – and a view. After so much flat land, a view across the low valleys, the exposed ridges of chalk, or up the lazy course of the Loire river as it sidles past from the south – any kind of view – and then I'm back into the square for a seat in the sun and a glass of cold, crisp white wine. Sancerre. Although the price of Sancerre has risen and its quality has just as frequently dipped as popularity has taken its toll, it can still be the epitome of thirst-quenching, tangy, tingly fresh, dry white wine.

In fact there is a family of five white wines (six, if we include the rare Coteaux du Giennois from a few miles downstream) that use the Sauvignon Blanc grape to excellent effect. This little patch of France also produces red and rosé wines, but it is the palate-teasing white from the Sauvignon Blanc that made the region famous, and that still produces its best wines.

WINE AREAS
Sancerre is the biggest and most important of these appellations, covering 14 communes on the west bank of the Loire, the best of which are clustered beneath the steep slopes close to the town of Sancerre itself. Pouilly-Fumé is a white-only appellation on the Loire's east bank, a couple of miles upstream from Sancerre. Its wines are of equal quality but sometimes they have slightly more weight, a little more coffee-bean smokiness and a little less gooseberry crunch.

Menetou-Salon makes red, white and rosé from ten different communes in the charmingly haphazard countryside between Sancerre and Bourges. Its whites, from the Sauvignon grape, are of a similar standard to Sancerre and are always cheaper. Quincy is a small appellation on sandy gravel just west of Bourges, producing white Sauvignon wines with a marked, but attractive, gooseberry

WHERE THE VINEYARDS ARE *Look at that tiny town of Sancerre, perched on its hill, and surrounded by a tight little clutch of slopes and valleys as the limestone rears briefly but dramatically out of the dull, flat farmland of the centre of France. The steep south-facing slopes of these hills are crammed with vineyards. Then look across the river Loire and down a mile or two towards Pouilly. From a landscape of bland cereal fields and meadows, suddenly there is a rash of vineyards. These two vineyard areas make similar wine which is seen by many as the most perfect example of the tangy, grassy-gooseberry dry styles that are the hallmark of good Sauvignon Blanc the world over.*

Both wines are only this good because of the soil type and the mesoclimate. The open spaces of this part of France would usually not be warm enough to ripen Sauvignon, or Pinot Noir, which Sancerre uses for rosé and red. Limestone is the basis for the soil, though Pouilly, around St-Andelain, and St-Satur north of Sancerre have a good deal of flint that is supposed to influence the flavour of the wine. Indeed, you should be able to recognize a good Pouilly Fumé by its smoky, flinty whiff.

Pouilly's vineyards slope gently south and south-west and are warmed by the Loire. Sancerre's best vineyards, in Bué, Chavignol, Verdigny and Menétréol, cling to those crevices cut into the limestone hills that offer protection from wind and rain and full exposure to the sun. Chavignol is also famous for a goats' cheese called Crottin.

aggression. A couple of miles further west is the even smaller Reuilly, which makes good whites on its chalky soil, adequate reds, and surprisingly good pale rosés from Pinot Gris and Pinot Noir. One of the local growers rejoices in the name of Olivier Cromwell, but there are no other outward signs of anti-royalist feeling.

All of these smaller appellations are now benefiting from the rise in popularity of Sancerre and Pouilly-Fumé. However, this rise is extremely recent. Until the 1950s, these were country wines no-one had ever heard of. Luckily, a merry band of Parisian journalists and restaurant-owners, enjoying a few jaunts from the capital, took to these sharp, tangy whites gulped down with their lunch on the banks of the Loire. Sancerre and Pouilly-Fumé consequently became chic first in Paris, and then throughout the world.

Yet Sancerre and Pouilly weren't even white wine areas to start with. The present increased interest in red Sancerre is a reminder of the situation before the phylloxera bug destroyed the vineyards in the late 19th century. In pre-phylloxera days, because of the area's proximity to Paris, the fields were intensively farmed and mostly packed with high-yielding, low-quality vines whose vast volumes of hooch disappeared down a million uncritical Parisian throats. A further 2000ha (4942 acres) or so made reasonable red from Pinot Noir. After the phylloxera scourge, Sauvignon Blanc was chosen as the grape variety to replant, both because it was a high yielder, and because it was easier to graft onto phylloxera-resistant rootstocks.

Pinot Noir was generally replanted only in the less suitable, exposed, north-facing plots in Sancerre, and not at all in Pouilly. There are now 2770ha (6845 acres) of vines in Sancerre, about one

SANCERRE AND POUILLY

TOTAL DISTANCE
NORTH TO SOUTH
18KM (11 MILES)

VINEYARDS

N

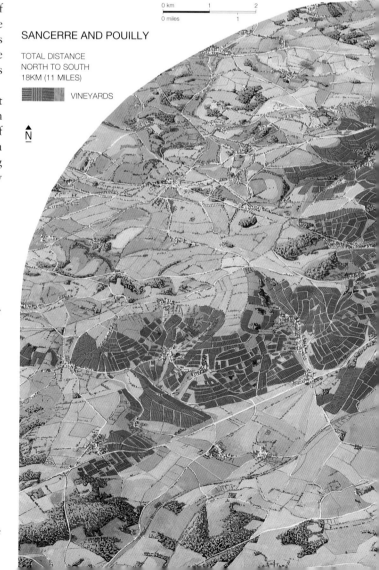

fifth of which are planted to Pinot Noir; and 1200ha (2965 acres) in Pouilly. Though one or two Sancerre producers now give some of their good land to Pinot Noir, most of the best sites are planted with Sauvignon Blanc. I'm sure this is correct. Sancerre Pinot Noir rarely achieves more than a rather wispy cherry fragrance although a few are more serious; Sancerre and Pouilly Sauvignon Blanc, on the other hand, can mix hedgerow and meadow scents with memorable intensity. They can reek of freshly roasted beans in a coffee shop on a December morning. They can have a thrilling new cut grass, blackcurrant leaf and gooseberry attack that taunts your taste buds. They can – but too high yields often undermines their quality.

In Sancerre, the best wines come from the villages near Sancerre town, usually from the steep south-facing slopes. Shelter from wind and exposure to sun are all-important, often more so than the different types of soil. Even so, soil does matter – the more limestone the better, in general, and the Kimmeridgian limestones and clay that produce the best Chablis reappear here and give very perfumed wine.

There are also patches of limestony gravel and a few scattered outcrops with flints. In Pouilly the vineyards cover less land, but are more dense and compact. The same limestone-dominated clays constitute most of the vineyard land, but there is also a patch of flinty, silex soil near St-Andelain which is sometimes said to be responsible for weightier, correspondingly more minerally wines.

AC WINE AREAS

POUILLY = AC WINE AREAS

—— AC BOUNDARIES

THE RHÔNE VALLEY

Right at the end of the season the leaves on the Syrah vines of Côte-Rôtie glow gold in the evening sun. The vines here are attached to stakes because of the steep slopes and the fierce winds.

ONE OF MY FAVOURITE PLACES in France is directly after the cacophonous, frightening, fume-filled tunnel that burrows through the centre of Lyon and emerges in a tumult of overheated, angry drivers and conflicting road signs next to the main railway station. It's a seedy, grubby, mistrustful part of town. So why do I like it so? Just a second. Patience, please. I like it because here I turn right, down the Rhône Valley. This is where I turn my back on the last of the glum North and travel towards the broad open skies, the balmy evening air, and the glittering Mediterranean. For me, this urban wasteland is the divide, after which I head into the sweet embrace of the South.

All that tells you precisely nothing about the vineyards of the Rhône Valley, but bear with me. I had to get it off my chest, because the Rhône is as much an emotional destination for me as it is a geographical one, and so it has been for every northern traveller, ever since we began making the long trek south to the welcoming Mediterranean world. This is the artery running down the centre of France, a surging flood sweeping us towards all the pleasures of the South. Anyone who spends long winter hours wrapped up tight against the chilly damp, anyone who searches the leaden summer skies longingly for a glimpse of golden sunshine, will know what I mean.

The Rhône river powers its way through Lyon with the urgency of an express train, churning through the deep channels it has cut itself against the eastern crust of the Massif Central, south of Vienne, before it sweeps out into the parched open spaces south of the hill of Hermitage at Tain. Taking a more languid course, it still gathers awesome power, only half-controlled by the engineering skills of man, and spreads itself across the increasingly arid red landscape past Avignon. It finally ripples out like a fan, its eastern estuary beckoning me past Marseille and Toulon to Provence. Its numerous western streams create a haunting delta of marshes and lagoons backed by the wild hills and valleys of Languedoc, of Minervois and Corbières and the distant Pyrenees. The Rhône, with its great peacock tail of Provence and Languedoc, is one of the parts of France that I came to love late but I've come to love well.

The Rhône rises way up in the Swiss Alps, and vines are grown along its banks almost continuously from here down to the confluence with the river Durance, just north of the marshy Rhône delta on the borders of Provence and Languedoc. Along its upper reaches, the Rhône spawns some of the most featherlight, wispy white wines of Europe, as well as some surprisingly beefy reds and whites on the steep, sun-trapping slopes of the Valais. But after melting into the broad, calm waters of Lake Geneva, it re-emerges on the other side of the French border ready for the dash to the Mediterranean. Its first wines on this side, still Alpine and snow-white in character, are those from the Savoie and Bugey regions. Some of the best whites are made from Roussanne (locally called Bergeron) from Chignin, near Chambéry (see page 99). The reds are led by the peppery, robust Mondeuse grape.

NORTHERN RHÔNE

Some 48km (30 miles) of industrial suburbs sprawl to the south of the city of Lyon, and little to tax the wine drinkers' taste buds occurs until after the town of Vienne. The exit off the autoroute marked Ampuis should quicken your pulse. Take a look down the river towards the vines of Côte-Rôtie. The east-facing slopes you'll see are as steep as any in the wine world, and they sport a patchwork of vines that looks as though they must be tacked or glued to the rock. Surely no human being could work this near-cliff-face? Surely no vines could establish a toe-hold on the scree and slate that shifts and slithers on these scarps? But a growing band of dedicated winemakers does tend such vertiginous slopes as these, and the vines that manage to establish a root system produce wines that are as great as any in France.

These steep slopes are the heart and soul of what we call the northern Rhône, a stretch of the river between the towns of Vienne and Valence, whose great vineyard sites are all characterized by the steepness of their crystalline, rocky hillsides and by the particular grape varieties they use. Life isn't easy here, and the struggle and commitment required to make great wine is mirrored in the passionate flavour of the reds and the wild, heady perfumes of the whites.

Above all, the Syrah grape finds perfect expression here. Syrah vines may have been planted in the region as long ago as 600BC, if local traditions concerning the hill of Hermitage are to be believed. If so, the savagery of the Syrah's wines, allied to perfumes that seem to have their beginnings in an altogether different, less predictable time, are a fitting and impressive testament. Côte-Rôtie, Hermitage and Cornas are the greatest reds of the northern Rhône, but St-Joseph and Crozes-Hermitage are also capable of fine, fruit-filled wines.

The most immediately thrilling of northern Rhône whites are those of the Viognier grape from the rocky terraces of Condrieu and Château-Grillet. At their best these wines are as overwhelmingly perfumed as a hothouse in summer, but a breathtaking freshness as open and welcome as mayblossom wafting on a spring day's breeze breaks through the aroma of peach and apricot. The Viognier, with its low and unpredictable yields, used to be one of the world's rarest grapes. Now it is the height of fashion. Reclaimed vineyard plantations in Condrieu and large-scale new plantings in Languedoc and overseas in the United States, Australia, Chile and Argentina have almost (but not quite) made it commonplace. But despite its worldwide spread few of these growers achieve the glories of the best Condrieu wines.

The Marsanne and Roussanne are not such eye-catching performers, but they provide the white wines of Hermitage, Crozes-Hermitage, St-Joseph and St-Péray. Usually a little flat and broad to start with, they can develop impressive layer upon layer of rich, viscous flavours if you have the patience to wait. St-Péray marks a natural break in the Rhône Valley. Until this point, most of the fine wine has been produced on east- and south-facing slopes of granite marking the edge of the Massif Central. From now on, as the Rhône Valley spreads broad and wide, the emphasis changes.

SOUTHERN RHÔNE

In the southern Rhône, it is the eastern bank of the river that hosts all the fine wines and, with the exception of Châteauneuf-du-Pape, all the truly exciting flavours come from the vineyards in the lee of Mont Ventoux and the Dentelles de Montmirail.

But the natural break isn't just in the wines: it's in the air you breathe, the scorched feel of the soil under your feet, and in the stark difference in vegetation as pear, apricot and cherry orchards and vegetable gardens give way to olive and peach groves, lavender and melon fields, and herb-strewn outcrops of rock, bleached as white as a desert corpse's bones.

The sun doesn't necessarily shine for longer periods here, but the whole character of this wide river basin is open and exposed. And once the Mistral starts, the word 'exposed' takes on an entirely new meaning. The Mistral is the fierce north-westerly gale that rakes the people and the crops of the southern Rhône for up to 300 days a year. On the remaining days, don't be surprised to find the Sirocco blowing from the south. The vines are mostly trained close to the ground as little bushes, to defend them against the wind and also to soak up extra warmth from the stony soil. The Mistral is reckoned to send a fair number of people mad each year, but in compensation it does wonders in drying out the crops after a rainfall; rot is rarely a problem down here.

While the northern Rhône specializes in small amounts of high-quality reds and whites, the southern Rhône's chief job is to churn out vast quantities of predominantly red Côtes du Rhône. The Rhône region is, along with Bordeaux and Burgundy, one of three major producers of appellation wine, and 85 per cent of this is basic Côtes du Rhône, almost all of it from the south between the towns of Montélimar and Avignon. In the last ten years the quality in general has risen and many smaller domaines truly shine despite their humble Côtes du Rhône AC.

And there are other highlights, too. The little appellation of Clairette de Die, way up the Drôme tributary, makes delightful fizz. There are some unctuously sweet fortified wines, led by Muscat de Beaumes-de-Venise, and there are some truly grand table wines, headed by the fabulous reds of Châteauneuf-du-Pape. These are followed by the reds of Gigondas, Vacqueyras, Lirac, Beaumes-de-Venise and the best Côtes du Rhône-Villages like Cairanne, Valréas and Rasteau, and sometimes supported by decent rosé in Tavel and Lirac and whites in Châteauneuf-du-Pape.

The dominant grape is the fleshy, alcoholic red Grenache which thrives in hot, dry climates such as that of the southern Rhône. However, most wines produced here are blends. Châteauneuf-du-Pape allows no fewer than 13 different varieties, and most southern Rhône reds will include at least Syrah, Cinsaut or Mourvèdre in their blends. Grenache Blanc, Clairette, Bourboulenc and Roussanne are the most important white varieties planted and usually blended too.

VINS DOUX NATURELS

Rasteau and Beaumes-de-Venise are the names of two leading communes producing red wine in the southern Rhône. But if you're after a slug of gutsy, dry red wine, check that label closely. Beaumes-de-Venise is actually more famous for a golden sweet wine than for its red. Rasteau is more infamous for a sweet red wine than for a dry one. In the torrid heart of the southern Rhône Valley, after a day spent toiling through the vineyards and the wine villages, I find the latter distinctly unappealing, yet the former, nicely chilled and served outside in the welcome shade of a plane tree, is one of the most delectable sweet wines on earth.

These two oddballs in the heart of sturdy red wine country are called *vins doux naturels* – which translates as natural sweet wines. Unnatural is more like how I'd describe them, because they are made by whacking in a hefty dose of almost 100 per cent alcohol spirit when the fermentation is only partially completed. This 'muting' as it's called stops the fermentation in its tracks and all the remaining unfermented grape sugar is left in the wine as sweetness.

At Rasteau they use the red wine grape Grenache and although the resulting wine – either in its peppery, jammy but relatively fruity young style, or its tired, oxidized *rancio* style – *seems* to be a throwback to some antediluvian wine culture, sweet Rasteau has only been made since 1932. It has never achieved a more than strictly local following and is now in entirely merited decline. Latest figures show that production is now only a fraction of what it was at the beginning of the 1980s.

Muscat de Beaumes-de-Venise has been made as a sweet wine since the beginning of the 19th century, but it has only been a fortified wine since World War Two. The excellent Muscat à Petits Grains, in both white and black forms, is the variety of Muscat grape used. This rich, syrupy fruit has a heady orchard and floral aroma; the winemakers' objective, often triumphantly achieved, is to marry these flavours with a very subtle alcoholic kick, despite the muting taking the strength to 21.5 degrees. As an apéritif or dessert wine, in a sorbet or served with one, Muscat de Beaumes-de-Venise is a delight.

The ruined papal château of Châteauneuf-du-Pape bakes in the high summer sun. The large, smooth stones, by reflecting the heat and preserving it after sundown, make the vineyards of Châteauneuf-du-Pape some of the hottest in France.

Cairanne, in the sprawling southern Rhône, makes powerful, brooding reds based on Grenache, Syrah and Cinsaut grapes.

NORTHERN RHÔNE

 RED GRAPES
Syrah is the only grape.

 WHITE GRAPES
Viognier, once a rare variety, is now the main grape, with some Marsanne and Roussanne grown too.

CLIMATE
The continental climate with its Mediterranean influence brings burning summer sun. The occasionally violent Mistral wind increases the effect of cold in springtime but is useful in drying out a wet harvest. Hail can be a problem.

SOIL
The slopes are crystalline and rocky, with a very fine topsoil of decomposed mica-schist or granite, and a subsoil of granite. Topsoil washed down the hillside by heavy rain over the growing season is carried back up and replaced within the terraces.

ASPECT
Steep, well-drained, south- to south-east-facing terraces etched into the hillsides provide difficult conditions for winemakers, though more alluvial land is now being brought into production. The region's main vineyards cover the slopes along the banks of the Rhône between the towns of Vienne and Valence.

Côte-Rôtie is made from Syrah grapes, although some growers add a small amount of the perfumed white Viognier – perfectly legal if the two varieties ferment together.

FROM COTE-ROTIE AT AMPUIS way south to Cornas and St-Péray 60km (37 miles) south opposite Valence, the Rhône River has hurled its bulk against the crystalline and granite cliffs of the Massif Central and created a dipping, weaving pattern of dauntingly steep slopes. Where these face south to south-east, they provide brilliant sites for vineyards, but require superhuman effort to exploit them to the full. There have been long periods in history when the terraces of Côte-Rôtie, Condrieu, St-Joseph and Cornas have lain rank and overgrown, deserted by dispirited *vignerons* after a lifetime of toil that gained them no respect. Each of these great vineyard sites has faced extinction because the human toll exacted was too great and the material reward too scant.

One of the most heartening movements of the 1980s and 1990s was the recognition of the great vineyards of the northern Rhône. Nature has provided great sites, but more than anywhere else in France, these have demanded tremendous sacrifice and commitment from the men and women who work their soil. Until the 1980s, few wine lovers knew of these treasures and even fewer would pay a fair price for them. But during the 1980s and the early 1990s the prices more than tripled, and these days a top Côte-Rôtie will outstrip all but the most expensive red Bordeaux, while a Condrieu will equal the price of a top Premier Cru Meursault.

For the products of the finest steep terraced slopes, with their low yields and astonishing concentrated flavours, this is just reward. But take a look at the map. See those steep cliffs at Ampuis, at Condrieu, and at Château-Grillet? These are subject to the special local climates that can make great wine. Then see the broad rolling uplands above the slopes. Here you'll find dairy farms and orchards full of cherries, pears and plums. Fertile, agricultural land such as this is never great vineyard land. Unfortunately you can now find brand new vineyards there too. There is no way these plateaux can produce a great red wine like Côte-Rôtie or a great white like Condrieu, yet they are still allowed the appellation.

Perhaps one shouldn't be too harsh after generations have toiled here for almost nothing. But if the insipid wines of these young, windswept plateau vines is allowed to dilute the quality of the great wines from the steep slopes, then everyone – consumer and producer – will eventually suffer.

Fashion is rightly fêting these northern Rhône wines now, but there are plantings of the red Syrah grape all over southern France and, increasingly, in the New World, as well as enormous new plantings of the white Viognier grape in the Ardèche and in the Rhône and Languedoc further south. It is only by being better than this new competition that Côte-Rôtie, Condrieu, Château-Grillet, St-Joseph and other top northern Rhône wines will command a premium.

These wines rely on just two grapes for their remarkable flavours and they equal any varieties in France or elsewhere in the world for quality. The red grape is the Syrah, clearly as fine a variety as the Cabernet Sauvignon of Bordeaux, or Burgundy's

Pinot Noir, but until recently quite unforgivably overlooked as a grape of international stature. The Viognier is the quality white grape of the northern Rhône, making delicious apricot-scented wine, but it has the two major drawbacks of being a poor yielder and prone to disease.

CÔTE-RÔTIE, CONDRIEU AND CHÂTEAU-GRILLET

I can't seriously believe that anyone stood at the bottom of what is now the Côte-Rôtie and said – ooh, that looks nice, let's have a few vines up there. The slopes of Côte-Rôtie get as steep as 55 degrees. I'm not joking. I've still got the scars. They soar off into the sky above Ampuis like the death-defying first drop of a ski jump. Except this ski jump is a garbled mass of single vines, each tethered to a quartet of posts bound together to look like a tepee; and it's criss-crossed with terraces made of dry stone, or even hewn out of the stark face of the rock itself, shoring up the scant soil that gives these vines the bare minimum of nourishment they need.

Vines may have been grown at Côte-Rôtie for as many as 24 centuries, and certainly 2000 years ago one of the Roman travel writers described the steep slopes on both sides of the Rhône as being covered with vines. But I doubt that this was the prime objective. I suspect the farmers at Ampuis simply got fed up with their vines being swamped yet again by the capricious Rhône in full flood. And so they chipped a few terraces higher up into the mica-schist hillsides, and a few years later everyone kept turning up at their place for a snifter before Sunday lunch.

Why? Because straight away this wine – from slopes much more exposed to the sun, better protected from the fierce northerly Mistral winds and able to benefit from the warmth of the river through reflection of light and hot air rising – tasted infinitely more exciting than the thin, flat old river bank stuff they'd had to put up with before. So generation after generation of *vignerons* scrambled their way higher and higher up this half-vertical cliff-face, hacking away at the rock, risking dreadful vertigo attacks as they gazed down on the rooftops and river beneath, assuredly developing arthritis in their embattled limbs long before their time. And all because the flavours of the wine were steeped in spice and perfume, the ruby-red fruit was as rich as nectar and a flagon or two inflamed their brains with passion and fantasy.

Syrah thrives on the steep, sun-baked slopes of Côte-Rôtie, and anywhere else in the northern Rhône as far down as

AC WINE AREAS

1. Côte-Rôtie
2. Condrieu
3. Château-Grillet
4. St-Joseph/Condrieu

— AC BOUNDARIES

Cornas in the south where it can find well-exposed, granite slopes. From such sites the wines will be dark, complex and capable of aging for 20 years or more in a good vintage. Meanwhile, more growers are producing Vin de Pays and increasingly rich, red table wines from the Syrah on the off-limit areas just west of the river and now in replanted ancient vineyard sites north of Vienne. Vin de Pays des Collines Rhodaniennes is a wine worth trying from well-reputed growers.

Similarly, at Crozes-Hermitage, the arable plain of Les Chassis, south of Tain, has been much more widely planted with vines. Cherries and apricots provide less return; their trees have been taken out. The largely clay subsoil gives fleshy, blackcurrant-flavoured wines, which lack the decisive tannic edging of the Syrahs from granite-based sites, but are still a delicious drink in the short term.

WHERE THE VINEYARDS ARE   *This map shows why the wines of the northern Rhône are so magnificent and yet so rare. Just look at how steep those slopes are on the north and west banks of the river. But what beautiful exposure to the sun, what marvellous drainage on those granite slopes and what free circulating air to avoid the development of rot and fungal diseases. And when the fierce Mistral wind blows, the worst of the gales won't catch the vines on the best slopes. Even so, such slopes are extremely difficult to cultivate and the yields are restricted. Côte-Rôtie covers only 224ha (553 acres), the best grapes coming from the steep slopes around Ampuis. Recent plantings on the plateau land behind produce markedly inferior wine. (That the flat land has been planted at all is a sign of the wine's growing popularity.) Condrieu has expanded more than tenfold since 1965, and too much of that expansion has been on exposed, upland fields that can produce pleasant white Viognier wine, but not something deserving the renown and price of Condrieu. Château-Grillet occupies its own sheltered little amphitheatre of vines just outside the village of Vérin.*

NORTHERN RHÔNE – CÔTE-RÔTIE TO ST-JOSEPH

TOTAL DISTANCE
NORTH TO SOUTH
20KM (12½ MILES)

VINEYARDS

N

The white Viognier is used for the Condrieu and Château-Grillet appellations, and is also found in Côte-Rôtie where it can be blended with Syrah, up to a maximum of 20 per cent. Viognier is a difficult vine, taking far longer than usual to produce high-quality grapes and then being very erratic in yield, but the unctuous texture of its wine, like apricots coated in crème fraîche, and the heady mayblossom perfume, make it all worthwhile.

Château-Grillet, one of France's smallest appellations with under 4ha (10 acres) of vines, is rare and overpriced and has long failed to live up to its reputation. Recent vintages are better, but many top Condrieu wines taste better and cost less.

HERMITAGE

No one's absolutely sure, but as you stand at the base of the hill of Hermitage, wedged in between the railway line and the rapidly ascending vineyard slopes in front of you, you just may be gazing up at the oldest vineyard in the Rhône Valley. There is a strong local belief that the Phocaeans, travellers from southern Greece in ancient times, who worked their way up the Rhône from Marseille, were carrying vines with them. The vine, it seems, could have been the Syrah. The towering hill of Hermitage clearly impressed them, and the locals say that sometime after 600BC a few Phocaeans stopped off and planted a vineyard there. Which would make Hermitage not only the oldest vineyard in the Rhône Valley, but almost certainly the oldest vineyard in France.

I hope the story's true, because Hermitage deserves the accolade. It's a magnificent vineyard site and when Virgil wrote a couple of thousand years ago that 'vines love an open hill', he couldn't have found a better one than the hill of Hermitage. It is capable of

The terraces of Côte-Rôtie above Ampuis: each vine is tied to four posts in some of the most labour-intensive planting to be found anywhere in the world.

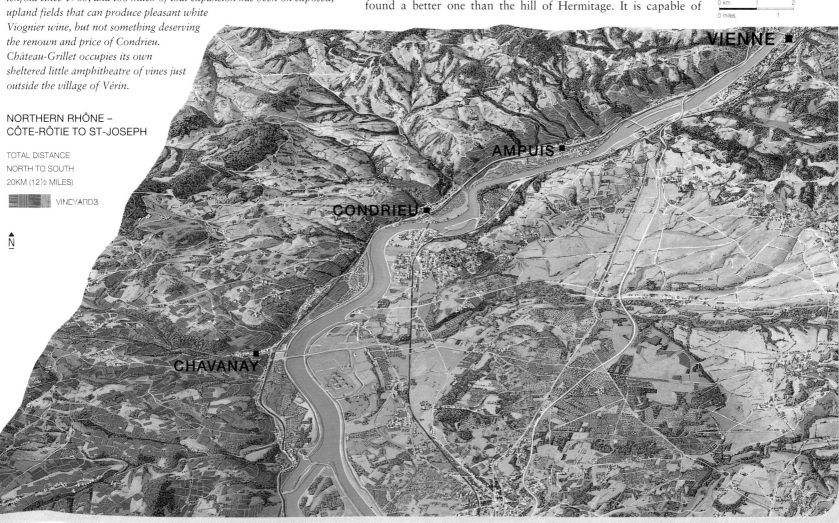

VIENNE

AMPUIS

CONDRIEU

CHAVANAY

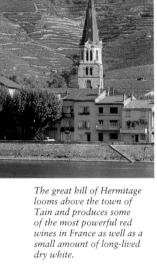

producing majestic reds and intriguing whites, which are able to stand the test of time as well as any other French wines. The red wines manage to combine a rough-hewn, animal power with a sweetness of fruit and wildness of perfume. This may be less academically correct than great Bordeaux and less sensually explicit than great Burgundy, but it catches you unawares and spins you in a dizzy pirouette in a way that no other red wine can.

White Hermitage lacks the immediate charm and fragrance of all France's other great white wines, and may seem fat and sulky almost before it's bottled, and its pudgy sullenness is surely no candidate for making old bones. I don't think many Rhône winemakers can explain it either, but good white Hermitage, often made solely from the Marsanne grape, but generally with a little Roussanne added, appears to get a second, third, and even a fourth wind, and seems to get younger as its red brother gets older. It can develop a leaner, fresher, flinty mineral tone, but it never loses its rich, ripe core of honey, nuts and buns, streaked with spice and topped with crystal sugar.

The Hermitage hill only has 130ha (321 acres) of vines, and on the map you can see how wonderfully exposed to the sun these are. The locals say the sun always sets last on these granite slopes of Hermitage, but it's obvious that the sun rises there first as well! The generally granite soils and the numerous terrace walls heat up in the warmth of the sun's rays, and help promote the ripening of the grapes. The drainage is clearly excellent and the Mistral wind will blow away any excess moisture in any case – yes, Virgil would have liked Hermitage. Over two-thirds of the Hermitage vines are red Syrah. The burliest, most virile red wines come from the most forbidding granite plots, Les Bessards and Le Méal.

The great hill of Hermitage looms above the town of Tain and produces some of the most powerful red wines in France as well as a small amount of long-lived dry white.

AC WINE AREAS

1. St-Joseph
2. Cornas
3. St-Péray
4. Crozes-Hermitage
5. Hermitage

━━━ AC BOUNDARIES

CROZES-HERMITAGE

All round the Hermitage hill, to the north, east and south, is the large appellation of Crozes-Hermitage. This is increasingly one of the Rhône's most satisfying red wines (although there is also some white) because the smoky, dark-fruited character of the Syrah is well to the fore, and the wines are ready for drinking when still quite young. Two styles come from Crozes-Hermitage's expanding 1358-ha (3355-acre) vineyard. The granite slopes of Gervans and Erôme produce structured, finely tannic wines with some mineral and red fruit in their texture. The more clay soils of Les Chassis, the plain near La-Roche-de-Glun, give softer, more overtly fruit-filled wines; these are bursting with exuberant black berry fruit. Most growers make a fruity wine for drinking inside four years or so, and select a more wood-raised cuvée for longer keeping and greater complexity.

ST-JOSEPH

The St-Joseph appellation, on the other hand, has suffered from expansion. It was originally based on a single hillside – the south-east-facing terraces you can see either side of Tournon, the town facing Tain l'Hermitage – but in 1969 the six original communes were expanded to 25, spreading over 50km (31 miles) of the right bank of the Rhône. Many of the new vines were planted on the flat, fertile banks of the Rhône rather than on the original steep, hillside terraces, and the reputation of the wonderfully perfumed, fruity reds and the weighty, ripe whites from the original granite slopes

was sadly eroded by the newcomers. The appellation has since exploded to 988ha (2441 acres) but measures were introduced in 1992 to downgrade wine from poorer sites over a period of 20 years to vins de pays and to forbid future planting on unsuitable sites. The original terraces above Mauves, Tournon and St-Jean-de-Muzols are being restored, and with them comes the restoration of St-Joseph's reputation as one of France's most delightful rich, fruity, perfumed and approachable reds.

CORNAS AND ST-PÉRAY

Cornas should be immune from expansion fever. The name Cornas means 'burnt earth' and applies to the steep amphitheatre of Syrah vines that cups the little village of Cornas in its suntrap palm. That almost claustrophobic shell of south-east-facing vines, protected even from the destructive Mistral winds that roar down the valley from the north-west, is a cauldron of heat in summertime. The Cornas vineyards produce the blackest, most torrid red wine in the Rhône, perhaps in the whole of France, its dark, essential flavours wrested from deep inside the earth.

Yet even here expansion looms. The use of higher-yielding Syrah clones unable to produce the dense black tarry liquid that marks out great Cornas, and the gradual increase of low-lying plantings of vines to a present total of 100ha (247 acres) do threaten Cornas' role as provider of France's most famously old-fashioned red. Luckily there's a long way to go yet, as I still haven't come across a Cornas light enough for me to see through. When young the wines

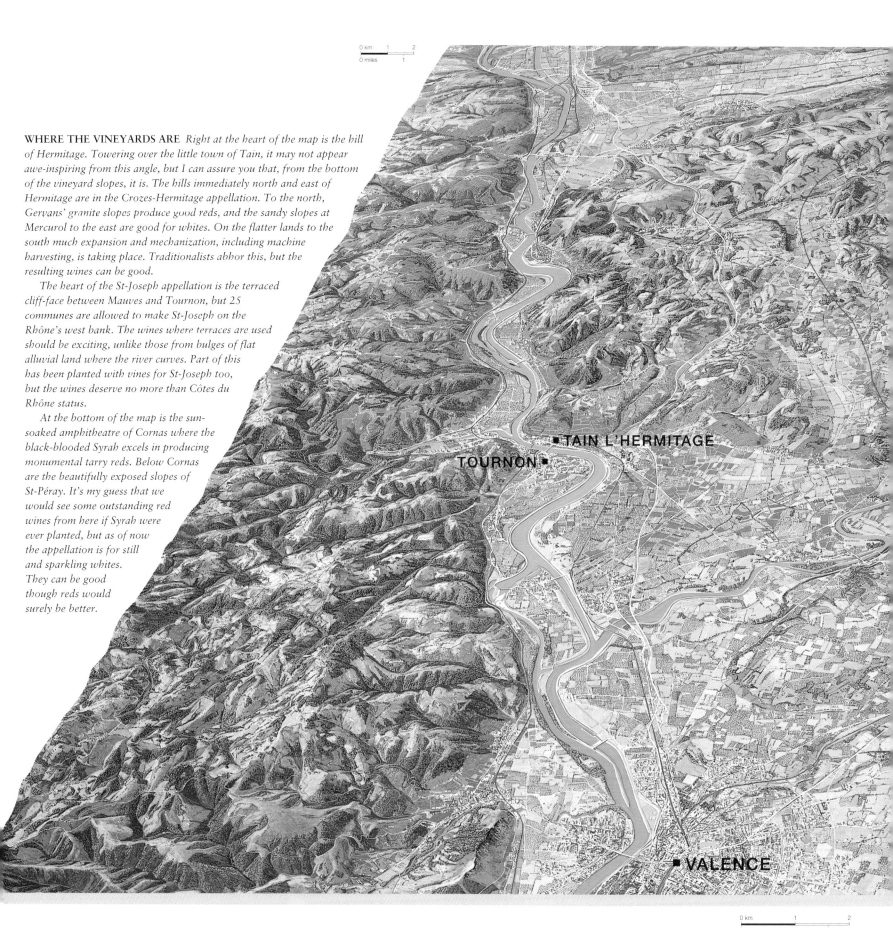

WHERE THE VINEYARDS ARE *Right at the heart of the map is the hill of Hermitage. Towering over the little town of Tain, it may not appear awe-inspiring from this angle, but I can assure you that, from the bottom of the vineyard slopes, it is. The hills immediately north and east of Hermitage are in the Crozes-Hermitage appellation. To the north, Gervans' granite slopes produce good reds, and the sandy slopes at Mercurol to the east are good for whites. On the flatter lands to the south much expansion and mechanization, including machine harvesting, is taking place. Traditionalists abhor this, but the resulting wines can be good.*

The heart of the St-Joseph appellation is the terraced cliff-face between Mauves and Tournon, but 25 communes are allowed to make St-Joseph on the Rhône's west bank. The wines where terraces are used should be exciting, unlike those from bulges of flat alluvial land where the river curves. Part of this has been planted with vines for St-Joseph too, but the wines deserve no more than Côtes du Rhône status.

At the bottom of the map is the sun-soaked amphitheatre of Cornas where the black-blooded Syrah excels in producing monumental tarry reds. Below Cornas are the beautifully exposed slopes of St-Péray. It's my guess that we would see some outstanding red wines from here if Syrah were ever planted, but as of now the appellation is for still and sparkling whites. They can be good though reds would surely be better.

• **TAIN L'HERMITAGE**

TOURNON •

• **VALENCE**

are a thick impenetrable red, almost black in the ripest years, and many need at least eight years' aging. They make attractive alternatives to the pricier Hermitage and Crozes-Hermitage.

Directly south of Cornas lies another range of beautifully exposed vineyard slopes. They look as though they would continue to paint the brilliant tapestry of dark, heady Rhône reds from the great Syrah grape, yet in fact they are planted with white Roussanne and Marsanne, and 40 per cent of their wine is a gently sparkling wine made by traditional methods. St-Péray is a curiosity, certainly, but efforts to raise the quality of the still wine

have started, including the involvement of new wave growers like Jean-Paul Colombo. Wagner apparently ordered a hundred bottles of the fizzy stuff to help him break through a writer's block in the middle of composing *Parsifal*. It's a matter of opinion whether or not the St-Péray did the trick.

Already, houses for people commuting to the nearby towns are being built among the vines to capitalize on the magnificent view of the river valley. Now, if they were allowed to plant Syrah on these splendid slopes, I'd almost support a move to expand the Cornas appellation!

**NORTHERN RHÔNE –
ST-JOSEPH TO
CROZES-HERMITAGE**

TOTAL DISTANCE
NORTH TO SOUTH,
50KM (30 MILES)

 VINEYARDS

N

SOUTHERN RHÔNE

IN THE NORTHERN RHÔNE you need to look upwards if you want to understand the unique qualities of the best vineyards, soaring towards the sky at crazy angles. But in the southern Rhône, you need to look down at your feet. The best vineyards here are virtually flat, but covered with stones so closely packed that there is no soil in sight. In the south's top wine area, Châteauneuf-du-Pape, it is almost as difficult to keep your balance as it is on the sheer slopes of Côte-Rôtie. The reason is not steepness, though, but smooth white and rust-coloured stones, often as hot to the touch as an oven door, which slither beneath your feet at every step. These act as a natural storage heater and rainwater sieve and allow the low-yielding vines to give a wine as heady and alcoholic as any in France, yet which is packed with perfume and fruit richness.

The south is far more dominated than the north by red wines, and these are almost always blends. The Grenache grape, which doesn't figure at all in the north, is the dominant variety, and this is usually blended with Cinsaut and Syrah, and maybe Carignan and Mourvèdre as well. Châteauneuf-du-Pape can be a blend of 13 grape varieties – eight red and five white. Three of the red grapes – Counoise, Vaccarèse and Muscardin – are virtually extinct elsewhere, but have excitingly unusual personalities whose potential heights are only just beginning to be explored. Grenache Blanc and Clairette are the chief white varieties.

WINE AREAS

Between Valence, in the northern Rhône, and Montélimar, the nougat capital of France, there is a gap of 44km (27 miles) in which there is hardly a vine. From Montélimar southwards, however, the vine increasingly becomes the dominant crop, grown on all types of terrain apart from the over-fertile alluvial flatlands down near the river Rhône itself. The sun beats down so relentlessly during a typical southern Rhône summer that extra exposure to its rays seems pointless. However, there are some sloping vineyards – the best ones being in villages like Gigondas, Vacqueyras and Cairanne in the

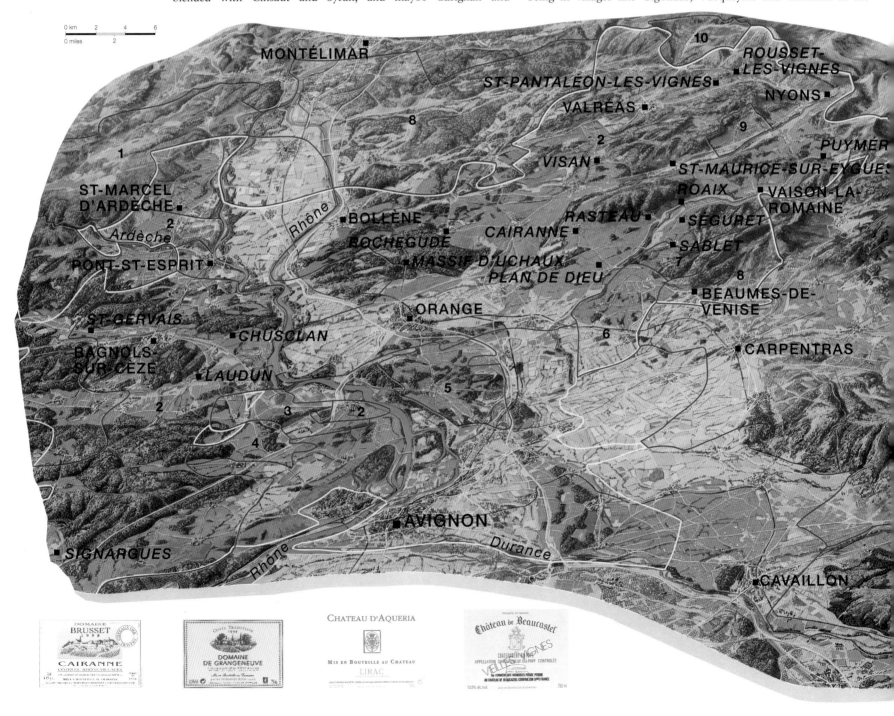

eastern foothills. The best Châteauneuf vineyards are on a plateau – and such conditions do help these places' ability to super-ripen their grapes. The soil types in the major Rhône villages are also varied, and they affect the ability of different varieties to ripen. The Mistral wind is combated by windbreaks and by training the compact vines low in bush form, although more modern training on wires is becoming common in lesser appellations to allow mechanization.

CÔTES DU RHÔNE & CÔTES DU RHÔNE-VILLAGES

Côtes du Rhône is a blanket appellation covering vines in 171 communes in six departments, from Vienne in the north to Avignon in the south. Eighty-five per cent of all the wine made between these two points is simple Côtes du Rhône and most of it comes from the sprawling vineyards that straddle the Rhône from St-Marcel-d'Ardèche and Bollène to south of Tavel. It is overwhelmingly red and, along with basic Bordeaux and Beaujolais, is France's favourite red quaffer. Generally it is a decent drink, but happily more single estates and reliable merchants like Guigal are raising the tempo a bit.

Côtes du Rhône-Villages supposedly applies to the wines of superior communes that will graduate to their own appellations. So far four have done so – Gigondas, Vacqueyras, Beaumes-de-Venise and Vinsobres. There are now 18 communes that can add their own name to 'Côtes du Rhône-Villages' on the label and a total of 95 communes that can use the Villages appellation. The Villages growers must accept a tighter control over their choice of grape varieties, yields per hectare and minimum alcohol levels. In the top Villages this is probably worthwhile, but in the more anonymous communes, growers frequently choose

to stick with straight Côtes du Rhône regulations and accept the lower price for fewer restrictions and a higher yield.

Grenache is the chief red variety and provides a rich, heady heart to the wine. For this you need dry, stony soil and a little inclination to the sun, as in the best Villages on the eastern slopes. The Syrah grape can overripen in many parts of the southern Rhône, but find it some moister, cooler soil and it will add a gorgeous dark-fruited, serious depth to the reds. Most of the top Villages like Cairanne have good chunks of moist clay soil gently sloping towards the plain. The late-ripening Mourvèdre adds a crucial, almost rasping, herb-leaf perfume and wild berry fruit to the more corpulent Grenache. Rich clay soil in a warm, protected spot suits it just fine.

COTEAUX DU TRICASTIN

The first vineyards south of Montélimar are some of the most recent in the valley, those of Côteaux du Tricastin. There had been vines

WHERE THE VINEYARDS ARE *Speeding through the flat, fertile plains on the valley floor towards the Mediterranean, it is easy to lose sight of the grandeur of this southern part of the Rhône Valley. With a mirage of an azure sea, glistening bronzed bodies and the perfect beach-side restaurant filling your mind, it is perfectly possible not to give this sprawling, arid landscape a second thought. But this map shows the Rhône Valley's majesty as it eases into the final stretch on its trip to the Mediterranean. To the west are the tumbling hills and hidden valleys of the Ardèche, where very tasty vins de pays are made. To the east are the splendours of Mont Ventoux and the sub-alpine foothills. These create high, fertile valleys whose vast wine potential is gradually being exploited by the Côtes du Ventoux and Côtes du Luberon appellations.*

The best vineyards are a lot less scenic, and only start appearing between Montélimar and Bollène, with the Coteaux du Tricastin and the beginnings of the Côtes du Rhône. Most of the best Côtes du Rhône-Villages communes hug the eastern slopes between Bollène and Carpentras and the very best ones huddle under the jagged fangs of the Dentelles de Montmirail. But there are some decent villages across the Rhône below Pont St-Esprit, notably St-Gervais. Further south both Lirac and Tavel are high class but the heart of the southern Rhône, however, is Châteauneuf-du-Pape, south of Orange. With an increasing number of top-quality estates Châteauneuf is one of France's top red wines today.

 RED GRAPES
Grenache is the most important of the many red varieties, followed by Syrah and Cinsaut, then Carignan and Mourvèdre, but there are many minor varieties.

WHITE GRAPES
Whites are far less important than reds: the main grapes are Clairette, Grenache Blanc, Bourboulenc, Roussanne and also Muscat.

 CLIMATE
The region enjoys a true Mediterranean climate: hot dry summers and warm wet winters. The planting of wind-breaks helps mitigate the force of the Mistral blowing chill blasts down the valley from the Alps.

 SOIL
This huge area has a wide variety of soil types, ranging from the heavy clays of the upper slopes of Gigondas to the stony alluvial deposits of the plains around Châteauneuf-du-Pape.

ASPECT
Unlike more northern wine areas of France, ripening the grapes properly this far south is not a problem, and many of the best vineyards, for example those of Châteauneuf-du-Pape, are on the flat land of the valley floor.

AC WINE AREAS

1. Côtes du Vivarais
2. Côtes du Rhône-Villages
3. Lirac
4. Tavel
5. Châteauneuf-du-Pape
6. Vacqueyras
7. Gigondas
8. Beaumes-de-Venise
9. Vinsobres
10. Coteaux du Tricastin
11. Côtes du Ventoux
12. Côtes du Luberon

CÔTES DU RHÔNE AC BOUNDARY

AC BOUNDARIES

RASTEAU = CÔTES DU RHÔNE-VILLAGES COMMUNE

TOTAL DISTANCE NORTH TO SOUTH 152KM (94½ MILES)

VINEYARDS

APT

12

11

N

PERTUIS

Durance

0 km   2   4   6
0 miles   2

here in the 19th century, but a quick look at the weather and soil will show why the growers had given up. The Mistral wind is reckoned to be at its most furious here, reaching speeds of over 100km/h (62mph). The soil is rather like that of Châteauneuf-du-Pape – covered in round flat stones – but Châteauneuf-du-Pape was a famous wine whose renown made it worthwhile to cultivate such barren land. No-one had heard of Tricastin wine, though its black truffles were famous, so these vineyards were abandoned. In the 1960s, the Algerian War of Independence sent a flood of farmers, who were used to working under tough conditions, back to France. The French government was eager to offer them land and a chance to earn a living, and one of the areas that was singled out lay between Montélimar and Bollène. These settlers have done a remarkable job hewing vineyards out of this unpromising land, and now there are 2830ha (6993 acres) of vines producing strong ripe reds with real fruit intensity and little tannin, mainly from Syrah.

South of Coteaux du Tricastin, the vineyards rapidly dominate the landscape, but there is a very definite hierarchy governing their quality levels. At the top end of the scale are the communes that have managed to create a track record of better than average wines over the years. These have their own appellations, and are led by the world-famous Châteauneuf-du-Pape.

VACQUEYRAS AND GIGONDAS
Vacqueyras and Gigondas, on the slopes of the Dentelles de Montmirail, possess particularly suitable local climates and soils. Vacqueyras' soil is especially stony and produces a correspondingly dark, thick-textured wine with a pleasing dry, plummy finish. Gigondas' wine is rough-hewn red, but has a sweet core and a muscularity that manages to be inviting rather than daunting. The raw richness is largely due to Grenache, grown on high steep slopes of yellow clay, or slightly lower slopes of heat-retaining stones. Both Vacqueyras and Gigondas started out as named communes in the Côtes-du-Rhône-Villages appellation and now have their own appellations, as do Beaumes-de-Venise and Vinsobres, the two most recent communes to be promoted.

CHÂTEAUNEUF-DU-PAPE
Of all the southern Rhône reds, this is the one which oozes richness and succulent juicy fruit, but which wraps its perfumed sweetness in the heady, open-air fragrance of hillside herbs and baking southern sun. The Grenache is the main grape, capable of ripening to 15 degrees and more in hot years, and there are twelve other permitted grape varieties, seven red and five white, that can be used in red Châteauneuf. Few properties actually use more than four or five in their blends. A little white is made and is increasingly good. The headiest wines come from vineyards on the stony plateau just north of the town of Châteauneuf-du-Pape. Immediately east of the town are more vineyards larded with these round flat stones, but further east towards Courthézon and Bédarrides the stones give way to more sand and clay, while in the south the land is generally more gravelly.

TAVEL AND LIRAC
Across the Rhône, on the west bank, are two appellations that languish somewhat in Châteauneuf's shadow. Tavel's proud producers would claim they don't languish at all, making what they claim is France's best, and often highest priced, rosé. I would add, the most alcoholic one too, because these pale but heady, dry, rather fruitless, wines are pretty hefty. They are based on Grenache, but up to nine varieties in total are allowed. Strangely, Tavel rosés do gain depth of flavour after a few years. It's almost as though they wanted to be red wines, and resent their juice being whipped off the colour-

Châteauneuf-du-Pape bottles are embossed with the Papal coat of arms, in memory of the period of history when the popes resided at nearby Avignon.

and flavour-laden grape skins after a mere 24 hours or so. Perhaps they do. Many of the vineyards are covered in the same heat-retentive stones as at Châteauneuf, and the surrounding infertile hills certainly look like red wine country. But the subsoils here are basically sand and limestone and, especially on the hillsides to the west of Tavel and the Vallongue plateau to the north, the high alcoholic degree allied to the lightness of body imparted by the limestone soils do, I suppose, favour the production of rosé at least as much as red.

Lirac also has much soil that seems broadly similar to Châteauneuf's, comprising big, bleached stones which carpet many of the vineyards; some of the best vines here are grown on wide, stark plateaus. And Lirac's red wines often try to catch a little of Châteauneuf's grandeur and fame. But, despite a good ripe fruit style and an attractive herb-and-hilltop perfume, they have never really caught the public eye. That's a pity. There are some excellent reds here, and some decent rosés and whites. The whites from this west side of the river are more aromatic than the Vaucluse whites opposite.

There are several other wine areas bordering the Rhône that are mostly of minor importance – so far. The potential is enormous, but no-one has ever demanded anything of the myriad producers there, mainly co-operatives, other than the production of large amounts of cheap hooch.

But look on the map at that magnificent natural amphitheatre east of Carpentras, and at the impressive south-facing ridge above the town of Apt. This whole area is known as the Côtes du Ventoux. These wines, led by private domaines, are on the up and rate good value for money. The mountain ridge south of Apt, running parallel to the Durance river, is the Côtes du Luberon. The Ardèche mountains are to the west of the river Rhône, full of unsung but good vineyards, and south-west of Montélimar is the Côtes du Vivarais. But there's one outpost of the Rhône Valley that is already fulfilling its potential – a hidden patchwork of vines way up the Drôme Valley, east of Valence. These produce the heavenly scented sparkling wine from Muscat and Clairette called Clairette de Die Tradition.

CHÂTEAUNEUF

Châteauneuf-du-Pape was the first AC to forbid the landing of flying saucers inside the commune boundaries, back in 1954! The ruling, quirky as it may seem, was tacked on to the six articles formulated by Baron Le Roy of Château Fortia in 1923, which were designed to protect the integrity of the vineyard and its wines. They stated the criteria that had to be followed for Châteauneuf-du-Pape. A delineated area, specific grape varieties, viticultural regulations, a minimum alcohol level, a discarding of 5 per cent of the crop at harvest, no rosé wine, and a tasting test were among the rules. These still stand today, but, more importantly, they were taken as the starting point for the entire French appellation contrôlée system that came into being in 1935.

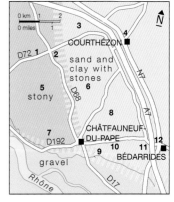

Wine Estates 1. la Vieille Julienne 2. Villeneuve 3. Beaucastel 4. la Janasse 5. Mont-Redon 6. Rayas 7. la Gardine 8. la Charbonnière 9. Fortia 10. la Nerthe 11. du Vieux Télégraphe 12. Font de Michelle. In Châteauneuf village: Beaurenard, Bois de Boursan, Henri Bonneau, Bosquet des Papes, les Cailloux, Clos du Mont Olivet, Paul Jeune/Monpertuis, Marcoux, Pegau, Roger Sabon, Pierre Usseglio, Le Vieux Donjon.

JURA & SAVOIE

MOUNTAIN PEOPLE ARE DIFFERENT. Isolation breeds individuality. This hostile, unpredictable environment, where life is a continual battle only partly compensated for by the thrill of a mountain peak glimpsed wreathed in cloud when the sun breaks briefly through, by falling water cascading over rocks, by the lonely echo of a night-bird's song rising up the valley. Both the Jura and Savoie reflect this individuality, but in different ways.

The Jura mountains run up the eastern side of France and act as a natural border with Switzerland. On the Swiss side the thickly wooded slopes fall dramatically down to the calm prosperity encircling Lake Geneva. The French side, staring balefully out west across the Saône Valley to Burgundy, is a mixture of high meadowland, dense forest, astonishing gorges and sudden splashes of tranquil vineyard. But few of the wines are tranquil.

The native Jura grapes are the surly, thick-witted red Trousseau, the indeterminate and pallid semi-red Poulsard and the vicious yet fascinating white Savagnin, used to make the flor-aged *vin jaune*. If the red and pink wines of Jura are merely sullen, this yellow wine is a freakish oddball. It has to be aged for six years in cask without topping up the evaporated wine. During this time a yeast film develops on the wine in the same way as in Jerez's *fino* sherry. The result is a wine with a raging, sour woody brilliance.

Château-Chalon is the centre of *vin jaune*, though it is made all over the Jura in small quantities. But there are signs of Burgundian influence from across the valley: an increasing amount of Pinot Noir is grown, making an attractive pale red. Chardonnay makes light dry whites so long as it's not made in casks that have held Savagnin, and the sparkling Crémant de Jura is particularly good. From a blend of, typically, Chardonnay, Savagnin, and the red Poulsard, production of the curious sweet wine, *vin de paille* is also increasing. Picked early, the grapes are hung from rafters or left in boxes in warm ventilated rooms until January. The grapes are then pressed and the nectar fermented and then matured in old wood for at least two years. Like *vin jaune*, these wines can age for decades.

SAVOIE

With just over 2000ha (4942 acres), slightly more than Jura, Savoie vineyards are scattered in distinct plots over a wide area, but most in sight of the Alps. Like Jura, Savoie has a range of native grapes, but the character of their wines couldn't be more different. Chasselas wine, from near Lake Geneva, is so ethereal as to be almost transparent, often in flavour as well as looks. The ubiquitous Jacquère variety makes wine that is also almost water-white but packs a tangy angelica and grapefruit pith punch.

But the best sites are reserved either for the dark, loganberry-scented Mondeuse or for the white Roussette, and in Chignin, near Chambéry, for Roussanne (locally called Bergeron). All three are capable of producing exceptional wines. The vines are restricted mainly to the southerly lower mountain slopes before they become too steep for any vine to cling to, or for any *vigneron* to work.

The tiny appellation of Crépy produces feather-light Chasselas white from vineyards near Lake Geneva; the local Crus of Ripaille and Marin are often a touch weightier. The vineyards of the slightly larger Seyssel appellation overlook the Rhône, and produce a fine still Roussette, and a good-value traditional method fizz from Roussette blended with the obscure variety, Molette. Towards Lake Bourget, Gamay, Chardonnay and Pinot Noir do well, while in Jongieux, Roussette is king, reaching its apogee in the spectacular vineyard slope of the tiny Cru of Marestel. It produces an almost rich, dry white with peach and apricot flavours, developing nuttiness after a couple of years.

But for me, the core of Savoie is near Chambéry, where the high peaks of the Alps jut out rudely into the valley, and then swing round to follow the Isère Valley up towards the skiing centre of Albertville. The Crus of Apremont and Abymes produce fresh dry whites from Jacquère grown in vineyards on the debris left from a disastrous landslide of Mont Granier in 1248. Jacquère also does well over in Chignin, but here Roussanne is revered to make sumptuously floral and peachy Chignin-Bergeron. From around Chignin and north-east towards Albertville in the Combe de Savoie, growers are giving increasing space to Mondeuse, a rich grape with formidable dark loganberry and woodsmoke flavours which, with low yields, gives enough intensity to partner a rich meat stew in front of a log fire.

To the west of Lake Bourget is the Bugey region which, in one of those quirks of fortune, has become trendy. Scattered patches of vines among woods and hills now total 500ha (1235 acres). All the Savoie and some Jura grape varieties are grown here but the pale, yet surprisingly intense, Chardonnay works best.

RED GRAPES

Poulsard is the main Jura grape with Pinot Noir and Trousseau increasing slowly. All may be made on their own or as a blend. Gamay is the most extensively planted red variety in Savoie, with the more interesting Mondeuse following behind. Some Pinot Noir is also grown.

WHITE GRAPES

Chardonnay is the most planted Jura grape, followed by Savagnin, the only permitted variety for *vin jaune*. Over 50 per cent of total plantings in Savoie are of Jacquère. Roussette (also called Altesse) follows, with small amounts of Chasselas, Roussanne (locally called Bergeron), Chardonnay and a few local obscurities.

CLIMATE

This is basically a continental climate, though with high rainfall and temperatures that decrease sharply with altitude. The severity in Savoie is moderated by the main lakes.

SOIL

In the Côtes du Jura the soil is mostly dark marly clay on the lower slopes, with limestone on the higher ones. In Bugey limestone and marly limestone predominate. Savoie vines are grown mostly on limestone-rich soils which are alluvial in origin.

ASPECT

In the Jura, the vines are grown on south- or south-west facing sites at an altitude of between 250 and 400m (820–1312ft), not dissimilar to Burgundy's Côte d'Or. In Bugey, vineyards are widely scattered on low hillsides. The vineyards in Savoie are also scattered, but may go as high as 600m (1968ft) in the foothills of the Alps and are often south- or south-east facing with a good aspect to the sun.

AC AND VDQS WINE AREAS

— Côtes du Jura	
— Arbois	
— Château-Chalon	
— l'Étoile	
— Vin du Bugey, Roussette du Bugey VDQS	
— Vin de Savoie, Roussette de Savoie	
— Seyssel	
— Crépy	
▭ OVER 500M (1640FT)	
▭ OVER 1000M (3280 FT)	

VIN DE SAVOIE CRUS

1. Ripaille
2. Marin
3. Marignan
4. Ayze
5. Chautagne
6. Jongieux
7. Apremont
8. Abymes
9. St-Jeoire-Prieuré
10. Chignin, (Chignin-) Bergeron
11. Montmélian
12. Arbin
13. Cruet
14. St-Jean de la Porte

ROUSSETTE DE SAVOIE CRUS

A. Frangy
B. Marestel
C. Monthoux
D. Monterminod

PROVENCE

IT IS DIFFICULT TO DISCUSS PROVENCE in simple unemotional wine terms. The Ancient Greeks planted vines here in the 6th century BC and the Romans produced wine supposedly fine enough to ship to Rome. But if this exotic, irresistible corner of France, stretching from the swooping slopes of the Montagne du Lubéron east of Avignon, from the chill, clear-scented meadows of the alpine pastures far up the Var Valley north of Nice, down through tumbling hills and forests and gorges full of pine trees, straggling herbs and olive groves, down to the azure and silver sea – if the inhabitants of this enchanted land thought that wine quality mattered, wouldn't they have done something about it by now?

Well, some people are doing something and increasingly so, prompted by a new generation or a change in ownership, often bringing foreign investment to the region. There are single estates sprouting in les Baux-de-Provence, around Aix-en-Provence, and among the myriad uninspired producers in the Côtes de Provence appellation, often hewn out of rock and garrigue to create new and fascinating flavours where nothing existed before. The established appellations of Bellet, Bandol, Cassis and Palette represent tiny

enclaves of individuality amid swathes of gutless land churning out shabby rosés, fruitless whites and scorched reds, not remotely redolent of the lavender, thyme and rosemary that surround the vines. Nevertheless, an easy-minded market of revellers, keen on indulgence, makes it easy for producers to forego the sacrifice and commitment needed to produce the great wine that is certainly possible here. And, yes, I've lazed under a sunshade at midday, gazing out over the shimmering sea, quaffing my icy whites and pinks, guzzling my *bouillabaisse*, my *aïoli monstre* and my *rouget* – and, yes, I've been as happy as can be and the devil take *my* critical faculties too.

But vines are crucially important in Provence because most of the land won't support much else. Almost half the cultivated land in Provence is vines, with those other hardy performers, olives and almonds, taking a substantial percentage of the rest. So, accepting that a large amount of Provençal wine is simply overpriced holiday hooch, let's see where things are better than this.

GRAPE VARIETIES

In general, pinks and reds come from the usual southern varieties of Grenache, Cinsaut and Carignan. Mourvèdre makes a big contribution at Bandol. Syrah and Cabernet Sauvignon are vital further inland, especially round Aix, while strange ancient grapes like Fuella in Bellet, Tibouren around St-Tropez and Manosquen in Palette add a certain spice.

AC WINE AREAS

1. Les Baux-de-Provence
2. Coteaux d'Aix-en-Provence
3. Palette
4. Côtes de Provence
5. Cassis
6. Bandol
7. Coteaux Varois

—— AC BOUNDARIES

TOTAL DISTANCE NORTH TO SOUTH 108KM (67 MILES)

 VINEYARDS

N

WHERE THE VINEYARDS ARE *If you're looking for the beaches of St-Tropez, Cannes and Nice I'm afraid you won't find them on this map – they're further to the east (as is the wine appellation of Bellet, in the hills behind Nice). But Provence is a vast region and this map shows plenty of its glory of coast, mountains and valleys as well as its main wine areas. The Alpilles hills between Arles and Cavaillon shelter the stark vineyards of les Baux-de-Provence, while Palette, one of the smallest appellations in France, is directly east of Aix. The large Coteaux d'Aix-en-Provence appellation is bounded in the north by the Durance River (across which are the vineyards of the Southern Rhône) and in the south by the Alpilles hills and Montagne Ste-Victoire, immortalized in the paintings of Cézanne. The Coteaux Varois lies to the east and is an area to watch. The Côtes de Provence vineyards are divided into five main sub-zones: the Bordure Maritime covers the vineyards east of Toulon along the coast to St-Raphaël (off the map); the Vallée Intérieure, north of the Massif des Maures inland of Hyères, produces nearly half of all Côtes de Provence wine; the Collines du Haut Pays vineyards lie around the town of Draguignan; the Bassin du Beausset vineyards, between Bandol and Cassis (two of Provence's best known appellations), enjoy cooling breezes from the sea; and finally there is the Massif Ste-Victoire zone just outside Aix-en Provence on the southern edge of Montagne Ste-Victoire.*

The whites are dominated by the southern varieties, Grenache Blanc, Clairette and Bourboulenc, with a growing amount of Rolle. And there are patches of Sémillon, Sauvignon, Roussanne and a certain amount of Chardonnay, too.

In such a vast area there are wide differences in soil, but in general the soils are poor and infertile, though there is some clay in the inland vineyards and some limestone too. Shale and quartz are common nearer the sea. However, Cassis and Bandol have a good deal of clay and limestone and Bandol has gravel too. In the west, the desolate moonscape of les Baux-de-Provence has vineyards planted amid the rubble of bauxite, and only a substructure of water-retentive limestone allows the vine to survive.

The climate differs too, but sun and wind are everywhere in the equation. The Mistral blows right through Provence, and though it barely troubles Bellet in the east, it whips through the low bush vines of Bandol and Cassis, and at les Baux-de-Provence the vines are trained north to south to minimize its force, while Palette rings its north-facing vineyard with pines. Yet with the fierce southern sun, the Mistral is crucial for cooling the grapes; at Bandol it is abetted by sea breezes too, and both these winds keep the vines remarkably free of rot. In fact, rot is rarely a problem in Provence because there is a serious shortage of rain, but if it does fall, it is frequently in the form of thunderous deluges in spring and autumn. With grapes near full ripeness, a good gust of warm dry wind does wonders in keeping disease at bay.

It isn't surprising that in such torrid conditions, red wines perform best. Les Baux-de-Provence has concentrated on reds based on Syrah and Cabernet Sauvignon, sometimes with a little Grenache. That would be thought of as an Australian combination today, but the idea came from a Dr Guyot, one of France's top wine experts in the 1860s. Domaine de Trévallon makes one of the most original and exciting reds in France from 60 per cent Cabernet and 40 per cent Syrah, but without any of the obligatory Grenache in the blend, it has been declassified to a *vin de pays*. Daft or what?

Coteaux d'Aix-en-Provence has a considerable reputation for red wines, but is dominated by under-achievers. I prefer the strange, pine-needle gauntness of Palette or the fascinating herbs and animal power of Bandol. Based largely on the Mourvèdre grape, Bandol is a prospering appellation whose wines seem to improve every year as the vines age and Mourvèdre increases its domination. There are good Côtes de Provence reds, usually from estates which have taken the bull by the horns and reduced the percentage of Carignan in favour of Syrah and Cabernet, and the Coteaux Varois is producing a growing number of good red wines.

Les Baux-de-Provence and Bandol produce the best pinks, Cassis and Palette, in their very different ways, the best white wines with some good Côtes de Provence from Rolle, Bourboulenc and Sémillon. But, I don't know – as the sun rises higher in the sky and the shade of the restaurant beckons, so long as the wine is ice cold, just about anything will do.

RED GRAPES
Typical southern varieties such as Grenache, Carignan and Cinsaut are most important, with significant amounts of Mourvèdre, Syrah and Cabernet Sauvignon.

WHITE GRAPES
The main grapes are Ugni Blanc and Clairette followed by Sémillon, Grenache Blanc, Sauvignon Blanc and Bourboulenc among others.

CLIMATE
The climate is classic Mediterranean – hot dry summers, warm wet winters with blasts from the Mistral helping to dry the grapes after the occasional deluge.

SOIL
A complex soil pattern includes stony limestone, sandstone, clay, shale and gravel underlying the plantings in different areas.

ASPECT
A diverse terrain has vines growing on slopes, foothills and lowland, especially where sheltered to the north by ridges and plateaux.

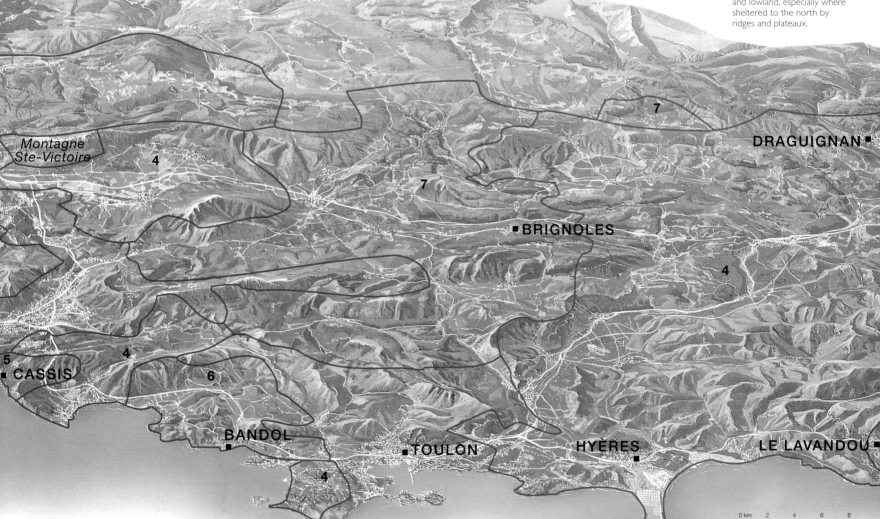

0 km   2   4   6   8
0 miles   2   4

LANGUEDOC-ROUSSILLON

LANGUEDOC-ROUSSILLON IS THE MOST COMPLETE wine region in France. It is also the most abused. It is France's largest by a long way, comprising more than one-third of France's total vineyard acreage, and yet it does not have one single world-famous wine style to show for it. It is one of the most old-fashioned, hidebound, reactionary parts of the French wine scene, and at the same time it is France's most exuberantly modern, most outward-looking, most international. Contradictions are at the heart of Languedoc-Roussillon. Let's look at a few of them.

I'm standing picking away at a strange, pinkish soil flecked with slivers of stone, crumbly, hardly able to prevent itself from disintegrating into dust. This is one of the most idiosyncratic and most perfect vineyard soils in France causing Bordeaux's greatest experts to collapse into paroxysms of excitement. It's in a tiny valley west of Montpellier in the Hérault Valley. It has no appellation contrôlée. When Aimé Guibert bought the property in 1971 there had never been a vine planted there. Now, 45 years later, his Mas de Daumas Gassac reds and whites are still impressive. They still have no appellation contrôlée and are sold as Vin de Pays.

Aimé Guibert remains the leading light, but every year sees more passionate, imaginative winemakers arrive in the South of France determined to create great wine their own way, outside the traditional strictures of the grand appellations where innovation is generally stifled and rules are strictly to be obeyed. Most of these

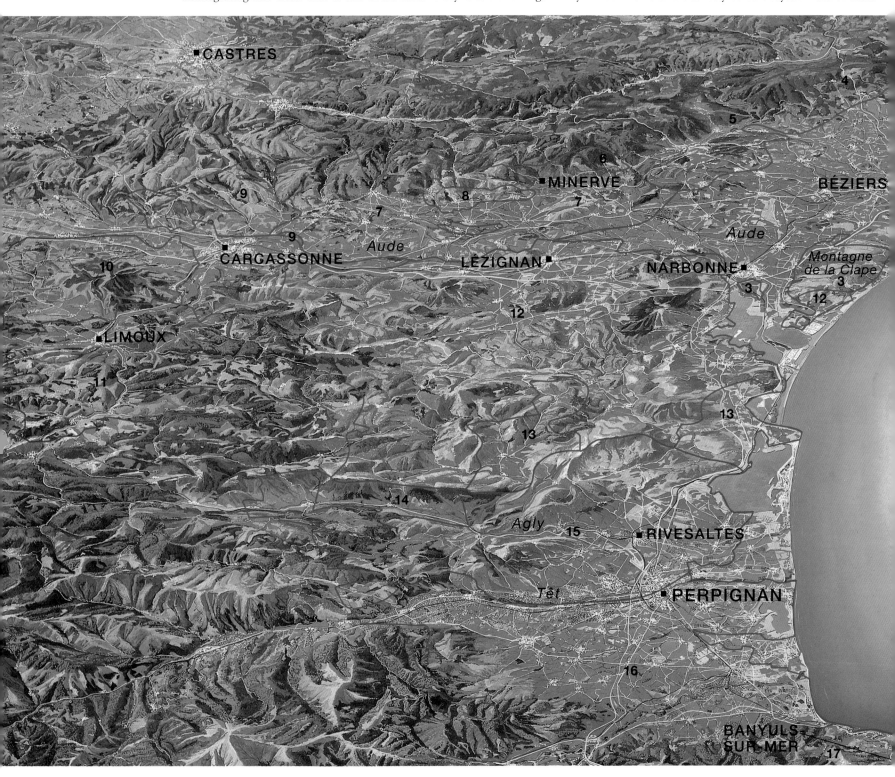

innovators are French, many of them refugees from such traditional and hidebound regions as Bordeaux and Burgundy, where types of vine variety and methods of growing grapes are strictly circumscribed. But people come from much further afield, from as far as California and Australia, seeking to put their New World ways to work in an Old World setting. In France, the Languedoc is the only alternative.

If we now head south-west across country, every second village we come to will have a co-operative winery. If we find one in ten where the wine is not stale and flat I should be surprised, but 30 years ago we would not have found one in 50. Still, it's not a co-operative we're after. It's a modern winery at Servian, north of

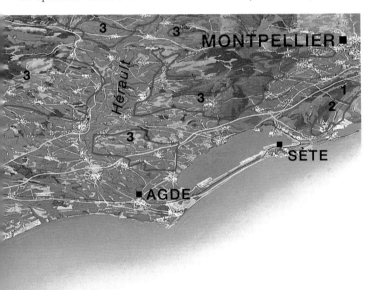

WHERE THE VINEYARDS ARE *Just about the only place on this map where there are no vines is along the ridge of mountain to the north. The higher you go, the cooler it is. But these mountains protect the vineyards from the northerly winds during the day, and at night, the warm air that has risen from the lowlands is pushed back downhill by the mountain air, dramatically cooling the foothill vineyards and ensuring balanced flavours in the fruit. Sea breezes temper the heat close to the coast, but the Mediterranean influence is basically very warm. Further west, this influence lessens and the climate cools and dampens as more temperate Atlantic influences take over. Most of the vineyards higher above sea level are on infertile, stony soil and are best suited to low yields of intensely flavoured black grapes. The lowlands areas are showing themselves highly suitable for the production of fresh whites and light reds.*

AC, VDQS AND VDN WINE AREAS

1. Muscat de Mireval VDN
2. Frontignan VDN, Muscat de Frontignan VDN
3. Coteaux du Languedoc, Clairette du Languedoc
4. Faugères
5. St-Chinian
6. Muscat de St-Jean-de-Minervois VDN
7. Minervois
8. Minervois la Livinière
9. Cabardès
10. Côtes de la Malepère VDQS
11. Blanquette de Limoux, Crémant de Limoux, Limoux

12. Corbières
13. Fitou, Rivesaltes VDN, Muscat de Rivesaltes VDN
14. Côtes du Roussillon-Villages, Maury VDN
15. Côtes du Roussillon-Villages, Rivesaltes VDN, Muscat de Rivesaltes VDN
16. Côtes du Roussillon, Rivesaltes VDN, Muscat de Rivesaltes VDN
17. Collioure, Banyuls VDN

— AC, VDQS AND VDN BOUNDARIES

▨ VINEYARDS

TOTAL DISTANCE NORTH TO SOUTH 144KM (89½ MILES)

Béziers. Here at Domaine de la Baume, originally set up by the giant Australian Hardy company in 1990, they're turning out crisp, scented dry whites and balanced fruity reds. The grapes come either from the estate or from local growers and the varieties are anything but regional – Chardonnay, Sauvignon Blanc, Merlot and Cabernet Sauvignon, and what about that 70/30 Viognier-Chardonnay blend they make, as well as a succulent scented and eminently affordable pure Viognier? The point is, with modern technology and know-how anything is possible in this sun-kissed corner of France. If more investment combined with imaginative management and winemaking were able to penetrate into the depths of the Languedoc, this really could be France's New World.

The *laissez-faire* attitude that characterizes the non-AC areas of Languedoc-Roussillon mirrors Australia. So does the hot sun, the dry earth and a reputation that owes nothing to the past but everything to the present and the future. What is 'local' when nothing but mediocrity or worse had ever characterized the vineyards whose grapes Domaine de la Baume now turns into pretty decent grog?

This is one side of what is so exciting in Languedoc-Roussillon. Innovation, excitement, lack of restrictions when transforming lead into gold. But there is another side. The side of some of the most ancient wines in France, some of the most ancient and distinctive styles, relying on ancient grape varieties like Carignan, Grenache, Syrah or Mauzac rather than Cabernet Sauvignon or Chardonnay.

If we go north from Béziers to Faugères, the road rises away from the plain towards the looming mountains of the Cévennes. The land is bleak but beautiful as we cut across through empty, twisting country lanes curling round the low slopes of the mountain range; the soil is barren, smothered in rock and stone, and only olive trees and vines survive.

But there are vineyards that go back to the 9th century at least, when monasteries planted these hills with vines knowing that only poor soil gives great wine. Good soil gives good fruit and vegetables. At Faugères, at St-Chinian, across the base of the towering Montagne Noire to Minerve, capital of the Minervois where the heretic Cathars were besieged during the Albigensian Crusade in 1210, but where vineyards had been established more than 1000 years before by the Romans, on and on, across the wide Aude Valley into the giddy mountain passes of the Corbières, last holdout of the Cathars, but planted with vines by the Romans too. These are great vineyards that have suffered centuries of neglect but that may justly be thought of as the true cradle of French viticulture, along with those of Hermitage.

Nowadays there is a ferocious, proud revival going on in these upland vineyards, and in many other parts of Minervois, and in Coteaux du Languedoc zones like la Clape, the rocky scrub-strewn mountain south of Narbonne that once used to guard its harbour mouth, in the days when Narbonne was the First City of Roman Gaul, and which is one of the coolest growing zones in the Midi. The wines are generally red, often still based on the Carignan grape, but old Carignan vines in poor stony soil can give excellent wine, especially when the blend is abetted by Grenache, Syrah, Cinsaut and Mourvèdre.

There are other great historic wines too. Limoux, high up in the Aude Valley south-west of Carcassonne, claims that its sparkling wine Blanquette de Limoux or Crémant de Limoux – based on the Mauzac grape which gives it its striking 'green-apple skin' flavour – is the oldest sparkling wine in the world. Certainly its wines were well-known in 1388 and the locals have set the date of their discovery of how to make them sparkle at 1531, more than a century before Champagne claims to have discovered the process.

New vineyards in Collioure, just north of the border with Spain. These vines are almost certainly destined to produce heavyweight red table wines, rather than fortified wines, in line with current fashion.

▦ **RED GRAPES**
There is a huge variety of grapes: traditional (e.g. Carignan, Grenache, Cinsaut, Syrah) and international (Cabernet, Merlot).

▦ **WHITE GRAPES**
Whites are less important, but include Grenache Blanc, Mauzac, Clairette, Muscat, Bourboulenc, Chardonnay, Viognier and Sauvignon Blanc.

▧ **CLIMATE**
The summers are hot and dry, winters cool and wet, with temperatures decreasing with increasing altitude. The chilly Mistral from the north, and mild sea breezes help cool the vines, and some varieties such as Carignan are drought-resistant.

▧ **SOIL**
This huge area displays a great diversity of soil types, some highly localized. Broadly they encompass the shale and marly limestone of the hills overlaid with clay in the best sites, red pebbly lateritic soil, and gravelly alluvial terraces among others.

▧ **ASPECT**
The rugged landscape provides numerous and varied sites for vine-growing, the broadly west-east orientation of the valleys combining protection from the north with good southern aspects.

The Coteaux du Languedoc appellation *covers a vast area between Montpellier in the east and Narbonne in the west. An increasing number of tasty red and white wines are being made in the region today and there are now plans for a new super-appellation, Languedoc, to cover the whole Languedoc and Roussillon region.*

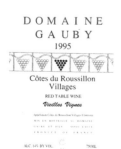

FORTIFIED WINES

Frontignan, on the shores of the salt lagoons near Montpellier, was known for its sweet Muscat wine in Pliny the Younger's time, and Arnaud de Villeneuve, a doctor at Montpellier, discovered how to make fortified wine here in the late 13th century. This discovery spread around Languedoc-Roussillon to Rivesaltes and on down to the foothills of the Pyrenees at Banyuls, where they applied it to the Grenache grape, baked to super-ripeness on the terraced hillsides overlooking the Mediterranean. At Banyuls they don't just fortify this heady purple juice, they age it and purposely oxidize it in large old oak barrels, or sometimes in smaller barrels left out exposed to the elements for at least thirty months. The result is a strange, exotic, dark treacle-chocolate wine, unlike any other to be found in France. And this is what I mean by Languedoc-Roussillon being the most complete region in France – it makes every conceivable sort of wine, and it makes them all increasingly well.

WINE AREAS

Looking at the landscape on the previous pages, it isn't difficult to imagine the whole region having a mass of different climatic and geological conditions, suitable for very different sorts of wine. It was the sheer ease of cultivation, and reliability of weather, that caused the great rolling plain stretching along from Montpellier to Narbonne to become the provider of France's cheap wine from the early 1800s onwards. It is this reliable weather and ease of cultivation that now makes these plains the heartland of the Vin de Pays d'Oc movement that is making *vins de cépage* – varietal wines – such a force in French wine. And their most important contribution is to show that modern vineyard and winery methods can make delicious white wines here – something never before achieved.

Yet this is not just prairie; the land dips and rises endlessly, providing myriad different soils and mesoclimates. Now, their potential is being explored. Previously, no-one had bothered. And there are a number of increasingly good appellation contrôlées. The best are for red wines – Costières de Nîmes, east of Montpellier in the Gard *département*; several of the top Coteaux du Languedoc Crus like la Clape, Pic St-Loup and Montpeyroux as well as

Minervois and Corbières. There is a group of good fortified *vins doux naturels* ACs led by Muscat de Frontignan, and one or two lonely white appellations like Picpoul de Pinet. The sun is never a problem – and the ever-present wind moderates the heat, the sea breezes being fairly humid and mild, the north winds, which sweep over the Montagne Noire, hard and dry. As we rise up towards this impressive southern bulwark of the Massif Central, the protected sites and the impoverished soil roast the red grapes to a dark, but sweet-hearted super-ripeness that, mixed in with the ever-present perfume of bay leaf, Angostura bitters and wild aromas of the hills, makes good modern wines from the appellations of St-Chinian, Faugères or Minervois (now with a new sub-zone entitled to its own appellation, Minervois-La Livinière).

Corbières and Fitou are sheltered by their mountain range, as the foothills of the Pyrenees south of the Aude slowly rise to lofty peaks on the Spanish border. Near the Mediterranean, the general effect is hot, but once past Carcassonne to the west, as the Mediterranean influence gives way to the Atlantic, increasingly cool conditions produce truly delicate reds and whites from grapes like Chardonnay, Sauvignon, Cabernet and Merlot.

The last great plain before reaching Spain is that of the Agly river. The sun is that bit hotter here, and the relentless Tramontane wind sears the vines. The late-ripening Carignan, helped by the widespread employment of carbonic maceration to extract colour and flavour, but not tannin, from the grapes and by a leavening of Cinsaut, Syrah and Grenache, produces sturdy Côtes du Roussillon and, largely in the southern foothills of Corbières, Côtes du Roussillon-Villages.

Rivesaltes makes good Grenache *vin doux naturel*, but better Muscat, while way down on the Spanish border overlooking the Mediterranean, Grenache reigns supreme in the sweet fortified wine of Banyuls. The tiny fishing port of Collioure has its own appellation which uses the usual southern red grapes but it is finding, above all, that low-yielding, sun-soaked terraces, with their awesome sea view and brow-cooling breeze, just could be one of the great sites for that most tricky but tempestuous of all the southern French varieties – the Mourvèdre, which is said to like its face in the hot sun and its feet in the water – exactly what it gets in Collioure.

VINS DOUX NATURELS

There are two main styles of *vins doux naturels* – the whites based on Muscat à Petits Grains or Muscat of Alexandria and the reds based on Grenache. Each of these naturally achieves very high sugar levels in the hot Mediterranean sun. But the object with the Muscat wines is to preserve their aroma and fruit, so they are sometimes given skin contact before a cool fermentation and, ideally, an early bottling and youthful drinking. Frontignan is the most famous, Mireval and Lunel fairly obscure, St-Jean-de-Minervois rare but good and Muscat de Rivesaltes the most up-to-date and attractive.

To make the Grenache wines of Rivesaltes, Maury and Banyuls, alcohol to 'mute' the wines is added either to free-run juice or to the skins and wine together, and the wines are then kept for between two and ten or more years in casks or vats, sometimes parked outside exposed to the air and the hot daytime temperatures, sometimes left not quite full if the traditional oxidized *rancio* style is being sought. Young, fresh aromas are not the point here: deep, dark, disturbing richness is.

How to cook a wine: the sun and heat are an essential treatment in the maturing process for these barrels of vins doux naturels *in Banyuls.*

CORSE

THE ANCIENT GREEKS called Corsica (Corse) the Beautiful Island and, my goodness, I can see why. It's a heavenly place. Well, most of it is. On my first visit the view from the aeroplane gliding down the west coast of the island was stunning: sun-baked ochre craggy peaks, mystical steep-sided valleys disappearing into rock, coves of dazzlingly pure sand and azure sea speckled with white sails. My thirst was building and my eyes scoured the parched terrain for tell-tale patches of soft, lush green that, even in the most arid of landscapes, denote a vineyard in leaf. I didn't see a vine. Not one. Even as we circled out into the Bay of Ajaccio and swooped round, down and on to the airport tarmac at Ajaccio. I knew the Ajaccio region had some of the island's best-regarded vineyards. I knew that Corsica had once been packed with vines and critics even now often say that the island has the perfect climate, with an average rainfall the same as Paris – that is, very high for the Mediterranean – and mountains and sea moderating the heat of the blazing sun.

Yet critics also say less kind things. They often say that splendid grapes are rarely turned into fine wine on this lovely island. My first general tasting of Corsican wines in London was marked by a melancholy acceptance that, while some interesting fruit flavours lurked in there somewhere, the standard of winemaking – excepting that of the Peraldi estate in Ajaccio – was dire. That first night, in my hotel, having finally located a few vines hidden away to the north of Ajaccio, I tried the red, the rosé and the white wines. I didn't finish a glass of any of them. Then I tried a couple of better-known single-estate wines. Rustic, rough, with a searing volatility. I switched to Campari-and-soda, and stuck to it.

MODERNIZATION AND TRADITION

But things have improved, both in the traditional low-yielding, difficult-to-find vineyards of the north, west and south, and in the extremely obvious large mechanized plantations on the flat prairie land in the east of the island. These two regions are attempting to do very different things, and both are having some success.

The reclaimed swampy plains of the east had been exploited by French settlers (*pieds noirs*) returning from Algeria in the 1960s. By 1973 they had planted 32,000ha (79,070 acres) of vines. Most *pieds noirs* had aimed merely to make rough hooch from the usual southern French grapes – Grenache, Cinsaut, Carignan and Alicante Bouschet. There's no demand any more for that kind of wine, and over 90 per cent of those plantations have been grubbed up, with just under 7000ha (17,297 acres) remaining. Today, the successful eastern vineyards are those making *vin de pays* from Chardonnay, Syrah and Cabernet, particularly around the Étang de Diane.

However, Corsica's tradition is based on less well-known grapes – the red Nielluccio (probably the same as Tuscany's Sangiovese), the red Sciacarello and the white Vermentino, all Italian varieties, reminding us that Corsica was Italian for 700 years before France took control in 1769. Corsica only received its first appellation contrôlée in 1968 – for Patrimonio – followed by Ajaccio in 1971, and most Corsican wine either doesn't qualify for (or does not seek) appellation contrôlée status. But there's a movement to implement the regulations of the Vin de Corse appellation, and in particular to raise the minimum percentage required of the three local grape varieties in the wines. This must be good for all the traditional vineyards. Yields are low and conditions difficult, so individuality is the only way to justify what will always be higher prices than those for wines produced in mainland southern France.

WINE AREAS

Patrimonio in the north is especially good at producing full-bodied, herb-scented reds dominated by Nielluccio grown on clay and limestone soils, as well as some rich, exotic Muscat du Cap Corse and fragrant Vermentino. Ajaccio to the west has granite soil that suits the Sciacarello; Comte Peraldi here also produces fine Vermentino.

Of the various Vin de Corse areas, Coteaux du Cap Corse has slaty soils which suit Vermentino, and strong winds and low rainfall, which encourage the production of some lovely sweet Muscat. Calvi makes good herb-scented rosé and decent gutsy red. The poor sandy or granite soils in Sartène, Figari and Porto-Vecchio could all be good for native varieties, yet Sartène and Porto-Vecchio have only one notable estate each – Domaine de Fiumicicoli and Domaine de Torraccia respectively – while Figari has suffered the attentions of *pieds noirs* returning from Algeria.

Corsica suffers, too, from its island mentality – mainland France is referred to as '*le continent*' – and all equipment, even bottles, is imported. A ready market of thirsty and not always discriminating tourists always encourages complacency. Nevertheless, a new generation is beginning to make its mark, with the gradual replanting of the vineyards with traditional Corsican varieties, and a marked improvement in cellar techniques (common throughout the Midi), to achieve some good modern, yet authentically Corsican wines.

AC WINE AREAS

- Ajaccio
- Patrimonio
- Vin de Corse
- Vin de Corse-Coteaux du Cap Corse
- Vin de Corse-Porto-Vecchio
- Vin de Corse-Figari
- Vin de Corse-Sartène
- Vin de Corse-Calvi
- Muscat du Cap Corse
- OVER 500M (1640FT)
- OVER 1000M (3280FT)

MEDITERRANEAN SEA

ROGLIANO
PATRIMONIO
BASTIA
L'ÎLE-ROUSSE
OLETTA
CALVI
CALENZANA
VESCOVATO
PONTE-LECCIA
CERVIONE
Golo
Tavignano
CORTE
PORTO
VIZZAVONA
Étang de Diane
Gravona
BOCOGNANO
ALÉRIA
Prunelli
BASTELICA
GHISONACCIA
AJACCIO
Bay of Ajaccio
Taravo
SOLENZARA
PETRETO-BICCHISANO
Rizzanèse
ZONZA
OLMETO
PROPRIANO
SARTÈNE
PORTO-VECCHIO
FIGARI
BONIFACIO

N
0 km 10 20
0 miles 10

SOUTH-WEST FRANCE

THE SOUTH-WEST OF FRANCE looks so easy to understand. There you have the great king Bordeaux lording it over the whole region, its robes spilling outwards from the Gironde. Vassal states like Bergerac, Côtes de Duras, Côtes du Marmandais and Buzet kneel at the hem imitating Bordeaux's styles, using the same grapes and generally making good wines, but not so good that they'll disturb the equanimity of Bordeaux. That's how it seems, but it's much more complicated than that. Not only do areas like Bergerac and the Marmandais have their own interesting features, but Buzet overlaps with an entirely different culture in the brandy-producing region of Armagnac. Cahors may base its wines on the Bordeaux grape Malbec – but as though in defiance of its long isolation up the winding Lot river, Cahors crafts from it an idiosyncratic, most un-Bordeaux-like wine. As the hills and valleys roll away from

Bordeaux, the Atlantic influence starts to be matched by that of the Mediterranean. And we enter a bewildering, fascinating world of ancient vineyards, ancient grape varieties and thrilling wine styles that the newly imaginative world of wine is only just discovering.

BERGERAC AND THE DORDOGNE

You wouldn't even know you'd left the Bordeaux region as you take the D936 through the Bordeaux town of Castillon-la-Bataille. The prosperous flat valley of the Dordogne is still a benign rural marriage of maize, meadow and vines. But although Cabernet and Merlot, Sauvignon and Sémillon are grown in virtually identical conditions, you've crossed the border between Gironde and Dordogne, and the wines aren't AC Bordeaux, but rather AC Bergerac or AC Montravel.

AC WINE AREAS

- 1. Bergerac, Côtes de Bergerac
  Bergerac sub-regions:
  - a. Côtes de Montravel
  - b. Haut-Montravel
  - c. Montravel
  - d. Saussignac
  - e. Monbazillac
  - f. Pécharmant
  - g. Rosette
- 2. Côtes de Duras
- 3. Côtes du Marmandais
- 4. Cahors
- 5. Marcillac
- 6. Gaillac, Gaillac Premières Côtes
- 7. Côtes du Frontonnais
- 8. Buzet
- 9. Madiran, Pacherenc du Vic-Bilh
- 10. Jurançon
- 11. Béarn
- 12. Béarn-Bellocq
- 13. Irouléguy

VDQS WINE AREAS

- A. Coteaux du Quercy
- B. Vins d'Entraygues et du Fel
- C. Vins d'Estaing
- D. Côtes de Millau
- E. Vins de Lavilledieu
- F. St-Sardos
- G. Côtes du Brulhois
- H. Côtes de St-Mont
- J. Tursan

OVER 500M (1640FT)

OVER 1000M (3280FT)

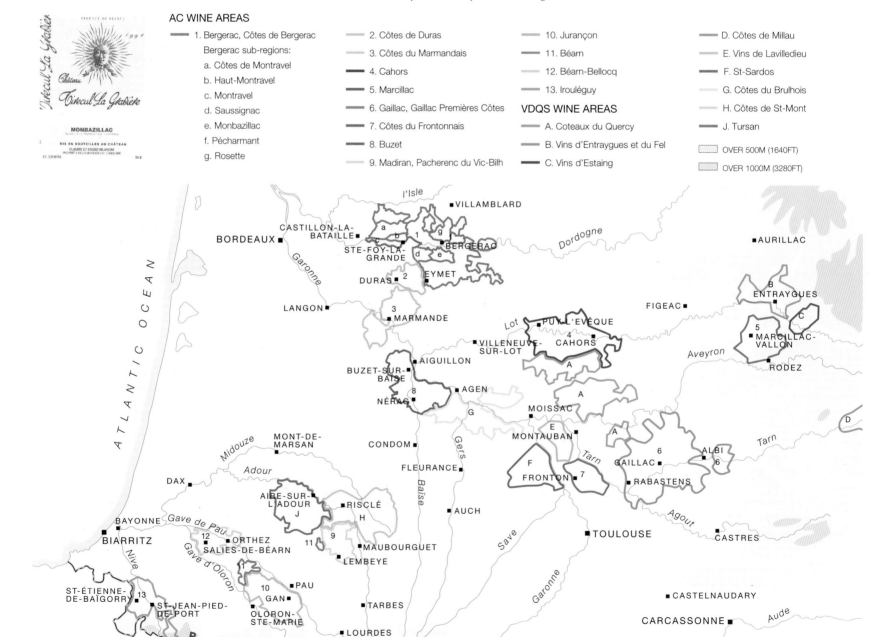

You wouldn't really know you'd left Bordeaux when you taste most Dordogne wines either. The soils are similar, generally tending towards the sandy clay types with some limestone outcrops. Sunshine and heat are similar, though rainfall is usually lower. The appellations can get a bit confusing, but most of the dry reds and whites will end up calling themselves Bergerac or Côtes de Bergerac and, at the western end, on the north bank of the Dordogne, the dry whites can call themselves Montravel, and the semi-sweets and fairly sweets, Côtes de Montravel and Haut-Montravel respectively. South-east of Ste-Foy-la-Grande, sweet wines can be called Saussignac but are generally called Côtes de Bergerac Moelleux and, north-west of the town of Bergerac, Rosette semi-sweet whites hardly ever appear under their own name. The appellation Bergerac wines themselves, produced in 79 different communes along the Dordogne, are mostly virtually indistinguishable from their Bordeaux counterparts.

Two sub-regions within Bergerac that outshine the rest and do usually use their own names are Pécharmant and Monbazillac. Pécharmant's vineyards are on a plateau mostly tilted towards the south, where a mixture of chalky and gravelly clays sit above an impermeable iron hardpan. These reds are often Bergerac's best: deep, dark but full of fruit and capable of aging. Monbazillac's vineyards frequently face north, sloping down to the river valley, losing heat, but gaining river mists that encourage noble rot and the production of sweet white wine. Most Monbazillac is mildly sweet, but more and more growers are prepared to let their grapes ripen sufficiently to make truly sweet wine.

GARONNE AND TARN WINES

Next to Bergerac lies the Côtes de Duras appellation, and, straddling the Garonne Valley further south, the Côtes du Marmandais. These wines are basically Bordeaux in all but name, though in the latter, the local grape Abouriou in small amounts along with Fer Servadou, Gamay and Syrah can add something to the red. Buzet, too, on the south banks of the Garonne and intertwined with the Armagnac brandy region, uses Bordeaux grapes to good effect.

But we have to push further up the Garonne, towards Toulouse, then branch east up the river Tarn to find an area that has truly broken away from Bordeaux's influence – the Côtes du Frontonnais, with its marvellous Negrette grape. The vines love the hot Toulouse weather and deep gravel beds and make a succulent, soft-centred red, velvet smooth and darkly sweet with liquorice and strawberries. Negrette is often blended with Malbec, Cabernet and Syrah, but I like as much Negrette as I can get.

Gaillac, a large area further up the Tarn, is dominated by giant co-operatives, and has tremendous potential. Six white grape varieties are used for a broad swathe of styles, from dry to sweet, from still to hinting at bubbles to fully foaming. Eight different red varieties contribute to wines that are often at their brisk best when peppery and young, but are sometimes made to age impressively.

THE LOT RIVER

The Cahors AC, 80km (50 miles) north-west of Gaillac, concentrates on one single wine – a fascinating, tobacco-scented, green apple-streaked, yet plum and prune-rich red made largely from the Malbec grape, here called the Cot or Auxerrois. Famous for 'black wine' that was much in demand for blending with pale Bordeaux reds during the years of English supremacy in Aquitaine – and for a good while after too – the region was devastated by phylloxera in the 19th century, and it was not until the 1970s that a band of local growers, along with a good co-operative,

rediscovered its former glories. Now, with vineyards planted on the high stony limestone plateau, or *causses*, and the sand and gravel alluvial terraces lower down in the Lot Valley, and a climate caught between the influences of the Atlantic and the Mediterranean, with the Lot twisting and turning like a demented serpent to create endless mesoclimates, Cahors is producing some of the most individual wines in the South-West.

Further along the Lot are three obscure wine areas. Marcillac, with its strong, dry reds, produced mainly from the Fer Servadou, is the best known.

THE PYRENEAN FOOTHILLS

Travelling south from Agen into the foothills of the Pyrenees, we come to Madiran. Viticulture here was virtually defunct after World War Two, but now there are about 1300ha (3212 acres) of vineyards. The chief variety is the Tannat, its tough, rugged style needing a while to come into focus – something many examples never achieve. However, modern winemaking and new oak barrels have helped smooth some of its rougher edges. A little white called Pacherenc du Vic-Bilh is made from a blend of four South-West grapes with the emphasis on the flinty, pear-skin-scented Ruffiac. Just to the north of Madiran, Côtes de St-Mont uses the same grape varieties to make attractive snappy reds and pleasant whites. The Tursan VDQS makes wines similar to Côtes de St-Mont.

Further up into the Pyrenees foothills are Béarn, an uninspiring region, and Jurançon, which uses Petit Manseng, Gros Manseng and Petit Courbu to make mostly dry white wines. But the many sheltered valley sites, where the vineyards lie at an average altitude of 300m (984ft), let the grapes bake in the sun. The low-yielding Petit Manseng often shrivels on the vines, concentrating its juice to make sweet wines dripping with honey and nuts, cinnamon and ginger, but always refreshingly cut with a slash of lemon acidity.

And if you continue into the chilly mountain valleys right to the border of Spain you'll find the tiny outpost of Irouléguy, whose strange gritty mountain red marks a final, defiant flourish of French tradition before the entirely different world of the Iberian peninsula takes over on the far side of the snowy peaks.

Vineyards in Jurançon, in the Pyrenean foothills, produce some of France's most individual flavours, especially the startling sweet wines from low-yielding Petit Manseng.

 RED GRAPES
The main grapes are the 'Bordeaux' varieties: Cabernets Sauvignon and Franc, Merlot and Malbec, with local specials, notably Tannat and Negrette.

WHITE GRAPES
Sémillon and Sauvignon Blanc predominate in the north, with Petit Manseng, Gros Manseng and other local varieties in the south.

CLIMATE
The climate is similar to Bordeaux with strong Atlantic influences, though with slightly higher temperatures and lower rainfall especially as you go south and east.

 SOIL
The great variety of soils include the sandstone and marly limestone of the Bergerac and Tarn regions, Kimmeridgian limestone in Cahors, alluvial sand and gravel in the South-West.

 ASPECT
Protection from Atlantic gusts can be important here favouring south-, east- and south-east-facing sites.

VINS DE PAYS

IT'S DIFFICULT NOWADAYS to realize quite how poor a vast amount of French wine used to be as recently as the 1970s. Wine for the most part in France was not anything exciting or unusual, it was simply the beverage you drank with your meals. Lunch, certainly, dinner, certainly, and in many rural and industrial communities, with your breakfast too, or on your way to work. What was necessary was that it should be cheap, it should have some sort of alcoholic strength to give you a bit of energy and a bit of a lift, and that it should aid your digestion. That it should taste good hardly ever entered the equation, because it hardly ever did.

And it hardly ever had a name except maybe for a fanciful brand name dreamed up by someone in a merchant's office who knew nothing of where the wine came from or which grape varieties contributed. *Pinard*, the French called it, or *onze degrés*, or *gros rouge*. *Pinard* is not politely translatable, *onze degrés* simply meant eleven degrees, its alcoholic strength, and *gros rouge* just means the big red, the rough red, neither adjective being complimentary. All of France contributed to this faceless lake of wine but by far the most important area was the Midi, the four *départements* of Gard, Hérault, Aude and Pyrénées-Orientales that are Languedoc-Roussillon. This area had enjoyed almost uninterrupted prosperity since the Industrial Revolution of the 1820s spawned a workforce millions strong, thirsty and uncritical. During the 1950s they were still drinking *pinard* in vast quantities. The average annual per capita consumption of wine hovered round 170 litres (45 gallons).

RADICAL RETHINK AS CONSUMPTION FALLS

In 1956 the annual wine consumption figure fell for the first time. By 1968 the figure had drifted down to 150 litres (40 gallons) per head and to 112 litres (30 gallons) by 1983. In 2004 a mere 54 litres (14 gallons) of wine per capita were drunk in France. These figures show a major crisis for French wine producers. But whereas almost all the areas apart from the South had traditions of quality enshrined by appellation contrôlée regulations and could afford to let the marginal vineyards be turned over to other crops, the Midi was a virtual monoculture of the vine, based solely on quantity, not quality. Nearly all the wine was red; useful, when the new generation of drinkers was demanding white. Appellations contrôlées in the Midi of the 1960s were as rare as snowflakes in summer.

Arriving from Australia, James Herrick sent shockwaves through the South of France when he planted these vineyards near Narbonne with Chardonnay. The locals didn't know what Chardonnay was. Now such Vins de Pays – labelled with their grape variety – form an important part of France's modern wine culture.

Throughout the 1960s it seemed that people were drinking less but better wine, so wines with some kind of geographical or historical individuality were increasingly in demand. The Midi's only reputation had been for anonymous mediocrity, so there was no geographical or traditional individuality you could attempt to improve. But if you could *give* them their own geographical identity, if you could formulate a set of regulations loose enough to encourage wine producers without any experience of quality to give them a try, yet tight enough in certain cases so as genuinely to improve the wine's flavour and – if money could be provided to support such a scheme – then economic disaster might be averted.

During the 1970s a framework of *vins de pays* was established to try to achieve this. *Vin de pays* means 'country wine' – an attractive name implying something local, even parochial – and it was exactly the right choice. French wine quality classification has always based itself on delimiting geographically precise vineyard areas. The top rung is the Controlled Appellation of Origin (AC). The second rung is the Delimited Wine of Superior Quality (VDQS). The *vin de pays* became the third rung, with very loose geographical strictures – any reasonable vineyard land in a set area could use it – but quite strict regulations for production, taking *vin de pays* way above *vin de table* in terms of quality.

There are three *vin de pays* levels. Regional is where a group of *départements* bands together under one name, the most important being Vin de Pays d'Oc, covering Languedoc-Roussillon. Each departmental *vin de pays* covers an entire *département*. And zonal *vins de pays* cover more precise regions.

In regions where there are also appellations contrôlées, the allowed yields are higher and the minimum alcohol lower than for appellation wines. Yet *vin de pays* requirements are far higher than for basic *vin de table*. This is crucial in all those swathes of the Midi that had never until recently produced anything but *vin de table*. Yields are between 80 and 90 hectolitres per hectare and minimum alcohol usually 10 degrees, whereas a *vin de table* producer might get 200 hectolitres per hectare, and was technically supposed to achieve 8.5 degrees alcohol. Choice of grape varieties here is crucial. The *vin de table* villains are varieties like Aramon, Alicante Bouschet and Carignan. Of these, only Carignan is allowed for *vin de pays*, while a whole variety of good quality grapes not permitted in local appellations contrôlées are allowed for *vins de pays*.

In the South this has meant the introduction of grapes like Cabernet Sauvignon, Merlot, Pinot Noir, Chardonnay, Sauvignon Blanc and Viognier. This has allowed growers to benefit from the current trend to label wine by grape variety, a practice being stamped on by the appellation contrôlée authorities, but applied with great international success by Vin de Pays d'Oc, and which can be seen as France's riposte to competition from the New World. These are the wines that have in turn attracted interest and investment from the New World.

The change is pretty impressive. Vineyard and cellar techniques have improved beyond recognition, with tighter controls of two of the most common wine faults – excessive volatile acidity and sulphur – and the increasing use of temperature control for fermentation, oak barrels for aging and insulated cellars for storage, all of which were rare in the Midi, 20, and even 15 years ago. The other achievements have been to encourage imaginative winemaking in areas like the Loire Valley, where the local appellations were inflexible and wedded to wine styles that simply weren't selling, and to inspire winemakers like Aimé Guibert at Mas de Daumas Gassac, north of Montpellier, who has created classic wines where nothing existed before, setting an example of quality, and also of price, to which many of his neighbours aspire.

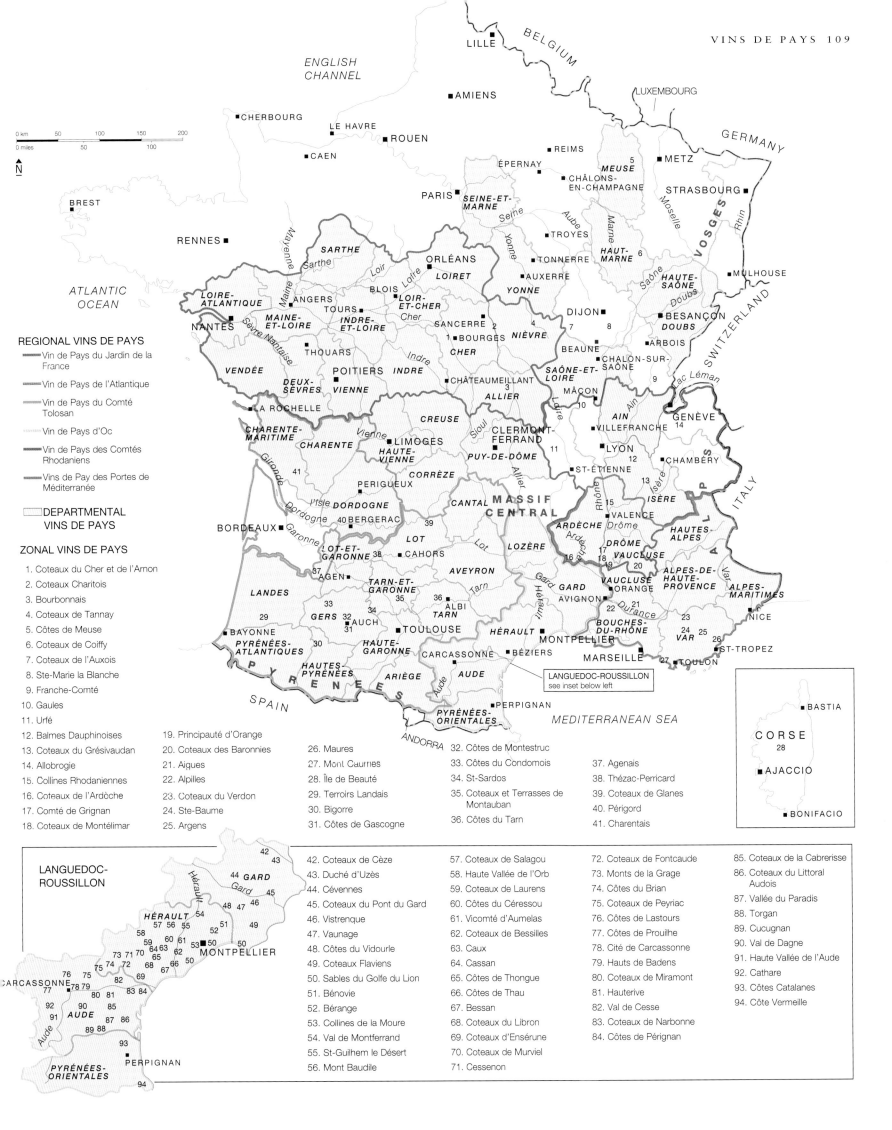

GERMANY

The heart and soul of German wine. An amphitheatre of golden-leaved vines, a tranquil river and a little village huddled on its banks. The sloping vines are those of the great Piesporter Goldtröpfchen vineyard in the Mosel Valley. And sundials – Sonnenuhren in German – are often placed in top vineyards, facing south to catch the sun.

If ever there were a country whose vinous treasures need cosseting, whose ability to thrill depends upon an annual dance along a climatic knife-edge, it is Germany. No country's growers must take greater risks to create the brilliant wines upon which their reputation relies. No vineyard sites need to be more carefully chosen for maximum exposure to sun and minimum exposure to wind, frost and rain. And in no other country are the most famous names betrayed more shamefully by vineyards with no right whatsoever to be associated with them.

Vineyards like those of the Mosel-Saar-Ruwer are pretty well as far north as you can go and still ripen any of the classic grapes. But the genius of the Riesling grape is that, if you allow it to ripen slowly through long, cool summers, and are lucky enough to have a balmy autumn, it is capable of a sublime balance between fruit acidity and fruit sweetness that is unique in the world – even at ridiculously low alcohol levels and scarily high levels of acid. Add a little noble rot and the result is even more remarkable.

Yet this is only possible on special sites. These should be as lovingly delineated and protected as are far less special sites elsewhere in Europe. Instead, such action was deemed elitist back in 1971, when Germany's current wine law was passed, while Germany's international reputation has been ruined by a misguided attempt at popularism in providing large amounts of innocuous, cheap wine. On the label there is no obvious difference between Piesporter Goldtröpfchen (see left) – one of Europe's great natural vineyard sites – and Piesporter Michelsberg, a name covering any wine from numerous inferior villages in the area. Bernkastel is a great wine village with some superb sites, yet wine from the whole Middle Mosel can call itself Bereich Bernkastel. What began as an attempt to simplify and update traditional practice has become one of the main reasons Germany's fine wine reputation is defiled. But there is hope: the best Rheingau sites now have an official classification – Erstes Gewächs. Other regions are evolving unofficial classifications, hoping that these, too, will become law.

One of the greatest changes in recent years is a growth in the awareness of terroir – something that the best growers have always understood. The other is the shift to red. In 1990 just 16 per cent of Germany's vineyards were planted with red grapes; but by 2005 the figure is 37 per cent. And while most of these wines are not of much interest to drinkers outside Germany, there is a notable minority of growers making exciting reds, mostly from Pinot Noir, which the Germans call Spätburgunder.

THE WINE REGIONS OF GERMANY

IN AN IDEAL WORLD the names on this map of Germany would echo with romance for all wine lovers. 'We're just popping to the Saar for the weekend,' people would boast. 'We try to go every year. We'll fit in an afternoon on the Ruwer, and say hello to the Bernkasteler Doctor as well.' Sounds absurd? It's how Europeans talk about Burgundy. You can see them driving along the main road through the Côte d'Or: they can't believe that they're seeing road signs to hallowed places they've only ever seen on wine labels.

But in fact sightseeing is every bit as crucial to understanding German wine as it is to understanding what makes one Burgundy taste different from another. Maybe even more so, since parts of Germany are as far north as grapes will ripen. Winemaking is only possible in much of Germany when four elements come together: site, climate, soil and grape. And the greatest of these is site.

Nearly all the vineyards are in the southern half of the country. The best vines are often grown where no other crops will flourish: on slopes too steep for cows, or where the soil is too poor for wheat. But steep slopes are good for vines. They offer shelter from the wind, particularly if they are crowned by woods or if there is a mountain range behind. Then again, they get stronger sunlight: on flat ground the sun's rays strike at an angle; on steeply sloping land they strike perpendicularly. (A great simplification, of course, but that is the principle.) That means fewer shadows and greater heat.

In order to maximize sunshine and warmth, in Germany the slopes must be south-, west- or east-facing. East-facing slopes catch the morning sun; those facing west get the afternoon sun, and this can be useful if fog is common, since it will usually have burnt off by the afternoon. And the best kind of slope of all is in a river valley, shutting out the wind, imprisoning the warmth.

Rivers are crucial to vine-growing in Germany. Nearly all the great wine areas are close to rivers and their tributaries: vines follow the progress of the Mosel and the Rhine, the Main and the Neckar and (to a lesser extent) the Elbe, Saale and Unstrut. The reason is that an expanse of water has the effect of moderating extremes of temperature. It helps to ward off frosts and it gives humidity in hot, dry summers; and the water surface reflects heat and light back on to the banks, particularly if they are steep.

Most wine areas are in the South, but there is an east-west division of climate, as well as a north-south one, with the climate becoming more continental as you travel east. Sachsen, Saale-Unstrut, Württemberg, Franken and parts of Baden are affected by this, and have a risk of both early and late frosts.

To the casual visitor the climate may not appear to vary much from Bonn down to Basel. It's not really that far, after all. But in Germany grape-growing is on the margin and every half degree counts. In the Pfalz, regarded as a relatively warm region, the mean annual temperature is 10.1°C (50°F); in the Mosel, considered distinctly cool, it is 9.8°C (49.6°F). Much of the time you'd hardly notice the difference. But the Pfalz also has an extra 138 hours of sunshine in the growing season, and produces wines that are rich and fat, whereas the wines of the Mosel are lean and delicate.

Soils in Germany are very varied. Some regions are famous for having a soil that gives its character to the wine – Mosel slate, say – but grapes are grown on limestone, sandstone, marl, loess and many other types. Generally, valley bottoms have richer, alluvial soil and produce richer wines; the slopes, where the soil is poorer, produce more elegant wines. What they have in common is the Riesling grape – the final clue to winemaking in Germany.

Great German wines don't have to be Riesling – Silvaner, the Pinot family and Scheurebe can all be first-class – but Riesling does have an uncanny ability to take advantage of all that German vineyards have to offer, and turn minuses into pluses at the same time. It thrives on a wide range of soils and its flavour reflects the character of the soil. It ripens late, so given a long, warm autumn and a south-facing slope, it will go on gathering complexity until well into October. It is resistant to cold. Even more remarkably, it can produce good wines at low levels of ripeness as well as when it is so overripe that the berries are shrivelled and brown.

This wine is from the Erdener Prälat vineyard, one of the great traditional Mosel vineyards.

THE CLASSIFICATION SYSTEM FOR GERMAN WINE

German wine law classifies all aspects of a wine: ripeness, sweetness and origin, but it does not grade vineyards in order of quality. German wine law is based on the premise that in a cool climate, the ripeness of the grapes is all. The quality categories are based on the amount of sugar in the grape juice, or must. This is measured in degrees Oechsle, which are a way of comparing the specific gravity of must with that of water. Water has a specific gravity of 1000, so grape juice with a specific gravity of 1100 has 100° Oechsle. Each quality category has a minimum required Oechsle degree, which may vary from region to region.

QUALITY CATEGORIES

- **Deutscher Tafelwein** Basic table wine from four main regions.
- **Landwein** Similar to France's *vin de pays* but it has not taken off in the same way. It can come from any of 17 regions.
- **Qualitätswein bestimmter Anbaugebiete (QbA)** Quality wine from designated regions. These wines are permitted to add sugar to the juice when natural ripeness has not produced enough and yields are high. The wines are usually pretty ordinary, though some producers choose QbA to allow them greater flexibility in levels of dryness, oak-aging etc.
- **Qualitätswein mit Prädikat (QmP)** [From 2007 this is being shortened to just Prädikatswein.] Quality wine with special attributes. Divided into six categories of ascending levels of ripeness: *Kabinett* Made from ripe grapes. Most are light, and may have as little as 7 per cent alcohol.

Spätlese From late-picked grapes. *Auslese* From selected bunches of late-picked grapes. Some are made from botrytis-affected grapes and are sweet. Many are made dry: good dry reds in particular may be labelled Auslese Trocken. *Beerenauslese* From individually selected berries affected by noble rot. The wine is very sweet. *Trockenbeerenauslese* From individually selected berries that are shrivelled with overripeness. The wines are intensely sweet. Very rare. *Eiswein* 'Icewine', from sound grapes, picked and pressed while naturally frozen.

- **Qualitätswein garantierten Ursprungs (QbU)** A new category: 100 per cent of the grapes and *Süssreserve* (unfermented grape juice for sweetening wine), if used, come from the area stated on the label.
- **Einzellage** A single vineyard. Most are at least 2.2ha (5.4 acres) in size, and many were enlarged under the 1971 wine law to meet the minimum size requirement laid down in that law. Most, but not all, of the finest wines will come from an *Einzellage*.
- **Grosslage** A group of *Einzellagen*. *Grosslagen* can cover large areas of indifferent land, and often take their name from their most famous vineyard. It is impossible to tell from looking at the label whether the name stated is an *Einzellage* or *Grosslage*.
- **Bereich** The next largest area. Sometimes a Bereich reflects the character of the wine of a district, sometimes it is drawn on political boundaries. A Bereich wine is unlikely to be exciting.
- **Anbaugebiet** A wine region, like Pfalz or Mosel-Saar-Ruwer.

PANORAMIC MAPS OF GERMANY

Mosel *pages 114–115*
Middle Mosel *pages 116–117*
Saar-Ruwer *pages 118–119*
The Rhine Valley *page 121*
Rheingau *pages 124–125*
Nahe *pages 126–127*
Rheinhessen *page 129*
Pfalz *page 130*
Franken *pages 132-133*
Baden *page 137*

OTHER MAPS

Ahr and Mittelrhein *page 122*
Franken *page 134*
Baden and Württemberg *page 135*

QUALITY WINE REGIONS

- Mosel
- Ahr
- Mittelrhein
- Nahe
- Rheingau
- Rheinhessen
- Pfalz
- Hessische Bergstrasse
- Franken
- Württemberg
- Baden
- Saale-Unstrut
- Sachsen

MOSEL

🍇 **RED GRAPES**
There is a tiny amount of Spätburgunder.

🍇 **WHITE GRAPES**
All the great Mosel wines come from Riesling. Müller-Thurgau is the other important grape but is on the decline.

☁️ **CLIMATE**
The Mosel is damp and cool but there are sheltering hills and dams along the river have improved the mesoclimates. The Saar and the Ruwer are cooler still.

⬜ **SOIL**
Different types of slate predominate in all areas apart from the Upper Mosel, which is largely limestone.

⛰️ **ASPECT**
The Mosel has many south, south-east and south-west-facing vineyards. The Saar flows north and has fewer ideal sites; the Ruwer's vineyards face mostly west-south-west. Vines are planted at 100–350m (328–1148ft).

YOU KNOW THAT FEELING. You look out of the window in the morning at blue skies. The trees are impossibly green and the river below the town glitters in the sun. You throw on jeans and a T-shirt and hurry out – and seconds later you hurry in again. You want a sweater, or two. This is May in the Mosel and it's cold.

Then you leave the town and cross the river – and you take off one of the sweaters. You're in the vineyards now, on the lowest slopes where the river reflects all that early morning sun back on to the vines. It's dazzlingly bright. It's not warm, precisely, but it's warmer, and you can see the town across the river, still in shadow. The vines around you are soaking up all the sun they can get, and you feel guilty about your shadow, spoiling the morning for at least three vines. You scramble up the slopes – and I mean scramble. It's so forbiddingly high and steep here that you wonder if Mosellaners are born with different legs to the rest of us. Each vine is tied to its own 2.5m (8ft) pole, and has its branches pulled back and down to spread the leaves to the sun; you can hang on to these poles as you climb, if you like, because they're embedded in solid rock. At the top of the slope you're glad of that second sweater again. It's cooler up here and the wind whistles round your ears.

This chilliness is the essence of the Mosel. In the best stretch, the Middle Mosel, where the river has carved out sheltered, steep slopes that face south, south-east or south-west, Riesling has an immensely long ripening time: between 120 and

150 days, compared with 105 to 115 for Cabernet in Bordeaux. These warm spots are responsible for the fame of the entire river. Elsewhere, and in inferior sites, vineyards are starting to fall out of cultivation: in 2005 there were 8094ha (22,000 acres) of vineyards, a decrease of about 3500ha (8648 acres) in a decade.

The Mosel enters Germany from France and for almost 40km (25 miles) it runs north along the border with Luxembourg. Here in the Upper Mosel, slopes are gentle, and the river much

KOBLENZ

KOBERN-GONDORF WINNINGEN *Rhein*

Mosel

COCHEM

ZELL

TLICH

2

Mosel

TRABEN-
TRARBACH

BERNKASTEL-
KUES

PIESPORT

N

TOTAL DISTANCE
NORTH TO SOUTH
132KM (82 MILES)

VINEYARDS

QUALITY WINE REGION AND BEREICHE

MOSEL
1. Bereich Burg Cochem
2. Bereich Bernkastel
3. Bereich Ruwertal
4. Bereich Saar
5. Bereich Obermosel
6. Bereich Moseltor

— BEREICH
BOUNDARIES

WHERE THE VINEYARDS ARE

I sometimes think it's a wonder that the Mosel ever reaches its confluence with the Rhine at all. The river has so many twists and turns on the way, trying first one direction and then another, and all because it keeps bumping into rock. The Mosel, over the millennia of its existence, has nudged and eased its way between walls of solid slate, and in doing so it has revealed some of the most diverse and perfect mesoclimates for the vine to be found in any wine region anywhere in the world.

Look at the way the vineyards hug the river and at the great amphitheatres of vines around Bernkastel-Kues: if there's a sun-trap along these banks, it will be thick with vines. And then look at the way the vineyards occasionally sprawl away from the water, on to flatter land or north-facing slopes. Are those vines going to be as good? The simple answer is, no, they're not. From the late 1960s to 1990, some 5000ha (12,355 acres) of these inferior vineyards were planted with grapes like Müller-Thurgau, Bacchus, Ortega and Optima, but these areas are gradually reverting to farmland.

narrower than it becomes later on – and thus less able to throw the sun's warmth back on to the vines. The river has an average width of only 7.5m (8 yards), although the main stretch from Trier up to Koblenz is wider. The slopes in the Upper Mosel are even a different colour: composed of shelly limestone, sandstone and red marl, they're softer and warmer in colour than the harsh, dark grey slate that takes over further downstream. The Elbling has been the main grape here since Roman times: it makes dry, brisk, acidic wines that seldom manage higher quality than QbA and are a godsend to the Sekt industry. Kerner gives high yields and is one of the reasons (along with 15 per cent Müller-Thurgau and tiny amounts of Elbling, Kerner, Bacchus, Grauburgunder, Optima, Ortega, Weissburgunder, Dornfelder and Spätburgunder) why Riesling, while covering 58 per cent of the Mosel vineyards, only yields 50 to 55 per cent of its wines. These are all, apart from Dorntelder and Spätburgunder, white grapes.

Red grapes don't ripen easily here: it's too cold. This coolness is recognized in law: Mosel wines require lower Oechsle readings at all QmP levels except *Trockenbeerenauslese* than do the wines of warmer regions like the Rheingau. Mosel Riesling Kabinett can have an Oechsle reading of 67°, for example, compared to 73° in the Rheingau. Yet the lightness and fragility of Mosel wines is deceptive and they can last and improve for years.

The six Mosel-Saar-Ruwer Bereichs, going north, are Moseltor on the French border; Obermosel (Upper Mosel); Saar and Ruwertal – named after two tributaries; Bernkastel – the whole of the Middle Mosel; and Burg Cochem between Zell and Koblenz, covering the Lower Mosel (Untermosel). Generally the Upper Mosel is cooler and windier than the Middle Mosel, though increasingly exciting wines are being made at the best sites here. In the northerly Lower Mosel, the Hunsrück hills press in close to the river leaving little room to live, never mind cultivate vines. Even so, there are some excellent sites here – steep, terraced slopes of sandy rocks that are even harder than the Devonian slate of the Middle Mosel. The villages of Winningen and Kobern-Gondorf would be better known were they closer to the clutch of famous villages further upstream.

This Riesling Spätlese from the Brauneberger Juffer Sonnenuhr, a perfectly sited south-east-facing vineyard, will need at least 10 years in bottle to show at its best.

MIDDLE MOSEL

THE SUNDIALS GIVE THE CLUE. In the Middle Mosel the most famous are at Wehlen, Zeltingen and Brauneberg, and they're right in the middle of the vines. The vineyards take their name – *Sonnenuhr* – from these intruders that squat in their midst. And what can you guess about a vineyard that has a sundial in it? It gets a lot of sun – which is so precious to vines in this northerly latitude that the towns and villages lie across the river on the shady side.

The tortuous bends of the Mosel specialize in such ideal sites. Vineyards rise to 200m (656ft) above the river, and beech and fir forests take over on the hilltops where it is too windy and cool for vines. The forests are home to wild boar, though, and boar are partial to grapes: one grower douses his fences in Lancôme's *Magie Noire* to keep them away.

The river is wider here than at any other point (broadened even more by the locks built since 1951) and that means more sunlight and warmth reflected back on to the vines, and more botrytis, too, since it means more early-morning fogs. Sometimes, as

at Wehlen, the town huddles on the north-facing bank and the sunny opposite bank is nothing but a wall of vines. Sometimes we find a twin town like Bernkastel-Kues linked by a bridge but the vines of the great Doctor vineyard press right to the back door of the gabled houses.

What's less ideal is when a town's north-facing slopes are also planted, and when an *Einzellage* name includes not only the south-facing slopes but also the much chillier north-facing ones, and even the flat ground by the river. These places were only planted with vines, mainly Müller-Thurgau, from the late 1960s to about 1990.

ENKIRCH TO KLÜSSERATH

TOTAL DISTANCE
NORTH TO SOUTH
22KM (13½ MILES)

▦ VINEYARDS

N

TRABEN
TRARBACH

BERNKASTEL-KUES

TRITTENHEIM

0 km   1   2
0 miles   1

WHERE THE VINEYARDS ARE

Bernkastel and Piesport are two of the most devalued names in the wine world – both names have been annexed to mass-produced wines, Piesporter Michelsberg and Bereich Bernkastel, neither of which bears the least resemblance to what made the villages famous (and made the mass-producers want to pinch the names in the first place). The map of the Middle Mosel shows you, though. Look at that great south-facing wall of vines at Piesport. Look at that spur of hill at Bernkastel – that's the world-famous Doctor vineyard. And beyond it the vines stretch in an almost unbroken wall, changing banks as the river turns, through Graach, through Wehlen, through Zeltingen and beyond Ürzig. And further important vineyard sites are provided by the tributaries of the Dhron, where the little-known Leiwener Laurentiuslay is making excellent wines, and of the Lieser, where, at Maring, there is yet another vineyard called Sonnenuhr (after one of the area's many sundials).

0 km   1   2
0 miles   1

Fruit trees were the original crop, and German wine would be in a better state if they were still there. Müller-Thurgau covers 15 per cent of the Mosel vineyards – less than in some German regions, but yields are far higher than the 30 to 40hl per hectare a top grower might take from old Riesling vines on the old, sloping terraces of, say, Zeltingen. Where terraces have been smoothed out by the Flurbereinigung programme of vineyard reshaping, the vines are often younger and yields are higher, perhaps 90hl/ha – though even Riesling will go up to 120hl/ha if it is allowed to (and encouraged with nitrogen fertilisers).

For the best growers, and in the best villages, the names of Middle Mosel and Riesling are synonymous. There's less agreement on what constitutes the Middle Mosel: the most conservative view has it beginning upriver at Trittenheim and continuing as far as Ürzig. But there are excellent sites both upriver and downriver of these points, for example the Bruderschaft site behind the village of Klüsserath. Downriver the top sites – like Kröver Steffensberg, Wolfer Goldgrube and Enkircher Batterieberg – become fewer.

MOSEL SLATE

The keys to the Middle Mosel are not just warmth and exposure: these enable the sun to ripen the grapes, but it is the soil that flavours them. The soil in the Middle Mosel is Devonian slate, dark and heat-absorbing, dry and instantly-draining, which decomposes into a thin topsoil that in the past was constantly replenished by the simple method of pulling chunks from the hillsides, breaking them up and scattering the shards. Nowadays this is too expensive, but because of slate's low pH it may be necessary to fertilize with lime every couple of years. Stand on these slopes and you'll feel them soft and flaky under your feet. The sun glints on the slate fragments and they slide as you move, bouncing down between the vines. Slate gives a particularly smoky taste to Riesling, a tang that, once tasted, is never forgotten. And when it rains the rain pours straight through like water through a sieve. More absorbent soil would hold the water, and in so doing would be washed down the slope. (More absorbent soil would also mean more water in the grapes and more risk of rot: free-draining slate is one reason why growers in the Mosel can pick so late.) Since Bernkastel gets twice as much rain as Geisenheim in the Rheingau, it's just as well that it can cope.

All the best Mosel vineyards are perilously steep, teetering above the river. This is the great Brauneberger Juffer.

WINE STYLES

Where the topsoils are thinnest, wines are more elegant; deeper soils make fuller wines. Ürzig gives spicy wine, particularly from its Würzgarten (spice garden) site and excels in dry years; so does Graach, where the slate is deep and rich in weathered clay-like soil. Erden has lighter soil and prefers wet years; Wehlen's best vineyards are at the base of the slope where it's 2°C warmer than at the top. Bernkastel gives smoky wines, rich and concentrated. But rich is a relative term in the Mosel. It's a region of *Kabinett* and *Spätlesen*, and sometimes *Auslesen* wines. A Mosel *Beerenauslese* is a rare bird, and even when the grapes are ripe and nobly-rotten enough, it won't have the lusciousness of a Rheingau. It's a paradox of the Middle Mosel that such a forbidding-looking place yields such delicate wines – but they're wines with a shining core of steel.

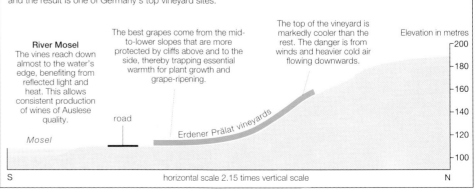

SELECTED VINEYARDS

1. Enkircher Batterieberg
2. Wolfer Goldgrube
3. Kröver Steffensberg
4. Erdener Treppchen
5. Erdener Prälat
6. Ürziger Würzgarten
7. Zeltinger Sonnenuhr
8. Wehlener Sonnenuhr
9. Graacher Josephshöfer
10. Graacher Himmelreich
11. Graacher Domprobst
12. Bernkasteler Lay
13. Bernkasteler Alte Badstube am Doctorberg
14. Bernkasteler Doctor
15. Lieserer Niederberg-Helden
16. Brauneberger Juffer Sonnenuhr
17. Brauneberger Juffer
18. Wintricher Ohligsberg
19. Piesporter Goldtröpfchen
20. Piesporter Domherr
21. Trittenheimer Apotheke
22. Trittenheimer Leiterchen
23. Trittenheimer Felsenkopf
24. Leiwener Laurentiuslay
25. Klüsserather Bruderschaft

— BEREICH BOUNDARIES

ERDENER PRÄLAT

The Middle Mosel's Erdener Prälat vineyard, located between the river Mosel and high cliffs above, provides ideal conditions for the Riesling grape. It became a single vineyard around the end of the 19th century, hived off from the Treppchen next door because its extraordinarily warm mesoclimate consistently produced riper grapes, although the higher parts are cooler than lower down. Add to this a perfect south-facing exposure, a high stone content in the iron-rich, red slate soil which retains heat and reflects warmth back onto the vines along with some old vines and the result is one of Germany's top vineyard sites.

River Mosel
The vines reach down almost to the water's edge, benefiting from reflected light and heat. This allows consistent production of wines of Auslese quality.

The best grapes come from the mid-to-lower slopes that are more protected by cliffs above and to the side, thereby trapping essential warmth for plant growth and grape-ripening.

The top of the vineyard is markedly cooler than the rest. The danger is from winds and heavier cold air flowing downwards.

Elevation in metres
—200
—180
—160
—140
—120
—100

road

Mosel

Erdener Prälat vineyards

S   horizontal scale 2.15 times vertical scale   N

SAAR & RUWER

THESE TWO TRIBUTARIES of the Mosel, flowing northwards to join the larger river either side of the Roman city of Trier, are, generally speaking, cooler and less promising than much of the Mosel. Thank goodness for that, their growers must say. Being less promising has meant that they escaped the drive to mass production in Germany that afflicted even the Mosel in the late 1960s and 1970s. In 1953 the Saar had 842ha (2080 acres) of vines; by 1998, it had increased to 1340ha (3311 acres), but now stands at 723ha (1786 acres). In the much smaller Ruwer region, the land under vine amounted to 304ha (751 acres) in 1953 and it has risen, fallen, risen and fallen again to a current figure of 190ha (469 acres).

The reason for this lack of planting mania is quite simple: these are not regions where a grower can make a quick buck. It takes the hardy Riesling vine to withstand the cold winds that blow far more strongly here than along the Mosel, and it takes an old-fashioned mentality on the part of the grower to put up with the low yields – lower than just about anywhere on the Mosel. These vary from grower to grower and from site to site, of course, and (to be honest) yields that pass for low in Germany would rarely be considered so in other top European regions.

The average yield for Riesling for the whole Mosel region is now about 80–85hl/ha – compare this with the massive average yield of 150hl/ha for the whole Mosel region in the 1980s and early '90s. Yields this high could not possibly produce concentrated Riesling wines. As to be expected there are big differences between the bulk wine producers and the top estates who often harvest at less than 40hl/ha or even 30 hl/ha.

Then there is the question of the slow, slow maturation of the wines in bottle. Saar and Ruwer wines are high in acidity and, in a cool year when the Riesling barely ripens, they can be low in fruit. But in long warm summers, when the sugar levels rise to meet the acidity, a Saar or Ruwer Riesling can be among the most exciting wines in Germany. But it will take its time. That razor-like acidity will need taming in bottle for several years before it is softened.

THE SAAR

Although they both flow in approximately the same direction and are not far apart, the two rivers produce wines of different character. The Saar wines probably show the greatest variation, both in vintage and in geological terms. The Saar can boast soils ranging from loam, quartzite and volcanic to hard and soft slate – and they are even stonier than those of the Mosel. And even though the Saar is less sheltered and more open to the wind than the Middle Mosel, and the valley therefore cooler, it doesn't look as harsh to the eye.

The vineyards don't wall the river in with the determination of those around Bernkastel on the Mosel; there is more pasture and forest, and the land tends to be gathered into large estates whose rambling manor houses sit among their woods and fields with a less mercantile air than do the solid riverside houses of the Mosel. But the Saar growers in their manor houses seem to be remarkably impervious to draughts; on a day when tourists are basking outside the bars of Bernkastel, a visitor will need a coat in the Saar. Here, where the Saar, and the Ruwer even more so, are not broad enough to have much tempering effect on the climate, the crucial questions of wine always come down to the weather.

For a small area the Saar's roster of excellent vineyard sites is astonishing – Scharzhofberg in Wiltingen, Ayler Kupp, Ockfener Bockstein, Saarburger Rausch, Serriger Schloss Saarstein (off our map to the south) and several others. This is even more so when only three or four times in a decade do they really produce wines to convert the sceptical.

THE RUWER

If the Saar is a backwater, the Ruwer is so small that you could overlook it completely. Rising in the Hunsrück hills, it's hardly more than a stream, yet its gently rounded hills offer some superb west-south-west-facing sites. Like the Saar, it's Riesling country, and the wine similarly needs a good year for its style of piercing acidity to come into its own. But Ruwer wines, even when young, are less intimidating than those of its neighbour. In the Ruwer the slate is often reddish in colour and is more decomposed into a friable soil than the rocky splinters of the Middle Mosel; it contributes to some superb vineyard sites. This richer soil also makes Ruwer wines more aromatic than their cousins from the Saar. The sharp variations in temperature can also play their part here: nights in the Ruwer can be colder than in Trier, but summer days can be hotter. Top sites include the Maximin Grünhaus estate at Mertesdorf and the Karthäuserhofberg estate at Eitelsbach – both, coincidentally, old monastic properties – and at Kasel there is the Nies'chen vineyard, with its perfect south-south-west exposure. The Avelsbacher Altenberg is in the valley of a tributary of the Ruwer: a tiny stream that joins an only just less tiny stream.

WINE STYLES

Riesling must be planted on the slopes, angled towards the sun, because it wouldn't ripen on flatter land here. Only the slopes can catch every bit of available sun. Even so, the proportion of QbA wine made here is far higher than in the Middle Mosel: only about 20 per cent of the crop reaches Spätlese or Auslese level. A Beerenauslese from the Saar or Ruwer would be a freak, but Eiswein is often possible. It is perhaps Kabinett wines that best express the taut delicacy of the wines from these valleys. In the trio of wonderful years which blessed Germany from 1988 to 1990, there was actually more wine of Prädikat level made in the Saar-Ruwer than there was of ordinary Qualitätswein. Low yields and low levels of ripeness, plus high production costs (many vines are still trained on individual stakes, which requires skilled labour), mean that only Riesling will fetch the high prices needed to keep at least some of the draughts out of the manor houses.

The growers, of course, are doing what they can to lower production costs: new vines tend to be trained on wires, and are easier to work than those on stakes, and the vines that are being planted nowadays are often planted further apart to enable narrow, compact vineyard tractors to trundle easily between the rows.

Riesling is increasing its share in both the Saar and the Ruwertal regions. In the Ruwertal it is now 90 per cent of the vineyards and in the Saar it has risen to 78 per cent. The less good vineyards, which were planted with inferior varieties such as Müller-Thurgau and Elbling, are being grubbed up.

The Saar Valley is decidedly cool and only in the best south-facing vineyards can the grapes fully ripen. Here the Scharzhofberg vines still catch the sun, while the winery below sinks into shadow.

SAARBURG

TRIER

SAAR & RUWER

TOTAL DISTANCE
NORTH TO SOUTH
26KM (16 MILES)

VINEYARDS

N

RUWER
EITELSBACH
MERTESDORF
KASEL
WALDRAC
TRIER
AVELSBACH
BEREICH RUWERTAL
Mosel
Ruwer
KONZ
BEREICH
OBERMOSEL
KONEN
BEREICH SAAR
KANZEM
OBEREMMEL
WILTINGEN
WAWERN
Saar
AYL
OCKFEN
SAARBURG

WHERE THE VINEYARDS ARE *The map shows how the Saar and the Ruwer wind northwards through the hills to join the Mosel, and all the best vineyards in the two Bereiche or districts of Saar and Ruwertal are in these two tiny river valleys. In this northerly climate the vines need all the warmth and shelter they can get, so the vineyards are angled towards the sun, ideally facing south and south-west, and sheltered from the wind by the woods on the hilltops. The Ruwer is the sort of tiny trickle that you could easily miss but for those great comma-shaped vineyards, arching down and away from the river in their search for the perfect exposure. Going downriver, Waldrach is the first wine village you reach: here, many vineyards have fallen out of cultivation leaving only the best sites, which keep the river company to the town of Ruwer itself. Saarburg is the main wine town along the Saar but the greatest vineyards are mostly further downstream towards Wiltingen. Notice, too, how the vineyards of both rivers are far less wedded to a river view than those of the Mosel: both rivers are pretty narrow and lots of the sites catch the sun best by leaning away from the water. They can even be found a long way from the main valleys, such as around the village of Oberemmel which has great sweeps of vines on three sides.*

SELECTED VINEYARDS

1. Avelsbacher Altenberg
2. Maximin Grünhäuser Herrenberg
3. Maximin Grünhäuser Abtsberg
4. Eitelsbacher Karthäuserhofberg
5. Kaseler Nies'chen
6. Kaseler Kehrnagel
7. Filzener Pulchen
8. Kanzemer Altenberg
9. Wiltinger Braune Kupp
10. Wiltinger Gottesfuss
11. Oberemmeler Hütte
12. Scharzhofberg
13. Wiltinger Braunfels
14. Schodener Herrenberg
15. Ockfener Bockstein
16. Ayler Kupp
17. Saarburger Rausch

BEREICH BOUNDARIES

THE RHINE VALLEY

Pfalz wines are often rich and dry, with more alcohol than those from vineyards further north.

Assmannshausen's beautiful vineyards, sloping down to the river Rhine on its north bank, are unusual in that they are best known for red wines from the Spätburgunder (Pinot Noir) grape.

THE RHINE (RHEIN) IS ONE OF THE MOST European of rivers. It rises in Switzerland and flows west along the northern border with Germany. At Basel it turns north to form the border between France and Germany for some 170km (106 miles) before setting off through the heartland of Germany. But Rhine wine is universally understood as being German. And if you wanted to get to grips with the nature of German wine, you could do a great deal worse than take a trip up the river from Basel to Bonn.

In fact, to understand German wine at all you have to look at Germany's river systems: it is the rivers that make viticulture an industry, and not just a hobby, in most of these cool climate regions. Even given that the Riesling is a grape that can resist the cold better than most; even given the long autumns that enable it to go on ripening well into October; in spite of all this, the growing of fine grapes in the more northerly vineyards of Germany would be a matter of chance, of reliance on the vagaries of the climate, if the rivers were not there to even up the odds a little. What the rivers do is temper the extremes of climate. They keep frosts at bay and, by reflecting sunlight and warmth, give the vines on their banks an added advantage. In addition, over the millennia they have carved deep gorges out of the rock through which they pass. Those steep banks, when planted with vines, catch all the available sunlight.

In the far south of the Rhine Valley (south of this map, and stretching up to meet it from the Swiss border) are the vineyards of Baden (see page 135), one of the few places in Germany warm enough for you to wander alongside a vineyard and pull cherries or apricots from the trees. The Kaiserstuhl area of Baden is Germany's warmest wine region, and the central part of the Pfalz is warm, too – warmer than much of Baden. Baden faces Alsace across the Rhine and uses many similar grapes such as the Pinot family, including Pinot Noir or Spätburgunder as it is generally called here, Riesling and Gewürztraminer. Since the 1990s, helped by good vintages, winemakers here have made considerable effort to produce serious Spätburgunder. Plantings have more than doubled in Germany since 1990 and it is now the most common grape by far in Baden. At Baden-Baden the Baden vineyards stop for a bit, and then continue on our right as we go northwards – while on our left, on the other side of the Rhine, the Pfalz begins.

THE PFALZ

The Pfalz is really a northerly continuation of Alsace. The southern Pfalz has never been considered to be as good quality as the north and taken overall it still isn't. It's a region of small-scale growers' co-operatives and one of the main sources of Liebfraumilch. But it is also home to some growers of ambition and great imagination, and some of the most exciting wines in Germany are emerging from these slopes – even if the vineyard names are still relatively unknown compared to those of Deidesheim, Forst and Ruppertsberg in the Mittelhardt. These are what made the Pfalz famous – and they're all between Neustadt and Bad Dürkheim on the map. So let's take a walk westwards over the wide agricultural plain, towards the wine villages north of Neustadt. It's quite a long way from the river – so far that the Rhine can't really be given much credit for the quality of their vineyards. Instead, it's the Haardt mountains, a continuation of Alsace's Vosges mountains, in the foothills of which the Pfalz vineyards shelter, that make a warm climate even warmer. Encouragingly, Riesling is on the increase here and now covers more than 20 per cent of the vineyards.

RHEINHESSEN

But as we wander away from the hills, heading north-east across the gentle slopes of the Rheinhessen, the Riesling all but disappears.

Instead there's Müller-Thurgau and Silvaner, plus Kerner and Scheurebe and a few others – and watch out as you cross the roads, or you'll be mown down by the tankers of simple, grapy, mass-produced wine on their way to the Liebfraumilch cellars. Only when we reach the riverside towns of Oppenheim, Nierstein and Nackenheim, and we find ourselves overshadowed by the rust-red hills of the Roter Hang, are we again in serious wine country. The soil here is sandstone and decomposed red slate, and the hills rear high enough to offer good south-east exposure across the Rhine – though still only a mere handful of growers take advantage of this.

RHEINGAU

We'll cross the river here, over to the right bank, and take a bus through the suburbs of Wiesbaden. We're now in the Rheingau, where we'll find many of Germany's most famous (but also, all too often, most underperforming) wine names. This, traditionally, is the culmination of the Rhine. The vineyards are crammed in on the foothills of the Taunus mountains between the river and the forest. As you go west from Wiesbaden the slopes get higher and steeper; the river reflects all the available warmth back on to the Riesling vines (because it is mostly all Riesling here, though there are increasing amounts of Spätburgunder) and the wines can be some of the weightiest, fieriest, most complex examples to be found.

MITTELRHEIN AND AHR

West of Bingen the Rhine resumes its northward course. There are fewer vineyards here in the Mittelrhein than there were 50 years ago; fewer even than ten years ago. The best vineyard sites are often tucked away in the side valleys, and the Sekt industry, with its need for light, lean wines, relies heavily on grapes from this region.

At Koblenz the Mosel joins the Rhine, and after that there is only one more wine region to go before Bonn. The tiny Ahr Valley, though, can spring surprises. Most of its wine is red, or at least pink; it used to be mainly sweetish, though dry wines are more in vogue now. At Bonn the Rhine vineyards stop. The local drink north of here is beer: the hop can ripen where even the hardy Riesling fears to tread.

WHERE THE VINEYARDS ARE *This is a bird's eye view of the greatest of Germany's wine regions (apart from the Mosel-Saar-Ruwer), and it also contains some of the most commonplace. The latter sprawl flatly across the centre of the map; the great ones are tucked into the corners, where you could easily miss them if you didn't know what you were looking for. The Rhine with its tributaries, the Nahe, Main and Neckar, is the artery of German wine; indeed before the advent of motorways it was the main artery of Germany itself. Even today it carries a heavy industrial traffic of barges as well as pleasure-boats, while clustered on its banks at irregular intervals are villages with some of the most famous names in German wine.*

On the lower lefthand side of the map are the Haardt mountains; the vineyards on their eastern foothills, sloping down to the plain, are the best parts of the Pfalz. Go north from there, to Bad Kreuznach on the Nahe, and you can just make out the remarkable vineyard slopes to the west of the town. And just north of the Rhine, where it heads westwards at Wiesbaden, and the wooded Taunus mountains take us off the map, that 32-km (20-mile) long strip of vineyards along the Rhine between the forest and the river is the main stretch of the Rheingau.

In contrast, look at the rich farmland enclosed within the great bend of the river at Mainz. This is the Rheinhessen region which produces soft, sweetish wine often sold in bulk, with one small exception, the heart of the Rheinfront between Nierstein and Nackenheim. The vine shouldn't be allowed to take life too easily: this map shows the difference.

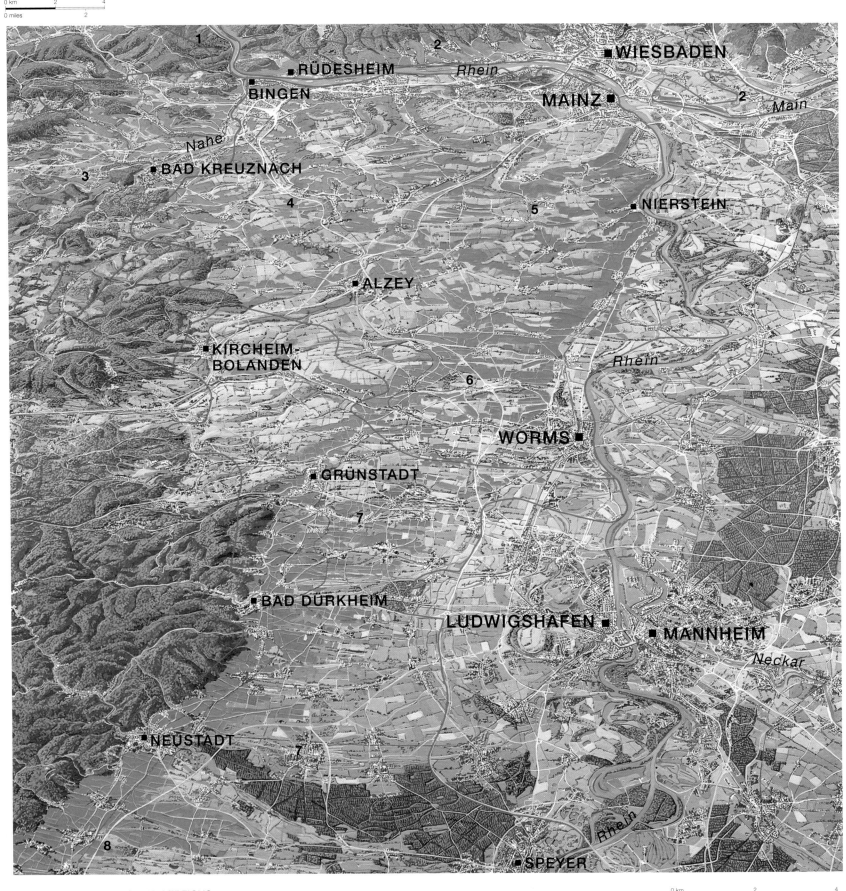

0 km 2 4
0 miles 2

1
2
WIESBADEN
Rhein
■ RÜDESHEIM
■ BINGEN
MAINZ ■
2 *Main*
Nahe
3
■ BAD KREUZNACH
4
5
■ NIERSTEIN
■ ALZEY
■ KIRCHEIM-
BOLANDEN
Rhein
6
WORMS ■
■ GRÜNSTADT
7
■ BAD DÜRKHEIM
LUDWIGSHAFEN ■
■ **MANNHEIM**
Neckar
■ NEUSTADT
7
8
Rhein
■ **SPEYER**

QUALITY WINE REGIONS AND BEREICHS

MITTELRHEIN	RHEINGAU	NAHE	RHEINHESSEN	PFALZ	
1. Bereich Loreley	2. Bereich Johannisberg	3. Bereich Nahetal	4. Bereich Bingen	7. Bereich Mittelhaardt/ Deutsche Weinstrasse	
			5. Bereich Nierstein		TOTAL DISTANCE NORTH TO SOUTH 89KM (55 MILES)
			6. Bereich Wonnegau	8. Bereich Südliche Weinstrasse	— BEREICH BOUNDARIES
					VINEYARDS

0 km 2 4
0 miles 2

AHR & MITTELRHEIN

RED GRAPES
Over 60 per cent of the plantings in the Ahr are Spätburgunder. Blauer Portugieser takes up 10 per cent. The Mittelrhein has 9 per cent Spätburgunder.

WHITE GRAPES
Riesling is the main white grape in the Ahr, but still comprises only 7 per cent of plantings. Mittelrhein vines are mostly Riesling and there is some Müller-Thurgau and Kerner.

CLIMATE
The climate is cool and northerly, but the Eifel hills to the north-west offer shelter in the Ahr, and steep valley sides provide shelter in the Mittelrhein.

SOIL
There is mainly loess in the Lower Ahr and Devonian slate in the Upper Ahr. The Mittelrhein is largely quartzite and slate on clay. There is some volcanic soil in the north.

ASPECT
In the Ahr most vines are on river valley slopes, on both the north and south banks, and are often terraced. Mittelrhein vines are on steep valley sides.

QUALITY WINE
REGIONS AND
BEREICHS
AHR

— Bereich
Walporzheim/
Ahrtal

MITTELRHEIN

— Bereich
Siebengebirge

— Bereich
Loreley

☐ OVER 500M (1640FT)

☐ OVER 200M (656FT)

W̲E̲ ̲W̲A̲N̲T̲ ̲D̲I̲F̲F̲E̲R̲E̲N̲T̲ ̲T̲H̲I̲N̲G̲S̲ ̲F̲R̲O̲M̲ ̲W̲I̲N̲E̲S̲ at different times. Sometimes we want a serious wine to sit over with friends, or something rich and complex for a special occasion. Sometimes we want something for gulping with pasta. And sometimes, particularly when we're on holiday, we want something local that we will see nowhere else, and we want to drink it as the sun sets over the hills and while the winemaker serves us some home-made sausage for supper.

Luckily, enough people in Bonn and Koblenz find themselves in this last mood pretty often, often enough to ensure the survival (so far) of the vineyards of the Ahr and Mittelrhein. They are both tourist areas kept alive by people drinking the wines on the spot. Happily both regions are wild and stunningly beautiful: the Rhine here is dotted with castles, the villages are old and often unspoilt and the air is full of legends of the Lorelei and of Siegfried. You'd feel cheated if the local wine wasn't pretty unusual.

AHR

In the Ahr, the wine is so unusual that it's red. To make red wine in what was, before re-unification, Germany's most northerly wine region, seems odd to say the least. Geography is the secret. Certainly, these are not big, beefy reds of the type one expects from, say, Spain or Italy, but there has nevertheless been a big change in styles here. Ahr reds used to be light, pale and sweetish: now they are bone dry, much deeper in colour and with decidedly more tannin. Indeed almost too serious to down by the jugful at a tavern table.

If the Ahr flowed in a straight eastwards line to join the Rhine it would be perfect: it would mean a wall of south-facing vines. As it is, the river takes a more convoluted path, flowing sometimes south to north and sometimes in any direction you care to name. Vines grow on both banks: some of the vineyards face south, some east, some west. And the soil, at least in the Upper Ahr, is the same Devonian slate that holds the heat in the Middle Mosel.

The equation is also the same: steep slopes plus slate soil plus warmth reflected off the river equals good wine. The difference is that in the Ahr the Spätburgunder gets the best spots. This is mostly because red wines are the Ahr's speciality: if a region has a speciality it doesn't change it lightly. The sites that are good for Spätburgunder would also be good for Riesling, but red wine has rarity value in Germany and Riesling doesn't. So Spätburgunder accounts for over half the vines in the Ahr; Blauer Portugieser has another 9 per cent and Riesling less than 7 per cent. The Portugieser, which makes more neutral reds than Spätburgunder, used to be more widely planted than the latter, but the trend towards tasty dry reds is driving it out of the region.

The biggest Spätburgunders come from the lower reaches of the Ahr, where the heat-retaining loess topsoil gives softer wines. Heppingen and Heimersheim produce notable examples. Further upstream the Devonian slate gives more structure and splendidly ripe wines. Overall, 93 per cent of vineyards in the Ahr slope 20 per cent or more and are often terraced: only four per cent are flat. These are advantages when it comes to wine quality, but today fewer and fewer young people want to commit their working lives to the unrelenting toil of such steep vineyards. Even so, while the tourists come you can make a good living, and in 2005 there were 520ha (1285 acres) planted, up from 478ha (1182 acres) in 1992.

MITTELRHEIN

The Mittelrhein must be dead envious. Here on the banks of the Rhine between just north of Bingen and Bonn, Riesling is the grape they most want to grow. It covers 68 per cent of these high, inaccessible, perching vineyards and, at its best, the wine can be very good. But the Mittelrhein has few of the advantages of the Ahr. For one thing, it is overshadowed by the fame of the nearby Rheingau. For another, the river here flows north-west or north, and often only where there are side valleys – at Bacharach, Oberwesel and Niederheimbach – are there really good south-facing slopes. Leubsdorf and Hammerstein, with their west- and south-west-facing sites, are also sheltered and warm. And the little tributary of the Lahn, where it flows north-west before joining the Rhine, provides some good sites.

In the southern part, between Boppard and Bacharach, things are easier. There is slate soil, and warmth and mist near the river even encourage the growth of noble rot. Bacharach has some good south and south-east-facing slopes and, from the Bopparder Hamm vineyard, Beerenauslesen wines are not unusual. There is indeed something of a quality renaissance in both Boppard and Bacharach.

Nevertheless, viticulture is a declining industry in the Mittelrhein. At the end of World War Two there were 1200ha (2965 acres) of vineyards planted on these impossibly steep slopes overlooking the river. By 1992 there were 700ha (1730 acres), and by 2005 there were just 455ha (1124 acres). The terraces are falling into disuse; the younger generation prefers to abandon winemaking and seek easier work in the cities. The industry is dying from the north, in the less favoured areas of the Mittelrhein, where the wines are leaner, more attentuated and more acidic.

However, the tourists keep coming, drawn by the legendary beauty of this part of the Rhine Valley. As in the Ahr, they want a drink when they get there and the vineyard area will presumably shrink to a level at which tourism can keep it going.

NORDRHEIN-WESTFALEN

BONN

KÖNIGSWINTER

DERNAU   MARIENTHAL
MAYSCHOSS   BAD NEUENAHR-AHRWEILER
HEIMERSHEIM   HEPPINGEN
Ahr   LEUBSDORF

HAMMERSTEIN
LEUTESDORF

ANDERNACH

RHEINLAND-PFALZ   Rhein

KOBLENZ   VALLENDAR

Mosel   LAHNSTEIN   DAUSENAU   Lahn
BRAUBACH
BOPPARD

ST GOAR   ST GOARSHAUSEN

OBERWESEL

STEEG   BACHARACH
OBERDIEBACH   HESSEN
NIEDERHEIMBACH

TRECHTINGSHAUSEN

N   Rhein
0 km   25   BINGEN
0 miles   10   Nahe

RHEINGAU

THE ROMANS WERE HERE. So, later, were the Cistercians. So, later still, was Queen Victoria, though she only stayed for lunch. Thomas Jefferson came as well, but unlike Queen Victoria he didn't get a vineyard named after him. One reason that the region attracted so many visitors down the centuries was because good wine could be made here. The reason they kept on coming was because great wine was being made, year after year, in the vineyards above and between a string of villages bordering one particular stretch of the Rhine – the great and historic Rheingau.

Standing high up the slopes on Kiedrich or clinging to the steep ledges above Rüdesheim, imagining the sun rising, reaching its zenith and then fading to a warm evening glow without ever once leaving the great Rheingau vineyards in the shade, it's easy to see why the ancients fell for it. 'The vine loves an open hill', Virgil wrote – and here the vine gets over 30km (19 miles) of consistently sun-soaked open slopes.

The Rheingau is all about slopes and it is a land of Riesling. These slopes, except in parts of Rüdesheim where the Rhine narrows as it turns northwards again, aren't as steep as they are in the Middle Mosel and there's not quite as much Riesling – 78 per cent of 3036ha (7502 acres) of vineyards. Just over 12 per cent of the vines in the Rheingau are Spätburgunder and this is mostly found in just one commune, Assmannshausen, the first village after the Rhine has turned north again. Just under 2 per cent of the vines are the commercial, high-yielding, accountant's delight, Müller-Thurgau. But grapes and slopes don't, on their own, produce great wine regions. The answer to what makes the Rheingau special is very simple: solid rock.

The Rhine flows more or less northwards through southern Germany until suddenly, at Wiesbaden, it comes up against the Taunus mountains. The river finds its route to the north blocked so it swings westwards and only 32km (20 miles) later, at Rüdesheim, is it able to turn north again. The heart of the Rheingau is here, along the stretch of the river that flows west with the vines planted on the south-facing slopes of the Taunus overlooking the river.

LOCAL CLIMATES AND WINE STYLES

It was the Cistercians, settled in the monastery at Kloster Eberbach at Eltville, who in the 12th and 13th centuries cleared much of the forest from these slopes above the Rhine. No vineyard is higher than 300m (984ft): and this altitude is only reached by the nearby Hendelberg vineyard in Hallgarten. This is about as high as you can get before the wind and the cold become too much for the grapes to ripen properly. But the steeper, higher vineyards do benefit from more sunlight than the lower ones. The Rheingau is fairly cool for viticulture, but the Taunus mountains keep the north and east winds off the vineyards, and the Rhine about 800m (half-a-mile) wide here, reflects the sun back on to the vines.

The river also encourages the formation of mists which, on warm autumn days, foster the development of *Botrytis cinerea*: nobly rotten sweet wines therefore tend to come from the lower vineyards. Some growers reckon that the middle part of the slope has the best of all possible worlds. It is still within range of the moderating effect of the Rhine – the very top vineyards miss out on this – but there is no danger, as there is at the foot of the slopes, of too much humidity (which can encourage rot of the wrong sort) or of the vines getting waterlogged in a wet year.

But if the nobly rotten wines come from the lower vineyards, so, paradoxically, do Eisweins, although the conditions that produce them are very different. For Eiswein, mists and noble rot are a distraction: what is needed are healthy grapes with no rot, plus frost. Lots and lots of frost – and the lower-lying vineyards here are the most susceptible to frost. The State Domaine at Eltville has indeed made a practice of making Eiswein every year, though for most producers it is a rarer treat. It is an expensive one, too: many growers admit that in spite of the high prices they can charge for Eiswein, since it is extremely fashionable in Germany, they still don't expect to make a profit from it. They make Eiswein as a badge of pride.

The lower slopes, too, yield the heaviest, richest wines; the upper slopes give more delicacy and elegance. Partly this is to do with temperature, and partly it is to do with soil, since the richer soils tend to be further down the slope. At the top of the slopes the soils are more eroded and weathered; there is quartzite and weathered slate here. In the middle there is marl, and at the bottom there is loam, loess, marl and sandy gravel. But with the Rheingau able to boast some 286 different soils (according to one estimate), all suitable for Riesling, generalizations are difficult. And, in spite of the fact that the Riesling grape tends to reflect the soil in its flavour, the wines of the Rheingau are marked more by their similarities than their differences.

WINE VILLAGES

The Rheingau begins just east of Wiesbaden with the large village of Hochheim, which is not on the Rhine at all. Instead it sits on the right bank of the Main river just before its confluence with the Rhine and, although it has lent an abbreviation of its name – 'hock' – to the English language as a name for all Rhine wine, it is by no means the most typical of Rheingau villages. For a start, Hochheim does not benefit from the shelter of the Taunus mountains, though it is nevertheless warm, partly because of the influence of two rivers, the Main and the Rhine, and partly because of its low altitude. Its vineyard slopes are gentle, and it has limestone in its soil as well as the more usual Rheingau sand and loess. Its wines are earthy and rich. This is where Queen Victoria stopped for a picnic to watch the harvesters at work, one fine day in 1850, and where a vineyard owner with a sharp eye for publicity asked if he could name a vineyard after her: the 5-ha (12-acre) Königin Victoriaberg which faces south over the Main.

 RED GRAPES
There is 12 per cent of Spätburgunder, mainly at Assmannshausen.

WHITE GRAPES
Rheingau Riesling has been famous for centuries and accounts for 78 per cent of the vineyards. There are tiny amounts of Müller-Thurgau and other varieties.

CLIMATE
The relatively cool climate benefits from the proximity of the Rhine which reflects heat back onto the vineyards.

SOIL
The Rheingau has a wide range of soils, partly depending on the altitude. The higher sites have quartzite and weathered slate; the mid slopes include patches of marl; and the lower sites have loam, loess, marl and sandy gravel. There is blue phyllite slate at Assmannshausen, Lorch, Kiedrich and Rauenthal.

ASPECT
The vineyards face south (south-west in Lorch and Assmannshausen) and are sheltered by the Taunus mountains.

The Rheingau's vineyards are spread out along gentle slopes to the north of the Rhine. Here the Klosterlay vineyard sits just above the village of Rüdesheim and is sheltered by the forest along the top of the slope.

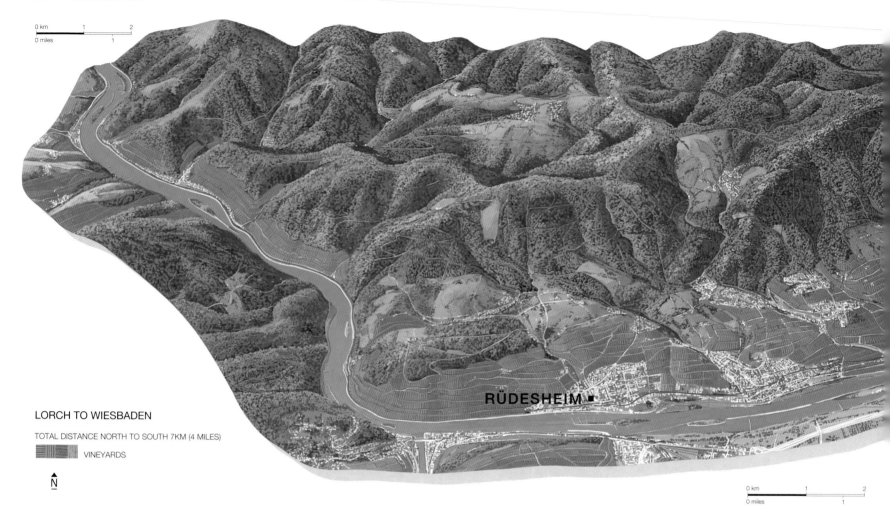

0 km 1 2
0 miles 1

LORCH TO WIESBADEN

TOTAL DISTANCE NORTH TO SOUTH 7KM (4 MILES)

VINEYARDS

RÜDESHEIM ■

N

0 km 1 2
0 miles 1

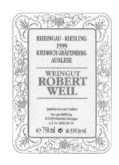

The curve of the river is occupied by Wiesbaden on one side and Mainz on the other and the two cities form a rather unlovely interruption to the landscape. But once out of Wiesbaden's suburbs it's a straight run westwards past some of the most famous names in German wine.

The Taunus range begins quietly, with shallow slopes above Walluf and Eltville, which is the home of the important State Domaine. But the great vineyards appear almost immediately, scattered here and there at different altitudes: Wallufer Walkenberg and Eltviller Sonnenberg are just above their respective towns, but Kiedricher Gräfenberg is right up high, and the suntrap of Erbacher Marcobrunn, a fine vineyard which has made some of the Rheingau's richest, weightiest Rieslings for centuries, is way down by the river. Oestricher Doosberg is low down but Schloss Vollrads is quite high. Schloss Johannisberg is situated about midway up the slope and Hattenheimer Rheingarten and Winkeler Jesuitengarten are so close to the river it's a wonder they're not standing in water.

The town of Johannisberg, with its historic Schloss Johannisberg wine estate, has long been famous – probably too famous for its own good in that it has involuntarily lent its name to the Americans who call Riesling 'Johannisberg Riesling', as well as having its name summarily adopted for the single Bereich, the Bereich Johannisberg, that covers the whole Rheingau.

By Geisenheim, home of a famous wine school and research institute that has devoted itself, among other tasks, to researching new grape crosses that can stand up to Germany's uncompromising climate, the slopes are distinctly steep. They continue to steepen all the way past Rüdesheim, while the river narrows and gathers itself for one final surge northwards. Here the Taunus mountains push in close to the river, forcing the vineyards onto steep terraces. These steepest vineyards take the name of Berg as a prefix: Berg Roseneck, Berg Rottland, Berg Schlossberg and Berg Kaisersteinfels. Here some of the richest, ripest wines in all the Rheingau are made. These hot vineyards that face south across the Rhine to Bingen are also very well

drained, making for low yields of around 50 hectolitres per hectare and the ability to shine in better years. The Rüdesheim hill is slate, but this is not the same Devonian slate of the Mosel. Nevertheless, it imparts its inimitable smoky taste to the wines.

After Rüdesheim the wines become lighter and slatier, sometimes with a flinty taste. This is where the river swings north again and we leave behind the remarkable south-facing stretch of vineyards that have lasted all the way from Wiesbaden. In Assmannshausen, Spätburgunder is the speciality. Local palates (and purses) rate it highly. The last village of the Rheingau is Lorch, where the wines (white again) begin to take on something of the lean acidity of the Mittelrhein that faces this part of the Rheingau across the river. The Rheingau straggles up the right bank for a few more miles past Lorchhausen.

GREAT WINE ESTATES

There is still one other reason why the Rheingau is so famous throughout the world, and it has nothing to do with geography and climate – at least, not directly. It is the presence of large, rich aristocratic estates, lying almost shoulder to shoulder along this stretch of the Rhine – estates like Schloss Johannisberg, Schloss Schönborn, Schloss Reinhartshausen and others, many of them dating back to the Middle Ages or even earlier. These are the Rheingau names that everyone knows and they do indeed have some splendid vineyards.

But there are around a thousand vine-growing families in the Rheingau, dividing a total of 3216ha (7947 acres) of vineyards between them, and with nearly all the aristocratic estates underperforming to some degree, and some shockingly so, it is the bourgeois estates that are currently forging ahead with first-class quality. The leading names in the Rheingau today are Georg Breuer, Peter Jakob Kühn, Johannishof, Josef Leitz, Franz Künstler, Robert Weil and Josef Spreitzer: and not a prince among them. And it's high time the great estates took note.

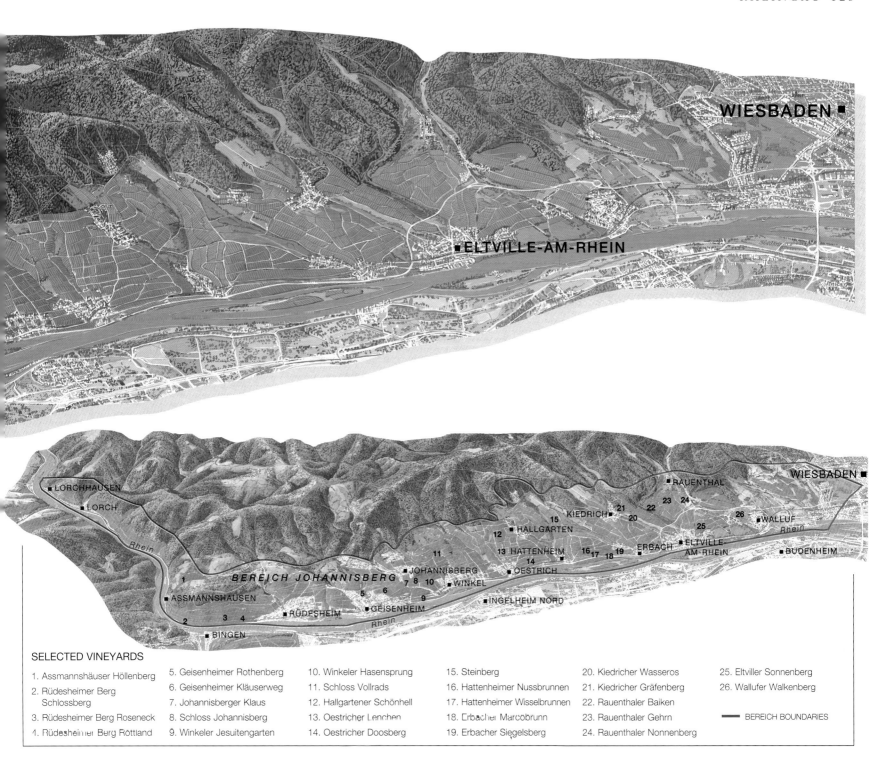

SELECTED VINEYARDS

1. Assmannshäuser Höllenberg	5. Geisenheimer Rothenberg	10. Winkeler Hasensprung	15. Steinberg	20. Kiedricher Wasseros	25. Eltviller Sonnenberg
2. Rüdesheimer Berg Schlossberg	6. Geisenheimer Kläuserweg	11. Schloss Vollrads	16. Hattenheimer Nussbrunnen	21. Kiedricher Gräfenberg	26. Wallufer Walkenberg
3. Rüdesheimer Berg Roseneck	7. Johannisberger Klaus	12. Hallgartener Schönhell	17. Hattenheimer Wisselbrunnen	22. Rauenthaler Baiken	
4. Rüdesheimer Berg Rottland	8. Schloss Johannisberg	13. Oestricher Lenchen	18. Erbacher Marcobrunn	23. Rauenthaler Gehrn	━━━ BEREICH BOUNDARIES
	9. Winkeler Jesuitengarten	14. Oestricher Doosberg	19. Erbacher Siegelsberg	24. Rauenthaler Nonnenberg	

WHERE THE VINEYARDS ARE *The map shows the heart of the Rheingau west of Wiesbaden. Here the Rhine is broad and dotted with islands, some of which have vines. But the river is the southern boundary of the Rheingau: any vines that creep up to the edge of the south bank near Bingen are in the Rheinhessen; the few on the map in the far south-western corner, on the left bank of the Nahe, are in the Nahe region.*

The Rheingau itself is a monoculture. As soon as the urban sprawl west of Wiesbaden comes to an end, vines begin, colonizing every likely slope. And just 3 or 4km (2 miles) away from the river the Taunus mountains begin in earnest, rearing high above the vineyards. Up here it is too cold for the vine; instead, the mountains shelter the lower slopes.

The list of top Rheingau vineyards on the map is not comprehensive and, just as in Burgundy, not all of every vineyard is of equal quality. Just 18ha (45 acres) of the 57-ha (140-acre) Lorcher Kapellenberg are top-ranking, and of Winkeler Hasensprung's 104ha (257 acres), only 20ha (49 acres) are first class. But all 5ha (12 acres) of Erbacher Marcobrunn make the grade. Other vineyards judged excellent throughout are Johannisberger Klaus and Hattenheimer Nussbrunnen. Some 30 per cent of the Rheingau is included in the new Erstes Gewächs (First Growth) classification of top sites.

THE RHEINGAU SOILS

Riesling is the predominant grape variety in the Rheingau region, producing particularly excellent wines on the higher slopes where the soil is well-drained. These wines, such as those from the famous Schloss Johannisberg, can take on a slaty taste from the soil. The lower slopes produce fuller-bodied Rieslings from the slightly heavier calcareous soils.

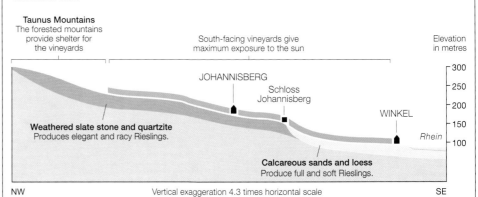

Taunus Mountains
The forested mountains provide shelter for the vineyards

South-facing vineyards give maximum exposure to the sun

Elevation in metres

JOHANNISBERG
Schloss Johannisberg
WINKEL
Rhein

Weathered slate stone and quartzite
Produces elegant and racy Rieslings.

Calcareous sands and loess
Produce full and soft Rieslings.

NW
Vertical exaggeration 4.3 times horizontal scale
SE

300 / 250 / 200 / 150 / 100

NAHE

RED GRAPES
There are tiny amounts of Spätburgunder, Portugieser and Domfelder.

WHITE GRAPES
Most Nahe wines are white – Riesling is one-quarter of all plantings. Müller-Thurgau, Silvaner and Kerner are other varieties.

CLIMATE
The Nahe is temperate and sunny. The vineyards are protected by the Soonwald forest and the Hunsrück hills to the north-west, but still get adequate rain.

SOIL
The region has many soil types: in the Middle and Upper Nahe there are porphyry, basalt, quartzite and coloured sandstone – the best for Riesling – and others. In the lower reaches soils include quartzite and slate.

ASPECT
Vines grow at 100–300m (328–984ft) and there are many protected south-facing sites on river valley slopes.

I'M ALWAYS PUZZLED BY THE NAHE. Some of the greatest German wines I've ever drunk have come from this tributary of the Rhine. They can be as complex and rich as the best of the Rheingau, with a flash of mineral fieriness, as though the metals once mined along these river banks have somehow got into the wine. The Nahe has vineyard sites as unlikely in their steepness, and growers as good as anywhere in Germany. So why do people forget about it?

I think it suffers from an identity crisis. The most famous German wine regions can be summarized in a few words: the Mosel is slate and floral delicacy, the Rheingau rich and complex, Baden is reds and the Pinot family, the Rheinhessen, all too often, is cheap bulk wine. Try and sum up the Nahe and all you can do is refer to other places. The wine is a bit like the Rheingau, but it's a bit like the Mosel, too. Riesling, with 25 per cent of the vineyard, has overtaken the undistinguished Müller-Thurgau as the most widely planted grape. Müller-Thurgau is now down to 13 per cent and the rest is made up of grapes like Silvaner and Kerner. In addition, Riesling wasn't planted there at all until the 19th century and, until the 1930s, most Nahe wine was sold under the generic heading of Rhine wine. Much of it was shipped to the Rhine and Mosel for blending, as well; in short, not much was bottled under its own regional name.

Many of the Nahe vineyards are scattered, though the stretch south-west of Bad Kreuznach, from the Traiser Rotenfels to the village of Schlossböckelheim, is the Nahe's answer to the great swathes of vineyard one sees in the Mosel

or Rheingau. The village of Norheim in the middle of this stretch used to be pretty uneven in quality, but these days excellent wines are being produced from its top sites.

Most of the vineyards are on quite gentle slopes, with only about a quarter managing real drama: the most spectacular wine scenery in the Nahe is around the villages of Traisen, with its dramatic Rotenfels precipice, and Schlossböckelheim. This is where most of the tiny band of well-known growers congregate. But the Nahe is a pretty big region stretching from the narrow valley above Schlossböckelheim to the broader reaches in the north near Bingen. Most village names, however, are all but unknown.

The Nahe rises in the Hunsrück hills and flows eastwards, then turns north to join the Rhine at Bingen. The Nahe's 4005ha (9896 acres) of vineyards are scattered here and there, not just along the Nahe itself, but also along and around some of its tributaries.

BINGEN TO SCHLOSSBÖCKELHEIM

TOTAL DISTANCE
NORTH TO SOUTH
22KM (13½ MILES)

VINEYARDS

N

BINGEN

BAD KREUZNACH

0 km   1   2
0 miles   1

The climate is warm and sunny and the vineyards are generally sheltered. It's an area of mixed farming, too, so the vine isn't considered to be God as it is in the Rheingau just across the Rhine from Bingen. But we must stick to the riverbanks to understand the character of Nahe wines.

WINE VILLAGES

In the uppermost reaches of the river the wines can be intense – particularly from producers such as Emrich-Schönleber. But they are less dramatic than those from further downstream, reflecting the gentler, less dramatic landscape – as the slopes steepen, so the wines become tenser and more taut, until suddenly, at Schlossböckelheim, they are as great as the very best in Germany. From here right up to Bad Kreuznach is the heart of the Nahe. This is where its spicy,

WHERE THE VINEYARDS ARE *This map shows the finest part of the Nahe. The Rhine is up at the top, with the Rheingau vineyards along the north bank. The Nahe vineyards, west of Bingen on the south bank, do their best to imitate the perfect southerly exposure of those Rheingau slopes in the river bend, but they don't have the advantage of a broad expanse of water to reflect heat back on to them.*

Going up the Nahe from Bingen, you can see how the vineyards seek out south-facing slopes along the small tributaries. Look at the ideal southerly exposure of Dorsheimer Pittermänchen or the south-west-facing expanses of Wallhäuser Felseneck or Johannisberg. The tributaries play a vital part; without them this smallish region would be tiny indeed. Only after Bad Kreuznach do the vines begin seriously to follow the Nahe itself – and from there until Schlossböckelheim they are virtually inseparable.

The little village of Traisen tucks itself just behind Norheim; it's not actually on the river at all. That way its best sites, the Bastei and the Rotenfels, have a clear river view: you can see on the map how dramatic they are, and how they rear high above the water. At Norheim the Dellchen and Kafels vineyards face south-west and catch the afternoon sun; at Niederhausen the Felsensteyer site faces south-east and warms up early in the morning sun. And further up the Nahe at Schlossböckelheim you can see the 14ha (35 acres) of the Kupfergrube vineyard, facing south-south-east and tremendously steep. It's sheltered by the woods above and around it and wines from the Kupfergrube are among the most expensive of the region.

minerally, fiery character is found, but as is so often the case, it's quite a small heart. For about 8km (5 miles) of river the wines are potentially great; on either side of this stretch of the Nahe they are, generally, merely very good.

The Kupfergrube vineyard at Schlossböckelheim used to be a copper mine (see photo) – it yielded ore until the beginning of the 20th century – and it must have taken a leap of the imagination on the part of the then director of what used to be the State Domaine of Niederhausen-Schlossböckelheim to see it as anything other than a sheer rockface of scrub and stone. Convict labour cleared the scrub and built the incredibly steep slopes out of the rocky hillside before a single vine could be planted. But the south-west exposure was always too good to waste on a mere mine, and the complex, heat-retaining soil – colourful, volcanic porphyry – produces long-lived Rieslings. The Kupfergrube is not, however, the region's top site. For this the laurels go to Niederhäuser Hermannshöhle, which was placed first in a Prussian classification of 1901 – second place in this classification was given to Schlossböckelheimer Felsenberg.

Porphyry and many other igneous rocks continue in the soil through Oberhausen and beyond, and the vineyards curve with the river, facing south-west, south or south-east, and sometimes crossing over to the south bank. It is, however, the north bank that supplies the suntraps and the wonderful Riesling sites of Schlossböckelheim, Niederhausen and Norheim. At Traisen the porphyry of the Traiser Rotenfels rears higher, it is said, than any other cliff in Europe north of the Alps and at its foot you will find a 2-ha (5-acre) ledge of extremely steep earth and scree: the leavings of the Rotenfels over the years, if you like, which is the perfect suntrap of the Traiser Bastei vineyard. Its Riesling vines yield as little as 14 supremely good hectolitres per hectare. Noble rot occurs in these warm vineyards, though not every year. Auslesen are not uncommon, Beerenauslesen and above rather rarer: they're not here for the taking as they can sometimes be in the Rheingau.

At Bad Kreuznach, which has some excellent vineyards jutting out above the town, we pass into the Lower Nahe where the hills are more gentle and the wines fuller, fatter and a little less focused. Many of the vineyards are along the tributaries to the west of the Nahe itself, such as the Guldenbach and the Gräfenbach. The villages of Wallhausen, Roxheim, Dorsheim and Münster-Sarmsheim have good sites, and some tremendous wines. One Bereich, the Bereich Nahetal, now covers the whole region.

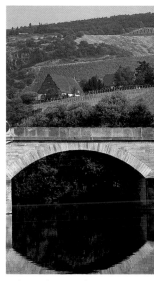

Nahe Rieslings are famous for their mineral tang: this would certainly make sense for Schlossböckelheim's Kupfergrube (copper mine) vineyard which was planted on the site of an old copper mine a century ago.

SELECTED VINEYARDS

1. Münsterer Dautenpflänzer
2. Münsterer Pittersberg
3. Dorsheimer Pittermännchen
4. Dorsheimer Goldloch
5. Dorsheimer Burgberg
6. Laubenheimer St Remigiusberg
7. Langenlonsheimer Löhrer Berg
8. Wallhäuser Johannisberg
9. Roxheimer Berg
10. Winzenheimer Rosenheck
11. Kreuznacher Brückes
12. Kreuznacher Krötenpfuhl
13. Kreuznacher Kahlenberg
14. Bad Münsterer Felseneck
15. Traiser Bastei
16. Traiser Rotenfels
17. Norheimer Kirschheck
18. Norheimer Dellchen
19. Norheimer Kafels
20. Niederhäuser Felsensteyer
21. Niederhäuser Hermannshöhle
22. Oberhaüser Brücke
23. Niederhäuser Hermannsberg
24. Schlossböckelheimer Kupfergrube
25. Schlossböckelheimer Felsenberg
26. Schlossböckelheimer Königsfels
27. Schlossböckelheimer in den Felsen

▬ BEREICH BOUNDARY

RHEINHESSEN

RED GRAPES
Dornfelder has overtaken
Portugieser to become the
most important red variety
(but is still only 13 per cent).
There is also some
Spätburgunder.

WHITE GRAPES
Müller-Thurgau dominates
with 16 per cent of the vines;
Riesling and Silvaner come
next, followed by Kerner and
Scheurebe.

CLIMATE
A temperate climate with
mainly dry autumns. The
Taunus mountains and the
Odenwald forest to the north
give some shelter, as do the
Hunsrück hills and Pfalzer
Wald to the west. The
Rheinfront sites are
particularly sheltered.

SOIL
A wide variety of fertile soils,
mainly loess but also limestone,
sandy marl, quartzite, red slate
and silty clay.

ASPECT
The Rheinfront faces east or
south-east with vines up to
150m (492ft); in hillier parts of
the hinterland they may go up
to 300m (984ft), but the rest
of the region is relatively flat.

I N THE FIRST EDITION OF THIS ATLAS I described the Rheinhessen as
a region being pulled in two directions. On the one
hand there is good quality: low yields, vines that are generally
Riesling or the potentially excellent Silvaner, steep sites and careful
viticulture, meticulous winemaking and a top grower's name on
the label. On the other hand there are (or were) the bulk blends:
usually Müller-Thurgau and Kerner, from flattish vineyards that
produced Germany's equivalent of the wine lake. Well, that
particular tug-of-war now seems to have been resolved – and for
once it's the bad guys who have landed in a heap in the mud.

What happened was that the bottom fell out of the market
for Liebfraumilch and the like – who'd have thought it,
after all these years? As a result, more and more producers have
been driven to start producing decent dry wine. These may
still come from a merchant house: merchant houses are vital in the
Rheinhessen. But bulk prices for the sugar-water sold under the
name of Liebfraumilch and its equivalents have fallen through the
floor, and there are now almost no buyers. Hip hip hooray. Now,
I'm not claiming that you'll never see another bottle of
Liebfraumilch. But that style is on its way out in a big way. Let's
hope it stays out.

That the Rheinhessen was so efficient at producing this style was
partly a result of its geography: it's a warm region, and because
mechanical harvesters are feasible on these gentle slopes,
production costs can be very low. These exact same factors also
make it efficient at producing inexpensive dry wines, which makes
me hope that what we're seeing is long-term change and not just a
blip in the market.

RHEINFRONT
The Rheinfront, Rheinhessen's best known area, is a string of
villages along the west bank of the Rhine, south of Mainz.
From the north, they are Bodenheim, Nackenheim, Nierstein,
Oppenheim, Dienheim, Ludwigshöhe, Guntersblum, Alsheim and
Mettenheim. These villages benefit from the fact that the land rises
along this stretch of the bank and provides sloping vineyards that
overlook the river to the east and south-east. The reddish soil is
also important. It's a kind of red slate known in German as
Rotliegendes, and it produces the great Rieslings of Nierstein and
Nackenheim from some of the best vineyards in the whole Rhine
Valley. It appears in other places in Germany too, notably in Erden
and Ürzig on the Mosel. Oppenheim also benefits from the
northern end of a ridge of limestone that runs north from Alsheim.
Vines are grown here at up to 150m (492ft) above sea level and the
slopes have a significant incline.

Rieslings from the Rheinfront can be as minerally
and complex as the best of the Rheingau, though there is always a
little extra breadth to them, an extra touch of softness. The sad
thing is that at the moment there is still only a handful of
growers exploiting the vineyards' great potential. In dry years
Oppenheim, with its more gently sloping vineyards and
greater access to moisture, is the best bet; Nierstein gains
concentration in wetter years.

OTHER WINE AREAS
After the Rheinfront the other quality areas in the
Rheinhessen are south-east of Bingen, in the
north-west corner of the region, where the
river Nahe meets the Rhine at Ingelheim,
and in Westhofen and Flörsheim-Dalsheim
in the south-east near the city of Worms (below the
right-hand corner of our map). The vineyards of Bingen don't

overlook either of the local rivers: instead they face south, on slopes
of red quartzite that gives the wines smoky depth and powerful
fruit. In nearby Ingelheim, facing the Rheingau, the Riesling and
Silvaner give way to Spätburgunder, though the red wines
that result are light and raspberryish, rather than dark and sturdy.
It was from his palace here that the Emperor Charlemagne is
reputed to have looked across at the slopes of Johannisberg, in
what is now the Rheingau, and noted the slopes where the snow
melted first. He then ordered vines to be planted there. The
Westhofen and Flörsheim-Dalsheim vineyards have started making
a name for quality much more recently, but their Rieslings, both
dry and sweet, are encouragingly good. In Westhofen look out for
Philipp Wittmann and for the Keller family in Flörsheim-Dalsheim.

Even apart from these villages, Rheinhessen's hinterland is not
devoid of good wines. But the inland hills are cooler than the river
valleys, the soil is not so quickly warmed by the sun, and good
wines tend to be more the result of an individual grower's
determination than an obvious gift of nature. Some good hillsides
are to be found in the west, which the locals regard, rather
optimistically, as their version of Switzerland. Vines can be found
up to 300m (984ft) here, which most definitely does not count as
'high altitude'. The central part of the Rheinhessen is known as
Hügelland or hill country and is where the three Bereichs (Bingen in
the north-west, Nierstein in the north-east and Wonnegau west of
Worms) meet.

GRAPE VARIETIES
Müller-Thurgau is the workhorse grape of the Rheinhessen;
although declining, it still covers 16 per cent of the vineyards.

SELECTED VINEYARDS

1. Nackenheimer Rothenberg
2. Niersteiner Pettenthal
3. Niersteiner Brudersberg
4. Niersteiner Hipping
5. Niersteiner Kranzberg
6. Niersteiner Glöck
7. Niersteiner Ölberg
8. Niersteiner Heiligenbaum
9. Niersteiner Orbel
10. Oppenheimer Herrenberg
11. Oppenheimer Sackträger
12. Oppenheimer Kreuz
13. Dienheimer Tafelstein

— BEREICH BOUNDARY

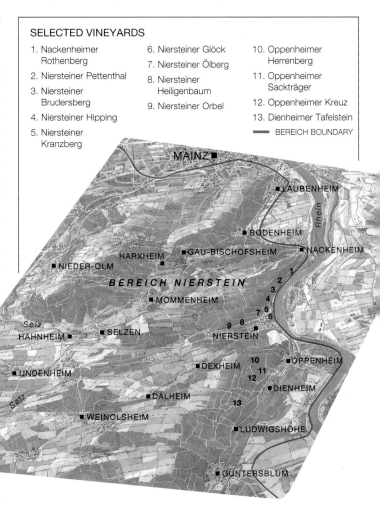

Riesling, in fact, covers just 10 per cent of the Rheinhessen's 25,179ha (62,216 acres), but tends to dominate the better sites. Next comes Silvaner (potentially of high quality, often made dry, but with a falling share – now only 9 per cent – of the land under vine) and the aromatic Kerner. Many of Germany's aromatic, early-ripening new crosses such as Scheurebe were actually developed in the Rheinhessen and as a result they are popular with the Rheinhessen growers, most of whom are part time with only a few hectares of vines and sell their grapes to co-operatives. But the new *trocken* or dry Rheinhessen wines tend to be made from Riesling, Silvaner, Müller-Thurgau (sometimes sold under its alias of Rivaner), Weissburgunder and Grauburgunder, so in the future we may see a decrease in the amount of more heavily scented grapes like Bacchus.

Ambitious growers realize the lazy gravy-train of the sweetish Liebfraumilch is past and a much better future is beckoning. Thirty-two per cent of the wine made in the Rheinhessen is now dry, compared to only 22 per cent in 2001. As well as Liebfraumilch the off-dry and sweeter wine styles are in decline here too.

WHERE THE VINEYARDS ARE *It all looks rather idyllic on the map. Once south of the urban sprawl of Mainz, the Rheinhessen becomes gentle and bucolic. There are fields of maize and other cereals; there are woods and small villages, and the broad Rhine ambles northwards along the eastern edge. Even the Rheinfront, probably the Rheinhessen's best-known area, doesn't look all that dramatic, compared to some wine landscapes.*

The villages facing the Rhine along the Rheinfront benefit from sloping land facing east and south-east over the river and soils on which Riesling thrives. Nierstein, the centre of the Rheinfront, has some wonderful vineyard sites. It is famous also because of the abuse of its reputation: Nierstein has had to give its name to the Bereich covering vineyards all over the east of Rheinhessen. The Bereich accounts for about one-third of the region's wines, almost all of them unmemorable, while the growers in Nierstein itself struggle to maintain their high reputation.

THE RHEINFRONT

TOTAL DISTANCE NORTH TO
SOUTH 22KM (13½ MILES)

▓▓▓ VINEYARDS

N

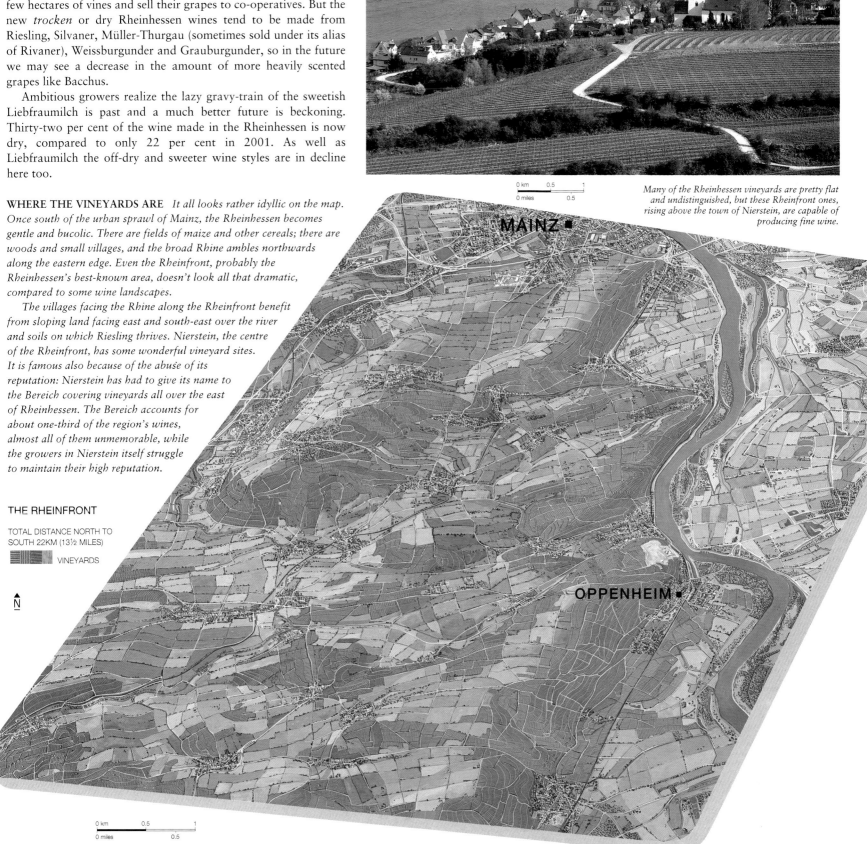

Many of the Rheinhessen vineyards are pretty flat and undistinguished, but these Rheinfront ones, rising above the town of Nierstein, are capable of producing fine wine.

MAINZ ■

OPPENHEIM ■

PFALZ

 RED GRAPES
Domfelder and Portugieser
are the main varieties with
some Spätburgunder.

 WHITE GRAPES
Mainly a white wine region,
the Pfalz has important
plantings of Riesling (21 per
cent). Müller-Thurgau is now
down to 10 per cent. Kerner
and Grauburgunder are other
important white varieties.

CLIMATE
This is Germany's sunniest and
driest wine region and it is
almost as warm as Baden.

 SOIL
The soils are very varied,
including loam, weathered
sandstone (especially near the
Haardt mountains), shelly
limestone, granite and slate.
The Südliche Weinstrasse has
heavier, more fertile soils than
the northern Mittelhaardt.

ASPECT
Vines are planted either on
the plain or on the gentle
east-facing slopes of the
Haardt mountains up to
250m (820ft).

*Many of the Pfalz vineyards
are on the flat but Schloss
Wachenheim's vineyard
slopes downward from the
castle crag.*

IE PFALZ – IT EVEN SOUNDS RICH and ripe and spicy. If you had
to guess, you might say it was a land of fertile soil and good
living, of rich food and rich wine to match. And you'd be right. In
fact, if you imagined something along the lines of Alsace you'd also
be right, because if you were to head due south off this map, you'd
soon find yourself crossing into France. The hills would be the
same and so would the river, (the Rhine), flowing northwards at
some distance from the hills. Many of the grapes would be the
same and many of the growers would have Germanic names, but
the language and the flavours, would be different.

The Haardt mountains, which rise up to the west of the Pfalz
vineyards and shelter them, are simply a northerly extension of
the Vosges. The soils are mixed as in Alsace and the villages as
picturesque, full of life-size gingerbread houses. Yet
something happens to the wines as you cross from France
into Germany. Even though today they are largely dry, they
are still indefinably German, just as Alsace wines, though
made from Germanic varieties, are indefinably French. Any
doubts that a winemaker's character is crucial to the wines
are dispelled on that short trip from Pfalz to Alsace. The
Pfalz is divided into two Bereichs, the Mittelhaardt/
Deutsche Weinstrasse north of Neustadt and the
Südliche Weinstrasse to the south. Traditionally, the
best wines come from the north.

SÜDLICHE WEINSTRASSE
The Südliche Weinstrasse was long viewed as the
home of fat, overcropped wines that quickly flopped
over into blowziness. More recently it was the source
of much Liebfraumilch: like the Rheinhessen, this part
of the Pfalz has flattish, easily worked vineyards and a large
proportion of high-yielding grapes like Müller-Thurgau and Kerner.
But times have changed, and those quiet, rural villages in southern
Pfalz are gaining a reputation for being among the most exciting
regions in Germany. Ambitious growers are determined to make
themselves a name for quality, while the collapse of the market for
Liebfraumilch and lookalikes is having its effect. Yes, high-yielding
vineyards are still there, but the discovery that field-grafting works in
the warm Pfalz climate means that good growers should soon be
grafting over to higher quality clones and varieties.

Generally it is even more fertile here than further north. Yields
can be high, often too high, from the heavy, lime-rich soils. When it
comes to grapes, think spiciness. There is not much Riesling,
therefore, but Weissburgunder, Pinot Gris (alias Grauburgunder)
and, particularly in the far south, Gewürztraminer. Silvaner, too, is
spicier here than elsewhere and Müller-Thurgau can be a veritable
pot-pourri. The best growers, of course, take only fairly low yields
from their grapes, ferment them dry, and then often break what used
to be an unwritten rule of German winemaking – they age their Pinot
family wines in new oak. But then oak suits the Pinot family well, so
long as it is applied with a light hand.

Gentle slopes (or no slopes at all) are usual for high-yielding
vineyards, but top ones, even in the South, are sloping, sometimes
steep. In Südliche Weinstrasse are small farmers who are only part-
time vine-growers (an average vineyard holding in the whole Pfalz is
less than a hectare); the big wine estates are in the Mittelhaardt.

THE MITTELHAARDT/DEUTSCHE WEINSTRASSE
Even though this is where the best Pfalz wine is made, results are still
mixed: the vineyards sprawl over the sandy river plain, and there's
plenty of bulk wine made here, too, but the stars are the string of
villages from Neustadt north to Wachenheim. Neustadt is not

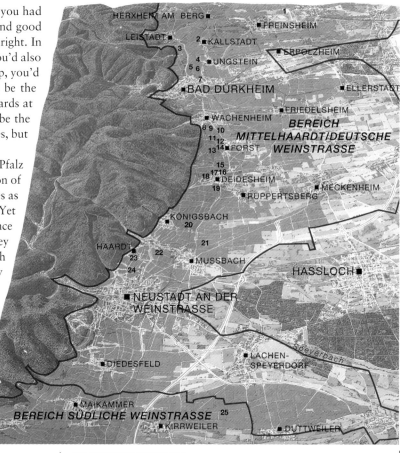

SELECTED VINEYARDS

1. Freinsheimer Goldberg
2. Kallstädter Saumagen
3. Kallstädter Annaberg
4. Ungsteiner Weilberg
5. Dürkheimer Spielberg
6. Ungsteiner Herrenberg
7. Dürkheimer Michelsberg
8. Wachenheimer Belz
9. Wachenheimer Rechbächel
10. Wachenheimer Goldbächel
11. Forster Pechstein
12. Forster Jesuitengarten
13. Forster Ungeheuer
14. Forster Kirchenstück

15. Deidesheimer Kalkofen
16. Deidesheimer Grainhübel
17. Deidesheimer Hohenmorgen
18. Deidesheimer Leinhöhle
19. Ruppertsberger Reiterpfad
20. Königsbacher Idig
21. Mussbacher Eselshaut
22. Gimmeldinger Mandelgarten
23. Haardter Herrenletten
24. Haardter Bürgergarten
25. Kirrweiler Mandelberg

—— BEREICH BOUNDARIES

particularly hilly. The vineyards continue on sandy-soiled slopes
through Ruppertsberg, suddenly steepening at Deidesheim. The
vines are planted up to 250m (820ft) and they're sheltered by hills;
here the Rhine is really too far away across the plain to make any
great difference. We're in Riesling country now; in the best parts of
the Mittelhardt Riesling covers around 70 per cent of the vineyard.
Nowhere else in the Pfalz is it so important: in fact, overall it only
accounts for 21 per cent, though the proportion is creeping up, while
Müller-Thurgau's share is fast shrinking.

At Forst the soil is varied by an outcrop of black basalt which
makes already warm soil even warmer; not surprisingly, growers
that don't have any basalt often import it, to the particular benefit of
the Mariengarten and Kirchenstück vineyards and those in
Deidesheim. The subsoil is water-retentive clay, which seems to give
the wines their fascinating backbone. But Forst's secret isn't just soil.
The vineyards are perfectly sheltered by the hills of the Haardt –

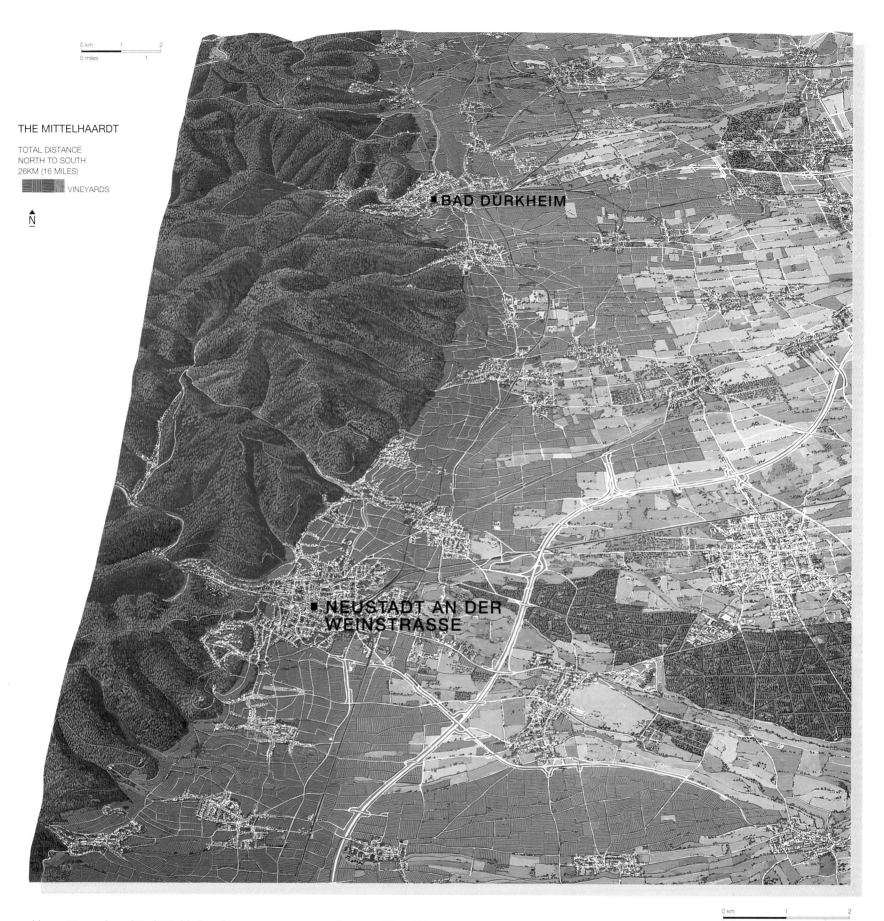

N

■ BAD DÜRKHEIM

■ NEUSTADT AN DER WEINSTRASSE

unlike at Neustadt and Bad Dürkheim, there are no gaps or valleys here. So while Forst has no steep slopes for vines, it has other compensating factors. The Kirchenstuck and Jesuitengarten are perhaps the most famous sites in the whole of the Pfalz.

Most of the great vineyards here and in Wachenheim are 100 per cent Riesling but, at Bad Dürkheim, except in the best sites, red grapes like Spätburgunder and Blauer Portugieser are favoured. The region's reputation is fairly recent: until the end of World War Two Pfalz wine was generally bottled elsewhere, much blended with Mosel wines. The Pfalz has been reinventing itself ever since.

WHERE THE VINEYARDS ARE *You could easily confuse this map of the Pfalz with that of Alsace. There's that same narrow, sheltered strip of vineyards, the same spilling of vines on to the plain towards the Rhine, and the Haardt mountains, a northerly continuation of Alsace's Vosges mountains, can be seen stretching away to the west. Even though the southern Pfalz proves time and time again that flat or flattish vineyards can make excellent wine, there is a clear distinction in the Mittelhaardt, the area shown on the map, between the plain and the hills. The plain, with its intensive farming and higher yields, is home to bulk wines and Riesling is concentrated on the east-facing slopes north of Neustadt.*

Dr. Bürklin-Wolf
1999
PECHSTEIN
FORST

FRANKEN

RED GRAPES
There is a tiny amount of
Spätburgunder.

WHITE GRAPES
Silvaner is at its best in
Franken, even though Müller-
Thurgau accounts for almost
one-third of the vineyards.
Other important varieties
include Bacchus, Rieslaner and
Kerner. There is a little
Riesling, Scheurebe, Perle,
Ortega and Traminer.

CLIMATE
Franken has a continental
climate, with a short growing
season, cold winters and
warm summers.

SOIL
The soils are very varied, with
heavy, weathered red marl
in the Steigerwald, clay/
limestone in the
Maindreieck and weathered
coloured sandstone in
the Mainviereck.

ASPECT
Most vines are planted on
south-facing slopes, usually in
river valleys and many
vineyards are fairly steep.

*This squat bottle shape has
been used for Franken wine
since the 18th century. It was
introduced in 1718 by the
leading Bürgerspital estate to
try to guarantee the
authenticty of their wine.*

There's something about Franken wine. It gives me the most
terrible thirst. I have done my best in snooping about the
cellars of Würzburg and those of the little villages around the city,
but I have to admit, after an hour or two of impressive but
relentlessly dry Silvaners and Müller-Thurgaus, only occasionally
relieved by something perfumed and rich, I am panting for a beer.
And luckily Würzburg does have more than its share of cellars
where the beer foams from the barrel and the platters are piled high
with sausages and gritty bread.

It's easy to forget that much of Germany finds it a struggle
to make wines suited to the traditionally robust German fare.
That's how Franken wines got their reputation – the earthy
Silvaner grape, not generally renowned for making wine of
much personality in its own right, comes into its own here, giving
wines of far weightier texture than most of Germany's other
'dry' wines. And that's why it's so difficult to find Franken
wines outside Germany – the Germans pay high prices for every
bottle they can get.

There's also another reason – the climate. Apart from the
even more easterly regions of Saale-Unstrut and Sachsen, it is the
only vine-growing region of Germany to have a truly continental
climate of cold, cold winters and warm summers. But it also has a
short growing season, and spring and autumn are unpredictable.
Early spring can be warm, encouraging the vines to bud early;
the weather can then turn, and a hard frost can destroy the crop.
In February 1985, for example, temperatures of –25°C (–13°F) for
several nights running killed two-and-a-half million vines in
Franken, with the southern part and Maindreieck the worst
affected areas. Autumns can be long and warm, making sweet
wines a possibility, or they can be cold and wet. As a result
yields can fluctuate here more than anywhere else in Germany –
and only the biggest estates can rely on having enough to
export, year after year.

Franken lies 80km (50 miles) east of the Rheingau and is centred
on the river Main. The vineyards are scattered, and sometimes
are so far apart that the bureaucrats haven't even bothered to
assign Grosslagen to them. As a result Bereich names are much
used – Bereich Mainviereck is in the west, where the Main
roughly describes two sides of a square (the name means 'Main
square'); Bereich Maindreieck ('Main triangle'), where the river
becomes two sides of a triangle, is in the centre; and in the east
is Bereich Steigerwald.

The soils are in fact very varied in Franken: there's a fair bit of
marl and sandstone and some loam, gypsum and clay, and
limestone in the Maindreieck. There are some top vineyard sites,
too: including the famous Würzburger Stein overlooking the Main
and benefiting from the river's warming influence, the steep,
south-south-west-facing Rödelseer Küchenmeister or, in Iphofen,
the Julius-Echter-Berg vineyard, again steep, and with excellent
south-south-west exposure.

GRAPE VARIETIES

Silvaner and, to a lesser extent, Riesling, are the star grapes.
Riesling is not greatly favoured in Franken: it's too late a ripener
for the region's short growing season, except in the most favoured
sites of all. But Silvaner attains heights it reaches nowhere else.
'Earthy' is the word usually used to describe it; it's minerally, too,
low in acidity and high in extract. Made dry (and Franken's wines
are always dry, except when noble rot makes one of its rare visits),
Silvaner is an ideal food wine.

Overall in Franken, Müller-Thurgau, with 32 per cent of the
vineyard, is the most common variety. It can be good here –

WÜRZBURG

**WHERE THE VINEYARDS
ARE** *For a map of a wine region, this
shows remarkably few vineyards. And yet this is
the heart of Franken: it's the part of the Maindreieck
where there are more vineyards than anywhere else. You
might be forgiven now for wondering why Franken is
regarded as a wine region at all. Winemaking is usually a sideline
here – at least half the growers take their grapes to the local
co-operative for vinification and most of the land is given over
to pasture and cereals.*

*The Main river flows, in this part of the region, first generally south
and then generally north-west through Würzburg. Just south of the city
there is a south-west-facing wall of vines: these are the Randersacker
vineyards rising above the river. Go a little further north, and just as the
city of Würzburg peters out there is another straight, south-facing cliff.
This is the Stein vineyard which has just about everything a vineyard
could ask from nature. The river and the city both keep it warm, and the
water reflects sun and heat back on to the vines. As a result temperatures
here in the summer can reach 40°C (104°F), and Auslesen wines and
above are not uncommon.*

certainly more distinguished than in most of Germany – but it's still
not as good as Silvaner, so it's a pity that so much land was planted
with it in the 1960s and 1970s at the expense of Silvaner.

Silvaner accounts for 20 per cent of Franken's 5914ha (14,613
acres), but after that it's largely a litany of newish grape crosses like
Bacchus and Kerner. These crosses don't do badly here, but frankly
they're never likely to be as interesting as a good Silvaner. The first
cross, Müller-Thurgau, was bred in 1882 but the drive to produce
ever more of them is new. The idea behind all the crosses is much
the same: the Riesling has many advantages, among them its
resistance to the cold of Germany's winters. But it yields relatively
meanly and ripens late in the year – just when the cold can be
setting in – and there is a risk of it not ripening at all. The ideal vine
would have all Riesling's advantages, as well as the sheer breed of
its wines, but would ripen earlier and yield more generously.

The new varieties that pass the stringent tests of the vine-
breeding stations and appear in the vineyards are, of course, only a
minute proportion of all the crosses that are bred and tried out.
Most of them have Riesling not too far back in their ancestry.
The most successful include Scheurebe (Riesling x Silvaner – the
same parents as used to be thought produced Müller-Thurgau,
though DNA fingerprinting has revealed the latter to be
Riesling x Chasselas de Courtillier), which makes excellent,

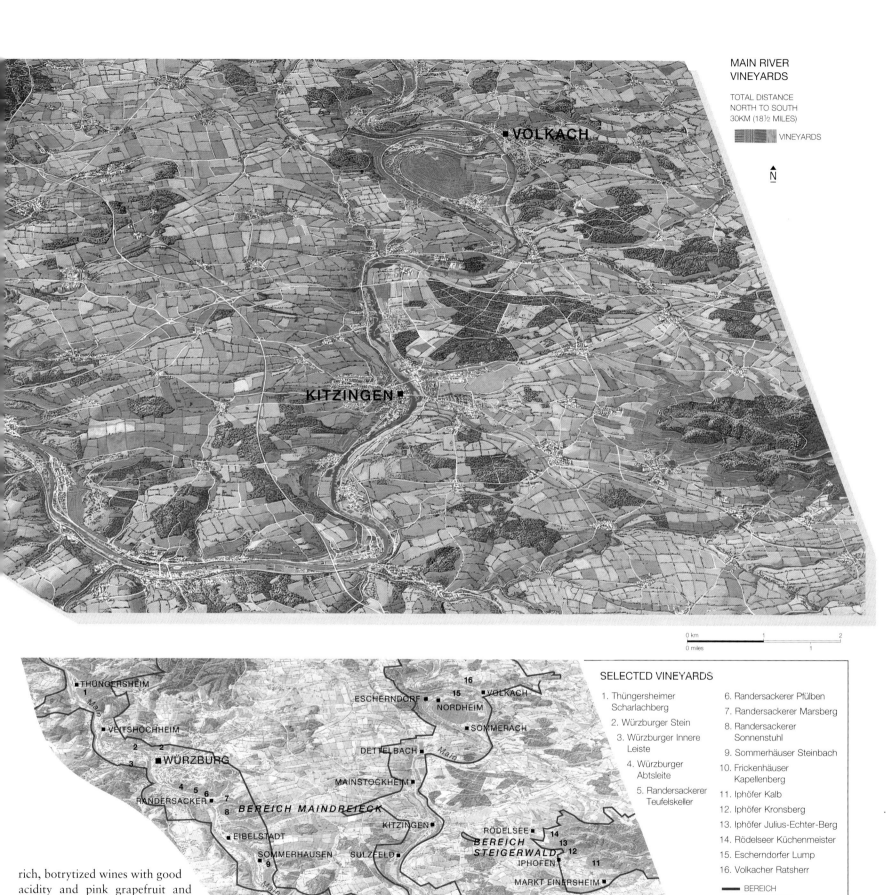

MAIN RIVER
VINEYARDS

TOTAL DISTANCE
NORTH TO SOUTH
30KM (18½ MILES)

VINEYARDS

N

VOLKACH

KITZINGEN

0 km   1   2
0 miles   1

SELECTED VINEYARDS

1. Thüngersheimer
Scharlachberg

2. Würzburger Stein

3. Würzburger Innere
Leiste

4. Würzburger
Abtsleite

5. Randersackerer
Teufelskeller

6. Randersackerer Pfülben

7. Randersackerer Marsberg

8. Randersackerer
Sonnenstuhl

9. Sommerhäuser Steinbach

10. Frickenhäuser
Kapellenberg

11. Iphöfer Kalb

12. Iphöfer Kronsberg

13. Iphöfer Julius-Echter-Berg

14. Rödelseer Küchenmeister

15. Escherndorfer Lump

16. Volkacher Ratsherr

BEREICH
BOUNDARIES

THÜNGERSHEIM
1

VEITSHÖCHHEIM

2   2

3   WÜRZBURG

4 5 6
7
RANDERSACKER
8   *BEREICH MAINDREIECK*

EIBELSTADT

SOMMERHAUSEN
9

FRICKENHAUSEN   10

OCHSENFURT

16
15   VOLKACH
ESCHERNDORF
NORDHEIM

SOMMERACH

DETTELBACH   Main

MAINSTOCKHEIM

KITZINGEN

SULZFELD

MARKTBREIT

RÖDELSEE   14
13
BEREICH   12
STEIGERWALD
IPHOFEN   11

MARKT EINERSHEIM

rich, botrytized wines with good acidity and pink grapefruit and pepper flavours.

Other crosses include Bacchus (Silvaner x Riesling) whose wines are rather soft, but can reach good sugar levels; and Kerner (Riesling x Trollinger), which has the advantage of being early-ripening. Quite well balanced, its wine has a whiff of Muscat. Perle (Gewürztraminer x Müller-Thurgau) and Ortega (Müller-Thurgau x Siegerrebe) are also aromatic. None is exciting, except for Scheurebe. But if you are a Franken grower selling your grapes to a co-operative and your big problem is early, cold winters, you can see the attraction of using crosses.

Political power and cultural beauty are closely intertwined in the baroque city of Würzburg. It is only fitting that the Marienberg fortress – home to a succession of prince-bishops until the 18th century – should have a vineyard, the Schlossberg, sited beneath its walls.

QUALITY WINE REGION AND BEREICHS

FRANKEN

━━━ Bereich Mainviereck

━━━ Bereich Maindreieck

━━━ Bereich Steigerwald

▭ OVER 200M (656FT)

▨ OVER 500M (1640FT)

BEREICH MAINDREIECK

In the Maindreieck the soil turns to limestone. Some 70 per cent of Franken wine comes from this central area, on what is if not quite the doorstep of the city of Würzburg, then certainly its back garden. Würzburg has the most famous of all Franken vineyards – the Stein – and the one that has given its name (unofficially) to all Franken wine: Steinwein, though, strictly speaking, this should refer only to the wine of the Stein vineyard, a great cliff of heat-retaining limestone that looks southwards over the city. Look for Silvaner from here, or Riesling, for the full Würzburger Stein experience.

Würzburg has more to offer than wine, however (more than beer, too), and it is undoubtedly one of the loveliest cities in Germany. The magnificent 18th-century Residenz of the Prince-Bishops who ruled Franken has a fresco by Tiepolo, among other treasures. There are more vines around Würzburg than anywhere else in Franken. Go to the villages north and south of the city: on both sides of the river Main, where slope and exposure allow, vines are planted. Further upriver, at Escherndorf, there is another top Silvaner spot, the very steep, south-facing Lump site, where marly clay overlays limestone.

BEREICH STEIGERWALD

This is the easternmost Bereich and the scattered vineyards lie away from the Main, on the western slopes of the Steigerwald. The climate here is more continental than in the rest of Franken and the deep, rich soils produce full-flavoured, fruity wines with a vigorous acidity. The best wine villages in the Steigerwald are Iphofen, Rödelsee and Castell, all on heavier gypsum marl.

BEREICH MAINVIERECK

The smallest and least ambitious of Franken's three regions is the Bereich Mainviereck. It has the fewest vineyards, scattered at intervals along the Main as it wends its way through Wertheim as far as Aschaffenburg. There are a few along the north bank of the river Rück, a tributary of the Main north of Klingenberg, and around Hörstein near the Hessen border. It's mostly Riesling here, though there's some Spätburgunder south of Aschaffenburg. The soils are largely sandstone and loam, the former used particularly for Spätburgunder. Red vines can be found along the Main south

of Rück, too, in Erlenbach, Klingenberg, Miltenberg, Grossheubach and Bürgstadt. And the wines? Showing dramatic improvements in recent vintages.

But if all this sounds as though winemaking is difficult, as though the growers only do it to make themselves suffer – think again. The vineyard area has increased by more than 54 per cent since the early 1980s to 5914ha (14,613 acres): in 1981 Franken had just 3847ha (9,506 acres). The region may suffer from cold winters – that's why the vineyards tend to huddle around the river, or in the shelter of woods, so they can gain whatever protection is going – but it also has hot summers and these allow it to make dry wines with the greatest of ease. Too much ease, perhaps: the popularity of Franken wine on the domestic market has taken a plunge lately, as other Germanic regions master the art of making dry wines and, sadly, Franken's famous flagship estates underperform.

THREE GREAT WINE ESTATES

Great in terms of size and importance, certainly, but at the moment rather coasting on old glories. Franken resembles the Rheingau in that it has splendid old aristocratic wine estates, but that the best wines come from smaller family affairs like Rudolf Fürst, Horst Sauer, Johann Ruck and Hans Wirsching. Those great estates have, since the Middle Ages, included charitable institutions similar to Burgundy's Hospices de Beaune. Their principle was the same: the poor and needy could be provided for out of the income from wine. The Bürgerspital zum Heiligen Geist, founded in 1319 to provide for the old people of Würzburg, is the oldest. In the Middle Ages, in fact, Franken was Germany's biggest wine region, with 40,000ha (98,839 acres) of vineyards at its peak.

The decline began in the 16th century, roughly at the time that Würzburg's other great charitable institution, the Juliusspital, was founded – 1576. This was a religious establishment, set up by the Prince-Bishop Julius Echter von Mespelbrunn. As you might expect from a Prince-Bishop, it was on a lavish scale. Both it and the lay Bürgerspital were endowed with prime vineyard sites and both acquired more over the years, so that now the Bürgerspital owns 110ha (272 acres), including the biggest chunk of the Stein vineyard, and the Juliusspital owns 170ha (420 acres), which makes it Germany's second largest wine estate. The Juliusspital owns part of the famous Stein and part also of Escherndorfer Lump and Iphöfer Julius-Echter-Berg, among others.

The other great Franken estate has the unromantic name of the Staatlicher Hofkeller – which sounds dull until you realize that its premises are in the cellars of the Residenz (Tiepolo didn't paint any ceilings that far down, sadly) and that this was the winery of the Prince-Bishops of Würzburg. In 1803, with the invasion of Napoleon and the subsequent secularization of church land, it was taken over by the Bavarian state and now owns 120ha (296 acres) of vineyards. The Juliusspital, however, managed to avoid being handed over to the state, and both it and the Bürgerspital survive.

Yet viticulture in Franken continued to decline. The increasing popularity of tea and coffee, competition from Bavarian beer, the industrial revolution, poor weather in the 19th century – all played their part. And then as now, Franken's lack of a market for its wines outside its borders told. Indeed, Franken's wine trade as a whole was poorly developed: in the 18th century there were even police rules against selling wine outside the region, ostensibly to prevent Würzburg from running out. The vinous disasters of the 19th century – oidium, mildew, phylloxera – completed the process of decline. Now Franken's vineyards are flourishing again, though at a less brilliant level – and they still keep most of the wine for themselves, four out of five bottles being consumed locally.

Map

HESSEN

Saale ■ HAMMELBURG

HASSFURT ■

SCHWEINFURT ■ *Main*

■ HÖRSTEIN

Main Wern

■ ASCHAFFENBURG

Elsava

THÜNGERSHEIM ■ ESCHERNDORF ■ ■ VOLKACH

BAYERN ■ SOMMERACH

RÜCK WÜRZBURG ■

■ ERLENBACH AM MAIN HOMBURG RANDERSACKER ■ ■ ABTSWIND

■ KLINGENBERG KITZINGEN ■ ■ CASTELL

GROSSHEUBACH WERTHEIM SOMMERHAUSEN ■ ■ RÖDELSEE

MILTENBERG ■ ■ BÜRGSTADT OCHSENFURT ■ ■ IPHOFEN

FRICKENHAUSEN ■ ■ NEUNDORF

IPPESHEIM ■

Tauber

BAD WINDSHEIM ■

BADEN-WÜRTTEMBERG

0 km 10 20
0 miles 10

N

BADEN-WÜRTTEMBERG

BADEN AND WÜRTTEMBERG are the odd ones out among the German wine regions. They make wines different in character from the rest of the country, and different even from each other. They are both remarkably diffuse in terms of styles and grapes, yet here they are, yoked together into the state of Baden-Württemberg and, while Baden's wines have for some years been trying to make an impact on foreign markets, the growers of Württemberg are only just beginning this process. It used to be that the locals could be relied upon to swallow every drop, but not now. Suddenly they're having to look elsewhere for their customers.

BADEN

It's easy to think of Baden as being a long, narrow strip of vineyards stretching for 130km (81 miles) between the spa town of Baden-Baden down the Rhine Valley to Basel in Switzerland. That's certainly the main part, as 80 per cent of its wines come from here. But wines labelled Baden also come from the Bereich Tauberfranken, tucked in between the south of Franken and the north of Württemberg – and only belonging to Baden at all because a political boundary says it does. South-west of that there's another chunk of Baden vineyards, this time wedged in south of Hessische Bergstrasse and west of Württemberg. And then right down in the south-east, south of the Danube (Donau), there's a little enclave of Baden vines on the banks of Lake Constance (Bodensee).

Even the bureaucrats recognize that, although these four are all counted as Baden, this doesn't make them the same. Accordingly, the five Bereichs in the main strip alongside the Rhine – that is, from the south, Markgräflerland, Tuniberg, Kaiserstuhl, Breisgau and Ortenau – have different, and generally higher, minimum must weights for each category of wine (Kabinett, Spätlese and so on) than do the others. Yet all of Baden is classified, in EU terms, as being in Region B (along with such places as the Loire and Champagne) instead of in the cooler region A along with the rest of Germany. It just shows how little most bureaucrats understand of the endlessly changing conditions that make up a wine area.

Well, it certainly is warmer here in Baden, even in winter. The average January temperature in the city of Freiburg is 1.1°C (34°F), which is warmer than Strasbourg in Alsace. The five Bereichs that make up the principal part of Baden are tucked in between the Rhine and the foothills of the Black Forest; they are effectively the mirror image of the Alsace vineyards just over the border. The climate is marginally less good than that of Alsace.

It's a little cooler and a little damper, though the vines are sheltered by the forest that crowns the hills, and the difference is not very great.

The Markgräflerland is where Swiss viticulture shades into German. The speciality of the gentle, fertile district is the Gutedel grape (alias Chasselas), which makes a crisp, somewhat neutral wine that is usually pretty unremarkable. It is not until near the beautiful medieval city of Freiburg that the typical style of Baden wine – dry, full, winey rather than flowery, and relatively low in acidity – begins to emerge. It reaches its peak in the twin areas of Kaiserstuhl and Tuniberg. The Kaiserstuhl is the stump of a three million-year-old volcano, partly covered with wind-blown loess, and its southern slopes, in particular the village of Ihringen, are Germany's warmest.

There is Riesling to be found here, as there is in most of Baden, but Riesling is not usually what Baden does best. This is the part of Germany where the Pinot family shines, with a depth and

Baden's warm climate produces fine, dry wines from Grauburgunder (Pinot Gris).

QUALITY WINE REGIONS AND BEREICHS

BADEN	WÜRTTEMBERG
Bereich Tauberfranken	Bereich Kocher-Jagst-Tauber
Bereich Badische Bergstrasse	Bereich Württembergisch Unterland
Bereich Kraichgau	Bereich Remstal-Stuttgart
Bereich Ortenau	Bereich Oberer Neckar
Bereich Breisgau	Bereich Württembergischer Bodensee
Bereich Kaiserstuhl	Bereich Bayerischer Bodensee
Bereich Tuniberg	OVER 500M (1640FT)
Bereich Markgräflerland	OVER 1000M (3280FT)
Bereich Bodensee	

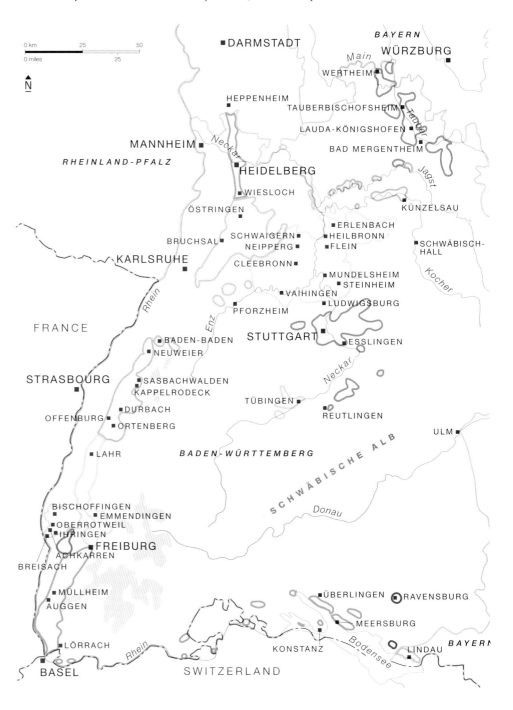

RED GRAPES
Baden has 50 per cent of all Germany's Spätburgunder. Trollinger is Württemberg's main red grape.

WHITE GRAPES
Müller-Thurgau, with 18 per cent of the vineyard, leads a long list of white varieties in Baden, followed by Grauburgunder (10 per cent), Riesling and others. Riesling (18 per cent) is Württemberg's main white grape, followed by Kerner and Müller-Thurgau.

CLIMATE
Baden is Germany's warmest wine region. Many of the vineyards are sheltered by the Odenwald mountains and the Black Forest. Württemberg is warm, and sheltered by river valleys and the Swabian Alps.

SOIL
Baden has mostly rich and fertile soils. There is gravel near the Bodensee, and limestone, clay, marl, loam, granite, loess and sandy marl elsewhere, plus volcanic soil on the Kaiserstuhl. Württemberg's soils are usually deep and well-drained. There is red marl, clay, loess, loam and shelly limestone.

ASPECT
Most Baden vineyards, except the Kaiserstuhl and Tuniberg, are on level or gently sloping land. In Württemberg they are on the gentle slopes of river valleys.

All of Germany has been involved in rebuilding its vineyards to reduce costs and increase productivity. These broad terraces on the slopes of the ancient Kaiserstuhl volcano were constructed during the 1970s.

weight that is akin to the wines of Alsace across the river. Grauburgunder or Pinot Gris, Weissburgunder or Pinot Blanc, and Spätburgunder or Pinot Noir all ripen well here – indeed, it's one of the few parts of Germany where Spätburgunder can be relied on to ripen just about every year. But not even the Kaiserstuhl, with its warm temperatures, makes much botrytized wine. It's too dry here for the fungus to flourish – and besides, the wines don't always have the high acidity needed to support such a concentration of sugar.

The Tuniberg is smaller than the Kaiserstuhl, at only 304m (997ft) high compared to the latter's 576m (1890ft). Almost every inch of it is covered with vines, but the soil is limestone, rather than volcanic, and it is slightly cooler and damper than its big brother, although like the Kaiserstuhl it has a topsoil of loess.

Loess, as well as shelly limestone and gneiss, is the rule in the Bereich Breisgau, as well, which runs up the Rhine Valley north of Freiburg, hugging the slopes of the Black Forest. There is slightly more rainfall here and slightly higher acidity in the wines. As elsewhere in Baden, the slopes were reorganized and re-terraced in the 1960s and 1970s under the Flurbereinigung programme and the vineyard area overall has doubled. Output also soared, until the Baden growers decided that enough was enough and that yields would simply have to be restricted. Accordingly, since the 1984 vintage onwards, they have been set at no more than 90 hectolitres per hectare; still fairly generous, but a definite improvement. There is an emphasis in Baden on organic viticulture, too, that tends to lower yields even further. Baden's yields are among the lowest in Germany. (This sort of collective decision is made easier by the fact that some 85 per cent of wine in Baden is made by the co-operatives, with individual estates being a rarity.)

The Bereich Ortenau is home to some of Baden's best Rieslings, particularly on the granite hills east of Offenburg. Durbach is the archetype: Riesling from here (they call the grape Klingelberger locally) is dry and minerally. There are little valleys running eastwards into the Black Forest, too; south-facing sites here regularly yield wines of Spätlesen and Auslesen quality. Rosé (or *Weissherbst*) wines used to be a speciality in much of Baden and particularly in Ortenau, but the demand for red means that rosé is currently out of favour. This is all very well, and the red wines (or *Ortenau*) are attractively fruity, but they certainly don't have the power of reds from the Kaiserstuhl.

The vineyards die away abruptly at Baden-Baden. South-east of Karlsruhe at Pforzheim they begin again: this is the Bereich Kraichgau, which runs north towards Heidelberg and another Bereich, Badische Bergstrasse. The vineyards are dotted here and there, taking their turn with wheat and other crops in the landscape, and occasionally finding good south or south-west exposure on the banks of the Neckar. In the Bereich Tauberfranken, the wines are Franconian in character, sappy and dry; they are grown along the little Tauber river, which joins the river Main at Wertheim.

Finally, the Seewein (or 'lake wine') of the Bodensee is made almost entirely from Müller-Thurgau or Spätburgunder which is frequently vinified as a rosé. The broad expanse of the lake modifies the cool climate, reflecting summer warmth back on to vines that, at up to 570m (1870ft) above sea level, are the highest north of the Alps. But the lake also gives rise to fog problems, which make it very difficult to ripen noble, classic grape varieties – hence the prevalence of Müller-Thurgau.

WÜRTTEMBERG

In Württemberg nearly half the vineyards are planted with red grapes, with Trollinger being the most widely planted. Sometimes red grapes may be mixed with white to make Schillerwein (allegedly named after the poet) and a Württemberg speciality. Schwarzriesling, alias Pinot Meunier, is also popular, with 16 per cent of the vineyard, as is Kerner among white grapes, though the favourite white grape is the Riesling, with 18 per cent of the vineyard. The wines are expensive and seldom better than foursquare. Good whites are particularly rare. The bulk is sold in litre bottles for drinking immediately, so most of the demand is for wine that is sound, fresh, dry and appealing, but not too complex or challenging. Reds may still be slightly sweet.

Württemberg is better suited than most German regions to making red wines. Its climate is more extreme than Baden's, with colder winters but sunnier summers and red grapes ripen well. The pity is that most growers opt for the light, easy-drinking Trollinger, rather than testing the limits with something more challenging like Dornfelder or Spätburgunder. Soils tend to be marl and limestone; here it is shelter and good exposure to the sun that determine where the vine can be grown and where it can't. Württemberg is a sprawling region and four out of five growers own less than 1ha (2½ acres), so the co-operatives are all important. Even in the central area, Bereich Württembergischer Unterland, where three-quarters of the vineyards are situated, they are scattered.

River valleys are the key to winemaking here. Some of the vineyards follow the river Neckar as it zigzags northwards to join the Rhine at Mannheim; others hug the narrower valleys of the Tauber, Jagst and Kocher, all tributaries of the Neckar. There are side valleys, too, planted with vines where a suitable spot presents itself, so the vine may be pushed far to the east into the Schwäbische Alb hills running north of the Danube.

Württemberg's other smaller Bereichs are the Oberer Neckar in the south, with only 60ha (148 acres) under vine; the Württembergischer and Bayerischer Bodensee, 6 ha (15 acres) nudging the Bodensee outpost of Baden; and Remstal-Stuttgart which includes 40ha (99 acres) of vines in the city itself.

FLURBEREINIGUNG

Flurbereinigung, or the remodelling of vineyards, is possibly the most radical project to take effect in the vineyards of Germany since the Romans began to plant them. It is done only at the express wish of every village, with every grower, part-time or not, having an equal vote. If the vote is yes, then all the vines are uprooted, all the centuries-old terraces are bulldozed and the boundaries that separate plot from plot are temporarily eradicated. The bulldozers smooth their way over the slopes and new, larger terraces are created; new access roads are built and drainage is improved. The land is then reallocated.

The process started in the 19th century, was given a boost in the 1920s by the replanting that became necessary with phylloxera, speeded up in the 1950s and by the 1970s was at work almost everywhere. It is an expensive business, initially: it means four years without a profitable crop, though government subsidies are available. Up to 15 per cent of the land is lost to new roads, but labour costs fall by up to 25 per cent and yields can rise dramatically. Over 60 per cent of Germany's vineyards have now been remodelled, with a huge 80 per cent adopting the scheme in Baden, a region that has embraced the scheme enthusiastically.

THE KAISERSTUHL

TOTAL DISTANCE NORTH TO SOUTH
18KM (11 MILES)

 VINEYARDS

N

WHERE THE VINEYARDS ARE *Three million years ago the Kaiserstuhl was an active volcano. Then, gradually, it died and over the millennia the elements wore it down, a bit here, a bit there, until it was ready to be tamed. Terraces were built and vines planted; they thrived on the rich, volcanic soil and now there are vines on every suitable slope. The villages are clustered in the valleys and forest covers the hilltops, but otherwise this horseshoe-shaped volcanic rock, 576m (1889ft) high, is given over to viticulture, orchards and grazing. The higher slopes are a nature sanctuary, home to many rare plants, butterflies and birds.*

See how perfect the exposure is on these south- and south-west-facing slopes. The mesoclimate is dry and the river is just about close enough to help to moderate extremes of temperature. The grapes don't roast here, but develop richness and complexity during a long growing season. Even so, it gets pretty warm. Summer days when the thermometer reaches a Mediterranean 30°C (86°F) or more are common and Ihringen, tucked into the southern slopes, is accounted the warmest village in Germany. Wines from the Kaiserstuhl frequently achieve 13–14° alcohol without help from sugar additions.

The Tuniberg, in comparison, looks like small fry. The hill reaches 304m (997ft), which means that this limestone outcrop (that it is here at all is pure coincidence; the Tuniberg does not have volcanic origins) can be entirely planted with vines and no point is too high and cool to be left to forest. Indeed, its southern tip is almost as warm as Ihringen. The vineyards on both hills have been completely rebuilt as part of the Flurbereinigung *programme (see photo left) and new terraces have been constructed to replace the old.*

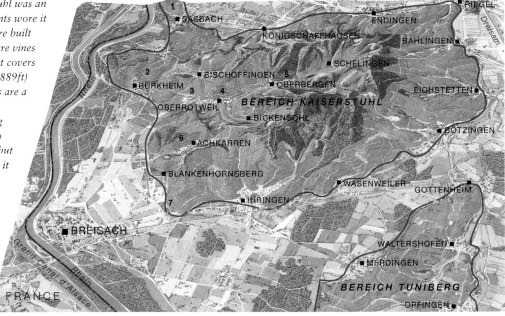

SELECTED VINEYARDS

1. Sasbacher Limburg
2. Burkheimer Feuerberg
3. Oberrotweiler Henkenberg
4. Oberrotweiler Eichberg
5. Oberbergener Pulverbuck
6. Achkarrer Schlossberg
7. Ihringer Winklerberg

━━━ BEREICH BOUNDARIES

HESSISCHE BERGSTRASSE

 **RED GRAPES**
Spätburgunder accounts for 10 per cent of the vines.

WHITE GRAPES
Riesling accounts for 50 per cent. Müller-Thurgau (11 per cent) and Grauburgunder (8 per cent) are also important.

CLIMATE
The climate is mild, and spring comes very early.

SOIL
There are various weathered light soils, including loess, gravel, gneiss and basalt.

ASPECT
Vines are planted on the south-facing slopes of east-west valleys as well as on the west-facing slopes. The Odenwald shelters the vines from the east wind.

An old-fashioned polyculture still thrives in the pretty hillsides of Hessische Bergstrasse, vines having to take their place among cherry, apricot and peach trees. This is the Streichling vineyard at Bensheim.

BERGSTRASSE: THE MOUNTAIN WAY. What picture does that name conjure up? Sunday hikers in shorts and boots and backpacks, threading their way along the crest of a hill. Or going back a century or more, travellers from the university city of Heidelberg in the south, wending their way north to Darmstadt and on to Frankfurt. Going back still further, monks journeying to and from their monastery at Lorsch, south-west of Bensheim, and their vineyards; and before that, Roman centurions, since this road, the Strata Montana, was built by the same Romans who planted the vineyards and indeed brought the vine to Germany.

The Bergstrasse continues south of Heidelberg as well, but nowadays lies within the state of Baden – and is accordingly known as the Badische Bergstrasse. The part of the Bergstrasse vineyards that fall into the state of Hessen have their very own region, the Hessische Bergstrasse.

Until reunification when the two wine regions of the former GDR (Saale-Unstrut and Sachsen) came to join the party, Hessische Bergstrasse had the distinction of being Germany's smallest wine region. It was probably also its least-known outside the country; in fact, it is likely only due to the fact that hiking is thirsty work that the vineyards thrive as much as they do. But the hikers continue to come and they need refreshment; and the reason they come is that Hessische Bergstrasse is particularly pretty. It is planted with fruit trees, which are interspersed with vines along its main 16-km (10-mile) stretch. Vines and fruit trees compete all along the slopes of the Odenwald that runs along the crest of the hills and in the spring the profusion of blossom brings out the tourists.

The Rhine, flowing north through a flat, fertile valley, is to the west of the region. To the east is the Odenwald, and the vine is planted on the south-west-facing slopes of the foothills, and also on the south-facing slopes of the small side valleys. Logically Hessische Bergstrasse is a northerly extension of Baden, but the *Flurbereinigung* programme that has transformed Baden's vineyards over the past three decades from labour-intensive terracing to more manageable gentler slopes, workable by tractors, has hardly touched the region. Here there are still small terraces laboriously cut into the hillsides, each terrace supporting a few rows of vines, and needing enormous and expensive upkeep. This is the way most German vineyards used to look, a generation or two ago.

GRAPE VARIETIES

There are two Bereichs in the region: Starkenburg, which encloses the 16-km (10-mile) stretch of hillside that is the main part of Hessische Bergstrasse, and Umstadt, a more isolated area east of Darmstadt and north of the main vineyards in Starkenburg. In Umstadt, Müller-Thurgau, Silvaner and Riesling are grown; in Starkenburg, Riesling dominates. Riesling is given the best, warmest, most sheltered sites and the wines can reach *Spätlese* and *Auslese* level and even occasionally beyond, but they are usually on the delicate side. They have good fruit flavours, and though these Rieslings could never be mistaken for the structured richness of the Rheingau, the lean elegance of the Mosel or the broad fatness of the Pfalz, there is certainly good quality and good value to be found here. The less-regarded Müller-Thurgau is simple, everyday wine, fresh and attractive.

Numerous other grape varieties are planted in much smaller quantities: Silvaner, Grauburgunder (or Pinot Gris), Kerner, Ehrenfelser (a new cross), the grapefruit-scented Scheurebe and Traminer. The red Spätburgunder (or Pinot Noir) is on the increase, though though the percentage is much smaller than in Baden to the south of Hessische Bergstrasse. Here it makes light wines that are little more than curiosities.

Yields, generally speaking, are fairly low – on a par with, say, the Nahe as opposed to the huge number of hectolitres per hectare from the Rheinhessen and the Pfalz, and lower than in Baden to the south, where the climate is warmer and the soil more fertile.

WINE VILLAGES

There are some very good vineyard sites, though none of them are famous beyond the region's boundaries. At Heppenheim there are the Centgericht and the Steinkopf vineyards, the former owned in its entirety by the Staatsweingüter Domaine Bergstrasse or State Domaine, the region's largest vineyard owner. It is particularly good for Riesling *Kabinett Trocken* or *Halbtrocken*. Bensheim is the other leading commune with the good south-facing, sloping Streichling vineyard. The village of Schönberg has the Herrnwingert vineyard, also owned by the State Domaine.

Apart from the State Domaine there are few other individual producers. With around 1000 growers owning just 422ha (1043 acres) of vines, vineyard holdings are often tiny and most of the wine is made by the Bergsträsser Winzer, the regional co-operative in Heppenheim. Some of the growers mix vines with other crops and are full-time farmers; others tend their vines at weekends and commute to town during the week; and there is increased pressure on the land from housing.

CLIMATE AND SOIL

The Riesling thrives here because of the mild climate and the long growing season. Hessische Bergstrasse notches up more hours of summer sunshine than the warm Pfalz across the Rhine, and it's nearly as warm as Baden to the south. Hence all the fruit trees, which in spring are the first in Germany to come into flower. Hessische Bergstrasse isn't known as the spring garden of Germany for nothing. Its late-harvest wines can be delicious but it doesn't make much over *Spätlese* level. Following the modern trend, it prefers to use the advantages of a warm climate to make *Trocken* and *Halbtrocken* wines of pretty good quality.

The soils vary, but are generally fairly light. Indeed it is these light soils that help to keep the yields down. North of Bensheim there is decomposed granite stretching north to Zwingenberg; Heppenheim has loess and yellow sandstone, and elsewhere there is mostly sand or light loam.

SAALE-UNSTRUT & SACHSEN

WHAT A LOT HAS CHANGED in just a few years. In the immediate aftermath of the Berlin Wall's disappearance nobody thought much about wine. The two wine regions of the former East Germany (GDR) sounded as run-down as so much of that country, and the Easterners, it seemed, all wanted to drink Coca-Cola. And in fact they'd never had much chance to drink their local wine anyway. East German wine was either a privilege for Party bosses, or it was useful for trading in situations where money alone wouldn't get you the car spares or whatever it was you needed. What the wine tasted like wasn't tremendously important, especially since there was nothing good coming into the country to compare it with.

After reunification both Saale-Unstrut and Sachsen were given a ten-year release from the EU ban on planting new vineyards (this ban, designed to prevent – or at least control – wine surpluses, applies to every other AC or equivalent region in member countries). Some of the ancient vineyard land in Saale-Unstrut and Sachsen had lain fallow for decades – certainly since the 1930s. It has now been replanted to give Saale-Unstrut 654ha (1616 acres) of vineyards, and Sachsen 383ha (946 acres); still tiny compared to the Rheinhessen's 25,000ha (61,774 acres), but nevertheless a big percentage increase, though it is unlikely to reach anything like the level of the Middle Ages, when 5000–6000ha (12,400–14,800 acres) were planted in Sachsen alone.

Change was dramatic at the moment of formal reunification. In 1990 these two regions found themselves pretty well overnight under the umbrella of the 1971 German wine law. The West sent them experts on viticulture, experts on winemaking, experts on this, that and the other. The Easterners learnt quickly. At first their main aim was to produce as much as possible, as fast as possible. Now there are some seriously good producers in both regions: look for Schloss Proschwitz and Klaus Zimmerling in Sachsen, and Lützkendorf in Saale-Unstrut. All make their wines dry.

Yields are tiny in both regions – 30 to 40 hectolitres per hectare – partly because the vines are planted far apart; partly because the vine clones were poor, and imported from Hungary and Czechoslovakia since the GDR had no vine nurseries of its own; and partly because of the weather. Such yields are in themselves a reflection of high quality; it's the yield per vine that counts for the taste in the glass.

CLIMATE AND SOIL

The weather can be harsh in these regions, but it's only because it's so extreme that viticulture is possible at all. Summers are hot and sunny and bring plenty of extract to the wines to balance their decidedly high acidity; conversely, winters are long and cold. Saale-Unstrut is the most northerly wine region of Germany and Sachsen, the most easterly, is not far behind; in Saale-Unstrut late frosts, hitting the vines roughly three years in every ten, cut the crop by 20 to 80 per cent. In Sachsen the cold is even harsher, and spring frosts, a threat until mid-May, can reduce the harvest by up to 90 per cent.

In both regions, then, it is only the most sunny and sheltered sites that have any chance of ripening grapes. South-facing slopes in river valleys are generally the only option: the rivers Saale and Unstrut provide these, generally south-east-facing along the Saale and south-west-facing along the Unstrut. Freyburg, on the Unstrut, is the main focus for vineyards; steep, south- or west-facing limestone slopes offer the vine some of the best opportunities to be had in the whole region. In Sachsen it's the southern reaches of the Elbe that are the

focus, with the greatest concentration of vineyards being around the city of Meissen. Tourists coming here and to Dresden are likely to remain Sachsen's main market in the near future.

The main difference between the regions is soil and with better viticulture and winemaking real character will develop in the wines. Saale-Unstrut's vines are planted on limestone and occasionally on sandstone; the wines are fruity, full-bodied and generous, even if they're backed up by fairly high acidity. Sachsen's are on granite subsoil and are sleeker and more racy. They often seem to taste less alcoholic than they are, but can go from 11 per cent to as high as 14 per cent. Topsoils here are of loam, loess, sandstone or porphyry, with sand on low-lying sites by rivers. There is plenty of sandstone here, but on the whole it is not planted with vines.

In both regions the best and warmest sites are planted with Riesling, although autumns are really too early and cold for this late-ripening grape to show at its best. The early-ripening and reliable Müller-Thurgau is the main grape and gains some structure from the low yields (which, even with better clones and better management probably won't go much above 50 or 60 hectolitres per hectare). There's some good Silvaner in Saale-Unstrut and both regions have small amounts of Weissburgunder, Traminer and Gutedel. There are tiny plantings of red varieties (Portugieser, Spätburgunder and Dornfelder) but nobody expects any great colour or ripeness. In Saale-Unstrut the wines are usually vinified dry; Sachsen makes a softer, lighter style which undoubtedly appeals to the tourists who gravitate to the region. Spätlese and Auslese wines can only be produced in exceptionally warm years.

VITICULTURE

The steep, labour-intensive vineyards are terraced but had fallen into disrepair under the GDR. Now the stone walls supporting the terraces are being repaired and the aim is to retain them: there is, so far, no move to smooth them out in the manner of the rest of Germany. The Freyburger Schlufterburg in Saale-Unstrut is being turned into a model vineyard under the guidance of the Geisenheim Viticultural Institute. The idea is that the terraces will be a tourist attraction and part of the character of each region – indeed, both regions have already established tourist wine routes, including cycle and hiking trails.

RED GRAPES
There are small amounts of Portugieser, Spätburgunder and Domfelder.

WHITE GRAPES
Müller-Thurgau accounts for 20 per cent of the vines in both areas and Weissburgunder between 10 and 15 per cent. Silvaner takes up 9 per cent in Saale-Unstrut; while Riesling covers 15 per cent in Sachsen, but little in Saale-Unstrut. Both areas have some Grauburgunder, Gutedel and Traminer and there's a little Kerner in Sachsen.

CLIMATE
This is a continental climate, with cold winters, late spring frosts and hot summers.

SOIL
Saale-Unstrut has limestone and red sandstone on the slopes and deeper fertile soils in the valleys. In Sachsen there is loam, loess, granite and weathered porphyry.

ASPECT
In Saale-Unstrut vines are planted up to 200m (656ft), along the banks of the Saale and Unstrut rivers and on hills near Freyburg. Most of Sachsen's vines are on south-east-facing slopes along the Elbe river valley.

The revival of vineyards in the East has been a slow business since reunification. Here the little wine town of Freyburg in the Unstrut Valley sits beneath the Neuenburg castle and the Edelacker vineyard.

SWITZERLAND

Switzerland and skiing? Yes. Switzerland and cheese? Sure. Switzerland and glorious Alpine peaks glistening with fresh-fallen snow, Switzerland and steep-sided valleys, waterfalls and mountain streams cascading into deep glacial lakes, Switzerland and yodelling if you must – but how many of us think of Switzerland and wine? Go into most neighbourhood shops and I challenge you to find a single bottle of Swiss wine.

There are two reasons. The Swiss do in fact make rather a lot of wine, but they drink even more than they make, and there's hardly ever any available for export. And if there were, the prices, for what are usually at best pleasant light wines for drinking young, would shock most non-Swiss into abstention.

But that shouldn't surprise us. Everybody knows that Switzerland is an expensive country. The cost of manual labour is 20 to 30 per cent more than in neighbouring countries, and the cost of producing wine can be four times as high as in France, because of the steepness of the slopes and the expense of maintaining the terraces. The vineyards are also small: the average holding is less than half a hectare. But while the wine often has charm, while it may have individuality and go well with food, it's mostly not great wine. The most unusual wines are the Petite Arvines of the Valais, which can age in bottle for a good few years, but most Swiss wine is best drunk young, like most wine, in fact. French-speaking Switzerland probably makes better Chasselas than most places (not

many other places make it, actually), but Chasselas is never going to be earth-shaking. The Valais is now making some surprisingly good Syrah, which is usually better than the often muddy Pinot Noir. Italian-speaking Switzerland makes good Merlot and this has got much better – more concentrated and serious – in recent years. German-speaking Switzerland concentrates on Pinot Noir (or Blauburgunder), of which the best examples come from the canton of Graubünden, and Müller-Thurgau (which the Swiss call Riesling-Sylvaner: this was long believed to be its parentage, but DNA fingerprinting has revealed that a fling between Riesling and Chasselas de Courtillier was to blame instead).

Three-quarters of Switzerland's vineyards are in the French-speaking part of the country – 11,221ha (27,726 acres) of the country's 14,885ha (36,780 acres) of vineyards are here, compared to 2595ha (6412 acres) in the German-speaking part and only 1069ha (2641 acres) in Ticino, the Italian-speaking part. The vineyards tend to be squeezed round the edges of the country and in the corners, with only a few isolated patches in the more mountainous centre and eastern section. With the exception of some of the scattered vineyards in the German-speaking cantons, all Swiss vineyards depend on the beneficial influence of water for their existence. That water may be a river, such as the Rhône which runs through the Valais; quite often it's a lake, such as Lake Geneva (Lac

Swizerland is the only country to make a speciality of Chasselas and, if drunk young, the wines can be very pleasant. Chasselas assumes different names in different regions: in the Valais it is known as Fendant.

CANTONS AND MAIN WINE SUB-REGIONS

JURA

NEUCHÂTEL
1. Bielersee

FRIBOURG
2. Vully

VAUD
3. Vully
4. Bonvillars

5. Côtes-de-l'Orbe
6. La Côte
7. Lavaux
8. Chablais

GENÈVE
9. Mandement
10. Arve-et-Rhône
11. Arve-et-Léman

VALAIS
12. Vouvry
13. Monthey

TICINO AND MISOX
14. Sopraceneri
15. Sottoceneri

CANTONS OF EASTERN SWITZERLAND
16. Bündner-Herrschaft
17. Walensee
18. St Galler Rheintal
19. Zürichsee
20. Weinland

21. Limmattal
22. Klettgau
23. Rheintal
24. Thunersee

PANORAMIC MAP OF SWITZERLAND
Valais *pages 142–143*

Léman) and there are lots of these here. But a large body of water to moderate extremes of temperature and reflect the ample sunshine back on to the vines is vital here, particularly where the vines grow at altitudes of 350m (1148ft) or more. That's already higher than most vines in Europe, but here it's nothing.

The other climatic factor affecting Swiss viticulture is the wind – and usually it's benevolent. In the eastern part of the country the Foehn wind blows up the valleys from the south, warming and drying the grapes. This is particularly important in the Upper Rhein Valley around Chur, which is the warmest place in German-speaking Switzerland, in spite of all its mountains. Neuchâtel and Geneva are subject to a north wind, which is less good news, and in Zürich and points north of here the prevailing wind is westerly and the vineyards need to be planted on sheltered slopes.

In such a mountainous country shelter is not hard to come by. Every vineyard region has its protecting range. In Geneva, where the vineyards are relatively flat, there is a whole collection of them, including the Jura and the Salève, which send the rain clouds off into France. Neuchâtel also has the Jura and the Valais has the Alps.

WINE REGIONS
Of all the Swiss wine cantons, the Valais is the most important and it also has the greatest variety of grapes (see page 142). The Vaud, in terms of area under vine, comes next. Two-thirds of the Vaud's wine is white, nearly all of it Chasselas which, since this grape reflects the soil on which it is grown, changes in character according to whether it is planted on the scree of Chablais, the moraine of Lavaux and La Côte or the puddingstone of Dézaley in Lavaux (Vaud's top village appellation), where the wine is more structured.

The vineyards of Côtes-de-l'Orbe, Bonvillars and Vully are influenced by Lake Neuchâtel. La Côte, on the banks of Lake Geneva, is planted half with red (Gamay and Pinot Noir) and half with white grapes. Swiss red wines used to be low in acidity and high in yield, but now steps are being taken to reverse that situation. Yields are certainly lower than they were, but, judging from the average quality, could come down still further, with good results. The vines are also being planted in cooler sites so that the grapes gain more acidity. In the case of Chasselas, avoiding or limiting the malolactic fermentation, which changes the green

apple-tasting malic acid in wine to the creamy tasting lactic acid, has improved quality. But the majority of Swiss wines still nearly always tend to be light in colour and body. A few producers are experimenting with aging their reds in new oak, but the majority of the wines – even those from the warm Valais – just don't have the guts needed for this sort of treatment.

Reds are on the increase in the canton of Geneva, where they're mostly Gamay. Chasselas is still in the majority, though. This is calm, rolling, fertile land, with most of its vineyards scattered amid fields of other crops. In Neuchâtel half the vineyards are of Pinot Noir and there is even a special clone called Cortaillod. Chasselas is the next most important grape, growing on soil that is mostly limy, with alluvial soil lower down the slopes. The region is dry and sunny, though not quite as sunny and not quite as dry as the Valais.

A prevailing fault of Swiss wines used to be the flabbiness and wateriness that result from over-production, and matters reached a head in 1982 and 1983, when there was a surplus and the wine just didn't sell. Neuchâtel was the first canton to limit yields, and in 1992 they were restricted all over the country by a Federal Decree – and not before time. The legal limit is now 1.4 kilograms of grapes per square metre for white grapes, and 1.2 kg/m² for reds, which is still quite high. Even 1 kg/m² is equivalent to 75 hectolitres per hectare – pretty high for cool-climate vineyards. Individual cantons may also impose their own, tighter rules if they so wish.

Fribourg, with vineyards at Vully, has varying amounts of sandstone in the soil; again, the vineyards are lake-influenced. And Jura has only recently rectified its record of being the only French-speaking canton with no vineyards at all, by planting just 7ha (17 acres). The canton of Bern is mainly German-speaking but the vineyards are mostly in the French-speaking part, the Lac de Bienne. Here they're happy to grow Chasselas (which they call Gutedel in German). The canton includes the vineyards of Lake Thun, looking rather lonely all by themselves in the middle of Switzerland, but they don't do so badly. They're south-facing, the Pinot Noir and Riesling-Sylvaner vines grow up to 600m (1968ft) and Switzerland's favourite warm wind, the Foehn, keeps the chill off.

In the 19 German-speaking wine cantons of eastern Switzerland we're further north, almost at the limit of vine cultivation, and the climate is cooler and often wetter. The average minimum annual temperature is 9°C (48°F), which is as low as you can happily go for viticulture, and spring, as well as autumn frosts can be a problem. But the vines are grown at up to 600m (1968ft) in parts of Graubünden and the growers seek out sheltered south-facing sites and pray for the Foehn. The soil varies: there is chalky limestone in the Jura foothills, sandstone in the middle and limestone, moraine and schist elsewhere, with alluvial cones in parts of Graubünden. The best vineyards of Graubünden are on slate; effectively scree from the mountains above them. The cool climate here doesn't stop them growing red wine. Over 80 per cent of the Graubünden vines are red, mainly Pinot Noir. Whites are mostly Riesling-Sylvaner.

In the Italian-speaking canton of Ticino, the architecture is increasingly Italian the further south you go. Here, south of the Alps, the climate too is more influenced by the Mediterranean. That means lots of sun and plenty of rain and even the rain has an Italian temperament: it arrives in short, violent storms. The region south of Mount Ceneri, the Sottoceneri, is the viticulture centre, with Merlot as its flagship wine. Quality is increasingly good, with new methods of viticulture and up-to-date, even international, winemaking being used to good effect.

You'd expect Switzerland to have some of Europe's highest vineyards. Well, these ones are at a height of 1100m (3609ft) at Visperterminen on the road up to Zermatt.

THE CLASSIFICATION SYSTEM FOR SWISS WINE

Switzerland has federal and and a plethora of cantonal regulations, and uses three different languages. From 2008 its wines will fall into three different categories.

• **Appellation d'origine contrôlée** These wines come from an individual canton or region within a canton. They may bear a place name, a combination of place and grape name, or a generic name (for example, Fendant). There are currently over 650 appellations.

• **Vin de pays** These wines come from an area larger than a canton, for example, Chasselas Romand, for Chasselas from the Suisse Romande.

• **Vin de table** These wines are usually sold by the litre.

OTHER CANTONAL REGULATIONS

The canton of Geneva also has Grand Cru and Premier Cru wine, which are more precisely delimited and have to meet stricter requirements. In the German-speaking cantons there is a seal of quality – Winzer-Wy or Vintner's wine – awarded by a tasting panel, and Ticino in Italian-speaking Switzerland labels its best Merlots with the VITI seal. The French-speaking cantons also have quality seals, called Terrain in the canton of Vaud and La Gerle in Neuchâtel.

VALAIS

N

RIDDES TO LEUK

TOTAL DISTANCE NORTH TO
SOUTH 12KM (7½ MILES)

 VINEYARDS

For a wine enthusiast, the train from Geneva through the Simplon tunnel into Italy has to be one of the greatest journeys in the world. Heading out along the idyllic north shore of Lake Geneva to Lausanne, the Vaud vineyards crowd in on the track. Turning east and south past Vevey and Montreux on to Yvorne and Martigny, the tranquil beauty of the lake is matched by the increasing grandeur of the mountains and the strips of vineyards reaching down into the valley floor.

At Martigny the railway track does a right-angle turn to the left, and stretching up to Sion and Sierre are the south-east-facing slopes of the Bernese Alps. Glue your face to the lefthand windows of the train. I don't know anywhere else where the monoculture of the vine is more beautiful or more startling. Vines seem to climb vertically up the spectacular mountain faces, tiny villages perch on plateaux cut off from every other manifestation of life except their vines and, even in the height of summer, the great mountain peaks glow with luminous snow as this Alpine suntrap bakes its perfectly exposed vines to a quite

remarkable degree of ripeness. Past Sierre, the vines need to seek nooks and crannies to ripen fully and at Visp, just before the Simplon tunnel, a little narrow gauge railway trails off up to Zermatt past the death-defying terraces of Visperterminen, some of the highest vines in Europe at 1100m (3609ft).

But you have to step off the train and actually trek up the mountainsides themselves to understand fully quite how remarkable these vineyards are. And it's only by braving the elements in person that the unique character of the Valais vineyards makes sense. The sun and the steep angle of the vineyard slopes you can gauge from the train. The wind, you can't. And however perfect those slopes, they still wouldn't be able to ripen grapes at these altitudes without the wind. This wind is called the Foehn – and it is Switzerland's godsend. It blows from the south down the mountain slopes, and it blows east–west along the Rhône Valley, crucially raising the temperature, and helping the grapes to ripen.

0 km   1   2
0 miles   1

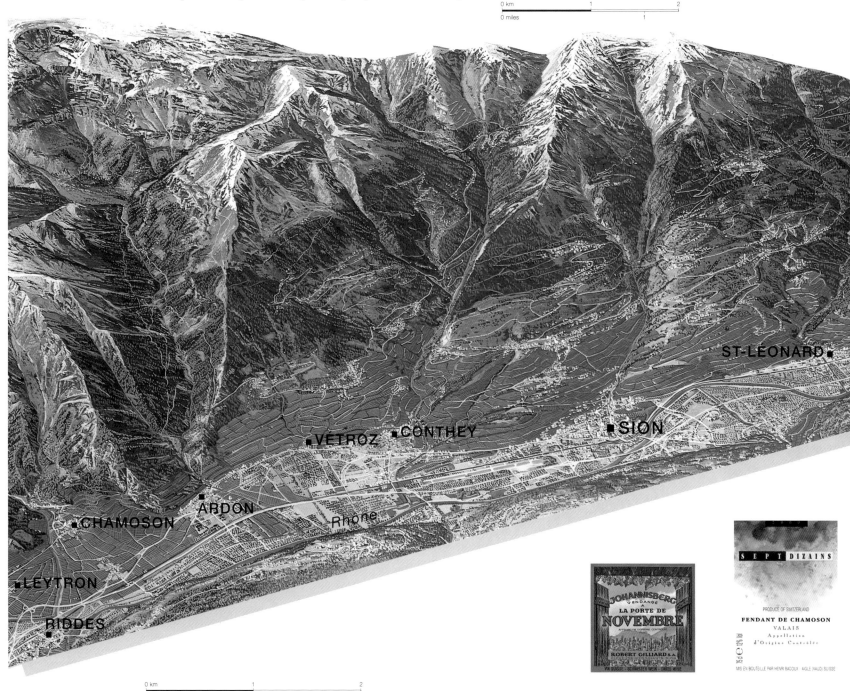

GRAPE VARIETIES AND WINE STYLES

This Rhône is, of course, the same Rhône that produces massive, tannic Syrah reds a long way downstream in France. Here, though, in the Valais one-third of the wines are white, from Chasselas, Sylvaner, Marsanne , Pinot Gris, Arvine, Amigne, Muscat, Riesling and a few others, including increasing amounts of Chardonnay. The reds are principally from Pinot Noir and Gamay, often blended into that Valais speciality, Dôle, which must be a blend of at least 80 per cent of these two varieties. Blends from less ripe grapes can be sold as Goron. Pinot Noir is also sometimes bottled on its own. Sometimes it's perfumed and good, and generally speaking Valais reds are the fullest-bodied in Switzerland. There's even some Syrah, and while the Swiss can often overdo the hype here, there are a few genuinely very good examples – as good even as a decent St-Joseph from the northern Rhône. And finally don't forget the very Valais red grapes like Humagne Rouge and Cornalin.

Some of the vines here, like Petite Arvine, are found nowhere else in Switzerland. They thrive in the Valais because this long gorge, where the Rhône flows approximately south-west for about 50km (31 miles) and then north-west into the more isolated vineyards of the Bas Valais, is one of the sunniest parts of the country, with 2100 hours of sunshine per year. Most of the vineyards are on the right bank, facing south and catching all the sun. It's dry,

too, with between 400 and 700mm (16 and 28in) of rain per year – in fact, since the soils are light and well-drained it's sometimes rather too dry for comfort, and irrigation has to be used. The vignerons used to have little canals called *bisses* cut into the hillsides to carry melted snow down to the vines, but now you're more likely to see the draped hoses of drip irrigation.

You might think that getting any water up or down these mountains would be a feat of engineering, but the Swiss, to judge from their vineyards, are good at engineering. Some of these slopes have gradients of as much as 85 per cent, and there's no way you can cultivate anything except ivy on a slope that steep. So the mountains are terraced, with the neatest dry stone walls I've seen anywhere. Even the supporting walls tower high above your head: the Swiss have taken mountains and they've fortified them. Now, if that's not devotion to the vine I'd like to know what is. It also requires an enormous communal effort. There are 5136ha (12,690 acres) of vines in the Valais, and around 22,700 growers; that's not many vines each. Only about 700 growers bottle their own wine; the rest take their grapes to the co-operatives or sell to the merchant houses, and the wines are sold mostly by grape name or by style. Village names, with the exception of a few like Sion, the capital of the Valais, don't feature all that much.

Sion is famous for its Fendant (or Chasselas), a variety which, rather like the Riesling, reflects the character of its soil in its flavour. Sion has schist; elsewhere in the Valais there is limestone

The vineyards of the Valais are some of the most inspiringly beautiful in Europe and their steep terraces angled towards the sun produce surprisingly alcoholic wine. These vineyards are at Chamoson.

WHERE THE VINEYARDS ARE
The map shows the main part of the Valais, the broad expanse of south-facing vineyards on the north bank of the Rhône from Riddes to Leuk. Eight-five per cent of the Valais' vineyards are in this stretch. The vineyards here are dwarfed by the mountains: altitudes that sound fantastically high when compared to other vineyards elsewhere in the world look pitifully low compared to peaks that are snow-covered all the year round. But look how the vineyards creep just a little bit higher into the warmer side valleys and how the flatter land on the valley floor has only a few vineyards. Instead there are orchards – the Swiss are fond of fruit brandy to polish off a meal.

On the south bank of the Rhône and further west off the map, where the river takes an abrupt turn for the north-west, there are a few vineyards, but these are found in small pockets, rather than in a continuous band – a reflection of their less good exposure. But look how all the vineyard land twists in and out, ducking round an outcrop here, nudging the water's edge there and then drawing back as the sun and the shadows and the changing soil alter the balance for the vine. Deciding which vines to plant in which spots in an area like this has taken the growers centuries of trial and error.

in a long stretch from Leuk in the east to Leytron and Saillon in the west, with the greatest concentrations of limestone at Leuk and Sierre. West of Saillon, at Fully and Martigny, there is hardly any limestone, which makes these prime areas for Gamay. And at Saillon and the villages to the east, Leytron, Chamoson and Ardon, there is gravel. The growers have put it there themselves as it retains the heat admirably and reduces water evaporation. Chamoson also has the largest alluvial cone of the region which provides good conditions for Sylvaner, here called Johannisberg. Leuk, set in a position where it catches all the sun, makes good Dôle; Salgesch (Salquenen in French) also makes good reds. Val d'Anniviers, facing Sierre, is the home of a local speciality, Vin des Glaciers, made originally from the now all-but-extinct Rèze grape, but nowadays usually from Arvine and other white varieties. The wine is aged at high altitude in a modified solera system.

But there are two other parts of the Valais. There is the Bas Valais, the stretch of the river leading to Lake Geneva (Lac Léman), where the vines face mostly west or south-west. But even including the vineyards in Martigny and Entremont, the region can boast only 217ha (536 acres) of vines – just four per cent of the total. Then there are the vineyards east of Sierre, the traditional dividing point between the German-speaking Haut-Valais and rest of the Valais – and they really are *haut*. There are only 150ha (371 acres) of vines here, but they include the ones at steepling Visperterminen.

 RED GRAPES
Pinot Noir is found throughout the Valais and takes up over 60 per cent of the vineyard area. Gamay is the other main variety. The Valais has Switzerland's only plantings of Humagne Rouge.

WHITE GRAPES
Nearly 60 per cent of the white wine varieties are Chasselas (called Fendant in the Valais), with Sylvaner (called Johannisberg) being restricted to the best sites. There are also small amounts of other varieties, including Chardonnay, Pinot Gris (called Malvoisie here) and the indigenous Amigne, Arvine, Humagne Blanc and Rèze.

 CLIMATE
The Valais is Switzerland's sunniest wine region. It is always windy, and the Foehn wind helps to raise the temperature. Rainfall is low.

SOIL
The soil is generally light and well-drained and warms up rapidly. There is limestone, gravel, schist, as well as various alluvial cones along the Rhône.

 ASPECT
Vines grow as high as 1100m (3609ft) at Visperterminen; elsewhere they grow to 750m (2460ft), mostly on south-facing slopes overlooking the Rhône. The slopes are usually terraced and irrigated.

AUSTRIA

I CAN'T THINK OF A EUROPEAN NATION where the wine culture has changed as dramatically over a generation as it has in Austria. Up till 1985 Austria's quality reputation rested largely on her sweet wines from the Burgenland. Dry, or dryish whites were usually just for local consumption. Liebfraumilch lookalikes were the staple export commodity. And everyone seemed to eat vast plates of ham, sausage, black pudding and *speck* (fat bacon) for every single meal. Vegetables and fresh fruit? Well, I barely saw them.

And then there's now. Austria still makes great sweet wine, but the so-called 'anti-freeze' scandal, where a handful of producers were caught sweetening their wine with diethylene glycol, acted like an electric shock juddering through the body of Austrian wine, nearly killing the whole culture off. Eventually, however, it had the opposite effect, creating an entirely new order based on world-class dry whites and increasingly fine reds. Suddenly Austria seems sleek and positively New World in its ambition and innovativeness.

Ah, but is that the real Austria? Only partly. Spend a day out wine tasting in the cellars of the Wachau, or Burgenland, or Styria (Steiermark) – above all, Styria – and at every turn you'll be offered plattersful of sausage and ham and *speck* and rye bread smeared with smoked lard (delicious, by the way) as your palate slowly learns to judge a wine through the smog of pork fat and pepper. And lunch will probably be in a *Buschenschenke*, a family-owned country inn, in which the food and the wine are all home-produced.

The ones I'm talking about are in the east of the country, since that's where the vineyards are – the Austrian vineyards have a climate influenced, in the main, by the warm, dry climate of the Pannonian plain, to the east. Further west it's too mountainous and the climate too extreme.

A lot of winemaking families own *Buschenschenken*: in Styria (Steiermark), for example, there are 4000 growers, which includes (for tax purposes) mothers, fathers, grandparents and children, and some 800 *Buschenschenken*. One effect of this used to be that nearly all Austrian growers grew as many different grape varieties as they could – Grüner Veltliner, Weissburgunder, Welschriesling, Traminer, Müller-Thurgau, Rhine Riesling, Sauvignon Blanc, Blauburgunder and Blaufränkisch. But things have changed a lot in

recent years, and growers are increasingly focusing on what they and their regions do best. For example, most Wachau growers have ceased to grow red grapes; and in Styria many have uprooted their Riesling and Grüner Veltliner.

WINE REGIONS

In the northern part of Burgenland, the shallow Neusiedl lake makes great sweet wines possible; south Burgenland makes increasingly good reds; Lower Austria (Niederösterreich) makes the best Grüner Veltliner (this grape is an Austrian speciality) and Styria makes high acid but keenly flavoured wines which have achieved cult status in Austria. Vienna (Wien) has a wine region to itself and is a bit of a Jack-of-all-trades, with whole villages on the outskirts of the city apparently dedicated solely to serving wine to tourists.

It is the climate that makes Austrian viticulture feasible and, where the wine rises above everyday quality, it is because of a better mesoclimate. Indeed so favourable is the climate in eastern Austria that vineyards are scattered everywhere, rising up on odd south-facing slopes, while maize or pumpkins or orchards occupy the lower ground. There is none of the feeling of battling against the elements that one gets in parts of Germany – and accordingly there is no skeleton of moderating rivers to be found underlying the wine map. The Danube (Donau) runs west to east through Lower Austria, but only in the Wachau is the river genuinely necessary to the vine.

The Wachau lies at the western end of Lower Austria. Here the banks of the Danube rise into cliffs of rock and scrub, and the landscape is as beautiful and uncompromising as any in the Mosel. Some of Austria's finest dry whites come from these vineyards

WINE ZONES AND REGIONS

NIEDERÖSTERREICH
- Wachau
- Traisental
- Kremstal
- Kamptal
- Weinviertel
- Donauland
- Carnuntum
- Thermenregion

WIEN
- Wien

BURGENLAND
- Neusiedlersee
- Neusiedlersee-Hügelland
- Mittelburgenland
- Südburgenland

STEIERMARK
- Süd-Oststeiermark
- Südsteiermark
- Weststeiermark

PANORAMIC MAPS OF AUSTRIA
Niederösterreich *pages 146–147*
Burgenland *pages 148–149*

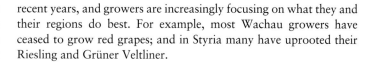

overlooking the river, just as her finest sweet whites come from the lush, low-lying, misty Neusiedlersee region in Burgenland. This is the other place where water plays a major part in Austrian wine – the large, shallow Neusiedl lake encourages the botrytis fungus to attack the grapes with a ferocity that is seen nowhere else in Europe – and consequently, it's possible to make great sweet wines here every year.

Most of the rest of vinous Austria is gently hilly or flattish. The hilliest region is Styria, down on the border with Slovenia, where the vines grow between 350 and 600m (1148 and 1968ft) on the Alpine foothills, partly to avoid the frost in the valleys, partly to get more sun and partly to benefit from the greater temperature fluctuations from day to night, that give acidity and finesse to the white grapes that dominate.

In spite of the high rainfall here – 900–1000mm (35–40in) a year – drought can be a problem on the well-drained sandy or stony soils, as can erosion. Finding the right sheltered, south-facing site is the key in Styria, and the best wines have elegance and taut balance combined with good levels of ripeness. Between 13 and 13.5 per cent alcohol, without chaptalization, is not uncommon for the top wines. But even the botrytis-affected sweet wines (and they may get botrytis as many as six years out of ten) don't taste as rich and as fat as those of Burgenland.

The fashion, though, is for the dry wines. Austria as a whole makes dry wines rather than sweet or semi-sweet, and the Austrian taste for dryness and acidity really took off with the Austrian wine scandal of 1985, when a small number of growers in Burgenland were caught adding the chemical diethylene glycol to their sweet wines to make them taste even richer. The Austrians have long since put this scandal behind them, but it was of great importance in changing national tastes in subsequent years, and in bringing Austrian wine up to its current high standard. The very strict wine laws are another legacy of the scandal.

Styria is divided into three regions – West, South and South-East Styria – of which the South-East is the largest in area and has 1300ha (3212 acres) under vine. The hills are lower here and the climate less extreme than elsewhere in Styria. South Styria looks the smallest area on the map, but has 1950ha (4818 acres) of vines, mainly around Leibnitz and down to the Slovenian border. The

specialities are Chardonnay (here called Morillon), Sauvignon Blanc and Gelber Muskateller. West Styria has a mere 450ha (1112 acres), nearly all given over to a fearsome rosé called Schilcher, made from the Blauer Wildbacher grape and notable for its tooth-piercing acidity. The slate soil and the climate, with its hot days and cold nights, are the key to making Schilcher – that and the hordes of tourists who will buy a grower's entire stock within four months of the harvest.

Vienna's vineyards are concentrated to the west of the city, though there are also some within the city itself. But it is the suburbs of Grinzing, Nussberg, Heiligenstadt and Stammersdorf that flourish on the proceeds of the vine. It's a short journey for the Viennese and for the tourist buses to these vine-covered courtyards where the accordionist plays until late into the evening – and you might even get some vegetables with your pork.

Most of the great vineyards of northern Europe need a river valley to provide heat and protection from wind and frost. At Weissenkirchen in the Wachau, the Danube sparkles in the afternoon sun, reflecting light and warmth on to the vines.

THE CLASSIFICATION SYSTEM FOR AUSTRIAN WINE

Austria's wine categories are basically similar to those of Germany although different, usually higher, must weights (the amount of original sugar in freshly picked grapes) are required for each category in acknowledgment of the more favourable climate. Must weights in Austria are measured in degrees KMW (Klosterneuburger Mostwaage), and each quality category of wine sets a minimum number of KMW: as a rule of thumb, KMW multiplied by five gives the Oechsle measurement used in Germany.

- **Tafelwein** Basic table wine of at least 10.6 degrees KMW.
- **Landwein** Country wine from a specific region, with at least 14 degrees KMW.
- **Qualitätswein** Quality wine from one of the 16 regions; may be chaptalized; minimum KMW 15 degrees; maximum KMW 19 for whites and 20 for reds.
- **Kabinett** This is not a Prädikat category, unlike in Germany. The wine may not be chaptalized; minimum KMW 17 degrees; must be dry.
- **Prädikatswein** As in Germany quality wines may additionally have a special category, but since most Austrian wines are dry, these categories

count for less here. The wines may not be chaptalized nor be sweetened with *Süssreserve* (natural grape juice). The Wachau has a ripeness scale for dry whites: Steinfeder wines are for early drinking; Federspiel wines can last three years or so; and the top wines are called Smaragd. SPÄTLESE Made from fully ripe grapes with at least 19 degrees KMW. AUSLESE Made from fully ripe grapes with a minimum KMW of 21 degrees. EISWEIN Made from grapes picked and pressed when frozen, with a minimum KMW of 25 degrees. BEERENAUSLESE Made from overripe or nobly rotten grapes, with a minimum KMW of 25 degrees. AUSBRUCH An Austrian category for wine made from overripe, nobly rotten or shrivelled grapes, with a minimum KMW of 27 degrees. TROCKENBEERENAUSLESE Made from overripe, nobly rotten or shrivelled grapes, with a minimum 30 degrees KMW.

- **DAC** This is the new Austrian appellation system based on identifying typical regional wine styles which was introduced in 2002. The Weinviertel DAC was the first one, covering Grüner Veltliner wines. Others are Mittelburgenland for Blaufränkisch and Traisental for Riesling and Grüner Veltliner wines.

Grüner Veltliner is Austria's speciality and makes very individual dry whites with a peppery tang.

NIEDERÖSTERREICH

RED GRAPES
Blauer Portugieser and Zweigelt are the most popular red grapes, taking up roughly one-third each of the vineyards. There are small amounts of Blauburgunder (Pinot Noir) and St Laurent.

WHITE GRAPES
Niederösterreich produces Austria's best Grüner Veltliner, and nearly half the vineyards are planted with it. Next comes Müller-Thurgau, Riesling and Welschriesling.

CLIMATE
The climate is generally dry, but Niederösterreich is a large area and there is great variation. Most parts are fairly warm; the eastern Weinviertel can be cooler and damper.

SOIL
Gneis subsoil is common, particularly in the Wachau. Topsoils include stony schist, limestone, gravel, loess in Krems and occasionally loam.

ASPECT
Most Niederösterreich vineyards are on plains or gently rolling hills. In the Wachau the Danube Valley is the focus, with the banks of the river getting steeper west of Krems.

NIEDERÖSTERREICH (Lower Austria), situated on the fertile Danube (Donau) plain, is one of the loveliest parts of Austria. It is a land of hills crowned with vast baroque monasteries and tunnelled with troglodyte wine cellars, of terraced slopes and fertile fields, of picturesque villages and, of course, the broad Danube: calm, powerful and yes, blue. Well, on a good day, anyway.

The map shows the heart of the area, where four wine regions gather along the Danube's banks. In the west, on both sides of the river, is the Wachau, home of Austria's best Rieslings. Next comes Kremstal. Kamptal is centred on the river Kamp and the important wine town of Langenlois, while Donauland stretches away to the east along the Danube as far as Vienna. All these regions make dry whites.

The Wachau Rieslings both are and are not like German Rieslings. Coming from a relatively warm climate, the wines are dry, full of extract and minerally, rather than flowery. They age well, although the Austrian taste is for young wine and they seldom get the chance. The grapes grow in conditions as demanding as those of any German vineyard: about half the Wachau is terraced, and the vines have to work hard for their living on shallow, stony soil that is often only 50cm (20in) deep; underneath there is gneiss. The Wachau receives about 450mm (18in) of rain a year, but the summers are very dry, and the only concession the vine gets is irrigation, though not much: six days in any growing season is the maximum allowed.

The eastern end of the Wachau makes more opulent wines, but only where the soil is shallow and poor is Riesling planted, on slopes up to 300m (984ft). On the flatter land and the sandy soil nearer the river, Grüner Veltliner is grown and, in the right hands and providing yields are kept down to around 40 hectolitres per hectare, the wines can be intense and powerful, with good structure and even the ability to age for a few years. There is Weissburgunder here, too, but it's the Riesling that gets the prime south-facing sites.

Growers say the terraces are three to five times more work than the flat vineyards and the flatter vineyards, as mechanization increases, are getting cheaper to work. But the effort and expense of keeping these remarkable vineyards going is rewarded by an array of brilliant whites. Kremstal is less spectacular but the wines are also seriously good. Niederösterreich generally is the home of Austria's best Grüner Veltliner (it's too warm in Burgenland and too cold elsewhere in the country) and Kremstal produces Grüner Veltliners as good as those of the Wachau, again providing the yields are kept low. The climatic influence is from the south-east – the great Pannonian plain stretches across into Hungary, where it is warm and dry – and Krems gets less than 500mm (20in) of rain per year.

The town of Krems is the wine capital of these parts and the town of Stein, next door, has some of Austria's best vineyard sites. Most famous is the Steiner Hund, steep and terraced and ideal for Riesling, followed by Pfaffenberg, which is every bit as good, and Kögl and Kremsleiten, which are almost in the same class. Then there is the Krems Valley, winding down from the north-west; and to the east a great swathe of vineyards around Rohrendorf on loess soil.

Kamptal's wine centre is Langenlois, which before 1986 had a whole wine region named after it. Now its fame rests mostly on the high-quality grapes (the usual Austrian cocktail of varieties – Grüner Veltliner, Ruländer, Chardonnay, Weissburgunder, Blauburgunder, Merlot and both Cabernets) – coming from the great curve of south-facing vineyards that arches around the town plus some good growers to make the most of it all.

Traisental consists of some 700ha (1730 acres) along the valley of the Trais between St Pölten and the Danube to the north. Donauland looks to the town and old monastery of Klosterneuburg as its capital: the monastery is the largest single vineyard owner in Austria, and the town is the home of Austria's first viticultural institute and the inventor of Klosterneuburger Mostwaage or KMW, the Austrian system for measuring must weight. Carnuntum lies south-east of Vienna and runs up to the Leitha Hills, which separate it from Burgenland. The climate here is warm and dry and, especially near the Burgenland border, fairly similar to that of Burgenland itself.

Thermenregion is a region of spas and hot springs. It's sunnier and drier here than in Vienna, and as warm as you'd expect from a place with its own inbuilt central heating. But it is windy, and it's this wind that prevents much noble rot settling on the grapes. So its wine capital, Gumpoldskirchen, developed its own speciality: semi-sweet wines made from a blend of two local grapes, Rotgipfler and Zierfandler, and it was precisely this style of wine that went out of fashion overnight when the Austrian wine scandal broke in 1985.

The growers turned to dry wines, often made from Welschriesling, but now there are signs that the traditional style could make a comeback. The Zierfandler is planted on the higher slopes of the hills, where it develops plenty of acidity, and the Rotgipfler lower down. Red wines are the speciality in the south of Thermenregion and the most successful ones come from vineyards planted on the stony soils of the villages of Tattendorf and Teesdorf.

Niederösterreich's biggest region, the Weinviertel, also produces good reds, particularly on the granite soil around Retz near the Czech border, where there is less rain than in any other Austrian wine region. In the north-east of the Weinviertel the climate is damper and the vineyards here are a source of good Grüner Veltliner. In some of these villages there are wonderfully pretty Kellergassen, tiny pedimented cellars built in a row into the hillside, along narrow lanes running between high banks. Anyone on a wine tour of Austria really should try to get an invitation to one of these cellars, if only to get a glimpse of a winemaking tradition that goes back centuries. At regular intervals along the lanes are front

WEISSENKIRCHEN

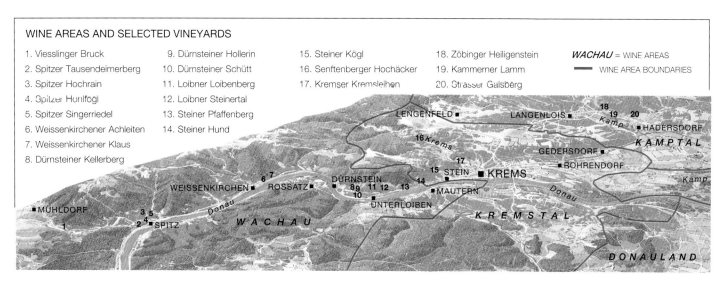

WINE AREAS AND SELECTED VINEYARDS

1. Viesslinger Bruck
2. Spitzer Tausendeimerberg
3. Spitzer Hochrain
4. Spitzer Honifogl
5. Spitzer Singerriedel
6. Weissenkirchener Achleiten
7. Weissenkirchener Klaus
8. Dürnsteiner Kellerberg

9. Dürnsteiner Hollerin
10. Dürnsteiner Schütt
11. Loibner Loibenberg
12. Loibner Steinertal
13. Steiner Pfaffenberg
14. Steiner Hund

15. Steiner Kögl
16. Senftenberger Hochäcker
17. Kremser Kremsleihen

18. Zöbinger Heiligenstein
19. Kammerner Lamm
20. Strasser Galsberg

WACHAU = WINE AREAS
—— WINE AREA BOUNDARIES

doors leading straight into the hillside, like a scene out of a fairy tale. Inside, the cellars are deep and narrow, each one wide enough for only one row of barrels on each side and a pathway down the middle.

As you go further into the hill the temperature drops dramatically; and in these emerald- or scarlet-hooped black barrels is the entire harvest of one small-scale grower. Hopefully, he'll take some samples of wine for you to try. The wine will be cold and fresh, high in acidity and with a piercing fresh fruit. There'll be Grüner Veltliner, Müller-Thurgau, Welschriesling and three or four others and just when your teeth are beginning to chatter and you've lost all feeling in your feet, he'll lead you back outside to the sun.

Most of the grapes for Austria's Sekt industry come from east of the Weinviertel, though the Sekt companies have their offices in or near Vienna. Austrians tend to have a sweeter tooth for sparkling wines than for still, and most Austrian Sekt tastes heavy and over-sweetened to a foreign palate. Some is made by the traditional method (like Champagne).

WHERE THE VINEYARDS ARE *This map shows why the Wachau is Niederösterreich's leading quality region. To the west of Krems the banks of the Danube (Donau) begin to rise into steep hills, and by the pretty town of Dürnstein (where Richard the Lionheart was imprisoned: the ruins of the castle built with his ransom are still there today) they are high, rugged and arid. The vineyards here, facing south or south-west across the river, get all the sun they need, and the Danube does its bit by reflecting all that warmth back on to the slopes. The great rocky outcrops and stony soils found around here hold the heat, too. The warm days and cool nights mean that the grapes retain their acidity and have lots of flavour, as well as getting nicely ripe.*

There are lots of little tributaries flowing into the Danube through these hills. The Krems and the Kamp rivers offer good sites along their banks, but really it's the Danube itself that is the focus of viticulture in this part of Niederösterreich. East of Krems is a flatter area of mixed farming. Here the vineyards spread away from the river, both north and south, clustering around the villages. South of the Danube the vineyards spread over gently rolling hills, alternating with other forms of agriculture.

WACHAU, KREMSTAL AND KAMPTAL

TOTAL DISTANCE NORTH TO SOUTH 21KM (13 MILES)

 VINEYARDS

N

0 km   1   2
0 miles   1

BURGENLAND

 RED GRAPES
Blaufränkisch, with 17 per cent of the vineyard, is the main red variety. There is also a significant amount of Zweigelt (13 per cent) but only tiny amounts of Cabernet, St Laurent, Blauburgunder (Pinot Noir) and Blauburger.

 WHITE GRAPES
The Austrian speciality, Grüner Veltliner, has 19 per cent of the vineyard area. Muskat-Ottonel and Neuburger, along with Welschriesling and Weissburgunder, are much used for Ausbruch and other sweet wines.

CLIMATE
This is the warmest and driest wine region in Austria. The average annual temperature at Illmitz is 10.9°C (51.5°F).

SOIL
The soil is very varied, with sand around the Neusiedl lake and loam further away. There is limestone in the Leitha Hills and the Rosalien Hills to the west of the lake. Elsewhere there is gravel and deep loam.

ASPECT
The region is generally flat. Neusiedlersee-Hügelland is gently undulating, with good south and south-east-facing slopes, and there are occasional ranges of hills in Mittelburgenland. In the north-east of Südburgenland the Eisenberg faces east and south-east over the plain.

FOR LOVERS OF LUSCIOUSLY SWEET botrytis-affected wine, the marshy, reedy corner of Austria that is mapped here is one of the most remarkable places on earth. Nowhere else does *Botrytis cinerea* attack the grapes so reliably every year; nowhere else is it so easy to make great sweet wines, and in such quantities. In Germany and France growers watch their grapes anxiously for the first signs of the fungus that will shrivel and brown the grapes and impart its distinctive flavour to the wines. In the vineyards bordering the Neusiedl lake (Neusiedler See) they seldom need to worry. This reliability has a produced a surge in quality in recent years, as producers have focused on refining their techniques. Wines that were once safe and inexpensive, and then fell out of favour after the wine scandal of 1985, are now world-class, and (inevitably) rather more expensive.

The Burgenland has had a chequered history. Until 1921 it was part of Hungary, and joined Austria just in time for the economic hardship of the 1920s and 1930s. After the end of World War Two the Burgenland was part of the Russian zone of occupation, and it

WHERE THE VINEYARDS ARE *It's difficult to see the Neusiedl lake from a distance: the land is so flat, especially on the eastern side, that the reed beds hide the shimmer of the water. Only the brightly coloured sails of the pleasure boats mark where the water is deep enough to sail. At its deepest point the lake only reaches about 2m (6ft) – the shallow water heats up quickly and, since this is the hottest part of Austria, the water temperature can be as high as 30°C (86°F) in late summer. The whole of the western side of the lake, the Neusiedlersee-Hugelland, is more undulating. It is thickly planted with vines towards the south, but where the Leitha hills, one of the last foothills of the Alps, rise up in the north the vines climb a little way up the slopes.*

The eastern side is flat all the way into the vast Hungarian plain. The Neusiedlersee or Seewinkel is an area dotted with hundreds of ponds and small lakes; some of these dry up in the summer, but there are enough to make this a remarkably humid area. This humidity combines with the warmth that has given the Podersdorf region the nickname of Hölle (hell) to make Podersdorf, Illmitz and Apetlon centres of sweet wine production. Further north, around Gols, dry whites and reds are made: look how the little lakes of the Seewinkel don't reach that far.

The same is true of the west side of the lake: sweet wines are made only where humidity can reach the vines. Beyond a narrow strip running alongside the lake, the vineyards produce dry whites and reds, which have greater acidity (since the nights are cooler) as the vines rise up the slopes of the Leitha Hills. The centre for sweet wines here is Rust, a picturesque village crammed with tourist coaches in the summer and nesting storks in the spring.

was only when the Russians left in 1956 that the way was clear for investment in the vineyards. So while fine sweet wines have been made around the Neusiedl lake since the beginning of the 17th century, it is only in recent decades that they have been made in such large quantities. The southern shores of the lake, indeed, are still part of Hungary and form part of the Sopron wine region. But unlike the Austrian vineyards around the lake, these Hungarian vineyards are largely planted with red varieties, both Cabernets, Merlot and Pinot Noir.

The eastern shore, a shallow expanse of water that imparts humidity to the area, has only a recent history of viticulture. This was a largely forgotten part of the country, given over to cattle farming until the late 1950s, when the local chamber of commerce suggested that the farmers plant bulk vines like Grüner Veltliner and Müller-Thurgau for basic blending wine. Neither is remotely suited to this hot, humid, flat region where grapes ripen early and can lack acidity unless care is taken in the winemaking process; it has only been with the planting of aromatic varieties like Traminer,

THE NEUSIEDLER SEE

NEUSIEDLERSEE = WINE AREA

━━ WINE AREA BOUNDARY

TOTAL DISTANCE NORTH TO SOUTH 19 KM (12 MILES)

VINEYARDS

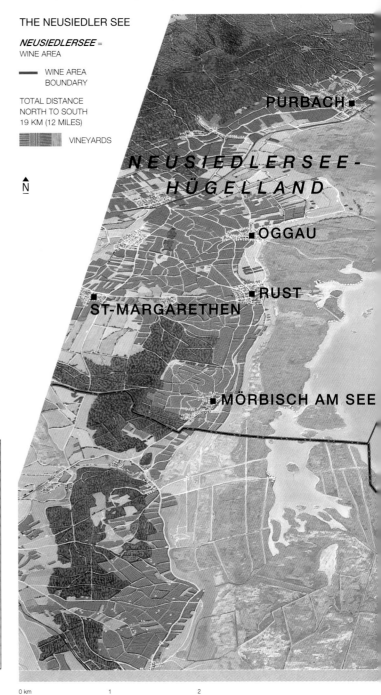

PURBACH

NEUSIEDLERSEE-HÜGELLAND

OGGAU

RUST

ST-MARGARETHEN

MÖRBISCH AM SEE

0 km   1   2
0 miles   1

NEUSIEDLER SEE

The shallow Neusiedl lake is one of the most perfect mesoclimates in the world for the development of *Botrytis cinerea* or noble rot. As the autumn draws in after the long, hot continental summer the falling temperatures cause night fogs and early morning mists over the warm waters of the lake and the surrounding vineyards. Later in the morning the bright autumn sunshine burns off the fogs and mists and this alternation of humidity and sunshine provides ideal conditions for botrytis.

Upper vineyards Further away from the lake there is less humidity. Botrytis infection occurs only occasionally, perhaps about twice a decade.

Lower vineyards The warmth and humidity in this low-lying area near the lake and in the Seewinkel, with its hundreds of small ponds and lakes, mean that it is almost impossible for ripe grapes not to be infected with botrytis in the late autumn.

Elevation in metres

RUST

Neusiedler See   Seewinkel

200
150
100

W   Vertical exaggeration 11.4 times horizontal scale   E

and traditional Burgenland vines like Welschriesling and Weissburgunder, that fine wines have emerged.

The soil on both sides of the lake is sandy, since the lake itself once covered an even larger area than its current 152 square kilometres (59 square miles). Away from the immediate lake area the soil is loam, which tends not to heat up quite as fast, and there is limestone in the foothills to the west. The eastern side of the lake is even warmer; the grapes ripen here some two weeks earlier, and in late September 1989, when the grapes were still green on the western side, the first grapes for Trockenbeerenauslesen wines were picked on the eastern side. Yields on the eastern side are fairly high, at around 60 or 70 hl/ha, though nobly rotten grapes are more likely to give half that figure.

However, Burgenland is not all sweet wines. The region extends in a knobbly strip south-west of the lake along the Hungarian border through the flat Mittelburgenland down to Südburgenland and the border with Slovenia. The Mittelburgenland is red wine country. Over eighty per cent of the grapes are red and most of them are Blaufränkisch. The more enterprising growers follow an international path of dry wines, sometimes aged in new oak, and often given extra backbone with some Cabernet Sauvignon. Yields from such growers are around the 50hl/ha mark. Horitschon, Neckenmarkt and Deutschkreuz are the most important villages.

Südburgenland is an altogether quieter place. It is a region of summer rain and relatively late ripening, and of mixed farming except in the best spots, which include the villages of Deutsch Schützen and Eisenberg. The village of Rechnitz, too, produces good whites. The grapes are mainly Blaufränkisch and Zweigelt for reds and Welschriesling for whites – plus rarities such as Concord, Noah, Otello, Seibel and Ripatella which are grown for wine in only a few places in Europe; darkest Südburgenland is one of these places and the wine is known as Uhudler. I rather wish it were exported as it has a long and by no means disproven reputation as an aphrodisiac. In the USA these vines are commonplace, since they are the names of native American vines of the sort bred for rootstocks of European vines.

Alois Kracher makes some of Austria's greatest sweet botrytized wines at Illmitz in the Neusiedlersee region.

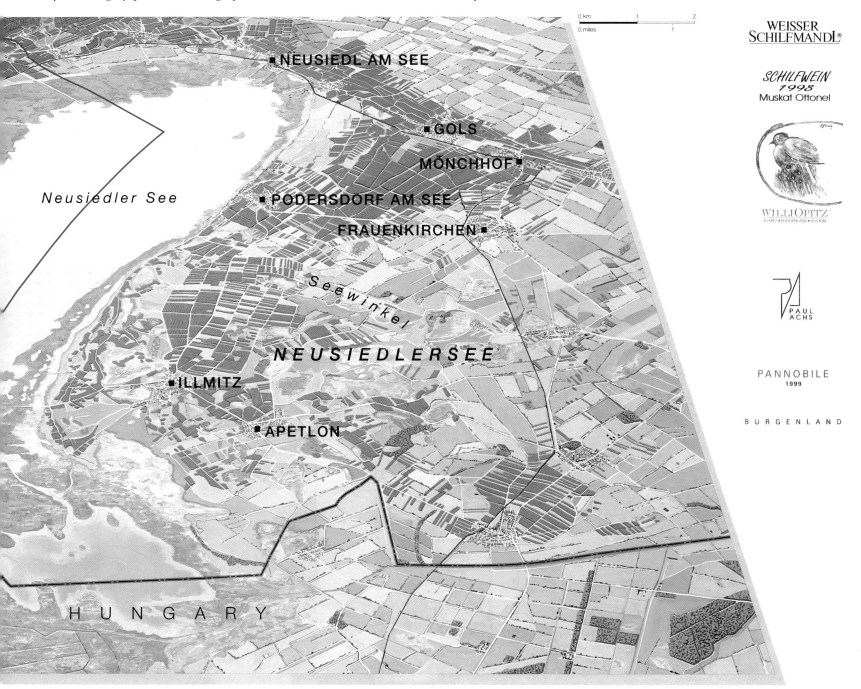

ITALY

The Chianti vineyards of Rampolla in Tuscany near Panzano, left, and newly picked Nebbiolo grapes from Roberto Voerzio in Barolo country in Piedmont, above. For many years these two regions and styles of wine were the twin poles of quality in Italian red wines. Now, I'm happy to say, they are being challenged by new ideas all over the country.

Italy. What an exasperating country. No other nation can so easily fill my eyes with tears at the sheer beauty of its human achievements, yet no other country makes steam shoot from my ears in fury at the wholesale squandering of nature's gifts. But, I wonder, is it possible to have it any other way? There are countries where you can easily understand the potential and range of their wines, good or bad. Reliable, conformist, unlikely to let you down. Unlikely to thrill you either. Italy's not a bit like that. Some of her most famous vineyards produce some of her worst wines. Some of her greatest wines had no legal standing at all until 1995. The DOC system, set up in 1963 to try to make sense of the anarchy that was Italian wine, has spent as much time enshrining mediocrity and protecting incompetence as it has promoting and preserving quality and regional character. In an area such as Tuscany, where great wine names like Chianti and Vino Nobile di Montepulciano had come to be meaningless, the region's innovative, quality-conscious producers were forced to go outside the law rather than submit to regulations that had nothing to do with excellence and everything to do with political expediency.

And yet, and yet. From the northern terraces in the snowy embrace of the Tyrolean Alps to the southern islands that are mere specks on the horizon within hailing distance of Africa, Italy has more continuous vineyard land than any other country. Italians are also the world's leading drinkers of wine, but they still have enough spare to be the world's main exporter of wine too. The Apennine backbone running down the centre of the country means that increasing sunshine can almost always be countered with altitude. The surrounding seas provide calm, soothing maritime influences to all the wine regions except those of the far north. And most of the grape varieties are Italian originals.

It all sounds like a wine paradise on earth. Well it hasn't been, not recently, maybe not ever, as generation after generation failed to make the best of this bounty. But Italy now swarms with enthusiastic, talented young vine growers and winemakers passionate in their desire to test just how good her wines can be. The timing is perfect. The new wave of wines across the world has been based largely on French role models and French grape varieties. But the 21st century has brought with it a hunger for new directions and new flavours. Italy, with her maverick mentality, her challenging wine styles and her jungle of grape varieties, is at last ready to take on the role of leadership she has avoided for so long.

THE WINE REGIONS OF ITALY

VINES AND ITALY DO GO TOGETHER. Indeed, given the amount of wine that Italy produces, a first-time visitor to the country might expect every imaginable nook and cranny to be planted with vineyards. But they'd be wrong. There are vast tracts of vines in Italy, but these tend to be concentrated in a few regions: Piedmont (Piemonte) in the north-west, Veneto and Friuli in the north-east, Tuscany (Toscana) and Emilia-Romagna in west central Italy, Marche and Abruzzo in the centre-east, Puglia in the south and the islands of Sicily and Sardinia. In between you often don't see a vine.

Even so, there are more vines growing in Italy than in almost any other country on earth (only France and Spain have more) and when you remember how long Italy is, it's obvious that there will be enormous differences of wine styles. In the Alpine valleys of the Aosta Valley you are far closer to London than you are to the tiny island of Pantelleria, which almost touches the African shores of Tunisia. And from the Alps to Sicily runs the great spine of the Apennines. Indeed 80 per cent of the country is hilly or mountainous and the endless twists and turns provide a vast array of beautifully exposed slopes on which the vine can bask. Their altitude is important too. While the northern Alpine slopes allow wines of delicate crystalline purity, as we head south their craggy heights are crucial in tempering the blazing southern sun.

Proximity to water is also vital, and Italy's long thin body means that many vines benefit from the cooling effects of the Adriatic and Tyrrhenian seas on the eastern and western flanks. Inland lakes like Lake Garda in the north-east create local climates that greatly influence wine styles. And then there are the rivers. From the Adige, tumbling out of the Dolomites in the north-east, to Piedmont's Tanaro creating the boundary between the Roero and Langhe hills, on to the Po bisecting northern and central Italy, to Tuscany's Arno and Lazio's Tiber. In some cases, these rivers serve to moderate the climate, but with others, most notably the Po, they provide fertile valleys in which the vine performs like an athlete on steroids.

Given the great climatic and topographical diversity, it is hardly surprising that Italy has such a wide range of native grape varieties, most of which are suited only to their local growing conditions.

The Nebbiolo, for instance, only seems to flourish in Piedmont, and nowhere better than on the limestone rich soil of the Langhe hills; the white Moscato grape, though grown throughout the peninsula, excels in the white, chalky soils around Canelli in Piedmont's Monferrato hills.

Further east, around Verona, the white Garganega and red Corvina flourish in the Dolomite foothills, while in the hills along the Slovenian border, international varieties like Pinot Grigio and Sauvignon do battle with natives like Tocai Friulano and Ribolla. On the eastern coast the Montepulciano grape holds sway, but attempts to transport it across the Apennines to Tuscany have been thwarted by the cooler climate there. Sangiovese, however, produces meagre wines on the eastern coast, but in Tuscany rises to great heights. It is planted throughout the peninsula, as are Barbera and the white Trebbiano, the latter still being Italy's most widely planted white grape, accounting for almost 10 per cent of all the vineyards. But while Barbera and Sangiovese can produce great wines in the right sites, Trebbiano is prized only for its resistance to disease and prodigious yields, and is today rapidly losing ground.

Moving south, we encounter varieties first brought to the peninsula by the Greeks 3000 years ago – Negroamaro, Uva di Troia, Aglianico, Gaglioppo and Greco di Tufo – all of which perform brilliantly in southern conditions. When northern varieties like Sangiovese and Trebbiano are planted in the south they ripen as early as August and, as a result, produce wines of ineffable neutrality, but the native southern grapes, more accustomed to the hot summers, have a much longer growing season, which allows them time to develop interesting and complex perfumes and tastes.

The islands, too, have their own varieties. In Sicily the Nero d'Avola is unrivalled, while in Sardinia, evidence of Spanish domination in the Middle Ages is still to be found in grape varieties like the red Cannonau (Spain's Garnacha) and Carignano (Cariñena) and the white Vermentino (said to be a strain of Malvasia). Here, as elsewhere in Italy, the importance of matching these grape varieties with suitable terrain and climate cannot be underestimated.

Gaja is arguably Italy's most famous producer. Sperss is a top Barolo vineyard but Gaja has chosen to use the less restrictive Langhe regional denomination.

THE CLASSIFICATION SYSTEM FOR ITALIAN WINE

Italy's wine laws evolved out of the chaos of the 1950s and in 1963 the Italian government set up a system of *denominazione di origine*, or denomination of origin, which was based loosely on the French appellation contrôlée system. Until recently only about 10 per cent of the enormous Italian wine harvest was regulated by wine laws. This is now changing as new wine laws passed in 1992, known as the Goria law, continue to incorporate more wines into the various categories.

QUALITY CATEGORIES

Wine is divided into two categories – quality wine (DOCG and DOC) and table wine (IGT and VdT).

▪ **Denominazione di Origine Controllata e Garantita (DOCG)** This top tier of Italian wine started off as a tighter form of DOC, as a way of recognizing the finest Italian wines. There were more stringent restrictions on grape types and yields and the wine had to be analyzed and tasted by a special panel before being granted its coveted seal. It acknowledges the evident superiority of wines like Barbaresco, Barolo, Brunello di Montalcino and Vino Nobile di Montepulciano. Although wines are made under stricter standards that have favoured improvements, the best guarantee of quality remains the producer's name. Thirty-five zones have been granted DOCG status.

▪ **Denominazione di Origine Controllata (DOC)** This level applies to wines made from specified grape varieties, grown in specified zones and aged by prescribed methods. To a certain extent the DOC rules serve to preserve existing traditions which have more of an eye to quantity than quality at the expense of progress, and do not always guarantee good quality. Nearly all the traditionally well-known wines are DOC. Recently the laws have become more flexible, encouraging producers to reduce yields and modernize techniques while bringing quality wines under new appellations that allow for recognition of communes, estates and single vineyards. There are now over 315 DOCs.

▪ **Indicazione Geografica Tipica (IGT)** This is a higher level of table wine and designed as an Italian version of the successful French *vin de pays* category. The wines can use a geographical description on the label followed by a varietal name. Because some individual producers have become disillusioned with the strict DOC laws, some of Italy's greatest wines carry the humble IGT designation.

▪ **Vino da Tavola (VdT)** This is the most basic classification and no geographical or varietal distinctions can be made on the label. Particularly cunning is the prohibition of the mention of vintage, forcing most producers upward at least into the IGT category.

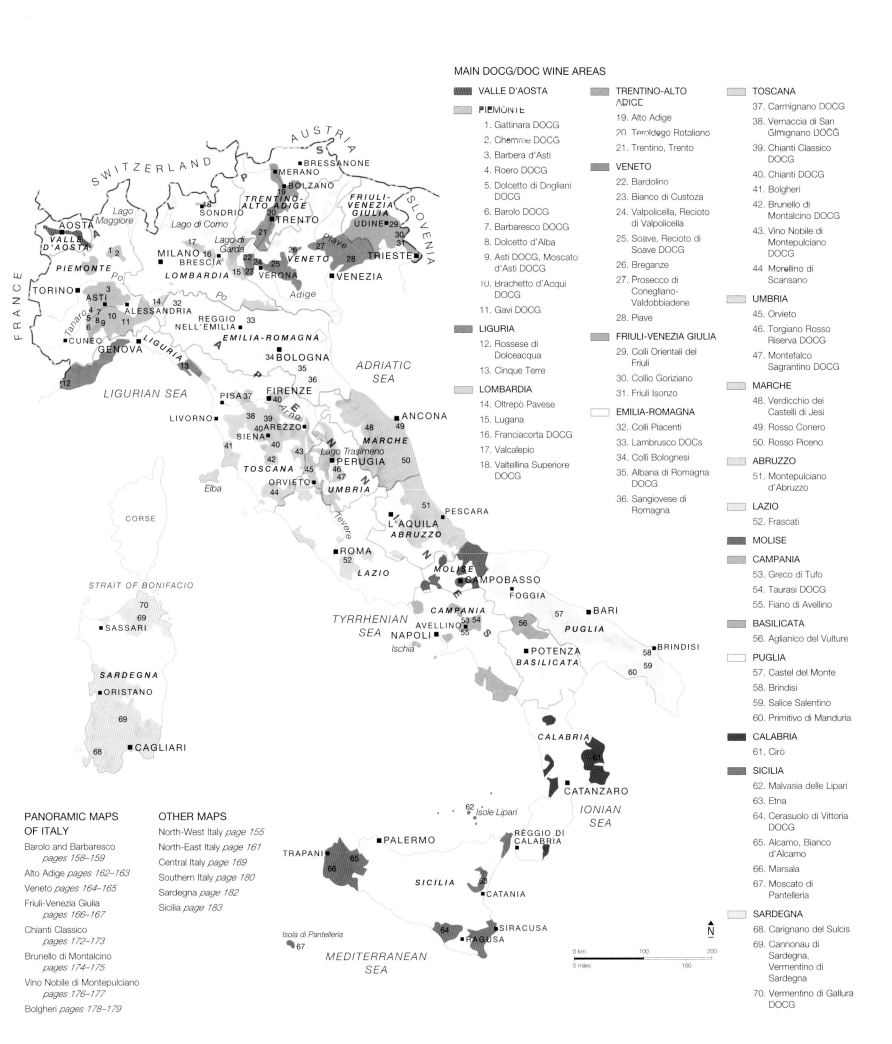

MAIN DOCG/DOC WINE AREAS

VALLE D'AOSTA

PIEMONTE

1. Gattinara DOCG
2. Ghemme DOCG
3. Barbera d'Asti
4. Roero DOCG
5. Dolcetto di Dogliani DOCG
6. Barolo DOCG
7. Barbaresco DOCG
8. Dolcetto d'Alba
9. Asti DOCG, Moscato d'Asti DOCG
10. Brachetto d'Acqui DOCG
11. Gavi DOCG

LIGURIA

12. Rossese di Dolceacqua
13. Cinque Terre

LOMBARDIA

14. Oltrepò Pavese
15. Lugana
16. Franciacorta DOCG
17. Valcalepio
18. Valtellina Superiore DOCG

TRENTINO-ALTO ADIGE

19. Alto Adige
20. Teroldego Rotaliano
21. Trentino, Trento

VENETO

22. Bardolino
23. Bianco di Custoza
24. Valpolicella, Recioto di Valpolicella
25. Soave, Recioto di Soave DOCG
26. Breganze
27. Prosecco di Conegliano-Valdobbiadene
28. Piave

FRIULI-VENEZIA GIULIA

29. Colli Orientali del Friuli
30. Collio Goriziano
31. Friuli Isonzo

EMILIA-ROMAGNA

32. Colli Piacenti
33. Lambrusco DOCs
34. Colli Bolognesi
35. Albana di Romagna DOCG
36. Sangiovese di Romagna

TOSCANA

37. Carmignano DOCG
38. Vernaccia di San Gimignano DOCG
39. Chianti Classico DOCG
40. Chianti DOCG
41. Bolgheri
42. Brunello di Montalcino DOCG
43. Vino Nobile di Montepulciano DOCG
44. Morellino di Scansano

UMBRIA

45. Orvieto
46. Torgiano Rosso Riserva DOCG
47. Montefalco Sagrantino DOCG

MARCHE

48. Verdicchio dei Castelli di Jesi
49. Rosso Conero
50. Rosso Piceno

ABRUZZO

51. Montepulciano d'Abruzzo

LAZIO

52. Frascati

MOLISE

CAMPANIA

53. Greco di Tufo
54. Taurasi DOCG
55. Fiano di Avellino

BASILICATA

56. Aglianico del Vulture

PUGLIA

57. Castel del Monte
58. Brindisi
59. Salice Salentino
60. Primitivo di Manduria

CALABRIA

61. Cirò

SICILIA

62. Malvasia delle Lipari
63. Etna
64. Cerasuolo di Vittoria DOCG
65. Alcamo, Bianco d'Alcamo
66. Marsala
67. Moscato di Pantelleria

SARDEGNA

68. Carignano del Sulcis
69. Cannonau di Sardegna, Vermentino di Sardegna
70. Vermentino di Gallura DOCG

PANORAMIC MAPS OF ITALY

Barolo and Barbaresco *pages 158–159*

Alto Adige *pages 162–163*

Veneto *pages 164–165*

Friuli-Venezia Giulia *pages 166–167*

Chianti Classico *pages 172–173*

Brunello di Montalcino *pages 174–175*

Vino Nobile di Montepulciano *pages 176–177*

Bolgheri *pages 178–179*

OTHER MAPS

North-West Italy *page 155*

North-East Italy *page 161*

Central Italy *page 169*

Southern Italy *page 180*

Sardegna *page 182*

Sicilia *page 183*

0 km   100   200
0 miles   100

NORTH-WEST ITALY

IF I'VE GOT TIME – and if the mountain pass is open – I like to enter Italy the hard way, driving the long tortuous route over the small St-Bernhard pass from Bourg St-Maurice and down into the Aosta Valley getting ever more excited as the valley opens out and the whole of Italy beckons. Such excitement is, in part, the reaction of a sun-starved northern European arriving in the luminous landscapes of Italy, but there is also, for the wine lover, the added attraction of Italy's greatest wine zone just over an hour's drive away in Piedmont's Langhe hills around the town of Alba.

The corrugated sub-Alpine hills and the clay and limestone soils of the Langhe provide the perfect environment for the cultivation of the vine, and the growers' dedication results in some of the most exciting wines in Italy. But it's only relatively recently that the thought of the Langhe has been able to set my tastebuds tingling in anticipation. Once my gums would have trembled at the prospect of tasting the hard wines that Barolo and Barbaresco used to be. But today I find myself increasingly drawn to the new style of delicately balanced wines emerging from this region, wines which, far from betraying their ancient reputation for power and thrilling hauteur, are transforming, then rebuilding it in a most remarkable way. None of the arrogance of old Barolo and Barbaresco has been lost; there's no hail-fellow-well-met open-handed New World bonhomie about these wines. Yet there is a core of sweet fruit and beguiling perfume coiled within the surly exterior that used to be destroyed by years of aging in ancient wood, yet which now bursts through the tannic shield with a firework display of blackberries and tar, wild mountain strawberries and the sweet fragrance of rose petals.

The Langhe hills no longer form an island of quality in a sea of mediocrity, as was the case a few years ago. True, historic names like Gattinara and Ghemme consistently underperform, but underperformers of the recent past, like the Barberas of the Asti and Monferrato zones, are responsible today for wines of real excellence and excitement. There are, too, some extraordinarily tasty and adventurous blends coming from various parts of Piedmont, bringing together not just local Nebbiolo and Barbera (incidentally a potentially blissful marriage) but also one or other of these – or both – with Cabernet, Merlot, even Pinot Noir.

The international varieties are spreading their influence in the white wine department too – with Chardonnay, Sauvignon Blanc and even Viognier coming increasingly into contention not just in Piedmont but indeed more so in Lombardy's Franciacorta and Oltrepò Pavese zones – the former being perhaps the world's closest rival to Champagne in the quality sparkling wine stakes.

There is indeed no reason why north-west Italy shouldn't produce good wine, since it has all the necessary natural attributes. Mountains – the Alps to the north and west, the Apennines to the south – form a protective semi-circle, and act as a natural border between Piedmont (its name is derived from the fact that it lies at the foot of the mountains) and the coastal region of Liguria to the south. Rivers like the Po, Tanaro and Bormida irrigate the lush, low-lying valleys that produce some of Italy's best fruit, while hills like the Langhe and Monferrato, and the Alpine foothills of Lombardy, provide the vine with ideal growing conditions.

The Po, Italy's longest river, rises in the Alps near the French border before cutting a swathe through the plains of Piedmont, Lombardy and the Veneto, dividing northern Alpine Italy from Emilia-Romagna and central Italy. The broad, fertile Po valley, unsuitable for viticulture (though its very fertility has tempted many a greedy grape grower), is bordered to the north by an outcrop of limestone and dolomite (calcium magnesium carbonate) that forms the foothills of Lombardy's Alps. These extend into the

This bright, breezy label is a far cry from the ultra-serious labels of traditional Barolo, but Cerequoio is a single-vineyard wine from Roberto Voerzio, one of Barolo's leading modernists.

Veneto, hosting the Classico zones of Valpolicella and Soave, but in Lombardy are largely responsible for the wines of Franciacorta.

While the Alps act as a protective helmet for Italy's head, the Apennines – curving eastwards along the southern border of Piedmont before turning south – act as the top of her spine. And, like the Alps, their presence has an influence on the region's viticulture with the vines clothing suitable slopes on both sides of the range, those on the Ligurian slopes tumbling headlong towards the sea, and producing wines like Cinque Terre and Vermentino that quench the thirst of legions of tourists.

Italy has few landlocked regions, yet in the north-west of the country only Liguria has contact with the sea. This nearness to the water gives this slight, crescent-shaped region a more moderate climate than Piedmont, Lombardy or the mountainous Aosta to the north. Inland, winters are bitterly cold, summers long and hot and autumns generally fine until thick fogs descend for days on end in early October. The prospects for a fine vintage are greatly increased if the fogs hold off or are counterbalanced by sunny afternoons.

PIEDMONT (PIEMONTE)
In Piedmont, Italy's largest region, the Langhe and Monferrato hills (together accounting for over 90 per cent of the region's wine production) are often wreathed in thick swirls of fog. Known as *nebbia* in Italian, the fog has given its name to one of Piedmont's – indeed Italy's – greatest grape varieties: Nebbiolo. This fickle variety, the sole component of Barolo and Barbaresco, ripens late, and is quite often struggling to reach maturity when the fogs cover the valleys and the lower slopes. When Nebbiolo wins the battle, the results are splendid; when the fog wins, the growers are left with a rather insipid, raw and rasping red wine that leaves tasters grimacing and wondering what all the fuss is about.

But as I said above, Piedmont has more weapons in its armoury than just the noble Nebbiolo. Other red grapes like Barbera and Dolcetto produce greater volumes of wine. Barbera is a prodigious variety that appears to flourish wherever it is planted, and it has the great virtue of ripening easily to produce a rich, black-fruited wine that is high in acid and mercifully low in tannin. In recent years Barbera has been found to have an amazing affinity for barrel-aging, as well as responding remarkably successfully to crop limitation to make wines of impressive concentration and stylishness. Dolcetto, for its part, was always considered to be at its best a vibrant, purple-red wine, packed with plummy fruit and spice – unsophisticated, undemanding, and marvellously gluggable. Today, however, Dolcetto is being driven upmarket by crop-thinning and aging in oak barrels.

Though noted for its red wines, Piedmont also produces large volumes of white, primarily from the Moscato grape grown in the Monferrato hills. Its heavenly scent, all elderflowers and white peaches, is found in the best Asti and Moscato d'Asti, and it makes it a perfect antidote to the Langhe's brooding reds. Less reliable, but marvellously scented with a fruit that veers between pears and white peaches, are still wines from the Arneis and Favorita varieties.

OTHER REGIONS
The remainder of north-west Italy's wines are dwarfed by the colossus of Piedmont. Liguria's wine, which accounts for less than a half of one per cent of Italian production, is consumed mainly by the summer tourists, and generally suffers the fate that easy popularity and a thirsty tourist trade always brings to a region – carelessly mediocre quality and sky-high prices. But the potential for quality in Liguria is good. The overriding sensation I've got from good examples of wines like Ormeasco, Rossese, Pigato and

MAIN DOCG/DOC WINE AREAS

VALLE D'AOSTA
— Valle d'Aosta

PIEMONTE
— Carema
— Gattinara DOCG
···· Ghemme DOCG
— Erbaluce di Caluso, Caluso Passito

— Barbera d'Asti
···· Monferrato
— Barbera d'Alba
— Langhe
···· Roero DOCG, Roero Arneis DOCG
······ Dolcetto d'Alba
— Asti DOCG, Moscato d'Asti DOCG

— Gavi DOCG
— Colli Tortonesi
1. Barbaresco DOCG
2. Barolo DOCG
3. Dolcetto di Dogliani DOCG
4. Brachetto d'Acqui DOCG

LOMBARDIA
— Oltrepò Pavese
— Valcalepio
— Franciacorta DOCG, Terre di Franciacorta
— Lugana
······ Garda, Riviera del Garda Bresciano
····· Valtellina, Valtellina Superiore DOCG

LIGURIA
····· Riviera Ligure di Ponente
— Rossese di Dolceacqua
— Cinque Terre
— Colli di Luni
☐ OVER 300M (984FT)
☐ OVER 600M (1968FT)

Vermentino is of the fat, round, ripe body so often missing in Italian wines, allied to some fascinating flavours. This all makes sense, because the vines are mostly grown on warm mountain slopes with a strong maritime influence. There aren't that many good examples, but they are worth seeking out.

Aosta has the same problem – a thirsty tourist trade from the ski resorts willing to hoover anything down at high prices. However, it's a high, cool alpine valley, where ripening the grape is by no means easy. I've had good, herb-scented Gamays and Nebbiolos, some rather good Moscatos and some exceptional unusual reds and whites from local grapes, so I would go out of my way to find Aostan wines, but chances are few and far between.

In terms of area and output, only Lombardy can even attempt to challenge Piedmont. Unfortunately, much of what is produced in the prolific zone of Oltrepò Pavese, in the south-west of Lombardy, is merely sound but uninspiring wine, and is in any case soaked up by Milan, Italy's industrial centre and the nearest large city. But Franciacorta, between the cities of Breganze and Brescia, is today increasingly admired for its French-style wines, while right in the north Valtellina, the sole significant outpost of Nebbiolo outside of Piedmont, is making a quality comeback after decades in the doldrums. The best wines are made under the Valtellina Superiore DOCG as Grumello, Inferno, Sassella and Valgella.

PIEMONTE

IF, LIKE ME, YOUR FIRST EXPERIENCE of Piedmont (Piemonte) was the great city of Turin (Torino), then you might be excused for wondering where the vineyards are in this, one of the three classic Italian wine regions. The heart of Turin is beautiful – in the discreet, industrious style that sets the Piedmontese apart from their fellow Italians – but as you move away from the centre, it becomes an urban jungle set in the centre of a flat, monotonous terrain.

This land-locked region is supposed to have cold, bright winters and hot, bright summers – well… the people who write the travel guides have clearly never been there at the same time as me. In summer, the heavy, clammy warmth reduces any distant view to a haze, while in autumn or winter, a thick, eerie fog can suddenly descend and limit visibility to about five yards. On a clear spring or winter day, however, the Alps are visible to the north and west and all seems well with the world, but anyone in search of vineyards is left wondering in which direction they might lie.

Right, let's use my common sense; head west, towards the mountains and the border with France, working on the assumption that the foothills will offer plenty of sites ideally suited to the cultivation of the vine. But it's not quite as simple as that. The mountains of eastern Savoy are surprisingly lacking in vineyards, and the hills to the south-west are equally bare.

A foolhardy soul who struck out east towards Vercelli would soon find themselves ankle deep in paddy-fields, for this part of the Po Valley grows most of the sticky arborio rice for the risottos that are found on menus throughout the country.

So we'll head north from the paddy-fields and at last we stumble upon some vineyards – not great swathes of them but, unlike the Alpine foothills to the west, those to the north are at least lightly dappled with vines. These northern foothills rise up from the unremitting flatness of the Po Valley, and they do provide superb south-facing slopes for vines, but that doesn't mean their potential is realized to the full.

SÉSIA VALLEY

The Sésia Valley lies to the north of Vercelli's paddy-fields cutting its course between the industrial town of Biella and the moneyed resorts around Lake Maggiore. The Nebbiolo grape – Piedmont's greatest but most capricious red variety – has reigned supreme in the glacial soil of the hills that flank the Sésia river for centuries now, yet its fabled past sits uneasily with the current reality. Out of the many wine zones in this area, only Gattinara, a typically controversial DOCG, can make even a feeble claim to rank among the region's most noted wines. Many of the other zones here – Lessona, Bramaterra, Boca, Ghemme, Sizzano and Fara – dine out, like an aging film star, on the fact that they were once more famous than the new kids on the block, Barolo and Barbaresco. But that was a long, long time ago.

DORA BALTEA VALLEY

To the west of the Sésia lies the Dora Baltea, another river valley carved by the glaciers that swept down from the Alps during the last Ice Age to sculpt the face of northern Italy. Here, on the border between Piedmont and the Valle d'Aosta, is some of the steepest vineyard terrain in Europe. These mountain terraces form the Carema DOC zone, comprising about 40ha (100 acres) of Nebbiolo, planted wherever the sheer granite face gives way to a patch of arable land.

It is only in the longest, hottest summers that wines with even a reasonable degree of ripeness are produced, and even then they are more prized for their delicate perfumes than for their somewhat skeletal structure.

To the south of the town of Carema, as the hills soften and the flatlands of the Po Valley once again come into view, the Nebbiolo's dominance is momentarily relaxed. Here, around the town of Caluso, a small amount of both dry and acidic, and rich, golden, sweet white wine is produced from the Erbaluce grape. After such a circular journey from Turin, through about 10 per cent of Piedmont's wine production area, a glass of white wine is a welcome relief, but the relief is genuine – these rare whites have got real substance to them from a good producer.

Well, this has all been very interesting so far, but we really haven't got into the mainstream yet. No problem. We still have 90 per cent of Piedmont's vineyards to explore and, since all other directions have been tried with only limited success, there's nothing for it but to head south-east. At first, the vineyards of Chieri and Castelnuovo Don Bosco seem nothing more than fool's gold, but after a while, as we move into the hills around the town of Asti, it is obvious that we have finally struck a rich, and surprisingly diverse, seam of the real thing.

MONFERRATO HILLS

As the Po and the Tanaro rivers edge southwards, finally joining up just north of the city of Alessandria, they embrace the steep, calcareous Monferrato hills. The southern, eastern and western slopes are covered with vineyards as far as the eye can see and the vines are trained low. Many of them are the Moscato Bianco variety, for this is Asti country, and local growers until fairly recently enjoyed rocketing sales of this sparkling wine – known these days simply as Asti rather than Asti Spumante. Indeed prices for Moscato Bianco grapes were among the highest of any variety in Italy.

Those halcyon days now seem an awfully long time ago and Asti producers recently suffered the indignity of having some of their precious juice compulsorily distilled by the EU. Fashion is cruel, but anyone who thinks Asti is an innocuous frothy fizz to keep

The famous Barolo region is based on a series of hills, all giving different ripening conditions. These vineyards, showing the first hint of autumn mists, are sited between the villages of Barolo and La Morra.

troublesome maiden aunts quiet should buy a bottle from a good producer, or perhaps a bottle of the sweeter, semi-sparkling Moscato d'Asti, search out a shaded bower on a blisteringly hot afternoon, pour themselves a cool glass of this lovely wine and quietly contemplate how lucky they are to be alive. I mean it – the wine is that good.

The local red wine comes from the Barbera grape which, around Nizza Monferrato and Castel Boglione, is planted on the best vineyard sites and produces red wines of intense colour, soft tannins and, usually, mouthwatering acidity. Between them, Barbera and Moscato account for about 80 per cent of the wine produced in the Monferrato hills. But that's not the whole story. Piedmont is such a land of paradoxes and surprises. Barbera can certainly make pretty serious wine if it wants to – full, burly, broad-shouldered stuff.

But what about Freisa, Brachetto, Malvasia, or Ruché? These are four red varieties that make wine as carefree and happy-go-lucky as any in the world – as though they are determined to undermine the solemnity of many of Piedmont's reds. Freisa generally makes fizzy and lighter reds and has a delightful raspberry scent. Brachetto fairly bubbles with a joyous Muscat candyfloss and rose scent. Malvasia can also sparkle coyly and fill the room with the perfume of roses, while Ruché is still, pale red and quite shockingly grapy. In comparison, the gushing purple-proud Dolcetto and the pale, rather herb-harsh Grignolino seem almost serious.

The same producers who have ridden the Moscato wave have cautiously set their sights on Chardonnay, but with only limited success. They should persevere, however, for the other native white grape, the Cortese, seldom produces anything other than an acidic, neutral, at best appetizing seafood white even in Gavi, its most successful spot in the south-east corner of the Monferrato hills. But it does say something about the shortage of so-called 'serious' dry whites in this red wine hunting ground that its frankly unmemorable wines have become excessively chic and expensive despite their lack of any discernible character.

LANGHE AND ROERO HILLS

This lack of decent dry whites has affected the Roero hills just north of Alba on the Tanaro river's left bank. Both the Arneis and the Favorita have suddenly sprung to prominence after generations of neglect, because, in the right hands, they – especially the Arneis – can produce light, orchard-scented whites for a local market that is starved of them and, indeed, an increasingly international audience seems to be taking to them. Good ones can be expensive but the cheaper versions rarely work.

In any case, the light, sandy Roero soils are just as suited to Nebbiolo, but generally in a lighter, more perfumed style than over the river in Barbaresco and Barolo. A good Nebbiolo d'Alba, or Roero as it is today more often called, can be thirst-quenching and delightful. Today, from clay-based soils reminiscent of the Langhe, some growers are making big full wines to rival even Barolo.

On the opposite side of the Tanaro Valley, south of the towns of Asti and Alba, lie the Langhe hills. Though smaller than the Monferrato hills in terms of their territory and quantity of wine produced, the Langhe are far more important than the Monferrato with regard to quality. Thanks largely to the renown of Barolo and Barbaresco, these hillside plots of clay and limestone are Italy's most expensive vineyard land. Though excellent Dolcetto and Barbera, and now Chardonnay, are to be found in the Langhe, the best sites are reserved for the Nebbiolo, which here rises to the full height of its remarkable powers.

Like any maestro, the Nebbiolo grape is a sensitive creature. Within the almost 1700ha (4200 acres) of vineyard that make up the Barolo zone are many minor variations in soil, altitude and exposure, each of which coaxes out a different facet of Nebbiolo's character. On the lighter chalky soils of the commune of La Morra in the north-west of the zone, for instance, the Nebbiolo displays the gentler, more graceful side of its nature, while on the heavier soils of Serralunga d'Alba in the south-east, rich in iron and limestone, its dark, brooding and explosively powerful character is more often to the fore. The same subtleties exist in the Barbaresco zone, where some 700ha (1730 acres) of Nebbiolo are planted. Such a complex character, in such diverse zones, warrants further exploration (see pages 158–159).

The Nebbiolo grape takes its name from the fogs or nebbie that creep through the vineyards every autumn. These Barbaresco vineyards now have a winter dressing of snow but still the fog lingers.

RED GRAPES
There are several distinctive varieties including Barbera and Dolcetto and the famous Nebbiolo of Barolo and Barbaresco. Grignolino has a dedicated following and Freisa is returning to favour.

WHITE GRAPES
Moscato is most widely known, but Cortese and Arneis are more fashionable. Erbaluce is declining as Chardonnay increases.

CLIMATE
The continental climate has long cold winters, slightly moderated by the influence of rivers. Summers are warm while autumn is plagued by fog.

SOIL
Subsoils are generally calcareous marl with some areas of glacial moraine. Topsoils are clay, sand and gravel and can be very fertile.

ASPECT
Nearly half of Piedmont is mountainous with vineyards frequently planted on high, steep slopes and terraces carefully angled to take best advantage of exposure.

ALBA AND TRUFFLES

Any town that can boast two wines of such renown as Barolo and Barbaresco is fortunate indeed. Alba, however, is not content with just its wine. This small town of about 30,000 inhabitants is also noted for its food – which ranks with Italy's best – and the legendary white truffle found in the countryside around. This small white fungus is dug up near the roots of oak trees by specially trained dogs that cost almost as much as a plot of vines in the Langhe. Early morning hunts are followed by discreet trafficking in Alba's truffle market.

In October and November, the restaurants and hotels are packed, booked months in advance by those keen to undertake a culinary pilgrimage here. Each restaurant tends to have its own suppliers, and there are subtle yet noticeable variations in quality between truffles. Truffle can be grated over raw meat, risotto, pasta or in some cases, scrambled eggs.

At its best, the truffle's memorable perfume is perfectly complemented by the equally evocative aromas of the best Barolos and Barbarescos, although the modern wines have more fruit and floral aroma and less mushroomy smell.

BAROLO & BARBARESCO

 RED GRAPES
Nebbiolo rules supreme in both Barolo and Barbaresco, but it needs careful siting. Dolcetto and Barbera are more accommodating.

 WHITE GRAPES
Although considered chiefly a red wine area, Moscato, Chardonnay and Sauvignon Blanc also thrive here.

CLIMATE
The continental climate is tempered by air currents flowing along the Tanaro Valley, bringing slightly cooler summer temperatures and allowing formation of autumn fog which causes Nebbiolo's slow ripening.

 SOIL
The soil is generally fertile with calcareous bluish-grey marl in the west, and an iron-rich sand and limestone conglomerate in the east.

ASPECT
Most vineyards here face south-west to south-east on steep to very steep hills. The Barolo vineyards, at 250 to 450m (820 to 1476ft) are higher than those of Barbaresco, which lie at between 200 and 350m (656 and 1148ft).

I USED TO THINK THAT BURGUNDY was the most difficult wine to understand until I visited Barolo and Barbaresco. Before that, and despite the urging of friendly Italophiles, I had failed to find the magic they purported to divine in a glass of Barolo. All I found was a hard, tannic wine, its fruit eviscerated by long aging in large, old oak casks. Throughout the 1980s, I searched many times for the complexity and greatness said to reside in the Nebbiolo grape. More often than not, though, I ended up in need of a dentist, my teeth and gums suffering from the full-frontal assault of tannin and acidity. But as the decade progressed things changed. My doubts, and Nebbiolo's wall of tannin, seemed to crumble at the same rate. In 1986, when the 1982s were released, I first glimpsed something of the magic of the Nebbiolo. By the time I tried the '85s in 1989, I sensed that the producers were bottling the wine in time to capture those perfumes of roses, liquorice, violets, mint, cherries and game. When the great 1997s were released I knew for certain.

As the wines improved, the differences between producers became more marked. Previously the stylistic variations had been masked by tannin and oxidation. Now I began to find that the new approach in the vineyards brought lower yields with better ripeness and riper tannins. In the cellar, the extraction of better tannins meant less aging in barrel and more in bottle, which in turn ensured greater freshness, releasing the many beautiful notes Nebbiolo is capable of sounding.

In the early 1990s, I visited the town of Alba for the first time. First stop was Barolo. Alba lies on the banks of the Tanaro river, and the first slopes of the Langhe hills rise up from the narrow plain just south of the town. The road out of Alba is straight, but once you reach the small town of Gallo d'Alba it begins to twist and climb. It then splits into three, heading off towards Serralunga d'Alba, Castiglione Falletto and Monforte d'Alba, or La Morra and Barolo. Being a moderate soul, I took the middle road and began climbing towards Castiglione Falletto. I got a sore neck, and almost drove into the ditch several times, as I tried to get my bearings and distinguish the south- and south-west-facing slopes. Those vineyards with the finest exposure are planted with Nebbiolo. Those with an easterly or south-east aspect are planted with Dolcetto and Barbera, or with white grapes like Chardonnay.

As the road evens out, you get a spectacular view of the whole of Barolo. To your right are the La Morra and Barolo vineyards, while to your left are those of Serralunga. Snow-capped mountains loom behind the hilltop town of La Morra and the lighter, whiter chalky soil of the vineyards that stretches below seems to reflect the snow.

The soil in the western part of Barolo is a Tortonian calcareous marl, while in the east, there is Helvetian marl with higher levels of lime and iron. Because of Nebbiolo's sensitivity to soil, the wines from the former tend to be lighter and more fragrant than the powerful, tannic wines that characterize Serralunga. The spur running through Castiglione Falletto to the southerly vineyards in Monforte d'Alba produces wines that combine the power of Serralunga with some of the grace of La Morra and Barolo.

Barolo's 1686ha (4166 acres) are split between some 1200 growers. Such fragmentation results in as many different approaches to winemaking as there are plots of land, producing a confusing picture. Old-timers remember when Nebbiolo, the last grape to be harvested in the Langhe, would be left in its fermentation vat, in contact with its skins, until after Christmas. The resulting wines were so tough that they needed aging in large *botti* (casks) for anything up to ten years before the tannins had softened enough for the wine to be bottled. But by that time the wine would have oxidized.

In the 1960s, changes took place as younger producers like Renato Ratti, Angelo Gaja and Aldo Conterno travelled to France and saw a different approach to winemaking. Fresher and softer wines were the aim, though disputes raged about how to achieve them. Some proposed little contact with the skins and even less with oak; others suggested substituting small oak barriques for large *botti*; others simply said, reduce yields and clean up your act in the cellar. Top producers split into traditionalist and modernist camps. But the complexity of the zones and of Nebbiolo itself, and the approach of different growers, defies such a simplistic solution. And in Barbaresco, where lower vineyards and a closer proximity to the Tanaro mean a warmer mesoclimate and an earlier harvest, the wines are, in any case, different in character.

However, debate has been healthy. Not only are the wines much better than they were 20 or 30 years ago, but the growers have established themselves as a great force in the region. In the

BAROLO'S TERRA BIANCA

Barolo's famous *terra bianca*, or white earth, is a milky calcareous marl bearing reflective and alkaline qualities. To the west of the town of Barolo, near the impressively sited Castello della Volta, the younger Tortonian soil is bluish in colour from magnesium and manganese, which stimulate growth and flavour, producing elegant, early drinking wines. The land to the east has the older Helvetian soil, more beige-yellow in colour from rust, producing powerful, long-lasting reds. Between these, running north-east from the town, is the Cannubi ridge (*connubio* means marriage or union), with the perfect combination of soil producing wines with the finest characteristics of both areas, the strength and staying power of the east mixed with the finesse and delicacy of the west. Owning vines here is a mark of prestige.

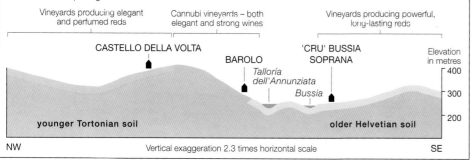

CHERASCO

0 km 1 2
0 miles 1

past, merchants would buy wines from numerous growers and blend them together to make a wine of a house style. Improvements in the vineyard and cellar have led to a new emphasis on the wines of individual communes and, within these communes, single vineyards. Specific terms such as *Bricco* (hilltop), *Sorì* (slope), and *Vigna* (vineyard) now appear on labels – with a grape like Nebbiolo, the importance of provenance cannot be overstated. The future looks bright and growers are trying non-Italian varieties like Syrah, Cabernet Sauvignon, Sauvignon Blanc and Chardonnay. But success has brought

conservatism. Many younger growers think there is only one way to make a good Barolo: early picking and short maceration followed by barrique-aging, all too often resulting in those subtle grape aromas being overwhelmed by those of toasty oak. It would be sad if this resulted in a lack of diversity, and I can only hope there is no slowing down in the experimentation which, in the past couple of decades, has improved these wines beyond all recognition.

DOCG WINE AREAS, SELECTED TOP 'CRUS' AND VINEYARDS

BAROLO

1. La Serra
2. Cerequio
3. Brunate
4. Rocche dell'Annunziata
5. Arborina
6. Monfalletto/Gattera
7. Conca dell'Annunziata
8. Cannubi Boschis
9. Cannubi
10. Bussia Soprana
11. Fiasco

12. Monprivato
13. Villero
14. Rocche di Castiglione
15. Ginestra
16. Francia
17. Vigna Rionda
18. Marenca-Rivette (including Sperss vineyard)

BARBARESCO

19. Roncagliette (including Costa Russi and Sorì Tildin vineyards)

20. Rio Sordo
21. Secondine (including Sori'San Lorenzo vineyard)
22. Asili
23. Moccagatta
24. Martinenga
25. Rabajà
26. Santo Stefano
27. Gallina
28. Basarin
29. Serraboella
30. Bricco di Neive

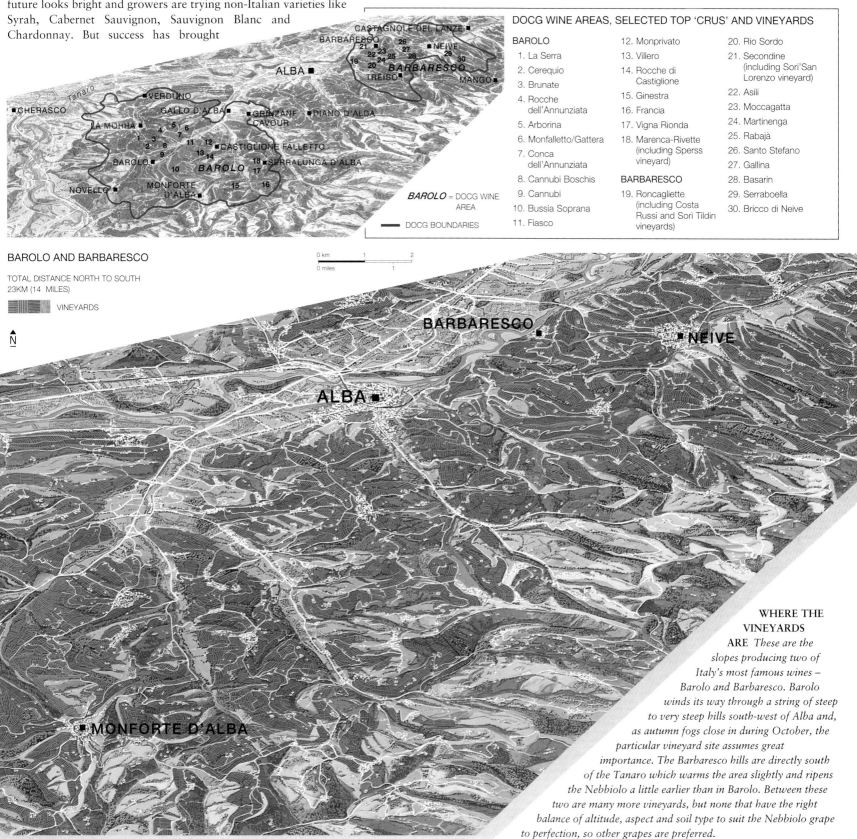

BAROLO AND BARBARESCO

TOTAL DISTANCE NORTH TO SOUTH
23KM (14 MILES)

VINEYARDS

BAROLO = DOCG WINE AREA

—— DOCG BOUNDARIES

WHERE THE VINEYARDS

ARE *These are the slopes producing two of Italy's most famous wines – Barolo and Barbaresco. Barolo winds its way through a string of steep to very steep hills south-west of Alba and, as autumn fogs close in during October, the particular vineyard site assumes great importance. The Barbaresco hills are directly south of the Tanaro which warms the area slightly and ripens the Nebbiolo a little earlier than in Barolo. Between these two are many more vineyards, but none that have the right balance of altitude, aspect and soil type to suit the Nebbiolo grape to perfection, so other grapes are preferred.*

NORTH-EAST ITALY

SOAVE, VALPOLICELLA, PINOT GRIGIO. Each of these wines, virtually synonymous with Italian wine as a whole, is produced in north-east Italy – yet this is perhaps the least Italian of any part of the country. To the north is Austria, to the east Slovenia, and both have contributed to the diversity of culture, peoples, food and wine that exists in north-east Italy. Names of winemakers like Gravner and Haas hardly evoke images of pasta and Chianti, but the vagaries of 20th-century politics have made them Italian, though perhaps not quite as Italian as pasta and Chianti, I admit.

North-east Italy is a region that has been at the crossroads of Europe since at least Roman times. Merchants, scholars and soldiers coming from the north or east would pass through this part of the country on their way to Rome, Florence or Milan, as would the great traders of Venice, the city that controlled much of the world's commerce in the 14th and 15th centuries. Each of these visitors left a legacy that we are enjoying today. The Malvasia grape of Friuli was undoubtedly brought back from Greece by Venetian merchants, as perhaps was Ribolla, which today can still be found on the Ionian island of Kefallonia (as Robola). And the French varieties so prevalent here, Chardonnay, Cabernet and Merlot, owe their presence not to the fact that they fell off a passing bandwagon in the past decade, but that they were brought from France by horse and cart in the wake of the Napoleonic invasion over two centuries ago.

All the best Valpolicella vines are grown on hillside sites to the north-west of Verona.

Even earlier than that, other 'foreign' varieties were being planted in what is today part of north-east Italy: before the early part of the 20th century both Friuli-Venezia Giulia and the Alto Adige were part of the Austro-Hungarian Empire. The hills of Friuli were filled with varieties like Riesling, Müller-Thurgau and, later, Sauvignon Blanc and the Pinots Blanc and Noir (called Pinot Bianco and Nero in Italy). Wines made from these grapes were particularly highly regarded by the Habsburg court in Vienna. Such a ready market for their wares gave the grape growers of Friuli an early incentive to produce quality, though this was rudely removed when the region joined Italy in 1919.

The quality of the wines from the North-East shot back up to its previous peak when, in the 1960s and 1970s, increasing wealth among the people of prosperous cities like Milan and Venice created a clamouring market for the varietals from the hills of Collio and the Colli Orientali. The same factors – climate, soil and grape variety – that produced the wines enjoyed by the Habsburg monarchs successfully came back into play.

Alto Adige – or Süd-Tirol as most of the inhabitants prefer to call their region to this day – wasn't at all happy to be detached from Austria in 1919 as part of the peace treaty. They were even less happy as the determined attempt to Italianize their towns and villages by Mussolini meant great train-loads of immigrants from further south in Italy being dumped on their doorsteps. Place names were Italianized and the Tirolean German that had been spoken for hundreds of years was banned.

Nowadays this mountain province seems a charming and contented place, but there is even still a simmering undercurrent of Tirolean nationalism, and the majority of the people still prefer to speak German, and follow Austrian customs. One benefit of being detached from Austria could perhaps be seen in Alto Adige's tourist industry as German, Swiss and Austrian holidaymakers crowd through the Brenner Pass and fill the locals' coffers with gold. But an adverse side-effect of this is that the majority of Alto Adige's vineyards grow red grapes in an area that would seem brilliantly suited to high-quality whites.

It's those tourists again. With traditions of very light, mild reds in their own countries, they have encouraged the wholesale plantation of the Vernatsch or Schiava grape to produce enormous volumes of semi-red wine of completely forgettable quality. But the white wines are gaining ground both in Italy, which suffers from a shortage of fresh, fragrant whites, and abroad. And South Tyrol reds from Cabernet, Merlot, Pinot Nero and the local Lagrein are being taken increasingly seriously.

North-east Italy is protected from cool north winds by the Julian pre-Alps to the north. From the hills just outside Gorizia the snow-capped peaks of this protective barrier can be seen standing guard on the border with Austria. In the east, the tree-covered hills were once bisected by the southern reaches of the Iron Curtain, while to the south lies the Adriatic, its gentle waters providing a moderating influence on the continental climate that would otherwise prevail here. The hills of Gorizia and Collio are the source of the best wines in this region: rich and perfumed varietals like Pinot Grigio, Tocai Friulano and Pinot Bianco that often stake competing claims to the title of Italy's best dry white wine – and rightly so.

Moving further west, away from the hills and onto the plains, the soil becomes more fertile, the vines more prodigious and the wines increasingly insipid. This trend continues and reaches its lowest point in the Piave Valley. The Piave, one of the two great rivers in the north-east (the other is the Adige), flows from the Alps through an alluvial plain in the eastern Veneto into the Adriatic north of Venice. Its fertile plain produces a great deal of the bulk

wine used to pad out the blends of the Veronese merchants to the west, and a fair amount of the light, lean but refreshing mealtime reds glugged and forgotten in the cafés and restaurants of Venice.

THE VENETO

Bordered to the south by the Po river and to the west by Lake Garda, the Veneto accounts for about 10 per cent of Italy's wine, ranging from the gushing torrents of Piave to the intense trickles that emerge from the hills of Valpolicella. As well as Valpolicella, historically one of Italy's best-known red wines, the region is also home to Soave, Bardolino, Breganze, Bianco di Custoza and huge amounts of Pinot Grigio (see pages 164–165).

The best wines of the Veneto, including the Classico (or hilly) areas of Soave and Valpolicella, come from the chain of hills that rises from the northern rim of the Po Valley. The valley itself is the home of most of the basic stuff that makes the region such an important player in the wine mass-market. Important in volume, that is, not in quality. Very little of the valley floor Soave or Valpolicella deserves its name. The heat here in summer is unbearable, the temperatures often rising higher than those in the low-lying Salento peninsula 900 km (560 miles) to the south. It is only as you move into the hills that relief from the heat is granted, not only for people but also for vines. The cooler night time temperature up in the hills is one of the factors behind the finer wines produced here.

In the hills on the western shores of Lake Garda, the shimmering leaves of olive trees give a rare Mediterranean touch to this northerly region. While most of north-east Italy labours under the hot summers and cold winters that characterize a continental climate, the proximity of Lake Garda moderates the winter temperatures here so that this is the most northerly point in Europe that the olive is cultivated.

FRIULI-VENEZIA GIULIA

The vineyards of Friuli-Venezia Giulia may be a great deal closer to the Mediterranean, with many of the vines planted on low land running down towards the Adriatic and the Gulf of Trieste, but they don't feel balmy too often. With the Julian and the Carnic pre-Alps directly to the north there is a non-stop seesaw of air currents between the cold, wet mountains and the sea that keeps the region mild and damp by Italian standards, with fairly continual breezes (see pages 166–167).

TRENTINO-ALTO ADIGE

The Mediterranean influence quickly recedes once past the northern shores of Lake Garda. The same glacier that carved the lake also cut an almighty swathe through the Dolomites to the north. The result – the Adige river and its valley – is for the most part cast in shadow by the steep, granite walls of the mountains. This fertile valley runs south from the border with Austria, taking in Alto Adige and Trentino. For political purposes, the region is known as Trentino-Alto Adige, but the two have little in common. A strong Germanic influence remains in Alto Adige, still often called the Süd Tirol, but traditional German grapes like Riesling, Sylvaner and Müller-Thurgau are slowly giving way to Chardonnay and Pinot Grigio and, though Schiava (Vernatsch to the locals) remains the most widely planted variety – thanks to an Austrian affinity for the light, innocuous reds that this variety excels in producing – it too is steeply on the decline.

The snow-dusted Dolomites often serve to convince people that this is an area to which the term 'cool-climate viticulture' must be applied. Anybody checking the temperature chart in

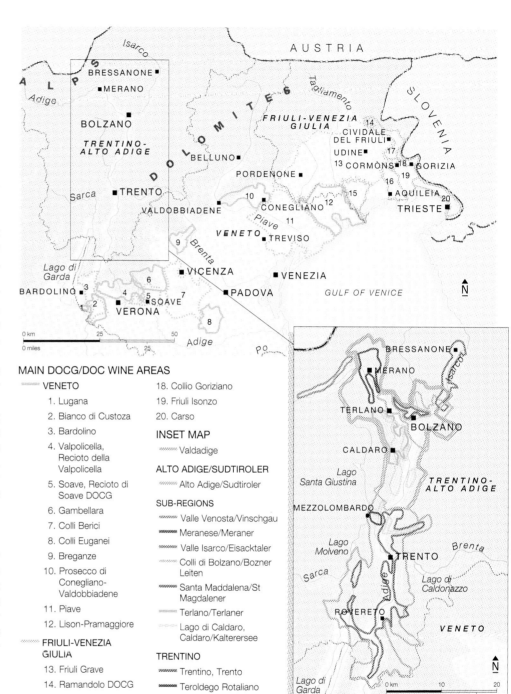

MAIN DOCG/DOC WINE AREAS

VENETO
1. Lugana
2. Bianco di Custoza
3. Bardolino
4. Valpolicella, Recioto della Valpolicella
5. Soave, Recioto di Soave DOCG
6. Gambellara
7. Colli Berici
8. Colli Euganei
9. Breganze
10. Prosecco di Conegliano-Valdobbiadene
11. Piave
12. Lison-Pramaggiore

FRIULI-VENEZIA GIULIA
13. Friuli Grave
14. Ramandolo DOCG
15. Friuli Latisana
16. Friuli Aquileia
17. Colli Orientali del Friuli
18. Collio Goriziano
19. Friuli Isonzo
20. Carso

INSET MAP
Valdadige

ALTO ADIGE/SUDTIROLER
Alto Adige/Sudtiroler

SUB-REGIONS
Valle Venosta/Vinschgau
Meranese/Meraner
Valle Isarco/Eisacktaler
Colli di Bolzano/Bozner Leiten
Santa Maddalena/St Magdalener
Terlano/Terlaner
Lago di Caldaro, Caldaro/Kalterersee

TRENTINO
Trentino, Trento
Teroldego Rotaliano

OVER 300M (984FT)
OVER 600M (1968FT)

an Italian newspaper in July will know that this need not be the case: Bolzano is often the hottest place in the whole country. As elsewhere in Italy, altitude can play an important role in moderating extreme temperatures but, unfortunately, too many of the vineyards here are on the valley floor. One reason Trentino wines often seem flat and dull is that so many of the vineyards are on fertile valley floor land: most of the valley floor in Alto Adige is given over to apples.

At their best, Süd-Tirol wines are fragrant and intense, but often lack the weight that the same varietals display in other parts of Italy, but frankly there are too many modern wines where weight and power are everything. Wines that can be delicate yet intense and fragrant are rare and special – and this region can produce them (see pages 162–163 for more detail).

Superb red, it is made unusually from just one of the Valpolicella grape varieties, Corvina.

TRENTINO-ALTO ADIGE

RED GRAPES
The most significant local varieties are Vernatsch (Schiava), Lagrein, Teroldego and Marzemino. Cabernet Sauvignon is making ground as are Cabernet Franc, Merlot and Pinot Noir.

WHITE GRAPES
Although native Traminer and Nosiola remain locally important, Chardonnay and Pinot Grigio continue their relentless march. Müller-Thurgau, Sauvignon Blanc and Moscato also produce wines of good quality.

CLIMATE
The north has a continental Alpine climate with great temperature fluctuations. Summers can be very hot, especially on the valley floor. Trentino is less extreme though slightly warmer overall.

SOIL
Soils of sub-regions vary, but generally they are infertile, light and well-draining. The subsoil is limestone with alluvial deposits of gravel, sand or clay.

ASPECT
The mountainous terrain means that most vineyards are found in river valleys where they are often planted on steep terraces.

IN A PERFECT WORLD the most beautiful wines would come from the most beautiful vineyards. In which case, Italy's reputation for wine would probably soar over that of any other nation because she has more heavenly vineyard sites than any other country I can think of. There's a reasonable chance that, if sheer scenic splendour were relevant, the Trentino-Alto Adige region would be looked upon as the greatest wine region in the world. The Dolomites and the southern Alps exert such a glorious heart-stopping influence that I don't believe there is a single bad view in the entire province. Certainly I can't think of one vineyard that isn't a scenic delight, either because it's nestling beneath the steep peaks, or because it's clinging improbably to scraps of land halfway up the giddy slopes.

In such circumstances, it's easy to bask in the midday sun on the shores of Lake Caldaro, or perch precariously among the vine pergolas of Santa Maddalena so high above the roofs of Bolzano that the hubbub of this busy city is lost in the still mountain air, and think – I don't care what the wine tastes like, I'm just glad to be alive. If it's easy for the visitor, it's even easier for the grower. Such is the tourist trade, especially in Alto Adige, the northern half of the

region, and so thirsty are the visitors who throng south from Austria, Germany and Switzerland, that until a few years ago scarcely any producers ever felt the need to strike out for excellence. They could make more money the easy way – by maximizing their yields and selling pleasant, but light and dilute wines for healthy sums to the tourists. Today that view is at last being reversed not only by small and medium-sized growers but by large co-operatives (for example those of St Michael Eppan and Colterenzio) as well. This, at least, is true for Alto Adige. Trentino, alas, remains in thrall to the makers of huge volumes of plonk and, though the number of enterprising growers is growing here, there is nothing like the buzz you'll find in Alto Adige.

Yet Trentino, like Alto Adige, has all the prerequisites for a great wine region. Perhaps it's unfair to link them: they are two regions really, with different histories and personalities. Trentino runs from Lake Garda north to the Dolomites above the town of Trento. Its historic links are with northern Italy, in particular the ancient republic of Venice, and before that the Etruscans. The boundary between the two is very precise, as the Adige Valley

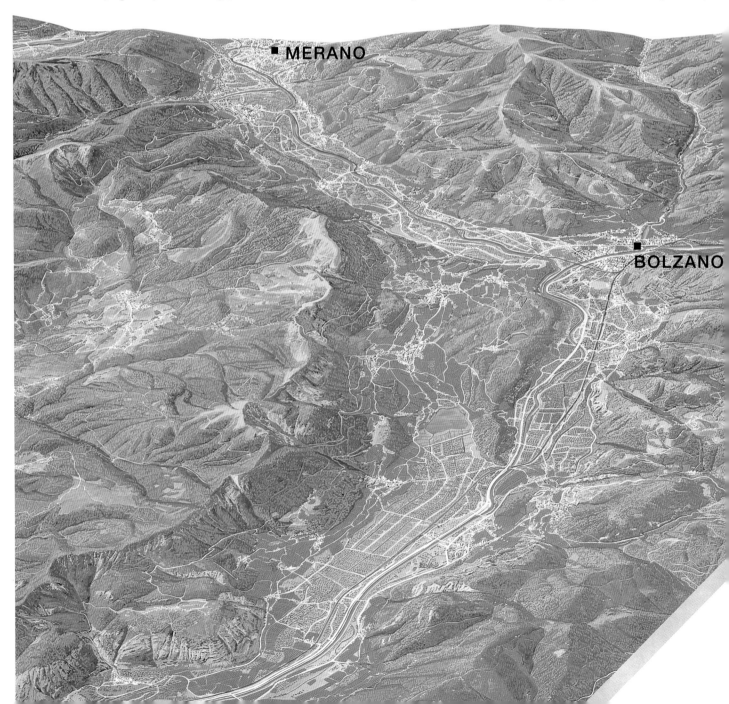

MERANO

BOLZANO

0 km   1   2
0 miles   1

closes in like a pincer at Salorno, the high mountain walls warning off intruders from the south. North of here, most of the inhabitants don't use the title Alto Adige – they call their homeland Süd-Tirol (South Tyrol), because until 1919 when it was traded to Italy as part of the spoils of World War One, Süd-Tirol belonged to the Austro-Hungarian Empire, and to this day it is bilingual, with a strong inclination towards German. All the towns have Italian and German names and, travelling round the region, you notice German featuring more prominently on road signs than Italian. Was that really someone wearing *Lederhosen* and a Tyrolean hat I just saw? It almost certainly was. And dumplings, smoked pork belly and *Sauerkraut* are indeed what you see on the menu. All the wines are labelled in Italian and German too, but since much of the wine trade is with German speakers from the north (although Italy's share is rapidly increasing), many of the bottles sport German titles in far bigger letters than their Italian ones.

And the Alto Adige wine tradition is strongly Germanic. The most widely planted grape is the Schiava or Vernatsch. This makes a soft, mild, light red that can be delightful from a good grower,

but is normally sold off in large bottles as the most innocuous of red table wines. White grapes like Riesling, Sylvaner, Müller-Thurgau and Traminer – named after the local town Tramin (or Termeno) – abound. There is also the French Pinot family, red and white, plus Chardonnay, Cabernet and the excellent local Lagrein. But as you can see, this is a wine region with a culture little related to the Italy of further south, except that yields are very high, and co-operatives and merchants dominate production. Alto Adige was the very first Italian area to react to the wave of modern ideas and techniques that swept the world in the 1970s and 80s. Blessed with an endless variety of infertile, well-drained, south-facing mountain slopes, long sunshine hours, yet altitudes stretching from 250 to 1000m (820 to 3280ft), leading to warm days and chilly nights during the ripening season, it seemed that Alto Adige, with its aromatic white grape varieties, and Trentino, a little warmer and lower and ideally suited to international varieties like Chardonnay, Pinot Bianco and Merlot, were set to lead the Italian Renaissance.

As late as the mid-90s it looked as if it was never going to happen. Friuli, to the north-east of Venice, took over the characterful white wine mantle – you have to remember that most Italians, who only drink at mealtimes, don't like their white wines to be too aromatic, which could be one reason for the apparent false dawn in Alto Adige. Although it had seemed that the protected south-facing suntraps in the hills and the warm gravel banks on the valley floor would produce thrilling reds, few materialized and Tuscany and Piedmont easily saw off any challenge to their authority by the end of the 1980s. Alto Adige's finer reds, from its own Lagrein grape as well as, increasingly, from Cabernet, Merlot and Pinot Nero, only started coming through in any volume in the last few years of the 20th century.

In Trentino, on the other hand, many of the most interesting reds still come from the local Marzemino and Teroldego grapes. It's lovely to see indigenous varieties surviving, but the potential is there for so much more. Apart from a few gorgeous sweet wines from the Nosiola grape, the only area of activity in which Trentino has made as much of its potential as it should is in sparkling wines which are some of the best in Italy. Certainly conditions are ideal, both in the vineyard and for the winemaker, during those long cold winters when the wines can slowly evolve.

All the best wines in Trentino-Alto Adige come from mountain slopes and many growers still use this old-fashioned overhead pergola system of training. These vines are near Bolzano.

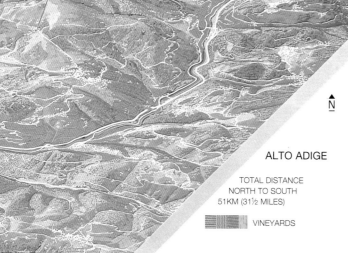

ALTO ADIGE

TOTAL DISTANCE
NORTH TO SOUTH
51KM (31½ MILES)

VINEYARDS

WHERE THE VINEYARDS ARE

This map shows the Alto Adige region: Trentino begins at Salorno and, as you travel south, the mountains become less commanding and the fertile valley floor is planted more frequently with high-yielding vines. But in the Alto Adige, one of the points of pride is that the valley floors are given over to fruit crops, primarily apples, while the slopes are dominated by vines. The southern part of this map shows this well: vineyards cram the western slopes south of Termeno and seek out the sunny nooks to the east above Salorno as far as Ora, and down on the flat fertile plain are packed some of the most important apple orchards in the EU. The ancient pergola system of vine-training makes for picturesque vineyards here, but gives high yields of grapes that are not always fully ripened. More modern, quality-conscious training systems are slowly being introduced, but it shows how well suited the area is to the vine that the best wines can still be so good. Delicious snappy light whites are grown at the top of the Isarco Valley near the Brenner Pass. The sunbaked slopes above Bolzano produce fragrant Santa Maddalena reds; and the Adige Valley up towards Merano produces masses of lighter reds, while the mountainsides reaching down to Salorno can produce exciting whites.

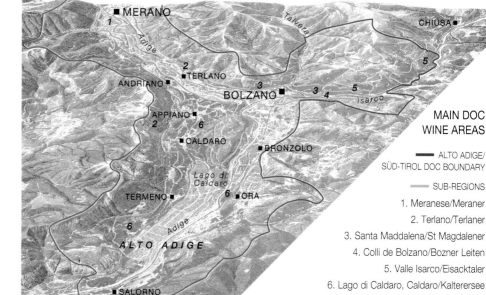

MAIN DOC
WINE AREAS

— ALTO ADIGE/
SÜD-TIROL DOC BOUNDARY

— SUB-REGIONS

1. Meranese/Meraner
2. Terlano/Terlaner
3. Santa Maddalena/St Magdalener
4. Colli de Bolzano/Bozner Leiten
5. Valle Isarco/Eisacktaler
6. Lago di Caldaro, Caldaro/Kalterersee

VENETO

IT IS LIKELY THAT one of your first experiences of Italian wine was a bottle of Veneto wine. It could have been Soave, Bardolino or Valpolicella, or Bianco, Rosso, Merlot or Tocai del Veneto, or even a Pinot Grigio, Chardonnay or Cabernet. For not only does the Veneto produce a vast array of wines, it also churns out a huge volume, from the shores of Lake Garda in the west to the Piave Valley in the east, from the Alpine foothills in the north to the dull flatlands of the Po valley to the south. Quality varies from anonymous whites and weedy reds to a few outstanding wines produced in the Valpolicella and Soave Classico zones in the hills that flank Verona.

Although, by and large, greater Italian reds are found in Tuscany and Piedmont, no other region makes such a range of styles at such a decent average level of quality and charges relatively so little for them. The wine styles, from native grapes in the west like red Corvina and white Garganega, to international stars like Chardonnay and Pinot Grigio, Cabernet and Merlot, are generally soft, accessible and reassuringly recognizable, while consistent quality comes from the presence of one of Italy's wine schools at Conegliano in north-east Veneto. The school has trained a generation of winemakers who have transformed the region's bountiful crop into clean, faultless wines. And, even if it may be coupled with anonymity, this consistency has been popular.

Names like Valpolicella and Soave are world famous and, seen as good-value wines in the 1960s, they soon helped forge Italian wine's cheap-and-cheerful image. Despite this image, the Classico vineyards of both zones, up in the Alpine foothills that spring suddenly from the northern lip of the vast Po Valley, remain the finest in the region, in terms of current quality and future potential. But both Classico zones must be distinguished from the wines of the plains which can only use the straight Valpolicella and Soave names. On the plains the soil is more gravelly, irrigation is more widely used and yields are higher. The wines, particularly those of Valpolicella, are consequently a pale shadow of those from the stony, limestone hills of the Classico zones.

In Soave Classico, the Garganega grape is king. Traditionally supplemented with Trebbiano di Soave to add perfume, it may now be blended with Chardonnay or Sauvignon, though most top producers stick to Garganega. Soave wines from the best producers have an attractive purity of fruit and understated perfumes, and are never better than when drunk with fresh seafood. Soave Superiore, also known as Soave Classico, is now DOCG as is the sweet Recioto version, from dried grapes.

The quality of Soave has increased more rapidly than that of Valpolicella Classico in recent years, though from a lower base, and the potential for quality in the latter zone far outstrips that in Soave. The steep slopes of the Valpolicella Classico zone, the climate of which is tempered by its proximity to Lake Garda, are ideally suited to the Corvina and Corvinone grapes. Unfortunately, Corvina became diluted by lesser grapes in the post-war years. The high percentage of Molinara used and the fact that the vines are traditionally trained high in a pergola form that usually leads to excessive yields and a further dilution of quality are why many people think of Valpolicella as a light red wine. But that image is fading as more and more growers bring out outstanding table wines like Allegrini's La Poja and La Grola.

Indeed in sites where the proportion of Corvina Classico is high, or where good viticulture is practised, the wines have marvellous depth and intensity, and can rival a good Chianti for concentration. Traditionally, such concentration has been achieved

VALPOLICELLA CLASSICO AND VALPANTENA

— VALPOLICELLA DOC BOUNDARY

VALPOLICELLA CLASSICO = VALPOLICELLA ZONES

— VALPOLICELLA ZONAL BOUNDARIES

TOTAL DISTANCE NORTH TO SOUTH 16KM (10 MILES)

▨ VINEYARDS

0 km   1   2
0 miles   1

N

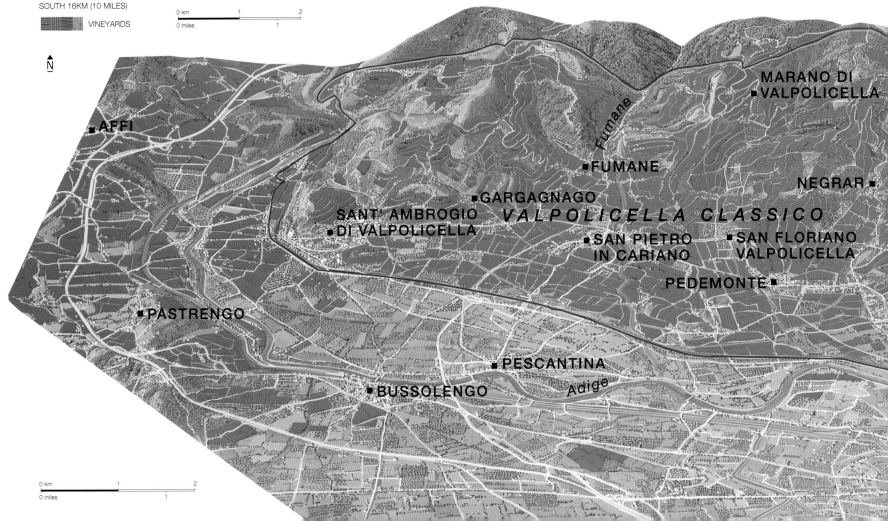

AFFI

FUMANE

MARANO DI VALPOLICELLA

NEGRAR

GARGAGNAGO

SANT' AMBROGIO DI VALPOLICELLA

VALPOLICELLA CLASSICO

SAN PIETRO IN CARIANO

SAN FLORIANO VALPOLICELLA

PEDEMONTE

PASTRENGO

PESCANTINA

BUSSOLENGO

Adige

Fumane

0 km   1   2
0 miles   1

by refermenting the young wines on the skins of the dried grapes used in the production of Amarone and Recioto. These refermented wines, known as *ripasso*, have better alcohol and weight than the younger wines and are often smoother with higher viscosity, since the refermentation releases more glycerine into the wine as well as increased concentration and complexity.

The great wines of Valpolicella, however, are the dry Amarone and sweet Recioto. The grapes (primarily Corvina) are picked early and laid out on mats to dry until any time from the December to the February following the vintage. This drying process concentrates sugars, acids and flavours, and the resulting wines – rich, intense and alcoholic – are, at their best, unique in the world of wine.

To the west of Valpolicella, across the Adige in the western corner of Veneto, the glacial shores of Lake Garda are carpeted with vines. Here, a similar mix of red grapes to those in Valpolicella are used to make Bardolino, which is lighter in style than its more illustrious neighbour, thanks to the glacial soil. The white wine of the zone is Bianco di Custoza which can be surprisingly characterful blend of Garganega, Tocai, Trebbiano and Cortese grapes. Garda is a catch-all DOC for a range of wines in the provinces of Verona and Mantova and Brescia across the border in Lombardy.

East of Valpolicella, again in the Alpine foothills, is the Breganze DOC. North of Vicenza it incorporates a diverse range of varietals including Tocai, Pinot Grigio, Pinot Bianco, Vespaiolo, Merlot, Cabernet and Pinot Nero. Further east, around Conegliano, the Prosecco grape makes a soft, creamy fizz that charms the tired palates of Venice. South of Vicenza, the volcanic hills are home to the Colli Berici and Colli Euganei DOCs, where a similarly wide range of varietals is used to make wines that have, at their best, more intensity than Breganze achieves. In the far eastern Veneto, hills give way to the broader plains of the Piave valley, which produces a boundless source of Merlot and Cabernet. Beyond Piave, astride the border with Friuli, the Lison-Pramaggiore zone makes reliable wines from Cabernet, Merlot, Tocai and Pinot Grigio.

WHERE THE VINEYARDS ARE

The best Valpolicella vineyards are in the steep hills north of Verona in the Classico and Valpantena and Val d'Illasi zones. The altitude in these hills ranges from 100 to 400m (328 to 1312ft) above sea level and the soil is full of limestone pebbles. The Classico zone consists of three main valleys: Negrar, Marano and Fumane. All the valleys are open to the north and act as funnels for the cool wind that blows off the Lessini mountains to the north. Fumane is the most open of the three valleys, and as a result it receives more light, which helps the grapes to achieve greater ripeness, producing wines that are more robust in style. Marano is the most closed valley and, because far fewer of its vineyards have southerly exposures, the wines are lighter and finer, and tend to have a higher level of acidity. Negrar has some of the best vineyard sites (Jago and Moron) in the whole Classico zone, but a higher percentage of Molinara in the vineyards here tends to obscure the true quality of the sites which, at their best, produce fine, powerful wines that age wonderfully. To the west, Sant'Ambrogio is classified as a semi-valley and its vineyards are more exposed to the moderating effect of nearby Lake Garda (just off the left of the map) than to the northerly winds.

To the east, Valpantena and Val d'Illasi (off the map) are the only valleys that have similar climatic and soil conditions to those in the Classico zone. The cool breeze blowing down the Valpantena helps to produce supremely elegant wines, the best of which have always been from Bertani, whose estate at Grezzana has some outstanding vineyards. Dal Forno, considered by some to be Valpolicella's greatest producer, though his vineyards are far from the Classico zone, is the best-known producer of the Val d'Illasi.

RED GRAPES
Corvina, Molinara and Rondinella are used for Valpolicella and Bardolino. Merlot and Cabernet are popular in the Veneto.

WHITE GRAPES
Garganega is grown everywhere but is best known in Soave. Trebbiano di Soave, a superior sub-variety of Trebbiano, is widely used for blending, and Prosecco makes sparkling wines of great popularity

CLIMATE
The influence of Lake Garda and protection of the Alpine foothills combine to produce a generally mild climate, but the plains can be hot in summer. Hail is a constant problem.

SOIL
Around Lake Garda is a mixture of moraine, sandy gravel and clay. Further east there is calcareous clay and limestone. Piave has sand and clay over gravel with finer loam near the Adriatic.

ASPECT
The best vineyards are on hillsides as the plains are too fertile for good quality wine production.

FRIULI-VENEZIA GIULIA

Tucked into the north-eastern corner of the country, stretching from the plains of the eastern Veneto to the borders with Austria and Slovenia, Friuli is a relative newcomer to united Italy as it was, until 1919, part of the Austro-Hungarian Empire. Perhaps because of this, the locals take a view of themselves as hard-working, constant northerners who are different from their more fickle, flighty neighbours elsewhere in Italy.

There is a certain truth in this as far as making wine goes. Over the past couple of decades, Friuli white wines (which account for approximately two-thirds of DOC production in the region) have become a byword for modernity and consistency. Seventy-five per cent of all wine produced here is entitled to DOC status (the national average is 10 per cent). Thanks to its Austro-Hungarian legacy and its proximity to Eastern Europe, Friuli has a wide range of both imported and native grape varieties. And, as an added bonus, it has some outstanding vineyard sites, mainly in the Collio and Colli Orientali hills. Friuli's northern borders are defined by the Julian and Carnic pre-Alps, which make up just over 40 per cent of the total land area. These inhospitable peaks

hold no prospects for the vine, although, as well as forming a stunning backdrop to the vineyards, they do trap the cool wind, the Bora, that blows off the Gulf of Trieste. The Bora blows from the south across the rest of Friuli, which is comprised largely of the Venetian Plain and the gentle hills along the Slovenian border which are home to the Collio Goriziano and Colli Orientali zones. The cool Tramontana wind that blows off the mountains from the north also moderates the climate.

The two zones, though geographically identical, are divided by provincial boundaries. The sandstone and marl hills are flecked with limestone, the soil being nicely friable, well-drained and easy to work. Terraces, known as *ronchi*, have been carved into the hills in order to pander to the vine's temperamental nature and to make work easier in the vineyards.

The numerous cultural influences to which Friuli has been subjected over the centuries have resulted in a multitude of primarily white grape varieties of German, French, Italian and Eastern Europe origins. Riesling and Traminer perform well – though, rather like a beetroot-red northerner on a sun-drenched beach, they seem to hanker for the cooler reaches of their

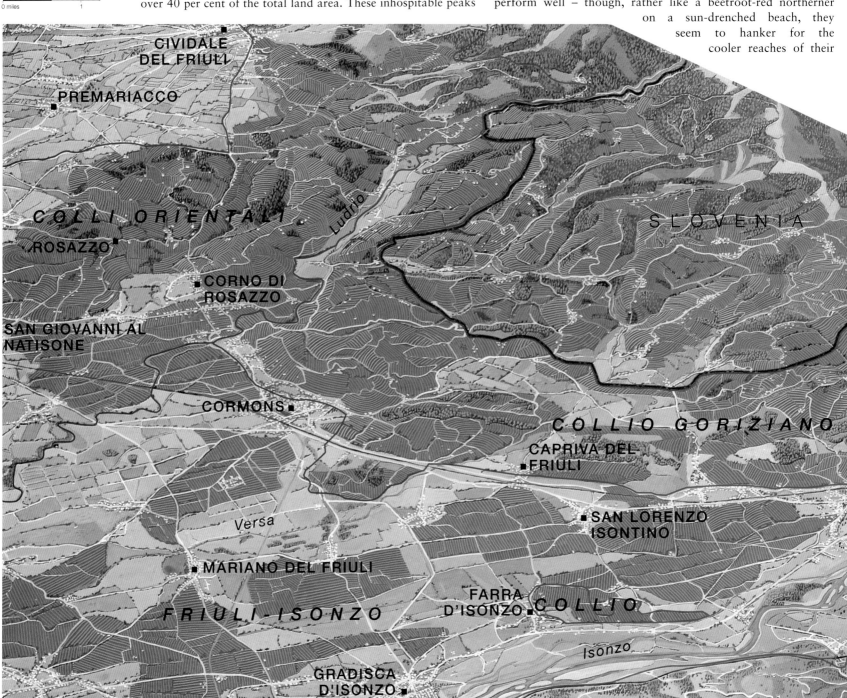

German homeland. Pinot Grigio, Pinot Bianco, Chardonnay and Sauvignon have had no such problem adapting – reflecting, perhaps, the greater similarities that exist between the growing conditions in France and northern Italy.

The native Ribolla Gialla is currently enjoying something of a revival, although its waxy nature and tangy acidity do not endear it to palates with a greater affection for the richer, more rounded styles of Australian and Californian wines, while the Tocai Friulano can produce some of the most interesting of Friuli's dry whites.

Other natives include Picolit and Verduzzo, both of which are highly regarded locally for the quality of their sweet wines, but their erratic quality means we rarely see them off their home patch. Of the reds, Refosco dal Peduncolo Rosso can, at its best, be as much of a mouthful to drink as it is to pronounce, while Schioppettino produces lighter wines. Neither, however, produces wines of the stature of the whites.

In Collio and Colli Orientali, producers like Mario Schiopetto and Vittorio Puiatti began producing fresh, modern varietals in the 1960s when the rest of the peninsula was still churning out wines that bore a greater resemblance to poor-quality sherry. Others, like Jermann, Gravner, Livio and Marco Felluga, Abbazia di Rosazzo, La Castellada and Radikon followed, making this a rare area in Italy where small growers and merchants outnumbered the large merchants and co-operatives.

Their success was immediate though, it must be said, easy, while the rest of Italy lagged behind. These largely unoaked whites very firmly emphasized the primary fruit aromas of the varietal and were supported by a viscous richness on the palate derived from the warm growing conditions and low yields. Such wines were immeasurably more characterful than those made from

Trebbiano or other grapes elsewhere in Italy. As a result, Friuli in general, and Collio and Colli Orientali in particular, acquired this great reputation for quality, something that was reflected in the prices the wines fetched. Despite (or perhaps because of) these prices, the wines soon came to be seen as rather one-dimensional and, in an attempt to add complexity, growers like Gravner began experimenting with oak and a partial malolactic fermentation.

As you move on to the plains, the quality and price both descend, and the differences between the zones become far less pronounced. In the far west, the Friuli Grave zone produces more red than white wine. The soil on this large alluvial plain consists mainly of gravel, which results in reds of decent weight and colour. A great deal of this wine is sold in bulk, though there are some attractively herbal Merlots and some rather weedy Cabernets. However, as elsewhere in north-east Italy, Pinot Grigio and Chardonnay are on the increase.

Red wines also predominate between Grave and the Adriatic, in the Annia and Latisana zones. Here, however, the soil is more fertile, and the wines lack the weight that the best in Grave can attain, though they are usually eminently drinkable. A similar drinkability prevails in the Aquileia zone, but in Isonzo, situated between Aquileia and Collio, more intensity creeps into the wines as the hills begin rolling towards Gorizia.

In all areas, the grape mix is similar to that in Collio and Colli Orientali. The region's predilection for the varietal has proved a very useful marketing tool, but times change, and all over Italy producers are jumping on the varietal bandwagon, often with considerable success, and frequently at lower prices. If Friuli wants to hold on to its pre-eminent spot in Italian whites in particular, we'll want to see a wider diversity of styles and a greater intensity of flavour to justify those prices.

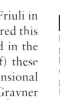

RED GRAPES
Red varieties are no longer predominant in the region but Merlot still counts for one-third of vineyard plantings. Cabernet Franc and Refosco are losing ground to Cabernet Sauvignon. There is some Carmenere.

WHITE GRAPES
Tocai Friulano remains the most planted white grape, but Chardonnay, Pinot Bianco, Pinot Grigio and Sauvignon are on the increase. Picolit and Verduzzo are two ancient Friuli varieties.

CLIMATE
To the north, the Carnic Alps have the heaviest rainfall in Italy but generally the Friulian climate is mild and fine. The coastal plains can be hot and dry in the summer.

SOIL
Hillside vineyards are often planted on crumbly marl and sandstone. Elsewhere soils range from clay, sand, and gravel to the alluvial deposits of the Isonzo river, and famous limestone formations of the Carso.

ASPECT
The best vineyards lie on well-sited slopes between the Alps to the north and the Venetian plain to the south and west.

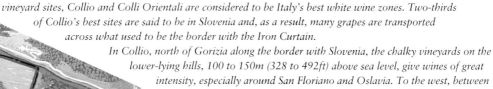

WHERE THE VINEYARDS ARE *Thanks to modern technology, excellent raw materials and some fine vineyard sites, Collio and Colli Orientali are considered to be Italy's best white wine zones. Two-thirds of Collio's best sites are said to be in Slovenia and, as a result, many grapes are transported across what used to be the border with the Iron Curtain.*

In Collio, north of Gorizia along the border with Slovenia, the chalky vineyards on the lower-lying hills, 100 to 150m (328 to 492ft) above sea level, give wines of great intensity, especially around San Floriano and Oslavia. To the west, between Gorizia and Cormons and especially on the slopes west of Capriva, the wines combine richness and perfume. It is here that many of the best producers (among them, Schiopetto, Jermann and Puiatti) are situated.

South of Cormons the soil consists of more gravel than limestone, and we move into the Isonzo zone. The climate, though, is similar to Collio's and some producers, notably Gianfranco Gallo of Vie di Romans and Alvaro Pecorari of Lis Neris, are showing that the wines can have similar stuffing, if slightly less refinement than the best Collio can offer – but only if the approach to viticulture is equally rigorous. North of Cormons, the slightly cooler climate gives Collio wines with more delicate aromas.

Colli Orientali is merely a north-easterly extension of Collio and virtually all its best vineyards are along the border of the two zones, around Rosazzo.

CIVIDALE DEL FRIULI TO GORIZIA

COLLIO GORIZIANO = DOC WINE AREA

—— DOC BOUNDARIES

TOTAL DISTANCE
NORTH TO SOUTH
24KM (15 MILES)

▦▦▦ VINEYARDS

N

0 km   1   2
0 miles   1

CENTRAL ITALY

Single-vineyard Chiantis like Selvapiana's Bucerchiale are a sign of the region's new focus on quality.

THE DISPARATE COLLECTION OF REGIONS lumped together as central Italy separates the sub-Alpine landscapes of the north from the ancient hills and plains of the southern part of the country. Bisected by the Apennines, central Italy begins on the southern bank of the Po river and stretches to an imaginary line, running from the Gargano Massif to the Gulf of Gaeta, that separates Lazio from Campania and Molise from Puglia.

In vinous terms, there is a thin thread of cohesion that links the wines of central Italy. Grapes like the ubiquitous Trebbiano, Sangiovese, Montepulciano and Lambrusco dominate the vineyards, but only in a few places do they result in knolls of quality in a complacent sea of mass-produced quantity. Some grapes – notably Trebbiano and Sangiovese – straddle the Apennines but appear in distinctly different guises on the eastern and western flanks, but most others, in typically Italian fashion, are local heroes rather than national figures. Tuscany, because of its great wealth of wines, is covered separately on page 170.

The climate in central Italy varies greatly, depending upon proximity to either the eastern or western coast. Within these confines, climatic differences can be attributed to altitude or latitude, since more than 500km (310 miles) separate Piacenza, in the north-west, from the border with Puglia. In general, the eastern coast benefits from the Adriatic's benign influence. Further inland, the Apennines take over and here the winters are colder and the summer heat less tempered by cool maritime breezes but eased by altitude. In the western half – Tuscany excepted – there is a less even coastal strip, with the vertebrae of the Apennine spine more of a home to vines than any verdant Mediterranean paradise.

EMILIA-ROMAGNA
The lush, fertile plains of the Po valley are among the most intensively farmed land in Italy. Most of this is orchard, but the land around Modena, Reggio nell'Emilia and Bologna is carpeted with Lambrusco vines. The vast if diminishing Lambrusco production – dominated by several enormous co-operatives – is not all destined for large, screw-top bottles of red wine: there are, if you happen to be in the region, any number of bottles that contain the genuine article. Whether from the DOC zones of Grasparossa di Castelvetro, Salamino di Santa Croce, Reggiano or Sorbara, real Lambrusco is a frothing, purple drink with high acidity and usually a touch of sweetness that perfectly complements the rich cooking of Emilia.

The rest of Emilia-Romagna's wine tends to come from the Apennine foothills that cut across the southern part of the region. To the west, the Piacenza hills form the basis for the Colli Piacentini DOC, while those around Parma and Bologna are known respectively as the Colli di Parma and Colli Bolognesi. In each of these zones, up to ten different varietals or blends are designated separately under the DOC umbrella. In general, quality from grapes such as Trebbiano, Barbera, Malvasia and even Chardonnay, Sauvignon and Cabernet, is sound rather than exciting.

To the east of Bologna, the Romagnan hills form the nucleus for the Sangiovese, Trebbiano and Albana di Romagna zones. The Albana grape produces a decent dry and an excellent sweet white wine, while the former two, once notable only for their lack of distinction, are today throwing up wines of increasing quality (especially Sangiovese), even if those remain somewhat isolated in a sea of mediocrity.

MARCHE
The wines of the Marche are an altogether more interesting lot. While Sangiovese and Trebbiano are still prevalent, if you're interested, you can seek out some excellent Verdicchio and Montepulciano. The former, undoubtedly one of Italy's best native white grape varieties, has had to overcome the reputation it acquired when it was bought more for its amphora-shaped bottles than for the intrinsic merit of the wine. The best Verdicchio – from producers like Bucci, Garofoli and Umani Ronchi – has a richness and viscosity that is seldom found in Italian white wines.

This richness is matched by the reds from Montepulciano, most notably Rosso Conero, which at its best shows the generosity that the Montepulciano grape can lend to wines.

ABRUZZO AND MOLISE
Unfortunately, much of Abruzzo's wine is symptomatic of poorly grown Montepulciano. This great grape, which can make wines with irresistible dark chocolate flavours, and which is traditionally trained low in the *alberello* or bush system (*gobelet* in France), was twisted into ill-conceived configurations by wayward bureaucrats in the 1960s, when it was recommended that the vine be trained high in a pergola or *tendone* system. Such stupidity has conspired to rob the bulk of Montepulciano wines of their stuffing, though there are increasing exceptions. Trebbiano is Abruzzo's sole white variety and even in the best of hands, its indomitable neutrality makes temperance an appealing prospect.

Continuing south into mountainous Molise, most viticulture is near the coast, where hot summer temperatures are moderated by cool sea breezes. The only important DOC, Biferno (reds from Montepulciano and whites from Trebbiano), accounts for less than a quarter of one per cent of the region's total production. With the odd exception, the remainder is drunk locally or sent north for blending. It is still too early to see whether the newer Molise DOC, which allows a whole range of Italian and international varietals, will turn things round. Meanwhile, the occasional grower like di Majo Norante demonstrates that interesting wines can come from alternative varieties like Falanghina, Greco and Aglianico.

LAZIO
Though the temptation here is to push further south into Puglia, we must complete our journey through central Italy by wending our way across the Apennine mountains into southern Lazio. The mountains form Lazio's eastern border, while the Tyrrhenian Sea serves to moderate the climate of the hot, arid plains that comprise 20 per cent of the region. Most of Lazio's wine production is concentrated on the hills south-east of Rome, where most of it is consumed. The wines are based on a blend of Trebbiano and Malvasia grapes, and the predominance of the former ensures wines of supreme neutrality. A similar situation exists in northern Lazio where Est! Est!! Est!!! di Montefiascone dominates production. Today, however, producers both in Frascati (Castel de Paolis) and Montefiascone (Falseco) are using alternative grapes like Viognier and Chardonnay to conjure up wines of real interest out of what is generally a pretty uninspiring hat.

UMBRIA
Over the border in Umbria, Orvieto boasts a more diverse blend, which improves proportionately as the percentage of grapes like Grechetto, Chardonnay and Sauvignon increases. Nearly all of Umbria consists of hills or mountains, ensuring that the vine has many a felicitous spot in which to flourish. The higher altitude of the 'green heart of Italy' compensates for the land-locked nature of the region, which would normally render it too hot for viticulture. Grechetto is the most characterful native white variety, producing wines of good depth and breadth

MAIN DOCG/DOC WINE AREAS

EMILIA-ROMAGNA
1. Colli Piacentini
2. Colli di Parma
3. Lambrusco DOCs
4. Colli Bolognesi
5. Trebbiano di Romagna
6. Albana di Romagna DOCG
7. Sangiovese di Romagna

TOSCANA
8. Colline Lucchesi
9. Montecarlo
10. Carmignano DOCG, Barco Reale di Carmignano
11. Chianti DOCG
12. Pomino
13. Chianti Classico DOCG
14. Vernaccia di San Gimignano DOCG, San Gimignano
15. Montescudaio
16. Bolgheri Sassicaia
17. Bolgheri
18. Val di Cornia
19. Elba
20. Monteregio di Massa Marittima
21. Morellino di Scansano
22. Brunello di Montalcino DOCG, Rosso di Montalcino, Sant'Antimo
23. Vino Nobile di Montepulciano DOCG, Rosso di Montepulciano

UMBRIA
24. Colli del Trasimeno
25. Torgiano, Torgiano Rosso Riserva DOCG
26. Montefalco, Montefalco Sagrantino DOCG
27. Colli Martani
28. Orvieto

MARCHE
29. Colli Pesaresi
30. Falerio dei Colli Ascolani
31. Verdicchio dei Castelli di Jesi
32. Conero DOCG, Rosso Conero
33. Verdicchio di Matelica
34. Vernaccia di Serrapetrona DOCG
35. Rosso Piceno

ABRUZZO
36. Montepulciano d'Abruzzo
37. Trebbiano d'Abruzzo
38. Montepulciano d'Abruzzo Colline Teramane DOCG

LAZIO
39. Est! Est!! Est!!! di Montefiascone
40. Cerveteri
41. Montecompatri Collona
42. Frascati
43. Marino
44. Colli Albani
45. Colli Lanuvini
46. Velletri
47. Castelli Romani

MOLISE
48. Molise
49. Biferno

OVER 300M (985FT)
OVER 600M (1968FT)

in the Colli Martani DOC, that borders Montefalco to the west. Its red counterpart, Sagrantino, is one of Italy's great red grape varieties, but it is only found around the town of Montefalco, where the Montefalco Sagrantino DOCG is located. It produces deep-coloured, tannic wines of great intensity and length. As small barrels become a more regular part of the production process, so is Sagrantino softening in style, sometimes, alas, at the expense of having to take in excessive wafts of oak.

Umbria's other noted red is the Sangiovese-based Torgiano. This wine is the monopoly of the Lungarotti family, pioneers in Umbrian viticulture. But whereas 30 years ago they were ahead of the game, recent years have seen them creep forward while others raced ahead. Not surprisingly, Torgiano seems less exciting as a result, though the oak-aged Riserva DOCG has a certain appeal.

0 km 25 50
0 miles 25

TOSCANA

RED GRAPES
The chief grape of Tuscany is the Sangiovese, also known as Brunello, Prugnolo Gentile, and Sangioveto. Canaiolo Nero and Mammolo are other local varieties nowadays joined by Cabernet Sauvignon and Merlot.

WHITE GRAPES
Vernaccia produces the best white wine but high-yielding Trebbiano is much more common. International varieties are led by Chardonnay, Pinot Bianco Sauvignon Blanc and increasingly Viognier.

CLIMATE
The temperate climate of the central hills is in complete contrast to the river basins which trap summer heat and damp, and the drier, hotter coastal regions. Hail can be a threat to fruiting vines.

SOIL
Soil is generally calcareous, with tufa and some sandy clay. The flaky marl called *galestro* is highly desirable and features in Montalcino and the Chianti Classico and Rufina zones. Near Pitigliano, soils are volcanic.

ASPECT
The best vineyards are carefully sited on slopes and steep hills, often interspersed with olive groves and woodland.

HOW IMPOSSIBLE IT IS to look at Tuscan wine objectively. For anyone born and brought up in Western culture, imbued as it is with the Renaissance, for anyone who has ever looked at those Renaissance landscapes, all blue hills forming a backdrop to a Madonna or a Medici – well, do you think they didn't drink? Of course they did, and Tuscan wine is what they drank. Every time I pick up a glass of Vernaccia, I expect it to meet Michelangelo's description of a wine that 'kisses, licks, bites, thrusts and stings', rather than the dim, dull brew it usually is today. Was it really that good then? How did it kiss? How did it sting? Ah, not knowing is such sweet certainty.

But at least the modern Tuscany (Toscana) looks quite remarkably like its pictures look. You know the sort of thing – cypresses, rounded green hills, old farmhouses with carved stone doorways and cool, dark interiors, the brilliance of the sun, the vast blue distances. It is a place where civilization seems unimaginably old and intensely alive. Everything is done with grace and beauty, and a timeless beauty drifts on the breeze.

It affected me the first time I actually went to look at vineyards there, as it affects everybody. I'd gone to try to elope with a very beautiful girl, and we headed for the hills above Florence to escape from prying eyes. And without even noticing it we began to go native and soon we were wishing we'd never have to leave. And it happens to everyone. You can't go to Tuscany without wanting to be more like the Tuscans: you crave that easy knack of producing the most delicious meal imaginable from the simplest ingredients; of pouring local wine, harvested less than a year ago from slopes that your hostess can point out to you just across the valley – there, do you see? Where the last of the evening sun is catching the vines and where the grey-green olive trees further round the hill are already in brooding shadow.

So no, I can't be objective about Tuscan wine. I become disproportionately angry when the Tuscans get it wrong, and irrationally ecstatic when they get it right. And whenever I go there I imagine myself in a painting – although reason tells me that the landscape is very different now from what it was. But then I look around and I say – no it isn't. Dress me up in some local finery. Take up your palette and your oils… and no one would ever know.

But first, the basics. To the west of Tuscany is the Mediterranean sea, in which basks the island of Elba with its echoes of Napoleon. To the east lie the Apennines, arching round to the north; while to the south there's Lazio, Rome and the Mezzogiorno. The land lies flat near the coast, as if to let the Mediterranean climate as far inland as possible, but most of Tuscany is hilly. Not necessarily seriously hilly, although you'll find white grapes cultivated up to 700m (2300ft) and reds up to 550m (1800ft), but often just gently rolling. The hills are essential for viticulture because summers here can be long and hot, and hills that rise high enough to temper the heat or catch a cooling breeze can make all the difference between a baked, flat white wine and one with perfume and fruit.

For reds, the slopes provide the concentration of heat that the sun-loving Sangiovese grape needs to ripen. So it's the hills that provide the mesoclimates that serious winemakers want. Which is just as it should be. Tuscany without its hills is just any old place. Tuscany with its hills is rare and unforgettable.

And serious winemakers love Tuscany. You don't have to be a Tuscan to make good wine here. You can be a rich immigrant from Rome, Lombardy, Milan, or just about anywhere; the main thing, from the point of view of the hardheaded locals, is that you're investing – and it's your sort that has done a lot to repair the desolation that spread throughout the region in the 1950s. The

land was farmed then by a system of sharecropping, in which the peasants who worked the land divided the harvest with those who owned it. This meant riches for the landowners and poverty for the peasants, and the frosts of 1956, which left dead olive groves and vines in their wake, were the final straw. The peasants fled the land for jobs in factories. And when Tuscany's vineyards were replanted, largely between 1965 and 1975, it was with quantity rather than quality in mind.

High-yielding clones of Sangiovese from Romagna to the north and a rash of dull, thin white Trebbiano sprang like disease from the hillside slopes. But they did produce copious quantities of simple, gluggable red, and that seemed to be where the market lay: people craved light, fresh, zippy reds, sold as often as not in straw-covered *fiaschi*. Today it couldn't be more different. A remarkable sense of seriousness and endeavour pervades the wineries and the vineyards. New estates brimful of pride and determination appear with every new vintage, and the work done on the quality of the grapes, epitomized by the Chianti Classico 2000 movement that set out to provide the best clones and plant them in the best sites, is everywhere apparent.

SANGIOVESE AND OTHER GRAPES

Tuscany's main grape is the Sangiovese. To put it in perspective, 72 per cent of the region's wine is red and if it's red, it's probably at least 75 per cent Sangiovese. The rest of the blend may be any of several grapes: Cabernet Sauvignon, Cabernet Franc, Merlot, Syrah, Canaiolo Nero, Mammolo, Colorino, Ciliegiolo; or white grapes like Trebbiano, Vermentino, Canaiolo Bianco or Malvasia. (You might think that adding white grapes to a wine that is meant to be red can do little for its colour or extract. You would of course be right: the best producers haven't done it for years, even if laws saying that they should have changed only comparatively recently).

Some 14 sub-varieties of Sangiovese are well-known, and some even have their own names, like the Brunello of Montalcino or the Prugnolo Gentile of Montepulciano. These two are among the best, and one reason why the Sangiovese-based wines of these two places have established such a reputation for themselves. Consistency, however, is not Sangiovese's strong point. Other clones, often those planted in the 1960s and 1970s, when over-produced lack colour, extract, flavour and just about everything else and are favoured solely for the large crops they are capable of yielding. Sangiovese needs low yields to produce grapes of quality.

Sangiovese is extremely sensitive to soil and climate, so alters its guise to suit its surrounding environment. In Chianti, for example, the sandy clay soils of Colli Aretini yield wines with good colour and robust, generous fruit that is best drunk young. These are plump, pasta wines compared to the sleek, lean, aristocratic and intense characters produced further north in Rufina, where the soils are clay and limestone and the climate is cooler. In the best parts of the Colli Senesi, around Sinalunga, the Sangiovese metamorphoses into a burly, muscular beast that intimidates the thin, rather insubstantial weaklings from Pisa and Montalbano. Fortunately, in recent years there has been widespread replanting with new clones arising out of viticultural programmes like Chianti Classico 2000 and quality is rising dramatically, with further big leaps expected in the future as new vineyards mature.

Tuscan whites are mainly from the Trebbiano, in whole or in part, although as quality consciousness increases along with the drift from white to red, numerous hectares of this variety are being field-grafted to black grapes or simply ripped out and replaced. With the popularity of Tuscan wines increasing internationally, more and more vineyards of excellence are coming into production, but for all that, vines do not dominate the landscape except in parts of Chianti Classico. Even prestigious Montalcino is half given over to forest, and there is more land planted with olive groves there than with vines. Tuscany for the most part is still a region of mixed farming. Wine has traditionally been a part of everyday life here and traditions, in Italy, are slow to change.

It is the ready availability of sun-drenched slopes that makes Sangiovese the most popular planting in Tuscany. The further north you go, the lower down the slopes you find the best Sangiovese: as low as 50 to 200m (165 to 656ft) in northerly Carmignano, and in the south, in Montepulciano, from 250 up to 550m (820 to 1800ft). Other grape varieties, mostly white but also Pinot Noir, may be planted at higher altitudes where it gets too cold for Sangiovese. Marl soil high in calcium seems to suit the vine best, but there are big variations, with, for instance, more sand in Montepulciano. What gives the wines their finesse, though, is the difference between the warm daytime temperatures and the cool nights. Most noticeable inland in Chianti and Montepulciano, this difference evens out towards the coast, and the wines of the Maremma are accordingly richer, beefier and higher in alcohol.

SUPER-TUSCANS

It all started in the early 1970s. Tignanello and Sassicaia were the first so-called 'super-Tuscan' wines, and wineries piled on to the bandwagon faster than you could count. The idea was to thwart the more restrictive aspects of Italian wine law by producing wines that flaunted their supposedly lowly *vino da tavola* status – and their extremely high prices. Tignanello comes from the Chianti Classico zone but is nearly all Sangiovese; Sassicaia, from Bolgheri near the coast, is a blend of Cabernet Sauvignon and Cabernet

Franc. Both are aged in small oak barrels, a move that, to its detractors, smacked of distinctly un-Italian activity. The wines that followed were either entirely Sangiovese or from both Cabernets and/or Merlot and often a blend of all of them. The idea spread out of Tuscany to Piedmont and elsewhere in Italy and white wines took it up, particularly Chardonnay and Sauvignon Blanc.

But with the passing of the Goria Law in 1992 the option of a *vino da tavola* tag disappeared. The super-Tuscans must now, if they want to display a vintage or provenance on the label, come under the wing of either the IGT or DOC laws. Sassicaia, ever the first, became DOC (as Bolgheri Sassicaia) with the 1994 vintage.

VIN SANTO

When you step from the blazing sun into the cool of a Tuscan farmhouse, this is what, according to tradition, you should be offered. Literally 'holy wine', *vin santo* is made by everyone with some spare Trebbiano grapes and room under the rafters in which to dry them on straw mats.

Most people think Malvasia actually makes better *vin santo*: DOC laws specify that the wine may be made from either or both, together along with up to 30 per cent of other grapes, including Sangiovese. The grapes are left to shrivel before crushing, usually between November and March (the longer they are left, the more concentrated the sugars will be and the sweeter the wine). After fermentation, the wine is aged in small sealed barrels for at least three years and sometimes for more than ten.

There are several DOCs, or parts of DOC, which may overlap geographically and leave parts of Tuscany out, but *vin santo* is made everywhere, DOC or not. The resulting wines can be very sweet, bone dry or anything between. Quality varies just as widely.

Tuscany's reputation has been made by wines like Chianti, Brunello di Montalcino and Vino Nobile di Montepulciano. However, the whole region is buzzing with activity and the area of the Maremma, south-west of Siena, already known for soft Sangiovese reds called Morellino, is receiving heavy investment. This is Castello di Montepo' owned by the family of famous Brunello producer Biondi-Santi.

Cepparello, made by the leading Chianti Classico estate Isole e Olena, is one of the most famous 'super-Tuscan' wines, created as a 100 per cent Sangiovese wine during the 1980s.

CHIANTI

CHIANTI CLASSICO:
GREVE TO SIENA

TOTAL DISTANCE
NORTH TO SOUTH
28KM (17½ MILES)

▨▨▨ VINEYARDS

▲
N

THE AREA OF CHIANTI SEDUCED ME from the first second. I alighted from the train at Florence station, marvelled at the city and then, within a few hours, headed off south into the hills of what I now know were the northern reaches of Chianti Classico. But the wine? Well my first mouthful of gushing, prickly sour red-fruited wine on that trip – from an unmarked bottle in some farmer's field by the side of a silent road – that was a revelation. Yet the vast majority of Chianti wine that I drank until at least the mid-1990s tottered between dull and disgraceful. The change in quality and attitude at the end of the 20th century and the start of the new millennium has been nothing short of remarkable.

Chianti first came to prominence around the beginning of the 13th century. At the time, Florence was the banking capital of the world. Its bankers – the Medici and Frescobaldi families, among others – funded the wayward campaigns of most of the rulers of medieval Europe and became rich in the process. This wealth spilled out of the city into the countryside, where the great villas and estates that now lure tourists to these verdant hills in summer were developed into agricultural properties. Because of the rocky soil, only the olive tree and the vine flourished, yet its products were greatly appreciated in affluent Florentine society.

This wealthy market provided the impetus to the development of Chianti as a quality wine zone. By the beginning of the 15th century, Chianti's name was already established and, as has happened the world over when a certain area attains fame, others tried to pass off their usually inferior products as the real thing. This led, in 1716, to the Grand Duke of Tuscany mapping out the borders of the zone in an attempt to prevent fraud. While delimiting the area, the Grand Duke also pushed the borders north from their original area towards Greve and Panzano. Such elasticity, however, did little to staunch the flow of ersatz Chianti that increased towards the end of the 19th century, when Chianti enjoyed a boom thanks to the shortage of wine created by phylloxera. By this time, virtually every Tuscan red wine, no matter what its provenance or history – and some, like those from Rufina, Carmignano and Montepulciano, had histories every bit as noble – was being sold as Chianti.

There were many, then, who argued that some legal definition was required to protect the name of Chianti, but this was generally ignored in the rush for sales. It was only several decades later, during the slump that inevitably followed the boom, that people began to think along these lines. This resulted in the Dalmasso commission, whose report in 1932 led to new boundaries being established.

The original zone was doubled in size to take in the lower-lying, clay-clogged hills closer to Florence and was renamed Chianti Classico. This new name distinguished it from the six new Chianti zones that were created by appending to the name a broad geographical designation. In most cases, this was simply a matter of mopping up all the vineyards in a particular province like Florence or Siena that weren't already covered by another zone. It is an

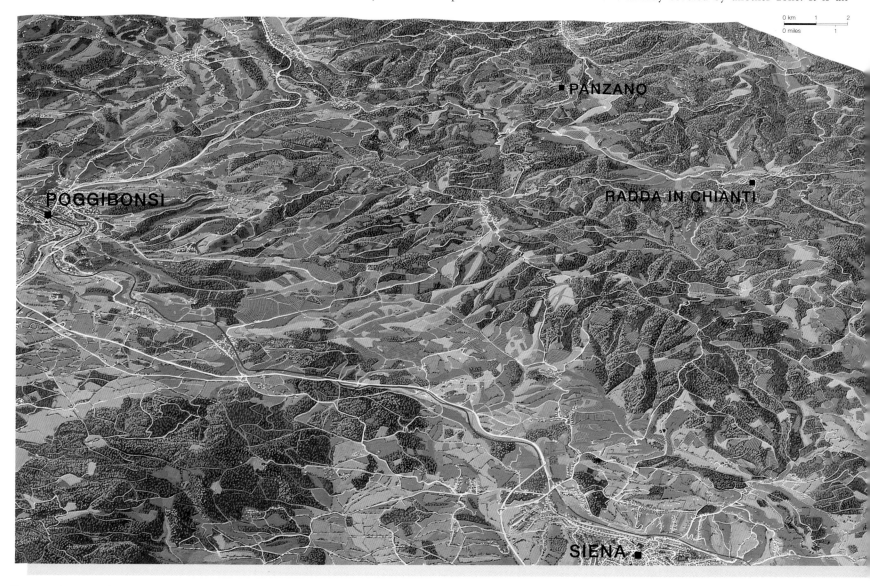

idiotic basis upon which to define a wine, yet it was confirmed by the DOC laws of 1967, reaffirmed when the DOCG was introduced in 1984 and remains in practice to this day.

In the province of Siena, for instance, any appropriate grapes grown outside the Sienese part of Classico, or beyond the borders of the Montepulciano and Montalcino zones, are entitled to the name Chianti Colli Senesi. Never mind that the zone covers a wide variety of soils and mesoclimates, it's just that the area fits neatly into the politically defined borders of the province of Siena. Similarly in Florence, all areas under vine not covered by Rufina, Pomino, Carmignano, Montalbano and Chianti Classico is delimited as the Chianti Colli Fiorentini, despite the fact that this takes in two such diverse zones as the Val d'Arno and the Val d'Elsa. Now whether you believe in the sanctity of *terroir* or not, it is manifestly stupid that wines produced in such distinctive zones as these should bear the same name. By extending the name of Chianti over vast tracts of Tuscany, from the green rolling hills of central Classico to the arid Sienese slopes, from the cool reaches of Rufina to the low-lying vineyards of the Colline Pisane, the Italian authorities have succeeded not only in confusing the adventurous wine drinker, but also in robbing the growers of their individual identities.

There are something like 7000 growers in the seven Chianti zones and it is likely, given the diversity of soil, altitude, climate and, to a lesser extent, varietal composition, that there are as many

WHERE THE VINEYARDS ARE *This map shows the southern half of the Chianti Classico zone and the three communes – Radda, Castellina and Gaiole – that comprised historic Chianti, the area noted for the quality of its red wines since the 13th century. In 1932 the zone was extended to take in the lower-lying hills that spread further north towards Florence, but generally, the best vineyards are still in these southern Sienese hills. Soils vary greatly within the zone and this, along with Sangiovese's chameleon-like character, results in wines that range from aristocrats to peasants. The clay of Greve and the northern part of the zone gives way, in Panzano, to galestro, a*

different styles of wine. Even within Classico, altitude varies between 150 and 550m (492 and 1800ft), resulting in great temperature variations. The vineyards in the central Classico hills are higher and cooler than those on the coast, one factor that gives finer, more perfumed wines.

Proximity to forests, valleys or rivers throws another complicating variable into the equation. Those vineyards on the western flank of Classico, for instance, produce fuller wines than do their neighbours several miles nearer the central part of the zone, largely because of the warmth generated by the Val d'Elsa. In the Rufina zone, on the other hand, the cool breeze funnelled down the Sieve Valley from the Apennines sets this tiny area apart, creating a unique mesoclimate and a distinctive style of wine.

But through all the variations in climate, soil and altitude within the Chianti zone there is one constant factor: the Sangiovese grape (see page 170). This grape forms the mainstay of Chianti, being used on its own in some of the best wines, or blended with native varieties like Canaiolo and Colorino, or international ones like Merlot and Cabernet, in others. In lesser wines, white grapes such as Trebbiano and Malvasia still occasionally find their way into the blend, remnants of the lean times in Tuscany when they were used to boost production and render the wine lighter, and ready for drinking sooner. As vineyards are replanted, however, their numbers are diminished, at least among the quality producers.

friable, shaly clay that, along with the limestone alberese, which begins to appear also at this point, provides the ideal growing conditions for the Sangiovese grape. Both galestro and alberese dominate the vineyards of Radda and Gaiole and in the south, around Castelnuovo Berardenga, the potent mixture of tufaceous rock and galestro gives some of the greatest wines of Chianti at estates like Felsina. Yields from these sites are invariably low.

In the past 15 years, in the search for quality, many estates, including Fontodi, Rampolla and Isole e Olena, have replanted their higher vineyards, which had been abandoned in the 1960s and 1970s in favour of lower-lying, more easily worked sites.

RED GRAPES
The most important grape is Sangiovese (locally also called Sangioveto). Canaiolo Nero and Colorino are also sometimes used in Chianti as well as increasing amounts of Cabernet and Merlot.

WHITE GRAPES
Trebbiano is widely planted, but rapidly decreasing in importance. Malvasia del Chianti is also in decline as Chardonnay and Sauvignon Blanc become more fashionable in varietal wines.

CLIMATE
The central hills of the Chianti Classico zone are cooler and more temperate than the coast. Hail can sometimes be a problem in summer and the occasional frost can be quite severe and damaging.

SOIL
Stony calcareous soils are varied by parcels of limestone, sand, clay and schist. In the heart of Chianti Classico the shaly clay known as galestro gives wine with notably good body. The Colli Senesi and Colli Aretini zones have clay and towards the coast the soil becomes lighter and sandier.

ASPECT
The region is characterized by sloping vineyard plots among woods and groves of olives. Altitude plays a key role in determining the style and quality of Chianti produced.

CHIANTI CLASSICO DOCG WINE AREA AND SELECTED ESTATES

1. Badia a Passignano (Antinori)
2. Poggio al Sole
3. Vecchie Terre di Montefili
4. Querciabella
5. Villa Cafaggio
6. La Massa
7. Castello dei Rampolla
8. Fontodi
9. Casa Emma
10. Isole e Olena
11. Monsanto
12. Castello della Paneretta
13. La Brancaia
14. Castellare
15. Rocca delle Macie
16. Castello di Fonterutoli
17. Terrabianca
18. Castello di Volpaia
19. Montevertine
20. Poggerino
21. Badia a Coltibuono
22. Riecine
23. Castello di Ama
24. Rocca di Castagnoli
25. Cacchiano/Rocca di Montegrossi
26. Ricasoli/Castello di Brolio
27. San Giusto a Rentennano
28. San Felice
29. Fattoria di Felsina

— DOCG BOUNDARY

BRUNELLO DI MONTALCINO

 RED GRAPES
Brunello is another name for the Sangiovese of Chianti. Some producers have also made experimental plantings of Merlot and Cabernet for use in alternative wines.

 WHITE GRAPES
Moscato Bianco is grown to produce Moscadello di Montalcino. Chardonnay and Sauvignon Blanc are also beginning to be planted.

CLIMATE
The temperate hill climate benefits from the influence of the Tyrrhenian Sea, while nearby Mount Amiata offers protection from storms.

 SOIL
The best vineyards are on the prized *galestro* (shaly clay). Elsewhere sandy clay is often combined with limestone.

ASPECT
The longest-lived wines come from the relatively cooler, higher vineyards found on the four major slopes which dominate Montalcino. Further plantings have recently been made on lower-lying terrain.

Castello di Argiano is on the lower slopes of Montalcino – you can see the higher slopes behind the castle – and this contributes to the rich, ripe fruit quality of its wines.

LEAVING BEHIND THE WOODED HILLS of Chianti and the ancient towers of Siena, and heading south towards Rome, I could be forgiven for thinking that I have seen the last of Tuscany's vines. The hills of the Val d'Orcia are parched brown, the heavy, clay soil proving more suitable to the cereals swaying in the southerly breeze than to the vine. The horizon is open, with only a few gentle hills occasionally providing relief from an otherwise unbroken vista.

Then, just past Buonconvento, I turn to my right and, as the road winds uphill, clay gives way to *galestro*, vines replace wheat and, at 600m (1968ft) altitude, I arrive in Montalcino, the town famed for its Brunello, Italy's longest-lived and, some would say, greatest wine. This is a town that lives on and for wine. On the main street, there is a wonderful bar, the Fiaschetteria, serving any number of Brunellos by the glass, as well as a wide selection of other wines. Since extended aeration used to be regarded as vital for drawing out the aromas of Brunello, you could well strike lucky with some sullen old brute finally cracking a smile after a couple of days open behind the bar. With modern Brunellos, I'd want one opened on the day I drank it.

The renown enjoyed by Brunello is a rather recent development. Indeed, it was only in the 1960s that whispers reached the outside world of wines of incredible longevity from the cellars of one producer in Montalcino called Biondi-Santi. The legendary 1891, tasted by few but lauded by all, put first Biondi-Santi and then Montalcino on the map. A legend was created, and the prices of Biondi-Santi wines climbed higher than Mount Olympus. Some producers, able to sell their wines at half the price (still double what the better bottles of Chianti fetched), were happy to let Biondi-Santi make all the running. Others, keen to jump on the bandwagon, planted vineyards, increasing the area under vine from less than 100ha (247 acres) in 1968 (soon after the Biondi-Santi-drafted DOC regulations came into force) to over 2000ha (4942 acres) today.

Despite this growth the legend lives on, but there is no doubt that Montalcino is a zone with a great vocation for viticulture. Rising from a sea of clay, it is ringed by a protective wall of valleys – the Ombrone to the west, the Orcia to the south and east – and mountains, with the forbidding face of Mount Amiata standing guard on Montalcino's southern flank. These protect the vineyards from nasty weather and help to make the Brunello zone the most arid of all Tuscany's wine areas, with about 500mm (20in) of rainfall a year. But cooling breezes blowing off the sea, a luxury neither Chianti nor Montepulciano enjoy, provide a bit of relief.

The dry, hot climate brings the grapes to maturity quicker than in Chianti or Montepulciano. There are years when producers in Montalcino have their grapes safely in the fermenting vats, while their colleagues to the north are still struggling to complete the harvest amid the onset of autumn rains. In overly hot years, however, the wines of Montalcino can be brutish in character, and lacking any of the gentler tones found in the best Chiantis.

Perhaps because of their stature, Montalcino wines have traditionally been aged in large old oak barrels for a protracted period in order to temper their ferocious tannins. A compulsory wood-aging period of four years was inserted into the DOC law in 1966, reduced in 1998 to two years in oak before release, followed by a minimum of four months in bottle. Even so the total aging period before release remains four years. This lengthy period may have been fine a generation or so ago when tastes were different, but in today's market it all too often results in the wines' freshness perishing under the onslaught of wood. True, Biondi-Santi's great old wines (made as recently as 1975 and 1964) were able to withstand this aging, and their high acidity also enabled them to age well in bottle. But what about the lighter years, when elegance

is prized above structure? Four years in oak would kill whatever elegance the wine may initially have had. There are those today who reckon that even two years is too long in wood in a light vintage, and that the total of four is absurd – why shouldn't the consumer take responsibility for bottle-aging the wines, they demand, as in the case of Bordeaux? Relaxing of regulations would more closely reflect the already widely diverging styles of Brunello, though traditionalists already feel they've moved far enough.

WINE STYLES

Brunello's original claim to greatness was based on the wine's longevity (and an inflated price), and the so-called classic style – as exemplified by Biondi-Santi – is still made by producers in the centre of the zone where the soil is *galestro*-rich and the vineyards are relatively high, at 400–500m (1310–1640ft) above sea level.

On new estates in the north-west and north-east of the zone, producers like Castiglion del Bosco, Caparzo and Altesino have planted vineyards on clay soils not previously cultivated with vines. Though these wines are good, they often need to be given polish by adding a little something from vineyards around Sant' Angelo in Colle in the south or from the *galestro*-rich ones around Montosoli.

This diversity of wine styles illustrates the limitless number of masks the old trouper Sangiovese has at its disposal. As part of the myth management process, Montalcino producers, led by Biondi-Santi, propagated the theory that their particular sub-variety of Sangiovese, called Brunello, was distinctive from, and superior to those found elsewhere in Tuscany. But independent research showed that there were numerous clones of Sangiovese in

WHERE THE VINEYARDS ARE

As Montalcino has expanded, areas not previously cultivated have come under vine, and there is now a much greater diversity of wine styles than ever before. What might be termed the classic Biondi-Santi style lives on, not only at the family's Il Greppo farm, but also among other producers in the high central section around Montalcino. Here the soil has more galestro *than clay, which, combined with the higher altitude, results in wines that have more acidity and a leaner, steelier fruit than those from lower-lying vineyards nearer the zone's perimeter. This style is best exemplified by Costanti's Colle al Matrichese estate and, when they are good, Biondi-Santi.*

In the south around Sant'Angelo Scalo, a different style is produced. There is more clay and limestone in the soil, and warmth from the nearby Val d'Orcia gives richer wines with a lower acidity that tend to be fleshier and more accessible when young, yet ceding none of their aging ability.

MONTALCINO

TOTAL DISTANCE NORTH TO SOUTH
19KM (12 MILES)

▦▦▦ VINEYARDS

0 km   1   2
0 miles   1

Montalcino vineyards, so the growers adopted a new position, claiming that Brunello was a local name for the Tuscan grape stemming from the fact that, in the hot, arid Montalcino summers, the grapes often acquired a brownish hue at ripening, hence Brunello, or 'little brown one'. Moves by California growers to cash in on Montalcino's success by labelling their wines 'Brunello' have since forced the Italian growers to renounce Brunello as a grape name, and today it is officially viewed by them as just a wine.

However that may be, the sole use of Sangiovese for their wines did make the producers of Montalcino unique in Tuscany. But now that others in Chianti and beyond are adopting the same approach and improving the quality of their raw materials, the Montalcino producers are having to fight to retain their pre-eminent position.

Realizing that selling their wines at high prices brings with it a certain responsibility with regard to quality, as far back as 1984 they set up a 'junior' DOC called Rosso di Montalcino, followed in 1996 by a much broader and more inclusive DOC called Sant' Antimo. These 'junior' DOCs have proved particularly successful, not only in maintaining the generally high standard of quality but also in giving a modern and more attractive range of red wines to widen the choice in Tuscany. And of course if you can sell the wine younger, you get your money earlier.

BRUNELLO DI MONTALCINO DOCG WINE AREA AND SELECTED ESTATES

1. Castiglion del Bosco	15. Pian delle Vigne (Antinori)
2. Altesino	16. Case Basse/Soldera
3. Caparzo	17. Poggio Antico
4. Casanova di Neri	18. Pieve Santa Restituta
5. Cantina di Montalcino	19. Mastrojanni
6. Siro Pacenti	20. Ciacci Piccolomini d'Aragona
7. Val di Suga	21. Lisini
8. Salvioni	22. Talenti
9. Fuligni	23. Il Poggione
10. Costanti	24. Argiano
11. Biondi-Santi	25. Banfi
12. Poggio Salvi	26. Col d'Orcia
13. Castelgiocondo	
14. Barbi	—— DOCG BOUNDARY

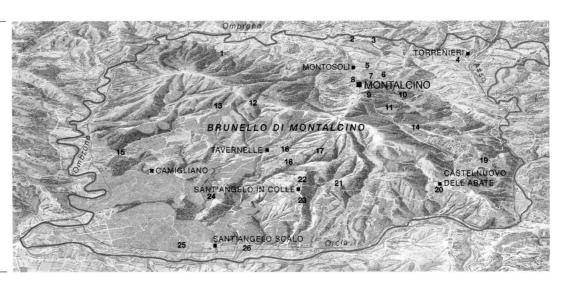

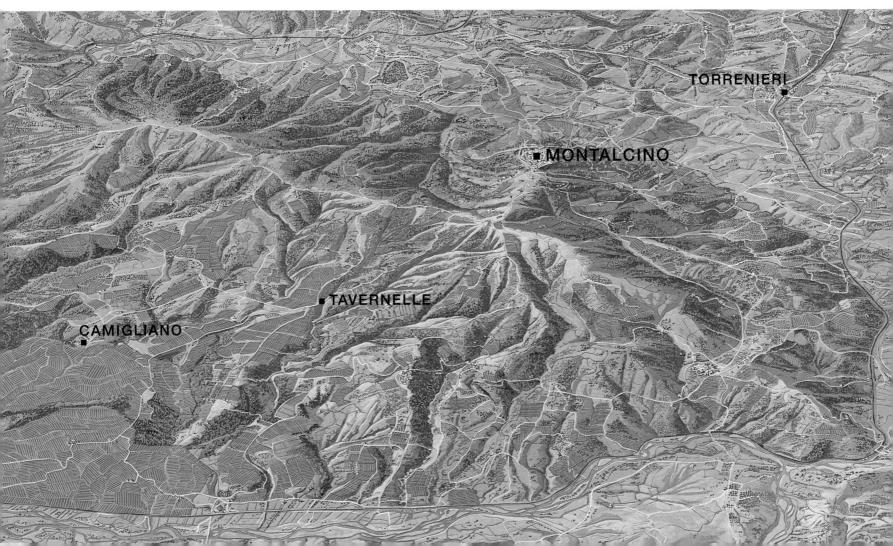

VINO NOBILE DI MONTEPULCIANO

RED GRAPES
Sangiovese, under the name Prugnolo Gentile, is king. Canaiolo is allowed to 20 per cent, as are Cabernet Sauvignon and Merlot.

WHITE GRAPES
A blend of Chardonnay and Sauvignon Blanc make the best whites. Trebbiano and Malvasia are becoming less popular, except for Vin Santo.

CLIMATE
Quasi-continental with hot summers and cold winters, mitigated to a modest extent by the proximity of Lake Trasimeno.

SOIL
Predominantly the classic *albarese* with prized *galestro* (shaly clay), but in parts with a higher proportion of sand.

ASPECT
The majority of the Vino Nobile vineyards face east or south east, occasionally at altitudes up to 550m (1800ft).

THE TOWN OF MONTEPULCIANO (and let's be quite clear – we are not talking about the grape Montepulciano, which is barely grown in Tuscany) is one of the most seductively attractive in all of Italy. Steeped in history and personality, Montepulciano was the home town of Lorenzo de' Medici's favourite poet, Poliziano. It stands in a commanding position on a steep hill, and from its medieval walls you can gaze out over rolling vineyards and olive groves and a distant blue horizon – a view that probably hasn't changed for centuries.

Montepulciano (from the Latin *Mons Politianus*) is situated 40 minutes' drive east of Montalcino in the province of Siena and is the most inland of Tuscany's classic zones. It has the most continental climate and its vineyards are at a generally higher altitude than those of its rivals. Like Montalcino, it is a zone which runs on Sangiovese – here called Prugnolo Gentile, though this historic name is retained mainly for marketing purposes as the Sangiovese clones grown here are, for the most part, the same as those cultivated in Montalcino and Chianti.

Montepulciano was a papal favourite as far back as the 14th century and much of its production used to be controlled by the local nobility – hence the name Vino Nobile di Montepulciano. In 1680 Francesco Redi (poet and physician to the Dukes of Tuscany) went so far as to hail Montepulciano 'of every wine the king', an accolade that other wine-producing zones of Tuscany, let alone the rest of Italy, might dispute today. But by the end of the 1970s, if not much earlier, this 'king' had lost most of his royal trappings, and was left with 'nobility' in name only. By then, the grandly named Vino Nobile had descended to the humble level of ordinary Chianti.

As with Chianti, local rules let winemakers put a hefty proportion of white grapes into the blend – almost a third was allowed and 10 per cent was mandatory – more than enough to ruin any red wine with pretensions to class. Worse still, the wine had to contain at least 10 per cent Canaiolo (a coarser red variety) and its excessive aging processes were conducted in old barrels, finally killing off any quality or freshness that might have survived to that point.

The granting of DOCG status in 1980, although it seemed a travesty at the time, turned out to be just the stimulus the winemakers needed. While the new law still allowed white grapes into the blend, and required Canaiolo, it seemed more flexible and the best producers, in time-honoured Italian tradition, started to ignore the law's stupidities and began writing their own script. This led to the development of wines made with 100 per cent Sangiovese, or Sangiovese blended with Cabernet or Merlot, all officially illegal until further changes to the law were made.

Perhaps the first producer to rise from the ashes and gain an international reputation was Avignonesi. This company became known not only for a classier version of Vino Nobile, but also for more international style wines like Grifi – a now defunct super-Tuscan blend of Sangiovese and Cabernet and Il Marzocco (Chardonnay). It also produced the most sought-after Vin Santo of all Tuscany (theirs is a non-botrytized sweet wine, barrel-aged and produced in tiny quantities).

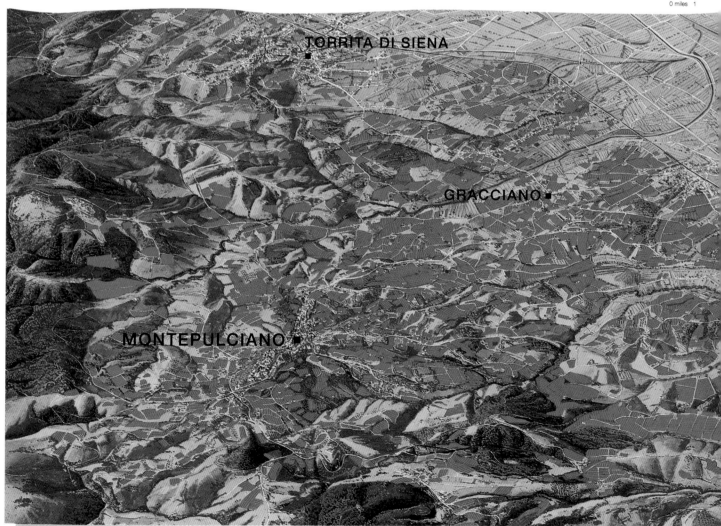

0 km 1 2
0 miles 1

TORRITA DI SIENA

GRACCIANO

MONTEPULCIANO

MONTEPULCIANO

TOTAL DISTANCE NORTH TO SOUTH 13KM (8¼ MILES)

VINEYARDS

0 km 1 2
0 miles 1

The key to Vino Nobile's revival, though, lay in the taming of tannins and acids which, while making the wine one of Tuscany's longest-lived (before they started adding white grapes), also made it impossibly tough when young. Since the early 1990s techniques learned from the French – in the vineyard, during fermentation and in the aging process (particularly the use of barriques) – have enabled more and more producers to make wines which are concentrated and full of extract, yet approachable within two to five years of vintage.

Today's Vino Nobile is not yet on a par with either Montalcino or Chianti Classico, the former doing a better job with pure Sangiovese and the latter, if you include the IGT super-Tuscans, putting out superior blends as well as varietals. There are, on the other hand, fewer producers here, and far fewer that have a quality track-record. But the

signs are very encouraging and the feeling is that Vino Nobile di Montepulciano is finally coming back into its own in the early years of the 21st century. As in Montalcino nearby, the introduction of the Rosso di Montepulciano DOC as essentially a second wine has given producers the chance of improving the selection for the grander Vino Nobile wine.

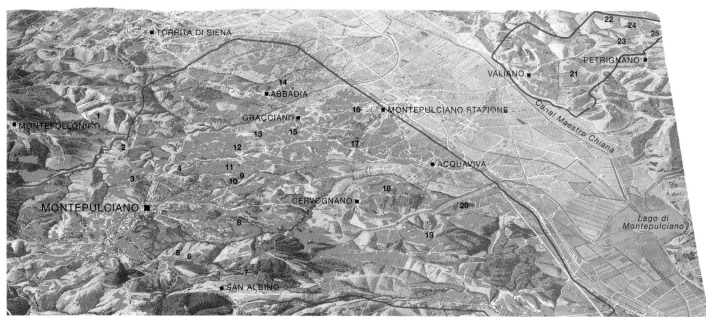

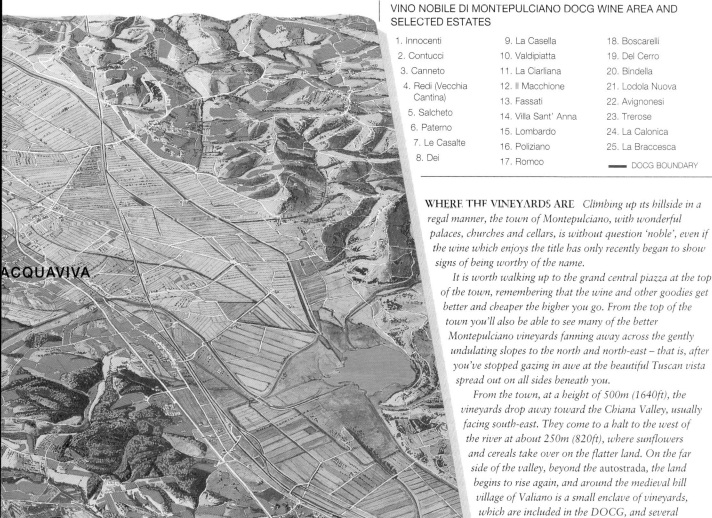

ACQUAVIVA

VINO NOBILE DI MONTEPULCIANO DOCG WINE AREA AND SELECTED ESTATES

1. Innocenti	9. La Casella	18. Boscarelli
2. Contucci	10. Valdipiatta	19. Del Cerro
3. Canneto	11. La Ciarliana	20. Bindella
4. Redi (Vecchia Cantina)	12. Il Macchione	21. Lodola Nuova
5. Salcheto	13. Fassati	22. Avignonesi
6. Paterno	14. Villa Sant' Anna	23. Trerose
7. Le Casalte	15. Lombardo	24. La Calonica
8. Dei	16. Poliziano	25. La Braccesca
	17. Romeo	—— DOCG BOUNDARY

POLIZIANO
Vino Nobile di Montepulciano

WHERE THE VINEYARDS ARE *Climbing up its hillside in a regal manner, the town of Montepulciano, with wonderful palaces, churches and cellars, is without question 'noble', even if the wine which enjoys the title has only recently began to show signs of being worthy of the name.*

It is worth walking up to the grand central piazza at the top of the town, remembering that the wine and other goodies get better and cheaper the higher you go. From the top of the town you'll also be able to see many of the better Montepulciano vineyards fanning away across the gently undulating slopes to the north and north-east – that is, after you've stopped gazing in awe at the beautiful Tuscan vista spread out on all sides beneath you.

From the town, at a height of 500m (1640ft), the vineyards drop away toward the Chiana Valley, usually facing south-east. They come to a halt to the west of the river at about 250m (820ft), where sunflowers and cereals take over on the flatter land. On the far side of the valley, beyond the autostrada, the land begins to rise again, and around the medieval hill village of Valiano is a small enclave of vineyards, which are included in the DOCG, and several superlative wine estates.

BOLGHERI

 RED GRAPES
Primarily Cabernet Sauvignon for the top wines with smaller plantings of Cabernet Franc, Petit Verdot and Merlot, the other Bordeaux red varieties, plus Syrah and Sangiovese.

WHITE GRAPES
Traditionally the quality white grape here is Vermentino, but Chardonnay and Sauvignon Blanc are making progress.

 **CLIMATE**
It is significantly hotter here on the low-lying coast than inland Tuscany, but with mitigating sea breezes.

 SOIL
The key to Bolgheri's quality is drainage, helped by the gravel and sand mixed in with the marl.

ASPECT
Most vineyards are on very gently rising ground facing west and south; there are a few hillside sites.

I N 1974, A SIX-YEAR-OLD SASSICAIA WINE won an astonishing victory over an assortment of illustrious Bordeaux Grands Crus in a tasting organised by *Decanter* magazine. It put Bolgheri on the map. Before that no-one would have dreamt that a Cabernet, let alone a great one, could conceivably hail from central Italy, nor that a high quality wine of any sort could be produced from the once-malarial, low-lying Tuscan coast known as the northern Maremma or Costa degli Etruschi. Nor had anyone ever heard of the quiet village of Bolgheri, in the province of Livorno, other than a few artists and tourists, or horse-lovers keen to admire the fine beasts reared and trained on the vast properties of the della Gherardesca and other noble families.

Bolgheri itself is an insignificant parish or 'frazione' of the commune of Castagneto Carducci, a zone named after a pretty hilltop town a few kilometres to the south. The fact that the region's prototype wine, Sassicaia, comes from an estate situated near Bolgheri is no doubt the reason for the honour of DOC being bestowed on the *frazione* rather than the commune. Bolgheri DOC wines can, in fact, come from anywhere in the commune of Castagneto, except the part nearest the sea, west of the Via Aurelia. But the influence of Sassicaia and Bolgheri extends much further, spreading along the coast northwards to Montescudaio, in the province of Pisa, and south to Suvereto-Val di Cornia in Livorno.

The land near the sea is flat, rising gradually until you reach the first slopes of the Colline Metallifere, a few kilometres inland,. The DOC vineyards are both on the flat and on slopes and some producers, including the producers of Sassicaia, make wine blended from grapes grown in both terrains. Soils contain varying amounts of marl, sand and gravel, the drainage is similar to that of Bordeaux and the climate, which one might have thought impossibly hot for Bordeaux grapes, is modified by the nearness of the sea. And there are plenty of umbrella pines, cypresses and even eucalyptus trees to break up the sometimes brisk breezes whipping off the water.

In terms of a history, this wine zone hasn't really got one. It was known largely for rosés made principally from Sangiovese. This grape ripens well here (some say too well) producing a jammy, blowsy product, unless care is taken in both vineyard and winery. Some excellent Sangiovese reds now come from Bolgheri: Michele Satta's Vigna al Cavaliere is an outstanding example. But once the Marchesi Incisa della Rocchetta – of Sassicaia fame – along with their advisers, Giacomo Tachis and Professor Emile Peynaud, had shown Bolgheri to be ideal for Cabernet, it was to Bordeaux varieties that growers turned, to a rising crescendo of applause.

First to take the plunge in the early 1980s was Lodovico Antinori (brother of Piero, and cousin of Niccolò Incisa of Sassicaia through their della Gherardesca mothers). Lodovico planted Cabernet Sauvignon, Cabernet Franc, Merlot and Sauvignon at his Ornellaia estate. He showed the world how well both Merlot (the wine is called Masseto) and Sauvignon Blanc (Poggio alle Gazze) could perform here. His brother Piero followed suit at Tenuta Belvedere with a Cabernet/Merlot blend, Guado al Tasso. And a few years ago another big name, Angelo Gaja, from Piedmont, also bought an estate in Bolgheri – Ca' Marcanda.

The Bolgheri DOC, approved in 1994, has a broad scope: its red wines are based on Cabernet Sauvignon (up to 80 per cent) or Merlot or Sangiovese (up to 70 per cent), topped up with other varieties. Bolgheri Sassicaia, for example, is a blend of 85 per cent Cabernet Sauvignon and 15 per cent Cabernet Franc (interestingly, this was the first Italian estate wine to have its name attached as a sub-zone to a DOC). Whites can be based on Sauvignon Blanc, Vermentino or Trebbiano (to 70 per cent), with the remainder being other white grapes, such as Chardonnay or Viognier.

BOLGHERI AND MONTESCUDAIO

TOTAL DISTANCE
NORTH TO SOUTH
22.5KM (14 MILES)

VINEYARDS

N

Cabernet Franc vines, just outside the fortified village of Bolgheri, belonging to Tenuta dell'Ornellaia. Count Lodovico Antinori, a member of the famous Tuscan wine dynasty, established the estate in the 1980s to create world-class Bordeaux-style reds. The estate now belongs to the famous Tuscan wine dynasty, the Frescobaldis.

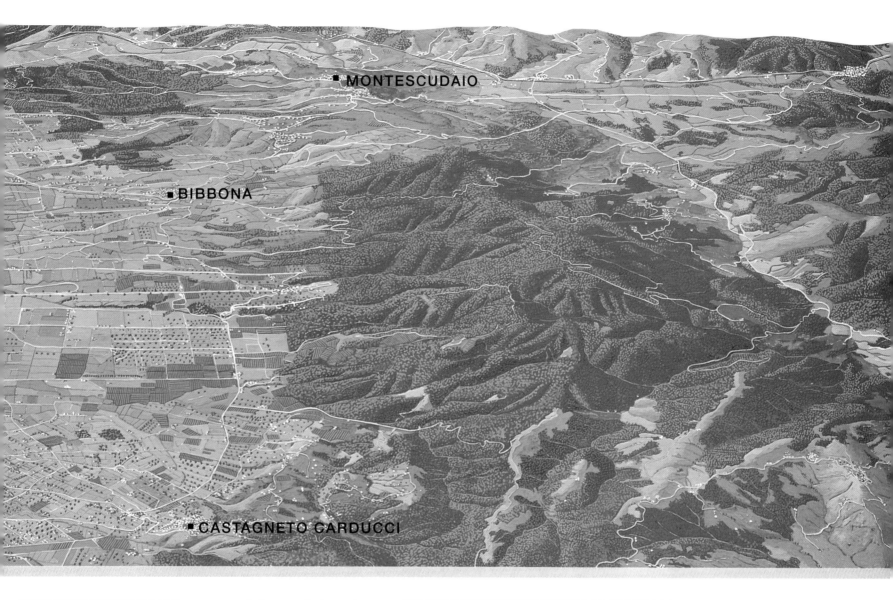

WHERE THE VINEYARDS ARE *It was years before I worked out what was so special about Bolgheri and its more inland neighbour, Montescudaio. The landscape between Livorno and Piombino along this part of the Tuscan coast is of such unrelenting drabness that there had to be something else – and luckily there is.*

Lack of any significant grape-growing and winemaking traditions and no restrictive regulations about which grape varieties could be used were a crucial part of the area's success. But the poor, infertile soils of those vineyards huddled up against the hills (the 1-hectare patch of rocky hillside that was the first Sassicaia vineyard is actually several kilometres up into the hills) are also important.

Sea breezes moderate the strong Tuscan summer sun, yet yields on these generally poor soils are so low that ripening is usually two to three weeks ahead of central Tuscany. There aren't many producers, even today, despite the number of local success stories – the area's estates are large and the amount of land suitable for viticulture is limited.

Montescudaio's vineyards, like the earliest tiny Sassacaia vineyard, are mostly some 300m (985ft) above sea level, and the altitude and sea breezes allow a remarkable array of white grapes to flourish, as well as some exciting reds.

DOC WINE AREAS AND SELECTED ESTATES

MONTESCUDAIO
1. Poggio Gagliardo
2. La Regola
3. Merlini

BOLGHERI
4. Tenuta San Guido (Sassicaia)
5. Sassicaia vineyard
6. Tenuta Guado al Tasso (Antinori)
7. Guado al Tasso vineyard

8. Le Macchiole
9. Tenuta dell'Ornellaia
10. Ca' Marcanda (Gaja)
11. Grattamacco
12. Michele Satta

BOLGHERI = DOC WINE AREA
— DOC BOUNDARIES

SOUTHERN ITALY

 RED GRAPES
Local grapes, such as Negroamaro, Primitivo, Uva di Troia, Gaglioppo and Aglianico still feature.

WHITE GRAPES
Native varieties include Greco di Tufo, Fiano, Falanghina and Greco di Bianco.

CLIMATE
The plains can be bakingly hot and arid, but in the Apennines the climate is almost alpine.

SOIL
Soils vary from calcareous, alluvial and volcanic to clay, sand and marl.

ASPECT
Altitude is important in determining vineyard sites and methods of vine-training.

MAIN DOCG AND DOC WINE REGIONS

CAMPANIA
▬▬ Falerno del Massico
▬▬ Solopaca
▬▬ Greco di Tufo DOCG
▬▬ Taurasi DOCG
▬▬ Fiano di Avellino DOCG
▬▬ Campi Flegri
▬▬ Ischia
▬▬ Capri

PUGLIA
▬▬ Aleatico di Puglia DOC covers all DOC zones in the region
▬▬ San Severo
▬▬ Moscato di Trani
▬▬ Rosso Canosa
▬▬ Rosso Barletta
▬▬ Castel del Monte
▬▬ Locorotondo
▬▬ Brindisi
▬▬ Primitivo di Manduria
▬▬ Salice Salentino
▬▬ Squinzano
▬▬ Copertino
▬▬ Leverano

BASILICATA
▬▬ Aglianico del Vulture

CALABRIA
▬▬ Cirò
▬▬ Donnici
▬▬ Savuto
▬▬ Greco di Bianco

☐ OVER 300M (984FT)
☐ OVER 600M (1968FT)

SOUTHERN ITALY is the spiritual home of Italian wine. The vine's first foothold on the peninsula was said to have been in the south, where it thrived as never before in any Mediterranean habitat. Indeed, such was its affinity for the hills and plains of southern Italy – whether the lower slopes of Mount Vulture in Basilicata, Puglia's Salento plains or Calabria's Cirò – that the Greeks called their new colony *Enotria Tellus* or 'Land of Vines'.

An eerie sense of history pervades southern wines, both in the vineyard and in the cellar. The vines tend to be trained low in the free-standing *alberello* or bush system, a configuration said to have been imported by the Greeks; and the generous and exotic flavours of figs and spices found in grapes like Negroamaro, Gaglioppo and Aglianico evoke the vine's Mediterranean origins to a much greater extent than the cooler, northern Italian wine flavours ever can, reflecting a tangible sense of an unbroken tradition stretching back 3000 years and beyond.

Phoenicians, Greeks, Romans, Normans and Bourbons have all been seduced by the Mezzogiorno, Italy's south. It is a land of incomparable light, unbearable heat, unencumbered plenty, immovable indolence and unbelievable corruption, a land blessed by the gods with opportunities squandered by man.

To people from the north – whether from Italy or Europe – it is a foreign land, full of scents of musk and sensuality. The industriousness that pervades northern European culture is lacking here, and life under the searing sun is taken at a more relaxed pace. Such a languid approach is often confused with lassitude, yet it is, along with a diet of fresh vegetables and pasta, responsible for giving modern southern Italians the longest life expectancy of any Europeans.

Unfortunately this lackadaisical, if healthy, approach to living has meant that the southern vineyards were easy prey to focused, aggressive northerners. Historically, the Bourbon royal family, based in Naples (Napoli), had supported local quality wines, but Italy's unification in 1861 saw northern merchants, intent on sourcing dark, ripe reds to bolster their pale northern brews, invade the south, and many ancient, heady, exotic wines disappeared into blending vats in Verona, Florence and Alba. In addition, the traditional, low-yielding, bush-trained vines were often replaced over the century following unification by high-yielding, wire-trellised ones, and the great southern grapes were ripped up and replaced by the unsuitable Trebbiano and Sangiovese from further north. Grapes from high-trained Trebbiano and Sangiovese vines produce enormous amounts of wine, but little worth drinking. Not only are yields too high, but these northern varieties ripen too quickly in the south, in the process never developing any of the desirable fruit flavours and perfumes that might have blossomed if the grapes had been grown in a cooler climate.

And in the 1980s and 90s, the EU embarked on one of its periodic attempts to reduce wine production by initiating a scheme to finance the uprooting of vineyards. This was *supposed* to reduce the amount of high-yielding vines that did nothing but pump dilute swill into the wine lake. Who were they kidding? Certainly not the majority of local peasant farmers who enthusiastically ripped out those difficult, low-yielding ancient bush vines on the hillsides that gave such backache whenever they had to be pruned or picked. But a fair number of growers resisted the lure of EU cash and they, with today's modern winemaking technology, are now in a prime position to capitalize on the superior nature of their raw materials. Indeed, the rich inheritance of native grape varieties is now the South's greatest strength: few other wine regions grow such a range of individual varieties – including Aglianico, Falanghina, Fiano, Gaglioppo, Greco di Tufo, Mantonico, Montepulciano, Moscato, Negroamaro, Piedirosso, Primitivo and Uva di Troia. These varieties, as

the Greeks observed, are ideally suited to the varied terrain and climate of the south. Altitude, topographical features and proximity to the sea can all exert profound moderating influences on latitude and result in mesoclimates considerably cooler than one might predict in such a southern environment. On the slopes of Basilicata's Mount Vulture, for instance, Aglianico vines planted at 500 to 600m (1640 to 1968ft) are, in late October, among the last in Italy to be harvested. Such a long growing season results in wines which, with their fascinatingly complex flavours, belie their southern origins. In Campania's Apennine foothills, altitude similarly influences Taurasi (also made from Aglianico) and whites like Greco di Tufo.

In other areas, however, it is proximity to the sea that tips the scales in favour of quality wine production. In Calabria's Cirò zone, for instance, cool breezes blowing off the Ionian Sea refresh the low-lying Gaglioppo vines, extending their growing season and resulting in the wonderful flavours of licorice, figs and cumin found in the best wines. Similarly in Puglia, on the flat Salento peninsula that comprises the heel of Italy's boot, the winds blowing between the Adriatic and Ionian seas alleviate what would otherwise be desert conditions and produce the ideal climate for strapping reds – Salice Salentino, Copertino and Brindisi, among others – that can be some of Italy's most satisfying wines.

WINE REGIONS

Puglia is the South's most important wine region. Stretching almost 400km (250 miles) into the Adriatic, this mostly flat landscape produces some 17 per cent of all Italian wine. Much of this bulk comes from the northern part of the region, where high-trained Montepulciano, Sangiovese and Trebbiano vines in the San Severo zone account for about 30 per cent of Puglia's total DOC production. In central Puglia, the Uva di Troia grape forms the base for the Castel del Monte, Rosso Barletta and Rosso Canosa DOCs, all of which have yet to realize their full potential. Quality remains patchy, yet just occasionally I sample a really sumptuous mouthful so, as I've been saying for a few years now, the promise for the future is great.

Further south, in the Salento peninsula itself, the bush-trained Negroamaro grape reigns supreme. Because Negroamaro produces, as its name suggests, wines that are dark and bitter, the Malvasia Nera is used to soften its rough edges and make the wines more supple and aromatic. This successful partnership works well in DOCs like Salice Salentino, Copertino, Squinzano, Leverano and Brindisi, where flavours of game, chocolate and prunes are all wrapped up in a velvety texture and brushed with herb scent. And thanks to this partnership and some inspired winemaking, this once backwards part of Puglia is now, along with the best areas of Sicily, the south's standard-bearer for quality wines.

In theory, this accolade should go to Aglianico del Vulture, Basilicata's best known DOC. The Aglianico grape is one of Italy's finest red varieties, and the long growing season in the hills south of Melfi provides it with an ideal stage on which to perform. But while the script is a classic, the performance tends to be amateurish. The young wines often have a thrillingly vibrant flavour but, by the time they are bottled, they have become dull and flaccid. Only producers such as D'Angelo and Paternoster, plus relative newcomers like Basilico and Cantina del Notaio score the odd hit.

Calabria forms the toe of the Italian boot, kicking out into the Ionian and Tyrrhenian seas and only missing Sicily by the 3km (2 miles) that are the Straits of Messina. With the exception of its 780-km (485-mile) coastline, the whole region is wild and mountainous. But although such a terrain should provide many

Most of Italy's best wines come from hillside vineyards. However, much of Puglia is flat and easy to develop for low cost (but not low quality) vineyards. These vineyards, on the Rivera estate near Andrea, are about to be planted with Uva di Troia.

ideal vineyard sites – and in Greek times Calabria was noted for its high quality wines – little quality wine is produced here today other than by Librandi of Cirò on the Ionian side and Odoardi of Cosenza on the Tyrrhenian.

More than 90 per cent of Calabria's DOC wine comes from the Cirò zone on the Ionian coast. The reds from the Gaglioppo grape tend to have less colour and more tannin than those from Puglia's Negroamaro, but display a similar broad range of exotic flavours. In recent years the great advance here has been the introduction of temperature control in winemaking, resulting in wines with fresher, more defined flavours. The white wines of Cirò, made from an undistinguished member of the Greco family of grapes, have benefited to an even greater extent, although they are less distinctive than their red counterparts.

To the north of Calabria is Campania, bordered to the east by Basilicata and northern Puglia, to the north by Lazio and to the west by the Tyrrhenian Sea. Campania is better known for the beautiful Bay of Naples and Mount Vesuvius than for the intrinsic quality of its wines, but in the Apennine foothills that slope gently from the inland mountainous peaks to the flat shoreline there exists great potential that today is rapidly being turned into a reality. The grapes – reds like Aglianico and Piedirosso, and whites like Fiano, Greco and Falanghina – are in place, and the cool hills of northern and central Campania provide ideal conditions for them to flourish. For most of the past four decades the venerable Mastroberardino was the only decent producer in Campania, creating the reputation of the Taurasi DOCG and the Aglicanico grape; but today we are witnessing an explosion of good to outstanding producers in Campania producing some exciting wines, led by Feudi di San Gregorio and including Antonio Caggiano, De Conciliis, Galardi, Montevetrano, Terredora, the Cantina del Taburno and Villa Matilde. Even one of the ancient Romans' star wines Falernian has been revived as the Falerno del Massico DOC and the wines look promising.

Taurasi is the leading red wine of the Campania area, made from Aglianico grapes grown inland from Naples.

SARDEGNA

RED GRAPES
Cannonau, Monica and Carignano are the most important traditional varieties.

WHITE GRAPES
Vermentino in Gallura produces the best wine, but Nuragus accounts for a third of vineyard plantings. Other significant varieties are Torbato, Vernaccia di Oristano and Malvasia Sarda.

CLIMATE
Sardinia has ample sunshine. The south and west are exposed to hot winds from Africa. Drought can be a problem away from the influence of the mountains.

SOIL
Most of Sardinia comprises granite and volcanic rock. The remainder includes calcareous deposits, alluvial sand, gravel and clay.

ASPECT
The better wines come from the hills, but many new vineyards are regions that are flat and dry.

MAIN DOCG AND DOC WINE REGIONS

Cannonau di Sardegna, Monica di Sardegna, Moscato di Sardegna and Vermentino di Sardegna DOCs cover the whole island

— Vermentino di Gallura DOCG

— Alghero

— Malvasia di Bosa

— Vernaccia di Oristano

— Giro di Cagliari, Malvasia di Cagliari, Moscato di Cagliari, Monica di Cagliari, Nasco di Cagliari, Nuragus di Cagliari

— Carignano del Sulcis

☐ OVER 300M (984FT)

☐ OVER 600M (1968FT)

CONSIDERING THAT IT IS the second largest island in the Mediterranean, Sardinia (Sardegna) remains relatively unknown to outsiders. It is also remarkable, given its strategic importance, that while often subjected to long periods of foreign domination, the island was never conquered. The feeling of strangeness often experienced by visitors is enhanced by the local use of the Sardo dialect – an amalgam of Spanish, Catalan and Arabic on a Latin foundation. Equally mysterious, especially to the tourists who descend on the island every summer from the maritime nations of northern Europe, is that the people of Sardinia resolutely eschewed the lure of the sea and its wealth and remained hill and mountain dwellers until very recently. The root of this conundrum must reach back into antiquity as do the odd stone towers called *nuraghi* which dot the landscape for no known purpose.

Nowadays the island is known for its rugged coastline and shimmering sea, in places the colour of lapis lazuli. The beaches of the lovely Costa Smeralda peninsula have been adopted by the rich and famous, but elsewhere you can still find beautiful secluded bays. Not many tourists venture into Sardinia's wild, mountainous interior where people scrape a living by tending their goats and sheep. These mountains, hills and plateaux which make up 85 per cent of the island would be well-suited to quality winemaking, but most of Sardinia's vineyards are planted by growers who choose the easy option

offered by the Campidano plain between Cagliari and Oristano, or else the flatlands near Alghero. As vines need to struggle to produce their best, it is obvious that this lazy approach contributed to the flow of unexciting and even poor wine which once bore down like a tidal wave from the co-operatives.

In the north the terrain varies between cork oak wooded hills with a quasi-continental climate where grapes grown on granite-based soil can produce appealing, well-balanced red and, especially, white wines (including the potentially excellent Vermentino di Gallura DOCG), to the plain of Alghero where the hot, dry conditions mean that only the most serious producers avoid overcropping and overripening. The western vineyards tend to produce grapes of high sugar content. Malvasia di Bosa comes from steep volcanic hill sites, whereas the grapes for the sherry-like Vernaccia di Oristano benefit from the rich alluvial sand and gravel of the Tirso valley, whose hot, dry climate allows the grapes to reach staggering levels of ripeness. The eastern vineyards benefit from cooling north-easterly winds coming from the Gennargentu mountains. Up in the coastal hills the climate becomes somewhat hotter and drier, and the mixed granite soil generally renders comparatively (and mercifully) low yields. The fertile soils of the south, allied with hot, dry conditions, best suit fuller, strapping reds like Cannonau. The steamy conditions of the low-lying south-west corner favour the production of potentially high-quality Carignano on *alberello*-trained vines.

GRAPE VARIETIES AND WINE STYLES

The strong sense of separation from the rest of Italy is reflected in the grapes grown here – though several varieties are indigenous, some of the most important come from Spain, fostered by the Aragonese who arrived on the island in the 13th century. Most of these confirmed the popular wisdom that a hot maritime climate is best suited to big strong aperitif and dessert wines and strapping reds. Here Sardinia has one of its few points in common with Sicily.

But as times and tastes changed, export markets demanded light table wines. The co-operatives, which account for 60 per cent of Sardinia's production, jumped on the bandwagon with ill-considered haste and began pumping out rivers of anonymous white. Now, however, a number of fresh, dry fruity whites are being made from Nuragus and Vermentino, the best of the latter coming from the stony soils of inland Gallura.

Putting new trends aside, the most distinctive wines continue to be those traditional oddities for which Sardinia was once best known. Vernaccia di Oristano develops a light film of flor yeast in cask, similar to that found in sherry production, which prevents spoilage, while imparting a distinctive spiced and nutty character. The history of this wine dates back at least to the 16th century when it was widely appreciated throughout Italy, and it can come either fortified or not. Nasco, made from the grape of the same name, is another rare delight which can also be fortified and comes in dry, medium-dry or sweet styles.

Malvasia di Bosa, too, can be vinified in different ways: it depends on the winemaker. It may be a sweet or dry aperitif or else a fortified wine. Sometimes, like Vernaccia di Oristano, a film of flor yeast might be allowed to develop in cask for added flavour and complexity. Malvasia di Cagliari can likewise be made sweet or fortified but is generally considered best as a delicate dry aperitif. The red Cannonau is usually made into a dry table wine, but it can make a glorious, sweet, mouth-filling dessert wine of real quality, the best known example of which is Sella & Mosca's Anghelu Ruju. Apart from these fascinating specialities, most wine from the island is fairly run-of-the-mill.

SICILIA

When I think of Sicily (Sicilia) I am transported back to the haunting ancient Greek temple and theatre at Segesta, near Alcamo, or I can see again the inspiring medieval mosaics in Monreale cathedral above Palermo. And my first ever job offer was as a baritone with Opera Massima in Palermo. They don't know how lucky they are that I turned to wine. But, sadly, ask anyone what they associate with this beautiful island with its lovely beaches and remarkable art and architecture, and nine out of ten people will probably mention the Mafia.

The traditions of winemaking on the island go back to antiquity and reached dizzy heights in the late 18th century, when the English first created Marsala. But as fortified wines became less fashionable, Sicily was sidetracked. Now its fortunes are looking up again with the advent of some of Italy's most individual table wines.

The north of Sicily is dominated by the tail end of the Apennines which sweep down through the entire length of Italy. Here it can be cool with good rainfall, but enough sun to ensure ideal conditions for grapes to ripen. The south consists mainly of arid, scrubby hills where irrigation is essential, and the east is dominated by the brooding presence of the volcano Mount Etna, so it is not surprising that much of the island's soil is volcanic. The south and east are less well-favoured, lying in the path of hot winds blowing straight from North Africa. Paradoxically, the coolest vineyards, on the slopes of Etna, overlook Catania, one of the hottest cities in Italy. The heart of Sicily provides first-class conditions for vines with cool, high altitudes and mixed volcanic, clay and limestone soils. In the west lies the greatest expanse of vineyards, not only in Sicily, but in all Italy. Here the hot, dry climate and generally arid conditions lead to highly concentrated wines ideal for Marsala.

Sicily's wine reputation was built on its dessert and fortified wines and these still show the greatest depth, style and complexity. Best known until it declined in both popularity and quality was Marsala, now once more achieving great heights after an overhaul of the rules governing its production. Try dismissing all thoughts of Marsala as a wine fit only for sauce in some local Italian restaurant, and taste a dry or *vergine* version. It will come as a revelation. Marsala comes in various styles and levels of sweetness, and can be made from different grapes including Grillo, Catarratto, Inzolia and Damaschino. Grillo is thought to have migrated to Sicily only in the 19th century, but the others have been around since early times.

The sweet tradition is further reflected in a fascinating range of luscious wines made from either Moscato or Malvasia. The most northerly of these comes from the Aeolian or Lipari Islands and is called Malvasia delle Lipari. It is naturally sweet, with an exquisite bouquet. On the other side of Sicily lies the sun-baked volcanic island of Pantelleria. Here the rich, intense wine is made from dried and concentrated Moscato grapes of a variety known locally as Zibibbo. In between these two geographic extremes come Moscato di Noto and Moscato di Siracusa, but sadly these extraordinary sweet wines are made only in tiny quantities in some years, if at all.

Table wines have improved out of all proportion in the last few years, to the extent that some of Italy's finest red wines are now made here. The best tend to be based on the native Nero d'Avola and the best whites on Inzolia. In a region where 90 per cent of the output comes from co-operatives it is usually the private producers who achieve the best quality. It is refreshing to find that Sicilians remain largely faithful to their traditional vine types, although Cabernet, Merlot and Chardonnay have all made inroads and Syrah, reckoned by Sicilians to be the cousin of, if not derived from Nero d'Avola, is clearly going to be the next big thing. The downside is that only a tiny percentage of Sicilian wine qualifies for DOC (in some cases by choice of the producers). One of the best that does is Cerasuolo di Vittoria from the south-east of Sicily, a deep cherry-coloured red made mainly from Frappato and Nero d'Avola grapes, and promoted to DOCG in 2005. Some of the better known DOCs include Bianco d'Alcamo which can show real class, although it is often watery and anonymous. Faro, further north, was undistinguished until the excellent Palari came on the scene, while both red and white Etna can be terrific in the hands of a dedicated producer like Benanti.

The combination of numerous co-operatives, political corruption, and lack of quality has meant that, until recently, the two wine names most widely known outside Sicily were Corvo from the state-owned Duca di Salaparuta – large volumes of adequate red and white plus some excellent special selections – and Regaleali from Tasca d'Almerita, capable of world-class wines. Sicily is emerging with a renewed spirit and firms like Planeta, Donnafugata and Abbazia Santa Anastasia have also achieved deserved international recognition.

RED GRAPES
The best red variety is Nero d'Avola (Calabrese), followed by Nerello. Others are Frappato di Vittoria and Perricone (Pignatello).

WHITE GRAPES
Forty per cent of Sicily's vineyards are planted with Catarratto Bianco. Trebbiano Toscano is also widespread. Inzolia and Camicante thrive, but Grecanico is declining and Zibibbo is often grown as a table grape.

CLIMATE
Rainfall is scarce throughout much of the island, and the south is particularly arid. The north and east are cooler and less prone to drought.

SOIL
Near Etna, soils, naturally, are volcanic. Elsewhere, they range from chalky clay to limestone.

ASPECT
The best vineyards are found on the cooler slopes in the north and east. The most extensive vineyard area in Italy is on the plain and low hills surrounding Trapani.

DOCG AND MAIN DOC WINE REGIONS

- Marsala
- Alcamo, Bianco d'Alcamo
- Contessa Entellina
- Contea di Sclafani
- Faro
- Etna
- Moscato di Siracusa
- Moscato di Noto
- Cerasuolo di Vittoria DOCG
- Malvasia delle Lipari
- Moscato di Pantelleria
- OVER 300M (984FT)
- OVER 600M (1968FT)

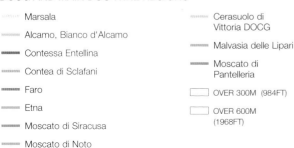

Isola di Pantelleria

SPAIN

Green and gold, the colours of Spain: vast expanses of arid cereal land punctuated by the bright fresh green of vines. These are the vines of Bodegas Nekeas, one of Navarra's most forward-looking wineries. Above are 60-year-old Tinto Fino vines at harvest time, their grapes carefully laid in small modern plastic boxes, before being taken to the Dominio de Pingus winery in Ribera del Duero, one of Spain's top red wine regions.

The late 1990s provided a dramatic turnaround in the quality of Spain's long-neglected wines, and also in the international perception of the many Spanish regions that had long been overshadowed by the indomitable duo of Jerez and Rioja. A drastic modernization of winemaking technology has finally allowed regions like Priorat, Ribera del Duero, La Mancha, Rueda and Toro to muscle into the limelight with potent fruit-driven wines with the impact and style to convert the modern consumer.

Spain is basically far hotter and drier than its more famous wine neighbour, France, so the variation in local climates is less and the range of grapes that find conditions ideal is limited. It has taken her a long while to appreciate the need to search out mesoclimates influenced by altitude and by maritime cooling conditions. And it has taken her some time to realize that hot-climate grapes like Garnacha, Cariñena, Tempranillo, Verdejo and Monastrell can produce delicious flavours if approached with up to-the-minute New World technology and attitudes.

The lush, hilly north-west is heavily influenced by cool, damp Atlantic conditions and the fragrant whites and tangy, juicy reds are marvellously individual. Further south along the Duero river are some of Spain's most exciting reds and whites.

Andalucía in the south-west doesn't have much to offer in terms of table wines, but the fortified wines of Jerez and Montilla-Moriles can be among the world's greatest. Málaga's fame has faded since the 19th century, but occasional bottles still show how exciting her wines can be. The large area of the Levante stretching between Alicante and Valencia and the vast plateau of La Mancha and Valdepeñas inland, to the south of Madrid, used to be synonymous with cheap, coarse flavours that filled the flagons of forgettable international brands owned by brewers and distillers. Yet the enormous potential for low-priced, attractive wine is at last being realized as the giant wine companies modernize their wineries, their techniques and their desire to please.

The north-east has traditionally been seen as the quality wine capital of Spain, with famous reds and whites from Rioja and Penedès, and Cava sparklers. But here, too, the winds of change are blowing, and areas like Navarra, Somontano, Campo de Borja and Costers del Segre are making thrilling contributions to the new, exciting Spain. After a long wait in the shadows of nations like Italy and France, the 21st century could finally be Spain's century.

THE WINE REGIONS OF SPAIN

HOWEVER MUCH THE NEW WORLD bewitches the dedicated follower of wine fashion, Spain somehow manages to cling to its reputation as one of the most exotic countries to grow the grape. How is this? There was a time in the 1980s when much of Spain's wine was desperately mediocre and we turned right round and headed east to Central Europe for wine bargains. But in the 1990s, across the Iberian peninsula, new equipment, the replanting of vineyards with better varieties as well as disease-free vines and the use of highly trained enologists, some from abroad, all helped to give a kick-start to Spanish winemaking. Yet we still grumbled about the quality and embraced the delights of the New World, even though the vinous tradition and heritage of Spanish winemaking never quite lost its magic.

We can't really put this down to Spain's rich treasure trove of native grapes (Tempranillo, under a variety of local pseudonyms, and Albariño are the best of the bunch), or her assortment of unique wine styles – only sherry, maybe red Rioja and Priorat and Galicia's whites are truly original.

But there is the varied landscape of the wine regions: the broad Duero valley, the rocky foothills of the cool Pyrenees, the hillside pastures of Galicia, the scorching, stony central plains of La Mancha or the baked white plains of Jerez in Andalucía. It seems that, however much the landscape and climate alter, there are always vineyards – indeed, Spain has the world's largest acreage under vine. But it is not its largest wine producer. Spain long relied on very low-yielding, dry-farmed old vineyards. New plantings and the now legal drip irrigation have changed all that, to the extent that Rioja production more than doubled between 1990 and 2000 and excessive yields became, for the first time, a cause for concern.

Spain's main geographical features are the huge plateau or *meseta* in its centre and high mountains rising steeply from the coast around and across this plateau – the Pyrenees, the Cantabrian mountains, the Iberian range and the sierras Nevada, Guadarrama and Morena are the main ones. Not surprisingly, there are several climates in this large, diverse country, from cool uplands to coastal Mediterranean and Atlantic belts and, inland in the high *meseta*, arid semi-desert with its extremes of temperature.

Variety is the key to Spain's wine regions and starting in the north-east, important vineyard areas are found within Navarra, Aragón and Catalunya. The large region of Navarra is an important producer of acclaimed reds and *rosados*, and Aragón's little Somontano DO is a picturesque spot in the Pyrenean foothills, where winemaking is progressing at a cracking pace. Further south,

both Campo de Borja and Calatayud are now waking up to the modern world. Over to the east in Catalunya, vineyards are divided between small, demarcated areas: Alella's sea-facing vineyards produce good white wine, while craggy Priorat has benefited immensely from better techniques being applied to its powerful reds. Nestling up to Navarra is La Rioja, with its world-famous Rioja wine from the upper Ebro valley.

The north-west is known as 'green Spain' because of its Atlantic climate and high rainfall. Perched above the Portuguese border are the rainy regions of Rías Baixas, producing some of Spain's most fragrant whites from Albariño, and Ribeiro, a pretty, hilly area with rapidly improving wines. On the north coast the traditional wine of the Basque seaboard, Txakolí, is produced in three País Vasco DOs. In Castilla y León, through which the Duero river makes its way to Portugal, is the flat region of Toro, best for its red wines, and Rueda, producer of fresh whites. Just beyond this is the tiny Cigales DO, where the *rosado* flows fresh and plentiful, and Ribera del Duero, literally 'the banks of the Douro', a high pine-strewn, undulating red wine region of increasing renown and popularity.

Down in central Spain, the land is as hot and baked as you will find anywhere in Europe. Castilla-La Mancha stretches out to form a huge, arid plateau of windmills and vines, alternately whipped by cold winters and scorched by impossibly hot summers. It is dry and mostly inhospitable, but here lie more than half of Spain's vineyards. La Mancha also encompasses the DO of Valdepeñas, increasingly known for highly drinkable red wines.

Over to the east of La Mancha are the regions of Valencia and Murcia, once just known for grapy Moscatels and blending wines, but now showing real potential for reds. In particular the excellent local grape, Monastrell (known as Mourvèdre in France) has been rediscovered and there are now some 40,500ha (100,075 acres) of it in Alicante and Murcia. To the west, the sweet Malaga wines are, alas, becoming less and less important these days. Montilla-Moriles is another sunbaked area where white soil and Pedro Ximénez grapes create sherry look-alikes. The real thing is, of course, produced further west in Jerez and Manzanilla where vast, gently sloping vineyards cover areas of chalky white *albariza* soil. Jerez's neighbour, Condado de Huelva, used to sell its fruit to the sherry producers; now it is turning its attention to light white wines.

Finally, there is wine produced on the holiday islands. Binissalem is the main Balearic wine area, while the winemakers in the Canaries have recently gained DO status in several areas.

CLOS ERASMUS
1997

PRIORAT

Pesquera is one of the top estates in Spain's Ribera del Duero region, producing rich, ripe reds from the Tinto Fino (Tempranillo) grape.

THE CLASSIFICATION SYSTEM FOR SPANISH WINE

Spanish wine law is administered by the Agriculture Ministry and increasingly by the autonomous regions and run by local Consejos Reguladores. Rioja was the first region to set up a Consejo Regulador in 1926, followed by Jerez and Málaga. Legislation is based on a DO (*denominación de origen*) system, revised when Spain joined the EU in 1986. Spain's wine, in common with that of all EU countries, is split into two levels: quality wine – Vino de Calidad Producido en Región Demarcada (VCPRD), and table wine – Vino de Mesa.

QUALITY WINES

• **Denominación de Origen (DO)** Roughly equivalent to French ACs, these are the best-known classic wines of Spain. There are now more than 60 DOs, each with its own Consejo which, together with the local government, decides on quality control issues like permitted yields and grape varieties.

• **Denominación de Origen Calificada (DOCa)** This new super-category

came into being in 1991 with the award of a DOCa to Rioja and then Priorat in 2001. It is reserved for wines which have a long tradition of high quality. Regulations are more stringent and include rigorous tasting.

TABLE WINES

• **Vino de la Tierra (VdlT)** This category roughly corresponds to French *vin de pays* and denotes a wine from a demarcated region which does not have a DO at present but which has a distinctive local character. At least 60 per cent of the wine must come from the stated region.

• **Vino Comarcal (VC)** This is the next stage down in quality. These areas have no great pretension to quality. Producers may put a vintage on the label.

• **Vino de Mesa (VdM)** This is the equivalent of France's *vin de table*. It is made from grapes from unclassified vineyards, or wine which has been declassified by blending from different classified regions. The label has no vintage.

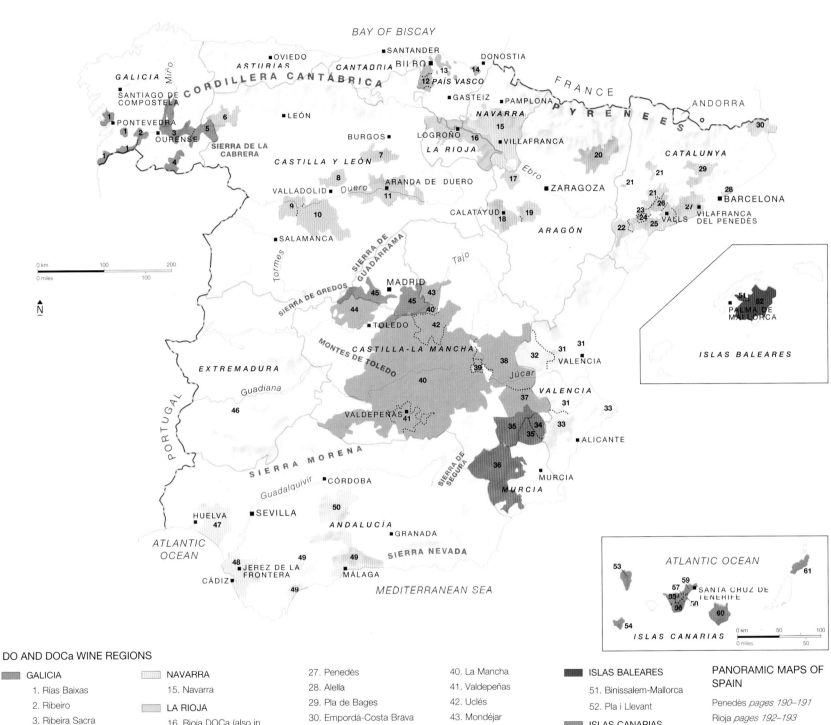

BAY OF BISCAY

GALICIA
ASTURIAS CANTABRIA
OVIEDO ■SANTANDER ■BILBAO
■DONOSTIA
CORDILLERA CANTÁBRICA
13
12 PAÍS VASCO
14
FRANCE
ANDORRA
SANTIAGO DE COMPOSTELA
■GASTEIZ ■PAMPLONA
■PONTEVEDRA
■LEÓN
NAVARRA
1
6
5
OURENSE
3 2
3
SIERRA DE LA CABRERA
1
1
4
BURGOS■
LOGROÑO■ 16
LA RIOJA
15
■VILLAFRANCA
20
30
CATALUNYA
CASTILLA Y LEÓN
7
17
Ebro
21
29
21
28
ZARAGOZA
21 26
23 27
24
22 25
■BARCELONA
VALLS VILAFRANCA DEL PENEDÈS
8
VALLADOLID■ Duero
11
ARANDA DE DUERO
9
10
CALATAYUD■ 19
18
ARAGÓN
■SALAMANCA
Tormes
SIERRA DE GUADARRAMA
Tajo
SIERRA DE GREDOS
MADRID
44 45
43
45
40
42
TOLEDO■
MONTES DE TOLEDO
CASTILLA-LA MANCHA
39
38
32
31 31
VALENCIA
51 52
PALMA DE MALLORCA
ISLAS BALEARES
EXTREMADURA
Guadiana
40
Júcar
VALENCIA
37
31
46
VALDEPEÑAS■ 41
35 34
35
33
33
■ALICANTE
SIERRA MORENA
36
SIERRA DE SEGURA
MURCIA
■MURCIA
Guadalquivir ■CÓRDOBA
50
HUELVA■ 47
■SEVILLA
ANDALUCÍA
■GRANADA
SIERRA NEVADA
53
ATLANTIC OCEAN
59
57
55 SANTA CRUZ DE TENERIFE
56
58
61
ATLANTIC OCEAN
48 49
CÁDIZ■ JEREZ DE LA FRONTERA
49
MÁLAGA
49
MEDITERRANEAN SEA
54
60
ISLAS CANARIAS

0 km 100 200
0 miles 100

0 km 50 100
0 miles 50

N

PORTUGAL

DO AND DOCa WINE REGIONS

GALICIA
1. Rías Baixas
2. Ribeiro
3. Ribeira Sacra
4. Monterrei
5. Valdeorras

CASTILLA Y LEÓN
6. Bierzo
7. Arlanza
8. Cigales
9. Toro
10. Rueda
11. Ribera del Duero

PAÍS VASCO
12. Arabako Txakolina
13. Bizkaiko Txakolina
14. Getariako Txakolina

NAVARRA
15. Navarra

LA RIOJA
16. Rioja DOCa (also in País Vasco and Navarra)

ARAGÓN
17. Campo de Borja
18. Calatayud
19. Cariñena
20. Somontano

CATALUNYA
21. Costers del Segre
22. Terra Alta
23. Montsant
24. Priorat DOCa
25. Tarragona
26. Conca de Barberá
27. Penedès
28. Alella
29. Pla de Bages
30. Empordá-Costa Brava

VALENCIA
31. Valencia
32. Utiel-Requena
33. Alicante (also in Murcia)

MURCIA
34. Yecla
35. Jumilla (also in Castilla-La Mancha)
36. Bullas

CASTILLA-LA MANCHA
37. Almansa
38. Manchuela
39. Ribera del Júcar
40. La Mancha
41. Valdepeñas
42. Uclés
43. Mondéjar
44. Méntrida (also in Madrid)

MADRID
45. Vinos de Madrid

EXTREMADURA
46. Ribera del Guadiana

ANDALUCÍA
47. Condado de Huelva
48. Jerez-Xérès-Sherry and Manzanilla de Sanlúcar de Barrameda
49. Málaga and Sierras de Málaga
50. Montilla-Moriles

ISLAS BALEARES
51. Binissalem-Mallorca
52. Pla i Llevant

ISLAS CANARIAS
53. La Palma
54. El Hierro
55. Ycoden-Daute-Isora
56. Abona
57. Valle de la Orotava
58. Valle de Güímar
59. Tacoronte-Acentejo
60. Gran Canaria
61. Lanzarote

PANORAMIC MAPS OF SPAIN

Penedès *pages 190–191*
Rioja *pages 192–193*
Ribera del Duero *pages 198–199*
Jerez *pages 204–205*

OTHER MAPS

North-East Spain *page 189*
North-West Spain *page 196*
Central Spain *page 201*
Southern Spain *page 203*

NORTH-EAST SPAIN

RED GRAPES
Tempranillo, Garnacha Tinta, Cariñena, Monastrell, Moristel and Graciano are the main ones. Cabernet Sauvignon and Merlot are also grown.

WHITE GRAPES
Macabeo (Viura), Garnacha Blanca, Xarel-lo, Parellada, Malvasía are the principal varieties, with some Chardonnay.

CLIMATE
This varies, from the damp northern Basque coastline to the pleasant moderate conditions of Rioja and the Catalan coastline, to the semi-arid parts of southern Aragón and inland Catalunya.

SOIL
These are very varied, from the reddish-brown limestone of Navarra and Cariñena to the calcareous clay of parts of Rioja and Penedès chalk.

ASPECT
Vineyards are found on flat plateau land, coastal hills and high inland terraces.

Priorat is an ancient vineyard area near Barcelona, whose powerful, heady reds are in great demand once more, due to wines such as L'Ermita, made from 100-year-old Garnacha vines grown in a rocky amphitheatre on a slope of 45°.

I MUST HAVE WANDERED THROUGH north-eastern Spain more than most parts of Europe. Our first ever family holiday abroad was on the Costa Brava and the first time I escaped from the family for my own holiday I ended up very excited and nervous in Barcelona railway station late at night en route for Tarragona and Tangier. I was all of sixteen. My parents thought I was on a cosy campsite in Normandy. I wish. A year or two later, I had my first, not entirely pleasurable taste of Chacolí (or Txakoli, in local Basque dialect) in San Sebastián (Donostia) – I *was* on a campsite this time. Usually anything tastes good on a campsite but this didn't. My first experience of Rioja must have been more successful because I don't really remember bedding down for the night in a ravine near Cenicero where I almost got run over by a train just before dawn (always a sign that the local wine was good and you drank deep).

Since then, though I've usually been in a bit more of a rush, I have made time to traverse the Pyrenees – west to east, not north to south – in and out of France and Spain, along tiny mountain roads, touching on Navarra and Huesca, but every time the broad, flat prairies of the Ebro Valley get too oppressive, I hightail it back to the hills. And I have struck out into the lean and mournful hinterland west of Barcelona, beyond Lleida and Zaragoza, greeting its infrequent and forgettable towns with quite unreasonable enthusiasm, and in passing marvelling at what prescient force drove the Raventós family to establish the Raïmat estate in this remote saltbrush purgatory.

Raïmat has carved its impressive estate out of some of the least promising land in Spain, but the north-east in general is endowed with widely differing conditions. You couldn't get much more different than the straggly dribs and drabs of vines that half-ripen in the damp, cool hills near San Sebastián and suck their moisture directly off the Bay of Biscay. The thin, weedy Txakoli made here once had a strictly local following, although it has improved markedly since 1990 and is almost beginning to taste ripe.

Just south of these Basque vines the Sierra de Cantabria mountains soar, soaking up most of the rest of the moisture that rolls in from the Bay of Biscay. They act as vital protection for Rioja's and Navarra's vineyards, without which grapes like Tempranillo and Garnacha would never ripen.

The Pyrenees, which act as the border with France, aren't so much a protective range, since the ice-cold winds that whip southwards through the valleys originate in their chilly peaks. But they do provide water for irrigation from the many rivers that hurtle out of the foothills before joining the Ebro and heading east for the Mediterranean. Without them, much of Aragón and western Catalunya would be near-desert. Indeed, it's surprising how close you get to the Mediterranean before the landscape relaxes and the hills become less jagged. It's a fairly narrow coastal strip from the French border down through Barcelona to the mouth of the Ebro below Tarragona, but the Catalans characteristically make use of every inch of land they've got.

PAÍS VASCO

Where better to start for a tour around north-east Spain than in the country's tiniest DOs, those of Getariako Txakolina (Chacolí de Guetaria in Spanish), Bizkaiko Txakolina (Chacolí de Vizkaia) and Arabako Txakolina (Chacolí de Álava) in the Basque country of País Vasco. Here, on Spain's Cantabrian coast, the climate is exceedingly damp – about 1600mm (63in) of rain falls each year. It's also pretty cool, but that doesn't stop the locals farming a small number of vines of the local grape, Ondarribi Zuri, from which they make the traditional cider-like Basque white wine usually quaffed locally with fresh Atlantic seafood. A small amount of red

wine is also made, from Ondarribi Beltza. In this damp region where fungal diseases quickly take hold, the vines are traditionally grown on overhead trellises.

The finest Basque vineyards lie in the south of the region in the Alava province. Indeed, the Rioja Alavesa sub-region, which, unlike the rest of Rioja, is in the Basque country, has some of the best Rioja vineyards of all (see page 192).

NAVARRA

This large region used to be best known for its *rosado* wine from the Garnacha grape, but Navarra's progress over the past decade has been an example to the rest of Spain. New technology, plus better vineyard management on Navarra's soft, deep, fertile soils, has begun to coax excellent results out of traditional red Garnacha and, increasingly, Tempranillo, Merlot and Cabernet Sauvignon (see page 195). The officially funded experimental winery, Evena, at Olite, is one of the most important in Europe. Navarra has the potential to rival neighbouring Rioja and, with a wider range of grape varieties, perhaps to outshine it.

LA RIOJA

The region of La Rioja has just one classified wine – Rioja – but in 1991 it was the first in Spain to be awarded the new super-category of DOCa, higher than DO. Rioja's three sub-regions span a segment of the upper Ebro Valley between Haro and Alfaro, with Rioja's capital Logroño marking its centre point. I deal with Rioja in more detail on pages 192–193.

South of the Sierra de Cantabria mountains, the climate feels more Mediterranean and Rioja is sunny enough to merit a high number of second homes for those who live in the large industrialized cities of Bilbao (Bilbo) and San Sebastián north of the mountains. But it remains a surprisingly peaceful part of world, and even Logroño is relatively unspoilt considering the fact that it sits in the centre of one of the world's best-known wine regions.

ARAGÓN

The former kingdom of Aragón covers a wide sweep of land below the central Pyrenees, with the long Ebro river running south-eastwards through the region. Around the edges of the wide, flat Ebro valley are the vineyards. Aragón used to churn out uninspiring stuff, but standards are on the up (see page 194). Directly below Rioja lies Campo de Borja and here, as in Rioja, the Ebro plays an important part in forming the landscape.

In Campo de Borja, and also in Cariñena further south, the climate is distinctly continental – in other words, the summers are baking hot and the winters potentially very cold. Add to that a dry wind from the north and you've got some pretty tough conditions for the vine, and wines made from red Garnacha here are cranked up full on the alcohol front. Calatayud, cut off from the Ebro valley by several small mountain ranges, is a little more humid than Cariñena.

However, Aragón's most interesting DO is north from here across the Ebro. Somontano is a pretty spot in the Pyrenean foothills. Little mountain streams and high rainfall keep this area greener than those to the south, and its mild continental climate in the protective shadow of the Pyrenees helps it to make exciting wines, some from the traditional local red grapes Moristel and Parraleta, and some from international varieties such as Cabernet Sauvignon, Merlot and Chardonnay.

CATALUNYA

The thriving city of Barcelona and its hinterland has made Catalunya one of Spain's most prosperous regions, whose

independence of spirit and strong cultural tradition is symbolized by the existence of an official second language, Catalan. The cluster of wine regions along the coastal belt show Catalunya, with its warm Mediterranean climate, to be an important part of Spain's wine story (see pages 190–191). Much of its wine prosperity is based on Cava, but Penedès, as well as being the heart of Cava production, is also well-known for good reds and whites.

CAVA

Catalunya's Champagne-method sparkling wines were colloquially called *Champaña* but, after a few legal tussles with the Champagne producers of northern France, the Spanish agreed in 1970 to change the name to Cava, meaning 'cellar' in Catalan. The first Cava was made in the town of Sant Sadurní d'Anoia in the heart of Penedès by José Raventós of the firm Codorníu. Raventós had visited Champagne in 1872 and he returned to Spain determined to use the local grapes – Macabeo, Parellada and Xarel-lo – to make a similar sparkling wine. The same varieties are still used today: Macabeo is rather neutral-tasting, though sharpish, making it a good base for sparkling wine; Xarel-lo provides an earthy flavour and higher alcohol; while Parellada is finer and flowery.

Chardonnay was authorized in 1986 and plantings have rapidly increased since Spanish Chardonnay fizz can have lovely fruit and nutty-buttery flavours, as well as a softer character than Champagne.

Cava differs from all the rest of Spain's DOs in that it's not confined to one geographical area and the grapes can be sourced from 159 specified villages all over northern Spain, although most of them are from Penedès in Catalunya.

South-west of Penedès, Terra Alta and Priorat mark out the high ground and are ruggedly beautiful places. In both regions, the old, coarse reds are now giving way to a fascinating new style with power and concentration tamed by modern winemaking, and with some international grape varieties – led by Cabernet Sauvignon and Syrah – lending a new-found complexity to the Garnacha- and Cariñena-based wines. The scattered Costers del Segre DO, in the arid west of Catalunya, is famous for the Raïmat estate; the cool, high-altitude Conca de Barberá produces aromatic white grapes for Cava as well as increasingly good international varieties, and Tarragona, the largest Catalan DO, churns out some fairly basic wine, except in the favoured Falset sub-region, which has recently gained its own new DO of Montsant, where Priorat-like reds are now made. North of Barcelona lies Alella which produces some good fresh white wines, and right in the north is Empordà-Costa Brava. In addition, an all-encompassing Catalunya DO was added in 2001, aiming to play the same role as the basic Bordeaux AC does in France for cheaper blends or wines from lesser areas of the Bordeaux region.

BALEARIC ISLANDS (ISLAS BALEARES)

The tourists on the Costa Brava aren't the only ones who frolic near a wine industry. Mallorca also has a wine industry, Binissalem DO, which lies north of Palma de Mallorca, and Pla i Llevant on the island's rolling central plateau. To the north the Sierra de Alfabia shelters the vineyards from wet northerly winds. Hot summers, mild winters and limestone in the light soils all add up to good conditions for vines and the grapes can become extremely ripe. In the 19th century, sweet Malvasía wine from Binissalem was popular; today the native varieties Manto Negro and Callet make dry reds, while Moll (or Prensal) is used for light whites.

CATALUNYA

IT'S ALMOST LIKE CROSSING the border into another country. With its separate language (Catalan) much in evidence, its thriving capital city of Barcelona and an independence of spirit unmatched anywhere else in Spain, Catalunya is like a little kingdom of its own. Catalunya has always been a prosperous place, and Cava, Spain's traditional-method sparkling wine, and the mould-breaking winemaker, Miguel Torres, have contributed to that wealth.

Catalunya has a great deal of rugged mountain landscape: the Pyrenees dominate the north region, and mountains hem in the Mediterranean coast all the way south. The coastal zone, where many of the vineyards are situated, some even within sight of the glistening sea, enjoys a mild Mediterranean climate but, as you travel inland towards the border with Aragón, the climate becomes more continental, with hotter summers and colder winters.

PENEDÈS

The Penedès DO provides the widest variety of wine styles in this part of Spain. More than 40 years ago it was no better known than any other of the Catalan wine areas, but that was before Miguel Torres returned from winemaking studies in France in 1961 to work at the family bodega at Vilafranca del Penedès in the heart of the region. Since then he has brought a host of international grape varieties into the extensive Torres vineyards – not just Cabernet

Sauvignon and Chardonnay but also Riesling, Gewürztraminer, Muscat Blanc à Petits Grains, Sauvignon Blanc and Pinot Noir – as well as using vine-trellising systems, higher planting densities, organic methods and mechanical pruning quite unknown in Spain before. Not only a pioneer in the vineyard, Torres has experimented in the bodega – earlier bottling of red wines, temperature-controlled stainless steel fermentation, single-variety wines and blending local Parellada and Tempranillo with international varieties are just a few examples.

The Torres influence is not confined to Penedès – in neighbouring Conca de Barberá the Milmanda (Chardonnay) and Grans Muralles (Catalan varieties) vineyards make sought-after wines. The only pity is that Catalunya in general has failed to progress along the path set out by Torres a generation ago, though the whites still stand out for their perfume and finely balanced fruit. About 90 per cent of Penedès wine is white, mainly from Xarel-lo, Macabeo and Parellada (the best for quality), and Chardonnay has been allowed since 1986. Some of the whites, particularly those from Chardonnay, Sauvignon and the aromatic varieties, can be individual and exciting. As a result of the Cava boom, red wine has been rather neglected in Penedès. Poor winemaking far too often mars what seems to be good quality fruit, and even the mould-breaking Torres reds no longer lead the pack. The Catalunya DO

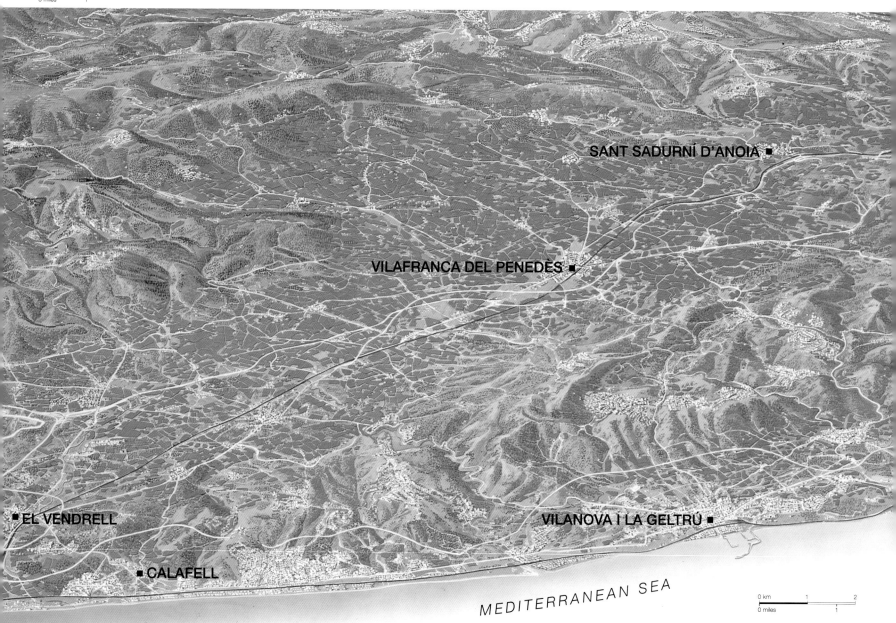

SANT SADURNÍ D'ANOIA ■

VILAFRANCA DEL PENEDÈS ■

■ EL VENDRELL

VILANOVA I LA GELTRÚ ■

■ CALAFELL

MEDITERRANEAN SEA

0 km   1   2
0 miles   1

was introduced in 2001 for blends from anywhere in the region. Once again, Torres has been one of the driving forces and some producers are now using this DO for their new wave wines as it offers greater flexibility.

Penedès is the most important region for Cava production (see page 189). Many of the big name producers are based at Sant Sadurní d'Anoia, where several make still wine as well as sparkling. Winemaking in Penedès revolves around two regional centres, Sant Sadurní d'Anoia and Vilafranca del Penedès – you'll see signs for bodegas in every lane and alley surrounding the residential areas of both these towns. The wealth and expertise generated by the prosperous Cava industry have kept Penedès way ahead of the rest of Catalunya, but Penedès' problem is that it is so well known for Cava, and Torres is so famous as a brand, that the region itself lacks identity

OTHER CATALAN WINE AREAS

One important development is at Lleida, in the parched wastelands between Barcelona and Zaragoza. Here the Raïmat winery, owned by the giant Codorníu group, was the force behind the granting of a DO in 1988 to several patches of vineyard in the area, now called Costers del Segre. Raïmat owns over 2450ha (6051 acres), over half of the total DO plantings, which are irrigated and include a

wide range of varieties, both Spanish and international. None of the region's traditional wines were previously up to much but Raïmat's wines, both still (especially the Chardonnay, Cabernet Sauvignon and Tempranillo) and sparkling, have shown that excellence is possible in these unpromising conditions.

Right up in the north of Catalunya the tiny Empordà-Costa Brava DO hugs the border with France, squeezed in by the Mediterranean and the Pyrenees. Here the mountains come almost down to the sea and the lower foothills are covered in vines. But it isn't all a holiday-making idyll along this beautiful rocky coastline – you'll notice the vines here are firmly tied to stakes, standing up bravely against a dreaded wind locally known as *tramontana*, which can blow for days on end. The wines here are mostly reds from Garnacha and Cariñena and the whites come from Macabeo and Xarel-lo. Nevertheless, along with many other areas of Catalunya such as Pla de Bages, new international grape varieties, mainly Cabernet Sauvignon, Merlot and Chardonnay, are creeping into the vineyards.

Further south in Catalunya the wine regions cluster around Barcelona and Tarragona. Down by the coast near Barcelona is Alella, rapidly becoming a victim of expanding urbanization. As the city grows, so the poor Alella vineyards, which are capable of producing rather tasty fresh white wines, disappear under new buildings. The DO was extended in 1989 to include land at higher altitudes so that Alella now runs from the coast inland to the foothills of the Cordillera Catalana. The new areas are cooler because they are higher, and are based on a limestone bedrock in the shelter of the mountains. Down on the coast the vines are mainly Garnacha Blanca; in the new, higher vineyards you'll find Pansa Blanca (Xarel-lo) and quite a bit of decent Chardonnay.

For spectacular mountain scenery head for Priorat and Terra Alta, relatively inaccessible inland areas in Catalunya's south. Weave round their precipitous twisting roads, and you're sure to emerge green and shaky for the experience – but it's worth it. These are among the most dramatically sited vineyards in Europe. Rugged mountains form a backdrop to the small terraced vineyards cut into the steep hillsides and interspersed with almond and olive trees. Priorat has a special soil known as *llicorella* which glints with mica particles: its heat retaining qualities help create monstrously powerful and alcoholic red wines. A group of new producers moved into the area around the village of Gratallops in the heart of Priorat in the 1980s, planted French varieties such as Cabernet Sauvignon alongside the native Garnacha and Cariñena, introduced modern winemaking techniques and new French oak barrels and created a new style of Priorat which took the world by storm. As a result of these rare, expensive wines Priorat has now been promoted to DOCa (the only region other than Rioja to be awarded Spain's highest wine category). Terra Alta, literally 'high land', had little contact with the rest of the country until the beginning of the 20th century, and it shows. The southernmost Catalan DO, it is chequered with green vineyard oases nestling between the mountains.

Elsewhere in Catalunya, the DOs fan out towards the dusty Tarragona plain. The large Tarragona DO sprawls in a wide sweep around Tarragona city. The Falset sub-region, bordering Priorat and enjoying the same advantages of low-yielding vineyards and a slightly cooler climate, now makes quality reds and was promoted to its own DO of Montsant in 2001. Conca de Barberá sits in a natural basin protected by the rolling Tallat, Prades and Montsant mountain ranges and produces vast amounts of hazelnuts and almonds, as well as much of the base wine for Cava. It is also the home of Torres' Milmanda and Grans Muralles vineyards.

Old Garnacha vines after harvest planted near Gratallops, the heart of Priorat, in intensely stony, schist soils (llicorella).

 RED GRAPES
Garnacha Tinta, Cariñena, Monastrell and Tempranillo (locally called Ull de Llebre) are the main traditional grapes, with increasing amounts of Cabernet Sauvignon, Merlot, Syrah and even Pinot Noir.

WHITE GRAPES
Macabeo, Garnacha Blanca, Xarel-lo and Parellada are the chief varieties, with decreasing amounts of Malvasía. New wave whites use Riesling, Muscat, Chardonnay, Gewürztraminer and Sauvignon Blanc.

CLIMATE
Coastal Catalunya enjoys a Mediterranean climate and it becomes drier and more extreme further inland.

SOIL
This varies, depending on whether you are in the rugged mountainous areas or nearer the coast. There is some limestone in the northern coastal regions. The Penedès lowlands have sand, while the highlands have clay. Quartzite and slate make up a special soil called *llicorella* in hilly Priorat and parts of Conca de Barberá.

ASPECT
There are low-lying vineyards on the coast at between sea level and 200m (656ft), while inland the vines can be set into terraces on the sides of steep foothills, up to 800m (2625ft) in Priorat and Terra Alta, or on alluvial river valley floors, as in Tarragona.

WHERE THE VINEYARDS ARE *The map shows the heart of Penedès, around the towns of Sant Sadurní d'Anoia, the thriving centre of Cava production, and Vilafranca del Penedès, where Torres has its ultra-modern vinification plant.*

The Penedès vineyards are arranged in three tiers, moving up in steps from the coastline, and these provide a wide range of growing conditions.

The strip of hot, flat coastal vineyards is known as the Bajo Penedès. The vineyards here are planted traditionally with Moscatel but hardy red varieties that can cope with the blazing summer sun are taking over.

Across the ridge of hills in the broad valley around Vilafranca del Penedès is the Medio Penedès, where 80 per cent of the Penedès vineyards are found. It's still fairly hot here but a mixture of varieties (mainly Xarel-lo and Macabeo for Cava but also some red ones) benefit from the cooler, higher altitude, between 250m (820ft) and 500m (1640ft) above sea level.

Further inland and higher still, up to 800m (2625ft), is the Penedès Superior with a climate almost as cool as Bordeaux. When you climb higher there's not much in the way of villages but the scattered vineyards are highly prized. Here are found the high-quality white grapes, mostly aromatic Parellada for Cava, but also experimental plantings of international varieties such as Chardonnay, Gewürztraminer, Muscat and Riesling.

MARTORELL

SITGES

RIOJA

 RED GRAPES
Tempranillo is the most important variety, followed by Garnacha Tinta and a little Mazuelo and Graciano. There is some experimental Cabernet Sauvignon.

 WHITE GRAPES
Viura (Macabeo) is the main white grape. There are tiny amounts of Malvasía and Garnacha Blanca.

CLIMATE
The Sierra de Cantabria protects most of the vineyards from the Atlantic weather, and for the most part, Rioja is sunny and temperate. Rioja Baja, to the south-east, has a Mediterranean climate and is hotter and more arid.

SOIL
Rioja Alavesa has yellow calcareous clay soils, as do parts of Rioja Alta. Rioja Alta and Rioja Baja are mainly alluvial silt, with ferruginous clay on the higher ground.

ASPECT
Vines are planted on relatively high ground in the Alavesa and Alta sub-regions, usually between 400 and 800m (1312 and 2625ft). In the Baja the ground slopes down to nearer 300m (985ft) and the vines are planted on the flat, fertile valley floor.

I THINK WE SOMETIMES FORGET what life was like before Rioja. Even I have to keep reminding myself. But I can remember the wonderful flavour of strawberry and blackcurrant swathed in soft, buttery vanilla of the first Rioja reds I tasted. So soft, so enjoyable. Red wine wasn't supposed to be this irresistible, this easy to understand. In the days before the New World wine revolution taught us that it was OK to have fun with fine wine, Rioja was preparing the way. And as such it was effortlessly Spain's leading table wine. It's still the most famous, but despite being granted Spain's first supposedly superior DOC classification, the 1990s were a fraught time for the region with too much inferior land planted, overproduction common and made worse by the introduction of irrigation in the late 1990s, and seesawing prices. However, a majority of producers are now going back to basics – good fruit and gentle use of oak – and even many commercial Riojas are reassuringly reminiscent of the good old days.

Rioja was originally the name for the basin of land formed by the small Oja river which flows into the Tirón near Haro. The Tirón eventually joins the Ebro river, and it is a chunk of the much larger Ebro valley that Rioja has come to stand for – the part that lies 100km (62 miles) south of the Atlantic and is bounded by mountains to north and south. It would be easy if the autonomous region of La Rioja corresponded to the Rioja DOCa winemaking region, but parts of La Rioja have no vines in them at all, while the Rioja DOCa veers off across the regional boundary into both País Vasco and Navarra and, on a few hundred acres, Burgos.

The Rioja DOCa is divided into three sub-regions: Rioja Alavesa lies north of the Ebro in the province of Alava in País Vasco; Rioja Alta is in the west and lies entirely within the province of La Rioja;

WHERE THE VINEYARDS ARE *The map shows the western half of the Rioja DOCa, the Rioja Alavesa and Rioja Alta sub-regions – the flatter, more arid Rioja Baja begins further east of Logroño. The Alavesa vineyards are north of the Ebro river and extend from the foothills of the Sierra de Cantabria down to the river. The Rioja Alta vineyards lie to the south of the river, with one small enclave north-east of Briones on the other side. The whole DOCa is closely concentrated on the Ebro valley, the mountains forming a dramatic backdrop along the northern edge and protecting the vineyards from the Atlantic weather to the north. Note how dense the vineyards are in this part of Rioja where vines are the most important crop. Much of the valley floor land used to be farmland, and cannot produce top quality grapes. Small vineyard plots are common – 87 per cent are 1ha (2 1/2 acres) or less.*

Rioja Baja lies to the east of Logroño, taking in land on both sides of the Ebro, as well as the Navarra and Burgos enclaves. Logroño, Rioja's capital city with a population of 120,000, lies just west of the point where the three sub-regions meet, roughly halfway along the 120-km (75-mile) west-to-east stretch of the Rioja DOCa.

Although Rioja is relatively close to the sea, the mountain ranges, especially the Sierra de Cantabria, protect its northern edge and shelter the vineyards from the cold Atlantic winds, and you can find yourself standing in warm sunshine among the vines, while in the distance, clouds gather threateningly over the mountain tops.

RIOJA ALAVESA AND RIOJA ALTA
The Rioja Alavesa vineyards start at 800m (2625ft) above sea level, among the foothills of the Sierra de Cantabria and descend in terraces down to the steep north bank of the Ebro river at just below 400m (1312ft). Cross the Ebro and you are in Rioja Alta, which mostly follows its south bank – apart from the Sonsierra, an important enclave on the north bank. These two sub-regions aren't radically different from one another, the line between them simply follows provincial boundaries rather than soil types, but the differences in soil do matter – Alavesa reds are generally a little lighter and more scented than Alta wines.

We're still on fairly high ground, especially in the south of Rioja Alta where the land climbs to 700m (2300ft) again. Despite the mountains' embrace, cool breezes meander in from the Atlantic, moderating summer temperatures and creating frosty winters. In general, the further east you go, the warmer and drier the climate. Haro's average annual temperature is 12.8°C (55°F), but further east in Alfaro, at the extreme end of the DOCa, it is 13.9°C (57°F).

THE SOILS OF RIOJA

Rioja has three main types of soil. The best wines come from clay with limestone soil found all over the Rioja Alavesa sub-region and in some parts of Rioja Alta. This yellowish-looking soil is densely planted with vineyards and Tempranillo flourishes here in the limestone, producing grapes with high acidity and a rich concentration of flavours. The second type, ferruginous clay, is found south of the Ebro in pockets of land on higher ground within larger areas of alluvial soil, the third Rioja soil type. Ferruginous clay produces good, sturdy wines with high levels of alcohol. Large parts of Rioja Baja and Rioja Alta are alluvial silt, much of it too fertile for good-quality grapes. Wines from this soil type tend to be high in alcohol and are used mostly for strengthening wines of lighter quality from the Alavesa and Alta.

Ferruginous clay · Alluvial soils · Clay with limestone · Sierra de Cantabria

River Ebro

Elevation in metres
900
800
700
600
500
400

S · Vertical exaggeration 9.5 times horizontal scale · N

RIOJA ALAVESA

LABASTIDA

HARO

OLLAURI

BRIONES

SAN ASENSIO

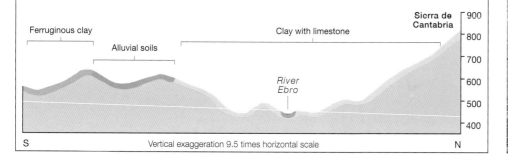

0 km 1 2
0 miles 1

Some of the region's most delicately scented and elegant red wines come from the yellow calcareous clay soils of Rioja Alavesa, which extend into Rioja Alta. Rioja Alta's more varied soils include patches of ferruginous clay and alluvial silt, and tend to produce firmer wines (though traditionally, Rioja producers have put little emphasis on soil types – the style of wine has long been more a product of aging in the winery than of *terroir* – and I'd say it was time for a rethink). Both sub-regions are widely planted with Tempranillo, the great grape of red Rioja, which thrives on chalky and clay soils and in the relatively cool climate. Rioja Alta also has a little Garnacha Tinta – great for heady Rosado – but the principal growing area for this variety is the third sub-region, Rioja Baja.

RIOJA BAJA

East of Logroño, the lower-lying Rioja Baja has a much warmer Mediterranean climate than the rest of Rioja and parts are even classified as semi-arid. Vines compete for space on the fertile, alluvial clay with red peppers, artichokes, asparagus. Garnacha Tinta does well here and in a long, hot autumn reaches high levels of ripeness, making chunky, fat wines of up to 15 per cent alcohol. Tempranillo is increasingly grown in the higher, hillier areas.

RED AND WHITE RIOJA

Much Rioja red is a blend from all three sub-regions, and a blend of different grapes. Once, over 40 varieties were grown here, but today the rules allow just seven, with some experimental varieties, including Cabernet Sauvignon. Tempranillo accounts for over 60 per cent of all plantings; it is responsible for the graceful strawberry flavour of red Rioja and is well suited to long aging. Garnacha Tinta

is added to flesh out the blend, and there may be a splash of Graciano and Mazuelo, too. The myriad combinations offered by the different sub-regions and varieties allow merchant bodegas to blend a unique house style. A little white Viura was traditionally added to help the acid balance and lighten the colour; this sometimes still happens in the Alavesa. White Rioja is made largely from Viura.

The vines are densely planted and pruned in bush shaped *gobelet* style to protect them from the elements. A few decades ago a jumble of varieties were all grown and harvested together. Now each variety is planted and picked separately, often in small plots that characterize the region. And if the patches of low-lying bush vines tell you you're in Rioja, so will the coopers. There can be few winemaking regions in the world that use so much oak. The casks (generally 225-litre *barricas*) are traditionally American oak, with its butter and vanilla flavours, but French is increasingly used.

Rioja joven sees little or no wood, and some fresh, unoaked whites are made, but much of the red wine is *Crianza*, released in its third year having spent a year in oak, or *Reserva*, released in its fourth year after at least a year in oak and two in bottle, or *Gran Reserva*, traditionally made only in exceptional years, and not released until its sixth year, after least two years in oak and three in the bottle. White Crianza must have spent six months in cask.

ARTADI

1997

AVRVS

RIOJA

RIOJA ALTA AND RIOJA ALAVESA

TOTAL DISTANCE NORTH TO SOUTH
24KM (15 MILES)

RIOJA ALTA = RIOJA SUB-REGION

━━━ RIOJA DOC BOUNDARY

━━━ SUB-REGIONAL BOUNDARIES

▦ VINEYARDS

0 km 1 2
0 miles 1

LAGUARDIA

RIOJA ALAVESA

Ebro

ELCIEGO

Ebro

CENICERO

FUENMAYOR

LOGROÑO

RIOJA ALTA

NAVARRETE

ARAGÓN & NAVARRA

RED GRAPES
Red varieties predominate in this northern part of Spain. Garnacha Tinta is the main grape and there is some Graciano too. Increasing amounts of Tempranillo, Cabernet Sauvignon, Merlot and Mazuelo are being grown for blending with Garnacha. There is even some experimental Merlot and Pinot Noir. Moristel and Passaleta are exclusive to Somontano.

WHITE GRAPES
Macabeo (Viura) is the most common white grape variety. There are also plantings of Parellada, Malvasía, Moscatel and Chardonnay.

CLIMATE
In the north, vineyards benefit from the cooling influence of the Pyrenees. The further south you go, the more continental and even semi-arid the climate becomes.

SOIL
Both Aragón and Navarra have generally reddish-brown soil over limestone, with stony, well-drained subsoil.

ASPECT
In the north the vineyards are situated in the green valleys of the Pyrenean foothills. Further south they are mainly along rivers and tributaries.

REMEMBER THE PROUD RULERS of Aragón from history lessons at school? King Ferdinand of Aragón, who married Queen Isabella of Castilla in the 15th century, uniting their two kingdoms, and their daughter, poor Catherine of Aragón, who suffered so badly at the hands of her husband King Henry VIII of England. Aragón is a place heaving with ancient feuds and romances, but today it is also another of Spain's exciting wine regions making an effort to realize its potential.

Most of the traditional wines from Aragón were strong reds from Garnacha. Garnacha ripens easily and becomes very sweet, and all that sugar in the grapes turns into head-thumping degrees of alcohol levels, as high as 17 or 18 per cent, unless the grapes are picked at the very first sign of them being ripe – usually at something like 13 degrees. Serious efforts are being made by some of the large co-operatives that dominate wine production in Aragón to cater for modern tastes by lowering the alcohol levels, making the wine using modern methods to maximize the brawny, mouthfilling fruit of the Garnacha, and selling the wines younger. Garnacha is now often blended with other varieties such as Tempranillo, Spain's best native red grape, which is grown all over the north of the country.

Aragón takes in a good part of the Spanish Pyrenees in the far north of Spain and reaches south as far as Valencia and Castilla-La Mancha. You'll come away with an impression of scenery that changes as often as a kaleidoscope. In the cool Pyrenean foothills there are rivers and forests. Creep further south into a little more warmth and you'll find the hilly landscape of Somontano, followed by flatter plateau land with patches of vines and finally the harsher, continental climate of the flat, broad Ebro valley.

Tucked onto the southern end of the large Navarra DO, along the right bank of the Ebro river, is the Campo de Borja DO. The area is named after the land, or *campo*, surrounding the old town of Borja. Borja was also the original name of a local family who emigrated to Italy in the 14th century and changed their name to Borgia, giving an entirely new meaning to the phrase, 'What's your poison?' when being offered a drink. Campo de Borja remained obscure for centuries but, today, as the world begins to clamour for big, juicy reds, it at last finds itself in the right place at the right time.

Campo de Borja has a harsh continental climate. In winter temperatures can fall as low as –7°C (19°F), while summers are hot and dry, with temperatures soaring to 40°C (104°F). That's not all the poor vines have to put up with: late spring frosts crack the ground and threaten the buds and, to cap it all, there's a harsh north wind – *El Cierzo* – that blows down from the Pyrenees. Perhaps it was in order to escape the wind that farmers used to build labyrinthine cellars under their hill villages – cellars that are still used today for storing wine. But it's not all bad news for vines here. The brown, sandy soils also have a stony character, so they are well drained – if there's any rain to drain, that is – and the mists coming off the river Ebro offer some protection against drought. The area is, in fact, versatile enough for the vines of Borja to be farmed alongside olive trees, beans and asparagus.

They do love their Garnacha Tinta here and it occupies 75 per cent of the vineyard. Tempranillo, grown on slopes and higher plateaux, is on the increase. There is also some Mazuelo and Cabernet Sauvignon both of which, like Tempranillo, are used for blending with Garnacha. Although the trend here (as elsewhere in Aragón) is towards wines with lower levels of alcohol and less wood aging, DO regulations stipulate a minimum of 13 per cent for reds and *rosados*, so these will never be light wines. Happily, white wines with an alcohol level of only 10.5 per cent have been allowed

New plantings at Larraga, Navarra. The plastic greatly speeds up the growth of these young vines, as well as stopping them from being eaten by rabbits.

in the DO since 1989, and these are made using Macabeo (Viura) and Moscatel Romano grapes.

South of Campo de Borja is the Cariñena DO, a pretty name which also gave the title to the Carignan grape of southern France. (In northern Spain this grape is called Mazuelo.) Like Campo de Borja, there are fiercely hot summers and cold winters here, and the *El Cierzo* wind plays its part in making conditions seem extreme. Cariñena's vineyards stretch south of Zaragoza along the Huerva river to the Sierra de la Virgen. Most of the vineyards are on undulating plateaux with reddish-brown limestone soils.

Traditionally, Cariñena's wine has, like Campo de Borja's, been made from Garnacha, with pretty high levels of alcohol and an inky deep red colour. Although Garnacha still rules the vineyards here, there has been a move recently to plant other varieties, and it's now possible to find quite a lot of Tempranillo, as well as Cabernet Sauvignon, Merlot and some Mazuelo. White vines are much less important, accounting for just one-fifth of the vineyards, and are almost always Macabeo.

Just west of Cariñena, cordoned off by several mountain ranges, lies the Calatayud DO, where life is a slightly easier for the winemakers since it rains a little more here and is generally a degree or two cooler than elsewhere in Aragón. It shows in the wines which, in general, have a brighter, juicier fruit than the other Aragón wines – but the reds still pack a serious punch at 13 degrees and over. As you might expect, this is more fertile land – most of the small valleys with tributaries flowing into the Jalón river are planted with fruit trees, producing rich crops of peaches, pears and cherries, and the vineyards are found around the valley edges. The DO, only granted in 1990, limits the grapes to traditional Spanish varieties. Garnacha Tinta is the main red grape, with some Tempranillo and a little Monastrell and Mazuelo. Macabeo (known here as Viura) is the main white grape, with a little Malvasía, Moscatel and Garnacha Blanca.

The final – and the prettiest – Aragón DO is Somontano. Its name means 'under the mountain' and so it is, lying far over to the north-east of the region in the green foothills of the central Pyrenees, isolated on the north side of the river Ebro from the other Aragón DOs. It's a little wine paradise – relatively cool because of its altitude, with a rainfall nearly twice as high as the other Aragón wine regions, and watered by a network of tiny mountain streams that criss-cross the region. Mountains loom up to 1100m (3600ft) high, forming a dramatic backdrop to the vineyards and sheltering them from inclement weather from the north. Vines are grown on the slopes of the foothills as well as lower down in the valleys of tributaries running down to the Ebro. Almond trees and silvery olive trees colour the landscape and, perched high on a rocky hill, is a striking landmark, the ancient Monasterio de Pueyo.

Enchanting indeed and, to add to its beauty, Somontano is Aragón's most promising DO, since the milder continental climate means progressive winemakers can experiment with different grape varieties. The local grape Moristel (which may or may not be the same as Monastrell) is still important for red wines with Macabeo for whites, but the regional government has encouraged experimental planting. There is now almost as much Tempranillo as Moristel and hundreds of acres are being planted with Cabernet Sauvignon, Merlot, Pinot Noir, Chardonnay and Gewürztraminer, while the interesting Parraleta (a clone of Rioja's Graciano, as shown by DNA testing) has been saved from extinction at the very last minute.

NAVARRA

The region of Navarra is famous for the ancient festival of San Fermín that takes place in its capital Pamplona in July, with the world-famous bull running spectacle. Fine for building up a thirst, but are the local wines up to the job? Well yes and no. The potential is massive, the local government has, for once, been positively helpful in vineyard and winery innovations. Yet results are infuriatingly haphazard. It's certainly had long enough to practise, because this was the original site of Spain's winemaking industry; archaeologists have found a 2nd-century Roman site on the Arga river, built to make wine for Roman soldiers based in Spain. Wine from Navarra was certainly well-known by the 11th century, when the kingdom stretched from Bordeaux as far south as Rioja. Yet it has taken until relatively recently for Navarra's vineyards to pull themselves back from the devastation caused by phylloxera in the late 19th century.

The region sits between Aragón and the País Vasco, bounded to the north by the Pyrenees and to the south by the Ebro river that forms a boundary with La Rioja. Up in the mountains sheep scramble across the grey rocks – they are kept for their milk which produces Navarra's famous Roncal cheese. In between the Pyrenean foothills are soft, green valleys clothed in vineyards and fields. In the north, mountain peaks rise to over 1400m (4595ft), while in the fertile Ebro Valley in the south of the DO the land is only 275m (900ft) above sea level. Here vegetables are cultivated (especially asparagus, for which Navarra is famous) and, of course, vines.

Some of the Rioja DOC lies within Navarra (see map page 189) but here we are interested in the Navarra DO. Vineyards are spread across five zones which lie south of Pamplona. The three hilly northern zones, Baja Montaña, Valdizarbe and Tierra de Estella, are influenced by the Pyrenees, so they escape drought and extremes of temperature; some of the new Chardonnay plantings here are doing well. In the two southern zones, Ribera Alta and Ribera Baja, the land flattens out towards the Ebro plain, and here the climate is hotter and more arid.

The soil is fairly uniform throughout the region, deep and fertile topsoil over gravel with a chalky bedrock – great conditions, in fact, for viticulture. Vineyards are planted at between 250 and 550m (820 and 1800ft) above sea level. The southern zones produce most of Navarra's grapes, which are mainly Garnacha. Tempranillo – the most widely-grown grape in neighbouring Rioja – is on the increase in Navarra due to a rigorous replanting scheme organized by the local Consejo Regulador. You'll also find Graciano and the white Viura (Macabeo).

What do you do with all that Garnacha? Traditionally, you turned it into a pretty robust pink wine, and *rosado* is still often the best wine made at the less forward-looking wineries. But what Navarra wants to be known for is its modern, international-style reds and whites – full, ripe, oaky Chardonnays and well-structured, but fruity and complex reds, mixing Tempranillo with such global stars as Cabernet Sauvignon and Merlot.

There have been some great successes and there are a handful of well-known quality wineries. But progress has been nothing like as fast as I'd hoped, especially since Navarra's was probably the first regional government to make a conscious effort to modernize its wine industry, instigating ambitious schemes for research and experimentation in the area. Sharing the applause is Evena, the Estación de Viticultura y Enología de Navarra, which used to be a humble local co-operative at Olite. Evena is largely responsible for the vine nurseries, experimental vineyards, modern laboratories and state-of-the-art equipment now commonplace in Navarra.

All of which should have Navarra challenging and perhaps even bettering the reputation of Rioja next door. Isolated examples of reds and whites are thrilling. But I'm still waiting for the cavalry charge of quality and it hasn't happened yet.

Somontano is a small but promising region within sight of the Pyrenees. This is a Cabernet-Merlot blend from Enate, one of the area's best producers.

NORTH-WEST SPAIN

RED GRAPES
There are many varieties of varying quality, but Galicia's best red is Mencía. In Castilla y León Tempranillo (Tinto Fino), Garnacha Tinta (Alicante) and Mencía do well.

WHITE GRAPES
Although there is lots of high-yielding Palomino, Albariño and Godello are Galicia's leading whites for quality wines. Rueda's Verdejo is the star of Castile and has more character than most Spanish white varieties.

CLIMATE
It is very wet and cool on the coast in Galicia and the climate becomes increasingly warm and dry as you travel inland past the mountains.

SOIL
Soils are very varied, from the alluvial deposits found in Galicia's Rías Baixas and Ribeiro, to Rueda's sandy and chalky soils, the ferruginous soil of Bierzo and the stony land of Cigales.

ASPECT
Because of the reliance on river valleys for viticulture in both regions, the vineyards are characterized by terracing from the river level up the hillsides; they are also on plateaux in Castilla y León.

DO WINE REGIONS

GALICIA
- Rías Baixas
- Ribeiro
- Ribeira Sacra
- Monterrei
- Valdeorras

CASTILLA Y LEÓN
- Bierzo
- Toro
- Rueda
- Cigales
- Arlanza
- Ribera del Duero

▭ OVER 500M (1640FT)
▨ OVER 1000M (3280FT)

I SOMETIMES FEEL AS THOUGH I'm in Australia when I'm in the north-west of Spain. No, that's not as daft as it sounds. Australia has a precious narrow coastal strip where the rain falls and flowers bloom. But cross the Great Dividing Range and the blazing red hot heart of Australia stretches merciless and parched for thousands of miles. Spain isn't that bad, of course, but Galicia is so verdant, almost shimmering with lush plant life in the damp seaside air, that the speed with which you reach the austere, arid Spain of popular legend as you climb through the mountains is still something of a shock. And from there across to the Mediterranean, in whatever direction you aim, you'll be in the hot, harsh heart of Spain.

The regions of Galicia and Castilla y León are quite different from one another. Galicia, with Cape Finisterre (Cabo Fisterra) at its extreme westerly point, is unlike anywhere else in Spain, and the fact that it is separated from the rest of the country by the Cantabrian mountains has helped to create a fierce spirit of independence in the region. Further inland, gentle hills start to appear and, as you approach Castilla y León, these grow more impressive and arid as the influence of the Atlantic on the climate lessens. Rivers play an important part in the landscapes of both regions and their valleys are essential for crop farming.

GALICIA
No wonder it's called 'green Spain'. The rain in Spain doesn't fall mainly on the plain, as the winemakers of the La Mancha plain know only too well; here in Galicia it drenches the craggy coastline and rolling forested hills. We're right up at the top of Spain's north-west corner, surrounded by the sea on two sides and this explains why there is so much rain here – it sweeps up and drops nearly 1300mm (50in) a year on to the land, with the result that Galicia is far more verdant and forested than the rest of Spain.

Galicia is strikingly beautiful too, and in a surprising way. Its characteristically un-Spanish coastal landscape is cut through with low, wide fjord-like inlets known as *rías*. Dotted along the coast are tiny fishing communities huddled into rocky Atlantic coves, while

further inland hilltop roads plunge through thick forests and deep river valleys, past dramatically impressive fortified castles. In parts, Galicia looks and feels a little like a warmer version of Scotland, and the culture bears a similarity too, for the people of this region claim ancient Celtic origins. There's even a form of the bagpipes played here called *gaita*. And, as in Catalunya, there is an official second language (a cross between Spanish and Portuguese) which says something about the region's independence.

Galician winemaking has only recently become even a little sophisticated. The vineyards are scattered between grain fields and plots of kiwi fruit, and modern viticultural practices have taken their time to catch on. In the past visitors to the agricultural areas were more likely to notice the *hórreos*, strange stone granaries raised high on squat legs to repel hungry rats, than anything going on in the vineyard or winery.

But since the introduction of modern technology in the mid-1980s, Galicia has made some smashing discoveries. First came the realization that its Rías Baixas DO was capable of making whites that rank among the best in the country, thanks to the Albariño grape. However, an eight-fold increase in the size of the Rías Baixas vineyard since it was awarded its DO in 1988 means, inevitably, that quality is uneven. Reds and whites are rapidly improving in Ribeiro DO, while Valdeorras DO, albeit slower to improve, is making more use of the scented Godello grape, although Godello still accounts for just 3 per cent of the vineyard. Galicia's progress is also marked by an increased ability to use its traditional varieties, rather than to adopt internationally fashionable grapes as is happening in some other parts of Spain.

Still less developed, but full of beguiling potential, are the two newest DO regions. Monterrei, from the Portuguese border to north of Verín, is Galicia's driest region, but it still produces fragrant whites from the Godello and Dona Branca grapes, and pungent sharp reds from Mencía and Brancellao. But it's in the Ribeira Sacra DO to the north, near Lugo, with its precipitous schist hillsides that are an Atlantic replica of the Priorat, that the

finest reds (from Mencía grapes) in the whole of Galicia are made – or, at least, will be made one day.

Rías Baixas (literally, the 'lower inlets') covers five zones near the coast around Pontevedra and Vigo. It's cool here since any potentially harsh temperatures are moderated by the Atlantic. Not surprisingly, this is also one of Spain's wettest areas and fungal diseases pose a constant threat. So the vines are trained high on pergola systems, with branches pulled up on to granite posts to keep them well aired. This is how you'll see the prized Albariño grapes growing, and they are used to make the acidic, aromatic whites that Rías Baixas is increasingly famed for. You'll also find the white grapes Loureiro and Caiño and the red grape Brancellao here, but it was for Albariño that Rías Baixas was awarded the DO in 1988, and this has given the area new impetus, and a programme of rapid vineyard planting.

Inland from Rías Baixas, around Ribadavia, is the DO region of Ribeiro. Less rain falls here than on the coast, but at 800 to 1000mm (31 to 40in) a year it's still a lot more than in most parts of Spain. The word *ribeiro* means 'riverbank', and that's exactly where the grapes grow here, in the alluvial soils of three river valleys of the Miño, Avía and Arnoya, often on low terraces cut into the hillsides. Gentle winds blow from the Portuguese mountains, keeping the region relatively temperate, and flowers, especially carnations, are grown alongside the vines, which have churned out cheap and cheerful wine for centuries. The quality is improving, though, especially now that vineyards are being replanted with more aromatic whites, such as Treixadura and Torrontes, instead of the high-yielding Palomino, and fresher, juicier reds are being made from Garnacha.

Valdeorras is the fifth Galician DO, and the furthest inland, about 150 km (93 miles) from the coast. As you might expect, the Galician rain starts to dry up here, and temperatures are not moderated by the Atlantic – the summers can be blindingly hot, at up to 44°C (111°F). Most of Valdeorras' vineyards lie in the valley of the Sil river, where about half the grapes are the heavy-cropper Alicante, a local name for Garnacha Tintorera (Alicante Bouschet). At their best these wines are inky and intense, but many are sold in bulk. Mencía, one of Galicia's best grape varieties and a close relation of Cabernet Franc, produces better results. Whites are usually made from the aromatic Godello.

CASTILLA Y LEÓN

Castile, to give it its English name, was one of the original Spanish regions to unite against the Moors in the Middle Ages and thus became the north-west stronghold of the Catholics. Now, although it's the largest *autonomía* in the country, covering one-fifth of the land, it's sparsely populated. The historic towns with their castles, ancient fortifications and royal residences contrast strongly with the visually unexciting landscape – most of Castile consists of plateaux with rolling terrain used for grain and the occasional grazing flock of sheep.

The weather is much harsher in Castile than in Galicia, with hot summers and cold winters. The DO wine areas stretch west as far as Bierzo, on the Galician border, and east to Ribera del Duero in the provinces of Valladolid, Segovia, Burgos and even Soria to the east, where the scenery starts to grab your attention again.

Apart from Ribera del Duero, with its worldwide reputation (see page 198), there are five DO wine regions in Castile. Bierzo in the west marks the transition from Galicia; it lies between the Cantabrian mountains and the Montes de León, sheltered by these mountain ranges from any extremes of temperature. In fact, Bierzo is altogether suitable for winemaking, with plenty of sunshine but less rain than Galicia, and an iron-rich reddish-brown soil which

Vineyards above the Miño river in the Ribeiro region of Galicia. This is the greenest part of Spain and its wines, both red and white, are light and aromatic.

the vines like. Its producers have lagged behind, however, and Bierzo is only now raising the profile of its Mencía wines. About time – they're delicious.

Rueda, with its sleepy little villages scattered across flat plains and low hills, is probably the most famous Castile DO after Ribera del Duero, and rightly so, for it now produces very good whites. Around the town of Rueda are extensive cellars that date back to the 14th century – it is here that wine is traditionally made and stored. Some have been restored and can be visited, particularly at Bodegas Antaño with its amazing miles-long maze of galleries. The Rioja bodega, Marqués de Riscal, has been making white wine here since the 1970s, concentrating on the local Verdejo grape and Sauvignon Blanc grown in sandy and chalky soils, with a dash of gravel in the best vineyards: Rueda now leads the way in Castilian white wine.

The Toro DO borders Rueda to the north-west. Pilgrims who took this route to Santiago de Compostela in Galicia used to stop off in Toro and quench their thirst on the local wines. It's still a thriving wine centre and suddenly, since the late 1990s, a fashionable hot spot as many of Spain's best wineries open Toro subsidiaries to exploit some outstanding old vineyards. Toro's best wine comes from the Tinta de Toro (alias Tempranillo as usual) grape, which makes powerful blockbuster reds.

Right in the middle of Castilla y León is Cigales which follows the course of the Pisuerga river north from Valladolid. The DO, granted in 1991, was mostly due to Cigales' pleasant *rosados*, although the most promising developments have all been in red wines. Again as in Rueda, there are cellars running under the town of Cigales, with ventilators sticking up like small domes in the surrounding fields. Go over to take a look but watch where you step. If you are wearing open-toed sandals, the whopping great stones that litter the vineyard could give you a holiday souvenir in black and blue you won't appreciate. South of Burgos, Arlanza is the newest Castilian DO, mainly for reds from Tempranillo.

Dark, elegant reds from the Ribera del Duero region are now some of the most fashionable wines in the whole of Spain.

RIBERA DEL DUERO

 RED GRAPES
Nearly 95 per cent of the plantings are Tinto Fino or Tinta del País, a local variant of Tempranillo. There is also a tiny amount of Cabernet Sauvignon, Merlot, Garnacha Tinta and Malbec.

WHITE GRAPES
White wines are not included in the Ribera del Duero DO but sometimes included in the red blend.

CLIMATE
The climate is a mixture of continental and temperate – hot, dry summers and long, cold winters with a serious risk of frost as late as May due to the high altitude.

SOIL
There is clay and alluvium near the river Duero and more limestone on higher slopes.

ASPECT
This is high-altitude viticulture, with vineyards at 700 to 850m (2300 to 2790ft). Vineyards start near the river and climb the valley slopes.

VALBUENA TO FUENTECÉN

━━━ DO BOUNDARY

TOTAL DISTANCE NORTH TO SOUTH 24KM (15MILES)

▩▩▩ VINEYARDS

JUST WHAT IS IT that makes the wines of Ribera del Duero so exciting? The landscape is not as spectacular as in some regions of Spain: apart from the flat-topped mountains and an occasional striking landmark such as the imposing castle of Peñafiel, Ribera mostly stretches out in rolling plateaux and forested hills. We're in a relatively moderate climate but, because of the high altitude, frosts can be a daunting threat to the vines. And until the late 20th century there were only a couple of show estates in the region that could boast truly magnificent wines.

Yet Ribera del Duero now ranks among the greatest of all Spain's DOs, outstripping its neighbours in Castilla y León for the quality of its red wines and sheer breathless rate of progress. The region simply buzzes with life as more and more winemakers invest and experiment, cashing in on Ribera's rising star.

Ribera del Duero means 'the banks of the Duero', the river best known as the Douro – its name when it flows through port country across the border in northern Portugal. The region lies in the heart of Castilla y León, 190km (118 miles) north of Madrid, in the broad Duero valley, which traverses the provinces of Burgos, Valladolid and Soria. There are also some vines in the northern province of Segovia, making a total of over 20,000ha (49,419 acres), more than half of which have been planted since 1990. The area forms part of Spain's central plateau or *meseta*, so the vineyards are high, at between 700 and 850m (2300 and 2790ft).

The altitude – pretty near the upper limits for viticulture – plays a large part in Ribera's success. Although the summer daytime temperatures are hot – it can soar to 40°C (104°F) – at night they drop dramatically, giving the grapes marvellous intensity and enhanced aromas. Add to this a perfect soil for viticulture (poor quality, yet easy to work) and you'll get vines that work hard to cram a great deal of concentrated flavour and high acidity levels into what little fruit they can produce. The continental climate is tempered by an Atlantic influence – rainfall is moderate and mists from the nearby Duero River provide welcome humidity.

Ribera's success story is typical of many modern wine regions, only more dramatic than some. Although red wine had

been produced here for centuries, it was mostly sold in bulk, just like in any other second-rate Spanish wine region. No-one really understood its potential. Ribera's rise to fame began in the mid-19th century when Don Eloy Lecanda Chaves set up a bodega just south of Valbuena de Duero. The estate was called Pago de la Vega Santa Cecilia y Carrascal – a bit of a mouthful, eventually shortened to Vega Sicilia. Breaking with local tradition, the vineyards were planted with the red Bordeaux varieties, Cabernet Sauvignon, Merlot and Malbec, as well as with more traditional white Albillo and Tinto Fino. Tinto Fino is said by proud locals to be their very own unique clone of Tempranillo, and it has clearly adapted to the rough conditions, producing small berries with great fruit concentration. For more than a century, Vega Sicilia was renowned as one of the best bodegas in Spain, and the prices of its powerful, complex red wines vied with those of a top Bordeaux – even the King of Spain had to stand in line to await his allocation – yet it remained the sole estate with any clout in Ribera.

Then in the late 1970s Alejandro Fernández set up a successful bodega making a red wine called Pesquera from Tinto Fino. He discovered that Ribera's high altitude meant that Tinto Fino grew thick-skinned with high levels of acidity and the resulting rich, aromatic red wines were a revelation. Importantly, the wines seemed to age brilliantly, something that caught the attention of international critics, with subsequent rave reviews in the mid-1980s. In 1982 the region was awarded the DO. Ribera del Duero had arrived.

The region makes a little *rosado* wine too, mostly from Garnacha, but the best ones have about 50 per cent Tinto Fino. There is a little white Albillo planted, which is sometimes added to the red wine blend to make the wines more fragrant and to dilute their inky

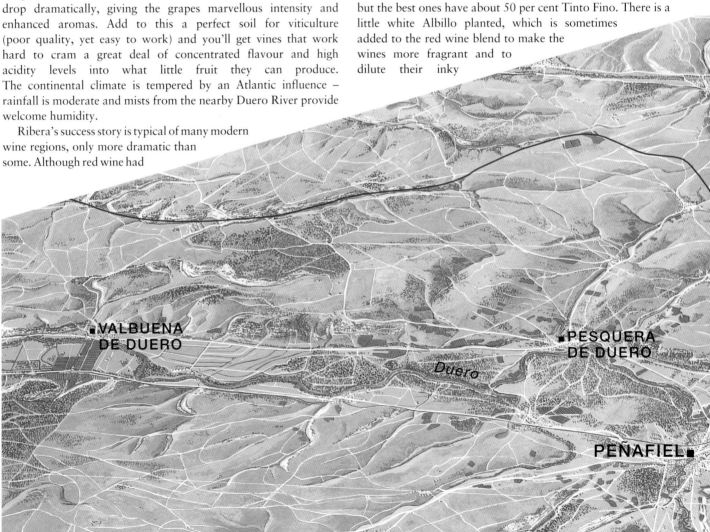

VALBUENA DE DUERO

Duero

PESQUERA DE DUERO

PEÑAFIEL

0 km   1   2
0 miles   1

N

colour, as well as being used for dessert grapes. White wines are made in the region but are not yet allowed to be part of the DO. Nearly 95 per cent of the vineyards are planted with Tinto Fino, and several bodegas have followed Vega Sicilia's example by planting Cabernet Sauvignon and Merlot. Wines with the Ribera del Duero DO must be made with at least 75 per cent Tinto Fino.

Many of these vineyards are at the upper limits of 850m (2788ft) in altitude, for the river itself lies only just below this level. The character of the vineyards changes as you move away from the river and, at each stage, there is a name for the type of land you come to. The lower-lying plots on the banks of the river are called *campiñas*, and these are based on more clayey, alluvial soil with some sand. Climb a little, and you reach the *laderas*, or higher slopes, with more limestone in the soil. In places these vineyards are so chalky-white they start to resemble the famous *albariza* vineyards of Jerez in southern Spain. These are the best plots of land, and the local Consejo Regulador is seeing to it that much of the vineyard investment takes place here. Next come the *cuestas*, and here viticulture starts to peter out as the land gets less easy to work. The highest land, on steepest slopes and flat-topped mountain peaks, is known as *páramos*, and tends to be too exposed for anyone to want to plant vines, although Alejandro Fernández has – and with good results.

The most renowned Ribera vineyards are to the north-west of Peñafiel where the Vega Sicilia and Pesquera are located. However, many of the remaining old vines and certainly many of the best sites are in the central Ribera around La Horra and Roa de Duero.

Further east, the area near Aranda de Duero used to produce *rosados*, but it is rapidly becoming home to many of the most progressive red wine producers.

Right across Ribera it's a jumble of small and large plots of land, with over 14,000 active vineyards. The smaller ones – those under a hectare – are vital to the region as a whole, for they account for nearly 90 per cent of the vineyards. Inevitably this means there are several important co-operatives in Ribera and, equally inevitably, it means that even as quality increases, it will not increase uniformly. Prices, however, will.

WHERE THE VINEYARDS ARE *The map shows the central and western parts of the Ribera del Duero region. The west around the town of Peñafiel is the traditional heartland of the DO where two of Ribera's best-known wine estates are located – the world famous Vega Sicilia vineyards are at Valbuena on the south bank of the Duero and Alejandro Fernández's Pesquera vineyards are just to the east of Pesquera. See how the Ribera vineyards spread out along the Duero river valley. Many of them are close by the river, on both the north and the south banks, but the wine region stretches out up to 35km (22 miles) from the Duero. A great deal of development is taking place across the region as a whole, but most interesting is the central area – particularly the north central area – where you can see the vineyards clustered near Roa and La Horra. This part of the region used to produce basic fruit for* rosado *wine, but is now a hive of activity, with producers experimenting with more modern techniques, sometimes using American oak barrels for aging, sometimes French. Alejandro Fernández has established his second bodega and vineyard in Roa, which is fast becoming Ribera del Duero's new wine capital.*

A magnificent castle dominates the town of Peñafiel. Some of the many tunnels beneath it are used as cellars by wine companies, and this strange little construction is a ventilation shaft.

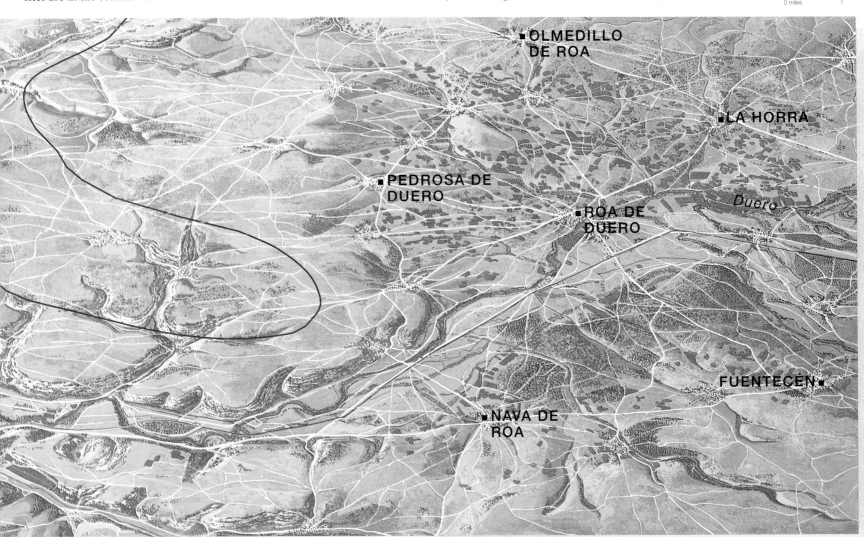

CENTRAL SPAIN

 RED GRAPES
Tempranillo (locally called Cencibel) is the best quality grape. Others include Monastrell, Garnachas Tinta and Tintorera, and Bobal.

 WHITE GRAPES
Airén is the dominant grape in Castilla-La Mancha and Merseguera in the Levante.

CLIMATE
The high central plain has a continental, semi-arid climate. Further east in Levante it is wetter and less extreme.

 SOIL
Sandy clay throughout but rich in limestone in places.

ASPECT
On the high central plain the vines are planted in large plots. The vineyards are more scattered further south-east in the rolling Levante hills.

These Cencibel (Tempranillo) vines are at Casa de la Viña in Valdepeñas. The red topsoils cover a limestone subsoil that holds enough moisture for the vines to survive the torrid summers.

SPAIN'S VAST LANDLOCKED CENTRAL PLATEAU, Castilla-La Mancha, and Murcia and Valencia to its east, contain the country's most important regions for table wine. Even if this part of Spain does not produce the finest Spanish wines, the sheer volume that comes from here is astonishing. There is still a little old-style wine, mostly white from the Airén grape, but progress is being made, especially with oak-aged reds from Cencibel (Tempranillo's local name), as well as Cabernet Sauvignon and, increasingly, Shiraz.

CASTILLA-LA MANCHA AND MADRID

All I can see are vines, reaching right up to the horizon on every side. No, wait a minute, there's a row of windmills, their black arms stretching up out of the vast plain to punctuate the skyline. I'm in the southern half of Spain's central *meseta*, in Castilla-La Mancha, the huge, high, flat table of land that makes up the heart of the country and supplies more than half of its wine. I'm at least 500m (1640ft) above sea level but there are no hills in sight. Castilla-La Mancha is entirely bordered by rivers and mountains and just occasionally you can see a faint, misty outline of mountain tops over the horizon across the vast plain.

I rather like it here, though it's pretty inhospitable. Despite being bordered by rivers and mountains, the region is so wide that these natural defences can do nothing to protect it from freezing cold winters and scorching, relentless summers. The temperature veers wildly between extremes, from as much as 42°C (108°F) in the high summer to –8°C (18°F) during the long winter, delivered with a bitingly cold wind. And although electric storms occasionally bring slanting rain in the autumn and spring, the desolate plateau is generally arid, hence the Arabic name *al-Manshah* or 'dry land'.

It's easy to be overwhelmed by the size of such a seemingly endless landlocked region. Here and there small groups of whitewashed homes huddle together, or a straggling flock of sheep bleats about a lone tree. The windmills, at which Cervantes' hero Don Quixote tilted, stride across the plain, reminding the visitor that this was once useful grain country. But apart from the windmills and the odd castle, all you'll see are row after row of vines, planted in grid patterns and pruned with their canopy draped over the ground to retain as much moisture as possible.

Then again, you might spy shiny new wine tanks, for investment in modern wine technology is happening even here. Castilla-La Mancha used to supply Spain with most of its cheap table wine, or base wine for distillation. Now almost all of the sub-standard stuff goes to alcohol distillation, but only one-tenth of the total wine produced in the region has DO status. Huge efforts are being made to improve the wine in many parts of the region, with EU subsidies providing an impetus. In the region's largest DO, La Mancha, vastly improved new-style wine, pale, fresh and fruity, rather than yellowy-orange, flat and dull, is now being made for export markets. It's a gradual change, rather than a revolution, but Castilla-La Mancha's hot sunshine and healthy aridity means that potential exists for an ocean of decent stuff if they can overcome a lack of irrigation and rainfall.

La Mancha is Spain's largest DO, with over 300 bodegas and 190,980ha (471,905 acres) of vineyards stretching north almost as far as Madrid and covering areas rich in limestone. Airén is the major white grape and although decreasing it still covers 80 per cent of the vineyards – down from 90 per cent. With its thick skin and heavy leaf canopy, it's ideally suited to the climate. New, higher quality grape varieties, new technology and early picking mean that the wines are becoming light, fresh and faintly aromatic, rather than dark and heavy. There is also an increasing amount of Cencibel, producing light and fruity or richer red wines.

The Valdepeñas DO is a hot, dry enclave on the southern border of Castilla-La Mancha, where the central plain begins to descend towards Andalucía. A small basin surrounded by sheltering hills, there are excellent vineyard areas in its Los Llanos ('the plains') and Las Aberturas ('the open spaces') sub-regions. Airén is again the main grape, some of it blended into the red wine. The amount of Cencibel for quality reds is rapidly increasing and Chardonnay and Cabernet Sauvignon are being used experimentally by several progressive local winemakers. However, overall, quality is making slower progress than in La Mancha.

In the north of Castilla-La Mancha, and with a few vineyards across the border in Madrid, is the large Méntrida DO, making dull, tannic reds and heavy *rosados* mainly from Garnacha. There is still a long way to go before the region justifies its DO but things are beginning to stir. The Vinos de Madrid DO covers the vineyard communes around the southern edge of the capital city. Created in 1990, it has finally begun to justify its DO status, with some well-made reds from Cencibel and Cabernet Sauvignon. East of Madrid, the new Mondéjar DO is a mystery for now – no wines of any quality have emerged from there yet.

Overshadowed by La Mancha and Valdepeñas, the Almansa DO is right down in the south-east where the great La Mancha plain gives way to the Murcian plateau. Its easterly position means its climate is a little less extreme than the rest of Castilla-La Mancha. Although most of the vineyards are on fairly flat terrain down on the plain, there are some on the rolling foothills. (Thank goodness – I was beginning to think I'd never spy a bump in the landscape again.) The wines are mainly dark reds, from Monastrell (Mourvèdre) and Garnacha Tintorera, with some of the better ones including Cencibel in the blend.

Manchuela ('little Mancha') is a vast DO covering 75,000ha (185,322 acres) between La Mancha, Almansa and Utiel-Requena. Its scattered vineyards covering just 4150ha (10,255 acres) of vines are on high, sloping clay-limestone soil, climbing to over 800m (2625ft) in altitude and show Castilla-La Mancha's best potential for fine reds. The unglamorous Bobal grape, which still dominates here, is a negative factor, as is the lack of small private bodegas. But some new investment and the widespread planting of better quality

varieties (Cencibel, Cabernet Sauvignon, Syrah and even Petit Verdot and Touriga Nacional) should make for some interesting changes. Several of Castilla-La Mancha's best estates (Dominio de Valdepusa and Dehesa del Carrizal in the Toledo mountains, and Finca Elez and Guijoso in Albacete) lie entirely outside any DO boundaries, and a new law has created single-estate appellations (Viño de Pago DOs) for each of them.

VALENCIA AND MURCIA

Bordering Castilla-La Mancha to the east, this part of Spain is also known as Levante. The scenery is a good deal more varied, if less dramatic – its green fertility is soothing after the desolate plain, as low mountains that cut off the *meseta* give way to the *huertas*, pleasant irrigated tiers of land covered in apple trees, apricots, olives and peaches which form a giant stairway down to the coast. Here you come to the huge bays adjoining the cities of Valencia and Alicante, with the resort of Benidorm in between. I'm hurtling back into civilization, if you can call it that – there are tourists, millions of them, and ugly industrialization around the ports.

Within Levante there are six main wine districts. Valencia, with its pretty blue ceramic tiles covering the church roofs, is more famous for orange trees than grapes. Here the *huerta* is covered in brightly-coloured citrus trees, but hilly vineyard areas grow mainly Merseguera which makes rather boring whites. There is also some red and *rosado* from Monastrell and Garnacha Tintorera. None of these are great grapes but the bodegas are some of the most modern in Spain, equipped with the latest technology. Look at wine labels and see for yourself how many Spanish 'own label' wines hail from Valencia. Valencia's most famous and most attractive wine is a lusciously sweet fortified white made from Moscatel (the Spanish name for Muscat). Although in no way a sophisticated dessert wine, good ones have an appealing crunchy table-grape character.

Driving west from Valencia along the ridge between the *meseta* and the coast, you pass through a rockier terrain where vines peek out from between the pine forests. This promising region is Utiel-Requena, where the important Valencian bodegas have large holdings. The vines are likely to be Bobal, normally used for making *rosado*, which can be some of Spain's best, and there are increasing amounts of decent reds from Tempranillo and Garnacha as well as French varieties. Macabeo is the main white variety, making promising wines, but no more than that for the moment.

Further south lie Alicante, Yecla and Jumilla, forming a line of DOs marching progressively inland from the city of Alicante to the regional boundary. To find a vineyard here you have to scale the hills inland, cross the *huerta*, and emerge the other side in cooler wine country. To be fair, some dessert grapes (mostly Moscatel) are grown down by the coast, but up on the higher ground, expect Monastrell, Tempranillo and experimental Cabernet Sauvignon. Yecla and Jumilla, further inland, are hard to tell apart, their terrain marked by low hills, chalky soil and a more dramatic mountain range, the Sierra del Carche, in the distance. Monastrell, a great grape variety when it goes by its adopted French name of Mourvèdre, has only recently begun to be mastered by winemakers in its native land. There is also some Garnacha here.

Which leaves us trailing south to Bullas, a district around the historic town of Lorca, and a fruitful part of the region – literally – for here farmers effortlessly grow heaps of apples, apricots, nuts and peaches. Monastrell dominates the hilly vineyards and, at last, we are in wetter territory: Bullas' higher land receives 500mm (20in) of rain a year. Most of the wine is basic *rosado*, but Bullas is a quietly promising region. And, after the wind-whipped plain of Castilla-La Mancha and the sweaty tourist resorts of the Costa Blanca, it's as refreshing and relaxing a place as any to end up in.

DO WINE REGIONS

MADRID
Vinos de Madrid

CASTILLA-LA MANCHA
Méntrida (also in Madrid)
La Mancha
Valdepeñas
Mondéjar
Manchuela
Almansa
Uclés
Ribera del Júcar

VALENCIA
Utiel-Requena
Valencia
Alicante (also in Murcia)

MURCIA
Yecla
Jumilla (also in Castilla La Mancha)
Bullas

EXTREMADURA
Ribera del Guadiana

Single-estate DOs
1. Dominio de Valdepusa
2. Dehesa del Carrizal
3. Finca Elez
4. Guijoso

OVER 500M (1640FT)
OVER 1000M (3280FT)

SOUTHERN SPAIN

RED GRAPES
There is a little experimental Cabernet Sauvignon and Tempranillo in Montilla-Moriles and several international grape varieties around Ronda.

WHITE GRAPES
Palomino Fino is the classic sherry grape, while Pedro Ximénez (PX) is grown throughout Andalucía's wine regions.

CLIMATE
Cooling Atlantic breezes moderate the hot summer temperature in Condado, and Málaga's coastal vineyards also benefit from sea breezes. Inland Montilla-Moriles has a hot continental climate.

SOIL
Jerez has its famous chalky *albariza* soil and Montilla-Moriles also benefits from limestone soils. There is reddish sandy soil in Condado and varied soils in Málaga.

ASPECT
Condado's vineyards start at just 25m (82ft) above sea level. The land rises to gentle slopes in Jerez and Málaga, and up to 300 to 700m (985 to 2300ft) in Montilla-Moriles.

THIS IS HOW EVERYONE IMAGINES SPAIN TO BE – a picture postcard of sun-filled vistas with golden beaches, whitewashed villages perched on hilltops and proud flamenco dancers. And don't forget seven centuries of Moorish influence: the Moors made their capital first at Córdoba, then at Seville (Sevilla), and for centuries these cities were the cultural focal point of southern Europe. Their influence lives on in the food, customs and architecture of the region. Andalucía is also the home of *tapas*, light snacks of cold meat, seafood, olives, salted almonds and bread, eaten while you stand in a small, cool bar, washing down your fare with a *copita* of chilled sherry.

Andalucía is Spain's second largest region, covering the whole of the southern part of the country. It is hemmed in by the Atlantic in the south-west, and beyond the Straits of Gibraltar by the Mediterranean. In the north the Sierra Morena forms a natural boundary between Andalucía and the high plateau of Castilla-La Mancha, while to the east the Sierra Nevada – the highest mountain range on Spain's mainland – rises between Granada and the coast. In fact, much of Andalucía is mountainous and the remainder of the region is dominated by the basin and delta formed by the Guadalquivir river between Seville and Cádiz.

Being so far south, the climate is hot, but not uncomfortably so, because the cooling breezes from the Atlantic act as an effective air-conditioner. In the areas where crops are cultivated, the soil is relatively fertile, thanks to the Guadalquivir as well as to a history of ingenious water engineering started by the Moors. So where you might expect dry baked plains with little vegetation, what you get are rolling plains and plateaux clothed in silvery olive trees, citrus groves, cornfields, almond orchards and, of course, vineyards.

Winemaking has long been an important industry here. Indeed, between the 17th and 19th centuries, Andalucía's fortunes were predominantly founded on its wine trade. All eight provinces produce some wine, although the eastern ones, especially Almería, are more famous for their dessert grapes. Led by the world-famous

sherries from the Jerez region (see page 204), the style of wine in Andalucía traditionally has been fortified, with the wine aged in a solera system. But a worldwide fashion for light, dry table wines has resulted in several of Andalucía's winemakers changing direction towards lighter wines.

CONDADO DE HUELVA

Situated near the border with Portugal, this is Andalucía's most westerly DO. To the south it borders the Atlantic and includes the Coto de Doñana national park, an area of wetland at the southern end of the Guadalquivir estuary renowned for its bird population. Most of the vineyards sit on low-lying plains, sometimes as little as 25m (82ft) above sea-level around the town of Bollullos par del Condado on the road between Seville and Huelva. The soils are predominantly reddish sand, although the best plots also have a high lime content. The climate is almost identical to that of Jerez further south along the coast, with hot, dry summers, and relatively mild, wet winters. The sherry-style wines of the area were once world famous – even being mentioned in the 14th century by Chaucer in *The Pardoner's Tale*. But a decline set in around the 17th century, largely because Condado's wines were mostly ending up in the bodegas of Jerez. Gradually, inexorably, the area found itself in the shadow of its more famous neighbour.

Now the sherry producers have more wine of their own than they can cope with and some of the Condado vineyard has been turned over to strawberries, grain, sugar beet and olives. Local winemakers have attempted to diversify away from fortified wine by making light table wine or *joven afrutado* (literally 'young and fruity') from the bland local Zalema grape which still occupies 80 per cent of the vineyard. Areas are being turned over to sherry's classic grape, Palomino Fino (locally called Listán) and Garrido Fino, neither variety being renowned for wild displays of character, although both a little more interesting than the stultifyingly neutral Zalema and experimental plantings of Chardonnay, Sauvignon

All the best sherry grapes are grown on pale, chalky albariza soil that soaks up the winter rainfall and then preserves it underground to give the vine nourishment during the fiercely hot summers.

Blanc and many other international varieties for lighter table wines are gaining ground. Making light white wines in a climate where the average annual temperature is 18°C (64°F) is not easy and, despite early harvesting in August, the Zalema often oxidizes and spoils unless great care is taken between picking and winemaking. The traditional fortified Condado Viejo (*olorosos*, ranging from dry to sweet) and Condado Pálido (aged for at least two years under a film of flor, like *fino* sherry, but less fine in style) are drunk locally.

MÁLAGA

Across the Serranía de Ronda from Jerez lies the Málaga DO, another region with a glorious past that has found itself out of fashion at the start of the new millennium. Poor Málaga. Its sweet toffee-and-nuts style of wine used to be among the most prized of southern Spain's 'sack', more famous even than sherry but, at end of the 19th century, it became the first area in Spain to be attacked by the vine louse phylloxera. The devastation of the vineyards – which then covered a staggering 113,000ha (279,220 acres), the destruction of the city of Málaga during the Spanish Civil War, and changing habits in wine drinking have meant that it is now one of Spain's smallest DOs at just 1215ha (3002 acres). Indeed, if it weren't for the fact that Málaga is one of Spain's main tourist airports and holidaymakers love to take back a bottle of something to remind them of their break, I believe the vineyard would be smaller still.

Most of the vineyards are split between two sub-regions: one in the west around Estepona on the coast, an area more famous for its Moscatel table grapes; and the other around the city of Málaga. A few lie in the coastal areas around Nerja, east of Málaga, and also inland along the border with the province of Granada, but most of the grapes for Málaga grow on the rolling Antequera plateau around the village of Mollina. Here, in this hot inland area, about half the vineyards are planted with Pedro Ximénez (abbreviated to PX).

There is a huge range of wine styles with varying degrees of sweetness – PX is the main grape in traditional Málaga wine, although vineyards are also planted with what's known locally as *vidueno*, a jumble of neutral varieties, usually high-yielding Airén (here called Lairén) or Doradillo. The Moscatel de Málaga can be used for Málaga wine too, but is usually found only in the cooler coastal vineyards. Lairén is also used to make basic white wine.

The fortified wine is matured for at least two years in single barrels or a solera system in the city of Málaga down on the coast: it is cooler here than in the inland vineyards where the wines are fermented. Its distinctive burnt-toffee style is due to the complex blend of different wines and grape juices, including *arrope*, a dark grape juice concentrate, and *vino tierno*, sweet wine made from sun-dried grapes. Classic Málaga is aged in wood, but the Moscatel version is not and tends to be lighter, fresher and more grapy.

The newer Sierras de Málaga DO covers still wines in the provinces of Málaga (at Ronda), Granada and Almería. Some of these high-altitude vineyards are making very interesting reds.

MONTILLA-MORILES

Montilla-Moriles, directly north of Málaga, covers the southern part of the province of Córdoba. Montilla-Moriles was classified as part of the sherry area until well into the 20th century, not being recognized as a separate wine region until 1933. The wine is made in the same way as sherry, and in a similar range of styles from very dry to very sweet, but it is produced from PX, rather than from the sensitive Palomino Fino, the main sherry grape.

Montilla's gentle landscape consists of low hills and small plains carpeted with vines and olive and almond trees. Villages are usually

DO WINE REGIONS

ANDALUCÍA

▬▬ Condado de Huelva	▬▬ Montilla-Moriles
▬▬ Jerez-Xérès-Sherry and Manzanilla de Sanlúcar de Barrameda	▬▬ Málaga, Sierras de Málaga
	☐ OVER 500M (1640FT)
	☐ OVER 1000M (3280FT)

built on hilltops and occasionally a rugged rock like the famous La Lengue ('the Tongue') interrupts the calm scenery. The most inland of Andalucía's wine regions, its climate is continental: at the height of summer temperatures can reach 45°C (113°F); winters are short and cold. The vines huddle together under the trees that help to retain some precious moisture and offer shade – something the hot and bothered pickers must be grateful for at harvest time.

The vineyards with the best soils – *zonas de superior calidad* – lie east of the whitewashed town of Montilla up in the slightly cooler Sierra de Montilla, and in the sub-region called Moriles Alto around the village of Moriles. Here the off-white soils contain large amounts of limestone and resemble the best chalky soils or *albarizas* of Jerez. In summer, the hot sun bakes a hard crust on the surface of the soil and this not only reflects the heat back onto the grapes from underneath, but also helps prevent the rainwater that falls in winter from completely evaporating during the long hot summer. Other vineyard areas in the DO have inferior reddish sandy soil with clay and limestone, and are known as *ruedos*.

Almost 90 per cent of the grapes grown here are PX, a vine that copes better with the searing heat than Palomino Fino, and small amounts of Airén and Torrontés are also grown. These last two varieties are used either to produce a slightly less alcoholic blend (PX grown here can make a wine of 15 per cent alcohol, no problem), or for making the new-style *joven afrutado* wines. Yes, it's the same story here as in Condado – fortified wines aged in soleras are in decline, despite the best being of very good quality, while progressive winemakers make other styles to boost their flagging fortunes. The sad thing is that the *finos*, *amontillados*, *olorosos* and *palo cortados* of Montilla-Moriles are what it does best; dry white table wines are made so much better elsewhere in Spain – in Rueda and Rías Baixas in the cooler north-west, for example. I love some of the vibrant fortified wines of Andalucía, and not just the famous ones of Jerez either. Let's just hope the sweeping tide of fashion comes round again before we lose them for good.

'Mountain' used to be a famous wine from the Málaga region. Almost extinct, it has been resurrected by super-talented roving winemaker Telmo Rodriguez.

JEREZ

 WHITE GRAPES
Palomino is the classic sherry grape. Palomino Fino is by far the better variety and is planted in most of the vineyards. There is also some Palomino de Jerez and Pedro Ximénez, with Moscatel grown for the sweet wines.

CLIMATE
The long hot summers (at times up to 40°C/104°F) are moderated by the influence of the Atlantic. The humidity near the coast is crucial to the development of flor and the production of sherry. In the winter there is fairly heavy rainfall in the region.

 SOIL
Chalky *albariza* soil with smaller amounts of clay and sand is the best type for sherry grapes. The less good soils contain large amounts of clay, mud or sand.

ASPECT
The vineyards lie mainly on bare, rolling hills, up to 150m (492ft) high, or else on flat land.

Valdespino is one of Jerez's great companies, dating back over 700 years. Inocente is a beautiful bone-dry fino *from the outstanding Macharnudo vineyard north-west of Jerez de la Frontera.*

IF I VENTURE INTO SHERRY COUNTRY, I make sure I pack my sunglasses. It isn't that it's desperately hot; in August the temperature can reach 40°C (104°F), but gentle, cooling breezes from the nearby Atlantic Ocean keep things comfortable. No, it's the effect of the sun glinting off the bleached land that dazzles me and makes me screw up my eyes in pain. The vineyards of Jerez look as though someone has cut down all the trees, then taken a big pot of whitewash and splashed it over the scenery before marking out the green vines against the bright canvas. This effect is caused by the special chalky soil of region, called *albariza* – literally 'snow white'. It's one of the keys to the unique character of sherry, the fortified wine that has spawned a thousand imitations, but which only truly comes from this corner of south-west Spain near Cádiz.

It surprises many who imagine southern Spain to be baked and arid to discover that Jerez has a relatively high rainfall – much higher, at 635mm (25in) a year, than Rioja right up in the north-east of Spain, for example. March is the wettest month, but rain falls frequently during the winter, sweeping inland from the Atlantic. And this is where *albariza* comes in handy, for it soaks up the rain and stores it away in its subsoil like an underground camel's hump. This large amount of water will see the vines through the long hot summer months. During the rainy season the vineyards are ploughed in such a way that the water is soaked up and doesn't roll away down the gentle slopes. In summer, the sun bakes a smooth crust on the surface of the chalk, which stops too

much water from evaporating. *Albariza* is also good for ripening grapes; the hot sun reflected off the bright white soil helps the maturing process along nicely. All this makes for very contented, high-yielding vines. And that's true especially of the white Palomino Fino, a heavy cropper even in poor conditions.

Palomino Fino now covers 95 per cent of the Jerez vineyards. If you make table wine from these grapes (and many sherry companies do) it's pretty dull, insipid stuff. But the neutral must, with its relatively low acidity, is perfect for undergoing the magical transformation that turns Jerez wine into sherry.

The creation of sherry calls for a clever performance by Mother Nature. Humidity from the nearby Atlantic encourages a yeast growth called flor to form on the surface of the new wine, though usually only when the wine has been made from the more acidic grapes and given a light fortification with *aguardiente* (grape spirit). At first the flor just looks like a sprinkling of powder, but this soon spreads and thickens to form a creamy protective layer, which prevents oxidation and adds its own sour cream, bread dough character to the wine maturing in the cask. The bone-dry, pale straw sherry that emerges from this process is *fino*.

Fino is made in large volumes at bodegas in the towns of Jerez de la Frontera and El Puerto de Santa María. At Sanlúcar de Barrameda, a coastal fishing port, the humidity means that the flor layer on the casked wine grows thicker and denser than elsewhere in Jerez. Sanlúcar produces a particular type of *fino* known as

0 km 1 2
0 miles 1

Guadalquivir

SANLÚCAR DE BARRAMEDA

CHIPIONA

ATLANTIC OCEAN

ROTA

0 km 1 2
0 miles 1

manzanilla – lighter and more delicate than *fino* – some tasters even find it salty. *Amontillado* is *fino* that has been allowed to mature and oxidize developing a more rounded, nutty flavour. *Oloroso* has had no protective layer of flor, so it develops a dark colour, marked oxidized flavours and greater richness. All sherry is matured in a solera system – a stack of casks containing progressively older wines, which are continually refreshed by blending with younger wines creating greater complexity. Commercial sherry is sweetened by adding concentrated grape juice.

In recent years the Consejo Regulador of Jerez-Xérès-Sherry and Manzanilla de Sanlúcar (Spain's oldest *consejo*) has offered financial incentives to growers in poorer areas to persuade them to grub up their vineyards and replant in Jerez Superior. Some have done so, while others have opted out of the DO altogether and stopped making sherry. As a result, the area under vine in Jerez Superior is growing, but overall vineyard holdings are decreasing. It's good news, as a boom in the sherry market during the 1970s had led to a doubling of vineyard area and the inevitable use of some duff patches of land. Today, as quality rises volume decreases, with the better, chalkier soils being used more and more to provide better quality Palomino Fino grapes.

So what does sherry country look like? If you can stop squinting in the brightness, cast your eye over huge vistas of very gently sloping land with rows and rows of neatly pruned vines. They are nearly all Palomino Fino. This wouldn't have been so a century ago when the traditional local grape was Palomino de Jerez or Palomino Basto. Both this and the grape used for sweetening sherry, Pedro Ximénez, have yielded most of their territory to Palomino Fino. Here and there a shimmering white building stands out on the soft brow of a hill. It will doubtless belong to a bodega – everything does here. You won't see much else, although further afield in the region you'll catch a glimpse of patches of bright yellow sunflowers.

Sanlúcar and El Puerto de Santa María lie on lower, flatter land on the coast. Sanlúcar's vineyards are mostly on *albariza* soils, while Puerto's soil is less chalky. The grapes are not necessarily used in their home town – they may be used by bodegas all over the region. But for a sherry to qualify as a *manzanilla*, it must have been matured in Sanlúcar. The town's seafront, with its little blue-and-white fishing boats pulled up on the beach and traditional bars all serving the chilled sherry straight from the cask, is one of the most delightful spots in the region. After this, drinking sherry back at home is never the same again…

The character of fino *sherry depends on the growth of a thin layer of yeast or flor on the surface of the wine. Bodegas Domecq have created this glass-ended barrel for visitors to see the flor for themselves.*

JEREZ SUPERIOR

TOTAL DISTANCE NORTH TO SOUTH
28KM (17½ MILES)

 VINEYARDS

N

JEREZ DE LA FRONTERA ■

■ **EL PUERTO DE SANTA MARÍA** *Guadalete*

WHERE THE VINEYARDS ARE *The three important centres for sherry production, Jerez de la Frontera, Sanlúcar de Barrameda and El Puerto de Santa María, form a rough triangle north of the Guadalete river. Most of the vineyards fan out around Jerez and Sanlúcar in rolling countryside. Jerez has always been the most important of the three, and its Moorish name, Seris, is the origin of the English word, sherry. The shippers' headquarters and bodegas are concentrated in these towns and the wine is no longer made in the* caserios *(country houses) out in the vineyards.*

Centuries ago the vineyards were sited more to the east of Jerez, but over the years they have crept gradually westwards to occupy the albariza *or chalkier soils to the west of the town. The road between Jerez and Sanlúcar takes you past some of the finest vineyards. Others lie further afield, to the north and the south, but the ones on the map between the three sherry towns make up Jerez Superior, the best zone for sherry vines, and where 83 per cent of the vineyards are found. Most lie on huge, very gently sloping hillsides with few buildings and almost no trees to break up the landscape. As the aspect of the vineyards does not matter in such a southerly latitude, the hills are usually planted with vines on all sides. A few of the big sherry companies have large vineyard holdings, but most of the vineyards are small and divided between 2600 growers.*

DEL DUQUE
Amontillado Muy Viejo
Jerez-Xérès-Sherry
Gonzalez Byass

ALBARIZA CHALK

The finest sherry vineyards are located on *albariza* chalk soil which contains between 60 and 80 per cent chalk. This soil can appear almost as white as snow in summer and is very high in calcium. It is finely grained and this even texture is very important in the Jerez climate where there are heavy rains in winter and early spring. The deep *albariza* soil absorbs the rain like a sponge and this then sustains the vines during the long summer drought.

Most of the *albariza* soil is found in two areas between Sanlúcar and Jerez and the more outlying vineyards are mainly on poorer, darker soils which contain less chalk: *barros rojos* or clay soils contain up to 30 per cent chalk and *arenas* or sandy soils have about 10 per cent chalk. In an effort to improve quality the proportion of vineyards on the *albariza* soil has grown from 50 per cent in 1960 to over 80 per cent today.

Guadalquivir

ATLANTIC OCEAN

■ SANLÚCAR DE BARRAMEDA

■ JEREZ DE LA FRONTERA

Guadalete

■ EL PUERTO DE SANTA MARÍA

CÁDIZ ■

N

0 km 5 10
0 miles 5

Albarizas ☐

Barros rojos and Arenas ☐

PORTUGAL

Portugal at its most traditional: terraced vineyards in the Douro Valley (left), and painted tiles at the railway station at Pinhão, one of the main towns of the Douro Valley. For centuries the steepness of the slopes has meant that everything has to be done by hand. However, the terraces shown to the right of picture are new ones, cut into the hillsides wide enough to accommodate a small tractor.

It isn't so long ago that I would have approached Portugal's table wine world with exasperation at lost opportunities easily outweighing the pleasure I gained from its occasional triumphs. There seemed to be so much potential from its myriad native grape varieties, and yet the producers seemed supremely unconcerned about what we foreigners might like to drink. Well, that's half the story. She did have some wines that we liked to drink – and which were always intended for export – the great fortified wines of port and Madeira were invented by traders, largely from Britain; the medium-sweet, lightly sparkling rosé wines of Mateus and Lancers were created after World War Two with the export market very much in mind. The rest of Portugal's wines, however, were mostly lapped up by the domestic market along with countries like Brazil and Angola which had strong Portuguese connections.

This has meant that many wine producers have begun only recently to bring their methods and machinery close to accepted modern standards. But it also meant that the rush to uproot old vine varieties and replace them with international favourites like Chardonnay and Cabernet only happened on a very small scale. For which we should give thanks because Portugal is a jewel house of ancient vine varieties. In a world of increased standardization, Portugal is a beacon of individuality. Careful application of modern methods to these varieties, far from spoiling their character, is demonstrating just how good they are. Portugal has been through several Golden Ages as a fortified wine producer. Its Golden Age as a table wine producer is only just beginning. As it is, Portugal, with the tempering influence of the Atlantic affecting all her coastal regions, already offers a fascinating array of wines. These range from the fiercely acidic yet fragrant Vinho Verdes of the Minho in the north, through the majestic ports and succulent soft reds of the Douro Valley, past the rudely impressive reds of Bairrada and the potentially magnificent reds and whites of Dão, and on to the areas of the centre and the south, where the transformation from simple bulk producer merely satisfying local thirsts to international player creating some of the most original and thrilling flavours in Europe has been astounding. Much poor wine is still made, especially in the Estremadura and the tourist honeypot of the Algarve, but in the low hills of Alenquer, in the broad acres of the Ribatejo inland from Lisbon, in the area around Setúbal to the east and in the torrid plains of the Alentejo, good whites and great reds are beginning to appear, and frequently there isn't a Chardonnay or Cabernet Sauvignon vine in sight.

THE WINE REGIONS OF PORTUGAL

IMAGINE TWO GLASSES OF WINE standing side by side. The first, a Vinho Verde, is almost water-white with a few rather lazy bubbles clinging to the side of the glass. It smells vaguely citrous and it knocks you sideways with its acidic rasp. Then on to the second, a port, with its deep impenetrable colour. A heady aroma of super-ripe fruit wafts from the glass and its rich flavours warm and soothe, conjuring up images of a homely winter's evening by the fireside. It is hard to believe that the two wines, with at least ten degrees of alcohol separating them, come from the same country, let alone adjacent regions, but Vinho Verde and port live cheek by jowl in the north of Portugal. It's not as if we're talking about a large area. Port and Vinho Verde cohabit in a country that is little more than 160km (100 miles) wide. You're driving along, you turn a corner and you go from one wine region to a neighbour who could not be more different, just like that.

That's the beauty of Portugal. For such a small country she has a strong regional feel and the climate plays a vital role in this. With its prevailing westerly winds, the Atlantic Ocean exerts a strong influence on the coastal belt, but this diminishes sharply as you journey inland. As you cross a mountain range, grey rain-bearing clouds scudding inland from the sea suddenly disappear. Taking a straight line across the north of the country, climate statistics illustrate this dramatic change. The Atlantic coast north of Porto is drenched by over 1200mm (47in) of rainfall a year. This rises to 2000mm (79in) on the mountains inland, a figure comparable with Bergen on the fjord coast of Norway. Then in the rain-shadow to the east of the mountains the figure falls progressively to as low as 400mm (16in) near the frontier with Spain, drought conditions by any standard. Between these two extremes is the heart of the Douro Valley with around 700mm (28in) of rainfall, the perfect climate for ripening the grapes that make port, Portugal's most famous wine. As you travel across Portugal, the landscape, architecture and traditions change dramatically too. As mountains rise and subside, the temperate maritime climate with its lush vegetation gives way further south and east to more extreme temperatures and arid scrub. Sturdy grey granite houses built to withstand wind and rain become flimsy shelters painted white to reflect the burning sun.

This regional identity is reflected in the breadth of Portugal's wines. Two fortified wines, port and Madeira, are world-famous. Others like Setúbal and Carcavelos, popular in the 19th century, virtually gave in to the commercial pressures of the 20th century. Apart from light, spritzy Vinho Verdes, the north of the country also produces reds that are earning very different reputations for

themselves. The Douro's best reds have a luscious, perfumed, soft-textured depth; Bairrada demands a sterner reaction to her aggressive, but impressive wines; and Dão is now showing why it was so well regarded generations ago. Modern vinification methods produce some increasingly attractive fresh whites. In the centre and the south ripeness is the key, with healthy red grapes that would be the envy of many a cool-climate Frenchman being turned into wines packed with ripe berry-fruit flavours. It is here that Portugal shows the most promise, having attracted the attention of several international winemakers.

But long-standing traditions, often deeply rooted in rural culture, are only reluctantly cast aside. Nowhere is this better illustrated than in Portugal's rather muddled vineyards. In the past, the same grape variety was frequently christened with four or five names depending on where it was planted. The Portuguese authorities (egged on by the EU) have banged a few heads together and decided on a principal name for each of Portugal's grape varieties. For example Castelão Francês, once variously known as João de Santarem and Periquita, is now simply known as Castelão. It won't really affect the smaller farmers, as many have no idea what grapes they are growing but it will have an impact on the larger growers, most of whom have now replanted their vineyards with each variety carefully delineated.

Following examples set elsewhere in the world, the Portuguese have set out on a varietal path. Varieties like the deeply coloured, scented Touriga Nacional, traditionally planted in the Douro and Dão, are now appearing on wine labels up and down the country. Likewise Tinta Roriz (which also still travels under the name of Aragonez and is better known outside Portugal under its Spanish name of Tempranillo), Trincadeira, Tinto Cão and Castelão – all unfamiliar names on the international circuit. Portugal has woken up to the potential of these grapes to make world class wines. Some native white grapes have also come to the fore. In Vinho Verde there is the triumvirate of Alvarinho, Loureiro and Trajadura, each now being made into varietal wines. Then there's Bical, Fernão Pires and in southern Portugal Arinto, a variety that hangs on to its crisp acidity in spite of the warm sun. Red or white, the future's bright in Portugal.

The Portuguese only began to sort out their chaotic vineyards in the mid-1980s after the country joined the EU. Much has changed since. Impressive roads now link remote inland regions with the coast where most of the country's population lives. The result is that the new stainless steel wineries in land-locked regions like Dão and the Douro are now just a commute from Porto; in the past the journey would take half a day.

Quinta do Crasto have led the way in creating exciting new Douro table wines, often from single-grape varieties: this is Touriga Nacional.

THE CLASSIFICATION SYSTEM FOR PORTUGUESE WINE

Portugal's wine laws have been in a state of flux ever since the country joined the European Union in 1986. That's the polite way of describing the chaos that has resulted from bureaucrats in Brussels meeting bureaucrats in Lisbon. The new wine regions are now beginning to settle into a framework, but recent shenanigans rather detract from the fact that Portugal mothered the modern appellation system over two centuries ago. After a period of fraud and scandal in the fledgling port industry, in 1756 Portugal's forward-thinking prime minister, the Marquis of Pombal, drew a boundary around the Douro vineyards to protect the wine's authenticity – one of the world's first examples of vineyard delimitation. Nothing more happened until the early 20th century, when several other wine regions were similarly demarcated. The situation then remained static until after the 1974 Revolution, when Bairrada's vineyards were finally awarded demarcated status. On joining the EU, Portugal's wine classification was brought into line with that of other EU countries.

QUALITY CATEGORIES

- **Denominação de Origem Controlada (DOC)** This is the top tier and parallels the French Appellation d'Origine Contrôlée (AC). It has expanded considerably in recent years as newer regions make the grade up from IPR.
- **Indicação de Proveniência Regulamentada (IPR)** Intermediate category of regions. Most have now been promoted to DOC.
- **Vinho Regional** This is an increasingly important category, particularly in the south where wines are often made from grapes grown over a wide area. These large regions parallel the French regional *vins de pays* and allow similar flexibility, making them more popular with winemakers than many of the more obscure DOCs and IPRs.
- **Vinho de Mesa** The most basic category, table wine, is commercially important as so much off-dry to medium-dry rosé is exported under this label.

WINE REGIONS

A journey around Portugal's wine regions can hardly ever be whistle-stop. From the Minho province that marks the border with Spain in the north-west to the Algarve in the south may be just under 650km (400 miles) as the crow flies but there are over 30 officially recognized wine regions in between, as well as a tier of Vinhos Regionais (VR) or regional wines that cover most of the country. Almost everywhere you go in Portugal, apart from the highest mountain peaks where viticulture is simply not feasible, it seems that someone somewhere is making wine.

The largest region is Vinho Verde which covers the entire soggy north-west of the country, including the lower reaches of the Douro Valley. The Douro region itself, delimited both for port and table wine, begins 80km (50 miles) or so upstream and extends east to the Spanish border. In the granite mountains immediately to the south, the Dão spreads over three river valleys, the vineyards climbing into the foothills of the Serra da Estrêla, Portugal's highest mountain range, which rises to a lofty 1993m (6539ft). Bairrada, with its tannic red wines, occupies the flat coastal strip between the misty Aveiro lagoon and the ivory-towered university town of Coimbra.

Stretching along the rolling coastal hills to the south, Estremadura (known as the *Oeste* or 'west') is a colourful region making bulk wines for the thirsty local market. For many years the area was best known for its historic enclaves of Bucelas, whose white wines were drunk by Wellington's army during the Peninsular War nearly 200 years ago, and Colares, with its centenarian, phylloxera-free vines growing in the sand. More recently, the town of Alenquer has lent its name to a new enclave, which is being taken seriously by a number of forward-thinking single estates.

The Tagus or Tejo river, which flows into the Atlantic near Lisbon, marks the divide between the hilly north and the great plains of the south. Inland the Ribatejo region spans the broad river valley, its fertile alluvial soils producing fat, juicy tomatoes and large crops of ripe grapes. The Setúbal peninsula south-east of Lisbon (Lisboa) is one of the few Portuguese regions to embrace foreign grape varieties, which have found a niche on the limestone slopes of the Serra da Arrábida. East and south the undulating Alentejo plain sweeps to the Spanish border with vineyards concentrated around the small whitewashed towns of Portalegre, Borba, Granja-Amareleja, Moura, Redondo, Reguengos and Vidigueira, not forgetting Évora – the regional capital. Last, and probably least, on the Portuguese mainland, the Serra de Monchique separates the Alentejo from the Algarve whose warm maritime climate is ideal for sun-seeking tourists, but few winemakers have yet exploited it.

But there's more to Portugal than the mainland, or *continente* as it is known. The Portuguese are custodians of a number of volcanic Atlantic islands, which their early navigators were the first to discover. Vines were introduced to the Azores by Portuguese settlers in the 15th century. Two islands in this remote archipelago, Pico and Graciosa, exported fortified wines, but the industry was all but wiped out by oidium and phylloxera in the 19th century. Madeira, 1100km (680 miles) south-west of Lisbon, has been home to a flourishing wine industry ever since it was first discovered in the 15th century, and by the end of the 17th century there were already 30 wine shippers on the island. It too suffered oidium and phylloxera but the wine industry underwent a slow and painful recovery. The island's humid subtropical climate and the manufacturing process of heating the wine sets it apart from the rest of Portugal; the process of modernization is slower and more difficult, too.

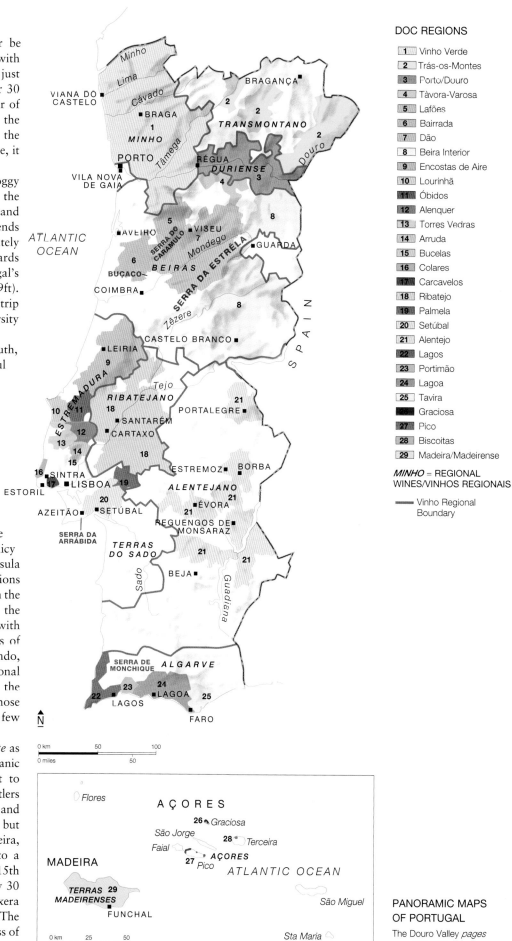

DOC REGIONS

1 Vinho Verde
2 Trás-os-Montes
3 Porto/Douro
4 Távora-Varosa
5 Lafões
6 Bairrada
7 Dão
8 Beira Interior
9 Encostas de Aire
10 Lourinhã
11 Óbidos
12 Alenquer
13 Torres Vedras
14 Arruda
15 Bucelas
16 Colares
17 Carcavelos
18 Ribatejo
19 Palmela
20 Setúbal
21 Alentejo
22 Lagos
23 Portimão
24 Lagoa
25 Tavira
26 Graciosa
27 Pico
28 Biscoitas
29 Madeira/Madeirense

MINHO = REGIONAL WINES/VINHOS REGIONAIS

— Vinho Regional Boundary

PANORAMIC MAPS OF PORTUGAL

The Douro Valley *pages 212–213*

Madeira *pages 216–217*

NORTHERN PORTUGAL

 RED GRAPES
The best varieties are Touriga Nacional, Touriga Franca, Tinta Roriz, Jaén and Tinta Cão, as well as Bairrada's Baga.

WHITE GRAPES
Alvarinho, Loureiro, Trajadura, Viosinho and Gouveio are the main grapes.

CLIMATE
Near the coast there is ample rainfall and a long warm ripening season. The inland Douro Valley has harsh winters and hot summers.

SOIL
The sandy clay of Bairrada gives way to granite with schist in the Douro and granite in Dão.

ASPECT
Mountainous inland with steeply terraced vineyards in the Douro. Flatter land on the narrow coastal strip.

Many of the top port houses were founded by northern Europeans. The Niepoorts from Holland founded this house in 1842.

I**T'S ALL TOO EASY TO LOSE YOUR WAY** in northern Portugal. On the road map there's a maze of country lanes linking tiny villages, but when you're driving you'll see very few road signs. That means that only locals use the roads. And not always for driving: you'll pass creaking ox carts full of hay, or with the whole family and a dog peering over the side. You'll pass women balancing baskets of live chickens on their heads, or earthenware jars of water, and you'll have to avoid dogs who take an afternoon snooze in the middle of the road. But beware: next thing you know, a shiny new BMW is carving you up on a blind corner. Portugal's rural idyll is changing.

Anyway, what seems like a rural idyll to the casual visitor can be more like grinding poverty when you actually live it. North-west Portugal, alongside neighbouring Galicia over the border in Spain, is one of the most densely populated parts of the Iberian Peninsula. It must have seemed like paradise to the early settlers, browned off with the barren wastes of central Iberia. Rivers and streams, and the warm, rain-bearing Atlantic westerlies that fill them, support a riot of vegetation. But over centuries, with successive generations staking their rightful claim, land holdings have diminished in size to such an extent that many can offer only the barest subsistence. Just imagine making a living from a plot of land smaller than a suburban back garden. As you peer from the roadside into the jungle of greenery, count the number of different crops that you can see within a stone's throw. Depending on the time of year, the chance is that you will spy a few tall cabbages growing alongside olive and almond trees, some maize, a tethered goat or a cow, some hens, and across the top of all this, trained off the ground because of the damp climate, there'll be a lush canopy of vines dripping with grapes.

VINHO VERDE
The grapes you see here are destined for Vinho Verde, Portugal's famous 'green wine'. For most people outside Portugal Vinho Verde conjures up an image of a light, slightly sparkling, medium-dry white wine. But back in its country of origin, ask for a glass of Vinho Verde in one of the numerous rough and ready roadside bars and you are likely to be shocked into the truth: that a substantial chunk of the region's production is not the widely exported white wine but a dark, rasping, fizzy red drunk only in northern Portugal. Even the authentic Vinho Verde white will taste different. The lack of any of the residual sweetness, which is believed to be necessary to mollycoddle foreigners, exposes the searing acidity that is the hallmark of true Vinho Verde. High yields conspire with the damp climate to produce low alcohol, high acid wines.

But Vinho Verde is moving on, albeit at its own pace. The vines grown on pergolas along the borders of fields, which used to form the core of Vinho Verde production, can still be found, as can the primitive training of vines up poplar trees – you can spot the latter in parts of Italy, too. But remember that a fair bit of home winemaking goes on. That's probably the roughest sort of wine, and you're unlikely to come across it. Next in quality will be wine from the local co-ops: this, too, can lack finesse. But the big private companies train their vines on wires in proper vineyards, and get higher degrees of ripeness as a result. There is also a move towards growing vines on slopes rather than on the flat. And even though there's a lot of water around – some 1500mm (60in) per year – it can be very dry in summer, and vines can actually suffer from water stress. The climate is not the easiest of conundrums to solve. Those with an interest in selling higher priced wine to export markets – the private companies and the single *quintas* – are, predictably, the ones doing the most work on the canopy management techniques that give greater ripeness and flavour to their grapes.

The Alvarinho grape growing along the river Minho in the extreme north of the region heads the varietal tree, producing a relatively full but delicate dry white wine, with an aroma and flavour akin to a fresh Cox's apple. Further south in the Lima and Cavado valleys around Braga, the Loureiro grape makes a lighter, crisper style, more typical of Vinho Verde which sometimes has a minerally, floral whiff reminiscent of Riesling. Trajadura, often used alongside Loureiro, makes a slightly softer style of wine, while inland along the lower reaches and tributaries of the Douro river, the tangy Avesso grape ripens to produce fuller, riper flavours.

Vintages only tend to appear on the labels of single-*quinta* wines, very few of which have the capacity to age. Other wines are just assumed to be from the most recent harvest, hence the name Vinho Verde, so called because it should be drunk 'green', or in its first flush of youth. From time to time, appallingly wet years like 2002 force up prices and remind us that these vineyards are at the mercy of the fickle Atlantic weather. But an ice-cold bottle of prickly, bone dry Vinho Verde still makes a great picnic wine.

TRÁS-OS-MONTES
Mountain ranges separate the high, barren country of north-east Portugal – which deserves its name of Trás-os-Montes or 'behind the mountains' – from the heavily populated north-western coast. The climatic extremes of this high, inland area make agriculture difficult and the mountain slopes offer more to walkers than to farmers. The three wine regions here, Chaves, which is better known for its cured hams or *presunto*, hot, dry Planalto-Mirandês along the border with Spain, which only has a few scrubby vineyards, and Valpaços, whose co-operative is one of the north-east's better ones, have recently been promoted from IPR status to form the new Trás-os-Montes DOC. The wine is made from some of the same grapes as in the Douro Valley just to the south, but, in general, it's the old Portuguese story of growers sending their good grapes to be made into mediocre wine at the local co-operative.

DÃO
Until recently the Dão region in the heart of Portugal around Viseu was in a time warp. For over 30 years dowdy co-operatives had a stranglehold on the region's winemaking, leaving anyone with a jot of initiative standing with apoplexy on the sidelines as Dão wines went from bad to worse. The rules and regulations that perpetuated this monopoly situation were blown away by Brussels when Portugal joined the EU in 1986 and Dão has been given a new lease of life. The potential is certainly there. Bottles that predate the dark ages have lasted well, retaining their powerful, spicy concentration of flavour, and some recent wines from the huge Sogrape company – which has taken it upon itself to reinvigorate the region – share some of the same character. Touriga Nacional has been accepted as the best red grape variety for Dão, with the better runners-up including Tinta Roriz, Jaen and Alfrocheiro Preto, but most vineyards are still in a muddle.

Like much of northern Portugal, Dão is made up of thousands of tiny plots planted in clearings in the pine and eucalyptus forests that clothe the granite hills. Dão is almost completely surrounded by wild, forbidding mountains, with a narrow gap south of the Serra do Buçaco through which Portugal's largest homegrown river, the Mondego, drains towards the coast. The mountains tend to protect this eyrie from the unpredictable onslaught of Atlantic storms and summer months tend to be warm – August in particular can be very dry – although winter temperatures often plunge well below freezing. Spring frosts can be a problem, too: frost can strike here until mid-May, and there is really no economical way of preventing frost damage, although the occasional vineyard sports a wind machine. The best way of avoiding it is to stick to the sites that have been planted for longest: our ancestors were not stupid, and could identify a frost-free pocket as well as anyone can today. Away from the new highway that slices through the granite hills, remote villages specialize in the pungent local cheese, Queijo da Serra, which is a good foil for a glass of peppery red Dão.

The Serra do Buçaco with its pine forests marks the boundary between Dão and the coastal strip of fertile clay known as Bairrada. The 19th-century Buçaco Palace Hotel, just outside Luso, buys in grapes from Dão and Bairrada to make its own reds and whites, which rank as some of Portugal's best to those who favour ultra-traditional flavours. Whether more recent vintages will ever attain the quality of the much older wines that made the hotel's reputation must be open to question. In any case the wines are only available to guests prepared to endure the hotel's archaic plumbing and dismal cooking (and to guests at other hotels in the same group).

BAIRRADA

Like the Vinho Verde region, Bairrada is at the mercy of the Atlantic, with frequent sea mists and annual rainfall reaching 1000mm (40in). The countryside is mainly flat and featureless, with tall pine and eucalyptus trees sheltering small plots of land planted with cereals, beans and knotty old vines. Bairrada is unusual in Portugal in that it is very nearly a one-grape region and Baga's small, dark berries produce fiercely tannic red wines. Other varieties like Castelão and even Cabernet Sauvignon are being planted to make wines that are softer and more approachable when young. However, the best wines, from traditional producers like Caves São João, Casa de Saima and Luís Pato, reward patience. A small amount of aromatic dry white wine is produced, most of which is used by the local sparkling wine industry. It's worth turning off the Lisbon-Oporto highway to sample a firm-flavoured red Bairrada with the local delicacy, *leitão* or suckling pig.

DOURO VALLEY

After the Tagus, the Douro is the most important river in Portugal (and its importance continues over the border into Spain, as the Duero). The Douro Valley (see pages 212–13) is a wild and beautiful part of Portugal and the poverty of its natural resources has driven the inhabitants to ingenious extremes in order to wrest a living out of what can only just be called soil. The vineyards here must be some of the most labour-intensive in the world. Until recently, in order to grow anything on these slopes of schistous rock, terraces had to be carved out of the hillsides, sometimes to support no more than a row or two of vines. Hillside profiles like step pyramids make you think that the Douro should be one of the wonders of the world. Indeed, UNESCO has made part of the Douro a World Heritage Site. Mechanization of the vineyards was impossible until a replanting programme began in the early 1980s. Now there are there four different methods of vine cultivation in use along the Douro Valley (see diagram, right). Mechanical pruning, on the other hand, will always be impossible, except on the gentler slopes.

Demarcated for port in the 18th century, the Douro Valley is now recognized as a source of some increasingly good table wines. Made from the same varieties used for port, many of these red table wines would be hard and unapproachable – probably not very far removed from the so-called 'blackstrap' wines that were first exported from the Douro over 300 years ago – if it were not for modern methods of viticulture and winemaking. Ferreira's Barca Velha, made in the upper reaches of the Douro near the Spanish border, is the most famous example of what can be done, while properties downstream

like Quinta do Côtto, Quinta do Crasto, Quinta de la Rosa, Quinta Vale Dona Maria, Quinta de Gaivosa and Niepoort's Redoma have followed suit with supple wines that capture the port-like flavours of ripe Douro grapes, yet add a brilliant fragrance.

Some properties make both table wines and port with equal aplomb, only deciding at the last minute which grapes will go to which, and sometimes using the very best grapes for table wines (there's an annual quota for port production, which may not be exceeded). Sometimes, though, it's the grapes with higher acidity and lower sugar content which are directed towards table wine, and these tend to come from the very highest vineyards, where the grapes ripen later and make lighter wines that are less well rated for port production. In some cases, grapes that are used for making good table wines today would, in the past, have simply been sent for distillation as being surplus to requirements.

In the spring after the harvest, the young wines are brought downstream to Vila Nova de Gaia which faces Oporto at the mouth of the Douro river. There the wines are put into barrels, where they age in the relative cool and calm of long, low buildings called lodges. It is here that the wines evolve into their different styles.

Ruby port is the simplest, bottled young while it retains its spicy personality and its dark, purple-ruby colour. Reserve wines or premium ruby (sometimes called Vintage Character) are left to age for five years or so before bottling. Tawny ports are left for longer until they become smooth and silky, sometimes up to 20 or 30 years. Vintage port is a wine from a single exceptional year and bottled after spending a short time in wood. The wine continues to age for 20 years or more in bottle, throwing a 'crust' or sediment as it loses colour and gains complexity with age. Late Bottled Vintage or LBV is a port from a single year, bottled ready to drink after spending between three and six years maturing in wood. Crusted port is a blend of two or three vintages bottled at between three and five years. A small amount of white port is also made from white grapes.

Traditional picking baskets in the Douro Valley. These ones are waiting to be taken to the winery at Quinta do Seixo, just south of Pinhão (seen in the background).

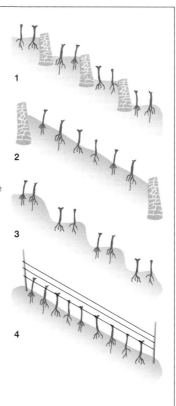

TERRACING IN THE DOURO

Since the late 19th century, experiments have been made with different terracing systems in the Douro in an effort to minimize costs.

1. shows traditional *Socalcos*. These narrow, walled terraces built around hill contours were established mainly in the 19th century when labour was abundant and cheap. Since mechanization is impossible, labour costs have made this traditional method increasingly expensive.

2. shows newer-style *Socalcos*. These inclined terraces became more popular early in the 20th century but are similarly costly to maintain.

3. shows *Patamares* or contour terraces. These unwalled terraces have well-positioned tracks for small tractors. The system, devised in the 1970s, is widely used because of lower labour costs but it is wasteful of land and unsightly.

4. shows vertical planting up-and-down the slope or *vinha ao alto*. This 1980s technique allows easier maintenance and therefore reduces costs. Although soil erosion is not as adverse as predicted, it is limited to slopes of less than 30°.

THE DOURO VALLEY

RED GRAPES
Up to 80 varieties are permitted, but Touriga Nacional, Touriga Franca, Tinto Roriz and Tinta Cão have been identified as the four best varieties.

WHITE GRAPES
Varieties for white port include Codega, Rabigato, Gouveio and Viosinho.

CLIMATE
The humid Atlantic climate in Oporto is ideal for aging port. Further east it is more arid.

SOIL
Port vines are only planted on schistous soils.

ASPECT
The Douro is famous for its steep terraces which follow the narrow river valleys.

TAKE MY ADVICE and leave the car behind. I'm not suggesting it because of the port but because going by train is much the best way to see the Douro. Yes, there's a smart new road linking the Douro with Porto, the city that has given its name to 'Vinho do Porto' or port wine, and it will get you to Pinhão in half the time taken by the train – but what's time? The train offers one of the great railway journeys of the world. The little single-track line runs alongside the river for much of the journey, so if you want a pre-taste of the Douro – the winding, contoured terraces, the high, perching villages, the tethered fishing boats – this is the way to do it. But before you set off, look down from the two-tier bridge that links Porto and Vila Nova de Gaia on the opposite bank. You'll see the black roofs of the port lodges and the waterfront lined with *barcos rabelos*, boats which once brought the young wines downstream, before the river was dammed in the 1970s, on an unnerving journey through the rapids. Thank goodness for the train.

The Douro vineyards are between 80 and 200km (50 and 125 miles) upstream from Porto. As you leave the murky suburbs and the sea mist behind, the train passes through chaotic Vinho Verde country with characteristic tall crops growing beneath pergolas of vines. About an hour into the journey the Douro comes into view and from there on to the end of the line the train snakes alongside the river. It's not uncommon for passengers to sit with the door open on the steps of the carriage and there are places along the track where you can almost dangle your feet in the still waters.

The train rounds a bend and the landscape changes. Hard grey granite gives way to flaky, silver-coloured schist. This is where the port vineyards begin, today as they did in the mid-18th century when Portugal's prime minister, the forward-thinking Marquis of Pombal, first drew a boundary around the Douro Valley vineyards to protect the authenticity of port wine.

The Douro DOC divides unofficially into three sub-regions. The most westerly one, Baixo Corgo, is centred on the town of Régua. Here the climate is cooler and wetter than further upstream and the wines from here tend to be lighter and less substantial – ideal for young rubies and light tawnies that supply the insatiable French taste for cheap port. Indeed, half of all port comes from the Baixo Corgo. The train pauses at Régua but it is worth continuing upstream as far as Pinhão. This is the heart of the Cima Corgo sub-region, and from Pinhão's station you can see Cálem's Quinta da Foz, Ferreira's Quinta do Seixo, Dow's Quinta do Bomfim and Royal Oporto's Quinta das Carvalhas. The Pinhão valley is where you'll find Quinta do Noval and properties belonging to Taylor, Warre and other famous shippers. As the train climbs towards Tua more celebrated names come into view, including Croft's Quinta da Roêda and Graham's Quinta dos Malvedos.

Upstream from Tua the vineyards cease for a while. A massive outcrop of granite squeezes the river into a forbidding gorge. The railway disappears into a tunnel only to reappear once again among terraced vineyards carved from the schist. This, the most easterly of the three sub-regions, is known as the Douro Superior. It has attracted port shippers like Cockburn, Ferreira and Ramos Pinto who have pioneered vineyards on the relatively flat land

WHERE THE VINEYARDS ARE *This map of the Douro Valley shows the Cima Corgo and part of the Douro Superior sub-regions where the best port vineyards are located. The finest tawny, vintage and late bottled vintage ports are sourced from the Cima Corgo where all the major port shippers have large vineyard holdings. The little town of Pinhão is surrounded by steep terraces of vines, with some of the most famous names in port emblazoned on the high retaining walls shoring up these terraces. Vineyards are graded officially from A to F according to 12 different factors, among them altitude, aspect, locality and soil. Nearly all the best A and B grade quintas are within sight of the Douro or one of its tributaries, the Tedo, Távora, Torto and Pinhão. The higher vineyards around the towns of Sabrosa, Alijó and São João da Pesqueira are awarded lower grades (C, D, E and F) and a much smaller proportion of their production is made into port. They can, however, produce good table wines with lighter body and higher acidity than are needed for port: there can be two to three weeks difference in ripening between high sites like São João da Pesqueira and vineyards down by the river.*

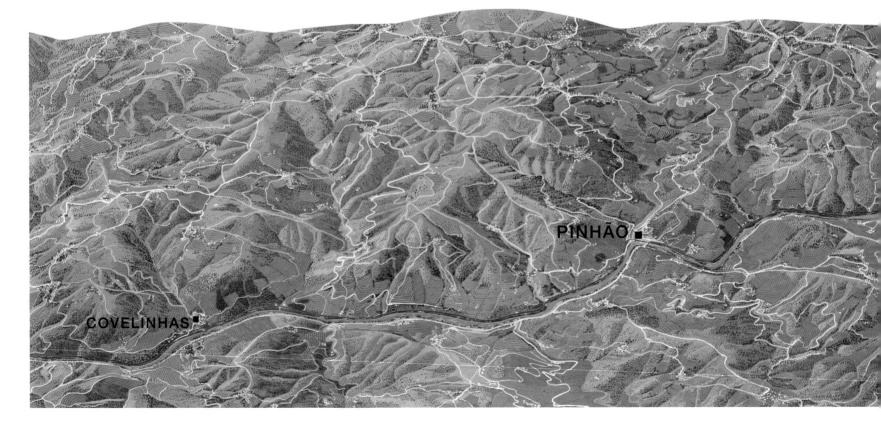

PINHÃO

COVELINHAS

towards the Spanish frontier. The train crosses the river and two of the grandest of all vineyard properties can be spied: first Taylor's Quinta de Vargellas, then Symington's Quinta do Vesúvio, both of which have their own railway stations. Beyond here the landscape begins to look increasingly arid and vineyards tend to be planted on high land out of sight of the river. Just before the train reaches the end of the line Quinta do Vale do Meão appears, former home of Portugal's legendary red wine, Barca Velha. Production has since moved to a new property, Quinta da Leda, away from the river. At Pocinho the driver shunts the engine to the other end of the carriages and the train returns to Porto.

Few visitors, however, get this far. To most of us the Cima Corgo around Pinhão is the epitome of port country: steep schist slopes with vineyards facing north or south, east or west: there's no shortage of heat here. The shortage, instead, is of water. The lower slopes are more schistous and retain water well, as do the old, pre-phylloxera terraces, the ones with hand-built dry-stone walls that need constant maintenance. Irrigation is being discussed and, used properly, could improve quality. In the Douro Superior the climate is the most constant, but the climate in the Pinhão and Torto valleys is better balanced with slightly more rainfall. Further upriver, irrigation could definitely help improve the balance. The remote Douro Superior is where the landscape departs from the stereotype. Go within spitting distance of the Spanish border and you'll find vineyards that are rolling rather than mountainous – and vineyards that are mechanized. (Mechanization here in the Douro really only means perhaps pre-pruning by tractor and then finishing by hand.) The trouble is that labour costs are rising, so technology is aimed at replacing even the labour used for treading grapes – with robots. But no-one can change the soil.

To plant in dense Douro schist you must break up the rock to a depth of 1.5m (5ft) to give the roots a chance. After five years the roots reach the bedrock where finding water gets easier. The soil is pretty homogeneous throughout the valley: there are pockets of other soils, but schist rules. What varies here and makes one wine different from its neighbour is exposure, altitude and climate. And, of course, winemaking.

SELECTED QUINTAS

1. Qta. de Nápoles	6. Qta. da Boa Vista	11. Qta. das Lages	16. Qta. do Noval
2. Qta do Crasto	7. Qta. do Porto	12. Qta. de la Rosa	17. Qta. da Cavadinha
3. Qta. da Água Alta	8. Qta. da Côrte	13. Qta. da Foz	18. Qta. de Terra Feita
4. Qta. de São Luiz	9. Qta. do Seixo	14. Qta das Carvalhas	19. Qta. do Cruzeiro
5. Qta. do Panascal	10. Qta. do Bom Retiro	15. Qta. do Bomfim	20. Qta. do Passadouro
			21. Qta. de Santo António
			22. Qta. da Roêda
			23. Qta da Gricha
			24. Qta. dos Malvedos
			25. Qta do Tua
			26. Qta. de Vargellas
			27. Qta. dos Canais
			28. Qta. do Vesúvio

- - UNOFFICIAL SUB-
REGION BOUNDARY

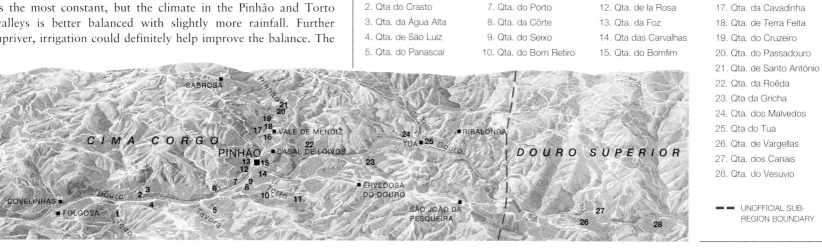

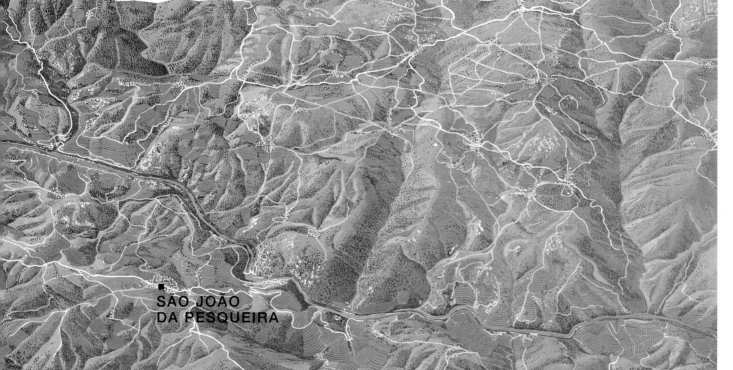

SÃO JOÃO DA PESQUEIRA

FOLGOSA TO VESUVIO

TOTAL DISTANCE
NORTH TO SOUTH
17 KM (11 MILES)

 VINEYARDS

CENTRAL & SOUTHERN PORTUGAL

 RED GRAPES
Castelão is found throughout the region, along with Tinta Miuda in Estremadura and Trincadeira in the Ribatejo and Alentejo. There is some Cabernet Sauvignon and Merlot in the Ribatejo and on the Setúbal Peninsula.

WHITE GRAPES
Arinto has the potential for good wines. Femão Pires is widely planted in the Ribatejo, where there is also some Chardonnay. Roupeiro and Antão Vaz are the best white grapes in the Alentejo and there is Muscat on the Setúbal Peninsula.

CLIMATE
The influence of the Atlantic is important in the west. Inland, the arid Alentejo can be very hot in summer.

SOIL
Estremadura has calcareous clay and limestone, Ribatejo clay, sand and fertile alluvial soils and Alentejo granite, limestone and red clay.

 ASPECT
The Ribatejo and Alentejo plains contrast with the hillier Torres Vedras, Alenquer and Arruda areas.

João Portugal Ramos is one of a new breed of winemaker/consultants, concentrating on single varietal wines.

THE MUDDY TEJO or Tagus river flows south-west through central Portugal dividing the country into two roughly symmetrical halves. Just north of the river the mountains subside and as you drive south the roads straighten out and the patchwork of poor, intensively farmed smallholdings of the north gives way to vast estates or *latifúndios*, some of which cover thousands of acres of low-lying plain.

ESTREMADURA

This strip of rolling countryside, stretching from Lisbon's populated hinterland along the wild and windy western Atlantic coast, is known colloquially as the Oeste (pronounced 'wesht', a rather drunken-sounding version of the word 'west' which is what it means). Although Estremadura produces more wine than any other single region in Portugal, until recently there were few wines of any quality. It has been divided into several DOCs but, apart from Alenquer, few are going to hit the headlines. Most of the wines emanate from a number of huge co-operatives which have benefited from significant investment since Portugal joined the European Union. Although Estremadura produces little that could be classed as truly fine, it is the source of some large volumes of simple, easy-to-drink red and white wine.

The picturesque towns and villages are considerably more memorable than most of the wines. Lush, high-yielding vineyards are predominantly planted with bland white grape varieties which used to produce large quantities for distillation, but now find their way onto the local market as wine. Ripening can be difficult in this relatively cool maritime climate and red wines, made predominantly from the ubiquitous Castelão grape, often taste mean and thin.

But there is hope for the Estremadura region. A number of properties around Alenquer are making increasingly good red wines from grapes like Touriga Nacional and Tinta Roriz as well as Cabernet, Merlot and Syrah. Quinta de Pancas, Quinta da Cortezia, Quinta do Carneiro, Quinta do Monte d'Oiro, Quinta das Setencostas and Casa Santos Lima are names to look out for. The region has also been taken by storm by José Neiva who through his work at D F J Vinhos made large volumes of very drinkable wine, predominantly with quality conscious export markets in mind. Many of these wines are bottled under the Vinho Regional Estremadura designation.

Two tiny enclaves in Estremadura are worth a special detour. The windswept, seaside vineyards of Colares just 35km (22 miles) west of the centre of Lisbon grow in the sandy soil on the clifftops, their roots anchored in the clay below. This sand protected the vines from the phylloxera louse which attacked vineyards throughout Europe in the 19th century. Consequently, the local Ramisco vine is one of the only European varieties that has never been grafted onto phylloxera-resistant American rootstock. Cultivating vines in the sand is difficult and expensive today and the region has been in slow decline for the last 30 years. Still, the few gnarled old vines that remain are a pilgrimage for incurable wine romantics who like to sample these strangely wild, tannic reds within sight and smell of the great ocean.

Inland, shielded from the damp, misty Tagus estuary by a low range of hills, the Bucelas region produces dry white wines from two grape varieties, the Arinto and the aptly named Esgana Cão meaning 'dog strangler'. Both grapes, especially the latter, retain plenty of natural acidity in a relatively warm climate producing crisp, dry white wines that became popular in Britain in the nineteenth century under the title 'Portuguese Hock'. Mention that name to a Brussels legislator today and it would send him into paroxysms. Carcavelos, a rich, raisiny, fortified wine with a nutty,

port-like length, enjoyed a moment of glory in the 18th century, but it's hard to find any vineyards today. With the relentless expansion of Lisbon along the Tagus estuary, most of the Carcavelos vineyards have disappeared under roads and blocks of apartments.

RIBATEJO

Journeying inland, the broad Tagus Valley, known as the Ribatejo, serves the capital as a kitchen garden. Ripe, fat tomatoes, curly beans, maize and grapes compete for space on the fertile alluvial flood plain which is regularly irrigated by the swollen river. Like neighbouring Estremadura it has been subdivided into a number of smaller sub-regions – Tomar, Santarém, Chamusca, Almeirim, Cartaxo and Coruche – but the whole of the Ribatejo has been raised to one DOC, with the confusing designation of 'Ribatejano' permitted for wines that fall into the Vinho Regional category (mostly those made from international grape varieties).

Ribatejo wines reflect their soils. The fertile alluvial flood plain alongside the Tagus known as the *leziria* yields large volumes of light insubstantial red and white wine. Away from the river the wines from the *charneca* or heathland are more substantial, particularly towards the south-east of the region where they tend to resemble those of the Alentejo.

Although the Ribatejo is still dominated by large co-operatives, there are a number of single quintas making increasingly good wines. Casa Cadaval, Falcoaria, Falua, Quinta da Lagoalva da Cima, Casa de Alorna and Quinta do Santo André are all labels to look out for. Australian winemaker Peter Bright (of Bright Brothers) sources Sauvignon Blanc, Chardonnay, Cabernet and Merlot for much of his wine from the giant Fiúza estate and makes wines with more than a hint of the New World.

SETÚBAL PENINSULA

Two elegant suspension bridges span the Tagus linking the north bank of the river to the densely populated Setúbal Peninsula on the south. After a while, Lisbon's high suburbs finally subside and you find yourself travelling through a forest of fragrant umbrella pines growing on the warm, sandy plain. Around Setúbal to the south, the rugged Arrábida hills rise out of the plain and then shelve steeply to the Atlantic. The region around Setúbal is home to some of Portugal's most enterprising winemakers making wines from a wide variety of Portuguese and foreign grape varieties. The two leading companies are the internationally minded J P Vinhos (formerly known as João Pires and famous for its dry Muscat) and José Maria da Fonseca, who make a series of powerful reds as well as some superb Moscatel de Setúbal.

The large fishing port of Setúbal at the mouth of the river Sado lends its name to an unctuous, raisiny fortified wine made mainly from Muscat grapes from vineyards on the limestone hills behind the city. In recent years this traditional sweet Muscat has been upstaged by other wines from the region, including the light, dry, João Pires Muscat, first made in 1981 from a surplus of Moscatel grapes, and Quinta de Bacalhôa, a ripe, minty red made from a Bordeaux blend of Cabernet Sauvignon and Merlot. Chardonnay also seems to be well suited to the north-facing limestone soils of the Arrábida hills and the warm maritime climate.

But foreign grape varieties still have some way to go before they oust native grapes like Castelão (still unofficially known as 'Periquita') which thrives on the broad, sandy plain around the walled town of Palmela. José Maria da Fonseca's raspberryish Periquita is one of Portugal's best known red wines and they also produce some excellent *garrafeiras* (reserve wines) labelled with curious code names like 'CO' and 'TD'.

Vines as far as the eye can see in the Arruda region of Estremadura, north of Lisbon. Traditionally just producers of bulk wine, many parts of the Estremadura are rapidly modernizing, with some impressive results.

ALENTEJO

In Setúbal stop briefly at José Maria da Fonseca's old winery in the main street at Azeitão and then it's time to head east towards the walled city of Évora and the heart of the Alentejo. After a few miles batting down a long straight road – what a change after the winding roads of northern Portugal – the landscape begins to change and a giant, undulating plain unfolds before our eyes. This is the Alentejo. Golden wheatfields extend for almost as far as the eye can see, dotted by deep evergreen cork oak and olive trees that provide shade for small nomadic herds of sheep, goats and black pigs. Green in spring, the landscape turns an ever deeper shade of ochre with summer temperatures that frequently soar over 40°C (104°F) and rainfall that barely reaches 600mm (24in) a year. The open vista is broken only by the occasional dazzling whitewashed town or village and perhaps the jagged outline of a ruined castle on the crest of a low hill.

As we approach Évora rows of vines stretch out before us. Until fairly recently cork was the Alentejo's main connection with wine – cork oaks, stripped of their bark, are a common sight as you travel around – but this is now one of Portugal's fastest improving red wine regions. Alentejo is the name of the DOC as well as the province and there are eight sub-regions: Borba, Évora, Granja-Amareleja, Moura, Portalegre, Redondo, Reguengos and Vidigueira. The Vinho Regional wines, from the entire province stretching from the Tagus in the north to the Algarve in the south, use the name Alentejano.

The Portuguese used to deride the Alentejo as 'the land of bad bread and bad wine'. Conventional wisdom dictated that climate was against it. It seemed healthy, fault-free wine was impossible when the summer temperatures were high enough to force the indolent locals indoors out of the relentless sun. This wasn't helped in 1974 when the south was the most determined and aggressive part of Portugal in overthrowing the dictatorship. Having been a land primarily of absentee landlords – unlike the Douro where relationships between landowner and worker were close and the revolution was a positively gentlemanly affair – the peasants and workers relished occupying the large estates. Unfortunately they weren't interested in making them work, even on a co-operative basis. But now, with a bit of gleaming stainless steel technology, the Alentejo has begun to prove that it can produce fine wines, especially reds from evenly ripened native grapes.

Among the red grapes, Trincadeira and Aragonez are the best performers and both the white Arinto and scented Roupeiro manage to hang on to good, crisp natural acidity in spite of the heat. The best Alentejo vineyards are over to the east, not far from the Spanish border – Cartuxa near Évora, Quinta do Carmo and Quinta da Moura at Estremoz, Esporão near Reguengos, Cortes de Cima at Vidigueira, and Herdade do Mouchão at Sousel are just a few of the best properties. João Portugal Ramos is one of the country's top winemakers and from his base at Estremoz produces a superb range of wines, both pricy reds and juicy, affordable reds and whites. Co-operatives at Borba, Redondo and Reguengos are turning out some sound, full-flavoured reds.

ALGARVE

The title 'land of bad wine' should probably have passed to the Algarve where two large co-operatives bottle headaches for the tourists that flock here each year. Cliff Richard has shown what can be done by planting vines and producing something pretty serious which he calls Vida Nova ('New Life'), and top winemaker José Neiva is also in the region. The Lagoa co-operative makes an intriguing dry aperitif wine aged like *fino* sherry under a veil of flor.

MADEIRA

RED GRAPES
Tinta Negra Mole is Madeira's most widely planted variety.

WHITE GRAPES
White grapes all planted in fairly small quantities: Sercial, Verdelho, Bual and Malvasia.

CLIMATE
A warm, damp subtropical climate means that oidium and botrytis can be a problem. Rainfall varies from 3000mm (118in) inland to about one-third of that on the coast.

SOIL
The soil is volcanic. The pebbles of basalt have often weathered red.

ASPECT
The vineyards are planted on terraces up to 1000m (3280ft) in the south of the island and lower down in the north.

IT'S DIFFICULT TO GET a really good look at Madeira. The early Portuguese navigators who saw a bank of black cloud billowing over the Atlantic thought that they had reached the end of the world and steered well clear. Approaching the island's precarious airport today with a view of dark, cloud-covered mountains on one side and the ocean on the other, you could be forgiven for thinking the same.

There are two ways to appreciate Madeira when you have safely reached land. First of all, clamber down to the rocky shore that passes for a beach, turn your back on the sea and stare inland. Behind the subtropical shoreline with its decorative palms and exotic flowers, tiny shelf-like terraces stack up the mountainsides until they seem to be subsumed in the clouds. Then drive up one of the tortuous roads from the coast to Pico de Arieiro which, at 1818m (5965ft) above sea level, is nearly the highest point on the island. On the way you pass through a belt of dank mist, only to emerge in bright sunlight before the summit. From here you can see volcanic peaks poking through the cloud, but on a rare clear day you might glimpse the ocean.

On the face of it Madeira is an unlikely place to make wine. This humid, subtropical island 700km (435 miles) from the coast of North Africa has long, warm winters and torrid summers and a mean annual temperature in Funchal of 19°C (66°F) – hardly the temperate clime of the world's best wines. But Madeira wine certainly has individuality and there's no lack of finesse in a glass of venerable Malmsey. The answer is that the character of Madeira comes from the aging process: it may be wrong to say that the geography of the island has little effect, but when viticulture is geared to high yields of barely ripe grapes from vines under 15 years old, as it is here, you cannot expect even the faintest whiff of *terroir* to show through.

Like so many of the best inventions, Madeira wine came about almost by accident. Soon after the island was discovered, it became an important supply point for ships en route for Africa and the east. Wine was one of many goods to be taken on board and a generous drop of local brandy was added to prevent it from spoiling on its long voyage. The pitching and rolling across the tropics seemed to suit Madeira and it often tasted better when it reached its destination than at the start of the journey. The taste caught on and demand grew for *vinho da roda*, wine that had crossed the equator and back.

As Britain and the United States emerged as important customers for Madeira in the 19th century, merchants looked for ways to simulate the long but costly tropical sea voyages that had proved to be so beneficial to the wine. They built *estufas*, store rooms with huge vats heated by fires to produce the maderized aromas and flavours that the world had become accustomed to.

But Madeira's isolated island economy has suffered from a catastrophic cycle of boom and bust. The boom began in the eighteenth century when demand for Madeira began to outstrip supply. It lasted until the 1850s when oidium (powdery mildew) reached the island and spread rapidly through the vineyards encouraged by the warm, humid climate. Eventually, sulphur dusting of the vine leaves was found to cure the problem, but not before the island's monocrop economy had been devastated.

Worse still, 20 years later phylloxera struck, destroying entire vineyards in its wake. Shippers left the island, and the wine trade never really recovered.

Bananas replaced vines as the island's most important crop and the vineyards that remained were planted with disease-resistant hybrids which produced large amounts of dreary wine. In 1913 a number of shippers merged to form the Madeira Wine Association,

MADEIRA

TOTAL DISTANCE
NORTH TO SOUTH
21.5KM (13½ MILES)

VINEYARDS

PORTO MONIZ

RIBEIRA DA JANELA

ATLANTIC OCEAN

SEIXAL

SÃO VICENTE

PIC ARI

SERRA DA ÁGUA

CALHETA

JARDIM DA SERRA

PONTA DO SOL

CÂMARA DE LOBOS

RIBEIRA BRAVA

CABO GIRÃO

0 km   1   2
0 miles   1

precursor of the Madeira Wine Company which produces most Madeira today, as well as controlling more than half the exports. Few of the shippers own any vineyards, and land is now too expensive to buy. Instead they buy their grapes from myriad tiny smallholdings perched on little terraces, or *poios*, carved out of the mountainsides; with approximately 2000 growers owning only 1800ha (4448 acres) of vines, the average vineyard holding is tiny, covering only about half a hectare and the largest single vineyard on the island is less than 4ha (10 acres). This is hardly conducive to good or progressive viticulture.

Along with vines most farmers grow other crops, including bananas, avocados, lemons and, especially in the east of the island, willow for baskets and other tourist items. The warm, damp climate means that the vines have to be trained off the ground so as to lessen the risk of fungal diseases and this makes backbreaking work in the vineyards as the labourers duck beneath the lattice of straggly vines to apply treatments or harvest the grapes.

Agriculture is only really possible on Madeira because of the high annual rainfall on the inland mountains – more than three times as much as falls in Funchal down on the coast. This water is diverted into a complex network of over 2000km (1243 miles) of manmade channels called *levadas* which ensure an even distribution to every tiny property.

Most Madeira goes to the French market, for cooking rather than for drinking. It is made from the versatile, but dull local red *vinifera* grape, Tinta Negra Mole. The pale, pinky-red wine is fortified with grape brandy and heated in an *estufa* to between 40° and 50°C (104° and 122°F) for a minimum of 90 days. The cheaper wines made in this heavy-handed manner often smell and taste coarse and stewed and are a poor imitation of the real thing.

The finest Madeiras, usually produced from one of four top-quality or 'noble' grapes: Sercial, Verdelho, Bual and Malvasia, are made without any *estufagem* or artificial heating at all. They age slowly on *canteiros* or racks under the eaves in lodges in the island's capital, Funchal.

Warmed naturally by the sun, they gradually develop a unique pungency and intensity of flavour. Having been subject to this long, slow, controlled maturation, fine Madeira stands the test of time like no other wine.

Traditionally, different styles of Madeira have been distinguished from each other by the grapes from which the wines were made, and the styles range from dry to sweet. Of the four traditional 'noble' grape varieties, Verdelho and Malvasia are the most planted, and there are smaller amounts of Sercial and Bual. However, all the noble grapes together comprise anywhere between seven and 20 per cent of the total: nobody knows the true figure.

Sercial likes the coolest vineyards and grows on the north side of the island and at the highest altitudes in the south. With a lower accumulation of sugar it makes the driest wine with a distinctly sharp, acidic tang. Verdelho is also planted on the cooler, north coast, but in slightly warmer locations and it ripens more easily than Sercial, producing a wine that is softer and medium-dry. Bual is found growing on the warmer, steamy south side of the island where it produces richer, medium-sweet wines.

Finally, Malvasia (better known in English as Malmsey) grows in the warmest, low-altitude locations on the south coast, like the spectacular vineyards at the foot of the island's highest cliff, Cabo Girão. The darkest and sweetest Madeira, a good Malmsey will be raisiny and smoky, still retaining a characteristic tang of acidity which prevents the wine from cloying.

The productive American hybrid grapes which crept into the vineyards, following the destruction of the island's best vineyards by phylloxera, can no longer be used for bottled wine and most Madeira now comes from Tinta Negra Mole. Madeira producers have been obliged to comply with EU legislation which states that a varietal wine must be made from at least 85 per cent of the variety named on the label.

A replanting programme is currently underway in the Madeira vineyards to increase production of the four 'noble' varieties which are in short supply, but for the moment most Madeira blends are labelled only with the terms *seco* (dry), *meio seco* (medium-dry), *meio doce* (medium-sweet) and *doce* (sweet or rich).

Terraces are the only way of cultivating land in Madeira. Here vines rub shoulders with cabbages and other crops.

WHERE THE VINEYARDS ARE

Agriculture on this small, densely populated island is confined to the narrow coastal fringe, where banana plants compete with vines and other crops for precious space in the tiny terraced fields. Vineyards tend to be concentrated around the capital, Funchal, on the warmer south side of the island, where the best Malvasia and Bual vineyards are situated. In recent years, bananas have ousted vines from some of the best land above the picturesque fishing village of Câmara de Lobos. There are plots of Sercial at Jardim da Serra ('mountain garden') lying at around 900m (2952ft) above the south coast, but grapes for the drier styles of wine come mainly from the cooler vineyards clinging to the near-vertical slopes on the north side of the island. Here, the spectacular vineyards have to be protected from the fierce northerly winds by high bamboo and broom windbreaks. A few varietal wines are now being made from non-traditional grapes on the north side of the island and are sold under the Madeirense DOC.

ENGLAND & WALES

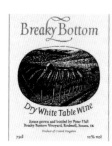

Wine production in England and Wales is no longer the domain of retired army officers, hobbyists and eccentrics. Although today's winegrowers still have to contend with apathy from the home market, a government which gives little help and the reliably unreliable weather, they are a much more professional bunch than they were 20 years ago. Many of the vineyards set up in the 1960s and '70s either no longer exist or just concentrate on grape-growing, leaving the winemaking to those better at it. Today's industry leaders, such as Chapel Down Wines, Denbies and Three Choirs, are as commercially run as any in the world. Many of the most successful winemakers have benefited from experience abroad and are well aware that their wines have to compete on the shelf with those from around the world. Even so the industry is tiny, with around 800ha (2000 acres) of vines, 330 vineyards (many very small), 115 wineries and an annnual average output of 2 million bottles.

While vines are planted as far north as Leeds and York, most lie below a line drawn from the Wash to the Bristol Channel. The counties of Kent, East Sussex and West Sussex are the most heavily planted. Vineyards in Britain are at the northern extreme of wine production and only possible due to the tempering influence of the Gulf Stream. Even so, summers have become much warmer during the last decade, and the UK now averages seven days a year over 30°C. Twenty years ago the average was 1½ days. Traditionally, Bordeaux only got seven days above 30°C! This has improved ripening, brought forward the harvesting date by several weeks and greatly improved vineyard yields, though they are still well below mainland European levels.

In the vineyards, the various subsoils include limestone, gravel, chalk (south Kent), clay (Essex, north Kent) and Kimmeridgian limestone clay (Dorset). Much of southern England has significant amounts of chalk or limestone, and the challenge is to find sheltered south-facing sites at below 100m (328ft). The grape varieties grown have changed dramatically in the last few years, and when all the new plantings are bearing fruit, the Champagne varieties of Chardonnay and Pinot Noir will outnumber the traditional German

crosses developed for cool climates. This is because of the remarkable success of English sparkling wines – not totally surprising when you consider that the chalk soils of Kent, Surrey and Sussex are the same as those of Champagne – just a couple of hours drive away across the Channel. Of the German varieties Müller-Thurgau is the most widely planted, followed by the black Reichensteiner, the Sauvignon-like Bacchus and the spicy Schönburger. Seyval Blanc is a French hybrid which makes some of Britain's best dry whites.

The style of white wines varies more between wineries than between regions, and depends on factors such as the ripeness of the grapes and winemaking techniques. The best are delicate and aromatic, with flavours of apples, grapefruit, elderflower, grapes and hints of smoke, with enough ripeness and depth to balance the crisp acidity. Wines from varieties such as Bacchus, Reichensteiner and Schönburger can be drunk young and one vineyard, Three Choirs, produces a 'nouveau', released in November after the harvest. In the past, sweetness was sometimes added to counter excess acidity, but that is changing. Clean, grapy fruit has replaced clumsiness in the better wines, with residual sweetness being retained from fermentation, rather than added later. Some excellent late-harvest botrytized dessert wines are also made. Sparkling wines have made remarkable strides too, with suitable clones of Chardonnay and Pinot Noir being increasingly used to make top quality products. The best whites, both still and sparkling, can be long lived.

Ripening red varieties can be a problem, but today, with better varieties and techniques, including the occasional use of top quality French and American oak *barriques*, results can be impressive. Although grown less widely than whites, red varieties are becoming more popular, with Regent, Rondo, Dornfelder and Pinot Noir being the most widespread. The best are produced by Chapel Down, Denbies and Valley Vineyards.

Regulations now require growers to submit their wines for testing before they can label them 'English' or 'Welsh'. Wines labelled 'UK table wine' should be avoided.

• SELECTED VINEYARDS

1. Astley	26. Breaky Bottom
2. Heart of England	27. Hidden Spring
3. Frome Valley	28. Davenport
4. Three Choirs	29. Sandhurst
5. Llanerch	30. Chapel Down (English Wine Group)
6. Glyndwr	31. Tenterden (English Wine Group)
7. Camel Valley	32. Biddenden
8. Sharpham	33. Leeds Castle
9. Yearlstone	34. Barnsole
10. Wylye Valley	35. New Hall
11. A'Beckett's	36. Mersea
12. Beaulieu Abbey	37. Carters
13. Danebury	38. Warden Abbey
14. Northbrook Springs	39. Chilford Hall
15. Wickham	40. Shawsgate
16. Priors Dean	
17. Bothy	
18. Chiltern Valley	
19. Stanlake Park	
20. Nutbourne	
21. Nyetimber	
22. Denbies	
23. Bookers	
24. RidgeView	
25. Plumpton	

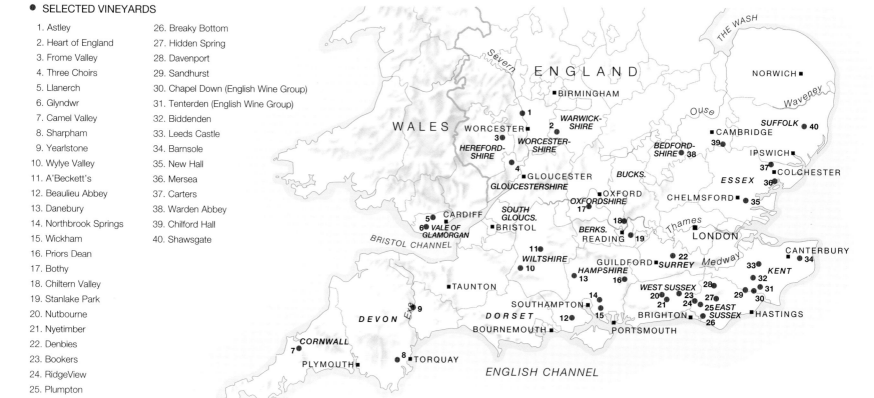

CZECH REPUBLIC & SLOVAKIA

W HEN CZECHOSLOVAKIA WAS ONE NATION there was a pretty natural divide: Slovakia made the wine, the Czechs brewed the beer. Yet this divide is simplistic. Slovakia generally has better conditions for viticulture; indeed in the far east of the country, some of the original villages for the famous sweet Hungarian wine, Tokaji (or Tokay in English), lie within its borders. But the Czech vineyards of Morava are almost as good. Nevertheless, if I had to choose the wines from either country that have given me most pleasure, they would be the violet-scented, damsony St-Laurent, the boudoir-perfumed Irsay Oliver and the crackly, peppery, celery stick Grüner Veltliner – all from Slovakia.

Despite the gluggability of that St-Laurent – and the occasional Frankovka – both countries are better suited to white, rather than red wine production. There's huge potential for quality here: the latitude is virtually the same as that of Alsace and many of the best wines have the same spicy fatness; most companies are run on a refreshingly human scale; and Australian and French winemakers, there to advise, say that the winemaking equipment in several cellars is pretty good.

After the division of the country into two in 1989, Slovakia found itself with two-thirds of the former nation's vineyards. Nonetheless, talk to the café drinkers of Prague (Praha) and they all swear that the best wines come from the Morava region on the Czech side of the border. Well, Prague cafés may be very seductive places in which to drink, but I'll stick with Slovakia for now, especially as the flying winemakers there are making a fair go of raising standards without sacrificing individuality.

Both countries enjoy a settled continental climate: warm and dry in the growing season, with cool, dry autumns and little variation between regions, though Slovakia is slightly warmer. If we start in the west, most of Čechy's 500ha (1235 acres) of vineyards are clustered round the Elbe (Labe) and its tributaries. These wines, seldom seen outside the region, resemble their Sachsen counterparts across the border in Germany, being dry with marked acidity – you begin to see why most people drink the beer. Moving south-east, Morava's 11,500ha (28,416 acres) of vineyards are planted in the valleys of the Dyje, Svratka and Morava rivers, which flow into the Danube (Dunaj). The grapes are mainly Grüner Veltliner, Müller-Thurgau, Welschriesling, Ryzlink Rynsky (Riesling) and Pinot Blanc for whites, and the spicy, plummy, St-Laurent and Lemberger for reds. The wines from around Znojmo have a good reputation, and sparkling wines are made in Mikulov and Bzenec.

Slovakia's 12,000ha (29,652 acres) of vineyards are located mainly around the Váh, Nitra and Hron tributaries of the Danube. The vines are planted on undulating land around Bratislava or on the foothills of the Tatry mountains, although there are several smaller vine-growing regions as you travel east along the border with Hungary, each producing mainly perfumed whites such as Irsay Oliver, Veltliner and Riesling, and a few light reds. Slovakia's most important producer is the state winery at Nitra, while Western investment is improving quality in the smaller wineries to the south and west, such as Gbelce and Hurbanovo near the Hungarian border at Komárno. The grape varieties grown here are virtually the same as the Czech ones, with the addition of some tasty Grüner Veltliners, the fruity Frankovka red and the local Ezerjó and Leányka. In Tokai, at Slovakia's eastern extreme, Furmint, Hárslevelü and Muscat Ottonel can produce wines of similar character to the more famous Tokaji wines of neighbouring Hungary.

The loss of the Soviet market in the late 1980s meant that the wineries need more than ever to export to the West, and this will have been helped by both countries' accession to the EU in 2004. Governmental organization seems to have progressed slightly more quickly in the Czech Republic than in Slovakia, but foreign companies – and indeed domestic wine producers – are still waiting for the dust to settle before investing.

SLOVAKIA WINE REGIONS

- 17 Malokarpatský
- 18 Južnoslovenský
- 19 Nitriansky
- 20 Strodoslovenský
- 21 Východoslovenský
- 22 Tokai

CZECH REPUBLIC WINE REGIONS AND AREAS

ČECHY REGION
- 1 Mostecká
- 2 Žernosecká
- 3 Roudnická
- 4 Mělnická
- 5 Pražská
- 6 Čáslavská

MORAVA REGION
- 7 Znojemská
- 8 Brněnská
- 9 Mikulovská
- 10 Velkopavlovická
- 11 Podluží
- 12 Mutěnická
- 13 Kyjovská
- 14 Bzenecká
- 15 Strážnická
- 16 Uherskohradištská

HUNGARY

Vines high above Lake Balaton looking down towards the castle of Szigliget. The warmth of the lake and good sandy/volcanic soil combine to produce some of Hungary's best white wines, the most exciting being from the Szürkebarát and Kéknyelu.

I THINK I'VE ONLY DONE IT ONCE. Given a perfect score to a wine: 20 out of 20. A 1957 Tokaji. Somehow this bottle had escaped the process of homogenization that the Hungarian wine industry suffered after the Soviet invasion of 1956. Of all Eastern Europe's nations, Hungary's traditions were the proudest and most individual, and they died slowly under the Soviet system of state-run farms and wineries.

In the 1960s, fine reds were still being released under the Bull's Blood or Egri Bikavér label. Indeed it was international distributors clamouring for the rights to such a marketable name that encouraged the authorities to debase what was a splendid wine. At the end of the 1960s, you could still find marvellous yet fiery golden whites, almost viscous lanolin in texture, with sparks of spicy perfume. Historic white wines such as Hárslevelű (meaning 'linden leaf') from Debrő, an old wine region now part of Mátra, and Szürkebarát (Pinot Gris) and Kéknyelű from Badacsony, fell into a sleep through the 1970s and '80s. The 1990s saw a reawakening of Hungary's pride and energy and the rebirth of Hungary as a great wine producer began again at breakneck speed. EU membership in 2004 can only accelerate this further.

The wine export boom in the 1990s was led by international grape varieties – full of flavour and extremely cheap, in particular Chardonnay, Sauvignon Blanc, Pinot Gris, Cabernet and Merlot – and the country enthusiastically welcomed the Antipodean 'flying winemakers'. But top Hungarian winemakers, such as Akos Kamocsay and Vilmos Thummerer, are emerging, determined to put New World principles into practice, as well as to rediscover Hungary's great past: they are set to produce gorgeous wines from both international and indigenous varieties. The Tokaj region has already attracted multinational wealth and expertise. Other regions, well stocked with international grape varieties, plus a clutch of marvellous indigenous ones, are ideally placed for the 21st century.

White plantings still dominate, but red varieties are increasing and now account for 29 per cent of the vineyards. There are now 85,260ha (210,675 acres) of vineyards split into 22 regions. Most of the country's output – easy-drinking styles made from Olasz Rizling and Kékfrankos grapes – comes from the Great Plains (Alföld)

between the Danube (Duna) and Tisza rivers, where the sandy soil is suitable for little but viticulture. Hungary's climate is similar to much of inland Europe, warm and dry, with altitude bringing the only variation. However, the vineyards around Lake Balaton enjoy the tempering effect of central Europe's largest lake.

AROUND LAKE BALATON

On the north shore, Badacsony and Balatonfüred-Csopak produce some of Hungary's best whites. They benefit from well-drained soil – a mix of sand and volcanic rock – and gain heat from the sun's reflection off the lake. Badacsony produces good to excellent Olasz Rizling (Welschriesling), Szürkebarát and Traminer, as well as its own local variety, the spicy but increasingly rare Kéknyelű. East of Badacsony, Balatonfüred was a vineyard and spa town in Roman times. The vineyards, on the south-facing lower slopes of the Bakony hills, are planted with 60 per cent Olasz Rizling, more's the pity.

Balatonboglár on the southern shore of the lake is one of the country's newest regions. The wines are mainly whites made from familiar varieties such as Chardonnay, Sauvignon Blanc, Olasz Rizling, Rhine Riesling and Traminer, as well as less well-known Irsai Olivér and Királyleányka. You may find a Chasselas-based sparkling wine, as well as the occasional red made from Merlot, Pinot Noir, Cabernet Sauvignon, Kékfrankos, Zweigelt and Kékoportó. Heavy investment is paying off with noticeable quality increases.

THE SOUTH

Located between the Danube and Tisza rivers, the region of Kunság has one-third of Hungary's vines but most are everyday whites for local consumption. Better for reds is Villány, down on the Croatian border, with its loam and limestone soil. The eastern end of the region produces lovely, juicy, soft red wines made from Kékoportó, Kékfrankos, Cabernet Sauvignon and Merlot, while further west around Siklós is better for whites: Chardonnay, Olasz Rizling, Traminer and Hárslevelű.

The Pécs region has Chardonnay and good Olasz Rizling, while Szekszárd has its own Bikavér as well as Ovörös – old red wine – made mainly from Kékfrankos, popular in Hungary but rarely seen abroad.

THE NORTH-EAST

The south-facing vineyards of Eger are famous for Egri Bikavér (Bull's Blood of Eger), once a hearty blend of Kadarka, Kékfrankos, Cabernet Sauvignon, Kékoportó and Merlot. While vinous anaemia may have diluted much of the current output, especially where Kadarka has been replaced, good examples can still be found, particularly those made by winemakers such as Vilmos Thummerer. And new stringent regulations controlling varieties, release and quality are correcting the overall situation.

There are interesting white wines made from Leányka, Hárslevelű and Cserszegi Füszeres, but the increasing presence of Chardonnay and Olasz Rizling means that these are becoming harder to find.

In the foothills of the Mátra mountains, the Nagyréde co-operative has a reputation for reds and rosés made from Kadarka, but the best wines have been whites made by visiting international winemakers like Hugh Ryman and Kym Milne.

THE NORTH-WEST

Mór's speciality has long been a high-alcohol white from the Ezerjó grape (*ezerjó* means 'a thousand good things'), of which the locals have long been proud; but it is most definitely not my favourite style of wine. To the north, Ászár-Neszmély is best known for white wines, including Olasz Rizling, Chardonnay and Irsai Olivér.

TOKAJI WINE

Wine from the region of Tokaj is truly the stuff of legend. A Commission for Hungarian wines was set up in St Petersburg to ensure regular supplies for the Tsars, and bottles of the precious nectar were kept by the bedside to revive ailing monarchs. The communist regimes of the 20th century succeeded in removing most traces of greatness from the region by blending the top wines with the mediocre, achieving something which, while perfectly drinkable, was hardly remarkable. New ownership is beginning to restore much of the wine's former glory.

The wine has been produced since the middle of the 16th century and in 1700, 56 years before the demarcation of the Douro vineyards in Portugal, the Rákóczi family, one-time princes of Transylvania (now part of Romania), made the first appraisal of the Tokaji vineyards, which were spread out between 28 villages north-west of the town of Tokaj at the confluence of the Tisza and Bodrog rivers. A subsequent classification in 1804 defined three Great First Growths, followed by First, Second, Third and Unclassified Growths. The three Great First Growths were all on the slopes of Mount Kopaszhegy or 'Bald Mountain' near the village of Tarcal, north-west of Tokaj. Of these, only Mézesmály remains, the rest having been amalgamated with various other First Growth areas.

Most of the vineyards are on south-east to south-west-facing slopes, but what makes the great vineyards great is their soil. Vineyards with fast-draining loess north-west of Tokaj, near Tarcal and Mad, are considered the best. The other Tokaji soils are largely stony clays. Vines on loess ripen faster and give the richest, most aromatic wines. Those on clays tend to produce wines of higher acidity (and possibly longer life). The best vineyards have slopes of 15 per cent or more, the middle part of the slope being the best.

The region is sheltered by the Carpathian mountains to the north-east, while warm winds off the Great Plains maintain a reasonably high temperature. Indeed, drought at vintage time can be a problem. Mists rising from the Bodrog river in autumn encourage the onset of noble rot in the Furmint grapes, which make up around two-thirds of a typical Tokaji with the balance being the sugar-rich Hárslevelű and Muskotály (Muscat Ottonel).

The botrytized grapes, known as *aszú*, spend about a week in a bucket, during which time an unctuous juice known as *eszencia* seeps out. This precious fluid is so rich in sugar that, even with special strains of yeasts, it can take years to ferment. Pure Eszencia is usually used to bolster lesser wines, but bottles do appear occasionally. In spite of all that sugar, Eszencia does not taste hugely sweet – colossal acidity levels balance it out nicely. But it's so thick it's virtually impossible to drink – you almost have to chew it.

After the removal of the Eszencia, the remaining grapes are mashed to a syrupy paste, and then added to dry base wine. The quality of the wine is determined by the number of *puttonyos* (30-litre tubs) of paste added to each *gönc* (136-litre barrel) of dry wine. Two-*puttonyos* wine is never made; three, four and five are reasonably easy to find; six is only made in good years. The 'Aszú Eszencia' available today is about an eight-*puttonyos* wine, while 'Szamorodni' (literally 'as it comes') is a wine to which no *aszú* has been added, and can come as either a sweet (*édes*) or dry (*száraz*) wine. Neither form is particularly attractive, having a rather sherry-like character that cries out for sweetening from the *aszú* grapes.

After the grape paste has steeped in the base wine for around a week, the wine is racked off to begin its long, slow fermentation in barrel. In the past, the state-owned casks were not always topped up and the oxidized styles that resulted became the norm. Now, non-oxidized styles are taking over, allowing the botrytized flavours of the wine to shine through. In addition, a flor-like fungus attacks the wine, giving it further complexity. The resulting flavours – a perfumed cocktail of apricots, marzipan, blood oranges, smoke, spice, tea and tobacco – do take some getting used to, but they are certainly unique in the world of wine, and Tokaji clearly deserves a place among the world's great sweet wines.

Most Tokaji is sweet, and its intensity is measured in puttonyos. *Five* puttonyos *wine, such as this one, is very sweet but by no means the sweetest.*

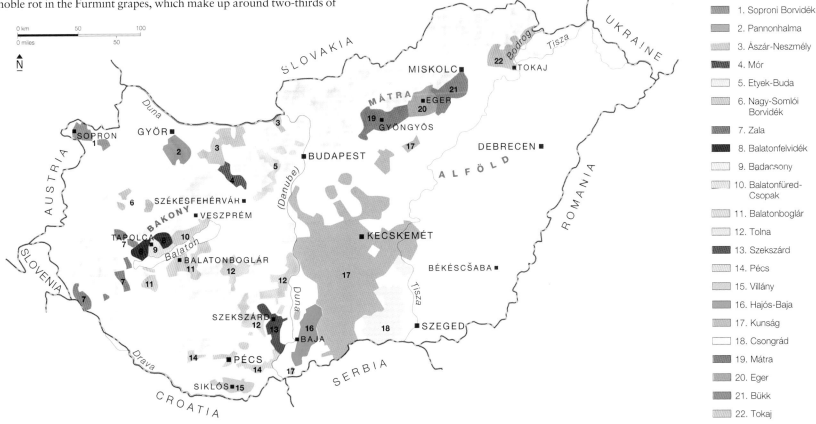

WINE REGIONS

1. Soproni Borvidék
2. Pannonhalma
3. Ászár-Neszmély
4. Mór
5. Etyek-Buda
6. Nagy-Somlói Borvidék
7. Zala
8. Balatonfelvidék
9. Badacsony
10. Balatonfüred-Csopak
11. Balatonboglár
12. Tolna
13. Szekszárd
14. Pécs
15. Villány
16. Hajós-Baja
17. Kunság
18. Csongrád
19. Mátra
20. Eger
21. Bükk
22. Tokaj

BLACK SEA STATES

I'M NOT SURE THE WINEMAKING PICTURE since the collapse of the Soviet Union is any clearer than it used to be. A few old certainties have been replaced by a swarm of uncertainties, and only a handful of them have so far done anything to improve the wine.

MOLDOVA

One of my most startling wine discoveries of the 1990s was a wine that needed to be opened about ten hours before drinking, that came in dusty, misshapen bottles with labels hand-scrawled in Cyrillic and tasted as though it was some great old Pauillac – Latour, perhaps, or Lafite. Negru de Purkar 1967. A dark, dauntingly dry wine, it seemed to be fatally cocooned in cobwebs and neglect at first sip, but after half a day's patient wait, it developed an aroma of cedarwood, the cherished volumes of an old bachelor's library, mingled with blackcurrants with all their sugar lost in time, but their essence and intensity preserved for eternity. Based on the local Saperavi grape and mellowed with a bit of Cabernet Sauvignon and Rara Niagra, this was the cream of the Moldovan crop, to be broached only when the local Party bosses went feasting. These bottles of Negru de Purkar – and several others like them – showed that Moldova really did deserve its great 19th-century reputation and that the glories could be recreated.

Winemaking is a major part of the Moldovan economy and 7.5 per cent of agricultural land is planted with vines, tended by over 70,000 smallholders. Moldova used to provide one-fifth of the wine for the former Soviet Union but it is still suffering dreadfully in the wake of its emergence as an independent state with chaotic social conditions and poor infrastructure; and then Moldova's major export market, Russia, temporarily banned imports of their wine in 2006.

At the invitation of Tsar Alexander, French winemakers brought their grapes and expertise to Moldova in the early 19th century. The result is a long history of growing 'noble' European grapes such as Chardonnay and Sauvignon Blanc, Cabernet Sauvignon, Pinot Noir (here known as Pinot Franc) and Merlot, and these varieties still account for 70 per cent of the plantings. The vineyards are shrinking year by year, and are down to about 146,300ha (361,502 acres), with white grape plantings leading by about three to one. Standards of winemaking and equipment still leave much to be desired, but the quality of the fruit is good, and international players, including Jacques Lurton, Alain Thiénot and Southcorp Wines have all reported on the great potential here. Now local winemakers are carrying on the good work.

Although the country has no coastline, the Black Sea still has a tempering effect on the continental climate. Summers are dry and reasonably warm, although enough rain falls in the rest of the year to prevent the need for irrigation. Well-drained loess and loam soils cover three-quarters of the country, with the southern regions having more clay and more northerly areas having some limestone and marl.

There are four main wine regions: Bălţi in the north, Codru in the centre, Cahul in the south and Nistreana in the south-east. Codru has 60 per cent of Moldova's vines and suits varieties like Sauvignon Blanc and Chardonnay. The vineyards in the warmer, drier south and south-east are better for reds. There has been a massive replanting since the millennium and investment is now on the increase too, following some turbulent years when few outsiders were willing to risk their money or, indeed, their lives making any great investment in Moldova.

WINE AREAS

- MOLDOVA
- UKRAINE
- RUSSIA
- GEORGIA
- ARMENIA
- AZERBAIJAN

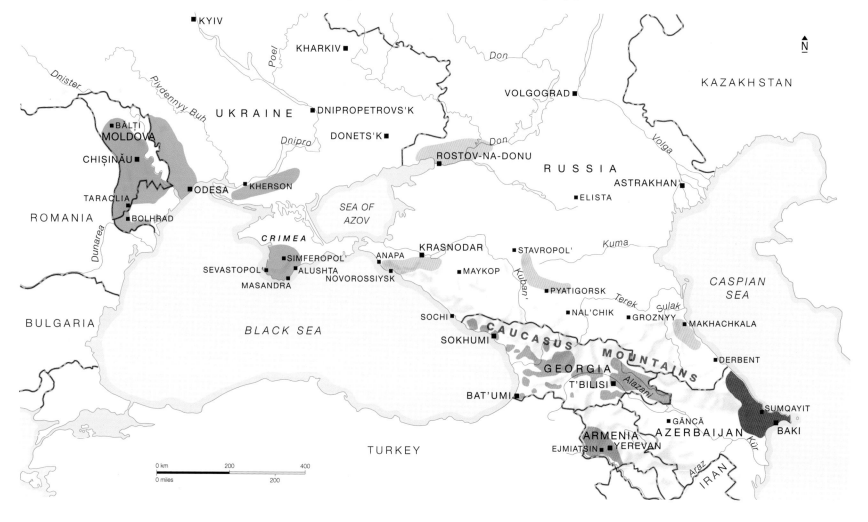

The most important white grapes are Aligoté (used mainly for sparkling wine), Rkatsiteli, Sauvignon Blanc, Feteasca, Chardonnay and Traminer. The leading reds are Merlot, Cabernet Sauvignon, Pinot Franc and Saperavi, the great Georgian grape. Malbec and Syrah are now also being planted.

The vineyard area around Bălţi in the north is mainly white grape country destined for fortified wines and brandies. The south-eastern zone is home to the historic Purkari winery, and reds, especially Cabernet, are important here. Negru de Purkar, a blend of Cabernet and Saperavi plus an occasional dollop of Rara Niagra, can age remarkably well into something similar to fine old-fashioned Médoc, despite corks the size of thimbles. Romaneşti, from north of Chişinău, is another good red, and takes its name from the former owners of a vineyard here, the Romanovs. Cricova produces good Cabernet, although it is better known for its sparkling wines. Made mainly from Chardonnay and Pinot Franc, these are among the best traditional-method wines from the Black Sea countries: they mature in vast underground cellars linked by a 65km (40 mile) road network complete with road signs and traffic lights. Cahul, the southern region, does best with red wines and sweet whites.

UKRAINE

Viticulture accounts for one fifth of the Ukraine's agricultural economy. It is based on three principal wine-growing regions: Crimea (Krym) in the south, Odesa to the south-west, and the shrinking area of Kherson on the Dnipro river. Crimea's vineyards are mostly along the coast of the Black Sea peninsula, since inland temperatures can be too cold in winter. Here sparkling and sweet table wines predominate, of which Cagur, a port-like wine, is the most popular locally. Ruby of Crimea, a hearty blend of Saperavi, Matrassa, Aleatica, Cabernet and Malbec, also has a good reputation, but I've never been brave enough to finish the bottle when I've encountered it abroad.

Odesa, the largest region, has about 40,000ha (98,839 acres) of vines on the Black Sea coast, and has a long tradition of sparkling wine production. This dates back to 1896 when a member of the Roederer family established a Russian-French company to produce sparkling wine from local grapes. Today, Aligoté, Rkatsiteli, Sukhul Lamanski – meaning 'dry sea' – and Cabernet Sauvignon are the major varieties grown.

The most interesting wine region, though, is Crimea. The best wines ever to have come from the area were those produced at the Masandra winery, near Yalta. Originally destined for the Tsar's summer palace at Livadia, these superb dessert and fortified wines started being made in the early 19th century. The quality of current releases does not appear to be up to the splendid level of these museum pieces (some of which, at over a hundred years old, caused quite a stir when they were auctioned by Sotheby's in London in 1990), but the potential for a return to those glory days clearly exists. In the main, present day winemaking seems regrettably aimless. A little foreign investment is trickling through, however.

GEORGIA

More than 5000 years of wine history make Georgia a front runner for the title of birthplace or cradle of wine. Today this former Soviet republic, sitting between Russia and Turkey, is an independent state, reeling from 70 years of Soviet rule and the political upheavals of the 1990s. With its subtropical to moderate continental climate, frost-free winters and hugely diverse soils, the five vine-growing regions (Kakheti, Kartli, Racha-Leckhumi, Imereti and the subtropical zone around the Black Sea, embracing several smaller regions) produce a

great diversity of styles. The area under vine has decreased to about 64,000ha (158,142 acres) in Georgia, with the vast majority of winemaking grapes (some 70 per cent) coming from Kakheti, which spans the south-eastern foothills of the Caucasus Mountains in the east of the country. Kakheti wines can be fragrant but tannic. Most recognizably 'European' style wine comes from the central Kartli area, around Georgia's capital, T'blisi.

There are hundreds of different grape varieties at the disposal of the country's winemakers, but only 38, both indigenous and international, are approved for wine production. Of the indigenous varieties, Saperavi, an ancient red making brawny, peppery, Syrah-like wines, holds out the most promise. Saperavi has health-giving properties, reputedly giving drinkers 'more flexible blood vessels', thanks to its high potassium content – and it's one of the reasons Georgians are so famously long-lived. The obscure Matrassa grape makes rather solid reds. Two of Georgia's best known white wines, Gurjaani and Tsinandali, are Rkatsiteli-Mtsvane blends aged in oak for three years. Other important white varieties are Chinuri (particularly for sparkling wine), Krakhuna, Tsitska and Tsolikauri.

Georgian wine comes in every colour and degree of sweetness imaginable. Most wines, originally destined for the sadly depleted Russian market, leave much to be desired, although new investment is slowly having an impact. The country's major producer and exporter is the Georgian Wines & Spirits Company (GWS). Established in 1993 as a joint venture with Pernod Ricard and now 75 per cent owned by them, it owns 700ha (1730 acres) of vineyards and a highly modernized winery in the Kakhetian city of T'elavi, and was set on the right path by Australian winemaker David Nelson incorporating a little New World flair.

The challenges for the industry in the coming years are the resistance to change, an unhealthy interest in counterfeiting and the lack of very necessary wine production and vineyard quality control regulations. But the tourist industry is vibrant and helping to introduce Georgian wines to a wider audience.

RUSSIA

Climate dictates viticultural success here. Russia has two main vineyard regions, both in areas where the presence of a mass of water tempers the effect of the icy winters. Around Krasnodar on the Black Sea coast, Riesling, Aligoté, Sauvignon, Sémillon, Pinot Gris and Cabernet Sauvignon are used for still and sparkling wines, with the best coming from vineyards around Anapa, just along the coast to the north. Further north at Rostov, where the Don river runs into the sea of Azov, sparkling wines of varying hues and sweetness levels are made from Plechistick, giving backbone, and the Black Tsimlyansky grape. The area near Stavropol has a reputation for dry Riesling and Silvaner and sweet Muscat. There are also vineyards producing reds and dessert wines on the Caspian Sea coast around Makhachkala.

KAZAKHSTAN, AZERBAIJAN AND ARMENIA

Heading north along the same coast, Kazakhstan has a long tradition of dessert wines and Riesling. Further south, the vineyards of Azerbaijan grow Bayan Shirey, Matrassa, Isabella and several other indigenous varieties. The Sadilly white and Matrassa red from near the city of Baku (Baki) on the Caspian Sea are the not-too-bright stars twinkling dimly in a firmament of Azerbaijani dessert wines, port-like only in their alcohol levels. The similarly alcoholic reds and fortified wines of Armenia are equally uninspiring, although the wines of the Ejmiatsin region are reputed to be quite good. But frankly, how would I know? The political situation in such areas as these is so unstable that I don't get in, and the wines don't get out.

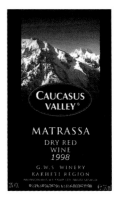

ROMANIA

Although surrounded on most flanks by people of Slavic origin, the proud brown eyes of the Romanian burn with a definite Latin fire. The capital Bucharest, even after the ravages of Ceauçescu and subsequent turmoil and unrest, still has much of the ambience and architecture that earned it the soubriquet 'Little Paris'. It comes as no surprise, then, to learn that grapes have been grown in the country for more than 6000 years.

Romania covers much the same latitudes as France, but its climate is very different, being generally continental, with hot summers and cold winters. The Black Sea exerts a moderating influence, while the Carpathian mountains act as a barrier to cooler weather systems from the north. In general, the northern regions of the country, especially Moldova and Transylvania, favour white wine production, while the best reds come from the south, from Muntenia and Dobrogea.

Major replanting programmes, both at the end of the 19th century after phylloxera, and in the 1960s under the communists, have meant that Romania now produces more wine than any other Balkan state, and has the fifth-largest area under vine – 222,000ha (548,554 acres) – in Europe (after Spain, France, Italy and Portugal). The first set of replantings introduced French varieties to the country, notably Cabernet Sauvignon, Merlot and Pinot Noir. The second was mainly of indigenous varieties. As a result, Romania now has some of the best raw materials in Eastern Europe, in the form of mature, reasonably healthy vines of a wide range of familiar and unfamiliar grape varieties, and some superbly sited vineyards.

Such a state of affairs should have led to a major Romanian assault on the world wine market, but the political situation hinders progress, while the wine industry here desperately lacks investment. EU membership from 2007 may shake things up: both in the build-up to joining the EU and since there has been large-scale replanting in the vineyards, to replace the large amounts of prohibited hybrid vines with *Vitis vinifera* varieties such as Pinot Noir, Cabernet Sauvignon, Merlot and the native Feteascǎ Neagrǎ for the reds, Pinot Gris and Chardonnay for the whites, and to increase the amount of quality wine produced (currently less than 10 per cent). A disastrous harvest in 2005 which cut production by 50 per cent did not help the situation.

Modern winemaking, along with winemaking expertise from abroad and new equipment, is beginning to make a difference, but bottle shortages, conflicting tax regulations and limited ownership of local companies don't help. International-backed ventures such as Cramele Recas, Halewood and Carl Reh are a sign of the mini-revolution but challenges remain as over one-third of the vineyard plots are 1ha (2½ acres) or less in size. Neither do local tastes help. Romanian wine drinkers still take the age of a wine as a sign of quality, and tannin as a defect in reds as well as in whites. Their preference for strong sweet wines, especially reds, needs to adapt if the production of wines attractive to world markets – and currencies – is to become the order of the day. Having said that, there's no doubt that where temperature can be regulated and where there is some residual sugar, the whites can certainly be good, if not great. Dessert styles, whether botrytis-affected or not, can be excellent. The tendency to high acidity means

WINE REGIONS AND MAIN SUB-REGIONS

MOLDOVA
1. Cotnari
2. Iaşi
3. Bohotin
4. Huşi
5. Dealu Bujorului
6. Nicoreşti
7. Panciu
8. Odobeşti
9. Coteşti

DOBROGEA
10. Sarica-Niculitel
11. Babadag
12. Murfatlar

DANUBE TERRACES
13. Oltina

MUNTENIA-OLTENIA
14. Pietroasa
15. Dealul Mare
16. Stefaneşti
17. Sambureşti
18. Drǎgǎşani
19. Dealurile Olteniei

BANAT
20. Banat
21. Recaş

CRIŞANA-MARAMURES
22. Minis
23. Crisana

TRANSYLVANIA
24. Lechinţa
25. Aiud
26. Alba Iulia
27. Sebeş-Apold
28. Târnave

that wines of 30 years old or more still taste remarkably fresh, although more fruit flavours might be welcome.

The same could be said for much of the red wine, where softness is the desired attribute, and there is frequently a degree of sweetness, although this is disappearing. Warm fermentations bring out jammy characteristics in many, and long aging in oak does nothing to promote freshness. Some offerings are particularly rustic. The fruit could be of sufficiently high quality to mask winemaking defects but, infuriatingly, just as we are starting to see wines that are made to reasonably modern standards, they've started ripping all the grapes off the vines before they're ripe. The new dawn has produced a trickle of correct but fruitless wines, and I rather pine for the old-fashioned versions which at least were packed with flavour.

GRAPE VARIETIES

Of the native grape varieties, herby, rustic Fetească Neagră is the best red, producing deep-coloured, robust wines that are full and fruity when young, but which can age for decades. Babeașcă Neagră and Crimpiosa produce lighter wines, while Cadarca (the same as Hungary's Kadarka) is used for more basic glug in the west of the country.

For dry whites, the spicy, grapefruity Fetească Albă and Fetească Regală are the most interesting grapes, while the ubiquitous Riesling is always the inferior Riesling Italico, rather than Rhine Riesling. The best sweet wines usually come from Grasă and Tămîioasă (both Alba and Româneasca) – Tămîioasă is the Romanian name for Muscat and it is known as the frankincense grape due to its aroma – while Traminer, Tămîioasă Ottonel (Muscat Ottonel) and Kékfrankos, here known as Burgund Mare, are used for wines of all degrees of sweetness and quality.

Most successful of the international varieties are Cabernet Sauvignon, Pinot Noir and Merlot for reds, Chardonnay and Pinot Gris for whites. An increasing number of plantings that were thought to be other varieties are, on closer inspection, turning out to be Sauvignon Blanc which means, happily for the growers, that both demand and price are increasing.

ROMANIA'S WINE REGIONS

Like its neighbours, Romania had to redefine its wine legislation on joining the EU. These are the current classifications: VM for table wine and VMS for superior table wine; quality wines are divided into VS or Country wines, equivalent to France's vin de pays system; wines from a controlled area of origin are DOC, with quality grades similar to German ripeness categories: wines from fully ripe grapes are labelled DOC-CMD; late harvested grapes, DOC-CT; nobly rotten grapes, DOC-CIB – a strange hybrid of French and German ideas of classification.

The appellations fall within seven main wine regions. Moldova, in the north-east, is predominantly white wine country. At Bucium, near Iași, whites made with Aligoté and Traminer can be especially good. Merlot is the best of the reds, demonstrating a minty, eucalyptus character, and sparkling wines are also made. Nicorești is known for its Babeașcă Neagră, and the Pinot Noir from Cotești has a good reputation. But a sweet wine known as the Pearl of Moldova is the region's pride and used to be Romania's most famous wine. Cotnari is a sweet, botrytis-affected white which at one time enjoyed the same prestige as Hungary's Tokaji. Cotnari is sheltered from the cold east winds by a range of hills. It enjoys warmth and mist, and the harvest continues as late into the year as November. In good years, sugar levels can reach 300g per litre, and the wines, bursting with raisin, honey and orange peel flavours, taste fantastic and can last almost indefinitely.

Murfatlar, with 2000ha (4942 acres) of vineyards in the centre of the Dobrogea region, produces some of Romania's best reds, full and fruity. The 210 days of sunshine a year are tempered by cool winds from the nearby Black Sea, permitting an extended growing season. Long, warm autumns encourage the development of noble rot in the Tămîioasă, Pinot Gris and Chardonnay grapes, producing the prized sweet wines. Once Romania gets itself sorted out, there is every reason to hope that this could become a really classic vineyard region.

Muntenia's main wine district, Dealul Mare, in the foothills of the Carpathian mountains, is one of the largest – at 14,500ha (35,829 acres) – and most important regions, where the warm climate allows the production of good, and not excessively tannic, red wines. It is particularly known for Pinot Noir, Cabernet Sauvignon and Merlot. There is a sporadically brilliant white wine made in Pietroasa to the east, whose vines thrive in the calcareous, stony soil, and whose Tămîioasă grapes are often affected by botrytis.

Stefanești, on the Argeș, produces reasonable dry and sweet white wines, as does Drăgășani on the left bank of the Olt. The Cabernet Sauvignon from the Olt's opposite bank at Samburești is highly regarded.

Transylvania's premium wine area is Târnave, surrounding the Târnava Mare and Târnava Mică rivers. The high altitude means a cool climate, although the rivers act as a tempering influence. White grapes predominate, and Traminer makes particularly good wines at several levels of sweetness.

In the west, Banat produces a large output of drinkable whites and everyday reds but, so far, it has not excelled itself in either colour. Crișana-Maramures, towards the border with Hungary, is best known for its white wines.

The label design may seem a bit dated, but Cotnari wine was once famous throughout Europe and is still an intensely sweet impressive mouthful.

Romania has suffered much turbulence in the last generation, but Transylvania, caught in the crook of the Carpathian mountains, has survived better than most. This tranquil street in the town of Ernea is in the Tarnave region where the Feteasca and Traminer grapes make fresh, fragrant whites, both dry and sweet.

WESTERN BALKANS

T HE WESTERN BALKAN STATES – torn by civil war in the early 1990s and still troubled in many areas – are working hard to rebuild their wine industry and infrastructure. The good news is Slovenia is now well-established as a separate nation, and is beginning to realize her considerable potential.

The western Balkans lie roughly across the same latitudes as Italy, with similar viticultural conditions, and yet the two wine industries share few characteristics. Austria, due north of Slovenia, provides more of a comparison with its aromatic, sometimes sweet, wines. And strong links in wine styles cross from Hungary to parts of Croatia and Slovenia.

The large area of Croatian vineyards are now recovering following the war, with many being replanted. They can be split geographically into two distinct areas. Inland Croatia or Kontinentalna Hrvatska runs south-east along the Drava tributary as far as the Danube. This is mainly white wine country, growing Traminer, Welschriesling (here known as Graševina), Muscat Ottonel and Pinot Blanc, often on terraces. The best wines are said to come from the slopes of Baranja, in the Danube Valley north of Osijek, and known as 'The Golden Hill' since Roman times. Along the strip of coastal Croatia – Primorska Hrvatska – the sun, sea and rocky soil combine to produce good reds, particularly those made from the characterful and ageworthy Plavac Mali grape. The best-known wines are Postup and Dingač from the Peljesac peninsula

and Faros from the island of Hvar, although Plavac of varying quality and sweetness is produced all along the beautiful Dalmatian coast. Plavac Mali leapt to unexpected renown during the 1990s when it was thought that Californian Zinfandel was in fact Plavac Mali. Now it seems that both Zinfandel and Italian Primitivo are the same as the obscure Croatian variety, Crljenak, which itself probably comes from Albania or Greece. That's what the DNA experts say, but I say this one will run and run.

West of Split, another native variety, Babic, produces a light red wine for everyday drinking. The Istrian peninsula produces Motovunski Teran, a tart, herbal-tasting red wine (the grape Teran is believed to be related to Refosco). Istria also grows Malvasia, Pinot Blanc, Merlot, Cabernet Sauvignon and Gamay. Mike Grgich, of Californian fame, has set up a small winery on the Peljesac peninsula to bring modern technology back to his homeland. This is what is needed now: more investment, more technology in vineyard and winery and a fair price for the grapes. An origin-based quality wine scheme, linked to a tasting system, is used for premium wines.

Bosnia-Herzegovina, with its Muslim traditions, has never been a strong wine-producing area. A few wines, such as the red Blatina and the dry, unusually full-flavoured white Zilavka, had built up a good reputation. But rebuilding is slow, and it's hardly a mecca for investment. If there was stability there would be some potential here. Serbia and Kosovo, thrown into disarray by the war, must now rebuild and move forward technologically. This was an area with potential. The large winemaking area of central Serbia included the vineyards of Župa in the Kruševac area – some of the former Yugoslavia's oldest – which

WINE AREAS

SLOVENIA

PRIMORSKA
1. Goriška Brda
2. Vipavska Dolina
3. Kras
4. Slovenska Istra

POSAVJE
5. Bela Krajina
6. Dolenjska
7. Bizeljsko-Sremič

PODRAVJE
8. Stajerska-Slovenija
9. Prekmurski

CROATIA

KONTINENTALNA HRVATSKA
10. Plešivica
11. Zagorje-Medimurje
12. Prigorje-Bilogora
13. Moslavina
14. Pukuplje
15. Slavonija
16. Podunavlje

PRIMORSKA HRVATSKA
17. Istra
18. Hrvatsko Primorje
19. Sjeverna Dalmacija
20. Dalmatinska Zagora
21. Srednja i Južna Dalmacija

BOSNIA-HERZEGOVINA

HERZEGOVINA

SERBIA

SUBOTICA-HORGOS DESERT

SREM

BANAT

POCERINA

SUMADIJA-GREAT MORAVA RIVER
22. Beograd
23. Mlava River
24. Oplenac
25. Jagodina

TIMOK VALLEY
26. Krajina
27. Knjaževac

NISAVA AND SOUTHERN MORAVA RIVERS
28. Aleksinac
29. Toplica River
30. Niš
31. Nišava River
32. Leskovac
33. Vranje

WESTERN MOROVA RIVER
34. Cacak
35. Kruševac

MONTENEGRO

MONTENEGRO

KOSOVO

KOSOVO

F.Y.R.M. (MACEDONIA)

PELAGONIJA-POLOG

POVARDARJE

PCINJA OSOGOVSKE

ranked among Serbia's finest. Red grapes predominated, particularly the native Prokupac, which was often blended with Pinot Noir and Gamay. The poor soils of Kosovo were only good for viticulture. Reds predominated: Pinot Noir, Cabernet Franc, Prokupac, Merlot and Gamay. Whites included Welschriesling, Rhine Riesling and Zilavka.

Macedonia is the latest casualty in this troubled Balkan region. Sad, because Macedonia's mild winters and dry subtropical summers are ideal for viticulture. The best wine is red, made from Kratosija and Vranac.

In Montenegro, red Vranac, with its bitter cherry flavour, predominates. The best-known vineyards are those in the sparse, pebbly soil on the southern and south-western slopes surrounding Lake Skadar. A similar quality system to Croatia applies.

SLOVENIA

The relative calm of the new independent Slovenia, established in 1991, is testimony to the common heritage of the Slovenian people and there was little dissent when their application to join the EU was accepted in 2004. Wine has always been part of its heritage. It comes as no surprise to discover Roman writers praising the wines from the Devin area of Kras in the first century AD. Today, Slovenia has around 22,952ha (56,714 acres) of vineyard with more designated for development. This is far less than the 50,000ha (123,548 acres) at the end of the 19th century, when the country was part of the Austro-Hungarian empire.

A well-policed quality wine scheme allows only the best wines to be bottled and exported. These normally carry a seal of approval. A drive towards quality is still needed for Slovenia to fulfil its potential.

The country has three defined wine districts and the style of each looks to its neighbour. Littoral (or Primorska) touches the Adriatic for a stretch of the coast around Koper and extends north along the Italian border. This is hilly country with a *karst* plateau – a limestone region with many underground caves and passages formed by the dissolution of the rock – and many of the vineyards lie in the valleys between the mountains and the plateau. The proximity of the Alps tempers the Mediterranean climate. The most famous vineyards of this area straddle the rather artificial border around Dobrovo, Nova Gorica and the area called Goriška Brda or Collio Goriziano in Italian. Grapes such as Refosco (known here as Refosk or Teran), Ribolla (Rebula), Tocai Friuliano (Tocay) and Picolit (Pikolit) highlight the shared culture between this region and neighbouring Friuli-Venezia Giulia. Also grown are Malvasia, Muscat Blanc à Petit Grains (for dessert wines), Chardonnay, Sauvignon Blanc, Pinots Blanc and Gris, Merlot, Cabernets Franc and Sauvignon and Barbera. Vipava's indigenous white specialities are Zelen and Pinela. The white wines from Slovenska Istra can also be good. For Slovenians the most noted wine is the red Kraski Teran, made from Refosco grapes grown around Sezana in the Kras region, where *terra rossa* (literally, 'red earth') overlays the *karst*. Vipava and Brda are forward-looking areas with go-ahead co-operatives.

The country's best whites come from Posavje, the Sava Valley, in the south-east. This is the meeting point of three different weather systems – alpine, continental and Mediterranean – resulting in a climate with showers in spring, hot summers and warm sunny autumns. High sugar levels are possible, and a recent development has been the production of Eiswein in the Metlika district. The vineyards, mainly on steep slopes, grow Laski Rizling, Traminer, Sauvignon Blanc, Chardonnay, Pinot Blanc, Sipon (Hungary's Furmint) and Silvaner. Rumeni Plavac, a white relation

of Dalmatia's Plavac Mali, is grown around Bizeljsko, although its lack of character often means that it is blended with grapes such as Laski Rizling. The speciality of the Dolenjska region is the light red Cviček, and other reds and rosés are made from Blaufränkisch, Zametovka (or Kîlner Dark), Blauer Portugieser, Pinot Noir, Cabernet and Merlot.

Podravje, or the Drava Valley, has similar climate, grape varieties and winemaking practices to those of the Austrian Steiermark region just across the border, producing young, fresh, tangy whites. Best known is Ljutomer Laski Rizling, once, as Lutomer Riesling, the top-selling wine in the UK, although the Gewürztraminer (known here as Traminec), Sauvignon Blanc and Chardonnay are much better. The semi-sweet 'Tiger Milk' is made from Bouvier, or Ranina as it is locally known. In Gorna Radgona, Pinot Blanc can be used to make sparkling wines by the traditional method.

In many ways the success of Lutomer Riesling, and the consequent flow of hard currency into the region, did as much harm as good. Lutomer Riesling was initially an extremely enjoyable full, soft, rather fruity white. It was the first white wine to cross my lips, and in fact it was usually the only white wine we had in the house when I was a kid. But, as its success grew, rather than use the profits to create ever larger amounts of good wine, the quality got worse and worse. Those of us who had enjoyed it did increasingly violent U-turns to avoid it, and inevitably, its success faded and with it the whole reputation of the old Yugoslavia as a producer. This was quite unfair, but Lutomer's place in the easy dry white pantheon was then taken by Liebfraumilch – initially a pleasant, fruity German wine that was wildly popular. As Liebfraumilch's quality slumped, the whole of Germany's reputation in the export markets suffered exactly the same way as Yugoslavia's had done.

The vineyards of the Drava Valley in eastern Slovenia are squashed in between those of Hungary and Austria and closely follow the contours that weave in and out of the wooded hills. The prospect of mechanization here is very distant indeed.

BULGARIA

I'VE HAD A LOVE-HATE RELATIONSHIP with Bulgarian wine right from the beginning. The first tasting I did was when Jancis Robinson asked me at zero hour minus one minute's notice to 'guest edit' the *Which?* wine monthly newsletter for her. We organized a tasting of Bulgarian wines. These were some of the first samples to hit British shores, at the very beginning of the 1980s. There were some remarkable hefty, violent, scabrous reds – strange, soupy and thick on the tongue. But there was fruit there too, a proud, rip-roaring essence of blackcurrant, quite unlike the delicate, lacy perfume of old Bordeaux, quite unlike the bright, keen flavours of Chilean Cabernet.

The reds were infinitely preferable to the whites, whose blend of searing acidity, reckless sulphur and building-site dust made them painful to the lips and dangerous to one's sanity. Since then, although the red wines still easily outshine the whites in Bulgaria, the flavours have changed. The stentorian old Cabernets are no longer so impressive, but the bright young Cabernets and Merlots are infinitely better.

One gets the sense that in the 1980s, Bulgarian Cabernet Sauvignon was made for an export market that was starved of new and exciting affordable flavours. New World offerings then came along in the 1990s and filled the gap just as the Bulgarian success story of the 1980s fell into disarray. Free market reforms followed, in particular, land reforms which gave Bulgarian wineries the opportunity to buy their own vineyards. In the past few years there have been huge changes for the better: rationalization, positive restructuring and better control over the huge variation in fruit quality bode well for the future and entry into the EU in 2007 with accompanying new wine legislation and huge inward investment for modernizing wineries and replanting vineyards should encourage a more positive attitude.

Although Bulgaria has been cultivating vines for 3000 years, its immediate past doesn't stretch back much past the end of World War Two. Between 1396 and 1918, Turkish Islamic domination brought winemaking to a commercial halt. Hillside plantings were established after the end of Turkish rule but it was the Soviet

WINE REGIONS

DANUBIAN PLAIN
1. Novo Selo
2. Vidin
3. Pleven
4. Lovech
5. Lositza
6. Svishtov
7. Pavlikeni
8. Suhindol
9. Lyaskovets
10. Russe
11. Türgovishte
12. Veliki Preslav
13. Varbitsa
14. Khan Kroum
15. Novi Pazar
16. Evksinograd
Black Sea Region

THRACIAN LOWLANDS
17. Pomorie
18. Karnobat
19. Slavyantzi
20. Soungourlare
21. Yambol
22. Sliven
23. Shivachevo
24. Nova Zagora
25. Oryahovitsa
26. Stara Zagora
27. Karlovo
28. Septemvri
29. Hissarya
30. Plovdiv
31. Peroushtitsa
32. Brestnik
33. Assenovgrad
34. Haskovo
35. Stambolovo
36. Lyubimets
37. Sakar
38. Ivailovgrad
39. Melnik
40. Harsovo
41. Sandanski

South Black Sea Region

Strouma Valley Region

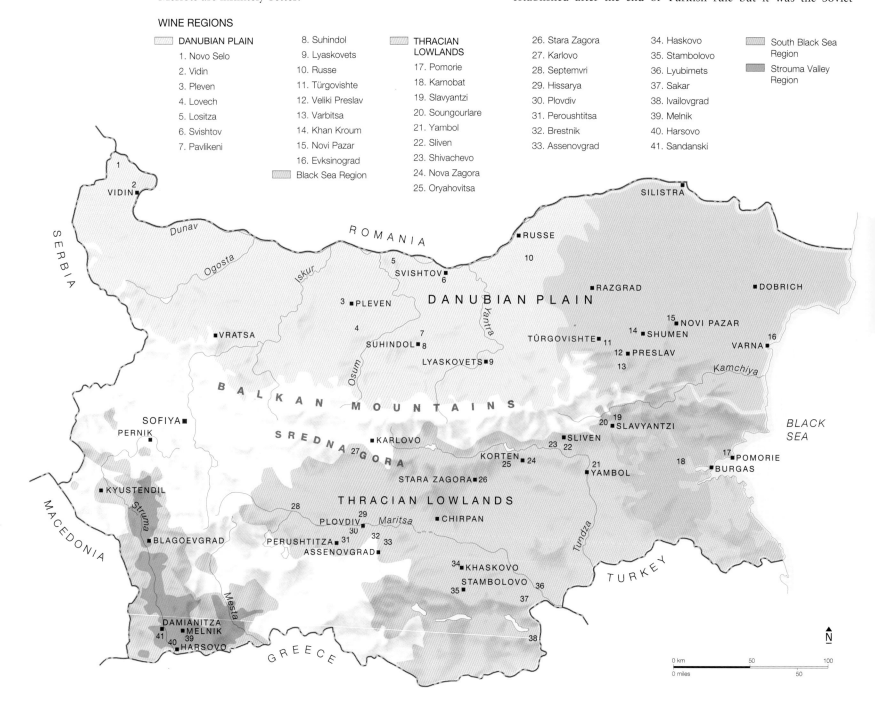

decision that Bulgaria should be a massive modern vineyard to supply the USSR that triggered the planting of all the fertile flatland vineyards that now mark out Bulgaria. And it was some canny bartering with American cola companies that gained her the vast acreage of international grape varieties upon which she has made her export reputation.

GRAPE VARIETIES

The grape most readily associated with Bulgaria, and which is one of the country's most widely planted, is Cabernet Sauvignon. The wines first appeared in the West in the early 1980s, and they were a revelation at that time – unassuming, but tasty and affordable. Since their debut the easy, ripe, plummy, well-priced Bulgarian offerings arguably have done as much as anything from Australia or California to establish the variety as the world's most famous red grape. Those first Bulgarian wines, rich, creamy and blackcurranty, with some oak and some bottle age, were virtually identikit pictures of what wine drinkers were seeking, and we lapped them up. In a rush to provide us with more of what we were clamouring for, production increased and quality slipped. It may just be nostalgia, but all these years later, current releases still don't seem as good as those first Suhindol Cabernets from vintages of the late 1970s.

Merlot is almost as widely planted as Cabernet and can also be good, particularly from Stambolovo. Gamza (the same grape as Hungary's Kadarka) is vigorously fruity when young, but can age to a meaty richness, while the similarly sturdy, plummy Mavrud also produces wines of character. Pamid is the most widely planted native red variety, but generally its wines are thin and lacking in character, though modern winemaking may yet produce bright gluggers from this variety. Much better is the Shiroka Melnishka Ioza, usually just called Melnik, which is grown almost exclusivley in the south-west in the Strouma Valley region and produces a powerful, fruity red wine which takes to oak aging very well.

Native white varieties include Dimiat, which manages to maintain a fairly aromatic, soft-centred character even from quite high yields, and Red Misket, a musky, grapy variety which one might think had some relation to the Muscat family but it doesn't. Rkatsiteli is the most widely planted white, and there are also significant amounts of Muscat Ottonel, Chardonnay, Ugni Blanc, Aligoté, Riesling and Sauvignon Blanc.

While the reds have thrived, the whites have been, on the whole, disappointing. The reds have been developed along French lines, and have been able to cope with some pretty rudimentary winery conditions. The whites initially followed Germanic models, with Riesling and Welschriesling being prominent. But Germanic models require positively aseptic conditions to succeed. In Bulgaria, grapes were frequently unhealthy and the wineries simply not clean enough: even today, sulphurous brews outnumber attractive drinks, although there is now a handful of perfectly good 'international' Chardonnays being made.

According to the latest survey in 2006 there are some 135,000ha (333,580 acres) under vine, but there are doubts about how many of these hectares are still in production and at least 50,000ha (123,548 acres) of this total are young vines. There are over 26,000 grape growers, many of whom own tiny, fragmented holdings, but the industry is still dominated by large wineries such as those at Suhindol and Khan Kroum. Many of the old state-owned wineries are now private companies owning increasing amounts of their own vineyards in an attempt to control the quality of the fruit. Two of the largest newer operations are Stork Nest, the former Svishtov winery on the Danube, and Bessa Valley, near Plovdiv. The largest

company, Domaine Boyar started life in 1991 as an export company for several large wineries and now has wineries at Schumen and Korten as well as a new state of the art, Australian-designed winery at Blueridge, outside Sliven. Boyar now sells more than 65 million bottles of wine a year and not surprisingly quality is erratic: many of the reds are raw and tannic and the whites are merely decent. On the whole Bulgarian wines have still not re-established any real individuality, rather just a vague and acceptable modernness. The next step must surely be movement up the quality ladder and the creation of regional pyramids of quality for specific wines. There are signs of small producers beginning to emerge.

As part of the process of joining the EU the wine laws have been revised. The country is now divided into two main table wine areas, the Danubian Plain, the northern half of the country, and the Thracian Lowlands, the southern part, with a over 40 quality wine areas.

WINE REGIONS

The Black Sea region in eastern Bulgaria enjoys a more moderate continental climate than the rest of the country with long warm autumn days. White grapes do best here and the most widely grown are Muscat Ottonel, Dimiat and Chardonnay.

Reds and whites are made in roughly equal amounts in the Danubian Plain Region, although the reds are the real gems. Suhindol's best-known wine is the Cabernet Sauvignon, although the Merlot and Gamza are also good. Suhindol was the first Bulgarian area to become famous with its Cabernet Sauvignon. New technology and judicious use of oak have restored the quality in recent years. Ready to snatch the crown for Bulgaria's top wine when the quality at Suhindol slipped were the Cabernet and Merlot from the foothills around Russe in the north-east of the region. Another decent Cabernet comes from the Svishtov region on the border with Romania.

Cabernet Sauvignon is also important south of the Balkans in the Thracian Lowlands, both on its own or blended with Merlot or Mavrud. That from Plovdiv is good, although nearby Assenovgrad produces a better version, as well as impressive chunky Mavrud. The vines are planted in rich black and red carbonated soils on gentle slopes chosen for their low susceptibility to frost.

The hilly districts of Sliven, Oryahovitsa and Stara Zagora, just south of the Balkan mountains, are also sources of good Cabernet Sauvignon. The vineyards enjoy a sheltered southerly exposure and the soils are mostly well-drained sand and clay. Sliven also produces a very drinkable, clean Chardonnay and a fine cheap blend of Merlot and Pinot Noir. In the hilly regions of the south, Merlot from Stambolovo can be excellent. The Merlot from Sakar is also good, as is the Cabernet Sauvignon.

The Strouma Valley on the border with Greece is the warmest area in the country. The continental climate is modified by warm air rising from the Strouma river and has a distinctly Mediterranean feel, although the altitude prevents temperatures from rising too high for viticulture. This is the home of Melnik, a variety which thrives on the clay and sand soils around Damianitza and Harsovo: a wine to watch. Even in such warm conditions, Melnik ripens late, and autumn rains can give rise to problems with rot before harvest in October. Experiments are under way, particularly with Melnik, to produce new strains of grape designed to require a growing period two to three weeks shorter than other varieties, so that they can be harvested before the rains begin, thus avoiding damage to the crop. Cabernet Sauvignon, Merlot, Rkatsiteli and Muscat Ottonel are also important here.

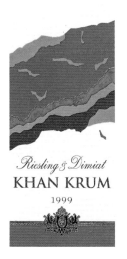

Bulgaria has several tasty indigenous grape varieties. Mavrud makes powerful, plummy reds.

GREECE & EASTERN MEDITERRANEAN

THIS REGION HAS BEEN MAKING WINE FOR THOUSANDS OF YEARS. Heavy, oxidized wines that pleased local drinkers are rapidly disappearing in favour of modern, clean wines. The best are very good, though the rest have a long way to go yet. The country which is leading the charge is unquestionably Greece, where a new generation of winemakers and grapegrowers, many of them trained in France, California or Australia, have looked in horror at the decay of a wine culture stretching back thousands of years and resolved to do something about it. Technological upgrading of wineries has been matched by the revival of old vineyards and the creation of new ones, especially in the relatively rare cooler parts of the country. But above all, these modern Greeks have a vision of the flavours they want to achieve, and a reassuring pride in Greece itself. Many of the newer estates, that could have just planted a swathe of Cabernet and Chardonnay, have in fact covered the majority of their vineyards with native varieties, and the wines are modern, but marvellously original too. Established companies such as Boutari, Kourtakis and Tsantalis, together with a new band of small, quality-minded producers – Gaia, Gentilini, Gerovassiliou, Hatzimichalis, Constantin Lazaridi, Papaïoannou, Strofilia and the younger members of the Boutaris family – are upping the quality stakes every vintage.

NORTHERN GREECE

Along the wine roads of Makedonia, the Xinomavro grape is responsible for the dark, spicy powerful Naousa and, when blended with Negoska, the softer, rounded Goumenissa. The best producers of Naousa are Boutari, Tsantalis, Katoghi-Strofilia and Kyr-Yanni. In Goumenissa, Aïdarinis is a winery to watch. On the Chalkidiki peninsula, Tsantalis leases vineyards from the Mount Athos monastery and produces red wines that blend the native Limnio with Cabernet and Grenache. Evanghelos Gerovassiliou, a former pupil of Bordeaux's Professor Peynaud, is Greece's most respected enologist; he now has his own eponymous state-of-the-art winery in the rolling hills near Epanomi. Terrific Rhône-like reds and a fine Condrieu-style Viognier are among his impressive offerings.

CENTRAL GREECE

Other parts of Greece make equally good wines, particularly the Hatzimichalis estate north-west of Athens where a diverse collection of grape varieties is grown. The Cabernet Sauvignon, Merlot, Chardonnay, and the Ambelon Estate white – 100 per cent Robola – are all good, if a little pricy. Robola plays second fiddle to the Savatiano grape further east on the island of Evvoia. Savatiano is the source of most retsina, which gets its particular character from Aleppo pine resin added during fermentation. Love it or loathe it, retsina when fresh and young is a brilliantly individual drink, but retsina sales are falling fast, both domestically and internationally.

The Ionian island of Kefallonia is best known for its dry white Robola. Most exciting are the Gentilini wines made by Gabrielle Beamish. Her Classico white, reminiscent of Australian Semillon, with its crisp lemon acidity and mineral perfume, is a blend of Robola and another local grape, Tsaoussi, together with small amounts of Moschofilero and Muscat. The Fumé is an oak-aged blend of Chardonnay and Sauvignon Blanc.

PELOPONNISOS

The best wine of the Peloponnese (Peloponnisos) is the dark, spicy Nemea, made from Aghiorghitiko. Vineyards are found between 250 and 800m (820 and 2600ft) with the best ones on slopes below the plateau of Asprokambos. (Wines from Antonopoulos, Cambas, Gaia, Kokotos, Papaïoannou and Skouras are worth seeking out.) Further west, the aromatic white Moschofilero produces Mantinia, one of Greece's most promising whites; those produced by Cambas, Achaïa Clauss, Spyropoulos and Tselepos are especially good. Elsewhere in the Peloponnese, Patras dry whites are made from rather dull Roditis – but the Kouros brand from Kourtakis is good. The two vins doux naturels – Muscat of Patras and Mavrodaphne of Patras, made mainly from the red Mavrodaphne grape supplemented by Korinthiaki, can be deliciously exciting, especially when aged.

GREEK ISLANDS

In the Aegean, Crete (Kriti) produces an awful lot of awful wine, but Kourtakis has begun to produce remarkable reds from ungrafted vines as well as crisp clean whites. Boutari also has a decent white. Better wines can be found in Rhodes (Rodos), particularly the Muscat, although better still is the Muscat from Samos. The unfortified Samos Nectar from the Samos co-op is a marvellous mouthful. The white wines from the volcanic island of Santorini (Thira) are made from the Assyrtiko and Aidani grapes, with the vines trained like coils of rope to resist the wind. They have the minerally grip and tang of Sémillon matching an intense baked-apple fruit (especially Gaia's Thalassitis); a magnificent old-fashioned sweet vin santo is also produced.

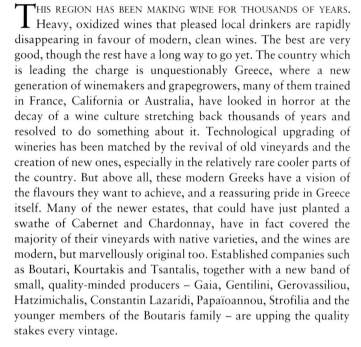

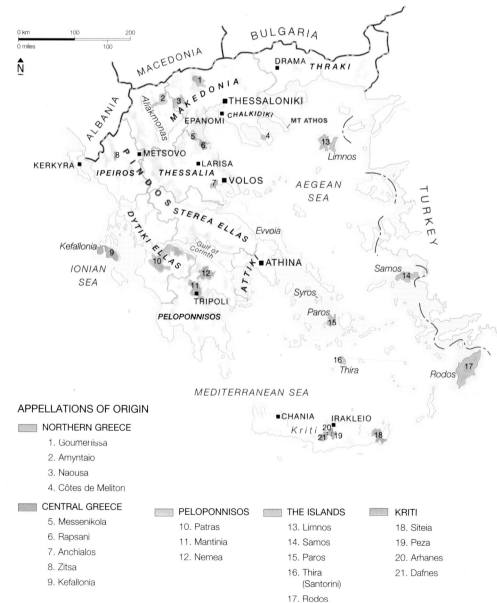

APPELLATIONS OF ORIGIN

NORTHERN GREECE
1. Goumenissa
2. Amyntaio
3. Naousa
4. Côtes de Meliton

CENTRAL GREECE
5. Messenikola
6. Rapsani
7. Anchialos
8. Zitsa
9. Kefallonia

PELOPONNISOS
10. Patras
11. Mantinia
12. Nemea

THE ISLANDS
13. Limnos
14. Samos
15. Paros
16. Thira (Santorini)
17. Rodos

KRITI
18. Siteia
19. Peza
20. Arhanes
21. Dafnes

TURKEY

Only three per cent of the huge acreage of Turkey under vine is used for wine production; the rest is table grapes. Turks who do drink – and 99 per cent of them, being Muslim, are not supposed to – do so for the effect, rather than the flavour, and the oxidized, high-alcohol style of many wines find few devotees in today's wine world.

Most famous of the red wines is Buzbag from Eastern Anatolia, made from the native Öküzgözü and Bogazkere grapes. It can be good, or plain- awful. Turkey's better producers include Diren from Tokat in Eastern Anatolia, Kavaklidere near Ankara and Doluca in Thrace: here modern technology, French oak barrels and local and international varieties come together in a very drinkable way.

LEBANON

After 25 years of war, peace has brought a new generation of producers and improved quality from the older companies. Modernization has even gripped Château Ksara, Lebanon's oldest and largest winery. Its new releases of such modern wines as Chardonnay Cuvée du Pape, the Cabernet-Cinsaut-Syrah mix Réserve du Couvent or indeed the straight Cabernet, are a world removed from what they were offering only a few years ago. The other most important wineries are Château Musar and Château Kefraya, both of whose vineyards lie on the east-facing slopes of Mount Barouk, overlooking the beautiful Bekaa Valley. The high altitude, over 1000m (3280ft) above sea level, keeps temperatures low. Clos St Thomas is a high-quality smaller producer in the valley whose top red is stunning. Massaya, a Franco-Lebanese project, is another producer to watch.

Château Musar, established in 1930 by Gaston Hochar, is the most internationally famous of the Lebanese wine producers and was for a long time the shining star in Lebanon's wine sky. The red, based on between 50 and 80 per cent Cabernet Sauvignon, the balance being largely Cinsaut, and only released after its fifth year, used to be a thrilling, exotic, kasbah-scented mishmash of flavours, unlike any other. The flavours are now more mainstream, but recent vintages still look pretty good – and old ones are superb. Musar Blanc is also full-bodied and is a blend of the local Obaideh and Merwah – Chardonnay and Sémillon lookalikes respectively.

ISRAEL

Most of Israel's best wines to date have come from the Galilee region, which counts the Golan Heights as its best sub-region. The Golan Heights Winery makes good dry whites under the Yarden and Gamla labels, and also produces Yarden bottle-fermented sparkling wines. The vineyards, in the foothills of Mount Hermon, are on well-drained soils over basalt and other volcanic rocks, hence the success with Cabernet Sauvignon, Merlot, Muscat, Chardonnay and Sauvignon. The altitude keeps daytime temperatures below 25°C (77°F). Israel's oldest and largest producer, Carmel, makes 55 per cent of the country's total output, but in the 1990s numerous new boutique wineries opened, making good use of modern technology, but often producing tiny quantities. Some of Israel's most promising wines now come from Castel in the Judean Hills, Galil Mountain in Galilee and Tishbi in Shomron. Let us hope the continuing conflict in this area does not stall innovation and expansion.

CYPRUS

Until recently the Cypriot wine industry was known for little other than bulk and fortified wines. After the triple whammy of the collapse of the Russian wine market, the banning of the name 'sherry' from the island's fortified wines, and a severe drought through much of the 1990s the industry had to rethink and act pretty quickly. Accession to the EU in 2004, with the ending of subsidies and a free market for grape prices, was another shock. The large companies – ETKO, KEO, LOEL and SODAP – have been forced to take quality more seriously, restructuring the vineyards with better grape varieties and building regional press houses close to the vineyards to avoid trucking fruit for hours in the hot sun. In the process thousands of hectares have been grubbed up – the total in 2005 was 14,305ha (35,347 acres), a 50 per cent reduction since 1990.

Native grape varieties, Mavro (black) and Xynisteri (a white grape better and more subtle than Mavro), still cover around 70 per cent of vineyard plantings, but there are now small but significant amounts of international varieties being grown, generally on the slopes of the Troodos mountains, where the melting snow provides much-needed water for irrigation in this parched island. For the first time we are seeing varietal wines being made in Cyprus, and early efforts with grapes like Cabernet Sauvignon and Sémillon are impressive. Commandaria, Cyprus's dark, sweet and often fortified wine, is still the most famous wine from the island. It is made with sun-dried Mavro and Xynisteri grapes, and aged in solera systems.

The Bekaa Valley was once the frontline in Lebanon's civil war. These vineyards belong to Château Kefraya, an important producer.

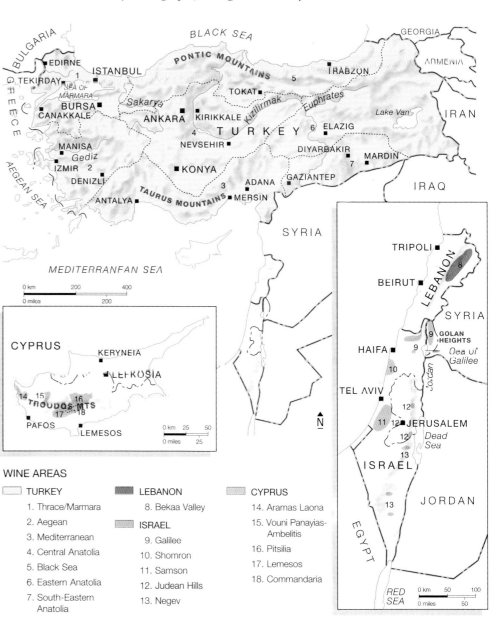

WINE AREAS

TURKEY
1. Thrace/Marmara
2. Aegean
3. Mediterranean
4. Central Anatolia
5. Black Sea
6. Eastern Anatolia
7. South-Eastern Anatolia

LEBANON
8. Bekaa Valley

ISRAEL
9. Galilee
10. Shomron
11. Samson
12. Judean Hills
13. Negev

CYPRUS
14. Aramas Laona
15. Vouni Panayias-Ambelitis
16. Pitsilia
17. Lemesos
18. Commandaria

NORTH AMERICA

A vineyard doesn't need to be centuries old to be famous. Bien Nacido (left) in the Santa Maria Valley was only planted in 1973 but various wineries, especially Au Bon Climat, whose winery is in the background, have made a string of great wines from its Pinot Noir, Chardonnay and Syrah grapes. Napa Valley is full of ultra-modern wineries, but a little history remains like this old water tower (above) at Franciscan Vineyards' Oakville Estate.

An event in Paris on 26 May 1976 proved to be a watershed in North America's winemaking history, the date with destiny the country had been heading towards since 1619 when Lord Delaware had tried to establish a vineyard of French wine grape varieties in Virginia. That sounds pretty sensationalist, I know, but that day has had a more far-reaching effect on the world's perception of fine wine than any other in the modern era.

Stephen Spurrier, a young British wine merchant, held a tasting in Paris for the most finely tuned French palates of the day. Ostensibly a Bordeaux and Burgundy tasting, it also included a few Californian wines, which the French judges then proceeded to denigrate in pretty condescending terms.

Except that this was a blind tasting. The wines they were denigrating turned out to be French, some of the top names in Bordeaux and Burgundy. The wines they were praising as typical examples of great French wines… weren't. The top white was Chateau Montelena Chardonnay 1973 from California's Napa Valley, which trounced wines from vineyards in Burgundy planted a thousand years before. The top red was Stag's Leap 1973 Cabernet – only the second vintage of this Napa Valley wine – which beat off the challenge of wines like Bordeaux's Château Haut-Brion and Château Latour which had the benefit of being rooted in hundreds of years of history.

Until that moment, France had reigned supreme in the world of wine, and had generally behaved as though its hallowed wines had a God-given right to be the best. No more. The astonishing victory at the blind tasting gave Americans the confidence to believe that they could match the best of the Old World, but on their own terms, and it inspired the other nations of the world that now produce world class wines – ranging from Australia and New Zealand to South Africa, Chile and others – to do the same.

It also fashioned the approach taken by many Americans to making wine. With the exception of the bulk producers, there are winemakers in California, Oregon, Washington, Texas, Virginia, New York – and now Ontario and British Columbia in Canada, too – who take 'the best' as their goal, the top wine as their role model, and buy the finest equipment to achieve their aim. Sometimes sheer ambition is their downfall. But more often their efforts sing with the excitement of a new industry turning the tables on old, revered institutions, and the whole world has cause to be grateful for that.

THE WINE REGIONS OF NORTH AMERICA

THERE ARE NUMEROUS TALES about the cradle of winemaking being in the Eastern Mediterranean, in Mesopotamia, Asia Minor or Persia – and they make sense. Grapes grow well there, and probably always did. More to the point, they've kept written records there for thousands of years for archaeologists and historians to discover.

But what about the Americas? Two 12th- and 13th-century Norse sagas tell of Leif Ericsson who established the colony of Vinland ('Wine Land') in north-east America, named after the wild vines which grew in profusion. Did he find bushes laden with grapes? And did he make these into wine? If so, surely the Indian tribes had discovered the grape's ability to ferment centuries – if not millennia – before, just as the Mesopotamians had. There is evidence that fermented grape juice was offered to the gods of Native American tribes such as the Seneca and Cayuga. How long had this been going on? Maybe for as long as in the courts of Cairo and Baghdad.

But, since Europeans arrived in force in the 16th and 17th centuries, extensive records have been kept that show a relentless determination to establish vineyards and wineries in almost every state of the Union. Also, the fact that American wines didn't break into the premier league until the 1970s is evidence of the succession of natural and man-made obstacles that winemakers had to overcome. On the east coast, the combination of a difficult climate and the presence of the indigenous vine-chomping phylloxera louse baffled generations of winemakers trying to make European-style wine from European grape varieties. In the centre and the south, climatic conditions defeated all but the hardiest pioneers. On the west coast, a brighter start with European grape varieties was unceremoniously cut short by the invasion of phylloxera from the east.

To cap it all, Prohibition, like an angel of doom, overshadowed the entire nation. From 1919 to 1933 alcohol was an illegal drug in the States. People still drank – they probably drank more than ever before – but the whole concept of wine as a noble, uplifting beverage went out of the window. By the time Prohibition laws were repealed, the Great Depression was stifling interest in the finer things of life, and then there was a World War to fight. By the 1950s, two generations had grown up with no experience of wine as anything other than a sweet, fortified drink to be consumed for effect rather than flavour.

The picture only began to change in the late 1960s, when Robert Mondavi established his Napa Valley winery, filling what was a virtual quality vacuum. During the 1970s and 1980s, winemaking spread to every suitable nook and cranny in California and the Pacific Northwest. The 1980s and 1990s saw the south-western and the eastern seaboard states at last conquer their difficult climate and now there are almost 5000 wineries in all 50 states – what some of them use for raw material hardly bears thinking about. And during the 1990s, the Canadians of Ontario and British Columbia threw over their mediocre wine traditions and struck out for the title of newest New World kid on the block, to startling effect.

INDIGENOUS VINE SPECIES

Back in the 17th and 18th centuries, every European visitor who travelled along the east coast commented on the vines, which flourished from New England right down to Florida. But all efforts to make decent wine from them failed, largely because the prevailing vine species, *Vitis labrusca*, simply will not make pleasant-flavoured wine. So generation upon generation of colonists imported European *Vitis vinifera* varieties – with conspicuous lack of success. The most obvious reasons for this failure were the very cold winters and hot humid summers, which either killed off the vines or provided perfect conditions for fungal diseases. But there was another hazard – the tiny phylloxera louse, indigenous to north-east America. Phylloxera could munch the roots of the hardy *Vitis labrusca* without weakening the vine, but *Vitis vinifera* had no natural tolerance to phylloxera and every vineyard succumbed within a few years.

THE EASTERN SEABOARD

The whole pattern of vineyards in the north-east was fixed by these sets of circumstances. Wine was and still is made from *labrusca* grapes from New England down to the Carolinas and across to the Great Lakes, yet even now no-one has managed to make it taste very good. However, some natural hybrids with phylloxera resistance and a less offensive flavour did evolve, and others were bred specifically.

When in the late 19th century the French were desperate for rootstocks and phylloxera-resistant plants for their own devastated vineyards, a large number of so-called French hybrids were

Santa Maria Valley is reckoned to produce some of California's best Chardonnay – and some elegant labels too.

THE CLASSIFICATION SYSTEM FOR AMERICAN WINE

Wine laws are a relatively new phenomenon in the United States, as the provenance of grapes for wine made in North America was unimportant up until the 1980s. About the most specific labels ever got was to mention the county of origin, but this didn't tell the consumer anything about quality. As US wine began to hold its own at international level it competed in export markets against wine from countries with more developed methods of quality control. The need for home-grown wine legislation led to the introduction of officially recognized American Viticultural Areas (AVAs) in 1983, roughly modelled on the French principle of Appellation Contrôlée. AVA boundaries are based on topographic and climatic zones and soil types, but unlike their European counterparts, they don't yet involve restrictions on the grape varieties that may be grown, or on yields and, as in Europe, they do not guarantee quality. Further restrictions may come in the future, as growers have the chance to observe where particular varieties do best, and can pinpoint the optimum crop yields for quality wine. There are currently over 150 AVAs in the US, more than 100 of which are in California.

MAJOR REQUIREMENTS OF THE LABELLING LAWS

• **Labelling by grape variety** American wines are most commonly labelled by the dominant grape variety used in the blend. The wine must contain at least 75 per cent of the named variety (except in Oregon where the minimum is 90 per cent, with an exception of 75 per cent for Cabernet Sauvignon to allow for the Bordeaux style of blending, common with this variety). If an AVA is named, at least 85 per cent of the grapes must come from that AVA.

• **Region of origin** The winery and the region of origin also appear on the label. At the most basic level this may be stated simply as 'America', used for a blend of wine from two or more states, or the label can mention a state or a county name. If the wine has only the name of a state, the grapes must be 100 per cent from that state; if only the county is named, at least 75 per cent must be from that county, regardless of variety.

• **Health warnings** Various health warnings are mandatory on US labels, as well as warnings about the dangers of alcohol and the presence of sulphites (used as a preservative) and of any other additives.

developed. These now dominate plantings in the eastern and central states, although classic *vinifera* varieties are at last succeeding on the east coast and provide the bulk of the crop in such places as Virginia and Long Island, New York.

CALIFORNIA AND THE SOUTH
The southern United States is largely unsuitable for *vinifera* grapes, because of the humid summers and insufficiently cold winters; the best known wine is from a non-*vinifera* vine called Scuppernong. But French and German immigrants did establish thriving wine businesses in Arkansas and Missouri, using a wide spectrum of grape varieties, and it was from Mexico, in the early 17th century, that *Vitis vinifera* grapes made their gradual progress north, Franciscan missionaries planting the first Californian vines in 1779. The 1849 Gold Rush drew the centre of attention in California north from Los Angeles to San Francisco, and saw the establishment of the great vineyard regions of Sonoma and Napa, north of San Francisco, as well as Livermore and Santa Clara to the south and east of the city, and the huge San Joaquin Valley in the interior.

By the late 19th century, California had more than 800 wineries, growing over 300 different *vinifera* varieties. Phylloxera, two World Wars, Prohibition and the Great Depression doused the bright flame of Californian wine for almost a hundred years, until progress in the last quarter of the 20th century changed the face of North America's, and the world's wine, for good.

THE PACIFIC NORTHWEST
Further north, however, in Oregon, Washington and Idaho, winemakers set out to change the face of American wine as defined by the Californians. But it was the rekindling of fires in California that sent sparks north to these states. Although Washington State had a wine industry of sorts based on hybrids and *labrusca*

varieties, and there are references to 19th-century wineries in places like Oregon's Willamette Valley, things only really got moving in 1966 when a couple of university professors making wine in their garage were noticed by a leading American wine critic. This coincided with the arrival of several 'refugees' from the heart of California who were prodding about in Oregon, trying to establish a vineyard for Pinot Noir. And it wasn't until the 1970s that some Idaho fruit farmers decided to diversify into wine grapes. The wine industries of the Pacific Northwest and Idaho are as recent as that.

CANADA
Far from being new to winemaking, Canada has been a producer since the 19th century, and in 1916 stole a march on the rest of North America by partially avoiding the Canadian Prohibition ban on alcohol. Grape growers negotiated an exemption from the Act, and by 1927 when their Prohibition ended, more than 50 wineries had a licence to operate. Wine is now produced in Ontario, Nova Scotia and Québec in the east and in British Columbia in the far west.

Despite harsh winter weather conditions, producers have moved away from the *labrusca* varieties which used to go into sweet 'port' and 'sherry' and are having success with *vinifera* varieties from Chardonnay to Pinot Noir. Robust hybrids such as Seyval Blanc, Vidal, Maréchal Foch and Baco Noir are still popular for their ability to withstand the alternate freezes and thaws of the Canadian spring, and winemakers have turned one major climatic factor to their advantage: the conditions that enable grapes to freeze on the vine occur every year here and luscious, perfumed, sweet Icewine results. Quality is controlled by the Vintners Quality Alliance (VQA), set up in 1988 to do a similar job to the AVAs south of the border.

PANORAMIC MAPS OF THE USA

California North Coast *pages 238–239*

North Sonoma *pages 240–241*

Russian River Valley *pages 242–243*

Napa Valley, Sonoma Valley and Carneros *pages 244–245*

Heart of Napa *pages 246–247*

California South Central Coast *page 251*

Santa Maria and Santa Ynez Valleys *pages 252–253*

Washington State *pages 258–259*

Oregon *pages 260–261*

New York State *pages 264–265*

OTHER MAPS

California *page 236*

California North Central Coast *page 248*

Pacific Northwest *page 257*

East Coast *page 262*

British Columbia *page 267*

Ontario *page 269*

CALIFORNIA

ON MY FIRST TRIP TO THE USA, I never got anywhere near California. But as a student actor with a notable thirst, I did get to the very heart of Californian wine as it then was. Draining flagon after flagon of brews with such names as Hearty Burgundy or Mountain Chablis – neither in any way related to the famous wine areas of France – I got my first ever experience of good, cheap wine. Until then, cheap had invariably meant filthy. But that was in Europe. In California, the world's first inexpensive, juicy, beverage wines were widely available. Winemakers had harnessed the vast, sun-baked desert of her Central Valley, and irrigated its parched soils with the limitless streams running off the Sierra Nevada mountains to produce these enjoyable wines in bulk. They were way ahead of their competitors, for this was when Australia was still stumbling out of a long period when beer and fortified wines were the national drinks, and before Spain, southern France and Eastern Europe had even grasped the concept that people might actually want a basic table wine to taste good.

That's one side of the Californian story, the side that has influenced the producers of basic wines across the world in the last twenty years, and that will eventually make obsolete bad wine at any price. But there's another even more inspirational side to the story.

This begins in the 1970s, around the time of my second trip to the US, when I did get to California and I immersed myself, without realizing it, in the fine wine revolution that had been gathering pace since the 1960s. I didn't know it then, but the bottles I used to pick off the wine shop shelves with names like Mondavi, Heitz, Sterling, Freemark Abbey and Schramsberg, were in the process of changing the face of the world of wine. These were the new wineries of the Napa Valley, north of San Francisco, that had thrown down the gauntlet to the classic French regions of Bordeaux, Burgundy and Champagne.

Not only that, but they were trying to emulate these ancient wines not at their basic level, but at the level of the greatest Grand Cru or De Luxe Cuvée they offered. They used the same grape varieties, the same methods of production as far as they could, and they bought equipment that only the very best French producers could afford. The wines they produced were stunning. They were so clearly related to the great French models, yet were so startlingly, thrillingly different. And they set the tone for this other side to California that has been avidly pursued ever since in the cooler vineyards of the state.

And there's the crux. Cooler. The Central Valley is a broad, torrid, irrigated, mass producer of grapes, making wines that never manage to achieve greatness, because the climatic conditions, here don't bring about exciting enough fruit. You need less sun, less heat, longer ripening seasons and lower yields. Yet if

MAIN AVA WINE AREAS

NORTHERN CALIFORNIA
1. Seiad Valley
2. Willow Creek

NORTH COAST AVA
3. Redwood Valley
4. Potter Valley
5. Clear Lake
6. Mendocino
7. Anderson Valley
8. Mendocino Ridge
9. Sonoma Coast
10. Northern Sonoma
11. Russian River Valley
12. Dry Creek Valley
13. Alexander Valley
14. Knights Valley
15. Sonoma Valley
16. Carneros
17. Napa Valley

CENTRAL VALLEY
18. Dunnigan Hills
19. Clarksburg
20. Merritt Island
21. Lodi
22. Diablo Grande
23. River Junction
24. Madera

SIERRA FOOTHILLS AVA
25. North Yuba
26. El Dorado
27. Fair Play
28. California Shenandoah Valley
29. Fiddletown

CENTRAL COAST AVA
30. San Francisco Bay
31. Livermore Valley
32. Santa Clara Valley
33. Santa Cruz Mountains
34. Monterey
35. Carmel Valley
36. Arroyo Seco
37. Chalone
38. Paso Robles
39. Edna Valley
40. Arroyo Grande Valley
41. Santa Maria Valley
42. Santa Ynez Valley

SOUTH COAST AVA
43. Malibu-Newton Canyon
44. Cucamonga Valley
45. Temecula
46. San Pasqual Valley

OVER 500M (1640FT)
OVER 1000M (3280FT)

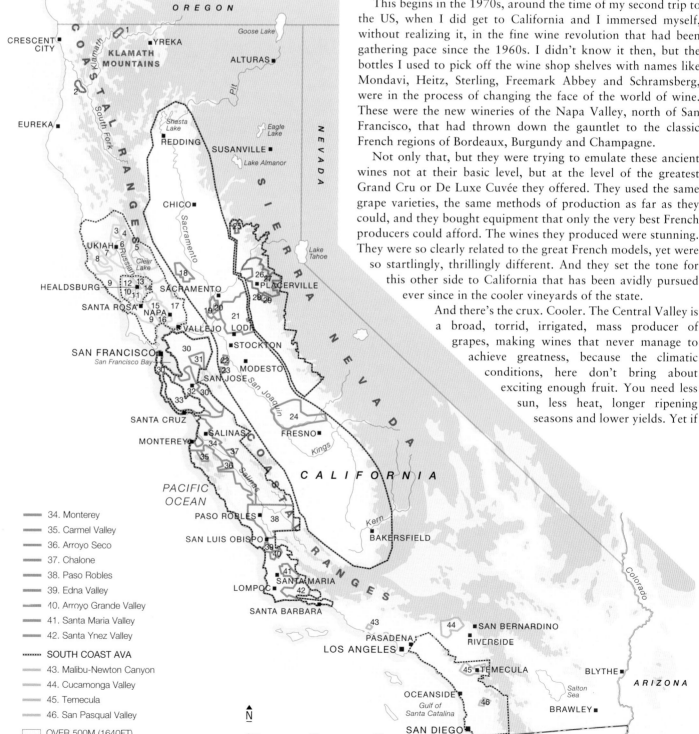

you look at the map, the Central Valley stretches from above Sacramento almost to Los Angeles, and that's exactly the same latitudes covered by all the California vineyard regions that manage to produce some of the world's most thrilling wine. The one factor they enjoy that the Central Valley doesn't, being tucked inland between the coastal ranges and the Sierra Nevada, is that they're all near to the sea. Even that wouldn't be enough by itself. The California coastline, however, produces unique climatic conditions, and with the help of some cold Pacific currents, the coastal ranges and the Central Valley itself, creates every conceivable vineyard climate, often within the space of just a few miles.

It works like this. There's an extremely cold current from Alaska that runs right down the California coast, and every summer this causes bodies of ice-cold water to well up from depths of several hundred feet. Being −7° to −9°C (12° to 16°F) colder than the surface water it replaces, it causes the warm air above the sea to condense and cool, forming huge fog banks. Meanwhile, over 160km (100 miles) inland, the Central Valley is baked every day in summer by the blazing sun. The hot air rises and creates a vacuum. There's no replacement air available from the east because of the high Sierras, so it has to come from the west.

At the top of the valley, the San Joaquin River creates a gap as it flows westwards into San Pablo Bay and out to sea through the mile-wide Golden Gate gap. As the Central Valley heats up, cold air and fog are sucked through the Golden Gate gap and over dips in the coastal ranges. Most of the fog is drawn towards the San Joaquin Valley, but some sweeps over Carneros and heads up both the Napa and Sonoma valleys. All the way along the coast south to Santa Barbara and north to Mendocino, wherever a dip in the hills or a river valley creates a gap in the coastal ranges, fogs and cold winds sweep in.

On the coast itself it's too cold to ripen any grape. But as the fog and wind sweep inland they gradually lose their force and it is reckoned that for every mile you travel up one of the valleys, the temperature can rise by one degree Fahrenheit. So Carneros, right down by San Pablo Bay is quite cool, yet Calistoga, 48km (30 miles) up the Napa Valley, is very warm. There are climatic quirks in all the valleys, and there are sites where altitude plays

more of a part than fog and sea breezes, but this relationship between cool Pacific and warm interior is the most important influence on vineyard quality in California.

GRAPE VARIETIES

It is only recently that the relationship between different grape varieties and their suitability for the various Californian soil and climatic conditions has begun to be properly explored. Before the 1960s, the number of acres planted with bulk varieties dwarfed those growing top-quality grapes. Since then, with the birth of California's fine wine tradition, things have changed so dramatically that Chardonnay is the most widely planted variety of all, and Cabernet Sauvignon the most common red. But there is a danger here. Because Chardonnay and Cabernet Sauvignon – and, more recently, Merlot – fetch the best prices, they have often been planted in inappropriate places, where other varieties would have been much more suitable.

In the late 1980s, growers had the perfect chance to re-evaluate what was planted in their vineyards, when phylloxera (or, as some people believe, a mutation called Biotype B phylloxera) reappeared. This led to the uprooting and replanting of almost all the vineyards in the state. A great opportunity, one would have thought, to replace inefficient vineyards and unsuitable varieties with modern systems and ideal grape varieties. If this had happened, we would now be seeing a lot more Sangiovese, Mourvèdre, Grenache, Marsanne, Viognier...

But what we are seeing is a lot more Chardonnay, Cabernet Sauvignon and Merlot, as market forces rather than the relationship between *terroir* and variety lead the way. Only Syrah, of the hot climate varieties, is on the march. That's a pity, but even so, some areas have proved themselves to be particularly suitable for certain varieties. Carneros is good for Pinot Noir and Chardonnay, as is the Santa Maria Valley, while Santa Ynez is good for Pinot Noir and Edna Valley for Chardonnay. Cabernet and Merlot have proved to work particularly well in the mountainside vineyards in Napa and Sonoma, and Zinfandel pops up in the most surprising places in many different guises.

Early morning fog blanketing the floor of Napa Valley at Calistoga plays a crucial role in cooling the vineyards.

THE CALIFORNIA CLIMATE

The very cold summer water along the west coast of the United States has a direct influence on the making of fine wine in coastal California. The cold ocean current running down the Pacific coast from Alaska wells up off north California, partly as a result of the strong coastal winds turning the water over. The colder water below comes to the surface and meets the warmer surface air, causing it to cool and condense into massive fog banks.

Meanwhile, on land, the baking morning sun heats up the interior valleys, where the hot air rises and pulls the cooler air and the fogs from the coast inland, through any gaps in the coastal ranges, to fill its space. The temperature falls, fogs roll in throughout the night only to disperse again the next day with the midday heat. If it weren't for this cooling influence, the coastal areas would be too hot for fine wine grapes. As it is, the influence lessens gradually as the breezes and fog banks travel inland. There is as much as an 18°F difference in temperature on a typical summer day between cool Carneros and warmer Calistoga, 48km (30 miles) up the Napa Valley.

'SLV' stands for Stag's Leap Vineyard, one of Stag's Leap Wine Cellars' finest sites on the east side of the Napa Valley.

NORTH COAST

IT'S A GOOD IDEA to start with Mendocino way up in northern California, because we're going to have to get used to the wild fluctuations in climate that afflict – or bless, depending on how you look at it – every single coastal wine region down to Santa Barbara. Up in Mendocino are some of California's hottest high-quality vineyards (I'm excluding the bulk-producing San Joaquin or Central Valley regions), best suited to grand, old-style, rip-roaring, throaty Zinfandel reds. But there are fog-draped, drizzly, chilly sites in Mendocino as well, that can just about coax Chardonnay and Pinot Noir to some sort of ripeness, and that make the eyes of a winemaker from the windswept Champagne region of northern France well up with tears of homesickness.

MENDOCINO AND LAKE COUNTY

The climatic variations found in Mendocino are all to do with those cold air currents rising up from the Pacific Ocean, and their accompanying fogs. The Anderson Valley which slices north-west through the towering redwood forests, feels them right to the bone. This is fascinating backwoods country, with vastly contrasting vineyard conditions, depending upon whether you are above or below the fog line. It is perhaps the most dramatic of Mendocino's various vineyard areas.

Up on the ridges above the valley, way above the fog line at between 400 and 700m (1300 and 2300ft), are some great old Zinfandel vineyards, their origins dating back to the sites that were first planted by Italian immigrants back in the closing decade of the 19th century. With a surfeit of sun, but cooled by their elevation above sea level, these mature vines give some thrilling flavours. New plantings of Zinfandel, Pinot Noir, Syrah and Merlot are also going on in the new AVA – known as Mendocino Ridge – for the scattering of vineyards in the west of the county sited at least 370m (1200ft) up.

Down below in the valley, though, things couldn't be more different. Even the early pioneers in the 1970s planted cool-climate grapes like Gewürztraminer and Riesling, and all the recent action

Flowers Winery vineyards at Cazadero, in the cool Sonoma Coast region. The netting is to stop birds eating the grapes.

is to do with Pinot Noir and Chardonnay destined for sparkling wine that has proved to be some of California's best and is uncannily similar to Champagne itself in character.

But generally most of Mendocino just sits and sizzles in the heat. Whereas further south in California I talk endlessly about how gaps in the Coast Ranges allow maritime breezes into the interior to cool everything down, up in the north in Mendocino, none of the little river valleys reach far enough inland to make much difference, because the Coast Range mountains here are 600 to 900m (1970 to 2953ft) high. And at that height, you are not going to get even a sniff of cooling breeze coming in from the Pacific. Indeed, the main valley here runs north-south, carved out by the Russian River (though the Russian River Valley AVA wine region doesn't appear until further south, in Sonoma County), which has to head right down to Healdsburg before it can

WHERE THE VINEYARDS ARE

On this map you only catch sight of a sliver of the Pacific Ocean to the west, and a tiny inlet or two of San Pablo Bay to the south, but keep a good eye on those two splashes of water: they're crucial to an understanding of the vineyards that lie north of San Francisco. Also take a note of the Coast Ranges. These are the mountains that run down to the edge of the Pacific. In general, they're not particularly high, but they are high enough to act as a barrier to most of the fog and icy wind that would otherwise sweep in from the ocean.

On the other hand, the areas inland from the sea would be far too hot for growing good wine grapes were it not for some cooling influence. And this is provided by the sea. In Mendocino County, the Anderson Valley; in Sonoma County the Russian River Valley; and in Sonoma, Napa and other counties east, the Golden Gate gap allows fog and cold air to be sucked in to the warm interior day by day. Without this effect, there would be no fine wine industry in California. With this effect, we have cool vineyards near the sea, gradually warming as the maritime influence weakens further inland.

Areas cut off from the maritime influence, like Potter Valley and Clear Lake, rely on altitude to keep their vines cool. There are also areas that rely upon altitude to moderate the heat as they are above the fog line. Howell Mountain, Atlas Peak, Spring Mountain, Mount Veeder and Sonoma Mountain are the best known.

find a low enough gap in the Coast Ranges to force a way through to the sea. Up in Mendocino, we're at the river's source. So the maritime influence which affects things further downstream has been pretty well played out, and the whole upriver basin is simply left to bake.

The results are strong, ripe reds from the north around Ukiah – mainly from Cabernet Sauvignon and Zinfandel, but there are also encouraging results from Italian and Rhône varieties. Following the Russian River south, the red wines are still quite hefty; and the beginnings of cooler conditions produce some fair whites down by Hopland. To the north of Ukiah, the Redwood Valley produces good whites and some excellent reds, while Potter Valley, further inland, is that bit warmer, but its elevation helps in providing cool nights. McDowell Valley, east of Hopland, is a high, sloping benchland that still has ancient planting of Grenache and Syrah, and is also getting good results from Viognier and Marsanne.

Further east is Lake County, where vineyards around Clear Lake, mostly at sites above 400m (1300ft), experience scorching days with ice-cold nights, and produce both red and white fruit of considerable intensity.

NORTH SONOMA
If Mendocino is relatively simple to understand, Sonoma County, directly to the south, is the most complex but also the most intriguingly satisfying of the other main wine counties north of San

SELECTED AVA WINE AREAS

1. Mendocino Ridge
2. Anderson Valley
3. Mendocino
4. Potter Valley
5. McDowell Valley

6. Clear Lake
7. Sonoma Coast
8. Northern Sonoma
9. Guenoc Valley
10. Sonoma Valley

11. Napa Valley
12. Carneros

RED GRAPES
Certain districts are associated with particular grape varieties, such as Dry Creek Valley Zinfandel, Napa Cabernet and Carneros Pinot Noir. Merlot also features.

WHITE GRAPES
Chardonnay is most widely planted. Sauvignon Blanc shows regional variations in style. There is also Pinot Blanc, Gewürztraminer and Riesling.

CLIMATE
The two-season climate of short, mild winters and long, dry, hot summers is dramatically influenced by summer fogs coming off the Pacific.

SOIL
An extraordinary variety of soils ranges from well-drained gravel and loam to infertile gravel and rock, volcanic ash with quartz and sandy loam.

ASPECT
Hill slopes are favoured for important vineyard sites, though much of the Napa Valley is flat.

CALIFORNIA NORTH COAST AVA BOUNDARY

OTHER AVA BOUNDARIES

TOTAL DISTANCE NORTH TO SOUTH
139KM (86 MILES)

VINEYARDS

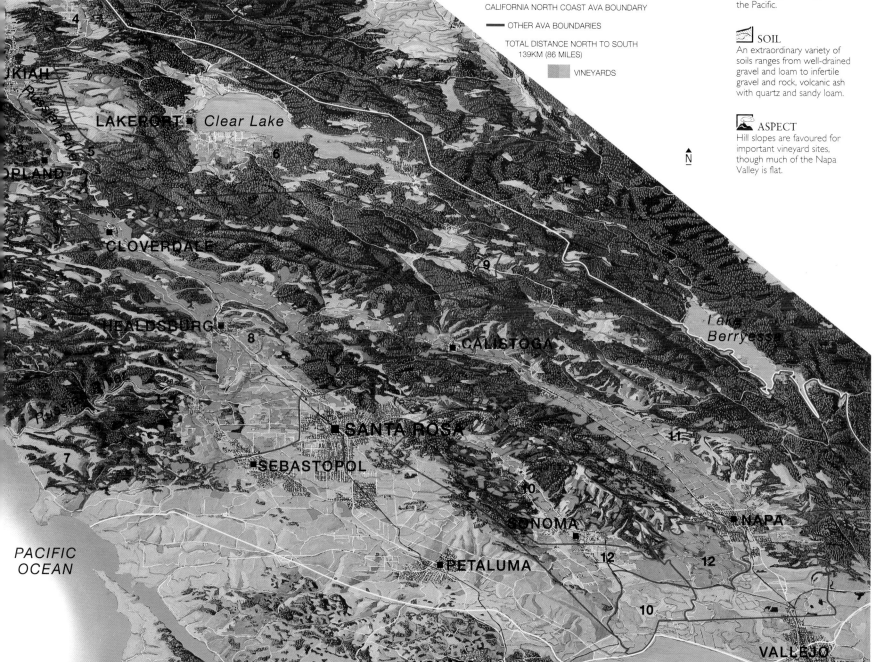

Francisco. Again, the dominant factor is the cooling effect of sea fogs and breezes, both as they push inland through the Russian River Valley, and as they flow off the northern slopes of San Pablo Bay at the southern end of the county – although, obviously, different soils, different elevations and different exposures to the sun also count.

Coming south from Mendocino on Highway 101, the Alexander Valley opens out north of Cloverdale; it's warm here, and both Zinfandel and the Rhône varieties ripen easily. However, the valley doesn't really begin to show its form until you get south of Geyserville. The broad fertile swathes of gravelly loam encourage vines to run riot, but modern methods of pruning, trellising and yield restraint now produce wonderfully soft-edged, yet mightily flavoured Cabernets that are a joy in youth and yet age with grace. Of slightly more concern are the swathes of high-yielding Chardonnay that carpet much of the southern section around Jimtown. One wonders quite who is going to buy it all. The small Knights Valley AVA, further east on the road to Calistoga in the Napa Valley, used to be very much a one-horse domaine – Beringer bottled a delicious fruity Cabernet from Knights Valley grapes, but apart from that the area was a vinous backwater. It isn't now. Much former pastureland is now strewn with vines and the big

players like Gallo have significant plantings here. Chardonnay is much more important than it was. The most encouraging sign is that there are some significant plantings on the low-yielding hillsides, rather than just on the valley floor.

Dry Creek Valley was planted with Zinfandel by Italian immigrants during the 1870s and it is still Zinfandel, in the breezeless, baking northern half of the valley, that makes Dry Creek special and gives you a feeling that the old rural America is still hanging on in here, amid the ever increasing dominance of the large companies. On both sides of the river are deposits of reddish rocky, gravelly soil, well-drained but able to retain the higher than average rainfall the valley receives. Cabernet is encroaching on these sites, but it is the Zinfandel that makes me want to shout for joy. On the valley floor, well-drained gravels produce surprisingly good Sauvignon Blanc and Chenin Blanc and, at the cooler southern end of the valley, some fine Chardonnay is grown.

It's really only south of Healdsburg in the Russian River Valley AVA that Sonoma County changes from a warm environment with a few cooling influences to a cool environment with warm patches, especially in the areas affected by the river. Technically, it should be too cold for Zinfandel along this stretch of the Russian River, but some marvellous examples crop up, frequently in vineyards that

NORTH SONOMA

TOTAL DISTANCE
NORTH TO SOUTH
32KM (20 MILES)

VINEYARDS

also grow superb Pinot Noir – no, don't ask me why, but you get the same paradox in Australia, where fine Shiraz and Riesling can grow in neighbouring fields. There's also lovely Gewürztraminer (albeit too little), Syrah and Merlot. Intensely flavoured Sauvignon Blancs (most notably from Rochioli) perfectly capture the grape's freshly cut hay and citrus peel aromas and, now that Sauvignon is becoming trendy in the US – thanks to the arrival of superb examples from New Zealand, patches of land with proven Sauvignon performance are going to be in demand.

But it is for Chardonnay and Pinot Noir that the cooler reaches have become famous. The Chardonnays have tropical fruit flavours backed by healthy oak and really fill your mouth. Most are naturally high in acid, so winemakers generally put them through malolactic fermentation. Yet, thanks to a long growing season, they maintain their pinpoint fruit character without ever being flabby.

RUSSIAN RIVER VALLEY

Russian River Valley has been seen as one of the premier appellations for Pinot Noir in California for more than a decade. At first, these wines grabbed our attention for their ripeness and boldness, a style far removed from the delicate, pretty examples that areas like Carneros were striving for at that time. Yet today there's been something of a U-turn. Areas like Carneros, Santa Maria and Anderson Valley in California, and Willamette Valley in Oregon to the north, are achieving richer, more succulent styles, just as the Russian River growers seem on the whole to be easing back. The typical Russian River style based on sweet black cherry fruit is being replaced by wild strawberry and a whiff of Coca Cola – sounds strange, but it's not uncommon in good Pinot Noir. Does it work? Yes it does, and so long as the wines retain their delightful lush texture, I'm pretty happy with what is yet another manifestation of Pinot Noir's increasing brilliance on the West Coast of America. If this implies Russian River is just about

Pinot – well, it isn't. Chardonnay for a start is renowned here. This is the heart of the fruit that goes into famous brands like Sonoma-Cutrer, and as you crisscross the areas west of Healdsburg and Windsor, you get a sense of an insatiable thirst for more and more Chardonnay. But there's Zinfandel too – brilliantly different, juicier, fresher than much other Zin, because those fogs travelling up the Russian River Valley from the sea have cooled things sufficiently to allow the grapes up to two weeks extra ripening time on the vine.

The early morning mist is still clearing from the ancient Lytton Springs Vineyard in Dry Creek Valley. Ridge use the fruit for a famous Zinfandel, but there's also some old Carignan as well as some Petite Sirah.

WHERE THE VINEYARDS ARE *It doesn't look like much, that little thread of Russian River Valley in North Sonoma, curling in from the west, but even a small gap like the Russian River Valley can let enough cold maritime winds and fogs creep inland to have a dramatic cooling effect on what would otherwise be an extremely hot growing environment.*

There are now vineyards planted so far out west they are within sight of the coast, that are producing exciting Pinot, Chardonnay and sparkling wine. The vineyards you can see here, at the extreme left of the map, are for sparkling wines; follow the river east and you will come to Green Valley, whose vineyards are still strongly affected by fog and wind; these produce both sparkling wines and good Chardonnay and Pinot Noir.

The climate is a little warmer looking across to Santa Rosa, although surprisingly Pinot Noir can still be excellent in places, as can Zinfandel. The Chalk Hill area to the east has shown form with Chardonnay and with Sauvignon Blanc. Healdsburg is the hub for two other areas. Dry Creek Valley is an excellent warm region lying in a short, north-west-running valley. And to the north of Healdsburg, Alexander Valley provides some of the most approachable Cabernet wines in California.

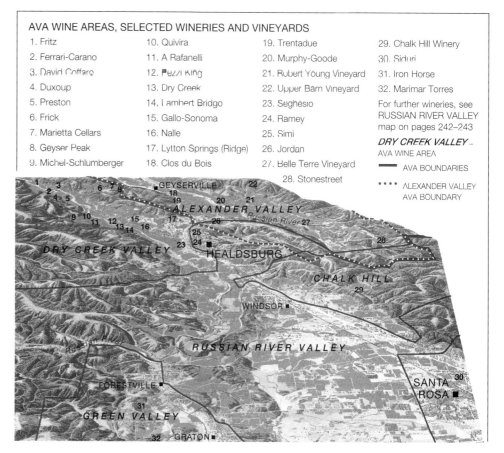

AVA WINE AREAS, SELECTED WINERIES AND VINEYARDS

1. Fritz	10. Quivira	19. Trentadue	29. Chalk Hill Winery
2. Ferrari-Carano	11. A Rafanelli	20. Murphy-Goode	30. Siduri
3. David Coffaro	12. Pezzi King	21. Robert Young Vineyard	31. Iron Horse
4. Duxoup	13. Dry Creek	22. Upper Barn Vineyard	32. Marimar Torres
5. Preston	14. Lambert Bridge	23. Seghesio	For further wineries, see
6. Frick	15. Gallo-Sonoma	24. Ramey	RUSSIAN RIVER VALLEY
7. Marietta Cellars	16. Nalle	25. Simi	map on pages 242–243
8. Geyser Peak	17. Lytton Springs (Ridge)	26. Jordan	*DRY CREEK VALLEY* –
9. Michel-Schlumberger	18. Clos du Bois	27. Belle Terre Vineyard	AVA WINE AREA
		28. Stonestreet	

— AVA BOUNDARIES

• • • • ALEXANDER VALLEY AVA BOUNDARY

SANTA ROSA

0 km   1   2
0 miles   1

There has been an interesting debate going on in Russian River recently about redefining the AVA so that it would only apply to areas affected by the cool coastal fogs. Since most AVAs are politically motivated rather than being based on the special characteristics of vineyard land, it was very heartening when at the end of 2005 the Russian River Valley AVA was formally changed to include all of Green Valley, all of Santa Rosa Plains and a cool southerly section known as Sebastopol Hills. Hopefully this will set a precedent for other AVAs and will open the door for numerous other areas to put a proper vineyard-sensitive definition on the books. The whole concept of 'Appellation' in California will be greatly enhanced.

Green Valley is a sub-AVA south of Forestville, and is even cooler – a prime site for Chardonnay, Pinot Noir and sparkling wine. Interestingly, examples of Pinot Noir from here are darker in colour than the rest of Russian River Valley, with more intense acidity and greater concentration. The sparkling wines, aided by these slow-ripening tasty grapes, are full and fleshy, but age extremely well.

SONOMA COAST

The Sonoma Coast appellation is a mish-mash that covers all of Russian River, along with parts of Sonoma Valley and Carneros. This boundary definition came about, as did several other AVAs in California, through political grandstanding. Basically, it means that the appellation has no signature style, although there are a few sites that display special characteristics with Pinot Noir. The vineyards around the town of Cazadero, only a few miles inland

from the Pacific Ocean, are among the most prized in Sonoma. At a height of some 350–450 metres (1150–1475ft) above sea level, they are above the fog line, enabling the grapes to ripen fully in the bright sunlight. Yet the proximity to the ocean means very cool temperatures, which can make optimal ripening a problem in certain years.

These struggles allow for deeply coloured – well, purple really –, massively concentrated Pinot Noirs that are Californian versions of Chambertin. Flowers Winery is the leading estate here, while the Hirsch Vineyard has been the source for remarkable Pinot Noir for several of Sonoma's finest estates. But the State's trendsetters are also flooding in to the region. Marcassin's Chardonnays and Pinot Noirs, grown on a site 460m (1500ft) up but only one bluff in from the sea, are producing thrilling flavours, and Pahlmeyer and Marimar Torres have headed towards the coast, and Failla-Jordan, whose owner makes wine for Turley in Napa Valley, has even planted Syrah. Not all the vineyards are as high as 460m (1500ft) – Coastlands to the south, for instance, is significantly lower – and not all the vineyards are quite so close to the sea – it's a 11-km (7-mile) hike from the new Torres Dona Margarita site – but over the next few years, we're going to see some remarkable wines from the gullies, bluffs, creeks and forest glades that make up the Sonoma Coast region.

SONOMA VALLEY

The Sonoma Creek rises south-east of Santa Rosa and the Sonoma Valley AVA stretches southwards, taking in the lower slopes of the Mayacamas mountains, and bordering the Carneros AVA down

Vineyards in the Russian River Valley. The green of the pine forest implies a cool climate and, indeed, the vines are cooled by breezes running up the river valley from the Pacific.

RUSSIAN RIVER VALLEY

 VINEYARDS

TOTAL DISTANCE NORTH TO SOUTH 24KM (15 MILES)

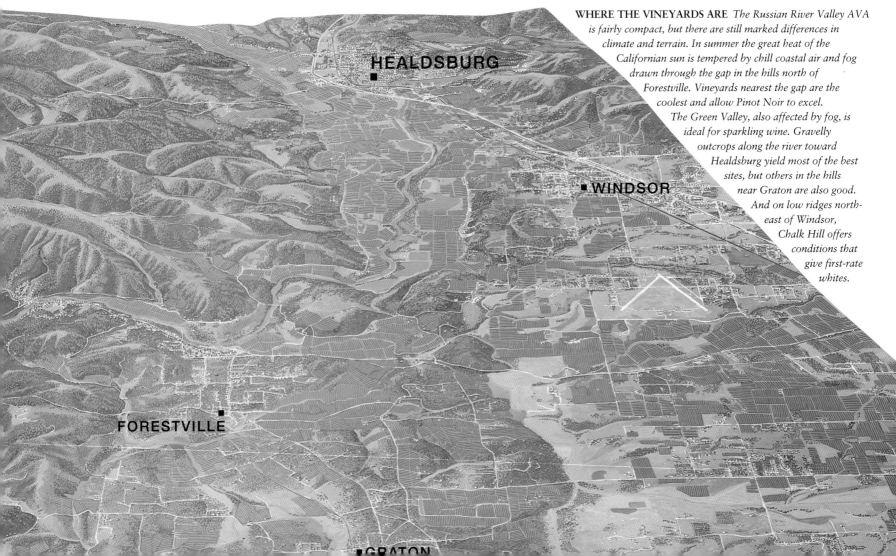

WHERE THE VINEYARDS ARE *The Russian River Valley AVA is fairly compact, but there are still marked differences in climate and terrain. In summer the great heat of the Californian sun is tempered by chill coastal air and fog drawn through the gap in the hills north of Forestville. Vineyards nearest the gap are the coolest and allow Pinot Noir to excel. The Green Valley, also affected by fog, is ideal for sparkling wine. Gravelly outcrops along the river toward Healdsburg yield most of the best sites, but others in the hills near Graton are also good. And on low ridges north-east of Windsor, Chalk Hill offers conditions that give first-rate whites.*

HEALDSBURG

WINDSOR

FORESTVILLE

GRATON

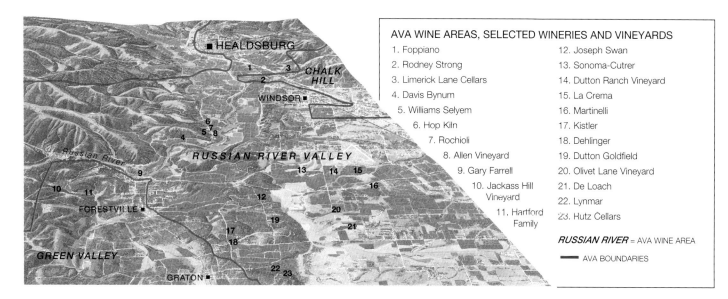

AVA WINE AREAS, SELECTED WINERIES AND VINEYARDS

1. Foppiano
2. Rodney Strong
3. Limerick Lane Cellars
4. Davis Bynum
5. Williams Selyem
6. Hop Kiln
7. Rochioli
8. Allen Vineyard
9. Gary Farrell
10. Jackass Hill Vineyard
11. Hartford Family
12. Joseph Swan
13. Sonoma-Cutrer
14. Dutton Ranch Vineyard
15. La Crema
16. Martinelli
17. Kistler
18. Dehlinger
19. Dutton Goldfield
20. Olivet Lane Vineyard
21. De Loach
22. Lynmar
23. Rutz Cellars

RUSSIAN RIVER = AVA WINE AREA

━━━ AVA BOUNDARIES

towards San Pablo Bay. From Santa Rosa south to Kenwood, some of the cooling fog and ocean air from Russian River can still be felt, but the more powerful tempering forces are the fog banks and wind that have roared through the Golden Gate gap at San Francisco, howled across Carneros and still had enough chilly life in them at Kenwood to see off any fog from the north.

This double influence does make for unpredictable, if cool, conditions, particularly south of Glen Ellen, where the Mayacamas and Sonoma mountains crowd in on the valley from the east and west. Good Chardonnay, Pinot Noir and Merlot are grown in these cooler climates – as you might expect with Carneros nudging the southern border. Zinfandel, which you might not expect, also performs well here; these versions are pure blackberry as opposed to the rich raspberry jam and dates of Dry Creek Valley.

Conditions change dramatically when you climb above the fog line. On the west-facing slopes of the Mayacamas, the greater intensity of afternoon sunshine produces deep-fruited, dark-hearted Cabernets and Zinfandels. Sonoma Mountain is also above the fog line, but has more vineyards angled east-to-north-east to avoid direct exposure to the midday and afternoon rays. With relatively warm nights due to the fogs on the valley floor pushing warmer air up the mountainsides, equally intense, but more thrillingly fragrant and soft-hearted Cabernets and Zinfandels are produced, as well as a famous Chardonnay at McCrea vineyard south-west of Glen Ellen.

CARNEROS

Carneros extends right across the bottom of the map on pages 244 to 245; to its south is the San Pablo Bay and, over its border to the north east, is the city of Napa. It is one of the most important vineyard areas in California. In the search to make wines of a supposedly European delicacy and finesse, Carneros was singled out as long ago as 1938 by Californian wine wizard André Tchelistcheff, but the region had been growing vines for maybe a century before that. It was the very un-California-ness that attracted Tchelistcheff – small crops and small grapes struggling manfully to survive in difficult soil, with not enough rain, and with fog and wind a virtual certainty throughout the growing season.

The Carneros wine region slithers across the southern end of Napa and Sonoma, the Mayacamas and Sonoma mountains splaying their feet into a series of rumpled hummocks that gradually subside into San Pablo Bay. Farmers have always known that this was difficult soil to grow anything on, and traditionally most of it was consigned to grazing. With the lowest annual rainfall in both Napa and Sonoma counties – usually about 560mm (22in) – and a shallow, silty soil, often only a couple of feet above impenetrable, dense clay, few people felt inclined to plant anything in the area.

And then, when the search for a cool-climate vineyard began, they were converted. The Golden Gate gap at San Francisco is the only place that the Pacific Ocean actually breaches the Coast Ranges, to form the long enclosed sea of San Francisco Bay and San Pablo Bay. And as the fogs and the winds are sucked inwards by the baking heat of the inland valleys, the first land they come to is Carneros. Fogs blanket Carneros on summer nights. These clear by late morning to be replaced by bright sunshine – and then up comes the afternoon breeze, merely strong or positively howling depending on the conditions that day. The net result of this combination of hot sun and clammy fog is a very long, cool ripening period, from early March until well into October. The wind cools the vines, but its strength can also cause the vines' photosynthetic system to shut down temporarily, delaying ripening. This is almost too much for most grape varieties, but remember, even if the warmth of Carneros is not hugely different from somewhere like Chablis in Burgundy, we're at latitude 38° North here: that's the equivalent of the toe of Italy in Europe. This means that the intensity of sunshine, warm or not, is much greater in southern Italy than it is in northern France. And it's the same in Carneros. These conditions are ideal for zingy, crisp Chardonnays and tartly refreshing sparkling wines and, of course, expressive Pinot Noirs. While these Pinots were delicate wines at first, the introduction of new clones plus careful canopy management to ensure riper fruit, has resulted in a bigger, meatier and, frankly, much more exciting style.

There is the occasional Cabernet and some fine Syrah emerging from Carneros as well, particularly from vines that are set back from the Bay, but the newest star is Merlot. Just as Pomerol is better suited for Merlot than Pauillac or St-Julien in the Haut-Médoc, so too does Carneros suit this variety. Two factors are at work here: cooler temperatures and clay soils. Merlot likes both and the examples from here, as opposed to those from the middle of the valley, have greater intensity and higher acidity. Black cherry flavours and soothing textures dominate these wines, instead of the simple raspberry or cranberry fruit and, frequently, rough unripe edges, that characterize Merlot from the warmer reaches of the valley.

As virtually every inch of available land in Napa Valley seems to be under vine, growers are always on the lookout for new sites. South and east of the city of Napa, thousands of acres have been planted around American Canyon. Cool temperatures and gently rolling hillsides make the area ideal for Merlot and Chardonnay, as these grapes, used by many of the valley's premium producers, add structure and backbone to final blends. Less reassuring are plantings in the low-lying land west of Napa River as it approaches the Bay and also down towards the naval base of Skaggs Island, on land that seems barely better than swamp.

NAPA VALLEY

The Napa valley runs north-west to south-east for only about 48km (30 miles), but the difference in conditions along this short distance is dramatic. Calistoga, at the head of the valley, has a daytime climate hot enough to ripen every known red variety, and is only saved from being a cauldron in which to bake the life out of its fruit by the ice-cold air that drains down the high mountains, hemming it in on three sides. Yet down at the mouth of the valley is Carneros, chilled by fogs and gales, only able to ripen its cool-climate Pinot Noir, Merlot and Chardonnay because of the brief bursts of sun that separate the morning fogs from the afternoon wind.

And throughout most of the valley, it is still the climatic conditions that govern what types of grape are grown and what wines excel, rather than the soils and their exposure to the sun. There are, in fact, more soil types in Napa, I'm told, than in the whole of France, and some committed growers are trying to match grape variety with soil conditions as they replant. But, with a few brilliant exceptions, such as the well-drained fans of soil around Rutherford and Oakville, much of the soil on the Napa Valley floor

NAPA VALLEY,
SONOMA VALLEY
AND CARNEROS

TOTAL DISTANCE NORTH TO
SOUTH 49KM (30 MILES)

VINEYARDS

N

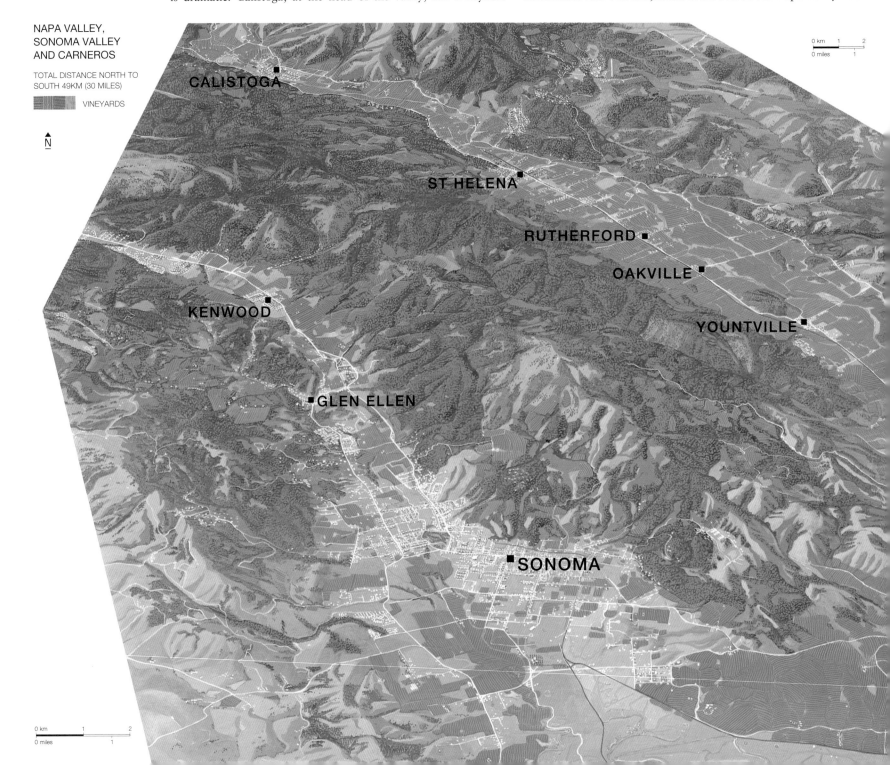

CALISTOGA

ST HELENA

RUTHERFORD

OAKVILLE

KENWOOD

YOUNTVILLE

GLEN ELLEN

SONOMA

0 km 1 2
0 miles 1

0 km 1 2
0 miles 1

is heavy, clayish, over-fertile and difficult to drain, and certainly unfit to make great wine. There's no shame in this, because much of Bordeaux's great Médoc region cannot spawn a decent grape. The only shame is in pretending that this isn't so. The trouble is that the wines made from the good soil have been so good that every man and his dog wanted a piece of the action. When two Napa wines, a Chardonnay and a Cabernet Sauvignon, won the famous 'Judgement of Paris' tasting in 1976 against Grand Cru white Burgundy and Premier Cru Bordeaux, Napa became a promised land – for those with ambition and money.

Vineyards were planted and wineries sprang up like mushrooms after rain; a couple of dozen wineries at the end of the 1960s had become nearly 400 by 2005. And, sadly, this traffic jam of growers and producers, many blending grapes and wines from sites all over the valley and outside it as well, led to a blurring of personality and a dilution of recognizable flavours. But a clutch of fine vintages at the end of the 1990s and beginning of the 2000s, and a greater maturity among winemakers who initially were slavishly following

college textbook winemaking methods, rather than allowing themselves and their grapes free rein, has begun to signal an upturn in Napa quality.

Brilliant conditions do exist in the Napa Valley, and there are more committed owners and gifted winemakers at work today than ever before, but as quality reaches an all-time high, the chief point of distress is that prices are at an all-time high too. So let's see where they grow their fruit. We'll work from north to south. And we'll stick to the valley floor first, and then look into the mountains where some of the most exciting fruit is grown.

Calistoga at the head of the valley has a touch of the frontier town about it, with a more rough-hewn feel than the other wine towns and villages, and I always head here to try to dissolve some of the black Cabernet tannin off my teeth with draughts of local ale. But it has good vineyards too. One or two mesoclimates like Storybook Mountain to the north-west of Calistoga produce startling Zinfandel; otherwise, the rocky outcrops and sandy loams produce good results with Cabernet and Merlot.

This is one of the most expensive wines produced in America. Harlan Estate's Napa Valley red is made from the Bordeaux varieties.

WHERE THE VINEYARDS ARE *So many great Californian vineyards are packed into the flatlands of Sonoma, Carneros and Napa and up on the surrounding mountains, that I hardly know where to start. But I'll try. Let's begin with Carneros at the bottom of the map. To the south, just off the map, is San Pablo Bay, whose roaring winds and billowing fogs affect all the vineyards. Their cooling influences extend up the Sonoma and Napa Valleys, lessening as they go. In the north-west are Sonoma Mountain's fine vineyards and, directly north, the Mayacamas mountains boast equally good sites. East of the Mayacamas, Spring Mountain, Mount Veeder and Howell Mountain all have fine, high-altitude vineyards. There are also excellent sites in Stags Leap and on the hills near Napa itself. Vines carpet the valley floor, from cool Napa right up to warm Calistoga, while the most famous sites are at Oakville and Rutherford.*

AVA WINE AREAS, SELECTED WINERIES AND VINEYARDS				
SONOMA VALLEY AVA	16. Buena Vista	31. Stony Hill	48. Newlan	64. Acacia
1. Matanzas Creek	17. Gundlach-Bundschu	32. El Molino	49. Monticello	65. Saintsbury
2. Landmark		33. Burgess	50. Altamura	66. Bouchaine
3. St Francis	**NAPA VALLEY AVA**	34. Viader	51. Jade Mountain	67. Kent Rasmussen
4. Chateau St Jean	18. Storybook Mountain	35. Dunn	52. Luna	
5. Kenwood	19. Chateau Montelena	36. Liparita	53. Atlas Peak	For further wineries, see HEART OF NAPA map on pages 246–247
6. Kistler Vineyard	20. Diamond Creek	37. La Jota	54. Pahlmeyer	
7. Laurel Glen	21. Reverie	38. Seavey	55. Robert Biale	
8. Benziger	22. Clos Pegase	39. Neyers		**NAPA VALLEY** = AVA WINE AREA
9. Kunde	23. Araujo/Eisele Vineyard	40. Green & Red Vineyard	**CARNEROS AVA**	
10. Wellington Vineyards	24. Cuvaison	41. Bryant Family Vineyard	56. Durrell Vineyards	▬ AVA BOUNDARIES
11. Arrowood	25. Sterling	42. Harrison	57. Sangiacomo Vineyards	
12. B R Cohn	26. Schramsberg	43. Chateau Potelle	58. Gloria Ferrer	▬ ▬ CARNEROS AVA BOUNDARY
13. Monte Rosso Vineyard	27. Barnett	44. Mayacamas	59. Richardson	
14. Moon Mountain	28. Robert Keenan	45. Mount Veeder	60. Artesa	
15. Ravenswood	29. Philip Togni	46. Hess Collection	61. Truchard	
	30. Cain	47. Havens	62. Domaine Carneros	
			63. Carneros Creek	

Just above St Helena, the Napa Valley changes direction: instead of running east-south-east, it alters to something more like south-south-east and keeps this orientation more or less until Carneros. As it begins to broaden out, vineyards stretch right across the valley floor, though the best, like Spottswoode and Grace Family, are still tucked into the base of the mountain slopes on either side.

The only time when there seems to be a general consensus about valley floor conditions being truly excellent over one great swathe rather than just in dribs and drabs, is at Rutherford and Oakville. All the great original Cabernet Sauvignon vineyards were planted here, some of them over a century ago, mostly on the so-called Rutherford Bench. Two alluvial fans spread out at Rutherford and at Oakville, though Rutherford attached its name to the Bench first. They are well-drained in Napa terms, though also heavy enough to hold moisture during summer, and they slope just perceptibly towards Highway 29, which is crucial for drainage. Whether or not these soils go beyond the road is one of those arguments to keep lawyers and pedants happy for generations. Suffice to say that Napa Valley Cabernet made its reputation on fruit from these Rutherford and Oakville acres.

But was it just the soil? I personally think the soil gets heavier and more cloddish east of the road, but fine Cabernets still turn up from sites not only east of the road, but east of the river too. Nevertheless, the Rutherford Bench and Oakville vineyards do seem to have struck the right balance between water-holding and drainage, between vigour and restraint, for the climatic conditions of this particular part of the Napa Valley. Imprecise, sure. But there's more than a century of experience that says it's so. This imprecise but definable balance of elements affecting the grape is what the French would call *terroir*. It took them quite a while to work it out, too.

Oakville and Rutherford are separate AVAs, and while there are fine examples of Chardonnay and Sauvignon Blanc made here, Cabernet is what both do best. As more new money has been invested in replanting and research, a separate style is starting to emerge from these districts. Rutherford, being further north, is slightly warmer and produces wines that feature black cherry and black olive fruit and a dusty, grainy, tannic flavouring, known as Rutherford Dust.

Oakville, being cooler, gets more hangtime in the vineyards, consequently producing wines that display a wider and more intriguing array of black fruits. It is these flavours, from estates such as Screaming Eagle, Opus One and Harlan, that have created such a stir over the last decade. However, even within Oakville, two styles emerge. As the district runs the entire east-west width of the valley, wines vary according to where the grapes are grown.

The vineyards on the east side that receive the hotter afternoon sun (Dalla Valle) produce wines that are riper and softer in tannins than those from the west side. Wines from this cooler mesoclimate (Harlan, Far Niente) are tighter and not as sumptuous on release. These wines also show more herbaceousness and often a slight mintiness in the aroma, at least partly due to the effect of the prominent eucalyptus trees in the area.

When you drive past the bluffs in the middle of the valley, just north of Yountville, you're driving past a barrier to the fog and wind that brings about a discernible dip in temperature to their south. Yountville is decidedly cooler than Oakville and it gets even cooler down by the town of Napa. They do grow reds here, but the most impressive results are from Chardonnay.

The Mayacamas Range to the west is a collection of gaunt, thinly populated peaks, where coyotes, rattlesnakes and wild deer are as likely to impede your progress as people. But they do harbour some smashing vineyards, especially on Mount Veeder, Spring Mountain and, further north off our map, Diamond Mountain. We're talking primarily incisive, focused, powerful red wines from low-yielding volcanic soils at heights that can go past 600m (1970ft).

Stags Leap District spreads out onto the valley floor towards Yountville and up the sides of several small hillocks about a mile away from the eastern mountains proper, and produces Cabernets that are rich and pinging with fruit, yet artfully balance tannin and acidity. Many of California's wine regions have acquired their fame through relentless marketing efforts. Stags Leap is famous because its wines taste better. Higher up the eastern mountains are Atlas Peak, Chiles Valley, Pope Valley and above them all, Howell Mountain, whose vineyards have been famous since the 19th century and whose coppery red volcanic soil, exposed to the sun but cooled by its altitude of 420–600m (1378–1970ft) regularly produces some of the sturdiest but most deliciously scented reds in Napa.

0 km   1   2
0 miles   1

ST HELENA ▪

RUTHERFORD ▪

OAKVILLE ▪

YOUNTVILLE ▪

HEART OF NAPA

TOTAL DISTANCE
NORTH TO
SOUTH 18.5 KM (11½ MILES)

▨▨▨ VINEYARDS

▲
N

0 km   1   2
0 miles   1

You know spring is near when the mustard begins to flower. These vines, that are framed by the low ranges of the Mayacamas Mountains, are in the Rutherford area of the Napa Valley, which has been prime Cabernet territory over the last 70 years or so. The flat, benchland soils are deep and well drained, giving rich wines with lovely black cherry fruit, touched with a supple spiciness.

WHERE THE VINEYARDS ARE

The heart of the Napa Valley is really California's promised land for one great variety – Cabernet Sauvignon. The character of the wines can be refreshingly diverse, depending on whether the grapes come from the valley floor or from the surrounding mountain slopes.

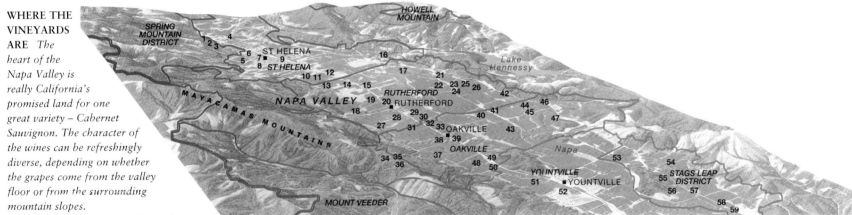

On the valley floor, conditions become gradually warmer as you head north-west, away from the fogs and cold winds. Yountville's cooler conditions can produce fine Chardonnay, but Oakville and Rutherford, appreciably warmer and with well-drained vineyard sites, have long been famous for Cabernet Sauvignon.

Mount Veeder, Spring Mountain and Diamond Mountain provide a fascinating array of steeply angled, low-yielding sites on volcanic soils, well above the fog belt, but cooled by altitude. Stags Leap is a famous Cabernet stronghold, benefiting from just enough of the cool breezes off San Pablo Bay, while the grapes planted on its wide, well-drained alluvial fan ripen to perfection.

AVA WINE AREAS, SELECTED WINERIES AND VINEYARDS

1. Colgin
2. Grace Family
3. Vineyard 29
4. Duckhorn
5. Newton
6. Beringer
7. Cafaro
8. Spottswoode
9. Merryvale
10. Abreu
11. Flora Springs
12. Heitz Cellars
13. Livingston
14. Whitehall Lane
15. Franciscan Oakville Estate
16. Joseph Phelps
17. Quintessa
18. Rubicon Estate
19. Grgich Hills
20. Beaulieu Vineyard
21. Conn Creek
22. Frog's Leap
23. Caymus
24. Bacio Divino
25. Mumm Napa
26. ZD
27. Staglin Family
28. Swanson
29. St. Supéry
30. Cakebread
31. Robert Mondavi
32. Turnbull
33. Opus One
34. Harlan Estate
35. Oakford
36. Martha's Vineyard
37. Far Niente
38. To Kalon Vineyard
39. Etude
40. Saddleback
41. Groth
42. Miner Family
43. Silver Oak
44. Rudd
45. Plumpjack
46. Dalla Valle
47. Screaming Eagle
48. Paradigm
49. Cardinale
50. Lokoya
51. Dominus
52. Domaine Chandon
53. S. Anderson Vineyard
54. Shafer
55. Silverado Vineyards
56. Pine Ridge
57. Stag's Leap Wine Cellars
58. Chimney Rock
59. Clos du Val

NAPA VALLEY = AVA WINE AREA

— AVA BOUNDARIES

NORTH CENTRAL COAST

RED GRAPES
Cabernet Sauvignon, Pinot Noir and Zinfandel are widely planted, while the minor varieties include Petite Sirah and Merlot.

WHITE GRAPES
Chardonnay and Sauvignon Blanc are ever-present, along with some Chenin Blanc, Riesling and Pinot Blanc.

CLIMATE
This ranges from cool and foggy when influenced by San Francisco and Monterey bays, to dry and very hot. Strong, incessant winds can also represent a threat to the vineyards. Rainfall is low.

SOIL
A wide variety of soils includes gravel, stones of considerable size, clay and loam, with occasional granite and limestone outcrops. These can be mixed, even within single vineyards.

ASPECT
Vineyard exposure is very important in order to ensure the correct ripening of the grapes. Elevation varies widely, which causes great differences in the influence of fog, wind and sunshine.

Clos LaChance

THERE AREN'T MANY OF MY FAVOURITE VINEYARDS that I can say I prefer to visit at night, but Ridge, high in the Santa Cruz Mountains, is one of them. Climb to the top of the rise above the tasting room on the night of a full moon. As the moon hangs heavy in the vast night sky, its cloak of silver stars spreadeagled across the purple blackness, the dark crags of the forested mountain peaks pierce the pale night light to the west. And to the east, 600m (1970ft) below me, lies the bustling city of San Jose, so far below that the brilliant city lights are just twinkling patterns on the valley floor. The sullen drone of its cars and businesses fades to silence halfway up my mountain slope, and away to the north, San Francisco Bay glows with a faint pewter sheen.

Ridge is the most famous of the wineries that are sprinkled sparsely around San Francisco Bay itself. There used to be many more, but as the Bay area's urban sprawl reaches further into the hinterland, few wineries or vineyards have been able to resist the temptation of the easier profits to be gained by selling up to housing developers. But that doesn't mean the companies have all gone out of business. They haven't. They've simply moved their vineyard interests further south. This North Central Coast region divides neatly into the old regions of Livermore, Santa Clara and Santa Cruz, where wineries outnumber vineyards, and the great new tracts of land centered on Monterey County, where wineries are few and far between, but contract vineyards can stretch as far as the eye can see.

You have to use your imagination in the Livermore Valley to see it as one of the original great vineyard sites of California. Getting there, either from the north or the south, is a seemingly endless trek through industrial parks and housing subdivisions that don't let up till you're right in the vineyards themselves, glancing nervously at the nuclear facility to one side and the futuristic wind generator farms to the other. But Livermore is a fine vineyard site, albeit one that has its back to the wall as the start of the new millennium decides its land is more useful for houses and factories. There are still about 2023ha (5000 acres) of vines, mostly owned by the Wente family who are staunchly leading a fight against urbanization. It is relatively warm, because hills to the west block off most of the chill Pacific winds, and the gravelly Médoc-like soils promise good results from grapes like Cabernet Sauvignon. Curiously, reds are not that special, but white Bordeaux specialities – Semillon and Sauvignon Blanc – can be outstanding.

Santa Clara County's vines have been pushed relentlessly south by San Jose's suburbs, and it is really only around Gilroy that you get a sense of a wine culture still hanging on. Gilroy is the self-dubbed 'garlic capital of the world' and, boy, can you smell it when you stop on Highway 101 to fill up with gas. But good fruit is grown to the east of the town and wineries pay good money for Pinot Noir, amongst others. If you turn west off 101 and head up through the Hecker Pass, you'll find remnants of the old farmgate Italian wineries that used to pepper Santa Clara and Santa Cruz counties, and you'll find scrubby patches of bush vines of varieties like Grenache, that are at last beginning to be appreciated.

Santa Cruz County is important for its wineries, as well as its vineyards – there are some 542ha (1340 acres) of vines sprinkled through the majestic forested hills that rear up on this Pacific Coast between San Francisco and the resort of Santa Cruz. Some of these vines – as those belonging to Mount Eden, David Bruce and, of course, Ridge – produce stunning wines, especially long-lived Chardonnay and Cabernet Sauvignon, but much fruit is bought in from other areas. There is also some robust Pinot Noir. It is impossible to characterize the Santa Cruz conditions: vineyards range in height from over 600m (1970ft) high down to fog level, and their aspects can be east, south, north or west facing; the only relatively consistent features are the soil, which is largely infertile, impoverished shale – keeping yields low and contributing to the startling flavours in many of the local wines – and the likelihood of an earthquake disturbing your slumbers: the San Andreas Fault lies right alongside Ridge's winery.

Startling flavours were nearly the undoing of the other part of the North Central Coast – the vast, flat, supremely fertile, dark-soiled acres of Monterey County. The 'Monterey veggies' these unripe, green flavours were called, and since, as I head down for Santa Cruz, I pass through Watsonville, Prunedale, Castroville, Salinas and so on – towns which variously proclaim themselves World Capital of the artichoke kingdom, or prunes, or broccoli, lettuces and pretty well anything else a starving vegetarian might crave – I suppose I shouldn't be too surprised.

The Salinas Valley, in Monterey County, does have every reason to proclaim itself the Salad Bowl of America, and most of its flat valley floor is given over to intensive vegetable and fruit cultivation. However, as long ago as 1935, experts were suggesting it would be a good area for

MAIN AVA WINE AREAS

- •••• Central Coast AVA
- —— 1. San Francisco Bay
- —— 2. Livermore Valley
- —— 3. Santa Cruz Mountains
- —— 4. Ben Lomond Mountain
- —— 5. Santa Clara Valley
- —— 6. San Ysidro District
- —— 7. Pacheco Pass
- —— 8. Mount Harlan
- —— 9. Cienega Valley
- —— 10. Lime Kiln Valley
- ═══ 11. San Benito
- ═══ 12. Paicines
- ═══ 13. Montcroy
- ═══ 14. Carmel Valley
- ═══ 15. Santa Lucia Highlands
- ═══ 16. Chalone
- ═══ 17. Arroyo Seco
- ═══ 18. San Lucas
- ═══ 19. Hames Valley
- ☐ OVER 500M (1640FT)
- ▨ OVER 1000M (3280FT)

planting grape vines and, when vineyards in the Bay area were squeezed by urban development in the late 1950s and 1960s, big companies like Masson and Mirassou upped sticks and headed south to the Salinas Valley, planting like fury as they came.

Monterey County now has over 16,188ha (40,000 acres); one vineyard alone near King City is 14 by 8km (9 by 5 miles). The only problem is they mostly planted the wrong grapes, and in the wrong places, and in particular, too many red grapes, too near the sea.

Let me explain. The first point is, as usual in California, the influence of the Pacific Ocean. Monterey Bay is about 56km (35 miles) wide and acts as an enormous funnel at the mouth of the Salinas Valley. Its waters stay a chilly 13°C (55°F) all year round. Looking south-east up the valley, the Santa Lucia mountains lie between the ocean and the valley, virtually without a break along their 138km (86 mile) length.

On the inland side, the Gavilan mountains are much more broken up, with large gaps leading through into the Central Valley. The Central Valley bakes daily under the sun, its hot air rises creating a thirsty vacuum, which then sucks the cold Monterey Bay air up the valley with sometimes terrifying ferocity. The closer to the sea, the colder and more violent the wind. It's cold enough to destroy any vine's chance of ripening, and it's violent enough to rip the branches off a tree, let alone a young vine trying to set its first crop. A lot of those first vines never even got as far as boasting a single grape.

As we move further up the Salinas Valley, the winds become milder and warmer. At Gonzales, you can just about ripen white grapes, you can ripen most red grapes by Soledad and Greenfield, and by King City, with the wind dropping to a pleasant breeze, you can ripen anything, although, so far, nobody's been thrilled by the result. There is very little rainfall throughout the valley – an average of 250mm (10in) a year – and, with the eternal sunshine, some growers claim that the valley has the longest ripening period in the world. With budbreak as early as February due to the mild winters, and an autumn that can linger on into December, they may well be right, though you'll hear the same claim from growers in Edna Valley and Santa Maria Valley further south (see page 250).

But where's the Salinas River? Right under your feet. In fact, the Salinas River is California's largest underground river and is fed by the Santa Lucia, Gavilan and Diablo ranges. Given that the soil is mostly deep, free draining silt and sandy loam, I can see why the early pioneers saw it as a paradise for the vine. But the vine is a greedy plant, and the early plantations suffered from massive over-irrigation, leading to vigorous vines pushing out forests of foliage – and producing grapes of a decidedly green vegetable flavour that made wines with an equally vegetal taste. If we wine-enthusiastic humans were going to gain any benefit from this paradise, we were going to have to take the vine firmly in hand.

Vineyard management is now far more advanced. The areas too close to the sea have been abandoned to the vegetable farmers. The cooler areas, a bit further inland, are left to white grapes, irrigation is properly controlled, and areas away from the valley floor have been developed for higher quality whites and reds – indeed, all the really exciting wines so far have come from these sites. Facing north-east towards Gonzales and Soledad are the Santa Lucia Highlands slopes. Thanks to a few growers – mainly the irreverent Gary Pisoni – this AVA has become one of the state's most revered for Pinot Noir. Once again, it's the passion of the Pinot Noir enthusiasts that pushes back the limits in California, while the producers of the easier-to-grow, easier-to-sell Merlot and Cabernet are more likely to settle contentedly in the mainstream. The wines here share a meaty, spicy, muscular character that is attracting

wineries from Sonoma, Napa and Santa Barbara to buy this fruit. Carmel Valley and Arroyo Seco have some favoured spots; and high up on the arid eastern slopes of the Gavilan range, the producers Chalone and Calera make world-class Pinot Noirs and a variety of whites in splendid limestone isolation.

A gruff old Frenchman, André Noblet, the legendary winemaker at Domaine de la Romanée-Conti at Vosne-Romanée in the heart of Burgundy, would murmur 'limestone, limestone' under his breath in response to the endless questions from callow young Americans about his marvellous wines, and the magic ingredient that made them so special. This belief in the power of limestone so devotedly held by Burgundy's top winemaker, provided the spur for Calera and Chalone, which are now two of California's most famous – and most individual – wines.

Limestone isn't easy to find in California, but is at the heart of the greatest sites in Burgundy – places where finesse usually wins over power. In the 19th century a roving Frenchman called Curtis Tamm searched along the Californian coast for years for limestone soil to make sparkling wine. He finally found what he wanted on a parched wilderness 600m (1970ft) up in the Gavilan range below the Pinnacles peaks, the site of present-day Chalone. A dozen miles north, 670m (2200ft) up on the north-east-facing slopes of Mount Harlan, Josh Jensen established Calera in 1974 on limestone soils that he first had to clear of virgin scrub. Calera is still one of the highest and coldest vineyards in California.

This being California, neither winery manages to make wines of Burgundian delicacy, but what they do achieve is something more exhilarating – the savage, growling, unfathomable, dark beauty of the great red wines of Burgundy's Côte de Nuits. In land that deserves a desert rating for its aridity, the grape yields are tiny (as they have to be with Pinot Noir), the methods of winemaking are traditional to a fault and, as is the case of their Burgundian role models, the Chalone and Calera Pinot Noirs are of an unpredictable yet brilliant magnificence.

Vineyards seem to stretch for ever in the Salinas Valley in Monterey County. These are at Soledad. The milk cartons in between the vines protect new plantings from rodents and, when summer comes, sunburn. The soil is very fertile and crops are planted between the rows to provide competition for the vine.

This label proudly boasts that Chardonnay grapes for this wine were grown 610m (2000ft) above the valley floor, in the Santa Cruz Mountains.

SOUTH CENTRAL COAST

 RED GRAPES
While Cabernet Sauvignon has greater acreage in Santa Barbara, Pinot Noir is better suited to local conditions. In San Luis Obispo, Cabernet and Zinfandel are planted extensively.

 WHITE GRAPES
Chardonnay is widely planted, with lesser amounts of Sauvignon Blanc, Riesling and Gewürztraminer.

CLIMATE
Differences are huge, being largely related to the influence of the Pacific sea fogs.

SOIL
Alkaline sandy and clay loams, with some rich limestone.

ASPECT
Paso Robles vineyards are on a valley floor, sheltered by mountains. Santa Maria has half its vines on benchlands above the fog line.

Byron Vineyards in Santa Maria Valley. A part of the vineyards – the Nielson Block – was planted in 1964 and is the oldest commercial planting in the valley, and still one of the best sites.

I'M AFRAID I ONLY GET TO SEE PASO ROBLES, the northernmost wine region of the so-called South Central Coast, if I'm in a hurry. There it is, straddling Highway 101 right at the source of the Salinas River; it seems easy enough to get to. But there's another road southwards from Santa Cruz and Monterey. Highway 1. Hugging the coastline, dipping and diving in and out of the cliff face and soaring up above the crashing ocean waves, and – I'm a '60s boy remember – traversing Little Sur, Point Sur and Big Sur. What am I supposed to do? Hurry down boring old 101, or bask in the glory of this wild Pacific coast?

Well, I take Highway 1, don't I? Not a vine in sight, and no passing places. I once left Santa Cruz to try to make a lunch appointment in Santa Barbara County. Unwisely, but inevitably, I took Highway 1. And I got behind a band of six camper vans, laden with spaced-out hippies dawdling contentedly down the coast, drinking in every second of the majesty of Big Sur and its stuff of dreams. Lunch? I just about made dinner. Luckily my host was a dreamer, a romantic – and an ace winemaker. He understood.

Paso Robles, though, is a good wine area. Right next door to the rather underperforming San Lucas region, it should really be taken as the southern outpost of North Central Coast rather than the northern outpost of South Central Coast. I know, I know. Does it really matter? No. Do I care? No. It's just another example of the AVA system doggedly and unfortunately following political boundaries, rather than geological ones. Paso Robles is the high point in the Salinas Valley that runs north-west through Monterey County to the sea. And its hot, dry climate is the natural progression from foggy and cold at the seaward end to baking and arid at its head as the influence of Monterey Bay's chilly waters is finally dissipated under the burning sun. But the San Luis Obispo County line crunches across the map about 14km (8 miles) north of Paso Robles, so Paso Robles is lumped into the South Central Coast region.

Never mind that a 460-m (1500-ft) high pass has to be traversed to get down to the sea level of San Luis Obispo. Nor that San Luis Obispo's reputation is for some of the coolest-climate fruit produced in the whole of California, as the fog and sea breezes chill Edna Valley and Arroyo Grande so successfully that some of the most Burgundian-style Chardonnay

in the state comes from Edna Valley, and some of the most characterful Pinot Noir comes from Arroyo Grande. Well, that's the way it is. So let's turn back up 101 as it heads away from the sea at San Luis Obispo and climbs to the hot inland gaps at Paso Robles.

There are several reasons why Paso Robles makes an increasing amount of red wine. It is divided from the Pacific to the west by the 900-m (2950-ft) Santa Lucia Range. Even the California fogs and sea winds can't get over these mountains, although a stiff breeze sometimes works its way up to Templeton along Highway 46 and even causes ripening difficulties for Cabernet in one or two spots south of Templeton.

To assist the last gasps of ocean breeze puffing up the valley from Monterey or along Highway 46, you've got altitude. The vineyards are sited at heights between 180 and 300m (590 and 985ft), though the small, cool York Mountain area west of Paso Robles reaches 500m (1640ft) above sea level. And being protected from the maritime influence means that the temperature plummets at night. In the scorching months of July and August, the difference between day and night temperatures is usually over 28°C (50°F). That's great for the flavour of the fruit. And it is fruit quality that makes Paso Robles exciting. That, and a willingness to break the stranglehold of Cabernet Sauvignon. Paso Robles does have a lot of Cabernet, almost one-third of its total plantings. Cabernet grows mostly on its east side, on river terraces and the rolling grassland of the Estrella Prairie to the north-east, but the wine has a joyous ripe quality and minimal tannic intrusion that makes for some of California's eminently approachable examples.

The limestone soils to the west of Paso Robles are home to numerous old Zinfandel plantings, and both sides of the valley are becoming more interesting for their plantings of the now fashionable Rhône and Italian varieties. The creation of an estate, Tablas Creek, to grow Rhône varieties near Adelaida to the west of Paso Robles by the Perrin Brothers, who own the top estate of Château de Beaucastel in Châteauneuf-du-Pape in the southern Rhône, is a clear indication that things are getting exciting down here. Interestingly, it was their Rhône-style whites which shone first, rather than the reds, as the brothers discovered that a headstrong area like the Paso Robles takes a few vintages to reveal how to grow the grapes and make the wine.

WHERE THE VINEYARDS ARE *This map shows in dramatic manner the way that the sea's influence makes great vineyards possible in California. The sea may look nice and blue on the map, but more likely it will be covered with a thick blanket of fog during the summer and, wherever there is a break in the mountains for a river to force its way to the sea, this blanket will stream inland for between 16 and 32km (10 and 20 miles). But that wouldn't have looked so nice, so we chose a rare sunny summer's day.*

Right at the top of the map, look how dry and parched the land seems to be around Paso Robles. It is parched, and the vineyards here are only slightly cooled by air currents from the Salinas Valley to the north and the odd breeze from the west, that comes up from the sea through what is known as the Templeton Gap. Most of the vineyards are in the dry lands, east of Paso Robles, but there are some excellent sites in the wooded hills to the west.

However, near San Luis Obispo, Edna Valley and Arroyo Grande are both strongly influenced by maritime cool, and the vineyards just east of Arroyo Grande are some of the coolest for Pinot Noir in the state. It's far too cold for vines west of Santa Maria, but south and east, the conditions are perfect. Many people think this may prove to be one of California's top vineyard regions for Chardonnay and Pinot Noir – and I'm one of them. Lompoc is also too cold, but a few miles east along the Santa Ynez Valley are some of the best cool-climate vineyards in California, gradually warming up as the valley opens out at Santa Ynez and Los Olivos.

EDNA VALLEY AND ARROYO GRANDE

On into the real San Luis Obispo, and the areas of Edna Valley and Arroyo Grande. Neither is big, neither is well known, but both are exceptional. Edna Valley's forte is Chardonnay, and I can vividly remember the first example I tried. It was a 1979 or 1980 – it's not important, really – from Edna Valley Vineyards, made by Dick Graff, winemaker at Chalone. It was dry yet luscious, lean yet viscous with a heavenly savoury quality: butter melting on toast or hazelnuts lightly grilling over a log fire. Such wine was rare enough from Puligny-Montrachet; from California, it was a revelation.

Sparkling wine used to be the strong point for Arroyo Grande, but as sales of domestic bubbly have been less than buoyant, much of that production has shifted to still Chardonnay and Pinot Noir. Of the two, Pinot Noir is the star varietal in Arroyo Grande; the ripe plum and black cherry fruit and fine structure make this one of the state's most underrated regions for the grape.

The climate has much to do with the quality of Pinot Noir here. While it is obviously warmer than Burgundy's Côte d'Or, it is cool and temperate by Californian standards, with an early February budbreak and flowering, yet a long, gentle ripening period and,

0 km 2 4
0 miles 2

AVA WINE AREAS

1. York Mountain
2. Paso Robles
3. Edna Valley
4. Arroyo Grande Valley
5. Santa Maria Valley
6. Santa Rita Hills
7. Santa Ynez Valley

TOTAL DISTANCE NORTH TO
SOUTH 137KM (85 MILES)

CALIFORNIA CENTRAL COAST
AVA BOUNDARY

OTHER AVA
BOUNDARIES

VINEYARDS

SAN MIGUEL
ESTRELLA
ADELAIDA
PASO ROBLES
SANTA LUCIA RANGE
TEMPLETON
ATASCADERO
MORRO BAY
SAN LUIS
OBISPO
GROVER
CITY
Twitchell
Reservoir
SANTA
MARIA
LOS ALAMOS
LOS OLIVOS
LOMPOC
SANTA YNEZ
BUELLTON
PACIFIC
OCEAN

N

0 km 2 4
0 miles 2

interestingly, the morning fogs become more frequent in autumn, making the grapes susceptible to noble rot – which, for Chardonnay, adds that touch of magical richness in the finished wine as harvest sometimes lingers on as late as November.

Arroyo Grande also has marine deposits in its soil, which improves fruit quality, along with a fair bit of clay loam. Laetitia, which bought out the pioneering winery here, sparkling wine producer Maison Deutz, has the area's vineyards that are nearest to the ocean, planted with Pinot Noir, Chardonnay and Pinot Blanc. The highest part of the valley is hot enough to ripen Zinfandel – from a patch of vines planted in 1879 – and in between, excellent Pinot Noir and Chardonnay are grown by Talley Vineyards and a dozen or so other wineries. All in the space of less than 16km (10 miles).

SANTA MARIA VALLEY

Onward down the 101, and over another county line into Santa Barbara County, and the Santa Maria Valley region. I'm beginning to pine for Highway 1 and Big Sur again, because this is monotonous country. As I swoop into the wide valley, the dusty anonymous town of Santa Maria sprawls away to my right, and to the left, inland, it looks like yet another sub-'East of Eden' lettuce prairie spreading gloomily away to the distant hills. It may not look much, but the Santa Maria Valley is one of California's most important fine wine regions, in particular producing Chardonnay

that frequently puts better-known vineyard areas north of San Francisco to shame, as well as exciting Pinot Noir and Syrah.

There are several parallels with the development of Monterey's Salinas Valley further north. During the 1960s and 1970s, as demand for wine boomed, various farmers decided to give grapes a try, and planted what rapidly became vast spreads of grapes grown almost entirely for purchase by wineries in other regions which were desperate for a decent supply. This was fine while the demand for grapes outstripped supply, but the 1980s saw a serious over-supply situation develop, just as the region was finally proving its worth and the reputation for Santa Maria Chardonnay and Pinot Noir was rocketing. With banks and insurance companies repossessing the land, but not at all keen to get into the grape-growing business, three of California's most important quality wineries – Mondavi, Beringer and Kendall-Jackson – put their money where their mouths were and snapped up vast tracts of prime vineyard land to stop any of their rivals getting their hands on it. We consumers have been the beneficiaries of greatly improved Chardonnays from these three players. So, as in the Salinas Valley, most of the vineyard land is owned in large blocks, and there are very few local wineries. But in terms of quality, Santa Maria has won hands down over the Salinas Valley so far.

Sea fogs play a part, yet again. Santa Maria must be one of the least pleasant of all wine towns to live in – it gets on average 87 days a year of heavy fog, generally in the late summer to autumn

This wine isn't shy of telling us how good it is – 'Incredible Red' it's called. With some reason, because Peachy Canyon in warm Paso Robles does produce powerful Zinfandel.

SANTA MARIA AND SANTA YNEZ VALLEYS

TOTAL DISTANCE
NORTH TO
SOUTH 45KM
(28 MILES)

VINEYARDS

■ SANTA MARIA

LOS OLIVOS ■

■ BUELLTON

SOLVANG ■

period. The late summer is particularly bad when deep, cold ocean currents well up and are carried landward as the summer progresses, and are pushed southwards along the California coast. By August these cold currents are icing up the shoreline as far south as Santa Barbara County. The wet off-shore winds are cooled right down and head inland to meet warm inland air head on – *et voilà* – fog. Loads of it.

But remember we're a long way south here. The sun is incredibly powerful; glance up at the hilltops on both sides of the Santa Maria Valley and they are scorched and windswept. So the fog may ooze in from the sea, but it is burnt off by the sun. Yet as soon as that happens, cool ocean breezes take up the slack. So there's loads of sun, but it is always being tempered by the ocean.

The average summer temperature is only 24°C (75°F), but the crucial thing is that the heat peak is at 1.30pm, after which up come those chilly ocean breezes that get to work sparing the grapes from the danger of roasting under a hot afternoon sun. (North of San Francisco in the better-known areas of Sonoma and Napa counties, the heat peak is often about 4pm.) Add to that an early budding and flowering in Santa Maria – and, because of the more southerly latitude, a long, reliable autumn giving the grapes extra time to hang on the vine – along with the odd touch of noble rot again, and you've got Chardonnay nirvana if it's handled properly.

Mostly it is. The soil here is a mix of sandy loam and marine limestones which don't encourage foliage vigour, and lead to yields that can be as little as two or three tons an acre – that's low for California. Most of the vines are managed extremely competently by farmers who know that – stuck in the middle of a not very attractive nowhere as they are – quality is everything. With average rainfall running at between just 300 and 380mm (12 and 15in) a year, irrigation is essential, but so far, it hasn't been abused.

Most of the 2000ha (4940 acres) or so of vineyards lie on a curious ledge to the north of the Santa Maria river, though there are a few excellent properties quite close to Santa Maria township on the south side of the river. Chardonnay is the clear favourite, but Pinot Noir can be spectacular (from Au Bon Climat and others)

and the Bien Nacido ranch was one of the earliest sites in California to show superb results with the Rhône varieties Syrah and Viognier. And a few miles further south, over the Solomon Hills, there are considerable plantings – of about 3050ha (7539 acres) – in Los Alamos, an area without an AVA, but with a good reputation for Chardonnay and for Pinot Noir.

SANTA YNEZ VALLEY

While the Santa Maria Valley goes from ultra-cool to, well, mild at best, the Santa Ynez Valley goes from equally cool to hot, so much so that it's hot enough for Cabernet Sauvignon, Merlot and the Rhône varieties to ripen easily in the upstream vineyards. But whereas the Santa Maria Valley is very broad-mouthed, rapidly narrowing as it turns from west to south, Santa Ynez is narrow near the sea, opening out and fragmenting inland above Solvang.

The whole feeling of the valley, only a short distance north of the city of Santa Barbara, couldn't be more different from that of Santa Maria. There are numerous small estates, fine homes, ancient trees and paddocks sporting handsome stallions. It's wealthy country with more than a sprinkling of Hollywood and Los Angeles glamour about it, and this can't have hindered its entry into the limelight during the 1970s as the source of California's supposedly finest Pinot Noirs.

In fact, those early Pinot Noirs were pretty weird, but underlying the maverick winemaking there was a core of exciting fruit, most of all from the Sanford & Benedict Vineyard west of Buellton. Located at between about 25 and 40km (15 and 25 miles) from the sea, this area is known as the Santa Rita Hills, and has been planted with Pinot Noir and Chardonnay by more than a dozen of the county's finest producers. A combination of north-facing slopes avoiding the direct strong afternoon sun along with fog and sea breezes shrouding the vines have convinced some that this may be the greatest site for Pinot Noir in the whole of California. How many 'greatest sites' does that make, you may ask. I don't know, but the wonderful thing is that when it comes to Pinot Noir and excellence, so many people care.

Machine-harvesting is common in California, but many producers prefer to trust human pickers. These vines are at Sanford's La Rinconada vineyard, near Buellton in the Santa Ynez Valley.

WHERE THE VINEYARDS ARE *Santa Barbara County is virtually unique on the US west coast, because its river valleys run east to west. Being so far south, Santa Barbara would be too hot were it not for the influence of the cold ocean currents that run along the coast and send cooling fogs and winds inland up the valleys.*

The town of Santa Maria is at the top of the map and is just too cold for grapes, but as you move up the valley, the effect of the fogs and breezes lessens, and vineyards start to appear. The most important section is the ledge of continual vineyard to the north of the river between Au Bon Climat and Rancho Sisquoc. Just to the south, vineyards along the course of the San Antonio Creek, west of Los Alamos, are similarly impressive, despite not having their own AVA.

The Santa Ynez Valley is very cool at the western end and is a prime site for Pinot Noir. At Solvang the valley splays out, and becomes much warmer, particularly to the east and the south. However, there are numerous good sites to the north of Solvang. These are still warm, but are helped by their altitude and what remains of the cool air systems of the Santa Maria Valley to the north-west.

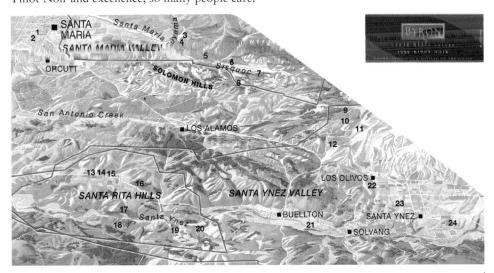

AVA WINE AREAS, SELECTED WINERIES AND VINEYARDS

1. Whitcraft	8. Foxen	15. Babcock	21. Hitching Post
2. Lane Tanner	9. Zaca Mesa	16. Foley	22. Longoria
3. Au Bon Climat/Qupé	10. Andrew Murray	17. Sea Smoke	23. Beckmen
4. Bien Nacido Vineyard	11. Fess Parker	18. Sanford & Benedict Vineyard	24. Gainey
5. Cambria	12. Firestone	19. Lafond	
6. Byron	13. Clos Pepe	20. Sanford	
7. Rancho Sisquoc	14. Melville		

SANTA MARIA VALLEY = AVA WINE AREA

—— AVA BOUNDARIES

0 km 1 2
0 miles 1

CENTRAL & SOUTHERN CALIFORNIA

We're looking at some of California's highest vineyards at Lava Cap winery. Vines here in El Dorado County, up in the foothills of the Sierra Nevada, are planted as high as 1000m (3300ft), almost at the limit of grape-growing.

I SUPPOSE I SHOULD APOLOGIZE for allowing the region that produces four out of every five bottles of California's wine less than a full page to itself, but the trouble is, there's not a lot to say about most of the wine, and there's not a lot to say about most of the region. A minute proportion of the wine actually proclaims its provenance as California's Central Valley – or, more correctly, the San Joaquin Valley – and my chief problem in driving around the interminably flat, sunbaked and over-irrigated land is trying to stay awake.

Yet the valley is a triumph of agro-industry, even if glamour is signally absent, and indeed an air of moody secretiveness hangs over not only the massive wine complexes, but the other enormous vegetable and fruit concerns that dominate the landscape. The Central Valley is not a place to linger in; strangers don't receive too warm a welcome down here.

Technically, there are two parts to the Central Valley – the San Joaquin Valley and the Sacramento River Valley – and there is a significant difference between the two, because around Sacramento, and pushing just a little south towards Lodi, the cool maritime breezes can still make their way up through the gap the Sacramento River has forged in the Coast Ranges. At Lodi, at Clarksburg below the daunting levees of the Sacramento River delta, and in parts of Solano County just above San Pablo Bay, interesting table wines can be produced.

However, the awesome vastness of the Central Valley starts south of Lodi. This is where a substantial amount of the United States' vegetables and fruit are produced, as well as the massive majority of its wine. There are wineries that would dwarf oil refineries, producing more than many serious wine-producing nations. Gallo, the world's second largest wine company, has four plants, with a combined output of about 7.1 million hl (156 million gallons) per annum, more than Chile's current annual output, and not far off Portugal's 7.5 million hl (165 million gallons).

The vineyards run right down to Bakersfield, a distance of 370km (230 miles) and the deep fertile soils can spread as wide as 110km (70 miles) between the Coast Ranges and the Sierra Nevada. There is almost no moderating influence for the overpowering heat, and there's precious little rain, but two reservoir and canal systems based on 19th-century irrigation schemes draw off all the water from the Sierra Nevada range for hundreds of miles making rain irrelevant.

Few producers have made a name for quality wine, although, given the torrid conditions, there have been some high-quality fortified wines created. Andrew Quady at Madera makes the best of these, and his imagination was fired by a batch of Zinfandel grapes from Amador County in the Sierra Foothills in the early 1980s. If the Central Valley can seem like a new millennium nightmare, the attractive Sierra Foothills towns can just as easily seem like a delightful leftover from more than a century ago.

SIERRA FOOTHILLS

This is where the great goldrush began in 1848 and, just as gold fever gripped the nation in Australia, so it did in California. Gold miners have massive thirsts and, by the 1870s, there were more than 100 wineries, largely in El Dorado and Amador counties. Some of the ancient Zinfandel vines still bear fruit and, though more fashionable varieties have made their mark, and Sangiovese, of all things, is now attracting attention, dark, alcoholic, massively flavoured Zinfandels are still what the Sierra Foothills does best.

The vineyards can be as high as 900m (2950ft) around Placerville in El Dorado, but are likely to be just over 300m (985ft) in the main Amador area of the Shenandoah Valley and anywhere from 450 to 750m (1476 to 2460ft) in Fiddletown.

The highest vineyards attract rainfall of up to 1150mm (45in) a year, the lower ones less than 760mm (30in). Differences between day- and night-time temperatures are similarly more extreme in the higher vineyards, helped by night-time mountain breezes and the tail end of maritime breezes off San Francisco Bay. But in the ripening season, daytime temperatures usually hover between 27 and 38°C (80 and 100°F) and the resulting mix of tannin and intensity of fruit makes for some of California's most impressive and traditional wines.

SOUTHERN CALIFORNIA

South of Santa Barbara, the coast takes a long lurch eastward, and the effects of the ice-cold waters are largely lost. There is only one more vineyard region of significance along this coast – Temecula. Situated 38km (24 miles) inland to the south-east of Los Angeles, it's a strange spot. Its high elevation – 430m (1400ft) – gives it a welcome cool edge and the mild Pacific breezes also help, but even so, this far south, you'd expect red wine to be the major player. In fact, almost all Temecula's best wine is white.

As in the Livermore Valley, east of San Francisco Bay, urban expansion is squeezing the vineyard areas, although local politicians and property developers regard vineyards as part of the lifestyle they are trying to promote. Disastrously, though, the area has been hit by a deadly vine ailment called Pierce's Disease. The bacterial infection has no known cure and is spread by the glassy-winged sharpshooter. While researchers race to find ways to combat the disease, vine damage has been so significant over the last few years that the future of Temecula viticulture is in question.

Pierce's Disease has, in fact, been present in California for over 100 years, and even the leading areas of Napa and Sonoma accept losses. Temecula's sad notoriety is based upon it being the entry point for the glassy-winged sharpshooter, brought over from Florida on ornamental plants. With no known predators on the West coast and an ability to travel considerable distances per day, all of California's vineyards are at risk. The Central Valley already has infestations, and the probability is that the insect and its deadly disease will travel inexorably northwards.

SOUTHERN & MID-WEST STATES

NEW MEXICO LIKES TO CLAIM that it is the original wine state of what is now the USA. The conquistadores headed up from Mexico along the Rio Grande – and it makes sense to me that they'd have planted vines to rectify the extremely haphazard supply of sacramental wine from Spain. They'd have found it tricky, though. Rainfall is very sparse – as little as 200mm (8in) a year around Albuquerque – and the height of the Rio Grande Valley, rising to 2000m (6560ft) at Santa Fe, not only makes for savage winter frosts, but also extremely cold summer nights and, consequently, very acid grapes.

Nowadays, all these factors are considered to be advantages when trying to grow grapes with good flavours. Irrigation water is now readily available, winter frosts can be countered by piling up earth round the vines as protection and, without the high-altitude cold, it would be too hot to grow decent *vinifera* grapes. Wineries like Anderson Valley produce remarkably good Cabernet Sauvignon, but that ability to ripen grapes in the relentless sun yet preserve high acids has, not surprisingly, led to some excellent fizz from producers such as Gruet. In the 1990s the wine industry enjoyed a rebirth and there are now about 20 boutique wineries.

The high altitude of the Rockies has also attracted winemakers to Colorado, where the vineyards, ranging from heights of 1200–2100m (3000–4000ft), are some of the highest in the world. Along the Grand Valley of the Colorado River a clutch of wineries make intense, rather piercing *vinifera* wines for a chic and well-heeled holiday crowd. Syrah and Viognier are doing well here. Higher altitude vineyards in the West Elks AVA, along the North Fork of the Gunnison River, are showing promise for Riesling, Pinot Noir, Gewurztraminer and Pinot Gris. High altitude is also what makes decent wine possible in Arizona. Most of the vineyards so far are in the south-east corner near Tucson. Plantings here go as high as 1460m (4800ft): Callaghan Vineyards at Elgin exploit the relentless sunshine tempered by mountain coolness and dramatic differences between day and night temperatures to produce not only memorable reds based on Zinfandel, Syrah and the Bordeaux varieties, but also thrilling white blends based on anything from Riesling to Viognier.

But the slumbering giant of south-west wine is Texas where there has been a 25 per cent increase in the number of acres of vines since 2000. I've been tasting these wines since the boom-time days of the 1983 vintage, when even then the volume of production was doubling every year, and you could catch vintners like Bobby Cox of Pheasant Ridge making gobsmacking assertions like, 'If half the cotton fields on the high plains around Lubbock were planted to grapes, we could produce as much wine as all of France'. I'm sure you could, Bobby, but you'd have to make sure the stuff tasted decent if you weren't going to oversee the biggest bust in viticultural history. And the trouble throughout the 1980s was that ambitious vineyard developments simply weren't matched by good winemaking skills and most of the wines ranged from dreary to worse.

Somehow you would expect Texans to be able to conquer all their problems simply through money, effort and sheer self-belief. Perhaps, therefore, it is humbly reassuring to realize that establishing a wine culture is considerably more complicated than that. There do seem to be several areas that are suitable for viticulture. The Texas High Plains near Lubbock in north-west Texas, at around 1200m (4000ft) above sea level, have dramatic shifts between day and night-time temperatures, deep, fairly loose, limestone soil and low humidity, yet a reasonable amount of rainfall. The West Texas Mountains are surprisingly cool. And the Texas Hill Country around Austin is, indeed, vaguely hilly, and there's a fair amount of decent limestone and sandy loam soil there as well as some cool mesoclimates.

Scattered through these vast and isolated regions are more than 1500ha (3700 acres) of vines, with over 70 per cent planted to Chardonnay, Cabernet Sauvignon, Merlot, Zinfandel, Colombard and Pinot Noir. The growth of wineries has been spectacular, doubling in just two years from 2003 to 2005 – there are now nearly 140, with one, Ste Genevieve at Fort Stockton, producing over 60 per cent of Texas wine. Because the growth of wineries has outpaced the grapes available about one quarter of the wine made in Texas still comes from grapes grown outside the state.

In general, the south-eastern states find it pretty difficult to grow decent grapes. But that doesn't mean that they haven't had a damn good try. Napoleon's soldiers planted Cabernet Sauvignon vines in Alabama when they were left at a loose end after the French defeat at the Battle of Waterloo. Mississippi, which kept Prohibition on the statute books until as recently as 1966, understandably hasn't been a hotbed of activity and even in 2007 had only two wineries. But there is still a wine industry, and in several of the states, they've made a virtue out of necessity by championing non-*vinifera* wine. Scuppernong isn't exactly a poetic title for a grape variety, but it is the leading member of the Muscadine varieties of *Vitis rotundifolia* that manage to survive the humidity and heat on the Gulf of Mexico and round to the southern Atlantic seaboard. These are massive vines – a single wild Scuppernong vine can cover an acre – and the grapes, which can be 2.5cm (1in) in diameter, grow in loose clusters, so resisting the rot that is the scourge of tightly bunched *vinifera* grapes down here. The wine flavour is musky and distinctly fruity, and was the basis for Virginia Dare – for some years after Prohibition the bestselling wine in the US. Down in the humid Gulf, a chilled tumbler of Scuppernong makes a really pleasant drink.

Even so, there are some *vinifera* plantings, and the wine industry is increasing almost everywhere, thanks to the growth of local tourism. The magnificent Biltmore Estate in North Carolina has a 32-ha (80-acre) vineyard and despite problems ranging from hurricanes to frost, even produces Champagne-method fizz. Swiss, German and Italian immigrants planted vines in Arkansas in the 19th century and, particularly around Altus in the state's north-west, vines still do well. Further north, Missouri has a rich tradition of grape and wine production and had the first AVA granted – for Augusta in 1980 – though most of the state's wineries grow hybrids and *labrusca*, rather than *vinifera* grapes.

All the states bordering the Great Lakes in the north have some sort of wine industry. Even Minnesota and Wisconsin squeeze a few wines out of mainly hybrid vines. Indiana has a mix of hybrid and *vinifera* plantations struggling along. But Michigan and Ohio do better than that. Michigan is the USA's tenth biggest wine producer, and though a lot of it is hybrid and *labrusca*, this is a state that exemplifies America's 'can do' philosophy – remarkably tasty *vinifera* wines coming from a clutch of wineries on the south-eastern shores of Lake Michigan, as well as some delicious Riesling from the Leelanau peninsula further north. In the 19th century, Ohio used to grow more grapes than California and, while those days are long gone, the conditions that prevail along the south shore of Lake Erie and on the offshore islands to the north of Sandusky, aided by the warm waters of this shallow lake, are good enough to produce some excellent Chardonnay and Riesling as well as those hybrids and *labruscas*.

This looks more like a blasted heath than a vineyard, but these high-altitude vines near Elgin, Arizona produce excellent grapes.

Arizona Zinfandel: Callaghan's mountain vineyards, mixing bright sunshine with cool temperatures, produce startling, intense reds and whites.

PACIFIC NORTHWEST

QUILCEDA CREEK

CABERNET SAUVIGNON

Woodward Canyon Winery

WASHINGTON CHARDONNAY

KEN WRIGHT CELLARS

GUADALUPE VINEYARD
2000

IT'S HARD TO IMAGINE TWO more totally different wine regions than those of Washington's Columbia River Valley and of Oregon's Willamette Valley. The Willamette Valley has a gentle, long-settled rural quality, with quietly prosperous, self-contained families that run back generations tending the farm. It's more like New England than the next-door state to California, or more like one of the bucolic counties of Old England, such as Gloucestershire or Herefordshire.

The Columbia Valley is a desperate desert of a place – wild, empty, and far too savage for most people to settle in, however hardy they are. And through this inhospitable desperado's backyard runs the great Columbia River and, here and there along its banks, are vast spreads of green gardens sprouting in the desert. Not people, not nice friendly communities, gabled barns and paddock fences – just the raw bones of fields and crops, against an eerie wilderness of bleached sagebrush ranges.

Yet both owe their existence to the same geographical phenomena. And both owe their rise from obscurity to international renown to a desire to prove that California and its particular styles of wine, based in the 1960s and 1970s upon big, ripe, assertive flavours, weren't the only valid American styles, and maybe weren't even the best.

The best place to read the geological tale is in Ted Jordan Meredith's *Northwest Wine* (out of print but available in libraries), where the author makes the activities of the earth's plates, volcanoes and rivers over millions of years sound as fresh and immediate as a news report. I'll just précis the story – but it's a vital story since the activities of the tectonic plates in America's Pacific Northwest are still visible today. Remember Mount St Helens exploding in 1980? That was the tectonic plates in action.

What has been happening for millions of years in the Pacific Northwest is that the Oceanic plate has been crunching up against the Continental plate and sinking beneath it, at the same time depositing sedimentary layers on the Continental crust and pushing it upwards.

This uplift has pushed the Willamette area above sea level and created the Coast Ranges, which ward off just enough of the cold Pacific influences to make the Willamette Valley an ideal cool-climate vineyard area. Meanwhile, the Oceanic plate keeps on pressing inland, deeper and deeper below the Continental plate, until it melts. And about 160km (100 miles) inland the molten basalt forces itself upwards creating the series of volcanic peaks known as the Cascades.

As the Mount St Helens eruption showed, this process is ongoing, and parts of the volcano are only 2000 years old. The youth of the Cascades explains the majestic soaring beauty of the major peaks and the overall height of the range, often reaching 3650m (12,000ft). Almost all the ocean influences – the breezes, fogs and rain – get stopped by this mountain barrier. To its east is the virtual desert of the Columbia River basin – endless sunshine, almost no rain. All it took was human ingenuity to harness the Columbia's mighty flow for irrigation and you had one of the world's great unnatural vineyards.

There's a lot more to the story than this – massive floods of lava sweeping across thousands of square miles of landscape at some 50km (30 miles) an hour; these enormous lava flows being buckled into ridges as the west coast itself moves northward; vast glacial floods up to 300m (985ft) deep scouring the landscape during the last ice age. If you want to get excited about geology and geography, the Pacific Northwest is the place to do it. And it explains the almost primeval desolation of so much of the land east of the Cascades.

THE FIRST VINEYARDS
The Willamette Valley has been settled since the first migrants arrived along the Oregon trail, and parts of the Columbia, the Yakima and Snake River valleys have been exploited agriculturally for the best part of a century, but none had been exploited for classic wine grapes. Western Oregon was reckoned to be too cool and damp for *vinifera* varieties. The Columbia Valley in

This may not look like a vineyard yet, but these plastic 'grow-tubes' accelerate the growth of new vines by as much as a year. This is a new vineyard of Sangiovese vines at Kiona Vineyards in Washington's Yakima Valley. Sangiovese – more at home in central Italy – is proving a tricky variety to get right in the United States.

eastern Washington was simply too far over the Cascades from any sizeable market and, although moderating winter influences did come from the Columbia River, these weren't always able to combat periodic bouts of intense winter frost, as freezing weather from Alaska got caught in the Columbia River basin.

And yet, beginning in the 1960s and continuing through the 1970s, these two totally different wine regions grew and flourished together. Oregon's cool, wet Willamette Valley was sought out by Californians keen on cool-climate grapes like Pinot Noir, Riesling and more recently Pinot Gris, and by refugees from the big, brash California way of living.

In Washington State in the early 1960s, a group of university professors founded a little wine company (Associated Vintners) to produce homemade wine from some *vinifera* grapes they'd located in the Yakima Valley. At the time, the state was suffering from archaic liquor laws and its wine industry was based on cheap, sweet fortified wine made out of *labrusca* grapes. Within a decade the company – now renamed Columbia – was fashioning new vineyards out of the sagebrush along the Yakima and Columbia rivers, together with a big new operation based on a Yakima growers' co-operative called Chateau Ste Michelle, owned and generously financed by US Tobacco. Chateau Ste Michelle came here looking for an alternative to the wine regions further to the south – land was expensive and egos were big in the California of the 1970s.

Columbia and Chateau Ste Michelle studied the figures for eastern Washington and saw a healthy bottom line, based not on cheap bulk but on high-quality wine grown in controlled conditions at a latitude similar to that of Bordeaux. With slower ripening fruit, and the combinations of long sunny days and chilly nights giving higher acids than California, yet ample sugar, Washington wine producers realized that perhaps they could approach the European ideal of a balanced wine more easily than their California colleagues, and they have based their business on this argument ever since.

The European card has worked for both states. Oregon's Eyrie Vineyard's 1975 Pinot Noir equalled Burgundy's greatest reds in a 1979 'Olympiad' held in Paris, and since then Pinot Noir has been Oregon's greatest achievement. However, some 50 years after the first planting of Pinot Noir in the Willamette Valley, consistent success has not yet been achieved. Which is fair enough. It's a very marginal climate. It took Burgundy a thousand years to get sorted. Thirty-five years is early yet.

Washington's first great success came with Riesling, but the market moved quickly on, and first Semillon and Sauvignon and now Chardonnay dominate white plantings. But the market moved again – to red – and now Cabernet Sauvignon and Merlot with Syrah in hot pursuit are making all the running. The red varieties have taken to Washington conditions with enthusiasm, and give fruit of a powerful, individual style. Not all the wines have so far matched fruit quality, but each year produces more star performers. Yakima and Columbia flavours needed taming. Sorting out how to grow the fruit wasn't difficult, but Washington, like Oregon, learns with each vintage how to make the best wine from some of America's best vineyards.

IDAHO

There is a third member of the Pacific Northwest wine family – Idaho. Idaho's winemaking tradition actually goes back to the 19th century, when European immigrants brought winemaking ambitions with them, and an Idaho wine won a prize at the 1898 Chicago World Fair. But Idaho was a keen prohibitionist state, and for most of the 20th century the potato saw off the grape without too much difficulty. But there's something catching about the wine bug. Idaho now has 728ha (1800 acres) of vineyards, 15 wineries, over 40 vineyards, and a brand new AVA, Snake River Valley, a tiny portion of which crosses over the border in Oregon. The AVA covers a massive area but most of the plantings so far are near the cities of Nampa and Caldwell. Even so, if it weren't for fruit farms wanting to diversify, Idaho wouldn't seem a perfect spot for a wine industry. The Snake River does allow some moderating maritime influence to flow up from the Columbia Valley, which is necessary, because the vineyards are high, at 610–914m (2000–3000ft) above sea level. They enjoy hot bright summer days, but intensely cold nights – and are continually at risk from frost. Full ripening of the grapes only comes with extended hang time. There is some extremely good Idaho sparkling wine, however – but then, the best sparklers tend to come from not fully ripe grapes. So far, Idaho has been best known for white wines but some wineries are now making successful reds from classic Bordeaux and Rhône varieties.

Andrew Will is one of Washington's top winemakers, but his winery is on the forested Vashon Island west of Seattle. His Merlot grapes, however, come from some of the state's best vineyards east of the Cascade Mountains.

WASHINGTON STATE

 **RED GRAPES**
Cabernet Sauvignon and Merlot are the main grapes, followed some way behind by Syrah and Cabernet Franc. Other grapes such as Sangiovese, Pinot Noir, Grenache, Malbec, Mourvedre and Petit Verdot are beginning to take off. The hardy Lemberger, once popular in the Yakima Valley, is now in decline.

WHITE GRAPES
Riesling was the first success in Washington State but has now been overtaken by Chardonnay. Following way behind but gaining in popularity are Sauvignon Blanc, Pinot Gris and Viognier.

CLIMATE
There can be very dramatic contrasts between summer and winter temperatures. The region west of the Olympic Mountains has a maritime climate with high rainfall. East of the Cascades, the pattern is continental and some areas are semi-desert. Wahluke Slope has one of the driest, warmest climates in the state.

SOIL
Most of the Columbia Valley is basaltic sand with some loess and occasional river gravel. The Yakima Valley has sandy soils with low water retention, making irrigation essential.

ASPECT
Vineyards are few and far between. All plantings have been made on either low ridges, the south-facing slopes of hills, or near rivers. The most important factor is avoiding damaging winter cold, rather than excessive summer heat and many vineyards are located on ridges and terraces with good air drainage.

Y OU'VE GOT A CHOICE for the most unlikely, inhospitable vineyard site ever. The Australian Outback. Or the moon. You get both in the Columbia River Valley basin, to the east of the towering Cascade Range in Washington State, up in the cold, foggy Pacific Northwest corner of the United States. But there are two vastly different landscapes in Washington State: the part where people live, make money, support football teams and go to the opera is cool and foggy, lies to the west of the Cascades and is open to the influence of the northern Pacific Ocean that, in 1579, had Sir Francis Drake reeling, beaten back by 'the most vile, thick and stinking fogges'. They're still there, around Puget Sound, Seattle and the mouth of the Columbia River.

But take Interstate 90 south-east out of Seattle, away from the leafy suburbs, through the Snoqualmie Pass and over the Cascades into the head of the Yakima Valley at Ellensburg. You'll feel you've moved to a completely different world of clear, dry mountain air, barren ridges and uneasy civilization. Here you have a choice. Take Interstate 90 further east across the Columbia River, across Moses Lake way across to Ritzville. You wanted moonscape? You've got it. Windswept sagebrush ranges, like the great hunched backs of vast animals, spread out over the plain, and as signs of habitation get less and less, the vast sky loses its charm and starts to threaten you with its emptiness. You find yourself nervously checking your fuel gauge every ten minutes. Then the plains flatten and spread, lifeless, inhospitable, useless. That's eastern Washington.

But take the right turn just after Ellensburg and head south. Sure the mountain ridges are still as desolate and gaunt as you could wish, but you'll suddenly see the Yakima Valley open out beneath you, a brilliant splash of dappled greens like a lush turf carpet laid on a sun-bleached earthen floor. Someone wasn't too clever with the carpet shears, though: the neatly defined edges are erratically cut, and the fertile greens come to razor-sharp edges, then nothing but parched bleached uplands, the hills like the vertebrae of some giant fossilized lizard. This is eastern Washington too. That spread of bright green is agro-industry at its most intense, the jagged edges marking out the

limits of irrigation water rights. Without human resourcefulness there'd be little more growing here than out in the empty vastness towards Ritzville and beyond.

Eastern Washington is desert. The curtain of volcanic peaks making up the Cascade Range runs north to south only 80km (50 miles) east of Seattle, and continues to rise inexorably towards the Rocky Mountains of Idaho and Montana. Nothing much grows there except firs. But there's one vast bowl gouged out between the mountains and skirted by the mighty Columbia River as it hurls its mighty flow against the Cascades, turns unwillingly south until, aided by the extra volume of the Snake and Yakima rivers, its torrent forces its way back west and out to the ocean.

This is the Columbia River basin, all 60,000 square km (23,000 square miles) of it. And among the millions of empty acres lie most of Washington's 12,546ha (31,000 acres) of vines. They're not here by chance, but because the Cascade Range, rising to 3650m (11,975ft), creates a virtual rain-shadow to its east, guaranteeing minimal rainfall and maximum sunshine. Not

WHERE THE VINEYARDS ARE *You're looking here at one of the most remarkable landscapes in the world of wine. Without human effort, this whole vista would be a drab, sun-parched expanse, only saved from being a wilderness by the mighty Columbia River to the right, and the Yakima River running across the map left to right. Irrigation has changed the Yakima Valley into a prolific grower of vegetables, fruit and, today, wine grapes. Most of the valley floor is taken up with orchards and crops other than grapes – but look at those watercourses that appear to be running across, rather than down, the Rattlesnake Hills in the north and the Horse Heaven Hills in the south. These take off water from the Yakima and its tributaries and pump it to the hillside properties where nearly all the wine grape vineyards are found. The hills are two examples of the buckled basalt ridges that crop up in the Columbia River basin and afford protection from severe Alaskan weather patterns, as well as south-facing slopes for vines. To the west is the new Rattlesnake Hills AVA, but the majority of the plantings are further east in the Yakima Valley AVA. The most exciting results, especially for dark, intense reds, are coming from the Red Mountain AVA near Benton City at the mouth of the valley.*

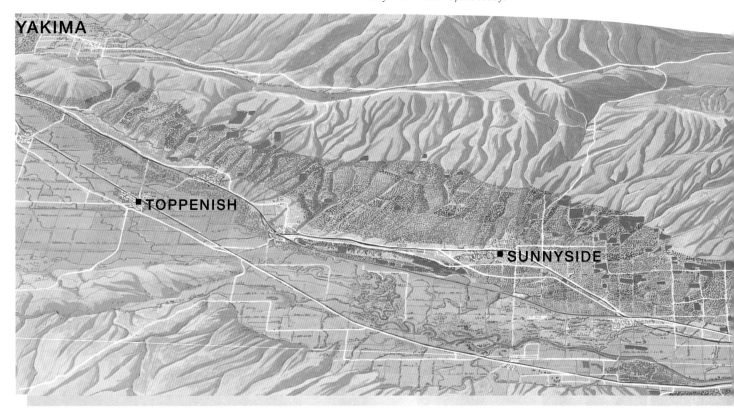

YAKIMA

TOPPENISH

SUNNYSIDE

0 km 4 8
0 miles 4

maximum heat though. Columbia Valley can get incredibly hot, but all its vineyards are in mesoclimates that are warm at best. Yet being so far north – most vineyards are between 46° and 47° North – you can get up to two hours more sun daily than in California's Napa Valley. Vital, as it's photosynthesis, powered by sunlight, that ripens grapes, not blasts of midday heat. And, since this is a continental climate, temperatures plummet at night. So you get grapes full of sugar because of long, sun-filled days, yet chilly nights keep acids high…the perfect recipe for wine grapes.

One more thing – there's almost no rain. So you irrigate. The Columbia is America's second river in terms of volumes of water shifted. The Yakima and Snake Rivers are two other significant performers. On the Columbia and Snake Rivers, vineyards are either planted right on the banks to reduce the very real threat of winter and spring frosts, or on low, south-facing ridges close to the water. Irrigation is simply a case of obtaining water rights.

Most of the Yakima valley floor, protected by hills to the north-east and south-west, is taken up with horticulture other than vines. But vineyards occupy the irrigated low ridges, especially on south-facing patches of the Rattlesnake Hills east of the city of Yakima.

Washington's wine industry used to be based on orchard fruits, *labrusca* vines and a few vineyards of varieties like Müller-Thurgau in the west near Seattle, in the area now called Puget Sound. Several major wine concerns are still based there, including the two biggest, Chateau Ste Michelle and Columbia, and there are 52ha

(130 acres) of vines. Pinot Gris and Pinot Noir are showing some promise here. But most of the vines are east of the Cascades in the Columbia Basin. Although the whole of Washington's acreage under vine is only two-thirds that of the Napa Valley the state has the second largest planting of classic *vinifera* varieties in the United States after California and new plantings keep coming thick and fast. The overall AVA is Columbia Valley which encompasses all the vineyards east of the Cascades. Yakima Valley, including Red Mountain and Rattlesnake Hills, has about one-third of the state's plantings. Horse Heaven Hills, Walla Walla and Wahluke Slope are other top areas with large plantings.

Initially, Washington was seen as white wine country because of its relatively cool climate, but long sunlight hours have started to produce superb Merlots as the vines mature, and the rare Lemberger makes excellent crunchy reds in the Yakima Valley. Reds now dominate, with Cabernet Sauvignon and Merlot between them accounting for one-third of the vines. Syrah is another red variety doing well in eastern Washington and plantings are increasing fast. Both Riesling and Semillon positively shine, while Chardonnay flares brightly in places such as Woodward Canyon, but is more often pleasant than exciting.

Leonetti makes Washington's most sought-after Merlot – its succulent fruit showing the great potential of Columbia Valley fruit.

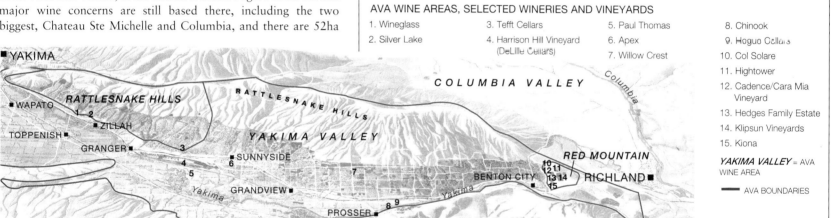

AVA WINE AREAS, SELECTED WINERIES AND VINEYARDS

1. Wineglass
2. Silver Lake
3. Tefft Cellars
4. Harrison Hill Vineyard (DeLille Cellars)
5. Paul Thomas
6. Apex
7. Willow Crest
8. Chinook
9. Hoguo Cellars
10. Col Solare
11. Hightower
12. Cadence/Cara Mia Vineyard
13. Hedges Family Estate
14. Klipsun Vineyards
15. Kiona

YAKIMA VALLEY = AVA WINE AREA

—— AVA BOUNDARIES

YAKIMA VALLEY

TOTAL DISTANCE NORTH TO SOUTH 44KM (27 MILES)

VINEYARDS

N

OREGON

RED GRAPES
Pinot Noir rules in Oregon, especially in the Willamette Valley, with nearly 50 per cent of the state's plantings. Merlot is also present, as well as small amounts of Cabernets Sauvignon and Franc, Syrah, Zinfandel and even Tempranillo.

WHITE GRAPES
Pinot Gris and Chardonnay are dominant, with Riesling a distant third. Sauvignon Blanc, Gewürztraminer and Müller-Thurgau have a following.

CLIMATE
The lower Willamette Valley is cooler than the upper part, which in turn is cooler than Umpqua, itself cooler than Rogue Valley down on the Californian border. Frequent rainfall in the north declines in a similar sequence. The Rogue Valley acts as a heat trap, with long hot spells, but sunshine is generally less reliable than in California.

SOIL
In the Willamette Valley, particularly the 'red' Dundee Hills, the soil is of volcanic origin and rich in iron. The Rogue Valley is more mixed with some granite.

ASPECT
Most vineyards are planted on slopes, to avoid spring frosts and to make the most of summer sun, but the Rogue Valley also has plantings on the valley floor.

There wouldn't have been an Oregon wine industry if it weren't for the bloody-mindedness of its pioneers. But by pioneers, I don't mean the settlers who followed the Oregon trail out west in the 1850s or the first wave of Californians who trekked north a bit later and began planting grapes just over the state line. No. I'm talking about the second wave of Californians. The 1960s wave, which has continued to this day and results in many of Oregon's wineries being owned by people who, for whatever reason, couldn't hack California any longer and decided to head north.

Nowadays, there's good reason to forsake the easy life in California for the damp, cool Oregonian hills. Nearly 50 years of pioneering winemaking has finally proven that Oregon can make some remarkable wines, quite unlike anything that is being produced in California.

Back in the 1960s a betting man wouldn't even have offered odds on such a dumb proposition. But a few people took the gamble all the same. Although California's astonishing growth didn't begin before 1966 at the earliest, when Robert Mondavi set up shop, the University of California at Davis already boasted the most important winemaking and vineyard management course in the nation. The aim of the course was then – and to some extent still is – to teach students how to raise huge crops of healthy grapes in warm climates, and how to avoid foul ups, rather than encouraging them to strive for something difficult and unique.

But a few of the graduates didn't simply want to head off to warm fertile valleys and effortlessly produce copious amounts of adequate wines. Above all, they had visions based on two great European wine styles that California had never mastered: the stylish Rieslings of the Rhine and Mosel valleys in Germany, and the classic Pinot Noir red wines of Burgundy. One of the Davis professors is said to have told David Lett, a young student passionate about Pinot Noir, 'You'll be frosted out in the spring and fall, rained on all summer and you'll get athlete's foot up to your knees.' Given that Oregon's own State University was warning that quality *vinifera* wine varieties would not ripen, you did have to be pretty pig-headed to give Oregon a go. Richard Sommer of Hillcrest and David Lett of Eyrie were just that. In the early 1960s Richard Sommer established a Riesling vineyard in the Umpqua Valley in southern Oregon, then in 1965 David Lett headed further north for cooler, more unpredictable weather – more like Burgundy, in fact. That's exactly what Lett wanted, and exactly what he got.

PINOT NOIR RULES

The reputation of Oregon has been made on Pinot Noir. Lacking local expertise, many grape growers did turn to the University at Davis and, in general, they got advice on methods of cultivation and ground preparation, and choice of clones, especially in the case of Chardonnay, that might have suited California, but that weren't relevant to the situation in Oregon. Big winery mentality simply didn't suit Oregon because, of all the American wine regions, Oregon is based on small family units. Five acres, ten acres, maybe twenty-five is typical, anything much bigger is rare. The total state plantings of 6313ha (15,600 acres) is still only about one-third of those in California's Napa Valley.

The parallels with Burgundy don't end there. The sun often doesn't shine, and rain frequently falls before the grapes are ripe. And in Oregon, as in Burgundy, mesoclimate is everything in the battle to ripen grapes. Uniquely, among the great red varieties, Pinot Noir needs cool spots rather than hot ones.

Let's look at the Willamette Valley first, since almost all the well-known Oregon wines come from here. The long valley stretches from north-west of Portland to just below Eugene, with the Coast Ranges to the west and the Cascades to the east. The crests of the rather haphazard Coast Ranges allow a fair amount of maritime influence through, usually in the form of cloud cover and damp, cool air. While the latitude may be similar to that of Bordeaux, the daytime summer temperatures are actually slightly warmer on average, but the nights here are considerably cooler.

Though its wine history is very short, a surprising number of sub-regions are already staking a quality claim and now have their own AVAs. Almost all of these are based on small ridges of hills running down the west side of the Willamette Valley, which afford protected south and south-east-facing slopes. The Tualatin Valley has a group of good, primarily white, vineyards in the north, and there are good vineyards almost within Portland's suburbs. Heading south, the east-west Chehalem Mountains, including Ribbon Ridge, grow some of Oregon's finest fruit; the Dundee Hills with their red volcanic soil are still the most heavily planted area, while the Eola-Amity Hills, south of McMinnville have also produced top material.

The climate slowly warms as you head south, and so, though there are vineyards right down south of Eugene to the border with California, the real cool-climate action is between the Tualatin River and the Eola Hills.

WHERE THE VINEYARDS ARE *This map shows less than half of the Willamette Valley, but the northern half of the valley does include nearly all the important quality vineyard sites. If you think the Willamette landscape looks a bit cool and green to be a major wine region, you'd not be far wrong – it is chilly and damp here. That's why there are no grand swathes of vines; the growers here have to search out the few little pockets of land that will manage to ripen their grapes.*

Virtually all of the vineyards are on low hillsides, facing south-east to south-west. It's a marginal climate in the Willamette Valley. The Coast Ranges to the west of the valley cut off most of the foggy, wet Pacific influence, but can't exclude it completely. The Cascades to the east cut off the worst of the continental winters that could otherwise kill the vines.

The most important grouping of vineyards is on the Dundee Hills, just to the south-west of Newberg. Here are many of the original plantings, as well as more recent additions like Domaine Drouhin, established by Robert Drouhin from Burgundy in the late 1980s. North-west of Newberg, the Chehalem Mountains have good, well-protected sites. There are some vineyards right up next to Portland, but the other important area on the map is in the north-west, where the Coast Ranges offer good protected sites. At the top-left corner is Montinore, Oregon's first large-scale vineyard development.

NORTH WILLAMETTE

TOTAL DISTANCE
NORTH TO SOUTH
32KM (20 MILES)

▨▨▨ VINEYARDS

0 km _____ 1 _____ 2
0 miles _____ 1

N

The Umpqua Valley, squeezed between the Coast Ranges and the Cascades, is warm enough to grow fair Cabernet Sauvignon alongside Pinot Noir. On the California border the Rogue Valley sites, though higher than 300m (1000ft), are still fairly warm and dry. The Illinois Valley, cooled by Pacific influences, can take even longer than the Willamette to ripen its fruit. In the north-east, along the Columbia River, there are now irrigated plantings of a similar character to the Washington vineyards on the far bank of the river. In the far east is the new Snake River Valley AVA, most of which lies in Idaho.

SELECTED WINERIES

1. Elk Cove
2. Montinoro
3. Oak Knoll
4. Cooper Mountain
5. Ponzi
6. WillaKenzie
7. Beaux Frères
8. Brick House
9. Adelsheim
10. Rex Hill
11. Chehalem
12. Ken Wright
13. Domaine Serene
14. Erath Vineyards
15. Cameron
16. Argyle
17. McKinlay
18. Sokol Blosser
19. Domaine Drouhin
20. Archery Summit
21. Panther Creek
22. Torii Mor
23. Eyrie

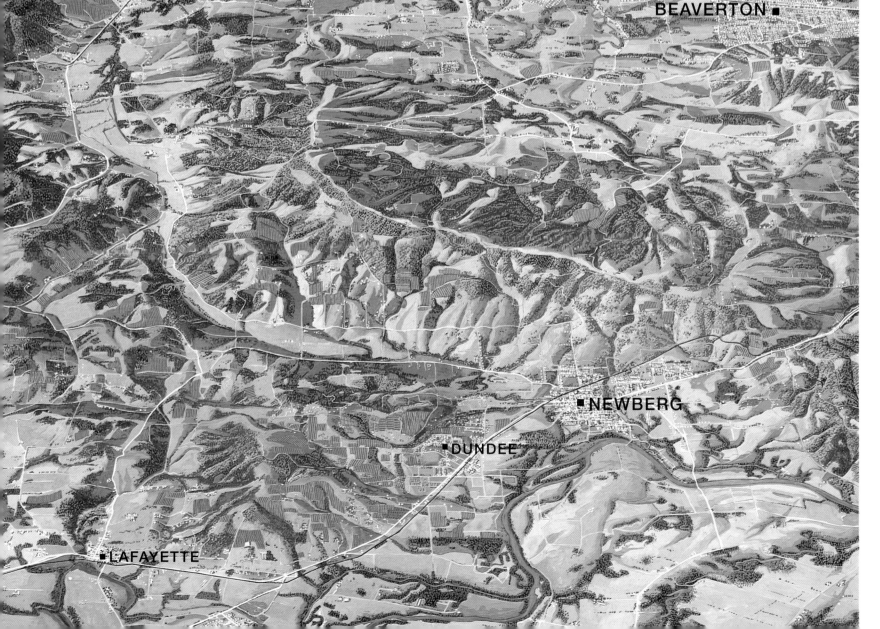

EAST COAST

THE EAST COAST IS WHERE the American wine industry started, but it took a long time to work out how to make anything half-decent. America must have seemed to be a winemaker's paradise, when the first settlers arrived to find fat, juicy grapes hanging off the trees at every turn in New England and Virginia. But, as early as 1606, a certain Captain Smith was complaining that while they might be good to eat, these native varieties made horrendous wines.

In 1619 Lord Delaware brought over French vine cuttings and French vignerons to try to emulate French wines. No go. The vines simply died in droves, and the vignerons weren't any more successful at making a drinkable wine out of the native vines than the original guys. Moses 'the Frenchman' Fournier was having a go on Long Island and Peter Stuyvesant, governor of what was then called New Amsterdam, was planting vines on Manhattan. And his successor helped French Huguenot settlers to plant vineyards futher north up in the valley of the Hudson River. But nothing worked.

The chief problem was phylloxera. This is a tiny aphid that preys on the roots of vines, sucking out their sap and eventually killing the vine. It is endemic throughout North America, and so domestic varieties of vine evolved that could thrive even in soils that were seething with phylloxera. The imported European vines, from the *Vitis vinifera* family, had no such tolerance and immediately succumbed. The only legacy they left is that some of these doomed vines may have cross-bred with native species. These resultant so-called hybrids gained an immunity to phylloxera's depredations and, at the same time, ameliorated the strange, sickly, sweet-scented yet sour-edged fruit of the local grape varieties, in particular those of the *Vitis labrusca*.

This is probably how the first well-known American hybrid – the Alexander or Cape – came into being, and this led on to such varieties as Isabella, Catawba and Concord in the early 19th century. These hybrids produced good crops and could cope with the East Coast's fierce north-eastern winters without rotting in the humid, sticky summers, but, unfortunately, they produced wine that was, well, barely drinkable at worst, with a flavour usually referred to as 'foxy' – the sickly-sweet *labrusca* parentage still showed and it was a long way from any wine aroma familiar to drinkers of *vinifera* wines. But if it was made into 'sherry', 'port' or sparkling wine, it was really quite palatable.

Throughout the 19th and 20th centuries, a reasonably thriving wine industry grew up on the East Coast, led by New York State. It was dominated by wine made from hybrids such as Concord. During the years of Prohibition, between 1920 and 1935, this reliance on Concord served the industry well. The grapes and their juice could be sold for eating or drinking just as they were.

If you had to print such helpful instructions on what were called 'grape bricks' (blocks of pressed grapes) as 'To prevent fermentation add one-tenth per cent Benzoate of Soda' – well, sometimes you just happened to forget, and then sometimes the damned thing did ferment. And it seemed such a waste to throw it

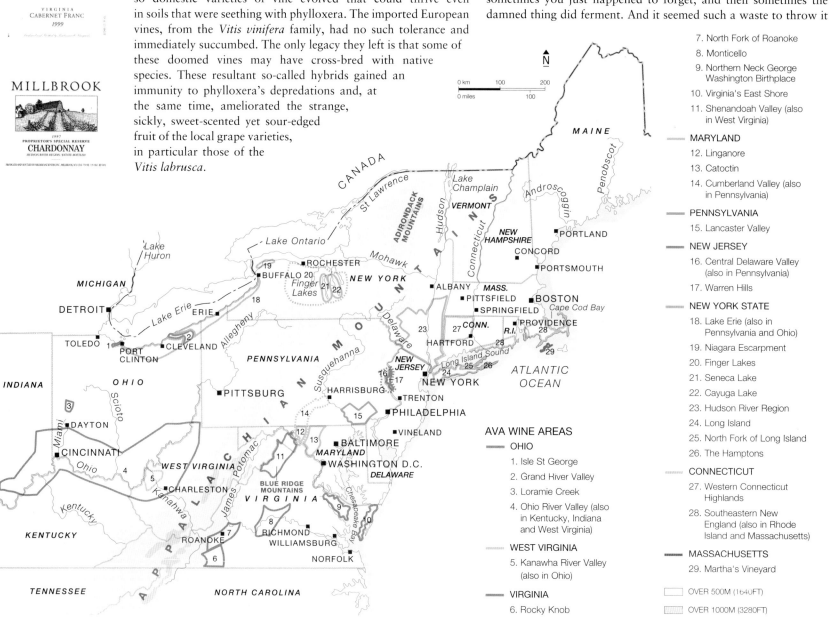

7. North Fork of Roanoke
8. Monticello
9. Northern Neck George Washington Birthplace
10. Virginia's East Shore
11. Shenandoah Valley (also in West Virginia)

MARYLAND
12. Linganore
13. Catoctin
14. Cumberland Valley (also in Pennsylvania)

PENNSYLVANIA
15. Lancaster Valley

NEW JERSEY
16. Central Delaware Valley (also in Pennsylvania)
17. Warren Hills

NEW YORK STATE
18. Lake Erie (also in Pennsylvania and Ohio)
19. Niagara Escarpment
20. Finger Lakes
21. Seneca Lake
22. Cayuga Lake
23. Hudson River Region
24. Long Island
25. North Fork of Long Island
26. The Hamptons

CONNECTICUT
27. Western Connecticut Highlands
28. Southeastern New England (also in Rhode Island and Massachusetts)

MASSACHUSETTS
29. Martha's Vineyard

AVA WINE AREAS
OHIO
1. Isle St George
2. Grand River Valley
3. Loramie Creek
4. Ohio River Valley (also in Kentucky, Indiana and West Virginia)

WEST VIRGINIA
5. Kanawha River Valley (also in Ohio)

VIRGINIA
6. Rocky Knob

OVER 500M (1640FT)

OVER 1000M (3280FT)

away, so you simply drank it. It may not have tasted all that good, but in the era of bathtub gin, who really cared what it tasted like?

It wasn't until a few tentative moves in the 1960s, followed by a slow push first towards quality hybrids and then towards classic European *vinifera* grapes grafted onto American rootstocks, that things began to really hum. New York State has been the leader in this movement, but a surprising number of other states have managed to produce attractive *vinifera* wines before the fading sunlight and icy air of Maine kill off the grape's chance of ripening in the north, or the humid climes of South Carolina and Florida rot it on the vine to the south.

New Hampshire grows just a few vines (8ha/20 acres at the last count) and Massachusetts grows rather more (283ha/700 acres), with the most attractive efforts produced so far being those wines made from grapes grown on the island of Martha's Vineyard – proving that the sea's tempering influence does allow *vinifera* vines to survive at such a northern latitude. Rhode Island claims a similar climate to Bordeaux – but then an awful lot of maritime vineyard regions do. I wouldn't go that far, but good mesoclimates do abound here, the sea helps moderate the extremes of climate, and certainly Sakonnet Vineyards has produced some pretty fair Chardonnay. Connecticut benefits from the mild influence of Long Island Sound. There are wines made upstate, but the climate gets pretty continental away from the maritime influence, and all the best ones I've had, like Chamard Chardonnay, have come from vines grown down near the Sound. Skirting round New York State, New Jersey is struggling to put her past as a *labrusca* producer behind her, and West Virginia produces some wine up in her north-east corner, but the important wine-producing states, after New York State, are Pennsylvania, Virginia and Maryland.

Maryland's chief claim to fame is its oldest winery, Boordy Vineyards, founded in 1945, where Philip Wagner planted America's first French-American hybrids – just as resistant to the cold winters, the scorching summers and the phylloxera as the American versions, but with a much more European flavour. Until recently, most of the best East Coast wines came from these hybrids – Vidal and Chambourcin are two of the best known – and though there are an increasing number of *vinifera* success stories from wineries like Boordy and Basignani, producers such as these generally continue with their share of hybrids. Overall, however, Maryland has not yet lived up to the potential it showed in the 1980s and it has been largely surpassed by its neighbours, Pennsylvania to the north and Virginia to the south.

Pennsylvania divides its vineyards between the shores of Lake Erie in the north-west, where long, but cool days suit some of the northern European varieties like Riesling and Pinot Noir, and the south-east, in the Lancaster and Cumberland valleys, where a new generation of winemakers are having particular success with Chardonnay, though the hybrid, Chambourcin is also producing surprisingly good dark-coloured reds from wineries like Chaddsford and Naylor.

Some winemakers say south-east Pennsylvania reminds them of Burgundy, but Virginia, which shares the same sweep of mountain slopes that run down to the west of Washington DC, actually offers a more realistic comparison. This was where Captain Smith tried and failed to make wine from vinifera varieties in the 17th century, and where Thomas Jefferson, a great admirer of Bordeaux wines, suffered the same fate in the 18th on his estate at Monticello.

Things got so bad, that in 1960 Virginia grew only 6.5ha (16 acres) of vines – and all for table grapes. Now there are some 769ha (1900 acres) of vines, more than two-thirds of which are

vinifera varieties with Chardonnay leading the way. That almost goes without saying, since to build up a cellar-door trade you have to offer a Chardonnay, and Virginia is perfectly placed not only for Washington D.C. but also for a thriving tourist trade – even colonial Williamsburg has its own winery now. Luckily Chardonnay has taken well to Virginia. But that hasn't stopped people experimenting, not only with obvious choices like Riesling, Merlot or Cabernet Franc, but also with such long shots as Viognier (now some of the best in the US) and Barbera.

Things still aren't easy, however. Phylloxera may have been conquered, but the warm climate still poses a constant threat. With most of the vineyards being planted inland on the eastern slopes of the Blue Ridge Mountains, away from the tempering effects of Chesapeake Bay, and with a latitude similar to that of southern Italy and southern Spain, the winemakers are lumbered with all the classic problems of a continental climate – cold winters, spring frosts, tremendous heat and possible excessive humidity and summer rainfall. Even the soils are by no means perfect, consisting largely of fertile red clays and clay loams.

But they do manage a certain amount of success. By planting the vineyards at mostly between 335 and 460 metres (1100 and 1500ft) up on slopes, the grape-growers can provide drainage for excess water and good air circulation. This is vital in order to combat spring frosts and to reduce the incidence of grape rot when the humidity starts to climb. Wide spacing of vines and an open trellis canopy also help to circulate air and minimize rot.

Some of the more cold-sensitive *vinifera* varieties find the winters too harsh in Virginia, but white wines from Viognier, Riesling, Sauvignon Blanc and Chardonnay, and reds from Cabernet (especially Cabernet Franc), Merlot, and even Petit Verdot, from wineries like Barboursville, Linden, Tarara, Horton, White Hall, Valhalla and even Williamsburg, down on sandy soils near the coast, point the way to Virginia challenging New York for East Coast quality in the not-too-distant future.

The aromatic grape varieties do well in New York's cool conditions. This highly perfumed Gewürztraminer is from the Finger Lakes in northern New York State.

It would be impossible to grow grapes this far north in New York State were it not for a group of deep glacial lakes, called the Finger Lakes after their long, thin appearance. This is Seneca Lake, the deepest at 193m (632ft), and able to store heat so effectively that the vintage can sometimes continue until November.

NEW YORK STATE

 **RED GRAPES**
Native American and hybrid varieties continue to dominate, with Concord accounting for 75 per cent of total plantings, but nearly 80 per cent of this is used for juice, not for wine. *Vinifera* vines include Cabernet Sauvignon, Merlot, Cabernet Franc and Pinot Noir.

WHITE GRAPES
Chardonnay is the leading *vinifera* variety, followed by Riesling, Gewürztraminer and Sauvignon Blanc. *Vinifera* grapes now exceed all other varieties with the exception of Niagara, much of which goes into sweet juice.

CLIMATE
The Lake Erie vineyards benefit from the proximity of the Great Lakes which warm up the cold Arctic air. The Finger Lakes have a short, humid growing season, followed by severe winters. The Hudson River is milder, while Long Island benefits from the moderating influence of water on three sides: the Atlantic Ocean, Long Island Sound and Great Peconic Bay separating the two forks. Right up on the Canadian border in the new Niagara Escarpment area the long limestone ridge or escarpment, Lake Ontario and the Niagara River all help to moderate the climate and protect the vines from the cold winters.

SOIL
Soils are varied. By Lake Erie there is gravelly loam and around the Finger Lakes calcareous shale. The Hudson River has shale, slate, schist and limestone. Long Island is sandy with silt and loam and quick-draining. The Niagara Escarpment benefits from well-drained soils.

ASPECT
The Allegheny plateau, a ridge of hills parallel to the south shore of Lake Erie, traps the warmth from the lake. Vineyards in the Finger Lakes and the Niagara Escarpment are on slopes to avoid frost and the steep Hudson River Valley is an efficient conduit for warm Atlantic air. The Long Island vineyards are on the flatlands along the seashore.

I KNOW THEY SAY THAT LONG ISLAND is the closest vineyard area to New York City, but it depends on when you visit. Don't do it in June, or July, or August, or any time when it's sunny, or weekends – and don't drive. If you do, you'll need to leap out of bed before dawn, slam the hire car into 'drive', hare through the Midtown Tunnel, out through Queens on Interstate 495 and in no time – well, even obeying the speed limit, in about an hour-and-a-half – you should be at Riverhead, with time for some leisurely vineyard visits. Except for me it didn't work out like that: I visited in summer. Four hours to Riverhead, every appointment missed, and then the long drive home. Too much sea and sand. Too popular.

Well, that's Long Island for you. It's the reason everyone rushes there as soon as the sun comes out. It's also the reason that it is seen increasingly as America's answer to its quest for a Bordeaux-like wine region. It's got similarities, I'll grant you, and is making a good stab at Cabernet and Merlot, although most of its best wines are Chardonnays, as is often the case on the East Coast. And the vineyards laying claim to a slice of Bordeaux's glory are virtually all on the North Fork. The South Fork has the Hamptons: they throw better parties there, the houses are bigger, the limos longer, but in wine terms its soil is rather heavy, leading to waterlogging when summer and autumn rains get excessive. Its spring frosts can strike as late as May, prevailing winds are cooler and the ripening period is two or three weeks shorter than on the North Fork. Makes you wonder why the socialites didn't choose the North Fork.

Long Island is New York's newest wine area. A few vines were planted here in the 17th and 18th centuries, but nothing really happened until 1973 when Alex and Louisa Hargrave uprooted a vegetable patch at Cutchogue, a couple of miles up the North Fork from Riverhead, and planted vines. So? So the vines they planted were the French classics of Bordeaux and Burgundy, together with Riesling. Until then New York's reputation, such as it was, had been based on native American vines and French hybrids: a few plantations of classic *vinifera* grapes existed upstate. Everyone said they couldn't survive the bitter winters and short, fiery summers.

WHERE THE VINEYARDS ARE *We're looking at a tiny sliver of land here. Riverhead to Southold is a mere 19km (12 miles), and Jamesport north to Long Island Sound is only 5km (3 miles). But dotted about among the scarcely undulating fields, full of lush market produce, are about 1200 ha (3000 acres) of vineyards that many experts think will prove to be some of the best in the USA. Indeed you can narrow things down even more to the area around Cutchogue, where most of the best vineyards are and which people have begun whispering about as the Médoc of America.*

There are some vines on the South Fork of Long Island (just 40ha/100 acres or so), but the North Fork clearly has better potential; the South Fork's soils are heavier, the climate is a little cooler and the risk of spring frosts catching you unawares lasts a little longer. Long Island's soils were formed by retreating Wisconsin glaciation about 10,000 years ago, but the North Fork's thin claw has grabbed the freest draining, more gravelly and sandy soils. It has also grabbed the better climate.

Stretching north-east into Long Island Sound, with Peconic Bay to its south, the North Fork is surrounded on three sides by relatively warm water. The prevailing westerlies reach the North Fork after blowing across the Sound. This helps to create a mild growing period of up to 230 days, although the relative air humidity requires fairly strict anti-fungal spray regimes as does the likelihood of late season rain. The climate during September and October mirrors that of Bordeaux, and winemakers in the North Fork can experience the same heartbreak that a sudden downpour in the middle of harvest causes their French counterparts.

But if they really want to be thought of as this transatlantic Médoc, they're going to have to get used to dreams of 'Vintage of the Century' turning to ashes far more frequently than they become glorious reality.

This didn't bother the Hargraves. They realized that the waters of Long Island had a moderating effect on the North Fork, cooling the summer heat and warding off the worst of the north-east winter cold. They'd also found that the gently undulating farmland around Cutchogue – sitting on deep sand and gravel subsoils – was ideal for decent drainage and reasonable water retention. And their thoughts turned to Bordeaux, and to the Médoc especially, which juts out into the Bay of Biscay on its tongue of low-lying land. They checked the growing season temperatures and found that, though the season starts a little later than in Bordeaux, slightly warmer summer temperatures bring both areas' grapes to ripen at much the same time, between mid September and mid October. And the well-drained soil means that a slightly higher rainfall isn't that much of a problem and lessens the chance of late season rot.

But it hasn't been an easy ride. Fungicide sprays are crucial to control rot caused by the humidity. The soils are more fertile than those of Bordeaux's best properties and pruning and trellising must be adapted accordingly. And New York City has been slow to take Long Island's wines to its heart. I remember on an early trip trying to persuade the city's gastronomic glitterati of Long Island's brilliant potential. I might as well have been extolling the friendly nature of the Great White Shark to a group of scuba divers. But at last, the quality of Long Island Chardonnay, the fine Merlots, Cabernets and, occasionally Sauvignon Blancs and late-harvest Rieslings, have become hot enough in the Big Apple that on a recent trip, every restaurant I ate in boasted at least one Long Island wine. In the past few years, Long Island's wine industry has been transformed. Some of the original owners have now sold on for vast sums of money and I hope this infusion of capital and new plantings – the area under vine had reached about 1214ha (3000 acres) in 2007, all of it *vinifera* – will lead to higher quality, rather than profiteering. The area is an attractive weekend destination and it's certainly worth trying some of that Chardonnay with the famous local lobsters.

But other parts of the state have a longer grape-growing tradition and contribute the bulk of the volume that makes New York the

RIVERHEAD

second state for wine production after California with some 12,950ha (32,000 acres) of vines. The Lake Erie region, also known as Chatauqu, has 7649ha (18,900 acres), yet few have heard of it because most of its vineyards grow Concord, which makes great grape juice but pretty duff wine. The Finger Lakes region also relies upon the effects of water in tempering a climate that would otherwise be far too harsh for wine grapes. Its 11 narrow, deep lakes, running north to south just below Lake Ontario, were gouged out of rock by glaciers in the last Ice Age. The three biggest – Keuka, Seneca and Cayuga – have the majority of the region's total 4209ha (10,400 acres) of vineyards. Initially, the region was seen as suitable only for native varieties and hybrids, but a visionary called Konstantin Frank believed that vines such as Riesling and Chardonnay could survive icy winters if grafted on to sufficiently hardy rootstocks. He eventually proved his point (using rootstock from a convent in Quebec) and there are now increasing numbers of delicate, delicious white wines being made on the shale-dominated soils. Leading producers such as Fox Run and Lamoreaux Landing now make some delicate Pinot Noir, spicy Cabernet Franc and juicy Merlot but, in general, reds still struggle to ripen fully. The lower altitude and greater depth of Seneca and Cayuga lakes, allowing a slightly longer protection from frost, are regarded as the best sites and they now have their own separate AVA designations.

The Hudson River Valley, directly north of New York City, has the longest unbroken grape-growing tradition in the USA. Only recently have the 202ha (500 acres) of vines begun producing good *vinifera* wines, including of some the state's best Chardonnay and Pinot Noir, as growers realized that the steep Pallisades through which the Hudson flows south act as a conduit for warming maritime influences from the Atlantic Ocean. The state's newest wine area is the Niagara Escarpment up on the Canadian border, with 162ha (400 acres) of vines dominated by native and hybrid vines.

AVA WINE AREA AND SELECTED WINERIES

1. Palmer
2. Marth Clara
3. Paumanok
4. Macari Vineyards
5. Shinn Estate
6. Pellegrini
7. Galluccio
8. Castello di Borghese
9. Peconic Bay
10. Bedell
11. Pindar
12. Lenz

NORTH FORK = AVA WINE AREA

— AVA BOUNDARY

LONG ISLAND SOUND

SOUTHOLD
PECONIC
NORTH FORK
MATTITUCK
CUTCHOGUE
NEW SUFFOLK
Robins Island
GREAT PECONIC BAY
AQUEBOGUE
JAMESPORT
RIVERHEAD
Peconic River
THE HAMPTONS

NORTH FORK OF LONG ISLAND

TOTAL DISTANCE NORTH TO SOUTH 23KM (14 MILES)

0 km   1   2
0 miles   1

VINEYARDS

N

SOUTHOLD

MATTITUCK

CANADA

I MUST ADMIT, I'D NEVER GIVEN IT a second thought. The first vineyards I visited were those of Bordeaux when I was a student. But I wonder, I wonder. Before I went to university, I trailed across Canada, hanging out and playing the guitar. Tired of thumbing lifts, I snuggled down one late afternoon in a sun-bathed orchard just north of Peachland in British Columbia's Okanagan Valley, and drifted off to sleep. It wasn't a vineyard then but, looking at the map, could it be the site of what is now Chateau Ste Claire or Hainle? It just could. And a little later when I visited my parents in Ontario, I drove down to Vineland, and tramped through the rows of vines below the Niagara Escarpment before getting my first samplings of Maréchal Foch, De Chaunac and Vidal Blanc, while gazing out over the sullen grey waters of Lake Ontario. I was warmed and cheered up by a smashing 'port' made from *labrusca* grapes, and I concluded, upon this evidence alone, that perhaps Ontario was fortified wine country at best. Had I been to Bordeaux yet? Or was Ontario first?

I don't really know, but there's no doubt that Bordeaux captured my imagination more than the Niagara Peninsula or the Okanagan Valley for the next decade or two. Which is fair enough. The New Age of wine was scarcely drawing its first breath in the Canada of the early 1970s. By the mid-1990s, however, Canada was, albeit timidly, knocking on the door and asking to be regarded as the newest New World wine nation.

To be taken seriously, any new country has to have a product that other people are not already doing better. Australia without Chardonnay, or New Zealand without Sauvignon Blanc, would have had a far greater struggle for recognition. For Canada, it wasn't the grape variety that mattered – it was the type of wine. One of the rarest, most difficult styles of wine to achieve in the world can be made every single year in Canada – sweet Icewine – and all because of her terrible sub-Arctic winter weather. But if the numbing winter weather makes Icewine possible, the rapid onset of winter and the late arrival of spring make life perennially difficult for anyone attempting to make any other sort of wine. For a long time it was thought to be virtually impossible to ripen *vinifera* grapes satisfactorily in Canada, and to prevent them being killed during the worst of the cold spells.

In British Columbia and Ontario, these problems have to a large extent been sorted out and there has been enormous progress in the most important regions in recent years where the move from hybrid to vinifera grape varieties has been rapid (see British Columbia pages 267–268 and Ontario page 269); and Icewine still remains Canada's trump card. However, there is another side to Canada's wine industry, too – the eastern seaboard. Here they reckon they've had a wine industry going in fits and starts – but mostly fits – since, well, since one summer circa AD1000, when Leif Ericsson, the Viking who discovered the Americas long before Christopher Columbus, settled in for a long, cold winter.

Ericsson was stuck in a place now called L'Anse aux Meadows, in northern Newfoundland and there, it is reported, he discovered – grapes. Ericsson knew what to expect from a Newfoundland winter – he originated from Norway, after all – and it seems entirely likely that he did find native vines bearing grapes and that he made them into wine. The first chronicler of Leif's transatlantic adventure – Adam of Bremen – says Leif christened the place Vinland, because the vines he found yielded 'the best of wine'. Two things. First, it's horrifically cold in northern Newfoundland in winter. Any kind of wine would have tasted fantastic as they huddled together for warmth and watched the icefloes jostle and crunch. Secondly, the wine couldn't have been that good, because as soon as spring came, they upped sticks and returned to Norway.

And that – apart from the presence of one tiny 'fruit' winery today – was it for Newfoundland wine.

But even though it isn't easy there is a modern wine industry in the eastern seaboard, in Québec and Nova Scotia. You wouldn't think that Québec was suited to viticulture by the look of the climate and the soils. Most of the vines are about 80km (50 miles) south-east of Montreal, down near Lake Champlain and the US border. It's a glacial plain, mostly covered in the worst sort of soil for cool climate viticulture – clay. But there are pockets of slate and gravel, and producers assidously seek these out and exploit them. As for weather – summers are short and humid, you may have snow until April, frost until May and by October the snow and frost are back again. And talking of frost – the winter temperatures can go as low as –30°C (–22°F). The vines just split open at that temperature, so they have to cover them with soil after every harvest. There are 142ha (350 acres) of vines, all being winter-hardy French and American hybrids.

Better known for its fishing fleets than its wines, Nova Scotia does have a fledgling wine industry too. The vineyards are mostly in the Annapolis valley, next to the relatively protected waters of the Bay of Fundy, though there are also some vines further north overlooking the Northumberland Strait, the warmest salt waters north of the Carolinas, across to Prince Edward Island – an area that calls itself 'The Sunshine Coast of Nova Scotia'. All things are relative. Most of the 132ha (325 acres) of vines are French hybrid but there are a few acres of Chardonnay and Pinot Noir. As in Québec there really isn't enough heat and some of the wineries have to blend imported grapes with their own produce. But one fascinating oddity is that they use *Vitis amurensis* varieties – Michurinetz and Severny – from the frozen wastes of the Amur river on the Chinese-Russian border – and, understandably, these hardy vines find it quite balmy down in sunny Nova Scotia.

BURROWING OWL
vineyards
Pinot Gris
1999
Estate Bottled
VQA Okanagan Valley VQA

PELEE ISLAND WINERY
2000
VQA Ontario VQA
RIESLING DRY

Riesling Icewine: Canada can produce this style every year without fail.

VINTNERS QUALITY ALLIANCE

I really like the description that the wine producers of Ontario and British Columbia have given to their strict Vintners Quality Alliance (VQA) scheme, that was created in 1989 and has been a powerful force, both for change and for good, ever since. They describe it as 'a contract between the vintners and the consumer'. If only the appellation systems that are used in Europe and in other parts of North America held dear to such a contract.

I am, in general, critical of appellation schemes, since they rapidly become catch-all descriptions, with the unintentional result of both inhibiting the talented winemakers as well as protecting the mediocre. But in countries with marginal climates, like Canada, where the classic grape varieties will only ripen in the very best mesoclimates, a proactive scheme like the VQA, which lays down guidelines on geographical designations, minimum ripeness levels and grape types, really begins to make sense.

• Each potential VQA wine is subjected to a tasting panel – the judging takes place blind and the award of a VQA medallion marks out the best of the bunch. The VQA has a refreshingly high rate of rejection – around 20 per cent.

• The majority of wines in the VQA scheme are made from *vinifera* grapes (though Icewine often uses hybrids, like Vidal).

• Table wines that are labelled as originating from one of the Designated Viticultural Areas of Ontario – Pelee Island, Lake Erie North Shore, Niagara Peninsula and now Prince Edward County – must be made from 100 per cent *vinifera* grapes.

BRITISH COLUMBIA

IT WAS WHEN I DISCOVERED AN Okanagan Valley Syrah, that I knew British Columbia was ready to join in the ever lengthening line of serious New World producers. Not simply because Syrah is a smashing grape. Not only because many intelligent growers are now realizing that Syrah, despite having been thought of as solely a warm-climate grape, can actually ripen in dry but cool areas better than Cabernet Sauvignon. New Zealand is proving this. Switzerland is proving this, for goodness sake. So why not Canada?

But there's more. Alex Nichol thought carefully when he established his vineyard on the east side of Okanagan Lake, looking out across to Summerland. He planted his vines at the base of a granite cliff which, as the afternoon sun heats up, reflects blistering amounts of heat right down on to his vines and yet still manages to retain heat as the sun's glow fades away in the evening. And by doing so, he was demonstrating the maturity that marks out a new area on the up. Because he didn't just say – 'Where has everyone else planted? I'll plant there too.' He started to seek out the nooks and crannies, the sheltered spots, the infertile soils that the grape vine flourishes in – all the things that will turn a marginal area into something special.

Marginal? Able to grow Syrah, and yet marginal? Yes. Most areas of Okanagan won't be able to grow Syrah – though more sites, one or two down in the south near the USA border, are looking promising. Quite a few areas will find red wines in general pretty difficult to ripen, especially as things cool down, moving up towards Kelowna and beyond. And many growers, especially those who have come from a traditional farming background – after all, the Okanagan Valley is a paradise for growing fruit (you don't call

one your towns down by the lake Peachland for nothing) – will find it difficult to accept the fundamental rule of producing decent, ripe, wine grapes in a marginal area: that you must keep the yield down or the fruit won't ripen and the wine will taste sour.

There's that 'marginal' word again. And it is deserved. So let's look at some basics. Lake Okanagan runs pretty much north-south from Vernon in the north to Penticton in the south. Below Penticton, the area called South Okanagan continues down to the USA border, which actually cuts across Osoyoos Lake – Canada's warmest lake – on the 49th parallel. Well, if we look round the rest of the world to see which vineyards lie between 49° and 50.5° north, as Okanagan's do, we don't get much of a choice. The Rheingau and Mittelrhein in Germany hover around 50°; the northernmost vineyards of Champagne in France are at about 49°. In Europe, very few grapes ripen that far north, and Champagne is famous for sparkling wine precisely because its grapes are basically too acid to make into palatable table wine. But there are some crucial reasons why Okanagan can ripen a decent array of grapes – both red and white – so far north.

The first of these is rain. Or lack of it. Northern Europe gets a lot of rain, which means two things – vigorous vines and large crops – especially when it rains near vintage, which it usually does. And less sunshine. Well, think of it. The sky is full of rain-bearing clouds, so how are the sun's rays going to get through them and warm up the vines?

The Okanagan Valley is lucky. In the north, the rainfall is only about 400mm (16in) a year, but it is cooler too, so once you get up to Kelowna and Vernon, the crisp, lighter wines are the most likely styles. But as you head south, down through Penticton to Okanagan Falls and Oliver and Osoyoos Lake, the rainfall drops right down to 152mm (6in) a year. This little region is the only part

RED GRAPES
Merlot is by far the most important variety, with 40 per cent of the red plantings. Early plantings of Pinot Noir and Merlot have been joined by Cabernet Sauvignon, Cabernet Franc, Gamay and even a little Syrah.

WHITE GRAPES
Whites dominate, particularly those early ripening varieties that are most successful in northern Europe. The quality whites are Chardonnay with over a quarter of white plantings. Pinot Gris and Pinot Blanc follow, with 13 per cent each. There are smaller amounts of Gewürztraminer, Riesling and Sauvignon Blanc.

CLIMATE
In the Okanagan Valley, the long, deep lake is critical in moderating the worst extremes of hot and cold. Lying to the west of the Cascade Range, the area receives scant rainfall, and very little during the short growing season, with its long hot days. Similkameen also has an arid climate and can be colder in winter than the Okanagan because of the absence of a major lake to moderate temperatures. The weather in the coastal regions is more variable, with very wet winters, large storms and increased humidity.

SOIL
Soils in the Okanagan Valley vary from gravelly benchlands above the lake to sandier soils in the expanding areas that lie to the south of the lake. Drainage is good, but combines with summer heat and low rainfall to make irrigation essential.

ASPECT
At this latitude vineyards need to face south, although those actually sited on the lake slope more markedly east or west, towards the margins of the lake. Similkameen is a long narrow valley with steep mountainsides. The Fraser Valley is generally flat with rolling hillsides.

BRITISH COLUMBIA VQA WINE AREAS

- Vancouver Island
- Gulf Islands
- Fraser Valley
- Similkameen Valley
- Okanagan Valley
- OVER 500M (1640FT)
- OVER 1000M (3280FT)

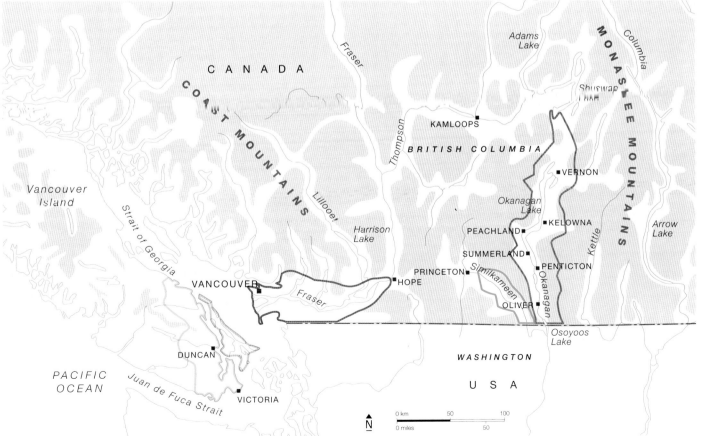

The Okanagan Valley is one of Canada's top resort areas and vines have to share the land with holidaymakers. Here Quails' Gate Vineyard slopes down to the holiday homes and jetties on Okanagan Lake, just below Kelowna.

not heat, that builds up the sugar in those grapes. No wonder that a strip of land just south-west of Oliver in this southern stretch has been called 'The Golden Mile', and that it is packed full of vineyards that are sprouting Cabernet Sauvignon, Cabernet Franc and Merlot, proving that you can ripen reds like these above the 49th Parallel. And they do taste special. Those very hot days are followed by very cool nights up here by the Columbia Mountains. High acids are the result, and this, combined with high sugar levels makes for some very interesting wines. Of course, there are a few problems. About every decade, an almighty winter freeze threatens to destroy your vines. And despite the torrid high summer conditions, winter closes in very fast here come mid-October. You can't let the grapes hang around for extra flavour, as you can in somewhere like New Zealand. If you're not intending to make Icewine, those grapes have simply got to come off – ripe or not.

There are now 3075ha (7599 acres) of wine grapes planted in British Columbia, compared to just 405ha (1000 acres) in 1989, and the figure goes on increasing each year. Over 93 per cent of the province's total production comes from the Okanagan, with most vineyards located south of Penticton. But there are also a few other areas to note.

West of Oliver lies the Similkameen Valley, described as 'high desert cattle country' with hot, dry summers and low humidity. It sounds good for grapes, and there are already over 120ha (300 acres) of vines. Down the Fraser Valley towards Vancouver, where it's cooler and wetter, there are over 40ha (100 acres). And, more importantly, out on the heavily wooded lumber and leisure centre of Vancouver Island, with a mild climate that is tempered by the sea, there are a number of small vineyards and wineries that cater to an eager tourist trade. Finally, the Gulf Islands region with its mild climate, like the Okanagan and Fraser valleys, had an established fruit and market gardening tradition in the 19th century and new vineyards are being planted on many of these small islands.

of Canada officially designated as 'desert', and irrigation is a must if vines are to survive and flourish. And think – only 152mm (6in) of rain a year. That means clear skies and endless summer sunshine. And being so far north, they reckon they get about two hours longer of sunshine per day during high summer than the vineyards of California do. Not as hot, maybe, but it's sunshine,

Harvesting frozen Vidal grapes for Icewine in mid-January at Inniskillin.

ICEWINE

Every winter, the temperatures in the vineyards of Ontario and British Columbia (from the Okanagan and Similkameen valleys only) drop way below freezing and frequently stay there for weeks, if not months, on end. If your grapes are still on the vine in late November and December, they freeze. This doesn't sound good. But if you gather these grapes, frozen, (harvesting must take place at temperatures of –8°C/46°F) and take them, still frozen, to the winery and delicately press them – still frozen – you'll discover that the water which constitutes more than 80 per cent of the grape juice has turned into ice crystals, and the sugar has separated out into a thick, gooey, sludgy syrup that is ridiculously sweet. Remove the ice from the syrup and you've got the basis for one of the most distinctive flavours in the wine world – the phenomenally rich Icewine. Once or twice a decade, a few German vineyards attempt this wine style, and sell their minute production at astronomical prices. In Canada, they can make it every year.

The first Icewine was made by Hainle in British Columbia in 1973, and though British Columbia produces a small but growing amount, Ontario produces nearly five times the amount, with over 400,000 litres (105,669 gallons) on average per year. Things really took off in 1991 at the Vinexpo World Wine Show in France, when a 1989 Inniskillin Icewine won the Grand Prix d'Honneur. Most Icewine is made from Riesling and Vidal but there are red versions too, from varieties such as Pinot Noir.

ONTARIO

Ontario's 6475ha (16,000 acres) of vineyards lie on the shores of Lake Ontario and Lake Erie, between 42° and 43.5° North – on the same band of latitude as Corsica and the Languedoc vineyards of southern France. That sounds extremely promising for some fairly gutsy flavours, but it isn't as simple as that. Those European vineyards are strongly influenced by the perenially warm Mediterranean sea. Even in the middle of winter you can still jump into the sea at Ajaccio or Marseilles and experience, at worst, a mildly bracing immersion. Jump into the sea off Canada's 44th parallel in midwinter and you'll be nursing some extremely nasty cold bruises from the icebergs. And that's only half the story. Proximity to the sea tempers any region's extremes, but Ontario's vineyards are hundreds of miles inland. Long, numbing winters and short, searing summers would rule out any chance of winemaking – if it weren't for the lakes.

It's the lakes that make viticulture possible in Ontario, by storing up the summer heat to release it slowly though the winter, yet also providing breezes that help cool the fierce, if short-lived, summer sun. We end up with summer temperatures that are higher than both Bordeaux and Burgundy – a crucial point, because until the end of May, Ontario is appreciably cooler, and by September her temperature drops below that of Bordeaux once again. But in between, Niagara is hotter than Bordeaux in June, July and August, and it's hotter than Burgundy right up to the middle of October, when there's a dramatic drop. In the south, Pelee Island, 18km (11 miles) out in Lake Erie, has a ripening period 30 days longer than the Canadian mainland, helped by the southerly latitude and the warming effect of the shallow Lake Erie. That warming effect only lasts till winter comes. Then, the extreme shallowness of the lake means it frequently freezes over and Pelee Island is encased in ice. So, despite the potential of a much longer ripening period, vintages are erratic. Lake Erie North Shore, near Windsor, also benefits from the water's warm surface temperature and suffers less from the winter freeze.

However, the heart of Ontario viticulture – and indeed the engine room for Canadian wine in general, since it produces 80 per cent of the country's wine grapes – is on the Niagara Peninsula. The most important part of this is a narrow strip of land running for about 56km (35 miles) east from Hamilton to Niagara-on-the-Lake and comprising the south-western shore of Lake Ontario, but there's also a stretch following the Niagara River south to the Niagara Falls. It would be easy to dismiss this as one homogenous small region, but when you are in marginal conditions, little things matter, and they do here. The general view is that this slim peninsula, bounded by the two Great Lakes – Ontario and Erie – is protected from the worst of the winter weather because of the heat those great bodies of water hold. This is broadly true, but there seem to be three distinctly different parts to the Niagara vineyard region, all tightly meshed together. Right on the Lake Ontario shore, there's no doubt the continual movement of air does ward off frost, but these constant breezes also cool the air down in spring, delaying the whole development of the vine. That's fine for avoiding spring frosts, but not so good for completing ripeness, especially when you're faced with a cold October.

A mile or two south of Niagara-on-the-Lake is the Niagara Plain – it's not very big but, being further from the Lake, you lose some of the breezes and immediately encounter a problem with spring frosts. But the plus point is that the vines start to develop sooner, and the higher summer temperatures give fatter, richer flavours and an earlier harvest.

And running east-west just south of the Lake Ontario shoreline is the Niagara Escarpment – or the Niagara Bench, as wine people like to call it. This reaches up to 175–185m (574–607ft) in height. Vineyards here are cooler than those on the Plain, but drainage is good on the slopes. It needs to be. There's a lot of fairly heavy clay loam soil mixed in with the sandy loam, and the continual air movement minimizes frost danger, and helps to balance out loss of heat by eliminating the fungal diseases that bedevil humid areas at the end of the ripening season. The wines in general have higher acidity but, year by year, become better balanced.

And which is the best? Hard to say. Some people like the St David's Bench near Niagara Falls. Others like the Beamsville Bench further to the west, past St Catharine's. Time and commitment from the growers will sort it all out.

And what types of wine will they be producing? Well, even the best hybrids are in retreat, except for Vidal, which due to its ability to produce startling Icewines with the exotic flavours of mango, guava and lychee – and yet keep the acid up – has earned itself its place. The first wave of *vinifera* plantings presumed that Ontario had to be white wine country – fair enough, and of course this was in the late 1980s to mid-1990s, when the world was mad for white. Early concentration on Riesling and Gewürztraminer was quickly superceded by the realization that you could grow the superstar Chardonnay here. Inniskillin and Chateau des Charmes led the way and everyone followed, with considerable success. But now the world wants red – and Ontario shows it can do that too – from Cabernet Franc, Gamay and Zweigeltrebe right up to that talisman of New-Age red – Syrah. And, of course, there's Icewine. Where would Canada be without Icewine?

 RED GRAPES
Pinot Noir seems most suited, but Cabernet Franc, Cabernet Sauvignon, Merlot and even Syrah are on the increase, though there are few sites that can ripen them successfully, and then only in the warmest years.

WHITE GRAPES
Chardonnay leads, followed by Gewürztraminer, Pinot Blanc and Riesling. The hybrid Vidal remains important, particularly for Icewine.

CLIMATE
A cool region, it depends on the moderating effect of its lakes for successful viticulture. Rainfall is moderate, and snow in December and January favours Icewine production.

SOIL
Soils range from free-draining sandy loams, gravels and sand to heavier soils with varying amounts of clay.

ASPECT
There is a mixture of flat and sloping vineyards. Those close to the shore of Lake Ontario and on the Niagara plain are basically flat. Those on the Niagara Bench reach up to 185m (607ft) in altitude and the best sites are on the relatively steep, north-facing slopes.

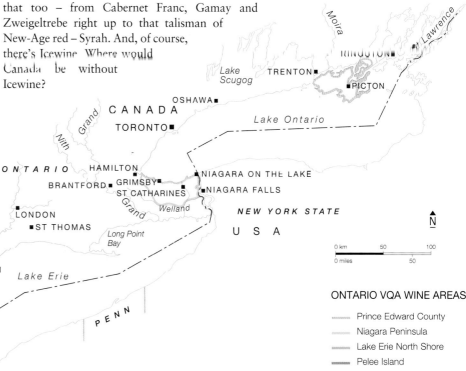

ONTARIO VQA WINE AREAS
- Prince Edward County
- Niagara Peninsula
- Lake Erie North Shore
- Pelee Island

SOUTH AMERICA & MEXICO

THE PAN-AMERICAN HIGHWAY makes for the geographical ride of a lifetime: a great, long road running south from the US border, it takes you through a political, cultural and economic landscape of incredible diversity. Mad drivers and the impressive mountainous spine of the Andes are almost the only constants on a road which connects the heat of Mexico with the chill blasts of Patagonia. Apart from football, one of the major forces that provides any cohesion or unity on this southward trek is religion. Early missionaries propagated Christianity in the mid-16th century, beginning their journey in Mexico and spreading throughout South America. With them came the *vinifera* vine from Europe, and the traditional view is that they made wine in order to celebrate the Eucharist.

Wine for normal consumption was also made by the *conquistadores* – importing wine from back home was far too risky. Few wines reacted well to the long sea voyage across the Atlantic, even less to the hot, bumpy overland journey to the Pacific coast, followed by yet another stage by sea down to Chile and Peru. Subsequent dispersal of settlers and missionaries took winemaking from the mile-high plateau of Mexico to the Río Negro in Argentina. Various waves of largely European immigrants have had their effect on the development of both the wine industry and the culture that supports it, in particular the influence of the French in Chile and the Italians in Brazil and Argentina. These days, winemaking techniques are a blend of local knowledge and international expertise. This expertise is increasingly bringing out remarkable quality, especially in parts of Chile and Argentina, which enjoy warm, dry conditions, ideal for the vine, and are well away from the influence of the tropics.

TOPOGRAPHY AND CLIMATE

Latitude and climate are the most obvious restrictions on winemaking in South America and Mexico. From the Tropic of Cancer which bisects Mexico, to the Tropic of Capricorn which cuts across Argentina's northern border, high temperatures and humidity alternately rot the grapes or bake them, making it difficult in many places to produce quality wine. Clever use of altitude, together with stubborn persistence, do, however, create exceptions. French winemaker Michel Rolland has exploited the benefits of being over 1700m (5577ft) above sea level at Cafayate to make award-winning red Malbec and white Torrontés wine in the Argentine region of Salta, barely 150km (93 miles) from the tropics. And Venezuela, too, has made a substantial investment in tropical wine experiments.

The massive Andean chain and cooling breezes off the Pacific are the most important physical influences on viticulture. These maritime breezes help regulate excessive temperatures the length of the coast, from Baja California, down through the Ica region of Peru and on into Chile's Central Valley. In the case of Chile, the cold Humboldt Current creates an additional chilling factor, which benefits white wine areas such as Casablanca. On the eastern side of the continent, vineyards in Uruguay and parts of southern Brazil are influenced by the problematic combination of warm, wet oceanic weather off the Atlantic, and regular blasts from the cold *Pampero* wind that originates in the Argentine pampas.

The effect of the Andean mountain chain is most evident in South America's two most important wine regions: Chile's Central Valley and Argentina's Mendoza region. Just 150km (90 miles) separate the two yet, because the Andes lie between them, shielding Argentina from the moist Pacific breezes, temperature and rainfall differences are enormous. Mendoza gets almost no rain and would be a virtual desert were it not for abundant irrigation from rivers fed by mountain run-off. The Andes has had a dramatic effect on soil, too. Over the millennia, silt washed down onto the alluvial plains has created rich, fertile soils, which, as Chile demonstrates, creates ideal conditions for most kinds of horticulture. Vines love it too, but produce enormous crops if not rigorously controlled. Top wines rarely come from high yielding vines.

CHILE

In South America, Chile continues to lead the way. Since the mid-1980s, its winemakers have been returning from France, California, Australia and New Zealand, bringing with them ideas and technology. Foreign investors have been attracted by the political and economic stability, with the result that Chile now boasts more than 200 exporting wineries with a total annual export income of US$1 billion, compared with US$23 million in 1988.

Like the country itself, the wine industry is squeezed into a long, narrow, north-south strip either side of the capital, Santiago, with vineyards never more than 100km (60 miles) from the coast or the Andes, and with considerable climatic variation between Elqui and Limari in the north and Malleco in the south. Matching grape varieties with subtle differences in soils and mesoclimates has resulted in an exciting range of wine styles (see pages 273–279).

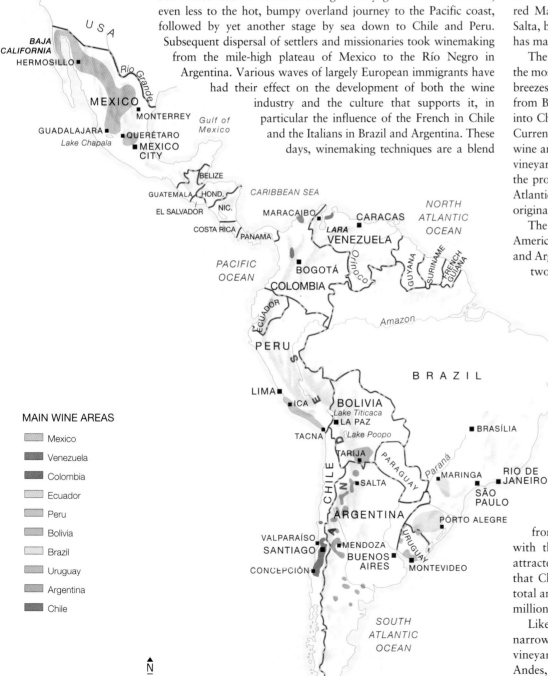

MAIN WINE AREAS

- Mexico
- Venezuela
- Colombia
- Ecuador
- Peru
- Bolivia
- Brazil
- Uruguay
- Argentina
- Chile

0 km 1000 2000
0 miles 1000

N

ARGENTINA

Over to the east, a previously sleeping giant is at last stirring into action. Who would have thought the world's fifth largest producer of wine, with over 550 wineries in the Mendoza area alone, could have remained so quiet on the international scene for so long? The reason for this was a thirsty Argentine population, ready to drink most of what was produced, and triple to quadruple figure inflation that made any economic activity problematic. However, stability arrived in the late 1980s, when the banks found new ways to deal with the country's huge debt crisis. There was another debt crisis in 2002 but the general feeling is that the Argentinians are determined to stop this boom-bust culture. If they're ever going to punch their weight in the international market, that's a must (see pages 280–283).

URUGUAY

Uruguay's wine culture was developed at the end of the 19th century, mainly by Basque settlers, and it is now the fourth biggest South American wine producer. About 9000ha (22,240 acres) are planted, mostly near Montevideo, and we are just starting to see experimental plantings in other areas that may prove more suitable. Compared to Chile and Argentina, Uruguay is a small player, but could well flourish by being definably different (see page 272).

BRAZIL

Brazil is such a vast country that it seems to squeeze all the others in South America into margins of the continent and you think – there must be some ace places to plant vineyards. Well, there aren't. From Uruguay at 33° South of the equator to Venezuela at 5° North, there doesn't seem to be anywhere that isn't too humid or too hot, or both. That hasn't stopped people trying. There are 74,000ha (182,851 acres) of vines, – mostly on the Uruguayan border and just north of Porto Alegre – but even there the twin evils of damp and heat make it extremely difficult to ripen *vinifera* grapes without them rotting on the vine. I've had some decent Cabernet Franc, Chardonnay, Sauvignon and Gewürztraminer, and the fizz isn't bad, but most vines are hybrids or American varieties that survive the conditions but don't make good wine. The San Francisco valley in the north is now producing decent stuff from two crops a year. The economies of scale are such that these sub-tropical vines could soon be producing half of Brazil's wine. The prospect is not desperately appetizing.

VENEZUELA

Surely Venezuela is far too close to the Equator to be able to grow grapes. Wrong. The vine loves it so much that at around 10° North, near Maracaibo, it can obligingly give three crops a year – and two is perfectly normal! Labels often tell you not only the vintage but also the month – there are discernible differences in flavour and quality between each harvest. The only quality vineyards are in Lara State, where the Pomar winery, owned by the giant Polar Brewery, has had some success with Syrah, Petit Verdot and Tempranillo.

BOLIVIA

Bolivia is a difficult country to comment on, since her small volume of wine is nearly all consumed locally. But the vineyards appear to be good. There are about 3000ha (7413 acres), mostly near Tarija in the south-east, and they are high, mainly at 1800m (5900ft) to 2500m (8202ft). These certainly used to be the highest in the world, though new plantings near Cafayate in northern Argentina seemed to have surpassed even this awesome height. The word is that the grape quality is excellent.

OTHER SOUTH AMERICAN COUNTRIES

Peru used to have a relatively important wine industry, but its vineyards have now slumped to about 11,000ha (27,180 acres), and most of the grapes are used for distilling Pisco, the local spirit. Still, there are vineyards sprinkled down the coast of Peru, whenever a valley from the Andes breaks up the desert and allows irrigation. And just inland the Ica Valley has some important wineries, such as Tacama who have employed French specialists for decades, but I've never enjoyed the wines very much. I haven't enjoyed Cuba's wines much either and wines from such countries as Ecuador, Colombia and Paraguay have left me in little doubt that I do not need to investigate them very fully yet.

MEXICO

Mexico ought to play a much more important role in this atlas, since the whole Central and South American wine industry, as well as that of California, stems from the Spanish arriving in Mexico and making wine from native vines. It wasn't long before they were planting imported Spanish vines and establishing wineries. The oldest winery in the Americas was established here towards the end of the 16th century, and is still going. But Mexicans have never taken to wine and, although the country has 42,000ha (103,780 acres) of vines, over 90 per cent of the grapes go for brandy, or just for eating. The few quality vineyards are mostly in the Baja California peninsula, just south of the USA border, where a number of east-west valleys mimic the Californian conditions – considerable heat tempered by mists and cooling breezes, sucked in from the cold Alaska current that lies just offshore. Two companies – Domecq and L A Cetto – dominate production and make some good reds from Petite Sirah, Nebbiolo, Tempranillo and Zinfandel. On the other side of the country, west of the city of Monterrey in the Parras Valley, Casa Madero has had some success with Cabernet Sauvignon.

Catena's highest Merlot vineyard is sited at an altitude of 1450m (4757ft), in Tupungato, Mendoza. Behind lies arid scrubland and the magnificence of the Andes.

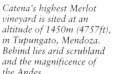

URUGUAY

VINEYARD AREAS

URUGUAY IS A COUNTRY unsure of its identity. Is it part of South America, and should its wine styles ape those of Chile and Argentina? Or should it look east, back to the south-west of France, where its most evident wine traditions come from? And should it try to muscle in on the four-lane, international grape-varieties highway of Chardonnay, Cabernet, Merlot and Shiraz? Or should it realize that the historical chance that has left over 15 per cent of its vineyards planted to the obscure, but undoubtedly high quality, Tannat grape – a beefy, burly contender from the Madiran region of south-west France – is a fantastic stroke of luck to be exploited. And for that matter – are its vineyards in the right place, crowded round the fringes of its capital, Montevideo? Most wine cultures start on the outskirts of major cities, so as to supply the population easily. And most wine cultures have then discovered the better vineyards are further away from town. In the 19th century, there was the excuse of poor transport to explain the original plantings. That won't wash in the 21st century. And are the vineyards using the right trellising and pruning systems? And are the winemakers using the right methods of vinification? And on and on and on.

The open-minded uncertainty of Uruguay is positively refreshing. In most established wine countries, any well-meaning visitor bold enough to question the wine styles, the pruning systems or the location of vineyards gets very short shrift. But Uruguay is at a crossroads – and at just the right time. Most so-called 'New World' countries have pretty much sorted out what they're best at, although this doesn't stop the more adventurous from pushing back any frontiers they can find. So Uruguay can look at them and see how she compares. At the same time, the famous wine nations of Europe are having to radically reappraise how they grow their grapes and make their wine. And Uruguay can listen, look and learn. Which is exactly what she does.

So, to basics. Uruguay is small – in South American terms, that is. At 176,215 sq km (68,042 sq miles),

that's considerably bigger than many important European countries – about twice as big as places like Austria or Hungary, for a start. But the country is largely empty – less than 3.5 million people live there, and most of them in Montevideo – so there is a large amount of land just sitting around being grazed by the odd cow. If someone wants to start a vineyard in the middle of Uruguay, prices are little more than $1000 a hectare. So far, hardly anyone has, but experimental plantings are popping up in the north, the centre and the west.

And you can't see the Andes from Uruguay. In Chile and Argentina, the Andes dominate the vineyards. But it's pretty hard to even find a hill in ultra-flat Uruguay. So the Andes have no effect on Uruguay. But the ocean does. Chile benefits from the Pacific Ocean, but Uruguay has the unpredictable, rain-bearing Atlantic as its sea, and the effect is dramatic. Rows of vineyards, clustered round Montevideo, are on about 34–35° South, much the same latitude as southern Mendoza in Argentina or the Colchagua Valley in Chile, or Stellenbosch in South Africa and Barossa in South Australia for that matter – all of them dry, warm vineyard areas. But Uruguay is wet, and it's wet throughout the year, not just in winter. There are usually 1000mm (40in) of rain a year in its southern areas. February–March rains are common, especially around the equinox. That's when they're preparing the vintage or actually picking it. Some years the rain doesn't come and everyone rejoices. Of course, that's exactly what happens in Bordeaux. Most vintages there are also afflicted with autumn rains, that come piling in from the Atlantic. Only a few lucky ones aren't.

So is Uruguay more like Bordeaux than, say, Chile? Yes, although it's warmer and the grapes ripen more easily. But there are major differences, apart from the welcome open-mindedness of Uruguay wine professionals. The soils, for a start. The best in Bordeaux are the Médoc's gravel banks or St-Émilion's limestone plateaux. Clay only stars in Pomerol. In the southern parts of San José, and in Canelones where 90 per cent of Uruguay's vineyards are, it is almost all clay. Clay is cold, holds water and encourages vigorous growth. Not what's wanted in a wet climate. But visit the vineyards, and it sort of makes sense. They're on gentle slopes – not steep, but enough for most of the water to run off. And there are patches of limestone, and calcareous subsoil. But gravel? Well, about 60km (37 miles) north of San José, there's gravel – indeed land so stony, it's never even grown fruit. Minas, north-east of Montevideo, is stony, and, at around 400m (1312ft), just about Uruguay's highest patch of vineyard. And on the sea shore, down at Rocha, like the Médoc, there's gravel aplenty, buffeted by the Atlantic winds. Alternatively, head north – there's sandy soil on the Brazilian border at Rivera, and alluvial soils at Salto – both giving wines of encouraging quality – but with an annual rainfall of up to 1600mm (63in), this isn't classic vineyard country.

Then there's the Tannat. Is it the great red hope? Well, it'll take work. It's a bit of a brute of a grape: thick-skinned, tannic and requiring time in cask and bottle to soften and show delightful raspberry and blueberry fruit. It lacks the charm of Argentine Malbec or Chilean Carmenère, but can survive damp conditions, and is different, in a world increasingly looking for difference. But it isn't the only grape that will work here. Cabernet Franc might be more suited, and its softer, fruitier wine is easier to sell. A strong Italian influence means varieties like Nebbiolo (60,000 vines at one Carmelo vineyard!) and Sangiovese will make a mark. And old favourites like Sauvignon and Chardonnay will work, if they can cope with the damp. But for it all to come together, wineries must be modernized, vineyards modified and yields lowered. They've started, but there's still a way to go. Then Uruguay should emerge as a strong niche player among New World wine countries.

BRAZIL

BELLA UNIÓN
ARTIGAS

RIVERA

SALTO SALTO

RIVERA

TACUAREMBÓ

PAYSANDU

TACUAREMBÓ

PAYSANDU

Embalse del Rio Negro

MELO

URUGUAY

RIO NEGRO

Negro

DURAZNO

CUCHILLA GRANDE

TREINTA Y TRES

MERCEDES

SORIANO

FLORES

FLORIDA

CARMELO
COLONIA

SAN JOSÉ

FLORIDA LAVALLEJA

ARGENTINA

Uruguay

SAN JOSÉ

CANELONES
CANELONES

MINAS

ROCHA

COLONIA DEL SACRAMENTO JUANICÓ
LAS PIEDRAS PROGRESO

MALDONADO

Rio de la Plata

MONTEVIDEO

ATLANTIC OCEAN

0 km   50   100
0 miles   50

N

CHILE

D AWN IN CHILE'S CENTRAL VALLEY is spectacularly slow. The silhouette of the Andes appears like some giant frozen wave of water, swelling in colour and shape as the sun struggles over the ridge. As more light filters through, the older but lower Coastal Range comes into view to the west, and you realize you're caught in a lush, green trough between two immense walls of stone. Shielding your eyes from the brilliant Chilean light, there's just fruit and vines as far as the eye can see. If wines were judged solely on the beauty of their vineyards, this country would be hard to beat.

Pedro de Valdivia, founder of the capital Santiago, arrived in 1541 and in his day, before the region was shrouded in smog, it must have been a near perfect place in which to live. Cool winters and long dry summers make it climatically similar to California, but with a more spectacular backdrop of snow-covered mountains.

For the first 300 years of its colonial life, the valley grew only País, an unremarkable black variety identical to the Mission of California. Modern winemaking began as recently as the 1860s, when wealthy landowners around Santiago imported French winemakers, increasingly out of work after phylloxera had destroyed Europe's vineyards, and employed them to tend newly imported *Vitis vinifera* varieties, partly as an experiment in improving the quality of their own vineyards, partly as a status symbol. Chile has managed to stay phylloxera-free because of its geographical isolation, with the Atacama Desert, the Andes and the Pacific Ocean all forming natural barriers against the pest. In fact, when Europe was ready to replant its vineyards, Chile supplied many of the scions to be grafted on to phylloxera-resistant American rootstock.

Chile has a fledgling Denominación de Origen (DO) system, which divides the country into five regions, with further sub-divisions. The Atacama (further north, off our map) and Coquimbo regions largely produce the grape spirit Pisco. The three table wine regions are Aconcagua, Central Valley and the Southern Region.

CLIMATE

The Andean range is one of the most influential forces affecting Chile's viticultural zones, that now extend from Copiapó, 665km (413 miles) north of Santiago, down to the Bío Bío river, 490km (305 miles) south of the capital. From the singeing heat bouncing off the Elqui Valley, north in Coquimbo province, to the glacial chill slipping down from the Maipo Canyon, south-east of Santiago, these mountains make their presence felt in every vineyard and wine.

Although vineyards extend for about 930km (578 miles) north to south, the most important climatic disparities are in the opposite direction, east to west across Chile's meagre breadth. This is due to the presence of the Andean and the Coastal Ranges which, together with the maritime climate, have a critical effect on temperature and rainfall in each vineyard area. The extent of this influence depends very much on where, east-to-west, the vineyards are located.

Those on the east–facing slopes of the Coastal Ranges are in a rain-shadow and receive lower rainfall and warmer temperatures than vines situated closer to the Andes. Vineyards in the Andean foothills benefit from big variations between night-time and daytime temperatures, with great downdrafts of cold night air producing high levels of grape acidity and a good concentration of fruit. Just north of Rancagua, the Coastal Ranges and the Andes squeeze together and then diverge, and gaps appear further south in the lower Coastal Ranges, allowing the cooling effect of Pacific Ocean breezes to influence most vineyards further inland. Plentiful Andean

WINE REGIONS AND SUB-REGIONS

COQUIMBO
- Elqui Valley
- Limarí Valley
- Choapa Valley

ACONCAGUA
- Aconcagua Valley
- Casablanca Valley
- San Antonio Valley

CENTRAL VALLEY
- Maipo Valley
- Rapel Valley/ Cachapoal Valley
- Rapel Valley/ Colchagua Valley
- Curicó Valley
  1. Teno Valley
  2. Lontue Valley
- Maule Valley
  3. Claro Valley
  4. Loncomilla Valley
  5. Tutuven Valley

SOUTHERN REGION
- Itata Valley
- Bío Bío Valley
- Malleco Valley

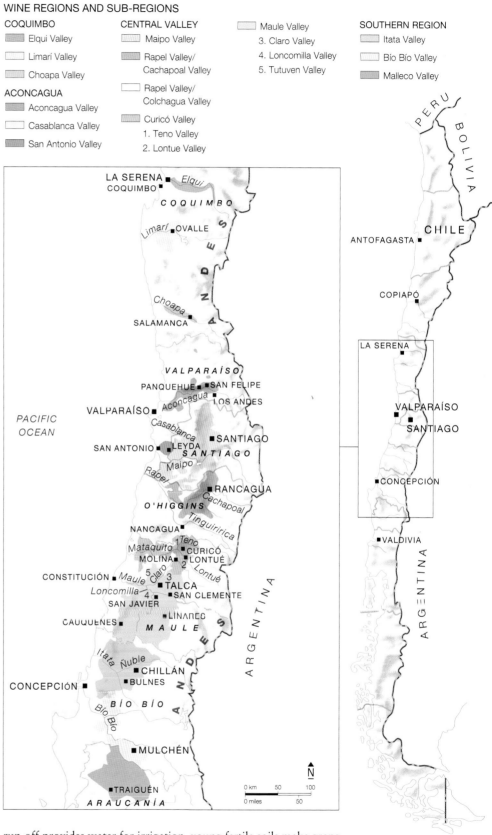

run-off provides water for irrigation, young fertile soils make grape growing child's play, and dry conditions help to prevent most pests and diseases. Add to this the fact that this is the only country without phylloxera, and you realize that a struggling Chilean vine is an exception, not the rule. Maybe Chilean winemakers could do with a few challenges in the vineyard, because this would force change, which could lift Chilean wines to far greater recognition than they currently enjoy. The use of irrigation should certainly be

PANORAMIC MAPS OF CHILE

Maipo Valley *pages 276–277*

Rapel Valley *pages 278–279*

examined, as the all-too-common sound of gurgling water as you walk through most Chilean vineyards would seem to indicate overuse of this readily available resource.

RED AND WHITE WINES

At their best, Chilean wines are packed with exhilarating, youthful fruit that almost kicks its way out of the bottle. País used to be the most widely planted variety, doing the same humdrum job of providing large amounts of cheap wine as Criolla in Argentina. But domestic wine drinking in Chile, especially at the bottom end, has slumped considerably, and now producers realize their future lies in exports – or at the top end of the Chilean market. The grape that has taken over as leader is Cabernet Sauvignon. It was Cabernet Sauvignon from the Maipo Valley that launched Chile's reputation in the 19th century, and the mixture of luscious ripe black fruit, low tannin and, often, an intriguing whiff of eucalyptus that Maipo Cabernet possesses makes it still Chile's most famous wine. But it isn't just Maipo. Cabernet is grown in the north in the Elqui and Limarí valleys, in the south at Bío Bío, and absolutely everywhere else in between – even in ultra cool Casablanca.

The new star in Chile's portfolio is Merlot. Or rather, the wines are labelled Merlot, but all the best ones, the ones that marry lush black cherry fruit with an unexpected but delicious savouriness of capsicum, coffee beans and soy sauce, have a heavy dose of Carmenère in them. Carmenère was one of the numerous French varieties brought out to Chile in the mid-19th century. And it's Carmenère which is the real star: very few of Chile's pure Merlots are particularly thrilling. Carmenère is the great lost grape of Bordeaux. It used to play an important role in most of the top wines, but was not replanted after the phylloxera scourge in the 19th century because it didn't give a regular crop and ripened after all the other varieties. That's a problem in Bordeaux, where poor spring and autumn weather is common, but it isn't a problem in Chile, where weather is consistent and fine year by year. Sometimes you have to wait until May (that's November in the northern hemisphere) for Carmenère to be ready but, since the sun is still shining, such a late harvest doesn't pose an enormous risk.

We're now seeing an increasing number of wines labelled as Carmenère, and most Chilean winemakers are taking its potential very seriously. They're also very serious about Syrah/Shiraz – Aconcagua and Colchagua are producing excellent examples. Pinot Noir is beginning to shine, especially in Casablanca and the Leyda zone of San Antonio, while a reasonably wide selection of other reds like Malbec, Cabernet Franc, Petit Verdot, Zinfandel and

others show that criticism of Chile as having a narrow range of wine styles is quite unfounded.

The white wine revolution has happened more recently, with the discovery of cool climates, such as Casablanca and Leyda, and the implementation of up-to-the-minute winemaking techniques. Chardonnay has a lush, tropical yet well-balanced quality but Sauvignon Blanc is the new star, tangy and challenging. Also good are citrous Riesling, apple-packed Chenin Blanc and Gewürztraminer, whose lychee-spiced personality has shone in Casablanca and, more recently, in the southern area around Mulchén. There's quite a lot of good, unfashionable Semillon, and ultra–fashionable Viognier has also been planted, with mixed results so far.

WINE REGIONS

Chile's viticultural areas are often divided into the Irrigated Zone, fed by Andean riverwater, and the Unirrigated Zone. The latter involves areas to the west of the Coastal Ranges, and those in the wetter southern areas of Chillán and Bío Bío. This was fine in the old days when the only irrigation used was from the Andean rivers. But development of bore technology now means that irrigation is available to many areas where it would have been impractical to plant. Casablanca is the most obvious example, where today's highly successful vineyard cultivation would be impossible without water pumped from bore holes. But each year brings new examples, especially since coastal regions are so cool and Chilean winemakers crave cool conditions. However, a statute passed by the Chilean government in 1995 has created regions and sub-regions based on the huge river valleys which slice through the country, and these are the ones shown on our map. But our map can only show the heart of Chilean wine. In this country that stretches 4274 kms (2656 miles) north to south, there are already vines growing for about a third of that distance, touching on the Atacama Desert to the north, and hardly a bottle's throw from the lush green Lake District in the far south. Let's look at the north first.

Right up in the Atacama region, the only grapes grown are those used for distillation into the national spirit, Pisco. Pisco Sour is an entirely lethal and irresistible drink after a long day researching the vineyards. South of Atacama there are three river valleys – the Elqui, Limari and Choapa, all of which are making a name for cool, ripe reds and whites. Limari, at 30° South leads the way with summer temperatures that rarely top 30°C (86°F) due to the icy Humboldt current just offshore. The vineyards are only 30km (19 miles) from the sea and get regular morning mists and afternoon breezes to keep the heat down. There are over 1800ha (4448 acres) of vines here, with more than half of them Cabernet Sauvignon, but Syrah is also showing promise. There's almost no rain, so reservoirs need to catch every drop as well as keep themselves supplied from bore holes, but quality is remarkably good so far.

We need to go down to 35° South – only 100km (62 miles) north of Santiago for the next important area – Aconcagua. Its reputation has been built by a single winery – Errázuriz – though there is now rapid expansion into its coolest zones nearer the coast. The Aconcagua Valley is the main pass over the Andes into Argentina. Its prime activity has always been orchards and fruit, including table grapes, and frankly, it should be too hot for wine grapes, except that around the town of Panquehue, the valley opens up out towards the sea – and its wind. The mixture of downdraughts from the Andes and stiff breezes from the coast that seem to arrive on the dot of midday keeps things surprisingly cool. Errázuriz, having created its reputation with Cabernet, came out with Chile's first commercial Syrah in 1996 – from vineyards at Panquehue. The

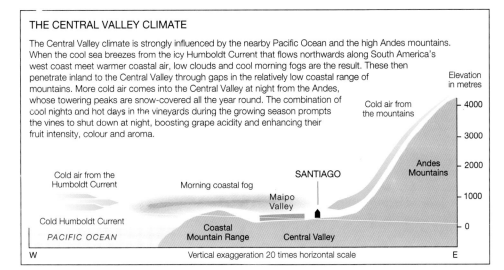

THE CENTRAL VALLEY CLIMATE

The Central Valley climate is strongly influenced by the nearby Pacific Ocean and the high Andes mountains. When the cool sea breezes from the icy Humboldt Current that flows northwards along South America's west coast meet warmer coastal air, low clouds and cool morning fogs are the result. These then penetrate inland to the Central Valley through gaps in the relatively low coastal range of mountains. More cold air comes into the Central Valley at night from the Andes, whose towering peaks are snow-covered all the year round. The combination of cool nights and hot days in the vineyards during the growing season prompts the vines to shut down at night, boosting grape acidity and enhancing their fruit intensity, colour and aroma.

Elevation in metres

Cold air from the mountains

Cold air from the Humboldt Current

Morning coastal fog

SANTIAGO

Andes Mountains

Maipo Valley

Cold Humboldt Current

Coastal Mountain Range

Central Valley

PACIFIC OCEAN

4000
3000
2000
1000
0

W

Vertical exaggeration 20 times horizontal scale

E

Aconcagua Valley now has over 850ha (2100 acres), with over half being Cabernet Sauvignon. Technically in the same region, but vastly different in character, are the Leyda Valley, forming part of the San Antonio zone, and the Casablanca Valley. Both these areas are new, but Leyda is very new, lying about 15km (9 miles) inland from the port of San Antonio. A series of ridges, either wide open to the sea, or protected by low bluffs, and a mixture of gravel and clay soils create conditions as ultra-cool as the coolest in Casablanca. So far exciting Sauvignons, Chardonnays and thrilling Pinot Noirs suggest that the struggle to ripen the grapes is worth it.

And talking of ultra-cool – well, in Chilean terms so far this means Casablanca. There's no question that it's a struggle growing grapes here, but it *is* worth it. Many of Chile's best Sauvignons and Chardonnays come from here and increasingly some top Pinot Noirs. Add in the odd spectacular Cabernet and Merlot, and an occasional tip-top Gewürztraminer and Viognier, and you can see the talent that lies in this land.

But it's difficult. For a start, there's no water all summer. The Casablanca River doesn't rise in the Andes and thus doesn't benefit from floods of snowmelt every year. It rises in the Coastal Range: there's no snowmelt, and it's a pretty feeble river anyway. There are over 500mm (20in) of rain each year, almost all in the winter, but most of it goes into subterranean aquifers. Nowadays these can be exploited, but until they developed the technology for pumping subterranean water, Casablanca was just a distinctly unprosperous grazing area. The first plantings were in 1982, but it wasn't until everyone saw the stunning intensity of these first white wines that a stampede for land occurred. There are nearly 4000ha (9884 acres) – and there could be twice that, if there was water. Well, there could be water. So far there are 1000 wells feeding Casablanca, and water is the biggest cost in the valley. Yet because of the cool conditions, vines only need a third of the water they need in the Central Valley between the Coastal Range and the Andes. And a lot of the land is still used for maize. Maize uses five times as much water as vines. Now, if the maize farmers could be persuaded...

And those cool conditions. Well, they're a blessing and a curse. The Casablanca Valley is about 80km (50 miles) west of Santiago, and between 20km (12 miles) and 35km (22 miles) from the coast. It is distinctly cooler at the coastal end, partly because as early as 10am every morning in summer a breeze is being sucked up from the cold Pacific. The upper end of the valley can be warmer. I say can be, because though Cabernet and Carmenère vines can ripen higher up on the slopes, the valley floor, where the sea breezes only survive right next to the river and where cold air from the east tumbles down every evening, is cool enough for snappy Sauvignon. Fifty metres in height can make all the difference between a warm red and an ice-cool white. And it can make the difference between keeping your crop and losing it to frost. Spring frosts are regular as clockwork and in September and October, as the vine is budding and putting forth young shoots, the whole valley is on frost alert. Frosts in midsummer and before harvest aren't uncommon either. When you think that the Chardonnay harvest usually lasts from 20 March to 30 April, and the reds might not be ripe till May, you can see why there are wind machines all over the valley to counteract frost. Despite all this, Casablanca fruit is superb. It used to be mostly Chardonnay, but Chardonnay is now only 47 per cent, with the other major players being Sauvignon Blanc, Pinot Noir, Merlot and Carmenere.

Casablanca is very much the modern face of Chilean wine. If we head back through the mountains to Santiago, and in particular to the Maipo Valley just to the south, we get to the heart of traditional Chilean wine (see pages 276–277). And if we hit the Pan-American

The cactus might imply heat, but these vineyards, owned by Veramonte, are at the top of the Casablanca Valley, one of Chile's coolest growing regions. But it's also very dry – which perhaps explains the cactus, after all.

Highway and head south for a couple of hours, we get to Rapel and the areas of Cachapoal and Colchagua (see pages 278–279).

And we'll keep going, south to the Curicó Valley, Chile's second largest wine region, after Maule, with nearly 14,000ha (34,594 acres) of vines. You'd expect it to be getting colder as we head south. Well, not yet it isn't, because the Coastal Range rears up a good deal higher in Curicó between the vineyards and the sea, and you lose most of the effect of the cold breezes. The coolest part of Curicó is up the Teno Valley towards the Andes (where you get a fairly cold downdraught) but most of the vines are on the rich, fertile soils around the river Lontué. All the big companies have cellars or vineyards down here, but relatively few exciting wines appear, largely because it is so easy to overcrop in these warm valley-floor conditions. Chile's largest plantations of Sauvignon Blanc are here – 3775ha (9328 acres) – mostly in the cooler eastern sections, but Casablanca quality is clearly higher.

And at last, it does get cooler. And wetter. The Maule Valley directly south of Curicó has almost a quarter of Chile's vines – 25,443ha (62,869 acres) out of a total of 114,448ha (282,797 acres). Cabernet Sauvignon has now overtaken the native País, at its best in areas warm enough in the centre and west of the Valley. Close to the Andes rainfall can rise up to 1000mm (39in) per year, and it does get a bit cold. Out towards the sea, at Cauquenes, there are some very good old, dry-farmed vines, as well as some new ones – Californian giant Kendall-Jackson has planted 700ha (1730 acres), attracted by reports of good Syrah, Mourvèdre and Cabernet Franc.

There are just a few more areas even further south. Itata is mostly given over to smallholdings of grapes like Moscatel and País. But Bío Bío, over 500km (310 miles) south of Santiago at 37° South, with stony soils, over 1300mm (50in) of rain a year and Chile's coolest inland conditions, has produced good Gewürztraminer, Chardonnay and Sauvignon, and Pinot Noir is promising. The Malleco Valley is Chile's southernmost appellation with a few hectares of Chardonnay and Pinot Noir, although experimental vineyards have been planted even further south in Osorno.

The Maipo Valley is the traditional centre for Cabernet Sauvignon in Chile.

CENTRAL VALLEY/MAIPO VALLEY

I WAS LOOKING FOR THE COUSIÑO MACUL VINEYARDS. I headed out east from Santiago city centre through endless suburban streets, their boredom only relieved by the spectacular Andes mountains, looming directly ahead. 'Here we are,' said my guide. But it's a car park. Not only that, it's two car parks and two supermarkets, Carrefour and Easy, slugging it out in a ring-road shopping mall. 'That's one of Cousiño Macul's best vineyards,' said my guide. Or it was. The urban pressure of Santiago, sandwiched as it is between the Andes and the Coastal Ranges, is now so intense that a mere vineyard, however famous, can't stand in its way. Cousiño Macul, perhaps Chile's most famous and definitely most traditional wine company, has sold off all but 25ha (62 acres) of its old vineyards and planted new ones at Buin, safely south of Santiago.

The Maipo Valley is the core of old Chile, stretching from the Macul area, huddled between Santiago and the Andes, down through Puente Alto and Pirque to Buin and Isla de Maipo, some 50km (31 miles) further south. It has been at the heart of Chilean wine ever since the mid-19th century, when the wealthy of Santiago began to build French-style estates and vineyards as proof of their riches. They brought French experts and French grape varieties to Chile – above all from Bordeaux. And of these, Cabernet Sauvignon has adapted quite brilliantly to Maipo. Out of the Valley's 10,784ha (26,647 acres), 60 per cent are Cabernet.

And, despite Cousiño Macul's problems, the Macul region still has vineyards left, and extremely talented winemakers exploiting them at Aquitania and Quebrada de Macul. The vineyards are pushed right up to the edge of the Andes Cordillera, reaching almost 1000m (3280ft) above sea level. Soil is poor – you hit gravel and rock at only 60cm (24in) below the surface, and water is difficult to find, especially since the city consumes more and more. Sometimes it's difficult to find the sun as well. Not because of cloud – rainfall is only 300mm (12in) plus a year – but because of smog and dust. Santiago is notoriously polluted and a haze can hang over the city all summer. As for dust – well, Aquitania used to wash their grapes after picking, they were so dusty. The plus point is a long ripening period. The vintage is usually mid-April – they're just starting when everyone else is having their vintage party – and the flavours of the wines are astonishing, blending blackcurrant fruit, eucalyptus fragrance and soft, silky tannins.

That mix of eucalyptus or mint and blackcurrant continues to dominate red-wine flavours further south, though the eucalyptus does become less marked. You will have barely left the southern suburbs when you arrive at the vineyards

of Puente Alto just to the north of the Maipo River, and Pirque just to the south. But we've already dropped around 300m (984ft) in height – the vineyards of Puente Alto are between 640m (2100ft) and 680m (2230ft) – and we've drifted further away from the Andes. Puente Alto has some of Chile's greatest Cabernet vineyards – used for Concha y Toro's Don Melchor and the Chilean-French blockbuster Almaviva. The soils here are infertile alluvial clays, that quickly turn into deep stony, rocky subsoils. With a very low water-table – you may have to drill 200m (656ft) to find water – the conditions favour low yields and intense flavours, and that's exactly what you get. At Pirque, the Maipo River runs into a kind of gorge and both easterly and westerly winds funnel into it, especially at night when temperatures are several degrees lower than at the Don Melchor vineyard and the vines shut down, considerably lengthening the ripening season. Santa Isabel, right by the mountains, is colder still and you can't ripen Cabernet there. Not on the flat anyway! Patrick Valette from Bordeaux has a west-facing slope at 740m (2428ft), and the extra afternoon sun he gets does ripen his Cabernet. Just.

Just 10km (6 miles) west of Valette's vines, a thin spur of hills called the Alto Jahuel claws its way out north-west from the main Andes, and in a large west-facing horseshoe provides some of Maipo's best conditions, both on the slope and on the flat. The vines belong primarily to Carmen and Santa Rita and produce exciting results, from Cabernet Sauvignon and the other red Bordeaux varieties, from Syrah, and from the rare Petite Sirah. Altitude is about 500m (1640ft), and these soils on the south of the Maipo River are richer than those to the north – there can be a couple of metres of sandy clay and loam topsoil – but below that we're back to rock and stones. Old vines give the best fruit with their roots well down in the rocky subsoil, and the marvellously seductive reds from here are picked ten days earlier than those further north.

TALAGANTE

MAIPO VALLEY

TOTAL DISTANCE
NORTH TO SOUTH 40KM (25 MILES)

 VINEYARDS

N

0 km   2   4
0 miles   2

There are a couple of other important areas of Maipo. To the west, where the Maipo River loops round below an isolated mountain, is the Isla de Maipo. In general the soils are non-fertile stones and gravels, but there's also clay, sand and alluvial soils – it depends on where the old river flowed. And although lots of the soils seem good, that old riverbed means an incredibly high water table, so it's difficult to control yields. Add heavy doses of cold winds from the west and foggy mornings and it isn't quite the red wine paradise you'd hoped for. Cabernet ripens four weeks later than at Puente Alto. Results from top players like Santa Inés are good, but you can see why Tarapacá has decided to site its new plantings of heat-seeking varieties on the hills.

Finally, there are some good but warm vineyards further north around Talagante. And several large companies have planted vines out in the Coastal Ranges themselves.

WHERE THE VINEYARDS ARE *This is the Maipo Valley, the most famous wine valley in Chile. It relies for irrigation on the Maipo River, that tumbles off the foothills of the Andes, watering the vineyards flanking its banks. Without this thread of glacial water, the area would be a dustbowl.*

There are considerable differences across the area, however. In the top right-hand corner, the vineyards of Quebrada de Macul and Cousiño Macul are almost swamped by suburban development. As the Maipo River flows out of the Andes, the great Don Melchor and Almaviva vineyards

are just to the north of Puente Alto. Nestled into the spine of hills east of Buin are the outstanding vineyards of Carmen and Santa Rita. And across the river, to the west of Maipo are the cool vineyards of Santa Inés in the Isla de Maipo, with some good warm vineyards sited just further to the north, around Talagante.

SELECTED WINERIES

1. Odfjell	8. Viñedo Chadwick	14. Santa Rita	18. Santa Inés/De Martino
2. Canepa	9. Concha y Toro	15. Antiyal	19. Terramater
3. Santa Carolina	10. William Fèvre	16. Portal del Alto	20. Santa Ema
4. Cousiño Macul	11. El Principal	17. Undurraga	21. Tarapacá
5. Aquitania	12. Haras de Pirque		
6. Quebrada de Macul	13. Carmen		
7. Almaviva			

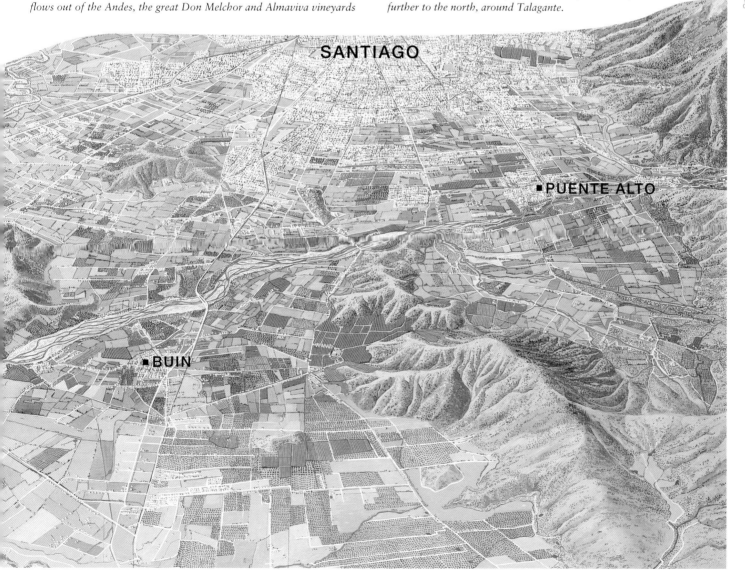

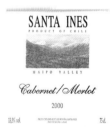

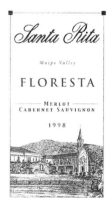

CENTRAL VALLEY/RAPEL VALLEY

RED GRAPES
Despite the valley's reputation for Merlot and Carmenère, Cabernet Sauvignon still takes up 50 per cent of the vineyards. Malbec and Cabernet Franc are here too, and Syrah is an important new variety, especially in Colchagua.

WHITE GRAPES
Chardonnay and Sauvignon Blanc are the dominant whites, but only here and there have wines been produced with good levels of natural acidity. Gewürztraminer, Semillon and Viognier are also present in small quantities.

CLIMATE
Warm and dry, even in the most westerly part of the Coastal Ranges. Only very near the Pacific is it markedly cooler. Even so, there is a range of mesoclimates determined by elevation, slope and exposure. River mists also have an influence near Chimbarongo.

SOIL
Soils are very mixed. But there is clay here as well as the usual Chilean patchwork of loam, limestone and sand. The fertile soils on the plain have been eroded from the surrounding mountain ridges, becoming more sandy and gravelly towards the river's edge. The rivers fed by Andean snows feed the high water-table, often very close to the surface. Away from the river, on low slopes, the soils are thinner and less fertile, and drip irrigation is the norm.

ASPECT
Rapel is criss-crossed by hills or mountains; there are no extensive flat areas, common to the other subregions of the Central Valley. There is only a relatively narrow break between the Andes proper and the Coastal Ranges. While many vineyards are on the river plains of the Colchagua and Cachapoal valleys, much of the recent spate of planting has been on low slopes through to quite steep hillsides.

THE FIRST COUPLE OF TIMES I VISITED THE Colchagua Valley, I had no idea I'd done so. I'd turned right at San Fernando and headed off down a river valley towards the coast. The river was called the Tinguiririca. There were vines here and there –always on the fertile valley floor – but there were far more fruit trees and maize fields, and I only remember noting one tired-looking winery before we finally got to the elegant spread of Los Vascos, about 60km (37 miles) to the west. The whole valley seemed a pleasant, rather indolent, mild-mannered place, with very little ambition to be anything else. And the name Colchagua was never mentioned.

How things change in just a few years. Now Colchagua is a powerhouse. Grape growers have decided to become wine producers. Those sleepy wineries have given themselves a radical makeover and have not only begun to produce wine infinitely finer than anything they'd ever made before, but they've also taken the lead in challenging the old belief that the Colchagua Valley's rich soil and high water-table could only produce large volume bulk. They've shown that you can make thrilling wines even with super-fertile conditions – if your vines are old enough and you're strict enough with them – but they've also led the flight to the hills, and to the sea. In other words, away from the easy life and headlong into the challenge of wresting great quality from far more taxing conditions.

Colchagua Valley is the principal, but not the only part of the Rapel Valley section of the Central Valley. And if you're looking for the Rapel River, you won't have much more luck than with the Colchagua River – it doesn't start until after Lake Rapel, outside the vineyard area to the west. The river at the top of the map is called the Cachapoal and, not surprisingly, its valley is called Cachapoal Valley. It's less important than Colchagua, and at 10,027ha (24,776 acres) it has just under half the plantings of Colchagua, but it does have some strong points.

Requínoa, huddled underneath the Andes, right to the east of the valley, is one of them. Historically this area has always produced a fresher, fruitier Cabernet Sauvignon (not quite half of Cachapoal's

vines are Cabernet) because the proximity to the Andes brings about extreme day-night differences of temperature. Add to this free-draining gravelly soil and a very low water-table, and it adds up to superb red wine conditions, reminiscent of the Médoc in Bordeaux. A series of French and Bordeaux-financed properties in the area reinforce this impression.

Cachapoal's other important area is between Peumo and Las Cabras, where the river curls round a limb of the Coastal Range and heads north-west to Lake Rapel. The lake provides continuous cooling breezes, which are necessary because the sloping vineyards are well exposed to the afternoon sun, but a mixture of gravels, red clays and a high water-table produce exceptionally fresh but ripe reds. On the valley floor here, the water-table is so high that during the winter you can find crayfish in the vineyards, but, remarkably, Sauvignon Blanc thrives.

Colchagua is directly to the south of Cachapoal, separated from it by some fairly serious mountains. Again, its strength is red wines. Of the 22,527ha (55,663 acres) of vines planted, over 11,000ha (27,181 acres) are Cabernet Sauvignon. There are also large plantings of other reds, especially Merlot and Carmenère, but also Syrah, Zinfandel and Sangiovese. There are some decent whites, mainly Chardonnay, but they are generally soft and mild, betraying their fertile-soil and hot-climate origins.

But Colchagua isn't all hot. The centre of the valley floor certainly is, but to the east and west, things are less torrid. It's possible to divide the valley up into three areas, though only in very general terms. The east is the easiest. North of San Fernando, the Andes and the Coastal Range almost converge on Angostura, and there are good vineyards, old and new, on both sides of of the narrow pass. Day-night differences in temperature are very marked with the Andes and their ice-cold air so close – up to 22°C (40°F) in the ripening period – and morning fogs temper the fierce afternoon heat, allowing not only Cabernet and Carmenère to thrive, but also such unlikely bedfellows as Chardonnay and Sangiovese. South of San Fernando, Chimbarongo is renowned for its river mists drifting off the

WHERE THE VINEYARDS ARE
Of the various rivers on the map, the two most important are the Cachapoal, which enters the map from right of top centre, then curls round to reach Lago Rapel, upper left off the map, and the Tinguiririca, which sweeps across the bottom of the map, before turning north to join the Cachapoal at Lago Rapel.

The Cachapoal has two main vineyard areas. The well-drained area of Requínoa benefits from considerable day-night temperature differences by being so close to the Andes to the east. The area round Peumo, nestling against a limb of the Coastal Ranges and cooled by westerly breezes, is successful for both reds and whites.

The area irrigated by the Tinguiririca is called the Colchagua Valley. It has three main areas. To the east, there are vineyards north and south of the river between the Andes and the Coastal Ranges. The closeness of the Andes creates a day-night temperature difference of around 22°C (40°F) and the morning mists cool things still further. In the centre, round Nancagua and Cunaco, though spreading right across to Peralillo, are traditional valley-floor vineyards. These have always been exploited by Chile's wine companies as the source of soft, ripe reds from fertile soils, nourished by a very high water-table. Consequently, there are a lot of mature vines here, and today's producers are learning to make the best of them, despite the fertile conditions. But look at the hillsides, both north and south. These are difficult, steep, stony sites, quite unlike the typical Chilean vineyards, but all the best local producers are now planting them to create powerful reds. The many plantings west of Peralillo near Marchihue are mostly new, on clay-rich soils, but far enough away from the river to require bore-hole irrigation. Red wines from here are powerful yet scented.

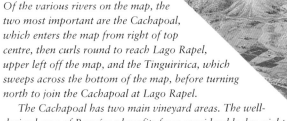

SANTA CRUZ

0 km 2 4
0 miles 2

0 km 2 4
0 miles 2

SELECTED WINERIES & VINEYARDS

1. La Rosa
2. Château Los Boldos
3. Las Casas del Toqui
4. Córpora (Gracia/Porta)
5. Anakena
6. Altair
7. Torreón de Paredes
8. Morande
9. Casa Silva
10. Santa Helena
11. Cono Sur
12. Emiliana Orgánico
13. Luis Felipe Edwards
14. Viñedos Emiliana
15. Viu Manent
16. Casa Lapostolle
17. Montes Apalta Vineyards
18. Caliterra La Arboleda Winery
19. Santa Laura/Laura Hartwig
20. MontGras
21. Bisquertt
22. Los Vascos

with vines on its steep south-facing slopes. The Ninquen Hill juts out of the valley north-west of Santa Cruz and it too is covered, top and sides, with vines. And out towards Peralillo, those southern hills sprout one vineyard after another. A new style of Colchagua wine. A new mood. These vineyards are the exact opposite of those in the valley. There's no ground-water up there to dilute the fruit. You get breezes at that height to cool the vines. And the soils are fierce – barren and infertile, boulders as big as beasts littering the edges of the new plantations. Montes prised out 700 truckloads of boulders to plant their Apalta vineyards. First indications are a triumphant vindication of the effort. Late-ripening grapes like Syrah, Cabernet and Carmenère have produced thrilling, dense flavours from tiny yields. And at high prices. All very different to the past.

The third part of Colchagua is out towards the sea. In particular north-west of Peralillo, around Marchihue, where parched, undulating grazing land is being transformed by bore-hole irrigation. It's pretty warm here, though breezes do get through from the Pacific. Thousands of hectares are being planted, mostly with warm-climate reds, but I've already seen surprisingly fragrant Viognier as well. West of Santa Cruz, through a gap in the hills, Lolol is being touted as another top red area, with Syrah already showing form. And way out towards the coast, chilly conditions have already produced attractive Chardonnay and Riesling, of all things.

Viña La Rosa's aptly named La Palmería vineyard hugs the Coastal Range mountains in Cachapoal Valley.

Tinguiririca every morning and keeping the deep, stony, sandy soils and their fruit cool. Until the emergence of Casablanca, all Chile's decent Pinot Noir came from here.

But the centre of the Valley is traditionally the heart of the action. The Tinguiririca runs west from San Fernando before turning north and heading for Lake Rapel after Santa Cruz. To start with, both north and south, high hills hem the valley in creating a canyon effect. The result is a very warm area, with very fertile river soils. That's why it was so popular in the old days – you could ripen enormous crops of decent tasting wines here every year. By Cunaco the valley is widening, and the heat is only maintained because the southern range of hills swings round and heads north, deflecting the cold Pacific breezes. And something else is happening. Look closely left and right at those mountain slopes. They're not all bare any more. North of Cunaco, the great horseshoe of Apalta is cross-hatched

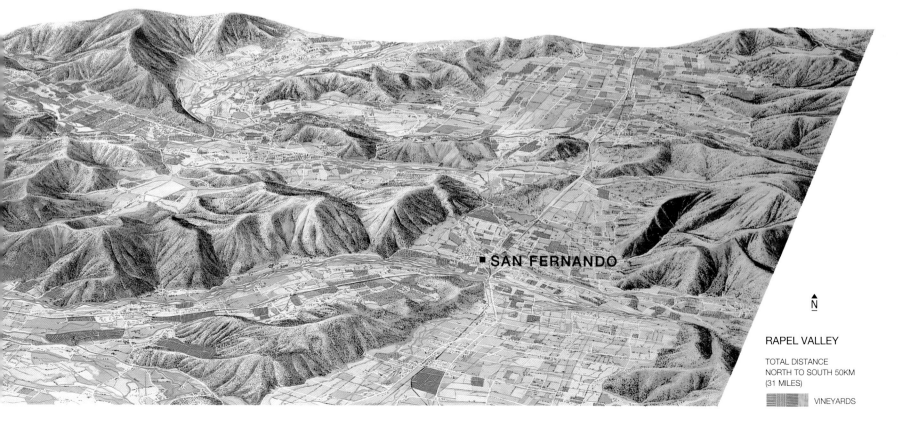

RAPEL VALLEY

TOTAL DISTANCE
NORTH TO SOUTH 50KM
(31 MILES)

VINEYARDS

ARGENTINA

Snow-melt water from the Andes is so plentiful in Mendoza that the traditional irrigation method is simply to flood the rows between the vines. These are young vines at Norton's Luján de Cuyo property.

IN ARGENTINA, EVERYTHING SEEMS TO COME BIG – distances, hailstones and steaks all give the impression that you've arrived in the land of the giants. The wine industry is equally gargantuan in proportion: Argentina is the fifth-largest producer of wine in the world, and used to be a top consumer too, though annual consumption in 2004 had dropped to a mere 29 litres (8 gallons) per head from 96 litres (25 gallons) per head in 1979! This, more than anything, explains why Argentina is now so determined to improve the quality of its wines and succeed in the export markets.

If your local population will drink everything you make, it's not difficult to decide that exports don't matter, and when you've got a very uncertain political and economic climate – inflation peaking at about 5000 per cent a year – as Argentina had for so many years, export markets are not that keen on doing business with you in any case. Indeed, for a long time Argentina was virtually a closed society, and it wasn't until the 1990s, with important political change and some serious restructuring of the economy, that it could finally start to do business on the rest of the world's terms. It's no coincidence that during the second half of the 1990s, wine quality improved dramatically, and heavyweight investors from Europe and America began a whole range of vineyard and winery projects, especially in Mendoza where 70 per cent of the country's wine is made. Sadly, 2002 saw Argentina's economy lurch back into crisis again, but by then the new Argentine wine fraternity was too set on its determined way to be deterred. The wine industry now seems to be emerging as one of the brightest stars in the global firmament. Wine exports rose by more than 36 per cent in volume just in 2006 and the overall quality and range of wines has never been better.

GRAPE VARIETIES

Back in 1557, the Spanish started planting Criolla, the pink-skinned grape used to make huge quantities of deep-coloured, oxidized white wine. Since then, the vine has spread out over a distance of 1700km (1050 miles), from the Río Negro in the south, up to the Calchaquí Valley, close to the far northern town of Salta. Better quality international varieties are fast replacing local grapes like Criolla, Pedro Giménez (sic) and Ceresa. Of the 209,000ha (516,430 acres) under vine, over 75 per cent are now planted with international varieties. However, walk into any wine shop in Argentina, and you'll still see lines of bottles labelled Borgoña or Chablis; both are comprised of unknown blends and demand little in the way of tasting notes.

Of the European varieties, the intense black, liquorice-lined Malbecs and ripe, spicy Syrahs show the most potential for red wines. Italian immigration has brought in varieties such as Sangiovese, Bonarda and Barbera, and the Spaniards have brought in Tempranillo, but their flavours traditionally have been fused together in blends. Now they are starting to appear under their own names and are showing how suited they are to Argentine conditions. Even so, Malbec is undoubtedly the grape best suited to the hot continental climate, producing wines which are packed with blackcurrants, damsons and spice – vastly superior to its European counterpart from South-West France.

Of the white grape varieties, the highly aromatic Torrontés – probably a distant relative of the Spanish Malvasia family – is the most widely planted quality variety (Pedro Giménez is still first by a long way), and there's a lot of Muscat of Alexandria. Chardonnay, predictably, is rapidly increasing, and has now overtaken the less good varieties, Ugni Blanc and Chenin. Viognier looks as though it may be good in the warm areas, but Argentina, with the exception of cooler areas like Cafayate, Río Negro and Tupungato, is still without question a red wine country.

The Andes form the most important physical influence on Argentine vineyards. This barrier removes all moisture from the Pacific winds, thus creating bone-dry conditions and 320 days of sunshine every year, but also providing plentiful water for irrigation. A more negative role played by the mountains helps to explain why nets are strung over many vines in the Mendoza region. High-altitude thunderstorms formed over the Andes regularly drop golfball-sized hailstones just before the harvest, and this is more of a hazard than frost.

Unlike Chile, Argentina does not have the natural barriers to protect it from phylloxera, which is now widespread in the country, but which appears to cause little concern among winemakers. Most argue that poor soils and the use of flood irrigation keep the louse at bay. In general, soils are arid and stony with very little humus, creating stressful conditions for the vines.

CLASSIFICATION OF ARGENTINE WINE

There is no official classification system and there is little enthusiasm for one at present among Argentine winemakers. Some wineries, mainly in the region of Luján de Cuyo, use a Denominación de Origen Controlada (DOC) system, but this is more as a way of guaranteeing certain standards in production.

In Mendoza, if you're looking for the best white grape conditions, you have to head up towards the Andes foothills, using altitude as your cooling system. But if you head south of Mendoza, well south, right down to Patagonia itself, you come to the small, but highly promising Río Negro region. It doesn't look promising as you press your face against the window of the tiny plane that carries you south from San Rafael. Endless barren scrub is relieved only by minimal signs of human endeavour, and even these offer little reassurance. A settlement laid out near the Río Colorado is now nothing but rectangular scars scratched into the parched sandy soil. But then the greenery returns – the gash of fertility that marks the Río Negro. Yet again, you realize how most of Argentina would be mere desert if it weren't for irrigation. And if you climb up to the ridge on the south bank of the Río Negro, you are looking at the beginning of Patagonia, the stone-strewn, inhospitable terrain in front of you which spreads south towards Cape Horn for 2500 km (1553 miles). Turn back and look north towards the river, and you can see poplars swaying in the evening breeze, dark green fruit trees packed tight next to vineyards, and the odd cloud of dust as a rare car hurries along the unpaved roads. And below the ridge on the northern side of the valley, the reason for this verdancy – the Valle Alto irrigation channel that runs from the main town of Neuquén and waters all the plantations between the northern ridge and the Río Negro itself.

There are about 5000ha (12,355 acres) under vine in Patagonia, though local producers are talking ambitiously of increasing this to 25,000ha (61,774 acres) within 10 years. The Río Negro could very easily become Argentina's best white-wine region, with its long ripening seasons and cool conditions, giving grapes that are naturally high in acidity. But for now this is primarily red-wine country, and certainly the Malbec is marvellously scented and deep in colour. Noemía de Patagonia, owned by the Countess Noemi Cinzano of the historic Castello di Argiano estate in Tuscany's Montalcino zone, makes remarkable Malbec east of Neuquén, while several companies led by Familia Schroeder, NQN and Fin del Mundo are successfully taming the area west of Neuquén.

OTHER REGIONS

North of Mendoza, there are still substantial vineyards, but their wines are far less known than those of Mendoza itself. San Juan, directly north of Mendoza, grows about 22 per cent of the national grape crop, most of it in the Tulum Valley. We don't hear much about it for two reasons. The majority of grapes there are pretty dull varieties, and most of them end up as grape concentrate. Secondly, we are only just beginning to see the emergence of private estates. Until now, most of the wine has been processed at co-operatives and has ended up in anonymous blends. However, the potential of this warm area is good, especially in the cooler El Pedernal Valley down towards Mendoza, where there are vineyards planted as high up as 1350m (4429ft).

The Famatina Valley in La Rioja, around Chilecito, is hot and dry, with mainly poor, sandy soil. Most grapes here are white and processed by local co-ops, which are luckily pretty good, especially with Torrontes. Clearly this is an area that suits reds, but it's a slow process trying to persuade smallholders to uproot healthy white vines and replant with red. In any case, expansion may be hindered by shortage of water, which would be a pity because there are promising sites going up to 1200m (3937ft).

North of La Rioja, the high-altitude desert of Catamarca has some vineyards, including a new one at 2000m (6562ft), planted by

a group led by Peñaflor, Argentina's biggest producer, but the real action is in Salta province, particularly in the mountain resort of Cafayate, sitting at 1700m (5577ft) in splendid isolation in the midst of what is virtually a desert. A new airport has made access easier, but I'd still recommend driving from the city of Salta to Cafayate through the Rio de las Conchas Valley for some of the most breathtakingly beautiful mountain scenery you will ever encounter. Vineyards go well past 2000m (6562ft) here – there are plantings at up to 3100m (10,170ft) north of Cafayate, though most are sited at around 1700m (5577ft). The speciality is a wonderfully scented version of Torrontés, though all whites are good, as is the purple-hued Malbec. The height clearly cools things down, and although temperatures can rise to 38°C (100°F), in February, they generally drop back at night to 12–15°C (54–59°F). But Cafayate gets 350 days of sun a year – so an important extra bonus for the grapes is a breeze that starts every day between 2 and 3pm and blows until about 8pm, when the sun has already gone down. So far any investment here has been hindered by the region's remoteness, but as more and more producers crave cool-climate sites, this is sure to change.

Malbec is Argentina's most famous red; and Mendoza is the centre of production.

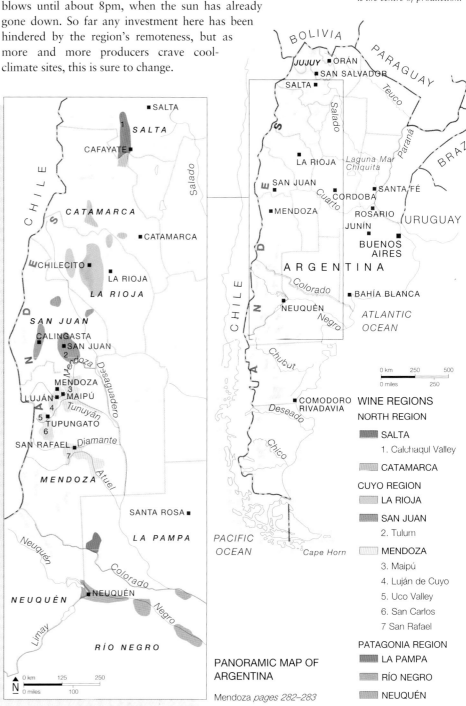

PANORAMIC MAP OF ARGENTINA

Mendoza *pages 282–283*

WINE REGIONS

NORTH REGION

SALTA
1. Calchaquí Valley

CATAMARCA

CUYO REGION

LA RIOJA

SAN JUAN
2. Tulum

MENDOZA
3. Maipú
4. Luján de Cuyo
5. Uco Valley
6. San Carlos
7 San Rafael

PATAGONIA REGION

LA PAMPA

RÍO NEGRO

NEUQUÉN

MENDOZA

RED GRAPES
Malbec is the leading quality variety, but the inferior Bonarda, and then Cabernet Sauvignon, are close behind. On the increase are Syrah, Merlot and Tempranillo.

WHITE GRAPES
Pedro Giménez is still the most planted white variety but Chardonnay has become the dominant quality variety associated with Mendoza, in particular with the high-altitude Tupungato subregion. Torrontés, more associated with Salta, is also here, while there is only a little Sauvignon Blanc, Sémillon, Riesling and other northern European whites. Viognier, as elsewhere, is likely to continue to increase.

CLIMATE
A continental climate, it is dry everywhere, with little or no rainfall in places. Summers are hot, but excessive heat is avoided at altitude, where spring frosts become an increasing threat. Winters are cold, but generally only markedly so at heights of 1000m (3280ft) or more.

SOIL
The topsoil is typically thin, alluvial and often sandy, though in places it is more stony, particularly at greater depths. Irrigation is essential, but the water supply is plentiful, given a system of canals and channels, as well as bore holes to complement that brought by rivers. Once common flood irrigation has now given way to drip irrigation in most vineyards.

ASPECT
A great variation in altitude is a feature of Mendoza, as it pushes into the foothills of the Andes. Even within individual subzones, altitudes can vary quite considerably.

WHEREVER YOU ARE IN MENDOZA, you can't escape the mountains. And you don't want to. The majestic Andes give everything to Mendoza, not only its weather, its water, its very earth, but also its heart. At dawn they glow cherry pink above the city, by midday they gleam white as models' teeth above the urban fug of the town and, as the sun arcs west into the evening, the mountains are bleached of their form, the cotton clouds blending with the snow to create what seem like streams of molten silver flowing down the blue-grey mountainside. And you can't get lost. East, south, west and north, just look up to the Andes, and you'll know where you are.

Mendoza needs the mountains. Face them, and you are in a beautiful and stunning wineland. Turn your back on them and the vista in front of you is relentlessly flat. And find yourself on a spit of land where the irrigation channels don't go, and you're in a parched, scrubby desert. Which is exactly what Mendoza province would be if the surging waters of four mighty rivers hadn't been tamed and their torrents of snow-melt channelled into irrigation systems, spreading out across the arid shrubland and creating hundreds of thousands of hectares of horticulture. The broad Mendoza River valley, east of the city, has just a thin dribble of water trailing through: all the rest is nourishing crops. Yet even so, only 3 per cent of Mendoza province is cultivated.

But that provides a substantial vineyard area – almost 150,000ha (370,645 acres) in all – with the bulk of it in a ring round the city of Mendoza. There are five main areas. North Mendoza is the least important, except for the fact that at Las Heras they've got Malbec vines going right back to 1861. Whether they came from France, or over the Andes from Chile is unclear, but since that time Malbec has become Argentina's flagship wine.

Much more important is East Mendoza. There are over 11,216ha (27,715 acres) of vines, spreading out along the Tunuyán River as far as La Paz. And it does seem hot and flat out here. But there is a slope – only 1° or so, but that's important because Mendoza is at 700m (2297ft) above sea level, Santa Rosa, 80km (50 miles) east is at 610m (2000ft) and La Paz, 135km (84 miles) east, is at 560m (1837ft). The lower you get, the hotter it gets. From the 560m (1837ft) of La Paz up to Tupungato, south-west of Mendoza, you can rise imperceptibly to 1500m (4920ft) above sea level. Those high vineyards will ripen up to four weeks after the low ones, if they ripen at all.

Out east, ripening is not a problem – everything, even notorious late ripeners like Bonarda, will ripen. But they often ripen too fast. One way of controlling this is by the trellising system. Most systems are designed to aid ripening. But all over the east, and to a lesser extent elsewhere in Mendoza, you'll find vast spreads of overhead pergolas called Parrals. Here the grapes hang above your head under a canopy of leaves. These Parrals can support impressive crops – 30 tonnes to the hectare is regarded as very restrained – but the crop does ripen slowly, which is exactly what you need in the blazing heat of the east. And the leaf canopy has another use. Ultra-violet penetration is very high in Mendoza, and the leaves protect the grapes from sunburn and keep them cool. The biggest advocate of this system, José Alberto Zuccardi also conducts trials into different irrigation techniques, organic growing and with grape varieties like Viognier, new to Mendoza. One of the great strengths of the east is that it already has considerable plantings of grapes like Bonarda, Sangiovese and Tempranillo which, in a world thirsty for change and new wines, could be a great boon.

The Central Mendoza region covers a lot of vineyards, spreading out south of Mendoza city and along the Mendoza River. Many of the older vineyards have been grubbed up for urban development, but those of Maipú to the south-

MENDOZA

TOTAL DISTANCE
NORTH TO SOUTH 40KM (25 MILES)

VINEYARDS

east are resisting the housing estates, at least partly, because many are owned by large companies able to spurn offers that can equal up to $100,000 a hectare! Very few smallholders could resist that kind of money. Catena have some outstanding old Malbec at Lunlunta and, on the south side of the river at Barrancas, Finca Flichman have vineyards where the soil is virtually pure stone, that remind me of those of Châteauneuf-du-Pape, and grow good Syrah to prove it.

West of Maipú is Luján de Cuyo, the heart of Malbec in Mendoza, but it's not just Malbec, because there are considerable differences in the various subdistricts. The whole area is higher than Maipú, going from 850m (2789ft) at Drummond, close to the city, up to more than 1060m (3478ft) at Las Compuertas, where the land visibly begins to rise towards the Andes. That's worth a harvesting date 10 to 14 days later. South of the Mendoza River, the areas of Perdriel and Agrelo have some of the best vineyards, particularly for reds, and some of the top companies like Catena and Norton. Again, there's pressure from weekend homes, but west towards the mountains and south right down to Ugarteche, there are also numerous new plantings to compensate.

The Uco valley, and in particular Tupungato which lies over to the south-west, is much closer to the Andes, and significantly higher. There's nothing under 900m (2953ft) and all of the major vineyard development is between about 1000m (3280ft) and as much as 1500m (4920ft). The ripening season is much longer, often reaching well into April, and there's no doubt it's Argentina's top spot for Chardonnay. But reds like Malbec and Merlot, and perhaps Pinot Noir, are also excellent. Tens of millions of investment dollars from France, America, Holland and elsewhere demonstrate that Tupungato is Argentina's 'coolest' area in more ways than one.

SELECTED WINERIES

1. Domaine Vistalba (Fabre Montmayou)
2. Nieto Senetiner
3. Alta Vista
4. Weinert
5. Leoncio Arizu (Luigi Bosca)
6. Lagarde
7. Viniterra
8. Septima
9. Dominio del Plata
10. Terrazas de los Andes
11. Norton
12. Etchart
13. Chandon
14. Catena Zapata
14. Anubis
15. Navarro Correas
16. Medrano Estate
17. Lopez
18. Trapiche
19. Trivento
20. San Telmo
21. Finca Flichman
22. Pascual Toso
23. Alto Las Hormigas
24. Familia Zuccardi (Santa Julia/La Agrícola)

It's a dull 130-km (80-mile) drive south-east through lifeless shrub, before you get to the most southern part of Mendoza – San Rafael. This region is irrigated by the Diamante and Atuel Rivers, and the vines here are planted between 450m (1476ft) and 800m (2625ft) high. That means that it is getting hotter, and it is wines like Malbec and Barbera that excel down here. But only if they survive to harvest. Hail is a perennial threat in Argentina, but it is at its worst in San Rafael. The hailstones here can weigh up to 500g (1lb) and they don't just destroy vineyards – they destroy cars too! Nowadays, most of the vineyards are protected by hail nets. And the cars? Well, there is a thriving panel-beating industry in San Rafael.

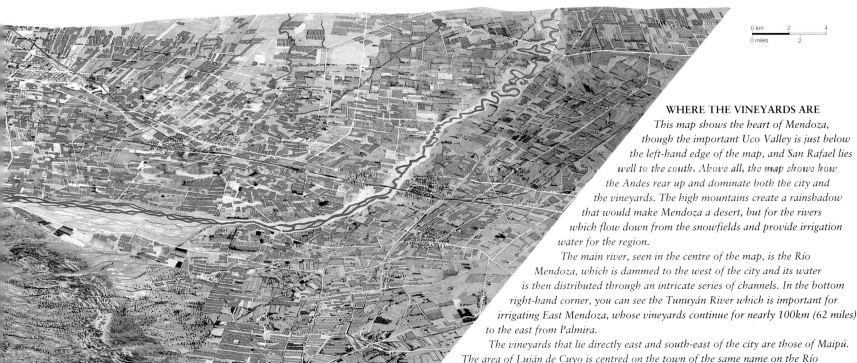

WHERE THE VINEYARDS ARE

This map shows the heart of Mendoza, though the important Uco Valley is just below the left-hand edge of the map, and San Rafael lies well to the south. Above all, the map shows how the Andes rear up and dominate both the city and the vineyards. The high mountains create a rainshadow that would make Mendoza a desert, but for the rivers which flow down from the snowfields and provide irrigation water for the region.

The main river, seen in the centre of the map, is the Río Mendoza, which is dammed to the west of the city and its water is then distributed through an intricate series of channels. In the bottom right-hand corner, you can see the Tunuyán River which is important for irrigating East Mendoza, whose vineyards continue for nearly 100km (62 miles) to the east from Palmira.

The vineyards that lie directly east and south-east of the city are those of Maipú. The area of Luján de Cuyo is centred on the town of the same name on the Río Mendoza, south of Mendoza City. Luján's original vineyards have largely been swallowed up by urban sprawl, but some excellent ones still survive just to the west, at Vistalba and Las Compuertas. South of the river at Perdriel and Agrelo and on past Ugarteche are some of Mendoza's other top-class vineyards, both established and new.

AUSTRALIA

In the foreground (left) sheep graze as they have done for generations and in the background vineyards reach up from the Barossa Valley floor on to the arid slopes above Tanunda. Ancient gum trees (above) stand guard over Mountadam's vineyards in the Eden Valley, South Australia and suck what moisture they can from the parched hillsides.

Australia didn't have many advantages when it came to establishing a wine industry. There was no history of wine among the aboriginal people because there weren't any native vines. None of Australia's trading partners in South-East Asia had ever had wine as part of their culture. And it didn't seem propitious that the nation which decided to colonize the vast continent was Britain. Now, if the French, or the Italians, or the Spanish…

We forget one thing. The British weren't much good at growing grapes at home, but they were the world's greatest connoisseurs when it came to appreciating the wine of other European countries, in particular the table wines of France and the fortified wines of Portugal and Spain. Since Australia was initially settled as a penal colony, the authorities were keen to establish a temperate wine-drinking culture, rather than one based on the more savage rum. And at the end of the 18th century, when New South Wales was gradually establishing itself, Europe was embroiled in war. The idea of a British Imperial vineyard not hostage to the recurrent political crises in Europe must have seemed enticing. Well, it almost did work out like that. For considerable portions of the 19th and 20th centuries, Australia provided a steady stream of unchallenging – and mostly fortified – wines that were lapped up by Britain. But by the last quarter of the 20th century the country had embarked on a remarkable voyage of wine discovery that has placed her at the forefront of all that is best in the New Age of wine – despite having a vineyard area that is dwarfed by the major European nations.

This position has been achieved without Australia enjoying many of the perceived benefits of Europe's classic regions, most of which are poised on the cusp between not being able to and being able to ripen their fruit. Unlike Europe, the general rule in Australia is more than enough sunshine and not nearly enough rain. Traditionalists say you can't make great wine under such conditions but Australia's winemakers have turned this to their advantage, using irrigation freely and highlighting the ripeness of the grapes in a succession of sun-filled, richly textured reds and whites. Despite the very different conditions these may initially have been inspired by the best of Europe, but they have created such a forceful identity of their own that Europe now often attempts to ape the style of these Down Under Wonders. In the meantime, a better understanding of how to bring grapes to optimum ripeness – not over- or underripe, but just so – have led to an explosion of cool-climate wine regions on the fringes of this parched continent that challenge, but in no way imitate, the old classic regions of Europe.

THE WINE REGIONS OF AUSTRALIA

WATER, WATER, WATER. That's the story of Australia. On this vast, parched continent, finding meagre supplies of moisture is an ever-present priority, and not just for grape-growers. The nation's population, let alone any vineyard development, is limited by the availability of water and little of the rain that does fall arrives when it is most needed – during the long, hot summers. Yet Australians show amazing resourcefulness and new vineyards spring up where no-one had dreamt vines could flourish.

At the beginning of the 1980s, when its thoughts turned winewards, the country was known abroad for little more than the odd bottle of Kanga Rouge red. Since then Australia has established a reputation for approachable, yet high quality, characterful wines of every possible style that is nothing short of astonishing.

All the major states manage to find a mixture of cool, warm and roasting conditions in which to grow their wines. All the major players, that is. The Northern Territory's Chateau Hornsby near Alice Springs probably qualifies as the hottest – and maddest – winery in the universe. Queensland is pretty torrid too, though some high-altitude vineyards down on the New South Wales border like to think of themselves as coolish. Tasmania endlessly seeks patches of land warm enough to ripen grapes in a climate once condemned by its own government as too cool for grapes and about right for apples, and most of its main vineyards, based in the north of the island, find life a struggle.

WESTERN AUSTRALIA

Western Australia is a vast state, virtual desert except for its south-western coastal strip. Its wine industry was one of the first to be established in Australia, but Perth's isolation kept it largely focused on supplying the local market, with the exception of the Swan Valley, whose Houghton White Burgundy was highly successful in the eastern states. This old-fashioned, sun-baked region was best suited to throaty reds and fortified wine. But winery and vineyard expertise is now so sophisticated that remarkably good dry whites are now emerging. Even so, the most exciting wines come from the secluded vales of the Margaret River and the Great Southern regions, where the continent's south-western tip turns away from the Indian Ocean towards the cold depths of the Southern Ocean.

SOUTH AUSTRALIA

South Australia was the last of the major wine states to be established in the 1840s, but more than made up for lost time. It dominates the Australian wine scene, growing the greatest tonnage of grapes, making the largest volume of wine – and housing most of its biggest wine companies. The bulk of its grapes are grown in the impressive vineyards along the banks of the Murray River where mechanization, sunshine and a historically plentiful supply of water have created some of the world's most efficient vineyards.

But South Australia has far more to offer than oceans of attractive, undemanding, gluggable wine. The single most important factor is that the phylloxera bug, which destroyed almost all the world's wines in the 19th century, never reached South Australia, so their vines, along with those of Chile, are planted on their own roots, not grafted. In the north, the verdant Clare Valley, scooped out of the parched grazing land that stretches away on all sides, is an unexpected but excellent producer of 'cool-climate' table wines. Not always that cool, however, because, as so often in Australia, local climates within an area provide a far broader range of styles than one would find in Europe. Clare Shiraz and Clare 'port' are just as good as delicate Clare Riesling.

The Barossa Valley is South Australia's heartland, where most of the big companies are based and much multiregional wine is processed. It is also home to some of the planet's oldest vines, and the blockbuster Shiraz and Grenache from these vines have made Barossa world famous. Eden Valley, in the hills east of Barossa, has a spectrum of wine styles, but it is the crisp, steely Rieslings that set it apart. Just south of Adelaide is the first wine area to be developed in South Australia, once famous for 'ferruginous' reds and fortified wines, which were shipped to England in vast quantities. Despite incursions from the expanding city, the area is now a major producer of high quality reds and whites.

Population explosion has never been a problem at Padthaway and Coonawarra – hardly anyone lives in this damp, forlorn corner of the state – but this has allowed the development of superb vineyards making thrilling wines, and the lack of a local populace has forced the region to become the world leader in the science of total vineyard mechanization.

There are vines over 140 years old in the Hill of Grace vineyard owned by Henschke in Eden Valley, South Australia. No wonder this Shiraz is one of Australia's most expensive wines.

THE CLASSIFICATION SYSTEM FOR AUSTRALIAN WINE

Australia's system for classifying wines on the labels of bottles for export stems from an 1994 agreement with the EU. In order to reach this agreement, it was necessary to define areas of origin, and the Geograpical Indications Committee was set up in 1993 to do this. It divided the wine-producing states into a number of zones, regions and sub-regions. The complete extent of all of them is yet to be agreed and the discussions, arguments and political wranglings that always accompany such decisions will be in full voice for some years yet.

The system has to encompass certain peculiarities. The main one is the widespread use of regional blending in Australia: that is, trucking grapes from several different areas, possibly in different states, for blending together. Five major wine groups (Fosters, Hardys, Orlando Wyndham, McGuigan Simeon and Casella) make over 60 per cent of Australia's wine, and they rely a lot on blending varieties and wines from different areas, especially for their big-selling brands, such as Koonunga Hill and Jacob's Creek, which are now important players in the wine scene. Whatever the origin of a wine, however, 85 per cent of its grapes must come from the area specified, whether it is a zone, region or sub-region, and it must be made of at least the same percentage of the named grape variety.

QUALITY CATEGORIES AND GEOGRAPHICAL INDICATIONS

- **The Label Integrity Program** This system (also called LIP) was introduced in 1990 and guarantees all claims made on the label, for example, the vintage, variety and region, by making annual checks and audits on specific regions, varieties and wineries.
- **Produce of Australia** This is the most general geographical designation. Any wine sold solely under this category will not be able to have a grape variety or a vintage on its label.
- **South-Eastern Australia** This is the next level, a category which covers, in fact, most of the wine-producing areas of Australia and is widely seen, particularly on the big-selling brand name wines.
- **State of Origin** This is the next most specific category.
- **Zones** Many of Australia's traditional wine areas are being incorporated into these new zones. For example, Barossa is a zone within the state of South Australia.
- **Regions** These are the next level, for example, Barossa is divided into the regions of Barossa Valley and Eden Valley.
- **Sub-regions** Some regions are divided into sub-regions, for example, Eden Valley consists of the High Eden and Springton sub-regions.

VICTORIA

Victoria's vineyards seem like they've been hurled into position with a scatter-gun. This is because they followed the Gold Rush, and when gold was exhausted odd vines were left all over the state. They can, however, produce some of the most exhilarating and distinctive Australian wines, albeit in tiny quantities. Victoria was Australia's major wine producer for most of the 19th century, until phylloxera devastated her vineyards. She has only recently reassumed her position as provider of some of the most startling Australian wines. Large amounts are produced in the Murray River area, but it's the stunning liqueur Muscats of Rutherglen and Glenrowan, the thrilling dark reds of Central Victoria, the urbane Yarra Valley and Mornington Peninsula reds and whites, and the lean, perfumed reds and whites that crop up in patches of cool vineyard land right across the state that leave their imprint on my mind.

NEW SOUTH WALES

Colonial Australia began in New South Wales (in the Hunter Valley), as did the wine revolution that propelled Australia to the front of the world stage. However, the state is a major bulk producer along the Murrumbidgee River, and a clutch of new wine regions in the Central Ranges are grabbing headlines.

PANORAMIC MAPS OF AUSTRALIA

Barossa *pages 290–291*
Coonawarra *page 293*
Clare Valley *page 295*
Yarra Valley *pages 298–299*
Hunter Valley *page 303*
Margaret River *page 306*

OTHER MAPS

South Australia *page 289*
Victoria *page 296*
New South Wales *page 301*
Western Australia *page 305*
Tasmania *page 308*
Queensland and Northern Territory *page 309*

WINE ZONES

WESTERN AUSTRALIA

1. Eastern Plains, Inland and North of Western Australia
2. Greater Perth
3. Central Western Australia
4. West Australian South-East Coastal
5. South-West Australia

SOUTH AUSTRALIA

- - - Adelaide (Super zone)
6. Far North
7. The Peninsulas
8. Mt Lofty Ranges
9. Barossa
10. Lower Murray
11. Fleurieu
12. Limestone Coast

VICTORIA

13. North-West Victoria
14. Central Victoria
15. North-East Victoria
16. Western Victoria
17. Port Phillip
18. Gippsland

NEW SOUTH WALES

19. Western Plains
20. Northern Slopes
21. Northern Rivers
22. Hunter Valley
23. Central Ranges
24. Big Rivers
25. Southern New South Wales
26. South Coast

QUEENSLAND

NORTHERN TERRITORY

AUSTRALIAN CAPITAL TERRITORY

TASMANIA

SOUTH AUSTRALIA

The bleakness of Coonawarra railway station surrounded by a sea of vines and not a house in sight illustrates the remoteness of the Limestone Coast.

THEY RECKON ADELAIDE'S DRINKING WATER is some of the worst in the civilized world. I do, too. But the beer is excellent, so, apart from brushing my teeth, I don't have a lot to do with it. However, throughout the state, water – or lack of it – is a hot topic. The only part of South Australia that has enough water is the southern tip where Coonawarra almost drowns in the stuff. In the rest of the state every drop counts.

Luckily, South Australia has one massive zillion-gallon water resource – the Murray River – which follows a tortuous route for nearly 2600km (1615 miles) between New South Wales and Victoria before arcing through South Australia and trickling out into the ocean at Lake Alexandrina. The exploitation of the Murray for irrigating hundreds of thousands of otherwise uncultivable barren acres was one of the great agro-industrial feats of the 20th century, but ever increasing exploitation of this finite resource and a disturbing rise in the salinity of the soils it nourishes is causing great concern.

This was not an issue in the early 1950s when the late Max Schubert, winemaker at Penfolds near Adelaide, produced his first experimental barrels of Grange – a wine that was to transform the perception of what quality was possible in the vineyards of the 'New World', and which is now as prized and appreciated as the greatest red wines of Europe. But when he set out to create Grange, Schubert didn't have a special vineyard to hand – he merely had a vision of flavour, great scientific expertise and a bloody-minded belief that if the French could do it, so could he. This approach is not approved of by the traditionalists of Europe, who maintain, through their systems of controlled appellation of origin, that great wines only come from special rare patches of land, pinpointed after centuries of trial and error. They've had a thousand or two years to fine-tune this principle of *terroir*, which lays all the emphasis for specialness on the place, and regards the men or women involved merely as transient guardians of the flame. But they're missing half the trick.

Australia hasn't had hundreds of years during which to gradually pick and choose her favourite spots. She hasn't had a hundred generations of inhabitants whose lives revolved around the vine, developing a fine wine tradition across the ages.

Max Schubert's success at creating a great wine is proof of Australia's greatest gift to the world of wine – the belief that everything is possible. And that the art of blending suitable wines to create a delicious flavour – regardless of where the vines grew and what varieties they were – is a truly noble art. You can do it from scratch, with whatever materials suit your purpose. You just have to believe. Of course, you can't guarantee what the end result will be like, but if you follow your vision with courage and determination, you can do it.

ADELAIDE'S FIRST VINEYARDS

As with the other states, vines were planted within a year of the first settlement in 1836 and, as with Sydney and Melbourne, these first vineyards have long since disappeared under the tarmac and brick of modern Adelaide, although a small patch of the original Penfolds vineyard at Magill is still producing grapes, hemmed in by suburbia. Vineyards were fairly quickly established in the northern reaches of the city, and the influx of German settlers to the Barossa Valley in the 1840s created a vineyard and winery community that has played a dominant role in Australian wine ever since, and left it with some of the world's oldest vines.

But the first moves out of Adelaide were in fact to the south: to Morphett Vale, Reynella, McLaren Vale and Langhorne Creek. Morphett Vale and most of Reynella have now largely disappeared

under the creeping tide of urban sprawl, but Adelaide is not only much smaller than Melbourne and Sydney, it is also more aware of the importance of wine to the state. Consequently the attractive neighbourhood of McLaren Vale has largely been able to resist the developers and to enjoy a burgeoning number of vineyards and wineries, both large and small.

RIVERLAND

Australia has two Californians to thank for much of the wine they drink today. The Chaffey brothers arrived in Australia at the end of the 1880s, having successfully established irrigation schemes in Californian desert conditions. They had the foresight and determination to utilize their experience to transform the annual flooding of the Murray River into the most important resource in Australian viticulture.

The headwaters of the Murray River are numerous streams fed by the melting snowfields of the Great Dividing Range. Every year the river used to bulge and burst with the thaw. The waters flooded vast expanses of empty, arid land that gratefully lapped up the moisture – but to no avail, since no-one knew how to exploit this annual bounty.

First at Renmark in South Australia, and then at Mildura further upstream in north-west Victoria, the Chaffeys built pumping stations, dams, locks and irrigation channels to harness the Murray River. As a result verdant market gardens and vineyards were planted where nothing but saltbush desert had existed before.

Both Renmark and Mildura went through tricky times but, by and large, they and the other Murray Valley regions of South Australia and Victoria flourished, and so did the Riverina region which lies on a Murrumbidgee River tributary in New South Wales. This large-scale irrigation has helped Australia to transform the quality of budget wine worldwide, but long term weather pattern changes have put the whole culture of irrigation farming in doubt as snowfalls evaporate and water flows dwindle along the Murray. In any case, the heart and soul of the South Australian wine industry is still in the water-starved, sun-soaked fields and vales to the north and south of Adelaide.

GRANGE

It was near Adelaide that Australia's fine wine tradition began, when Max Schubert, Penfolds' chief winemaker, began work in 1951 on what was to become one of the greatest wines in the world – known first as Grange Hermitage, now as Grange.

Schubert had returned from a trip to Europe's vineyards the year before, fired up most of all by the great red wines of Bordeaux's Médoc – a fine wine area with a lot of rain, barely enough sunshine, and a predominance of the Cabernet Sauvignon grape. The region produced wine that was aged in new French oak barrels and could mature for half a century. He was determined to make the same style of wine in South Australia – where there was tons of sunshine, hardly any rain, about one shopping basket full of Cabernet Sauvignon in the entire state, and not a new French oak barrel to be found. And until his visit to Bordeaux he had had no idea that a red wine could hope to age for more than ten years at the outside.

No worries. Schubert had the vision. He decided the Shiraz grapes – the same variety as Syrah in France's Rhône Valley – were the best South Australia could offer. So he'd use these. Different flavour from Cabernet, but if he picked them early from low-yielding vines and treated them with kid gloves from the moment of picking to the moment of bottling, he reckoned he could get the result he wanted. He managed to secure a few American rather than the more traditional French oak barrels, and decided they were in any case more suitable for his Shiraz.

Ah yes, the vineyards. Well, Schubert began with some vines at Morphett Vale, south of Adelaide, and some at Magill in the foothills fringing Adelaide. They weren't famous vineyards, but he knew them, he knew their soils, their ripening patterns, and the flavour of their fruit. They served him well for the first Grange. Later he added Kalimna, in the Barossa Valley, and when Morphett Vale was sold for housing he expanded into the Clare Valley. These days, with Southcorp, Penfold's parent company, controlling a massive amount of South Australia's top vineyards, Coonawarra fruit joins McLaren Vale, Barossa, Clare, indeed any fruit that is good enough. Simple as that. If the fruit is good enough it will be considered for Grange, though recent vintages have been increasingly Barossa dominant.

Whenever someone starts to lecture me about the necessity of colonizing the world with the self-serving, protectionist appellations that stifle so much of Europe's creativity, I triumphantly raise the case of Grange. All it claims on the Grange label is 'South Australian Shiraz'. That's a proud enough statement for me. I hope it never has to change.

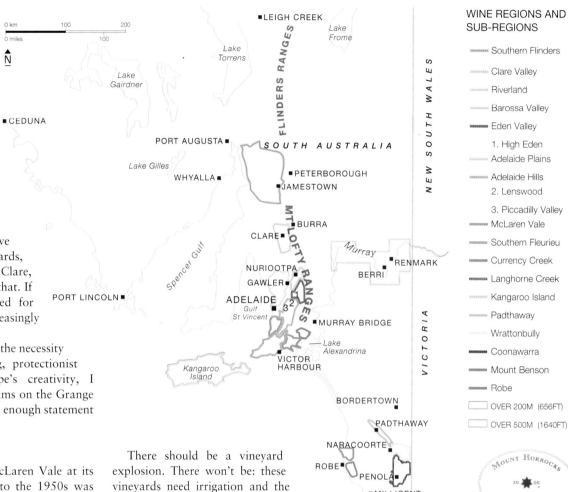

FLEURIEU
The region directly south of Adelaide, with McLaren Vale at its centre, is called Fleurieu. Its success right up to the 1950s was based on its ability to ripen black grapes sufficiently to create fortified 'ports' of high quality, or strapping great red table wines that boasted of their 'ferruginous' (iron-rich) character as being of medicinal quality. Generations of respectable British ladies supped happily on Tintara and Emu Burgundy, convinced they were imbibing for their health's sake. Well, well, perhaps they were.

In fact Fleurieu has proved a highly adaptable wine region. Although it is sunny, and McLaren Vale and further north is genuinely hot, most of the vineyards benefit from afternoon sea breezes cooling down the vines. Langhorne Creek on the eastern side of the Fleurieu Peninsula is positively cool and is also fairly heavily irrigated. Water is short in McLaren Vale and the Cabernet, Shiraz and even Grenache are rich and heady, but there are also surprisingly good Chardonnays and Sauvignons.

MOUNT LOFTY RANGES AND BAROSSA
Just inland from McLaren Vale you can see the southern tip of the Adelaide Hills. These hills head north, skirting Adelaide, to become part of the Mount Lofty Ranges, continuing up east of the Barossa Valley to Mount Pleasant, where they become the Eden Valley.

Just 30 minutes's drive east of Adelaide is the small exciting wine region of Adelaide Hills. Here, the hills around Piccadilly are high, even slightly damp, and this sub-region is now producing some exceptional 'cool-climate' whites and exciting sparkling wines. Lenswood, a little to the north, can also produce gorgeous reds; and southwards towards Mount Barker and Kuitpo it's also warmer and lower and lovely reds are the result. Adelaide Hills has attracted some of the greatest talents in the South Australian wine world and, with the recent vogue for cool- rather than warm-climate sites, they make a series of remarkable wines.

There should be a vineyard explosion. There won't be: these vineyards need irrigation and the hills are a crucial catchment area for Adelaide's water. The water may taste lousy, but thirsty citizens with votes win over vines every time. The tale is of water right through South Australia. Clare Valley in the north might also have expanded much more than it has done if there was enough water, but rainfall is low and subterranean water hard to come by. Meanwhile, Barossa growers have paid to build a massive new pipeline from the Murray River to boost its over-burdened bore water supply. Will the Murray have enough water for this increasing demand?

LIMESTONE COAST
Water dominates the cool far south of the state as well, but in a different way. The Great Artesian Basin stretches across the area towards the sea. The water table is so high that most of the land is far too swampy for viticulture. But there are a series of limestone ridges in the south-east of the state that offer brilliant conditions for vines. Coonawarra's exceptional qualities have been known about since the end of the 19th century, and it is now one of Australia's most sought after localities for vineyard land. Padthaway, 65km (40 miles) to the north of Coonawarra, is another fine region, and wherever limestone crops up we are seeing vineyards being developed – right out to the coast at Robe and Mount Benson, and around Naracoorte at Wrattonbully.

However, in order to preserve supplies of drinking water to Victoria in the east, South Australia has had to accept strict limitations on how much water she extracts on her side of the state border. Even when there is water, water everywhere, someone is going to stop you doing what you want with it.

WINE REGIONS AND SUB-REGIONS

- Southern Flinders
- Clare Valley
- Riverland
- Barossa Valley
- Eden Valley
  1. High Eden
- Adelaide Plains
  2. Lenswood
- Adelaide Hills
  3. Piccadilly Valley
- McLaren Vale
- Southern Fleurieu
- Currency Creek
- Langhorne Creek
- Kangaroo Island
- Padthaway
- Wrattonbully
- Coonawarra
- Mount Benson
- Robe
- OVER 200M (656FT)
- OVER 500M (1640FT)

MOUNT HORROCKS
20 00
Watervale
RIESLING

PETALUMA
1996 COONAWARRA
UNFILTERED
750ml
PRODUCE OF AUSTRALIA BOTTLED AT PICCADILLY SA

Charles Melton's Nine Popes from the Barossa Valley is a pun on France's Châteauneuf-du-Pape, and the wine is a rich, ripe red based on Grenache and Shiraz – just like Châteauneuf-du-Pape.

BAROSSA

RED GRAPES
Shiraz is the star red, not only dominating current plantings, but new vineyards as well. Cabernet Sauvignon is also important, but the next most precious resource is hundreds of hectares of old Grenache and a little ancient Mataro (Mourvèdre). There are also increasing quantities of Spanish, Italian and Portuguese varieties.

WHITE GRAPES
Semillon followed by Chardonnay are the most important white varieties in the Barossa Valley while Riesling still reigns supreme in the Eden Valley. There are also small amounts of Sauvignon Blanc and Viognier.

CLIMATE
The Barossa Valley is hot, with some drip irrigation used to counteract the arid summers. The Eden Valley and the Barossa Ranges are cooler with more rain, but it's winter rain when the vines are dormant, so irrigation is often necessary.

SOIL
Topsoils are varied, ranging from heavy loam with clay, to light sand; some soils need the addition of lime to counteract acidity. Subsoils are limestone, quartz-sand and clay, and red-brown loams.

ASPECT
Traditional valley floor estates are best at big reds; estates in the higher Eden Valley are excellent for cooler climate styles.

JUST LISTEN TO THESE NAMES – Kaiser Stuhl, Siegersdorf, Bernkastel, Gnadenfrei – the names of wineries and vineyards in the Barossa. And listen to these names – Johann Gramp, Johann Henschke, Peter Lehmann, Leo Buring – the names of Barossa winemakers, ancient and modern. Add to these a delightful assembly of old Lutheran bluestone churches, bakeries offering *Streusel* and *Kuchen*, rather than buns and cakes, delicatessens displaying *Mettwurst* and *Lacksschinken*, and the strains of lusty-lunged choirs and brass bands at practice cutting through the still warm air of a summer's evening – and you know the Barossa is different. It's in a time warp from the early days when Lutheran settlers from Silesia (now part of Poland) travelled halfway round the world to spread themselves across this valley just to the north of Adelaide, intent upon creating a new homeland.

Scratch the surface, though, and you find a different story. These days Kaiser Stuhl and Leo Buring are mere brand names within the giant Southcorp group. Many of Australia's largest-scale and most efficient wineries now cluster round the old settler towns of Nuriootpa, Tanunda and Angaston. Indeed, today more than half of all Australia's wine is made by these big Barossa-based companies. But not many of the grapes for these wines are grown in the Barossa by the descendants of the Silesian settlers who used to provide the fruit.

It was little short of a disaster for these ancient families in the late 20th century when, one by one, the famous old Barossa wine concerns grew into nationally important operations, and two things dawned on the money-men. First, the Barossa vineyards might produce good grapes, but their yields were low and their prices were high. Second, that the reverse was true of the vast easily irrigated vineyards that were springing up along the banks of the Murray River. These might not produce exciting grapes, but they have high yields and low prices.

These large companies concluded that if talented corporate winemakers could make perfectly good wines out of these inferior grapes, why use expensive local fruit? They showed a callous disregard for the welfare of the local Barossa growers, much of whose crop, during the 1980s, they were prepared to let shrivel, unpicked, on the vine. Beady-eyed financial ruthlessness pushed Barossa grape-growing to the brink, and many ancient Barossa families cursed the men in suits who now ran the companies their forebears had created. But by the beginning of the new millennium, the pendulum had swung the growers' way. Enthusiasts worldwide realized that some of the oldest pre-phylloxera vines still alive survive in Barossa – many over a century old. The incomparable flavours these centenarians offer has meant that 'boutique' small-scale, high quality wine production now flourishes in the Barossa. The big companies are still there, and put these precious grapes to far better use than before but now, when they try to browbeat a grower, the grower has somewhere better to turn.

The Barossa Valley was settled by a mixture of German and British pioneers in the 1840s and '50s. George Angas, a Scot, was one of South Australia's most important frontiersmen. To counteract the chronic shortage of labour to work his estate north of Adelaide, he paid for three shiploads of German Lutherans to emigrate from Silesia. They arrived in the Barossa Valley in 1842 and, though Anglo-Saxon families like the Hill-Smiths of Yalumba have thrived since, settling at Angaston in 1849, it was the Germans – or Barossa Deutsch – who moulded the character of the valley. Vineyards and wine companies were established, which, by the beginning of 20th century, already led South Australian production. With the abolition of interstate tariffs and the decimation of rival Victoria's vineyards by phylloxera, South Australia fast assumed the dominant position in Australian wine, and the efficient Barossa companies were the natural leaders.

BAROSSA VALLEY VINEYARDS

Vineyards were established in two main areas: the gently undulating valley floor, along the North Para River from Nuriootpa down to Lyndoch, and on the hills to the east. The valley floor is hot and dry; soils veer from infertile yellow clays to deep red loam, suited to the production of dark intense red wines. There's little rainfall, and there's little subterranean water suitable for irrigation. This seemed to satisfy all parties until the 1970s, when there was a huge swing in public taste towards fresh, fruity, white wines – not at all what the Barossa was suited to with its gnarled old Shiraz and Grenache. It becomes blindingly obvious why big companies gave up using Barossa grapes and began developing huge, mechanized vineyards on the Murray River.

The Barossa Valley as a grape-growing region might have sunk without trace. But luckily a local hero – Peter Lehmann – was around to rescue one of Australia's greatest wine heritages. He set up a company with the sole aim of saving vineyards from the plough. He's now surrounded by a prosperous grape-growing community, but they haven't forgotten who stood firm when it really mattered.

EDEN VALLEY

Up in the hills it is very different. Greater height means much cooler conditions. This has made Eden Valley and the surrounding hills one of Australia's top white wine producers: the Rieslings, in particular, with their steely attack and lime fragrance are often Australia's best. Big companies increasingly use Eden Valley fruit in their top wines, and it is significant that the French giant Moet Hennessey has taken over the trailblazing Mountadam. But the true glories still come from old family operations like Henschke.

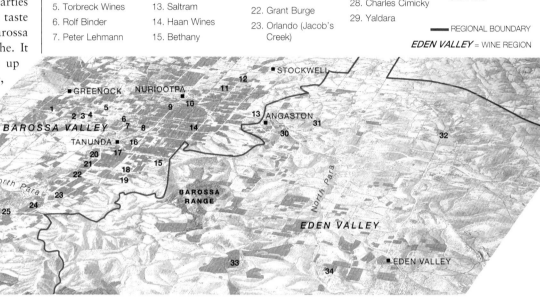

WHERE THE VINEYARDS ARE *This map is a marvellous panorama of the whole Barossa grape-growing region. One of the things that always strikes me in South Australia is how seemingly insignificant the mountains are. The inaptly named Mount Lofty Ranges stretch up the right of the map, yet these ancient hills have been worn away over the millennia into hummocks of storm-smoothed rock. But they are a vital few hundred metres above the valley floor, creating cooler, windier conditions for viticulture, and since they are some of the first obstacles the westerly winds have encountered since coming in from the Indian Ocean, whatever moisture there is will drop mainly in these hills.*

As you can see, most of the vineyards have lakes next to them. These are large catchment dams to catch winter rains for irrigation in the dry summers, when each vine may need 5 litres (2 gallons) of water a day.

The valley floor gets far less winter rain and almost none in summer. Not only that, subterranean water to the west of the North Para River is too salty to be of much use for irrigation. Consequently, most vineyards lie east of the river. But the dry land to the north and around Nuriootpa and Greenock can produce stunning reds from old, low-yielding vines: Penfolds' Grange is based on Kalimna fruit from north of Nuriootpa. Further south, wineries such as St Hallett, Rockford and Charles Melton have built enviable reputations. A new pipeline has been built from the Murray River, without which a lot of the new plantings west of the Para River could not survive. But with the Murray in the throes of serious drought, such non-core irrigation schemes may have to be abandoned in the future, and with it any attempts to spread Barossa outside its traditional boundaries.

In the Eden Valley hills, water is less of a problem – so long as you are prepared to build large catchment dams to hold the winter rains, as precious little falls in summer. It is distinctly cooler here, due to the height of the hills themselves: most vineyards are at 400–500m (1300–1640ft) high, and produce some of Australia's top white wines.

BAROSSA AND EDEN VALLEYS

TOTAL DISTANCE NORTH TO SOUTH 31KM (19 MILES)

▤▤▤ VINEYARDS

COONAWARRA

 RED GRAPES
Success with Cabernet Sauvignon makes this the predominant variety now, though there is a good deal of Shiraz and some Merlot.

 WHITE GRAPES
Chardonnay is the most widely planted variety, but there's also Riesling and some good Sauvignon Blanc.

CLIMATE
These are the southernmost, and, therefore, coolest, of South Australian vineyards. The easily accessible water table gives high yields of good quality. Vintage can take place from early March to as late as May.

 SOIL
An area of terra rossa (literally 'red soil'), or crumbly red loam, covers the low ridges, with both black cracking clay and sandy soils over a clay base on lower ground.

ASPECT
It is flat here – uniformly so, and with its long growing season, high light intensity and unique soil structure, it is ideal for vines.

Wynns was one of the earliest wineries in Coonawarra: this is its John Riddoch Cabernet, named in honour of the region's first grape-grower, the founder of the Coonawarra fruit colony in 1890.

MOST OF THE GREAT VINEYARDS of the world owe their presence to a river which has carved its path to the sea, creating a mixture of valley slopes and river plains that provide unique conditions for grapes to ripen. Coonawarra's uniqueness is the fact that there *aren't* any rivers: there are mountains to the east; there's sea to the west; but there are no rivers to connect one to the other.

There is a lot of water, though, falling in the mountains every winter. And it seeps, inch by inch, just below the surface across the bleak swathe of bogland that makes up the southern tip of South Australia. They call this the rump end of the Great Artesian Basin – at least, that's how I interpret their vernacular. Depending on who you talk to, the water has seeped from neighbouring Victoria or all the way from Queensland. And depending on how far the water has come, it could be thousands of years old or hundreds. Anyway, it's so pure you almost need to add salts to it to make it suitable for vines. And there's lots of it, just below the surface.

That's all very well. But what about what happens above ground? What about the climate; and, for that matter, what about the soil? So far this sounds like a graphic description of one of the world's all-time squelchy hell-holes. What's it to do with wine? Let's go back a bit. About 600,000 years.

The area was underwater then, with the shoreline marked by the Comaum Range east of Coonawarra. But two things happened. First, there was a reversal in the earth's magnetic field, followed by a slow but continual upheaval in the land that has by now raised Coonawarra 60m (200ft) above sea level. Second, about every 50,000 years, there has been an ice age and the seas have retreated. With each subsequent warm period, the seas have crept back to find the land sufficiently raised that a new beach is established, and a new ridge is built up of limestone over sandstone. There have been 12 ice ages in the last 600,000 years. There are 12 ridges between the Comaum Range and the sea – one for each ice age – running north to south, parallel to the shore. Between each ridge the land is a sullen mix of sandy soil over a clay subsoil, or black cracking clay. On the barely perceptible ridges, a thin sprinkling of fertile reddish soil sits above a tough limestone cap. Break through that cap and the limestone becomes so damp and crumbly you can poke your finger into it and waggle it about. And a yard or two further down, the pure mountain waters from the east seep slowly towards the sea.

The limestone ridges topped with *terra rossa* soil provide perfectly drained sites for vines, islands in a vast expanse of waterlogged land. And the underground water provides one of the best natural resources for irrigation that any wine area in the world possesses – that is, if the vines need it: many of the older vines' roots tap directly into the water. Given that Australia is a hot country, this should be a recipe for the efficient production of vast amounts of reliable, low cost wine.

CHILLY VINEYARDS

But there's one other thing. It's not hot in the south of South Australia. Coonawarra, 400km (250 miles) south of Adelaide, is surrounded by the chill Southern Ocean. The winters are cold and damp, with most of the rain dumping uselessly on the area during winter, often waterlogging all but the scattered limestone ridges. Springtime is squally, and often frosty too.

Summer starts out mild but dry, yet in February and March there are often hot spells that can scorch and exhaust the vines: then the bore holes pump day and night, providing life-saving irrigation. And as the grapes slowly ripen into April the weather can break into sour, joyless early winter before the harvest is in and stay unfriendly and raw until the following spring.

RED WINES

And yet some of Australia's greatest red wines are made on this thin strip of vineyard land, where the climate makes vines struggle all year but the famous red soil and subsoil cosset and spoil them.

Since its foundation as a vine-growing area in 1891, French-style reds, primarily from Shiraz and Cabernet, have dominated. But, it wasn't until the 1960s that the world began to appreciate the relatively light yet intensely flavoured qualities of Coonawarra reds. By the 1990s, Coonawarra's terra rossa acres had become some of the most sought after vineyard land in Australia. This has led to problems and infighting. On both sides of the terra rossa ridges are heavy clay plains, where hundreds of acres are planted with vines. Some decent white wine has been produced, but such damp cold soils cannot ripen Cabernet or Shiraz. Should their wines be allowed the name Coonawarra? More to the point, to the north, west and south there are outcrops of *terra rossa* rising a metre or so above the damp clay. Should these be allowed the Coonawarra name? Well, they've been bickering since 1984 about this. A decision in 2000 gave a tight, historically accurate definition of Coonawarra. But powerful interests were excluded, so in 2001 it went to appeal – and a larger area was validated. And a larger. And a larger. It all became

TERRA ROSSA

The diagram shows a vine root growing in Coonawarra red earth, commonly known as terra rossa. It is one of the best soils for growing vines in Australia, and covers a north-south strip 15km (9 miles) long and 2km (1 mile) wide. Although both red top soil and limestone have excellent drainage, it is not fully understood why this soil produces such fine grapes.

1. is the rich, red-brown topsoil, a freely drained earth, about 2–50cm (3/4–20in) deep.

2. is a band of hard calcrete of up to 15cm (6in) deep, a result of calcium carbonate being leached out of the topsoil and redeposited above the limestone. This layer needs to be broken up before planting to provide access for vine roots and passage through for water.

3. is a thick, free-draining limestone, an ideal environment for root nourishment.

4. is where the rock becomes saturated with ground water. The water table is unusually high in Coonawarra, at a depth of only 2–4m (6½–13ft) and the vine roots that extend deep enough can benefit from year-round water.

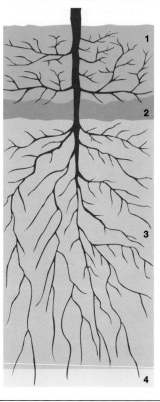

a tasteless farce. The core vineyards of Coonawarra are as good as ever, but you can grow grapes right to the Victorian border in the east, or well into the black clay swap to the west, and still call the wine Coonawarra.

OTHER VINEYARD AREAS

Of course, Coonawarra is only one ridge. There are other similarly good ones: St Marys, just to the west, Mount Benson on the coast, and various sites around Naracoorte to the north, in particular Wrattonbully, produce superb quality. Also the regional title 'Limestone Coast' is already achieving significant acceptance as a general description of the cool climate wines of the whole area. And Padthaway, 65km (40 miles) to the north, produces fantastic wines. The area wasn't developed with quality in mind. In the early 1960s, it was forecast that Australian wine consumption would triple in the next 30 years. So the big companies looked for land to buy and operate cheaply. Seppelt, Hardy and Lindemans have such efficient mechanized vineyards there that they reckon to need only one person per 40ha (99 acres). Planted with all kinds of varieties, at first superb Chardonnay, and now fine Shiraz and sweet wines have propelled this featureless plot to star status.

SELECTED WINERIES

1. Rymill
2. Penley Estate
3. Brand's
4. Wynns Coonawarra
5. Di Giorgio
6. Zema Estate
7. Jamieson's Run
8. Majella
9. Lawrence Victor Estate
10. Katnook Estate
11. Highbank
12. Leconfield
13. Murdock Wines
14. Yalumba (The Menzies)
15. Bowen Estate
16. Balnaves
17. The Blok Estate
18. Hollick
19. Punters Corner
20. Ladbroke Grove
21. Parker Coonawarra Estate
22. Lindemans

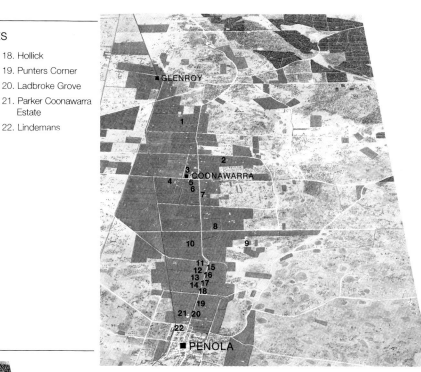

WHERE THE VINEYARDS ARE *Well, here it is – one of Australia's most famous vineyard areas in all its glory. It is a spectacular place to grow vines, but it just so happens to be dumped in the middle of what is virtually a swamp. When the rain starts, you keep to the roads or take a pair of water-wings. Penola – the little town at the bottom of the map – is aboriginal for 'big swamp'.*

But if you take the main road north out of Penola, for about 15km (9 miles) you travel along the low limestone ridge of Coonawarra. This slight increase in altitude raises the road and a thin strip of land either side a crucial few feet above the surrounding waterlogged clay soils, and provides brilliant conditions for growing an abundance of healthy vines.

The best land has a thin covering of red-brown topsoil which lies directly over a layer of calcrete and then limestone. This terra rossa topsoil is extremely fertile, so the best quality comes from thin coverings of as little as an inch or two on top of barely perceptible rises in the land.

However, those vines you can see to the west of the railway are on black clay soils, and many of the vines stretching east are on white clay, some of which (both black and white) is little more than partially reclaimed swamp. Neither is capable of properly ripening Cabernet or Shiraz grapes.

The underground water that nourishes the Coonawarra vines is remarkably pure, but as more and more water is drawn out of the Great Artesian Basin by Coonawarra and other nearby emergent wine areas, damaging salts are likely to be leached from further inland. A water-sharing agreement between South Australia and Victoria, only 20km (12 miles) east of here, aims to limit any water extraction in the future.

COONAWARRA

TOTAL DISTANCE NORTH TO SOUTH 24KM (15 MILES)

 VINEYARDS

CLARE VALLEY

RED GRAPES
The main plantings are Shiraz and Cabernet Sauvignon, with some Merlot, Malbec and Grenache. There are tiny amounts of Mourvedre, Sangiovese and Tempranillo.

WHITE GRAPES
Riesling is the principal variety, with significant amounts of Chardonnay and Semillon plus some Sauvignon Blanc.

CLIMATE
The heat should lower acidity and send sugars soaring, but instead produces light wines, especially Rieslings, with an unexpected natural acidity and delicacy.

SOIL
The main subsoil is of calcareous clay. In the north, there's a sandy loam topsoil, in the centre, red loam, and in the south, red clay.

ASPECT
Vineyards are planted at 400–500m (1300–1640ft) above sea level, in the narrow valleys running from north to south, and in the foothills to the west. Aspects vary, with twisting contours.

One of the remarkable things about Clare Valley is its suitability for both hot-climate grapes, like Shiraz, and cool-climate ones, like Riesling. Jeffrey Grosset's Riesling is one of the best in Australia.

IT DOESN'T MAKE SENSE. Here I am, heading out of Adelaide in South Australia, the hottest and driest of Australia's major winemaking states. And I'm heading north towards the parched centre of the continent. Yet I'm looking for a famous cool-climate vineyard area – the Clare Valley. It might make a little more sense if I were heading up into the Adelaide Hills I can see to the east, since a climb of a few hundred metres dramatically cools the air, and the craggy hills also attract whatever rainfall there might be.

But I'm driving along the flat northern highway out past Gawler and Tarlee, through arid, dun-coloured cereal fields interrupted by occasional grain silos. The vista of broad, bone-dry acres peppered with doughty gums makes my tongue stick to the roof of my mouth as I ache for an ice-cold beer. And suddenly, in a dip in the land just north of Auburn, there's a field of shocking green. There are vines – the first vines of the Clare Valley – healthy, vigorous, their leaves waving gently in the breeze.

The breeze? There wasn't any breeze when I stopped back at Tarlee for a beer. There is unmistakably one now, taking the harshness out of the hot afternoon sun. And the air feels fresh, hillside fresh. Without once realizing that I was climbing at all, I've reached over 400m (1300ft) above sea level. At last some of the reasons for Clare's reputation as one of Australia's great cool-climate vineyard regions are falling into place.

Don't worry. They'll fall out of place again. Clare may have a reputation for elegant, balanced Riesling, but it also produces some of the most startlingly concentrated, brawny Shiraz in South Australia. Its 'ports' and Liqueur Tokays are pretty exceptional, for that matter. In one vineyard Riesling grapes struggle to ripen by late April. A couple of miles north-east, another vineyard harvests the port variety Touriga Nacional in February. I'll try to explain.

I've seen Clare described as a frontier town and as the 'hub of the north' in its early days. I'll buy that. After the long trek up from Adelaide, nearly 130km (80 miles) away, Clare promises to offer the last relief before the endless parched plains that stretch away to the north towards Jamestown and Port Pirie. Since the town of Clare's establishment in 1846, it has always been a focal point both for trading and for the refreshment of tired limbs and parched throats for the whole area. It's been a boom town several times. Copper was discovered nearby in 1845. Clare serviced that boom. There were massive wheat plantations established during the 1870s. Clare serviced these too. World-class slate reserves were discovered at neighbouring Mintaro, and there was a silver rush leading to the formation of the Broken Hill Propriety Co – Australia's largest company – in 1855. Once again, this small town reaped its share of the benefits.

What is left now is a traditional, well-worn market town – still quietly prosperous long after those early frenzied years – and vines. Vineyards throughout much of Australia were established to slake the thirsts of wealth-crazed pioneers in the 19th century. Those of the Clare Valley were no exception, though one distinct novelty, for Australia, was the establishment of Sevenhill Jesuit monastery in 1851. Naturally they planted vines. Just as naturally, they are still making wine.

Clare was luckier than many areas in that there was a genuine effort made to plant only the better grape varieties – and particularly Cabernet Sauvignon, Malbec and Shiraz. But then, as elsewhere in Australia, these were largely supplanted by varieties planted for cheap fortified wine and brandy in the early 20th century. However, the re-establishment of Clare Valley as a quality region during the 1950s and 1960s saw the better red varieties dominate new vineyard plantings once more, along with the white grapes Riesling and (more recently) Chardonnay.

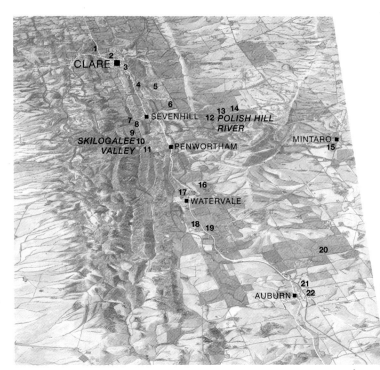

SELECTED WINERIES

1. Jim Barry Wines	9. Skillogalee Wines	17. Crabtree Wines
2. Knappstein Wines	10. Mitchell Winery	18. Brian Barry Wines
3. Leasingham Wines	11. Killikanoon Wines	19. Tim Gramp Wines
4. Tim Adams	12. Paulett Wines	20. Taylors Wines/
5. Wendouree	13. The Wilson Vineyard	Wakefield
6. Sevenhill Cellars	14. Pikes Wines	21. Grosset Wines
7. Stringy Brae Wines	15. Mintaro Wines	22. Mt. Horrocks Wines
8. Waninga Wines	16. Quelltaler Estate/	
	Annie's Lane	

VINEYARD AREAS

The trick was to have planted the vines in the right place. The term 'valley' isn't really an accurate description of this region. There are in fact three valley systems in Clare Valley, stretching both south and north with a watershed plateau in the middle at Penwortham. Incorporated into this are five sub-regions with differing soils at different heights above sea level – and differing mesoclimates too. Confusing, especially since Clare seems to get about as much heat as, and even less rain in the growing season than the impossibly hot Liqueur Muscat centre of Rutherglen in Victoria. Well, it does and it doesn't. Except in the valley bottom, it would be impossible to establish vineyards without irrigation. Storage dams for winter rain are the most effective source of water. And the tumbling landscape allows a wide variety of aspects to the sun, while nights are generally chilly and breezes arise to cool the vines during the day.

There is some disagreement about these cooling breezes because they have a fair way to travel inland from the sea, 50km (30 miles) to the west and south-west. It seems that, by and large, they only arise in the late afternoon, cooling the vines in the evening and at night, but not affecting the most intense heat of the early afternoon. So ripening is not hindered, but acid levels in the fruit remain high. Some locals say it is the daily fade-out, around 4pm, of the hot, northerly winds that is the crucial factor in cooling the vineyards, especially in the north-facing valleys above Penwortham. Altitude certainly seems to help. The excellent Enterprise and Petaluma vineyards, both giving outstanding Riesling, are over 500m (1640ft) high, facing west over the town of Clare. The vineyards of the

CLARE

SEVENHILL

WATERVALE

AUBURN

Skillogalee Valley, near Sevenhill, are not far short of 500m (1640ft) and protected from the north. Their fruit flavours are particularly fine and focused. Soil also plays a major role. Deep dark loams below Watervale produce ripe, fat reds and whites, yet the ridge of limestone north of Watervale provides white wines with an acid bite that such a warm climate should deny. In the Polish Hill River area an acidic slaty soil seems to retard ripening by as much as two weeks and the results are surprisingly delicate structured whites and reds. A paradoxical place, the Clare Valley? It certainly is. There are moves to divide Clare into sub-zones and I can see why.

WHERE THE VINEYARDS ARE *Clare Valley is only 25km (15 miles) long, but a surprising number of different growing conditions exist for its 5500ha (13,590 acres) of vines. To call it a valley isn't actually accurate, as the watershed at Penwortham forms a plateau from which three river systems run, two north – including the Clare – and one south. The area, however, with its remarkably crisp, fragrant whites and elegant reds, is baffling. It seems too hot and dry. Certainly altitude is very important. None of the vineyards seen here are at less than 400m (1300ft). But Clare has one of the lowest summer rainfalls of any Australian quality wine region and could do with more. And it relies on sea breezes from the west and south-west to cool the vines and would prefer to have an uninterrupted flow.*

CLARE VALLEY

TOTAL DISTANCE
NORTH TO SOUTH
33.5KM (21 MILES)

 VINEYARDS

N

VICTORIA

🍇 **RED GRAPES**
Shiraz, Cabernet Sauvignon, Merlot and Pinot Noir predominate.

🍇 **WHITE GRAPES**
The main quality variety is Chardonnay, followed by Riesling, Sauvignon Blanc and Semillon, but there are also small amounts of Marsanne, Muscat Blanc à Petits Grains and Muscadelle.

☁ **CLIMATE**
Coastal areas have a maritime climate. The north-east of the state, producing fortified wines, is hot and dry.

▱ **SOIL**
There is red loam in the north, quartzose alluvial soils in the Goulburn Valley, crumbly black volcanic soil at Geelong.

⛰ **ASPECT**
Steep, sloping, north-facing vineyards in cool-climate areas allow extended ripening. Most of the interior is pretty flat and featureless.

Morris's Old Premium, from Rutherglen in north-east Victoria, is intensely rich and will include a tiny proportion of treacly 100-year-old wine.

ROLL UP, ROLL UP to the Great Victorian Wine Show! All human life is here, with its triumphs, its tragedies, its noblest qualities and its greed. Especially greed. Swiss settlers were the first to make their mark, with toil and honest endeavour. Later, Gold Fever hit Victoria, bringing speculators with a mighty yet indiscriminate thirst. Soon after came the first attempts to harness the Murray River and turn desert into orchards and vineyards. Then came phylloxera, the world's most feared vine predator, followed by the Great Bank Crash, bankruptcies and ruin. The few remaining outposts of vines struggled for survival.

And then the new Victoria emerged. All the old vineyard areas have now been re-established and new ones have sprung into life, offering a wealth of styles more diverse than any in Australia, ranging from some of the richest, most succulent fortified wines in the world made at Glenrowan and Rutherglen in the torrid north-east, down to damp, windy Drumborg in the south-west tip, where the grape struggles to ripen enough even for sparkling wine. The amounts produced of many of these remarkable wines is pitifully small and, with few exceptions, the wineries are spread thinly across the state, rather than bunched together in comprehensible regional groups. But that just makes the effort to find them all the more rewarding.

FIRST PLANTINGS
Let's have a quick look at the history first. The vine arrived in 1834 from Tasmania, of all places. Melbourne itself, at the north of Port Phillip Bay, proved ideally suited to vine-growing: not too hot, with an attractive maritime climate easing the grape towards ripeness. But the city's expansion was, obviously, always going to push out the vineyards, and the two areas that thrived were out of town at Geelong and the Yarra Valley.

Geelong is to the west of Port Phillip Bay, and is challenging vineyard land. The best sites are on outcrops of deep, crumbly, black volcanic soil, and are water-retentive but not prone to waterlogging. Although it isn't that wet, it's rarely that hot either and the cold Antarctic gales haven't crossed any landmass to reduce their chilly force when they hit Geelong. The reason Geelong did well – by 1861 it was the most important vineyard area in the State – was largely due to the settlement of Swiss vignerons who knew how to coax good flavour out of cool surroundings. They did the same in the Yarra Valley and we look at that in more depth later (see page 298).

The next wave of vineyards was established not because the land was thought suitable, but because gold was discovered there in 1851. From all over the world men flocked to the heartland of Victoria, their minds giddy with dreams of untold wealth from these extensive, easily dug lodes of precious metal. And they were thirsty too. Avoca established vineyards in 1848, Bendigo followed suit in 1855, Great Western in 1858 and Ballarat in 1859. North-East Victoria already had vines near Rutherglen, but was equally boosted by the madhouse prosperity brought by gold. Wine could be sold for as much as £5 a gallon in the goldfields – 20 times the price it would fetch in New South Wales, southern Victoria or South Australia.

WINE REGIONS

Murray Darling	Pyrenees	Rutherglen	Glenrowan	Sunbury	Geelong
Swan Hill	Bendigo	Beechworth	Strathbogie Ranges	Yarra Valley	OVER 200M (656FT)
Henty	Heathcote	Alpine Valleys	Upper Goulburn	Mornington Peninsula	OVER 500M (1640FT)
Grampians	Goulburn Valley	King Valley	Macedon Ranges		

1. Nagambie Lakes

Eventually the Gold Rush died, and with it most, though not all, of the vines. But far worse was to come. Phylloxera arrived in Australia via Geelong in 1875. Geelong's vines were uprooted by government order, and so were those of Bendigo, but to no avail. Phylloxera spread through most of Victoria and by 1910 the state that was once the jewel in Australia's winemaking crown had seen her wine industry reduced to a withered rump centred on North-East Victoria, the Murray vineyards (whose founders, the Chaffey brothers, were paupered by the combination of the Great Bank Crash of 1893 and the Murray River inexplicably drying up) – plus a few vines at Tahbilk in the Goulburn Valley and at Great Western.

RED AND WHITE WINES

The rebirth of Victoria as a key wine region began with the re-establishment of vines at Geelong in 1966, but it really only began to take off in the 1980s. The result has been dramatic and triumphant. Among the wine areas to have enjoyed a resurgence, Geelong is no easier a place to grow vines in than it was 150 years ago, but it still manages to produce brilliantly focused, dark-hearted reds and attractive whites, when the sun stays out long enough. The Mornington Peninsula is still windy, but its position provides more maritime stability than Geelong, and any harsh north and north-east winds are cooled and dampened during their journey across the waters of the bay. The wines, especially the Chardonnays, Pinot Noirs and Rieslings, are light in texture but magnificently piercing in fruit intensity.

There are further cool-climate vineyards whose fruit intensity is remarkable near Portland in the south-west and at Gippsland in the south-east. Sunbury and Macedon, barely further north of Melbourne than its airport, combine fine sparkling wine with stunning lean but concentrated reds and whites. Bendigo is next stop north, but neighbouring Heathcote has turned most heads recently with joyfully dense, lush Shirazes. The central Goulburn Valley to the east is warm and principally famous for Chateau Tahbilk whose ancient vines provide palate-crunching reds and heady but approachable whites. Next door the Strathbogie Ranges grows small amounts of scented, focussed reds and whites. And way to the east, the hills and valleys of the Victorian Alps – especially the King and Ovens Valleys and the clifftop region of Beechworth are providing yet more fascinating original Victorian flavours.

CENTRAL AND WESTERN VICTORIA

Scattered sparsely across the Central and Western Victoria zones are the remnants of the great goldfield vineyards. The soils are mostly poor, producing a low yield of fruit, and rainfall is generally meagre. Although there is a considerable amount of sunshine, high altitudes, at places like Ballarat, the Pyrenees and much of the Grampians, moderate the heat and produce remarkable results from Shiraz, Cabernet Sauvignon, Chardonnay and even Riesling. If you think you spot a fascinating streak of eucalyptus and mint in these reds, you're not wrong – they were commenting on its presence 150 years ago. And since you'll have to make your way through miles of daunting eucalyptus forests to find most of the vineyards, you can guess where that scent of eucalyptus comes from.

MURRAY RIVER

The Murray River marks Victoria's northern border. The majority of Victoria's wine comes from the vast, irrigated fields that fan out from the lefthand banks of the river. An increasing amount is made to a high standard. Lindemans' Karadoc, the biggest winery in Australia, processes much of the fruit, and the giant Mildara plant at Merbein, just north of the town of Mildura, does a similar job.

NORTH-EAST VICTORIAN 'STICKIES'

There are two main regions in North-East Victoria noted for their sweet fortified wines or 'stickies': Glenrowan, where Baileys make fine sweet 'stickies' as well as startling reds; and Rutherglen. Here a host of winemakers, young and old, make a hotchpotch of styles but, above all, the magnificent 'stickies' that leave your lips smeared and stained, your palate shocked and seduced, and your soul uplifted by their unashamed richness. At Milawa, Brown Brothers also make top-quality 'stickies', often from Rutherglen fruit, but their more significant contribution has been the revival of King Valley as a top table wine area and the establishment of Whitlands, at 800m (2600ft), one of Australia's highest vineyards.

Red soils often crop up at the site of Australia's best vineyards, and it's the same in North-East Victoria. At Rutherglen all the finest wines come from a bank of red loam soil. At Glenrowan, Baileys grow their Muscat and Muscadelle (usually called Tokay) on a deep seam of pulverized red granite soil. Both of these soils are friable, but do hold water and allow the vines to develop a massive, deep root structure. Each vine is reckoned to want up to 5l (1 gallon) a day, and Baileys, with access to water from Lake Mokoan and the Broken River, prefer to irrigate, unlike many of the Rutherglen producers, who prefer to leave things to nature and have their small crops of intensely sweet fruit to prove their point.

North-East Victoria gets no cooling sea breezes, so grapes really do bake in the heat (though cold nights help preserve acid). Muscat and Muscadelle grapes often reach 20–22 per cent potential alcohol, as they shrivel in long warm autumns. When picked, they ooze richness, and the thick juice is barely fermented before being whacked with spirit to kill the yeasts. It's then left in barrels, virtually turning to treacle as it cooks under the winery eaves for anywhere between one year and a hundred. The best, from makers like Chambers, Morris, Baileys, Campbell and Stanton & Killeen, blend the bright floral grapiness of young Muscat with small amounts of thick and viscous ancient wines to give a uniquely 'sticky' experience.

Early morning mists are still lifting over the Yarra Valley. Coldstream Hills' vines slope down to Yarra Yering (on the left) and on to grazing land on the valley floor.

YARRA VALLEY

RED GRAPES
Pinot Noir is the leading red, with Cabernet Sauvignon and Merlot following some way behind. Shiraz is next and there are tiny amounts of Sangiovese and other reds, including Tempranillo.

WHITE GRAPES
Chardonnay dominates and is the Number One variety planted in the valley. Sauvignon Blanc is also important and there are small amounts of Pinot Gris and other whites.

CLIMATE
The cool climate allows extended ripening. Wind and rain can interfere with flowering and fruit-set in December and January.

SOIL
There are two main types of soil: grey, sandy clays or clay loams and deep, fertile, red volcanic soil.

ASPECT
The angle of slope and height above sea level vary greatly, with vineyards planted at 50–400m (165–1300ft).

I CAN SEE IT NOW, 1837, AND William Ryrie breasting the hills above Healesville in the blazing afternoon sun. He'd trekked over mountain and prairie all the way down from Cooma in New South Wales. He must have been parched and exhausted. Spreading out below him was a lush valley with a glistening, if sluggish, river curling its way down the centre. As the sweet air drifted up to him, he must have thought – yes, this'll do.

Ryrie did settle in the Yarra Valley, and he laid the foundations for both its wine industry and its cattle-rearing business. The two have been at odds with each other ever since. But the beauty and serenity that must have filled his heart with exultant joy in 1837 are still there. Eagles soar overhead, kingfishers race like arrows near the river, and gum trees rear majestically over the flat parkland and way up the mountain slopes, too. It's all too easy to forget that the tranquillity of this peerless landscape has been earned and created by its inhabitants.

The first people to thank are the Swiss. Ryrie employed a Swiss assistant to prune the vines he planted and to help make the wine. In 1845 he managed to produce a Burgundy-like red and a Sauternes-like white. This sounds an improbable combination, but it may say something about the Yarra's climate that has been proven time and again in recent decades. The valley is not at all hot by Australian standards, providing rare suitable conditions for the fussy Pinot Noir. And it's relatively humid, too, encouraging the noble rot which can produce brilliant sweet Yarra wines.

The Swiss straightaway took a leading role in the Yarra Valley, and their winemaking expertise quickly created a reputation for delicacy and balance that was uncommon in Australia. They even won a *Grand Prix* – the only one for a southern hemisphere wine – at the 1889 Paris International Exhibition.

But thirty years later, phylloxera and a series of financial and natural disasters put an end to all this. Not until the 1960s did vine leaves rustle once more in the valley breezes, and it was the 1980s before the big hitters of Australian wine remembered the valley's former reputation and wondered if Yarra could do it all again.

RED AND WHITE WINES

It could and it has; indeed, it has boomed. (Phylloxera has also returned, but, so far, is under control.) And the remarkable thing is that the Yarra Valley has shown an ability to produce virtually every type of classic cool-climate wine within its small boundaries in a way that would make French traditionalists, hemmed in with restrictive *appellations contrôlées*, wring their hands in envy and despair. Marvellous traditional-method sparkling wines are made by Domaine Chandon, and superb Burgundian-style reds and whites are made by such outfits as Coldstream Hills, De Bortoli, Diamond Valley, Yarra Ridge, Tarrawarra and Metier. Excellent Bordeaux styles also abound, particularly at Mount Mary, Oakridge and Yarra Yering,

which also excels in Rhône styles as does De Bortoli, while wonderful sweet wines are made by producers such as Seville Estate and St Huberts. Yet none of these wines taste like their European role models. They are, in general, softer in texture, fuller of fruit, equally well-structured but easy to appreciate at every stage of their lives. This is because the challenge of Yarra's cool conditions is attracting talented winemakers, sensitive enough to want to work in harmony with nature, rather than bludgeon and straitjacket her.

Certainly the Yarra Valley is cool – in Australian terms – but it neatly cuts across the conditions that might pertain for good vintages in Bordeaux and Burgundy. Generally not quite so warm as Bordeaux but warmer than Burgundy, Yarra's temperature during the ripening season is more consistent than either of the two. Rainfall, while it can disrupt flowering in late spring, almost always stops around the end of December and, except for the odd welcome shower, doesn't usually return until autumn, after the harvest. So you can let the fruit ripen gently on the vine, the prerequisite for delicate, perfumed wine.

But all this depends on where your vineyards are. Up in the hills it is often too cold for vines. The valley floor, a broad flood plain, has boggy soil that couldn't ripen grapes. Sites to the north of the valley ripen earlier than most to the south. And, depending upon whether your sites face north or south and catch the full force of the sun or only part of it, crops at the same altitude can ripen two weeks apart.

YARRA VALLEY SOILS

The two main soil types in the Yarra Valley are very different. The southern side of the valley, to the east and south of the Warramate Hills, is primarily deep, fertile red soil. Vines are extremely vigorous here, and whites and dessert wines are the speciality. The classic Yarra soils, spreading across the centre and north of the valley, are grey sandy clays and clay loams, often directly above a heavy clay pan. Vigour is restricted, vines struggle to establish themselves and often need help from irrigation during the summer, but it's these soils that first gave Yarra vines their reputation, and most of the greatest reds and whites still come off these sites.

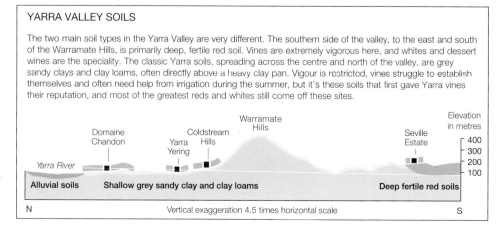

YARRA VALLEY

TOTAL DISTANCE NORTH TO
SOUTH 27.5KM (17 MILES)

▦ VINEYARDS

▲
N

0 km   1   2

0 miles   1

WHERE THE VINEYARDS ARE *That's the outskirts of Melbourne in the lower lefthand corner, and the Great Dividing Range of mountains is over on the right. The Yarra Valley is beautiful, and it's only a short journey via electric train from Lilydale to the city centre. Pressure from property developers is the biggest threat to face the Yarra Valley, and a flourishing wine industry is one of the best ways to combat it. Vineyard planting here has exploded and now totals 3600ha (8895 acres), with more vines still being planted. This is great news to halt urban development, but such rapid expansion in a cool area brings poor wine as well as good.*

The vineyards originally stretched north-east of Coldstream across the grey loam soils at St Huberts and Yeringberg, and a little further west towards Yarra Glen at Yering Station. Only well-drained banks are suitable for grapes on the valley floor. There has been a great deal of development around Dixons Creek in the north of the valley, but again only on the raised ground. The land around the Warramate Hills is high enough, and as is the case in the Coldstream Hills, it is steep enough for drainage not to be a problem.

East and south of the Warramate Hills, away from the flood plain, the soil changes to a highly fertile, deep red terra rossa. This continues into the wooded hills to the south (off the map) where large developments at locations like Hoddles Creek, are producing high-quality grapes, used primarily for sparkling wine.

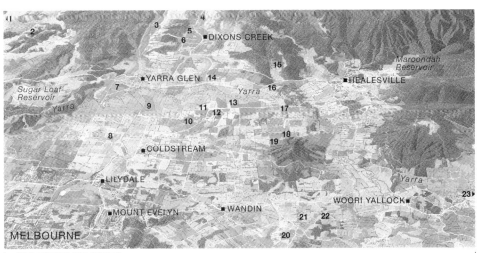

SELECTED WINERIES

1. Arthurs Creek	6. Fergusson	11. Domaine Chandon/Green Point	15. Long Gully	20. Five Oaks
2. Diamond Valley	7. Yarra Ridge		16. TarraWarra	21. Seville Estate
3. Yarra Yarra	8. Mount Mary	12. Yeringberg	17. Rochford	22. Lillydale
4. Shantell	9. Yering Station/ Yarra Bank	13. Oakridge	18. Yarra Yering	23. Yarra Burn/ Hoddles Creek
5. De Bortoli	10. St Huberts	14. Metier Wines	19. Coldstream Hills	

NEW SOUTH WALES

RED GRAPES
Shiraz, Cabernet Sauvignon and Merlot are widely planted. There are also a number of other reds, of which Pinot Noir is the most significant.

WHITE GRAPES
The main varieties are Semillon and Chardonnay, but Riesling and Traminer are also significant. In Riverina there are also substantial plantings of Trebbiano, Muscat, Verdelho and Colombard for everyday whites.

CLIMATE
It is hot, even by Australian standards, particularly in the Hunter Valley and Riverina. Wet, humid autumns encourage rot.

SOIL
Sandy and clay loams, along with some red-brown volcanic loams, granite and alluvial soils predominate.

ASPECT
Vines are planted on the gently undulating valley floors (Cowra, Riverina and Upper Hunter), or in the foothills of the Brokenback and Great Dividing Ranges (Lower Hunter Valley, Mudgee, Hilltops and Orange).

Unoaked Hunter Semillon, one of Australia's truly original wine styles, needs years in bottle to show at its best. Tyrrell's Vat 1 will continue to improve for a generation.

NEW SOUTH WALES is where I started my Australian wine odyssey. And I have to admit my first Australian hangover was in New South Wales, though it was the result of beer, not wine, but I wouldn't vouch for the genesis of numerous subsequent ones. It's where Australian wine started its journey, too. The very first vines to reach Australia sailed into Sydney Harbour with the First Fleet in 1788. They had been picked up in Rio de Janeiro and in the Cape of Good Hope on the long voyage out from England, and in no time the settlers had cleared some scrub by the harbour and planted vines. They weren't a great success – the humid atmosphere encouraged black spot disease, knocking out any grapes before they had a chance to ripen – but the scene had been set. All the main Australian settlements took the same line, establishing vineyards at the same time as establishing a community. And the reason usually given was to encourage sobriety. In a new, savage country where rough men became more savage and wild under the influence of fiery high-strength spirits, wine was seen as a moderating influence, a weapon against drunkenness and disorder.

These attempts in New South Wales to promote a benevolent, rosy-cheeked, wine-sipping society didn't work out too well, because there were very few places near Sydney suitable for vines. Close to the sea, the climate is too subtropical and vines routinely rotted. Further inland, around Bathurst, the cooler, high-altitude terrain looked promising, but harsh spring frosts simply made vine-growing economically unviable.

Although a few vineyards did survive near Sydney until modern times – at Camden, Rooty Hill and Smithfield – the story of wine in New South Wales is one of establishing vineyards well away from the main consumer market-place, with quality acting as the magnet drawing the attention of Sydney. This movement still continues today.

The crucial factors in New South Wales are excessive heat from the relatively northerly latitude; the presence of the sea close by; and the Great Dividing Range of mountains which separates the humid, populated seaboard from the parched, empty interior. The Great Dividing Range provides cool vineyard sites in some of its high hill passes, as well as the springs from which enough rivers flow inwards to irrigate some of the largest agro-industrial vineyards in Australia. Proximity to the sea brings with it advantages and disadvantages: the priceless bounty of cooling breezes but also the seasonal curse of cyclonic cloudbursts, frequently around vintage time.

HUNTER VALLEY

The first real success came with the Hunter Valley, which is about 130km (80 miles) north of Sydney and just inland from the major industrial city of Newcastle. Vineyards were being planted there as early as the 1820s, but it wasn't until the 1860s that the areas now thought of as best – those around the mining town of Cessnock – were planted. I cover the Hunter Valley more fully on page 302.

MUDGEE

At about the same time, pioneers pushed up into the mountains to the west of the Hunter and founded the community of Mudgee. Helped by an influx of German settlers and by a minor gold rush, vineyards were well-established by the end of the 19th century. But, as with the other New South Wales regions, the 1893 depression, then Federation in 1901 – with the lowering of trade barriers between States and the flood of cheap wines from South Australia – virtually did for the region. It wasn't until the 1960s that Mudgee began to get up on its feet again.

It all seems so idyllic here at the Broke Estate Vineyards in the Hunter Valley. The grapes ripen in the summer sun, the Brokenback mountains look on under a perfect azure sky. But the Hunter is subtropical and, more often than not, cyclonic storms will rage down the East Coast and drench the vines – normally just before harvest.

Now, its qualities are being realized. Hunter Valley wineries often used to rely on Mudgee wine for blending in the past, because the acid soils produce fat, strongly flavoured reds and whites. In addition, Mudgee's position at over 450m (1500ft) above sea level on the western slopes of the Great Dividing Range gives easily enough heat to ripen any grape variety, yet protects the vines from late summer rains. The growers were sufficiently proud of their individuality that they organized one of Australia's first appellation systems. My chief problem with Mudgee has not been with the fruit, but with the quality of the winemaking. Things look good in the vineyard, the grapes taste great on the vine, but the flavours in the bottle are solid at best and prehistoric at worst. Lack of leadership has meant lack of healthy competition. But Rosemount has at last kick-started the modern age with some fine wines called Hill of Gold and Blue Mountain. It is now up to the major players, like Orlando, as well as individual estates, to follow suit.

COWRA

Heading down off the mountains towards the interior, we come to the great irrigated vineyards of the State. The highest quality wine so far has come from Cowra on the Lachlan River, which has long been recognized as a prime source of fruit. The first Petaluma Chardonnays, beginning with the 1977, were made from Cowra fruit and immediately exhibited a fat, lush style – quite unlike the modern Petaluma Chardonnays, whose fruit is sourced in the ultra-cool Adelaide Hills. Even so, they lasted well, and their quality persuaded industry legend the late Len Evans to make the leap into Chardonnay when 40ha (99 acres) came up for sale in 1981. His Rothbury Cowra Chardonnay, with its rich, creamy style, became one of the winery's most successful wines.

One of the area's great virtues is its relentless reliability. The soil is sandy and free-draining, the sun shines throughout the summer, with almost no interruption from rain, and the Lachlan River has historically provided an abundant source of irrigation water. Total reliability. But there's more. The large irrigated vineyards along the Murray River, which provide the bulk of Australia's wine grapes, are generally owned by thousands of smallholders. Their sole objective is to produce as large a crop of reasonably healthy grapes as possible, get them picked as early as they can – regardless of whether or not the grapes are truly ripe – to minimize the risk of disease and bad weather, and bank the money. Much of the region's potential is thus never realized.

But Cowra has been developed largely by major wine companies like Rothbury and Orlando's Richmond Grove, or quality-orientated, large-scale growers. With the winemakers having full control over the ripeness of crop, Cowra fruit, and Chardonnay in particular, has created a totally recognizable style of its own.

RIVERINA

Riverina, in the new zone of Big Rivers, centred on the town of Griffith, way down in the scorched flatlands, is the most significant wine region in New South Wales in terms of the volume of wine it produces. It taps into the river system of the Murrumbidgee, a tributary of the Murray, to produce well over 100,000 tonnnes of grapes from about 5500ha (13,590 acres) of featureless land. It adjoins the large Sunraysia area which straddles the state of Victoria. Riverina's and Cowra's future will depend upon snowmelt waters continuing to fill the rivers in sufficient volume.

One special product of Riverina is the remarkable botrytis-affected sweet Semillon which the De Bortoli winery pioneered and others have followed. The grapes are left to hang on the vines for up to two months after the normal vintage date, and the quality often matches that of a top Sauternes from Bordeaux.

CANBERRA

With the transport efficiency of the late 20th century, Canberra – Australia's newest city, and its capital – didn't need its own vineyards unlike the cities developed in the 1800s, but that didn't stop a few impassioned inhabitants developing some in the 1970s.

Because you can't buy land freehold within the Australian Capital Territory (ACT), the vineyards have been developed just outside the ACT in New South Wales – mostly to the north-east near Lake George and to the north around Murrumbateman. The summer days are hot and dry, and not tempered by sea breezes, yet the nights are cold. The autumn, however, is cool and frequently wet. The soils and subsoils are not water retentive so irrigation is vital. Because of the cold night air moving north from the Australian Alps snowfields, sites have to be selected with care to avoid spring frosts that can occur as late as November. If this all sounds a bit negative, I'd have to say, if Canberra weren't there, these vineyards probably wouldn't be there either, but wineries like Lark Hill, Clonakilla and Doonkuna Estate have had success with Riesling, Chardonnay and, surprisingly, with Cabernet Sauvignon and Shiraz. And it is not all small-scale – Hardys has installed a sizeable vineyard and 2000-tonne winery here called Kamberra.

OTHER VINEYARD AREAS

Although Sunraysia on the Murray River does have substantial vineyards, most of the action is across the river in Victoria. Other developments in New South Wales have been more concerned with trying to locate high-quality sites, despite challenging climatic

WINE REGIONS AND SUB-REGIONS

Murray Darling	Gundagai	Southern Highlands	Hastings River
Swan Hill	Canberra District	Shoalhaven Coast	OVER 200M (656FT)
Riverina	Hilltops	Mudgee	OVER 500M (1640FT)
Perricoota	Cowra	Hunter	
Tumbarumba	Orange	1. Broke Fordwich	

conditions. In particular, the state's winemakers hanker after a source of cool-climate fruit, with the most successful attempts being in Tumbarumba, Hilltops and Orange.

Tumbarumba in the Snowy Mountains, way down south near the border with Victoria, is producing some outstanding Sauvignon Blanc and Chardonnay, and Pinot Noir has great potential. It has red volcanic soils planted at over 750m (2500ft), and granite soils in slightly warmer, yet still cool, sites at around 550m (1800ft). The reputation of Hilltops near Young has been established by McWilliam's Barwang wines. It is warm enough for most of the New South Wales varieties, but the higher altitude and the well-drained soils encourage a slow, regular ripening season with consequently intensified fruit flavours.

There are also successful vineyards around Orange, and though we're getting back into the spring frost problems that deterred settlers in the 19th century, the region has thrived. Bloodwood Estate were the pioneers in the 1980s producing remarkable cool reds and whites, and many have followed including ex-Rosemount whizzkid Philip Shaw whose reds and whites are the quintessence of cool. Big business is also here with the vast Little Boomey vineyard development.

Perhaps the most bizarre vineyard development is in the Hastings Valley near Port Macquarie, north of Newcastle. Here one of Australia's hottest vineyard sites combines with the highest recorded rainfall – most of it during the ripening season – but somehow Cassegrain manages to make interesting wine, mainly from the French hybrid Chambourcin which is resistant to mildew.

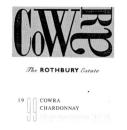

The ROTHBURY Estate

19 90 COWRA CHARDONNAY

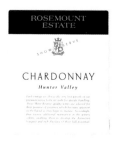

ROSEMOUNT ESTATE

CHARDONNAY
Hunter Valley

HUNTER VALLEY

RED GRAPES
Mainly Shiraz and Cabernet Sauvignon are grown, with some Merlot, Pinot Noir and Malbec.

WHITE GRAPES
Chardonnay and Semillon are the most important grapes, but there is some decent Verdelho and Sauvignon Blanc.

CLIMATE
The summer heat is tempered by cloudy skies. Autumn is often wet. The Upper Hunter Valley needs irrigation.

SOIL
The rich, red volcanic loams and the alluvial soils near the Goulburn River are the best. The poor-draining, heavy clay subsoils are tough going.

ASPECT
Vines are planted next to the Goulburn River in the Upper Hunter Valley. Lower Hunter vineyards are on the lower slopes of the Brokenback Range, or on the valley floor.

LAKE'S FOLLY
HUNTER VALLEY
1999
WINE OF AUSTRALIA
750 ml

MOUNT PLEASANT
ELIZABETH
HUNTER VALLEY SEMILLON 1996
PRODUCE OF AUSTRALIA

I STILL HAVE VIVID MEMORIES of the first time I realized just how special the Hunter Valley could be. Some roaming wine gypsy I knew had strayed far from his usual European pastures and ended up in Sydney. Eventually escaping with liver and limb more or less intact, he'd brought some wine back to London and decided to try it out on a group of us young whipper-snappers. Tyrrell's Vat 47 1973. A Chardonnay – well, mostly Chardonnay, with a little Semillon too, I shouldn't wonder. I can still see the astonishing day-glo, greeny-gold colour, all fiery-eyed and demanding of attention, and the sensual viscous texture of the wine that swirled lazily round the glass like a courtesan interrupted during her siesta.

And the flavour. I'd been brought up on French Chardonnay from Burgundy. I knew and understood the generally austere but fascinating, if intellectual, pleasure of those pale, oatmeal- and mineral-scented whites from the centre of France. Then there was my first mouthful of Vat 47. The explosion of peaches and honey, hazelnuts, woodsmoke and lime sent stars bursting over my palate. In that single split second I foresaw the greatness Australia could bring to Chardonnay, and Chardonnay could bring to Australia.

Yet what I was tasting was not some classic wine style, carefully honed over the generations. This was only the third vintage of the Hunter Valley's very first varietal Chardonnay. And its brilliance was even more astounding because you shouldn't really be able to create exciting wine in the Hunter at all. Ask any modern vineyard consultant about establishing a vineyard in the Hunter Valley, and he'd say you must be barmy even to consider it. So what's going on? Have all the great Hunter wines of the last 150 years been made by madmen? Or do they know something we don't?

For a start, you've got the heat against you, the rainfall patterns against you, and, except in a few charmed sites, the soils are against you, too. But, as Hunter winemakers have shown, if you're stubborn and obsessive – and, well, yes, slightly mad – you can produce wines of quite shocking individuality and quality.

UPPER HUNTER VALLEY
The Hunter Valley divides, in wine terms, into two parts as it snakes inland from Newcastle. The Upper Hunter is to the north around Denman. Its vineyards have to fight with powerful local coal-mining interests when they want to expand. Although initially planted in the 19th century, it only achieved any prominence in the 1980s and still has only a few major wineries, including Rosemount Estate and Arrowfield.

The area was heavily planted in the 1960s' and '70s' wine boom, mostly on rich, alluvial soil with irrigation keenly applied. But the grape most often planted was the black Shiraz, whose reaction to such fertile, high-yielding conditions was to produce limp, lifeless wine, only half-way to red. White wines fare much better under these conditions, and fleshy Chardonnays and Semillons are commonplace. But so far, only one vineyard has proven to be world-class – Rosemount's Roxburgh, a weathered limestone and basalt outcrop in the middle of pastureland between Denman and Muswellbrook. In the 1980s, early vintages of its sensational Chardonnay did more than any other wine to propel Australian Chardonnay – and therefore Australia itself – to the forefront of the New World wine revolution that was then unfolding.

LOWER HUNTER VALLEY
The drive southwards from the Upper Hunter to the Lower Hunter exposes the contradictions of this area as a grape-growing centre. You'll see more signposts to coal mines than vineyards. The black gold of coal or the white gold of Chardonnay? Until you descend into the heart of the Lower Hunter, the argument is still fierce. And

even then the area is centred around Cessnock, a town more dominated by coal than wine for most of its existence, though now the grape has pretty well won the battle of vine versus mine. Spread out to the west and north-west are numerous vines, the healthiest-looking being those that run up to the slopes of the Brokenback Range, and odd volcanic 'pimples' – ridges of weathered basalt typified by Lake's Folly and Evans Family vineyards. These red soils are fertile, well-drained and deep, and capable of producing good crops of high-quality red grapes.

The volcanic outcrops are marvellous soils, but vineyards still have to combat the heat and rain. Lake's Folly and Evans Family face south, away from the sun, and the best sites on the Brokenback slopes are those up as high as 400m (1300ft) at Mount Pleasant and the properties set back on the slopes of Mount View, west of Cessnock. These escape the warm westerlies, get a little more rain, but have the slopes to drain freely, and often ripen up to two weeks later than the vines on the valley floor.

FORMER VINEYARD AREAS
There are also some alluvial flats with sturdy-looking vines, but then you notice fields full of weary, stunted vines and great patches of barren land where you think – funny, I could have sworn there was a vineyard there. There was. But it's been ripped out after years of failing to provide a half-decent crop. The problem is that most of the good topsoil has been washed away. The thick, impermeable pug clays that remain are difficult to work and hardly support any crop, let alone the vine. Yet thousands of acres were planted in the mad Vine Rush of the 1960s on this hopeless yellow-orange clay. Rothbury Estate had a 180-ha (445-acre) vineyard here, which the late Len Evans, its founder and chief executive until the Mildara Blass 1998 takeover, admitted was 'a total cowpat' anyway.

HUNTER VALLEY CLIMATE
Because the Hunter is relatively far to the north and close to the hotter inland zones, the climate does at first glance seem oppressive. Yet the quality of wine made here means that there must be some compensating factors. There are. Though Cessnock would appear, statistically, to get appreciably more heat than Montpellier in the broiling south of France, the warm spring and autumn temperatures – that don't actually affect the grapes' ripening – distort the figures. Heat undeniably does build up fast until early afternoon, but because the Great Dividing Range dips to the north and west of Cessnock, the warm interior sucks cold air in up the Hunter Valley. Most summer afternoons there's cloud cover over the Hunter and, in any case, being closer to the equator than Montpellier means relatively shorter summer days. The humidity is also important in reducing vine stress.

But water is a problem in the Hunter. There's not enough when you want it and too much when you don't. The annual rainfall of 700mm (27in) would be fine if it fell at the right time, but it tends to get dumped at the end of summer, often just before the Shiraz grapes are ripe. You also need good winter rains to fill the irrigation dams, since borehole water here is far too saline, but winter droughts are frequent. When rain does arrive in January and February, cyclones come in off the Coral Sea and bang up against the mountains of the Great Dividing Range, dumping their watery load on the vines. When they hit Queensland, Hunter winemakers know they've got two or three days to harvest, regardless of ripeness, before the rains reach them. You can make great Semillon from underripe grapes, fair Chardonnay, and even passable Cabernet, but you just can't transform a rain-bloated Shiraz into a classy red, and no matter how hard you try, you'll only break your heart.

WHERE THE VINEYARDS ARE *The Hunter River is just visible on the map, snaking briefly in and out of the top righthand corner. It continues to run from the west, just above the top of the map. All the original important vineyards were established on these fertile river flats. You can see just one remaining example on the bend of the river at Wyndham Estate.*

However, from the 1860s onwards, plantings shifted south and west, towards the slopes of the Brokenback Range, an isolated ridge west of Cessnock, where rich, red, volcanic loams provide that unusual combination – high quality and high volume. Occasional outcrops of red volcanic soil in the Valley also offer these conditions, as at Lake's Folly and Evans Family vineyards (see map). The south-facing aspect also helps by reducing exposure to the hot sun.

The little Mount View Range, which lies directly to the west of Cessnock, is also particularly suited to vines.

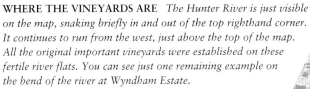

SELECTED WINERIES

1. Wyndham Estate	17. Meerea Park
2. Margan Family	18. Hope Estate
3. Pendarves Estate	19. Tower Estate
4. Tempus Two	20. Pepper Tree
5. Keith Tulloch	21. Evans Family
6. Rothvale	22. Lake's Folly
7. Bimbadgen	23. De Bortoli
8. Kulkunbulla	24. Allandale
9. De Iulliis	25. Capercaillie
10. Tyrrell's	26. Lindemans
11. Scarborough	27. Draytons Family
12. McGuigan Cellars	Wines
13. Brokenwood	28. McWilliam's Mount
14. Tamburlaine	Pleasant
15. Thomas Wines	29. Petersons
16. Glenguin	30. Saddler's Creek

LOWER HUNTER VALLEY

TOTAL DISTANCE NORTH TO SOUTH
25KM (15½ MILES)

VINEYARDS

WESTERN AUSTRALIA

RED GRAPES
Shiraz and Cabernet Sauvignon are the main varieties, with much smaller plantings of Merlot, Pinot Noir and Cabernet Franc.

WHITE GRAPES
Chardonnay, Sauvignon Blanc, Riesling and Semillon are used for white wines. In addition, the Swan Valley grows Chenin Blanc, Muscadelle and Verdelho.

CLIMATE
The coastal regions have a maritime climate. Regions further inland and to the north are hotter, drier and more continental.

SOIL
Mainly brown or grey-brown alluvial topsoil, frequently fairly sandy with some gravel.

ASPECT
Vineyards are concentrated on the valley floors or gentle slopes along the coast, although there are some vines in more hilly areas along the Darling Ranges.

Sweet, loveable kangaroos at play? That's not what you'd think if you're a grape-grower; they could have just chewed all the young buds off your vines.

'WINES SHOULD BE RESPLENDENT with generosity; unless a wine can be diluted with an equal volume of water, it wasn't worth making in the first place.' This wonderful remark was made by Jack Mann, the greatest of Western Australia's old-time winemakers. He made wines in the Swan Valley, the hottest serious vineyard area in Australia and one of the hottest in the world. He admitted he never picked his grapes until the sun-baked vine simply had nothing more to offer them, and I've tasted some of the old Houghton White Burgundy wines with which he made his reputation – deep, thick, viscous golden wines, oozing with over-ripeness.

SWAN VALLEY

Until the 1970s, Houghton White Burgundy was the only Western Australian wine to make any impact across the state line, and it is still one of Australia's most popular white wines. It was originally based on Chenin Blanc and contained a significant proportion of Muscadelle until the late 1980s. Now it is a blend of Chenin Blanc (50 per cent), Chardonnay (20 per cent), Semillon (15 per cent), the remainder being Verdelho, Riesling and Muscadelle.

It was about the only shooting star Western Australia had in wine between 1829, when the 'Parmelia' landed to establish the colony, and the late 1970s, when the pioneers of Margaret River began making waves. Yet in the 19th century the Swan Valley had more wineries than any other viticultural area of Australia. As Western Australia never succumbed to phylloxera, there was a boom in plantings during the 1890s as Victoria's vineyards fell to the rapacious aphid. And as usual the discovery of gold and the attendant influx of wealth-crazed, sun-parched prospectors in need of a bit of rest and recuperation didn't do any harm either.

After World War One, numerous Yugoslavs took refuge in Perth, much as they did in New Zealand's North Island. They were doughty winemakers and loyal consumers of their competitors' wares, and dominated the local wine scene which – until the late 1960s – was almost entirely centred on the hot Swan Valley.

And we are talking roasting: the Swan has January and February temperatures that can soar to 45°C (113°F) – hotter than any other serious Australian wine region. Air humidity is very low, further stressing the vines, and summer rainfall is the lowest of any Australian wine district – though occasionally the bulk of it falls in February, bang in the middle of vintage. The Swan gets the most sunshine hours per day as well.

People bake; grapes bake. It would all be too much if it weren't for the afternoon breezes that come belting across the bay from Fremantle, swoop into the Swan Estuary at Perth and then funnel north-east up the valley, sucked across the riverside vineyards by the heat of Australia's desert heart. The best of the Swan vineyards are on river terraces of deep, well-drained young alluvial soils, often with a sandy clay subsoil to conserve winter rains for high summer, though few vineyards nowadays get by without irrigation.

All of this, despite the sea breeze, still sounds a lot more like conditions for fortified wine, rather than table wine. And many experts have predicted that the future of the Swan is in fortifieds. Yet fortifieds belong to the past, not the future of Australian wine, and as Jack Mann proved with his Houghton White Burgundy, something pretty spectacular can be achieved with table wines too.

More technologically driven winemaking, more widespread use of stainless steel, better refrigeration and the use of classier oak has made for significant improvements in the quality of the region's reds over the past decade. Excellent examples can be seen in the wines of Lamont, Talijancich, Upper Reach, Faber, John Kosovich, Sandalford, Moondah Brook, and especially Houghton. The most surprising fact is that whites perform better here than reds. The

reason for this becomes clearer when we look at the varieties planted. Chenin Blanc has by far the largest acreage, followed by Chardonnay, Verdelho and Semillon. Chenin's great ability is to retain acidity under virtually any conditions. Indeed, it positively courts the heat it so rarely gets in its homeland of France's Loire Valley. Verdelho is used to make Madeira in Portugal, where it retains its attractive honeyed character, despite high temperatures. And Semillon is the best variety in New South Wales' near-subtropical Hunter Valley.

Houghton makes good use of all of these and is still the major Swan producer, but, just as in the other states, when the national and export palate shifts away from overripe or fortified wine styles, so the hotter areas go out of fashion. As the Barossa and McLaren Vale in South Australia show, they can, with a few adjustments to wine style, come back into fashion again. Houghton now sources many of the grapes for its excellent whites from the slightly cooler Moondah Brook vineyard, about 60km (37 miles) north of the Swan Valley at Gingin, as well as from the much cooler Pemberton, Margaret River and Great Southern regions way to the south.

These latter two are the areas now making the running for Western Australia. Both had been considered suitable for grape-growing before. The Lower Great Southern (as it was then called) impressed Jack Mann himself between the two World Wars, and earlier still the Western Australian government had tried to get Penfolds to establish a vineyard at Mount Barker. But Western Australia is a very sparsely populated state. Until recently in Australia, unless there was a decent centre of population nearby, you couldn't establish a wine industry. Perth, with its Swan Valley, was (and is) the only sizeable city in the state.

But the wine industry in the Swan hit trouble in the 1950s. The vineyards were decaying, yields were falling and in 1955 the government called in Professor Harold Olmo (of the University of California at Davis) to find the cause. He did (it was nematodes, a root-nibbling worm, and poor drainage), and he also remarked in passing that he thought the Swan was too hot anyway. He wrote a report in which he recommended planting vines around Mount Barker and Frankland, north of the port of Albany – sites now at the heart of the Great Southern. This was easier said than done.

GREAT SOUTHERN

We're talking about a big area here – the largest recognized agricultural area in Australia – and we're talking about some fairly diverse conditions, as well as taming a wild landscape of jarrah and red gum trees and scrub. Progress was slow, the first vines didn't go in at Forest Hill (near Mount Barker) until 1966, and progress hasn't exactly been quicksilver since. Small vineyards established themselves east of Mount Barker beneath the rounded granite Porongurup Hills, west around Frankland and down near the coast, inland from Denmark and Albany.

Most of these are on gravelly sandy loams, though these soils may well be underpinned by impermeable clay subsoils, inhibiting drainage. The temperatures around Mount Barker and Frankland are fairly similar to those of the Médoc in Bordeaux – which is as cool as Western Australia gets – and this results in good, dark but lean Cabernet styles and, interestingly, lovely lean Rieslings as well.

Porongurup vineyards are cooler because the slopes are planted up to 350m (1150ft) and this can slow ripening by a good week, which serves to intensify the fruit of the Cabernets and Rieslings. Coastal vineyards between Albany and just west of Denmark benefit from cooler days and warmer nights because of the ocean's influence, though some good vineyards near Denmark face north and are sheltered from the sea. The vines also get more rain, but this is a plus in a dry state, since the extra usually falls outside the March to April harvest period. Piercing cool flavours are again the order of the day, with even some good Pinot Noir rearing its head near Albany and Denmark.

A mixture of tax incentives, better understanding of how to marshal the meagre water supplies – and greatly improved transport systems – have encouraged a considerable increase in vineyards, few of which, except those near Albany, can expect much passing trade. Westfield at 100ha (247 acres) was the first big enterprise and grew fantastic fruit for Houghton. Alkoomi, Plantagenet and Goundrey were founded in the 1970s. But the real surge was in the late 1990s with Frankland leading the way, growing from 300ha (740 acres) to over 1500ha (3700 acres) in little more than five years.

PEMBERTON/MANJIMUP

The twin regions of Pemberton and Manjimup are almost directly to the west of Frankland (an hour's drive away) and just south-east of Margaret River (about two hours away). It was originally established in the late 1980s as Pemberton, but personal disagreements over the name led the Geographic Indicators Committee to split the region into two – a decision that has little support among local vignerons.

There are viticultural differences between them. Pemberton is cooler, has fewer sunshine hours, more rainfall and higher humidity. Manjimup has mostly gravelly soil. Pemberton has some gravel, but also a lot of slow-ripening fertile loams.

No clear picture has yet emerged about which varieties most suit which area. John Gladstones recommends the Cabernet varieties, Shiraz and Chardonnay for Manjimup, and Pinot Noir and the Cabernets (especially Franc) and Merlot for Pemberton. Brian Croser of Petaluma, which owns the large Smithbrook vineyard, is confident that the Bordeaux varieties will suit Pemberton. But Bill Pannell (now at Picardy, but founder of Moss Wood, one of Margaret River's great vineyards) believes Pinot Noir and Chardonnay will make the region's reputation. For now, Cabernet Sauvignon, Merlot, Pinot Noir and Shiraz are the most important reds, while Chardonnay dominates the whites, followed by Sauvignon Blanc, and small amounts of Semillon and Verdelho.

MARGARET RIVER

More crowded, more inhabited and more organized is the Margaret River region. Here Southern Ocean influences meet those of the Indian Ocean, and the natural potential which results has already been exploited by brilliant winemakers and self-publicists alike. As it is now Western Australia's most high-profile and successful area, I talk about it separately over the page.

GEOGRAPHE

This is a diverse region covering the coastal plain near Bunbury and Capel, the dairy country round Harvey, the Ferguson Valley in the Bunbury hinterland and the orchard and farmlands of Donnybrook between Bunbury and Bridgetown. In the last decade, vineyards have been planted apace – partly fuelled by tax incentives.

The coastal strip from Capel to Harvey has a mix of sandy soils and fertile, brown loams, and a climate tempered by the sea. Merlot, Chardonnay and Verdelho do best here. The Ferguson Valley and the hills behind Harvey have vineyards 250–300m (850–1000ft) above sea level, with a more moderate climate and about 10 per cent more rainfall than those on the flat. The soil is granitic gravel over clay loam and retains water better than the alluvial sands nearer the coast. Shiraz, Merlot, Chardonnay,

Semillon and Sauvignon Blanc are good – there's even some Nebbiolo. Near Donnybrook, vineyards occupy the gentle slopes of the Darling Ranges, where fertile soils contain granite and ironstone gravel. This warm area is particularly good for Shiraz, Cabernet Sauvignon, Zinfandel and Grenache. The region's major winery is Capel Vale which sources fruit from throughout the state. Willow Bridge is the major player in the Ferguson Valley.

BLACKWOOD VALLEY AND PEEL

The small Blackwood Valley region centred on Boyup Brook, Bridgetown and Nannup has about 50 vineyards, five of which produce wines under their own label. For now, the stand-out wines are red, especially Shiraz and Cabernet Sauvignon. Chardonnay is the most widely planted white, with small amounts of Sauvignon Blanc and Semillon. North of Geographe, Peel has vineyards of almost talcum powderiness on the grey Tuart sands, that run almost up to Perth's southern suburbs. There've been vines here since 1857, and Peel Estate grows an eclectic range of wines.

PERTH HILLS

The other small region is the Perth Hills which are, in effect, the Darling Range. These overlook Perth from 20–30km (12–18 miles) inland, and the wooded valleys have vineyards established at between 150–400m (500–1300ft) above sea-level. Sea breezes blowing in across the range's western escarpment reduce daytime temperatures; by contrast, warm sea air stops the temperature dropping too much at night. The hilly, irregular nature of the valleys creates widely differing mesoclimates that, at their coolest, ripen grapes two to three weeks later than those in vineyards in the nearby Swan Valley flats. Soils are good, with a fair amount of gravelly loam, and rainfall is high – but almost all of it is in the winter. If you've got storage dams for spring and summer irrigation, that's no problem; but if you haven't, those gravelly soils will be too free-draining to raise a crop.

Leeuwin Estate in Margaret River was one of the first Australian wineries to produce world-class Chardonnay. Its Art Series Chardonnay is still superb wine.

MARGARET RIVER

THE MARGARET RIVER might never have been discovered as a fine wine vineyard area had it not been for a clutch of beady-eyed local doctors. They saw a couple of reports in the mid 1960s by a Dr John Gladstones that the Margaret River had unusually close climatic analogies with Bordeaux, but with less spring frost, more reliable summer sunshine, and less risk of hail or excessive rain during ripening.

For some reason, Australian doctors right across the nation have never been able to resist such pronouncements. First Dr Tom Cullity at Vasse Felix, then fellow doctors Bill Pannell at Moss Wood and Kevin Cullen of Cullen Wines, planted vineyards that were to form the heart of the Margaret River region right from the start. Indeed, Margaret River went on to establish itself as a remarkably versatile, if somewhat capricious, cool-climate region which was good as any in Australia. But Bordeaux? Well, yes and no.

In fact Dr Gladstones was supposed to be doing research on lupins – rather the same as Cullity and Co. were supposed to be keeping the locals hale and hearty – but his good luck was that the legendary Jack Mann at Houghton vineyard in the Swan Valley let him use a spare couple of acres of land next to the winery cellars for his lupin experiments. Lupins are all very well, but the ever-open cellar door at his neighbour's winery began to weave its magic on the doctor and distract him from his original research. The possibilities in Western Australia for fine wine, as yet barely touched upon by winemakers in the torrid Swan Valley, began to take up more and more of Dr Gladstones' time.

A visiting Californian, Professor Olmo, had already suggested in 1956 that the far south of the state, near Mount Barker and Rocky Gully, would make a high-quality vineyard site. Gladstones thought the area on the south-west coast, about 130km (80 miles) further north, between Cape Leeuwin and Cape Naturaliste, would be warmer and more predictable in weather and more flexible in the varieties of grapes that could be grown. He felt the Great Southern Region, with its cool, southerly maritime influence could indeed match Bordeaux's cooler regions, but that the Margaret River, influenced by the Indian Ocean to the west, could match the warmer Bordeaux regions of Pomerol and St-Émilion. The added advantage for Margaret River was that it was an area free of the risk of frost and rain at vintage that so often spoiled things in Bordeaux. It was these thoughts that galvanized the local winemaking doctors into action.

Yet there are problems, and the most intractable is wind. Sea breezes are crucial for cooling down vines in many areas of Australia, but these are gales we're talking about – especially in spring – when salt-laden winds power in off the Indian Ocean and can crucially affect the vine as it attempts to flower and set a crop. Given the fact that the winters are some of the mildest in Australia, vines are likely to wake up early and the early-budding Chardonnay and Merlot often get into trouble.

And then there's the wildlife. Those lovely mysterious stands of tall Karri gums are home to legions of kangaroos. Delightful, shy little roos; how we Europeans wish they were less timid so that we could feed them lettuce leaves from the palms of

NORTHERN MARGARET RIVER

TOTAL DISTANCE NORTH TO SOUTH 39.5KM (24½ MILES)

▦ VINEYARDS

N

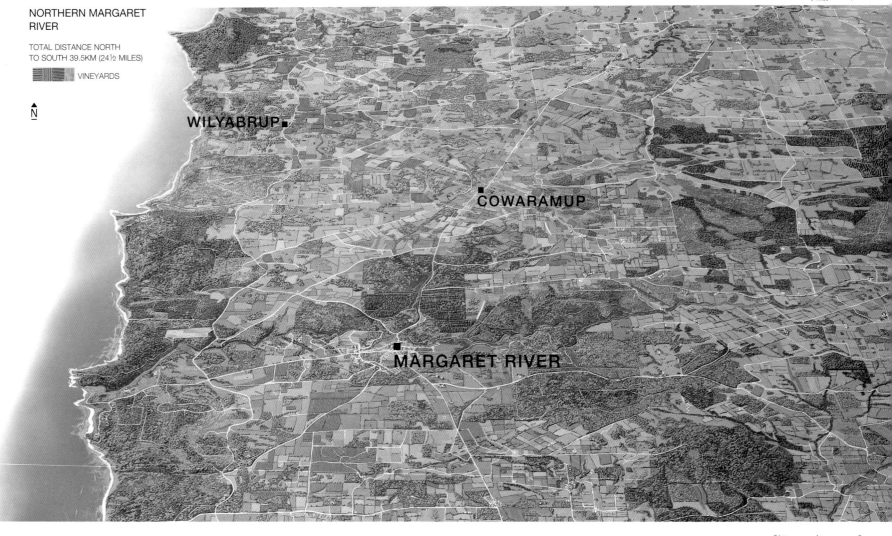

WILYABRUP ▪

▪ COWARAMUP

▪ MARGARET RIVER

0 km 1 2
0 miles 1

our hands. Try giving that sentimental tosh to a grape grower in springtime when the little fellas have nipped out overnight and chewed all the emerging buds off his vines. And don't talk to him about how divine those lime green parrots are fluttering and cawing among the vines. They are rapacious pests that munch away at the grapes for nourishment and then, replete with his best Cabernet, chew through the vine branches for recreation. And don't mention silver-eyes either, sweet little migratory birds that find the netting protecting the vines rather good for nesting in – and anyway they're tiny enough to wriggle through and devour the crop under the nets.

Such problems rarely occur in Europe – or in traditional Australian wine districts. But where new vineyards are carved from virgin land there are bound to be upsets. In such thinly populated regions as Margaret River, the relatively small areas of vines and grapes make easy targets for hungry wildlife. Interestingly, the only effective defence against the yearly silver-eye invasion is a natural one: their favourite refuelling food is the nectar of red gum blossom. When the gums flower on time, the silver-eyes relish this feast, but if flowering is late, they turn to the sugar-sweet grapes.

But it does all seem to be worth it. Although the region only contributes 3 per cent of Australia's wine grapes, it commands over 20 per cent of the premium wine market. Across a wide spectrum of wines, the quality of Margaret River fruit sings out loud and clear: from mighty, gum-scented Pinot Noirs to classic Cabernets and Chardonnays, from unnervingly French, yet tantalizingly individual Semillons and Sauvignons to positively un-Australian Shiraz and Zinfandel, and even to vintage 'port'.

WHERE THE VINEYARDS ARE *You shouldn't have too much trouble getting casual labour around vintage time in Margaret River. But be warned – it may be very casual, depending on the size of the waves, rather than the ripeness of the grapes, because that long, inviting coastline that you see on the left of the map is one of the greatest surfing beaches in the world. So don't expect the pickers to stay bent over the vines when the waves get up.*

The sea's influence, though, is one of the crucial aspects of Margaret River. That's the Indian Ocean there. It's a warm sea, and the difference between summer and winter temperatures is smaller here than anywhere else in the whole of Australia. But this isn't always a bonus: early-flowering varieties, like Chardonnay, often get lashed by westerly gales just when they are trying to set a crop, and the winds can carry salt miles inland; grapes and salt don't get on. On the other hand, those long, baking, sun-soaked autumns will ripen most varieties of grape to perfection.

The first group of vineyards, those that were established by those doctors in the 1960s, are the ones you can see in the middle of the map. They are still the most important group. It becomes cooler as you head south to below the Margaret River itself, but some of the most famous vineyards are those shown right at the bottom of the map.

At the top, inland from Cape Clairault, is the latest wave of new wineries and vineyards.

VINEYARD AREAS

There were intermittent attempts in the 19th century to plant the area, but Doctors Cullity, Pannell and Cullen really showed the way in the late 1960s and early '70s, when they planted small vineyards in the locality of Wilyabrup, about 15km (9 miles) north of the township of Margaret River, an area which still boasts the most flagship estates in the region. However, some of the highest profile estates – Cape Mentelle, Leeuwin, Voyager and Xanadu – are actually south of the Margaret River around Witchcliffe and Forest Grove. There's also been a lot of vineyard development around Karridale in the extreme south of the region. Here summers are cooler than in the northern plots, although it also benefits from prolonged mild sunny weather into late autumn. And in the far north, around Yallingup, between Cape Clairault and Cape Naturaliste, are wineries such as Amberley, Clairault, Happs and Marri Wood Park. In general average temperatures rise as you move north, and leading estates south of the Margaret River definitely produce wines of a cooler fruit flavour than those to the north.

On the other side of the Bussell Highway, in the north-east, is the former potato-growing area of Jindong. Ex-potato fields are not famous for producing high-quality grapes but these are good, and if they weren't muscling in on the Margaret River name everyone would acknowledge the fact. Several big wine companies have taken advantage of its flat, largely fertile land, plentiful water and moderate climate to plant large vineyards here.

CLIMATE AND SOIL

Soils in the region do differ, but most good vineyard sites in Margaret River are either located on gravels or sands over clay. These tend to drain well – which is fine as long as you've built plenty of dams to store your irrigation water. Of the area's annual 1160mm (46in) rainfall, just 200mm (8in) falls in the all-important growing season – between October and April – when the vines need it most. Efficient irrigation is vital. The intensity of the fruit, and the acid and tannin structure in the wines are the best rebuttal I can think of when people suggest that you can't make great wines using irrigation. With a few outstanding exceptions, such as the excellent Moss Wood, Cullen and Leeuwin, in the Margaret River region you can't make great wines without it.

 RED GRAPES
The main varieties are Cabernet Sauvignon, Shiraz and Merlot.

 WHITE GRAPES
There are substantial amounts of Semillon and Sauvignon Blanc, which are often blended together, and Chardonnay is a close second. There is also some Chenin Blanc and Verdelho.

 CLIMATE
This is a maritime climate, with a coolish growing season and a mild, wet winter. Cold Antarctic currents flowing south of the land mass and westerly winds from the Indian Ocean cool this region and make it more temperate than Perth to the north. Sea breezes are good for preventing overheating, but bad for drying out the soil, sometimes making irrigation necessary. In spring the breezes may reach gale force, damaging early bud break.

 SOIL
The topsoil tends to be sand or gravel, the subsoil is often clay loam. These subsoils have the capacity to retain water, but irrigation is still often necessary.

ASPECT
Vines are planted on low, gentle slopes, at around 40m (130ft) above sea level.

SELECTED WINERIES
1. Amberley Estate
2. Clairault
3. Moss Wood
4. Evans & Tate
5. Woodlands
6. Brookland Valley
7. Pierro
8. Gralyn
9. Cullen Wines
10. Vasse Felix
11. Howard Park
12. Ashbrook Estate
13. Sandalford
14. Willespie
15. Hay Shed Hill
16. Woody Nook
17. Cape Mentelle
18. Xanadu Wines
19. Redgate
20. Voyager Estate
21. Stella Bella
22. Leeuwin Estate
23. Devil's Lair
24. Suckfizzle

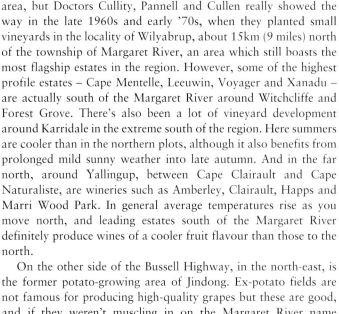

Cape Clairault
JINDONG
WILYABRUP
COWARAMUP
GRACETOWN
Margaret
MARGARET RIVER
PREVELLY
WITCHCLIFFE

TASMANIA

RED GRAPES
Pinot Noir is dominant, with some Cabernet Sauvignon and a little Merlot.

WHITE GRAPES
Chardonnay is the most popular white, followed by Riesling and Sauvignon Blanc.

CLIMATE
Temperatures are lower and humidity higher than in most other Australian wine regions. Windbreaks on seaward slopes protect vines from sea winds.

SOIL
In the north, rich, moisture-retentive clays predominate, and in the south, peaty, alluvial soils.

ASPECT
Strong westerly winds tend to restrict vineyards to the east-facing slopes.

Not all of Australia is hot. You can almost feel the chill in the still air at the St Matthias Vineyard on the river Tamar near Launceston.

UNTIL RELATIVELY RECENTLY, the Tasmanian Department of Agriculture's view was that Tasmania was totally unsuitable for grapes, so why didn't the inhabitants put a bit more effort into somthing safe and traditional – like apples. I don't know whether Burgundy in France is particularly suitable for apples, but the view of Dr Andrew Pirie in the early 1970s, a view which earned him the first viticultural Ph.D. awarded by the University of Sydney, was that certain areas around the Pipers and Tamar rivers were the nearest thing Australia could find to Burgundy. The truth lies somewhere in between.

One of the most difficult facts to accept is that irregularity of vintage quality, ranging from sensational to dismal, has been the norm in the great French vineyards for centuries. But no one in the New World can set up a commercial venture with such a haphazard likelihood of harvesting good fruit. Such a scenario affects red grapes more than white in France, and so it does in Tasmania, particularly in the north, where frequently the red grape crop just doesn't get ripe enough to make good table wine.

A good base for sparkling wine, however, needs to be acidic and this is where Tasmania has really made its mark. Many of the very best Australian sparklers are coming from here – Pirie, Clover Hill, Jansz, Arras and Stefano Lubiana are all beautifully made, complex and exciting. But that wasn't what the pioneers intended to make.

VINEYARD AREAS

Vineyards were established in Tasmania in 1823, before either Victoria or South Australia, but they were short-lived and weren't revived until the 1950s. It was in 1974 that the modern era really began with Pirie's establishment of Pipers Brook on iron-rich but relatively exposed soils to the north-east of Launceston. The annual heat summation is generally similar to that of Burgundy's Côte de Nuits, but aggressive winds off the Bass Strait mean that only the best sites will really ripen grapes well. Within a few miles, temperatures as cool as Germany's Mosel Valley can be found. This would explain why the area is most successful at Riesling and sparkling wine base. Ah, sparkling wine base. You hear that phrase

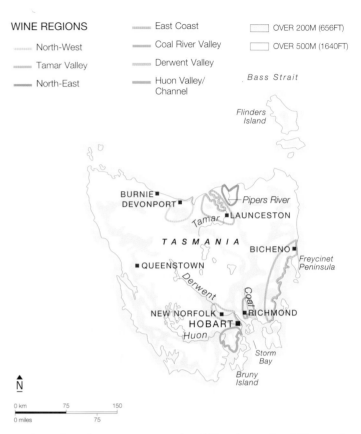

WINE REGIONS

East Coast

North-West

Coal River Valley

Tamar Valley

Derwent Valley

North-East

Huon Valley/Channel

OVER 200M (656FT)

OVER 500M (1640FT)

again and again as you tramp the chilly vineyards of Tasmania. 'What's that over there?' Pause. 'Sparkling wine base.' 'And what's that.' Pause. 'Er...sparkling wine base.' And then you spot some lovely protected, steep, north-facing slope, and before you can ask, the grower is bubbling over with excitement – this little precious patch makes his top Chardonnay, or Pinot Noir, or whatever. When you're up in the north of the island, you just have to stop dreaming about making the great Bordeaux and Burgundies of France and settle for making another French classic – Champagne, with an Aussie accent. Tassie fizz from the north is superb. And although there are also a few fine Chardonnays and Pinot Noirs, the other wines from these exposed vineyards that thrill me are the cool-climate stars Gewürztraminer, Pinot Gris and Riesling, all wonderfully fresh and irresistibly fragrant.

The Tamar River running north of Launceston is protected from the winds and warmed by the estuary. This, combined with lower rainfall, allows red grapes to ripen reasonably well now and then, but I've had few convincing examples. In the far south, both the Derwent River Valley and the Huon Valley seem to defy latitude by ripening grapes at least as well as the north, but the power of the southern sun and protection from wind and frost in the river-warmed valleys are the crucial factors. Even so it is still sparkling wine, Riesling and delicate Chardonnays that perform best here.

The only places to ripen Cabernet and Pinot Noir satisfactorily, even excitingly, on a regular basis, are on the east coast and on the Coal River to the south. Eastern vineyards near Bicheno, notably Freycinet, are squeezed behind a bluff that deflects coastal winds and allows the long sunshine hours to have maximum effect. The Coal River is in a rain-shadow north of Hobart, and the long sunshine hours, balanced by cool nights, bring about full-coloured, ripe-flavoured reds and intense whites. With their own Tasmanian Appellation of Origin scheme, the growers are determined to promote their regional individuality but, unless global warming dramatically changes their climate, their best bet for lasting fame remains as a world-class producer of sparkling wine grapes.

QUEENSLAND

THERE WAS A TIME when Queensland produced more than twice as much wine as Western Australia, and even a quarter as much as volume leader South Australia. I don't know what the wine was like, but since it mostly came from Roma, north-west of Brisbane, where the temperature would make a Sahara camel gasp, I suspect it was pretty fierce stuff. There are still a few hectares of vineyards there today, but the centre of Queensland winemaking has long since settled on the high valleys of the Granite Belt, south of Stanthorpe and right on the New South Wales border, which regards itself as a cool-climate area. Well, there's cool and there's cool. If you look at the amount of heat the area generally gets, it's hotter than Rutherglen in North-East Victoria whose torrid conditions are turned to good account, producing sweet fortified wines. The Granite Belt manages to be seen as a table wine region, however, because of the height of its vineyards. Ranging between 700m and 1250m (2296ft and 4101ft) on high plateau land these are some of the highest in Australia.

The growers here also have a fairly late vintage, often from mid-March to mid-April, which is something of an advantage since the same cyclonic storms that drench the Hunter Valley further south in New South Wales often sweep in here, too. The rains can arrive late, in March, in which case they'll cause vintage rain dilution and disruption. But they are just as likely to be earlier, in February or even January, when they cause havoc in the Hunter Valley but don't do too much harm here. In any case, the rolling landscape of the Granite Belt allows winemakers to choose mesoclimates on slopes facing away from the sun and, where these are of the prevalent decomposed granite, they are sufficiently free-draining to cope. Despite all this, the Granite Belt produces some good, rather four-square wines. It may sound fanciful, but I do detect a stony,

mineral quality, in particular in the Cabernet Sauvignons. However, the Shiraz, which was the first classic variety planted here, seems to be more successful, giving quite a beefy, occasionally even scented performance at its best. Semillon leads the whites, but Chardonnay, and interestingly, Verdelho are also very tasty. Granite Belt is by far the largest of Queensland's wine regions, with 890ha (2200 acres) of vines and 55, mostly small wineries.

Considerable plantings have also taken place elsewhere in Queensland so that the state now has a total of 1600ha (3954 acres) of vines. South Burnett, north-west of Brisbane and centred on Kingaroy, is the second most important region. Since the 1990s this area has seen the most most vineyard growth in Queensland, with hundreds of new hectares being planted on land that used to support dairy farming. Quality so far is pretty good and the conditions here are much easier than up in the Granite Belt. Even so it's pretty hot and in summer water stress can be a danger for the vines. The Darling Downs region south of Toowoomba also grows good grapes, particularly reds like Shiraz and Petit Verdot. Then there are occasional tourist area vineyards like Mount Tamborine and Albert River south of Brisbane. Some wineries, particularly on the Gold Coast and Sunshine Coast, either don't grow grapes or buy in grapes or wine from further inland, because it is fairly subtropical out on the coast. And remember – Queensland has 18 million tourists a year and wine tourism is one of the best ways to sell your wine for a decent price. Most of the 180 or so wine producers are located within an easy drive of Brisbane and the tourists on the Sunshine Coast.

With production levels now having overtaken those of Tasmania, perhaps it is time to start taking the state seriously in wine terms.

Preston Peak's steep vineyards south of Toowoomba are over 650m (2133ft) above sea level. The beautiful mountains in the background run for hundreds of miles south into New South Wales and provide numerous excellent sites for vines.

RED GRAPES
Shiraz is the principal red grape, with significant plantings of Cabernet Sauvignon and Merlot.

WHITE GRAPES
Chardonnay, Semillon, Sauvignon Blanc and Verdelho are the most important quality grapes.

CLIMATE
Many of the vineyards are in regions with sub-tropical climates. The coastal vineyards have to contend with humidity and summer heat while the high-altitude ones have to contend with spring frosts. The late vintage avoids the worst of the rains but frost and hail can damage the crop.

SOIL
The soils are generally slightly acid. They can be granitic and sandy grey, or brown-grey soils over a subsoil of white sand and clay. Around Roma, the soil is a rich, sandy, alluvial loam.

ASPECT
The Granite Belt vineyards in the hilly area around Stanthorpe are some of the highest in Australia.

Map

TIMOR SEA

DARWIN

Gulf of Carpentaria

CORAL SEA

TANAMI DESERT

NORTHERN TERRITORY

MACDONNELL RANGES

ALICE SPRINGS

Lake Amadeus

SIMPSON DESERT

SOUTH AUSTRALIA

CAIRNS

TOWNSVILLE

CHARTERS TOWERS

MOUNT ISA

HUGHENDEN

MACKAY

QUEENSLAND

LONGREACH

ROCKHAMPTON

Great Barrier Reef

GREAT DIVIDING RANGE

MARYBOROUGH

Burnett

CHARLEVILLE

ROMA

KINGAROY

TOOWOOMBA

DARLING DOWNS

BRISBANE

MOUNT COTTON

MOUNT TAMBORINE

Barwon

STANTHORPE

WALLANGARRA

N

0 km 250 500
0 miles 250

WINE REGIONS

— South Burnett

▦ Granite Belt

☐ OVER 200M (656FT)

☐ OVER 500M (1640FT)

NEW ZEALAND

Ata Rangi makes Martinborough's most sumptuous Pinot Noir.

The Tutaekuri River in Hawkes Bay borders Sacred Hill vineyard. Warm gravelly soil and sheltering hills crucially aid ripening.

THE DRAMATIC TRANSFORMATION of New Zealand during the 1990s was nothing short of astonishing. From being thought of as a rather quaint, introverted nation at the far side of nowhere down towards the South Pole, New Zealand has become a vibrant, self-confident, exciting place to be. Yes, *exciting*. Has anyone but a sheep farmer ever called New Zealand *exciting* before? *Has* New Zealand ever been exciting before? I can't vouch for what the early settlers thought 200 years ago, but even the most venerable of my present-day New Zealand acquaintances are enjoying the current mood of excitement, while remaining ever so slightly bemused by it all.

And the same goes for its wine industry. Strangely, it seems to have started off well enough. A visiting Frenchman in 1840 enjoyed the local product – which he described as a 'light, white wine, very sparkling, and delicious to taste' (not bad praise from a Frenchman) – an early hint that light whites and sparklers were the styles most likely to succeed. During the 19th century, other good reports of vines and their wines surfaced from time to time but, by the 1860s, temperance societies were lobbying for laws that hedged the wine producer round with more and more restrictions, with the ultimate aim of prohibiting alcohol altogether.

There was a brief period in the 1890s when Hawkes Bay produced some supposedly good-quality wines, but districts were already starting to vote for local prohibition. Indeed, the whole country voted for prohibition in 1919, only for the result to be overturned by the narrowest of majorities, thanks to the votes of servicemen who were returning home from World War One.

Clearly New Zealand society had little regard for its wine industry, so how on earth could it flourish? It didn't. Vine diseases like *oidium* (powdery mildew) were already making life hell in the warmer, more humid areas, and phylloxera was laying waste to vineyards on all sides. Replanting, when it occurred, was either with *Vitis labrusca* – Albany Surprise was the most widely planted variety until the 1960s – or French hybrids, and the production was mostly of thoroughly mediocre fortified wines.

Good fortified wines all come from warm, dry vineyard conditions. Most of New Zealand just isn't like that. When a Royal Commission after World War Two stated that a 'considerable quantity of wine made in New Zealand would be classified as unfit for human consumption in other wine-producing countries', it was a reflection on how low the quality of New Zealand wine had sunk.

But look at the way New Zealand society treated drinking: there were restrictions on every side. You couldn't drink on trains until 1968, in theatres until 1969, at airports until 1970, or at cabaret shows until 1971. It wasn't until 1976 that caterers were allowed to serve drink, or that wineries themselves could sell a glass of wine. The first wine bar licence was granted in 1979, and, good grief, sports clubs couldn't sell drink until 1980!

Although legislation against the 'demon drink' gradually eased, a whiff of disapproval still lingered over the New Zealand wine industry well into the 1980s. Close economic relations with Australia in the late '80s finally forced New Zealand to liberalize its drinking rules at much the same time as a new wave of freemarket politics was sweeping through the country and galvanizing society in general. In 1990, 'dry' areas were abolished, licensing laws were relaxed so that anyone could start a wine business if they wanted to, and supermarkets were given permission to sell wine: they now sell around half of all wine drunk in New Zealand. At last the past is being left behind – a wine past with nothing of value to cherish, a prim colonial legacy with a long expired sell-by date.

If ever there was a wine nation that should look forward and not back, it is New Zealand. Having a past that you are ashamed of can be a marvellously liberating experience. There are no fusty old traditions that you have to try and drag into the modern world; and no cobwebby wine styles stubbornly clung to by faithful consumers. But if you are going to make a fresh start, you have to take care choosing where and how you're going to do it; and New Zealand didn't get it quite right the first couple of times around.

They got the idea right – a cool climate – well, a lot cooler than their near, or rather only, neighbour Australia, in any case. And they realized that no-one in the dispirited industry itself seemed to have much idea about what to do – so they'd better call in a foreign expert. In 1895 an Italian-trained Dalmatian called Romeo Bragato arrived. He gave lots of good advice over the next few years, little of which seems to have been taken.

THE CLASSIFICATION OF NEW ZEALAND WINE

Wine labelling legislation in New Zealand has remained relatively relaxed until now. This is set to change with the introduction of a system to win international confidence by guaranteeing the geographic area stated on a wine label.

- **Geographical denominations** The broadest designation is New Zealand, followed by North Island, South Island or East Coast. These cover regional blends. Next come the 10 or so regions, such as Canterbury, followed by specific localities, and then vineyards.

In the 1960s they once again decided to go for top advice, and this time to act upon it. Not unreasonably, they looked to Germany as their model. The German influence had been important in teaching Australia how to make delicious, dry Riesling wines under difficult conditions. German wine was highly thought of at the time and it seemed that a Southern Ocean Rheingau or Mosel was a feasible objective.

Dr Helmut Becker, their chosen adviser, was an excellent fellow, and a first-rate scientist. But his life's work was to prove that cross-bred grape varieties could be produced which would give the quality of Riesling without any of its drawbacks. He might have recommended wholesale plantings of Riesling, which would probably have led to many outstanding wines. But he didn't. He chose Müller-Thurgau. So the brave new dawn for New Zealand wine, which could have concentrated on creating a new Bernkasteler Doctor, instead set about creating a better Liebfraumilch. Well, they succeeded there. New Zealand Müller-Thurgau pretty quickly became the best in the world – and I wouldn't be surprised if it still is.

But the advice to go for light, Germanic white wines can be seen, in retrospect, to have been short-sighted in the extreme. It is possible superficially to equate cool South Island regions like Central Otago and Canterbury, maybe even parts of Marlborough, with some parts of Germany. But no grapes were planted in these South Island regions in the 1960s. Instead, all the plantings took place in the North Island, whose climate goes from pleasantly Burgundian in the south to subtropical in the north. Of course you can grow Müller-Thurgau in these conditions – and get massive crops of simple flavoured wine from it – but you're never going to create a drink fit for heroes.

New Zealand's heroes were late in coming. The country's social revolution was a tortuously slow affair, and long after Australian and Californian winemakers were touring the world, drinking up every wine experience they could learn from, New Zealanders were still poking about at home. It wasn't until the 1970s that visionaries like John Buck of Te Mata, or the Spence Brothers of Matua Valley began to establish vineyards, and when they did, it wasn't Müller-Thurgau they had in their sights – it was the classic grapes of Burgundy and Bordeaux.

It soon became clear that Chardonnay and Pinot Noir could ripen easily, indeed, that the North Island was mostly too hot for Pinot Noir. Buck was convinced that he could find ways to ripen Cabernet Sauvignon and Merlot in Hawkes Bay. The Spences hit lucky straight away with Sauvignon Blanc. And by 1973, the new era of New Zealand wine was finally ushered in with the planting of the first vines at Marlborough in South Island.

By 1986, there was such a glut of grapes that the government paid growers NZ$6175 per hectare to rip up their vines. Too many people had rushed into the grape-growing market and had mostly chosen to plant high-yielding bulk varieties in fertile soils. As many as 507ha (1252 acres) of Müller-Thurgau alone were grubbed up. Gisborne, Hawkes Bay, Auckland, even the brand new plantations in the South Island, lost substantial areas; all in all, a quarter of the total national vineyard area – 1517ha (3748 acres) – was pulled out.

After the vinepull, the wine industry regrouped and licked its wounds. By the end of the 1980s New Zealand was becoming known worldwide for the quality of its wines and, in particular, its Sauvignon Blancs and Chardonnays, although Riesling, Pinot Noir, Cabernet and Merlot were also making their mark.

Despite the success of other varieties it is undoubtedly the Sauvignon Blancs from those early Marlborough vines that have taken the world by storm and created a new classic wine style so thrillingly different that it has been the standard-bearer for New Zealand ever since. No New Zealand wine had ever tasted like those Sauvignon Blancs from the

South Island. But then, no wine anywhere in the world had ever tasted like them. No previous wine had shocked, thrilled, offended, entranced the world before with such brash, unexpected flavours of gooseberries, passionfruit and lime, or crunchy green capsicum and asparagus spears. They catapulted New Zealand into the front rank of New World wine producers, and the gift she brought to the party was something that even California and Australia had been unable to achieve – an entirely new, brilliantly successful, wine style that the rest of the world has been attempting to copy ever since. New Zealanders now often prefer to talk of their Chardonnays, Rieslings, Merlots or Pinot Noirs, but the world is still thanking them for their Sauvignon Blanc.

PANORAMIC MAPS OF NEW ZEALAND

Hawkes Bay *pages 314–315*
Marlborough *pages 318–319*

WINE REGIONS

NORTHLAND

AUCKLAND

1. Great Barrier Island
2. Matakana
3. Kumeu/Huapai/ Waimauku
4. Henderson
5. Waiheke Island
6. Clevedon/Ihumatao

WAIKATO/BAY OF PLENTY

GISBORNE

HAWKES BAY

WELLINGTON

7. Te Horo

WAIRARAPA

MARLBOROUGH

NELSON

CANTERBURY

8. Waipara

CENTRAL OTAGO

OTHER WINE AREAS

NORTH ISLAND

RED GRAPES
Merlot is comfortably in the lead, with Pinot Noir second and Cabernet Sauvignon a distant third. Syrah is increasing and Cabernet Franc and Malbec follow some way behind.

WHITE GRAPES
Chardonnay rules, covering three times the acreage of second place Sauvignon Blanc. Next come Pinot Gris, Gewürztraminer, Viognier and Riesling.

CLIMATE
The North Island is generally warmer than the South Island, but overall the climate in both is maritime. Rainfall is plentiful and is often a problem during the ripening season when it can lead to rot.

SOIL
Soils range from glacial and alluvial at Hawkes Bay, to loam and clay in the north, and friable gravelly silt around Martinborough.

ASPECT
Vineyard site selection is now carefully considered, after a boom period when poor varieties were planted in many unsuitable places. Most vines are found on flatlands or gently rolling hills, where too high yields are controlled by skilled vine canopy management. And growing numbers of premium-focused vineyards are appearing on sun-drenched, north-facing slopes.

W HAT'S ALL THIS ABOUT NEW ZEALAND being a cool-climate wine region? That's a bit like saying France is a cool-climate wine region: some bits are, to be sure, but some bits are as hot as Hades. And it's the same with New Zealand. Way down in the South of Central Otago it's as cool as Germany's Mosel Valley. But that's 1000km (620 miles) south of the vineyards that lie just north of Auckland. And don't try to draw any conclusion from latitude. Central Otago's latitude is 45° South, about the same as some of the warmer parts of that not particularly cold area, Bordeaux, in the northern hemisphere.

As for the furthest vineyards of the Northland, above Auckland, they're at about latitude 34° South. In the northern hemisphere 34° slices across the top of Tunisia and Algeria. Now it isn't like Tunisia north of Auckland, but there are a fair few vineyards that struggle under the sort of warm, humid conditions that verge on the subtropical, so I think I'm going to leave most of this cool-climate chat until we get to the South Island.

If you want to suggest that New Zealand is a wet-climate wine region, I'll go for that. With the exception of the tiny Wairarapa area near Wellington, which behaves as though it were a virtual extension of Marlborough on the other side of the Cook Strait, and perhaps Waiheke Island out in the bay less than an hour's ferry ride from Auckland, the North Island is a wet place to grow grapes.

And if you want to suggest that it is a wonderfully fertile landscape ideally suited to growing vines, I'll say, yes – fertile soils, lots of sun, lots of rain: you can grow vines the size of peach trees in no time at all. But don't expect a crop of decent grapes fit for making fine wine. The best wines come from small crops, off vines grown in dry areas with infertile, impoverished, free-draining soil, and just the right amount of sun. That's not too much of a problem in the South Island, but in the North, these conditions are few and far between. And the story of how to find such sites – and if you can't, what to do instead – is very much the story of the North Island's wine industry.

Many producers actually started out in the 19th century by growing their grapes in greenhouses. That seems a bit extreme, and could explain why hardly any wineries grew to any size during the 19th century! But the early growers may not have been so dumb. Most of the vines in the North Island do suffer from the weather, particularly around Auckland where most of the early plantings were located.

Though the latitudes should imply hot to very hot conditions, things aren't as simple as that. In Europe, the main maritime influences are the warm Gulf Stream and the warm Mediterranean. New Zealand is set alone among seas strongly influenced by the icy Antarctic currents. Strong prevailing westerly winds continually pummel the west coast. Until you get down to the central mountain ranges that protect Gisborne and Hawkes Bay on the east coast, there is no protection from the westerlies, and the rain clouds happily deposit their loads on the vineyards around Auckland and Northland.

You might get away with this if you were guaranteed a dry autumn. But that's one thing you're not guaranteed in the North Island. If the westerlies don't keep drizzling down on you, you've got the cyclonic depressions of the Pacific to think about. These are likely to move in from the east in the early autumn. Some years you'll have picked your crop, some years you won't have. These cyclonic rainstorms are a particular problem over to the east in Gisborne and Hawkes Bay, which are otherwise well-protected from westerly rain.

Lots of rain, lots of sun – all you need is fertile soil for vines to grow like jungle. Well, with a couple of exceptions in parts of Hawkes Bay and Wairarapa, North Island soil goes from fertile to supremely fertile and that makes it very difficult indeed for quality-minded grape growers. Fertile soils rarely drain well, and they encourage large crops of grapes. Large crops take longer to ripen and – you've got it – up roll those cyclonic depressions brimful of rain just when you're not quite ready!

North Island has a history of autumn downpours, so you have to pick early even if the crop isn't really ripe. For all the negative aspects of having Müller-Thurgau as your major grape variety, it will at least provide you with adequate, mildly fruity wine at low alcohol levels from high crops. Not very ambitious, I admit, but until the 1980s, when producers began to realize something more exciting was possible, it was the mainstay of North Island vineyards.

CANOPY MANAGEMENT
Fertile soils also encourage vigorous leaf growth, and this is a serious problem if you want to progress from hybrids and Müller-Thurgau to the classic grape varieties. Excessive leaf growth shades your fruit, retarding physical maturity in the grapes and causing a lean, green streak to dominate red wine flavours even when the alcohol levels seem acceptable. For a long time, a green leafy streak of acidity was one way of identifying even the best New Zealand reds. To be honest, it can be rather a nice taste, but modern New Zealand winemakers are mostly determined to stamp it out.

Heavy foliage also reduces air movement. In the frequently damp North Island climates, this causes outbursts of bunch rot (*botrytis*) which can ruin the harvest. The desire to make wines suitable for competing in international markets, along with an increasingly demanding domestic market, forced New Zealand's wine industry to look for solutions to these problems. Led by Dr Richard Smart, New Zealand has become the world leader in developing trellising and pruning systems for fertile, warm-air, high-humidity vineyard conditions.

The results have been dramatic. For almost the first time we are seeing red wines of a fully ripe, yet memorably individual, style coming from all parts of the North Island – Auckland, Hawkes Bay, Wairarapa and even, in a few cases, from Gisborne. White wines are achieving far better ripeness without the accompanying botrytis tinge that used to be a mark of much New Zealand Chardonnay and Müller-Thurgau, and the prevailing acidity of the fruit is far better integrated in the wine. Even in cool years like 1995 and 2000, which, throughout most of New Zealand, were about as difficult as vintages can get, those vineyards using modern vineyard techniques still produced fair fruit. With the wholesale replanting necessitated by phylloxera infestation, we're seeing more and more vineyards adapting to the challenging conditions of New Zealand's North Island.

AUCKLAND AND WAIKATO
Nowhere are conditions more challenging than around Auckland. There are now very few plantings in Northland, where subtropical conditions make it difficult to ripen *vinifera* grapes before they rot on the vine. However, the Dalmatians who came to New Zealand to work the Kauri gumfields were good, old-fashioned thirsty Europeans, and many, having saved a bit of money, migrated nearer to Auckland and set up as winemakers. Almost all the traditional wine companies in Northland, as well as several of the newer ones, were founded by families of Dalmatian origin.

The hot, humid weather and the mostly heavy clay soils didn't matter too much when the chief product was fortified sherries and ports. But the swing to fine table wine production has found most of the go-ahead Auckland area wineries sourcing the bulk of their grapes from elsewhere – Gisborne, Hawkes Bay and Marlborough. Even so, there are some vineyards over by the airport to the south, rather more at Henderson just to the north, and a good deal more further up the road at Huapai, Kumeu and Matakana. But finding ways to produce a balanced wine isn't easy. Availability of superior clones helps, as do de-vigorating rootstocks on these soggy clay soils, and various farming methods and trellising systems are designed to control the vines' vigour and produce healthy fruit. All these efforts are producing some outstanding estate-grown wines from companies like Kumeu River and Matua Valley, but most of Auckland's top wines are nonetheless made from bought-in grapes.

Auckland's newest wine region is in Clevedon, about 40 minutes drive south of the city in rolling, verdant farmland near the eastern coast. Here, a few 'lifestyle' producers have established small micro-boutique wineries with a strong focus on Bordeaux-style reds and Chardonnay. Results are variable but, at best, promising. The soils are largely heavy clay, the weather warm, and with the Tasman Sea on one side and the Pacific on the other, humidity is high, but at least that gives cloud cover against the harsh effects of the sun. If we're looking for the region's most consistently exciting estate-grown wines, we may well have to look offshore, out into the Hauraki Gulf to Waiheke Island, a paradise of a place where you can sit on the bluffs above the bay and watch the ferries plying calmly between the island's tiny quays and the bustling port of Auckland – close enough to commute, yet a world away. Vineyards were established here as long ago as 1978, but it was only in the 1990s that the tempo picked up and a swarm of hopefuls began to plant the island's slopes. They were tempted by the nagging New Zealand dream of producing great red wine from the Bordeaux varieties of Cabernet Sauvignon and Merlot. Both Goldwater Estate and Stonyridge were consistently creating deep dry reds with an uncanny Bordeaux-like structure and taste, but it was the 1993 vintage – so cold and mean in most of New Zealand, so deep and lush and intense on Waiheke Island – that persuaded doubters that this truly was an exceptional vineyard site. The remarkable thing is that Waiheke has such a warm dry climate within spitting distance of humid, rain-swept Auckland, but it does. There's very little summer rain, the soils are infertile and free draining, and the surrounding seas create a balmy maritime climate. And it's such a heavenly place to live. Who wouldn't give it a go?

There's even a vineyard out on Great Barrier Island at Okupu Beach. Here, the guy only produces about 100 cases of wine, but hey, if he made any more, he might have to don a suit and tie and leave the reef to try to sell it. Some guys have all the luck.

The small Waikato region south of Auckland is one of the North Island's historic regions, but this rather damp, humid spot is probably better suited to dairy farming. Though there are some large vineyards here, there are few wineries, and much of the crop is made into grape juice. Even so, the Rongopai winery has used the warm, clammy conditions to make some superb botrytis-affected sweet wines.

GISBORNE
Heading east below the Bay of Plenty, there are several wineries but few vineyards, though there is a small vineyard on the pumice soils of Galatea to the south. But it is Gisborne, on Poverty Bay, that we are looking for. Most of the vineyards are sprawled across the Gisborne plains where a deep bed of alluvial silt supplies such fertile soil conditions that varieties like Müller-Thurgau can easily produce 30 tonnes per hectare of acceptable fruit. But the excessive fertility isn't as suitable for higher quality varieties, since it

encourages dense foliage and hefty crops that retard ripening. Chardonnay has still managed to produce high yields of decent fruit due to plenty of sunshine hours and protection from wet westerlies by the Huiarau Mountains. That protection counts for nothing, however, when cyclonic depressions form to the east in autumn. Gisborne has unacceptably high rainfall in the vintage period of February to April, a fact that has deterred most growers from trying red grapes. However, state-of-the-art vineyard management, replacement of phylloxera-infected vines with better clones, and a move into the less fertile hillside sites is turning Gisborne's reputation around. For years people have been talking of the area as New Zealand's Chardonnay capital; some of Auckland's top wineries make their best Chardonnays from selected Gisborne vineyards, and the soft, gentle, ripe quality of most recent releases shows that they may well be right.

WAIRARAPA
Hawkes Bay is way down the coast from Gisborne, and I cover it more fully over the page. But there is one more booming area – Wairarapa just north-east of Wellington. This is centred on the little town of Martinborough, though vineyards are now appearing on the river terraces above Martinborough, as well as further north towards Masterton. If the North Island's weak points are too much rain and excessively fertile soil, the Martinborough region has the answer. Surrounded by mountains to the south-west, west and north-east, it is protected from both summer and autumn rains. And although the land down by the river flats is heavy clay, a series of flat-topped river terraces to the north-east around Martinborough are shallow, gravelly silt over deep, free-draining, virtually pure gravel.

Add to this relatively cool and windy, but rainless, summers and autumns, and a bit of drip irrigation and you have positively Burgundian conditions for great Chardonnay and Pinot Noir. That, despite there being a reasonable amount of Sauvignon Blanc, plus a splash of Pinot Gris, Riesling and a handful of other varieties, is increasingly exactly what you get.

It's not just grape-growing which draws you to Waiheke Island with its warm, dry climate: the yachts in Te Whau Bay show lifestyle is equally important. But just across the water are the vineyards of Goldwater, one of New Zealand's top producers.

Few New Zealand reds get as ripe as this Hawkes Bay blend of Malbec, Merlot and Cabernet Franc from The Terraces, a tiny suntrap of a vineyard above Esk Valley's winery.

HAWKES BAY

 RED GRAPES
Merlot is by far the most widely planted red grape, ahead of Cabernet Sauvignon and Pinot Noir, followed by Syrah.

WHITE GRAPES
Chardonnay is by far the most important white grape, with Sauvignon Blanc in second place. Pinot Gris is catching up.

CLIMATE
This is ideal for high-quality wine production. Regular sunshine ensures full ripening of the grapes and there's optimum rainfall.

SOIL
Almost all the vineyards are planted on alluvial plains, but soil types still vary from well-drained gravel and sandy loam, to fertile, heavier silty loam.

ASPECT
The best vineyards are on free-draining soils of low fertility. Most Hawkes Bay plantings hitherto have been made on flat land, but nearby limestone hills may be found superior in the future.

'WELCOME TO SUNNY HAWKES BAY' the sign says, and they're not kidding. A while ago, I arrived here in March – straight from the heartland of Australia where I'd been boiled and bullied by the merciless sun day after day, but where Factor 30 cream had kept my face, neck and hands a hue somewhere between blancmange pink and butterscotch orange, and not a blister in sight. I had wondered, well, as New Zealand is so much cooler than Australia, will I really need sun lotion in March? But I'd slapped some on anyway and gone off to my first meeting. By late morning I was uncomfortable. By lunchtime I was hurting. By evening my hands were a welter of bright red blisters, so sore I could neither bear the sunlight on them nor soothe them with anything but cool water. Sunny Hawkes Bay? There should be a health warning.

But it's a serious point I'm making here. The sun may not feel hot, but it shines relentlessly at Hawkes Bay. New Zealand is known as the Land of the Long White Cloud, and you can see the clouds piling up near Gisborne to the north. You can watch them follow the coastline down towards Napier, yet a mile or two before the Bay, they head inland to hug the mountain range until, south of Havelock North and Te Mata, they return to the coast. More importantly, the ozone layer is presently extremely thin over the southern Pacific. I've been told that ultraviolet penetration round Hawkes Bay is higher than in any other populated area in the Southern hemisphere. It isn't known precisely what effect this has on grape ripening, whether it aids or impedes photosynthesis, the development of pigment, and the physical maturing of the grapes.

But long before ozone layers were even discovered, Hawkes Bay's blend of long sunshine hours, reasonable rainfall that usually fell at the right times, and availability of large tracts of suitable vineyard land, had made the area New Zealand's most exciting vineyard region. That was at the end of the 19th century. Various vineyards were established, mostly on good, infertile land, and mostly with classic grape varieties, and by 1913 Hawkes Bay was producing a third of New Zealand's wine. Bernard Chambers' Te Mata vineyard in Hawkes Bay was the largest in New Zealand.

However, as elsewhere in New Zealand, phylloxera, prohibition and lack of interest took their toll, vineyards were turned over to *Vitis labrusca* and hybrid varieties, and the heavy Heretaunga river flats were planted in preference to the low-yielding gravel beds. One

man, Tom McDonald, kept the flame of Chardonnay and Cabernet Sauvignon flickering, though mostly in the high-yielding, unsuitable black soils of the plain. But when John Buck visited Tom McDonald in the 1960s, Tom had pointed over to the Te Mata peak and said, 'That's the best Cabernet land you'll get in Hawkes Bay – frost-free, facing north, and free-draining.'

So John bought the old Te Mata property in 1974, and released a Cabernet in 1980 that I remember to this day, and which sparked the revival of Hawkes Bay as a great vineyard area, rather than a provider of bulk grapes like Müller-Thurgau. Hawkes Bay could, once more, enter the contest for New Zealand's premier wine region. It's a battle that can't ever be decisively won, though, because other large areas like Marlborough produce such completely different styles, and tip-top areas like Nelson, Wairarapa or Waiheke Island are a fraction of its size, and so don't bear comparison. Hawkes Bay's reputation relies increasingly on its ability to fully ripen the red Bordeaux varieties and Syrah – not easy in New Zealand – plus an impressive performance in the less challenging arenas of Chardonnay and Sauvignon Blanc. There is still a significant amount of planting on the heavy river flats, but Hawkes Bay's reputation depends on three different areas.

The warmest of these is Bay View and the Esk Valley. It is also the least planted, so far. Nevertheless, conditions are excellent. The bay swoops inwards north of Napier and presses up against the hills. There's not much land, but it's warm: apricot trees are all around and bud-burst comes as much as two weeks ahead of the rest of the Bay. The grapes can really fry on the terraces cut into the hillside, and red Bordeaux varieties romp to ripeness. The Esk Valley joins the sea just north of Bay View, and its well-protected, sandy alluvial soils over gravel enjoy daily sea breezes.

The heart of the Hawkes Bay revival lies in the gravel beds left behind by various rivers flowing into the Bay. Most important of

WHERE THE VINEYARDS ARE *The centre of the valley, between Hastings and Napier, is where most vineyards used to be, but with fertile soils and a high water table, quality was never good and most of the land has reverted to fruit and vegetables. One of the commonest sights now is a long line of poplars acting as a windbreak for kiwi fruit orchards. North of the airport, Bay View and the Esk Valley don't have that many vines, but Bay View is a sun-trap, and the sandy alluvial soils over gravel in the sheltered Esk Valley are excellent for grapes.*

The real action is happening along the Tutaekuri and Ngaruroro rivers. Their rushing waters have scoured parts of the valley floor clean of soil and silt until there's almost nothing but gravel left, and the rivers have also changed paths in the past, leaving great swathes of gravel ripe for vineyards. This is particularly obvious in the Gimblett Gravels area where 65 per cent of the total plantable area of 800ha (1977 acres) is now filled with vines as planting fever runs its course. The best southern sites are east of Havelock North below the Te Mata peak, where several of the vineyards for Te Mata's outstanding wines are situated, but there are also good largely unexploited sites in the Tukituki Valley where, once again, the river has scoured the land of its topsoil, leaving bare gravel beds.

SELECTED WINERIES

1. Sileni Estates
2. Alpha Domus
3. Ngatarawa
4. Trinity Hill
5. Te Awa Farm
6. Unison
7. Stonecroft
8. Sacred Hill
9. Matariki
10. Crossroads
11. C J Pask
12. Church Road (Montana)
13. Mission
14. Crab Farm
15. Esk Valley
16. Brookfields
17. Vidal
18. Askerne
19. Te Mata
20. Clearview
— GIMBLETT GRAVELS AREA

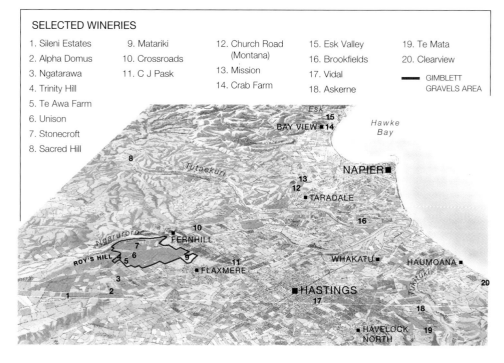

these are the Tutaekuri and the Ngaruroro. It's worth driving along and across these rivers to gaze on some of the purest gravel beds you are ever likely to see. Only the best bits of Margaux in Bordeaux get anywhere near them and yet here they stretch, mile upon mile, westwards up into the hills. Get out of the car and tramp through the vineyards next to Highway 50 and the Gimblett Road and you're walking along the old river-bed itself. Half the time there's no soil at all – just ashen gravel everywhere, with an aquifer running beneath to provide as much irrigation as you could want.

In 2001 a group of 34 wineries and grape growers banded together to define their own appellation based on an 700-ha (1730-acre) plot of this gravelly soil that produces some of Hawkes Bay's finest wines. 'Gimblett Gravels', as the new area is known, is claimed to be up to three degrees warmer than most other areas in the Bay during the day in summer and autumn. If you see 'Gimblett Gravels' on a wine label, at least 95 per cent of the grapes must be from there.

Gimblett Gravels' spokesman, Steve Smith MW, describes the area – which includes land along Gimblett Road, Highway 50, Fernhill and Roy's Hill – as 'the G-spot of Hawkes Bay'. Land prices here have increased 15-fold in the past decade. There's an air of feverish activity along the Ngaruroro at the moment as all the major players in New Zealand are planting like mad to make sure of their share of what they rightly see as Kiwi red wine heaven. Much of the land is virtually hydroponic and nothing survives without irrigation. Indeed, the gravel can be so pure that nutrients sometimes have to put back to avoid the wines turning out with all the right technical figures, but tasting dull.

The thing about such free-draining soil is that it hands control back to the winemaker: crops can be regulated and vines trellised to maximize the sun. But the weather still comes into it. Normal weather patterns at Hawkes Bay are like Bordeaux in a good year, albeit with slightly lower maximum temperatures, but a larger spread of sunny days and less rain. You can pretty much rely on a dry warm autumn (though cyclones in 1988 and 2001 deluged the vineyards at vintage time). The real cauldron is around Fernhill where even Syrah ripens, and there's a tiny parcel of Zinfandel. As you head up the valley past Roy's Hill and west to Riverview (off the map), the cooling influence of the mountains delays budding and ripening by a good week, but means increasingly good conditions for Pinot Noir and Riesling.

The Tutaekuri river cuts its way through the hills north of the Ngaruroro and much of its course is protected from maritime winds. The same gravelly conditions exist here and also in the Tukituki Valley to the south-east and in outcrops near Havelock North and the Te Mata peak. But the south side of the bay is typically shallow alluvial soils over impenetrable pug clays. This terrain is harder to control than pure gravel, but restricts yields and can produce fine wines. Te Mata's best vineyards are either on tan-coloured, gravelly terraces ('red metal'), or loess over limestone and sandstone.

HAWKES BAY

TOTAL DISTANCE
NORTH TO SOUTH
35KM (21½ MILES)

VINEYARDS

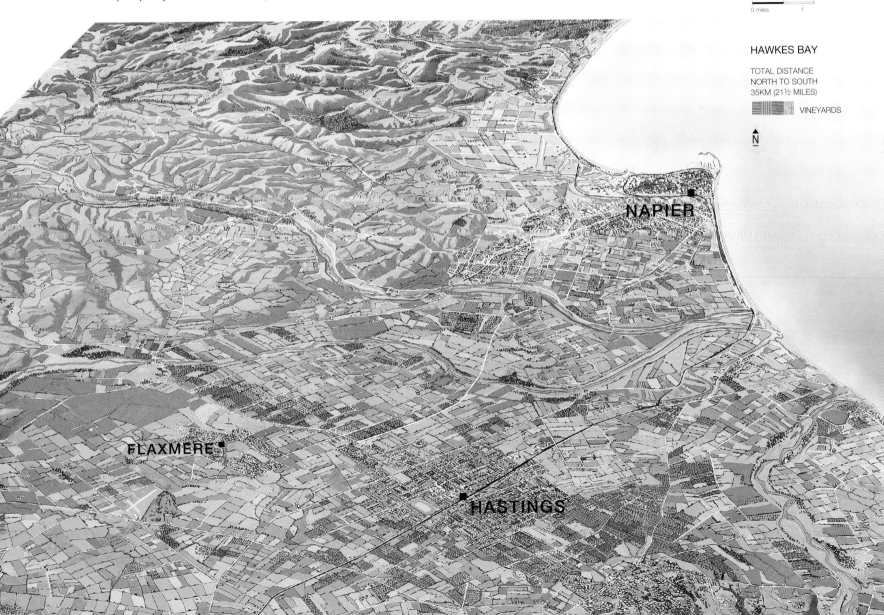

SOUTH ISLAND

The snow-capped peak of Mount Tapuaenuku reminds you that Vavasour's Awatere Valley vineyard is in one of New Zealand's top cool spots.

WINEMAKING IN THE SOUTH ISLAND is a lot older than you might think. It's true that when the large-scale producer Montana began planting in Marlborough in 1973 it was generally seen as the beginning of the modern industry there – the modern industry, yes, but of the centres of winemaking now spread across the island, Marlborough was the only place that hadn't had a proper wine industry before. Well, perhaps wine industry is stretching the point, since none of the original wine producers survived very long.

But Nelson, to the north-west of Marlborough, was visited in 1843 by boat-loads of Germans who, looking at the steep hills covered in virgin bush, thought the place looked too tough for them, and sailed on to Australia. Standing on the low hills running down to the sparkling waters of Tasman Bay, while a long white cloud, piled high with meringue fluff and with a base as flat as a smoothing iron, hangs motionless in the warm sky, I find it inconceivable anyone could ever want to leave this paradise. But there you go. Eventually some sort of winemaking got going there in 1868 and continued fitfully until 1939.

The French showed a bit more nerve in 1840 when they landed at Akaroa, south of Canterbury, and planted vines around their homes on the mountainous Banks Peninsula. But there are no records of them doing anything more than make enough wine for their own consumption, and when they died, so did their vineyards.

Further south, in Central Otago, was born that perennial fair-weather friend of the winemaker, a Gold Rush. It didn't spawn vineyards on the same scale as the Australian or Californian gold fevers, but there's no doubt that a Frenchman called Jean Desiré Feraud was doing good business in 1870 selling his wine and liqueurs to speculators. Yet this waned as the lustre of precious metal faded, and the island reverted to sheep, cattle and fruit – to quiet, unobtrusive, unpolluted prosperity, lost in the southern seas.

Until 1973, that is. That's when Marlborough, now New Zealand's leading wine region, was born out of nothing. At the time Montana, New Zealand's biggest wine company, was looking to expand and wanted cheap, easy land. Hawke's Bay was NZ$4800 per hectare. Marlborough was between NZ$600 and $1200 per hectare, depending on whether it was good for nothing but pasture or good for almost nothing but pasture. Montana bought 14 farms – 1600ha (3954 acres) – and before the locals had even woken up to what was happening, they had planted 390ha (964 acres) of vines, mostly Müller-Thurgau. But they took a punt and planted 24ha (60 acres) of Sauvignon Blanc – just a hunch after tasting an early New Zealand Sauvignon – but what a hunch.

Without Marlborough Sauvignon Blanc, New Zealand might still be struggling for acceptance in the World Premier League of wine. With Marlborough Sauvignon Blanc, it created a classic flavour that no-one had ever dreamed of before, and set a standard for tangy, incisive, mouth-watering dry wines as crunchy as iceberg lettuce, and as aggressive as gooseberries and lime, that the rest of the world has been trying to copy ever since.

SOUTH ISLAND'S GROWTH SPURT

Startling changes in the South Island wine industry have happened over the last generation, not least in the development of new wine regions such as Marlborough. Back in 1960 the total vineyard area for the whole of New Zealand was 388ha (960 acres) The South Island didn't have a single vine, and the most widely planted in the North Island was the *labrusca* variety, Albany Surprise, followed by a clutch of hybrids like Baco 22A and Seibel 5455.

By 1975, when there was massive vineyard expansion in the North Island, with six times as much land under vine as there had been in 1960, the first South Island vines were only just being planted. The hybrids had increased their acreage in the North Island, but the German influence was evident with Müller-Thurgau being nationally the most widely planted variety, and some 649ha (1604 acres) yielding fruit. Expansion continued at a breakneck pace and, although North Island led the way, Marlborough on South Island was rapidly proving its worth. By 1982, New Zealand's total vineyard area stood at 5901ha (14,580 acres); Auckland and Waikato still had the same area of vineyard as before, but the leaders now were Gisborne with 1922ha (4749 acres), Hawkes Bay with 1891ha (4673 acres) and Marlborough with a remarkable 1175ha (2904 acres). Small areas like Nelson and Canterbury in South Island, and Wairarapa in North Island, had now begun planting grapes, too.

The dramatic government-sponsored vinepull of the mid-1980s led to a sea-change in the industry and the significant growth since then has been entirely in high quality areas. By 2007, the total area of New Zealand vineyards totalled over 24,000ha (59,300 acres), with Marlborough being the largest and most important at 12,709ha (31,403 acres), followed by Hawkes Bay covering 4597ha (11,360 acres) and Gisborne 2056ha (5080 acres). And new areas of high-quality vines, especially in South Island, are bursting out and catching up fast. On South Island, Central Otago – invisible in 1982 – now has 1454ha (3592 acres) and more than doubled its vineyard plantings just between 2003 and 2007. Canterbury now has just over 1000ha (2471 acres), a figure that has more than doubled since 2002.

It's interesting to look at grape varieties, too. In 1970, the hybrid Baco 22A was the top variety with 217ha (536 acres). It is now officially extinct. Müller-Thurgau had 194ha (479 acres) in 1970, but by 1983 was easily the leader with ten times this amount. However, by 2007 this had dropped to 108ha (266 acres). There was no Sauvignon Blanc in 1970, but by 2002 it had overtaken Chardonnay and moved into the Number One slot. By 2007, there were 10,024ha (24,768 acres) and it accounted for 42 per cent of

all New Zealand's plantings. Pinot Noir is the second most planted grape, with 4405ha (10,884 acres). White grape varieties presently account for 70 per cent of the total planting area.

NELSON

Back in the South Island's early days, one of the first regions to stir was Nelson, 75km (45 miles) north-west of Marlborough. The tiny Victory Grape Wines vineyard at Stoke, a mile or so south-west of the city of Nelson, produced its first vintage in 1973, and in 1974 Hermann Seifried established what is Nelson's largest vineyard; others have since joined.

Yet development has been relatively small scale. The Waimea Plains, on flat but well-drained land running across to Rabbit Island and Tasman Bay, could have become another Marlborough, except that land prices and start-up costs are significantly higher. So much of the development has been in the beautiful Upper Moutere hills, just a few miles further to the north-west. The soils are mostly clay loam, but well-drained on these slopes, as they need to be, because Nelson is cooler than Marlborough and gets more concentrated periods of rain in autumn. Yet overall it has more rain-free days and long hours of sunshine, with the west coast taking the brunt of the westerlies. Despite the grapes ripening a week later than in Marlborough, and with the attendant risk of rain during vintage, some of the South Island's best Pinot Noir, Riesling and Chardonnay come from here.

CANTERBURY AND WAIPARA

Three hours' drive to the south from Marlborough, Christchurch sits at the heart of the Canterbury region on the shores of Pegasus Bay. The local Lincoln University began grape trials in 1973, despite the fact that all the traditional indicators said the area had to be too cold for grapes. There appears to be less heat here than in Champagne in France, hardly as much as on the Rhine in Germany and yet, and yet... One of my most vivid 'road to Damascus' tasting experiences ever was the St Helena Pinot Noir 1982, grown on an old potato field twenty minutes' drive north of Christchurch, and only its second vintage. Startling, intense, brimming with passionate fruit and heady perfume, it could have held its own with many of the Côte de Nuits' Grands Crus.

From a standing start, Canterbury suddenly became New Zealand's promised land for Pinot Noir. But it's not as simple as that: Wairarapa on North Island and Central Otago way to the south would dispute this claim, and Canterbury does have several different mesoclimates. The most regularly exciting Pinot Noirs and Chardonnays are now coming from Waipara, 40km (25 miles) north of Christchurch, where the Teviotdale range of hills protects the vines from the sea breezes and create an average temperature 2–3°C warmer than to the south around Canterbury.

Loess and gravel river terraces and their stressed low crops create a wine style that is lush and warm for Pinot Noir and Chardonnay, and thrillingly lean for Riesling. It's difficult to say if the area is really warm enough for Bordeaux varieties, but I've had some marvellous austere yet satisfying examples off the stoniest vineyards, as the grapes creep to ripeness in the long dry autumns, finally being harvested as late as May. Vines near Christchurch are battered by wind, none more so than Giesen's, which nonetheless manages to produce fabulously concentrated Rieslings, the wind's aggression being offset by low rainfall and reliably long, dry autumns. And to the south, French Farm is giving the Banks Peninsula another go, but that's nothing to what's happening along the Waitaki River, even further south, where several serious plantings are already yielding exciting results. A new north Canterbury area, around Pyramid Valley, is another recently planted district that shows great promise. The overriding influences allowing grapes to ripen are low rainfall and free-draining soils. Long, dry summer days lead to a dry, mild autumn, letting grapes hang on the vine until May – if April frosts don't strike. But then long, slow ripening is what brings flavour intensity – just like northern Europe, but without the vintage rains.

CENTRAL OTAGO

Even so, you do have to have a certain amount of heat for flavour intensity. Won't Central Otago, the world's most southerly wine region and stunningly beautiful too, way down near Queenstown in the heart of New Zealand's skiing region, be too cold? When you fly into Queenstown's tiny airport, wobbling between mist-wreathed mountain peaks, you feel as though you're in Scotland, not New Zealand. And on the ground the feeling remains – those raw, gaunt hillscapes are too Scottish for vines, surely? Well, on paper, yes. But this is the one Continental climate among South Island's wine regions. After all, Latitude 45° South lies on the same parallel as the heart of the northern Rhône Valley as well as Bordeaux in the northern hemisphere. And there are hot spots here and there – on the shores of lakes, beneath sheer rock faces that reflect heat and retain it in the chilly summer nights – where heat readings rocket upwards.

This far south the summer days are very long and the rainfall frequently the lowest in New Zealand; between December and February, the number of cloudless days with temperatures hour upon hour over 20°C (68°F) – and often peaking at over 30°C (86°F) – is exceptional. Equally important, and a major factor in the remarkable intensity of Central Otago fruit, are the fiercely cold nights. Hot days equal high ripeness; cold nights equal high acid. Result: memorable fruit flavours in the wines. Chardonnay, Pinot Gris, Riesling and Sauvignon Blanc all show promise here, but the star is Pinot Noir, covering 80 per cent of the region's vineyards. The Bannockburn district, a north-facing ridge riddled with abandoned gold mines, and the driest area in New Zealand, is the star performer. Nearby Lowburn, Bendigo and Earnscleugh are also special, as are cooler Wanaka and Gibbston.

 RED GRAPES
Pinot Noir is best suited to South Island's cool conditions and accounts for the lion's share of red plantings. Merlot and tiny amounts of Cabernet Sauvignon and Syrah are also grown.

 WHITE GRAPES
Sauvignon Blanc covers nearly seven times the vineyard area of Chardonnay, in second place. Riesling, Semillon and rising star, Pinot Gris, follow behind.

 CLIMATE
The climate is cool with abundant sunshine to help the ripening process. Autumn rainfall is low, but wind and frosts can be troublesome.

 SOIL
Soil types are variable. Alluvial gravel, or alluvial silt loams over gravel subsoils, are free-draining. In addition there are areas of chalky, limestone-rich loams and patches of loess.

 ASPECT
Much of the vineyard land is flat and quite low-lying. Nelson is more hilly with some sunny, sheltered sites.

MARLBOROUGH AND NELSON CLIMATES

Protected from the strong sea winds, Marlborough is one of the few South Island regions warm enough for large-scale viticulture. The Southern Alps dissipate the prevailing westerly winds and help to create a rain shadow in the region, reducing rainfall over the vineyards as well as cloud cover, which, in turn, increases the amount of valuable sunshine. The southern tip of North Island protects the vineyards from the cyclonic autumn storms that come in from the Pacific Ocean. The only winds that affect the Marlborough vineyards down on the flat Wairau River Valley are warm and dry and they help to boost grape ripening. Like Marlborough, Nelson also has warm summers and promisingly high sunshine hours, but as the harvest approaches there is a strong risk of damaging autumn rains.

Probably the most famous Sauvignon Blanc in the world: Cloudy Bay which comes from Marlborough in the South Island.

MARLBOROUGH

RED GRAPES
Pinot Noir is by far the most planted red grape variety in Marlborough, with most of it still used in still table wine. Merlot and Cabernet Sauvignon are minor players.

WHITE GRAPES
Sauvignon Blanc rules with about two-thirds of the region's total vineyard area. Chardonnay is next, with Pinot Gris and Riesling following well behind.

CLIMATE
The climate is cool, but sunshine is abundant. Rainfall is scarce between October and April, and frost and wind can cause problems.

SOIL
Soil varies from clay to stony gravel. Very stony districts are so well-drained that irrigation is essential.

ASPECT
Generally low and flat, but the Awatere Valley benefits from protected terraces allowing maximum exposure to the sun.

I DON'T HAVE MANY REGRETS IN LIFE, but one thing I would like to have done is to see the Marlborough region in New Zealand's South Island at the beginning of the 1970s. What would I have seen? Pastureland, sheep, garlic, cherry trees, sheep, a dozy market town… and maybe some more sheep. Nothing much really. But I would like to have seen it precisely because it was so ordinary, so unmemorable, so dull. And because it didn't boast one single vine.

Now, in the new millennium, it grows more vines than any other area of New Zealand and is expanding at an exhilarating but scary rate that gives the entire region a real Klondike feel. For every vast field of vines, their lush foliage glistening in the summer sunshine, there seems to be another vast field of raw earth being straddled and stretched by posts and wires as the land is prepared for yet another carpet of vines. And there's only one reason for all this: Marlborough is such a damned good place to grow vines. In fact, I'll go further than that. It's one of the greatest places on earth to grow them, producing some of the world's most remarkable wines. And I would love to have been in on it right from the start. But is Marlborough just about Sauvignon Blanc? No, it isn't; and it isn't just about Montana either (though the company owns or controls between a third and half of Marlborough's grapes). There are other higher-profile labels, led by the super-chic Cloudy Bay – one of the world's most sought after wines – whose first vintage was as recent as 1985.

The whole spectrum of grapes has been planted as people have tried to establish precisely what limits there are to Marlborough's abilities. Well, there are limits. Like any other great vineyard area, Marlborough is not all-purpose, because then you'd have to trade memorable brilliance for overall reliability. Most of Marlborough can't do much with Cabernet Sauvignon, for example, though where the soil is rocky and well-drained and yields are kept low, warm years will ripen it. But Merlot gives good results. People thought the cool conditions were tailor-made for Pinot Noir, but it took until the 2003 vintage for people to work out the best ways to grow and vinify it. Chardonnay, too, was expected to be uniformly brilliant. It isn't. Much of it ends up as fizz but, that said, there are already some stunning luscious, buttery, intense Chardonnays.

Sauvignon Blanc was world-class virtually from its first vintage and every year new examples appear. I love Marlborough Sauvignon. You may hate it. No problem. It's that sort of wine: it demands a reaction. It would be nice if Riesling one day demanded a reaction again, because Marlborough makes superb Riesling too, usually dry, occasionally lusciously sweet. But I suspect Pinot Gris will wow them in the aisles before Riesling struggles back to centre stage.

WHERE THE VINEYARDS ARE *Well, here it is. One of the world's newest fine wine regions in all its glory. Every vine you see here has been planted since 1973. And a lot more of those wide open spaces that gaze out so invitingly from the map will be filled with vines in the next few years. Already the silty land towards the sea is sprouting large vineyards that give yet another take on Sauvignon Blanc flavours. Even so some of the land is just too silty. To the left valleys running south are filling with vines, but they have to cope with a serious spring and autumn frost risk.*

Conditions are quite different on the two sides of the Wairau plains. In the north, near the river itself, the ground is mostly very stony and well-drained, with ample water supplies for irrigation. The land is generally flat, but there are dips which hold more fertile soil. Vines in the dips ripen more slowly than vines on the stony ridges. This is primarily white wine country. The south side has more fertile, water-retentive soils, but less available water, and grapes ripen up to two weeks after those near the Wairau River, but Pinot Noir thrives here. The important and rapidly expanding Awatere Valley is just off the bottom right-hand corner of the map. Up river it's pretty warm, yet down by the sea it's brilliantly cool and the result is an array of pungent flavours, red and white.

Right. So where does all this flavour intensity come from? A long, slow ripening season is the key. Blenheim, the main town, often gets more sunshine hours than any other town in New Zealand. Over a ripening season, Marlborough gets about the same amount of heat as Burgundy, and slightly less than Bordeaux. But the average daily temperature is lower than either as the sunny ripening season spreads into April, or even into May, with cold nights helping to preserve acidity.

This is fine if you can guarantee a dry autumn. Almost always, you can. Most of New Zealand's bad autumn weather comes in from the Pacific in the east and is soaked up by the North Island. The southerlies get headed off by the Southern Alps, and the wet westerlies during the growing season are fended off by the mountains to the west. Rainfall from February to April is lower than in any other New Zealand wine region, while March is the driest month. Given that it is relatively cool, it is vital that the growers have the confidence to let their fruit hang, and the dry autumns give them that (though an autumn frost occasionally wreaks havoc). A lack of rain also allows growers to minimize anti-disease programmes, with substantial cost savings but also means irrigation is essential. The valley's north side has as much water as it needs from the Wairau River and its aquifers. The south side is more barren and water often needs to be pumped from the north. Nevertheless it needs less water as its soils are more fertile and water-retentive. The vineyards in the north are mostly shallow silt over virtual free-draining gravel. In some vineyards you can't even see the soil for the stones. Add to this a drying northerly wind aiding transpiration from the leaves, and you need irrigation all right.

South-east of Blenheim on Highway One, the north side of the Awatere Valley has a series of stony, flat-topped river terraces with

RENWICK

0 km 1 2

0 miles 1

the loess topsoil struggling to make itself visible between the stones. Beneath the thin topsoil there's a deep gravel subsoil before the vines reach tough but mineral-rich mudstone at the bottom. With low yields and good protection from north-westerly winds, though occasional exposure to southerly winds, Vavasour (off the bottom right-hand corner of the map) has already produced the region's best Cabernets and excellent whites too, but the area has undergone a raft of new plantings, both near the sea and up to 25km (16 miles) inland and on the more fertile southern banks, by producers who crave the marvellous pungency of Awatere fruit.

Marlborough is renowned for great Sauvignon and Riesling, and excellent sparkling wine and Chardonnay. That's not bad, I'd say. Yet people there keep asking me to predict the next flavour fad in Britain, and I'm sure they want me to say, oh, Viognier, Marsanne, Malvasia – anything they haven't got so that they can fret like mad. But Marlborough must build on what it has already achieved. As my friend the late Auberon Waugh once said, 'It's very difficult to be best in the world at anything, but New Zealand has achieved that distinction with Sauvignon Blanc. You should simply get on with the job of making more of it.' I'll drink to that.

SELECTED WINERIES

1. Seresin Estate
2. Grove Mill
3. Isabel Estate
4. Cellier Le Brun
5. Forrest Estate
6. Framingham Wine
7. Nautilus
8. Clifford Bay
9. Wairau River
10. Huia
11. Le Grys Vineyard/ Mud House
12. Lake Chalice
13. Fromm Winery
14. Fairhall Downs
15. Villa Maria Estate
16. Wither Hills
17. Jackson Estate
18. Cloudy Bay
19. Allan Scott
20. Hunter's
21. Drylands Estate
22. Saint Clair
23. Whitehaven
24. Lawson's Dry Hills Wines
25. Montana Brancott Winery

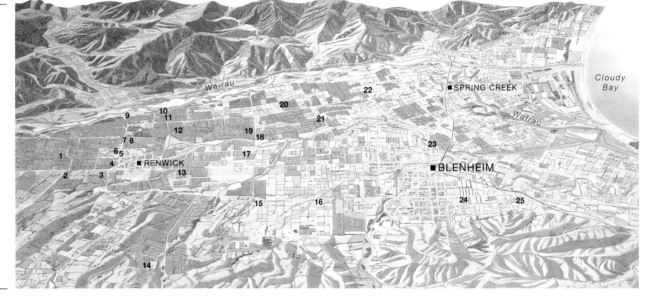

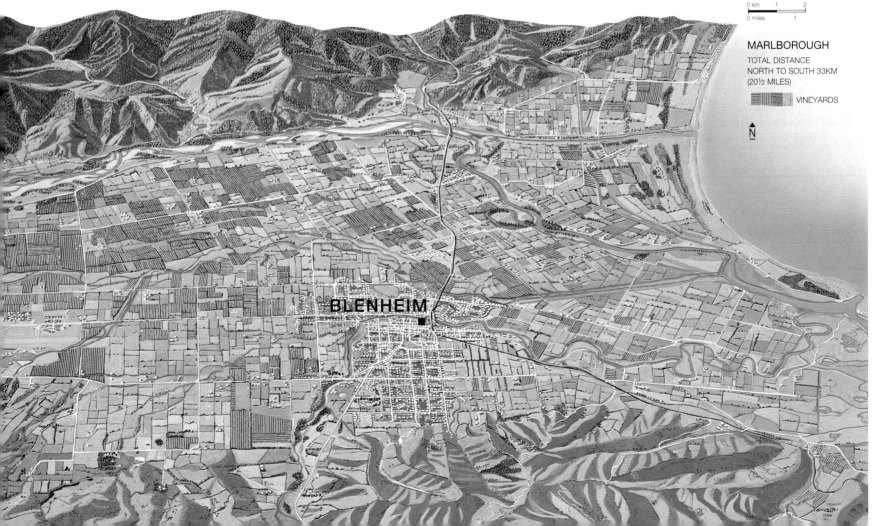

MARLBOROUGH

TOTAL DISTANCE NORTH TO SOUTH 33KM (20½ MILES)

VINEYARDS

SOUTH AFRICA

PANORAMIC MAP OF SOUTH AFRICA

Stellenbosch, Paarl and Franschhoek *pages 324–325*

F OR AS LONG AS I'VE BEEN WRITING ABOUT WINE – and that stretches right back into the 1980s – it's never quite seemed the right time to be writing about South Africa, her vineyards and her wines. In the '80s, it was tricky anyway, because it was difficult to find out what was actually going on. The wine industry's attitude during those last years of apartheid was extremely defensive and almost entirely controlled by giant groups like the KWV – it sounds like a secret police force but, in fact, was a little less sinister, merely an all-powerful organization of grape co-operatives that ruled most of the Cape's wine industry with a rod as hard and inflexible as Kryptonite. They and their PR outfits sold a single story – that all was well and that the oldest vineyards in the New World – we're talking a foundation date of 1655 here! – were flourishing and producing classic wines like they had always done. Well, this was tosh. Most of the vineyards were virus-infected. Most of the vines in any case were Chenin Blanc, Colombard and other grapes that basically went straight to the distillery. Not surprising, really, because hardly any of the grape growers drank wine – a brandy and Coke was the preferred tipple. And most of the winemaking was stuck in a time-warp of outdated equipment and a mentality of wine production that owed everything to the risk-averse, control-freak philosophy of the German wine schools of the 1960s and 1970s, and looked on the mould-breaking, rule-rewriting leap for freedom and flavour that marked out California and Australia with a mixture of fear and contempt. The 1980s saw more progress in technology, winery knowledge and thrilling ambition, unfettered by tradition, than in any previous decade. Winewise, the '80s were the most experimental decade of the 20th century – except in South Africa. The wine world was becoming a boisterous, babbling global village. South Africa was still the hermit on the hill.

The 1990s changed all that. With Mandela's release from jail, the winds of change finally began to blow through the Cape. There was enormous international goodwill towards South Africa in the 1990s and wine exports soared. But this success was two-edged. Few of the vineyards could do more than produce oceans of bland quaffing wine. Wines that had been stars of the previous era were now seen as outdated and stale in the bright new World of Wine. And right through the decade, a war was being waged between the reactionary old guard – unwilling to change, unwilling to cede their privilege and authority – and a new wave of youngsters who had sneaked off abroad, being made welcome for the first time in living memory by the wine producers of other countries, and had returned bristling with enthusiasm and ideas.

So, I think the beginning of the 21st century is, at last, the right time to write about South Africa. There is a mood of optimism and confidence that no longer seems arrogant – more often it is inspiring and believable. The changes being wrought in the vineyards are dramatic, yet, thankfully, lack the sense of Klondike opportunism that concerns me in countries like Australia, New Zealand and the USA. And the wines? Transformed. Bursting with vibrant fruit, sensitively tempered by oak and actually starting to speak of a sense of place. A Sauvignon from Constantia, a Riesling from Elgin, a Pinot Noir from Walker Bay, a Shiraz from Wellington, a Malbec from Paarl Mountain, a Pinotage from Simonsberg, and a bush-vine Chenin from the mountain slopes of Malmesbury. All special. All different from what the rest of the world might do with these varietals. All of them saying – this is just the beginning.

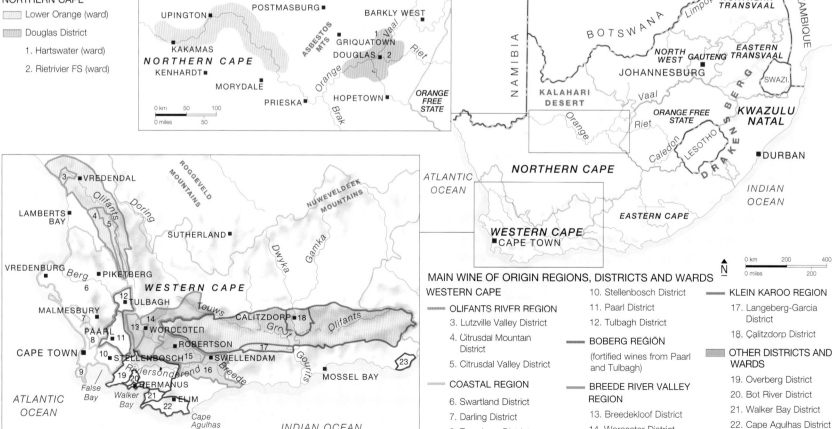

NORTHERN CAPE

- Lower Orange (ward)
- Douglas District
  1. Hartswater (ward)
  2. Rietrivier FS (ward)

MAIN WINE OF ORIGIN REGIONS, DISTRICTS AND WARDS

WESTERN CAPE

- **OLIFANTS RIVER REGION**
  3. Lutzville Valley District
  4. Citrusdal Mountain District
  5. Citrusdal Valley District

- **COASTAL REGION**
  6. Swartland District
  7. Darling District
  8. Tygerberg District
  9. Cape Point District

  10. Stellenbosch District
  11. Paarl District
  12. Tulbagh District

- **BOBERG REGION**
  (fortified wines from Paarl and Tulbagh)

- **BREEDE RIVER VALLEY REGION**
  13. Breedekloof District
  14. Worcester District
  15. Robertson District
  16. Swellendam District

- **KLEIN KAROO REGION**
  17. Langeberg-Garcia District
  18. Calitzdorp District

- **OTHER DISTRICTS AND WARDS**
  19. Overberg District
  20. Bot River District
  21. Walker Bay District
  22. Cape Agulhas District
  23. Plettenberg Bay District

And I believe it is. After a generation of being unable to decide whether they are Old World or New World in the fairest Cape, they're showing that they are precisely that – neither! Or, when it suits them, both.

THE CONCEPT OF *TERROIR*

And this mixture of new generation open-mindedness, allied to a sympathy which does lean more to France than Australia, has meant that the French idea of 'terroir' is firmly at the heart of the new South African agenda. This entails studying the geography of their country. This entails learning to match grape variety to site. It's a long process; it can't happen overnight – but, unlike in most New World countries, it's persuaded the authorities to base the demarcation of smaller areas on – wait for it – *terroir*.

Terroir? In the New World? Well, it's true that producers the world over are focusing more and more on the combination of soil, climate and exposure that go to make up the notion of *terroir*. But all too often either they're chary of admitting that that's what they're doing, or they fling the word around with all the gay abandon of a marketing department with a new toy.

In South Africa, before a new ward, as these smaller areas are called, is demarcated, there are considerations that must be taken into account. These include uniformity of soil and climate; ecological factors; the geography of the area; any existing cultural practices that may affect wine character or distinguish one area from another; existing evidence of the area's ability to produce unique wine, and the traditional name of the area. This would seem to include elements other than *terroir* – but, hang on, who really knows what *terroir* is? It's the land, climate, but it's also all the human aspects that influence nature. And that is pretty much what this ragbag of regulations is all about. Certainly there is much more reference to *terroir* as a defining factor than there ever was when the larger districts or regions were demarcated: these were drawn up along geopolitical lines. And because of that visible unifying topography, you can drive through the wards and see that they make sense.

South Africa is the world's ninth-largest wine producer, though its position of only 14th in actual vineyard area shows you how high some of the vineyard yields are – as much as 350hl (and more) per hectare in the most irrigated regions like Olifants River and Orange River, though not all these dilute grapes will end up as wine. In Orange River, wine only accounts for 28 per cent of grape production: the rest is distilled, concentrated or turned into sultanas. And if you look at Stellenbosch or Paarl – well, the vines there can yield as little as 20hl per ha, and other areas determined to improve quality – which means, fundamentally, reducing yields – include Robertson, Walker Bay, Elgin, Constantia, Durbanville, Swartland, Wellington and Franschhoek.

If you are trying to persuade a grape grower in a producer cellar, as co-operatives are now called, to reduce his yields, you will have to change his entire farmer's mindset that equates success with a big crop. However, the drive for quality in the last ten years is being led by a relatively new phenomenon in the Cape – a flood of new private producers. Between 2000 and 2006 about 220 new wineries were started up. Even so, they're still a minority and producer cellars still process some 80 per cent of the crop. (Official figures for co-operatives include those that have turned themselves into companies, like KWV.)

One of the glories of South Africa's vines is that you are never out of sight of the awesome mountain ranges. Here, Seidelberg's vines hug the sides of Paarl Mountain, looking across to the imposing backbone of the Simonsberg.

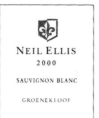

Pinotage is South Africa's very own grape, capable of making highly individual reds when handled carefully.

MOVE OVER, CHENIN BLANC

Around 70 per cent of this annual crop ends up as table wine, and white accounts for about 64 per cent of production. Chenin Blanc is still the dominant variety, though it has been declining for years and has now dipped to under 19 per cent of the total vineyard area. It is followed by Colombard and Cabernet Sauvignon, with Shiraz, Sauvignon Blanc, Chardonnay and Pinotage now registering more strongly on the dial. Although simple, fruity white wines still account for 43 per cent of South African wine exports for 2006, the classic red varieties (Cabernet Sauvignon, Shiraz, Merlot) plus Pinotage (which is not officially considered a classic variety), accounted for nearly 19 per cent of exports in 2006.

If Chardonnay and Sauvignon Blanc have levered themselves from nowhere to be a small but significant blip on the map, Cabernet Sauvignon, Merlot and home-bred Pinotage have overtaken all lesser red varieties. Shiraz, on producers' enthusiasm alone, would probably top the lot, but supply of vine material is still having trouble keeping up with demand. The swing towards classic, international varieties now includes small quantities of Viognier, Mourvèdre, Malbec, Nebbiolo and Sangiovese. The Cape's favourable climate, and the worldwide interest in all things Rhôneish, has also put the spotlight on the likes of Grenache, though little is currently grown here, and old bush-vine plantings of Cinsaut.

WINE REGIONS

The first experimental grape plantings took place in Cape Town in 1655, and it was from just three of the vines in this experimental nursery in the gardens of the Dutch East India Company that the first South African wine was made. Virtually the whole industry has since confined itself to the south-western Cape area of South Africa from about 32° to just over 34° South, since this is the only area that can at least partially boast a Mediterranean climate. There's good rainfall in the cold wet winters, and the long hot summers, which stretch from November right through to May, would actually be too hot for really fine wines were it not, on the west coast, for the Benguela Current of chilly water that surges up from the Antarctic and sends cooling breezes inland up the river valleys, and the prevailing south-easterlies that cool down most parts east of Paarl.

Increasingly, the best wines are from growers who have selected specific sites for specific varieties, some on the slopes of the ever-present mountain ranges in order to reduce temperatures even further. Grapes tend to ripen better there because, although there are numerous soil forms – Stellenbosch alone has 20 – they tend not to be overcropped like those on the alluvial, very fertile, lower and flatter sites. But there's another point, too: growers who planted very high up discovered that because heat rises, the vines failed to go into dormancy during the winter, and that's if they avoided being devoured by the baboons who roam the peaks. So it's the mid-slopes that are now considered the most desirable, with deep, well drained soils, often of decomposed granite, and good aspects being seen as just as important as those cooling breezes.

And vineyards are moving further south: there are vines south of Elim, towards Cape Agulhas, Africa's most southerly point. The vines here are planted on decomposed granite outcrops, and the plentiful and pure spring water keeps them going through the long, dry summer months. The chief problem is high humidity from the south-easterlies encouraging rot, but first results show brilliant Sauvignons and potentially fine reds.

Traditionally the best table wines have come from vineyards influenced by the cooling breezes of False Bay. Earliest and most famous are the wines of Constantia, just south of

Cape Town. Spectacular sweet wines were made here in the 18th and 19th centuries, as famous as Tokaji and Sauternes. In the mid-1980s, after a long gap, the tradition of Constantia dessert wine began to be revived, but it is the cool-climate, tangy, dry whites that excite me most.

The vast majority of the top wines have always come from Paarl and Stellenbosch. Many still do, but with new areas opening up and small, quality-minded producers operating in regions previously dominated by co-operatives, competition is increasing. Those intent on finding the coolest spots have headed south-east through the mountains towards the Overberg District and Hermanus. As you drive up over the mountain pass into this bowl-shaped highland, the vegetation and the air change from warm to cool climate at a stroke. Famous for apples and pears, the Elgin Ward is increasingly producing exciting Sauvignon, Chardonnay and Pinot Noir. Keep driving south-east and you'll come to Walker Bay, and in particular the Hemel-en-Aarde valley, behind the cliffs at Hermanus. This is where Tim Hamilton-Russell planted in the 1970s, hoping to find South Africa's coolest conditions and re-create Burgundian Chardonnay and Pinot Noir. He, his son and his neighbours have succeeded in doing precisely that.

But these vineyard areas are no longer South Africa's coolest. There are the Elim vineyards in the extreme south, and on the west coast sites cooled by fogs and breezes from the Benguela Current are also starting to shine, most notably Darling and its Groenekloof ward, whose Sauvignons are startlingly tart and tasty. Durbanville Hills, its vineyards fighting a pitched battle against urban encroachment from Cape Town's suburbs, is another fine cool area. A few kilometres inland, the temperature warms up at every step. Co-operatives dominate this landscape, but there are fine mountain slope sites at Piketberg, Riebeek and Perdeberg, where old Chenin vines share the parched soil with Pinotage, Cinsaut and Shiraz. And, as you head north to the Olifants River once again, co-operatives are battling to lower yields and improve quality, while north of Lamberts Bay, at Bamboes Bay, yet another windy cool site begins to flex its tiny muscles.

Inland areas, such as Worcester, Robertson and the Klein Karoo, are among the warmest in the winelands, although Robertson does benefit from afternoon winds blowing up the Breede River from the Atlantic. Worcester produces the most wine of any region, much of it quaffable, easy-priced white, though some similarly undemanding reds are showing their worth. Robertson's limestone soils and good access to properly utilized irrigation have proved to be excellent for both whites and sparklers, and the move now is to see whether they can repeat their success with reds. Calitzdorp in the Klein Karoo lays claim to be the port-style capital of South Africa; with the introduction of more Portuguese varieties and greater focus on the part of the producers, some real beauties are appearing. All three regions are known for other fortified wines as well, especially sweet Muscadels.

THE CLASSIFICATION OF SOUTH AFRICAN WINE

The Wine of Origin system is symbolized by the certificate or seal on a bottle (or other wine container). From the seal's number, the entire history of the wine can be traced back to its source, but quality is not guaranteed. Like many other New World wine countries, South Africa's labelling laws emphasize the grape variety, rather than the vineyard origin or wine style. Varietal wines must be made from at least 85 per cent of the named grape. To qualify as an 'estate' wine, the producer's vines must be grown on a single piece of land and the wine must be vinified, matured and bottled on the property.

STELLENBOSCH & PAARL

THE MOST ENDURING MEMORY of my first arrival in the Cape is of a colour. As I drove from the airport out to Somerset West, then turned north towards Stellenbosch along the banks of the Eerste River, a great carpet of purply crimson vines stretched out on both sides of the road, glinting in the evening sun and casting a rosy glow on to the slopes of the Helderberg that reared up to the east.

Yet that deep, dark red was nothing more than the colour of an entire vineyard region suffering from virus infection. It looked wonderful, but that crimson colour meant diseased leaves that had lost their ability to trap sunlight for photosynthesis and to ripen the crop. Some producers try to tell you that there's no longer a virus problem – but just look them in the eye and raise a quizzical eyebrow and they'll soon admit that the problem is still a major one, just as it has been in South Africa for as long as anyone can remember. Basically, the virus interferes with the natural progression of a grape towards sugar ripeness, and also the ripening of the stems and pips and the reduction in acid. This has meant that many traditional Cape red wines displayed raw green acidity and bitter tannins, and since everyone was stuck with virused vines, producers rather defiantly labelled this unappealing character the Cape Red style. But there's a new breed at work now in the Cape. The virus is now a problem to be solved, rather than endured. Better viticultural practices have shown that in cooler conditions you can coax vines to physiological ripeness and, in warm areas, good growers can actually use the virus to slow down the ripening process, allowing the grapes to hang longer on the vine and so develop more attractive complex flavours. That's the new South Africa for you. Gradually the vineyards will be replanted with virus-free material. Until this happens, they're coping.

There's another point worth mentioning amidst all this technical chat. I can't believe I've got this far without blurting it out, but this talk of lovely crimson leaves has forced my hand. The beauty of the vine leaves is nothing compared to the beauty of the land itself. The mountains that rear up at this southern tip of Africa are some of the most uplifting and majestic in the world. Almost every vineyard is within sight of them, but in Stellenbosch and Paarl they dominate your every thought, your every step, infusing you with calm and wonder – and, more mundanely, providing a rich variety of conditions in which to grow grapes. So, thank goodness for improved viticulture, then, because beneath the towering peaks of the Helderberg, Stellenbosch, Simonsberg and the Drakensteinberg mountains are some stunning vineyard sites that are at last starting to show the sort of quality at which they've always hinted.

Many of these sites are relatively warm, and have an annual rainfall of under 1000mm (40in), which is quite dry, but if your soils are right, it doesn't seem to be too much of a problem. In most of the major vineyard areas the soils are decomposed granites mixed with clay, often sufficiently deep that the vines hardly need the subsoils and shales. With the exception of super-cool areas like Elgin, that are prone to unwelcome summer rains, nearly all the rain falls in winter. The decomposed granite/clay soils, in particular, hold their water well and although many vineyards are irrigated, you can dry-farm in these conditions – especially with old bush vines – and many producers do. Which makes sense. Some wine growers see the Rhône Valley in France as having similar conditions to much of the Cape. When you drive through the

Rhône, you see mile upon mile of dry-farmed bush vines, clearly thriving in the arid conditions. Indeed, Stellenbosch is undergoing quite a bit of soul-searching at the moment. It sort of wants to believe it's relatively cool, but most of it isn't, and hopefully the tremendous quality of the new Shiraz wines now appearing will dampen the cries of the would-be cool-climate brigade.

Some areas, such as Bottelary and the Simonsberg around Kanonkop, acknowledge their warmth. Stellenbosch growers generally have to search quite hard for cooler mesoclimates, that are angled away from the sun and exposed to the maritime breezes off False Bay, directly to the south. As it happens, both reds and whites do well all over Stellenbosch, but the Simonsberg, further from the sea, is noted for richer, more muscular reds, while wines from the Helderberg, much nearer to False Bay, do tend to be finer-boned and more elegant, and some of the whites are first-class.

Well, ultra cool climate isn't quite so trendy as it was a few years ago, so Stellenbosch and Paarl with their generally warm conditions and long-established winery and vineyard infrastructure are well-placed to be the leaders of South Africa's wine world. The number of new wineries, virtually all independent, which have sprung up in the past ten years emphasizes both areas' importance. The 1991 *Platter Wine Guide* listed 55 wineries for Stellenbosch and 34 for Paarl; by 2007, they had 100 and 74 respectively. This escalation has meant that individual wineries have found it increasingly difficult to stand out from the crowd. One of the answers has been to demarcate Stellenbosch and Paarl into smaller areas. And, whereas the original district boundaries were drawn up along geo-political lines, these smaller areas, known as wards, come rather closer to the European concept of *terroir*.

THE WARDS OF STELLENBOSCH
Stellenbosch, at 43,347ha (107,110 acres), with 17,524ha (43,301 acres) under vine, covers less than a third of Paarl's area, and has a more unified look. Looking inland from False Bay, the mountains form an amphitheatre, with the Simonsberg being the furthest point from the Bay. The vineyards are dotted round the mountain slopes and straddle the lower ground in between.

The vineyards of Thelema catch the late evening sun on the Helshoogte Pass between Stellenbosch and the Franschhoek Valley.

RED GRAPES
The best red wines come from the classic grape varieties: Cabernets Sauvignon and Franc, Merlot and Shiraz. Pinotage also prospers here and there are isolated spots of good Pinot Noir.

WHITE GRAPES
Internationally popular Sauvignon Blanc and Chardonnay are widely planted. Semillon is showing great promise in various sites throughout both regions. Dry Chenin Blanc can be excellent, and both this and Riesling produce good dessert wine.

CLIMATE
The climate is Mediterranean in character, with most rainfall in winter and fairly hot, dry summers. The much-needed cooling winds of summer, known as the 'Cape Doctor', blow across the land from False Bay and the south-east.

SOIL
Stellenbosch alone has more than 20 soil forms, all of which are acidic; those in Paarl are, in general, more calcareous. Lower, flatter sites tend to be on very fertile alluvial soils.

ASPECT
Matching variety to site is what matters. Thus Sauvignon Blanc does best in cooler spots, preferably south-east facing; Shiraz will be planted on hotter north-west or west facing slopes.

The district now has seven wards. Many of the best-known wineries are in Simonsberg-Stellenbosch, the first ward to be demarcated and the furthest from the cooling sea breezes of False Bay. Vineyards go up to about 480m (1575ft), where mostly white varieties are planted in decomposed granite. Deep red soils in the lower, more sheltered sites give rich, structured reds, especially from Pinotage, Shiraz and Cabernet. Bottelary Ward is warm, and vineyards run up the hillsides to about 300m (985ft) just east of Stellenbosch town. Growers here have only just started to bottle their own wines; but new producers and revitalized old ones are creating exciting flavours here. On the top of the Bottelary Hills is a vineyard trail with panoramic views of Table Mountain, Cape Town, the Hottentots Mountains and the sea.

Climb over these hills and you drop down into Devon Valley, its gentle slopes forming an east-facing U-shape, down the middle of which runs a single meandering country lane that links the valley to Stellenbosch. More densely planted with vines than Bottelary, it too is mostly red wine country, though Chardonnay does well on the higher ground on the southern side of the U. Much of the soil is deep and red, and the valley has long been associated with Shiraz, though Cabernet does pretty well here. Generally wines are more restrained and less robust than those of Simonsberg or Bottelary. The new Polkadraai Ward is further on, running between Saxenburg in the west to Eikendal on the road south from Stellenbosch town to Somerset West.

As if the scenery all around here wasn't spectacular enough, if you really want to blow your mind, head for the

Jonkershoek Valley and, further on, the new Banghoek Ward. Once through the low-lying land near Stellenbosch town, you come to towering mountains which press ever closer to the narrow, winding road. The vines are almost all near the valley mouth and scrambling up to about 350m (1148ft) on the steep but cool, south-facing slopes. The south-easterly winds tear down this valley and steep peaks reduce the exposure to morning and evening sun, which would explain why initially Chardonnay was the chief grape. However, despite the conditions, the more exciting results are coming from Shiraz and Cabernet. The final ward is Papegaaiberg, or Parrot Mountain. Here, urban development and a pine forest restrict vineyards to just 180ha (445 acres). Other new developments are at the northern end of the Helderberg in the Blaauwklippen Valley, where some new estates are already excelling. And, just outside the Stellenbosch district, in the windswept Lourensford Valley, is Vergelegen, one of South Africa's top wineries.

THE WARDS OF PAARL
Paarl at 155,173ha (383,427 acres), with 18,029ha (44,549 acres) of them under vine, is by far the larger district, with a multitude of different mesoclimates, soils, altitudes and aspects.

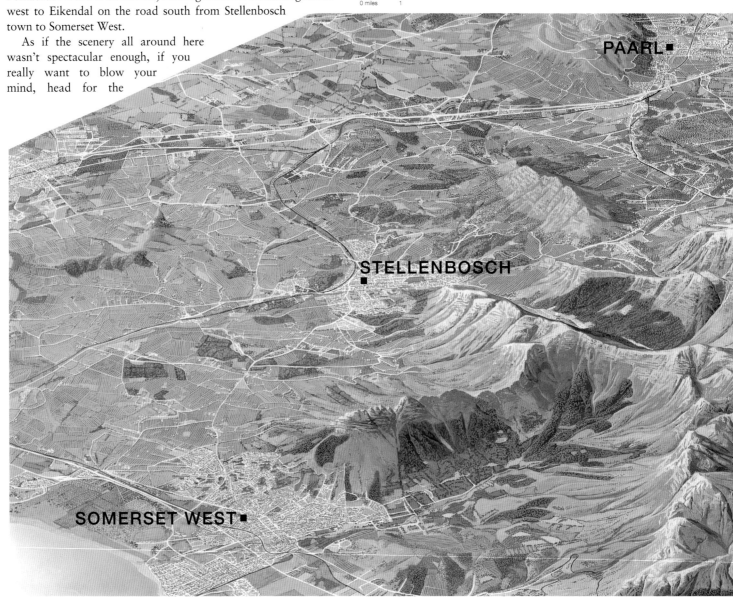

Mulderbosch's Sauvignon Blanc has acquired cult status since the early 1990s.

Unlike Stellenbosch, it has never claimed to be a cool area, and receives only the tail end of the False Bay breezes plus some Atlantic winds from the west. Consequently it's doing some storming stuff with the Rhône varieties and with Pinotage. But there are also spots where the fragile Pinot Noir puts in a good performance.

There are four wards in Paarl. Franschhoek, the most famous, is a long valley barricaded by mountains, but only a small part of the land is suitable for vines. Inaccessibility, forest, otherwise unsuitable land and other fruit orchards mean that only 1500ha (3700 acres) of its 11,000ha (27,180 acres) are planted with vines. Frankly, the alluvial and sandy soil of the valley floor has produced inferior wines for decades, but largely because, despite a spread of seemingly lovely estates, their fruit was processed at the co-op. You thought their wines tasted the same? They probably were the same. But now producers like Boekenhoutskloof are showing these soils can produce stunning Semillon and Cabernet if carefully farmed, and there's still a

huge variety of north-, south-, east- and west-facing slopes to be exploited. Plantings so far go as high as 420m (1378ft), and the chief problem is to maximize the cooling effect of the south-easterly winds that sweep down the valley without having your vines bludgeoned out of existence. Simonsberg-Paarl, on the northern and eastern foothills of the Simonsberg, has clearly got something special, because in a supposedly hot area Glen Carlou produces medal-winning Pinot Noir, while just across the valley on the south side of Paarl mountain, Fairview's Rhône and Bordeaux varieties bake to perfection in the afternoon sun. Wellington Ward is hotter, and well away from sea breezes. Its Chenin Blanc used to be a mainstay of Cape 'sherry', yet that's only half the story. There's a whole hillside of top quality, iron-rich Glen Rosa soil producing excellent reds, and the east-facing slopes of the Groenberg have some of the coolest conditions in the Western Cape – and stunning reds, of all things to show for it. The Voor Paardeberg Ward is west of Wellington and specializes in red wines.

WHERE THE VINEYARDS ARE *The most important feature on this map is down in the bottom left-hand corner, where you see False Bay. With Stellenbosch and Paarl vineyards lying at around 34° South, the sun would simply be too strong to produce fragrant, subtle wines. Even the Benguela Current, which runs along the west coast, barely*

affects False Bay. But every summer's day a south-easterly wind brews up from a high pressure zone over the continental shelf at the southern tip of Africa. It's the movement, rather than the temperature, of this wind, that is so effective in cooling the vines. The next most important feature on the map are the mountains. They provide excellent sloping vineyard sites up to about 600m (1970 ft), at which point slopes generally become too steep for cultivation, and soil gives way to bare rock. But even vineyards away from the slopes are not on flat land: most Stellenbosch ones grow on some sort of undulation, even if they are described as 'valleys'. In Paarl, there are a few riverbank vineyards, but these are mostly for table grapes.

STELLENBOSCH AND PAARL

TOTAL DISTANCE NORTH TO SOUTH
47KM (29 MILES)

▨▨▨ VINEYARDS

N

SELECTED WINERIES

STELLENBOSCH			
1. Hazendal	15. Mulderbosch	29. Le Riche	43. Morgenster
2. Kaapzicht	16. Beyerskloof	30. Neil Ellis	44. Vergelegen
3. Jordan	17. Bergkelder	31. Blaauwklippen	**PAARL**
4. Uiterwyk/DeWaal	18. L'Avenir	32. Vriesenhof	45. Nederburg
5. De Toren	19. Morgenhof	33. Stellenzicht	46. KWV
6. Meerlust	20. Delheim	34. Waterford	47. Fairview
7. Spier	21. Kanonkop	35. De Trafford	48. Welgemoend
8. Overgaauw	22. Warwick	36. Ernie Els	49. Glen Carlou
9. Neethlingshof	23. Le Bonheur	37. Rust en Vrede	50. Backsberg
10. Hartenberg	24. Lievland	38. Longridge	51. Rupert & Rothschild
11. Villiera	25. Rustenberg	39. Grangehurst	52. Plaisir de Merle
12. Meinert	26. Tokara	40. Avontuur	53. Boschendal
13. Middelvlei	27. Thelema	41. Ken Forrester	53. Nederburg
14. Simonsig	28. Delaire	42. Cordoba	

54. Graham Beck
55. La Motte
56. Boekenhoutskloof
57. Stony Brook
58. Cabrière

PAARL = WINE DISTRICT

—— WINE DISTRICT BOUNDARY

Franschhoek = WINE WARD

•••• WINE WARD BOUNDARY

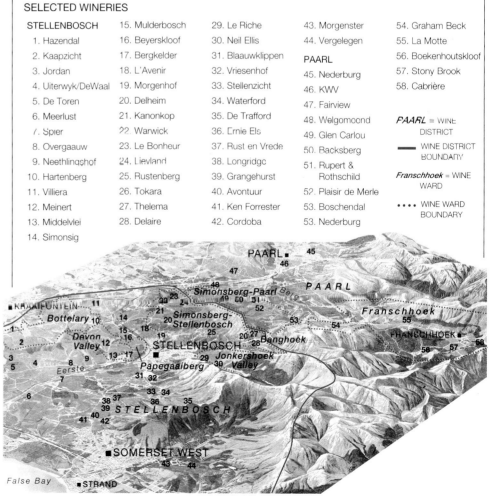

NORTH AFRICA

IT'S THE WASTED POTENTIAL that makes me want to cry. There are so many good vineyards here – or at least, vineyards that could be good, if anybody cared. Eighty per cent of the vines in Algeria are over 50 years old. Anywhere else – like Australia or Burgundy, say – they'd be jumping up and down with resources like that. They'd be making incredibly concentrated, brooding, spicy red wines and they'd have buyers queueing down the street. What happens here? Very little. The majority just go on making rough, fruitless, baked wines without flavour or acidity. There hasn't been a market for these wines since the French left in the 1950s and early 1960s. And as the French left their colonies, so did the best winemakers, heading for France's Midi.

France was North Africa's biggest market for wine from the early 1900s onwards, and in the 1950s between a half and two-thirds of the entire international wine trade was in North African wines. When the wine arrived in France, it was mostly blended with rather smarter French stuff, in a way that would be illegal now under EU rules. As the market fell away, so did the area under vine: Algeria, always the biggest producer of the three countries, had 400,000ha (988,387 acres) in 1938. By 2004, it hit a low of 95,000ha (234,742 acres). Three-quarters of Algeria's wine production is in the western coastal province of Oran, but much is still bottled and matured in France; and political uncertainty hinders progress. Tunisia's vineyards have also shrunk (to 23,000ha/56,832 acres), but there has been substantial foreign investment in recent years, such as the Italian Calatrasi operation in Khanguet involving an $8million investment, the grafting of new varietals, coupled with New World expertise. Tourism soaks up much of the production and little is exported.

Morocco was always the smallest producer of the three countries but produced the best quality wine. When the French left Morocco in 1956, the area under wine vines was about 55,000ha (135,900 acres); this had fallen to about 10,600ha (26,192 acres) by 2004. The phrase 'Moroccan wine' is no longer an oxymoron, though. Castel Frères' huge development is instigating a rebirth. Nearly 1200ha (2965 acres), split between Boulaouane and Meknès, the main vineyard areas, have been planted, and two large wineries are producing a range of decent offerings, including tasty Syrah and Cabernet reds.

So it's not all doom and gloom. The vines that have been uprooted were those on the hot plains: those that remain are on the cooler coastal ranges, where they are planted at up to 1200m (3937ft) above sea level – a relatively high altitude meaning cooler temperatures. Morocco benefits from an Atlantic coastline with its cooling breezes, although wind can be a problem: imagine being a vine in a near-desert country, with winds sweeping in from the Atlantic at 65km (40 miles) per hour. In Tunisia it's the hot, dry Scirocco wind that reduces the yields. What these countries need is advice on how to trellis and plant vines to protect them from wind. Because there's no reason why they couldn't be making brilliant wines. Sure, it's hot and dry – Algeria's vineyards only get 400–600mm (16–24in) of rain each year. But parts of Spain get less than that. Indeed, the 'Sahara Region' is now being officially extended to encompass southern Spain and Sicily.

GRAPE VARIETIES

Most of the grapes planted in North Africa are dull. Carignan is king, and shows over and over again just what reliably fruitless, tough red wine it can produce. Alicante Bouschet, Aramon and Cinsaut are equally uninspiring, though Cinsaut can do better if it's handled well. But Cabernet Sauvignon, Merlot, Mourvèdre and Syrah are becoming more widespread and growers should concentrate on these. Because sometimes when you taste the better reds, you get a glimpse – just a glimpse – of what they could achieve. Earthy, dusty, rustic (I'm not asking for miracles here), but with some ripe raspberry fruit. A bit of carbonic maceration could help no end in getting some juiciness and freshness into the wines.

As for whites, there's a fair bit of Clairette and Ugni Blanc, both contenders for the world's dullest wine grape, but Tunisia's sweet and dry Muscats are probably the best whites – pretty hefty, but at least they have perfume and fruit. Greater investment is the real key to improved quality. North Africans aren't great wine drinkers, and Islamic fundamentalism means attitudes to wine are ambiguous. The Koran forbids drinking alcohol, but the currency that can be earned from wine exports is a big attraction. Wine continues to be made and exported, so there must be a tiny ray of hope for the future.

WINE AREAS

▨ MOROCCO	▨ ALGERIA	▨ TUNISIA
APPELLATION D'ORIGINE GARANTIE WINE REGIONS	APPELLATION D'ORIGINE GARANTIE WINE REGIONS	APPELLATION D'ORIGINE CONTROLÉE WINE REGIONS
1. Doukkala	15. Côteaux de Tlemcen	22. Tibar
2. Sahel	16. Monts du Tessalah	23. 1er Cru Côteaux Tebourba
3. Zaer	17. Côteaux de Mascara	24. 1er Cru Côteaux d'Ultique
4. Zenata	18. Dahra	25. 1er Cru Muscat de Kelibia
5. Chellah	19. Côteaux du Zaccar	26. Mornag
6. Zemmour	20. Medéa	27. Sidi Salaam
7. Guerrouane	21. Ain Bessem-Bouira	28. Grand Cru Mornag
8. Beni M'tir		
9. Saiss		
10. Beni Sadden		
11. Zerhoun		
12. Rharb		
13. Angad		
14. Berkane		

ASIA

I WONDER, WOULD Cow's Nipple blend better with Cock's Heart or Dragon's Eye? And should I oak it? No, it's a serious question, and one which during the next generation, we might need to answer, because these are Asian grape varieties and they do produce wine. They sound unfamiliar: from the few examples I've had, they taste unfamiliar too, but the culture of wine is catching on in Asia. The economic boom at the end of the 20th century saw top-quality European wine reach higher prices in markets like Singapore, Hong Kong and Shanghai than anywhere else. Add to this the widespread evidence that red wine is good for your heart, and a greatly increased awareness of all things Western as globalization continues on its remorseless path, and we could be looking at the birth – or rather rebirth, since both China and India have long, though largely lapsed, wine traditions – of a globally significant wine culture, which will not be satisfied merely by importing European wine, but will want to manufacture its own.

CHINA

China's wine industry is growing like a weed now that official policy promotes wine. Although the majority of Chinese are reluctant to drink wine, demand for its wines is on the increase, particularly in the booming cities as the economy expands. China now ranks as the sixth biggest wine producer in the world with some 470,000ha (1,161,354 acres) of vines, but it is estimated that only 10 per cent of the grapes grown are crushed for wine. Inland regions, with their extreme climate, are best for dessert grapes or raisins, such as those grown in Xinjiang province in the north-west at 150m (492ft) below sea level. In the north-east, a maritime climate, moderate but for the occasional typhoon, produces the best wines, particularly in the coastal provinces of Shandong, Hebei and Tianjin. Many international varieties have been planted as well as traditional Chinese, German and Russian versions. And there is now a string of joint ventures between Western and Chinese companies, involving such companies as Rémy Martin and Pernod-Ricard of France, Torres of Spain and Sella & Mosca from Sardinia. I've had Chardonnays and Cabernet Francs, in particular from Shandong and Hebei, which were extremely good.

Western investment and involvement in wine production has led to a major change in style. Chinese taste in wine (really the Chinese taste is for rice wine or, better still, brandy) is for something sweetish and oxidized. There's no point in planting Chardonnay for that sort of wine – but anyway, what's wanted is wines to appeal to Western wallets. This means that, just like everywhere else in the world, the newest wines aim to imitate classic European styles. So far they show promise.

INDIA

India has a long winemaking history, though its recent fame as a wine-producer is due entirely to Omar Khayyam, a Champagne-method sparkler launched by Château Indage in 1985, and made for a time with technical assistance from Piper-Heidsieck of Champagne. Grapes for it are grown in the Maharashtra hills above Bombay, and it is these highland areas that come nearest to escaping India's

heat. Even so, massive irrigation is necessary, vines generally giving two crops a year; the monsoon crop is understandably less well regarded. Omar Khayyam is a blend of Chardonnay, Ugni Blanc, Pinot Noir, Pinot Blanc and Thompson Seedless: and while the white is good, the pink is fresh and excellent. There's also a sweeter fizz called Marquise de Pompadour, and red and white still wines. These bode well, as foreign winemakers get to grips with oak-aging Cabernet, Shiraz, Chardonnay and Ugni Blanc blends. Californian and French joint ventures are evidence of Indage's ambition, something Bangalore's Grover Vineyards also showed by using Bordeaux super-consultant Michel Rolland.

Vinifera vines have to be grafted in India, because phylloxera reached the subcontinent in the 1890s and wreaked as much havoc locally as it did elsewhere. The state of Maharashtra produces around 40 per cent of India's grapes, the rest coming from Karnataka, Andhra Pradesh and the Punjab, although less than one per cent of the total is made into wine.

JAPAN

In Japan, the problem is too much rain. There are spring and autumn monsoons, typhoons in summer, and icy winters. Land is either mountainous, or flat and waterlogged; there's little gently sloping terrain, beloved of vine growers. But a trellising system called *tana-zukuri* spreads vines out along wires, so they can dry. The Mount Fuji area, west of Tokyo, especially Yamanashi, is proving the best so far. The east coast is more extreme. In all, wine is made in 46 out of 47 provinces, tropical Okinawa being the odd one out.

Japanese varieties and hybrids account for most of the vineyards, but only about ten per cent of grapes are used to make wine, much of it blended with bulk imports. The favourite *vinifera* vine is Koshu, giving big, juicy dessert grapes and light white wines. High rainfall and high vine yields tend to make Japanese wines light in body. Suntory make some exceptions with Bordeaux varieties, as well as impressive Sauternes-like sweet wine. The smaller producers now appearing are spearheading a drive towards quality home produce, but too much is still imported bulk wine bottled in Japan.

The imitation of European styles is the aim of China's new export-oriented wine industry. This Chardonnay, at Hua Dong Winery in Qingdao, is likely to be made into table wine, rather than for brandy or dried fruit.

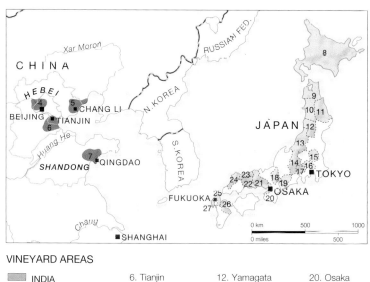

VINEYARD AREAS

INDIA	6. Tianjin	12. Yamagata	20. Osaka
1. Punjab	7. Qingdao	13. Niigata	21. Hyogo
2. Maharashtra	**JAPAN**	14. Nagano	22. Okayama
3. Karnataka	8. Hokkaido	15. Tochigi	23. Tottori
CHINA	9. Aomori	16. Saitama	24. Shimane
4. Sha Cheng	10. Akita	17. Yamanashi	25. Fukuoka
5. Chang Li	11. Iwate	18. Shiga	26. Oita
		19. Aichi	27. Nagasaki

Index

Note: D = Diagram, K = Map Key, M = Map, R = River

A

Aare R 140M
Aargau 140M
Abbadia 177M
Abbazia di Rosazzo 167
Abbazia Santa Anastasia 183
Abbey Vale 307
Abona DO 187K
Abreu 247K
Abruzzo 152, 168, 153K, 153M, 169K, 169M
Acacia 245K
Achaia Clauss 230
Achkarren 135M, 137M
Aconcagua R/Valley 24, 273, 274, 273K, 273M
Açores (Azores) 209, 209M
Açores VR 209M
Acquaviva 177M
Acqui Terme 155M
Adams, Tim 294K
Adelaida 250, 251M
Adelaide 13, 286, 288, 289, 292, 287M
Adelaide Hills 21, 289, 300, 289K
Adelaide (Super-zone) 287K
Adelsheim 261K
Adige (Etsch) R/Valley 152, 160, 161, 162, 163, 165, 153M, 161M, 163M, 164M
Affi 164M
Agde 103M
Agen 107, 31M, 106M, 109M
Aglianico del Vulture DOC 181, 153K, 180K
Agly R 104, 102M
Agout R 106M
Agrelo 283, 283M
Agrigento 183M
Água Alta, Quinta da 213K
Ahr R/Valley 120, 122, 113K, 113M, 122K, 122M
Aichi 327K
Aigle 140M
Aïdarinis 230
Aiguillon 106M
Ain R 31M, 99M, 109M
Aire-sur-l'Adour 106M
Aiud 224K
Aix-en-Provence 100, 31M, 100M
Aix-les-Bains 99M
Ajaccio 105, 31M, 105M, 109M
Ajaccio AC 105, 105K
Akaroa 316, 311M
Akita 327K
Alabama 255, 235M
Alava province 188, 192
Alba 154, 157, 158, 159, 155M, 159M
Alba Iulia 224K, 224M
Albacete 201M
Albana di Romagna DOCG 153K, 169K
Albany 304, 305, 257M, 262M, 305K, 305M
Albarine R 99M
Alberche R 201M
Albert River 309
Alberta 235M
Albertville 99, 99M
Albi 31M, 106M, 109M
Albuquerque 255
Alcamo 183, 183M
Alcamo DOC 153K, 183K
Alcantara R 183M
Alcobaça IPR 209K
Aleatico di Puglia DOC 180K
Alella DO 186, 189, 191, 187K, 189K
Alenquer DOC 209, 214, 209K
Alentejano VR 215, 209M
Alentejo DOC 8, 215, 209K
Aléria 105M
Alessandria 156, 153M, 155M
Alexander Valley 1, 240, 241, 241M
Alexander Valley AVA 236K; wineries and vineyards 241K
Alfaro 188, 189M
Alföld (Great Plains) 220, 221M
Algarve 215, 209M
Algeria 312, 326, 326M; wine regions 326K
Alghero 182, 182M
Alghero DOC 182K
Aliakmonas R 230M
Alicante 201, 187M, 201M
Alicante DO 201, 187K, 201K
Alice Springs 286, 309, 309M
Alijó 212
Allan Scott 319K
Allandale 303K
Allegrini 164
Allen Vineyard 243K
Allier R/Valley 83, 31M, 81M, 109M
Almansa DO 200, 187K, 201K
Almaviva 276, 277, 277K
Almeirim *see* Ribatejo
Almería 202
Alorna, Casa de 214
Aloxe-Corton AC 61, 62, 61D, 63K, 63M
Alpha Domus 314K
Alpine Valleys 296K
Alps 68, 99, 141, 145, 151, 152, 154, 156, 162, 164, 99M, 109M, 144M, 153M, 155M
Alsace AC 12, 22, 24, 30, 76-9, 120, 130, 131, 136, 31M, 76-7M, 78D, 79K; appellations and classifications 77, 78
Alsace Grand Cru AC 77, 78, 79K
Alsace Sélection de Grains Nobles AC 77, 78
Alsace Vendange Tardive AC 77, 78
Alsheim 128
Altair 279K
Alta Vista 283K
Altamura 245K
Altdorf 140M
Altesino 174, 175K
Alto Adige/Süd-Tirol DOC 22, 24, 160, 153K, 153M, 161K, 162-3M, 163K; *see also* Trentino-Alto Adige
Alto Las Hormigas 283K
Alto Jahuel 276
Altus 255
Alushta 222M
Alzey 121M
Ama, Castello di 173K
Amador County 254
Ambelon Estate 230
Amberley Estate 307, 307K
Amboise 86, 81M, 87M
Amboise, Ch. 83
Ambonnay 75, 75M
American Canyon 244
Ammerschwihr 79M
Ampuis 90, 92, 93, 92M
Amur R 266
Amyntaio AO 230K
Anahena 279K
Anapa 223, 222M
Ancenis 31M, 81M
Anchialos AO 230K
Ancona 153M, 169M
Andalucía 186, 202, 187K, 187M, 201M, 203M
Andernach 122M
Anderson, S, Vineyard 247K
Anderson Valley AVA (California) 238, 241, 236K, 239K
Anderson Valley (New Mexico) 255
Andes 270, 271, 272, 273, 274, 275, 276, 278, 280, 282, 283, 270M, 273M, 274D, 281M
Andhra Pradesh 327, 327M
Andrew Will 257
Andriano/Andrian 163M
Angaston 290, 291M
Angélus, Ch. 44, 50, 45K
Angers 80, 82, 85, 31M, 81M, 84M 109M
d'Angludet, Ch. 32, 37, 38K
Angostura 278
Angwin 245M
Anjou AC 81, 85, 81K
Anjou-Coteaux de la Loire AC 84, 81K
Anjou-Saumur (region) 81-2, 84-5, 81K, 85K
Anjou-Villages AC 82, 84, 81K
Ankara 231, 231M
Annapolis Valley 266
Annecy 99M
Annie's Lane 294K
Antaño, Bodegas 197
Antequera 203, 203M
Antinori, Lodovico & Piero 178
Antiyal 277K
Antonopoulos 230
Anubis 283K
Aomori 327K
Aosta 155, 153M, 155M
Aosta Valley *see* Valle d'Aosta DOC
Apalta 279
Apennines 151, 152, 154, 168, 170, 173, 181, 183, 153M, 169M, 180M
Apetlon 148, 149M
Apex 259K
Appenzell 140M
Appiano/Eppan 163M
Applegate Valley AVA 257K
Apt 98, 97M
Aquebogue 265M
L'Aquila 153M, 169M
Aquileia 161M
Aquitania 276, 277K
Arabako Txakolina DO 188, 187K, 189K
Arad 224M
Aragón 186, 188, 194-5, 187K, 187M, 189K, 189M, 201M
Aragón R 189M
Aramas Laona 231K
Aranda de Duero 199, 187M, 196M
Araujo/Eisele Vineyard 245K
Araz R 222M
Arbois 31M, 99M, 109M
Arbois AC 99K
d'Arche, Ch. 49K
Archery Summit 261K
Arcins 38M
Ardèche (mountains) 97, 98
Ardèche R 31M, 96M, 109M
Ardières R 69M
Ardon 143, 142M
Arezzo 153M, 169M
Arganda 201M
Argentina 22, 24, 270, 271, 280-3, 270M, 281M; classification system 280; wine regions 280-1, 281K; wineries 283K
Argeş R 225, 224M
Argiano, Castello di 174, 281, 175K
Argyle 261K
Arhanes AO 230K
Arizona 235M
Arizu, Leoncio 283K
Arkansas 255, 235M
Arlãza DO 197, 187K, 196K
Arles 100, 100M
Armagnac 106, 107
Armenia 223, 222K, 222M
Arno R 152, 153M, 169M
Arnoya R 197
Arrábida hills 214
Arras 308
Arrowfield 302
Arrowood 245K
Arroyo Grande Valley AVA 250, 251-2, 236K, 251K
Arroyo Seco AVA 249, 236K, 248K
Arroyo Seco R 248M
Arruda 215
Arruda DOC 209K
Arsac 36, 38M
Artesa 245K
Arthur's Creek 299K
Arve-et-Léman 140K
Arve-et-Rhône 140K
Aschaffenburg 134, 134M
Ascoli Piceno 169M
Asenovgrad 229, 228K, 228M
Ashbrook Estate 307K
Askerne 314K
Aspang 144M
Asprokambos 230
Assisi 169M
Assmannshausen 120, 123, 124, 125M
Associated Vintners 257
Asti 157, 153M, 155M
Asti DOCG 153K, 155K
Asturias 187M, 196M
Ászár-Neszmély 220, 221K
Ata Rangi 310
Atacama 273, 274
Atascadero 251M
Athina (Athens) 230, 230M
Atlas Peak AVA 246, 245M
Atlas Peak 245K
Atuel R 283, 281M
Au Bon Climat/Qupé 233, 253, 253K
Aubance Valley 82
Aube (Côte des Bar) (region) 70, 72, 73
Aube R 31M, 73M, 109M
Auburn 294, 294M
Auch 31M, 106M, 109M
Auckland 311, 312-13, 316, 311K, 311M
Aude *département* 8, 108, 109M
Aude R/Valley 103, 104, 31M, 102M, 106M, 109M
Vin de Pays de l'Aude 80
Auggen 135M
Augusta AVA 255
Aurillac 106M
Ausone, Ch. 45K, 46D
Austin 255, 235K
Australia 17, 18, 19: classification system 286; wine regions 286-309, 287K
Australian Alps 301
Australian Capital Territory (ACT) 301, 287M, 296M, 301M
Austria 24: classification system 145; wine regions 144-9, 144M
Auxerre 52, 53M, 109M
Auxey-Duresses AC 54, 62, 63K, 63M
Aveiro 209, 209M
Avellino 153M, 180M
Avelsbach 119K, 119M
Avenay-Val d'Or 75, 75M
Avignon 90, 91, 97, 98, 100, 31M, 96M, 100M, 109M
Avignonesi 176, 177K
Avize 75, 75M
Avoca 296, 296M
Avontuur 325K
Awatere Valley 316, 318
Ay 72, 75, 71M, 75M
Ayl 119K, 119M
Azay-le-Rideau 83, 86, 87M
Azé 55
Azeitão 215, 209M
Azerbaijan 223, 222K, 222M

B

Babadag 224K
Babcock 253K
Bacalhôa, Quinta de 214
Bacău 224M
Bacharach 122, 122M
Bacio Divino 247K
Backsberg 325K
Bad Dürkheim 120, 131, 121M, 130M
Bad Kreuznach 120, 126, 127, 121M, 127M
Bad Neuenahr-Ahrweiler 122M
Badacsony 220, 221K
Badajoz 201M
Baden (Austria) 144M
Baden (Germany) 112, 120, 135-6, 138, 113K, 113M, 135M; top vineyards 137K
Baden-Baden 120, 135, 136, 113M, 135M
Badia a Coltibuono 173K
Badia a Passignano 173K
Badische Bergstrasse, Bereich 136, 138, 135K
Bagnols-sur-Cèze 96M
Baileys 297
Bairrada DOC 208, 209, 211, 209K
Baixo Corgo 212
Baja (Hungary) 221M
Baja California 271, 270M
Baja Montaña 195
Bakersfield 254, 236M
Baki (Baku) 223, 222M
Bakony hills 220, 221M
Balatonboglár 220, 221K, 221M
Balatonfelvidék 221K
Balatonfüred-Csopak 220, 221M
Balearic Islands *see* Islas Baleares
Ballarat 296, 297, 296M
Balnaves 293K
Bălţi 222, 223, 222M
Bamboes Bay 322
Banat 225, 224K, 224M
Bandol 101M
Bandol AC 100, 101, 100K
Banfi 175K
Bangalore 327, 327M
Banghoek 324
Banks Peninsula 316, 317, 311M
Banksdale 21
Bannockburn 317, 311M
Banyuls VDN 30, 104, 103K
Banyuls-sur-Mer 102M
Bar-sur-Aube 73, 31M, 73M
Bar-sur-Seine 73, 31M, 73M
Baranja 226
Barbanne R 46, 47, 45M
Barbaresco 159M
Barbaresco DOCG 157, 158-9, 153K, 155K, 159M; crus and vineyards 159K
Barbastro 189M
de Barbe, Ch. 51
Barbera d'Alba DOC 155K
Barbera d'Asti DOC 153K, 155K
Barberino Val d'Elsa 175M
Barbi 175K
Barboursville 263
Barca Velha (211
Barcelona 13, 188, 190, 191, 187M, 189M
Barco Reale DOC *see* Carmignano
Bardolino 161M
Bardolino DOC 161, 165, 153K, 161K
Bari 153M, 180M
Barnett 245K
Barolo (village) 156
Barolo DOCG 157, 158-9, 153K, 155K, 158D, 159K, 159M; top crus and vineyards 159K
Barossa Range 14, 291M
Barossa and Barossa Valley 18, 272, 285, 286, 288, 289, 290-1, 287K, 289K, 290-1M; wineries 291K
Barossa Valley Estate 291K
Barrancas 283
Barry Wines, Brian 294K
Barry Wines, Jim 294K
Barsac 48, 49M
Barsac AC 35, 43, 32K, 49M
Barwang 301
Bas-Médoc 41
Bas Valais 143
Basedow 291K
Basel 120, 135, 113M, 135M, 140M
Basento R 180M
Basignani 263
Basilicata 180, 181, 153K, 153M, 180K, 180M
Basilico 181
Bastelica 105M
Bastia 31M, 105M, 109M
Bastor-Lamontagne, Ch. 49K
Bat'Umi 222M
Batailley, Ch. 41K
Bâtard-Montrachet AC 61, 63K
Bathurst 300, 301M
de la Baume, Dom. 103
les Baux-de-Provence AC 100, 101, 100K, 100M
Bay of Plenty 313, 311K 311M
Bay View 314, 314M
Bayerischer Bodensee, Bereich 136, 135K
Bayern 113M, 134M, 135M
Bayonne 31M, 106M, 109M
Beamsville Bench 269
Béarn AC 107, 106K
Béarn Bellocq AC 106K
de Beaucastel, Ch. 16, 250, 98D
Beaufort 99M
Beaujeu 69M
Beaujolais AC and Beaujolais-Villages AC 54-5, 68-9, 53K, 69K, 69M; Beaujolais Crus 55, 69, 69K
Beaujolais Nouveau 68
Beaulieu-sur-Layon 84M
Beaulieu Vineyard 247K
Beaumes-de-Venise AC 91, 97, 98, 97K
Beaumont-sur-Vesle 75M
Beaune 55, 62, 31M, 53M, 63M, 109M
Beaune AC 61, 62, 63K
de Beaurenard, Dom. 98D
Beauséjour, Ch. 45K
Beau-Séjour Bécot, Ch. 44
Beaux Frères 261K
Beaverton 261M
Beblenheim 79M
Beck, Graham 20, 325K
Beckmen 253K
Bédarrides 98, 98D
Bedell 265K
Beechworth 296K, 297
Bega R 224M
Beine 57M
Beira Interior 209K
Beiras 209M
Beja 209M
Bekaa Valley 231, 231K
Bel Air-Marquis d'Aligre, Ch. 38K
Belair, Ch. 45K
Belgrave, Ch. 41K
Belice R 183M
Bella Unión 272M
Belle Terre 241K
Bellet AC 100, 101
Belleville 55, 53M, 69M
Belley 99M
Bellingham 257M
Bellinzona 140M
Belvedere, Tenuta 178
Ben Lomond Mountain AVA 248K
Benalla 296M
Benanti 183
Bend 257M
Bendigo 296, 297, 296K, 296M, 317
Benidorm 201, 201M
Bennwihr 79M
Bensheim 138
Benton City 259M
Benziger 245K
Bergamo 155M
Bergerac 46, 31M, 106M, 109M
Bergerac AC 106-7, 106K
Bergères-lès-Vertus 71, 71M, 75M
Bergheim 79, 79M
Bergsträsser Winzer 138
Beringer Blass (Australia) 286
Beringer (USA) 240, 252, 247K
Berg R 320M, 325M
Bergkelder winery 325K
Bern 141, 140M
Bernese Alps 142, 140M
Bernkastel, Bereich 111, 115, 117, 118, 115K, 117M
Bernkastel-Kues 111, 115, 116, 117, 118, 115M, 117K, 117M
Bertani 165
Besançon 109M
Bessa Valley 229
Bethany 291K
Beychevelle, Ch. 39, 40, 41K
Beyer 78
Beyerskloof 325K
Béziers 103, 31M, 102M, 109M
Biale, Robert 245K
Bianco d'Alcamo DOC 153K, 183K
Bianco di Custoza DOC 153K, 161K
Biarritz 106M
Bibbona 179M
Bicheno 308, 308M
Bickensohl 139M
Bielersee 140K, 140M
Biella 156, 155M
Bien Nacido Vineyard 233, 253K
Bienvenues-Bâtard-Montrachet AC 63K
Bierzo DO 197, 187K, 196K
Biferno DOC 168, 169K
Biferno R 169M
Big Rivers 301, 287K
Big Sur 250, 252, 248M
Bilbao (Bilbo) 188, 187M, 189M, 196M
Biltmore Estate 255
Bimbadgen winery 303K
Bindella 177K
Binder, Rolf 291K
Bingen 122, 124, 125, 126, 127, 128, 121M, 122M, 125M, 127M
Bingen, Bereich 128, 121K, 127M
Bingerbrück 127M
Binissalem-Mallorca DO 186, 189, 187K, 189K
Bío Bío R/Valley 273, 274, 275, 273K, 273M
Biondi-Santi 171, 174, 175K
Biriad R 224M
Birs R 140M
Bischoffingen 135M, 137M
Biscoitos DOC 209K
Bisquertt 279K
Bizeljsko-Sremič 227, 226K
Bizkaiko Txakolina DO 188, 187K, 189K
Blaauwklippen Valley 324
Blaauwklippen 325K
Black Forest 135, 136
Black Sea Region 228K
Black Sea States 222-3, 222M
Blackwood R/Valley 305, 305K, 305M
Blagny 62, 63M
Blankenhornsberg 137M
Blanquefort 40, 41
Blanquette de Limoux AC 103K
Blass, Wolf 291K
Blaye 34, 35, 50, 32M, 38M
Blenheim 318, 311M
Blois 80, 83, 86, 31M, 81M, 109M
Blok Estate, The 293K
Bloodwood Estate 301
Blue Ridge Mountains 263, 262M
Boa Vista, Quinta da 213K
Boberg 320K
Boca DOC 156
Bodenheim 128, 128M
Bodensee, Bereich 135K
Bodrog R 221, 221M
Boekenhoutskloof 325, 325K
Bogotá 270M
Bohotin 224K
Bois de Boursan, Dom. de 98D
Boise 257M
Bolgheri (village) 178, 179M
Bolgheri DOC 178-9, 153K, 169K, 178-9M, 179K
Bolgheri Sassicaia DOC 171, 169K
Bolhrad 222M
Bolivia 271, 270M
Bollène 97, 98, 96M
Bollullos par del Condado 202, 203M
Bologna 168, 153M, 169M
Bolzano 161, 162, 163, 153M, 161M, 163M
Bom Retiro, Quinta do 213K
Bomfim, Quinta do (Dow) 212, 213K
Bommes 48, 49M
Bonifacio 31M, 105M, 109M
Bonn 120, 122, 113M, 122M
Bonneau, Henri 98D
Bonnes-Mares AC 60, 59K
Bonneville 99M
Bonnezeaux AC 82, 83, 85K
Bonny Doon 327
Bonvillars 141, 140K
Boonville 238M
Boordy Vineyards 263
Boppard 122, 122M
Borba *see* Alentejo
Bordeaux 22, 30, 32-51, 31M, 32-3K; appellations and classifications 35; 1855 Classification 36, 48; wine areas 36-51
Bordeaux AC and Bordeaux Supérieur AC 39, 51, 80, 32-3M
Bordeaux (city) 32, 36, 42, 43, 51, 31M, 32M, 43M, 106M, 109M
Bordeaux-Côtes de Francs AC 50, 32K
Bordeaux Haut-Benauge AC 32K
Bordeaux sweet wines 48-9
Borja 194, 189M
Bormida R 154, 155M
Bosa 182M
Boscarelli 177K
Boschendal 325K
Bosnia-Herzegovina 226, 226K, 226M
Bosquet des Papes 98D
Boston 235M, 262M
Bot River 320K
Bottelary 323, 324, 325M
Botzingen 137M
Bouchaine 245K
Boulaouane 326, 326M
Bourg 34, 35, 50, 32M
Bourg-en-Bresse 99M
Bourges 83, 88, 31M, 81M, 109M
Bourgneuf-Val d'Or 65, 64M
Bourgogne AC 52, 55, 59, 62, 61D
Bourgogne-Aligoté AC 59, 61D
Bourgogne-Côte Chalonnaise AC 65
Bourgogne Grand Ordinaire AC 55, 59, 62
Bourgogne-Hautes Côtes de Beaune AC 61D
Bourgogne-Hautes Côtes de Nuits AC 55
Bourgogne Passe-Tout-Grains AC 55, 59, 62
Bourgueil AC 80, 83, 86, 87, 81K, 86M, 87K
Boutari (Boutaris family) 230
Bouzeron 64, 65, 64K, 64M
Bouzy 72, 74, 75, 75M
Bowen Estate 293K
Boyup Brook 305, 305M
Bra 155M
La Braccesca 177K
Brachetto d'Acqui DOC 153K, 155K
Bradano R 180M
Bradley 248M
Braga 210, 209M
Bragança 209M
Bramaterra DOC 156
Branaire-Ducru, Ch. 40, 41K
La Brancaia 173K
Brancott 319K
Brands 293K
Brane-Cantenac, Ch. 36, 38K
Branne 45M
Branxton 303M
Bratislava 219, 219M
Braubach 122M
Brauneberg 115, 116, 117, 117K, 117M
Brazil 270, 271, 270M
la Brède 43M
Breede R 322, 320M
Breede River Valley Region 320K
Breedekloof 320K
Breganze 155
Breganze DOC 165, 153K, 161K
Breisach am Rhein 77M, 113M, 135M, 137M
Breisgau, Bereich 135, 136, 135K
Bremerton 257M
Brenner Pass 160, 163
Brenta R 161M
Brescia 155, 165, 153M, 155M
Bressanone 161M
Bressuire 81M
Brestnik 228K
Bretzenheim 127M
Breuer, Georg 124
le Breuil 75
Brick House 261K
Bridgetown 305, 305M
Brig 140M
Bright Brothers 214
Brignoles 101M
Brindisi 153M, 180M
Brindisi DOC 153K, 180K
Briones 192, 192M
Brisbane 287M, 309M
Brissac-Quincé 84, 84M
British Columbia 234, 235, 266, 267-8, 235M, 267M
Brno 219M
Brochon 59, 60, 59M
Broke Estate Vineyards 300
Broke Fordwich 301K
Broken R 297
Brokenback Range 300, 302, 303, 303M
Brokenwood 303K
Brolio, Castello di 173K

Bronzolo 163M
Brookfields 314K
Brookland Valley 307K
Brouilly AC 69, 69K
Brown Brothers 21
Bruce, David 248
Bruchsal 135M
Brunello di Montalcino DOCG 171, 174-5, 153K, 169K, 174-5M, 175K; top estates 175K
Bryant Family Vineyard 245K
Buçaco 209M
Buçaco Palace Hotel 211
Bucci 168
Bucelas DOC 209, 214, 209K
Bucerchiale 168
Bucium 225
Bucureşti (Bucharest) 224, 224M
Budapest 221M
Budenheim 125M
Bué 88, 89M
Buellton 253, 251M, 253M
Buena Vista 245K
Buenos Aires 270M
Buffalo 262M
Bugey 90, 99, 31M, 99M
Buin 276, 277, 277M
Bujori 224K
Bükk 221K
Bulgaria 228-9; wine regions 229, 228K
Bullas DO 201, 187K, 201K
Bunbury 305, 305M
Bündner-Herrschaft 140K
Buonconvento 174
Burg Cochem (formerly Zell), Bereich 115, 115K
Burg Layen 127M
Burge Family winemaker 291K
Burge, Grant 291K
Burgenland 144, 145, 148-9, 144K, 144M, 148-9M
Bürgerspital zum Heiligen Geist 132, 134
Burgess winery 245K
Burgos province 192, 197, 198
Bürgstadt 134, 134M
Burgundy 24, 30, 52-69, 31M; appellations and classifications 55; wine areas 56-69, 53M
Burkheim 137M
Burnett 309
Bussell Hwy 307
Busselton 305M
Butte de Saran 75
Buxy 64M
Buxy co-operative 55, 65
Buzău 224M
Buzet AC 106, 107, 106K
Buzet-sur-Baïse 106M
Bynum, Davis 243K
Byron 250, 253K
Bzenec 219, 219M

C

Ca' Marcanda 178, 179K
Cabardès AC 103K
Cabo Girão 217, 216M
Cabonne 301
Cabrière 325K
Cacchiano 173K
Caceres 201M
Cachapoal R/Valley 275, 278, 279, 273K, 273M, 279M
Cadaujac 43, 43M
Cadaval, Casa 214
Cadece/Casa Mia vineyard 259K
Cadillac 48, 51, 49M
Cadillac AC 49, 32K
Cádiz 202, 204, 187M, 203M, 205D
Cafaro 247K
Cafayate 270, 271, 280, 281, 281M
Caggiano, Antonio 181
Cagliari DOC 182, 153M, 182M
Cahors 22, 31M, 106M, 109M
Cahors AC 106, 107, 106K
Cahul 222
Calchaquí Valley 281K
Caillou, Ch. 49K
les Cailloux 98D
Cain Cellars 245K
Cairanne 91, 97, 96M
Cakebread 247K
Calabria 180, 181, 153K, 153M, 180K, 180M
Calafell 190M
Calatayud 187M, 189M
Calatayud DO 186, 188, 195, 187K
Calatrasi 326
Calchaquí Valley 280
Caldaro/Kaltern 161M, 163M; *see also* Lago di Caldaro DOC
Caldwell 257M
Calenzana 105M
Calera 249
Calheta 216M
California 12, 18, 24, 235, 236-54, 235M, 237D; main AVAs 236K, 239K; wineries 241K, 243K, 245K, 247K, 253K
California Shenandoah Valley AVA 254, 236K
Calingasta 281M
Calistoga 237, 240, 244, 245, 239M, 245M
Caliterra La Arboleda Winery 279K
Calitzdorp 322, 320M
Calitzdorp District 320K
Callaghan Vineyards 255
Calon-Ségur, Ch. 41K
La Calonica 177K
Caltanisetta 183M
Caluso 156, 155M
Caluso Passito DOC 155K
Calvi 105, 105M
Calzadilla 201
Câmara de Lobos 217, 216M
Cambas 230
Cambria 253K
Camden 300, 301M
Cameron 261K
Camigliano 175M
Campania 168, 181, 153K, 153M, 180K, 180M
Campbell 297
Campi Flegrei DOC 180K
Campo de Borja DO 186, 188, 194, 187K, 189K
Campobasso 153M, 169M
Canada 18, 235, 266-9; quality scheme 266
Canais, Quinta dos 213K
Canal Maestro Chiana 177M
Canale, Humberto 281
Canale (Piedmont) 155M
Canary Islands *see* Islas Canarias
Canberra 287M, 301M
Canberra District 301, 301K
Candelare R 180M
Canelli 152
Canelones 272, 272M
Canepa 277K
Canneto 177K
Cannonau di Sardegna DOC 153K, 182K
Canon, Ch. 45K
Canon-Fronsac AC 43, 47, 32K, 45M
Canon-la-Gaffelière, Ch. 50, 45K
Cantabria (region) 187M, 196M
Cantemerle, Ch. 36, 38K
Cantenac 36, 39, 38M
Cantenac-Brown, Ch. 36
Canterbury 311, 316, 317, 311K, 311M
Caparzo 174, 175K
Cape Agulhas 322, 320K, 320M
Cape Clairault 307, 305M, 307M
Cape Leeuwin 306, 305M
Cape Mentelle 307, 307K
Cape Naturaliste 306, 307, 305M
Cape Point 320K
Cape Town 13, 322, 324, 320M
Capel 305, 305M
Capel Vale 305
Capercaillie 303K
Capri DOC 180K, 180M
Capriva del Friuli 167, 166M
Carbonnieux, Ch. 43K
Carcassonne 103, 104, 31M, 102M, 106M, 109M
Carcavelos DOC 209K
Cardinale 247K
Carema DOC 155K
Carignano del Sulcis 153K, 182K
Cariñena DO 188, 195, 187K, 189K, 189M
Carl Reh 224
Carlton 261M
Carmel 231
Carmel Valley 249, 248M
Carmel Valley AVA 236K, 248K
Carmelo 272, 272M
Carmen 276, 277, 277K
Carmenet 245K
les Carmes Haut-Brion, Ch. 43K
Carmignano DOCG 171, 172, 153K, 169K
Carmo, Quinta do 215
Carneiro, Quinta do 214
Carneros AVA 8, 237, 241, 242, 243-4, 245, 236K, 237D, 239K, 244M, 245M; wineries and vineyards 245K
Carneros Creek 245K
Carnuntum 146, 144K
Carpathian (mountains) 221, 224, 225
Carpentras 97, 98, 96M
Carso DOC 161K
Cartaxo *see* Ribatejo
Cartegena 201M
Cartuxa 215
Carvalhas, Quinta dos (Royal Oporto) 212, 213K
Casa Lapostolle 279K
Casa Madero 271
Casa Silva 279K
Casablanca R/Valley 8, 18, 273, 274, 275, 273K, 273M
Casal de Loivos 213M
Le Casalte 177K
Casanova di Neri 175K
Las Casas del Toqui 279K
Cascade Range 256, 257, 258, 260, 261, 235M, 256M
Case Basse 175K
La Casella 177K
Casella 286
Caspian Sea 223, 222M
Cassegrain 301
Cassis 101M
Cassis AC 100, 101, 100K
Castagneto Carducci 178, 179M
Castagnole del Lanze 159M
Castel 231
Castel Boglione 157, 155M
Castel Frères 326
Castel del Monte DOC 181, 153K, 180K
Castel de Paolis 168
Castelbuono 183, 183K
Castelgiocondo 175K
Castell 134, 134M
La Castellada 167
Castellare 173K
Castelli Romani DOC 169K
Castellina in Chianti 173, 173M
Castello di Borghese 264, 265K
Castelnau-de-Médoc 38M
Castelnaudary 106M
Castelnuovo dell'Abate 175M
Castelnuovo Berardenga 173, 173M
Castelnuovo Don Bosco 156
Castelo Branco 209M
Castiglion del Bosco 174, 175K
Castiglione Falletto 158, 159M
Castilla-La Mancha 186, 200-1, 202, 187K, 187M, 189M, 196M, 201M
Castilla y León (Castile) 186, 196, 197, 198, 187K, 187M, 189M, 196K, 196M
Castillon-la-Bataille 50, 106, 33M, 106M
Castres 102M, 106M
Castroville 248
Catalunya (Catalonia) 186, 188-9, 190-1, 187K, 187M, 189K, 189M
Catalunya DO 190
Catamarca 281, 281M
Catania 183, 153M, 183M
Catanzaro 153M, 180M
Catena 282, 283, 283K
Catoctin AVA 262K
Catusseau 45M, 46D
Caucasus (mountains) 223, 222M
Cauquenes 275, 273M
Cava DO 189, 191
Cavadinha, Quinta da 213K
Cavado R/Valley 210, 209M
Cavaglia 155M
Cavaillon 100, 96M, 100M
Caymus 247K
Cayuga Lake AVA 262K
Cazadero 238, 242
Čechy 219, 219K
Cedar Creek 21
Cedrino R 182M
Cefalù 183M
Cellier le Brun 319K
Cenicero 188, 189M, 193M
Central Coast AVA (California) 248-53, 236K, 248K, 248M, 251K
Central Delaware Valley AVA 262K
Central Otago 8, 9, 14, 311, 312, 316, 317, 311K, 311M
Central Ranges (Australia) 287
Central Valley (Chile) 270, 273, 275, 276-9, 273K, 274D
Central Valley (USA) 236, 237, 238, 249, 254, 236K, 237D
Central Victoria 287K
Central Victorian High Country 296K
Central Western Australia 287K
Cerasuolo di Vittoria DOCG 153K183, 183K
Cernay 76, 76M
Cérons AC 43, 48, 49, 32K, 49M
Cervione 105M
Cervognano 177M
Cessnock 300, 302, 303, 301M, 303M
Cetto, L A 271
Cévennes 103
Chablais 141, 140K
Chablis 8, 56, 53M, 57M
Chablis AC 52, 55, 56-7, 53K, 56D; Grands Crus 56D, 57K; Premiers Crus 56D, 57K
Chacolí de Alava DO 188
Chacolí de Gueteria DO 188
Chacolí de Vizkaia DO 188
Chacras de Coria 283M
Chaddsford 263
Chagny 52, 54, 64, 53M, 63M, 64M
Chaintré 67M
Chalk Hill AVA 241, 242, 241M, 243M
Chalk Hill Winery 241K
Chalkidiki 230, 230M
Chalon-sur Saône 31M, 53M, 64M, 109M
Chalone AVA 236K, 248K
Chalone vineyards 249, 251
Chalonnes-sur-Loire 84, 84M
Châlons-en-Champagne 70, 31M, 109M
Chambave 155M
Chambers 297
Chambertin AC 59K
Chambertin-Clos de Bèze AC 59K
Chambéry 90, 99, 31M, 99M, 109M
Chambolle-Musigny AC 55, 58, 59, 60, 59K, 59M
Chambord, Ch. 86
Chamoson 143, 142M
Champagne AC 29, 30, 70-5, 31M, 70-1M, 72D, 73M, 74-5M; grand and premier cru villages 75M
Champignol-lès-Mondeville 73, 73M
Champillon 75M
Chamusca *see* Ribatejo
Chandon (Argentina) 283K
Chânes 66, 67M
Chang Li 327K, 327M
de Chantegrive, Ch. 43K
Chapelle-Chambertin AC 59K
la Chapelle-Vaupelteigne 57M
la Charbonnière, Dom. de 98D
Chardonnay (village) 66
Charleston 262M
Charmail, Ch. 41K
Charmes-Chambertin AC 59K
Charnay 67M
Charolles 52
Chassagne-Montrachet 61, 62, 63M
Chassagne-Montrachet AC 63K
Chasse-Spleen, Ch. 39, 38K
Chasselas 66, 67M
Château-Chalon 99M
Château-Chalon AC 99, 99K
Chateau des Charmes 269
Château Dauzac 38K
Château-Grillet AC 90, 92-3, 92K
Château la Gurgue 38K
Château Indage 327
Château Kefraya 231
Château Ksara 231
Château-du-Loir 81M
Chateau Los Boldos 279K
Château Mayne-Lalande 38K
Château Monbrison 38K
Chateau Montelena 233, 245K
Château Musar 231
Chateau Potelle 245K
Chateau St Jean 245K
Chateau Ste Claire 266
Chateau Ste Michelle 257, 259
Chateau Tahbilk 297
Château-Thierry 71, 70M
Châteaumeillant 31M, 109M
Châteaumeillant VDQS 81K
Châteauneuf-du-Pape AC 16, 91, 96, 97, 98, 96M, 97K; wine estates 98D
Chatham 269M
Chatillon-sur-Seine 73
Chaume AC 82, 83
Chavanay 92M
Chavignol 88, 89M
Chehalem Creek 261M
Chehalem 261K
Chemilly-sur-Serein 57M
Chénas AC 69, 69K
de Chenonceau, Ch. 80, 83, 86
Chenôve 60
Cher R 80, 86, 87, 31M, 81M, 87M, 109M
Cherasco 159M
Chesapeake Bay 263
Cheval-Blanc, Ch. 46, 47, 50, 45K, 46D
Chevalier, Dom. de 43, 43K
Chevalier-Montrachet AC 61, 63K
Cheverny AC 81K
Chiana Valley 177
Chianti DOCG 173, 153K, 169K
Chianti Classico DOCG 170-1, 172-3, 153K, 169K, 172-3M; top estates 173K
Chiclana de la Frontera 203M
Chico 236M
Chieri 156, 155M
Chieti 169M
Chigny-les-Roses 74, 75M
Chile 22, 24, 270, 273-9, 270M, 273M, 274D; wine regions 273K; wineries 277K, 279K
Chiles Valley 246
Chillán 274, 273M
Chimbarongo 278, 279M
Chimney Rock 247K
China 327, 327K, 327M; vineyard areas 327K
Chinon 82, 31M, 86M
Chinon AC 80, 83, 86, 87, 81K, 87K
Chinon, Ch. 86
Chinook 259K
Chipiona 204M
Chiroubles AC 68, 69, 69K, 69M
Chişinău 223, 222M
Chiusa/Klausen 163M
Choapa Valley 274, 273K
Cholet 31M, 81M
Chorey-lès-Beaune AC 63K, 63M
Chouilly 71, 71M, 75M
Christchurch 317, 311M
Chur 141, 140M
Church Road (Montana) 314K
Chusclan 96M
Ciacci Piccolomini d'Aragona 175K
La Ciarliana 177K
Cienega Valley AVA 248K
Cigales DO 186, 197, 187K, 196K, 196M
Cima Corgo 212, 213, 213M
Cimicky, Charles 291K
Cinca R 189M
Cinque Terre DOC 154, 153K, 155K
Cirò DOC 180, 181, 153K, 180K
Ciron R 33, 48, 49, 49M
Citrusdal Mountain 320K
Citrusdal Valley 320K
Ciudad Real 201M
Cividale del Friuli 161M, 166M
Cixerri R 182M
Clairault 307, 307K
Clairette de Die AC and Tradition AC 91, 98
Clairette du Languedoc AC 103K
la Clape 103, 104
Clare 294M
Clare Valley 8, 286, 289, 294-5, 289K, 295M; wineries 294K
Clarke, Ch. 39, 38K
Clark Fork R 257M
Clarksburg 254
Clarksburg AVA 236K
Claro R/Valley 273K, 273M
Claverie, Ch. 50
Le Clavoillon 21
Clayvin Vineyard 10
Clear Lake AVA 236K, 239K
Clearview 314K
Cleebronn 135M
Clemayne-Lalande 38K
Clerc-Milon, Ch. 41K
Clermont-Ferrand 31M, 81M, 109M
Clessé AC 55, 67
Clevedon 313, 311K
Cleveland 262M
Clifford Bay 319K
Climens, Ch. 49K
Clonakilla 301
Clos du Bois 241K
Clos Haut-Peyraguey, Ch. 49K
Clos des Lambrays AC 59K
Clos du Mont Olivet 98D
Clos de l'Oratoire 45K
Clos des Papes 98D
Clos Pegase 245K
Clos Pepe 253K
Clos Quebrada de Macul 276, 277, 277K
Clos de la Roche AC 60, 59K
Clos St-Denis AC 59K
Clos St-Fiacre 83
Clos St Thomas 231
Clos de Tart AC 59K
Clos du Val 247K
Clos de Vougeot AC 60, 59K
Cloudy Bay 319M
Cloudy Bay 317, 318, 319K
Clover Hill 308
Cloverdale 240, 239M
Cluj-Napoca 224M
Clutha R 311M
Coal R 308, 308M
Coast Ranges (USA) 238, 239, 243, 254, 256, 260, 261, 235M, 236M, 257M
Coastal Ranges (Chile) 273, 275, 276, 277, 278, 279, 274D
Coastal Region (South Africa) 320K
Coastlands 242
Cochem 115M
Codorníu 191
Codru 222
Coeur d'Alene 257M
Coffaro, David 241K
Coghinas R 182M
Cohn, B R 245K
Coimbra 209, 209M
Col d'Orcia 175K
Col Solare 259K
Colares DOC 209, 214, 209K
Colchagua Valley 272, 274, 275, 278, 273K
Coldstream 299, 299M
Coldstream Hills 297, 298, 299, 298D, 299K
Colgin 247K
Colle al Matrichese estate 174
Colli Albani DOC 169K
Colli Aretini 170
Colli Berici DOC 165, 161K
Colli Bolognesi DOC 168, 153K, 169K
Colli di Bolzano DOC 161K
Colli Euganei DOC 165, 161K
Colli Lanuvini DOC 169K
Colli di Luni 155K
Colli Martani DOC 168, 169K
Colli Orientali del Friuli DOC 167, 227, 153K, 161K, 166M
Colli di Parma DOC 168, 169K
Colli Pesaresi DOC 169K
Colli Piacentini DOC 168, 153K, 169K
Colli Tortonesi DOC 155K
Colli del Trasimeno DOC 169K
Colline Lucchesi DOC 169K
Colline Metallifere DOC 178
Colline Pisane DOC 173
Collio Goriziano DOC 167, 153K, 161K, 166M
Collioure AC 103, 104, 103K
Colmar 76, 78, 31M, 76M, 78D, 79M
Colombia 271, 270M
Colombo, Jean-Luc 95
Colorado 255, 235M
Colorado R (Argentina) 281
Colorado R/Valley (USA) 255, 235M
Colterenzio co-operative 162
Columbia Gorge AVA 257K
Columbia R/Valley 256, 257, 258, 259, 261, 235M, 257M, 259M
Columbia mountains 268
Columbia Valley AVA 257K, 259M
Comaum Range 292
Comblanchien 59M
Commandaria 231K
Commonwealth of Independent States (CIS) 222
Como 155M
Conca de Barberá DO 190, 191, 187K, 189K
Concepción 270M, 273M
Concha y Toro 276, 277K
Condado de Huelva DO 186, 202-3, 187K, 203K
Condrieu AC 90, 92-3, 94, 92K
Conegliano 164, 165, 161M
Conero DOCG 169K
Conn Creek winery 247K
Connecticut 263, 235M, 262K, 262M
Cono Sur 279K
la Conseillante, Ch. 45K
Constanţa 224M
Constantia 320, 321, 322, 320K
Contea di Sclafani DOC 183K
Conterno, Aldo 158
Contessa Entellina DOC 183K
Conthey 142M
Contucci 177K
Cooma 298
Coonawarra 9, 21, 286, 288, 289, 292-3, 289K, 293M; wineries 293K
Cooper Mountain 261K
Cootamundra 301M
Copertino DOC 181, 180K
Copiapó 273, 273M
Coquimbo 273, 273K, 273M
Corbières AC 90, 103, 104, 103K, 105K
Corcelles-en-Beaujolais 69M
Cordillera Cantábrica 186, 188, 197, 187M, 196M
Cordillera Catalana 191
Córdoba 202, 203, 187M, 203M
Cordoba 325K
Corgoloin 59, 59M
Cormons 167, 161M, 166M
Cornas AC 90, 92, 94-5, 94K, 94M
Corno di Rosazzo 166M
Córpora 279K
Corse (Corsica) 105, 31M, 107M, 109M, 153M
Corte 105M
Côrte, Quinta da 213K
Cortes de Cima 215
Cortezia, Quinta da 214
Corton AC 61, 62, 61D, 63K
Corton hill, 62, 61D, 63M
Corton-Charlemagne AC 61, 62, 61D, 63K
Cortona 169M
Coruche *see* Ribatejo
Cos d'Estournel, Ch. 10, 41, 41K
Cosenza 181, 180M
Cosne-sur-Loire 83, 89M
Costanti 174, 175K
Costers del Segre DO 189, 191, 187K, 189K
Costières de Nîmes AC 104
la Côte 141, 140K
Côte des Bar *see* Aube Region
Côte de Beaune 61-2, 53K, 62-3M, 63K; classifications 62
Côte de Beaune-Villages AC 55, 62
Côte des Blancs 70, 71, 72, 74, 75, 71M
Côte de Brouilly AC 69, 69K
Côte Chalonnaise 54, 55, 64-5, 53K, 64K, 65M
Côte de Nuits 58-60, 53K, 58-9M; classifications 58-60
Côte de Nuits-Villages AC 55, 60
Côte d'Or 8, 22, 24, 52, 54, 55
Côte Roannaise AC 80
Côte-Rôtie AC 8, 90, 92-3, 92K
Côte de Sézanne 70, 71, 72, 71M
Coteaux d'Aix-en-Provence AC 100, 101, 100K
Coteaux d'Ancenis VDQS 81K
Coteaux de l'Aubance AC 83, 81K, 85K
Coteaux du Giennois VDQS 88, 81K
Coteaux du Languedoc AC 104, 103K
Coteaux du Layon AC and Coteaux du Layon-Villages AC 83, 81K, 85K
Coteaux du Loir AC 81K
Coteaux du Quercy AC 106K
Coteaux de Saumur AC 85, 81K
Coteaux du Tricastin AC 97, 98, 97K
Coteaux Varois AC 100, 101, 100K
Coteaux du Vendômois VDQS 81K
Côtes d'Auvergne VDQS 81K
Côtes de Bergerac AC 107, 106K
Côtes de Blaye AC 50, 32K
Côtes de Bordeaux-St-Macaire AC 51, 32K, 49M
Côtes de Bourg AC 50, 32K
Côtes du Brulhois VDQS 106K
Côtes de Castillon AC 50, 32K
Côtes de Duras AC 106, 107, 106K
Côtes du Forez AC 80, 83
Côtes du Frontonnais AC 107, 106K
Côtes du Jura AC 99K
Côtes du Luberon AC 97, 98, 97K
Côtes de la Malepère VDQS 103K

Côtes du Marmandais AC 106, 107, 106K
Côtes de Meliton AO 230K
Côtes de Millau VDQS 106K
Côtes de Montravel AC 107, 106K
Côtes-de-l'Orbe 141, 140K
Côtes de Provence AC 100, 100K
Côtes du Rhône AC and Côtes du Rhône-Villages AC 91, 97, 97K
Côtes du Roussillon AC, Côtes du Roussillon-Villages AC 104, 103K
Côtes de St-Mont VDQS 107, 106K
Côtes du Ventoux AC 98, 97K
Côtes du Vivarais AC 98, 97K
Coteşti 225, 224K
Cotnari 225, 224K
Côtto, Quinta do 211
Couchey 60, 59M
Couhins-Lurton, Ch. 43K
Coulée-de-Serrant AC 85, 85K
Cour Cheverny AC 86, 81K
Courgis 57M
Courthézon 98, 98D
Cousiño Macul 276, 277, 277K
Coutet, Ch. 49K
Covelinhas 213M
Cowaramup 307M
Cowra 300-1, 301K, 301M
Coyote Creek 248M
Crab Farm 314K
Crabtree Wines 294K
Cramant 75, 75M
Cramele Recas 224
Crasto, Quinta do 208, 211, 213K
Crati R 180M
Crémant d'Alsace AC 77
Crémant de Bourgogne AC 52, 54, 55, 66, 67
Crémant de Limoux AC 103K
Crémant de Loire AC 83
Crème de Cassis 52
Cremona 155M
Crépy AC 99, 99K
Cresta Ranch 21
Crete *see* Kriti
Creuse 109M
Cricova 223
Crimea *see* Krym
Criots-Bâtard-Montrachet AC 63K
Crişana-Maramures 225, 224K, 224M
Crişul Repede R 224M
Croatia 24, 226, 226M; wine areas 226K
Crossroads 314K
Crozes-Hermitage AC 90, 91, 93, 94, 94K, 95M
Cru Barréjals 49
Cruzeau, Ch. de 43K
Cruzeiro, Quinta do 213K
Csongrád 221K
Cuba 271
Cucamonga Valley AVA 236K
Cuchilla Grande 272M
Cuchilla Lunlunta 283M
Cuddia R 183M
Cuis 74, 75M
Cullen Wines 306, 307, 307K
Culoz 99M
Cumberland Valley AVA 263, 262K
Cumières 75M
Cunaco 278, 279
Cuneo 153M, 155M
Curicó Valley 275, 273K, 273M
Currency Creek 289K
Cussac-Fort-Médoc 37, 38M
Cutchogue 264, 265M
Cuvaison 245K
Cuyama R 253M
Cyprus 231, 231M; wine areas 231K
Czech Republic 219, 219M; wine regions 219K

D

Dafnes AO 230K
Dakovica 226M
Dal Forno 165
Dalheim 128M
Dalla Valle 246, 247K
The Dalles 257M
Damery 71, 75, 71M, 75M
Damianitza 229, 228M
D'Angelo 181
Danube (Donau; Duna; Dunaj; Dunărea; Dunav) R 145, 219, 220, 219M, 221M, 222M, 224M, 226M, 228M
Danubian Plain 229, 228K, 228M
Danube Terraces 224K, 224M
Dão DOC 208, 209, 210-11, 209K
Darling (South Africa) 320K, 322
Darling Downs 309
Darling R 287M, 301M
Darling Ranges 305
Darmstadt 138, 135M
Dausenau 122M
Davayé 66, 67, 67M
Dayton 261M
De Bortoli winery 298, 301, 299K, 303K
De Conciliis 181
De Loach 243K
De Lulliis 303K
De Toren 325K
De Trafford 325K
De Waal 325K
Dealul Mare 224, 225, 224K
Deaulu Bujorului 224K
Deaulurile Olteniei 224K
Debrő 220
Dehesa del Carrizal 201, 201K
Dehlinger 243K
Dei 177K
Deidesheim 120, 130, 130K, 130M
Del Cerro 177K
Delaire 325K
Delatite 297
Delaware 262M
Delaware R 262M
Delheim 325K
DeLille Cellars 259K
Denbies 218, 218K
Denia 201M
Deniliquin 301M
Denman 302, 301M
Denmark (W. Australia) 304, 305, 305K, 305M
Dentelles de Montmirail 91, 97, 98
Derwent R (Tasmania) 308, 308M
Desmirail, Ch. 38K
Dettelbach 133M
Deutschkreuz 149
Deutschlandsberg 144M
Deutsch-Schützen 149
Deutz 252
Devil's Lair 307K
Devin 227
Devon Valley 324, 325M
Dexheim 128M
Dézaley 141
DFJ Vinhos 214
Dhron R 116, 117M
Di Georgio 293K
Di Majo Norante 168
Diablo Grande AVA 236K
Diablo Range 249, 248M
Diamante R 283, 281M
Diamond Creek 245K
Diamond Mountain 245, 246, 247
Diamond Valley 298, 299K
Diano d'Alba 159M
Diedesfeld 130M
Dienheim 128, 128M
Dijon 52, 58, 64, 73, 31M, 53M, 59M 109M
Diren 231
Dittanio R 183M
Dixons Creek 299, 299M
Dizy 75M
Dnipro R 223, 222M
Dnister R 222M
Dobrogea 224, 225, 224K, 224M
Dobrovo 227
Dogliano 155M
Doisy-Daëne, Ch. 49K
Doisy-Védrines, Ch. 49K
Dolcetto d'Alba DOC 153K, 155K
Dolcetto di Dogliani DOCG 153K, 155K
Dôle 99M
Dolenjska 227
Dolomites 152, 161, 162, 161M
Doluca 231
Domaine Boyar 229
Domaine Carneros 245K
Domaine Chandon (Australia) 298, 298D, 299K
Domaine Chandon (USA) 247K
Domaine Drouhin 260, 261K
Domaine Serene 261K
Domaine Vistalba 283K
Domecq 205, 271
Dominio del Valdepusa 201, 201K
Dominus 247K
Don Melchor 276, 277
Don R 223, 222M
Donauland 146, 144K, 147M
Donnafugatu 183
Donnici DOC 180K
Donnybrook 305
Donoratico 179M
Donostia 188, 187M, 189M
Doonkuna Estate 301
Dora Baltea Valley 156, 155M
Dora Riparia R 155M
Dordogne R/Valley 30, 33, 34, 44, 45, 46, 47, 50, 51, 106-7, 31M, 32M, 38M, 45M, 106M, 109M
Dorsheim 127, 127M
Doubs R 31M, 99M, 109M
Doué-la-Fontaine 81M, 85M
Douglas 320K, 320M
Douro DOC 209K
Douro R/Valley 8, 207, 208, 209, 210, 211, 212-13, 209M, 212-13M; terracing 211D; *see also* Duero R/Valley
Douro Superior 212, 213, 213M
Drăgăşani 225, 224K
Draguignan 100, 101M
Drakensteinberg (mountains) 323
Drava R/Valley 227, 221M, 226M
Draytons Family Wines 303K
Dresden 139, 113M
Drina R 226M
Drôme R 91, 98, 31M, 109M
Drumborg 296, 296M
Drummond 283
Dry Creek Valley AVA 8, 240, 241, 236K, 241K, 241M: wineries and vineyards 241K
Dry Creek 241K
Drylands Estate 319K
Dubrovnik 226M
Duckhorn 247K
Ducru-Beaucaillou, Ch. 41, 41K
Duero R/Valley 186, 198, 199, 187M, 196M, 198-9M; *see also* Douro R/Valley *and* Ribera del Duero
Duna; Dunaj; Dunărea; Dunav *see* Danube
Dundee (Oregon) 261M
Dundee Hills 260, 261M
Dunn 245K
Dunnigan Hills AVA 236K
Durance R 90, 98, 100, 31M, 96-7M, 100-1M, 109M
Duras 106M
Durbach 136, 135M
Durbanville 321
Durbanville Hills 322
Duriense VR 209M
Dürnstein 147, 147M
Durrell Vineyards 245K
Dutton Goldfield 243K
Dutton Ranch Vineyard 243K
Duttweiler 130M
Duxoup 241K
Dyje R/Valley 219, 219M
Dytiki Ellas 230M

E

Earnscleugh 317
East Coast (NZ) 310
East Coast (USA) 262-5; 263M; AVA wine areas 263K
Eastern Anatolia 231, 231K
Eastern Plains, Inland and North Western Australia 287M
Ebro R/Valley 186, 188, 192, 194, 195, 187M, 189M, 192D, 192-3M, 196M
Échézeaux AC 60, 59K
Echuca 296M
Ecuador 271
Écueil 74, 75M
Eden Valley 285, 286, 289, 291, 289K, 290-1M; wineries 291K
Edna Valley 237, 249, 250, 251-2
Edna Valley AVA 236K, 251K
Edwards, Luis Felipe 279K
Eerste R 323, 325M
Eger 220, 221K, 221M
l'Église-Clinet, Ch. 45K
Eguisheim 79M
Eibelstadt 133M
Eichstetten 137M
Eikendal 324
Eisenberg 149
Eisenstadt 144M
Eitelsbach 118, 119K, 119M
Ejmiatsin 223, 222M
El Dorado AVA 236K
El Dorado County 254
El Molino 245K
El Pedernal Valley 281
El Puerto de Santa María 204, 205, 203M, 205M, 205D
El Vendrell 190M
Elba 170
Elba DOC 169K
Elbe (Labe) R 219, 113M, 219M
Elche 201M
Elciego 193M
Elderton 291K
Eldridge 245M
Eleutero R 183M
Elgin (South Africa) 320, 321, 322, 323, 320K
Elgin (USA) 255
Elim 322, 320M
Elk Cove 261K
Ellensburg 258, 257M
Ellerstadt 130M
Ellis, Neil 325K
Elqui Valley 270, 273, 274, 273M, 273K
Els, Ernie 325K
Eltville-am-Rhein 123, 124, 125K, 125M
Eltville State Domaine 123, 124
Emilia-Romagna 24, 152, 168, 153K, 153M, 155M, 169K, 169M
Emiliana Orgánico 279K
Emma, Casa 173K
Empordà-Costa Brava DO 191, 187K
Emrich-Schönleber 127
Enate 195
Encostas de Aire IPR 209K
Endingen 137M
England 12, 218, 218M; selected vineyards 218K
Enkirch 117K, 117M
Enna 183M
Enterprise Vineyard 294
Entraygues 106M
Entre-Deux-Mers AC 35, 50-1, 32K
Entre-Deux-Mers Haut-Benauge AC 51, 32K
Entremont 143
Enz R 135M
Eola Hills 260
Epanomi 230, 230M
Épernay 71, 72, 73, 31M, 71M, 75M, 109M
Epineuil 52, 56, 53M
Erath Vineyards 261K
Erbach 124, 125, 125K, 125M
Erbaluce di Caluso DOC 155K
Erden 112, 117, 128, 117D, 117K, 117M
Erie 262M
Erlenbach 136M
Erlenbach am Main 134, 134M
L'Ermita 188
Ernea 225
Ernscleugh 317
Erôme 94, 94M
Errázuriz 19, 24, 274
Ervedosa do Douro 213M
Escherndorf 134, 133K, 133M, 134M
Esk Valley 314
Esk Valley 313, 314K
Esporão 215
Esslingen 135M
Essoyes 73, 73M
Est! Est!! Est!!! di Montefiascone DOC 168, 169K
Estepona 203, 203M
Estrella 251M
Estrella Prairie 250
Estremadura (Portugal) 209, 214, 215, 209M
Estremoz 215, 209M
Étang de Diane 105, 105M
Etchart 283K
ETKO 231
Etna DOC 153K, 183K
l'Étoile AC 99K, 99M
Etsch *see* Adige
Etude 247K
Etyek-Buda 221K
Euboea (Evvoia) 230, 230M
Eugene 260, 257M
l'Evangile, Ch. 45K
Evans Family 302, 303, 303K
Evans & Tate winery 307, 307K
Evena 188, 195
Evian 99M
Evksinograd 228K
Évora *see* Alentejo
Extremadura (Spain) 187K, 187M, 201K, 201M, 203M
Eymet 106M
Eyrie Vineyards 257, 260, 261K

F

Faber 304
Faenza 169M
Faial 209M, 217M
Failla-Jordan 242
Fair Play AVA 236K
Fairhill Downs 319K
Fairview Winery 325, 325K
Faiveley 64
Falcoaria 214
Falerio dei Colli Ascolani DOC 169K
Falerno del Massico DOC 180K
False Bay 322, 323, 324, 325, 320M, 325M
Falseco 168
Falset 189, 191, 189M
Falua 214
Familia Mundo 281
Familia Schroeder 281
Familia Zuccardi 283K
Far Niente 246, 247K
Far North 287K
Fara DOC 156
Fargues 48, 49M
de Fargues, Ch. 49K
Faro (Portugal) 209M
Faro DOC (Sicily) 183, 153K, 183K
Farra D'Isonzo 166M
Farrell, Gary 243K
Fassati 177K
Faugères AC 103, 104, 103K
Faye d'Anjou 83
Fecht R 79M
Felluga, Livio & Marco 167
Felsina, Fattoria di 173, 173K
Ferguson Valley 305
Fergusson 299K
Fernández, Alejandro 198, 199
Fernhill 315, 314M
Ferrara 169M
Ferrari-Carano 241K
Ferrer, Gloria 245K
Ferrière, Ch. 38K
Feudi di San Gregorio 181
Fèvre, William, winery 277K
Fiano di Avellino DOCG 153K, 180K
Fiddletown 254
Fiddletown AVA 236K
Fiefs Vendéens VDQS 81K
de Fieuzal, Ch. 43, 43K
Figari 105, 105M
Figeac 106M
Figeac, Ch. 44, 46, 45K
Figueras 189M
Filzen 119K
Finca Elez 201, 201K
Finca Flichman 283, 283K
Finger Lakes AVA 263, 265, 262K, 262M
Firestone 253K
Fitou AC 104, 103K
de Fiumicicoli, Dom. 105
Fiúza Estate 214
Five Oaks 299K
Fixin AC 59, 60, 59K, 59M
Flagey-Échézeaux 60, 59M
Flaxmere 314M
la Flèche 81M
Flein 135M
Fleurance 106M
Fleurie AC 69, 69K, 69M
Fleurieu Peninsula 289, 287K, 289K
la Fleur-Pétrus, Ch. 45K
Fleys 57M
Flinders Ranges 287M
Flora Springs 247K
Florence (Firenze) 172, 173, 153M, 169M
Flores 209M
Florida (Uruguay) 272M
Flörsheim-Dalsheim 128
Flowers Winery 238, 242
Focşani 224M
Foggia 153M, 180M
Foglia R 169M
Foix 106M
Foley 253K
Folgosa 213M
Fonseca, José Maria da 214, 215
Font de Michelle, Dom. 98D
Fontenil, Ch. 45K
Fonterutoli, Castello di 173K
Fontodi 173, 173K
Foppiano 243K
Forbes 301M
Forest Hill 304
Forestville 242, 241M, 243M
Forlí 169M
Forrest Estate 319K
Forrester, Ken 325K
Forst 120, 130, 131, 130K, 130M
Fortia, Ch. 98D
Fortore R 180M
Fosters 286
Fox Run 265
Foxen 253K
Foz, Quinta da (Cálem) 212, 213K
Framingham Wine 319K
France 24, 29: classification system 30; wine regions 30-109, 31M
France, South-West 106-7, 31M, 106M
Franciacorta DOCG 154, 155, 153K, 155K
Franciscan Vineyard 233, 247K
de Francs, Ch. 50
Frank, Konstantin 265
Franken 112, 132-4, 135, 113K, 113M, 132-3M, 134M; top vineyards 133K
Frankfurt 138,113M
Frankland 304, 305, 305M
Frankland River (region) 305K, 305M
Franschhoek 321, 323, 325, 325M
Frascati 169M
Frascati DOC 168, 153K, 169K
Fraser R 235M, 267M
Fraser Valley VQA 268, 267K
Frauenkirchen 149M
Fray de Beltrán 283M
Freemark Abbey 236
Freiburg 135, 136, 113M, 135M
Freinsheim 130M
Fremantle 304, 305M
French Farm 317
Fresno 236M
Freyburg 139
Freycinet 308
Fribourg 141, 140K, 140M
Frick 241K
Frickenhausen 133M, 134M
Friedelsheim 130M
Friesach 144M
Fritz 241K
Friuli Aquileia DOC 167, 161K
Friuli Grave DOC 167, 161K
Friuli Isonzo DOC 153K, 161K, 166M
Friuli Latisana DOC 167, 161K
Friuli-Venezia Giulia 152, 160, 161, 163, 153K, 153M, 161K, 161M
Frog's Leap winery 247K
Fromm Winery 319K
Fronsac AC 44, 45, 47, 32K, 44M, 45M
Frontignan VDN 104, 103K
Fronton 106M
Frosinone 169M
Fuenmayor 193M
Fuentecén 199M
Fuissé 66, 67M
Fukuoka 327K, 327M
Fuligni 175K
Fully 143
Fumane R 165, 164M
Funchal 216, 217, 209M, 217M
Fürst 134
Fürstenfeld 144M

G

Gaia 230
Gaillac 106M
Gaillac AC 107, 106K
Gainey 253K
Gaiole in Chianti 173, 173M
Gaivosa, Quinta de 211
Gaja, Angelo 152, 158, 178
Galatea 313, 311M
Galaţi 224M
Galicia 186, 196-7, 210, 187K, 187M, 196K, 196M
Galilee 231, 231K
Gallo, E & J 240, 254
Gallo, Gianfranco 167
Gallo d'Alba 158, 159M
Gallo of Sonoma 241K
Galluccio Family Wineries 265K
Gambellara DOC 161K
Gan 106M
Gâncă 222M
Gard *département* 108, 109M
Garda DOC 155K
la Garde, Ch. 43K
la Gardine, Ch. de 98D
Gargagnago 164M
Gargano Massif 168
Garilan Mountains 249, 248M
Garofoli 168
Garonne R 30, 34, 44, 48, 50, 51, 107, 31M, 33M, 38M, 43M, 49M, 106M, 109M
Gasteiz 187M, 189M
Gattinara DOCG 156, 153K, 155K
Gau-Bischofsheim 128M
Gavi 155M
Gavi DOCG 157, 153K, 155K
Gawler 294
Gazin, Ch. 45K
Gbelce 219
Gedersdorf 147M
Geelong 296, 297, 296K, 296M
Geisenheim 117, 124, 125M
Geisenheim Viticultural Institute 139
Gela 183M
Genève (Geneva) 141, 142, 31M, 99M, 109M, 140K
Genil, R 203M
Gennargentu Mountains 182, 182M
Genova (Genoa) 153M, 155M
Gentilini 230
Geographe 305, 305K
Georgia 223, 222K, 222M
Georgia (USA) 235M
Georgian Wines and Spirit Company 223
Germany 11, 24, 111: classification system 112; wine regions 112-39, 113M
Gerovassiliou 230
Gers R 106M
Gervans 94, 95, 94M
Getariako Txakolina DO 188, 187K, 189K
Gevrey-Chambertin AC 55, 59, 59K
Geyser Peak 241K
Geyserville 240, 241M
Ghemme DOCG 156, 153K, 155K
Ghisonaccia 105M
Gibbston 317
Gien 83, 81M
Giesen 317
Gigondas AC 91, 97, 98, 97K
Gijón 196M
Gilette, Ch. 49K
Gilroy 248, 248M
Gimblett Gravels 15, 314, 315, 314K
Gimblett Road 315
Gingin 304
Gippsland 297, 287K
Giro di Cagliari DOC 182K
Girona 189M
Gironde estuary 33, 34, 39, 41, 50, 106, 31M, 32M, 38M, 41M, 109M
Gisborne 311, 312, 313, 314, 316, 311K, 311M
Giscours, Ch. 38K
Givry AC 64-5, 64K, 64M
Glaetzer 291K
Glen Carlou 325, 325K
Glen Ellen 243, 245M
Glen Rosa 325
Glenguin 303K
Glenrowan 287, 296, 297, 296K, 296M
Glenroy 293M
Glun 94, 94M
Golan Heights 231, 231M
Golden Gate gap 237, 243
Goldwater Estate 313
Gols 148, 149M
Gonzales 249, 248M
Goriška Brda 227
Gorizia 160, 167, 161M, 167M
Gorna Radgona 227
Gottenheim 137M
Goulburn R/Valley 297, 296K, 296M
Goumenissa AO 230, 230K
Goundrey 305
Gourtis R 320M
Graach 116, 117, 117M
Gracciano 177M
Grace Family 246, 247K
Gracetown 307M
Gracia 274
Graciosa DOC 209, 209K, 209M
Gradisco d'Isonzo 166M
Gräfenbach R 127, 127M
Gralyn 307K
Gramp Wines, Tim, 294K
Grampians 296K, 297
Gran Canaria 187K
Granada 203, 187M, 203M
le Grand Colombier 99
Grand-Poujeaux 37, 39, 38M
Grand-Puy-Lacoste, Ch. 41, 41K
Grand Renouil, Ch. 45K
Grand River Valley AVA 262K
Grande-Rue AC 59K
Grands-Échézeaux AC 60, 59K
Grandview 259M
Grange 288-9, 291
Grangehurst 325K
Granger 259M
Granite Belt 309, 309K
Granja-Amareleja *see* Alentejo
Grans Muralles 190, 191
Grants Pass 257M
Grasparossa di Castelvetro DOC 168
Gratallops 191
Graton 242, 241M, 243M
Grattamacco 179K
Graubünden 141, 140M
Grauves 75, 75M
Graves AC 35, 42-3, 32K, 42M, 43K, 43M, 49M; 1959 classification 43
Graves de Vayres AC 51, 32K
Gravner 160, 167
Gravona R 105M
Graz 144M
Great Artesian Basin 289, 292, 293
Great Barrier Island 313, 311K
Great Dividing Range 288, 299, 300, 302,

309, 287M, 296M, 301M, 309M
Great Plains *see* Alföld
Great Southern (W. Australia) 304-5, 305K
Greater Perth 287K
Greco di Bianco DOC 180K
Greco di Tufo DOCG 153K, 180K
Greece 24, 230, 230M; appellations of origin 230K
Green & Red Vineyard 245K
Green Point 299K
Green Valley 241, 242, 241M, 243M
Greenfield 249, 248M
Greenock 291, 291M
Greenock Creek 291K
Il Greppo (Biondi-Santi) 174
Greta 303M
Greve 172, 173, 175M
Grevenmacher 114M
Grezzana 165, 165M
Grgich Hills 247K
Gricha, Quinta da 213K
Griffith 301, 301M
Grimsby (Ontario) 269M
Grinzane Cavour 159M
Grinzing 145
Griotte-Chambertin AC 59K
Groenberg 325
Groenekloof 322, 320K
Groot R 320M
Gros Plant du Pays Nantais VDQS 80, 81K
Grosset Wines 294, 294K
Grosseto 6, 169M
Grossheubach 134, 134M
Groth 247K
Grove Mill 319K
Grover City 251M
Grover vineyards 327
Groznyy 222M
Gruaud-Larose, Ch. 40, 41K
Gruet 255
Grünstadt 121M
Le Grys Vineyard 319K
Guadalajara 270M
Guadalete R 205, 205D, 205M
Guadalfeo R 203M
Guadalhorce R 203M
Guadalquivir R 202, 187M, 203M, 204M, 205D
Guadiana R 187M, 201M, 209M
Guado al Tasso, Tenuta 179K
Guarda 209M
Guardistallo 179M
Gueberschwihr 78, 79, 79M
Guebwiller 76M
Guenoc Valley AVA 239K
Guijoso 201, 201K
Guiraud, Ch. 49K
Guldenbach R 127, 127M
Guldental 127M
Gulf Islands VQA 268, 267K
Gumpoldskirchen 146
Gundagai 301K, 301M
Gundlach-Bundschu 245K
Guntersblum 128, 128M
Gutenberg 127M
Gyöngyös 221M
Györ 221M

H

Haan Wines 291K
Haardt 130M
Haardt Mountains 120, 130, 131
Haas 160
Hadersdorf 147M
Hahnheim 128M
Hainle Vineyards 266, 268
Hajós-Baja 221K
Halewood 224
Halle 113M
Hallgarten 125, 125K, 125M
Hames Valley AVA 248K
Hamilton (Australia) 296M
Hamilton (Canada) 269, 269M
Hamilton (New Zealand) 311M
Hammelburg 134M
Hammerstein 122, 122M
The Hamptons AVA 262K
Happs 307
Hardy Wine Company 103, 286, 293, 301, 305
Hargesheim 127M
Harlan Estate 245, 246, 247K
Haro 188, 192, 192M
Harrisburg 262M
Harrison Hill Vineyard *see* DeLille Cellars
Harrison 245K
Harsova 229, 228K, 228M
Hartenberg 325K
Hartford 262M
Hartford Family 243K
Hartswater 320K
Hartwig, Laura/Santa Laura 279K
Harvey 305, 305M
Harxheim 128M
Haskovo 228K
Hassfurt 134M
Hassloch 130M
Hastings 314, 311M, 314M
Hastings River (region) 301K
Hastings Valley 301
Hattenheim 125, 125K, 125M
Hattstatt 79M
Hatzimichali 230
Haumoana 314M
Hauraki Gulf 312, 313, 311M
Haut-Bailly, Ch. 43K
Haut-Batailley, Ch. 41K
Haut-Benauge *see* Entre-Deux-Mers Haut-Benauge AC
Haut-Bergey, Ch. 43K
Haut-Bertinerie, Ch. 50
Haut-Brion, Ch. 35, 42, 43, 43K
Haut-Gardère, Ch. 43K
Haut-Marbuzet, Ch. 41K
Haut-Médoc AC 10, 34, 35, 36, 41, 32K, 38-9M, 40M, 41M
Haut-Montravel AC 107, 106K
Haut-Poitou VDQS 81K
Haut-Rhin *département* 77, 78, 79
Haut-Valais 143
Hautes-Côtes de Beaune AC 55, 62, 53K, 62-3M, 63K
Hautes-Côtes de Nuits AC 58, 60, 53K, 58-9M
Hautvillers 75M
Havelock North 314, 315, 314M
Havens 245K
Hawke Bay 311M, 314M
Hawkes Bay 9, 12, 15, 20, 310, 311, 312, 313, 314-15, 316, 311K, 311M, 315K, 315M; wineries 314K
Hay Shed Hill 307K
Hazendal 325K
Healdsburg 238, 240, 241, 242, 236M, 239M, 241M, 243M
Healesville 298, 296M, 299M
Heathcote 296K, 296M, 297
Hebei province 327, 327M
Hedges Family Estate 259K
Heidelberg 136, 138, 113M, 135M
Heilbronn 113M, 135M
Heiligenstadt 145
Heimersheim 122, 122M
Heitz Cellars 236, 247K
Helderberg 323, 324
Helshoogte Pass 323
Hemel-en Aarde Valley 322
Henderson 313, 311K
Henschke 286, 291, 291K
Henty 296K
Heppenheim 138, 135M
Heppingen 122, 122M
Hérault *département* 108, 109M
Hérault R/Valley 102, 31M, 103M, 109M
Hérault, Vin de Pays de l' 80
Heretaunga R 314
Heritage 291K
Hermanus 322, 320M
Hermitage AC 91, 93-4, 94K
Hermitage hill 5, 93, 94, 95
Hermosillo 270M
Hess Collection 245K
Hessische Bergstrasse 129, 135, 138, 113K, 113M
El Hierro DO 187K
High Eden 279K
Highbank Estate 293K
Hightower 259K
Highway 50 (New Zealand) 315
Hill of Grace vineyard 286
Hillcrest vineyard 260
Hilltops 301, 301K
Hirsch Vineyard 242
Hissarya 228K
Hitching Post 253K
Hobart 308, 287M, 308M
Hochheim 123
Hoddles Creek 299
Hogue Cellars 259K
Hokkaido 327K
Holland (mountains) 322
Hollick 293K
Homburg 134M
Hop Kiln 243K
Hope 267M
Hope Estate 303K
Hopkins R 296M
Hopland 239, 239M
Horitschon 149
Hornád R 219M
La Horra 199, 199M
Horse Heaven Hills AVA 259, 257K
Hörstein 134, 134M
Horton 263
Hottentots 322, 324
Houghton 286, 304, 305, 306
Houston 235M
Howard Park 307K
Howell Mountain AVA 245, 246, 245M, 247M
Hron R 219, 219M
Hua Dong Winery 327
Huang He R 327M
Huapai 313, 311K
Hudson R/Valley 262, 265
Hudson River Region AVA 262K
Huelva 202, 187M, 203M
Huerva R 195, 189M, 203M
Huesca 188, 189M
Hugel 78
Huia 319K
Huiarau Mountains 313
Hunawihr 79M
Hungary 220-1, 221M; wine regions 221K
Hunsrück Hills 115, 118, 126
Hunter R 303, 301M, 303M
Hunter Valley, Upper and Lower 9, 287, 300, 302-3, 287K, 301K, 303M; wineries 303K
Hunter's 319K
Huon R/Valley 308, 308M
Hurbanovo 219
Huşi 224K, 224M
Hvar 226, 226M
Hyères 100, 101M
Hyogo 327K

I

Ialomiţa R 224M
Iaşi 225, 224K, 224M
Ica 270M
Ica Valley 270, 271
Idaho 235, 257, 235M, 257K, 257M
Igé 66
Ihringen 135, 137, 135M, 137M
Ihumatao 311K
Illats 49M
Illmitz 149, 149M
Illinois R/Valley 149, 261, 257M
Imereti 223
Imola 169M
Imperia 155M
India 327, 327M; vineyard areas 327K
Indiana 235M
Indre R 86, 31M, 81M, 87M, 109M
Ingelheim Nord 128, 125M
Ingersheim 79M
Inniskillin 268, 269
Innocenti 177K
Interlaken 140M
Iphofen 132, 134, 133K, 133M, 134M
Iraklion (Irakleio) 230M
Irancy 52, 56, 53M
Irminio R 183M
Iron Horse 241K
Irouléguy AC 107, 106K
Irvine 291K
Isabel Estate 319K
Isarco (Eisach) R/Valley 163, 161M, 163M
Ischia DOC 153M, 180K, 180M
Isère R/Valley 99, 31M, 94M, 99M, 109M
Isla de Maipo 276, 277, 277M
Islas Baleares 189, 187K, 187M, 189K, 189M
Islas Canarias 186, 187K, 187M
Isle R 34, 47, 31M, 33M, 45M, 106M, 109M
Isle St George AVA 262K
Isole e Olena 171, 173, 173K
Isonzo DOC 167
Israel 231, 231M; wine areas 231K
Issan 37, 38M
d'Issan, Ch. 38K
Istria 226
Italy 18, 24, 25: classification system 151, 152; wine regions 152-83, 153M
Itata R/Valley 275, 273K, 273M
Ivailovgrad 228K
Ivrea 155M
Iwate 327K

J

Jabalón R 201M
Jackass Hill Vineyard 243K
Jaén 203M
Jackson Estate 319K
Jade Mountain 245K
Jago 165
Jagst R 136, 113M, 135M
Jalle de Blanquefort 42
Jalle du Breuil 10, 41, 41M
Jalón R 195, 189M
Jamesport 264, 265M
Jamestown 294
Jamieson's Run 293K
la Janasse, Dom. de 98D
Jansz 308
Japan 327, 327M; vineyard areas 327K
Jardim da Serra 217, 216M
Jasnières AC 86, 81K
Jenke Vineyards 291K
Jerez de la Frontera 204, 205, 187M, 203M, 205D, 205M
Jerez-Xérès-Sherry DO 16, 186, 202, 204-5, 187K, 203K, 204-5M, 205D
Jermann 167
Jesi 169M
Jeune, Paul/Monpertuis 98D
Jimtown 240
Jindong 307, 307M
Joanicó 272M
Johannisberg 124, 128, 125D, 125K, 125M
Johannisberg, Bereich 124, 121K, 125M
Johannishof 124
John Day R 257M
Jongieux 99, 99K
Jonkershoek Valley 324, 325M
Jordan (California) 241K
Jordan (South Africa) 325K
J P Vinhos 214
Júcar R 187M, 201M
Judean Hills 231, 231K
Juliénas AC 69K
Juliusspital 134
Jumilla 201M
Jumilla DO 201, 187K, 201K
Jura (France) 30, 99, 31M
Jura (Switzerland) 141, 140K, 140M
Jurançon AC 107, 106K

K

Kaapzicht 325K
Kaiserstuhl, Bereich (Germany) 135, 136, 137, 135K, 137M; selected vineyards 137K
Kaitaia 311M
Kakamas 320M
Kakheti 223
Kalimna 289
Kallstadt 130M
Kamataka 327K
Kamberra 301
Kammern 147K
Kamp R 146, 147, 147M
Kamptal 146, 144K, 147M
Kanawha River Valley AVA 262K
Kangaroo Island 289K
Kanonkop 323, 325K
Kanzem 119M
Kappelrodeck 135M
Karadoc 297
Karlovo 228K
Karlsrühe 113M, 135M
Karnataka 327, 327K, 327M
Karnobat 228K
Karridale 307
Kartli 223
Kasel 118, 114M, 119K, 119M
Katnook Estate 293K
Katoghi-Strofilia 230
Kavaklidere 231
Kaysersberg 77, 79M
Kazakhstan 223, 222M
Kecskemét 221M
Keenan, Robert 245K
Kefallonia AO (Cephalonia) 230, 230K, 230M
Keller 128
Kellermeister/Trevor Jones 291K
Kelowna 267, 268, 267M
Kendall-Jackson 252, 275
Kennewick 257M
Kent 218, 218M
Kentucky 235M
Kenwood 243, 245M
Kenwood 245K
KEO 231
Kern R 236M
Khan Kroum 229, 228K
Khanguet 326, 326M
Kherson 223, 222M
Kiedrich 123, 124, 125K, 125M
Killikanoon Wines 294K
King City 249, 248M
King Valley 297, 296K
Kingaroy 309M
Kings R 236M
Kinheim 117M
Kiona Vineyards 256, 259K
Kircheim-Bolanden 121M
Kirrweiler 130M
Kirwan, Ch. 36, 38K
Kistler 243K, 245K
Kitzingen 133M, 134M
Klagenfurt 144M
Klamath Mountains 236M, 253M
Klein Karoo Region 322, 320K
Klettgau 140K
Klingenberg 134, 134M
Klipsun Vineyards 259K
Klosterneuburg 146
Klüsserath 117, 117K, 117M
Knappstein Wines 294K
Knights Valley AVA 240, 236K
Knjaževac 226M
Kobern-Gondorf 115, 115M
Koblenz 115, 120, 122, 113M, 115M, 122M
Kocher R 136, 113M, 135M
Kocher-Jagst-Tauber, Bereich 135K
Köflach 144M
Kokotos 230
Köln 113M
Komárno 219, 219M
Konen 119M
Königsbach 130M
Königschaffhausen 137M
Königswinter 122M
Konstanz 113M, 135M
Kontinentalna Hrvatska 226, 226K
Konz 114M, 119M
Koper 227
Korten 229, 228M
Koşice 219M
Kosovich, John 304
Kosovo 226, 227, 226K, 226M
Köwerich 117M
Kraalfontein 325M
Kracher, Alois 149
Kraichgau, Bereich 135K
Kras 227
Krasnodar 223, 222M
Krems 146, 147, 144M, 146K, 147M
Krems R/Valley 146, 147, 147M
Kremstal 146, 144K, 147M
Kriti (Crete) 230, 230K, 230M
Kröv 117K, 117M
Krym (Crimea) 223, 222M
Kruşevac 226, 226K, 226M
Kuban R 222M
Kues 117M
Kühn, Peter Jakob 124
Kuitpo 289
Kulkunbulla 303K
Kumanovo 226M
Kumeu 313, 311K
Kumeu River 313
Kunde 245K
Kunság 221K
Künstler, Franz 124
Kupa R 226M
KWV 320, 321, 325K
Kyneton 296M
Kyr-Yanni 230
Kyustendil 229

L

La Crema 243K
La Grande 257M
La Jota 245K
La Motte 325K
La Paz 282, 270M
La Rioja (Argentina) 281, 281M
La Rosa 279, 279K
Laa 144M
Labarde 36, 39, 38M
Labastida 192M
Labégorce-Zédé, Ch. 38K
Lachen-Speyerdorf 130M
Lachlan R 19, 300, 301, 287M, 296K, 301M
Ladbroke Grove 293K
Ladoix AC 63K
Ladoix-Serrigny 62, 61D, 63M
Laetitia 252
Lafaurie-Peyraguey, Ch. 49K
Lafayette (Oregon) 261M
Lafite-Rothschild, Ch. 10, 40, 41, 41K
Lafleur, Ch. 45K
Lafões DOC 209K
Lafon-Rochet, Ch. 41, 41K
Lafond 253K
Lagarde 283K
Lages, Quinta das 213K
Lago di Caldaro, Kalterersee DOC 161K, 163K
Lagoa DOC 215, 209K, 209M
Lagoalva da Cima, Quinta da 214
Lagos DOC 209K, 209M
Lagrange, Ch. 41K
Laguardia 193M
la Lagune, Ch. 36, 38K
Lahn R 122, 122M
Lahnstein 122M
Lahr 135M
Lake Chalice 319K
Lake County 238, 239
Lake Erie AVA (USA) 265, 262K
Lake Erie North Shore VQA (Canada) 266, 269, 269K
Lakeport 239M
Lake's Folly 302, 303, 303K
Lalande-de-Pomerol AC 47, 32K, 45M
Lamarque 37, 38M
Lambert Bridge 241K
Lambrusco DOC 153K, 169K
Lamont 304
Lamoreaux Landing 265
Lamothe-Guignard, Ch. 49K
Lancaster Valley AVA 263, 262K
Landmark 245K
Lane Tanner 253K
Langberg-Garcia 320K
Langeais 87M
Langenlois 146, 147M
Langenlonsheim 127M
Langhe DOC 155K
Langhe Hills 152, 154, 157, 158
Langhorne Creek 288, 289, 289K
Langoa-Barton, Ch. 41K
Langon 33, 42, 43, 31M, 33M, 49M, 106M
Languedoc 90, 92
Languedoc-Roussillon 30, 102-4, 31M, 102-3K, 109M
Lanzarote DO 187K
Lara State 271, 270M
Lark Hill 301
Larraga 194
Larrivet-Haut-Brion, Ch. 43K
Las Cabras 278, 279M
Las Compuertas 283
Las Heras 282
Lascombes, Ch. 38K
Latour, Ch. 34, 41, 41K
Latour-Martillac, Ch. 43K
Latour-à-Pomerol, Ch. 45K
Latricières-Chambertin AC 59K
Laubenheim (Rheinhessen) 128M
Launceston 308, 308M
Laurel Glen 245K
Lausanne 142, 140M
Lava Cap 254
le Lavandou 101M
Lavaux 141, 140K
L'Avenir 325K
Laville-Haut-Brion, Ch. 43, 43K
Lawrence Victor Estate 293K
Lawson's Dry Hills Wines 319K
Layon R/Valley 82-3, 84, 81M, 84M
Lazaridi, Constantin 230
Lazio 152, 168, 170, 153K, 153M, 169K, 169M
Le Bonheur 325K
Le Riche 325K
Leamington 269M
Leasingham Wines 294K
Lebanon 231, 231M; wine areas 231K
Lechinţa 224K
Leconfield 293K
Leda, Quinta da 213
Leeuwin Estate 7, 305, 307, 307K
Lehmann, Peter 291, 291K
Leibnitz 145, 144M
Leitha Hills 146, 148
Leitz, Josef 124
Leiwen 116, 117K, 117M
Lemesos 231K
Lengenfeld 147M
Leni R 182M
Lenswood 279K, 289, 289K
Lenz 265K
Léognan 42, 43, 43M
León 187M, 196M
Leonetti Cellar 259
Léoville-Barton, Ch. 41K
Léoville-Las-Cases, Ch. 41K
Léoville-Poyferré, Ch. 41K
Lesparre-Médoc 32M, 41M
Lessini Mountains 165
Lessona DOC 156
Leubsdorf 122, 122M
Leuk 143, 143M
Leuvrigny 75
Levante *see* Murcia and Valencia
Leverano DOC 181, 180K
Lewiston 257M
Leyda Valley 274, 275
Leynes 66, 67M
Leytron 143, 142M
Libourne 33, 44, 45, 46, 47, 31M, 33M, 45M
Librandi 181
Liebfraumilch 128, 129, 130
Lieser 117M
Lieser R 116, 117M
Lievland 325K
Liguria 154, 153K, 153M, 155K, 155M
Lillydale Estate Vineyards 299K
Lilydale 299, 299M
Lima R/Valley 210, 209M
Limarí Valley 274, 273K
Lime Kiln Valley AVA 248K
Limerick Lane Cellars 243K
Limestone Coast 8, 288, 289, 293, 287K
Limnos AO 230K, 230M
Limoux AC 103, 102M, 103K
Linares 273M
Lindau 135M
Lindemans 293, 297, 293K, 303K
Linden 263
Linganore AVA 262K
Linz 144M
Lipari 183, 153M, 183M
Liparita 245K
Lirac AC 91, 97, 98, 97K
Lis Neris 167
Lisboa (Lisbon) 209, 214, 209M
Lisini 175K
Lison-Pramaggiore DOC 165, 161K
Listrac-Médoc AC 35, 36, 37, 39, 32K, 38M
Litoměrice 219M
Little Boomey 301
Little Sur 250
Littoral *see* Primorska (Slovenia)
Livermore Valley AVA 235, 248, 254, 236K, 248K, 248M
Livingston 247K
Livorno 178, 179, 153M, 169M
Ljubljana 226M
Lleida 188, 191, 189M
Locarno 140M
Loché 66, 67M
Locorotondo DOC 180K
Lodi AVA 254, 236K, 236M
Lodola Nuova 177K
LOEL 231
Logroño 188, 192, 193, 187M, 189M, 193M
Loiben 147K
Loir R/Valley 86, 31M, 81K, 81M, 109M
Loire R/Valley 22, 30, 80-9, 31M, 81M, 84-5M, 87M, 89M, 109M; Central vineyards 83, 81K; sparkling wines 83, 85, 86; sweet wines 82-3, 85; Upper vineyards 83
Lokoya 247K
Lolol 279
Lombardia (Lombardy) 154, 155, 165, 153K, 153M, 155K, 155M
Lombardo 177K
Lompoc 250, 236M, 251M
Loncomilla Valley 273K
Long Gully 299K
Long Island 235, 262, 264, 262K, 264-5M; wineries 265K
Longoria, Richard 253K
Longridge 325K
Lontué 273M
Lontué R 275, 273M
Lontué Valley 273K
Lopez 283K
Loramie Creek AVA 262K
Lorca 201, 201M
Lorch 124, 125M
Lorchhausen 124, 125M
Loreley, Bereich 121K, 122K
Lörrach 135M
Lorraine 31M
Lorsch 138
Los Alamos 253, 251M, 253M
Los Andes 273M
Los Angeles 235, 237, 254, 235M, 236M
Los Gatos 248M
Los Llanos sub-region 200
Los Olivos 250, 251M, 253M
Los Vascos 278, 279K
Lositza 228K
Lot R 30, 106, 107, 31M, 106M, 109M
Louisiana 235M
Loupiac AC 48, 49, 51, 32K, 49M
Lourdes 106M
Lourensford Valley 324
Lourinhã DOC 209K
la Louvière, Ch. 43, 43K
Louvois 75M
Lovech 228K
Lowburn 317
Lower Great Southern Region (W. Australia) 286
Lower Murray 287K
Lower Orange 320K
Lubbock 255
Lubiana, Stefano 308
Lucca 169M
Lucia 248M

Ludon-Médoc 39, 38M
Ludwigshöhe 128, 128M
Lugana DOC 153K, 155K, 161K
Lugano 140M
Lugny 55
Lugo 196, 196M
Luján de Cuyo 283, 281M, 283M
Luján de Cuyo DOC 280, 281K
Luna 245K
Lungarotti 169
Lunlunta 283
Luso 211
Lussac-St-Émilion AC 46, 32K, 45M
Lützkendorf 139
Lutzville Valley 320K
Luxembourg 114, 113M, 114M
Luzern 140M
Lyaskovets 228K, 228M
Lynch-Bages, Ch. 41K
Lynch-Moussas, Ch. 36
Lyndoch 291, 291M
Lynmar 241K
Lyon 30, 52, 68, 90, 31M, 53M, 99M, 109M
Lytton Springs 8, 241, 241K
Lyubimets 228K

M

Macari Vineyards 265K
Macau 33, 36, 39, 38M
Le Macchiole 179K
Il Macchione 177K
Macedon 297
Macedon Ranges 296K
Macedonia (F.Y.R.M.) 227, 226K, 226M; wine areas 226K
Macerata 169M
Macharnudo vineyard 204
Machico 217M
Mâcon 52, 54, 67, 31M, 53M, 67M, 109M
Mâcon Blanc AC and Mâcon-Villages AC 67
Mâconnais 54, 66-7, 53K, 67M
Macquarie R 287M, 301M
Macul 276
Mad 221
Madeira DOC 209, 216-17, 209K, 209M, 216-17M
Madeira Wine Company 217
Madeirense DOC 217, 209K
Madera 254
Madera AVA 236K
Madiran AC 107, 106K
Madrid DO 187M, 201M
Magdelaine, Ch. 45K
Magill 288, 289
Maharashtra 327, 327K, 327M
Maikammer 130M
Mailly-Champagne 74, 75M
Main R 112, 120, 123, 132, 134, 136, 113M, 121M, 133M, 134M, 135M
Maindreieck, Bereich 132, 134, 133M, 134K
Maine R 81M, 84M, 109M
Mainstockheim 133M
Mainviereck, Bereich 132, 134, 134K
Mainz 120, 124, 128, 129, 121M, 128M
Maipo Canyon 273
Maipo R/Valley 8, 274, 275, 276-7, 273K, 273M, 274D, 276-7M; wineries 277K
Maipú (Argentina) 282, 283, 281K, 281M
Maipú (Chile) 277M
Majella 293K
Makedonia (Macedonia) (Greece) 230, 230K, 230M
Makhachkala 223, 222M
Málaga DO 186, 203, 187K, 187M, 203K, 203M
Malartic-Lagravière, Ch. 43K
Malescasse, Ch. 38K
Malescot-St-Exupéry, Ch. 38K
Malibu-Newton Canyon AVA 236K
Maligny 57M
de Malle, Ch. 49K
Malleco Valley 270, 275, 273K
Mallorca 186, 189, 187M, 189M
Malmesbury 320, 320M
Malvasia di Bosa DOC 182, 182K
Malvasia di Cagliari DOC 182, 182K
Malvasia delle Lipari DOC 183, 153K, 183K
Malvedos, Quinta dos (Graham) 212, 213K
Mambourg vineyard 78, 79, 79K
Mancey 66
La Mancha *see* Castilla-La Mancha
La Mancha DO 24, 25, 196, 200, 187K, 201K
Manchuela DO 200, 187K, 201K
Mancy 75, 75M
Mandel 127M
Mandement 140K
Manitoba 235M
Manjimup 305, 305K
Mannheim 136, 113M, 121M, 135M
Mannu R 182M
Mansfield 297, 296M
Mantinia AO 230K
Mantua (Mantova) 165, 155M
Manzaneque, Manuel 201
Manzanilla de Sanlúcar de Barrameda DO 203K
Mapocho R 277M
Maracaibo 271, 270M
Maranges AC 62, 63K, 63M
Marano di Valpolicella 164M
Marano Valley 165
Marcassin 242
Marche 152, 168, 153K, 169K, 169M
Marchihue 279, 279M
Marcillac AC 107, 106K
Marcoux, Dom. de 98D
Maremma 6, 171, 178, 169M
Mareuil-sur-Aÿ 71, 75, 75M
Margan Family 303K
Margaret River (region) 7, 286, 304, 305, 306-7, 305K, , 305M, 306M; wineries 307K
Margaux AC 8, 32-3, 35, 36-7, 40, 32K, 38K, 38M
Margaux, Ch. 20, 29, 37, 38K
Mariazell 144M
Marienthal 122M
Marietta Cellars 241K
Maring 116, 117M
Maringa 270M
Marino DOC 169K, 169M
Markgräflerland, Bereich 135, 135K
Marlborough 8, 10, 12, 16, 311, 312, 313, 316, 317, 318-19, 311K, 311M, 317D, 318-19M, 319K; wineries 319K
Marmande 106M
Marne R/Valley 70, 71, 75, 31M, 70-1M, 72D, 75M, 77M, 109M
Marqués de Riscal 197
Marsala DOC 183, 153K, 183K, 183M
Marsannay AC 58, 60, 59K, 59M
Marseille 90, 31M, 100M, 109M
Martha Clara 265K
Martha's Vineyard (California) 247K
Martha's Vineyard AVA (Massachusetts) 263, 262K
Martigny 142, 143, 140M
Martillac 43, 43M
Martinborough 313, 311M
Martinelli winery 243K
Martorell 191M
Maryland 263, 235M, 262K, 262M
Mas de Daumas Gassac 102
Masandra 222M
Masandra 223
Massa 169M
La Massa 173K
Massachusetts 263, 235M, 262K, 262M
Massaya 231
Massif Central 91, 92, 31M, 81M, 109M
Massif des Maures 100
Massif d'Uchaux 96M
Masson vineyards 249
Masterton 313
Mastroberardino 181
Mastrojanni 175K
Matakana 311K, 313
Matanzas Creek 245K
Matariki 314K
Matelica 169M
Matera 180M
Mátra 221K
Mátra (mountains) 220, 221M
Mátraalja 220
Mattituck 265M
Matua Valley 311, 313
Maubourguet 106M
Maucaillou, Ch. 39, 38K
Maule R/Valley 275, 273K, 273M
Maury VDN 104, 103K
Mautern 147M
Mauves 94, 95, 94M
Maximin Grünhaus 118, 119K
Mayacamas Mountains 242, 243, 245, 246, 247, 245M, 247M
Mayacamas 245K
Maycop 222M
Mayenne R 31M, 81M, 109M
Mayschoss 122M
Mazis-Chambertin AC 59K
Mazoyères-Chambertin AC 59K
McCrea Vineyard 243
McDowell Valley AVA 239, 239K
McGuigan Cellars 303K
McGuigan Simeon 286
McKinlay 261K
McLaren Vale 286, 288, 289, 289K
McMinnville 260, 261M
McWilliam's Mount Pleasant 301, 303K
Meckenheim 130M
Medford 257M
Mediterranean, Eastern 231, 231M
Médoc 22, 34, 36-41; soil 34D
Médoc AC 40, 32K, 41K, 40M, 41M
Medrano 283M
Medrano Estate 283K
Medway R 218M
Meerea Park 303K
Meerlust 325K
Meersburg 135M
Meinert 325K
Meissen 139, 113M
Meknès 326, 326M
Melbourne 296, 297, 299, 287M, 296M, 299M
Melfi 181
Melk 144M
Melnik (Bulgaria) 228K
Melnik (Czech Republic) 219M
Meloisey 63M
Melton, Charles 289, 253K, 291K
Melville 253K
Mendocino AVA 237, 238-9, 236K, 239K
Mendocino Ridge AVA 238, 236K, 239K
Mendoza City 283, 270M, 281M, 283M
Mendoza R/Valley 282, 283, 281M, 283M
Mendoza (region) 12, 18, 270, 271, 272, 280, 281, 282-3, 282-3M
Menetou-Salon AC 80, 83, 88, 81K
Ménétréol 88, 89M
Méntrida DO 200, 187K, 201K
Meranese/Meraner 161K, 163K
Merano 163, 153M, 161M, 163M
Merbein 297
Mercedes 272M
Mercurey AC 64, 65, 64K, 64M
Mercurol 95, 94M
Merdingen 137M
Mérida 201M
Mérignac 42, 43M
Merlini 179K
Merritt Island AVA 236K
Merryvale 247K
Mertesdorf 118, 119M
Mésima R 180M
Mesland 86
le Mesnil-sur-Oger 75, 75M
Messanges 59M
Messenikola AO 230K
Messina 183M
Metier Wines 298, 299K
Metlika 227
Mettenheim 128
Metz 31M, 109M
Meuilley 59M
Meursault AC 55, 61, 62, 63K, 63M
Mexico 24, 235, 270, 271, 270M
Mexico City 270M
Mézesmály 221
Mezzogiorno 170
Mezzolombardo 161M
Michel-Schlumberger 241K
Michigan 255, 235M
Middle Mosel 116-17, 116-17M; top vineyards 117K
Middlevlei 325K
Midouze R 106M
Mikulov 219, 219M
Milano (Milan) 155, 153M, 155M
Milawa 297, 296M
Mildara 297
Mildara Blass 302
Mildura 288, 297, 296M
Millicent 289M
Milly 57M
Milmanda vineyard 190, 191
Miltenberg 134, 134M
Minas 272, 272M
Miner Family 247K
Minerve 103, 102M
Minervois AC 90, 104, 103K
Minervois-la-Livinière AC 104, 103K
Minho province 209, 209M
Minis 224K
Minnesota 255, 235M
Miño (Minho) R 197, 210, 187M, 196M, 209M
Mintaro 294, 294M
Mintaro Wines 294K
Mirassou 249
Mireval 104
Misox *see* Ticino
Mission 314K
la Mission-Haut-Brion, Ch. 43, 43K
Mississippi 255, 235M
Missouri 235, 255, 235M
Mistelbach 144M
Mitchell 294K
Mittelburgenland 149, 144K
Mittelhaardt/Deutsche Weinstrasse, Bereich 120, 130-1, 121K, 130M, 131M
Mittelrhein 120, 122, 124, 113K, 113M, 121K, 122K, 122M
Modena 168, 169M
Modesto 236M
Moissac 106M
Moldova 222-3, 222K, 222M
Moldova (Romania) 224, 224K, 224M
Molina 273M
Molise DOC 168, 153K, 169K, 169M
Mollina 203, 203M
Molong 301
Mommenheim 128M
Monbazillac AC 107, 106K
Monbousquet, Ch. 45K
Monbrison, Ch. 37
Mönchhof 149M
Mondavi, Robert 234, 236, 250, 252, 260, 247K
Mondego R 210, 209M
Mondéjar DO 200, 187K, 201K
la Mondotte, Ch. 45K
Monferrato DOC 155K
Monferrato hills 152, 154, 156-7
Monforte d'Alba 157, 158, 159M
Monica di Cagliari DOC 182K
Monica di Sardegna DOC 182K
Monpertuis, Dom. 98D
Monprivato 159K
Monsanto 173K
MontGras 279K
Mont-de-Marsan 106M
Mont-Redon, Ch. 98D
Mont Ventoux 91, 97
Montagne de la Clape 102M
Montagne de la Combe Grizard 60
Montagne du Lubéron 100
Montagne Noire 103, 104
Montagne de Reims 70, 71, 72, 74-5, 71M, 72D
Montagne-St-Émilion AC 46, 32K, 45M
Montagne Ste-Victoire 100, 100M
Montagny AC 64, 65, 64K
Montagny-lès-Buxy 64M
Montalbano 170
Montalcino 174, 175M
Montalcino, Cantina di 175K
Montana (Switzerland) 143M
Montana (USA) 257M
Montana (NZ) 316, 318, 319K
Montauban 31M, 106M
Monte d'Oiro, Quinta do 214
Monte Rosso Vineyard 245K
Montecarlo DOC 169K
Montecello 245K
Montecompatri DOC 169K
Montefalco DOC 169
Montefalco Sagrantino DOCG 169, 153K, 169K
Montefiascone 168, 169K, 169M
Montefollónico 177M
Montélimar 91, 96, 97, 98, 96M
Montenegro 227, 226K, 226M
Montepo, Castello di 171
Montepulciano 170, 171, 172, 176, 177, 176M, 177M
Montepulciano d'Abruzzo DOC 153K, 169K
Montepulciano d'Abruzzo Colline Teramare DOCG 169K
Montérégie 266
Monteregio di Massa Marittima DOC 169K
Monteretiano 181
Monterey 250, 236M, 248M
Monterey AVA 236K, 248K
Monterey Bay 249, 250, 248M
Monterey County 248, 249, 252
Monteriggione 173M
Monterrei DO 196, 187K, 196K
Monterrey 271, 270M
Montes Apalta Vineyards 279, 279K
Montes de Léon 197, 196M
Montes de Toledo 187M
Montescudaio DOC 178, 179, 169K, 178-9M, 179K
Montevertine 173K
Montevideo 271, 272, 270M, 272M
Monthelie AC 63K, 63M
Monthey 140M
Monticello AVA 262K
Monticello 245K
Montilla 203, 203M
Montilla-Moriles DO 186, 203, 187K, 203K
Montinore 260, 261K
Montlouis AC 83, 86, 87, 81K, 87K, 87M
Montorio Veronese 165M
Montosoli 174, 175M
Montpellier 102, 104, 31M, 103M, 109M
Montpeyroux 104
le Montrachet AC 14, 61, 63K
Montravel AC 107, 106K
Montreal 266, 235M
Montreux 142, 140M
Montrose, Ch. 36, 41K
Monts Luisants 60
Montsant DO 189, 187K, 189K
Moon Mountain 245K
Moondah Brook 304
Mór 220, 221K
Morande 279K
Morava 219, 219K
Morava R 219, 219M, 226M
Mörbisch-am-See 148M
Morellino di Scansano DOC 153K, 169K
Morey-St-Denis AC 58, 60, 59K, 59M
Morgenhof 325K
Morgenster 325K
Morgex 155M
Morgon AC 69, 69K
Moriles 203, 203M ; *see also* Montilla-Moriles DO
Mornington Peninsula 21, 287, 297, 296K
Morocco 326, 326M; wine regions 326K
Moron 165
Morphett Vale 288, 289
La Morra 156, 157, 158, 159M
Morris 296, 297
Morro Bay 251M
Moscato d'Asti DOCG 153K, 155K
Moscato di Cagliari DOC 182K
Moscato di Noto DOC 183, 183K
Moscato di Pantelleria DOC 183, 153K, 183K
Moscato di Sardegna DOC 182K
Moscato di Siracusa DOC 183, 183K
Moscato di Trani DOC 180K
Mosel/Moselle R/Valley 15, 16, 21, 24, 112, 114, 115, 120, 31M, 109M, 113M, 114M, 115M, 117D, 117M, 119M, 122M
Mosel (-Saar-Ruwer) region 112, 114-19, 113K, 113M, 114-15M, 116-17M, 118-19M; top vineyards 119K
Moseltor, Bereich 115, 115K
Moses Lake 258, 257M
Moss Wood 305, 306, 307, 307K
Mostar 226M
Mouchão, Herdade do 215
Moulin-à-Vent AC 69, 69K
Moulins 81M
Moulis AC 35, 37, 39, 32K, 38M
Mount Athos 230, 230M
Mount Barker SA 289
Mount Barker WA 304, 306, 305K, 305M
Mount Benson 289, 293, 289K
Mount Cotton 309, 309M
Mount Eden vineyards 248
Mount Etna 183, 183M
Mount Harlan AVA 249, 248K
Mount Hermon 231
Mount Horrocks Wines 294K
Mount Kopaszhegy 221
Mount Lofty Ranges 289, 291, 287K, 289M
Mount Mary 298, 299K
Mount Pleasant 289, 302
Mount St Helens 256, 257M
Mount Tamborine 309
Mount Veeder AVA 245, 246, 247, 245M, 247M
Mount Veeder 245K
Mount View Range 302, 303, 303M
Mountadam 14, 285, 291, 291K
Moura *see* Alentejo
Mourm, Quinta da 215
Mouton-Rothschild, Ch. 35, 41K
Mud House 319K
Mudgee 300, 301K, 301M
Mühldorf 147M
Mulchén 274, 273M
Mulderbosch 324, 325K
Mülheim (Mosel) 117M
Mulhouse 78, 31M, 76M, 109M
Müllheim (Baden-Württemberg) 135M
Mumm Napa 247K
Münster-Sarmsheim 127, 127M
Muntenia-Oltenia 224, 225, 224K, 224M
Murcia 200, 201, 187K, 187M, 201K, 201M
Murdock Wines 293K
Murfatlar 225, 224K
Murphy-Goode 241K
Murray, Andrew 253K
Murray Darling 296K, 301K
Murray R/Valley 19, 288, 289, 290, 291, 296, 297, 301, 287M, 296M, 301M
Murray River (region) 286, 287
Murrumbateman 301, 301M
Murrumbidgee Irrigation Area 301
Murrumbidgee R 19, 287, 288, 287M, 296M, 301M
Muscadet ACs 81, 81K
Muscat de Beaumes-de-Venise VDN 91
Muscat du Cap Corse 105K
Muscat de Frontignan VDN 103K
Muscat de Lunel VDN 104
Muscat de Mireval VDN 103K
Muscat de Rivesaltes VDN 103K
Muscat de St-Jean-de-Minervois VDN 104, 103K
Musigny AC 58, 59K
Muswellbrook 302, 301M
Myrtleford 296M

N

Nackenheim 120, 128, 128M
Nagambie Lakes 296K
Nagano 327K
Nagasaki 327K
Nagy-Somlói Borvidék 241K
Nagyréde co-operative 220
Nahe 125, 126-7, 113K, 113M, 121K, 126M, 127M; top vineyards 127K
Nahe R 120, 126, 127, 128, 113M, 121M, 122M, 127M
Nahetal, Bereich 127, 121K, 127M
Nairac, Ch. 49K
Najerilla R 193M
Nal'chik 222M
Nalle 241K
Nalys, Dom. de 98D
Nampa 257M
Nancagua 278, 279M
Nannup 305, 305M
Nantes 80, 81, 31M, 81M, 109M
Nantoux 63M
Naousa AO 230K
Napa (city) 243, 224, 245, 236M, 239M, 245M
Napa R/Valley 9, 11, 17, 21, 233, 234, 235, 236, 237, 240, 244-7, 237D, 244M, 245M, 246M, 247M
Napa Valley AVA 236K, 239K, 245M, 247M; wineries and vineyards 245K, 247K
Napier 314, 311M, 314M
Nápoles, Quinta de 213K
Napoli (Naples) 153M, 180M
Naracoorte 289, 293, 289M
Narbonne 103, 108, 102M
Narrandera 301M
Nasco di Cagliari DOC 182, 182K
Naumburg 113M
Nautilus 319K
Nava de Roa 199M
Navarra 24, 186, 188, 192, 195, 187K, 187M, 189M
Navarra DO 194, 187K, 189K
Navarrete 193M
Navarro Correas 283K
Navia R 196M
Naylor 263
Néac 47, 45M
Nebrodi Mountains 183M
Neckar R 112, 136, 113M, 121M, 135M
Neckenmarkt 149
Nederburg 325K
Neethlingshof 325K
Negev 231K
Negotin 226M
Negrar (town) 165, 164M
Negrar Valley 165
Neipperg 135M
Neive 159M
Nekeovs, Bodegas 185
Nelson 317, 317D, 311K, 311M
Nemea AO 230K
Nepenthe 21
Nera R 169M
Nérac 106M
Neretva R 226M
Nerja 203, 203M
la Nerthe, Ch. 98D
Neto R 180M
Neuchâtel 141, 140K, 140M
Neumagen 117M
Neundorf 134M
Neuquén 281, 281K, 281M
Neusiedl am See 149M
Neusiedlersee-Hügelland 148, 144K, 148M
Neusiedlersee (region) 144, 145, 144K, 149M
Neustadt an der Weinstrasse 120, 130, 131, 113M, 121M, 130M
Neuweier 135M
Nevers 81M
Nevis Bluff 14
New Brunswick 235M
New England 234, 262
New Hampshire 263, 262M
New Jersey 263, 235M, 262K, 262M
New Mexico 255, 235M
New Norfolk 308M
New Orleans 235M
New South Wales 12, 287, 300-3, 287M; wine regions 287K, 301K; wineries 303K
New Suffolk 265M
New York City 265, 12M, 235M, 262M
New York State 24, 262, 263, 264-5, 262K, 262M
New Zealand 22, 24: classification system 310; wine regions 310-19, 311M; wineries 314K, 319K
Newberg 260, 261M
Newcastle (Australia) 300, 301, 302, 287M, 301M
Newfoundland 266
Newlan 245K
Newton 247K
Neyers 245K
Ngaruroro R 314, 315, 314M
Ngatarawa 314K
Niagara Bench 266, 269
Niagara Escarpment AVA 265, 262K
Niagara Peninsula VQA 266, 269, 269K
Nice 100, 31M, 109M
Nicoreşti 225, 224K
Nieder-Olm 128M
Niederemmel 117M
Niederhausen 127, 127K, 127M
Niederhausen-Schlossböckelheim State Domaine 127
Niederheimbach 122, 122M
Niederösterreich 144, 146-7, 144K, 144M; top vineyards 147K
Niepoort 210
Nierstein 120, 128, 129, 121M, 128M
Nierstein, Bereich 128, 129, 121K, 128M
Nieto Senetiner 283K
Niigata 327K
Nîmes 31M
Ninquen Hill 279
Niş 226M
Nistreana 222
Nitra 219, 219M
Nitra R 219, 219M
Nive R 106M
Nizza Monferrato 157, 155M

Noemía de Patagonia 281
Noizay 87
Nolay 63M
Nordheim 133M
Norheim 126, 127, 127K, 127M
North Africa 326, 326M
North Carolina 235M
North Coast AVA (California) 238-47, 236K, 239K
North-East Victoria 287K
North Fork of Long Island AVA 8, 264, 262K, 264-5M; wineries 265K
North Fork of Roanoke AVA 262K
North Island (NZ) 312-15; wineries 314K
North Para R 291, 291M
North Rothbury 303M
North-West Victoria 287K
North Yuba AVA 236K
Northern Cape 320K
Northern Neck George Washington Birthplace AVA 262K
Northern Sonoma AVA 236K, 239K, 240M
Northern Rivers 287K
Northern Slopes 287K
Northern Territory 286, 287K, 309M
Northland 312, 311K, 311M
North-West Victoria 287K
Norton 280, 283, 283K
Notaio, Cantina del 181
Nova Scotia 235, 266, 235M
Nova Zagora 228K
Noval, Quinta do 212, 213K
Novara 155M
Novato 239M
Nova Gorica 227, 226M
Nové Zámky 219M
Novello 159M
Novi Pazar 229, 228K, 228M
Novi Sad 226M
Novo Selo 228K
Novorossiysk 222M
Nowra 301M
NQN 281
Nuble R 273M
Nuits-St-Georges AC 55, 58, 60, 59K, 59M
Nuoro 182M
Nuragus di Cagliari DOC 182K
Nuriootpa 290, 291, 291M
Nürnberg 113M
Nussberg 145
Nyons 96M

O

Oak Knoll (California) 245M
Oak Knoll (Oregon) 261K
Oakford 247K
Oakland 248M
Oakmont 245M
Oakridge 298, 299K
Oakville AVA 246, 247, 245M, 247M
Oakville (town) 245M, 247M
Oakville Estate 233
O Barco 196M
Oberbergen 137M
Oberdiebach 122M
Oberemmel 119, 119M
Oberer Neckar, Bereich 136, 135K
Oberhausen 127, 127M
Obermorschwihr 79M
Obermosel, Bereich 115, 115K, 119M
Obernai 77M
Oberrotweil 135M, 137M
Oberwart 144M
Oberwesel 122, 122M
Óbidos DOC 209K
Oc, Vin de Pays d' 80
Oceanside 236M
Ochsenfurt 133M, 134M
Ockfen 118, 119K, 119M
Odenas 69M
Odenwald 138
Odesa 223, 222M
Odfjell 277K
Odoardi 181
Odobeşti 224K
Oestrich 125K, 125M
Ofanto R 180M
Offenburg 136, 113M, 138M
Oger 75M
Oggau 148M
Oglio R 155M
Ohio 255, 235M, 262K, 262M
Ohio River Valley AVA 262K
Ohre R 219M
Ohrid 226M
Oiry 75M
Oita 327K
Oja R 192
Okanagan R/Valley 21, 266, 267, 268, 257M, 267M
Okanagan Valley VQA 267K
Okayama 327K
Okinawa province 327
Oklahoma 235M
Okupu Beach 313
Olbia 182M
Oletta 105M
Olifants R 322, 320M
Olifants River Region 321, 320K
Olite 188, 195, 189M
Oliver 267, 268, 267M
Olivet Lane Vineyard 243K
Ollauri 192M
Olmedillo de Roa 199M
Olmeto 105M
Oloron-Ste-Marie 106M
Olt R 225, 224M
Oltet R 224M
Oltina 224K
Oltrepò Pavese DOC 154, 155, 153K, 155K
Olympia (Washington) 257M
Ombrone R/Valley 174, 169M, 175M
Ondava 219M
Ontario 12, 266, 269, 269M
Opfingen 137M
Oporto *see* Porto
Oppenheim 120, 128, 128M
Opus One 246, 247K
Ora 163, 163M
Oradea 224M
Orain 99M
Oran 326, 326M
Orange (Australia) 301, 301K, 301M
Orange (France) 97, 31M, 96M, 109M
Orange R (South Africa) 321, 320M
Orbe R 140M
Orcia R/Valley 174, 175M
Oregon 24, 235, 256, 260-1, 235M, 257K, 257M; wineries 261K
Orense (Ourense) 187M, 196M
Orinoco R 270M
Oristano 182, 153M, 182M
Orlando Wyndham 286, 300, 301, 291K
Orléans 80, 83, 86, 31M, 81M, 109M
Orléans VDQS 81K
les Ormes de Pez, Ch. 41K
Ornellaia, Tenuta dell' 178, 179K
Ortenau, Bereich 135, 136, 135K
Ortenberg 135M
Orthez 106M
Orvieto 168, 153M, 169M
Orvieto DOC 153K, 169K
Oryahovitsa 229, 228K
Osaka 327K, 327M
Osijek 226, 226M
Oslávia 167
Osorno 275
Östringen 135M
Osum R 228M
Otago *see* Central Otago
Otranto 180M
Ovada 155M
Ovens Valley 297
Overberg 320K
Overgaauw 325K
Oviedo 187M, 196M
Owyhee R 257M

P

Paarl (town) 320M, 325M
Paarl District 322, 323, 324-5, 320K, 324-5M; wineries 325K
Paarl Mountain 320, 321
Pacheco Pass AVA 248K
Pacherenc du Vic-Bilh AC 107, 106K
Padova (Padua) 161M
Padthaway 286, 289, 293, 289K, 289M
Pahlmeyer 242, 245K
Paicines (town) 248M
Paicines AVA 248K
País Vasco 186, 188, 192, 195, 187K, 187M, 189K, 189M, 196M
Palermo 183, 153M, 183M
Palette AC 100, 101, 100M
Pallisades 265
Palma de Mallorca 189, 187M, 189M
Palmela 214
Palmela DOC 214, 209K
Palmer, Ch. 38K
Palmer 265K
La Palmeria vineyard 279
Palmira 283, 283M
La Pampa 281K
Pamplona 195, 187M, 189M
Panascal, Quinta do 213K
Pancas, Quinta de 214
Panciu 224K
Paneretta, Castello della 173K
Pannonhalma 221K
Panquehue 274, 275, 273M
Pantelleria 152, 183, 153M, 183M
Panther Creek 261K
Panzano 151, 172, 173, 173M
Papaïoannou 230
Pape-Clément, Ch. 43, 43K
Papegaaiberg 324, 325M
Paradigm 247K
Paraguay 271
Paris 31M, 109M
Parker Estate 293K
Parker, Fess 253K
Parkfield 248M
Parma 168, 169M
Parma R 169M
Paros AO 230K, 230M
Parsac 45M
Pasadena 236M
Pasco 257M
Pascual Toso 283K
Pask, C J 314K
Paso Robles 236K, 236M, 251M
Paso Robles AVA 250, 251K
Passadouro, Quinta do 213K
Pastrengo 164M
Patagonia 281K
Paternoster 181
Pato, Luís 211
Patras AO 230K
Patrimonio AC 105, 105K, 105M
Pau 31M, 106M
Pauillac AC 35, 41, 41K, 41M
Paulett Wines 294K
Paulikeni 228K
Paumanok 265K
Pavia 155M
Pavie, Ch. 45K
Pavie-Macquin, Ch. 47, 45K
Pays Nantais 80-1, 81K
Paysandu 272M
Peachland 266, 267, 267M
Peachy Canyon 252
le Péage-de-Roussillon 92M, 94M
Pécharmant AC 107, 106K
Peconic Bay 264, 265M
Peconic Bay 265K
Peconic R 265M
Pecorari, Alvaro 167
Pécs 220, 221K, 221M
Pedemonte 164M
Pedrosa de Duero 199M
Peel 305K
Pegasus Bay 317, 311M
Pégau, Dom. de 98D
Pelee Island VQA 266, 269, 269K, 269M
Pellegrini 265K
Pelopennisos (Peloponnese) 230, 230K, 230M
Pemberton 304, 305, 305K
Peñafiel 198, 199, 196M, 198M
Peñaflor, Bodegas (Argentina) 281
Peñaflor (Chile) 277M
Pend Oreille R 257M
Pendares Estate 303K
Penedes DO 24, 190-1, 187K, 189K, 190-1M
Penfolds 21, 223, 288, 289, 304, 291K
Peninsulas, The 287K
Penley Estate 293K
Pennsylvania 263, 235M, 262K, 262M
Penola 293, 289K, 289M, 293M
Penticton 267, 268, 267M
Penwortham 294, 295, 294M
Pepper Tree 303K
Peraldi Estate 105
Peralillo 278, 279, 279M
Perdeberg 322
Perdriel 283, 283M
Perigueux 31M, 109M
Pernand-Vergelesses AC 61D, 63K, 63M
Pernod-Ricard 223, 327
Perpignan 76, 31M, 102M, 109M
Perricoota 301K
Peroushtitsa 228K
Perrin Brothers 250
Perth 13, 286, 304, 287M, 305M
Perth Hills 305, 305K
Pertuis 97M
Peru 270, 271, 270M
Perugia 153M, 169M
Pesaro 169M
Pescantina 164M
Pescara 153M, 169M
Pescare R 169M
Pesquera de Duero 199, 198M
Pesquera Estate 186
Pessac 42, 43, 43M
Pessac-Léognan AC 34, 35, 42-3, 32K, 42M, 43M
Petaluma (Australia) 294, 294K
Petaluma (USA) 239M
Petersons 303K
Petit Chablis AC 57, 56D, 57K
Petit-Village, Ch. 45K
Les Petits Musigny 55
Petreto-Bicchisano 105M
Petrignano 177M
Pétrus, Ch. 47, 45K
Peumo 278, 279M
de Pez, Ch. 41K
Peza AO 230K
Pezzi King 241K
Pfalz 112, 120, 130-1, 113K, 113M, 121K, 130M, 131M; top vineyards 130K
Pforzheim 135M
Pheasant Ridge 255
Phélan-Ségur, Ch. 41K
Phelps, Joseph 247K
Philadelphia 235M, 262M
Phoenix 235M
Piacenza 168, 169M
Pian delle Vigne 175K
Piave DOC 153K, 161K
Piave R/Valley 160, 161, 164, 165, 153M, 161M
Pic St-Loup 104
Picardy 305
Piccadilly Valley 279K, 289, 289K
Pichon-Longueville, Ch. 37, 41K
Pichon-Longueville-Comtesse-de-Lalande, Ch. 41K
Pico DOC 209, 209K, 209M
Pico do Arieiro 216, 216M
Picpoul de Pinet AC 104
Piemonte (Piedmont) 151, 152, 154, 155, 156-9, 163, 153K, 153M, 155K, 155M, 158-9M
Pierro 307K
Pierry 71, 75, 71M, 75M
Piesport 111, 116, 115M, 117K, 117M
Pietroasa 224K, 225
Pieve Santa Restituta 175K
Pikes Wines 294K
Piketberg District 322, 320K, 320M
Le Pin, Ch. 44, 45K
Pindar 265K
Pine Ridge 247K
Pingus, Dominio de 185
Pinhão 207, 212, 213M
Pinhão R/Valley 212, 213, 213M
Piombino 179, 169M
Piper-Heidsieck 327
Piper's Brook 308
Pipers R 308, 308M
Pirie 308
Pirque 276, 277M
Pisa 170, 178, 153M, 169M
Pisoni, Gary 249
Pistoia 169M
Pisuerga R 197, 196M
Piteşti 224M
Pitsilia 231K
Pittsfield 262M
Pivdennyy Buh R 222M
Pla de Bages 187K, 189K
Pla i Llevant DO 189, 187K, 189K
Placerville 254, 236M
Plaisir de Merle 325K
Plan de Dieu 96M
Planeta 183
Platani R 183M
Pleasanton 248M
Plettenberg Bay 320K
Ploieşti 224M
Plovdiv 229, 228K
Ploven 228K
Plumpjack 247K
Po R/Valley 152, 154, 156, 161, 164, 168, 153M, 155M, 169M
Pocinho 213
Podensac 43M, 49M
Podersdorf am See 148, 149M
Podgorica 226M
Podravje 227, 226K
Poel R 222M
Poggerino 173K
Poggibonsi 169M, 173M
Poggio Antico 175K
Poggio Gagliardi 179K
Poggio Salvi 175K
Poggio al Sole 173K
Il Poggione 175K
Poinchy 57M
Point Sur 250
Poitiers 31M, 81M, 109M
Poligny 99M
Polish Hill R 295, 294K
Polisy 73, 73M
Poliziano 177K
Polkadraai 324
Pollina R 183M
Pomar 271
Pomerol AC 34, 35, 44, 46-7, 32K, 44M, 45M
Pomino DOC 169K
Pommard AC 61, 62, 63K, 63M
Pomorie 228K
Poncey 64M
Ponferrada 196M
Pont-de-l'Isère 94M
Pont-St-Esprit 97, 96M
Ponta do Sol 216M
Pontarlier 99M
Ponte-Leccia 105M
Pontet-Canet, Ch. 36, 41, 41K
Pontevedra 187M, 196M
Ponzi 261K
Pope Valley 246
Pordenone 161M
Porongurup Hills 304, 305K, 305M
Port Clinton 262M
Port Macquarie 301, 301M
Port Phillip 287K
Port Phillip Bay 296, 297, 296M
Port Pirie 294
Porta 274
Portal del Alto winery 277K
Portalegre *see* Alentejo
Portes de Méditerranée 109K
Portets 43M
Portimão DOC 209K
Portland (Australia) 297, 296M
Portland (USA) 259, 260, 235M, 257M
Porto (France) 105M
Porto (Portugal) 211, 212, 209M
Porto, Quinta do 213K
Porto Alegre 271, 270M
Porto da Cruz 217M
Porto/Duoro DOC 208, 212-13, 209K; top quintas 213K
Porto Moniz 216M
Porto-Vecchio 105, 105M
Portugal 18, 207: classification system 208; wine regions 208-17, 209M
Posavje 227, 226K
Potensac, Ch. 41, 41K
Potenza 153M, 180M
Potter Valley AVA 239, 236K, 239K
Pouilly (Mâconnais) 66, 67M
Pouilly-Fuissé AC 54, 66, 67, 67K
Pouilly-Fumé AC and Pouilly-sur-Loire AC 83, 88-9, 81K, 89M
Pouilly-Loché AC 66, 67K
Pouilly-sur-Loire 31M, 81M
Pouilly-Vinzelles AC 66, 67K
Poujeaux, Ch. 39, 38K
Poverty Bay 313
Prades Mountains 191
Praha (Prague) 219M
Prahova R 224M
Preignac 48, 49M
Preizer, Josef 124
Premariacco 166M
Premeaux-Prissey 58, 59, 60, 59M
Premières Côtes de Blaye AC 50, 32K
Premières Côtes de Bordeaux AC 34, 51, 32K
Preston 241K
Prevelly 307M
Prieuré-Lichine, Ch. 36, 38K
Prigorje-Bilgora 226K
Primitivo di Manduria DOC 153K, 180K
Primorska (Slovenia) 227, 226K
Primorska Hrvatska (Croatia) 226, 226K
Prince Edward County VQA 269K
Prince Edward Island 266
Princeton 267M
Priorat DOCa 8, 22, 186, 191, 187K, 189K
Prissé 66, 67, 67M
Priština 226M
Progreso 272M
Prokuplje 226M
Propriano 105M
Prosecco di Conegliano-Valdobbiadene DOC 153K, 161K
Prosser 257M, 259M
Provence 90, 100-1, 31M, 100-1K
Providence 262M
Prunedale 248
Prunelli R 105M
Prut R 224M
Puente Alto 276, 277, 277M
Puget Sound AVA 257K
Puglia 152, 168, 180, 181, 153K, 153M, 180K, 180M
Puiatti, Vittorio 167
Puisieulx 75M
Puisseguin St Émilion AC 46, 32K, 45M
Pujols-sur-Ciron 49M
Pula 226M
Puligny-Montrachet AC 21, 61, 62, 63K, 63M
Punjab 327, 327K, 327M
Punters Corner 293K
Pupillin 99M
Purbach 148M
Purcari 223
Puy-l'Evêque 106M
Puygueraud, Ch. 50
Puymeras 96M
Pyatigorsk 222M
Pyramid Valley 317
Pyrenees (Australia) 297, 296K
Pyrenees (Europe) 90, 104, 107, 186, 188, 190, 194, 195, 109M, 187M, 189M

Q

Qingdao 327, 327K, 327M
Quady, Andrew 254
Quails' Gate Vineyard 268
Quarts de Chaume AC 82, 83, 85K
Québec 235, 266, 235M
Quebrada de Macul 277K
Queensland 286, 309, 287K, 309M
Queenstown 317, 311M
Queltaller Estate 294K
Querciabella 173K
Quincié-en-Beaujolais 69M
Quincy AC 83, 88, 81K
Quintessa 247K
Quivira 241K
Qupé *see* Au Bon Climat

R

Raab R 144M
Rabastens 106M
Rabaud-Promis, Ch. 49K
Rabbit Island 317
Racha-Lechkhumi 223
Radda in Chianti 173, 173M
Radikon 167
Rafanelli, A 241K
Ragusa 153M, 183M
Rahoul, Ch. 43K
Raïmat 188, 189, 191
Ramandolo DOCG 161K
Ramey 241K
Ramos, João Portugal 214, 215
Rampolla, Castello dei 151, 173, 173K
Rancagua 273, 273M
Rancho Sisquoc 253, 253K
Randersacker 132, 133M, 134M
Rangen de Thann 76
Rangitaiki R 311M
Rapel R/Valley 275, 278-9, 273K, 273M, 279M; wineries 279K
Rapsani AO 230K
Rasmussen, Kent 245K
Rasteau AC 91, 96M, 97K
Ratti, Renato 158
Rattlesnake Hills 258, 259, 259M
Rattlesnake Hills AVA 258, 259, 257K, 259M
Rauenthal 125M
Rauzan-Gassies, Ch. 36
Rauzan-Ségla, Ch. 37, 38K
Ravenna 169M
Ravensburg 135M
Ravenswood 245K
Rayas, Ch. 98D
Raymond-Lafon, Ch. 49K
Rayne-Vigneau, Ch. 49K
Recaş 224K
Rechnitz 149
Recioto di Soave DOCG *see* Soave DOC
Recioto della Valpolicella DOC *see* Valpolicella DOC
Red Mountain AVA 258, 259, 257K, 259M
Redding 236M
Redgate 307K
Redi 177K
Redoma 211
Redondo *see* Alentejo
Redwood City 248M
Redwood Valley AVA 239, 236K
Regaleali 183
Reggiano DOC 168
Réggio di Calabria 153M, 180M
Reggio nell'Emilia 168, 153M, 169M
Régnié AC 69, 69K
La Regola 179K
Régua 212, 209M
Reguengos *see* Alentejo
Reguengos de Monsaraz 209, 209M
Reims 70, 72, 73, 74, 31M, 71M, 75M, 109M
Remich 114M
Remstal Stuttgart, Bereich 135K
Rémy Martin 327
Rengo 279M
Renmark 288
Reno R 169M
Renwick 319M
la Réole 33M
Requena 201M
Requínoa 278, 279M
Retz 146
Reuilly AC 83, 88, 31M, 81K
Reuss R 140M
Reutlingen 135M
Reverie 245K
Rex Hill 261K
Reynella 288
Rhein (Rhin) R/Valley 24, 76, 112, 115, 120-31, 136, 138, 141, 31M, 77M, 109M, 113M, 121M, 122M, 124-31M, 125D, 135M, 137M, 140M
Rheinfront 128, 129, 129M
Rheingau 115, 117, 120, 122, 123-5, 127, 129, 113K, 113M, 121K, 124M, 125D, 125M ; top vineyards 125K
Rheinhessen 120, 125, 128-9, 130, 113K, 113M, 121K, 128M, 129M; top vineyards 128K
Rheintal 140K
Rhode Island 263, 235M
Rhône R/Valley 24, 90-8, 140, 142, 31M, 53M, 98D, 99M, 100M, 109M, 140M, 142M; Northern 30, 90-1, 92-5, 92M, 93M, 94M, 95M; Southern 91, 96-8, 96-7M
Rías Baixas DO 186, 196, 197, 187K, 196K
Ribadavia 196M
Ribalonga 213M
Ribatejano 209M
Ribatejo DOC 209, 214, 209K
Ribeauvillé 79M
Ribeira Brava 216M
Ribeira da Janela 216M
Ribeira Sacra DO 196, 196K
Ribeiro DO 186, 197, 187K, 196K
Ribera Alta 195
Ribera Baja 195
Ribera del Duero DO 8, 24, 185, 186, 197, 198-9, 187K, 196K, 198-9M
Ribera del Guadiana DO 187K, 201K
Ribera del Júcar 187K, 201K
Ricasoli 173K
les Riceys 73, 73M
Richardson 245K
Richebourg AC 59K
Richland 257M, 259M
Richmond 235M, 262M
Richmond Grove 301, 291K
Riddes 143, 142M
Ridge 248
Riebeek 322
Riecine 173K
Riegel 137M
Riet R 320M
Rieti 169M
Rietvivier FS 320K
Rieussec, Ch. 49K
Rijeka 226M
Rilly-la-Montagne 74, 75M
La Rinconarda 253
Río Colorado *see* Colorado R
Río de las Conchas Valley 281
Río Grande Valley 255, 235M
Río Negro (region) (Argentina) 280, 281K, 281M
Río Negro R (Argentina) 280, 281, 281M
Río Negro (region) (Uruguay) 272M
Rio Sordo 159K
La Rioja (Spain) 24, 186, 188, 192, 195, 187M, 189M, 196M
Rioja Alavesa 192-3, 192-3M
Rioja Alta 192-3, 192-3M
Rioja Baja 192, 193
Rioja DOCa 188, 192-3, 187K, 189K; soils 192D
Riquewihr 79M
Risclé 106M
Ritzville 258, 257M
River Junction AVA 236K
Rivera (Uruguay) 272, 272M
Rivera Estate (Italy) 181
Riverhead 264, 264M, 265M
Riverina 288, 301, 301K
Riverland 288, 289K
Riverview 315
Rivesaltes VDN 104, 102M, 103K
Riviera del Garda Bresciano 155K
Riviera Ligure di Ponente DOC 155K
Rizzanèse R 105M
Roa de Duero 199, 199M
Roaix 96M
Roanne 83
Roanoke 262M
Robe 21, 289, 289M

Robertson 320M
Robertson District 20, 321, 322, 320K
Roc de Cambes, Ch. 50
Rocca di Castagnoli 173K
Rocca delle Macie 173K
Rocca di Montegrossi 173K
Rocha 272, 272M
la-Roche-de-Glun 94, 94M
Roche-aux-Moines AC 85, 85K
la Roche-Vineuse 67M
la Roche-sur-Yon 81M
Rochegude 96M
de Rochemorin, Ch. 43K
la Rochepot 63M
Rochester 262M
Rochford Wines 299K
Rochioli 241, 243K
Rockford 291, 291K
Rocky Gully 306
Rocky Knob AVA 262K
Rocky Mountains 258, 235M
Rödelsee 134, 133K, 133M, 134M
Rodet 64
Rodez 106M
Rodos AO (Rhodes) 230, 230K, 230M
Roêda, Quinta da (Croft) 212, 213K
Roero Arneis DOCG 153K, 155K
Roero DOCG 153K, 155K
Roero hills 152, 157
Rogue R/Valley 261, 257M
Rogue Valley AVA 257K
Rohrendorf 146, 147M
Roma (Australia) 309, 309M
Roma (Rome) 170, 174, 153M, 169M
Romanèche-Thorins 69M
la Romanée AC 59K
la Romanée-Conti AC 21, 60, 59K
Romanée-St-Vivant AC 59K
Romaneşti 223
Romania 24, 224-5, 224M; wine regions 224K
Romeo 177K
Ronda 203M
Rongopai 313
Rooty Hill 300
Rosa, Quinta de la 211, 213K
Rosazzo 167, 166M
Rosé des Riceys AC 73
Roseburg 257M
Rosemount Estate 300, 301, 302
Rosette AC 107, 106K
Rossatz 147M
Rossese di Dolceacqua DOC 153K, 155K
Rosso Barletta DOC 181, 180K
Rosso Canosa DOC 181, 180K
Rosso Conero DOCG 168, 153K, 169K
Rosso di Montalcino DOC 175, 169K
Rosso di Montepulciano DOC 169K
Rosso Piceno DOC 153K, 169K
Rostov-na-Donu 223, 222M
Rota 204M
Roter Hang 120
Rothbury Estate 300, 301, 302
Rothvale 303K
Rotorua 311M
Rousse 229
Rousset-les-Vignes 96M
Roussette du Bugey VDQS 99K
Rousette de Savoie AC 99K
Roussillon 24
Rovereto 161M
Roxburgh (Rosemount) 302
Roxheim 127, 127M
Roy's Hill 315, 314M
Rubicon Estate 247K
Ruchottes-Chambertin AC 59K
Rück 134, 134M
Ruck, Johann 134
Rück R 134
Rudd 247K
Rüdesheim 123, 124, 121M, 125M
Rueda DO 186, 197, 187K, 196K, 196M
Rufina 170, 172, 173
Rully AC 55, 64, 65, 64K, 64M
Rümmelsheim 127M
Rupert & Rothschild 325K
Ruppertsberg 120, 130, 130M
Russe 228K
Russia 223, 222K, 222M
Russian R/Valley 238, 239, 240, 242, 236K, 239M, 241M, 243M
Russian River Valley AVA 238, 240, 241-2, 236K, 241M, 242M, 243M; wineries and vineyards 243K
Rust 148, 148D, 148M
Rust-en-Vrede 325K
Rustenberg 325K
Rutherford AVA 244, 246, 247, 245M, 247M
Rutherford (town) 245M, 247M
Rutherford Bench 246
Rutherglen 287, 294, 296, 297, 296K, 296M
Rutz Cellars 243K
Ruwer (town) 119M
Ruwertal, Bereich 115, 118, 119, 115K
Ruwer R 115, 118, 119, 114M, 119M
Rymill 293K

S

Saale R 112, 139, 113M, 134M
Saale-Unstrut 112, 132, 138, 139, 113K, 113M
Saar, Bereich 115, 119, 115K
Saar R/Valley 115, 118, 119, 113M, 114M, 119M
Saar-Ruwer *see* Mosel-Saar-Ruwer
Saarbrücken 113M
Saarburg 119, 114M, 119K, 119M, 120M
Šabac 226M
Sablet 96M
Sabon, Roger 98D
Sabrosa 212, 213M
Sachsen 112, 132, 138, 139, 113K, 113M
Sacramento 237, 236M
Sacramento R/Valley 254, 235M, 236M
Sacred Hill 310, 314K
Sacy 74, 75M
Saddleback 247K
Saddler's Creek 303K
Sado R 214, 209M
Saillon 143
Saima, Casa de 211
St-Amour (Côtes du Jura) 99M
St-Amour AC (Beaujolais) 69, 69K
St-Amour-Bellevue 66, 67, 69, 67M, 69M
St-Andelain 88, 89, 89M
St Andrä 144M
St-Aubin AC 62, 63K, 63M
St-Aubin de Luigné 83
St-Bris AC 52, 53M
St Catherines 269, 269M
St-Chinian AC 103, 104, 103K
St-Christophe-des-Bardes 45M
Saint Clair 319K
St-Cyr-en-Bourg 85M
St Davids Bench 269
St-Désert 64M
St-Émilion 44, 45M, 46D
St-Émilion AC and St-Émilion Grand Cru AC 34, 44-7, 32K, 44M, 45M, 46D; classification 47; satellites 46, 32K
St-Estèphe AC 10, 33, 35, 41, 32K, 41M
St-Étienne 31M, 109M
St-Étienne-de-Baïgorry 106M
St-Étienne-des-Ouillières 69M
St Francis 245K
St Gallen 140M
St Galler Rheintal 140K
St-Georges-de-Reneins 69M
St-Georges-St-Émilion AC 46, 32K, 45M
St-Gervais 97, 96M
St Goar 122M
St Goarshausen 122M
St Hallett 291, 291K
St Helena (California) 245, 246, 245M, 247M
St Helena (New Zealand) 317
St Huberts 298, 299, 299K
St-Jean-de-Muzols 94, 94M
St-Jean-Pied-de-Port 106M
St-Joseph AC 90, 91, 92, 94, 95, 92K, 94K, 95M
St-Julien AC 35, 37, 39-41, 32K, 41M
St-Laurent-Médoc 40, 41M
St-Laurent (Pouilly) 89M
St-Léonard 142M
St-Macaire 49M
St-Marcel-d'Ardèche 97, 96M
St-Margarethen 148M
St-Martin-sous-Montaigu 65, 64M
St Marys (vineyard area) 293
St Matthias Vineyard 308
St-Maurice-sur-Eygues 96M
St Michael Eppan co-operative 162
St-Morillon 43M
St Moritz 140M
St-Nazaire 80, 81, 31M, 81M
St-Nicolas-de-Bourgueil AC 80, 83, 86, 87, 81K, 86M, 87K
St-Pantaléon-les-Vignes 96M
St-Péray AC 91, 92, 95, 94K, 94M
St-Pierre, Ch. 41K
St-Pierre-de-Boeuf 92M
St Pölten 146, 144M
St-Pourçain VDQS 83, 81K, 81M
St-Raphaël 100
St-Rémy-de-Provence 100M
St-Romain AC 62, 63K, 63M
St-Sardos VDQS 106K
St-Satur 88, 89M
St-Seurin-de-Cadourne 40, 41, 41M
St-Supéry 247K
St-Tropez 100, 31M, 109M
St-Vallier 94M
St-Véran AC 66-7, 67K
St-Vérand 66, 67, 67M
St-Yzans-de-Médoc 41M
Ste-Croix-du-Mont AC 48, 49, 51, 32K, 49M
Ste-Foy-Bordeaux AC 51, 32K
Ste-Foy-la-Grande 107, 33M, 106M
Ste-Gemme-en-Sancerrois 89M
Ste-Genevieve 255
Saintsbury 245K
Saitama 327K
Sakar 229, 228K
Sakonnet Vineyards 263
Salamanca 187M, 196M
Salamino di Santa Croce DOC 168
Salaparuta, Duca di 183
Salcheto 177K
Salem 257M
Salento peninsula 161, 180, 181
Salerno 180M
Salève 141
Salgesch 143, 143M
Salice Salentino DOC 181, 153K, 180K
Salies-de-Béarn 106M
Salinas 248, 236M, 248M
Salinas R/Valley 248, 249, 236M, 248M
Salins-les-Bains 99M
Salmon R 257M
Salon-de-Provence 100M
Salorno 163, 163M
Salta (Argentina) 280, 270M, 281M
Salta (region) (Argentina) 270, 281, 281K
Salto (Uruguay) 272, 272M
Saltram 291K
Salvioni 175K
Sambuca di Sicilia 183, 183M
Sambureşti 225, 224K
Samos AO 230K, 230M
Samson 231K
San Albino 177M
San Antonio 273, 274, 275, 273K
San Antonio Creek 253, 253M
San Asensio 192M
San Benito AVA 248K
San Benito R 248M
San Bernardino 236M
San Bernardo 277M
San Clemente 273M
San Felice 173K
San Felipe 273M
San Fernando 278, 279, 279M
San Floriano del Collio 167, 167M
San Floriano Valpolicella 164M
San Francisco 13, 235, 236, 240, 243, 248, 12M, 235M, 236M, 237D, 248M
San Francisco Bay AVA 248, 254, 236K, 248K
San Gimignano DOC 169K, 169M
San Giovanni al Natisone 166M
San Giusto a Rentennano 173K
San Guido 179K
San Javier 273M
San Joaquin R/Valley 235, 237, 238, 254, 236M
San José (California) 248, 236M, 248M
San José (Uruguay) 272, 272M
San Juan 281, 281M
San Leonardo R 183M
San Lorenzo Isontino 166M
San Lucas (town) 248M
San Lucas AVA 250, 248K
San Luis Obispo (town) 236M, 251M
San Luis Obispo County 250, 251
San Miguel 251M
San Pablo Bay 237, 240, 243, 245, 247, 254, 237D, 239M
San Pasqual Valley AVA 236K
San Pietro in Cariano 164M
San Rafael DOC 280, 281, 283, 281K, 281M
San Sebastián *see* Donostia
San Severo DOC 181, 180K
San Telmo 283K
San Vicente de Talagante 279M
San Ysidro District AVA 248K
Sancerre 89, 31M, 81M, 89M, 109M
Sancerre AC 80, 83, 88-9, 81K, 88-9M
Sandalford 304, 307K
Sandanski 228K
Sandusky 255
Sanford 253, 253K
Sanford & Benedict Vineyard 253, 253K
Sangiacomo Vineyards 245K
Sangiovese di Romagna 153K, 169K
Sangro R 169M
Sankt Magdalener *see* Santa Maddalena
Sanlúcar de Barrameda 204, 205, 203M, 204M, 205D
Sant'Ambrogio di Valpolicella 165, 164M
Sant'Angelo in Colle 174, 175M
Sant'Angelo Scalo 174, 175M
Sant'Antimo DOC 175, 169K
Sant Sadurní d'Anoia 189, 191, 189M, 190M
Santa Barbara (city) 254, 236M
Santa Barbara County 237, 238, 252, 253
Santa Carolina 277K
Santa Clara Valley AVA 235, 248, 236K, 248K
Santa Cruz (Chile) 279, 279M
Santa Cruz (Portugal) 217M
Santa Cruz (USA) 250, 236M, 248M
Santa Cruz Mountains AVA 248, 236K, 248K
Santa Cruz de Tenerife 187M
Santa Ema 277K
Santa Fe 255, 235M
Santa Inés 277, 277K
Santa Laura 279K
Santa Lucia Highlands AVA 249, 248K
Santa Lucia Mountains 249, 250, 248M, 251M
Santa Maddalena/St Magdalener DOC 162, 163, 161K, 163K
Santa Maria (island) 209M
Santa Maria (town) 250, 252, 253, 236M, 251M, 253M
Santa Maria R/Valley 233, 237, 249, 250, 252-3, 252M, 253M
Santa Maria Valley AVA 234, 241, 236K, 251K, 253M: wineries and vineyards 253K
Santa Rita Hills AVA 253, 251K, 253M
Santa Rita 276, 277, 277K
Santa Rosa (Argentina) 282, 281M
Santa Rosa (California) 241, 242, 243, 236M, 239M, 241M
Santa Viñedos Emiliana 279K
Santa Ynez 250, 251M, 253M
Santa Ynez Valley AVA 250, 253, 236K, 251K, 252M, 253M
Santana 217M
Santander 187M, 196M
Santarém *see* Ribatejo
Santenay AC 62, 64, 63K, 63M
Santiago 270, 273, 275, 276, 12M, 270M, 273M, 274D, 277M
Santiago de Compostela 187M, 196M
Santo André, Quinta do 214
Sto António, Quinta do 213K
Santorini *see* Thira
Santos Lima, Casa de 214
São João, Caves 211
São João da Pesqueira 212, 213
São Jorge 209M
São Luiz, Quinta de 213K
São Miguel 209M
São Vicente 216M
Saône R/Valley 52, 54, 68, 99, 31M, 53M, 69M, 99M, 109M
Sarca R 161M
Sardegna (Sardinia) 152, 182, 153K, 153M, 182M
Sarica-Niculitel 224K
Sartène 105M
Sarthe R 31M, 81M, 109M
Sasbach 137M
Sasbachwalden 135M
Saskatchewan 235M
Sassari 153M, 182M
Sassicaia 171, 178, 179, 179K
Satta, Michele 178, 179K
Sauer, Horst 134
Sauldre R 81M
Saumur 31M, 81M, 85M
Saumur AC 82, 83, 84, 85, 81K, 85K
Saumur-Champigny AC 82, 85, 81K, 85K
Saumur Mousseux AC 83
Saussignac AC 107, 106K
Sauternes AC 35, 43, 48, 32K, 49M; 1855 classification 48
Sava R/Valley 227, 226M
Save R 106M
Savennières AC 80, 82, 84-5, 81K, 84M, 85K
Savigny-lès-Beaune AC 62, 63K, 63M
Savoie 30, 90, 99, 31M, 99M
Savona 155M
Savuto DOC 180K
Saxenburg 324
Sázava R 219M
Scarborough 303K
Schaffhausen 140K
Scharzhofberg 118, 119K
Schelingen 137M
Schild Estate 291K
Schiopetto, Mario 167
Schloss Johannisberg 124, 125D, 125K
Schloss Proschwitz 139
Schloss Reinhartshausen 124
Schloss Saarstein 118
Schloss Schönborn 124
Schloss Vollrads 124, 125K
Schlossböckelheim 126, 127, 127K, 127M
Schoden 119K
Scholls 261M
Schönberg 138
Schramsberg 236, 245K
Schrems 144M
Schwäbische Alb 136, 135M
Schwäbisch-Hall 135M
Schwaigern 135M
Schweinfurt 134M
Schweppenhausen 127M
Schwyz 140M
Screaming Eagle 246, 247K
Sea Smoke 253K
Seaside 248M
Seattle 257, 235M, 257M
Seavey 245K
Sebastopol (USA) 239M
Sebeş Apold 224K
Seewinkel 148, 148D, 149M
Seghesio 241K
Segovia province 197, 196M
Segre R 189M
Segura R 201M
Séguret 96M
Seiad Valley AVA 236K
Seidelberg 321
Seifried Estate 317
Seille R 99M
Seine R 31M, 73M, 109M
Seixal 216M
Seixo, Quinta do (Ferreira) 212, 213K
Sele R 180M
Sélestat 76M
Sella & Mosca 182, 327
Selvapiana 168
Selwyn 307
Selz R 128M
Selzen 128M
Seneca Lake AVA 265, 262K
Seppelt 293
Septemvri 228K
Septima 283K
Serbia 226, 226K, 226M; wine areas 226K
Serein R/Valley 56, 57, 53M, 56D, 57M
Seresin Estate 319K
Serra da Água 216M
Serra da Arrábida 209, 209M
Serra do Buçaco 210, 211
Serra do Caramulo 209M
Serra da Estrêla 209, 209M
Serra de Monchique 209, 209M
Serralunga d'Alba 157, 158, 159M
Serranía de Ronda 203, 203M
Serrig 118
Servian 103
Sésia R/Valley 156, 155M
Sète 103M
Setencostas, Quinta das 214
Setúbal 214, 209M
Setúbal DOC 208, 209K
Setúbal Peninsula 209, 214-15
Sevastopol' 222M
Sevenhill 294, 295, 294M
Sevenhill Cellars 294K
Sevilla 202, 187M, 203M
Seville Estate (Australia) 298, 298D, 299K
Sèvre Nantaise R 31M, 81M, 109M
Seymour 296M
Seyssel AC 99, 99K, 99M
Sezana 227
Sézanne 71M
Sha Cheng 327K
Shafer 247K
Shandong province 327, 327M
Shantell 299K
Shaw, Philip 301
Shenandoah Valley AVA (California) *see* California Shenandoah Valley AVA
Shenandoah Valley AVA (Virginia) 262K
Shepparton 296M
Shiga 327K
Shimane 327K
Shiner Estate 265K
Shivachevo 228K
Shoalhaven Coast 301K
Shomron 231, 231K
Shumen 229, 228M
Sicilia (Sicily) 152, 181, 183, 153K, 183M
Siduri 241K
Siebengebirge, Bereich 122K
Siena 171, 172, 173, 176, 153M, 169M, 173M, 175M
Sierra de Alfabia 189
Sierra de la Cabrera 187M
Sierra de Cantabria 192, 189M, 192D
Sierra del Carche 201, 201M
Sierra de la Demanda 196M
Sierra Foothills AVA (California) 254, 236K
Sierra de Gredos 187M
Sierra Guadarrama 186, 187M, 196M
Sierra de Montilla 203, 203M
Sierra Morena 186, 202, 187M
Sierra Nevada (California) 236, 237, 254, 236M
Sierra Nevada (Spain) 186, 187M, 203M
Sierra de Segura 187M
Sierra de la Virgen 195
Sierre 142, 143, 140M, 143M
Sieve Valley 173
Sigalas-Rabaud, Ch. 49K
Signargues 96M
Sigolsheim 78, 79M
Siklós 220, 221M
Sil R 197, 196M
Sileni Estates 20, 314K
Sillery 75M
Silverado Vineyards 247K
SilverLake 259K
Silver Oak 247K
Simeto R 183M
Simferopol' 222M
Simi 241K
Similkameen Valley VQA 268, 267K
Simonsberg 320, 321, 323, 325, 325M
Simonsberg-Paarl 325
Simonsig 325K
Simplon Pass 142
Sinalunga 170
Sinni R 180M
Sintra 209M
Sion 142, 143, 140M, 142M
Sioul R 31M, 81M, 109M
Siracusa 153M, 183M
Siran, Ch. 38K
Siret R 224M
Siro Pacenti 175K
Sisquoc R 253M
Siteia AO 230K
Sitges 19, 191M
Sizzano DOC 156
Skaggs Island 244
Skillogalee Valley 295, 294M
Skillogalee Wines 294K
Skopje 226M
Slavonski Brod 226M
Slavyantzi 228K, 228M
Sliven 228K, 229
Slovakia 219, 219M; wine regions 219K
Slovenia 16, 226, 227, 226M; wine areas 226K
Smederevo 226M
Smithbrook Vineyard 305
Smithfield 300
Smith-Haut-Lafitte, Ch. 43, 43K
Snake R/Valley 256, 257, 258, 259, 257M
Snake River Valley AVA 261, 257, 257K
Snoqualmie Pass 258, 257M
Snowy Mountains 301
Soave 161M
Soave DOC and Recioto di Soave DOCG 161, 164, 153K, 161K
Sochi 222M
Sociando-Mallet, Ch. 41K
SODAP 231
Sokhumi 222M
Sokol Blosser 261K
La Solana 201M
Solano County 254
Soldera 175K
Soledad 249, 248M
Solenzara 105M
Sologne 88
Solomon Hills 253, 253M
Solopaca DOC 180K
Solothurn 140M
Solutré 66, 67M
Solvang 253, 253M
Somerset West 324, 325M
Someş R 224M
Someşu Mic 224M
Somló 221K
Sommerach 133M, 134M
Somontano DO 186, 188, 194, 195, 187K, 189K
Sondrio 153M, 155M
Sonoma (town) 245, 239M, 245M
Sonoma Coast AVA 242, 236K, 239K
Sonoma County 235, 239-41
Sonoma Creek 242, 245M
Sonoma-Cutrer 241, 242, 243K
Sonoma Mountain AVA 243, 245, 245M
Sonoma Valley 237, 237D, 244M
Sonoma Valley AVA 242-3, 236K, 239K, 245M; wineries and vineyards 245K
Sonsierra 192
Sopraceneri 140K
Soproni-Borvidék 148, 221K, 221M
Sorbara DOC 168
Soria province 197, 198, 196M
Sosio R 183M
Sottoceneri 141, 140K
Soungourlare 228K
Soussans 37, 39, 38M
South Africa 12, 22, 24, 320-5; classification system 322; wine regions 320K; wineries 325K
South Australia 286, 288-95, 289M; wine regions 287K, 289K; wineries and vineyards 291K, 293K
South Black Sea Region 228K
South Burnett 309, 309K
South Carolina 235M
South Coast (Australia) 287K
South Coast AVA (California) 236K
South-Eastern New England AVA 262K
South Fork of Long Island 264
South Island (NZ) 316-19; wineries 319K
South-West Australia 287K
South-West France *see* France, South-West
Southern Alps (NZ) 311M
Southern Fleurieu 289K
Southern Flinders Ranges 289K
Southern Highlands 301K
Southern New South Wales 287K
Southern Oregon AVA 257K
Southern Region (Chile) 273, 273K
Southland 311M
Southold 264, 265M
Spain 18, 22, 24, 25; classification system 186; wine regions 185-205, 187M
Speyer 121M
Speyerbach R 130M
La Spezia 155M
Spier 325K
Spitz 147M
Split 226, 226M
Spokane 259, 257M
Spoleto 169M
Sponheim 127M
Spottswoode 246, 247K
Spring Creek 319M
Spring Mountain District AVA 245, 246, 247, 245M, 247M
Springfield 262M
Spyropoulos 230
Squarante R 165M
Squinzano DOC 181, 180K
Sredna Gora 228M

Staatliche Hofkeller 134
Staatsweingut Domaine Bergstrasse 138
Staglin Family 247K
Stags Leap District AVA 245, 246, 247, 245M, 247M
Stag's Leap Wine Cellars 233, 237, 247K
Stambolovo 229, 228K, 228M
Stammersdorf 145
Stanthorpe 309, 309M
Stanton & Killeen 297
Stara Zagora 229, 228K
Starkenburg, Bereich 138
Stavropol 223, 222M
Stawell 296M
Stefaneşti 225, 224K
Steiermark (Styria) 144, 145, 144K, 144M
Steigerwald, Bereich 132, 134, 133M, 134K
Stein 146, 147K, 147M
Steinberg 125K
Steinheim 135M
Stella Bella 307K
Stellenbosch 320M, 325M
Stellenbosch District 272, 322, 323-4, 320K, 324-5M; wineries 325K
Stellenzicht 325K
Sterling 236, 245K
Steyr 144M
Štip 226M
Stirling Range 305M
Stockerau 144M
Stockton 236M
Stockwell 291M
Stoke 317
Stonecroft 314K
Stoneleigh Vineyard 16
Stonestreet 241K
Stony Brook 325K
Stony Hill 245K
Stonyridge 313
Stork Nest 229
Storybook Mountain 245, 245K
Strand 325M
Strasbourg 135, 31M, 77M, 109M, 135M
Strass im Strassertal 147K
Strathbogie Ranges 296K, 297
Stringy Brae Wines 294K
Strofilia 230
Strong, Rodney 243K
Strouma Valley Region 229, 228K
Strumica 226M
Stura di Demonte 155M
Stuttgart 113M, 135M
Subotica 226M
Suckfizzle 307K
Südburgenland 149, 144K
Südliche Weinstrasse, Bereich 130, 121K, 130M
Süd-Oststeiermark 144K
Südsteiermark 144K
Süd-Tirol *see* Alto Adige/Süd Tirol
Suduiraut, Ch. 48, 49K
Sugar Loaf Reservoir 299M
Suhindol 229, 228K, 228M
Sulak 222M
Sulzfeld 133M
Summerland 267, 267M
Sumqayit 222M
Sunbury 296K, 297
Sunnyside 259M
Sunraysia 301
Suntory 327
Sury-en-Vaux 89M
Susquehanna R 262M
Sussex, East and West 218, 218M
Suvereto-Val di Cornia 178
Svishtov 229, 228K, 228M
Svratka R/Valley 219, 219M
Swan, Joseph 243K
Swan District 305K
Swan Hill 296K, 296M, 301K
Swan R/Valley 286, 304, 305K, 305M
Swanson 247K
Swartland District 321, 320K
Swellendam District 320K, 320M
Switzerland 24, 140; classification system 141; wine regions 141-3, 140K
Sydney 300, 287M, 301K, 301M
Szeged 221M
Székesfehérvár 221M
Szekszárd 220, 221K, 221M
Szigliget 220

T

Table Mountain 324
Taburno, Cantina del 181
Tacama 271
la Tâche AC 60, 59K
Tacna 270M
Tacoma 257M
Tacoronte-Acentejo DO 187K
Tacuarembó 272M
Tagliamento R 161M
Tagus (Tajo; Tejo) R/Valley 209, 211, 214, 187M, 201M, 209M
Tain-l'Hermitage 90, 94, 94M
Talagante 277, 277M
Talbot, Ch. 41K
Talca 273M
Talence 42, 43, 43M
Talenti 175K
Talijancich 304
Tallat Mountains 191
Talley Vineyards 252
Tamar R 308, 308M
Tambre R 196M
Tamburlaine 303K
Tâmega R 209M
Tanaro R 152, 154, 156, 157, 158, 159, 153M, 155M, 159M
Tanunda 285, 290, 291M
Tapolca 221M
Taraclia 222M
Taradale 314M
Taranaki 311M
Taranto 180M
Tarapacá 277, 277K
Tarara 263
Taravo R 105M
Tarbes 106M
Tarcal 221
Targu Jiu 224M
Târgu Mureş 224M
Tarija 271, 270M
Tarlee 294
Tarn R 30, 107, 31M, 106M, 109M
Târnava Mare R 225, 224M
Târnava Mică R 225, 224M
Târnave 225, 224K
Tarragona 188, 191, 189M
Tarragona DO 189, 191, 187K, 189K
Tarrawarra 298, 299K
Tasmania 286, 296, 308, 309, 287K, 287M
Tatry (mountains) 219, 219M
Tattendorf 146
Tauber R 136, 113M, 134M, 135M
Tauberbischofsheim 135M
Tauberfranken, Bereich 135, 136, 135K
Taunus Mountains 120, 123, 124, 125, 125D
Tauranga 311M
Taurasi DOCG 153K, 180K
Tauriac co-operative 50
Tavarnelle Val di Pesa 173M
Tavel AC 91, 97, 98, 97K
Tavernelle 175M
Tavignano R 105M
Tavira DOC 209K
Tàvora R 212, 213M
Tàvora-Varosa DOC 209K
Taylor's Wines 294K
T'bilisi 223, 222M
Te Awa Farm 314K
Te Horo 311K
Te Mata 311, 314, 315, 314K
Tedo R 212, 213M
Teesdorf 146
Tefft Cellars 259K
T'elavi 223
Tellaro R 183M
Temecula AVA 254, 236K, 236M
Temo R 182M
Templeton 250, 251M
Tempus Two 303K
Tennessee 235M
Teno R/Valley 275, 273K, 273M
Ter R 189M
Teramo 169M
Terek R 222M
Terlano 161M, 163M
Terlano/Terlaner DOC 161K, 163K
Termeno/Tramin 163, 163M
Terni 169M
Teroldego Rotaliano DOC 153K, 161K
Terra Alta DO 191, 187K, 189K
Terra Feita, Quinta de 213K 173K
Terrabianca 173K
The Terraces 313
Terras do Sado 214, 209M
Terras Madeirenses VR 209M
Terrazas 283K
Terre di Franciacorta 155K
Terre di Lavoro 181
Terradora di Paolo 181
Terremater 277K
du Tertre, Ch. 36-7, 38K
Tertre-Rôteboeuf, Ch. 45K
Têt R 102M
Tevere (Tiber) R 152, 153M, 169M
Texas 235M
Texas High Plains AVA 255
Texas Hill Country 255
Thames (New Zealand) 311M
Thelema 323, 325K
Thermenregion 146, 144K
Thessaloniki 230M
Thira AO (Santorini) 230, 230K, 230M
Thomas, Paul 259K
Thomas Wines 303K
Thonon les Bains 99M
Thorn-Clarke 291K
Thouarcé 84M
Thouars 31M, 81M, 109M
Thracian Lowlands 229, 228K, 228M
Thraki (Thrace) 231, 230M
Three Choirs 218, 218K
Thunersee 140K
Thüngersheim 133M, 134M
Thur R 140M
Thurgau 140M
Tianjin province 327, 327K, 327M
Tiber *see* Tevere
Ticino canton 141, 140K
Ticino R 140M, 155M
Tierra Estella 195
Timiş R 224M
Timişoara 224M
Tinguiririca R 278, 279, 273M, 279M
Tirnavou 230K
Tirón R 192
Tirso R/Valley 182, 182M
Tishki 231
Tisza R/Valley 220, 221M
Tivoli 169M
Tlemcen 326M
To Kalon Vineyard 247K
Tochigi 327K
Todi 169M
Togni, Philip 245K
Tokai (Slovakia) 219, 219K
Tokaj (Hungary) 220, 221, 221K
Tokara 325K
Tokat 231, 231M
Toledo 187M, 201M
Tolna 221K
Tomar *see* Ribatejo
Tonnerre 31M, 53M, 109M
Toowoomba 309, 309M
Topla R 219M
Toppenish 259M
Torbreck Wines 291K
Tordino R 169M
Torgiano DOC 169K
Torgiano Rosso Riserva DOCG 169, 153K, 169K
Torii Mor 261K
Torino (Turin) 156, 153M, 155M
Torlesse 20
Tormes R 187M, 196M
Toro 196M
Toro DO 186, 197, 187K, 196K
de Torraccia, Dom. 105
Torrenieri 175M
Torreón de Paredes 279K
Torres (Spain) 190, 191, 327
Torres, Marimar (USA) 242, 242K
Torres Vedras DOC 209K
Torrita di Siena 177M
Torto R/Valley 212, 213, 213M
Toscana 6, 24, 152, 163, 170-9, 153K, 153M, 155M, 169K, 169M
Tottori 327K
Toulon 90, 100, 31M, 101M, 109M
Toulouse 107, 31M, 106M, 109M
la Tour-Blanche, Ch. 49K
la Tour-Haut-Brion, Ch. 43K
la Tour Haut-Caussan, Ch. 41, 41K
la Tour-du-Haut-Moulin, Ch. 41, 38K
Touraine (region) 80, 86-7, 81K 86-7K
Touraine AC 83, 81K
Tournon 94, 95, 94M
Tournus 52, 54, 66, 53M
Tours 80, 86, 87, 31M, 81M, 87M, 109M
Tours-sur-Marne 75M
Touws R 320K
Tower Estate 303K
Traben-Trarbach 115M, 117M
Tracy-sur-Loire 89M
Trais Valley 146
Traisen 126, 127, 127K, 127M
Traisental 146, 144K
Transmontano VR 209M
Transylvania 225, 224K, 224M
Trapani 153M, 183M
Trapiche 18, 283M
Trás-os-Montes DOC 210, 209K, 209M
Trebbia R 169M
Trebbiano d'Abruzzo DOC 169K
Trebbiano di Romagna DOC 169K
Trechtingshausen 122M
Tréiso 159M
Trentadue 241K
Trentino DOC 153K, 161K
Trentino-Alto Adige 161-3, 153K, 155M, 161K, 161M
Trento DOC 162, 153K, 153M, 161K, 161M
Trenton 262M
Trerose 177K
Trévallon, Dom. de 101
Treviso 161M
Trieben 144M
Trier 115, 118, 113M, 114M, 119M
Trieste 153M, 161M
Trimbach 78
Trinity Hill 314K
Tripolis (Tripoli) 230M
Trittenheim 21, 117, 117M
Trivento 283K
Troodos (mountains) 231, 231M
Troplong-Mondot, Ch. 45K
Trotanoy, Ch. 47, 45K
Troyes 73, 109M
Truchard 245K
Tsantalis 230
Tselepos 230
Tua 212, 213M
Tua, Quinta do (Cockburn) 213K
Tualatin R/Valley 260, 261M
Tübingen 135M
Tuck's Ridge 21
Tucson 255
Tukituki R/Valley 314, 315, 314M
Tulbagh District 320K, 320M
Tulcea 224M
Tulloch, Keith 303K
Tulum 281K
Tumbarumba 301, 301K, 301M
Tundza R 228M
Tuniberg, Bereich 135, 136, 137, 135K, 137M, 139M
Tunisia 312, 326, 326M; wine regions 326K
Tunuyán R 282, 283, 281M, 283M
Tupungato 271, 280, 282, 283, 281M
Turckheim 79M
Türgovishte 228K
Turkey 231, 231M; wine areas 231K
Turkey Flat 291K
Turley 242
Turnbull 247K
Tursan VDQS 107, 106K
Tuscany *see* Toscana
Tutaekuri R 310, 314, 315, 314M
Tutuven Valley 273K
Twin Falls 257M
Twitchell Reservoir 251M
Two Hands 291K
Tygerberg District 320K
Tyrrell's 303K

U

Überlingen 135M
Uclés DO 187K, 201K
Uco Valley 281K, 283
Udine 153M, 161M
Ugarteche 283, 283M
Uiterwyk 325K
Ukiah 239, 236M, 239M
Ukraine 223, 222K, 222M
Ulla R 196M
Ulm 135M
Umani Ronchi 168
Umbria 168-9, 153K, 153M, 169K, 169M
Umpqua R/Valley 260, 261, 257M
Umpqua Valley AVA 257K
Umstadt, Bereich 138
Undenheim 128M
Undurraga 277K
Ungstein 130M
Union Auboise 73
Unison 314K
United States 233; classification system 234; wine regions 234-65, 235M
Unstrut R/Valley 112, 139, 113M
Unterloiben 147M
Untermosel *see* Burg Cochem, Bereich
Upington 320M
Upper Barn Vineyard 241K
Upper Klamath Lake 257M
Upper Moutere Hills 317
Upper Reach 304
Uruguay 270, 271, 272, 270M, 272M
Urville 73, 73M
Ürzig 15, 116, 117, 128, 117K, 117M
Usseglio, Pierre, Dom. de 98D
Utiel-Requena DO 200, 201, 187K, 201K

V

Vacqueyras AC 91, 97, 98, 97K
Váh R 219, 219M
Vaihingen 135M
Vaison-la-Romaine 96M
Val d'Anniviers 143
Val di Cornia DOC 169K
Val d'Illasi 165
Val di Suga 175K
Valais 90, 140, 141, 142-3, 140K, 142-3M
Valandraud, Ch. 45K
Valbuena de Duero 198, 199, 198M
Valcalepio DOC 153K, 155K
Valdadige DOC 161K
Valdeorras DO 196, 197, 187K
Valdepeñas 24, 187M, 201M
Valdepeñas DO 186, 200, 187K, 201K
Valdepusa, Dominio de 201
Valdespino 204
Valdipiatta 177K
Valdizarbe 195
Valdobbiadene 161M
Vale Dona Maria, Quinta 211
Vale do Meão, Quinta (Ferreira) 213
Vale de Mendiz 213M
Valençay AC 81K
Valence 80, 90, 92, 94, 96, 98, 31M, 94M, 109M
Valencia (region) 200, 201, 187K, 187M. 189M, 201M
Valencia DO 186, 201, 187K, 201K
Valeyrac 41
Valhalla 263
Valiano 177, 177M
Valladolid 187M, 196M
Valladolid province 197, 198
Valle Alto 281
Valle d'Aosta DOC 152, 154, 156, 153K, 153M, 155K, 155M
Valle Isarco/Eisacktaler DOC 161K, 163K
Valle de Güímar DO 187K
Valle de la Orotava DO 187K
Valle Venosta/Vinschgau 161K
Vallée de la Marne *see* Marne Valley
Vallejo 236M, 239M
Vallendar 122M
Valley Vineyards 218, 218K
Valli di Cornacchio 169M
Vallongue plateau 98
Valls 187M, 189M
Valpantena R/Valley 165, 165M
Valparaíso 270M, 273M
Valpolicella DOC and Recioto della Valpolicella DOC 161, 164, 165, 153K, 161K, 164-5M
Valréas 91, 96M
Valtellina DOC and Valtellina Superiore DOCG 155, 153K, 155K
Vancouver Island 268, 235M, 267M
Vancouver Island VQA 267K
Var R/Valley 100, 31M, 109M
Varbitsa 228K
Vardar R 226M
Varese 155M
Vargellas, Quinta de (Taylor) 213, 213K
Vashon Island 257
Vasse Felix 306, 307, 307K
Vaud 141, 142, 140K, 140M
Vaudieu, Ch. 98D
Vaux-en-Beaujolais 69, 69M
Vavasour 316, 319
Vayres 45M
Vecchia Cantina 177K
Vecchie Terre di Montefili 173K
Vega Sicilia 198, 199
Veitshöchheim 133M
Veles 226M
Veliki Preslav 228K
Velké Zernoseky 219M
Velletri DOC 169K
Vendôme 31M, 81M
Veneto 152, 154, 160, 161, 164-5, 153K, 153M, 155M, 161K, 161M
Venezia (Venice) 160, 162, 163, 165, 153M, 161M
Venezuela 270, 271, 270M
Veramonte 275
Vercelli 156, 155M
Verdicchio dei Castelli di Jesi DOC 153K, 169K
Verdicchio di Matelica DOC 169K
Verdigny 88, 89M
Verduno 159M
Vergelegen 324, 325K
Vergisson 66, 67M
Vérin (Rhône Valley) 93, 92M
Verín (Spain) 196, 196M
Vermentino DOC 154
Vermentino di Gallura DOCG 182, 153K, 182K
Vermentino di Sardegna DOC 153K, 182K
Vermont 266
Vernaccia di Oristano DOC 182, 182K
Vernaccia di San Gimignano DOCG 153K, 169K
Vernaccia di Serrapetrona DOC 169K
Vernon 267, 267M
Verona 152, 160, 164, 165, 153M, 161M, 165M
Versa R 166M
Vertheuil 41M
Las Vertientes vineyard 24
Vertus 75, 71M, 75M
Verzenay 70, 74, 75, 72D, 75M
Verzy 75M
Vescovato 105M
Vesúvio, Quinta do (Symington) 213, 213K
Veszprém 221M
Vétroz 142M
Vevey 142
Vézelay 52, 56
Viader 245K
Viana do Castelo 209M
Vicenza 165, 161M
Victoria 287, 296-9, 287M; wine regions 287K, 296K; wineries 299K
Victory Grape Wines 317
Vidal 314K
Vidigueira *see* Alentejo
Vie di Romans 167
la Vieille Julienne, Dom. de 98D
Vienna *see* Wien
Vienne (town) 90, 97, 31M, 92M
Vienne R 86, 87, 31M, 81M, 86M, 109M
Vierzon 81M
Viessling 147K
Vieux-Château-Certan 44, 50, 45K
Vieux-Château-Gaubert, Ch. 43K
le Vieux Donjon 98D
Vieux-Télégraphe, Dom. du 98D
Vigo 196M
Vila Nova de Gaia 211, 212, 209M
Vilafranca del Penedès 191, 187M, 189M, 190M
Vilanova i la Geltrú 190M
Villa Cafaggio 173K
Villa Maria Estate 319K
Villa Matilde 181
Villa Sant' Anna 177K
Villafranca del Bierzo 196M
Villafranca de Navarra 187M, 189M
Villamblard 106M
Villány 220, 221K
Villars-la-Faye 59M
Villedommange 74, 75M
Villefranche-sur-Saône 52, 31M, 53M, 109M
Villena 201M
Villenauxe-la-Grande 70M
Villeneuve, Dom. de 98D
Villeneuve-sur-Lot 106M
Villers-la-Faye 59M
Villers-Marmery 72, 75M
Villié-Morgon 69M
Villiera 325K
Vin du Bugey VDQS 99K
Vin de Corse AC 105, 105K
Vin de Pays 108-9, 109M;
Vin de Pays de l'Atlantique 109K
Vin de Pays du Comté Tolosan 109K
Vin de Pays des Comtés Rhodaniens 109K
Vin de Pays du Jardin de la France 109K
Vin de Pays d'Oc 104, 108, 109K
Vin de Pays des Portes de Mediterranée 109K
Vin Santo DOC 190M
Vin de Savoie AC 99, 99K; crus 99, 99K
Viña, Casa de la 200
Viñedo Chadwick 277K
Viñedos Emiliana 279K
Vineland (Canada) 266
Vineland (USA) 262M
Vineyard 29 247K
Vinho Verde DOC 209, 210, 212, 209K
Viniterra 283K
Vino Nobile di Montepulciano DOCG 176-7, 153K, 169K, 176-7M, 177K; top estates 177K
Vinos de Madrid DO 200, 187K, 201K
Vins Doux Naturels (VDN) 24, 91, 104, 230
Vins d'Entraygues et du Fel VDQS 106K
Vins d'Estaing VDQS 106K
Vins de Lavilledieu VDQS 106K
Vins du Thouarsais VDQS 31K
Vinsobres 91, 97, 98, 97K
Vinzelles 66, 67M
Vion 94, 94M
Vipava 227
Viré AC 55, 67
Virginia 235, 262, 263, 235M, 262K, 262M
Virginia's East Shore AVA 262K
Visan 96M
Viseu 210, 209M
Visp 142, 140M
Visperterminen 141, 142, 143
Vistalba 283
Viterbo 169M
Vitis Hincesti 223
Viu Manent 279K
Vizzavona 105M
Voegtlinshofen 79M
Voerzio, Roberto 154
Vojvodina 226M
Volga R 222M
Volkach 133M, 134M
Volnay AC 61, 62, 63K, 63M
Volos 230M
Volpaia, Castello di 173K
Volturno R 180M
Voor Paardeberg 325
Vorderrhein R 140M
Vosges Mountains 76, 77, 79, 120, 130, 131, 31M, 78D, 109M
Vosne-Romanée AC 21, 58, 59, 59K, 59M
Vougeot AC 58, 60, 59K, 59M
Vouni Panayias Ambelitis 231K
Vouvray AC 80, 83, 86, 81K, 87K, 87M
Vouvry 140K
Voyager Estate 307, 307K
Vranje 226M
Vrbas R 226M
Vredenburg 320M
Vredendal 320M
Vriesenhof 325K
Vrşac 226M
Vully 141, 140K

W

Wachau 144, 145, 146, 147, 144K, 146-7M
Wachenheim 130, 131, 130M
Wagga Wagga 301M
Wahluke Slope AVA 259, 257K
Waiheke Island 312, 313, 311K
Waikato 312, 313, 316, 311K, 311M
Waikato R 311M
Waimakariri R 311M
Waimauku 311K
Waimea Plains 317
Waipara 20, 317, 311K
Wairarapa 312, 313, 316, 317, 311K
Wairau Plains 318
Wairau R/Valley 16, 317, 318, 311M, 319M
Wairau River 319K
Waitaki R 317
Wakefield 294K
Waldböckelheim 127M
Waldrach 119, 119M
Walensee 140M
Wales 218; selected vineyards 218K
Walker Bay 320, 320K, 321, 322
Walla Walla 259, 257M
Walla Walla Valley AVA 257K
Wallangarra 309M
Wallhausen 127, 127K, 127M
Walluf 124, 125K, 125M
Walporzheim/Ahrtal, Bereich 122K
Waltershofen 137M
Wanaka 317
Wanganui R 311M
Wangaratta 296M
Waninga Wines 294K
Wapato 259M
Warramate Hills 299, 298D
Warren Hills AVA 262K

Warrnambool 296M
Warwick 325K
Wasenweiler 137M
Washington DC 235M, 262M
Washington Hills/Apex 259K
Washington State 12, 24, 235, 256, 257, 258-9, 235M, 257K, 257M; top wineries and vineyards 259K
Waterford 325K
Watervale 295, 294M
Watsonville 248
Waveney 218M
Wawern 119M
Wehlen 116, 117, 117M
Weill, Robert 124
Weinert 283K
Weinland 140K
Weinolsheim 128M
Weinsheim 127M
Weinviertel 146, 147, 144K
Weissenkirchen 226-7, 147M
Weiz 144M
Welgemeend 325K
Wellington (California) 245K

Wellington (New Zealand) 312, 313, 311M, 317D
Wasenweiler 137M
Wellington wine region (New Zealand) 311K, 311M
Wellington (South Africa) 320, 321, 325, 325M
Wendouree 294K
Wente 248
Wern R 134M
Wertheim 134, 136, 134M, 135M
West Australian South-East Coastal 287K
West Elks AVA 255
West Texas Mountains 255
West Virginia 263, 235M, 262K, 262M
Western Australia 22, 286, 304-7; wine regions 287K, 305K; wineries 307K
Western Balkans 226-7, 226M; wine areas 226K
Western Cape 320K
Western Connecticut Highlands AVA 262K
Western Plains 287K
Western Victoria 287K

Westhofen 128
Weststeiermark 144K
Wettolsheim 79M
Whakatu 314M
Whangarei 311M
Whistler Wines 18
Whitcraft 253K
White Hall 263
Whitehall Lane 247K
Whitehaven 319K
Whitlands 297
Wien 144, 145, 146, 147, 160, 144K, 144M
Wiesbaden 120, 123, 124, 125, 113M, 121M, 125M
Wiesloch 307K
Willakenzie 261K
Willamette R/Valley 235, 256, 257, 260, 257M, 260-1M
Willamette Valley AVA 241, 257K
Willespie 307K
Williams Selyem 243K
Williamsburg 262M
Williamsburg 263
Willow Bridge 305
Willow Creek AVA 236K
Willow Crest 259K
Willows Vineyard, The 291K

Wilson Vineyard, The 294K
Wiltingen 118, 119, 114M, 119M
Wilyabrup 307, 307M
Windesheim 127M
Windsor (Canada) 269, 269M
Windsor (USA) 241, 242, 241M, 243M
Wineglass 259K
Winkel 124, 125, 125D, 125K, 125M
Winningen 115, 115M
Winterthur 140M
Wintzenheim (France) 79M
Winzenheim (Germany) 127M
Wirsching 134
Wisconsin 255, 235M
Wissembourg 78
Witchcliffe 307M
Wither Hills 319K
Wittlich 115M
Wittmann, Philipp 128
Wolf 117, 177K
Wollongong 301M
Wonnegau, Bereich 128, 121K
Woodinville 257M
Woodlands 307K

Woodward Canyon 259
Woody Nook 307K
Worcester 320M
Worcester District 322, 320K
Worms 128, 113M, 121M
Wrattonbully 293, 289, 289K
Wright, Ken 261K
Württemberg 112, 135, 136, 113K, 113M, 135M, 137M
Württembergischer Bodensee, Bereich 136, 135K
Württembergisch Unterland, Bereich 136, 135K
Würzburg 132, 134, 113M, 133M, 134M, 133K, 135M
Wyndham Estate 303, 303K
Wynns 292, 293K

Y
Yakima 259, 257M, 259M
Yakima R/Valley 256, 257, 258, 259, 258-9M
Yakima Valley AVA 257K, 259M; wineries and vineyards 259K
Yaldara 291K
Yallingup 307
Yalta 223
Yalumba 290, 291, 291K
Yalumba (The Menzies) 293K
Yamagata 327K
Yamanashi 327, 327K
Yambol 228K
Yamhill 261M
Yantra R 228M
Yarra Bank 299K
Yarra Burn 299M
Yarra Glen 299, 299M
Yarra Ridge 298, 299K
Yarra R/Valley 287, 296, 297, 298-9, 296K, 296M, 298D, 298-9M, 299K
Yarra Yarra 299K
Yarra Yering 297, 298, 298D, 299K

X
Xanadu Wines 307, 307K
Xinjiang Province 327

Ycoden-Dante-Isora DO 187K
Yecla DO 201, 187K, 201K
Yerevan 222M
Yering Station 299, 299K
Yeringberg Estate 299, 299K
Yonne R 31M, 53M, 109M
Yonne (region) 52, 56, 53K, 53M
York Mountain AVA 250, 251K
Young (Australia) 301, 301M
Young, Robert Vineyard 241K
Yountville 245, 246, 247, 245M, 247M
d'Yquem, Ch. 35, 48, 49, 49K
Yreka 236M
Yverdon 140M
Yvorne 142

Zagreb 226M
Zala 221K
Zamora 196M
Záncara R 201M
Zaragoza 188, 191, 195, 187M, 189M
ZD 247K
Zell 115, 115M
Zell/Mosel, Bereich see Burg Cochem, Bereich
Zeltingen 116, 117, 117M
Zema Estate 293K
Zermatt 141, 142, 140M
Zêzera R 209M
Zillah 259M
Zimmerling, Klaus 139
Zitsa AO 230K
Znojma 219, 219M
Zöbing 147K
Zonza 105M
Zug 140M
Zūpa 226
Zürich 141, 140D
Zwingenberg 138

Z
Zaca Mesa 253K
Zadar 226M

ACKNOWLEDGMENTS

The publishers would like to thank the countless organisations and individuals all over the world who have given invaluable help and advice in preparing the maps and diagrams in this Atlas, and especially for the following sections:

FRANCE
Association Nationale Interprofessionelle des Vins de Table et des Vins de Pays (ANIVIT), Jean-Claude Audebert (Bourgueil), Domaine Baumard (Angers), Bureau Interprofessionel des Vins de Bourgogne, Bureau Interprofessionel des Vins du Centre, Cave de Tain l'Hermitage, Yves Chidaine (Montlouis), Comité Interprofessionel des Vins de Bordeaux, Comité Interprofessionel des Vins Côtes de Provence, Conseil Interprofessionelle des Vins d'Alsace, Georges Duboeuf (Beaujolais), GETEVAY (Chablis), Conseil Interprofessionnel des Vins du Languedoc, Olivier Humbrecht MW (Alsace), Institut National des Appellations d'Origine (INAO), Institut Technique du Vin, Inter Rhône, Maison du Vin (Saumur), Office International de la Vigne et du Vin, Alain Paret (St-Joseph), Lyn Parry (Rhône), René Renou (Bonnezeaux) Jean-Max Roger (Sancerre), Professor G. Seguin (Bordeaux University), SOPEXA (London), Syndicat Viticole d'Aloxe-Corton, Syndicat Viticole Médoc et Haut-Médoc, Syndicat Viticole de Pouilly, Syndicat Viticole St-Émilion, Union Interprofessionelle des Vins du Beaujolais, Les Vins du Val de Loire

GERMANY
Peter Anheuser (Nahe), Matthew Boucher, Bernard Breuer (Rheingau), Armin Diel (Nahe), German Wine Information Centre (London) Weingut Heyl von Herrnsheim (Rheinhessen), Karl-Heinz Johner (Baden), Weingut Juliusspital (Franken), Carl Koenen, Rainer Lingenfelder (Pfalz), Ernst Loosen (Mosel), Egon Müller Jr (Saar), Claus Piedmont (Saar), Rheinhessenwein, Dirk Richter (Mosel), Landwirtschaftskammer Rheinland-Pfalz, Verband Deutscher Prädikats und Qualitätsweingüter

SWITZERLAND
Swiss Wine Exporters' Association, Provins (Valais)

AUSTRIA
Arbeitsgemeinschaft Kartographie, Austrian Wine Marketing Board

ITALY
Richard Baudains, Dr Maurizio Castelli, Consorzio Bolgheri, Consorzio del Marchio

Storico (Chianti Classico), Consorzio per la Tutela dei Vini (Valpolicella), Consorzio del Vino Brunello di Montalcino, Consorzio del Vino Nobile di Montepulciano, David Gleave MW, Alois Lageder (Alto Adige), Paul Merritt, Produttori del Barbaresco, Pietro Ratti (Barolo), Servizio della Vitivinicoltura (ERSA, Friuli).

SPAIN
Consejo Regulador DO Jerez, Consejo Regulador DO Penedès, Consejo Regulador DO Ribera del Duero, Consejo Regulador DOC Rioja, Fedejerez, Joachin Galvez, Instituto Nacional de Denominaciones de Origen (INDO), Rioja Wine Exporters Group, The Sherry Institute of Spain (London), Miguel Torres SA (Penedes), Wines from Spain (London)

PORTUGAL
Peter Cobb, Joanna Delaforce (Douro), Direcção Regional de Agricultura (Região Autónoma da Madeira), Bruce Guimaraens (Douro), Instituto do Vinho da Madeira, Madeira Wine Company, The Symington Family Port Companies

ENGLAND
Stephen Skelton, John Worontschak

EASTERN EUROPE
Association of the Czech Vine Growers and Winemakers (CMVVU), Boyar Estates (Hungary), Mike Frumosu (Romania), Hungarian Food & Wine Bureau (London), Poslovna Skupnost za Vinogradništvo in Vinarstvo Slovenije (Slovenia), Premium Brand Corporation (Black Sea States), Alena Vitkovska (Slovakia)

EASTERN MEDITERRANEAN
Chateau Musar (Lebanon), Cyprus High Commission Trade Centre, Doluca Winery, Nico Manessis (Greece)

USA
Alexander Valley Vineyards, Rod Berglund (Russian River), California North Coast Grape Growers Association, Carneros Quality Alliance, Central Coast Winegrowers' Association, Chalone Wine Group, Chemeketa Vineyard Management and Winemaking Program (Oregon), Stan Clarke (Washington State), Edna Valley Arroyo Grande Vintners Association, Catherine Fallis (California), Lake County Winegrape Commission, Landmark Vineyards (Sonoma), McDowell Valley Vineyards (Mendocino), Mendocino Winegrowers Association, Mill Creek Vineyard (Sonoma),

Robert Mondavi Winery (Napa), Napa Valley Vintners Association, New York Wine & Grape Foundation, Oak Knoll (Oregon), Oregon Wine Advisory Board, Palmer Vineyards (Long Island), Paso Robles Vintners & Growers Association, David Petterson (cartographer, Oregon), Ponzi Vineyards (Oregon), Russian River Valley Winegrowers, Richard Sanford (Santa Barbara), Santa Barbara County Vintners' Association, Sonoma County Grape Growers Association, Sonoma Valley Vintners and Growers Alliance, Jonathan Swinchatt (EarthVision Inc., Napa), University of California at Davis, US Government Bureau of Alcohol, Tobacco and Firearms (BATF), Larry Walker, Dick Ward (Napa), Washington Wine Commission, Winegrowers of Dry Creek Valley, Wine Institute of California, Yamhill County Wineries Association

CANADA
British Columbia Wine Institute, Ontario Wine Institute

CHILE
Asociación de Exportadores y Embotelladores de Vinos A.G., Richard Neill, Alejandra Schultz, Christian Sotomayor, Patricio Tapia, Viñas de Colchagua, Viña Santa Rita (Maipo)

ARGENTINA
Catena Zapata (Mendoza), Familia Zuccardi (Mendoza), Instituto de Desarrollo Rural (Mendoza), Tom Pakenham, Pro Mendoza

AUSTRALIA
Australian Wine & Brandy Corporation, Australian Wine Bureau (London), Tony Brady (Clare), Clare Valley Winemakers Inc, Coonawarra Vignerons Association, Domaine Chandon (Yarra), Eden Valley Winemakers Association, Peter Forrestal (Margaret River), Hunter Valley Vineyard Association, Tony Keys, Tim Knappstein (Clare), Max and Stephen Lake (Hunter), Bob McLean (Barossa), Sally Marden (Barossa), Liz Morrison (Margaret River), Southcorp Wines, The Viticultural Council of the South East of South Australia, Wine Industry of Western Australia, Wynn's Coonawarra, Yarra Valley Winegrowers Association

NEW ZEALAND
Horticultural and Food Research Institute of New Zealand, Gus Lawson (Hawkes Bay), Montana Wines Ltd, Ollie Powrie (Hawkes Bay), John Stitchbury (Marlborough), Wine Institute of New Zealand, Wines of New Zealand (London)

SOUTH AFRICA
Dave Hughes, Dave Johnson, Angela Lloyd, South Africa Wine Industry Information & Systems (SAWIS)

NORTH AFRICA
Linda Domas, Tunisian Project Manager, Calatrasi

ASIA
Keith Grainger, Parmar Wines, Myoko Stevenson

GENERAL
Carpe Diem, The Royal Geographic Society Map Room, Westbury Communications

PICTURE CREDITS
Photographs of bottles by Nigel James.

Principal photo source by Cephas Picture Library. All photographs by Mick Rock except:
Kevin Argue 268 (below)
Nigel Blythe 47, 107, 118, 123, 184-5, 194
Stuart Boreham 80
Emma Borg 321
Andy Christodolo 5, 12, 14 (below right), 18, 21 (top row centre), 24, 139, 141, 143, 157, 255, 271, 279, 292
David Copeman 217
Chris Davies 327
Jeffrey Drewitz 21 (third row right), 300
Bruce Fleming 247, 249
Kevin Judd 7, 9, 10 (above), 14 (below left), 15 (right), 16 (top left), 20 (top left and second right), 21 (third row centre), 22, 237, 242, 268 (above), 288, 304, 310, 313, 316
Char Abu Mansoor 231
R & K Muschenetz 1, 11, 250
Alain Proust 20 (below), 323
H Shearing 308
Ted Stefanski 21 (top row left and right)

Other photographs by
Michael Bussellc 34 (left), 41, 64, 74, 90
Charmaine Grieger 82, 275
Janet Price 21 (second row centre and right), 44, 50, 120, 129, 134, 280
Kristian Reynolds 263
Scope (Jean-Luc Barde) 77, 202, 205; (Bernard Galeron) 160, 163; (Jacques Guillard) 20 (top right), 145, 156; (Noel Hautemaniere) 104
Tourism Queensland 309
David Williamson 220
Jon Wyand 54
Joco Znidarsic 16 (top row, left), 227